Strategic Management

Formulation, Implementation, and Control

Strategic Management

Formulation, Implementation, and Control

Twelfth Edition

John A. Pearce II

Villanova School of Business
Villanova University

Richard B. Robinson, Jr.

Moore School of Business
University of South Carolina

McGraw-Hill
Irwin

Published by McGraw-Hill/Irwin, a business unit of The McGraw-Hill Companies, Inc., 1221 Avenue of the Americas, New York, NY, 10020.
Copyright © 2011, 2009, 2007, 2005, 2003, 2000, 1997, 1994, 1991, 1988, 1985, 1982 by The McGraw-Hill Companies, Inc. All rights reserved.
No part of this publication may be reproduced or distributed in any form or by any means, or stored in a database or retrieval system, without the prior written consent of The McGraw-Hill Companies, Inc., including, but not limited to, in any network or other electronic storage or transmission, or broadcast for distance learning.

Some ancillaries, including electronic and print components, may not be available to customers outside the United States.

This book is printed on acid-free paper.

1 2 3 4 5 6 7 8 9 0 DOW/DOW 1 0 9 8 7 6 5 4 3 2 1 0

ISBN   978-0-07-813716-7
MHID   0-07-813716-0

Vice president and editor-in-chief: *Brent Gordon*
Publisher: *Paul Ducham*
Executive editor: *Michael Ablassmeir*
Director of development: *Ann Torbert*
Editorial assistant: *Andrea Heirendt*
Vice president and director of marketing: *Robin J. Zwettler*
Executive marketing manager: *Anke Braun Weekes*
Vice president of editing, design and production: *Sesha Bolisetty*
Lead project manager: *Pat Frederickson*
Senior production supervisor: *Kara Kudronowicz*
Cover designer: *Joanne Mennemeier*
Senior photo research coordinator: *Lori Kramer*
Photo researcher : *Ira C. Roberts*
Media project manager: *Suresh Babu, Hurix Systems Pvt. Ltd.*
Typeface: *10/12 Times New Roman*
Compositor: *MPS Limited, A Macmillan Company*
Printer: *R. R. Donnelley*

Library of Congress Cataloging-in-Publication Data

Pearce, John A.
    Strategic management : formulation, implementation, and control / John A. Pearce II,
Richard B. Robinson , Jr.—12th ed.
        p. cm.
    Includes index.
    ISBN-13: 978-0-07-813716-7 (alk. paper)
    ISBN-10: 0-07-813716-0 (alk. paper)
    1. Strategic planning. I. Robinson, Richard B. (Richard Braden), 1947–II. Title.
HD30.28.P3395 2011
658.4'012—dc22

                                        2009045538

To Susan McCartney Pearce, David Donham Pearce, Mark McCartney Pearce, Sage Ast, Rowan Ast, Anjali Ast, and Oakley Robinson—for the love, joy, and vitality that they give to our lives.

About the Authors

John A. Pearce II   *Villanova University*

John A. Pearce II, Ph.D., holds the Villanova School of Business Endowed Chair in Strategic Management and Entrepreneurship at Villanova University. In 2009, he received the Fulbright Senior Specialist Award for work at Simon Fraser University's Segal Graduate School of Business in Vancouver, Canada. In 2004, he was the Distinguished Visiting Professor at ITAM in Mexico City. Previously, Professor Pearce was the Eakin Endowed Chair in Strategic Management at George Mason University and a State of Virginia Eminent Scholar. He received the 1994 Fulbright U.S. Professional Award, which he served at INTAN in Malaysia. Dr. Pearce has taught at Penn State University, West Virginia University, the University of Malta as the Fulbright Senior Professor in International Management, and at the University of South Carolina where he was Director of Ph.D. Programs in Strategic Management. He received a Ph.D. degree in Business Administration and Strategic Management from the Pennsylvania State University.

Professor Pearce is coauthor of 36 books and has authored more than 250 articles and refereed professional papers. The articles have appeared in journals that include *Academy of Management Executive, Academy of Management Journal, Academy of Management Review, Business Horizons, California Management Review, Journal of Applied Psychology, Journal of Business Venturing, Long-Range Planning, Organizational Dynamics, Sloan Management Review,* and *Strategic Management Journal.* Several of these publications have resulted from Professor Pearce's work as a principal on research projects funded for more than $2 million.

Professor Pearce is the recipient of several awards in recognition of his accomplishments in teaching, research, scholarship, and professional service, including three Outstanding Paper Awards from the Academy of Management and the 2003 Villanova University Outstanding Faculty Research Award. A frequent leader of executive development programs and an active consultant to business and industry, Dr. Pearce's client list includes domestic and multinational firms engaged in manufacturing and service industries.

Richard B. Robinson, Jr.   *University of South Carolina*

Richard B. Robinson, Jr., Ph.D., is a Moore Fellow at the Moore School of Business, University of South Carolina. He also serves as Director of the Faber Entrepreneurship Center at USC. Dr. Robinson received his Ph.D. in Business Administration from the University of Georgia. He graduated from Georgia Tech in Industrial Management.

Professor Robinson has authored or coauthored numerous books, articles, professional papers, and case studies addressing strategic management and entrepreneurship issues that students and managers use worldwide. His research has been published in major journals including the *Academy of Management Journal, Academy of Management Review, Strategic Management Journal, Academy of Entrepreneurship Journal,* and the *Journal of Business Venturing.*

Dr. Robinson has previously held executive positions with companies in the pulp and paper, hazardous waste, building products, lodging, and restaurant industries. He currently serves as a director or adviser to entrepreneurial companies that are global leaders in niche markets in the log home, building products, animation, and visualization software industries. Dr. Robinson also advises more than 250 students each year who undertake field consulting projects and internships with entrepreneurial companies worldwide.

Preface

This twelfth edition of *Strategic Management: Formulation, Implementation, and Control* is designed to accommodate the needs of strategy students worldwide in our fast changing twenty-first century. These are exciting times, and they are reflected in this book and the accompanying McGraw-Hill supplements. This preface describes what we have done to make the twelfth edition uniquely effective in preparing students for strategic decisions in tomorrow's fast-paced global business arena. They include NEW or revised chapter material, cases, and illustrations examining:

- Business ethics and corporate social responsibility.
- Globalization as a central theme integrated and illustrated throughout this book and in a separate chapter on the global business environment every business faces.
- Fundamental ways strategists enable innovation and entrepreneurship to shape their companies' futures more proactively.
- Structuring networked, boundaryless organizational structures to face twenty-first-century challenges.

- The accelerating pace of global and technological change with frameworks that help managers adapt its impact on their companies, markets, and the industry dynamics that result.
- Ways for strategists to identify and leverage their firm's strengths in rapidly changing industry circumstances.
- Contemporary examination of the challenges and advantages using global supply chains and outsourcing of strategic parts of a firm's product or service offerings.

Top Strategist
Starbucks CEO Howard Schultz on CSR
Exhibit 3.9

Starbucks supports coffee farmers by paying premium prices for the highest quality coffee beans and by maintaining its position as the largest purchaser, roaster, and distributor of Fair Trade Certified™ coffee in North America (it is also among the largest worldwide). In addition, Starbucks is a long-time partner of Conservation International (CI). Together, the two organizations developed environmental and social practice standards (C.A.F.E. Practices) for coffee farmers and implemented a rewards system for farmers who adhere to these practices.

The partnership has had a major impact on coffee farmers worldwide. For example, the Association of Kilimanjaro Specialty Coffee Growers, an association of 8,000 smallholder coffee growers in Tanzania, receives support from Starbucks because it is C.A.F.E.-certified. As a result, the association is

able to add environmentally sustainable technology to increase coffee quality, which in turn improves the profitability of its farmer members.

Since he came out of retirement to be reappointed as Starbucks' CEO in January 2008, Howard Schultz has taken action to further solidify the company's support of coffee farmers. Schultz partnered with Peter Seligmann, CI's chairman and CEO, to take support of coffee farmers to the next level by protecting the land surrounding coffee farms. The effort involves an effort to help the farmers get a piece of the fast-growing $70 billion carbon finance business. Starbucks finances CI's efforts to work with local growers to protect the landscapes around the coffee farms. Farmers agree to preserve forests to replant trees so that they become eligible for carbon credits from companies that are voluntarily offsetting their emissions.

Under Schultz's leadership, Starbucks has also extended its direct financial support of coffee farmers. In 2008, Starbucks, Transfair USA, and the Fair-trade Labeling Organizations (FLO) International

Strategy in Action
Exhibit 4.3
Unions Seek Payback for Helping Obama

The labor unions that helped Barack Obama win the White House are looking for some payback. While Obama's support could help, unions' diminishing membership has made it tough to get their legislation passed. Unions represent about one in eight U.S. workers, down from about one in five 25 years ago.

The biggest labor-business donnybrook in the new Congress will be over a bill that would do away with employers' right to demand secret-ballot elections to recognize unions. Instead, a company would have to recognize and bargain with a union once union cards were signed by 50 percent of the company's eligible workforce plus one additional employee.

The House passed the measure in 2007, but it died under a Republican filibuster in the Senate. President Bush had vowed to veto it, but Obama made it part of his platform.

Labor leaders say employers have used secret-ballot elections, generally held on job sites, to coerce and intimidate workers into rejecting unions. Employers counter that workers are often coerced by their peers to sign union cards and that a secret-ballot election is the only way to determine their true desires.

- The increased and valued role of companies founded and/or run by women and minorities worldwide.

We are also pleased to offer:

- More than 20 new Top Strategist boxes highlighting leaders worldwide who are unique examples of good strategic leadership and thinking.
- 30 new, contemporary cases covering business situations from around the world in both large and small, entrepreneurial companies—6 short cases and 24 comprehensive cases are included in this twelfth edition's case selection.
- More than 50 new Strategy in Action boxes illustrating key concepts in each chapter.
- Literally hundreds of new, twenty-first-century examples woven into the text in each chapter.

The twelfth edition of *Strategic Management* is divided into 14 chapters. They provide a thorough, state-of-the-art treatment of the critical business skills needed to plan and manage strategic activities. While the text continues a solid academic connection, students will find the text material to be practical, skills oriented, and relevant to their jobs and entrepreneurial aspirations.

All of the material in this edition is based on a proven model-based treatment of strategic management that allows for self-study and an easy-to-understand presentation. We have also significantly reduced the page length in this edition, providing in turn a very focused presentation that is also the most cost-effective offering from McGraw-Hill/Irwin for twenty-first-century students and instructors of strategic management.

AN OVERVIEW OF OUR TEXT MATERIAL

The twelfth edition uses a model of the strategic management process as the basis for the organization of the text material. Adopters have identified this model as a key distinctive competence for our text because it offers a logical flow, distinct elements, and an easy-to-understand guide to strategic management. The model reflects strategic analysis at different organizational levels as well as the importance of innovation in the strategic management process. The model and parallel chapter organization provides a student-friendly approach to the study of strategic management.

Chapters

The first chapter provides an overview of the strategic management process and explains what students will find as they use this book. The remaining 13 chapters cover each part of the strategic management process and techniques that aid strategic analysis, decision making, implementation, control, and renewal. The literature and research in the strategic management area have developed at a rapid pace in recent years in both the academic and business press. The twelfth edition includes several upgrades designed to incorporate major developments from both these sources. While we include cutting-edge concepts, we emphasize straightforward, logical, and simple presentation so that students can grasp these new ideas without additional reading.

Strategy in Action Modules

Each chapter provides a key pedagogical feature, Strategy in Action modules, that have become standard in most strategy books. We have drawn on the work of prestigious business magazine field correspondents worldwide to fill more than 50 new Strategy in Action modules with short, hard-hitting current illustrations of key chapter topics. We are energized by the excitement, interest, and practical illustration value our students tell us they provide.

Top Strategists Boxes

Adding to the Strategy in Action modules, we have included one or more Top Strategist boxes in each chapter that tell the personal story about a company or industry leader whose behavior, practices, or actions illustrate a key concept in the strategic management process covered in that particular chapter. These boxes help personalize what we present in the chapter through a vignette about someone most students will recognize or have read about in the popular press.

CASES IN THE TWELFTH EDITION

We are pleased to offer 30 excellent cases in this edition. These cases present companies, industries, and situations that are easily recognized, current, and interesting. We have a good mixture of small and large firms; start-ups and industry leaders; global and domestically focused companies; and service, retail, manufacturing, technology, and diversified activities. We explore U.S.–based companies, European–based companies, Asian–based companies, and emerging Middle Eastern economies.

Six of the cases in this edition are short cases. They allow for flexibility in conducting class sessions where coverage of both a case and other material is desirable. We have found them useful at the start of a strategy course's case segment to jump-start students' grasp of what strategy is about—using short vignettes on companies very familiar to students presented as those companies face current strategic situations and decisions. So cases such as "Facebook vs. Twitter," "Microsoft vs. Mozilla," and "PetSmart vs. Petco" let students embark on case analysis in company settings with which they are already comfortable.

OUR WEB SITE

A substantial Web site has been designed to aid your use of this book. It includes areas accessible only to instructors and areas specifically designed to assist students. The instructor section includes supplement files, which include detailed teaching notes, PowerPoint slides, and case teaching notes for all 30 case studies, which keep your work area less cluttered and let you quickly obtain information. Students are provided company and related business periodical (and other) Web site linkages to aid and expedite their case research and preparation efforts. Practice quizzes are provided to help students prepare for tests on the text material and attempt to lower their anxiety in that regard. We expect students will find the Web site useful and interesting. Please visit us at www.mhhe.com/pearce12e.

SUPPLEMENTS

Components of our teaching package include a revised, comprehensive instructor's manual, test bank, Power Point presentation, and a computerized test bank. These are all available to qualified adopters of the text. Professors can also use a simulation game as a possible package with this text: the Business Strategy Game (Thompson/Stappenbeck). The Business Strategy Game provides an exercise to help students understand how the functional pieces of a business fit together. Students will work with the numbers, explore options, and try to unite production, marketing, finance, and human resource decisions into a coherent strategy.

Acknowledgments

We have benefited from the help of many people in the evolution of this project over twelve editions. Students, adopters, colleagues, reviewers, and business contacts have provided hundreds of insightful comments, suggestions, and contributions that have progressively enhanced this book and its supplements. We are indebted to the researchers and practicing managers who have accelerated the development of the literature on strategic management.

We are particularly indebted to the talented case researchers who have produced the cases used in this book, as well as to case researchers dedicated to the revitalization of case research as an important academic endeavor. First-class case research is a major avenue through which top strategic management scholars should be recognized.

Several reviewers provided constructive suggestions and feedback which helped facilitate useful revisions, the addition of numerous current examples throughout the text, and a new case selection we find compelling. We extend particular thanks to three who offered exceptionally comprehensive coverage:

Michele V. Gee
University of Wisconsin–Parkside

D. Keith Robbins
Winthrop University

Edward P. Sakiewicz
American Public University System

We are affiliated with two separate universities, both of which provide environments that deserve thanks. As the Villanova School of Business Endowed Chair at Villanova University, Jack is able to combine his scholarly and teaching activities with his coauthorship of this text. He is grateful to Villanova University, Dean James Danko, and his colleagues for the support and encouragement they provide.

Richard appreciates the support provided within the Moore School of Business by Dean Hildy Teegen, Deputy Dean Scott Koewer, Associate Dean Greg Neihaus, Dr. Brian Klaas, Mr. Dean Kress, Ms. Cheryl Fowler, and Ms. Carol Lucas.

We want to thank Dr. Ram Subramanian, Montclair State University, for his outstanding contributions in this instructor's manual and ancillaries for the twelfth edition. His dedication and attention to detail make this a better book. Likewise, we are most grateful to Dr. Amit Shah, Frostburg State University, for his excellent earlier contributions to this project.

Leaders at McGraw-Hill/Irwin deserve our utmost thanks and appreciation. Gerald Saykes, John Black, John Biernat, and Craig Beytein contributed to our early success. The editorial leadership of Michael Ablassmeir helps to assure that it will continue in this twelfth edition. Development Editor Kelly Pekelder and Editorial Assistant Andrea Heirendt helped us to produce a much improved book. The McGraw-Hill/Irwin field organization deserves particular recognition and thanks for their ongoing worldwide adoption results for this text. We particularly wish to express appreciation to and acknowledge the hard work and excellent support provided to us by Sandy Wolbers, Kathleen Sutterlin, Stacey Flowerree, Brooke Briggs, Nick Miggans, Kevin Eichelberger, Colin Kelley, Steve Tomlin, Bryan Sullivan, Clark White, Meghan Manders, Lori Ziegenfuss, Jessica King, Rosalie Skears, Lisa Huinker, Bob Noel, Adam Rooke, John Wiese, Carlin Robinson, Courtney Kieffer, Rosario Valenti, Anni Lundgren, Deborah Judge-Watt, Nate Kehoe, David Wulff, Kim Freund, Joni

Thompson, and Mary Park. Their professionalism and dedication to the professors and instructors they serve sets a standard we have worked very hard to match by making the twelfth edition a text deserving of their representation.

We hope that you will find our book and ancillaries all that you expect. We welcome your ideas and recommendations about our material, and we wish you the utmost success in teaching and studying strategic management.

Dr. John A. Pearce II
Villanova School of Business
Villanova University
Villanova, PA 19085–1678

Dr. Richard Robinson
Moore School of Business
University of South Carolina
Columbia, SC 29208

Brief Contents

Table of Contents

Part One

Overview of Strategic Management

The first chapter of this book introduces strategic management, the set of decisions and actions that result in the design and activation of strategies to achieve the objectives of an organization. The chapter provides an overview of the nature, benefits, and terminology of and the need for strategic management. Subsequent chapters provide greater detail.

The first major section of Chapter 1, "The Nature and Value of Strategic Management," emphasizes the practical value and benefits of strategic management for a firm. It also distinguishes between a firm's strategic decisions and its other planning tasks.

The section stresses the key point that strategic management activities are undertaken at three levels: corporate, business, and functional. The distinctive characteristics of strategic decision making at each of these levels affect the impact of activities at these levels on company operations. Other topics dealt with in this section are the value of formality in strategic management and the alignment of strategy makers in strategy formulation and implementation. The section concludes with a review of the planning research on business, which demonstrates that the use of strategic management processes yields financial and behavioral benefits that justify their costs.

The second major section of Chapter 1 presents a model of the strategic management process. The model, which will serve as an outline for the remainder of the text, describes approaches currently used by strategic planners. Its individual components are carefully defined and explained, as is the process for integrating them into the strategic management process. The section ends with a discussion of the model's practical limitations and the advisability of tailoring the recommendations made to actual business situations.

Chapter **One**

Strategic Management

After reading and studying this chapter, you should be able to

1. Explain the concept of strategic management.

2. Describe how strategic decisions differ from other decisions that managers make.

3. Name the benefits and risks of a participative approach to strategic decision making.

4. Understand the types of strategic decisions for which managers at different levels of the company are responsible.

5. Describe a comprehensive model of strategic decision making.

6. Appreciate the importance of strategic management as a process.

7. Give examples of strategic decisions that companies have recently made.

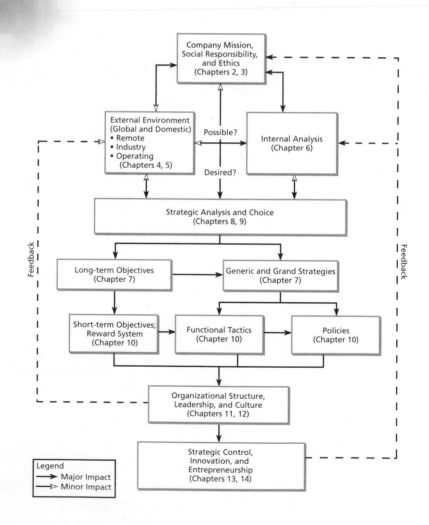

Strategic Blunder: Xerox's Sale of Insider Information to Apple

In the early 1970s, Xerox developed world-changing computer technology, including the mouse and the graphical user interface. (Modern GUIs include Microsoft Windows and Mac OS X.) One of the devices was called the Xerox Alto, a desktop personal computer that Xerox never bothered to market. A decade later, several Apple employees, including Steve Jobs, visited the Xerox PARC research and development facility for three days in exchange for $1 million in Apple's still–privately held stock. That educational field trip was well worth the price of admission (Apple stock was worth $3.5 billion in 2008), given that it helped Jobs build a company worth $110 billion in 2008. In the late 1980s, Xerox sued Apple for using GUI technology in its Macintosh computer, but the case was dismissed—the statute of limitations on the dispute had passed. Size of Blunder: $107 billion.

Source: Excerpted from Melanie Lindner, "The 10 Biggest Blunders Ever in Business," *Forbes*, March 25, 2008, http://www.msnbc.msn.com/id/23677510/

THE NATURE AND VALUE OF STRATEGIC MANAGEMENT

Managing activities internal to the firm is only part of the modern executive's responsibilities. The modern executive also must respond to the challenges posed by the firm's immediate and remote external environments. The immediate external environment includes competitors, suppliers, increasingly scarce resources, government agencies and their ever more numerous regulations, and customers whose preferences often shift inexplicably. The remote external environment comprises economic and social conditions, political priorities, and technological developments, all of which must be anticipated, monitored, assessed, and incorporated into the executive's decision making. However, the executive often is compelled to subordinate the demands of the firm's internal activities and external environment to the multiple and often inconsistent requirements of its stakeholders: owners, top managers, employees, communities, customers, and country. To deal effectively with everything that affects the growth and profitability of a firm, executives employ management processes that they feel will position it optimally in its competitive environment by maximizing the anticipation of environmental changes and of unexpected internal and competitive demands. For an intriguing example of how a failure to anticipate the consequences of competitive dynamics resulted in a major strategic blunder by Xerox, read Exhibit 1.1, Strategy in Action.

To earn profits, firms need to perfect processes that respond to increases in the size and number of competing firms; to the expanded role of government as a buyer, seller, regulator, and competitor in the free enterprise system; and to greater business involvement in international trade. Perhaps the most significant improvement in these management processes came when "long-range planning," "planning, programming, budgeting," and "business policy" were blended with increased emphasis on environmental forecasting and external considerations in formulating and implementing plans. This all-encompassing approach is known as strategic management.

strategic management
The set of decisions and actions that result in the formulation and implementation of plans designed to achieve a company's objectives.

Strategic management is defined as the set of decisions and actions that result in the formulation and implementation of plans designed to achieve a company's objectives. It comprises nine critical tasks:

1. Formulate the company's mission, including broad statements about its purpose, philosophy, and goals.

2. Conduct an analysis that reflects the company's internal conditions and capabilities.

3. Assess the company's external environment, including both the competitive and the general contextual factors.

4. Analyze the company's options by matching its resources with the external environment.

5. Identify the most desirable options by evaluating each option in light of the company's mission.

6. Select a set of long-term objectives and grand strategies that will achieve the most desirable options.

7. Develop annual objectives and short-term strategies that are compatible with the selected set of long-term objectives and grand strategies.

8. Implement the strategic choices by means of budgeted resource allocations in which the matching of tasks, people, structures, technologies, and reward systems is emphasized.

9. Evaluate the success of the strategic process as an input for future decision making.

strategy
Large-scale, future-oriented plans for interacting with the competitive environment to achieve company objectives.

As these nine tasks indicate, strategic management involves the planning, directing, organizing, and controlling of a company's strategy-related decisions and actions. By **strategy,** managers mean their large-scale, future-oriented plans for interacting with the competitive environment to achieve company objectives. A strategy is a company's game plan. Although that plan does not precisely detail all future deployments (of people, finances, and material), it does provide a framework for managerial decisions. A strategy reflects a company's awareness of how, when, and where it should compete; against whom it should compete; and for what purposes it should compete.

Dimensions of Strategic Decisions

What decisions facing a business are strategic and therefore deserve strategic management attention? Typically, strategic issues have the following dimensions.

Strategic Issues Require Top-Management Decisions   Because strategic decisions overarch several areas of a firm's operations, they require top-management involvement. Usually only top management has the perspective needed to understand the broad implications of such decisions and the power to authorize the necessary resource allocations. As top manager of Volvo GM Heavy Truck Corporation, Karl-Erling Trogen, president, wanted to push the company closer to the customer by overarching operations with service and customer relations empowering the workforce closest to the customer with greater knowledge and authority. This strategy called for a major commitment to the parts and service end of the business where customer relations was first priority. Trogen's philosophy was to so empower the workforce that more operating questions were handled on the line where workers worked directly with customers. He believed that the corporate headquarters should be more focused on strategic issues, such as engineering, production, quality, and marketing.

Strategic Issues Require Large Amounts of the Firm's Resources   Strategic decisions involve substantial allocations of people, physical assets, or moneys that either must be redirected from internal sources or secured from outside the firm. They also commit the firm to actions over an extended period. For these reasons, they require substantial resources. Whirlpool Corporation's "Quality Express" product delivery program exemplified a strategy that required a strong financial and personnel commitment from the company. The plan was to deliver products to customers when, where, and how they wanted them. This proprietary service uses contract logistics strategy to deliver Whirlpool, Kitchen Aid, Roper, and Estate brand appliances to 90 percent of the company's dealer and builder customers within 24 hours and to the other 10 percent within 48 hours. In highly competitive service-oriented businesses, achieving and maintaining customer satisfaction frequently involve a commitment from every facet of the organization.

Strategy in Action

Exhibit 1.2

Strategic Blunder: Seattle Computer Products' Sale of the DOS Operating System

In 1980, Tim Paterson, a 24-year-old programmer at Seattle Computer Products, spent four months writing the 86-DOS operating system. Meanwhile, Bill Gates was on a hunt for operating software that Microsoft could license to IBM; Big Blue had the money and factories to build computers, but not the operating system to run them. Gates bought the DOS system for a pittance: $50,000. When Seattle Computer figured out what it had let slip through its fingers, it accused Microsoft of swindling the company by not revealing that IBM was its customer; Microsoft settled by compensating Seattle Computer an additional $1 million in 1986. Big deal—the market for the rest of Microsoft's cool software had been born, and there was no looking back. Arguably, this key deal ultimately propelled Microsoft to software domination—and its current $253 billion valuation. Size of Blunder: $253 billion.

Source: Excerpted from Melanie Lindner, "The 10 Biggest Blunders Ever in Business," *Forbes,* March 25, 2008, http://www.msnbc.msn.com/id/23677510/

Strategic Issues Often Affect the Firm's Long-Term Prosperity Strategic decisions ostensibly commit the firm for a long time, typically five years; however, the impact of such decisions often lasts much longer. Once a firm has committed itself to a particular strategy, its image and competitive advantages usually are tied to that strategy. Firms become known in certain markets, for certain products, with certain technologies. They would jeopardize their previous gains if they shifted from these markets, products, or technologies by adopting a radically different strategy. Thus, strategic decisions have enduring effects on firms—for better or worse. For example, Commerce One created an alliance with SAP in 1999 to improve its position in the e-marketplace for business to business (B2B) sales. After taking three years to ready its e-portals, Commerce One and SAP were ready to take on the market in 2002. Unfortunately, the market changed. The "foolproof strategy" got to the market too late and the alliance failed.

For years, Toyota had a successful strategy of marketing its sedans in Japan. With this strategy came an image, a car for an older customer, and a competitive advantage, a traditional base for Toyota. The strategy was effective, but as its customer base grew older its strategy remained unchanged. A younger customer market saw the image as unattractive and began to seek out other manufacturers. Toyota's strategic task in foreign markets is to formulate and implement a strategy that will reignite interest in its image.

Strategic Issues Are Future Oriented Strategic decisions are based on what managers forecast, rather than on what they know. In such decisions, emphasis is placed on the development of projections that will enable the firm to select the most promising strategic options. In the turbulent and competitive free enterprise environment, a firm will succeed only if it takes a proactive (anticipatory) stance toward change. Microsoft's Bill Gates, who gained fame as a future-oriented strategic decision maker, often succeeds at the expense of short-sighted competitors as described in Exhibit 1.2, Strategy in Action.

Strategic Issues Usually Have Multifunctional or Multibusiness Consequences Strategic decisions have complex implications for most areas of the firm. Decisions about such matters as customer mix, competitive emphasis, or organizational structure necessarily involve a number of the firm's strategic business units (SBUs), divisions, or program units. All of these areas will be affected by allocations or reallocations of responsibilities and resources that result from these decisions.

Strategic Issues Require Considering the Firm's External Environment All business firms exist in an open system. They affect and are affected by external conditions that are largely beyond their control. Therefore, to successfully position a firm in competitive situations, its strategic managers must look beyond its operations. They must consider what relevant others (e.g., competitors, customers, suppliers, creditors, government, and labor) are likely to do.

Three Levels of Strategy

The decision-making hierarchy of a firm typically contains three levels. At the top of this hierarchy is the corporate level, composed principally of a board of directors and the chief executive and administrative officers. They are responsible for the firm's financial performance and for the achievement of nonfinancial goals, such as enhancing the firm's image and fulfilling its social responsibilities. To a large extent, attitudes at the corporate level reflect the concerns of stockholders and society at large. In a multibusiness firm, corporate-level executives determine the businesses in which the firm should be involved. They also set objectives and formulate strategies that span the activities and functional areas of these businesses. Corporate-level strategic managers attempt to exploit their firm's distinctive competencies by adopting a portfolio approach to the management of its businesses and by developing long-term plans, typically for a three- to five-year period. A key corporate strategy of Airborne Express's operations involved direct sale to high-volume corporate accounts and developing an expansive network in the international arena. Instead of setting up operations overseas, Airborne's long-term strategy was to form direct associations with national companies within foreign countries to expand and diversify their operations.

Another example of the portfolio approach involved a plan by state-owned Saudi Arabian Oil to spend $1.4 billion to build and operate an oil refinery in Korea with its partner, Ssangyong. To implement their program, the Saudis embarked on a new "cut-out-the-middleman" strategy to reduce the role of international oil companies in the processing and selling of Saudi crude oil.

In the middle of the decision-making hierarchy is the business level, composed principally of business and corporate managers. These managers must translate the statements of direction and intent generated at the corporate level into concrete objectives and strategies for individual business divisions, or SBUs. In essence, business-level strategic managers determine how the firm will compete in the selected product-market arena. They strive to identify and secure the most promising market segment within that arena. This segment is the piece of the total market that the firm can claim and defend because of its competitive advantages.

At the bottom of the decision-making hierarchy is the functional level, composed principally of managers of product, geographic, and functional areas. They develop annual objectives and short-term strategies in such areas as production, operations, research and development, finance and accounting, marketing, and human relations. However, their principal responsibility is to implement or execute the firm's strategic plans. Whereas corporate- and business-level managers center their attention on "doing the right things," managers at the functional level center their attention on "doing things right." Thus, they address such issues as the efficiency and effectiveness of production and marketing systems, the quality of customer service, and the success of particular products and services in increasing the firm's market shares.

Exhibit 1.3 depicts the three levels of strategic management as structured in practice. In alternative 1, the firm is engaged in only one business and the corporate- and business-level responsibilities are concentrated in a single group of directors, officers, and managers. This is the organizational format of most small businesses.

Alternative 2, the classical corporate structure, comprises three fully operative levels: the corporate level, the business level, and the functional level. The approach taken throughout

EXHIBIT 1.3
Alternative Strategic Management Structures

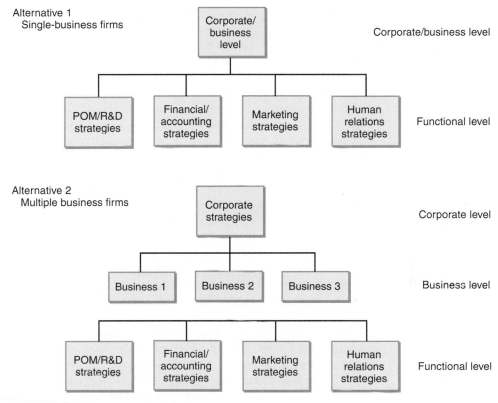

this text assumes the use of alternative 2. Moreover, whenever appropriate, topics are covered from the perspective of each level of strategic management. In this way, the text presents a comprehensive discussion of the strategic management process.

Characteristics of Strategic Management Decisions

The characteristics of strategic management decisions vary with the level of strategic activity considered. As shown in Exhibit 1.4, decisions at the corporate level tend to be more value oriented, more conceptual, and less concrete than decisions at the business or functional level. For example, at Alcoa, the world's largest aluminum maker, chairman Paul O'Neill made Alcoa one of the nation's most centralized organizations by imposing a dramatic management reorganization that wiped out two layers of management. He found

EXHIBIT 1.4   **Hierarchy of Objectives and Strategies**

		Strategic Decision Makers			
Ends (What is to be achieved?)	**Means (How is it to be achieved?)**	**Board of Directors**	**Corporate Managers**	**Business Managers**	**Functional Managers**
Mission, including goals and philosophy		✓✓	✓✓	✓	
Long-term objectives	Grand strategy	✓	✓✓	✓✓	
Annual objectives	Short-term strategies and policies		✓	✓✓	✓✓

Note: ✓✓ indicate a principal responsibility; ✓ indicates a secondary responsibility.

that this effort not only reduced costs but also enabled him to be closer to the front-line operations managers. Corporate-level decisions are often characterized by greater risk, cost, and profit potential; greater need for flexibility; and longer time horizons. Such decisions include the choice of businesses, dividend policies, sources of long-term financing, and priorities for growth.

Functional-level decisions implement the overall strategy formulated at the corporate and business levels. They involve action-oriented operational issues and are relatively short range and low risk. Functional-level decisions incur only modest costs, because they depend on available resources. They usually are adaptable to ongoing activities and, therefore, can be implemented with minimal cooperation. For example, the corporate headquarters of Sears, Roebuck & Company spent $60 million to automate 6,900 clerical jobs by installing 28,000 computerized cash registers at its 868 stores in the United States. Although this move eliminated many functional-level jobs, top management believed that reducing annual operating expenses by at least $50 million was crucial to competitive survival.

Because functional-level decisions are relatively concrete and quantifiable, they receive critical attention and analysis even though their comparative profit potential is low. Common functional-level decisions include decisions on generic versus brandname labeling, basic versus applied research and development (R&D), high versus low inventory levels, general-purpose versus specific-purpose production equipment, and close versus loose supervision.

Business-level decisions help bridge decisions at the corporate and functional levels. Such decisions are less costly, risky, and potentially profitable than corporate-level decisions, but they are more costly, risky, and potentially profitable than functional-level decisions. Common business-level decisions include decisions on plant location, marketing segmentation and geographic coverage, and distribution channels.

Formality in Strategic Management

The formality of strategic management systems varies widely among companies. **Formality** refers to the degree to which participants, responsibilities, authority, and discretion in decision making are specified. It is an important consideration in the study of strategic management, because greater formality is usually positively correlated with the cost, comprehensiveness, accuracy, and success of planning.

A number of forces determine how much formality is needed in strategic management. The size of the organization, its predominant management styles, the complexity of its environment, its production process, its problems, and the purpose of its planning system all play a part in determining the appropriate degree of formality.

In particular, formality is associated with the size of the firm and with its stage of development. Some firms, especially smaller ones, follow an **entrepreneurial mode.** They are basically under the control of a single individual, and they produce a limited number of products or services. In such firms, strategic evaluation is informal, intuitive, and limited. Very large firms, on the other hand, make strategic evaluation part of a comprehensive, formal planning system, an approach that Henry Mintzberg called the **planning mode.** Mintzberg also identified a third mode (the **adaptive mode**), which he associated with medium-sized firms in relatively stable environments. For firms that follow the adaptive mode, the identification and evaluation of alternative strategies are closely related to existing strategy. It is not unusual to find different modes within the same organization. For example, ExxonMobil might follow an entrepreneurial mode in developing and evaluating the strategy of its solar subsidiary but follow a planning mode in the rest of the company.

---

formality
The degree to which participation, responsibility, authority, and discretion in decision making are specified in strategic management.

entrepreneurial mode
The informal, intuitive, and limited approach to strategic management associated with owner-managers of smaller firms.

planning mode
The strategic formality associated with large firms that operate under a comprehensive, formal planning system.

adaptive mode
The strategic formality associated with medium-sized firms that emphasize the incremental modification of existing competitive approaches.

The Strategy Makers

The ideal strategic management team includes decision makers from all three company levels (the corporate, business, and functional)—for example, the chief executive officer (CEO), the product managers, and the heads of functional areas. In addition, the team obtains input from company planning staffs, when they exist, and from lower-level managers and supervisors. The latter provide data for strategic decision making and then implement strategies.

Because strategic decisions have a tremendous impact on a company and require large commitments of company resources, top managers must give final approval for strategic action. Exhibit 1.4 aligns levels of strategic decision makers with the kinds of objectives and strategies for which they are typically responsible.

Planning departments, often headed by a corporate vice president for planning, are common in large corporations. Medium-sized firms often employ at least one full-time staff member to spearhead strategic data-collection efforts. Even in small firms or less progressive larger firms, strategic planning often is spearheaded by an officer or by a group of officers designated as a planning committee.

Precisely what are managers' responsibilities in the strategic planning process at the corporate and business levels? Top management shoulders broad responsibility for all the major elements of strategic planning and management. They develop the major portions of the strategic plan and reviews, and they evaluate and counsel on all other portions. General managers at the business level typically have principal responsibilities for developing environmental analysis and forecasting, establishing business objectives, and developing business plans prepared by staff groups.

An executive who understands and excels at the strategic management process is Hewlett-Packard's CEO Mark Hurd. By cutting costs and restructuring to focus on core activities, Hurd led a three-year turnaround of Hewlett-Packard, resulting in a dramatic rise in sales revenue and profit. You can read about the challenges he faced, the strategies he led, and the successes he achieved in Exhibit 1.5, Top Strategist.

A firm's president or CEO characteristically plays a dominant role in the strategic planning process. In many ways, this situation is desirable. The CEO's principal duty often is defined as giving long-term direction to the firm, and the CEO is ultimately responsible for the firm's success and, therefore, for the success of its strategy. In addition, CEOs are typically strong-willed, company-oriented individuals.

However, when the dominance of the CEO approaches autocracy, the effectiveness of the firm's strategic planning and management processes is likely to be diminished. For this reason, establishing a strategic management system implies that the CEO will allow managers at all levels to participate in the strategic posture of the company.

In implementing a company's strategy, the CEO must have an appreciation for the power and responsibility of the board, while retaining the power to lead the company with the guidance of informed directors. The interaction between the CEO and board is key to any corporation's strategy. Empowerment of nonmanagerial employees has been a recent trend across major management teams. For example, in 2003, IBM replaced its 92-year-old executive board structure with three newly created management teams: strategy, operations, and technology. Each team combined top executives, managers, and engineers going down six levels in some cases. This new team structure was responsible for guiding the creation of IBM's strategy and for helping to implement the strategies once they were authorized.

Benefits of Strategic Management

Using the strategic management approach, managers at all levels of the firm interact in planning and implementing. As a result, the behavioral consequences of strategic

Top Strategist
Hewlett-Packard's CEO Mark Hurd Leads a Strategic Turnaround

Exhibit
1.5

Mark Hurd took over as CEO of Hewlett-Packard (HP) in March 2005, when the company was floundering from predecessor Carly Fiorina's 2001 Compaq merger, a deal that fell substantially short of meeting its projected returns and resulted in a chaotic organizational structure. HP was also struggling to grow market share in the Dell- and IMB-dominated personal computer (PC) and corporate server markets. Between 2001 and 2005, HP's stock price and profit growth were flat.

HP's turnaround began with retrenchment efforts, including reducing the workforce by 10 percent, freezing pension benefits, and raising executive accountability in budget management and sales issues. Hurd restructured the company into three main divisions: PCs, laptops, and handheld devices; printers and printing; and large-enterprise information technology (IT) services. HP's centralized sales and marketing force was then broken into corresponding divisions, removing redundant administrative layers and giving division heads control over their respective sales forces and budgets. In addition, significant investment was put into sales training and customer service.

In the 2005 annual report, Hurd wrote that the highly matrixed organization had contributed an excessive nine layers of management between the CEO and the customer and that utilizing a centralized sales team had given division heads control of only 30 percent of their budgets. Hurd therefore decentralized the HP structure, reducing the management layers between CEO and customer to six, and increased division-head budget control to 70 percent. Fewer sales layers enabled HP to form deals more quickly and win more bids because less time was tied up in administrative issues. Decentralization allowed for individual cost structures to better line up with HP's competitive businesses, which utilized HP's scales in pricing, operating expenses, and costs of goods sold. Employing scales simplified the cost system, provided greater flexibility, and more accountability.

Since turnaround efforts began in 2005, HP has demonstrated solid sales growth across all three divisions. By the end of 2007, gross profits rose by 25 percent and revenue rose by 20 percent to $104 billion. In market share of the personal computer global market, HP claimed the top position by 2007 with 17.6 percent to Dell's 13.9 percent. By 2008, HP climbed to second place behind IBM in corporate server market share, with 28.3 percent to IBM's 31.9 percent.

Sources: J. Fortt, "Mark Hurd, Superstar," *Fortune* 157, no. 12 (2008), p. 35; "A Fast Turnaround at Hewlett Packard: Quick, Easy Wins, or Long-Term Promise?" *Strategic Direction* 23, no. 2 (2007), p. 25; and P. Tam, "System Reboot—Hurd's Big Challenge at H-P: Overhauling Corporate Sales," *The Wall Street Journal*, April 3, 2006, p. A1.

management are similar to those of participative decision making. Therefore, an accurate assessment of the impact of strategy formulation on organizational performance requires not only financial evaluation criteria but also nonfinancial evaluation criteria—measures of behavior-based effects. In fact, promoting positive behavioral consequences also enables the firm to achieve its financial goals. However, regardless of the profitability of strategic plans, several behavioral effects of strategic management improve the firm's welfare:

1. Strategy formulation activities enhance the firm's ability to prevent problems. Managers who encourage subordinates' attention to planning are aided in their monitoring and forecasting responsibilities by subordinates who are aware of the needs of strategic planning.

2. Group-based strategic decisions are likely to be drawn from the best available alternatives. The strategic management process results in better decisions because group interaction generates a greater variety of strategies and because forecasts based on the specialized perspectives of group members improve the screening of options.

3. The involvement of employees in strategy formulation improves their understanding of the productivity-reward relationship in every strategic plan and, thus, heightens their motivation.

4. Gaps and overlaps in activities among individuals and groups are reduced as participation in strategy formulation clarifies differences in roles.

5. Resistance to change is reduced. Though the participants in strategy formulation may be no more pleased with their own decisions than they would be with authoritarian decisions, their greater awareness of the parameters that limit the available options makes them more likely to accept those decisions.

Risks of Strategic Management

Managers must be trained to guard against three types of unintended negative consequences of involvement in strategy formulation.

First, the time that managers spend on the strategic management process may have a negative impact on operational responsibilities. Managers must be trained to minimize that impact by scheduling their duties to allow the necessary time for strategic activities.

Second, if the formulators of strategy are not intimately involved in its implementation, they may shirk their individual responsibility for the decisions reached. Thus, strategic managers must be trained to limit their promises to performance that the decision makers and their subordinates can deliver.

Third, strategic managers must be trained to anticipate and respond to the disappointment of participating subordinates over unattained expectations. Subordinates may expect their involvement in even minor phases of total strategy formulation to result in both acceptance of their proposals and an increase in their rewards, or they may expect a solicitation of their input on selected issues to extend to other areas of decision making.

Sensitizing managers to these possible negative consequences and preparing them with effective means of minimizing such consequences will greatly enhance the potential of strategic planning.

THE STRATEGIC MANAGEMENT PROCESS

Businesses vary in the processes they use to formulate and direct their strategic management activities. Sophisticated planners, such as General Electric, Procter & Gamble, and IBM, have developed more detailed processes than less formal planners of similar size. Small businesses that rely on the strategy formulation skills and limited time of an entrepreneur typically exhibit more basic planning concerns than those of larger firms in their industries. Understandably, firms with multiple products, markets, or technologies tend to use more complex strategic management systems. However, despite differences in detail and the degree of formalization, the basic components of the models used to analyze strategic management operations are very similar.

Because of the similarity among the general models of the strategic management process, it is possible to develop an eclectic model representative of the foremost thought in the strategic management area. This model is shown in Exhibit 1.6. It serves three major functions: (1) It depicts the sequence and the relationships of the major components of the

EXHIBIT 1.6
Strategic
Management Model

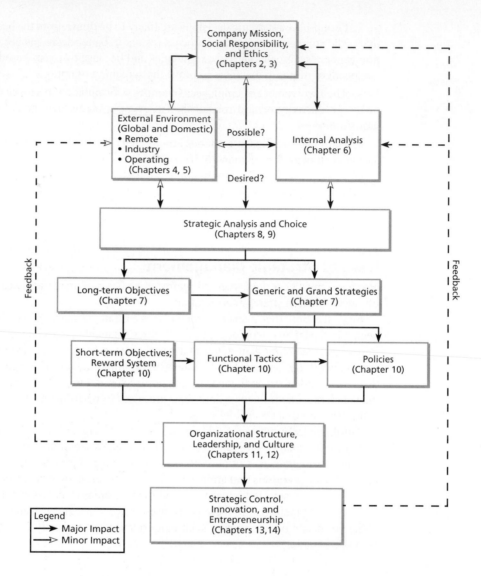

strategic management process. (2) It is the outline for this book. This chapter provides a general overview of the strategic management process, and the major components of the model will be the principal theme of subsequent chapters. Notice that the chapters of the text that discuss each of the strategic management process components are shown in each block. (3) The model offers one approach for analyzing the case studies in this text and thus helps the analyst develop strategy formulation skills.

Components of the Strategic Management Model

This section will define and briefly describe the key components of the strategic management model. Each of these components will receive much greater attention in a later chapter. The intention here is simply to introduce them.

Company Mission

company mission
The unique purpose that sets a company apart from others of its type and identifies the scope of its operations.

The mission of a company is the unique purpose that sets it apart from other companies of its type and identifies the scope of its operations. In short, the **company mission** describes the company's product, market, and technological areas of emphasis in a way that reflects the values and priorities of the strategic decision makers. For example, Lee Kun-Hee, the former chairman of the Samsung Group, revamped the company mission by stamping his own brand of management on Samsung. Immediately, Samsung separated Chonju Paper Manufacturing and Shinsegae Department Store from other operations. This corporate act of downscaling reflected a revised management philosophy that favored specialization, thereby changing the direction and scope of the organization.

Social responsibility is a critical consideration for a company's strategic decision makers because the mission statement must express how the company intends to contribute to the societies that sustain it. A firm needs to set social responsibility aspirations for itself, just as it does in other areas of corporate performance.

Internal Analysis

The company analyzes the quantity and quality of the company's financial, human, and physical resources. It also assesses the strengths and weaknesses of the company's management and organizational structure. Finally, it contrasts the company's past successes and traditional concerns with the company's current capabilities in an attempt to identify the company's future capabilities.

External Environment

A firm's external environment consists of all the conditions and forces that affect its strategic options and define its competitive situation. The strategic management model shows the external environment as three interactive segments: the remote, industry, and operating environments.

Strategic Analysis and Choice

Simultaneous assessment of the external environment and the company profile enables a firm to identify a range of possibly attractive interactive opportunities. These opportunities are *possible* avenues for investment. However, they must be screened through the criterion of the company mission to generate a set of possible and *desired* opportunities. This screening process results in the selection of options from which a *strategic choice* is made. The process is meant to provide the combination of long-term objectives and generic and grand strategies that optimally position the firm in its external environment to achieve the company mission.

Strategic analysis and choice in single or dominant product/service businesses center around identifying strategies that are most effective at building sustainable competitive advantage based on key value chain activities and capabilities—core competencies of the firm. Multibusiness companies find their managers focused on the question of which combination of businesses maximizes shareholder value as the guiding theme during their strategic analysis and choice.

Long-Term Objectives

long-term objectives
The results that an organization seeks to achieve over a multiyear period.

The results that an organization seeks over a multiyear period are its **long-term objectives.** Such objectives typically involve some or all of the following areas: profitability, return on investment, competitive position, technological leadership, productivity, employee relations, public responsibility, and employee development.

Generic and Grand Strategies

generic strategies
Fundamental philosophical options for the design of strategies.

Many businesses explicitly and all implicitly adopt one or more **generic strategies** characterizing their competitive orientation in the marketplace. Low cost, differentiation, or focus strategies define the three fundamental options. Enlightened managers seek to create ways their firm possesses both low cost and differentiation competitive advantages as part of their overall generic strategy. They usually combine these capabilities with a comprehensive, general plan of major actions through which their firm intends to achieve its long-term objectives in a dynamic environment. Called the **grand strategy,** this statement of means indicates how the objectives are to be achieved. Although every grand strategy is, in fact, a unique package of long-term strategies, 15 basic approaches can be identified: concentration, market development, product development, innovation, horizontal integration, vertical integration, joint venture, strategic alliances, consortia, concentric diversification, conglomerate diversification, turnaround, divestiture, bankruptcy, and liquidation.

Each of these grand strategies will be covered in detail in Chapter 7.

Short-Term Objectives

Short-term objectives are the desired results that a company seeks over a period of one year or less. They are logically consistent with the firm's long-term objectives. Companies typically have many **short-term objectives** to provide guidance for their functional and operational activities. Thus, there are short-term marketing activity, raw material usage, employee turnover, and sales objectives, to name just four.

Action Plans

Action plans translate generic and grand strategies into "action" by incorporating four elements. First, they identify specific actions to be undertaken in the next year or less as part of the business's effort to build competitive advantage. Second, they establish a clear time frame for completion of each action. Third, action plans create accountability by identifying who is responsible for each "action" in the plan. Fourth, each "action" has one or more specific, immediate objectives that the action should achieve.

Functional Tactics

Within the general framework created by the business's generic and grand strategies, each business function needs to undertake activities that help build a sustainable competitive advantage. These short-term, limited-scope plans are called **functional tactics.** A radio ad campaign, an inventory reduction, and an introductory loan rate are examples of tactics. Managers in each business function develop tactics that delineate the functional activities undertaken in their part of the business and usually include them as a core part of their action plan. Functional tactics are detailed statements of the "means" or activities that will be used to achieve short-term objectives and establish competitive advantage.

Policies That Empower Action

Speed is a critical necessity for success in today's competitive, global marketplace. One way to enhance speed and responsiveness is to force/allow decisions to be made whenever possible at the lowest level in organizations. **Policies** are broad, precedent-setting decisions that guide or substitute for repetitive or time-sensitive managerial decision making. Creating policies that guide and "preauthorize" the thinking, decisions, and actions of operating managers and their subordinates in implementing the business's strategy is essential for establishing and controlling the ongoing operating process of the firm in a manner consistent with the firm's strategic objectives. Policies often increase managerial effectiveness by standardizing routine decisions and empowering or expanding the discretion of managers and subordinates in implementing business strategies.

The following are examples of the nature and diversity of company policies:

A requirement that managers have purchase requests for items costing more than $5,000 cosigned by the controller.

grand strategies
The means by which objectives are achieved.

short-term objectives
Desired results that provide specific guidance for action during a period of one year or less.

functional tactics
Short-term, narrow scoped plans that detail the "means" or activities that a company will use to achieve short-term objectives.

policies
Predetermined decisions that substitute for managerial discretion in repetitive decision making.

The minimum equity position required for all new McDonald's franchises.

The standard formula used to calculate return on investment for the six strategic business units of General Electric.

A decision that Sears service and repair employees have the right to waive repair charges to appliance customers they feel have been poorly served by their Sears appliance.

Restructuring, Reengineering, and Refocusing the Organization

Until this point in the strategic management process, managers have maintained a decidedly market-oriented focus as they formulate strategies and begin implementation through action plans and functional tactics. Now the process takes an internal focus—getting the work of the business done efficiently and effectively so as to make the strategy successful. What is the best way to organize ourselves to accomplish the mission? Where should leadership come from? What values should guide our daily activities—what should the organization and its people be like? How can we shape rewards to encourage appropriate action? The intense competition in the global marketplace has made this traditionally "internally focused" set of questions—how the activities within their business are conducted—recast themselves with unprecedented attentiveness to the marketplace. *Downsizing, restructuring,* and *reengineering* are terms that reflect the critical stage in strategy implementation wherein managers attempt to recast their organization. The company's structure, leadership, culture, and reward systems may all be changed to ensure cost competitiveness and quality demanded by unique requirements of its strategies.

The elements of the strategic management process are evident in the recent activities at Ford Motor Company. In 2006, Ford undertook to create a strategy to lower costs, increase efficiency, improve designs, and increase brand appeal. These improvements were needed to keep cash flows up to cover rising pension costs. For Ford to accomplish this new strategy it had to improve operations. New executives were brought in to lead product development and financial controls. To break down the bureaucratic boundaries, a committee was created that included employees from the major functional areas, and it was given the assignment to reduce the time needed to develop a new-concept vehicle.

Strategic Control and Continuous Improvement

strategic control
Tracking a strategy as it is being implemented, detecting problems or changes in its underlying premises, and making necessary adjustments.

Strategic control is concerned with tracking a strategy as it is being implemented, detecting problems or changes in its underlying premises, and making necessary adjustments. In contrast to postaction control, strategic control seeks to guide action on behalf of the generic and grand strategies as they are taking place and when the end results are still several years away. The rapid, accelerating change of the global marketplace of the last 10 years has made continuous improvement another aspect of strategic control in many organizations. **Continuous improvement** provides a way for managers to provide a form of strategic control that allows their organization to respond more proactively and timely to rapid developments in hundreds of areas that influence a business's success.

continuous improvement
A form of strategic control in which managers are encouraged to be proactive in improving all operations of the firm.

In 2003, Yahoo!'s strategy was to move into the broadband and Internet search markets. However, even in its early implementation stages the strategy required revisions. Yahoo! had formed an alliance with SBC to provide the broadband service, but SBC had such limited capabilities that Yahoo! had to find new ways to reach users. Yahoo! also needed to continuously improve its new Internet search market, given competitors' upgrades and rapidly rising customer expectations. Additionally, for Yahoo! to increase its market share, it needed to continually improve its branding, rather than rely largely on its technological capabilities.

Strategic Management as a Process

process
The flow of information through interrelated stages of analysis toward the achievement of an aim.

A **process** is the flow of information through interrelated stages of analysis toward the achievement of an aim. Thus, the strategic management model in Exhibit 1.6 depicts a process. In the strategic management process, the flow of information involves historical, current, and forecast data on the operations and environment of the business. Managers evaluate these data in light of the values and priorities of influential individuals and groups—often called **stakeholders**—that are vitally interested in the actions of the business. The interrelated stages of the process are the 11 components discussed in the previous section. Finally, the aim of the process is the formulation and implementation of strategies that work, achieving the company's long-term mission and near-term objectives.

stakeholders
Influential people who are vitally interested in the actions of the business.

Viewing strategic management as a process has several important implications. First, a change in any component will affect several or all of the other components. Most of the arrows in the model point two ways, suggesting that the flow of information usually is reciprocal. For example, forces in the external environment may influence the nature of a company's mission, and the company may in turn affect the external environment and heighten competition in its realm of operation. A specific example is a power company that is persuaded, in part by governmental incentives, to include a commitment to the development of energy alternatives in its mission statement. The company then might promise to extend its research and development (R&D) efforts in the area of coal liquefaction. The external environment has affected the company's mission, and the revised mission signals a competitive condition in the environment.

A second implication of viewing strategic management as a process is that strategy formulation and implementation are sequential. The process begins with development or reevaluation of the company mission. This step is associated with, but essentially followed by, development of a company profile and assessment of the external environment. Then follow, in order, strategic choice, definition of long-term objectives, design of the grand strategy, definition of short-term objectives, design of operating strategies, institutionalization of the strategy, and review and evaluation.

The apparent rigidity of the process, however, must be qualified.

First, a firm's strategic posture may have to be reevaluated in response to changes in any of the principal factors that determine or affect its performance. Entry by a major new competitor, the death of a prominent board member, replacement of the chief executive officer, and a downturn in market responsiveness are among the thousands of changes that can prompt reassessment of a firm's strategic plan. However, no matter where the need for a reassessment originates, the strategic management process begins with the mission statement.

Second, not every component of the strategic management process deserves equal attention each time planning activity takes place. Firms in an extremely stable environment may find that an in-depth assessment is not required every year. Companies often are satisfied with their original mission statements even after a decade of operation and spend only a minimal amount of time addressing this subject.

A third implication of viewing strategic management as a process is the necessity of feedback from institutionalization, review, and evaluation to the early stages of the process. **Feedback** can be defined as the analysis of postimplementation results that can be used to enhance future decision making. Therefore, as indicated in Exhibit 1.6, strategic managers should assess the impact of implemented strategies on external environments. Thus, future planning can reflect any changes precipitated by strategic actions. Strategic managers also should analyze the impact of strategies on the possible need for modifications in the company mission.

feedback
The analysis of postimplementation results that can be used to enhance future decision making.

Strategic Blunder: The Merger of AOL and Time Warner

On February 11, 2000, Internet portal America Online, then valued at $108 billion, swallowed media stalwart Time Warner, worth $111 billion, for $164 billion in an all-stock deal. AOL owned 55 percent of the new, combined company; Time Warner, 45 percent. The tech wreck of 2001, followed by the rise of stiff competitors Yahoo! and Google, changed the competitive dynamics. As cultures clashed and the stock price tanked, the company in 2002 reported a one-time write-off of $99 billion—at the time, the largest corporate loss ever reported. At its nadir, the firm boasted a meager market cap of $48 billion—$171 billion less than at the time of the merger. Time Warner was worth only $53 billion in 2008. Size of Blunder: $196 billion.

Source: Excerpted from Melanie Lindner, "The 10 Biggest Blunders Ever in Business," *Forbes*, March 25, 2008, http://www.msnbc.msn.com/id/23677510/

dynamic
The term that characterizes the constantly changing conditions that affect interrelated and interdependent strategic activities.

A fourth implication of viewing strategic management as a process is the need to regard it as a dynamic system. The term **dynamic** characterizes the constantly changing conditions that affect interrelated and interdependent strategic activities. Managers should recognize that the components of the strategic process are constantly evolving but that formal planning artificially freezes those components, much as an action photograph freezes the movement of a swimmer. Since change is continuous, the dynamic strategic planning process must be monitored constantly for significant shifts in any of its components as a precaution against implementing an obsolete strategy. An example of the potentially devastating consequences of such dynamism is seen in the failure of the merger between AOL and Time Warner, as described in Exhibit 1.7, Strategy in Action.

Changes in the Process

The strategic management process undergoes continual assessment and subtle updating. Although the elements of the basic strategic management model rarely change, the relative emphasis that each element receives will vary with the decision makers who use the model and with the environments of their companies.

A recent study describes general trends in strategic management, summarizing the responses of more than 200 corporate executives. This update shows there has been an increasing companywide emphasis on and appreciation for the value of strategic management activities. It also provides evidence that practicing managers have given increasing attention to the need for frequent and widespread involvement in the formulation and implementation phases of the strategic management process. Finally, it indicates that, as managers and their firms gain knowledge, experience, skill, and understanding in how to design and manage their planning activities, they become better able to avoid the potential negative consequences of instituting a vigorous strategic management process.

Summary

Strategic management is the set of decisions and actions that result in the formulation and implementation of plans designed to achieve a company's objectives. Because it involves long-term, future-oriented, complex decision making and requires considerable resources, top-management participation is essential.

Strategic management is a three-tier process involving corporate-, business-, and functional-level planners, and support personnel. At each progressively lower level, strategic activities were shown to be more specific, narrow, short-term, and action oriented, with lower risks but fewer opportunities for dramatic impact.

The strategic management model presented in this chapter will serve as the structure for understanding and integrating all the major phases of strategy formulation and implementation. The chapter provided a summary account of these phases, each of which is given extensive individual attention in subsequent chapters.

The chapter stressed that the strategic management process centers on the belief that a firm's mission can be best achieved through a systematic and comprehensive assessment of both its internal capabilities and its external environment. Subsequent evaluation of the firm's opportunities leads, in turn, to the choice of long-term objectives and grand strategies and, ultimately, to annual objectives and operating strategies, which must be implemented, monitored, and controlled.

Key Terms

adaptive mode, *p. 8*
company mission, *p. 12*
continuous improvement, *p. 15*
dynamic, *p. 17*
entrepreneurial mode, *p. 8*
feedback, *p. 16*
formality, *p. 8*

functional tactics, *p. 14*
generic strategies, *p. 13*
grand strategies, *p. 14*
long-term objectives, *p. 13*
planning mode, *p. 8*
policies, *p. 14*
process, *p. 16*

short-term objectives, *p. 14*
stakeholders, *p. 16*
strategic control, *p. 15*
strategic management, *p. 3*
strategy, *p. 4*

Questions for Discussion

1. Read an article in the business press about a major action taken by a corporation. Be prepared to briefly describe this action to your professor and to name the key strategic management terms that the author used in the article.
2. In what ways do you think the subject matter in this strategic management–business policy course will differ from that of previous courses you have taken?
3. After graduation, you are not likely to move directly to a top-level management position. In fact, few members of your class will ever reach the top-management level. Why, then, is it important for all business majors to study the field of strategic management?
4. Do you expect outstanding performance in this course to require a great deal of memorization? Why or why not?
5. You undoubtedly have read about individuals who seemingly have given singled-handed direction to their corporations. Is a participative strategic management approach likely to stifle or suppress the contributions of such individuals?
6. Think about the courses you have taken in functional areas, such as marketing, finance, production, personnel, and accounting. What is the importance of each of these areas to the strategic planning process?
7. Discuss with practicing business managers the strategic management models used in their firms. What are the similarities and differences between these models and the one in the text?
8. In what ways do you believe the strategic planning approach of not-for-profit organizations would differ from that of profit-oriented organizations?
9. How do you explain the success of firms that do not use a formal strategic planning process?
10. Think about your postgraduation job search as a strategic decision. How would the strategic management model be helpful to you in identifying and securing the most promising position?

Part **Two**

Strategy Formulation

Strategy formulation guides executives in defining the business their firm is in, the ends it seeks, and the means it will use to accomplish those ends. The approach of strategy formulation is an improvement over that of traditional long-range planning. As discussed in the next eight chapters—about developing a firm's competitive plan of action—strategy formulation combines a future-oriented perspective with concern for the firm's internal and external environments.

The strategy formulation process begins with definition of the company mission, as discussed in Chapter 2. In this chapter, the purpose of business is defined to reflect the values of a wide variety of interested parties. In Chapter 3 social responsibility is discussed as a critical consideration for a company's strategic decision makers because the mission statement must express how the company intends to contribute to the societies that sustain it. Central to the idea that companies should be operated in socially responsible ways is the belief that managers will behave in an ethical manner. Management ethics are discussed in this chapter with special attention to the utilitarian, moral rights, and social justice approaches.

Chapter 4 deals with the principal factors in a firm's external environment that strategic managers must assess so they can anticipate and take advantage of future business conditions. It emphasizes the importance to a firm's planning activities of factors in the firm's remote, industry, and operating environments.

Chapter 5 describes the key differences in strategic planning among domestic, multinational, and global firms. It gives special attention to the new vision that a firm must communicate when it multinationalizes.

Chapter 6 shows how firms evaluate their company's strengths and weaknesses to produce an internal analysis. Strategic managers use such profiles to target competitive advantages they can emphasize and competitive disadvantages they should correct or minimize.

Chapter 7 examines the types of long-range objectives strategic managers set and specifies the qualities these objectives must have to provide a basis for direction and evaluation. The chapter also examines the generic and grand strategies that firms use to achieve long-range objectives.

Comprehensive approaches to the evaluation of strategic opportunities and to the final strategic decision are the focus of Chapter 8. The chapter shows how a firm's strategic options can be compared in a way that allows selection of the best available option. It also discusses how a company can create competitive advantages for each of its businesses.

Chapter 9 extends the attention on strategic analysis and choice by showing how managers can build value in multibusiness companies.

Chapter **Two**

Company Mission

After reading and studying this chapter, you should be able to

1. Describe a company mission and explain its value.

2. Explain why it is important for the mission statement to include the company's basic product or service, its primary markets, and its principal technology.

3. Explain which goal of a company is most important: survival, profitability, or growth.

4. Discuss the importance of company philosophy, public image, and company self-concept to stockholders.

5. Give examples of the newest trends in mission statement components: customer emphasis, quality, and company vision.

6. Describe the role of a company's board of directors.

7. Explain agency theory and its value in helping a board of directors improve corporate governance.

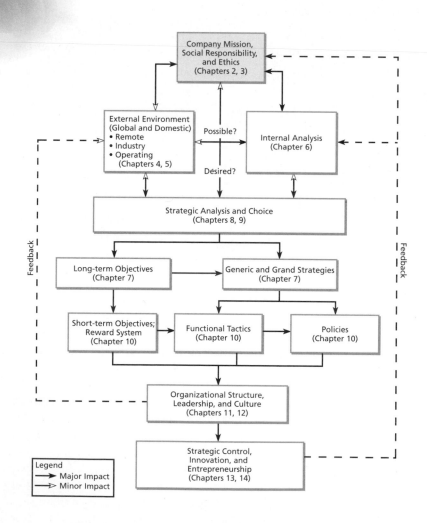

Mission Statement of Nicor Inc.

PREAMBLE

We, the management of Nicor Inc., here set forth our belief as to the purpose for which the company is established and the principles under which it should operate. We pledge our effort to the accomplishment of these purposes within these principles.

BASIC PURPOSE

The basic purpose of Nicor Inc. is to perpetuate an investor-owned company engaging in various phases of the energy business, striving for balance among those phases so as to render needed satisfactory products and services and earn optimum, long-range profits.

WHAT WE DO

The principal business of the company, through its utility subsidiary, is the provision of energy through a pipe system to meet the needs of ultimate consumers. To accomplish its basic purpose, and to ensure its strength, the company will engage in other energy-related activities, directly or through subsidiaries or in participation with other persons, corporations, firms, or entities.

All activities of the company shall be consistent with its responsibilities to investors, customers, employees, and the public and its concern for the optimum development and utilization of natural resources and for environmental needs.

WHERE WE DO IT

The company's operations shall be primarily in the United States, but no self-imposed or regulatory geographical limitations are placed upon the acquisition, development, processing, transportation, or storage of energy resources, or upon other energy-related ventures in which the company may engage. The company will engage in such activities in any location where, after careful review, it has determined that such activity is in the best interest of its stockholders.

Utility service will be offered in the territory of the company's utility subsidiary to the best of its ability, in accordance with the requirements of regulatory agencies and pursuant to the subsidiary's purposes and principles.

Source: Nicor Inc., http://www.nicor.com/

WHAT IS A COMPANY MISSION?

company mission
The unique purpose that sets a company apart from others of its type and identifies the scope of its operations in product, market, and technology terms.

Whether a firm is developing a new business or reformulating direction for an ongoing business, it must determine the basic goals and philosophies that will shape its strategic posture. This fundamental purpose that sets a firm apart from other firms of its type and identifies the scope of its operations in product and market terms is defined as the company mission. As discussed in Chapter 1, the **company mission** is a broadly framed but enduring statement of a firm's intent. It embodies the business philosophy of the firm's strategic decision makers, implies the image the firm seeks to project, reflects the firm's self-concept, and indicates the firm's principal product or service areas and the primary customer needs the firm will attempt to satisfy. In short, it describes the firm's product, market, and technological areas of emphasis, and it does so in a way that reflects the values and priorities of the firm's strategic decision makers. An excellent example is the company mission statement of Nicor Inc., shown in Exhibit 2.1, Strategy in Action.

The Need for an Explicit Mission

No external body requires that the company mission be defined, and the process of defining it is time-consuming and tedious. Moreover, it contains broadly outlined or implied objectives and strategies rather than specific directives. Characteristically, it is a statement, not of measurable targets but of attitude, outlook, and orientation.

The mission statement is a message designed to be inclusive of the expectations of all stakeholders for the company's performance over the long run. The executives and board who prepare the mission statement attempt to provide a unifying purpose for the company that will provide a basis for strategic objective setting and decision making. In general terms, the mission statement addresses the following questions:

Why is this firm in business?

What are our economic goals?

What is our operating philosophy in terms of quality, company image, and self-concept?

What are our core competencies and competitive advantages?

What customers do and can we serve?

How do we view our responsibilities to stockholders, employees, communities, environment, social issues, and competitors?

FORMULATING A MISSION

The process of defining the company mission for a specific business can perhaps be best understood by thinking about the business at its inception. The typical business begins with the beliefs, desires, and aspirations of a single entrepreneur. Such an owner-manager's sense of mission usually is based on the following fundamental beliefs:

1. The product or service of the business can provide benefits at least equal to its price.

2. The product or service can satisfy a customer need of specific market segments that is currently not being met adequately.

3. The technology that is to be used in production will provide a cost- and quality-competitive product or service.

4. With hard work and the support of others, the business can not only survive but also grow and be profitable.

5. The management philosophy of the business will result in a favorable public image and will provide financial and psychological rewards for those who are willing to invest their labor and money in helping the business to succeed.

6. The entrepreneur's self-concept of the business can be communicated to and adopted by employees and stockholders.

As the business grows or is forced by competitive pressures to alter its product, market, or technology, redefining the company mission may be necessary. If so, the revised mission statement will contain the same components as the original. It will state the basic type of product or service to be offered, the primary markets or customer groups to be served; the technology to be used in production or delivery; the firm's fundamental concern for survival through growth and profitability; the firm's managerial philosophy; the public image the firm seeks; and the self-concept those affiliated with the firm should have of it. This chapter will discuss in detail these components. The examples shown in Exhibit 2.2, Strategy in Action, provide insights into how some major corporations handle them.

Basic Product or Service; Primary Market; Principal Technology

Three indispensable components of the mission statement are specification of the basic product or service, specification of the primary market, and specification of the principal technology for production or delivery. These components are discussed under one heading because only in combination do they describe the company's business activity. A good example of the three components is to be found in the business plan of ITT Barton,

Identifying Mission Statement Components: A Compilation of Excerpts from Actual Corporate Mission Statements

1. Customer-market	We believe our first responsibility is to the doctors, nurses, and patients, to mothers and all others who use our products and services. (Johnson & Johnson)
	To anticipate and meet market needs of farmers, ranchers, and rural communities within North America. (CENEX)
2. Product-service	AMAX's principal products are molybdenum, coal, iron ore, copper, lead, zinc, petroleum and natural gas, potash, phosphates, nickel, tungsten, silver, gold, and magnesium. (AMAX)
3. Geographic domain	We are dedicated to total success of Corning Glass Works as a worldwide competitor. (Corning Glass)
4. Technology	Control Data is in the business of applying microelectronics and computer technology in two general areas: computer-related hardware and computing-enhancing services, which include computation, information, education, and finance. (Control Data)
	The common technology in these areas relates to discrete particle coatings. (NASHUA)
5. Concern for survival	In this respect, the company will conduct its operation prudently, and will provide the profits and growth which will assure Hoover's ultimate success. (Hoover Universal)
6. Philosophy	We are committed to improve health care throughout the world. (Baxter Travenol)
	We believe human development to be the worthiest of the goals of civilization and independence to be the superior condition for nurturing growth in the capabilities of people. (Sun Company)
7. Self-concept	Hoover Universal is a diversified, multi-industry corporation with strong manufacturing capabilities, entrepreneurial policies, and individual business unit autonomy. (Hoover Universal)
8. Concern for public image	We are responsible to the communities in which we live and work and to the world community as well. (Johnson & Johnson)
	Also, we must be responsive to the broader concerns of the public, including especially the general desire for improvement in the quality of life, equal opportunity for all, and the constructive use of natural resources. (Sun Company)

a division of ITT. Under the heading of business mission and area served, the following information is presented:

The unit's mission is to serve industry and government with quality instruments used for the primary measurement, analysis, and local control of fluid flow, level, pressure, temperature, and fluid properties. This instrumentation includes flow meters, electronic readouts, indicators, recorders, switches, liquid level systems, analytical instruments such as titrators, integrators, controllers, transmitters, and various instruments for the measurement of fluid properties (density, viscosity, gravity) used for processing variable sensing, data collecting, control, and transmission. The unit's mission includes fundamental loop-closing control and display devices, when economically justified, but excludes broadline central control room instrumentation, systems design, and turnkey responsibility.

Markets served include instrumentation for oil and gas production, gas transportation, chemical and petrochemical processing, cryogenics, power generation, aerospace, government, and marine, as well as other instrument and equipment manufacturers.

In only 129 words, this segment of the mission statement clearly indicates to all readers—from company employees to casual observers—the basic products, primary markets, and principal technologies of ITT Barton.

Often the most referenced public statement of a company's selected products and markets appears in "silver bullet" form in the mission statement; for example, "Dayton-Hudson Corporation is a diversified retailing company whose business is to serve the American consumer through the retailing of fashion-oriented quality merchandise." Such an abstract of company direction is particularly helpful to outsiders who value condensed overviews.

Company Goals: Survival; Growth; Profitability

Three economic goals guide the strategic direction of almost every business organization. Whether or not the mission statement explicitly states these goals, it reflects the firm's intention to secure *survival* through *growth* and *profitability*.

A firm that is unable to survive will be incapable of satisfying the aims of any of its stakeholders. Unfortunately, the goal of survival, like the goals of growth and profitability, often is taken for granted to such an extent that it is neglected as a principal criterion in strategic decision making. When this happens, the firm may focus on short-term aims at the expense of the long run. Concerns for expediency, a quick fix, or a bargain may displace the assessment of long-term impact. Too often, the result is near-term economic failure owing to a lack of resource synergy and sound business practice. For example, Consolidated Foods, maker of Shasta soft drinks and L'eggs hosiery, sought growth through the acquisition of bargain businesses. However, the erratic sales patterns of its diverse holdings forced it to divest itself of more than four dozen companies. This process cost Consolidated Foods millions of dollars and hampered its growth.

Profitability is the mainstay goal of a business organization. No matter how profit is measured or defined, profit over the long term is the clearest indication of a firm's ability to satisfy the principal claims and desires of employees and stockholders. The key phrase here is "over the long term." Obviously, basing decisions on a short-term concern for profitability would lead to a strategic myopia. Overlooking the enduring concerns of customers, suppliers, creditors, ecologists, and regulatory agents may produce profit in the short term, but, over time, the financial consequences are likely to be detrimental.

The following excerpt from the Hewlett-Packard statement of mission ably expresses the importance of an orientation toward long-term profit:

> To achieve sufficient profit to finance our company growth and to provide the resources we need to achieve our other corporate objectives.
>
> In our economic system, the profit we generate from our operation is the ultimate source of the funds we need to prosper and grow. It is the one absolutely essential measure of our corporate performance over the long term. Only if we continue to meet our profit objective can we achieve our other corporate objectives.

A firm's growth is tied inextricably to its survival and profitability. In this context, the meaning of growth must be broadly defined. Although product impact market studies (PIMS) have shown that growth in market share is correlated with profitability, other important forms of growth do exist. Growth in the number of markets served, in the variety of products offered, and in the technologies that are used to provide goods or services frequently lead to improvements in a firm's competitive ability. Growth means change, and proactive change is essential in a dynamic business environment.

AOL's strategy provides an example. In 2003, some analysts believed that AOL Time Warner should change to a survival strategy because of the amount of debt that it was carrying. They believed that AOL should try to reduce debt and regain some market share that it had lost over the previous year. AOL did decide to reduce its $7 billion debt by the end of 2004, but not simply to survive. AOL was trying to position itself for the acquisition of either Adelphia or Cablevision. AOL felt that if it could acquire one of these two companies or possibly both, it could increase its footprint in the market. AOL believed that growth for its company would have to come from the cable TV market and that the only way to grow was to serve more markets. Luckily, AOL's top competitor, Comcast, was in the same debt position as AOL and could not immediately preempt the acquisitions.

Hewlett-Packard's mission statement provides another excellent example of corporate regard for growth:

> Objective: To let our growth be limited only by our profits and our ability to develop and produce technical products that satisfy real customer needs.
>
> We do not believe that large size is important for its own sake; however, for at least two basic reasons, continuous growth is essential for us to achieve our other objectives.
>
> In the first place, we serve a rapidly growing and expanding segment of our technological society. To remain static would be to lose ground. We cannot maintain a position of strength and leadership in our field without growth.
>
> In the second place, growth is important in order to attract and hold high-caliber people. These individuals will align their future only with a company that offers them considerable opportunity for personal progress. Opportunities are greater and more challenging in a growing company.

The issue of growth raises a concern about the definition of the company mission. How can a firm's product, market, and technology be specified sufficiently to provide direction without precluding the exercise of unanticipated strategic options? How can a firm so define its mission that it can consider opportunistic diversification while maintaining the parameters that guide its growth decision? Perhaps such questions are best addressed when a firm's mission statement outlines the conditions under which the firm might depart from ongoing operations. General Electric Company's extensive global mission provided the foundation for its GE Appliances (GEA) in Louisville, Kentucky. GEA did not see consumer preferences in the world market becoming Americanized. Instead, its expansion goals allowed for flexibility in examining the unique characteristics of individual foreign markets and tailoring strategies to fit them.

The growth philosophy of Dayton-Hudson also embodies this approach:

> The stability and quality of the corporation's financial performance will be developed through the profitable execution of our existing businesses, as well as through the acquisition or development of new businesses. Our growth priorities, in order, are as follows:
>
> 1. Development of the profitable market preeminence of existing companies in existing markets through new store development or new strategies within existing stores.
> 2. Expansion of our companies to feasible new markets.
> 3. Acquisition of other retailing companies that are strategically and financially compatible with Dayton-Hudson.
> 4. Internal development of new retailing strategies.

Capital allocations to fund the expansion of existing Dayton-Hudson operating companies will be based on each company's return on investment (ROI), in relationship to its ROI objective and its consistency in earnings growth and on the ability of its management to perform up to the forecasts contained in its capital requests. Expansion via acquisition or new venture will occur when the opportunity promises an acceptable rate of long-term growth and profitability, an acceptable degree of risk, and compatibility with Dayton-Hudson's long-term strategy.

Company Philosophy

company creed
A company's statement of its philosophy.

The statement of a company's philosophy, often called the **company creed,** usually accompanies or appears within the mission statement. It reflects or specifies the basic beliefs, values, aspirations, and philosophical priorities to which strategic decision makers are committed in managing the company. Fortunately, the philosophies vary little from one firm to another. Owners and managers implicitly accept a general, unwritten, yet pervasive code of behavior

Saturn's Statement of Philosophy

We, the Saturn Team, in concert with the UAW and General Motors, believe that meeting the needs of customers, Saturn members, suppliers, dealers, and neighbors is fundamental to fulfilling our mission.

To meet our customer's needs . . .

- our products and services must be world leaders in value and satisfaction.

To meet our members' needs, we . . .

- will create a sense of belonging in an environment of mutual trust, respect, and dignity;
- believe that all people want to be involved in decisions that affect them, care about their jobs and each other, take pride in themselves and in their contributions, and want to share in the success of their efforts;
- will develop the tools, training, and education for each member, recognizing individual skills and knowledge;

- believe that creative, motivated, responsible team members who understand that change is critical to success are Saturn's most important asset.

To meet our suppliers' and dealers' needs, we . . .

- will strive to create real partnerships with them;
- will be open and fair in our dealings, reflecting trust, respect, and their importance to Saturn;
- want dealers and suppliers to feel ownerships in Saturn's mission and philosophy as their own.

To meet the needs of our neighbors, the communities in which we live and operate, we . . .

- will be good citizens, protect the environment, and conserve natural resources;
- will seek to cooperate with government at all levels and strive to be sensitive, open, and candid in all our public statements.

Source: Saturn Corp., http://www.saturn.com

that governs business actions and permits them to be largely self-regulated. Unfortunately, statements of company philosophy are often so similar and so platitudinous that they read more like public relations handouts than the commitment to values they are meant to be.

Saturn's statement of philosophy, presented in Exhibit 2.3, Strategy in Action, indicates the company's clearly defined initiatives for satisfying the needs of its customers, employees, suppliers, and dealers.

Despite the similarity of these statements, the intentions of the strategic managers in developing them do not warrant cynicism. Company executives attempt to provide a distinctive and accurate picture of the firm's managerial outlook. One such statement of company philosophy is that of AIM Private Asset Management, Inc. As Exhibit 2.4, Strategy in Action, shows, AIM's board of directors and executives have established especially clear directions for company decision making and action based on growth.

As seen in Exhibit 2.5, Global Strategy in Action, the philosophy of Nissan Motor Manufacturing is expressed by the company's People Principles and Key Corporate Principles. These principles form the basis of the way the company operates on a daily basis. They address the principal concepts used in meeting the company's established goals. Nissan focuses on the distinction between the role of the individual and the corporation. In this way, employees can link their productivity and success to the productivity and success of the company. Given these principles, the company is able to concentrate on the issues most important to its survival, growth, and profitability.

Exhibit 2.6, Strategy in Action, provides an example of how General Motors uses a statement of company philosophy to clarify its environmental principles.

Ronald A. Williams has led a multipronged strategy as CEO at Aetna since 2001 to provide affordable health care to the masses—the foundation of his company's mission. The

Growth Philosophy at AIM Private Asset Management Inc.

AIM's growth philosophy focuses on earnings—a tangible measure of a company's growth. Because stock prices can gyrate widely on rumors, we use earnings to weed out "high-flying" speculative stocks.

In selecting investments, we look for:

- Quality earnings growth—because we believe earnings drive stock prices.
- Positive earnings momentum—stocks with greater positive momentum will rise above the crowd.

Our growth philosophy adheres to four basic rules:

- Remain fully invested.
- Focus on individual companies rather than industries, sectors or countries.
- Strive to find the best earnings growth.
- Maintain a strong sell discipline.

Why growth philosophy?

- Investment decisions are based on facts, not guesses or big-picture economic forecasts.
- Earnings—not emotions—dictate when we should buy and sell.
- AIM's investment managers have followed the same earnings-driven philosophy for decades.
- This approach has proven itself in domestic and foreign markets.

Source: AIM Private Asset Management Inc., http://sma.aiminvestments.com/

components of his strategy include physician transparency acquisitions and communication among patients, employers, public officials and the health care industry, as is explained in Exhibit 2.7, Top Strategist.

Public Image

Both present and potential customers attribute certain qualities to particular businesses. Gerber and Johnson & Johnson make safe products; Cross Pen makes high-quality writing instruments; Étienne Aigner makes stylish but affordable leather products; Corvettes are power machines; and Izod Lacoste stands for the preppy look. Thus, mission statements should reflect the public's expectations, because this makes achievement of the firm's goals more likely. Gerber's mission statement should not open the possibility for diversification into pesticides, and Cross Pen's should not open the possibility for diversification into $0.59 brand-name disposables.

On the other hand, a negative public image often prompts firms to reemphasize the beneficial aspects of their mission. For example, in response to what it saw as a disturbing trend in public opinion, Dow Chemical undertook an aggressive promotional campaign to fortify its credibility, particularly among "employees and those who live and work in [their] plant communities." Dow described its approach in its annual report:

> All around the world today, Dow people are speaking up. People who care deeply about their company, what it stands for, and how it is viewed by others. People who are immensely proud of their company's performance, yet realistic enough to realize it is the public's perception of that performance that counts in the long run.

Firms seldom address the question of their public image in an intermittent fashion. Although public agitation often stimulates greater attention to this question, firms are concerned about their public image even in the absence of such agitation. The following excerpt from the mission statement of Intel Corporation is an example of this attitude:

> We are sensitive to our *image with our customers and the business community*. Commitments to customers are considered sacred, and we are upset with ourselves when we do not meet

Principles of Nissan Motor Manufacturing (UK) Ltd.

	People Principles **(All other objectives can only be achieved by people)**
Selection	Hire the highest caliber people; look for technical capabilities and emphasize attitude.
Responsibility	Maximize the responsibility; staff by devolving decision making.
Teamwork	Recognize and encourage individual contributions, with everyone working toward the same objectives.
Flexibility	Expand the role of the individual: multiskilled, no job description, generic job titles.
Kaizen	Continuously seek 100.1 percent improvements; give "ownership of change."
Communications	"Every day, face to face."
Training	Establish individual "continuous development programs."
Supervisors	Regard as "the professionals at managing the production process"; give them much responsibility normally assumed by individual departments; make them the genuine leaders of their teams.
Single status	Treat everyone as a "first class" citizen; eliminate all illogical differences.
Trade unionism	Establish single union agreement with AEU emphasizing the common objective for a successful enterprise.
	Key Corporate Principles
Quality	Building profitably the highest quality car sold in Europe.
Customer	Achieve target of no. 1 customer satisfaction in Europe.
Volume	Always achieve required volume.
New products	Deliver on time, at required quality, within cost.
Suppliers	Establish long-term relationship with single-source suppliers; aim for zero defects and just-in-time delivery; apply Nissan principles to suppliers.
Production	Use "most appropriate" technology; develop predictable "best method" of doing job; build in quality.
Engineering	Design "quality" and "ease of working" into the product and facilities; establish "simultaneous engineering" to reduce development time.

Source: Nissan Motor Co. Ltd., http://www.nissanmotors.com/

our commitments. We strive to demonstrate to the business world on a continuing basis that we are credible in describing the state of the corporation, and that we are well organized and in complete control of all things that determine the numbers.

Exhibit 2.8, Strategy in Action, presents a marketing translation of the essence of the mission statements of six high-end shoe companies. The impressive feature of the exhibit is that it shows dramatically how closely competing firms can incorporate subtle, yet meaningful, differences into their mission statements.

Company Self-Concept

A major determinant of a firm's success is the extent to which the firm can relate functionally to its external environment. To achieve its proper place in a competitive situation, the firm realistically must evaluate its competitive strengths and weaknesses. This idea—that

General Motors Environmental Principles

As a responsible corporate citizen, General Motors is dedicated to protecting human health, natural resources, and the global environment. This dedication reaches further than compliance with the law to encompass the integration of sound environmental practices into our business decisions.

The following environmental principles provide guidance to General Motors personnel worldwide in the conduct of their daily business practices:

1. We are committed to actions to restore and preserve the environment.

2. We are committed to reducing waste and pollutants, conserving resources, and recycling materials at every stage of the product life cycle.

3. We will continue to participate actively in educating the public regarding environmental conservation.

4. We will continue to pursue vigorously the development and implementation of technologies for minimizing pollutant emissions.

5. We will continue to work with all governmental entities for the development of technically sound and financially responsible environmental laws and regulations.

6. We will continually assess the impact of our plants and products on the environment and the communities in which we live and operate with a goal of continuous improvement.

Source: General Motors Corporation, http://www.gm.com/

---

the firm must know itself—is the essence of the company self-concept. The idea is not commonly integrated into theories of strategic management; its importance for individuals has been recognized since ancient times.

Both individuals and firms have a crucial need to know themselves. The ability of either to survive in a dynamic and highly competitive environment would be severely limited if they did not understand their impact on others or of others on them.

In some senses, then, firms take on personalities of their own. Much behavior in firms is organizationally based; that is, a firm acts on its members in other ways than their individual interactions. Thus, firms are entities whose personality transcends the personalities of their members. As such, they can set decision-making parameters based on aims different and distinct from the aims of their members. These organizational considerations have pervasive effects.

Ordinarily, descriptions of the company self-concept per se do not appear in mission statements. Yet such statements often provide strong impressions of the company self-concept. For example, ARCO's environment, health, and safety (EHS) managers were adamant about emphasizing the company's position on safety and environmental performance as a part of the mission statement. The challenges facing the ARCO EHS managers included dealing with concerned environmental groups and a public that has become environmentally aware. They hoped to motivate employees toward safer behavior while reducing emissions and waste. They saw this as a reflection of the company's positive self-image.

The following excerpts from the Intel Corporation mission statement describe the corporate persona that its top management seeks to foster:

Management is self-critical. The leaders must be capable of recognizing and accepting their mistakes and learning from them.

Open (constructive) confrontation is encouraged at all levels of the corporation and is viewed as a method of problem solving and conflict resolution.

Decision by consensus is the rule. Decisions once made are supported. Position in the organization is not the basis for quality of ideas.

A highly communicative, open management is part of the style.

Top Strategist
CEO Ronald A. Williams Leads to Fulfill Aetna's Mission

Exhibit
2.7

Ronald A. Williams joined Aetna in 2001 as chief of health operations and helped build the HealthFund network. The consumer-directed program consists of employer-funded health savings accounts; pretax employee-funded flexible spending accounts; and Aetna Navigator, where members can track expenditures. Williams's success in implementing this program catapulted his career, enabling him to oversee more initiatives in pursuit of the company's mission.

As president of Aetna, Williams guided his team to create Aexcel in 2003. Aexcel outlined physicians' effective care delivery and was crafted after obtaining feedback from various stakeholders and anonymous physician reviewers. The program was expanded to include physician-specific costs, clinical quality, and cost comparisons among hospitals, surgical centers, and free-standing health providers.

Williams's transition to CEO led him to use corporate acquisitions as a primary strategic tool. In August 2007, Aetna acquired Schaller Anderson, a health care management services company that specialized in Medicaid offerings. In October 2007, Aetna acquired Goodhealth Worldwide to provide expanded services to U.S. citizens working outside the country.

Company growth and member expansion bolstered Williams's health care reform agenda. He presented ideas for future expansion to the U.S. Senate in 2008, and outlined how to provide health care to more people. He stated, "Fundamentally it is about having a society in which everyone really has access to high-quality health care services."*

As an example of Aetna's commitment to its mission, Williams has, at critical times, temporarily lifted medical and pharmacy policy requirements for victims of natural disasters and relief workers who aid these victims. These victims and workers can obtain prescription refills without the normal 30-day restriction and are covered for doctor visits that are outside their network without referrals. This modification of Aetna policies has helped those exposed to hurricanes Katrina, Dolly, Rita, Wilma, Ike, and Gustav and to Southern California wildfires.

Sources: Aetna Mission & Values, http://www.aetna.com/about/aetna/ms/
*C. Freeland, "View from the Top," *Financial Times*, September 12, 2008, p. 10.

Management must be ethical. Managing by telling the truth and treating all employees equitably has established credibility that is ethical.

We strive to provide an opportunity for rapid development.

Intel is a results-oriented company. The focus is on substance versus form, quality versus quantity.

We believe in the principle that hard work, high productivity is something to be proud of.

The concept of assumed responsibility is accepted. (If a task needs to be done, assume you have the responsibility to get it done.)

Commitments are long term. If career problems occur at some point, reassignment is a better alternative than termination.

We desire to have all employees involved and participative in their relationship with Intel.

Newest Trends in Mission Components

Three issues have become so prominent in the strategic planning for organizations that they are now integral parts in the development and revisions of mission statements: sensitivity to consumer wants, concern for quality, and statements of company vision.

Mission Statements for the High-End Shoe Industry

ALLEN-EDMONDS

Allen-Edmonds provides high-quality shoes for the affluent consumer who appreciates a well-made, finely crafted, stylish dress shoe.

BALLY

Bally shoes set you apart. They are the perfect shoe to complement your lifestyle. Bally shoes project an image of European style and elegance that ensures one is not just dressed, but well dressed.

BOSTONIAN

Bostonian shoes are for those successful individuals who are well-traveled, on the "go" and want a stylish dress shoe that can keep up with their variety of needs and activities. With Bostonian, you know you will always be well dressed whatever the situation.

COLE-HAHN

Cole-Hahn offers a line of contemporary shoes for the man who wants to go his own way. They are shoes for the urban, upscale, stylish man who wants to project an image of being one step ahead.

FLORSHEIM

Florsheim shoes are the affordable classic men's dress shoes for those who want to experience the comfort and style of a solid dress shoe.

JOHNSTON & MURPHY

Johnston & Murphy is the quintessential business shoe for those affluent individuals who know and demand the best.

Source: "Thinking on Your Feet, the Johnston & Murphy Guerrilla Marketing Competition" (Johnston & Murphy, a GENESCO Company).

Customers

"The customer is our top priority" is a slogan that would be claimed by the majority of businesses in the United States and abroad. For companies including Caterpillar Tractor, General Electric, and Johnson & Johnson this means analyzing consumer needs before as well as after a sale. The bonus plan at Xerox allows for a 40 percent annual bonus, based on high customer reviews of the service that they receive, and a 20 percent penalty if the feedback is especially bad. For these firms and many others, the overriding concern for the company has become consumer satisfaction.

In addition many U.S. firms maintain extensive product safety programs to help ensure consumer satisfaction. GE, Sears, and 3M boast of such programs. Other firms including Calgon Corporation, Amoco, Mobil Oil, Whirlpool, and Zenith provide toll-free telephone lines to answer customer concerns and complaints.

The focus on customer satisfaction is demonstrated by retailer JCPenney in this excerpt from its statement of philosophy: "The Penney Idea is (1) To serve the public as nearly as we can to its complete satisfaction; (2) To expect for the service we render a fair remuneration, and not all the profit the traffic will bear; (3) To do all in our power to pack the customer's dollar full of value, quality, and satisfaction."

A focus on customer satisfaction causes managers to realize the importance of providing quality customer service. Strong customer service initiatives have led some firms to gain competitive advantages in the marketplace. Hence, many corporations have made the customer service initiative a key component of their corporate mission.

Quality

"Quality is job one!" is a rallying point not only for Ford Motor Corporation but for many resurging U.S. businesses as well. Two U.S. management experts fostered a worldwide emphasis on quality in manufacturing. W. Edwards Deming and J. M. Juran's messages were first embraced by Japanese managers, whose quality consciousness led to global dominance in several industries including automobile, TV, audio equipment, and electronic

Visions of Quality

CADILLAC

The Mission of the Cadillac Motor Company is to engineer, produce, and market the world's finest automobiles known for uncompromised levels of distinctiveness, comfort, convenience, and refined performance. Through its people, who are its strength, Cadillac will continuously improve the quality of its products and services to meet or exceed customer expectations and succeed as a profitable business.

MOTOROLA

Dedication to quality is a way of life at our company, so much so that it goes far beyond rhetorical slogans. Our ongoing program is one of continued improvement reaches out for change, refinement, and even revolution in our pursuit of quality excellence.

It is the objective of Motorola Inc. to produce and provide products and services of the highest quality. In its activities, Motorola will pursue goals aimed at the achievement of quality excellence. These results will be derived from the dedicated efforts of each employee in conjunction with supportive participation from management at all levels of the corporation.

ZYTEC

Zytec is a company that competes on value; is market driven; provides superior quality and service; builds strong relationship with its customers; and provides technical excellence in its products.

components manufacturing. Deming summarizes his approach in 14 now well-known points:

1. Create constancy of purpose.
2. Adopt the new philosophy.
3. Cease dependence on mass inspection to achieve quality.
4. End the practice of awarding business on price tag alone. Instead, minimize total cost, often accomplished by working with a single supplier.
5. Improve constantly the system of production and service.
6. Institute training on the job.
7. Institute leadership.
8. Drive out fear.
9. Break down barriers between departments.
10. Eliminate slogans, exhortations, and numerical targets.
11. Eliminate work standards (quotas) and management by objective.
12. Remove barriers that rob workers, engineers, and managers of their right to pride of workmanship.
13. Institute a vigorous program of education and self-improvement.
14. Put everyone in the company to work to accomplish the transformation.

Firms in the United States responded aggressively. The new philosophy is that quality should be the norm. For example, Motorola's production goal is 60 or fewer defects per every billion components that it manufactures.

Exhibit 2.9, Strategy in Action, presents the integration of the quality initiative into the mission statements of three corporations. The emphasis on quality has received added emphasis in many corporate philosophies since the Congress created the Malcolm Baldrige Quality Award. Each year up to two Baldrige Awards can be given in three categories of a company's operations: manufacturing, services, and small businesses.

Examples of Vision Statements

ALLIANCE CORPORATE VISION

Alliance is the most innovative and feature rich ACH processing platform available to client originators today and will remain on the cutting edge for electronic funds transfer services.

AMD CORPORATE VISION

A connected global population.

CUTCO CORPORATE VISION

To become the largest, most respected and widely recognized cutlery company in the world.

FEDERAL EXPRESS CORPORATE VISION

Our vision is to change the way we all connect with each other in the New Network Economy.

FIRSTENERGY CORPORATE VISION

FirstEnergy will be a leading regional energy provider, recognized for operational excellence and service; the choice for long-term growth, investment, value and financial strength; and a company committed to safety and driven by the leadership, skills, diversity, and character of its employees.

FORD MOTOR COMPANY CORPORATE VISION

Ford Motor Company's vision is to become the world's leading consumer company for automotive products and services.

GENERAL ELECTRIC CORPORATE VISION

We bring good things to life.

MAGNA CORPORATE VISION

Magna's corporate vision is to provide world class services that help maximize the customers ROI (Return on Investment) and promote teamwork and creativity. The company strongly believes in the corporate philosophy of fulfilling its commitments to its customers.

MICROSOFT CORPORATE VISION

Microsoft's vision is to enable people and businesses throughout the world to realize their full potential.

Vision Statement

Whereas the mission statement expresses an answer to the question "What business are we in?" a company **vision statement** is sometimes developed to express the aspirations of the executive leadership. A vision statement presents the firm's strategic intent that focuses the energies and resources of the company on achieving a desirable future. However, in actual practice, the mission and vision statement are frequently combined into a single statement. When they are separated, the vision statement is often a single sentence, designed to be memorable. For examples, see Exhibit 2.10, Strategy in Action.

vision statement

A statement that presents a firm's strategic intent designed to focus the energies and resources of the company on achieving a desirable future.

An Exemplary Mission Statement

When BB&T merged with Southern Bank, the board of directors and officers undertook the creation of a comprehensive mission statement that was designed to include most of the topics that we discussed in this chapter. The company updated its statement and mailed the resulting booklet to its shareholders and other interested parties. The foreword to the document expresses the greatest values of such a public pronouncement and was signed by BB&T's chairman and CEO, John A. Allison:

> In a rapidly changing and unpredictable world, individuals and organizations need a clear set of fundamental principles to guide their actions. At BB&T we know the content of our business will, and should, experience constant change. Change is necessary for progress. However, the context, our fundamental principles, is unchanging because these principles are based on basic truths.
>
> BB&T is a mission-driven organization with a clearly defined set of values. We encourage our employees to have a strong sense of purpose, a high level of self-esteem and the capacity to think clearly and logically.

We believe that competitive advantage is largely in the minds of our employees as represented by their capacity to turn rational ideas into action towards the accomplishment of our mission.

The Chapter 2 Appendix presents BB&T's vision, mission, and purpose statement in its entirety. It also includes detailed expressions of the company's values and views on the role of emotions, management style, the management concept, attributes of an outstanding employee, the importance of positive attitude, obligations to its employees, virtues of an outstanding credit culture, achieving the company goal, the nature of a "world standard" revenue-driven sales organization, the nature of a "world standard" client service community bank, the company's commitment to education and learning, and its passions.

BOARDS OF DIRECTORS

Who is responsible for determining the firm's mission? Who is responsible for acquiring and allocating resources so the firm can thoughtfully develop and implement a strategic plan? Who is responsible for monitoring the firm's success in the competitive marketplace to determine whether that plan was well designed and activated? The answer to all of these questions is strategic decision makers. Most organizations have multiple levels of strategic decision makers; typically, the larger the firm, the more levels it will have. The strategic managers at the highest level are responsible for decisions that affect the entire firm, commit the firm and its resources for the longest periods, and declare the firm's sense of values. In other words, this group of strategic managers is responsible for overseeing the creation and accomplishment of the company mission. The term that describes the group is **board of directors**.

board of directors
The group of stockholder representatives and strategic managers responsible for overseeing the creation and accomplishment of the company mission.

In overseeing the management of a firm, the board of directors operates as the representatives of the firm's stockholders. Elected by the stockholders, the board has these major responsibilities:

1. To establish and update the company mission.
2. To elect the company's top officers, the foremost of whom is the CEO.
3. To establish the compensation levels of the top officers, including their salaries and bonuses.
4. To determine the amount and timing of the dividends paid to stockholders.
5. To set broad company policy on such matters as labor–management relations, product or service lines of business, and employee benefit packages.
6. To set company objectives and to authorize managers to implement the long-term strategies that the top officers and the board have found agreeable.
7. To mandate company compliance with legal and ethical dictates.

In the current business environment, boards of directors are accepting the challenge of shareholders and other stakeholders to become active in establishing the strategic initiatives of the companies that they serve.

This chapter considers the board of directors because the board's greatest impact on the behavior of a firm results from its determination of the company mission. The philosophy espoused in the mission statement sets the tone by which the firm and all of its employees will be judged. As logical extensions of the mission statement, the firm's objectives and strategies embody the board's view of proper business demeanor. Through its appointment of top executives and its decisions about their compensation, the board reveals its priorities for organizational achievement.

AGENCY THEORY

agency theory
A set of ideas on organizational control based on the belief that the separation of the ownership from management creates the potential for the wishes of owners to be ignored.

Whenever there is a separation of the owners (principals) and the managers (agents) of a firm, the potential exists for the wishes of the owners to be ignored. This fact, and the recognition that agents are expensive, established the basis for a set of complex but helpful ideas known as **agency theory.** Whenever owners (or managers) delegate decision-making authority to others, an agency relationship exists between the two parties. Agency relationships, such as those between stockholders and managers, can be very effective as long as managers make investment decisions in ways that are consistent with stockholders' interests. However, when the interests of managers diverge from those of owners, then managers' decisions are more likely to reflect the managers' preferences than the owners' preferences.

In general, owners seek stock value maximization. When managers hold important blocks of company stock, they too prefer strategies that result in stock appreciation. However, when managers better resemble "hired hands" than owner-partners, they often prefer strategies that increase their personal payoffs rather than those of shareholders. Such behavior can result in decreased stock performance (as when high executive bonuses reduce corporate earnings) and in strategic decisions that point the firm in the direction of outcomes that are suboptimal from a stockholder's perspective.

agency costs
The cost of agency problems and the cost of actions taken to minimize them.

If, as agency theory argues, self-interested managers act in ways that increase their own welfare at the expense of the gain of corporate stockholders, then owners who delegate decision-making authority to their agents will incur both the loss of potential gain that would have resulted from owner-optimal strategies and/or the costs of monitoring and control systems that are designed to minimize the consequences of such self-centered management decisions. In combination, the cost of agency problems and the cost of actions taken to minimize agency problems are called **agency costs.** These costs can often be identified by their direct benefit for the agents and their negative present value. Agency costs are found when there are differing self-interests between shareholders and managers, superiors and subordinates, or managers of competing departments or branch offices.

How Agency Problems Occur

moral hazard problem
An agency problem that occurs because owners have limited access to company information, making executives free to pursue their own interests.

Because owners have access to only a relatively small portion of the information that is available to executives about the performance of the firm and cannot afford to monitor every executive decision or action, executives are often free to pursue their own interests. This condition is known as the **moral hazard problem.** It is also called shirking to suggest "self-interest combined with smile."

As a result of moral hazards, executives may design strategies that provide the greatest possible benefits for themselves, with the welfare of the organization being given only secondary consideration. For example, executives may presell products at year-end to trigger their annual bonuses even though the deep discounts that they must offer will threaten the price stability of their products for the upcoming year. Similarly, unchecked executives may advance their own self-interests by slacking on the job, altering forecasts to maximize their performance bonuses; unrealistically assessing acquisition targets' outlooks in order to increase the probability of increasing organizational size through their acquisition; or manipulating personnel records to keep or acquire key company personnel.

adverse selection
An agency problem caused by the limited ability of stockholders to precisely determine the competencies and priorities of executives at the time they are hired.

The second major reason that agency costs are incurred is known as **adverse selection.** This refers to the limited ability that stockholders have to precisely determine the competencies and priorities of executives at the time that they are hired. Because principals cannot initially verify an executive's appropriateness as an agent of the owners, unanticipated problems of nonoverlapping priorities between owners and agents are likely to occur.

The most popular solution to moral dilemma and adverse selection problems is for owners to attempt to more closely align their own best interests with those of their agents through the use of executive bonus plans. Foremost among these approaches are stock option plans, which enable executives to benefit directly from the appreciation of the company's stock just as other stockholders do. In most instances, executive bonus plans are unabashed attempts to align the interests of owners and executives and to thereby induce executives to support strategies that increase stockholder wealth. While such schemes are unlikely to eliminate self-interest as a major criterion in executive decision making, they help to reduce the costs associated with moral dilemmas and adverse selections.

Problems That Can Result from Agency

From a strategic management perspective there are five different kinds of problems that can arise because of the agency relationship between corporate stockholders and their company's executives:

1. Executives pursue growth in company size rather than in earnings. Shareholders generally want to maximize earnings, because earnings growth yields stock appreciation. However, because managers are typically more heavily compensated for increases in firm size than for earnings growth, they may recommend strategies that yield company growth such as mergers and acquisitions.

In addition, managers' stature in the business community is commonly associated with company size. Managers gain prominence by directing the growth of an organization, and they benefit in the forms of career advancement and job mobility that are associated with increases in company size.

Finally, executives need an enlarging set of advancement opportunities for subordinates whom they wish to motivate with nonfinancial inducements. Acquisitions can provide the needed positions.

2. Executives attempt to diversify their corporate risk. Whereas stockholders can vary their investment risks through management of their individual stock portfolios, managers' careers and stock incentives are tied to the performance of a single corporation, albeit the one that employs them. Consequently, executives are tempted to diversify their corporation's operation, businesses, and product lines to moderate the risk incurred in any single venture. While this approach serves the executives' personal agendas, it compromises the "pure play" quality of their firm as an investment. In other words, diversifying a corporation reduces the beta associated with the firm's return, which is an undesirable outcome for many stockholders.

3. Executives avoid risk. Even when, or perhaps especially when, executives are willing to restrict the diversification of their companies, they are tempted to minimize the risk that they face. Executives are often fired for failure, but rarely for mediocre corporate performance. Therefore, executives may avoid desirable levels of risk if they anticipate little reward and opt for conservative strategies that minimize the risk of company failure. If they do, executives will rarely support plans for innovation, diversification, and rapid growth.

However, from an investor's perspective, risk taking is desirable when it is systematic. In other words, when investors can reasonably expect that their company will generate higher long-term returns from assuming greater risk, they may wish to pursue the greater payoff, especially when the company is positioned to perform better than its competitors that face the same nominal risks. Obviously, the agency relationship creates a problem—should executives prioritize their job security or the company's financial returns to stockholders?

4. Managers act to optimize their personal payoffs. If executives can gain more from an annual performance bonus by achieving objective 1 than from stock appreciation resulting from the achievement of objective 2, then owners must anticipate that the executives will target objective 1 as their priority, even though objective 2 is clearly in the best interest of the shareholders. Similarly, executives may pursue a range of expensive perquisites that have a net negative effect on shareholder returns. Elegant corner offices, corporate jets, large staffs, golf club memberships, extravagant retirement programs, and limousines for executive benefit are rarely good investments for stockholders.

5. Executives act to protect their status. When their companies expand, executives want to ensure that their knowledge, experience, and skills remain relevant and central to the strategic direction of the corporation. They favor doing more of what they already do well. In contrast, investors may prefer revolutionary advancement to incremental improvement. For example, when confronted with Amazon.com, competitor Barnes & Noble initiated a joint venture Web site with Bertelsmann. In addition, Barnes & Noble used vertical integration with the nation's largest book distributor, which supplies 60 percent of Amazon's books. This type of revolutionary strategy is most likely to occur when executives are given assurances that they will not make themselves obsolete within the changing company that they create.

Solutions to the Agency Problem

In addition to defining an agent's responsibilities in a contract and including elements like bonus incentives that help align executives' and owners' interests, principals can take several other actions to minimize agency problems. The first is for the owners to pay executives a premium for their service. This premium helps executives to see their loyalty to the stockholders as the key to achieving their personal financial targets.

A second solution to agency problems is for executives to receive backloaded compensation. This means that executives are paid a handsome premium for superior future performance. Strategic actions taken in year one, which are to have an impact in year three, become the basis for executive bonuses in year three. This lag time between action and bonus more realistically rewards executives for the consequences of their decision making, ties the executive to the company for the long term, and properly focuses strategic management activities on the future.

Finally, creating teams of executives across different units of a corporation can help to focus performance measures on organizational rather than personal goals. Through the use of executive teams, owner interests often receive the priority that they deserve.

Summary

Defining the company mission is one of the most often slighted tasks in strategic management. Emphasizing the operational aspects of long-range management activities comes much more easily for most executives. But the critical role of the mission statement repeatedly is demonstrated by failing firms whose short-run actions have been at odds with their long-run purposes.

The principal value of the mission statement is its specification of the firm's ultimate aims. A firm gains a heightened sense of purpose when its board of directors and its top executives address these issues: "What business are we in?" "What customers do we serve?" "Why does this organization exist?" However, the potential contribution of the company mission can be undermined if platitudes or ambiguous generalizations are accepted in response to these questions. It is not enough to say that Lever Brothers is in the business of "making anything that cleans anything" or that Polaroid is committed to businesses that deal with "the interaction of light and matter." Only if a firm clearly articulates its long-term intentions can its goals serve as a basis for shared expectations, planning, and performance evaluation.

A mission statement that is developed from this perspective provides managers with a unity of direction transcending individual, parochial, and temporary needs. It promotes a sense of shared expectations among all levels and generations of employees. It consolidates values over time and across individuals and interest groups. It projects a sense of worth and intent that can be identified and assimilated by outside stakeholders, that is, customers, suppliers, competitors, local committees, and the general public. Finally, it asserts the firm's commitment to responsible action in symbiosis with the preservation and protection of the essential claims of insider stakeholders' survival, growth, and profitability.

Key Terms

adverse selection, *p. 35*	board of directors, *p. 34*	moral hazard problem, *p. 35*
agency costs, *p. 35*	company creed, *p. 25*	vision statement, *p. 33*
agency theory, *p. 35*	company mission, *p. 21*	

Questions for Discussion

1. Reread Nicor Inc.'s mission statement in Exhibit 2.1, Strategy in Action. List five insights into Nicor that you feel you gained from knowing its mission.
2. Locate the mission statement of a company not mentioned in the chapter. Where did you find it? Was it presented as a consolidated statement, or were you forced to assemble it yourself from various publications of the firm? How many of the mission statement elements outlined in this chapter were discussed or revealed in the statement you found?
3. Prepare a two-page typewritten mission statement for your school of business or for a firm selected by your instructor.
4. List five potentially vulnerable areas of a firm without a stated company mission.
5. Mission statements are often criticized for being lists of platitudes. What can strategic managers do to prevent their statements from appearing to be simple statements of obvious truths?
6. What evidence do you see that mission statements are valuable?
7. How can a mission statement be an enduring statement of values and simultaneously provide a basis of competitive advantage?
8. If the goal of survival refers to ability to maintain a specific legal form, what are the comparative advantages of sole proprietorships, partnerships, and corporations?
9. In the 1990s many Nasdaq firms favored growth over profitability; in the 2000s the goal of profitability is displacing growth. How might each preference be explained?
10. Do you agree that a mission statement provides substantive guidance while a vision statement provides inspirational guidance? Explain.

Chapter 2 Appendix

BB&T Vision, Mission, and Purpose

BB&T Vision

To create the best financial institution possible: *"The Best of The Best."*

BB&T Mission

To make the world a better place to live by: helping our clients achieve economic success and financial security; creating a place where our employees can learn, grow and be fulfilled in their work; making the communities in which we work better places to be; and thereby: optimizing the long-term return to our shareholders, while providing a safe and sound investment.

BB&T Purpose

Our ultimate purpose is to create superior long-term economic rewards for our shareholders.

This purpose is defined by the free market and is as it should be. Our shareholders provide the capital that is necessary to make our business possible. They take the risk if the business is unsuccessful. They have the right to receive economic rewards for the risk which they have undertaken.

However, our purpose, to create superior long-term economic rewards for our shareholders, can only be accomplished by providing excellent service to our clients, as our clients are our source of revenues.

To have excellent client relations, we must have outstanding employees to serve our clients. To attract and retain outstanding employees, we must reward them financially and create an environment where they can learn and grow.

Our economic results are significantly impacted by the success of our communities. The community's "quality of life" impacts its ability to attract industry for growth.

Therefore, we manage our business in a long-term context, as an integrated whole, with the ultimate objective of rewarding the shareholders for their investment, while realizing that the cause of this result is quality client service. Excellent service will be delivered by motivated employees working as an integrated team. These results will be impacted by our capacity to contribute to the growth and well-being of the communities we serve.

Values

"Excellence is an art won by training and habituation. We are what we repeatedly do. Excellence then is not an act, but a habit."—Aristotle

The great Greek philosophers saw values as guides to excellence in thinking and action. In this context, values are standards which we strive to achieve. Values are practical habits that enable us as individuals to live, be successful and achieve happiness. For BB&T, our values enable us to achieve our mission and corporate purpose.

To be useful, values must be consciously held and be consistent (noncontradictory). Many people have conflicting values which prevent them from acting with clarity and self-confidence.

There are 10 primary values at BB&T. These values are consistent with one another and are integrated. To fully act on one of these values, you must also act consistently with the other values. Our focus on values grows from our belief that ideas matter and that an individual's character is of critical significance.

Values are important at BB&T!

1. Reality (Fact-Based)

What is, is. If we want to be better, we must act within the context of reality (the facts). Businesses and individuals often make serious mistakes by making decisions based on what they "wish was so," or based on theories which are disconnected from reality. The foundation for quality decision making is a careful understanding of the facts.

There is a fundamental difference between the laws of nature (reality), which are immutable, and the man-made. The law of gravity is the law of gravity. The existence of the law of gravity does not mean man cannot create an airplane. However, an airplane must be created within the context of the law of gravity. At BB&T, we believe in being "reality grounded."

2. Reason (Objectivity)

Mankind has a specific means of survival, which is his ability to think, i.e., his capacity to reason logically from the facts of reality as presented to his five senses. A lion has claws to hunt. A deer has swiftness to avoid the hunter. Man has his ability to think. There is only one "natural resource"—the human mind.

Clear thinking is not automatic. It requires intellectual discipline and begins with sound premises based on observed facts. You must be able to draw general conclusions in a rational manner from specific examples (induction) and be able to apply general principles to the solution of specific problems (deduction). You must be able to think in an integrated way, thereby avoiding logical contradictions.

We cannot all be geniuses, but each of us can develop the mental habits which ensure that when making decisions we carefully examine the facts and think logically without contradiction in deriving a conclusion. We must learn to think in terms of what is essential, i.e., about what is important. Our goal is to objectively make the best decision to accomplish our purpose.

Rational thinking is a learned skill which requires mental focus and a fundamental commitment to consistently improving the clarity of our mental processes. At BB&T, we are looking for people who are committed to constantly improving their ability to reason.

3. Independent Thinking

All employees are challenged to use their individual minds to their optimum to make rational decisions. In this context, each of us is *responsible* for what we do and who we are. In addition, creativity is strongly encouraged and only possible with independent thought.

We learn a great deal from each other. Teamwork is important at BB&T (as will be discussed later). However, each of us thinks alone. Our minds are not physically connected. In this regard, each of us must be willing to make an independent judgment of the facts based on our capacity to think logically. Just because the "crowd" says it is so, does not make it so.

In this context, each of us is responsible for our own actions. Each of us is responsible for our personal success or failure; that is, it is not the bank's fault if someone does not achieve his objectives.

All human progress by definition is based on creativity, because creativity is the source of positive change. Creativity is only possible to an independent thinker. Creativity is not about just doing something different. It is about doing something better. To be better, the new method/process must be judged by its impact on the whole organization, and as to whether it contributes to the accomplishment of our mission.

There is an infinite opportunity for each of us to do whatever we do better. A significant aspect of the self-fulfillment which work can provide comes from creative thought and action.

4. Productivity

We are committed to being producers of wealth and well-being by taking the actions necessary to accomplish our mission. The tangible evidence of our productivity is that we have rationally allocated capital through our lending and investment process, and that we have provided needed services to our clients in an efficient manner resulting in superior profitability.

Profitability is a measure of the differences in the economic value of the products/services we produce and the cost of producing these products/services. In a long-term context and in a free market, the bigger the profit, the better. This is true not only from our shareholders' perspective (which would be enough justification), but also in terms of the impact of our work on society as a whole. Healthy profits represent productive work. At BB&T we are looking for people who want to create, to produce, and who are thereby committed to turning their thoughts into actions that improve economic well-being.

5. Honesty

Being honest is simply being consistent with reality. To be dishonest is to be in conflict with reality, which is therefore self-defeating. A primary reason that individuals fail is because they become disconnected from reality, pretending that facts are other than they are.

To be honest does not require that we know everything. Knowledge is always contextual and man is not omniscient. However, we must be responsible for saying what we mean and meaning what we say.

6. Integrity

Because we have developed our principles logically, based on reality, we will always act consistently with our principles. Regardless of the short-term benefits, acting inconsistently with our principles is to our long-term detriment. We do not, therefore, believe in compromising our principles in any situation.

Principles provide carefully thought-out concepts which will lead to our long-term success and happiness. Violating our principles will always lead to failure. BB&T is an organization of the highest integrity.

7. Justice (Fairness)

Individuals should be evaluated and rewarded objectively (for better or worse) based on their contributions toward accomplishing our mission and adherence to our values. Those who contribute the most should receive the most.

The single most significant way in which employees evaluate their managers is in determining whether the manager is just. Employees become extremely unhappy (and rightly so) when they perceive that a person who is not contributing is overrewarded or a strong contributor is underrewarded.

If we do not reward those who contribute the most, they will leave and our organization will be less successful. Even more important, if there is no reward for superior performance, the average person will not be motivated to maximize his productivity.

We must evaluate whether the food we eat is healthy, the clothes we wear attractive, the car we drive functional, etc., and we must also evaluate whether relationships with other people are good for us or not.

In evaluating other people, it is critical that we judge based on essentials. At BB&T we do not discriminate based on nonessentials such as race, sex, nationality, etc. We do discriminate based on competency, performance and character. We consciously reject egalitarianism and collectivism. Individuals must be judged individually based on their personal merits, not their membership in any group.

8. Pride

Pride is the psychological reward we earn from living by our values, that is, from being just, honest, having integrity, being an independent thinker, being productive and rational.

Aristotle believed that "earned" pride (not arrogance) was the highest of virtues, because it presupposed all the others. Striving for earned pride simply reinforces the importance of having high moral values.

Each of us must perform our work in a manner as to be able to be justly proud of what we have accomplished. BB&T must be the kind of organization with which each employee and client can be proud to be associated.

9. Self-Esteem (Self-Motivation)

We expect our employees to earn positive self-esteem from doing their work well. We expect and want our employees to act in their rational, long-term self-interest. We want employees who have strong personal goals and who expect to be able to accomplish their goals within the context of our mission.

A necessary attribute for self-esteem is self-motivation. We have a strong work ethic. We believe that you receive from your work in proportion to how much you contribute. If you do not want to work hard, work somewhere else.

While there are many trade-offs in the content of life, you need to be clear that BB&T is the best place, all things considered, for you to work to accomplish your long-term goals. When you know this, you can be more productive and happy.

10. Teamwork/Mutual Supportiveness

While independent thought and strong personal goals are critically important, our work is accomplished within teams. Each of us must consistently act to achieve the agreed-upon objectives of the team, with respect for our fellow employees, while acting in a mutually supportive manner.

Our work at BB&T is so complex that it requires an integrated effort among many people to accomplish important tasks. While we are looking for self-motivated and independent thinking individuals, these individuals must recognize that almost nothing at BB&T can be accomplished without the help of their team members. One of the responsibilities of leadership in our organization is to ensure that each individual is rewarded based on their contribution to the success of the total team. We need outstanding individuals working together to create an outstanding team.

Our values are held consciously and are logically consistent. To fully execute on any one value, you must act consistently with all 10 values. At BB&T values are practical and important.

The Role of Emotions

Often people believe that making logical decisions means that we should be unemotional and that emotions are thereby unimportant. In fact, emotions are important. However, the real issue is how rational are our emotions. Emotions are mental habits which are often developed as children. Emotions give us automatic responses to people and events; these responses can either be very useful or destructive indicators.

Emotions as such are not means of decision or of knowledge; the issue is: How were your emotions formed? The real question is, Are we happy when we should be happy, and unhappy when we should be unhappy, or are we unhappy when we should be happy?

Emotions are learned behaviors. The goal is to "train up" our emotions so that our emotions objectively reinforce the best decisions and behaviors toward our long-term success and happiness. Just because someone is unemotional does not mean that they are logical.

Concepts That Describe BB&T

1. Client-Driven

"World class" client service organization.
Our clients are our partners.
Our goal is to create win/win relationships.
"You can tell we want your business."
"It is easy to do business with BB&T."
"Respect the individual, value the relationship."

We will absolutely never, ever, take advantage of anyone, nor do we want to do business with those who would take advantage of us. Our clients are long-term partners and should be treated accordingly. One of the attributes of partnerships is that both partners must keep their agreements. We keep our agreements. When our partners fail to keep their agreements, they are terminating the partnership.

There are an infinite number of opportunities where we can get better together, where we can help our clients achieve their financial goals and where our client will enable us to make a profit in doing so.

2. Quality Oriented

Quality must be built into the process.

In every aspect of our business we want to execute and deliver quality. It is easier and less expensive to do things correctly than to fix what has been done incorrectly.

3. Efficient

"Waste not, want not."
Design efficiency into the system.

4. Growing Both Our Business and Our People

Grow or die.
Life requires constant, focused thought and actions towards one's goals.

5. Continuous Improvement

Everything can be done better.
Fundamental commitment to innovation.
Every employee should constantly use their reasoning ability to do whatever they do better every day. All managers of systems/processes should constantly search for better methods to solve problems and serve the client.

6. Objective Decision Making

Fact-based and rational.

BB&T Management Style

Participative
Team Oriented
Fact-Based
Rational
Objective

Our management process, by intention, is designed to be participative and team oriented. We work hard to create consensus. When people are involved in the decision process, better information is available to make decisions. The participant's understanding of the decision is greater and, therefore, execution is better.

However, there is a risk in participative decision making: the decision process can become a popularity contest. Therefore, our decision process is disciplined. Our decisions will be made based on the facts using reason. The best objective decision will be the one which is enacted.

Therefore, it does not matter whom you know, who your friends are, etc.; it matters whether you can offer the best objective solution to accomplishing the goal or solving the problem at hand.

BB&T Management Concept

Hire excellent people
Train them well
Give them an appropriate level of authority and responsibility
Expect a high level of achievement
Reward their performance

Our concept is to operate a highly autonomous, entrepreneurial organization. In order to execute this concept, we must have extremely competent individuals who are "masters" of BB&T's philosophy and who are "masters" in their field of technical expertise.

By having individuals who are "masters" in their field, we can afford to have less costly control systems and be more responsive in meeting the needs of our clients.

Attributes of an Outstanding BB&T Employee

Purpose
Rationality
Self-esteem

Consistent with our values, successful individuals at BB&T have a sense of purpose for their lives; that is, they believe that their lives matter and that they can accomplish something meaningful through their work. We are looking for people who are rational and have a high level of personal self-esteem. People with a strong personal self-esteem get along better with others, because they are at peace with themselves.

BB&T Positive Attitude

Since we build on the facts of reality and our ability to reason, we are capable of achieving both success and happiness.

We do not believe that "realism" means pessimism. On the contrary, precisely because our goals are based on and consistent with reality, we fully expect to accomplish them.

BB&T'S Obligations to Its Employees

We will do our best to:

Compensate employees fairly in relation to internal equity and market-comparable pay practices—performance-based compensation.

Provide a comprehensive and market-competitive benefit program.

Create a place where employees can learn and grow—to become more productive workers and better people.

Train employees so they are competent to do the work asked of them. (Never ask anyone to do anything they are not trained to do.)

Evaluate and recognize performance objectively, fairly and consistently based on the individual's contribution to the accomplishment of our mission and adherence to our values.

Treat each employee as an individual with dignity and respect.

Virtues of an Outstanding Credit Culture

Just as individuals need a set of values (virtues) to guide their actions, systems should be designed to have a set of attributes which optimize their performance towards our goals. In this regard, our credit culture has seven fundamental virtues:

1. Provides fundamental insight to help clients achieve their economic goals and solve their financial problems: We are in the high-quality financial advice business.

2. Responsive: The client deserves an answer as quickly as possible, even when the answer is no.

3. Flexible (Creative): We are committed to finding better ways to meet the client's financial needs.

4. Reliable: Our clients are selected as long-term partners and treated accordingly. BB&T must continue to earn the right to be known as the most reliable bank.

5. Manages risk within agreed-upon limits: Clients do not want to fail financially, and the bank does not want a bad loan.

6. Ensures an appropriate economic return to the bank for risk taken: The higher the risk, the higher the return. The lower the risk, the lower the return. This is an expression of justice.

7. Creates a "premium" for service delivery: The concept is to provide superior value to the client through outstanding service quality. A rational client will fairly compensate us when we provide sound financial advice, are responsive, creative and reliable, because these attributes are of economic value to the client.

Strategic Objectives

Create a high performance financial institution that can survive and prosper in a rapidly changing, highly competitive, globally integrated environment.

Achieving Our Goal

The key to maximizing our probability of being both independent and prosperous over the long term is to create a superior earnings per share (EPS) growth rate without sacrificing the fundamental quality and long-term competitiveness of our business and without taking unreasonable risk.

While being fundamentally efficient is critical, the "easy" way to rapid EPS growth is to artificially cut cost. However, not investing for the future is long-term suicide, as it destroys our capability to compete.

The intelligent process to achieve superior EPS growth is to grow revenues by providing (and selling) superior quality service while systematically enhancing our margins, improving our efficiency, expanding our profitable product offerings and creating more effective distribution channels.

The "World Standard" Revenue-Driven Sales Organization

At BB&T, selling is about identifying our clients' legitimate financial needs and finding a way to help the client achieve economic goals by providing the right products and services.

Effective selling requires a disciplined approach in which the BB&T employee asks the client about financial goals and problems and has a complete understanding of how our products can help the client achieve objectives and solve financial problems.

It also requires exceptional execution by support staffs and product managers, since service and sales are fundamentally connected and creativity is required in product design and development.

"World Standard" Client Service Community Banks

BB&T operates as a series of "Community Banks." The "Community Bank" concept is the foundation for local decision making and the basis for responsive, reliable and empathetic client service.

By putting decision making closer to the client, all local factors can be considered, and we can ensure that the client is being treated as an individual.

To operate in this decentralized decision-making fashion, we must have highly trained employees who understand BB&T's philosophy and are "masters" of their areas of responsibility.

Commitment to Education/Learning

Competitive advantage is in the minds of our employees. We are committed to making substantial investments in employee education to create a "knowledge-based learning organization" founded on the premise that knowledge (understanding), properly applied, is the source of superior performance.

We believe in systematized learning founded on Aristotle's concept that "excellence is an art won by training and habituation." We attempt to train our employees with the best knowledge/methods in their fields and to habituate those behaviors through consistent management reinforcement. The goal is for each employee to be a "master" of his or her role, whether it be a computer operator, teller, lender, financial consultant or any other job responsibility.

Our Passions

To create the best financial institution possible.

To consistently provide the client with better value through rational innovation and productivity improvement.

At BB&T we have two powerful passions. Our fundamental passion is our Vision: To Create The Best Financial Institution Possible—The "World Standard"—The "Best of the Best." We believe that the best can be objectively evaluated by rational performance standards in relation to the accomplishment of our mission.

To be the best of the best, we must constantly find ways to deliver better value to our clients in a highly profitable manner. This requires us to keep our minds focused at all times on innovative ways to enhance our productivity.

Chapter **Three**

Corporate Social Responsibility and Business Ethics

After reading and studying this chapter, you should be able to

1. Understand the importance of the stakeholder approach to social responsibility.

2. Explain the continuum of social responsibility and the effect of various options on company profitability.

3. Describe a social audit and explain its importance.

4. Discuss the effect of the Sarbanes-Oxley Act of 2002 on the ethical conduct of business.

5. Compare the advantages of collaborative social initiatives with alternative approaches to CSR.

6. Explain the five principles of collaborative social initiatives.

7. Compare the merits of different approaches to business ethics.

8. Explain the relevance of business ethics to strategic management practice.

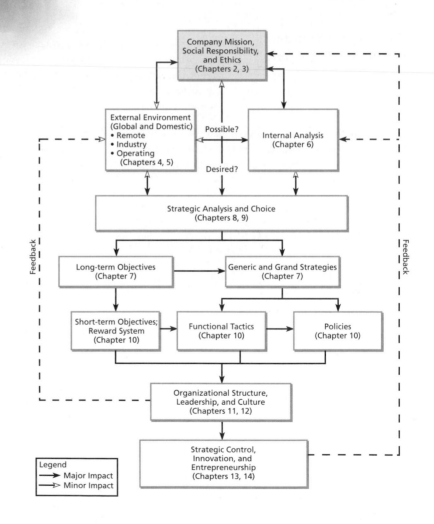

THE STAKEHOLDER APPROACH TO SOCIAL RESPONSIBILITY

In defining or redefining the company mission, strategic managers must recognize the legitimate rights of the firm's claimants. These include not only stockholders and employees but also outsiders affected by the firm's actions, sometimes referred to as stakeholders. Such outsiders commonly include customers, suppliers, governments, unions, competitors, local communities, and the general public. Each of these interest groups has justifiable reasons for expecting (and often for demanding) that the firm satisfy their claims in a responsible manner. In general, stockholders claim appropriate returns on their investment; employees seek broadly defined job satisfactions; customers want what they pay for; suppliers seek dependable buyers; governments want adherence to legislation; unions seek benefits for their members; competitors want fair competition; local communities want the firm to be a responsible citizen; and the general public expects the firm's existence to improve the quality of life.

According to a survey of 2,361 directors in 291 of the largest southeastern U.S. companies,

1. Directors perceived the existence of distinct stakeholder groups.
2. Directors have high stakeholder orientations.
3. Directors view some stakeholders differently, depending on their occupation (CEO directors versus non-CEO directors) and type (inside versus outside directors).

The study also found that the perceived stakeholders were, in the order of their importance, customers and government, stockholders, employees, and society. The results clearly indicated that boards of directors no longer believe that the stockholder is the only constituency to whom they are responsible.

However, when a firm attempts to incorporate the interests of these groups into its mission statement, broad generalizations are insufficient. These steps need to be taken:

1. Identification of the stakeholders.
2. Understanding the stakeholders' specific claims vis-à-vis the firm.
3. Reconciliation of these claims and assignment of priorities to them.
4. Coordination of the claims with other elements of the company mission.

Identification   The left-hand column of Exhibit 3.1 lists the commonly encountered stakeholder groups, to which the executive officer group often is added. Obviously, though, every business faces a slightly different set of stakeholder groups, which vary in number, size, influence, and importance. In defining the company, strategic managers must identify all of the stakeholder groups and weigh their relative rights and their relative ability to affect the firm's success.

Understanding   The concerns of the principal stakeholder groups tend to center on the general claims listed in the right-hand column of Exhibit 3.1. However, strategic decision makers should understand the specific demands of each group. They then will be better able to initiate actions that satisfy these demands.

Reconciliation and Priorities   Unfortunately, the claims of various stakeholder groups often conflict. For example, the claims of governments and the general public tend to limit profitability, which is the central claim of most creditors and stockholders. Thus, claims must be reconciled in a mission statement that resolves the competing, conflicting, and contradicting claims of stakeholders. For objectives and strategies to be internally consistent and precisely focused, the statement must display a single-minded, though multidimensional, approach to the firm's aims.

EXHIBIT 3.1
A Stakeholder
View of Company
Responsibility

Stakeholder	Nature of the Claim
Stockholders	Participation in distribution of profits, additional stock offerings, assets on liquidation; vote of stock; inspection of company books; transfer of stock; election of board of directors; and such additional rights as have been established in the contract with the corporation.
Creditors	Legal proportion of interest payments due and return of principal from the investment. Security of pledged assets; relative priority in event of liquidation. Management and owner prerogatives if certain conditions exist with the company (such as default of interest payments).
Employees	Economic, social, and psychological satisfaction in the place of employment. Freedom from arbitrary and capricious behavior on the part of company officials. Share in fringe benefits, freedom to join union and participate in collective bargaining, individual freedom in offering up their services through an employment contract. Adequate working conditions.
Customers	Service provided with the product; technical data to use the product; suitable warranties; spare parts to support the product during use; R&D leading to product improvement; facilitation of credit.
Suppliers	Continuing source of business; timely consummation of trade credit obligations; professional relationship in contracting for, purchasing, and receiving goods and services.
Governments	Taxes (income, property, and so on); adherence to the letter and intent of public policy dealing with the requirements of fair and free competition; discharge of legal obligations of businesspeople (and business organizations); adherence to antitrust laws.
Unions	Recognition as the negotiating agent for employees. Opportunity to perpetuate the union as a participant in the business organization.
Competitors	Observation of the norms for competitive conduct established by society and the industry. Business statesmanship on the part of peers.
Local communities	Place of productive and healthful employment in the community. Participation of company officials in community affairs, provision of regular employment, fair play, reasonable portion of purchases made in the local community, interest in and support of local government, support of cultural and charitable projects.
The general public	Participation in and contribution to society as a whole; creative communications between governmental and business units designed for reciprocal understanding; assumption of fair proportion of the burden of government and society. Fair price for products and advancement of the state-of-the-art technology that the product line involves.

Source: William R. King and David I. Cleland, *Strategic Planning and Policy,* © 1978 Litton Educational Publishing, Inc., p. 153.

There are hundreds, if not thousands, of claims on any firm—high wages, pure air, job security, product quality, community service, taxes, occupational health and safety regulations, equal employment opportunity regulations, product variety, wide markets, career opportunities, company growth, investment security, high ROI, and many, many more. Although most, perhaps all, of these claims may be desirable ends, they cannot be pursued with equal emphasis. They must be assigned priorities in accordance with the relative emphasis that the firm will give them. That emphasis is reflected in the criteria that the firm uses in its strategic decision making; in the firm's allocation of its human, financial, and physical resources; and in the firm's long-term objectives and strategies.

Coordination with Other Elements The demands of stakeholder groups constitute only one principal set of inputs to the company mission. The other principal sets are the managerial operating philosophy and the determinants of the product-market offering. Those determinants constitute a reality test that the accepted claims must pass. The key question is, How can the firm satisfy its claimants and at the same time optimize its economic success in the marketplace?

The Dynamics of Social Responsibility

As indicated in Exhibit 3.2, the various stakeholders of a firm can be divided into inside stakeholders and outside stakeholders. The insiders are the individuals or groups that are stockholders or employees of the firm. The outsiders are all the other individuals or groups that the firm's actions affect. The extremely large and often amorphous set of outsiders makes the general claim that the firm be socially responsible.

Perhaps the thorniest issues faced in defining a company mission are those that pertain to social responsibility. Corporate social responsibility is the idea that a business has a duty to serve society in general as well as the financial interests of its stockholders. The stakeholder approach offers the clearest perspective on such issues. Broadly stated, outsiders often demand that insiders' claims be subordinated to the greater good of the society; that is, to the greater good of outsiders. They believe that such issues as pollution, the disposal of solid and liquid wastes, and the conservation of natural resources should be principal considerations in strategic decision making. Also broadly stated, insiders tend to believe that the competing claims of outsiders should be balanced against one another in a way that protects the company mission. For example, they tend to believe that the need of consumers for a product should be balanced against the water pollution resulting from its production if the firm cannot eliminate that pollution entirely and still remain profitable. Some insiders also argue that the claims of society, as expressed in government regulation, provide tax money that can be used to eliminate water pollution and the like if the general public wants this to be done.

EXHIBIT 3.2
Inputs to the Development of the Company Mission

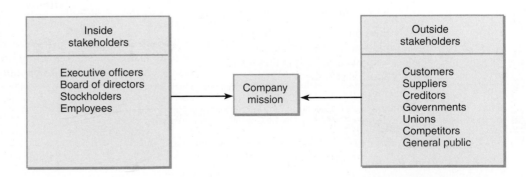

Inside stakeholders	Company mission	Outside stakeholders
Executive officers Board of directors Stockholders Employees		Customers Suppliers Creditors Governments Unions Competitors General public

Who's Doing Well by Doing Good

Automobiles

Toyota	The maker of the top-selling Prius hybrid leads in developing efficient gas-electric vehicles.
Volkswagen	A market leader in small cars and clean diesel technologies.

Computers and Peripherals

Toshiba	At forefront of developing eco-efficient products, such as fuel cells for notebook PC batteries.
Dell	Among the first U.S. PC makers to take hardware back from consumers and recycle it for free.

Health Care

Fresenius Medical Care	Discloses costs of its patient treatment in terms of energy and water use and waste generated.
Quest Diagnostics	Diversity program promotes businesses owned by minorities, women, and veterans.

Oil and Gas

Norsk Hydro	Cut greenhouse gas emissions 32 percent since 1990; strong in assessing social, environmental impact.
Suncor Energy	Ties with aboriginals help it deal with social and ecological issues in Canada's far north.

Retail

Marks & Spencer	Buys local product to cut transit costs and fuel use; good wages and benefits help retain staff.
Aeon	Environmental accounting has saved $5.6 million; good employee policies in China and Southeast Asia.

Communications Equipment

Nokia	Makes phones for handicapped and low-income consumers; a leader in phasing out toxic materials.
Ericsson	Eco-freindly initiatives include wind- and fuel-cell-powered telecom systems in Nigerian villages.

Financial Services

ABN Amro	Involved in carbon-emissions trading; finances everything from micro-enterprises to biomass fuels.
ING	Weighs sustainability in project finance; helps developing nations improve financial institutions.

Household Durables

Philips Electronics	Top innovator of energy-saving appliances, lighting, and medical gear and goods for developing world.
Matsushita Electric	State-of-the-art green products; eliminated 96 percent of the most toxic substances in its global operations.

Pharmaceuticals

Novo Nordisk	Spearheads efforts in leprosy and bird flu and is a leading player in lower-cost generics.
Glaxo-Smithkline	Devotes R&D to malaria and TB; first to offer AIDS drugs at cost.

Utilities

FPL	Largest U.S. solar generator.
Scottish & Southern	Aggressively discloses environmental risk, including air pollution and climate change.

Source: From "Beyond the Green Corporation," by Pete Engardino. Reprinted from January 29, 2007 issue of *BusinessWeek* by special permission. Copyright © 2007 by The McGraw-Hill Companies, Inc.

The issues are numerous, complex, and contingent on specific situations. Thus, rigid rules of business conduct cannot deal with them. Each firm *regardless of size* must decide how to meet its perceived social responsibility. While large, well-capitalized companies may have easy access to environmental consultants, this is not an affordable strategy for smaller companies. However, the experience of many small businesses demonstrates that it is feasible to accomplish significant pollution prevention and waste reduction without big expenditures and without hiring consultants. Once a problem area has been identified, a company's line employees frequently can develop a solution. Other important pollution prevention strategies include changing the materials used or redesigning how operations are bid out. Making pollution prevention a social responsibility can be beneficial to smaller companies. Publicly traded firms also can benefit directly from socially responsible strategies.

Different approaches adopted by different firms reflect differences in competitive position, industry, country, environmental and ecological pressures, and a host of other factors. In other words, they will reflect both situational factors and differing priorities in the acknowledgment of claims. Obviously, winning the loyalty of the growing legions of consumers will require new strategies and new alliances in the twenty-first century. Exhibit 3.3, Strategy in Action, discusses a wide range of socially responsible actions in which corporations are currently engaged.

Occidental Petroleum faces issues of corporate social responsibility in addressing the needs of the many stakeholders involved in the firm's oil exploration in developing countries. Many parties have the potential to be affected by the company's endeavors, including local inhabitants and government, environmental groups, and institutional investors.

Despite differences in their approaches, most American firms now try to assure outsiders that they attempt to conduct business in a socially responsible manner. Many firms, including Abt Associates, Dow Chemical, Eastern Gas and Fuel Associates, ExxonMobil, and the Bank of America, conduct and publish annual social audits. Such audits attempt to evaluate a firm from the perspective of social responsibility. Private consultants often conduct them for the firm and offer minimally biased evaluations on what are inherently highly subjective issues.

TYPES OF SOCIAL RESPONSIBILITY

To better understand the nature and range of social responsibilities for which they must plan, strategic managers can consider four types of social commitment: economic, legal, ethical, and discretionary social responsibilities.

economic responsibilities
The duty of managers, as agents of the company owners, to maximize stockholder wealth.

Economic responsibilities are the most basic social responsibilities of business. As we have noted, some economists see these as the only legitimate social responsibility of business. Living up to their economic responsibilities requires managers to maximize profits whenever possible. The essential responsibility of business is assumed to be providing goods and services to society at a reasonable cost. In discharging that economic responsibility, the company also emerges as socially responsible by providing productive jobs for its workforce, and tax payments for its local, state, and federal governments.

legal responsibilities
The firm's obligations to comply with the laws that regulate business activities.

Legal responsibilities reflect the firm's obligations to comply with the laws that regulate business activities. The consumer and environmental movements focused increased public attention on the need for social responsibility in business by lobbying for laws that govern business in the areas of pollution control and consumer safety. The intent of consumer legislation has been to correct the "balance of power" between buyers and sellers in the marketplace. Among the most important laws are the Federal Fair Packaging and

Labeling Act that regulates labeling procedures for business, the Truth in Lending Act that regulates the extension of credit to individuals, and the Consumer Product Safety Act that protects consumers against unreasonable risks of injury in the use of consumer products.

The environmental movement has had a similar effect on the regulation of business. This movement achieved stricter enforcement of existing environmental protections and it spurred the passage of new, more comprehensive laws such as the National Environmental Policy Act, which is devoted to preserving the United States' ecological balance and making environmental protection a federal policy goal. It requires environmental impact studies whenever new construction may threaten an existing ecosystem, and it established the Council on Environmental Quality to guide business development. Another product of the environmental movement was the creation of the federal Environmental Protection Agency, which interprets and administers the environmental protection policies of the U.S. government.

Clearly, these legal responsibilities are supplemental to the requirement that businesses and their employees comply fully with the general civil and criminal laws that apply to all individuals and institutions in the country. Yet, strangely, individual failures to adhere to the law have recently produced some of the greatest scandals in the history of American free enterprise. Probably the most disgraceful of these high-profile cases involved the Enron Corporation, an American company with headquarters in Houston, Texas. Enron was one of the world's largest electricity, natural gas, pulp and paper, and communication companies, before its bankruptcy in 2001. It had been named "America's Most Innovative Company" for six consecutive years and "100 Best Companies to Work For in America" by *Fortune* magazine. Its revenue in 2000 was $101 billion, making it the seventh largest corporation in the United States.

Enron's bankruptcy was caused by willful and creatively planned accounting fraud masterminded by three Enron executives. Kenneth Lay (founder, former chairman, and CEO), Jeffrey Skilling (former president, CEO, and chief operating officer [COO]), and Andrew Fastow (former chief financial officer [CFO]) received lengthy prison sentences for crimes including conspiracy, securities fraud, false statements, and insider trading.

It was revealed in court hearings that the majority of Enron's profits and revenue came from deals with special-purpose entities, while the majority of Enron's debts and losses were not reported in its financial statements. As the scandal was exposed to the general public, Enron's blue chip stock plummeted from more than $90 to pennies per share. Enron's accounting firm Arthur Andersen was found guilty of obstruction of justice for destroying documents related to Enron, was forced to stop auditing public companies, and suffered irreparable damage to its reputation. In 2007, Enron changed its name to Enron Creditors Recovery Corporation to reflect the reorganization and liquidation of remaining operations and assets of the company.

Exhibit 3.4, Strategy in Action, presents an overview of seven other major criminal or ethical violations that involved executives from Adelphia Communications, Arthur Andersen, Global Crossing, ImClone Systems, Merrill Lynch, WorldCom, and Xerox.

ethical responsibilities
The strategic managers' notion of right and proper business behavior.

Ethical responsibilities reflect the company's notion of right and proper business behavior. Ethical responsibilities are obligations that transcend legal requirements. Firms are expected, but not required, to behave ethically. Some actions that are legal might be considered unethical. For example, the manufacture and distribution of cigarettes is legal. But in light of the often-lethal consequences of smoking, many consider the continued sale of cigarettes to be unethical. The topic of management ethics receives additional attention later in this chapter.

An Overview of Corporate Scandals*

ADELPHIA COMMUNICATIONS

On July 24, 2002, John Rigas, the 77-year-old founder of the country's sixth largest cable television operator was arrested, along with two of his sons, and accused of looting the now-bankrupt company. Several other former Adelphia executives were also arrested. The Securities and Exchange Commission (SEC) brought a civil suit against the company for allegedly fraudulently excluding billions of dollars in liabilities from its financial statements, falsifying statistics, inflating its earnings to meet Wall Street's expectations, and concealing "rampant self-dealing by the Rigas family." The family, which founded Adelphia in 1952, gave up control of the firm in May, and on June 25 the company filed for bankruptcy protection. The company was delisted by NASDAQ in June 2002.

ARTHUR ANDERSEN

On June 15, 2002, a Texas jury found the accounting firm guilty of obstructing justice for its role in shredding financial documents related to its former client Enron. Andersen, founded in 1913, had already been largely destroyed after admitting that it sped up the shredding of Enron documents following the launch of an SEC investigation. Andersen fired David Duncan, who led its Houston office, saying he was responsible for shredding the Enron documents. Duncan admitted to obstruction of justice, turned state's evidence, and testified on behalf of the government.

GLOBAL CROSSING

The SEC and the Federal Bureau of Investigation (FBI) are probing the five-year-old telecom company Global Crossing regarding alleged swaps of network capacity with other telecommunications firms to inflate revenue. The company ran into trouble by betting that it could borrow billions of dollars to build a fiber-optic infrastructure that would be in strong demand by corporations. Because others made the same bet, there was a glut of fiber optics and prices plunged, leaving Global Crossing with massive debts. It filed for bankruptcy on January 28, 2002. Chairman Gary Winnick, who founded Global Crossing in 1997, cashed out $734 million in stock before the company collapsed. Global Crossing was delisted from the New York Stock Exchange (NYSE) in January 2002.

IMCLONE SYSTEMS

The biotech firm is being investigated by a congressional committee that is seeking to find out if ImClone correctly informed investors that the Food and Drug Administration (FDA) had declined to accept for review its key experimental cancer drug, Erbitux. Former CEO Samuel Waksal pled guilty in June 2003 to insider trading charges related to Erbitux and was sentenced to seven years in prison. Also, federal investigators filed charges against home decorating diva Martha Stewart for using insider information on the cancer drug when she sold 4,000 ImClone shares one day before the FDA initially said it would reject the drug.

MERRILL LYNCH

On May 21, 2002, Merrill Lynch agreed to pay $100 million to settle New York Attorney General Eliot Spitzer's charges that the nation's largest securities firm knowingly peddled Internet stocks to investors to generate lucrative investment banking fees. Internal memos written by Merrill's feted Internet analyst Henry Blodgett revealed that company analysts thought little of the Web stocks that they urged investors to buy. Merrill agreed to strengthen firewalls between its research and investment-banking divisions, ensuring advice given to investors is not influenced by efforts to win underwriting fees.

WORLDCOM

The nation's second largest telecom company filed for the nation's biggest ever bankruptcy on July 21, 2002. WorldCom's demise accelerated on June 25, 2002, when it admitted it hid $3.85 billion in expenses, allowing it to post net income of $1.38 billion in 2001, instead of a loss. The company fired its CFO Scott Sullivan and on June 28 began cutting 17,000 jobs, more than 20 percent of its workforce. CEO Bernie Ebbers resigned in April amid questions about $408 million of personal loans he received from the company to cover losses he incurred in buying its shares. WorldCom was delisted from NASDAQ in July 2002.

XEROX

Xerox said on June 28, 2002, that it would restate five years of financial results to reclassify more than $6 billion in revenues. In April, the company settled SEC charges that it used "accounting tricks" to defraud investors, agreeing to pay a $10 million fine. The firm admitted no wrongdoing. Xerox manufactures imaging products, such as copiers, printers, fax machines, and scanners.

*This section was derived in its entirety from "A Guide to Corporate Scandals," MSNBC, www.msnbc.com/news/corpscandal front.

discretionary responsibilities
Responsibilities voluntarily assumed by a business, such as public relations, good citizenship, and full corporate responsibility.

Discretionary responsibilities are those that are voluntarily assumed by a business organization. They include public relations activities, good citizenship, and full corporate social responsibility. Through public relations activities, managers attempt to enhance the image of their companies, products, and services by supporting worthy causes. This form of discretionary responsibility has a self-serving dimension. Companies that adopt the good citizenship approach actively support ongoing charities, public service advertising campaigns, or issues in the public interest. A commitment to full corporate responsibility requires strategic managers to attack social problems with the same zeal in which they attack business problems. For example, teams in the National Football League provide time off for players and other employees afflicted with drug or alcohol addictions who agree to enter rehabilitation programs.

It is important to remember that the categories on the continuum of social responsibility overlap, creating gray areas where societal expectations on organizational behavior are difficult to categorize. In considering the overlaps among various demands for social responsibility, however, managers should keep in mind that in the view of the general public, economic and legal responsibilities are required, ethical responsibility is expected, and discretionary responsibility is desired.

Corporate Social Responsibility and Profitability
CSR and the Bottom Line

corporate social responsibility (CSR)
The idea that business has a duty to serve society in general as well as the financial interest of stockholders.

The goal of every firm is to maintain viability through long-run profitability. Until all costs and benefits are accounted for, however, profits may not be claimed. In the case of **corporate social responsibility (CSR)**, costs and benefits are both economic and social. While economic costs and benefits are easily quantifiable, social costs and benefits are not. Managers therefore risk subordinating social consequences to other performance results that can be more straightforwardly measured.

The dynamic between CSR and success (profit) is complex. While one concept is clearly not mutually exclusive of the other, it is also clear that neither is a prerequisite of the other. Rather than viewing these two concepts as competing, it may be better to view CSR as a component in the decision-making process of business that must determine, among other objectives, how to maximize profits.

Attempts to undertake a cost-benefit analysis of CSR have not been very successful. The process is complicated by several factors. First, some CSR activities incur no dollar costs at all. For example, Second Harvest, the largest nongovernment, charitable food distributor in the nation, accepts donations from food manufacturers and food retailers of surplus food that would otherwise be thrown out due to overruns, warehouse damage, or labeling errors. In 10 years, Second Harvest has distributed more than 2 billion pounds of food. Gifts in Kind America is an organization that enables companies to reduce unsold or obsolete inventory by matching a corporation's donated products with a charity's or other nonprofit organization's needs. In addition, a tax break is realized by the company. In the past, corporate donations have included 130,000 pairs of shoes from Nike, 10,000 pairs of gloves from Aris Isotoner, and 480 computer systems from Apple Computer.

In addition, philanthropic activities of a corporation, which have been a traditional mainstay of CSR, are undertaken at a discounted cost to the firm since they are often tax deductible. The benefits of corporate philanthropy can be enormous as is shown by the many national social welfare causes that have been spurred by corporate giving. While such acts of benevolence often help establish a general perception of the involved companies within society, some philanthropic acts bring specific credit to the firm.

Mission Statement: Johnson & Johnson

"We believe our first responsibility is to the doctors, nurses and patients, to mothers and fathers and all others who use our products and services. In meeting their needs everything we do must be of high quality. We must constantly strive to reduce our costs in order to maintain reasonable prices. Customers' orders must be serviced promptly and accurately. Our suppliers and distributors must have an opportunity to make a fair profit.

"We are responsible to our employees, the men and women who work with us throughout the world. Everyone must be considered as an individual. We must respect their dignity and recognize their merit. They must have a sense of security in their jobs. Compensation must be fair and adequate, and working conditions clean, orderly and safe. Employees must feel free to make suggestions and complaints. There must be equal opportunity for employment, development and advancement for those qualified. We must provide competent management, and their actions must be just and ethical.

"We are responsible to the communities in which we live and work and to the world community as well. We must be good citizens—support good works and charities and bear our fair share of taxes. We must encourage civic improvements and better health and education. We must maintain in good order the property we are privileged to use, protecting the environment and natural resources.

"Our final responsibility is to our stockholders. Business must make a sound profit. We must experiment with new ideas. Research must be carried on, innovative programs developed and mistakes paid for. New equipment must be purchased, new facilities provided and new products launched. Reserves must be created to provide for adverse times. When we operate according to these principles, the stockholders should realize a fair return."

Source: Johnson & Johnson, http://www.jnsj.com

Second, socially responsible behavior does not come at a prohibitive cost. One needs only to look at the problems of A. H. Robbins Company (Dalkon Shield), Beech-Nut Corporation (apple juice), Drexel Burnham (insider trading), and Exxon (*Valdez*) for stark answers on the "cost" of social responsibility (or its absence) in the business environment.

Third, socially responsible practices may create savings and, as a result, increase profits. SET Laboratories uses popcorn to ship software rather than polystyrene peanuts. It is environmentally safer and costs 60 percent less to use. Corporations that offer part-time and adjustable work schedules have realized that this can lead to reduced absenteeism, greater productivity and increased morale. DuPont opted for more flexible schedules for its employees after a survey revealed 50 percent of women and 25 percent of men considered working for another employer with more flexibility for family concerns.

Proponents argue that CSR costs are more than offset in the long run by an improved company image and increased community goodwill. These intangible assets can prove valuable in a crisis, as Johnson & Johnson discovered with the Tylenol cyanide scare in 1982. Because it had established a solid reputation as a socially responsible company before the incident, the public readily accepted the company's assurances of public safety. Consequently, financial damage to Johnson & Johnson was minimized, despite the company's $100 million voluntary recall of potentially tainted capsules. CSR may also head off new regulation, preventing increased compliance costs. It may even attract investors who are themselves socially responsible. Proponents believe that for these reasons, socially responsible behavior increases the financial value of the firm in the long run. The mission statement of Johnson & Johnson is provided as Exhibit 3.5, Strategy in Action.

Performance To explore the relationship between socially responsible behavior and financial performance, an important question must first be answered: How do managers measure the financial effect of corporate social performance?

Critics of CSR believe that companies that behave in a socially responsible manner, and portfolios comprising these companies' securities, should perform more poorly financially than those that do not. The costs of CSR outweigh the benefits for individual firms, they suggest. In addition, traditional portfolio theory holds that investors minimize risk and maximize return by being able to choose from an infinite universe of investment opportunities. Portfolios based on social criteria should suffer, critics argue, because they are by definition restrictive in nature. This restriction should increase portfolio risk and reduce portfolio return.

CSR Today

CSR has become a priority with American business. In addition to a commonsense belief that companies should be able to "do well by doing good," at least three broad trends are driving businesses to adopt CSR frameworks: the resurgence of environmentalism, increasing buyer power, and the globalization of business.

The Resurgence of Environmentalism In March 1989, the Exxon *Valdez* ran aground in Prince William Sound, spilling 11 million gallons of oil, polluting miles of ocean and shore, and helping to revive worldwide concern for the ecological environment. Six months after the *Valdez* incident, the Coalition for Environmentally Responsible Economies (CERES) was formed to establish new goals for environmentally responsible corporate behavior. The group drafted the CERES Principles to "establish an environmental ethic with criteria by which investors and others can assess the environmental performance of companies. Companies that sign these Principles pledge to go voluntarily beyond the requirements of the law."

The most prevalent forms of environmentalism are efforts to preserve natural resources and eliminating environmental pollution, often referred to as the concern for "greening." The Heinz Corporation is a company that is praised for its strong green stance. Some details of its aggressive sustainability program are provided in Exhibit 3.6, Top Strategist.

Increasing Buyer Power The rise of the consumer movement has meant that buyers—consumers and investors—are increasingly flexing their economic muscle. Consumers are becoming more interested in buying products from socially responsible companies. Organizations such as the Council on Economic Priorities (CEP) help consumers make more informed buying decisions through such publications as *Shopping for a Better World,* which provides social performance information on 191 companies making more than 2,000 consumer products. CEP also sponsors the annual Corporate Conscience Awards, which recognize socially responsible companies. One example of consumer power at work is the effective outcry over the deaths of dolphins in tuna fishermen's nets.

Investors represent a second type of influential consumer. There has been a dramatic increase in the number of people interested in supporting socially responsible companies through their investments. Membership in the Social Investment Forum, a trade association serving social investing professionals, has been growing at a rate of about 50 percent annually. As baby boomers achieve their own financial success, the social investing movement has continued its rapid growth.

While social investing wields relatively low power as an individual private act (selling one's shares of ExxonMobil does not affect the company), it can be very powerful as a collective public act. When investors vote their shares in behalf of pro-CSR issues, companies may be pressured to change their social behavior. The South African divestiture movement is one example of how effective this pressure can be.

The Vermont National Bank has added a Socially Responsible Banking Fund to its product line. Investors can designate any of their interest-bearing accounts with a $500 minimum

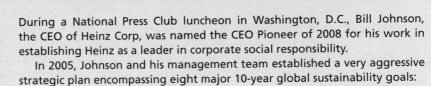

Top Strategist
Heinz CEO Bill Johnson Stresses Corporate Social Responsibility

Exhibit 3.6

During a National Press Club luncheon in Washington, D.C., Bill Johnson, the CEO of Heinz Corp, was named the CEO Pioneer of 2008 for his work in establishing Heinz as a leader in corporate social responsibility.

In 2005, Johnson and his management team established a very aggressive strategic plan encompassing eight major 10-year global sustainability goals:

Greenhouse gas	Emissions	Decrease by 20%
Energy use in manufacturing	Usage	Decrease by 20%
Water use in manufacturing	Water consumption	Decrease by 20%
Solid waste	Waste from Heinz operations	Decrease by 20%
Packaging	Total packaging	Decrease by 15%
Transportation	Fossil fuel consumption	Decrease by 10%
Renewable energy	Renewable energy resources	Increase by 15%
Sustainable agriculture	Carbon footprint	Decrease by 15%
	Water usage	Decrease by 15%
	Field yield	Increase by 5%

These environmental goals were viewed by Johnson as an extension of the original vision of Henry J. Heinz, who believed that food safety regulations made a significant contribution to society.

The overarching theme of Johnson's 2008 corporate social responsibility plan was a 20 percent reduction of greenhouse gas emissions by the year 2015. He stated, "To achieve these goals we are executing numerous global initiatives to reduce non-value-added packaging, increase the use of recycled materials, lower energy consumption, conserve water, and increase our use of renewable energy sources at some of our largest plants."* Examples of successes in achieving his plan included a European plastics consumption reduction of 340 tons and a solid waste reduction in an Ohio plant of 800,000 pounds.

* H.J. Heinz Corp. Web site, 2008, http://www.heinz.com/sustainability/environment.aspx
Source: 2008 Annual Report, H.J. Heinz Corporation, June 19, 2008, p. 14.

balance to be used by the fund. This fund then lends these monies for purposes such as low-income housing, the environment, education, farming, or small business development. Although it has had a "humble" beginning of approximately 800 people investing about $11 million, the bank has attracted out-of-state depositors and is growing faster than expected.

Social investors comprise both individuals and institutions. Much of the impetus for social investing originated with religious organizations that wanted their investments to mirror their beliefs. At present, the ranks of social investors have expanded to include educational institutions and large pension funds.

Large-scale social investing can be broken down into the two broad areas of guideline portfolio investing and shareholder activism. Guideline portfolio investing is the largest and fastest-growing segment of social investing. Individual and institutional guideline portfolio investors use ethical guidelines as screens to identify possible investments in stocks, bonds, and mutual funds. The investment instruments that survive the social screens are then layered over the investor's financial screens to create the investor's universe of possible investments.

Screens may be negative (e.g., excluding all tobacco companies) or they may combine negative and positive elements (e.g., eliminating companies with bad labor records while seeking out companies with good ones). Most investors rely on screens created by investment firms such as Kinder, Lydenberg Domini & Co. or by industry groups such as the Council on Economic Priorities. In addition to ecology, employee relations, and community development, corporations may be screened on their association with "sin" products (alcohol, tobacco, gambling), defense/weapons production, and nuclear power.

In contrast to guideline portfolio investors, who passively indicate their approval or disapproval of a company's social behavior by simply including or excluding it from their portfolios, shareholder activists seek to directly influence corporate social behavior. Shareholder activists invest in a corporation hoping to improve specific aspects of the company's social performance, typically by seeking a dialogue with upper management. If this and successive actions fail to achieve the desired results, shareholder activists may introduce proxy resolutions to be voted upon at the corporation's annual meeting. The goal of these resolutions is to achieve change by gaining public exposure for the issue at hand. While the number of shareholder activists is relatively small, they are by no means small in achievement: shareholder activists, led by such groups as the Interfaith Center on Corporate Responsibility, were the driving force behind the South African divestiture movement. Currently, there are more than 35 socially screened mutual funds available in the United States alone.

The Globalization of Business   Management issues, including CSR, have become more complex as companies increasingly transcend national borders: It is difficult enough to come to a consensus on what constitutes socially responsible behavior within one culture, let alone determine common ethical values across cultures. In addition to different cultural views, the high barriers facing international CSR include differing corporate disclosure practices, inconsistent financial data and reporting methods, and the lack of CSR research organizations within countries. Despite these problems, CSR is growing abroad. The United Kingdom has 30 ethical mutual funds and Canada offers 6 socially responsible funds.

One of the most contentious social responsibility issues confronting multinational firms pertains to human rights. For example, many U.S. firms reduce their costs either by relying on foreign manufactured goods or by outsourcing their manufacturing to foreign manufacturers. These foreign manufacturers, often Chinese, offer low pricing because they pay very low wages by U.S. standards, even though they are extremely competitive by Chinese pay rates.

While Chinese workers are happy to earn manufacturer wages and U.S. customers are pleased by the lower prices charged for foreign manufactured goods, others are unhappy. They believe that such U.S. firms are failing to satisfy their social responsibilities. Some U.S. workers and their unions argue that jobs in the United States are being eliminated or devalued by foreign competition. Some human rights advocates argue that the working conditions and living standards of foreign workers are so substandard when compared with U.S. standards that they verge on inhumane. A troubling twist on American corporations' role in the human rights debate about conditions in China arises from the sale of software to the Chinese government. Developed by Cisco, Oracle, and other U.S. companies, the software is used by China's police to monitor the activities of individuals that the Chinese government labels as criminals and dissidents.

SARBANES-OXLEY ACT OF 2002

Sarbanes-Oxley Act of 2002
Law that revised and strengthened auditing and accounting standards.

Following a string of wrongdoings by corporate executives in 2000 to 2002, and the subsequent failures of their firms, Washington lawmakers proposed more than 50 policies to reassure investors. None of the resulting bills were able to pass both houses of Congress until the Banking Committee Chairman Paul Sarbanes (D–MD) proposed legislation to establish new auditing and accounting standards. The bill was called the Public Company Accounting Reform and Investor Protection Act of 2002. Later the name was changed to the **Sarbanes-Oxley Act of 2002.**

On July 30, 2002, President George Bush signed the Sarbanes-Oxley Act into law. This revolutionary act applies to public companies with securities registered under Section 12 of the Securities Act of 1934 and those required to file reports under Section 15(d) of the Exchange Act. Sarbanes-Oxley includes required certifications for financial statements, new corporate regulations, disclosure requirements, and penalties for failure to comply. More details on the Act are provided in Exhibit 3.7, Strategy in Action.

The Sarbanes-Oxley Act states that the CEO and CFO must certify every report containing the company's financial statements. The certification acknowledges that the CEO or CFO (chief financial officer) has reviewed the report. As part of the review, the officer must attest that the information does not include untrue statements or necessary omitted information. Furthermore, based on the officer's knowledge, the report is a reliable source of the company's financial condition and result of operations for the period represented. The certification also makes the officers responsible for establishing and maintaining internal controls such that they are aware of any material information relating to the company. The officers must also evaluate the effectiveness of the internal controls within 90 days of the release of the report and present their conclusions of the effectiveness of the controls. Also, the officers must disclose any fraudulent material, deficiencies in the reporting of the financial reports, or problems with the internal control to the company's auditors and auditing committee. Finally, the officers must indicate any changes to the internal controls or factors that could affect them.

The Sarbanes-Oxley Act includes provisions restricting the corporate control of executives, accounting firms, auditing committees, and attorneys. With regard to executives, the Act bans personal loans. A company can no longer directly or indirectly issue, extend, or maintain a personal loan to any director or executive officer. Executive officers and directors are not permitted to purchase, sell, acquire, or transfer any equity security during any pension fund blackout period. Executives are required to notify fund participants of any blackout period and the reasons for the blackout period. The SEC will provide the company's executives with a code of ethics for the company to adopt. Failure to meet the code must be disclosed to the SEC.

The Act limits some and issues new duties of the registered public accounting firms that conduct the audits of the financial statements. Accounting firms are prohibited from performing bookkeeping or other accounting services related to the financial statements, designing or implementing financial systems, appraising, internal auditing, brokering banking services, or providing legal services unrelated to the audit. All critical accounting policies and alternative treatments of financial information within generally accepted accounting principles (GAAP), and written communication between the accounting firm and the company's management must be reported to the audit committee.

The Act defines the composition of the audit committee and specifies its responsibilities. The members of the audit committee must be members of the company's board of directors. At least one member of the committee should be classified as a "financial expert." The

The following outline presents the major elements of the Sarbanes-Oxley Act of 2002.

CORPORATE RESPONSIBILITY

- The CEO and CFO of each company are required to submit a report, based on their knowledge, to the SEC certifying the company's financial statements are fair representations of the financial condition without false statements or omissions.

- The CEO and CFO must reimburse the company for any bonuses or equity-based incentives received for the last 12-month period if the company is required to restate its financial statements due to material noncompliance with any financial reporting requirement that resulted from misconduct.

- Directors and executive officers are prohibited from trading a company's 401(k) plan, profit sharing plan, or retirement plan during any blackout period. The plan administrators are required to notify the plan participants and beneficiaries with notice of all blackout periods, reasons for the blackout period, and a statement that the participant or beneficiary should evaluate their investment even though they are unable to direct or diversify their accounts during the blackout.

- No company may make, extend, modify, or renew any personal loans to its executives or directors. Limited exceptions are for loans made in the course of the company's business, on market terms, for home improvement and home loans, consumer credit, or extension of credit.

INCREASED DISCLOSURE

- Each annual and quarterly financial report filed with the SEC must disclose all material off-balance-sheet transactions, arrangements, and obligations that may affect the current or future financial condition of the company or its operations.

- Companies must present pro forma financial information with the SEC in a manner that is not misleading and must be reconciled with the company's financial condition and with generally accepted accounting principles (GAAP).

- Each company is required to disclose whether they have adopted a code of ethics for its senior financial officers. If not, the company must explain the reasons. Any change or waiver of the code of ethics must be disclosed.

- Each annual report must contain a statement of management's responsibility for establishing and maintaining an internal control structure and procedures for financial reporting. The report must also include an assessment of the effectiveness of the internal control procedures.

- The Form 4 will be provided within two business days after the execution date of the trading of a company's securities by directors and executive officers. The SEC may extend this deadline if it determines the two-day period is not feasible.

- The company must disclose information concerning changes in financial conditions or operations "on a rapid and current basis," in plain English.

The SEC must review the financial statements of each reporting company no less than once every three years.

AUDIT COMMITTEES

- The audit committee must be composed entirely of independent directors. Committee members are not permitted to accept any fees from the company, cannot control 5 percent or more of the voting of

audit committee is directly responsible for the work of any accounting firm employed by the company, and the accounting firm must report directly to the audit committee. The audit committee must create procedures for employee complaints or concerns over accounting or auditing matters. Upon discovery of unlawful acts by the company, the audit committee must report and be supervised in its investigation by a Public Company Accounting Oversight Board.

The Act includes rules for attorney conduct. If a company's attorneys find evidence of securities violations, they are required to report the matter to the chief legal counsel or CEO. If there is not an appropriate response, the attorneys must report the information to the audit committee or the board of directors.

- the company, nor be an officer, director, partner, or employee of the company.
- The audit committee must have the authority to engage the outside auditing firm.
- The audit committee must establish procedures for the treatment of complaints regarding accounting controls or auditing matters. They are responsible for employee complaints concerning questionable accounting and auditing.
- The audit committee must disclose whether at least one of the committee members is a "financial expert." If not, the committee must explain why not.

NEW CRIMES AND INCREASED CRIMINAL PENALTIES
- Tampering with records with intent to impede or influence any federal investigation or bankruptcy will be punishable by a fine and/or prison sentence up to 20 years.
- Failure by an accountant to maintain all auditing papers for five years after the end of the fiscal period will be punishable by a fine and/or up to 10-year prison sentence.
- Knowingly executing, or attempting to execute, a scheme to defraud investors will be punishable by a fine and/or prison sentence of up to 25 years.
- Willfully certifying a report that does not comply with the law can be punishable with a fine up to $5,000,000 and/or a prison sentence up to 20 years.

NEW CIVIL CAUSE OF ACTION AND INCREASED ENFORCEMENT POWERS
- Protection will be provided to whistle-blowers who provide information or assist in an investigation by law enforcement, congressional committee, or employee supervisor.
- Bankruptcy cannot be used to avoid liability from securities laws violations.
- Investors are able to file a civil action for fraud up to two years after discovery of the facts and five years after the occurrence of fraud.
- The SEC can receive a restraining order prohibiting payments to insiders during an investigation.
- The SEC can prevent individuals from holding an officer's or director's position in a public company as a result of violation of the securities law.

AUDITOR INDEPENDENCE
- All audit services must be preapproved by the audit committee and must be disclosed to investors.
- The lead audit or reviewing audit partner from the auditing accounting firm must change at least once every five fiscal years.
- The registered accounting firms must report to the audit committee all accounting policies and practices used, alternative uses of the financial information within GAAP that has been discussed with management, and written communications between the accounting firm and management.
- An auditing firm is prohibited from auditing a company if the company's CEO or CFO was employed by the auditing firm within the past year.

A Public Company Accounting Oversight Board is established by the SEC to oversee the audits of public companies. The Board will register public accounting firms, establish audit standards, inspect registered accounting firms, and discipline violators of the rules. No person can take part in an audit if not employed by a registered public accounting firm.

Other sections of the Sarbanes-Oxley Act stipulate disclosure periods for financial operations and reporting. Relevant information relating to changes in the financial condition or operations of a company must be immediately reported in plain English. Off-balance-sheet transactions, correcting adjustments, and pro-forma information must be presented in the annual and quarterly financial reports. The information must not contain any untrue statements, must not omit material facts, and must meet GAAP standards.

Stricter penalties have been issued for violations of the Sarbanes-Oxley Act. If a company must restate its financial statements due to noncompliance, the CEO and CFO must relinquish any bonus or incentive-based compensation or realized profits from the sale of securities during the 12-month period following the filing with the SEC. Other securities

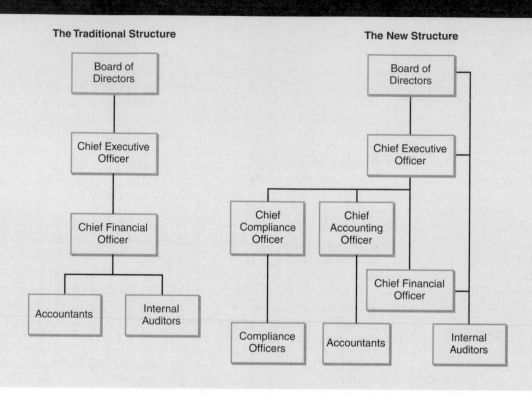

The Traditional Structure

The New Structure

fraud, such as destruction or falsification of records, results in fines and prison sentences up to 25 years.

The New Corporate Governance Structure

A major consequence of the 2000–2002 accounting scandals was the Sarbanes-Oxley Act of 2002, and a major consequence of Sarbanes-Oxley has been the restructuring of the governance structure of American corporations. The most significant change in the restructuring is the heightened role of corporate internal auditors, as depicted in Exhibit 3.8, Strategy in Action. Auditors have traditionally been viewed as performing a necessary but perfunctory function, namely to probe corporate financial records for unintentional or illicit misrepresentations. Although a majority of U.S. corporations have longstanding traditions of reporting that their auditors operated independently of CFO approval and that they had direct access to the board, in practice, the auditors' work usually traveled through the organization's hierarchical chain of command.

In the past, internal auditors reviewed financial reports generated by other corporate accountants. The auditors considered professional accounting and financial practices, as well as relevant aspects of corporate law, and then presented their findings to the chief financial officer (CFO). Historically, the CFO reviewed the audits and determined the financial data and information that was to be presented to top management, directors, and investors of the company.

However, because Sarbanes-Oxley requires that CEOs and audit committees sign off on financial results, auditors now routinely deal directly with top corporate officials, as shown in the new structure in Exhibit 3.8, Strategy in Action. Approximately 75 percent of senior corporate auditors now report directly to the Board of Directors' audit committee. Additionally, to eliminate the potential for accounting problems, companies are establishing direct lines of communication between top managers and the board and auditors that inform the CFO but that are not dependent on CFO approval or authorization.

The new structure also provides the CEO information provided directly by the company's chief compliance and chief accounting officers. Consequently, the CFO, who is responsible for ultimately approving all company payments, is not empowered to be the sole provider of data for financial evaluations by the CEO and board.

Privatization as a Response to Sarbanes-Oxley

privatization
A restructuring in which the ownership structure of a publicly traded corporation is converted into a privately held company.

A trend in financial restructuring that supports internal growth is **privatization,** in which the ownership structure of a publicly traded corporation is converted into a privately held company. There has been a dramatic upswing in the number of privatizations, due largely to negative manager and investor responses to the increased government regulation required by Sarbanes-Oxley Act of 2002. In 2006, a record number of 322 publicly traded companies with a combined value of $215.4 billion were taken private in the United States.

Some privatization deals are prompted by the huge funds attracted by private equity firms, which exceeded $280 billion in 2006, that allow a premium to be paid over the current stock price. However, the motivation in most cases of privatization is that privately held firms are not subject to the costs of complying with regulations for public companies stemming from the Sarbanes-Oxley legislation. Sarbanes-Oxley legislates that outside firms must audit a company's internal controls. The cost of hiring outside firms, maintaining systems to meet compliance standards, and establishing an audit committee on the board of directors to ensure that these activities are monitored is estimated to be $500,000 on average for the 16,000 publicly reporting companies.

Because of Sarbanes-Oxley, much more time is needed to manage reporting requirements for publicly traded companies. Managers must attest to the accuracy of quarterly financials and provide frequent releases of specified information, such as same-day notification of insider trades. In addition, general counsels are spending much more of their time on compliance activities, with 36 percent of companies incurring the cost and complication of hiring a chief compliance officer. Litigation costs have also risen because of the increased personal liability of board members and key executives, especially in the form of higher insurance premiums. The cost of directors' and officers' insurance premiums has risen nearly 40 percent for companies with solid sheets and clean financial histories.

Certain industry sectors are especially attractive for privatization strategies. In the technology sector, firms that were posting double-digit growth throughout most of the 1980s and 1990s are now having trouble growing their maturing businesses. Although Applied Materials, Dell, EMC, Intel, and Hewlett-Packard have considerable cash flow, equity investors have little interest in these slower-growing companies, cutting off a favorite source of equity funding and making them attractive privatization candidates.

Another active sector for privatization is real estate. In the first half of 2007, the stock prices for real estate investment trusts (REITs) were below the net asset value of their underlying real estate portfolios. This meant that investors believed that REITs were worth less as a company than the total value of their properties, creating an opportunity for investors to acquire the portfolio at a discount.

In the maturing technology sector, where slowing growth is lowering the price to earning multiples, executives look to other sources of funding outside of equity financing. Privatization offers a good alternative because it allows managers to avoid the distractions of short-term technical investors and traders, who react especially strongly to any unanticipated performance variation.

CSR's Effect on the Mission Statement

The mission statement not only identifies what product or service a company produces, how it produces it, and what market it serves, it also embodies what the company believes. As such, it is essential that the mission statement recognize the legitimate claims of its external stakeholders, which may include creditors, customers, suppliers, government, unions, competitors, local communities, and elements of the general public. This stakeholder approach has become widely accepted by U.S. business. For example, a survey of directors in 291 of the largest southeastern U.S. companies found that directors had high stakeholder orientations. Customers, government, stockholders, employees, and society, in that order, were the stakeholders these directors perceived as most important.

In developing mission statements, managers must identify all stakeholder groups and weigh their relative rights and abilities to affect the firm's success. Some companies are proactive in their approach to CSR, making it an integral part of their raison d'être (e.g., Ben & Jerry's ice cream); others are reactive, adopting socially responsible behavior only when they must (e.g., Exxon after the *Valdez* incident).

Social Audit

social audit
An attempt to measure a company's actual social performance against its social objectives.

A **social audit** attempts to measure a company's actual social performance against the social objectives it has set for itself. A social audit may be conducted by the company itself. However, one conducted by an outside consultant who will impose minimal biases may prove more beneficial to the firm. As with a financial audit, an outside auditor brings credibility to the evaluation. This credibility is essential if management is to take the results seriously and if the general public is to believe the company's public relations pronouncements.

Careful, accurate monitoring and evaluation of a company's CSR actions are important not only because the company wants to be sure it is implementing CSR policy as planned but also because CSR actions by their nature are open to intense public scrutiny. To make sure it is making good on its CSR promises, a company may conduct a social audit of its performance.

Once the social audit is complete, it may be distributed internally or both internally and externally, depending on the firm's goals and situation. Some firms include a section in their annual report devoted to social responsibility activities; others publish a separate periodic report on their social responsiveness. Companies publishing separate social audits include General Motors, Bank of America, Atlantic Richfield, Control Data, and Aetna Life and Casualty Company. Nearly all *Fortune* 500 corporations disclose social performance information in their annual reports.

Large firms are not the only companies employing the social audit. Boutique ice cream maker Ben & Jerry's, a CSR pioneer, publishes a social audit in its annual report. The audit, conducted by an outside consultant, scores company performance in such areas as employee benefits, plant safety, ecology, community involvement, and customer service. The report is published unedited.

The social audit may be used for more than simply monitoring and evaluating firm social performance. Managers also use social audits to scan the external environment, determine firm vulnerabilities, and institutionalize CSR within the firm. In addition, companies themselves are not the only ones who conduct social audits; public interest groups and the media watch companies who claim to be socially responsible very closely to see if they practice what they preach. These organizations include consumer groups and socially responsible investing firms that construct their own guidelines for evaluating companies.

The Body Shop learned what can happen when a company's behavior falls short of its espoused mission and objectives. The 20-year-old manufacturer and retailer of naturally based hair and skin products had cultivated a socially responsible corporate image based on a reputation for socially responsible behavior. In late 1994, however, *Business Ethics* magazine published an exposé claiming that the company did not "walk the talk." It accused The Body Shop of using nonrenewable petrochemicals in its products, recycling far less than it claimed, using ingredients tested on animals, and making threats against investigative journalists. The Body Shop's contradictions were noteworthy because Anita Roddick, the company's founder, made CSR a centerpiece of the company's strategy.[1]

SATISFYING CORPORATE SOCIAL RESPONSIBILITY

Corporate social responsibility has become a vital part of the business conversation. The issue is not whether companies will engage in socially responsible activities, but how. For most companies, the challenge is how best to achieve the maximum social benefit from a given amount of resources available for social projects. Research points to five principles that underscore better outcomes for society and for corporate participants.[2]

In 1999, William Ford Jr. angered Ford Motor Co. executives and investors when he wrote that "there are very real conflicts between Ford's current business practices, consumer choices, and emerging views of (environmental) sustainability." In his company citizenship report, the grandson of Henry Ford, then the automaker's nonexecutive chairman, even appeared to endorse a Sierra Club statement declaring that "the gas-guzzling SUV is a rolling monument to environmental destruction."

Bill Ford has had to moderate his strongest environmental beliefs since assuming the company's CEO position in October 2001, just after the Firestone tire scandal. Nevertheless, while he has strived to improve Ford's financial performance and restore trust among its diverse stakeholders, he remains strongly committed to corporate responsibility and environmental protection. In his words, "A good company delivers excellent products and services, and a great company does all that and strives to make the world a better place."[3] Today, Ford is a leader in producing vehicles that run on alternative sources of fuel, and it is performing as well as or better than its major North American rivals, all of whom are involved in intense global competition. The new CEO is successfully pursuing a strategy that is showing improved financial performance, increased confidence in the brand, and clear evidence that the car company is committed to contributing more broadly to society. Among Ford's more notable outreach efforts are an innovative HIV/AIDS initiative in South Africa that is now expanding to India, China, and Thailand; a partnership with the U.S. National Parks Foundation to provide environmentally friendly transportation for park visitors; and significant support for the Clean Air Initiative for Asian Cities.

Ford's actions are emblematic of the corporate social responsibility initiatives of many leading companies today. Corporate-supported social initiatives are now a given. For some time now, many *Fortune* 500 corporations have had senior manager titles dedicated to helping their organizations "give back" more effectively. CSR is now almost universally embraced by top managers as an integral component of their executive roles, whether motivated by self-interest, altruism, strategic advantage, or political gain. Their outreach is usually plain

[1] Jon Entine, "Shattered Image," *Business Ethics* 8, no. 5 (September/October 1994), pp. 23–28.

[2] This section was excerpted from J. A. Pearce II and J. Doh, "Enhancing Corporate Responsibility through Skillful Collaboration," *Sloan Management Review* 46, no. 3 (2005), pp. 30–39.

[3] "Ford Motor Company Encourages Elementary School Students to Support America's National Parks," www.ford.com/en/company/nationalParks.htm

Top Strategist
Starbucks CEO Howard Schultz on CSR

Exhibit 3.9

Starbucks supports coffee farmers by paying premium prices for the highest quality coffee beans and by maintaining its position as the largest purchaser, roaster, and distributor of Fair Trade Certified™ coffee in North America (it is also among the largest worldwide). In addition, Starbucks is a long-time partner of Conservation International (CI). Together, the two organizations developed environmental and social practice standards (C.A.F.E. Practices) for coffee farmers and implemented a rewards system for farmers who adhere to these practices.

The partnership has had a major impact on coffee farmers worldwide. For example, the Association of Kilimanjaro Specialty Coffee Growers, an association of 8,000 smallholder coffee growers in Tanzania, receives support from Starbucks because it is C.A.F.E.-certified. As a result, the association is able to add environmentally sustainable technology to increase coffee quality, which in turn improves the profitability of its farmer members.

Since he came out of retirement to be reappointed as Starbucks' CEO in January 2008, Howard Schultz has taken action to further solidify the company's support of coffee farmers. Schultz partnered with Peter Seligmann, CI's chairman and CEO, to take support of coffee farmers to the next level by protecting the land surrounding coffee farms. The effort involves an effort to help the farmers get a piece of the fast-growing $70 billion carbon finance business. Starbucks finances CI's efforts to work with local growers to protect the landscapes around the coffee farms. Farmers agree to preserve forests to replant trees so that they become eligible for carbon credits from companies that are voluntarily offsetting their emissions.

Under Schultz's leadership, Starbucks has also extended its direct financial support of coffee farmers. In 2008, Starbucks, Transfair USA, and the Fairtrade Labeling Organizations (FLO) International announced Starbucks' commitment to doubling its purchases of Fair Trade™ coffee to 40 million pounds in 2009. This commitment made Starbucks the worldwide largest purchaser of Fair Trade Certified™ coffee.

---

to see on the companies' corporate Web sites. CSR is high on the agenda at major executive gatherings such as the World Economic Forum. It is very much in evidence during times of tragedy—as seen in the corporate responses to the Asian tsunami of December 2004—and it is the subject of many conferences, workshops, newsletters, and more. "Consultancies have sprung up to advise companies on how to do corporate social responsibility and how to let it be known that they are doing it," noted *The Economist* in a survey on CSR.

Executives face conflicting pressures to contribute to social responsibility while honoring their duties to maximize shareholder value. They face many belligerent critics who challenge the idea of a single-minded focus on profits—witness the often violent antiglobalization protests in recent years. They also face skeptics who contend that CSR initiatives are chiefly a convenient marketing gloss. However, the reality is that most executives are eager to improve their CSR effectiveness. The issue is not whether companies will engage in socially responsible activities, but how. For most companies, the challenge is how best to achieve the maximum social benefit from a given amount of resources available for social projects.

Starbucks CEO Howard Schultz believes that he has found a way to make CSR produce benefits both for others and for his firm. Starbucks invests to support coffee farmers through a new initiative with partner Conservation International—and through Starbucks purchase commitments of premium coffee beans. The details are provided in Exhibit 3.9, Top Strategist.

Studies of dozens of social responsibility initiatives at major corporations show that senior managers struggle to find the right balance between "low-engagement" solutions such as charitable gift-giving and "high-commitment" solutions that run the risk of diverting attention from the company's core mission. In this section, we will see that collaborative social initiatives (CSIs)—a form of engagement in which companies provide ongoing and sustained commitments to a social project or issue—provide the best combination of social and strategic impact.

The Core of the CSR Debate

The proper role of CSR—the actions of a company to benefit society beyond the requirement of the law and the direct interests of shareholders—has generated a century's worth of philosophically and economically intriguing debates. Since steel baron Andrew Carnegie published *The Gospel of Wealth* in 1899, the argument that businesses are the trustees of societal property that should be managed for the public good has been seen as one end of a continuum with, at the other end, the belief that profit maximization is management's only legitimate goal. The CSR debates had been largely confined to the background for most of the twentieth century, making the news after an oil spill or when a consumer product caused harm, or when ethics scandals reopened the question of business's fundamental purpose.

The debates surfaced in more positive ways in the last 30 years as new businesses set up shop with altruism very much in mind and on display. Firms such as ice cream maker Ben & Jerry's argued that CSR and profits do not clash; their stance was that doing good led to making good money, too. That line of thinking has gained popularity as more executives have come to understand the value of their companies' reputations with customers—and with investors and employees. But only recently have business leaders begun to get a clearer understanding of the appropriate role of CSR and its effect on financial performance.

In the past, research on the financial effect of CSR produced inconsistent findings, with some studies reporting a positive relationship, others a negative one, and others no relationship at all. Since the mid-1990s, improvements in theory, research designs, data, and analysis have produced empirical research with more consistent results.[4] Importantly, a recent meta-analysis (a methodological technique that aggregates findings of multiple studies) of more than 10 studies found that on balance, positive relationships can be expected from CSR initiatives but that the primary vehicle for achieving superior financial performance from social responsibility is via reputation effects.[5]

There is no shortage of options with which businesses can advance their CSR goals. The greater challenge is finding the right balance. Philanthropy without active engagement—cash donations, for instance—has been criticized as narrow, self-serving, and often motivated to improve the corporation's reputation and keep nongovernmental organization (NGO) critics and other naysayers at bay.[6] However, redirecting the company toward a socially responsible mission, while seemingly attractive, may have the unintended consequences of

[4] J. J. Griffin and J. F. Mahon, "The Corporate Social Performance and Corporate Financial Performance Debate: Twenty-Five Years of Incomparable Research," *Business and Society* 36 (1997), pp. 5–31; R. M. Roman, S. Hayibor, and B. R. Agle, "The Relationship between Social and Financial Performance: Repainting a Portrait," *Business and Society* 38 (1999), pp. 109–125; and J. D. Margolis and J. P. Walsh, "Misery Loves Companies: Rethinking Social Initiatives by Business," *Administrative Science Quarterly* 48 (2003), pp. 268–305.

[5] M. Orlitzky, F. L. Schmidt, and S. L. Rynes, "Corporate Social and Financial Performance: A Meta-Analysis," *Organization Studies* 24, no. 3 (2003), pp. 403–441.

[6] B. Husted, "Governance Choices for Corporate Social Responsibility: To Contribute, Collaborate or Internalize?" *Long Range Planning* 36, no. 5 (2003), pp. 481–498.

EXHIBIT 3.10
Continuum of
Corporate Social
Responsibility
Commitments

Philanthropy/ gift giving	Collaborative social initiative	CSR- dominated mission
Peripheral CSR commitment	Balanced CSR commitment	Excessive CSR commitment

diverting both managers and employees from their core mission. Exhibit 3.10 presents a simple illustration of the range of options available to corporations as they consider their CSR commitments.

What managers need is a model that they can use to guide them in selecting social initiatives and through which they can exploit their companies' core competencies for the maximum positive impact. As a starting point, research confirms that a business must determine the social causes that it will support and why and then decide how its support should be organized.[7] According to one perspective, businesses have three basic support options: donations of cash or material, usually to a nongovernmental or nonprofit agency; creation of a functional operation within the company to assist external charitable efforts; and development of a collaboration approach, whereby a company joins with an organization that has particular expertise in managing the way benefits are derived from corporate support.[8]

Mutual Advantages of Collaborative Social Initiatives

The term *social initiative* describes initiatives that take a collaborative approach. Research on alliances and networks among companies in competitive commercial environments tells us that each partner benefits when the other brings resources, capabilities, or other assets that it cannot easily attain on its own. These *combinative capabilities* allow the company to acquire and synthesize resources and build new applications from those resources, generating innovative responses to rapidly evolving environments.

It is no different with collaborative social initiatives. While neither companies nor nonprofits are well-equipped to handle escalating social or environmental problems, each participant has the potential to contribute valuable material resources, services, or individuals' voluntary time, talents, energies, and organizational knowledge. Those cumulative offerings are vastly superior to cash-only donations, which are a minimalist solution to the challenges of social responsibility. Social initiatives involve ongoing information and operational exchanges among participants and are especially attractive because of their potential benefits for both the corporate and not-for-profit partners.

There is strong evidence to show that CSR activities increasingly confer benefits beyond enhanced reputation. For some participants, they can be a tool to attract, retain, and develop managerial talent. The PricewaterhouseCoopers (PwC) Project Ulysses is a leadership development program that sends small teams of PwC partners to developing countries to apply their expertise to complex social and economic challenges. The cross-cultural PwC teams collaborate with nongovernmental organizations (NGOs), community-based organizations, and intergovernmental agencies, working pro bono in eight-week assignments in communities struggling with the effects of poverty, conflict, and environmental

---

[7] N. C. Smith. "Corporate Social Responsibility: Whether or How?" *California Management Review* 45, no. 4 (2003), pp. 52–76.

[8] Husted, "Governance Choices for Corporate Social Responsibility."

Five Principles of Successful Corporate Social Responsibility Collaboration

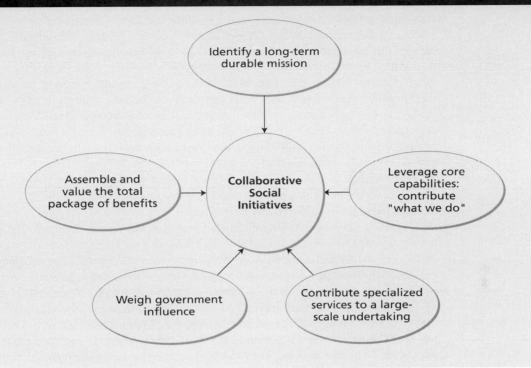

degradation. The Ulysses program was designed in part to respond to a growing challenge confronting professional services companies: identifying and training up-and-coming leaders who can find nontraditional answers to intractable problems.

All 24 Ulysses graduates still work at PwC; most say they have a stronger commitment to the firm because of the commitment it made to them and because they now have a different view of PwC's values. For PwC, the Ulysses program provides a tangible message to its primary stakeholders that the company is committed to making a difference in the world. According to Brian McCann, the first U.S.-based partner to participate in Ulysses, "This is a real differentiator—not just in relation to our competitors, but to all global organizations."

Five Principles of Successful Collaborative Social Initiatives

There are five principles that are central to successful CSIs, as shown in Exhibit 3.11, Strategy in Action. When CSR initiatives include most or all of these elements, companies can indeed maximize the effects of their social contributions while advancing broader strategic goals. While most CSIs will not achieve complete success with all five elements, some progress with each is requisite for success. Here are the five principles, along with examples of companies that have adhered to them well:

1. Identify a Long-Term Durable Mission

Companies make the greatest social contribution when they identify an important, long-standing policy challenge and they participate in its solution over the long term. Veteran *Wall Street Journal* reporter and author Ron Alsop argues that companies that are interested in contributing to corporate responsibility and thus burnishing their reputations should "own the issue."[9] Companies that step up to tackle problems that are clearly important to society's welfare and that require substantial resources are signaling to internal and external constituencies that the initiative is deserving of the company's investment.

Among the more obvious examples of social challenges that will demand attention for years to come are hunger, inadequate housing, ill health, substandard education, and degradation of the environment. While a company's long-term commitment to any one of those problems embeds that issue in the fabric of the company, it is more important that the company can develop competencies that allow it to become better at its social activities yet be able to keep investing in those outputs. It is also important to identify limited-scope projects and shorter-term milestones that can be accomplished through direct contributions by the company. Solving global hunger is a worthy goal, but it is too large for any individual company to make much of a dent.

Avon Products Inc., the seller of beauty and related products, offers a fine example of a long-term commitment to a pervasive and longstanding problem. In 1992, the company's Avon Foundation—a public charity established in 1955 to improve the lives of women and their families—launched its Breast Cancer Crusade in the United Kingdom. The program has expanded to 50 countries. Funds are raised through a variety of programs, product sales, and special events, including the Avon Walk for Breast Cancer series. The company distinguishes itself from other corporations that fund a single institution or scientific investigator because it operates as part of a collaborative, supporting a national network of research, medical, social service, and community-based organizations, each of which makes its own unique contribution to helping patients or advancing breast cancer research. The Crusade has awarded more than $300 million to breast cancer research and care organizations worldwide. In its first 10 years, The Avon Walks program raised more than $250 million for research, awareness, detection, and treatment.

Another example of a powerful CSI is found in IBM Corp.'s Reinventing Education initiative. Since 1994, IBM works with nonprofit school partners throughout the world to develop and implement innovative technology solutions designed to solve some of education's toughest problems: from coping with shrinking budgets and increasing parental involvement to moving to team teaching and developing new lesson plans. This initiative responds to a nearly universal agreement that education—especially education of young girls and women—provides the essential foundation for addressing a range of social and economic challenges in developing countries. Overcoming the existing educational deficit requires a long-term commitment to achieve school reform, such as methods for measuring learning.

One element of the Reinventing Education initiative is a Web-based "Change Toolkit" developed by IBM and Harvard Business School professor Rosabeth Moss Kanter, with sponsorship from the Council of Chief State School Officers, the National Association of Secondary School Principals, and the National Association of Elementary School Principals. The program has been lauded as a compelling model to systemic school reform.

The Home Depot has identified housing as its principal CSI. In 2002, the company set up its Home Depot Foundation with the primary mission of building "affordable, efficient, and healthy homes." Thirty million Americans face some sort of challenge in securing dependable housing, including living in substandard or overcrowded housing; lacking hot water, electricity, toilet, or bathtub/shower; or simply paying too high a percentage of their income on housing. Hence, Home Depot's long-term commitment in this area is unassailable. Its

---

[9] R. Alsop, *The 18 Immutable Laws of Corporate Reputation* (New York: Free Press, 2004).

Foundation works closely with Home Depot suppliers and with a variety of nonprofits, placing a strong emphasis on local volunteer efforts.

2. Contribute "What We Do"

Companies maximize the benefits of their corporate contributions when they leverage core capabilities and contribute products and services that are based on expertise used in or generated by their normal operations. Such contributions create a mutually beneficial relationship between the partners; the social-purpose initiatives receive the maximum gains while the company minimizes costs and diversions. It is not essential that these services be synonymous with those of the company's business, but they should build upon some aspect of its strategic competencies.

The issue was aired at the recent World Economic Forum gathering in Davos, Switzerland. "We see corporate social responsibility as part and parcel of doing business, part of our core skills," said Antony Burgmans, chairman of consumer-products giant Unilever NV. "The major value for Unilever is the corporate reputation it helps create."

The thinking is similar at IBM, where, as part of its Reinventing Education initiative, the company contributes financial resources, researchers, educational consultants, and technology to each site to find new ways for technology to spur and support fundamental school restructuring and broad-based systemic change to raise student achievement. In effect, IBM leverages its technological and systems expertise, and its experience providing systems solutions to educational clients, to meet a broader educational challenge. Says Stanley Litow, vice president of Corporate Community Relations at IBM: "IBM believes that a strong community is a key to a company's success . . . To this end, a key focus of our work has been on raising the quality of public education and bridging the digital divide."[10] IBM gains significant goodwill and brand identity with important target markets, in some ways repeating Apple Computer Inc.'s successful strategy in the 1980s under which it donated computers to schools as a way to gain recognition.

There are many comparable initiatives on the procurement side. Retailers such as Starbucks Coffee Company now source much of their bean supply directly from producers, thereby ensuring that those farmers receive fair compensation without being exploited by powerful middlemen. Many retail supermarkets have followed with their own versions of the "fair trade" model.

3. Contribute Specialized Services to a Large-Scale Undertaking

Companies have the greatest social impact when they make specialized contributions to large-scale cooperative efforts. Those that contribute to initiatives in which other private, public, or nonprofit organizations are also active have an effect that goes beyond their limited contributions. Although it is tempting for a company to identify a specific cause that will be associated only with its own contributions, such a strategy is likely to be viewed as a "pet project" and not as a contribution to a larger problem where a range of players have important interests.

A good example is The AES Corp.'s carbon offset program. AES, headquartered in Arlington, Virginia, is one of the world's largest independent power producers, with 30,000 employees and generation and distribution businesses in 27 countries. Some years ago, the company recognized that it could make a contribution to the battle against global warming—a significant environmental threat with serious consequences such as habitat and species depletion, drought, and water scarcity. AES developed a program that offsets

---

[10] "Reinventing Education," www.ibm.com/ibm/ibmgives/grant/education/programs/reinventing/re_school_reform.shtml

carbon emissions, creating carbon "sinks," a practical and effective means of combating this global problem.

Researchers have concluded that planting and preserving trees (technically "forest enhancement") provides the most practical and effective way to address the CO_2 emissions problem. Trees absorb CO_2 as they grow and convert it to carbon that is locked up (sequestered) in biomass as long as they live. AES leaders believed that if their company could contribute to increasing the standing stock of trees, the additional trees might be able to absorb enough CO_2 to offset the emissions from an AES cogeneration plant. This approach became one of the many mitigation measures now accepted in the global climate change treaty—the Kyoto Protocol—as a means of achieving legally binding emissions reduction targets.

For its part, packaged-foods giant ConAgra Foods Inc. helps to fight hunger in partnership with America's Second Harvest, an organization that leads the food recovery effort in the United States. Set up as the nationwide clearinghouse for handling the donations of prepared and perishable foods, ConAgra's coordination efforts enable smaller, local programs to share resources, making the food donation and distribution process more effective. In October 1999, ConAgra joined with food bank network America's Second Harvest in a specific initiative, the Feeding Children Better program, distributing food to 50,000 local charitable agencies, which, in turn, operate more than 94,000 food programs.

4. Weigh Government's Influence

Government support for corporate participation in CSIs—or at least its willingness to remove barriers—can have an important positive influence. Tax incentives, liability protection, and other forms of direct and indirect support for businesses all help to foster business participation and contribute to the success of CSIs.

For instance, in the United States, ConAgra's food recovery initiatives can deduct the cost (but not market value) of the donated products plus one half of the product's profit margin; the value of this deduction is capped at twice the cost of the product. To encourage further participation of businesses in such food recovery programs, America's Second Harvest generated a series of recommendations for the U.S. government. The recommendations seek to improve the tax benefits associated with food donation, including a proposal that tax deductions be set at the fair market value of donations. Tax deductions provide economic enticement for companies to consider participation, as Boston Market, KFC, and Kraft Foods have publicly acknowledged. Donating food also allows companies to identify the amount of food wasted because it is tracked for tax purposes.

Similar efforts are being applied to reforms that will ease businesses' concerns about their liability from contributing to social enterprises. The Bill Emerson Good Samaritan Food Donation Act, enacted in 1996, protects businesses from liability for food donations except in the case of gross negligence. Building on this federal U.S. act, all 50 states and the District of Columbia have enacted "good Samaritan" laws to protect donors except in cases evidencing negligence. Many companies and nonprofits would like to see more comprehensive tort reform to support their efforts.

Government endorsements are invaluable too. The Home Depot's partnership with Habitat for Humanity is actively supported by the U.S. Department of Housing and Urban Development (HUD). This support takes the form of formal endorsement, logistical facilitation, and implicit acknowledgement that the partnership's initiatives complement HUD's own efforts. Home Depot is assured that the agency will not burden the program with red tape. In the case of AES's efforts in the area of global warming, organizations such as the World Bank, the Global Environmental Facility, and the U.N. Environment and Development Program endorse and encourage offsets via grants, loans, and scientific research.

5. Assemble and Value the Total Package of Benefits

Companies gain the greatest benefits from their social contributions when they put a price on the total benefit package. The valuation should include both the social contributions delivered and the reputation effects that solidify or enhance the company's position among its constituencies. Positive reputation—by consumers, suppliers, employees, regulators, interest groups, and other stakeholders—is driven by genuine commitment rather than episodic or sporadic interest; consumers and other stakeholders see through nominal commitments designed simply to garner short-term positive goodwill. "The public can smell if [a CSR effort] is not legitimate," said Shelly Lazarus, chairman and CEO of advertising agency Ogilvy & Mather USA. Hence, social initiatives that reflect the five principles discussed here can generate significant reputation benefits for participating companies.

AES's commitment to carbon offsets has won it several awards and generates favorable consideration from international financial institutions such as the World Bank, International Finance Corporation, and Inter-American Development Bank, as well as from governments, insurers, and NGOs. In the consumer products sector, Avon receives extensive media recognition from the advertising and marketing of cancer walks, nationwide special events including a gala fund-raising concert, and an awards ceremony. Avon has become so closely associated with the breast cancer cause that many consumers now identify the company's commitment—and the trademark pink ribbon—as easily as its traditional door-to-door marketing and distribution systems.

While difficult to quantify precisely, the potential value of the pink ribbon campaign, and the brand awareness associated with it, generates economic benefits for Avon in the form of goodwill and overall reputation. Avon's strategy of focusing on a cause that women care about, leveraging its contributions, and partnering with respected NGOs has enabled it to gain trust and credibility in the marketplace. "There needs to be a correlation between the cause and the company," said Susan Heany, director for corporate social responsibility at Avon. "The linkage between corporate giving and the corporate product creates brand recognition. Both buyers and sellers want to achieve the same goal: improving women's health care worldwide."[11]

Assembling the Components

A range of corporate initiatives lend themselves to the CSI model because they share most of the five key attributes we have described here: they have long-term objectives, they are sufficiently large to allow a company to specialize in its contributions, they provide many opportunities for the company to contribute from its current activities or products, they enjoy government support, and they provide a package of benefits that adds value to the company. Exhibit 3.12, Strategy in Action, summarizes five very successful CSI programs and their performance against each of the five principles.

Of the five principles, the most important by far is the second one. Companies must apply what they do best in their normal commercial operations to their social responsibility undertakings. This tenet is consistent with research that argues that social activities most closely related to the company's core mission are most efficiently administered through internalization or collaboration. It is applicable far beyond the examples in this chapter; to waste management companies and recycling programs, for instance, or to publishing companies and after-school educational initiatives, or pharmaceutical companies and local immunization and health education programs.

---

[11] "Corporate Social Responsibility in Practice Casebook," *The Catalyst Consortium*, July 2002, p. 8. Available at www.rhcatalyst.org

Five Successful Collaborative Social Initiatives

Program	Pursue a Long-Term, Durable Mission	Contribute "What We Do"	Contribute Specialized Resources to a Large Scale Undertaking	Weigh Government Influence	Assemble and Value Total Package of Benefits
ConAgra Foods' Feeding Children Better	Individuals needing food from charity in the United States grew to more than 23 million in 2001. In the United Kingdom, the total was 4 million people in 2003.	ConAgra uses its electronic inventory control systems and refrigerated trucks to assist America's Second Harvest's food rescue programs.	ConAgra fights child hunger in America by assembling a powerful partnership with America's Second Harvest, Brandeis University's Center on Hunger and Poverty, and the Ad Council.	The Bill Emerson Good Samaritan Food Donation Act protects businesses from liability for food donations.	ConAgra's brand-sponsored support of food rescue programs sustains its image as provider of "the largest corporate initiative dedicated solely to fighting child hunger in America."
Avon's Breast Cancer Crusade	Breast cancer is the second-leading cause of death in women in the United States and the most common cancer among women.	Avon's commitment to being "the company for women" is shown by their 550,000 sales representatives who sell Crusade "pink ribbon" items.	Avon distinguishes itself by supporting a national network of research, medical, social service, and local organizations to advance cancer research.	Government agencies often match individual contributions; local governments provide logistical support for fundraising walks.	Avon receives media recognition from the advertising and marketing of cancer walks and nationwide special events, including a gala fundraising concert and awards ceremony.
IBM's Reinventing Education	Education in developing countries requires a long-term commitment to school reform, such as methods for measuring learning.	IBM uses its leading researchers, educational consultants, and technology to spur and support fundamental school restructuring.	IBM monitors the program with rigorous, independent evaluations from the Center for Children & Technology in conjunction with the Harvard Business School.	IBM teams with the U.S. Department of Education and the U.K. Department of Education and Employment on many reinvention projects.	IBM views a commitment to education as a strategic business investment. By investing in its future workforce and its customers, IBM feels that it promotes its own success.
Home Depot's In Your Community	30 million Americans face housing problems, such as overcrowding, no hot water, no electricity, and no toilet, bathtub, or shower.	Home Depot offers help with the construction of homes, plus donations and volunteers to help provide affordable housing for low-income families.	More than 1,500 Home Depot stores have Team Depot volunteer programs to support Habitat for Humanity, Rebuilding Together, and KaBOOM with the help of its 315,000 company associates.	Home Depot's partnership with Habitat for Humanity is actively supported by the U.S. Department of Housing and Urban Development.	Home Depot's volunteer programs and "how-to" clinics "invite the community into their stores." Hundreds of thousands of potential customers participate each year.
AES's Carbon Offsets Program	Global warming is an environmental threat. Carbon offsets or "sinks" are one proven, effective means of combating this problem.	AES is a leading international power producer with extensive knowledge of developing countries and their resources, including the dangers from cogeneration plants.	AES has teamed with the World Resources Institute, Nature Conservancy, and CARE to find and evaluate appropriate forestry-based offset projects.	The Environmental Protection Agency, European environmental organizations, U.N. Development Program, and other agencies support carbon offsets.	AES has committed $12 million to carbon offset projects to offset 67 million tons of carbon emitted over the next 40 years—the equivalent of the emissions from a 1,000-MW coal facility over its lifetime.

The Limits of CSR Strategies

Some companies such as Ben & Jerry's have embedded social responsibility and sustainability commitments deeply in their core strategies. Research suggests that such single-minded devotion to CSR may be unrealistic for larger, more established corporations. For example, some analysts have suggested that the intense focus on social responsibility goals by the management team at Levi Strauss & Co. may have diverted the company from its core operational challenges, accelerating the company's closure of all of its North American manufacturing operations.

Larger companies must move beyond the easy options of charitable donations but also steer clear of overreaching commitments. This is not to suggest that companies should not think big—research shows that projects can be broad in scale and scope and still succeed. Rather, it suggests that companies need to view their commitments to corporate responsibility as one important part of their overall strategy but not let the commitment obscure their broad strategic business goals. By starting with a well-defined CSR strategy and developing the collaborative initiatives that support that strategy by meeting the five criteria we have identified, companies and their leaders can make important contributions to the common good while advancing their broader financial and market objectives.

CSR strategies can also run afoul of the skeptics, and the speed with which information can be disseminated via the Web—and accumulated in Web logs—makes this an issue with serious ramifications for reputation management. Nike has been a lightning rod for CSR activists for its alleged tolerance of hostile and dangerous working conditions in its many factories and subcontractors around the world. Despite the considerable efforts the company has made to respond to its critics, it has consistently been on the defensive in trying to redeem its reputation.

Touching on this issue at the World Economic Forum, Unilever chief Antony Burgmans noted the importance of "making people who matter in society aware of what you do." His point was amplified by Starbucks CEO Orin Smith, who invited the authors of an NGO report critical of Starbucks' sourcing strategies to the company's offices and showed them the books. "In many instances we ended up partnering with them," he said.

The Future of CSR

CSR is firmly and irreversibly part of the corporate fabric. Managed properly, CSR programs can confer significant benefits to participants in terms of corporate reputation; in terms of hiring, motivation, and retention; and as a means of building and cementing valuable partnerships. And of course, the benefits extend well beyond the boundaries of the participating organizations, enriching the lives of many disadvantaged communities and individuals and pushing back on problems that threaten future generations, other species, and precious natural resources.

That is the positive perspective. The more prickly aspect of CSR is that for all of their resources and capabilities, corporations will face growing demands for social responsibility contributions far beyond simple cash or in-kind donations. Aggressive protesters will keep the issues hot, employees will continue to have their say, and shareholders will pass judgment with their investments—and their votes.

The challenge for management, then, is to know how to meet the company's obligations to all stakeholders without compromising the basic need to earn a fair return for its owners. As research shows, a collaborative approach is the foundation for the most effective CSR initiatives. By then adhering to the five key principles outlined in this section, business leaders can maintain ongoing commitments to carefully chosen initiatives that can have positive and tangible effects on social problems while meeting their obligations to shareholders, employees, and the broader communities in which they operate.

HR Professionals Believe Ethical Conduct Not Rewarded in Business

A major survey indicates that nearly half of human resources (HR) professionals believe ethical conduct is not rewarded in business today. Over the past five years, HR professionals have felt increasingly more pressure to compromise their organizations' ethical standards; however, they also indicate personally observing fewer cases of misconduct.

The Society for Human Resource Management (SHRM) and the Ethics Resource Center (ERC) jointly conducted the 2003 Business Ethics Survey, with 462 respondents. The survey results show the following:

- 79 percent of respondent organizations have written ethics standards.
- 49 percent say that ethical conduct is not rewarded in business today.

- 35 percent of HR professionals often or occasionally personally observed ethics misconduct in the last year.
- 24 percent of HR professionals feel pressured to compromise ethics standards. In comparison, 13 percent indicated they felt pressured in 1997.
- The top five reasons HR professionals compromise an organization's ethical standards are the need to follow the boss's directives (49 percent); meeting overly aggressive business/financial objectives (48 percent); helping the organization survive (40 percent); meeting schedule pressures (35 percent); and wanting to be a team player (27 percent).

Source: Society for Human Resource Management, www.shrm.org/press

MANAGEMENT ETHICS

The Nature of Ethics in Business

ethics
The moral principles that reflect society's beliefs about the actions of an individual or group that are right and wrong.

Central to the belief that companies should be operated in a socially responsive way for the benefit of all stakeholders is the belief that managers will behave in an ethical manner. The term **ethics** refers to the moral principles that reflect society's beliefs about the actions of an individual or a group that are right and wrong. Of course, the values of one individual, group, or society may be at odds with the values of another individual, group, or society. Ethical standards, therefore, reflect not a universally accepted code, but rather the end product of a process of defining and clarifying the nature and content of human interaction.

Unfortunately, the public's perception of the ethics of corporate executives in America is near its all-time low. A major cause is a spate of corporate scandals prompted by self-serving, and often criminal, executive action that resulted in the loss of stakeholder investments and employee jobs. The goal of every company is to avoid scandal through a combination of high moral and ethical standards and careful monitoring to assure that those standards are maintained. However, when problems arise, the management task of restoring the credibility of the company becomes paramount.

External stakeholders are not the only critics of the current state of business ethics. Exhibit 3.13, Strategy in Action, presents the findings of a major survey of human resource managers in which they indicate that strategic managers have much work to do to establish high ethical standards in their organizations.

Even when groups agree on what constitutes human welfare in a given case, the means they choose to achieve this welfare may differ. Therefore, ethics also involve acting to attain human goals. For example, many people would agree that health is a value worth seeking—that is, health enhances human welfare. But what if the means deemed necessary to attain this value for some include the denial or risk of health for others, as is commonly an issue faced by pharmaceutical manufacturers? During production of some drugs, employees are sometimes subjected to great risk of personal injury and infection. For example, if contacted

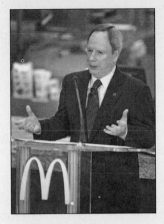

In 2005, the fast-food industry was blamed as a major contributor for the obesity epidemic in America. In response, McDonald's CEO James A. Skinner voluntarily introduced labeling of nutritional information on the packages of many McDonald's food items. The company introduced easy-to-read packaging in 20,000 of its 30,000 restaurants to educate their consumers on the content of McDonald's products.

Skinner predicted that the new labeling would encourage other fast-food restaurants to follow suit; "we would like to have our leadership be followed by others, because nutrition information is important in terms of how people pursue their balanced lifestyles."* With nearly one-third of the U.S. children ages 4 to 19 eating fast food, Skinner intended the new packaging to educate parents to be able to offer healthier options to their children.

Skinner expressed the view that, as mentioned in its corporate responsibilities statement, McDonald's demonstrated its regard for its consumer by providing high-quality foods and by conducting business with honesty and integrity by such actions as voluntarily disclosing nutritional information about its products.

*Melanie Warner, "McDonald's to Add Facts on Nutrition to Packaging," *New York Times*, October 26, 2005.

"Fast Food Linked to Child Obesity," *CBSNews*, January 5, 2003, http://cbsnews.com/stories/2004/01/05/health

"McDonald's Corporate Responsibility," *McDonald's Corporation*, November 7, 2008, http://www.mcdonalds.com/corporate

or inhaled, the mercury used in making thermometers and blood pressure equipment can cause heavy metal poisoning. If inhaled, ethylene oxide used to sterilize medical equipment before it is shipped to doctors can cause fetal abnormalities and miscarriages. Even penicillin, if inhaled during its manufacturing process, can cause acute anaphylaxis or shock. Thus, although the goal of customer health might be widely accepted, the means (involving jeopardy to production employees) may not be.

Although McDonald's faced a great deal of public criticism for the presumed poor nutritional balance of its food products that could contribute to poor consumer health, the law did not require the company or any of its competitors to disclose the exact nutritional contents of its products. However, in 2005, McDonald's broke ranks with its competitors and voluntarily provided the information on its labels. This act of CSR is described in Exhibit 3.14, Top Strategist.

The spotlight on business ethics is a widespread phenomenon. For example, a 2004 survey by the Institute of Business Ethics helps to clarify how companies use their codes of ethics.[12] It found that more than 90 percent of Financial Times Stock Exchange (FTSE) companies in the United Kingdom have an explicit commitment to doing business ethically in the form of a code of ethical conduct. The respondents also reported that 26 percent of boards of directors are taking direct responsibility for the ethical programs of companies, up from 16 percent in 2001. The main reasons for having a code of ethics were to provide guidance to staff (38 percent) and to reduce legal liability (33 percent). Many of the managers (41 percent) also reported that they had used their code in disciplinary procedures in the last three years, usually on safety, security, and environmental ethical issues.

[12] Accessed in 2005 from http://www.ibe.org.uk/ExecSumm.pdf

Approaches to Questions of Ethics

Managers report that the most critical quality of ethical decision making is consistency. Thus, they often try to adopt a philosophical approach that can provide the basis for the consistency they seek. There are three fundamental ethical approaches for executives to consider: the utilitarian approach, the moral rights approach, and the social justice approach.

utilitarian approach
Judging the appropriateness of a particular action based on a goal to provide the greatest good for the greatest number of people.

Managers who adopt the **utilitarian approach** judge the effects of a particular action on the people directly involved, in terms of what provides the greatest good for the greatest number of people. The utilitarian approach focuses on actions, rather than on the motives behind the actions. Potentially positive results are weighed against potentially negative results. If the former outweigh the latter, the manager taking the utilitarian approach is likely to proceed with the action. That some people might be adversely affected by the action is accepted as inevitable. For example, the Council on Environmental Quality conducts cost-benefit analyses when selecting air pollution standards under the Clean Air Act, thereby acknowledging that some pollution must be accepted.

moral rights approach
Judging the appropriateness of a particular action based on a goal to maintain the fundamental rights and privileges of individuals and groups.

Managers who subscribe to the **moral rights approach** judge whether decisions and actions are in keeping with the maintenance of fundamental individual and group rights and privileges. The moral rights approach (also referred to as deontology) includes the rights of human beings to life and safety, a standard of truthfulness, privacy, freedom to express one's conscience, freedom of speech, and private property.

social justice approach
Judging the appropriateness of a particular action based on equity, fairness, and impartiality in the distribution of rewards and costs among individuals and groups.

Managers who take the **social justice approach** judge how consistent actions are with equity, fairness, and impartiality in the distribution of rewards and costs among individuals and groups. These ideas stem from two principles known as the liberty principle and the difference principle. The *liberty principle* states that individuals have certain basic liberties compatible with similar liberties of other people. The *difference principle* holds that social and economic inequities must be addressed to achieve a more equitable distribution of goods and services.

In addition to these defining principles, three implementing principles are essential to the social justice approach. According to the *distributive-justice principle,* individuals should not be treated differently on the basis of arbitrary characteristics, such as race, sex, religion or national origin. This familiar principle is embodied in the Civil Rights Act. The *fairness principle* means that employees must be expected to engage in cooperative activities according to the rules of the company, assuming that the company rules are deemed fair. The most obvious example is that, in order to further the mutual interests of the company, themselves, and other workers, employees must accept limits on their freedom to be absent from work. The *natural-duty principle* points up a number of general obligations, including the duty to help others who are in need or danger, the duty not to cause unnecessary suffering, and the duty to comply with the just rules of an institution.

CODES OF BUSINESS ETHICS

To help ensure consistency in the application of ethical standards, an increasing number of professional associations and businesses are establishing codes of ethical conduct. Associations of chemists, funeral directors, law enforcement agents, migration agents, hockey players, Internet providers, librarians, military arms sellers, philatelists, physicians, and psychologists all have such codes. So do companies such as Amazon.com, Colgate, Honeywell, New York Times, Nokia, PricewaterhouseCoopers, Sony Group, and Riggs Bank.

Nike faces the problems of a large global corporation in enforcing a code of conduct. Nike's products are manufactured in factories owned and operated by other companies.

Nike Code of Conduct

Nike Inc. was founded on a handshake. Implicit in that act was the determination that we would build our business with all of our partners based on trust, teamwork, honesty, and mutual respect. We expect all of our business partners to operate on the same principles.

At the core of the Nike corporate ethic is the belief that we are a company comprised of many different kinds of people, appreciating individual diversity, and dedicated to equal opportunity for each individual.

Nike designs, manufactures, and markets products for sports and fitness consumers. At every step in that process, we are driven to do not only what is required by law, but what is expected of a leader. We expect our business partners to do the same. Nike partners with contractors who share our commitment to best practices and continuous improvement in:

1. Management practices that respect the rights of all employees, including the right to free association and collective bargaining.
2. Minimizing our impact on the environment.
3. Providing a safe and healthy workplace.
4. Promoting the health and well-being of all employees.

Contractors must recognize the dignity of each employee, and the right to a workplace free of harassment, abuse or corporal punishment. Decisions on hiring, salary, benefits, advancement, termination, or retirement must be based solely on the employee's ability to do the job. There shall be no discrimination based on race, creed, gender, marital or maternity status, religious or political beliefs, age, or sexual orientation.

Wherever Nike operates around the globe, we are guided by this Code of Conduct, and we bind our contractors to these principles. Contractors must post this Code in all major workspaces, translated into the language of the employee, and must train employees on their rights and obligations as defined by this Code and applicable local laws.

While these principles establish the spirit of our partnerships, we also bind our partners to specific standards of conduct. The core standards are set forth below.

FORCED LABOR

The contractor does not use forced labor in any form—prison, indentured, bonded, or otherwise.

CHILD LABOR

The contractor does not employ any person below the age of 18 to produce footwear. The contractor does not employ any person below the age of 16 to produce apparel, accessories, or equipment. If at the time Nike production begins, the contractor employs people of the legal working age who are at least 15, that employment may continue, but the contractor will not hire any person going forward who is younger than the Nike or legal age limit, whichever is higher.

To further ensure these age standards are complied with, the contractor does not use any form of homework for Nike production.

COMPENSATION

The contractor provides each employee at least the minimum wage, or the prevailing industry wage, whichever is higher; provides each employee a clear, written accounting for every pay period; and does not deduct from employee pay for disciplinary infractions.

BENEFITS

The contractor provides each employee all legally mandated benefits.

HOURS OF WORK/OVERTIME

The contractor complies with legally mandated work hours; uses overtime only when each employee is fully compensated according to local law; informs each employee at the time of hiring if mandatory overtime is a condition of employment; and, on a regularly scheduled basis, provides one day off in seven, and requires no more than 60 hours of work per week on a regularly scheduled basis, or complies with local limits if they are lower.

ENVIRONMENT, SAFETY, AND HEALTH (ES&H)

The contractor has written environmental, safety, and health policies and standards and implements a system to minimize negative impacts on the environment, reduce work-related injury and illness, and promote the general health of employees.

DOCUMENTATION AND INSPECTION

The contractor maintains on file all documentation needed to demonstrate compliance with this Code of Conduct and required laws, agrees to make these documents available for Nike or its designated monitor, and agrees to submit to inspections with or without prior notice.

Source: www.nike.com/nikebiz, 2009.

Nike's supply chain includes more than 660,000 contract manufacturing workers in more than 900 factories in more than 50 countries, including the United States. The workers are predominantly women, ages 19 to 25. The geographic dispersion of its manufacturing facilities is driven by many factors including pricing, quality, factory capacity, and quota allocations.

With such cultural, societal, and economic diversity, the ethics challenge for Nike is to "do business with contract factories that consistently demonstrate compliance with standards we set and that operate in an ethical and lawful manner." To help in this process, Nike has developed its own code of ethics, which it calls a Code of Conduct. It is a set of ethical principles intended to guide management decision making. Nike's code is presented in Exhibit 3.15, Strategy in Action.

Major Trends in Codes of Ethics

The increased interest in codifying business ethics has led to both the proliferation of formal statements by companies and to their prominence among business documents. Not long ago, codes of ethics that existed were usually found solely in employee handbooks. The new trend is for them to also be prominently displayed on corporate Web sites, in annual reports, and next to Title VII posters on bulletin boards.

A second trend is that companies are adding enforcement measures to their codes, including policies that are designed to guide employees on what to do if they see violations occur and sanctions that will be applied, including consequences on their employment and civil and criminal charges. As a consequence, businesses are increasingly requiring all employees to sign the ethics statement as a way to acknowledge that they have read and understood their obligations. In part this requirement reflects the impact of the Sarbanes-Oxley rule that CEOs and CFOs certify the accuracy of company financials. Executives want employees at all levels to recognize their own obligations to pass accurate information up the chain of command.

The third trend is increased attention by companies in improving employees' training in understanding their obligations under the company's code of ethics. The objective is to emphasize the consideration of ethics during the decision-making process. Training, and subsequent monitoring of actual work behavior, is also aided by computer software that identifies possible code violations, which managers can then investigate in detail.

Summary	Given the amount of time that people spend working, it is reasonable that they should try to shape the organizations in which they work. Inanimate organizations are often blamed for setting the legal, ethical, and moral tones in the workplace when, in reality, people determine how people behave. Just as individuals try to shape their neighborhoods, schools, political and social organizations, and religious institutions, employees need to help determine the major issues of corporate social responsibility and business ethics.

Strategic decisions, indeed all decisions, involve trade-offs. We choose one thing over another. We pursue one goal while subordinating another. On the topic of corporate social responsibility, individual employees must work to achieve the outcomes that they want. By volunteering for certain community welfare options they choose to improve that option's chances of being beneficial. Business ethics present a parallel opportunity. By choosing proper behaviors, employees help to build an organization that can be respected and economically viable in the long run.

Often, the concern is expressed that business activities tend to be illegal or unethical and that the failure of individuals to follow the pattern will leave them at a competitive disadvantage. Such claims, often prompted by high-profile examples, are absurd. Rare but much publicized criminal activities mask the meaningful reality that business conduct is as honest and honorable as any other activity in our lives. The people who are involved are the same, with the same values, ideals, and aspirations.

In this chapter, we have studied corporate social responsibility to understand it and to learn how our businesses can occasionally use some of their resources to make differential, positive impacts on our society. We also looked at business ethics to gain an appreciation for the importance of maintaining and promoting social values in the workplace.

Key Terms

corporate social
responsibility (CSR), *p. 52*
discretionary
responsibilities, *p. 52*
economic
responsibilities, *p. 49*

ethical responsibilities, *p. 50*
ethics, *p. 74*
legal responsibilities, *p. 49*
moral rights approach, *p. 76*
privatization, *p. 61*

Sarbanes-Oxley Act of
2002, *p. 57*
social audit, *p. 62*
social justice approach, *p. 76*
utilitarian approach, *p. 76*

Questions for Discussion

1. Define the term *social responsibility*. Find an example of a company action that was legal but not socially responsible. Defend your example on the basis of your definition.
2. Name five potentially valuable indicators of a firm's social responsibility and describe how company performance in each could be measured.
3. Do you think a business organization in today's society benefits by defining a socially responsible role for itself? Why or why not?
4. Which of the three basic philosophies of social responsibility would you find most appealing as the chief executive of a large corporation? Explain.
5. Do you think society's expectations for corporate social responsibility will change in the next decade? Explain.
6. How much should social responsibility be considered in evaluating an organization's overall performance?
7. Is it necessary that an action be voluntary to be termed socially responsible? Explain.
8. Do you think an organization should adhere to different philosophies of corporate responsibility when confronted with different issues, or should its philosophy always remain the same? Explain.
9. Describe yourself as a stakeholder in a company. What kind of stakeholder role do you play now? What kind of stakeholder roles do you expect to play in the future?
10. What sets the affirmative philosophy apart from the stakeholder philosophy of social responsibility? In what areas do the two philosophies overlap?
11. Cite examples of both ethical and unethical behavior drawn from your knowledge of current business events.
12. How would you describe the contemporary state of business ethics?
13. How can business self-interest also serve social interests?

Chapter **Four**

The External Environment

After reading and studying this chapter, you should be able to

1. Describe the three tiers of environmental factors that affect the performance of a firm.

2. List and explain the five factors in the remote environment.

3. Give examples of the economic, social, political, technological, and ecological influences on a business.

4. Explain the five forces model of industry analysis and give examples of each force.

5. Give examples of the influences of entry barriers, supplier power, buyer power, substitute availability, and competitive rivalry on a business.

6. List and explain the five factors in the operating environment.

7. Give examples of the influences of competitors, creditors, customers, labor, and direct suppliers on a business.

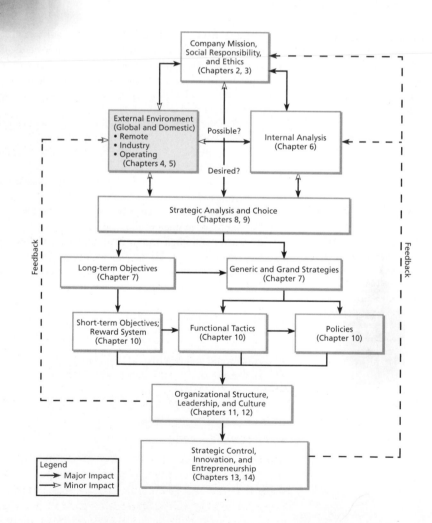

EXHIBIT 4.1
The Firm's External Environment

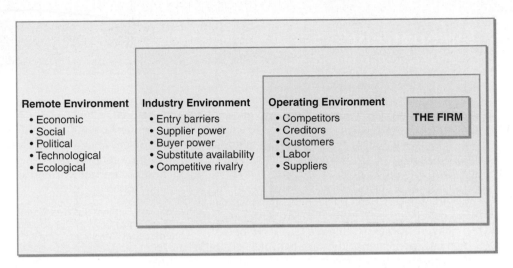

Remote Environment	Industry Environment	Operating Environment	
• Economic	• Entry barriers	• Competitors	THE FIRM
• Social	• Supplier power	• Creditors	
• Political	• Buyer power	• Customers	
• Technological	• Substitute availability	• Labor	
• Ecological	• Competitive rivalry	• Suppliers	

THE FIRM'S EXTERNAL ENVIRONMENT

external environment
The factors beyond the control of the firm that influence its choice of direction and action, organizational structure, and internal processes.

A host of external factors influence a firm's choice of direction and action and, ultimately, its organizational structure and internal processes. These factors, which constitute the **external environment,** can be divided into three interrelated subcategories: factors in the remote environment, factors in the industry environment, and factors in the operating environment. This chapter describes the complex necessities involved in formulating strategies that optimize a firm's market opportunities. Exhibit 4.1 suggests the interrelationship between the firm and its remote, its industry, and its operating environments. In combination, these factors form the basis of the opportunities and threats that a firm faces in its competitive environment.

REMOTE ENVIRONMENT

remote environment
Economic, social, political, technological, and ecological factors that originate beyond, and usually irrespective of, any single firm's operating situation.

The **remote environment** comprises factors that originate beyond, and usually irrespective of, any single firm's operating situation: (1) economic, (2) social, (3) political, (4) technological, and (5) ecological factors. That environment presents firms with opportunities, threats, and constraints, but rarely does a single firm exert any meaningful reciprocal influence. For example, when the economy slows and construction starts to decrease, an individual contractor is likely to suffer a decline in business, but that contractor's efforts in stimulating local construction activities would be unable to reverse the overall decrease in construction starts. The trade agreements that resulted from improved relations between the United States and China and the United States and Russia are examples of political factors that impact individual firms. The agreements provided individual U.S. manufacturers with opportunities to broaden their international operations.

Economic Factors

Economic factors concern the nature and direction of the economy in which a firm operates. Because consumption patterns are affected by the relative affluence of various market segments, each firm must consider economic trends in the segments that affect its industry. On both the national and international level, managers must consider the general availability of credit, the level of disposable income, and the propensity of people to spend.

Top Strategist
Glenn Murphy, CEO of Gap Inc.

Exhibit
4.2

Glenn Murphy took over as Gap Inc. CEO during the second quarter of 2007 following three years of declining corporate sales. Murphy's approach was to emphasize a turnaround strategy designed for " . . . improving results at our core brands, while pursuing strategic growth opportunities online and internationally."*

Gap's retrenchment efforts began paying off early. According to Gap CFO Sabrina Simmons, "Our focus on disciplined inventory and cost management has enabled us to achieve a 65 percent growth in earnings per share in the first half of 2008."** Gap also expected to generate about $1 billion in

free cash flow for the year. As part of its international growth plan, Gap signed franchise deals in 21 countries in 2008, including Mexico, Russia, and Japan. However, until the U.S. economy rebounds, it is difficult to predict if Gap Inc. can capitalize on its successful retrenchment and succeed with its turnaround strategy.

*"Gap Inc. Outlines Business Strategies for Brands and Highlights Growth Opportunities in Online and International Categories," Gap Inc. press release, October 16, 2008.
**Ibid.

Prime interest rates, inflation rates, and trends in the growth of the gross national product are other economic factors they should monitor.

For example, in 2003, the depressed economy hit Crown Cork & Seal Co. especially hard because it had $2 billion in debt due in the year and no way to raise the money to pay it. The down market had caused its stock price to be too low to raise cash as it normally would. Therefore, Crown Cork managers turned to issuing bonds to refinance its debt. With the slow market, investors were taking advantage of such bonds because they could safely gain higher returns over stocks. Not only were investors getting a deal, but Crown Cork and other companies were seeing the lowest interest rates on bonds in years and by issuing bonds could reorganize their balance sheets.

Some companies see opportunities arise during periods of national or global decline. For example, despite the downturn in the U.S. economy in 2008–2009, Gap Inc. hoped to leverage its ongoing retrenchment efforts to achieve its turnaround strategy, as described in Exhibit 4.2, Top Strategist.

The emergence of new international power brokers has changed the focus of economic environmental forecasting. Among the most prominent of these power brokers are the European Economic Community (EEC, or Common Market), the Organization of Petroleum Exporting Countries (OPEC), and coalitions of developing countries.

The EEC, whose members include most of the West European countries, eliminated quotas and established a tariff-free trade area for industrial products among its members. By fostering intra-European economic cooperation, it has helped its member countries compete more effectively in non-European international markets.

Social Factors

The social factors that affect a firm involve the beliefs, values, attitudes, opinions, and lifestyles of persons in the firm's external environment, as developed from cultural, ecological, demographic, religious, educational, and ethnic conditioning. As social attitudes change, so too does the demand for various types of clothing, books, leisure activities, and so on. Like other forces in the remote external environment, social forces are dynamic, with constant change resulting from the efforts of individuals to satisfy their desires and needs by controlling and adapting to environmental factors. Teresa Iglesias-Soloman hopes to benefit from social changes with *Niños*, a children's catalog written in both English and Spanish. The catalog features books, videos, and Spanish cultural offerings for English-speaking children who want to learn Spanish and for Spanish-speaking children who want to learn English. *Niños'* target market includes middle- to upper-income Hispanic parents, consumers, educators, bilingual schools, libraries, and purchasing agents. Iglesias-Solomon has reason to be optimistic about the future of *Niños*, because the Hispanic population is growing five times faster than the general U.S. population and ranks as the nation's largest minority.

One of the most profound social changes in recent years has been the entry of large numbers of women into the labor market. This has not only affected the hiring and compensation policies and the resource capabilities of their employers; it has also created or greatly expanded the demand for a wide range of products and services necessitated by their absence from the home. Firms that anticipated or reacted quickly to this social change offered such products and services as convenience foods, microwave ovens, and day care centers.

A second profound social change has been the accelerating interest of consumers and employees in quality-of-life issues. Evidence of this change is seen in recent contract negotiations. In addition to the traditional demand for increased salaries, workers demand such benefits as sabbaticals, flexible hours or four-day workweeks, lump-sum vacation plans, and opportunities for advanced training.

A third profound social change has been the shift in the age distribution of the population. Changing social values and a growing acceptance of improved birth control methods are expected to raise the mean age of the U.S. population, which was 27.9 in 1970, and 34.9 in the year 2000. This trend will have an increasingly unfavorable effect on most producers of predominantly youth-oriented goods and will necessitate a shift in their long-range marketing strategies. Producers of hair and skin care preparations already have begun to adjust their research and development to reflect anticipated changes in demand.

A consequence of the changing age distribution of the population has been a sharp increase in the demands made by a growing number of senior citizens. Constrained by fixed incomes, these citizens have demanded that arbitrary and rigid policies on retirement age be modified and have successfully lobbied for tax exemptions and increases in Social Security benefits. Such changes have significantly altered the opportunity-risk equations of many firms—often to the benefit of firms that anticipated the changes.

Cutting across these issues is concern for individual health. The fast-food industry has been the target of a great deal of public concern. A great deal of popular press attention has been directed toward Americans' concern over the relationship between obesity and health. As documented by the hit movie *Supersize Me*, McDonald's was caught in the middle of this new social concern because its menu consisted principally of high-calorie, artery-clogging foods. Health experts blamed the fast-food industry for the rise in obesity, claiming that companies like McDonald's created an environment that encouraged overeating and discouraged physical activity. Specifically, McDonald's was charged with taking advantage of the fact that kids and adults were watching more TV, by targeting certain program slots to increase sales.

McDonald's responded aggressively and successfully. The company's strategists soon established McDonald's Corp. as an innovator in healthy food options. By 2005, the world's largest fast-food chain launched a new promotional campaign touting healthy lifestyles, including fruit and milk in Happy Meals, activity programs in schools, and a new partnership with the International Olympic Committee. At the time of the announcement, McDonald's was enjoying its longest ever period of same-store sales growth in

Unions Seek Payback for Helping Obama

The labor unions that helped Barack Obama win the White House are looking for some payback. While Obama's support could help, unions' diminishing membership has made it tough to get their legislation passed. Unions represent about one in eight U.S. workers, down from about one in five 25 years ago.

The biggest labor-business donnybrook in the new Congress will be over a bill that would do away with employers' right to demand secret-ballot elections to recognize unions. Instead, a company would have to recognize and bargain with a union once union cards were signed by 50 percent of the company's eligible workforce plus one additional employee.

The House passed the measure in 2007, but it died under a Republican filibuster in the Senate. President Bush had vowed to veto it, but Obama made it part of his platform.

Labor leaders say employers have used secret-ballot elections, generally held on job sites, to coerce and intimidate workers into rejecting unions. Employers counter that workers are often coerced by their peers to sign union cards and that a secret-ballot election is the only way to determine their true desires.

Source: Excerpted from "Unions Seek Payback for Helping Obama," *The Associated Press*, November 10, 2008, http://www.msnbc.msn.com/id/27649167/. Reprinted with permission of The Associated Press, Copyright © 2008. All rights reserved.

25 years, with 24 consecutive months of improved global sales resulting from new healthy menu options, later hours, and better customer service, such as cashless payment options. McDonald's healthy options included a fruit and walnut salad, Paul Newman's brand low-fat Italian dressing, and premium chicken sandwiches in the United States and chicken flatbread and fruit smoothies in Europe.

Translating social change into forecasts of business effects is a difficult process, at best. Nevertheless, informed estimates of the impact of such alterations as geographic shifts in populations and changing work values, ethical standards, and religious orientation can only help a strategizing firm in its attempts to prosper.

Political Factors

The direction and stability of political factors are a major consideration for managers on formulating company strategy. Political factors define the legal and regulatory parameters within which firms must operate. Political constraints are placed on firms through fair-trade decisions, antitrust laws, tax programs, minimum wage legislation, pollution and pricing policies, administrative jawboning, and many other actions aimed at protecting employees, consumers, the general public, and the environment. Because such laws and regulations are most commonly restrictive, they tend to reduce the potential profits of firms. However, some political actions are designed to benefit and protect firms. Such actions include patent laws, government subsidies, and product research grants. Often, different stakeholders take different sides on important issues that affect business operations. They then work to influence legislators to vote for the position that they favor. The attempt of labor unions to influence President Barack Obama as payback for their support at the polls is an example, as described in Exhibit 4.3, Strategy in Action.

Political factors either may limit or benefit the firms they influence. For example, in a pair of surprising decisions, the Federal Communications Commission (FCC) ruled that local phone companies had to continue to lease their lines to the long-distance carriers at what the locals said was below cost. At the same time, the FCC ruled that the local companies were not required to lease their broadband lines to the national carriers. These decisions were good and bad for the local companies because, although they would lose money by leasing to the long-distance carriers, they could regain some of that loss with their broadband services that did not have to be leased.

Auto Dealership Meltdown Complicated by Tough State Franchise Laws

Amid the myriad problems facing the Big Three automakers is a costly, inefficient network of dealers. But while thousands of dealers are likely to disappear in coming years, there is little the auto industry can do to make its distribution more efficient, because dealers are well-protected by a byzantine network of state franchise laws.

The laws prevent automakers from owning dealers or selling directly to members of the public, ensuring that vehicle prices get a minimum markup before they reach consumers. "They can't take an order over the Internet for a made-to-order car like Dell because the states have made it illegal," said Peter Morici, professor of business at the University of Maryland. If automakers could sell over the Web, they could probably reduce inventory costs and "lop something like $1,000 off the cost of making one of their cars," he said.

But don't look for that to happen anytime soon. For one thing, auto dealerships are among the most powerful business groups in each state. They are politically well-connected and have been diligent in protecting the franchisee system or any attempt to cut them out of the car selling process, Morici said. Dealers defend the system, including laws that prohibit manufacturers from unfairly canceling or refusing to renew a dealer's franchise.

"Car dealerships are massively credit-intensive enterprises, and they are seen by lenders as more of a risk without state laws to protect them from being closed down," said Bailey Wood, a spokesman for the National Auto Dealers Association. He said the average individual dealership typically invests $11 million into a business over its life. "That money goes into inventory, buildings, tools and personnel," Wood said. "So if you suspended state franchise laws in general it would threaten the nation's economic stability."

A report from consulting firm Grant Thornton LLP says 3,800 dealers, or one in five, will need to close by the end of 2009 as weak sales, increased operational costs, and the credit crunch continue to take their toll.

State dealership laws make it difficult and costly for automakers to eliminate brands, as GM discovered when the automaker dissolved its 106-year-old Oldsmobile brand in April 2004. By discontinuing the Oldsmobile brand, GM had effectively broken is agreement with dealerships, and had to pay severance to each of its dealerships. "It cost GM between $1 billion and $2 billion to close down the Oldsmobile brand for the whole country, and the most expensive part of that was placating the dealers," said Aaron Bragman, an automotive analyst at consultancy Global Insight.

The decisions did not mean that the local carriers had to remove existing lines and replace them with broadband lines. Instead, the local carriers would have to run two networks to areas where they want to incorporate broadband because the long-distance carriers had a right to the conventional lines as ruled in the decision. These regulations caused the local carriers to alter their strategies. For example, they often chose to reduce capital investments on new broadband lines because they had to maintain old lines as well. The reduction in capital investments was used to offset the losses they incurred in subsidizing their current lines to the long-distance carriers.

Another important example of the political factor is its affect on law. In Exhibit 4.4, Strategy in Action, you can read how state legislation in the United States results in a number of consequences for automobile manufacturers, franchise dealers, and customers.

The direction and stability of political factors are a major consideration when evaluating the remote environment. Consider piracy. Microsoft's performance in the Chinese market is greatly affected by the lack of legal enforcement of piracy and also by the policies of the Chinese government. Likewise, the government's actions in support of its competitor, Linux, have limited Microsoft's ability to penetrate the Chinese market.

Political activity also has a significant impact on two governmental functions that influence the remote environment of firms: the supplier function and the customer function.

Supplier Function

Government decisions regarding the accessibility of private businesses to government-owned natural resources and national stockpiles of agricultural products will affect profoundly the viability of the strategies of some firms.

Customer Function

Government demand for products and services can create, sustain, enhance, or eliminate many market opportunities. For example, the Kennedy administration's emphasis on landing a man on the moon spawned a demand for thousands of new products; the Carter administration's emphasis on developing synthetic fuels created a demand for new skills, technologies, and products; the Reagan administration's strategic defense initiative (the "Star Wars" defense) sharply accelerated the development of laser technologies; Clinton's federal block grants to the states for welfare reform led to office rental and lease opportunities; and the war against terrorism during the Bush administration created enormous investment in aviation.

Technological Factors

The fourth set of factors in the remote environment involves technological change. To avoid obsolescence and promote innovation, a firm must be aware of technological changes that might influence its industry. Creative technological adaptations can suggest possibilities for new products or for improvements in existing products or in manufacturing and marketing techniques.

A technological breakthrough can have a sudden and dramatic effect on a firm's environment. It may spawn sophisticated new markets and products or significantly shorten the anticipated life of a manufacturing facility. Thus, all firms, and most particularly those in turbulent growth industries, must strive for an understanding both of the existing technological advances and the probable future advances that can affect their products and services. This quasi-science of attempting to foresee advancements and estimate their impact on an organization's operations is known as **technological forecasting.**

technological forecasting
The quasi-science of anticipating environmental and competitive changes and estimating their importance to an organization's operations.

Technological forecasting can help protect and improve the profitability of firms in growing industries. It alerts strategic managers to both impending challenges and promising opportunities. As examples: (1) advances in xerography were a key to Xerox's success but caused major difficulties for carbon paper manufacturers, and (2) the perfection of transistors changed the nature of competition in the radio and television industry, helping such giants as RCA while seriously weakening smaller firms whose resource commitments required that they continue to base their products on vacuum tubes.

The key to beneficial forecasting of technological advancement lies in accurately predicting future technological capabilities and their probable impacts. A comprehensive analysis of the effect of technological change involves study of the expected effect of new technologies on the remote environment, on the competitive business situation, and on the business-society interface. In recent years, forecasting in the last area has warranted particular attention. For example, as a consequence of increased concern over the environment, firms must carefully investigate the probable effect of technological advances on quality-of-life factors, such as ecology and public safety.

For example, by combining the powers of Internet technologies with the capability of downloading music in a digital format, Bertelsmann has found a creative technological adaptation for distributing music online to millions of consumers whenever or wherever they might be. Bertelsmann, AOL Time Warner, and EMI formed a joint venture called Musicnet. The ease and wide availability of Internet technologies is increasing the marketplace for online e-tailers. Bertelsmann's response to the shifts in technological factors enables it to distribute music more rapidly through Musicnet to a growing consumer base.

Ecological Factors

ecology
The relationships among human beings and other living things and the air, soil, and water that supports them.

pollution
Threats to life-supporting ecology caused principally by human activities in an industrial society.

The most prominent factor in the remote environment is often the reciprocal relationship between business and the ecology. The term **ecology** refers to the relationships among human beings and other living things and the air, soil, and water that support them. Threats to our life-supporting ecology caused principally by human activities in an industrial society are commonly referred to as **pollution.** Specific concerns include global warming, loss of habitat and biodiversity, as well as air, water, and land pollution.

The global climate has been changing for ages; however, it is now evident that humanity's activities are accelerating this tremendously. A change in atmospheric radiation, due in part to ozone depletion, causes global warming. Solar radiation that is normally absorbed into the atmosphere reaches the earth's surface, heating the soil, water, and air.

Another area of great importance is the loss of habitat and biodiversity. Ecologists agree that the extinction of important flora and fauna is occurring at a rapid rate and, if this pace is continued, could constitute a global extinction on the scale of those found in fossil records. The earth's life-forms depend on a well-functioning ecosystem. In addition, immeasurable advances in disease treatment can be attributed to research involving substances found in plants. As species become extinct, the life support system is irreparably harmed. The primary cause of extinction on this scale is a disturbance of natural habitat. For example, current data suggest that the earth's primary tropical forests, a prime source of oxygen and potential plant "cure," could be destroyed in only five decades.

Air pollution is created by dust particles and gaseous discharges that contaminate the air. Acid rain, or rain contaminated by sulfur dioxide, which can destroy aquatic and plant life, is believed to result from coal-burning factories in 70 percent of all cases. A health-threatening "thermal blanket" is created when the atmosphere traps carbon dioxide emitted from smokestacks in factories burning fossil fuels. This "greenhouse effect" can have disastrous consequences, making the climate unpredictable and raising temperatures.

Water pollution occurs principally when industrial toxic wastes are dumped or leak into the nation's waterways. Because fewer than 50 percent of all municipal sewer systems are in compliance with Environmental Protection Agency requirements for water safety, contaminated waters represent a substantial present threat to public welfare. Efforts to keep from contaminating the water supply are a major challenge to even the most conscientious of manufacturing firms.

Land pollution is caused by the need to dispose of ever-increasing amounts of waste. Routine, everyday packaging is a major contributor to this problem. Land pollution is more dauntingly caused by the disposal of industrial toxic wastes in underground sites. With approximately 90 percent of the annual U.S. output of 500 million metric tons of hazardous industrial wastes being placed in underground dumps, it is evident that land pollution and its resulting endangerment of the ecology have become a major item on the political agenda.

As a major contributor to ecological pollution, business now is being held responsible for eliminating the toxic by-products of its current manufacturing processes and for cleaning up the environmental damage that it did previously. Increasingly, managers are being required by the government or are being expected by the public to incorporate ecological concerns into their decision making. For example, between 1975 and 1992, 3M cut its pollution in half by reformulating products, modifying processes, redesigning production equipment, and recycling by-products. Similarly, steel companies and public utilities have invested billions of dollars in costlier but cleaner-burning fuels and pollution control equipment. The automobile industry has been required to install expensive emission controls in cars. The gasoline industry has been forced to formulate new low-lead and no-lead products. And thousands of companies have found it necessary to direct their R&D resources into the search for ecologically superior products, such as Sears's phosphate-free laundry detergent and Pepsi-Cola's biodegradable plastic soft-drink bottle.

Environmental legislation impacts corporate strategies worldwide. Many companies fear the consequences of highly restrictive and costly environmental regulations. However, some manufacturers view these new controls as an opportunity, capturing markets with products that help customers satisfy their own regulatory standards. Other manufacturers contend that the costs of environmental spending inhibit the growth and productivity of their operations.

Despite cleanup efforts to date, the job of protecting the ecology will continue to be a top strategic priority—usually because corporate stockholders and executives choose it, increasingly because the public and the government require it. As evidenced by Exhibit 4.5, the government has made numerous interventions into the conduct of business for the purpose of bettering the ecology.

Benefits of Eco-Efficiency

Many of the world's largest corporations are realizing that business activities must no longer ignore environmental concerns. Every activity is linked to thousands of other transactions and their environmental impact; therefore, corporate environmental responsibility must be taken seriously and environmental policy must be implemented to ensure a comprehensive organizational strategy. Because of increases in government regulations and consumer environmental concerns, the implementation of environmental policy has become a point of competitive advantage. Therefore, the rational goal of business should be to limit its impact on the environment, thus ensuring long-run benefits to both the firm and society. To neglect this responsibility is to ensure the demise of both the firm and our ecosystem.

Responding to this need, General Electric unveiled plans in 2005 to double its research funds for technologies that reduce energy use, pollution, and emissions tied to global warming. GE said it would focus even more on solar and wind power as well as other environmental technologies it is involved with, such as diesel-electric locomotives, lower emission aircraft engines, more efficient lighting, and water purification. The company's "ecomagination" plans for 2010 include investing $1.5 billion annually in cleaner technologies research, up from $700 million in 2004; and doubling revenues to $20 billion from environmentally friendly products and services.

eco-efficiency
Company actions that produce more useful goods and services while continuously reducing resource consumption and pollution.

Stephen Schmidheiny, chairman of the Business Council for Sustainable Development, has coined the term **eco-efficiency** to describe corporations that produce more-useful goods and services while continuously reducing resource consumption and pollution. He cites a number of reasons for corporations to implement environmental policy: customers demand cleaner products, environmental regulations are increasingly more stringent, employees prefer to work for environmentally conscious firms, and financing is more readily available for eco-efficient firms. In addition, the government provides incentives for environmentally responsible companies.

Setting priorities, developing corporate standards, controlling property acquisition and use to preserve habitats, implementing energy-conserving activities, and redesigning products (e.g., minimizing packaging) are a number of measures the firm can implement to enhance an eco-efficient strategy. One of the most important steps a firm can take in achieving a competitive position with regard to the eco-efficient strategy is to fully capitalize on technological developments as a method of gaining efficiency.

There are four key characteristics of eco-efficient corporations:

- Eco-efficient firms are proactive, not reactive. Policy is initiated and promoted by business because it is in their own interests and the interest of their customers, not because it is imposed by one or more external forces.

EXHIBIT 4.5
Federal Ecological Legislation

National Environmental Policy Act, 1969 Established Environmental Protection Agency; consolidated federal environmental activities under it. Established Council on Environmental Quality to advise president on environmental policy and to review environmental impact statements.

Air Pollution:

Clean Air Act, 1963 Authorized assistance to state and local governments in formulating control programs. Authorized limited federal action in correcting specific pollution problems.

Clean Air Act, Amendments (Motor Vehicle Air Pollution Control Act), 1965 Authorized federal standards for auto exhaust emission. Standards first set for 1968 models.

Air Quality Act, 1967 Authorized federal government to establish air quality control regions and to set maximum permissible pollution levels. Required states and localities to carry out approved control programs or else give way to federal controls.

Clean Air Act Amendments, 1970 Authorized EPA to establish nationwide air pollution standards and to limit the discharge of six principal pollutants into the lower atmosphere. Authorized citizens to take legal action to require EPA to implement its standards against undiscovered offenders.

Clean Air Act Amendments, 1977 Postponed auto emission requirements. Required use of scrubbers in new coal-fired power plants. Directed EPA to establish a system to prevent deterioration of air quality in clean areas.

Solid Waste Pollution:

Solid Waste Disposal Act, 1965 Authorized research and assistance to state and local control programs.

Resource Recovery Act, 1970 Subsidized construction of pilot recycling plants; authorized development of nationwide control programs.

Resource Conservation and Recovery Act, 1976 Directed EPA to regulate hazardous waste management, from generation through disposal.

Surface Mining and Reclamation Act, 1976 Controlled strip mining and restoration of reclaimed land.

Water Pollution:

Refuse Act, 1899 Prohibited dumping of debris into navigable waters without a permit. Extended by court decision to industrial discharges.

Federal Water Pollution Control Act, 1956 Authorized grants to states for water pollution control. Gave federal government limited authority to correct specific pollution problems.

Water Quality Act, 1965 Provided for adoption of water quality standards by states, subject to federal approval.

Water Quality Improvement Act, 1970 Provided for federal cleanup of oil spills. Strengthened federal authority over water pollution control.

Federal Water Pollution Control Act Amendments, 1972 Authorized EPA to set water quality and effluent standards; provided for enforcement and research.

Safe Drinking Water Act, 1974 Set standards for drinking water quality.

Clean Water Act, 1977 Ordered control of toxic pollutants by 1984 with best available technology economically feasible.

- Eco-efficiency is designed in, not added on. This characteristic implies that the optimization of eco-efficiency requires every business effort regarding the product and process to internalize the strategy.
- Flexibility is imperative for eco-efficient strategy implementation. Continuous attention must be paid to technological innovation and market evolution.

Top Strategist
CEO Jim McNerney of The Boeing Company

Exhibit
4.6

Jim McNerney, CEO of The Boeing Company, created a strategy to enable his company to lead the aerospace industry in environmental protection. Key components included the manufacturing of aircraft that produce significantly less pollution and getting Boeing production facilities certified as ISO 14001 to improve their environmental systems. ISO refers to the International Organization for Standardization, which is responsible for international management standards.

To implement his strategy to improve environmental awareness, McNerney created a group within Boeing in 2007 called Environment, Health, and Safety. This group was responsible for integrating environmental risk management into Boeing's processes and procedures. They were tasked with continuing Boeing's record of creating more environmentally friendly products through technological innovation, including a 70 percent reduction in carbon dioxide airplane emissions and noise footprint reduction of 90 percent over the past 40 years. McNerney believed that such efforts needed to be accelerated. For example, in 2008, he committed to improving fuel efficiency by an additional 15 percent in new commercial planes.

McNerney also provided direction for the company to become ISO 14001 certified by the end of 2008 in all major production facilities. This certification meant that each facility must create an environmental management system that will significantly reduce its footprint on the environment. Examples of environmental improvement efforts include lowering emissions, energy savings, and reducing water usage.

Sources: "2008 Environmental Report," The Boeing Company, November 9, 2008, http://www.boeing.com/aboutus/environment; "Boeing Portland Receives ISO 14001 Environmental Certification," The Boeing Company, November 9, 2007, http://www.boeing.com/news/releases/2007/q4/071107c_nr.html

- Eco-efficiency is encompassing, not insular. In the modern global business environment, efforts must cross not only industrial sectors but national and cultural boundaries as well.

The Boeing Company, lead by its CEO Jim McNerney, has implemented several successful initiatives designed to minimize the company's impact on the ecology, as described in Exhibit 4.6, Top Strategist.

International Environment

Monitoring the international environment, perhaps better thought of as the international dimension of the global environment, involves assessing each nondomestic market on the same factors that are used in a domestic assessment. While the importance of factors will differ, the same set of considerations can be used for each country. For example, Exhibit 4.7, Global Strategy in Action, lists economic, political, legal, and social factors used to assess international environments. However, there is one complication to this process, namely, that the interplay among international markets must be considered. For example, in recent years, conflicts in the Middle East have made collaborative business strategies among firms in traditionally antagonistic countries especially difficult to implement.

ECONOMIC ENVIRONMENT
- Level of economic development
- Population
- Gross national product
- Per capita income
- Literacy level
- Social infrastructure
- Natural resources
- Climate
- Membership in regional economic blocs (EU, NAFTA, LAFTA)
- Monetary and fiscal policies
- Wage and salary levels
- Nature of competition
- Currency convertibility
- Inflation
- Taxation system
- Interest rates

LEGAL ENVIRONMENT
- Legal tradition
- Effectiveness of legal system
- Treaties with foreign nations
- Patent trademark laws
- Laws affecting business firms

POLITICAL SYSTEM
- Form of government
- Political ideology
- Stability of government
- Strength of opposition parties and groups
- Social unrest
- Political strife and insurgency
- Governmental attitude towards foreign firms
- Foreign policy

CULTURAL ENVIRONMENT
- Customs, norms, values, beliefs
- Language
- Attitudes
- Motivations
- Social institutions
- Status symbols
- Religious beliefs

Source: From Arvind V. Phatak, *International Management,* South-Western College Publishing, 1997, p. 6. Reprinted with permission of Arvind V. Phatak.

INDUSTRY ENVIRONMENT

industry environment
The general conditions for competition that influence all businesses that provide similar products and services.

Harvard professor Michael E. Porter propelled the concept of **industry environment** into the foreground of strategic thought and business planning. The cornerstone of his work first appeared in the *Harvard Business Review,* in which Porter explains the five forces that shape competition in an industry. His well-defined analytic framework helps strategic managers to link remote factors to their effects on a firm's operating environment.

With the special permission of Professor Porter and the *Harvard Business Review,* we present in this section of the chapter the major portion of his seminal article on the industry environment and its impact on strategic management.[1]

HOW COMPETITIVE FORCES SHAPE STRATEGY

The essence of strategy formulation is coping with competition. Yet it is easy to view competition too narrowly and too pessimistically. While we sometimes hear executives complaining to the contrary, intense competition in an industry is neither coincidence nor bad luck.

Moreover, in the fight for market share, competition is not manifested only in the other players. Rather, competition in an industry is rooted in its underlying economics, and

[1] M. E. Porter, "How Competitive Forces Shape Strategy," *Harvard Business Review,* March–April 1979, pp. 137–45. Copyright © 1979 by the Harvard Business School Publishing Corporation; all rights reserved.

EXHIBIT 4.8 **Forces Driving Industry Competition**

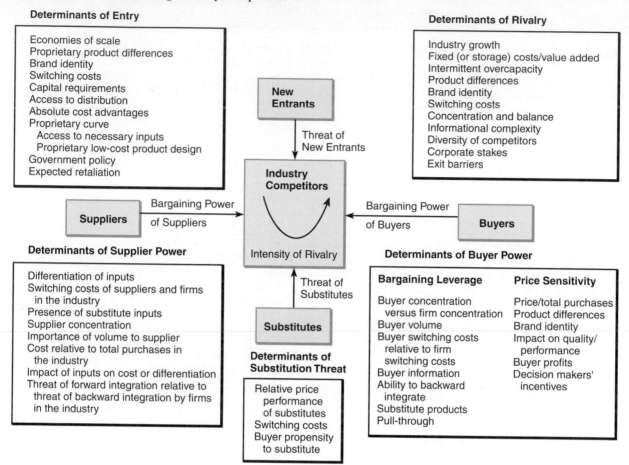

Determinants of Entry

Economies of scale
Proprietary product differences
Brand identity
Switching costs
Capital requirements
Access to distribution
Absolute cost advantages
Proprietary curve
  Access to necessary inputs
  Proprietary low-cost product design
Government policy
Expected retaliation

Determinants of Rivalry

Industry growth
Fixed (or storage) costs/value added
Intermittent overcapacity
Product differences
Brand identity
Switching costs
Concentration and balance
Informational complexity
Diversity of competitors
Corporate stakes
Exit barriers

New Entrants

Threat of New Entrants

Industry Competitors

Suppliers

Bargaining Power of Suppliers

Bargaining Power of Buyers

Buyers

Intensity of Rivalry

Threat of Substitutes

Substitutes

Determinants of Supplier Power

Differentiation of inputs
Switching costs of suppliers and firms
  in the industry
Presence of substitute inputs
Supplier concentration
Importance of volume to supplier
Cost relative to total purchases in
  the industry
Impact of inputs on cost or differentiation
Threat of forward integration relative to
  threat of backward integration by firms
  in the industry

Determinants of Substitution Threat

Relative price
  performance
  of substitutes
Switching costs
Buyer propensity
  to substitute

Determinants of Buyer Power

Bargaining Leverage	**Price Sensitivity**
Buyer concentration versus firm concentration	Price/total purchases
Buyer volume	Product differences
Buyer switching costs relative to firm switching costs	Brand identity
Buyer information	Impact on quality/ performance
Ability to backward integrate	Buyer profits
Substitute products	Decision makers' incentives
Pull-through	

competitive forces exist that go well beyond the established combatants in a particular industry. Customers, suppliers, potential entrants, and substitute products are all competitors that may be more or less prominent or active depending on the industry.

The state of competition in an industry depends on five basic forces, which are diagrammed in Exhibit 4.8. The collective strength of these forces determines the ultimate profit potential of an industry. It ranges from intense in industries like tires, metal cans, and steel, where no company earns spectacular returns on investment, to mild in industries like oil-field services and equipment, soft drinks, and toiletries, where there is room for quite high returns.

In the economists' "perfectly competitive" industry, jockeying for position is unbridled and entry to the industry very easy. This kind of industry structure, of course, offers the worst prospect for long-run profitability. The weaker the forces collectively, however, the greater the opportunity for superior performance.

Whatever their collective strength, the corporate strategist's goal is to find a position in the industry where his or her company can best defend itself against these forces or can influence them in its favor. The collective strength of the forces may be painfully apparent to all the antagonists; but to cope with them, the strategist must delve below the surface and analyze the sources of competition. For example, what makes the industry vulnerable to entry? What determines the bargaining power of suppliers?

Knowledge of these underlying sources of competitive pressure provides the groundwork for a strategic agenda of action. They highlight the critical strengths and weaknesses of the company, animate the positioning of the company in its industry, clarify the areas where strategic changes may yield the greatest payoff, and highlight the places where industry trends promise to hold the greatest significance as either opportunities or threats.

Understanding these sources also proves to be of help in considering areas for diversification.

CONTENDING FORCES

The strongest competitive force or forces determine the profitability of an industry and so are of greatest importance in strategy formulation. For example, even a company with a strong position in an industry unthreatened by potential entrants will earn low returns if it faces a superior or a lower-cost substitute product—as the leading manufacturers of vacuum tubes and coffee percolators have learned to their sorrow. In such a situation, coping with the substitute product becomes the number one strategic priority.

Different forces take on prominence, of course, in shaping competition in each industry. In the ocean-going tanker industry, the key force is probably the buyers (the major oil companies), while in tires it is powerful OEM buyers coupled with tough competitors. In the steel industry the key forces are foreign competitors and substitute materials.

Every industry has an underlying structure, or a set of fundamental economic and technical characteristics, that gives rise to these competitive forces. The strategist, wanting to position his or her company to cope best with its industry environment or to influence that environment in the company's favor, must learn what makes the environment tick.

This view of competition pertains equally to industries dealing in services and to those selling products. To avoid monotony, we refer to both products and services as *products*. The same general principles apply to all types of business.

A few characteristics are critical to the strength of each competitive force. They will be discussed in this section.

Threat of Entry

New entrants to an industry bring new capacity, the desire to gain market share, and often substantial resources. Similarly, companies diversifying through acquisition into the industry from other markets often leverage their resources to cause a shake-up, as Philip Morris did with Miller beer.

barriers to entry
The conditions that a firm must satisfy to enter an industry.

The seriousness of the threat of entry depends on the barriers present and on the reaction from existing competitors that the entrant can expect. If **barriers to entry** are high and a newcomer can expect sharp retaliation from the entrenched competitors, he or she obviously will not pose a serious threat of entering.

There are six major sources of barriers to entry.

Economies of Scale

economies of scale
The savings that companies achieve because of increased volume.

These economies deter entry by forcing the aspirant either to come in on a large scale or to accept a cost disadvantage. Scale economies in production, research, marketing, and service are probably the key barriers to entry in the mainframe computer industry, as Xerox and GE sadly discovered. **Economies of scale** also can act as hurdles in distribution, utilization of the sales force, financing, and nearly any other part of a business.

Economies of scale refer to the savings that companies within an industry achieve due to increased volume. Simply put, when the volume of production increases, the long-range average cost of a unit produced will decline.

Economies of scale result from technological and nontechnological sources. The technological sources of these economies are higher levels of mechanization or automation and a greater modernization of plant and facilities The nontechnological sources include better managerial coordination of production functions and processes, long-term contractual agreements with suppliers, and enhanced employee performance arising from specialization.

Economies of scale are an important determinant of the intensity of competition in an industry. Firms that enjoy such economies can charge lower prices than their competitors. They also can create barriers to entry by reducing their prices temporarily, or permanently, to deter new firms from entering the industry.

Product Differentiation

product differentiation
The extent to which customers perceive differences among products and services.

Product differentiation, or brand identification, creates a barrier by forcing entrants to spend heavily to overcome customer loyalty. Advertising, customer service, being first in the industry, and product differences are among the factors fostering brand identification. It is perhaps the most important entry barrier in soft drinks, over-the-counter drugs, cosmetics, investment banking, and public accounting. To create high fences around their business, brewers couple brand identification with economies of scale in production, distribution, and marketing.

Capital Requirements

The need to invest large financial resources to compete creates a barrier to entry, particularly if the capital is required for unrecoverable expenditures in upfront advertising or R&D. Capital is necessary not only for fixed facilities but also for customer credit, inventories, and absorbing start-up losses. While major corporations have the financial resources to invade almost any industry, the huge capital requirements in certain fields, such as computer manufacturing and mineral extraction, limit the pool of likely entrants.

Cost Disadvantages Independent of Size

Entrenched companies may have cost advantages not available to potential rivals, no matter what their size and attainable economies of scale. These advantages can stem from the effects of the learning curve (and of its first cousin, the experience curve), proprietary technology, access to the best raw materials sources, assets purchased at preinflation prices, government subsidies, or favorable locations. Sometimes cost advantages are enforceable legally, as they are through patents. (For analysis of the much-discussed experience curve as a barrier to entry, see Exhibit 4.9, Strategy in Action.)

Access to Distribution Channels

The new boy or girl on the block must, of course, secure distribution of his or her product or service. A new food product, for example, must displace others from the supermarket shelf via price breaks, promotions, intense selling efforts, or some other means. The more limited the wholesale or retail channels are and the more that existing competitors have these tied up, obviously the tougher that entry into the industry will be. Sometimes this barrier is so high that, to surmount it, a new contestant must create its own distribution channels, as Timex did in the watch industry.

Government Policy

The government can limit or even foreclose entry to industries, with such controls as license requirements, limits on access to raw materials, and tax incentives. Regulated industries

The Experience Curve as an Entry Barrier

In recent years, the experience curve has become widely discussed as a key element of industry structure. According to this concept, unit costs in many manufacturing industries (some dogmatic adherents say in all manufacturing industries) as well as in some service industries decline with "experience," or a particular company's cumulative volume of production. (The experience curve, which encompasses many factors, is a broader concept than the better-known learning curve, which refers to the efficiency achieved over time by workers through much repetition.)

The causes of the decline in unit costs are a combination of elements, including economies of scale, the learning curve for labor, and capital-labor substitution. The cost decline creates a barrier to entry because new competitors with no "experience" face higher costs than established ones, particularly the producer with the largest market share, and have difficulty catching up with the entrenched competitors.

Adherents of the experience curve concept stress the importance of achieving market leadership to maximize this barrier to entry, and they recommend aggressive action to achieve it, such as price cutting in anticipation of falling costs in order to build volume. For the combatant that cannot achieve a healthy market share, the prescription is usually, "Get out."

Is the experience curve an entry barrier on which strategies should be built? The answer is, not in every industry. In fact, in some industries, building a strategy on the experience curve can be potentially disastrous.

That costs decline with experience in some industries is not news to corporate executives. The significance of the experience curve for strategy depends on what factors are causing the decline.

A new entrant may well be more efficient than the more experienced competitors: if it has built the newest plant, it will face no disadvantage in having to catch up. The strategic prescription, "You must have the largest, most efficient plant," is a lot different from "You must produce the greatest cumulative output of the item to get your costs down."

Whether a drop in costs with cumulative (not absolute) volume erects an entry barrier also depends on the sources of the decline. If costs go down because of technical advances known generally in the industry or because of the development of improved equipment that can be copied or purchased from equipment suppliers, the experience curve is not an entry barrier at all—in fact, new or less-experienced competitors may actually enjoy a cost advantage over the leaders. Free of the legacy of heavy past investments, the newcomer or less-experienced competitor can purchase or copy the newest and lowest cost equipment and technology.

If, however, experience can be kept proprietary, the leaders will maintain a cost advantage. But new entrants may require less experience to reduce their costs than the leaders needed. All this suggests that the experience curve can be a shaky entry barrier on which to build a strategy.

like trucking, liquor retailing, and freight forwarding are noticeable examples; more subtle government restrictions operate in fields like ski-area development and coal mining. The government also can play a major indirect role by affecting entry barriers through such controls as air and water pollution standards and safety regulations.

The potential rival's expectations about the reaction of existing competitors also will influence its decision on whether to enter. The company is likely to have second thoughts if incumbents have previously lashed out at new entrants, or if

The incumbents possess substantial resources to fight back, including excess cash and unused borrowing power, productive capacity, or clout with distribution channels and customers.

The incumbents seem likely to cut prices because of a desire to keep market shares or because of industrywide excess capacity.

Industry growth is slow, affecting its ability to absorb the new arrival and probably causing the financial performance of all the parties involved to decline.

Powerful Suppliers

Suppliers can exert bargaining power on participants in an industry by raising prices or reducing the quality of purchased goods and services. Powerful suppliers, thereby, can squeeze profitability out of an industry unable to recover cost increases in its own prices. By raising their prices, soft-drink concentrate producers have contributed to the erosion of profitability of bottling companies because the bottlers—facing intense competition from powdered mixes, fruit drinks, and other beverages—have limited freedom to raise their prices accordingly.

The power of each important supplier (or buyer) group depends on a number of characteristics of its market situation and on the relative importance of its sales or purchases to the industry compared with its overall business.

A *supplier* group is powerful if

1. It is dominated by a few companies and is more concentrated than the industry it sells.

2. Its product is unique or at least differentiated, or if it has built-up switching costs. Switching costs are fixed costs that buyers face in changing suppliers. These arise because, among other things, a buyer's product specifications tie it to particular suppliers, it has invested heavily in specialized ancillary equipment or in learning how to operate a supplier's equipment (as in computer software), or its production lines are connected to the supplier's manufacturing facilities (as in some manufacturing of beverage containers).

3. It is not obliged to contend with other products for sale to the industry. For instance, the competition between the steel companies and the aluminum companies to sell to the can industry checks the power of each supplier.

4. It poses a credible threat of integrating forward into the industry's business. This provides a check against the industry's ability to improve the terms on which it purchases.

5. The industry is not an important customer of the supplier group. If the industry is an important customer, suppliers' fortunes will be tied closely to the industry, and they will want to protect the industry through reasonable pricing and assistance in activities like R&D and lobbying.

Powerful Buyers

Customers likewise can force down prices, demand higher quality or more service, and play competitors off against each other—all at the expense of industry profits.

A *buyer* group is powerful if

1. It is concentrated or purchases in large volumes. Large-volume buyers are particularly potent forces if heavy fixed costs characterize the industry—as they do in metal containers, corn refining, and bulk chemicals, for example—which raise the stakes to keep capacity filled.

2. The products it purchases from the industry are standard or undifferentiated. The buyers, sure that they always can find alternative suppliers, may play one company against another, as they do in aluminum extrusion.

3. The products it purchases from the industry form a component of its product and represent a significant fraction of its cost. The buyers are likely to shop for a favorable price and purchase selectively. Where the product sold by the industry in question is a small fraction of buyers' costs, buyers are usually much less price sensitive.

4. It earns low profits, which create great incentive to lower its purchasing costs. Highly profitable buyers, however, are generally less price sensitive (i.e., of course, if the item does not represent a large fraction of their costs).

MasterCard Faces Strong Buyer Power

MasterCard Inc. generates revenue by charging fees to process payments from banks to consumers who swipe MasterCard-brand credit and debit cards, making the banks, not individual consumers, MasterCard's customers. MasterCard issues 916 million cards through 25,000 financial institutions in more than 200 countries.

Rapid consolidation within the banking industry, combined with a 28 percent market share in global credit and debit card transactions compared with main-rival Visa's 68 percent share, means that MasterCard has to work hard to win and keep bank business. Further, MasterCard success depends on its four largest customers, which make up 30 percent of annual revenues: J.P. Morgan Chase, Citigroup, Bank of America, and HSBC.

MasterCard strategy focuses on two key elements—pricing and marketing. MasterCard carefully executed price increases between 2007 and 2008, with little customer pushback. At the same time, the company created MasterCard account teams that are tailored to fit the specific key customer needs. The teams drive the growth of customer usage, and thereby company growth. MasterCard's marketing talent was also reoriented from a dedication to strengthening MasterCard's brand identity to directly benefit these customers.

Sources: J. Kutler, "CEO Interview—Credit without the Crunch," *Institutional Investor* 4 (2008), pp. 30–32; T. Demos, "MasterCard's Keys to Survival," *Fortune* 158, no. 4 (2008), p. 159; and H. Terris, "MasterCard Results Show Pricing Power," *American Banker* 173, no. 22 (2008), p. 1.

5. The industry's product is unimportant to the quality of the buyers' products or services. Where the quality of the buyers' products is very much affected by the industry's product, buyers are generally less price sensitive. Industries in which this situation exists include oil field equipment, where a malfunction can lead to large losses, and enclosures for electronic medical and test instruments, where the quality of the enclosure can influence the user's impression about the quality of the equipment inside.

6. The industry's product does not save the buyer money. Where the industry's product or service can pay for itself many times over, the buyer is rarely price sensitive; rather, he or she is interested in quality. This is true in services like investment banking and public accounting, where errors in judgment can be costly and embarrassing, and in businesses like the mapping of oil wells, where an accurate survey can save thousands of dollars in drilling costs.

7. The buyers pose a credible threat of integrating backward to make the industry's product. The Big Three auto producers and major buyers of cars often have used the threat of self-manufacture as a bargaining lever. But sometimes an industry so engenders a threat to buyers that its members may integrate forward.

Most of these sources of buyer power can be attributed to consumers as a group as well as to industrial and commercial buyers; only a modification of the frame of reference is necessary. Consumers tend to be more price sensitive if they are purchasing products that are undifferentiated, expensive relative to their incomes, and of a sort where quality is not particularly important.

The buying power of retailers is determined by the same rules, with one important addition. Retailers can gain significant bargaining power over manufacturers when they can influence consumers' purchasing decisions, as they do in audio components, jewelry, appliances, sporting goods, and other goods.

Because its heavy reliance on a few large customers, MasterCard's corporate strategy is strongly influenced by buyer power, as discussed in Exhibit 4.10, Strategy in Action.

Substitute Products

By placing a ceiling on the prices it can charge, substitute products or services limit the potential of an industry. Unless it can upgrade the quality of the product or differentiate it somehow (as via marketing), the industry will suffer in earnings and possibly in growth.

Manifestly, the more attractive the price-performance trade-off offered by substitute products, the firmer the lid placed on the industry's profit potential. Sugar producers confronted with the large-scale commercialization of high-fructose corn syrup, a sugar substitute, learned this lesson.

Substitutes not only limit profits in normal times but also reduce the bonanza an industry can reap in boom times. The producers of fiberglass insulation enjoyed unprecedented demand as a result of high energy costs and severe winter weather. But the industry's ability to raise prices was tempered by the plethora of insulation substitutes, including cellulose, rock wool, and Styrofoam. These substitutes are bound to become an even stronger force once the current round of plant additions by fiberglass insulation producers has boosted capacity enough to meet demand (and then some).

Substitute products that deserve the most attention strategically are those that *(a)* are subject to trends improving their price-performance trade-off with the industry's product or *(b)* are produced by industries earning high profits. Substitutes often come rapidly into play if some development increases competition in their industries and causes price reduction or performance improvement.

Jockeying for Position

Rivalry among existing competitors takes the familiar form of jockeying for position—using tactics like price competition, product introduction, and advertising price-cutting. This type of intense rivalry is related to the presence of a number of factors:

1. Competitors are numerous or are roughly equal in size and power. In many U.S. industries in recent years, foreign contenders, of course, have become part of the competitive picture.

2. Industry growth is slow, precipitating fights for market share that involve expansion-minded members.

3. The product or service lacks differentiation or switching costs, which lock in buyers and protect one combatant from raids on its customers by another.

4. Fixed costs are high or the product is perishable, creating strong temptation to cut prices. Many basic materials businesses, like paper and aluminum, suffer from this problem when demand slackens.

5. Capacity normally is augmented in large increments. Such additions, as in the chlorine and vinyl chloride businesses, disrupt the industry's supply–demand balance and often lead to periods of overcapacity and price-cutting.

6. Exit barriers are high. Exit barriers, like very specialized assets or management's loyalty to a particular business, keep companies competing even though they may be earning low or even negative returns on investment. Excess capacity remains functioning, and the profitability of the healthy competitors suffers as the sick ones hang on. If the entire industry suffers from overcapacity, it may seek government help—particularly if foreign competition is present.

7. The rivals are diverse in strategies, origins, and "personalities." They have different ideas about how to compete and continually run head-on into each other in the process.

As an industry matures, its growth rate changes, resulting in declining profits and (often) a shakeout. In the booming recreational vehicle industry of the early 1970s, nearly every producer did well; but slow growth since then has eliminated the high returns, except for the strongest members, not to mention many of the weaker companies. The same profit story has been played out in industry after industry—snowmobiles, aerosol packaging, and sports equipment are just a few examples.

An acquisition can introduce a very different personality to an industry, as has been the case with Black & Decker's takeover of McCullough, the producer of chain saws. Technological innovation can boost the level of fixed costs in the production process, as it did in the shift from batch to continuous-line photo finishing.

While a company must live with many of these factors—because they are built into the industry economics—it may have some latitude for improving matters through strategic shifts. For example, it may try to raise buyers' switching costs or increase product differentiation. A focus on selling efforts in the fastest growing segments of the industry or on market areas with the lowest fixed costs can reduce the impact of industry rivalry. If it is feasible, a company can try to avoid confrontation with competitors having high exit barriers and, thus, can sidestep involvement in bitter price-cutting.

INDUSTRY ANALYSIS AND COMPETITIVE ANALYSIS

Designing viable strategies for a firm requires a thorough understanding of the firm's industry and competition. The firm's executives need to address four questions: (1) What are the boundaries of the industry? (2) What is the structure of the industry? (3) Which firms are our competitors? (4) What are the major determinants of competition? The answers to these questions provide a basis for thinking about the appropriate strategies that are open to the firm.

Industry Boundaries

industry
A group of companies that provide similar products and services.

An **industry** is a collection of firms that offer similar products or services. By "similar products," we mean products that customers perceive to be substitutable for one another. Consider, for example, the brands of personal computers (PCs) that are now being marketed. The firms that produce these PCs, such as Hewlett-Packard, IBM, Apple, and Dell, form the nucleus of the microcomputer industry.

Suppose a firm competes in the microcomputer industry. Where do the boundaries of this industry begin and end? Does the industry include desktops? Laptops? These are the kinds of questions that executives face in defining industry boundaries.

Why is a definition of industry boundaries important? First, it helps executives determine the arena in which their firm is competing. A firm competing in the microcomputer industry participates in an environment very different from that of the broader electronics business. The microcomputer industry comprises several related product families, including personal computers, inexpensive computers for home use, and workstations. The unifying characteristic of these product families is the use of a central processing unit (CPU) in a microchip. On the other hand, the electronics industry is far more extensive; it includes computers, radios, supercomputers, superconductors, and many other products.

The microcomputer and electronics industries differ in their volume of sales, their scope (some would consider microcomputers a segment of the electronics industry), their rate of growth, and their competitive makeup. The dominant issues faced by the two industries also are different. Witness, for example, the raging public debate being waged on the future of the "high-definition TV." U.S. policy makers are attempting to ensure domestic control of that segment of the electronics industry. They also are considering ways to stimulate "cutting-edge" research in superconductivity. These efforts are likely to spur innovation and stimulate progress in the electronics industry.

Second, a definition of industry boundaries focuses attention on the firm's competitors. Defining industry boundaries enables the firm to identify its competitors and producers of substitute products. This is critically important to the firm's design of its competitive strategy.

Third, a definition of industry boundaries helps executives determine key factors for success. Survival in the premier segment of the microcomputer industry requires skills that are considerably different from those required in the lower end of the industry. Firms that compete in the premier segment need to be on the cutting edge of technological development and to provide extensive customer support and education. On the other hand, firms that compete in the lower end need to excel in imitating the products introduced by the premier segment, to focus on customer convenience, and to maintain operational efficiency that permits them to charge the lowest market price. Defining industry boundaries enables executives to ask these questions: Do we have the skills it takes to succeed here? If not, what must we do to develop these skills?

Finally, a definition of industry boundaries gives executives another basis on which to evaluate their firm's goals. Executives use that definition to forecast demand for their firm's products and services. Armed with that forecast, they can determine whether those goals are realistic.

Problems in Defining Industry Boundaries

Defining industry boundaries requires both caution and imagination. Caution is necessary because there are no precise rules for this task and because a poor definition will lead to poor planning. Imagination is necessary because industries are dynamic—in every industry, important changes are under way in such key factors as competition, technology, and consumer demand.

Defining industry boundaries is a very difficult task. The difficulty stems from three sources:

1. The evolution of industries over time creates new opportunities and threats. Compare the financial services industry as we know it today with that of the 1990s, and then try to imagine how different the industry will be in the year 2020.

2. Industrial evolution creates industries within industries. The electronics industry of the 1960s has been transformed into many "industries"—TV sets, transistor radios, micro and macrocomputers, supercomputers, superconductors, and so on. Such transformation allows some firms to specialize and others to compete in different, related industries.

3. Industries are becoming global in scope. Consider the civilian aircraft manufacturing industry. For nearly three decades, U.S. firms dominated world production in that industry. But small and large competitors were challenging their dominance by 1990. At that time, Airbus Industries (a consortium of European firms) and Brazilian, Korean, and Japanese firms were actively competing in the industry.

Developing a Realistic Industry Definition

Given the difficulties just outlined, how do executives draw accurate boundaries for an industry? The starting point is a definition of the industry in global terms; that is, in terms that consider the industry's international components as well as its domestic components.

Having developed a preliminary concept of the industry (e.g., computers), executives flesh out its current components. This can be done by defining its product segments. Executives need to select the scope of their firm's potential market from among these related but distinct areas.

To understand the makeup of the industry, executives adopt a longitudinal perspective. They examine the emergence and evolution of product families. Why did these product families arise? How and why did they change? The answers to such questions provide executives with clues about the factors that drive competition in the industry.

Executives also examine the companies that offer different product families, the overlapping or distinctiveness of customer segments, and the rate of substitutability among product families.

To realistically define their industry, executives need to examine five issues:

1. Which part of the industry corresponds to our firm's goals?
2. What are the key ingredients of success in that part of the industry?
3. Does our firm have the skills needed to compete in that part of the industry? If not, can we build those skills?
4. Will the skills enable us to seize emerging opportunities and deal with future threats?
5. Is our definition of the industry flexible enough to allow necessary adjustments to our business concept as the industry grows?

Power Curves

Strategic managers have a new tool that helps them assess industry structure, which refers to the enduring characteristics that give an industry its distinctive character. According to Michele Zanini of the McKinsey Group, from whose work this discussion is derived, power curves depict the fundamental structural trends that underlie an industry.[2] While major economic events like the worldwide recession of 2008 are extremely disruptive to business activity, they do little to change the relative position of most businesses to one another over the long term.

What would you guess is the typical shape of the distribution of companies in an industry? Is it bell shaped, with a few superlarge firms, many companies of medium size, and a few extremely small competitors? Or, is it linear, with a few large companies and progressively larger numbers of smaller firms? Do you think that company strategies should be different if one of these models is right and the other wrong?

In many industries, the top firm is best described as a mega-institution—a company of unprecedented scale and scope that has an undeniable lead over competitors. Wal-Mart, Best Buy, McDonald's, and Starbucks are examples. However, even among these firms, there is a clear difference in size and performance. When the distribution of net incomes of the global top 150 corporations in 2005 was plotted, the result was a "power curve," which implies that most companies, even in the set of superstars, are below average in performance. This power curve is shown in Exhibit 4.11.

A power curve is described as exhibiting a small set of companies with extremely large incomes, followed quickly by a much larger array of companies with significantly smaller incomes that are progressively smaller than one another, but only slightly.

As Zanini explains, low barriers to entry and high levels of rivalry are positively associated with an industry's power curve dynamics. The larger the number of competitors in an industry, the larger the gap on the vertical axis usually is between the top and median companies. When entry barriers are lowered, such as occurs with deregulation, revenues increase faster in the top-ranking firms, creating a steeper power curve. This greater openness seems to create a more level playing field at first, but greater differentiation and consolidation tend to occur over time.

Power curves are also promoted by intangible assets such as software and biotechnology, which generate increasing returns to scale and economies of scope. By contrast, more labor- or capital-intensive sectors, such as chemicals and machinery, have flatter curves.

[2] Michele Zanini, "'Using Power Curves' to Assess Industry Dynamics," *The McKinsey Quarterly*, November 2008.

EXHIBIT 4.11
Common Shape of a
Power Curve

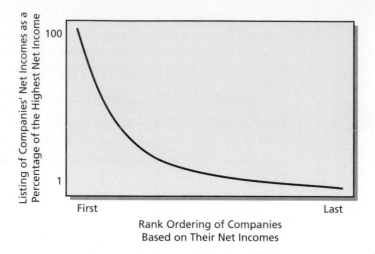

In industries that display a power curve—including insurance, machinery, and U.S. banks and savings institutions—intriguing implications suggest that strategic thrusts rather than incremental strategies are required to improve a company's position significantly. Zanini defends this idea with evidence from the retail mutual fund industry. The major players at the top of the power curve can extend their lead by exploiting network effects, such as cross-selling individual retirement accounts (IRAs), to a large installed base of 401(k) plan holders as they roll over their assets. A financial crisis, like the recession of 2008, increases the likelihood of this opportunity as weakened financial institutions sell their asset-management units to raise capital.

Power curves can be useful to strategic managers in understanding their industry's structural dynamics and in benchmarking its performance. Because an industry's curve evolves over many years, a large deviation in the slope can indicate some exceptional occurrence, such as unusual firm performance or market instability.

As Zanini concludes, power curves suggest that companies generally compete against one another and against an industry structure that becomes progressively more unequal. For most companies, this possibility makes power curves an important strategic consideration.

Competitive Analysis
How to Identify Competitors
In identifying their firm's current and potential competitors, executives consider several important variables:

1. How do other firms define the scope of their market? The more similar the definitions of firms, the more likely the firms will view each other as competitors.

2. How similar are the benefits the customers derive from the products and services that other firms offer? The more similar the benefits of products or services, the higher the level of substitutability between them. High substitutability levels force firms to compete fiercely for customers.

3. How committed are other firms to the industry? Although this question may appear to be far removed from the identification of competitors, it is in fact one of the most important questions that competitive analysis must address, because it sheds light on the long-term intentions and goals. To size up the commitment of potential competitors to the industry, reliable intelligence data are needed. Such data may relate to potential resource commitments (e.g., planned facility expansions).

Common Mistakes in Identifying Competitors

Identifying competitors is a milestone in the development of strategy. But it is a process laden with uncertainty and risk, a process in which executives sometimes make costly mistakes. Examples of these mistakes are:

1. Overemphasizing current and known competitors while giving inadequate attention to potential entrants.

2. Overemphasizing large competitors while ignoring small competitors.

3. Overlooking potential international competitors.

4. Assuming that competitors will continue to behave in the same way they have behaved in the past.

5. Misreading signals that may indicate a shift in the focus of competitors or a refinement of their present strategies or tactics.

6. Overemphasizing competitors' financial resources, market position, and strategies while ignoring their intangible assets, such as a top management team.

7. Assuming that all of the firms in the industry are subject to the same constraints or are open to the same opportunities.

8. Believing that the purpose of strategy is to outsmart the competition, rather than to satisfy customer needs and expectations.

OPERATING ENVIRONMENT

operating environment
Factors in the immediate competitive situation that affect a firm's success in acquiring needed resources.

The **operating environment,** also called the *competitive* or *task environment,* comprises factors in the competitive situation that affect a firm's success in acquiring needed resources or in profitably marketing its goods and services. Among the most important of these factors are the firm's competitive position, the composition of its customers, its reputation among suppliers and creditors, and its ability to attract capable employees. The operating environment is typically much more subject to the firm's influence or control than the remote environment. Thus, firms can be much more proactive (as opposed to reactive) in dealing with the operating environment than in dealing with the remote environment.

Competitive Position

Assessing its competitive position improves a firm's chances of designing strategies that optimize its environmental opportunities. Development of competitor profiles enables a firm to more accurately forecast both its short- and long-term growth and its profit potentials. Although the exact criteria used in constructing a competitor's profile are largely determined by situational factors, the following criteria are often included:

1. Market share.
2. Breadth of product line.
3. Effectiveness of sales distribution.
4. Proprietary and key account advantages.
5. Price competitiveness.
6. Advertising and promotion effectiveness.
7. Location and age of facility.
8. Capacity and productivity.
9. Experience.
10. Raw materials costs.
11. Financial position.
12. Relative product quality.
13. R&D advantages position.
14. Caliber of personnel.
15. General images.
16. Customer profile.
17. Patents and copyrights.
18. Union relations.
19. Technological position.
20. Community reputation.

EXHIBIT 4.12
Competitor Profile

Key Success Factors	Weight	Rating[*]	Weighted Score
Market share	0.30	4	1.20
Price competitiveness	0.20	3	0.60
Facilities location	0.20	5	1.00
Raw materials costs	0.10	3	0.30
Caliber of personnel	0.20	1	0.20
	1.00[†]		3.30

[*]The rating scale suggested is as follows: very strong competitive position (5 points), strong (4), average (3), weak (2), very weak (1).
[†]The total of the weights must always equal 1.00.

Once appropriate criteria have been selected, they are weighted to reflect their importance to a firm's success. Then the competitor being evaluated is rated on the criteria, the ratings are multiplied by the weight, and the weighted scores are summed to yield a numerical profile of the competitor, as shown in Exhibit 4.12.

This type of competitor profile is limited by the subjectivity of its criteria selection, weighting, and evaluation approaches. Nevertheless, the process of developing such profiles is of considerable help to a firm in defining its perception of its competitive position. Moreover, comparing the firm's profile with those of its competitors can aid its managers in identifying factors that might make the competitors vulnerable to the strategies the firm might choose to implement.

Customer Profiles

Perhaps the most vulnerable result of analyzing the operating environment is the understanding of a firm's customers that this provides. Developing a profile of a firm's present and prospective customers improves the ability of its managers to plan strategic operations, to anticipate changes in the size of markets, and to reallocate resources so as to support forecast shifts in demand patterns. The traditional approach to segmenting customers is based on customer profiles constructed from geographic, demographic, psychographic, and buyer behavior information.

Enterprising companies have quickly learned the importance of identifying target segments. In recent years, market research has increased tremendously as companies realize the benefits of demographic and psychographic segmentation. Research by American Express (AMEX) showed that competitors were stealing a prime segment of the company's business, affluent business travelers. AMEX's competing companies, including Visa and Mastercard, began offering high-spending business travelers frequent flier programs and other rewards including discounts on new cars. In turn, AMEX began to invest heavily in rewards programs, while also focusing on its strongest capabilities, assets, and competitive advantage. Unlike most credit card companies, AMEX cannot rely on charging interest to make money because most of its customers pay in full each month. Therefore, the company charges higher transaction fees to its merchants. In this way, increases in spending by AMEX customers who pay off their balances each month are more profitable to AMEX than to competing credit card companies.

Assessing consumer behavior is a key element in the process of satisfying your target market needs. Many firms lose market share as a result of assumptions made about target segments. Market research and industry surveys can help to reduce a firm's chances of relying on illusive assumptions. Firms most vulnerable are those that have had success with one or more products in the marketplace and as a result try to base consumer behavior on past data and trends.

Geographic

It is important to define the geographic area from which customers do or could come. Almost every product or service has some quality that makes it variably attractive to buyers from different locations. Obviously, a Wisconsin manufacturer of snow skis should think twice about investing in a wholesale distribution center in South Carolina. On the other hand, advertising in the *Milwaukee Journal-Sentinel* could significantly expand the geographically defined customer market of a major Myrtle Beach hotel in South Carolina.

Demographic

Demographic variables most commonly are used to differentiate groups of present or potential customers. Demographic information (e.g., information on sex, age, marital status, income, and occupation) is comparatively easy to collect, quantify, and use in strategic forecasting, and such information is the minimum basis for a customer profile.

Psychographic

Personality and lifestyle variables often are better predictors of customer purchasing behavior than geographic or demographic variables. In such situations, a psychographic study is an important component of the customer profile. Advertising campaigns by soft-drink producers—Pepsi-Cola ("the Pepsi generation"), Coca-Cola ("the real thing"), and 7UP ("America's turning 7UP")—reflect strategic management's attention to the psychographic characteristics of their largest customer segment—physically active, group-oriented nonprofessionals.

Buyer Behavior

Buyer behavior data also can be a component of the customer profile. Such data are used to explain or predict some aspect of customer behavior with regard to a product or service. Information on buyer behavior (e.g., usage rate, benefits sought, and brand loyalty) can provide significant aid in the design of more accurate and profitable strategies.

Suppliers

Dependable relationships between a firm and its suppliers are essential to the firm's long-term survival and growth. A firm regularly relies on its suppliers for financial support, services, materials, and equipment. In addition, it occasionally is forced to make special requests for such favors as quick delivery, liberal credit terms, or broken-lot orders. Particularly at such times, it is essential for a firm to have had an ongoing relationship with its suppliers.

In the assessment of a firm's relationships with its suppliers, several factors, other than the strength of that relationship, should be considered. With regard to its competitive position with its suppliers, the firm should address the following questions:

Are the suppliers' prices competitive? Do the suppliers offer attractive quantity discounts?

How costly are their shipping charges? Are the suppliers competitive in terms of production standards?

In terms of deficiency rates, are the suppliers' abilities, reputations, and services competitive?

Are the suppliers reciprocally dependent on the firm?

Creditors

Because the quantity, quality, price, and accessibility of financial, human, and material resources are rarely ideal, assessment of suppliers and creditors is critical to an accurate evaluation of a firm's operating environment. With regard to its competitive position with its creditors, among the most important questions that the firm should address are the following:

> Do the creditors fairly value and willingly accept the firm's stock as collateral?
>
> Do the creditors perceive the firm as having an acceptable record of past payment? A strong working capital position? Little or no leverage?
>
> Are the creditors' loan terms compatible with the firm's profitability objectives?
>
> Are the creditors able to extend the necessary lines of credit?

The answers to these and related questions help a firm forecast the availability of the resources it will need to implement and sustain its competitive strategies.

Human Resources: Nature of the Labor Market

A firm's ability to attract and hold capable employees is essential to its success. However, a firm's personnel recruitment and selection alternatives often are influenced by the nature of its operating environment. A firm's access to needed personnel is affected primarily by four factors: the firm's reputation as an employer, local employment rates, the ready availability of people with the needed skills, and its relationship with labor unions.

Reputation

A firm's reputation within its operating environment is a major element of its ability to satisfy its personnel needs. A firm is more likely to attract and retain valuable employees if it is seen as permanent in the community, competitive in its compensation package, and concerned with the welfare of its employees, and if it is respected for its product or service and appreciated for its overall contribution to the general welfare.

Employment Rates

The readily available supply of skilled and experienced personnel may vary considerably with the stage of a community's growth. A new manufacturing firm would find it far more difficult to obtain skilled employees in a vigorous industrialized community than in an economically depressed community in which similar firms had recently cut back operations.

Availability

The skills of some people are so specialized that relocation may be necessary to secure the jobs and the compensation that those skills commonly command. People with such skills include oil drillers, chefs, technical specialists, and industry executives. A firm that seeks to hire such a person is said to have broad labor market boundaries; that is, the geographic area within which the firm might reasonably expect to attract qualified candidates is quite large. On the other hand, people with more common skills are less likely to relocate from a considerable distance to achieve modest economic or career advancements. Thus, the labor market boundaries are fairly limited for such occupational groups as unskilled laborers, clerical personnel, and retail clerks.

Many manufacturers in the United States attempt to minimize the labor cost disadvantage they face in competing with overseas producers by outsourcing to lower-cost foreign locations or by hiring immigrant workers. Similarly, companies in construction and other labor-intensive industries try to provide themselves with a cost advantage by hiring temporary, often migrant, workers.

Labor Unions

Approximately 12 percent of all workers in the United States belong to a labor union; the percentages are higher in Japan and western Europe at about 25 and 40 percent, respectively, and extremely low in developing nations. Unions represent the workers in their negotiations with employers through the process of collective bargaining. When managers' relationships with their employees are complicated by the involvement of a union, the company's ability to manage and motivate the people that it needs can be compromised.

EMPHASIS ON ENVIRONMENTAL FACTORS

This chapter has described the remote, industry, and operating environments as encompassing five components each. While that description is generally accurate, it may give the false impression that the components are easily identified, mutually exclusive, and equally applicable in all situations. In fact, the forces in the external environment are so dynamic and interactive that the impact of any single element cannot be wholly disassociated from the effect of other elements. For example, are increases in OPEC oil prices the result of economic, political, social, or technological changes? Or are a manufacturer's surprisingly good relations with suppliers a result of competitors', customers', or creditors' activities or of the supplier's own activities? The answer to both questions is probably that a number of forces in the external environment have combined to create the situation. Such is the case in most studies of the environment.

Strategic managers are frequently frustrated in their attempts to anticipate the environment's changing influences. Different external elements affect different strategies at different times and with varying strengths. The only certainty is that the effect of the remote and operating environments will be uncertain until a strategy is implemented. This leads many managers, particularly in less powerful or smaller firms, to minimize long-term planning, which requires a commitment of resources. Instead, they favor allowing managers to adapt to new pressures from the environment. While such a decision has considerable merit for many firms, there is an associated trade-off, namely that absence of a strong resource and psychological commitment to a proactive strategy effectively bars a firm from assuming a leadership role in its competitive environment.

There is yet another difficulty in assessing the probable impact of remote, industry, and operating environments on the effectiveness of alternative strategies. Assessment of this kind involves collecting information that can be analyzed to disclose predictable effects. Except in rare instances, however, it is virtually impossible for any single firm to anticipate the consequences of a change in the environment; for example, what is the precise effect on alternative strategies of a 2 percent increase in the national inflation rate, a 1 percent decrease in statewide unemployment, or the entry of a new competitor in a regional market?

Still, assessing the potential impact of changes in the external environment offers a real advantage. It enables decision makers to narrow the range of the available options and to eliminate options that are clearly inconsistent with the forecast opportunities. Environmental assessment seldom identifies the best strategy, but it generally leads to the elimination of all but the most promising options.

Exhibit 4.13 provides a set of key strategic forecasting issues for each level of environmental assessment—remote, industry, and operating. While the issues that are presented are not inclusive of all of the questions that are important, they provide an excellent set of questions with which to begin. Chapter 4 Appendix, Sources for Environmental Forecasting, is provided to help identify valuable sources of data and information from which answers and subsequent forecasts can be constructed. It lists governmental and private marketplace intelligence that can be used by a firm to gain a foothold in undertaking a strategic assessment of any level of the competitive environment.

EXHIBIT 4.13
Strategic Forecasting
Issues

Key Issues in the Remote Environment Economy

What are the probable future directions of the economies in the firm's regional, national, and international market? What changes in economic growth, inflation, interest rates, capital availability, credit availability, and consumer purchasing power can be expected? What income differences can be expected between the wealthy upper middle class, the working class, and the underclass in various regions? What shifts in relative demand for different categories of goods and services can be expected?

Society and demographics

What effects will changes in social values and attitudes regarding childbearing, marriage, lifestyle, work, ethics, sex roles, racial equality, education, retirement, pollution, and energy have on the firm's development? What effects will population changes have on major social and political expectations—at home and abroad? What constraints or opportunities will develop? What pressure groups will increase in power?

Ecology

What natural or pollution-caused disasters threaten the firm's employees, customers, or facilities? How rigorously will existing environment legislature be enforced? What new federal, state, and local laws will affect the firm, and in what ways?

Politics

What changes in government policy can be expected with regard to industry cooperation, antitrust activities, foreign trade, taxation, depreciation, environmental protection, deregulation, defense, foreign trade barriers, and other important parameters? What success will a new administration have in achieving its stated goals? What effect will that success have on the firm? Will specific international climates be hostile or favorable? Is there a tendency toward instability, corruption, or violence? What is the level of political risk in each foreign market? What other political or legal constraints or supports can be expected in international business (e.g., trade barriers, equity requirements, nationalism, patent protection)?

Technology

What is the current state of the art? How will it change? What pertinent new products or services are likely to become technically feasible in the foreseeable future? What future impact can be expected from technological breakthroughs in related product areas? How will those breakthroughs interface with the other remote considerations, such as economic issues, social values, public safety, regulations, and court interpretations?

Key Issues in the Industry Environment

New entrants

Will new technologies or market demands enable competitors to minimize the impact of traditional economies of scale in the industry? Will consumers accept our claims of product or service differentiation? Will potential new entrants be able to match the capital requirements that currently exist? How permanent are the cost disadvantages (independent of size) in our industry? Will conditions change so that all competitors have equal access to marketing channels? Is government policy toward competition in our industry likely to change?

Bargaining power of suppliers

How stable are the size and composition of our supplier group? Are any suppliers likely to attempt forward integration into our business level? How dependent will our suppliers be in the future? Are substitute suppliers likely to become available? Could we become our own supplier?

EXHIBIT 4.13
(continued)

Substitute products or services

Are new substitutes likely? Will they be price competitive? Could we fight off substitutes by price competition? By advertising to sharpen product differentiation? What actions could we take to reduce the potential for having alternative products seen as legitimate substitutes?

Bargaining power of buyers

Can we break free of overcommitment to a few large buyers? How would our buyers react to attempts by us to differentiate our products? What possibilities exist that our buyers might vertically integrate backward? Should we consider forward integration? How can we make the value of our components greater in the products of our buyers?

Rivalry among existing firms

Are major competitors likely to undo the established balance of power in our industry? Is growth in our industry slowing such that competition will become fiercer? What excess capacity exists in our industry? How capable are our major competitors of withstanding intensified price competition? How unique are the objectives and strategies of our major competitors?

Key Issues in the Operating Environment

Competitive position

What strategic moves are expected by existing rivals—inside and outside the United States? What competitive advantage is necessary in selected foreign markets? What will be our competitors' priorities and ability to change? Is the behavior of our competitors predictable?

Customer profiles and market changes

What will our customer regard as needed value? Is marketing research done, or do managers talk to each other to discover what the customer wants? Which customer needs are not being met by existing products? Why? Are R&D activities under way to develop means for fulfilling these needs? What is the status of these activities? What marketing and distribution channels should we use? What do demographic and population changes portend for the size and sales potential of our market? What new market segments or products might develop as a result of these changes? What will be the buying power of our customer groups?

Supplier relationships

What is the likelihood of major cost increases because of dwindling supplies of a needed natural resource? Will sources of supply, especially of energy, be reliable? Are there reasons to expect major changes in the cost or availability of inputs as a result of money, people, or subassembly problems? Which suppliers can be expected to respond to emergency requests?

Creditors

What lines of credit are available to help finance our growth? What changes may occur in our creditworthiness? Are creditors likely to feel comfortable with our strategic plan and performance? What is the stock market likely to feel about our firm? What flexibility would our creditors show toward us during a downturn? Do we have sufficient cash reserves to protect our creditors and our credit rating?

Labor market

Are potential employees with desired skills and abilities available in the geographic areas in which our facilities are located? Are colleges and vocational/technical schools that can aid in meeting our training needs located near our plant or store sites? Are labor relations in our industry conducive to meeting our expanding needs for employees? Are workers whose skills we need shifting toward or away from the geographic location of our facilities?

Summary

A firm's external environment consists of three interrelated sets of factors that play a principal role in determining the opportunities, threats, and constraints that the firm faces. The remote environment comprises factors originating beyond, and usually irrespective of, any single firm's operating situation—economic, social, political, technological, and ecological factors. Factors that more directly influence a firm's prospects originate in the environment of its industry, including entry barriers, competitor rivalry, the availability of substitutes, and the bargaining power of buyers and suppliers. The operating environment comprises factors that influence a firm's immediate competitive situation—competitive position, customer profiles, suppliers, creditors, and the labor market. These three sets of factors provide many of the challenges that a particular firm faces in its attempts to attract or acquire needed resources and to profitably market its goods and services. Environmental assessment is more complicated for multinational corporations (MNCs) than for domestic firms because multinationals must evaluate several environments simultaneously.

Thus, the design of business strategies is based on the conviction that a firm able to anticipate future business conditions will improve its performance and profitability. Despite the uncertainty and dynamic nature of the business environment, an assessment process that narrows, even if it does not precisely define, future expectations is of substantial value to strategic managers.

Key Terms

barriers to entry, *p. 93*	external environment, *p. 81*	pollution, *p. 87*
eco-efficiency, *p. 88*	industry, *p. 99*	product differentiation, *p. 94*
ecology, *p. 87*	industry environment, *p. 91*	remote environment, *p. 81*
economies of scale, *p. 93*	operating environment, *p. 103*	technological, forecasting, *p. 86*

Questions for Discussion

1. Briefly describe two important recent changes in the remote environment of U.S. business in each of the following areas:
   a. Economic.
   b. Social.
   c. Political.
   d. Technological.
   e. Ecological.
2. Describe two major environmental changes that you expect to have a major impact on the wholesale food industry in the next 10 years.
3. Develop a competitor profile for your college and for the college geographically closest to yours. Next, prepare a brief strategic plan to improve the competitive position of the weaker of the two colleges.
4. Assume the invention of a competitively priced synthetic fuel that could supply 25 percent of U.S. energy needs within 20 years. In what major ways might this change the external environment of U.S. business?
5. With your instructor's help, identify a local firm that has enjoyed great growth in recent years. To what degree and in what ways do you think this firm's success resulted from taking advantage of favorable conditions in its remote, industry, and operating environments?
6. Choose a specific industry and, relying solely on your impressions, evaluate the impact of the five forces that drive competition in that industry.
7. Choose an industry in which you would like to compete. Use the five-forces method of analysis to explain why you find that industry attractive.
8. Many firms neglect industry analysis. When does this hurt them? When does it not?

9. The model below depicts industry analysis as a funnel that focuses on remote-factor analysis to better understand the impact of factors in the operating environment. Do you find this model satisfactory? If not, how would you improve it?

10. Who in a firm should be responsible for industry analysis? Assume that the firm does not have a strategic planning department.

Chapter 4 Appendix

Sources for Environmental Forecasting

Remote and Industry Environments

A. Economic considerations:
1. *Predicasts* (most complete and up-to-date review of forecasts)
2. National Bureau of Economic Research
3. *Handbook of Basic Economic Statistics*
4. *Statistical Abstract of the United States* (also includes industrial, social, and political statistics)
5. Publications by Department of Commerce agencies:
   a. Office of Business Economics (e.g., *Survey of Business*)
   b. Bureau of Economic Analysis (e.g., *Business Conditions Digest*)
   c. Bureau of the Census (e.g., *Survey of Manufacturers* and various reports on population, housing, and industries)
   d. Business and Defense Services Administration (e.g., *United States Industrial Outlook*)
6. Securities and Exchange Commission (various quarterly reports on plant and equipment, financial reports, working capital of corporations)
7. The Conference Board
8. *Survey of Buying Power*
9. *Marketing Economic Guide*
10. *Industrial Arts Index*
11. U.S. and national chambers of commerce
12. American Manufacturers Association
13. *Federal Reserve Bulletin*
14. *Economic Indicators*, annual report
15. *Kiplinger Newsletter*
16. International economic sources:
   a. *Worldcasts*
   b. Master key index for business international publications
   c. Department of Commerce
      (1) Overseas business reports
      (2) Industry and Trade Administration
      (3) Bureau of the Census—*Guide to Foreign Trade Statistics*
17. *Business Periodicals Index*

B. Social considerations:
1. Public opinion polls
2. Surveys such as *Social Indicators and Social Reporting*, the annals of the American Academy of Political and Social Sciences
3. Current controls: Social and behavioral sciences
4. Abstract services and indexes for articles in sociological, psychological, and political journals

5. Indexes for *The Wall Street Journal, New York Times*, and other newspapers
6. Bureau of the Census reports on population, housing, manufacturers, selected services, construction, retail trade, wholesale trade, and enterprise statistics
7. Various reports from such groups as the Brookings Institution and the Ford Foundation
8. World Bank Atlas (population growth and GNP data)
9. World Bank–World Development Report

C. Political considerations:
1. *Public Affairs Information Services Bulletin*
2. CIS Index (Congressional Information Index)
3. Business periodicals
4. Funk & Scott (regulations by product breakdown)
5. Weekly compilation of presidential documents
6. *Monthly Catalog of Government Publications*
7. *Federal Register* (daily announcements of pending regulations)
8. *Code of Federal Regulations* (final listing of regulations)
9. Business International Master Key Index (regulations, tariffs)
10. Various state publications
11. Various information services (Bureau of National Affairs, Commerce Clearing House, Dow Jones)

D. Technological considerations:
1. *Applied Science and Technology Index*
2. *Statistical Abstract of the United States*
3. Scientific and Technical Information Service
4. University reports, congressional reports
5. Department of Defense and military purchasing publishers
6. Trade journals and industrial reports
7. Industry contacts, professional meetings
8. Computer-assisted information searches
9. National Science Foundation annual report
10. *Research and Development Directory* patent records

E. Industry considerations:
1. *Concentration Ratios in Manufacturing* (Bureau of the Census)
2. *Input-Output Survey* (productivity ratios)
3. *Monthly Labor Review* (productivity ratios)
4. *Quarterly Failure Report* (Dun & Bradstreet)
5. *Federal Reserve Bulletin* (capacity utilization)
6. *Report on Industrial Concentration and Product Diversification in the 1,000 Largest Manufacturing Companies* (Federal Trade Commission)

7. Industry trade publications
8. Bureau of Economic Analysis, Department of Commerce (specialization ratios)

Industry and Operating Environments

A. Competition and supplier considerations:
1. Target Group Index
2. U.S. Industrial Outlook
3. Robert Morris annual statement studies
4. Troy, Leo *Almanac of Business & Industrial Financial Ratios*
5. *Census of Enterprise Statistics*
6. Securities and Exchange Commission (10-K reports)
7. Annual reports of specific companies
8. *Fortune 500 Directory, The Wall Street Journal, Barron's, Forbes, Dun's Review*
9. Investment services and directories: Moody's, Dun & Bradstreet, Standard & Poor's, Starch Marketing, Funk & Scott Index
10. Trade association surveys
11. Industry surveys
12. Market research surveys
13. *Country Business Patterns*
14. *Country and City Data Book*
15. Industry contacts, professional meetings, salespeople
16. *NFIB Quarterly Economic Report for Small Business*

B. Customer profile:
1. *Statistical Abstract of the United States*, first source of statistics
2. *Statistical Sources* by Paul Wasserman (a subject guide to data—both domestic and international)
3. *American Statistics Index* (Congressional Information Service Guide to statistical publications of U.S. government—monthly)
4. Office of the Department of Commerce:
   a. Bureau of the Census reports on population, housing, and industries
   b. *U.S. Census of Manufacturers* (statistics by industry, area, and products)
   c. *Survey of Current Business* (analysis of business trends, especially February and July issues)
5. Market research studies (*A Basic Bibliography on Market Review*, compiled by Robert Ferber et al., American Marketing Association)

6. *Current Sources of Marketing Information: A Bibliography of Primary Marketing Data* by Gunther & Goldstein, AMA
7. *Guide to Consumer Markets*, The Conference Board (provides statistical information with demographic, social, and economic data—annual)
8. *Survey of Buying Power*
9. *Predicasts* (abstracts of publishing forecasts of all industries, detailed products, and end-use data)
10. *Predicasts Basebook* (historical data from 1960 to present, covering subjects ranging from population and GNP to specific products and services; series are coded by Standard Industrial Classifications)
11. *Market Guide* (individual market surveys of over 1,500 U.S. and Canadian cities; includes population, location, trade areas, banks, principal industries, colleges and universities, department and chain stores, newspapers, retail outlets, and sales)
12. *Country and City Data Book* (includes bank deposits, birth and death rates, business firms, education, employment, income of families, manufacturers, population, savings, and wholesale and retail trade)
13. *Yearbook of International Trade Statistics* (UN)
14. *Yearbook of National Accounts Statistics* (UN)
15. *Statistical Yearbook* (UN—covers population, national income, agricultural and industrial production, energy, external trade, and transport)
16. *Statistics of (Continents): Sources for Market Research* (includes separate books on Africa, America, Europe)

C. Key natural resources:
1. *Minerals Yearbook, Geological Survey* (Bureau of Mines, Department of the Interior)
2. *Agricultural Abstract* (Department of Agriculture)
3. Statistics of electric utilities and gas pipeline companies (Federal Power Commission)
4. Publications of various institutions: American Petroleum Institute, Atomic Energy Commission, Coal Mining Institute of America, American Steel Institute, and Brookings Institution

Chapter **Five**

The Global Environment

After reading and studying this chapter, you should be able to

1. Explain the importance of a company's decision to globalize.

2. Describe the four main strategic orientations of global firms.

3. Understand the complexity of the global environment and the control problems that are faced by global firms.

4. Discuss major issues in global strategic planning, including the differences for multinational and global firms.

5. Describe the market requirements and product characteristics in global competition.

6. Evaluate the competitive strategies for firms in foreign markets, including niche market exporting, licensing and contract manufacturing, franchising, joint ventures, foreign branching, private equity, and wholly owned subsidiaries.

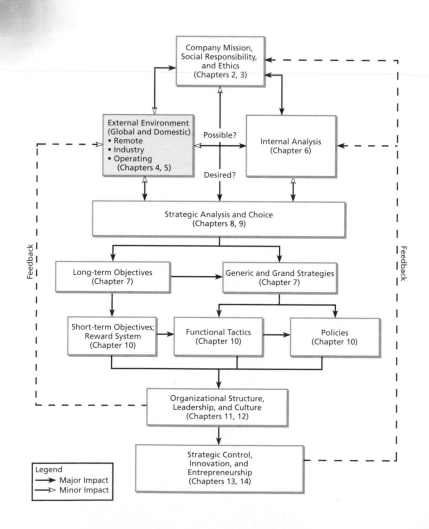

GLOBALIZATION

Globalization

The strategy of pursuing opportunities anywhere in the world that enable a firm to optimize its business functions in the countries in which it operates.

Globalization refers to the strategy of pursuing opportunities anywhere in the world that enable a firm to optimize its business functions in the countries in which it operates. A company with global sales may have its high value-added software design activity done in Ireland, while it may achieve its lowest manufacturing costs by outsourcing those activities to India.

There are two main theories concerning the introduction of a product globally: standardization and customization. Standardization is the use of a common product, service, and message across all markets to create a strong brand image. The constantly improving communication technology in the twentieth century led to an ever-more-homogenous global customer base that allowed for strategic success with a standardized product. Standardization performed well until the late 1990s, when global brand owners saw their share prices drop as consumers reached for local products that were better aligned with their cultural identities. The change in customer purchase behavior was the beginning of an evolution in international strategy.

Since then, standardization is steadily being replaced by customization, which is the development of modified products and services, and the use of somewhat tailor-made messages, to meet the demands of a local population.

Coca-Cola's CEO from 2000 to 2004, Douglas Daft, famously argued that globalization strategies had to adapt to the times, saying that multinational firms needed to "Think global. Act local." His approach, which combines global standardization with some local customization, is now widely accepted within the Coca-Cola Corporation, as well as by other global superstars, including McDonald's and Wal-Mart. The approach allows the company to build a global brand image while creating products to meet the local demands of the target market. For Coca-Cola, this strategy has resulted in a ranking as the number one global brand in carbonated beverages, while producing more than 450 localized brands in more than 200 countries. Refer to Exhibit 5.1, Global Strategy in Action, to read about Coke's recent major globalization efforts.

Awareness of the strategic opportunities faced by global corporations and of the threats posed to them is important to planners in almost every domestic U.S. industry. Among corporations headquartered in the United States that receive more than 50 percent of their annual profits from foreign operations are Citicorp, Coca-Cola, ExxonMobil, Gillette, IBM, Otis Elevator, and Texas Instruments. In fact, the 100 largest U.S. globals earn an average of 37 percent of their operating profits abroad. Equally impressive is the effect of foreign-based globals that operate in the United States. Their "direct foreign investment" in the United States now exceeds $90 billion, with Japanese, German, and French firms leading the way.

Understanding the myriad and sometimes subtle nuances of competing in global markets or against global corporations is rapidly becoming a required competence of strategic managers. For example, experts in the advertising community contend that Korean companies only recently recognized the importance of making their names known abroad. In the 1980s, there was very little advertising of Korean brands, and the country had very few recognizable brands abroad. Korean companies tended to emphasize sales and production more than marketing. The opening of the Korean advertising market in the 1990s indicated that Korean firms had acquired a new appreciation for the strategic competencies that are needed to compete globally and created an influx of global firms like Saatchi and Saatchi, J. W. Thompson, Ogilvy and Mather, and Bozell. Many of them established joint ventures or partnerships with Korean agencies. An excellent example

Coca-Cola-Follows Its Motto: "Think global. Act local."

In 2008, Coca-Cola Co. bought China Huiyuan Juice Group Ltd. for $2.4 billion. The price reflected a value for Huiyuan of 45 times the company's estimated annual earnings. This is a valuable asset for Coca-Cola due to Huiyuan's position as the leading fruit and vegetable juice company in China. Huiyuan Juice produces more than 220 brands of fruit and vegetable juice and enjoys an industry-leading market share of 10.3 percent, with Coca-Cola in second place with 9.7 percent of the market. Coca-Cola's strategy in China is a prime example of "Think global. Act local."

The acquisition of Huiyuan helps with the localization aspect of Coca-Cola's strategy in China. Although Coca-Cola is best known for its carbonated beverage,

the Chinese population prefers the tastes of juice to Coca-Cola's traditional products. The 2008 demand for juice in China was 10 billion liters compared to only 9.6 billion liters of soda. At the time, Euromonitor International estimated that fruit and vegetable juice sales would grow by 16 percent, which was more than double the growth of carbonated drinks. The projected growth was based on the health consciousness of Chinese consumers, who often opt for healthier teas and juices over carbonated beverages.

Source: Stephanie Wong, "Coca-Cola to Buy China's Huiyuan for $2.3 Billion," *Bloomberg.com*, September 3, 2008.

of such a strategic approach to globalization by Philip Morris's KGFI is described in Exhibit 5.2, Global Strategy in Action. The opportunities for corporate growth often seem brightest in global markets. Exhibit 5.3 reports on the growth in national shares of the world's outputs and growth in national economies to the year 2020. While the United States had a commanding lead in the size of its economy in 1992, it was caught by China in the year 2000 and will be far surpassed by 2020. Overall, in less than 20 years, rich industrial countries will be overshadowed by developing countries in their produced share of the world's output.

Because the growth in the number of global firms continues to overshadow other changes in the competitive environment, this section will focus on the nature, outlook, and operations of global corporations.

DEVELOPMENT OF A GLOBAL CORPORATION

The evolution of a global corporation often entails progressively involved strategy levels. The first level, which often entails export-import activity, has minimal effect on the existing management orientation or on existing product lines. The second level, which can involve foreign licensing and technology transfer, requires little change in management or operation. The third level typically is characterized by direct investment in overseas operations, including manufacturing plants. This level requires large capital outlays and the development of global management skills. Although the domestic operations of a firm at this level continue to dominate its policy, such a firm is commonly categorized as a true multinational corporation (MNC). The most involved strategy level is characterized by a substantial increase in foreign investment, with foreign assets comprising a significant portion of total assets. At this level, the firm begins to emerge as a global enterprise with global approaches to production, sales, finance, and control.

To get a more complete understanding of the many elements of a multinational environment that need to be considered by strategic planners, study the Chapter 5 Appendix. It contains lists of important competitive issues that will help you to see the complexity of the multinational landscape and to better appreciate the complicated and sophisticated nature of strategic planning.

The Globalization of Philip Morris's KGFI

Outside of its core Western markets, Kraft General Foods International's (KGFI) food products have a growing presence in one of the most dynamic business environments in the world—the Asia-Pacific region. Its operations there are expanding rapidly, often aided by links with local manufacturers and distributors.

Japan and Korea are important examples. In both countries, local alliances can be crucial to market entry and success. Realizing this fact in the early 1970s, General Foods established joint ventures in both Japan and Korea. These joint ventures, combined with Kraft General Foods International's (KGFI) stand-alone operations, generate more than $1 billion in revenues. In the aggregate, their combined food operations in Japan and Korea are larger than many *Fortune* 500 companies.

Whereas soluble coffee accounts for just over 25 percent of the coffee consumed in U.S. homes, it fills more than 70 percent of the cups consumed in the homes of convenience-minded Japan. Additionally, Japan is the origin of a unique form of packaged coffee—liquid—and a unique channel of distribution—vending machines. Japanese consumers have purchased packaged liquid coffee for years, and it amounts to a $5 billion category. Some 2 million vending machines dispense 9 billion cans of liquid coffee annually—an average of 75 cans per person.

Japan offers a culturally unique distribution channel for coffee products—the gift-set market. Many Japanese exchange specially packaged food or beverage assortments at least twice a year to commemorate holidays as well as special personal or business occasions. The gift-set business has helped Maxim products reinforce their quality image; it also will be a launching pad and support vehicle for Carte Noire coffees.

Outside the Ajinomoto General Foods joint venture, KGFI is developing a freestanding food business under the name Kraft Japan. It is building a cheese business with imported Philadelphia Brand cream cheese, the leading cream cheese in the Tokyo metropolitan market, as well as locally manufactured and licensed Kraft Milk Farm cheese slices. The cheese market is expected to grow approximately 5 percent per year. This is a rapid growth rate for a large food category. In addition to cheese, KGFI also imports Oscar Mayer prepared meats and Jacobs Suchard chocolates.

KGFI's joint venture in Korea, Doug Suh Foods Corporation, is one of the top 10 food companies in the country. Doug Suh manufactures coffees and cereals and has its own distribution network. One of Doug Suh's other businesses in Korea, Post Cereals, is also a strong number two, with a 42 percent category share.

Korea's $400 million coffee market is the fastest-growing major coffee market in the world, expanding at an average annual rate of 14 percent. Growing with the market, Maxim and Maxwell soluble coffees, in both traditional "agglomerate" and freeze-dried forms, account for more than 70 percent of the country's soluble coffee sales. The strength of these brands also brings the company a strong number one position in coffee mix, a mixture of soluble coffee, creamer, and sugar. In addition, its Frima brand leads the market in the nondairy creamer segment.

Beyond Japan and Korea, KGFI is targeting many other countries for geographic expansion. In Indonesia, for instance, KGFI has established a rapidly growing cheese business through a licensee and introduced other KGFI products. In Taiwan, the joint venture company, PremierFoods Corporation, holds a 34 percent share of the soluble coffee market and is aggressively developing a Kraft cheese and Jacobs Suchard import business. KGFI Philippines, a wholly owned subsidiary, has a leading position in the cheese and powdered soft-drink markets in its country. In the People's Republic of China, the company produces and markets Maxwell House coffees and Tang powdered soft drinks through two successful and rapidly growing joint ventures.

Some firms downplay their global nature (to never appear distracted from their domestic operations), whereas others highlight it. For example, General Electric's formal statement of mission and business philosophy includes the following commitment:

> To carry out a diversified, growing, and profitable worldwide manufacturing business in electrical apparatus, appliances, and supplies, and in related materials, products, systems, and services for industry, commerce, agriculture, government, the community, and the home.

A similar global orientation is evident at IBM, which operates in 125 countries, conducts business in 30 languages and more than 100 currencies, and has 23 major manufacturing facilities in 14 countries.

EXHIBIT 5.3 Projected Economic Growth

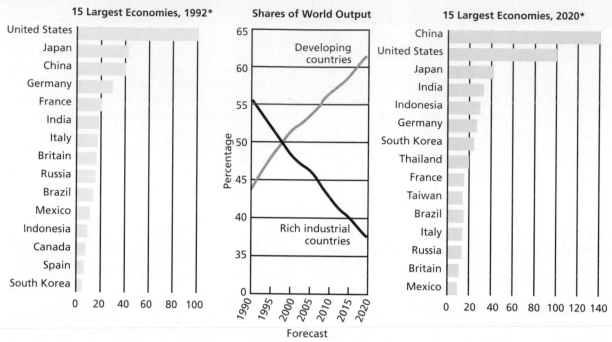

Forecast

Source: World Bank, *Global Economic Prospects and the Developing Countries.*

WHY FIRMS GLOBALIZE

The technological advantage once enjoyed by the United States has declined dramatically during the past 30 years. In the late 1950s, more than 80 percent of the world's major technological innovations were first introduced in the United States. By 1990, the figure had declined to less than 50 percent. In contrast, France is making impressive advances in electric traction, nuclear power, and aviation. Germany leads in chemicals and pharmaceuticals, precision and heavy machinery, heavy electrical goods, metallurgy, and surface transport equipment. Japan leads in optics, solid-state physics, engineering, chemistry, and process metallurgy. Eastern Europe and the former Soviet Union, the so-called COMECON (Council for Mutual Economic Assistance) countries, generate 30 percent of annual worldwide patent applications. However, the United States has regained some of its lost technological advantage. Through globalization, U.S. firms often can reap benefits from industries and technologies developed abroad. Even a relatively small service firm that possesses a distinct competitive advantage can capitalize on large overseas operations.

Diebold Inc. once operated solely in the United States, selling automated teller machines (ATMs), bank vaults, and security systems to financial institutions. However, with the U.S. market saturated, Diebold needed to expand internationally to continue its growth. The firm's globalization efforts led to both the development of new technologies in emerging markets and opportunistic entry into entirely new industries that significantly improved Diebold's sales.

In many situations, global development makes sense as a competitive weapon. Direct penetration of foreign markets can drain vital cash flows from a foreign competitor's domestic operations. The resulting lost opportunities, reduced income, and limited production can impair the competitor's ability to invade U.S. markets. A case in point is IBM's move to establish a position of strength in the Japanese mainframe computer industry before two key competitors, Fugitsu and Hitachi, could dominate it. Once IBM had achieved a substantial share of the Japanese market, it worked to deny its Japanese competitors the vital cash and production experience they needed to invade the U.S. market.

Firms that operate principally in the domestic environment have an important decision to make with regard to their globalization: Should they act before being forced to do so by competitive pressures or after? Should they (1) be proactive by entering global markets in advance of other firms and thereby enjoy the first-mover advantages often accruing to risk-taker firms that introduce new products or services or (2) be reactive by taking the more conservative approach and following other companies into global markets once customer demand has been proven and the high costs of new-product or new-service introductions have been absorbed by competitors?

Strategic Orientations of Global Firms

ethnocentric orientation
When the values and priorities of the parent organization guide the strategic decision making of all its international operations.

polycentric orientation
When the culture of the country in which the strategy is to be implemented is allowed to dominate a company's international decision-making process.

regiocentric orientation
When a parent company blends its own predisposition with those of its international units to develop region-sensitive strategies

geocentric orientation
When an international firm adopts a systems approach to strategic decision making that emphasizes global integration.

Multinational corporations typically display one of four orientations toward their overseas activities. They have a certain set of beliefs about how the management of foreign operations should be handled. A company with an **ethnocentric orientation** believes that the values and priorities of the parent organization should guide the strategic decision making of all its operations. If a corporation has a **polycentric orientation,** then the culture of the country in which a strategy is to be implemented is allowed to dominate the decision-making process. In contrast, a **regiocentric orientation** exists when the parent attempts to blend its own predispositions with those of the region under consideration, thereby arriving at a region-sensitive compromise. Finally, a corporation with a **geocentric orientation** adopts a global systems approach to strategic decision making, thereby emphasizing global integration.

American firms often adopt a regiocentric orientation for pursing strategies in Europe. U.S. e-tailers have attempted to blend their own corporate structure and expertise with that of European corporations. For example, Amazon has been able to leverage its experience in the United States while developing regionally and culturally specific strategies overseas. By purchasing European franchises that have had regional success, E*Trade is pursuing a foreign strategy in which they insert their European units into their corporate structure. This strategy requires the combination and use of culturally different management styles and involves major challenges for upper management.

Exhibit 5.4 shows the effects of each of the four orientations on key activities of the firm. It is clear from the figure that the strategic orientation of a global firm plays a major role in determining the locus of control and corporate priorities of the firm's decision makers.

AT THE START OF GLOBALIZATION

External and internal assessments are conducted before a firm enters global markets. For example, Japanese investors conduct extensive assessments and analyses before selecting a U.S. site for a Japanese-owned firm. They prefer states with strong markets, low unionization rates, and low taxes. In addition, Japanese manufacturing plants prefer counties characterized by manufacturing conglomeration; low unemployment and poverty rates; and concentrations of educated, productive workers.

External assessment involves careful examination of critical features of the global environment, particular attention being paid to the status of the host nations in such areas as economic progress, political control, and nationalism. Expansion of industrial facilities,

EXHIBIT 5.4 **Orientation of a Global Firm**

	Orientation of the Firm			
	Ethnocentric	**Polycentric**	**Regiocentric**	**Geocentric**
Mission	Profitability (viability)	Public acceptance (legitimacy)	Profitability and public acceptance (viability and legitimacy)	Same as regiocentric
Governance	Top-down	Bottom-up (each subsidiary decides on local objectives)	Mutually negotiated between region and its subsidiaries	Mutually negotiated at all levels of the corporation
Strategy	Global integration	National responsiveness	Regional integration and national responsiveness	Global integration and national responsiveness
Structure	Hierarchical product divisions	Hierarchical area divisions, with autonomous national units	Product and regional organization tied through a matrix	A network of organizations (including some competitors)
Culture Technology Marketing	Home country Mass production Product development determined by the needs of home country	Host country Batch production Local product development based on local needs	Regional Flexible manufacturing Standardize within region but not across regions	Global Flexible manufacturing Global product, with local variations
Finance	Repatriation of profits to home country	Retention of profits in host country	Redistribution within region	Redistribution globally
Personnel practices	People of home country developed for key positions in the world	People of local nationality developed for key positions in their own country	Regional people developed for key positions anywhere in the region	Global personnel development and placement

Source: From *Columbia Journal of World Business,* Summer 1985, by B.S. Chukravarthy and Howard V. Perlmuter, "Strategic Planning for a global Business," p. 506. Copyright © Elsevier 1985.

favorable balances of payments, and improvements in technological capabilities over the past decade are gauges of the host nation's economic progress. Political status can be gauged by the host nation's power in and impact on global affairs.

Understanding the political risk involved is a key element in the decision to do business in a foreign nation. Opportunities for fast growth and attractive profits often arise in countries with suspect political risk. The principal concern of foreign direct investors is whether the foreign government is able to implement its policies during a period of political, social, or economic upheaval. If it can, the country is judged to be stable. Stability provides investors with confidence that the country's regulatory environment will enable it to achieve the economic returns that it deserves.

A second issue that concerns investors is how the stability in a foreign nation is achieved. Strategists often place a country's openness along a simple continuum from closed to open. Closed countries maintain their stability by restricting the flow of money, goods, services, people, and information across their borders. Countries that tend toward this extreme include Cuba, Iran, and North Korea because their isolationist policies prevent their citizens from fully comprehending the conditions and options that are available in other countries.

The J-Curve on Country Stability and Openness

The J-curve represents the relationship between stability and openness as shown in the accompanying figure. Each country moves along its own J-curve and the curve itself shifts up and down with fluctuations in the economy. Nations higher on the graph are more stable; those lower are less stable. Nations to the right of the dip in the J are more open; those to the left less open. As a country that is stable because it is closed becomes more open, it slides down the left side of the curve toward the dip in the J, the point of greatest instability. So, for example, if Pakistan, Myanmar, or Cuba held elections next week, political turmoil would likely erupt. If North Koreans had access to South Korea media for a week, Kim Jong Il would have plenty to fear.

The irony is that the energies of globalization and growth in demand for key commodities are driving more businesses to contemplate ventures in politically closed countries, particularly China. But those same energies may destabilize the ground beneath unwary businesses' feet.

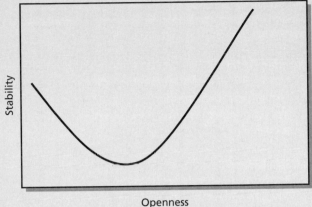

Openness

Source: From "Prepare to Lose It all? Read on . . . How to Calculate Political Risk," by Ian Bremmer, *Inc. Magazine*. Copyright © by Mansueto Ventures LLC. Reproduced with permission of Mansueto Ventures LLC via Copyright Clearance Center.

At the other extreme, many nations achieve their stability by allowing and encouraging exchanges among their and business and public institutions, and their citizens and those of other nations. Examples include the countries in Australia, Brazil, the European zone, Japan, and the United States.

Exhibit 5.5, Strategy in Action, describes the J-curve, a useful approach for evaluating the relationship between stability and openness and an important element in political risk assessment.

Internal assessment involves identification of the basic strengths of a firm's operations. These strengths are particularly important in global operations, because they are often the characteristics of a firm that the host nation values most and, thus, offer significant bargaining leverage. The firm's resource strengths and global capabilities must be analyzed. The resources that should be analyzed include, in particular, technical and managerial skills, capital, labor, and raw materials. The global capabilities that should be analyzed include the firm's product delivery and financial management systems.

A firm that gives serious consideration to internal and external assessment is Business International Corporation, which recommends that seven broad categories of factors be considered. As shown in Exhibit 5.6, Global Strategy in Action, these categories include economic, political, geographic, labor, tax, capital source, and business factors.

COMPLEXITY OF THE GLOBAL ENVIRONMENT

By 2003, Coke was finally achieving a goal that it had set a decade earlier when it went to India. That goal was to take the market away from Pepsi and local beverage companies. However, when it arrived, Coke found that the Indian market was extremely complex and smaller than it had estimated. Coke also encountered cultural problems,

Checklist of Factors to Consider in Choosing a Foreign Manufacturing Site

The following considerations were drawn from an 88-point checklist developed by Business International Corporation.

Economic Factors:
1. Size of GNP and projected rate of growth
2. Foreign exchange position
3. Size of market for the firm's products; rate of growth

Political Factors:
4. Form and stability of government
5. Attitude toward private and foreign investment by government, customers, and competition
6. Degree of antiforeign discrimination

Geographic Factors:
7. Proximity of site to export markets
8. Availability of local raw materials
9. Availability of power, water, gas

Labor Factors:
10. Availability of managerial, technical, and office personnel able to speak the language of the parent company
11. Degree of skill and discipline at all levels
12. Degree and nature of labor voice in management

Tax Factors:
13. Tax-rate trends
14. Joint tax treaties with home country and others
15. Availability of tariff protection

Capital Source Factors:
16. Cost of local borrowing
17. Modern banking systems
18. Government credit aids to new businesses

Business Factors:
19. State of marketing and distribution system
20. Normal profit margins in the firm's industry
21. Competitive situation in the firm's industry: do cartels exist?

in part because the chief of Coke India was an expatriate. The key to overcoming this cultural problem was promoting an Indian to operations chief. Coke also changed its marketing strategy by pushing their "Thums Up" products, a local brand owned by Coke. Then, they began to focus their efforts on creating new products for rural areas and lowering the prices of their existing products to increase sales. Once Coke had new products in the market, they focused on a new advertising campaign to better relate to Indian consumers.

Coke's experience highlights the fact that global strategic planning is more complex than purely domestic planning. There are at least five factors that contribute to this increase in complexity:

1. Globals face multiple political, economic, legal, social, and cultural environments as well as various rates of changes within each of them. Occasionally, foreign governments work in concert with their militaries to advance economic aims even at the expense of human rights. International firms must resist the temptation to benefit financially from such immoral opportunities.

2. Interactions between the national and foreign environments are complex, because of national sovereignty issues and widely differing economic and social conditions.

3. Geographic separation, cultural and national differences, and variations in business practices all tend to make communication and control efforts between headquarters and the overseas affiliates difficult.

4. Globals face extreme competition, because of differences in industry structures within countries.

5. Globals are restricted in their selection of competitive strategies by various regional blocs and economic integrations, such as the European Economic Community, the European Free Trade Area, and the Latin American Free Trade Area.

CONTROL PROBLEMS OF THE GLOBAL FIRM

An inherent complicating factor for many global firms is that their financial policies typically are designed to further the goals of the parent company and pay minimal attention to the goals of the host countries. This built-in bias creates conflict between the different parts of the global firm, between the whole firm and its home and host countries, and between the home country and host country themselves. The conflict is accentuated by the use of various schemes to shift earnings from one country to another in order to avoid taxes, minimize risk, or achieve other objectives.

Moreover, different financial environments make normal standards of company behavior concerning the disposition of earnings, sources of finance, and the structure of capital more problematic. Thus, it becomes increasingly difficult to measure the performance of international divisions.

In addition, important differences in measurement and control systems often exist. Fundamental to the concept of planning is a well-conceived, future-oriented approach to decision making that is based on accepted procedures and methods of analysis. Consistent approaches to planning throughout a firm are needed for effective review and evaluation by corporate headquarters. In the global firm, planning is complicated by differences in national attitudes toward work measurement, and by differences in government requirements about disclosure of information.

Although such problems are an aspect of the global environment, rather than a consequence of poor management, they are often most effectively reduced through increased attention to strategic planning. Such planning will aid in coordinating and integrating the firm's direction, objectives, and policies around the world. It enables the firm to anticipate and prepare for change. It facilitates the creation of programs to deal with worldwide development. Finally, it helps the management of overseas affiliates become more actively involved in setting goals and in developing means to more effectively utilize the firm's total resources.

An example of the need for coordination in global ventures and evidence that firms can successfully plan for global collaboration (e.g., through rationalized production) is the Ford Escort (Europe), the best-selling automobile in the world, which has a component manufacturing network that consists of plants in 15 countries.

GLOBAL STRATEGIC PLANNING

It should be evident from the previous sections that the strategic decisions of a firm competing in the global marketplace become increasingly complex. In such a firm, managers cannot view global operations as a set of independent decisions. These managers are faced with trade-off decisions in which multiple products, country environments, resource sourcing options, corporate and subsidiary capabilities, and strategic options must be considered.

stakeholder activism
Demands placed on a global firm by the stakeholders in the environments in which it operates.

A recent trend toward increased activism of stakeholders has added to the complexity of strategic planning for the global firm. **Stakeholder activism** refers to demands placed on the global firm by the foreign environments in which it operates, principally by foreign governments. This section provides a basic framework for the analysis of strategic decisions in this complex setting.

Multidomestic Industries and Global Industries

Multidomestic Industries

International industries can be ranked along a continuum that ranges from multidomestic to global.

multidomestic industry
An industry in which competition is segmented from country to country.

A **multidomestic industry** is one in which competition is essentially segmented from country to country. Thus, even if global corporations are in the industry, competition in one country is independent of competition in other countries. Examples of such industries include retailing, insurance, and consumer finance.

In a multidomestic industry, a global corporation's subsidiaries should be managed as distinct entities; that is, each subsidiary should be rather autonomous, having the authority to make independent decisions in response to local market conditions. Thus, the global strategy of such an industry is the sum of the strategies developed by subsidiaries operating in different countries. The primary difference between a domestic firm and a global firm competing in a multidomestic industry is that the latter makes decisions related to the countries in which it competes and to how it conducts business abroad.

Factors that increase the degree to which an industry is multidomestic include[1]

- The need for customized products to meet the tastes or preferences of local customers.
- Fragmentation of the industry, with many competitors in each national market.
- A lack of economies of scale in the functional activities of firms in the industry.
- Distribution channels unique to each country.
- A low technological dependence of subsidiaries on R&D provided by the global firm.

An interesting example of a multidomestic strategy is the one designed by Renault-Nissan for the low-cost automobile industry. Renault's strategy involves designing cars to fit the budgets of buyers in different countries, rather than being restricted to the production of cars that meet the safety and emission standards of countries in western Europe and the United States or by their consumer preferences for technological advancements and stylish appointments.

Global Industries

global industry
An industry in which competition crosses national borders on a worldwide basis.

A **global industry** is one in which competition crosses national borders. In fact, it occurs on a worldwide basis. In a global industry, a firm's strategic moves in one country can be significantly affected by its competitive position in another country. The very rapidly expanding list of global industries includes commercial aircraft, automobiles, mainframe computers, and electronic consumer equipment. Many authorities are convinced that almost all product-oriented industries soon will be global. As a result, strategic management planning must be global for at least six reasons:

1. *The increased scope of the global management task.* Growth in the size and complexity of global firms made management virtually impossible without a coordinated plan of action detailing what is expected of whom during a given period. The common practice of management by exception is impossible without such a plan.

2. *The increased globalization of firms.* Three aspects of global business make global planning necessary: *(a)* differences among the environmental forces in different countries, *(b)* greater distances, and *(c)* the interrelationships of global operations.

3. *The information explosion.* It has been estimated that the world's stock of knowledge is doubling every 10 years. Without the aid of a formal plan, executives can no longer know all that they must know to solve the complex problems they face. A global planning

---

[1]Y. Doz and C. K. Prahalad, "Patterns of Strategic Control within Multinational Corporations," *Journal of International Business Studies,* Fall 1984, pp. 55–72.

process provides an ordered means for assembling, analyzing, and distilling the information required for sound decisions.

4. *The increase in global competition.* Because of the rapid increase in global competition, firms must constantly adjust to changing conditions or lose markets to competitors. The increase in global competition also spurs managements to search for methods of increasing efficiency and economy.

5. *The rapid development of technology.* Rapid technological development has shortened product life cycles. Strategic management planning is necessary to ensure the replacement of products that are moving into the maturity stage, with fewer sales and declining profits. Planning gives management greater control of all aspects of new-product introduction.

6. *Strategic management planning breeds managerial confidence.* Like the motorist with a road map, managers with a plan for reaching their objectives know where they are going. Such a plan breeds confidence, because it spells out every step along the way and assigns responsibility for every task. The plan simplifies the managerial job.

A firm in a global industry must maximize its capabilities through a worldwide strategy. Such a strategy necessitates a high degree of centralized decision making in corporate headquarters so as to permit trade-off decisions across subsidiaries.

Among the factors that make for the creation of a global industry are

- Economies of scale in the functional activities of firms in the industry.
- A high level of R&D expenditures on products that require more than one market to recover development costs.
- The presence in the industry of predominantly global firms that expect consistency of products and services across markets.
- The presence of homogeneous product needs across markets, which reduces the requirement of customizing the product for each market. The presence of a small group of global competitors.
- A low level of trade regulation and of regulation regarding foreign direct investment.[2]

Six factors that drive the success of global companies are listed in Exhibit 5.7, Strategy in Action. They address key aspects of globalizing a business's operations and provide a framework within which companies can effectively pursue the global marketplace.

The Global Challenge

Although industries can be characterized as global or multidomestic, few "pure" cases of either type exist. A global firm competing in a global industry must be responsive, to some degree, to local market conditions. Similarly, a global firm competing in a multidomestic industry cannot totally ignore opportunities to utilize intracorporate resources in competitive positioning. Thus, each global firm must decide which of its corporate functional activities should be performed where and what degree of coordination should exist among them.

Location and Coordination of Functional Activities

Typical functional activities of a firm include purchases of input resources, operations, research and development, marketing and sales, and after-sales service. A multinational corporation has a wide range of possible location options for each of these activities and must decide which sets of activities will be performed in how many and which locations. A multinational corporation may have each location perform each activity, or it may center

[2]G. Hamel and C. K. Prahalad, "Managing Strategic Responsibility in the MNC," *Strategic Management Journal,* October–December 1983, pp. 341–51.

Factors That Drive Global Companies

1. Global Management Team

Possesses global vision and culture.

Includes foreign nationals.

Leaves management of subsidiaries to foreign nationals.

Frequently travels internationally.

Has cross-cultural training.

2. Global Strategy

Implement strategy as opposed to independent country strategies.

Develop significant cross-country alliances.

Select country targets strategically rather than opportunistically.

Perform business functions where most efficient— no home-country bias.

Emphasize participation in the triad—North America, Europe, and Japan.

3. Global Operations and Products

Use common core operating processes worldwide to ensure quantity and uniformity.

Produce globally to obtain best cost and market advantage.

4. Global Technology and R&D

Design global products but take regional differences into account.

Manage development work centrally but carry out globally.

Do not duplicate R&D and product development; gain economies of scale.

5. Global Financing

Finance globally to obtain lowest cost.

Hedge when necessary to protect currency risk.

Price in local currencies.

List shares on foreign exchanges.

6. Global Marketing

Market global products but provide regional discretion if economies of scale are not affected.

Develop global brands.

Use core global marketing practices and themes.

Simultaneously introduce new global products worldwide.

Source: Reprinted from *Business Horizons,* Volume 37, Robert N. Lussier, Robert W. Baeder and Joel Corman, "Measuring Global Practices: Global Strategic Planning Through Company Situational Analysis," p. 57. Copyright 1994, with permission from Elsevier.

an activity in one location to serve the organization worldwide. For example, research and development centered in one facility may serve the entire organization.

A multinational corporation also must determine the degree to which functional activities are to be coordinated across locations. Such coordination can be extremely low, allowing each location to perform each activity autonomously, or extremely high, tightly linking the functional activities of different locations. Coca-Cola tightly links its R&D and marketing functions worldwide to offer a standardized brand name, concentrate formula, market positioning, and advertising theme. However, its operations function is more autonomous, with the artificial sweetener and packaging differing across locations.

Location and Coordination Issues

How a particular firm should address location and coordination issues depends on the nature of its industry and on the type of international strategy that the firm is pursuing. As discussed earlier, an industry can be ranked along a continuum that ranges between multidomestic at one extreme and global at the other. Little coordination of functional activities across countries may be necessary in a multidomestic industry, since competition occurs within each country in such an industry. However, as its industry becomes increasingly global, a firm must begin to coordinate an increasing number of functional activities to effectively compete across countries.

Going global impacts every aspect of a company's operations and structure. As firms redefine themselves as global competitors, workforces are becoming increasingly diversified.

Market Requirements and Product Characteristics

Rate of Change of Product

Fast

Maintain differentiation
Computer chips
Automotive electronics
Color film
Pharmaceutical
Chemicals
Telecommunications
Network equipment

Operate an ever-changing "global warehouse"

Consumer   Watch cases
electronics   Dolls
Automobiles
Trucks

Toothpaste   Industrial
Shampoo   machinery

Standardized in All Markets

Customized Market-by-Market

Minimalize delivered cost
Steel
Petrochemicals (e.g., polyethylene)
Cola beverages
Fabric for men's shirts

Practice opportunistic niche exploration
Toilets
Chocolate bars

Slow

Source: Lawrence H. Wortzel, *1989 International Business Book* (Strategic Direction Publishers, 1989).

The most significant challenge for firms, therefore, is the ability to adjust to a workforce of varied cultures and lifestyles and the capacity to incorporate cultural differences to the benefit of the company's mission.

Market Requirements and Product Characteristics

Businesses have discovered that being successful in foreign markets often demands much more than simply shipping their well-received domestic products overseas. Firms must assess two key dimensions of customer demand: customers' acceptance of standardized products and the rate of product innovation desired. As shown in Exhibit 5.8, Global Strategy in Action, all markets can be arrayed along a continuum from markets in which products are standardized to markets in which products must be customized for customers from market to market. Standardized products in all markets include color film and petrochemicals, while dolls and toilets are good examples of customized products.

Similarly, products can be arrayed along a continuum from products that are not subject to frequent product innovations to products that are often upgraded. Products with a fast rate of change include computer chips and industrial machinery, while steel and chocolate bars are products that fit in the slow rate of change category.

Exhibit 5.8 shows that the two dimensions can be combined to enable companies to simultaneously assess both customer need for product standardization and rate of product innovation. The examples listed demonstrate the usefulness of the model in helping firms to determine the degree of customization that they must be willing to accept to become engaged in transnational operations. Starbucks has taken advantage of an industry with a slow rate of change in the product and relatively high standardization in all markets, namely, the retail coffee industry. Exhibit 5.9, Strategy in Action, provides some interesting details on how Starbucks' global success is achieved.

Starbucks' Global Expansion

Starbucks began its international expansion with two stores in Japan in the mid-1980s. By 2000, the company's non-U.S. operations reached 792 stores in 16 countries. Starbucks' global strategy included three key elements:

- Increase market penetration and focus on profitability in existing markets.
- Target long-term store potential of 15,000 locations beyond the United States.
- Focus on emerging markets—especially China, Brazil, and Russia—as a catalyst for long-term revenue and profit growth.

Starbucks was extremely successful with the global strategy. By 2007, Starbucks' 15,012 stores in 44 countries generated net revenues of $9.4 billion for the fiscal year, which was an increase of 21 percent over 2006. Its U.S. revenue grew by 19.4 percent and operating income grew by 12.1 percent. Even more impressive, Starbucks' international segment's revenue growth was 32.1 percent and its operating income grew 27.0 percent, principally because of aggressive expansion into new markets and a refocus on profitability in the large core markets of Canada and the United Kingdom.

In 2008, Starbucks undertook an even more aggressive global strategy. The plan is to accelerate expansion and increase the profitability of Starbucks outside the United States by redeploying a portion of the capital originally earmarked for U.S. store growth to the international business.

Sources: "Starbucks Outlines International Growth Strategy; Focus on Retail Expansion and Profitability," *Business Wire*, October 2004, p. 1; and "Starbucks Announces Strategic Initiatives to Increase Shareholder Value; Chairman Howard Schultz returns as CEO," Starbucks, news release, January 2008, p. 1.

COMPETITIVE STRATEGIES FOR FIRMS IN FOREIGN MARKETS

Strategies for firms that are attempting to move toward globalization can be categorized by the degree of complexity of each foreign market being considered and by the diversity in a company's product line (see Exhibit 5.10, Global Strategy in Action). *Complexity* refers to the number of critical success factors that are required to prosper in a given competitive arena. When a firm must consider many such factors, the requirements of success increase in complexity. *Diversity,* the second variable, refers to the breadth of a firm's business lines. When a company offers many product lines, diversity is high.

Together, the complexity and diversity dimensions form a continuum of possible strategic choices. Combining these two dimensions highlights many possible actions.

Niche Market Exporting

The primary niche market approach for the company that wants to export is to modify select product performance or measurement characteristics to meet special foreign demands. Combining product criteria from both the U.S. and the foreign markets can be slow and tedious. There are, however, a number of expansion techniques that provide the U.S. firm with the know-how to exploit opportunities in the new environment. For example, copying product innovations in countries where patent protection is not emphasized and utilizing nonequity contractual arrangements with a foreign partner can assist in rapid product innovation. N. V. Philips and various Japanese competitors, such as Sony and Matsushita, now are working together for common global product standards within their markets. Siemens, with a centralized R&D in electronics, also has been very successful with this approach.

The Taiwanese company, Gigabyte, researched the U.S. market and found that a sizable number of computer buyers wanted a PC that could complete the basic tasks provided by

Escalating Commitments to International Markets

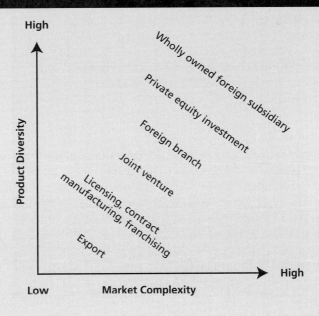

domestic desktops, but that would be considerably smaller. Gigabyte decided to serve this niche market by exporting their mini-PCs into the United States with a price tag of $200 to $300. This price was considerably less than the closest U.S. manufacturer, Dell, whose minicomputer was still larger and cost $766.

Exporting usually requires minimal capital investment. The organization maintains its quality control standards over production processes and finished goods inventory, and risk to the survival of the firm is typically minimal. Additionally, the U.S. Commerce Department through its Export Now Program and related government agencies lowers the risks to smaller companies by providing export information and marketing advice.

Licensing and Contract Manufacturing

Establishing a contractual arrangement is the next step for U.S. companies that want to venture beyond exporting but are not ready for an equity position on foreign soil. Licensing involves the transfer of some industrial property right from the U.S. licensor to a motivated licensee. Most tend to be patents, trademarks, or technical know-how that are granted to the licensee for a specified time in return for a royalty and for avoiding tariffs or import quotas. Bell South and U.S. West, with various marketing and service competitive advantages valuable to Europe, have extended a number of licenses to create personal computer networks in the United Kingdom.

Another licensing strategy open to U.S. firms is to contract the manufacturing of its product line to a foreign company to exploit local comparative advantages in technology, materials, or labor.

U.S. firms that use either licensing option will benefit from lowering the risk of entry into the foreign markets. Clearly, alliances of this type are not for everyone. They are used best in companies large enough to have a combination of international strategic activities and for firms with standardized products in narrow margin industries.

Two major problems exist with licensing. One is the possibility that the foreign partner will gain the experience and evolve into a major competitor after the contract expires. The experience of some U.S. electronics firms with Japanese companies shows that licensees gain the potential to become powerful rivals. The other potential problem stems from the control that the licensor forfeits on production, marketing, and general distribution of its products. This loss of control minimizes a company's degrees of freedom as it reevaluates its future options.

Franchising

A special form of licensing is franchising, which allows the franchisee to sell a highly publicized product or service, using the parent's brand name or trademark, carefully developed procedures, and marketing strategies. In exchange, the franchisee pays a fee to the parent company, typically based on the volume of sales of the franchisor in its defined market area. The franchise is operated by the local investor who must adhere to the strict policies of the parent.

Franchising is so popular that an estimated 500 U.S. businesses now franchise to more than 50,000 local owners in foreign countries. Among the most active franchisees are Avis, Burger King, Canada Dry, Coca-Cola, Hilton, Kentucky Fried Chicken, Manpower, Marriott, Midas, Muzak, Pepsi, and ServiceMaster. However, the acknowledged global champion of franchising is McDonald's, which has 70 percent of its company-owned stores as franchisees in foreign nations.

Joint Ventures

As the multinational strategies of U.S. firms mature, most will include some form of joint venture (JV) with a target nation firm. AT&T followed this option in its strategy to produce its own personal computer by entering into several joint ventures with European producers to acquire the required technology and position itself for European expansion. Because JVs begin with a mutually agreeable pooling of capital, production or marketing equipment, patents, trademarks, or management expertise, they offer more permanent cooperative relationships than export or contract manufacturing.

Compared with full ownership of the foreign entity, JVs provide a variety of benefits to each partner. U.S. firms without the managerial or financial assets to make a profitable independent impact on the integrated foreign markets can share management tasks and cash requirements often at exchange rates that favor the dollar. The coordination of manufacturing and marketing allows ready access to new markets, intelligence data, and reciprocal flows of technical information.

For example, Siemens, the German electronics firm, has a wide range of strategic alliances throughout Europe to share technology and research developments. For years, Siemens grew by acquisitions, but now, to support its horizontal expansion objectives, it is engaged in joint ventures with companies like Groupe Bull of France, International Computers of Britain, General Electric Company of Britain, IBM, Intel, Philips, and Rolm. Another example is Airbus Industries, which produces wide-body passenger planes for the world market as a direct result of JVs among many companies in Britain, France, Spain, and Germany.

JVs speed up the efforts of U.S. firms to integrate into the political, corporate, and cultural infrastructure of the foreign environment, often with a lower financial commitment than acquiring a foreign subsidiary. General Electric's (GE) 3 percent share in the European lighting market was very weak and below expectations. Significant increases in competition throughout many of their American markets by the European giant, Philips Lighting, forced GE to retaliate by expanding in Europe. GE's first strategy was an attempted joint venture with the Siemens lighting subsidiary, Osram, and with the British electronics firm, Thorn EMI. Negotiations failed over control issues. When recent events in eastern Europe opened the opportunity for a JV with the Hungarian lighting manufacturer, Tungsram, which was receiving 70 percent of revenues from the West, GE capitalized on it.

Although joint ventures can address many of the requirements of complex markets and diverse product lines, U.S. firms considering either equity- or non-equity-based JVs face many challenges. For example, making full use of the native firm's comparative advantage may involve managerial relationships where no single authority exists to make strategic decisions or solve conflicts. Additionally, dealing with host-company management requires the disclosure of proprietary information and the potential loss of control over production and marketing quality standards. Addressing such challenges with well-defined covenants agreeable to all parties is difficult. Equally important is the compatibility of partners and their enduring commitments to mutually supportive goals. Without this compatibility and commitment, a joint venture is critically endangered.

Foreign Branching

A foreign branch is an extension of the company in its foreign market—a separately located strategic business unit directly responsible for fulfilling the operational duties assigned to it by corporate management, including sales, customer service, and physical distribution. Host countries may require that the branch be "domesticated," that is, have some local managers in middle and upper-level positions. The branch most likely will be outside any U.S. legal jurisdiction, liabilities may not be restricted to the assets of the given branch, and business licenses for operations may be of short duration, requiring the company to renew them during changing business regulations. Gruma, Mexico's leading flour producer and the world's leading tortillas manufacturer, has manufacturing branches in 89 foreign countries and sales of $3 billion annually.

Equity Investment

private equity
Money from private sources that is invested by a venture capital or private equity company in start-ups and other risky—but potentially very profitable—small and medium-size enterprises

Small and medium-size enterprises with strong growth potential frequently have the need for additional funds to be able to grow further before deciding to trade their stock publicly in the marketplace. These firms often enlist the support of a venture capital firm or **private equity** company that invests its shareholders' money in start-ups and other risky but potentially very profitable small and medium-size enterprises. In exchange for a private equity stake, which is sometimes a majority or controlling position, the venture capital (VC) or private equity company provides investment capital and a range of business services, including management expertise.

Wholly Owned Subsidiaries

Wholly owned foreign subsidiaries are considered by companies that are willing and able to make the highest investment commitment to the foreign market. These companies insist on full ownership for reasons of control and managerial efficiency. Policy decisions about local product lines, expansion, profits, and dividends typically remain with the U.S. senior managers.

Fully owned subsidiaries can be started either from scratch or by acquiring established firms in the host country. U.S. firms can benefit significantly if the acquired company has complementary product lines or an established distribution or service network. For example, in 2007, PepsiCo's CEO Indra Nooyi led her company's large-scale global

Top Strategist
CEO Nooyi Spearheads PepsiCo's International Expansion Strategy

Exhibit
5.11

PepsiCo is one of the largest food and beverages companies in the world. It manufactures, markets, and sells a variety of salty, sweet, and grain-based snacks and carbonated and noncarbonated beverages. Indra Nooyi has been the chairman and chief executive officer of PepsiCo since 2007.

Nooyi wanted to become less reliant on the U.S. market, where sales growth has slowed for some of its flagship sodas and snacks. In 2008, 40 percent of PepsiCo revenue came from international business. About her strategic intention, Nooyi said, "Revitalizing this business is a huge priority for us and investments will be made to expand the company's footprint in fast-growing emerging markets."*

Nooyi planned to strengthen PepsiCo's presence in emerging high-growth markets—including China,

India, and Russia, where it has an established market in carbonated beverages and planned to expand with more focus on snack foods and other beverages.

PepsiCo planned to invest $1 billion in China between 2008 and 2011 to build more plants in western and interior areas of China, expand local R&D to develop products tailored to Chinese consumers, and build a larger sales force to expand marketing and distribution.

In an effort to expand its presence in the Russian juice category, PepsiCo bought a 75.53 percent stake in Russia's leading branded juice company, JSC Lebedyansky. PepsiCo also built a potato chip factory in southern Russia.

In 2008, Nooyi announced an investment plan of $500 million aimed at upgrading its manufacturing capacity, infrastructure, and R&D in India. With an established carbonated business, Pepsi India began to launch localized product offerings, such as the drink "nimbu paani."

*B. McKay and A. Cordeiro, "Pepsi Results Send Chills in Beverage, Snack Sector," *The Wall Street Journal,* October 15, 2008, p. B.1.

Source: B. McKay, "Pepsi to Boost China Outlay by $1 Billion," *The Wall Street Journal,* November 4, 2008, p. B. 3.

expansion based on developing wholly owned subsidiaries. The plan was to build brands in emerging markets to compensate for the slow growth in the United States, as described in Exhibit 5.11, Top Strategist.

U.S. firms seeking to improve their competitive postures through a foreign subsidiary face a number of risks to their normal mode of operations. First, if the high capital investment is to be rewarded, managers must attain extensive knowledge of the market, the host nation's language, and its business culture. Second, the host country expects both a long-term commitment from the U.S. enterprise and a portion of their nationals to be employed in positions of management or operations. Fortunately, hiring or training foreign managers for leadership positions is commonly a good policy, because they are close to both the market and contacts. This is especially important for smaller firms when markets are regional. Third, changing standards mandated by foreign regulations may eliminate a company's protected market niche. Product design and worker protection liabilities also may extend back to the home office.

The strategies shown in Exhibit 5.10 may be undertaken singly or in combination. For example, a firm may engage in any number of joint ventures while maintaining an export business. Additionally, there are a number of other strategies that a firm should consider before deciding on its long-term approach to foreign markets. These will be discussed in detail in Chapter 7 under the topic of grand strategies. However, the strategies discussed in this chapter provide the most popular starting points for planning the globalization of a firm.

Summary	To understand the strategic planning options available to a corporation, its managers need to recognize that different types of industry-based competition exist. Specifically, they must identify the position of their industry along the global versus multidomestic continuum and then consider the implications of that position for their firm.

The differences between global and multidomestic industries about the location and coordination of functional corporate activities necessitate differences in strategic emphasis. As an industry becomes global, managers of firms within that industry must increase the coordination and concentration of functional activities.

The Appendix at the end of this chapter lists many components of the environment with which global corporations must contend. This list is useful in understanding the issues that confront global corporations and in evaluating the thoroughness of global corporation strategies.

As a starting point for global expansion, the firm's mission statement needs to be reviewed and revised. As global operations fundamentally alter the direction and strategic capabilities of a firm, its mission statement, if originally developed from a domestic perspective, must be globalized.

The globalized mission statement provides the firm with a unity of direction that transcends the divergent perspectives of geographically dispersed managers. It provides a basis for strategic decisions in situations where strategic alternatives may appear to conflict. It promotes corporate values and commitments that extend beyond single cultures and satisfies the demands of the firm's internal and external claimants in different countries. Finally, it ensures the survival of the global corporation by asserting the global corporation's legitimacy with respect to support coalitions in a variety of operating environments.

Movement of a firm toward globalization often follows a systematic pattern of development. Commonly, businesses begin their foreign nation involvements progressively through niche market exporting, license-contract manufacturing, franchising, joint ventures, foreign branching, and foreign subsidiaries. |

Key Terms	ethnocentric orientation, *p. 119*	globalization, *p. 115*	regiocentric orientation, *p. 119*
	geocentric orientation, *p. 119*	multidomestic industry, *p. 124*	stakeholder activism, *p. 123*
	global industry, *p. 124*	polycentric orientation, *p. 119*	
		private equity, *p. 131*	

Questions for Discussion	1. How does environmental analysis at the domestic level differ from global analysis?
2. Which factors complicate environmental analysis at the global level? Which factors are making such analysis easier?
3. Do you agree with the suggestion that soon all industries will need to evaluate global environments?
4. Which industries operate almost devoid of global competition? Which inherent immunities do they enjoy?
5. Explain when and why it is important for a company to globalize.

6. Describe the four main strategic orientations of global firms.
7. Explain the control problems that are faced by global firms.
8. Describe the differences between multinational and global firms.
9. Describe the market requirements and product characteristics in global competition.
10. Evaluate the competitive strategies for firms in foreign markets:
    a. Niche market exporting
    b. Licensing and contract manufacturing
    c. Franchising
    d. Joint ventures
    e. Foreign branching
    f. Private equity investment
    g. Wholly owned subsidiaries

Chapter 5 Appendix

Components of the Multinational Environment

Multinational firms must operate within an environment that has numerous components. These components include the following:

1. Government, laws, regulations, and policies of home country (United States, for example)
   a. Monetary and fiscal policies and their effect on price trends, interest rates, economic growth, and stability
   b. Balance-of-payments policies
   c. Mandatory controls on direct investment
   d. Interest equalization tax and other policies
   e. Commercial policies, especially tariffs, quantitative import restrictions, and voluntary import controls
   f. Export controls and other restrictions on trade
   g. Tax policies and their impact on overseas business
   h. Antitrust regulations, their administration, and their impact on international business
   i. Investment guarantees, investment surveys, and other programs to encourage private investments in less-developed countries
   j. Export-import and government export expansion programs
   k. Other changes in government policy that affect international business

2. Key political and legal parameters in foreign countries and their projection
   a. Type of political and economic system, political philosophy, national ideology
   b. Major political parties, their philosophies, and their policies
   c. Stability of the government
      (1) Changes in political parties
      (2) Changes in governments
   d. Assessment of nationalism and its possible impact on political environment and legislation
   e. Assessment of political vulnerability
      (1) Possibilities of expropriation
      (2) Unfavorable and discriminatory national legislation and tax laws
      (3) Labor laws and problems
   f. Favorable political aspects
      (1) Tax and other concessions to encourage foreign investments
      (2) Credit and other guarantees

   g. Differences in legal system and commercial law
   h. Jurisdiction in legal disputes
   i. Antitrust laws and rules of competition
   j. Arbitration clauses and their enforcement
   k. Protection of patents, trademarks, brand names, and other industrial property rights

3. Key economic parameters and their projection
   a. Population and its distribution by age groups, density, annual percentage increase, percentage of working age, percentage of total in agriculture, and percentage in urban centers
   b. Level of economic development and industrialization
   c. Gross national product, gross domestic product, or national income in real terms and also on a per capita basis in recent years and projections over future planning period
   d. Distribution of personal income
   e. Measures of price stability and inflation, wholesale price index, consumer price index, other price indexes
   f. Supply of labor, wage rates
   g. Balance-of-payments equilibrium or disequilibrium, level of international monetary reserves, and balance-of-payments policies
   h. Trends in exchange rates, currency stability, evaluation of possibility of depreciation of currency
   i. Tariffs, quantitative restrictions, export controls, border taxes, exchange controls, state trading, and other entry barriers to foreign trade
   j. Monetary, fiscal, and tax policies
   k. Exchange controls and other restrictions on capital movements, repatriation of capital, and remission of earnings

4. Business system and structure
   a. Prevailing business philosophy: mixed capitalism, planned economy, state socialism
   b. Major types of industry and economic activities
   c. Numbers, size, and types of firms, including legal forms of business
   d. Organization: proprietorships, partnerships, limited companies, corporations, cooperatives, state enterprises
   e. Local ownership patterns: public and privately held corporations, family-owned enterprises

f. Domestic and foreign patterns of ownership in major industries

g. Business managers available: their education, training, experience, career patterns, attitudes, and reputations

h. Business associations and chambers of commerce and their influence

i. Business codes, both formal and informal

j. Marketing institutions: distributors, agents, wholesalers, retailers, advertising agencies, advertising media, marketing research, and other consultants

k. Financial and other business institutions: commercial and investment banks, other financial institutions, capital markets, money markets, foreign exchange dealers, insurance firms, engineering companies

l. Managerial processes and practices with respect to planning, administration, operations, accounting, budgeting, and control

5. Social and cultural parameters and their projections

a. Literacy and educational levels

b. Business, economic, technical, and other specialized education available

c. Language and cultural characteristics

d. Class structure and mobility

e. Religious, racial, and national characteristics

f. Degree of urbanization and rural-urban shifts

g. Strength of nationalistic sentiment

h. Rate of social change

i. Impact of nationalism on social and institutional change

Chapter **Six**

Internal Analysis

After reading and studying this chapter, you should be able to

1. Understand how to conduct a SWOT analysis, and be able to summarize its limitations.

2. Understand value chain analysis and how to use it to disaggregate a firm's activities and determine which are most critical to generating competitive advantage.

3. Understand the resource-based view of a firm and how to use it to disaggregate a firm's activities and resources to determine which resources are best used to build competitive advantage.

4. Apply four different perspectives for making meaningful comparisons to assess a firm's internal strengths and weaknesses.

5. Refamiliarize yourself with ratio analysis and basic techniques of financial analysis to assist you in doing internal analysis to identify a firm's strengths and weaknesses.

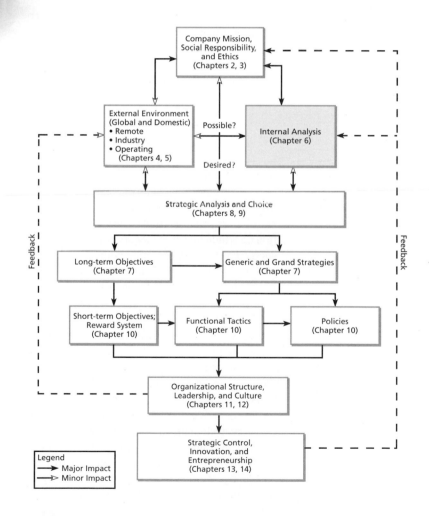

Company Mission, Social Responsibility, and Ethics (Chapters 2, 3)

External Environment (Global and Domestic)
• Remote
• Industry
• Operating
(Chapters 4, 5)

Possible?

Internal Analysis (Chapter 6)

Desired?

Strategic Analysis and Choice (Chapters 8, 9)

Long-term Objectives (Chapter 7)

Generic and Grand Strategies (Chapter 7)

Short-term Objectives; Reward System (Chapter 10)

Functional Tactics (Chapter 10)

Policies (Chapter 10)

Feedback

Organizational Structure, Leadership, and Culture (Chapters 11, 12)

Strategic Control, Innovation, and Entrepreneurship (Chapters 13, 14)

Legend
→ Major Impact
⇾ Minor Impact

The late R. David Thomas was once ridiculed by many restaurant industry veterans and analysts as he set about building "yet another" hamburger chain named after his young daughter, Wendy. While they thought the name was fine, critics argued that North America was already saturated with hamburger outlets such as McDonald's, Burger King, Hardees, Dairy Queen, White Castle, and others. Yet, as things turned out, Wendy's became the fastest-growing restaurant chain in the history of the world, having replaced Burger King as the second largest chain. Cisco, the global leader in networking equipment and switching devices linking wired and wireless computer systems worldwide, twice entered and tried to dominate the home-networking market. It failed each time, wasting more than $250 million in the process. Finally, just a few years ago, it acquired Linksys, the market leader, with the promise it would never try to bring Linksys into the normal Cisco company structure for fear of destroying the extraordinary success Linksys had achieved—not the least of which was vanquishing the much more powerful and wealthy Cisco twice in the last decade. Apple Computer was being written off in the increasingly competitive personal computer industry when it introduced, to a lukewarm reception, its new iPod device and iTunes service. Written off by many as a cute fad, that modest start pioneered a vast new global industry—much like Apple's original personal computer did three decades earlier.

Common to each of these diverse settings were insightful managers and business leaders who based their firm's pursuit of market opportunities not only on the existence of external opportunities but also on a very sound awareness of their firm's competitive advantages arising from the firm's internal resources, capabilities, and skills. A *sound, realistic awareness and appreciation of their firm's internally generated advantages* brought Wendy's, Apple, and Linksys immense success while its absence brought much the opposite to Cisco's home-networking ventures and to the competitors and critics of R. David Thomas and Steven Jobs. This chapter, then, focuses on how managers identify the key resources and capabilities around which to build successful strategies.

Managers often do this subjectively, based on intuition and "gut feel." Years of seasoned industry experience positions managers to make sound subjective judgments. But just as often, or more often, this may not be the case. In fast-changing environments, reliance on past experiences can cause management myopia—or a tendency to accept the status quo and disregard signals that change is needed. And with managers new to strategic decision making, subjective decisions are particularly suspect. A lack of experience is easily replaced by emotion, narrow functional expertise, and the opinions of others, thus creating the foundation on which newer managers build strategic recommendations. So it is that new managers' subjective assessments often come back to haunt them.

John W. Henry broke the most fabled curse in sports when his Boston Red Sox won their first World Championship since 1918. Most sports analysts, sports business managers, and regular fans (if they are honest now) would have bet a small fortune, based on their own subjective assessment, that there was no way the Boston Red Sox, having already lost three games, would win four straight games to beat the New York Yankees and then go on to win the World Series. That subjective assessment or "feel" would have led them to believe there were just too many reasons to bet the Red Sox could pull it out. At the same time, a seasoned global futures market trader, John W. Henry, relied on applying his systematic global futures market approach to baseball player selection along with selected other resources and capabilities unique to the Boston area and situation in his bet that the Red Sox could win it all. His very systematic approach to internal analysis of the Boston Red Sox sports enterprise and the leveraging of his/their strengths led to the World Series championship and perhaps many more, as described in Exhibit 6.1, Top Strategist.

Managers often start their internal analysis with questions like, How well is the current strategy working? What is our current situation? Or what are our strengths and weaknesses? The chapter begins with a review of a long-standing, traditional approach

Top Strategist
John W. Henry, CEO of the Boston Red Sox

Exhibit
6.1

John W. Henry, CEO of the Boston Red Sox, and Slugger David Ortiz

The return of pain and broken hearts for every Boston Red Sox fan with each new professional baseball season was legendary. Not since 1918 had they experienced winning the World Series, yet they had suffered through their arch nemesis, the New York Yankees, doing it 26 times over that lengthy spell. But something happened in the new millennium, and suddenly in 2004 and again in 2007 sports best-known curse was broken after almost a century of trying—the Boston Red Sox won two World Series titles.

It could not have happened in a more dramatic fashion. The Red Sox were down three games to none in the American League Championship series, once again, to the hated New York Yankees . . . and playing in New York for the deciding Game 4. Somehow, the Red Sox rallied to win that game, and then the next three, allowing them to go to the World Series. They won that too. Since then, the Sox have won another and are now in the championship hunt each year. What happened? John W. Henry became co-owner and CEO a few years before that initial win, and he took a different approach to charting the Red Sox's future. He may well have achieved immortality, at least in the Red Sox nation.

Henry set about a careful, internal analysis to determine the Red Sox's skills, resources, capabilities, and weaknesses. He set the tone by firing the manager during the 2003 playoff series for what he thought was a critical, poor decision in a decisive game. That set a tone of seriousness—and gained fan support. Henry had previously earned his fortune developing and building a business around his proprietary global futures trading system still widely used today. So he secondly approached internal assessments of the Red Sox player possibilities in a similar manner—he used a system called *sabermetrics* to mine baseball statistics about minor league and other young players, systematically finding undervalued players to bring into the Red Sox organization while also identifying when to avoid long-term contracts with aging stars.*

He further saw other underutilized capabilities, such as generating more revenue from Fenway Park, the oldest stadium in Major League Baseball, by squeezing in more seats and then charging the highest prices for home games. They always sold out. He started high-definition (HD) broadcasts of home games on their 80 percent–owned New England Sports Cable Network, broadening the fan base, increasing advertising revenue, and routinely winning regional prime-time ratings. The Red Sox quickly turned into the second-highest-earning MLB franchise, giving it the financial muscle to compete with the perennial highest payroll Yankees.

New York Times writer George Vecsey said about the Yankees: "They are becoming the Red Sox of old—25 players and a bunch of separate cabs." The Sox organization, led by Henry, has become a team of players, who get along, hang out, and play together. It all started with Henry's objective internal analysis, and he's now aiming for a dynasty.**

* "John Henry: Boston Red Sox," *BusinessWeek,* January 10, 2005.
** "Sports of the Times: Epstein to Red Sox Fans: This One's for You," *New York Times,* October 22, 2004.

managers have frequently used to answer these questions, SWOT analysis. This approach is a logical framework intended to help managers thoughtfully consider their company's internal capabilities and use the results to shape strategic options. Its value and continued use is found in its simplicity. At the same time, SWOT analysis has limitations that have led strategists to seek more comprehensive frameworks for conducting internal analysis.

Value chain analysis is one such framework. Value chain analysis views a firm as a "chain" or sequential process of value-creating activities. The sum of all of these activities represents the "value" the firm exists to provide its customers. So undertaking an internal analysis that breaks down the firm into these distinct value activities allows for a detailed, interrelated evaluation of a firm's internal strengths and weaknesses that improves upon what strategists can create using only SWOT analysis.

The resource-based view (RBV) of a firm is another important framework for conducting internal analysis. This approach improves upon SWOT analysis by examining a variety of different yet specific types of resources and capabilities any firm possesses and then evaluating the degree to which they become the basis for sustained competitive advantage based on industry and competitive considerations. In so doing, it provides a disciplined approach to internal analysis.

Common to all the approaches to internal analysis is the use of meaningful standards for comparison in internal analysis. We conclude this chapter by examining how managers use past performance, comparison with competitors or other "benchmarks," industry norms, and traditional financial analysis to make meaningful comparisons.

SWOT ANALYSIS: A TRADITIONAL APPROACH TO INTERNAL ANALYSIS

SWOT analysis
SWOT is an acronym for the internal Strengths and Weaknesses of a firm, and the environmental Opportunities and Threats facing that firm. SWOT analysis is a technique through which managers create a quick overview of a company's strategic situation.

SWOT is an acronym for the internal **S**trengths and **W**eaknesses of a firm and the environmental **O**pportunities and **T**hreats facing that firm. **SWOT analysis** is a historically popular technique through which managers create a quick overview of a company's strategic situation. It is based on the assumption that an effective strategy derives from a sound "fit" between a firm's internal resources (strengths and weaknesses) and its external situation (opportunities and threats). A good fit maximizes a firm's strengths and opportunities and minimizes its weaknesses and threats. Accurately applied, this simple assumption has sound, insightful implications for the design of a successful strategy.

Environmental and industry analysis in Chapters 3 and 4 provides the information needed to identify opportunities and threats in a firm's environment, the first fundamental focus in SWOT analysis.

Opportunities

opportunity
A major favorable situation in a firm's environment.

An **opportunity** is a major favorable situation in a firm's environment. Key trends are one source of opportunities. Identification of a previously overlooked market segment, changes in competitive or regulatory circumstances, technological changes, and improved buyer or supplier relationships could represent opportunities for the firm. Sustained, growing interest in organic foods has created an opportunity that is a critical factor shaping strategic decisions at groceries and restaurants worldwide.

Threats

threat
A major unfavorable situation in a firm's environment.

A **threat** is a major unfavorable situation in a firm's environment. Threats are key impediments to the firm's current or desired position. The entrance of new competitors, slow market growth, increased bargaining power of key buyers or suppliers, technological changes, and new or revised regulations could represent threats to a firm's success. The move by

Nokia to bundle free, unlimited music downloads for one year with its new Nokia phones has created a major new development in the digital-music-service market—heretofore essentially legitimized and dominated by Apple's iTunes. Nokia is one of the few global companies with the device capability and the muscle to challenge iTunes' domination of this global market. While Apple has a trinity—the iPhone, iPod, and iTunes—which most would say is a dominating strength, this move by Nokia must be considered a serious "threat" by Apple's management as they use a SWOT analysis to help them assess internal capabilities and craft a future iTunes' strategy.

Once managers agree on key opportunities and threats facing their firm, they have a frame of reference or context from which to evaluate their firm's ability to take advantage of opportunities and minimize the effect of key threats. And vice versa: once managers agree on their firm's core strengths and weaknesses, they can logically move to consider opportunities that best leverage their firm's strengths while minimizing the effect certain weaknesses may present until remedied.

Strengths

strength
A resource advantage relative to competitors and the needs of the markets a firm serves or expects to serve.

A **strength** is a resource or capability controlled by or available to a firm that gives it an advantage relative to its competitors in meeting the needs of the customers it serves. Strengths arise from the resources and competencies available to the firm. Southland Log Homes' southeastern plant locations (Virginia, South Carolina, and Mississippi) provide both transportation and raw material cost advantages along with ideal proximity to the United States' most rapidly growing second-home markets. Southland leveraged these strengths to take advantage of the moderate interest rates and rapidly growing baby-boomer second-home demand trend to become one of the largest log home companies in North America. This strength has continued to sustain Southland even as it navigates the recent economic depression in the U.S. housing market.[1]

Weaknesses

weakness
A limitation or deficiency in one or more resources or competencies relative to competitors that impedes a firm's effective performance.

A **weakness** is a limitation or deficiency in one or more of a firm's resources or capabilities relative to its competitors that create a disadvantage in effectively meeting customer needs. Limited financial capacity was a weakness recognized by Southwest Airlines, which charted a selective route expansion strategy to build the best profit record in a deregulated airline industry.

Using SWOT Analysis in Strategic Analysis

The most common use of SWOT analysis is as a logical framework guiding discussion and reflection about a firm's situation and basic alternatives. This often takes place as a series of managerial group discussions. What one manager sees as an opportunity, another may see as a potential threat. Likewise, a strength to one manager may be a weakness to another. The SWOT framework provides an organized basis for insightful discussion and information sharing, which may improve the quality of choices and decisions managers subsequently make. Consider what initial discussions among Apple Computer's management team might have been that led to the decision to pursue the rapid development and introduction of the iPod. A brief SWOT analysis of their situation might have identified:

Strengths

    Sizable miniature storage expertise
    User-friendly engineering skill

[1] www.SouthlandLogHomes.com

Reputation and image with youthful consumers

Brand name

Web-savvy organization and people

Jobs's Pixar experience

Weaknesses

Economies of scale versus computer rivals

Maturing computer markets

Limited financial resources

Limited music industry expertise

Opportunities

Confused online music situation

Emerging file-sharing restrictions

Few core computer-related opportunities

Digitalization of movies and music

Threats

Growing global computer companies

Major computer competitors

It is logical to envision Apple managers' discussions evolving to a consensus that the combination of Apple's storage and digitalization strengths along with their strong brand franchise with "hip" consumers, when combined with the opportunity potentially arising out of the need for a simple way to legally buy and download music on the Web would be the basis for a compelling strategy for Apple to become a first mover in the emerging downloadable music industry.

Exhibit 6.2 illustrates how SWOT analysis might take managerial planning discussions into a slightly more structured approach to aid strategic analysis. The objective is identification of one of four distinct patterns in the match between a firm's internal resources and

EXHIBIT 6.2
SWOT Analysis Diagram

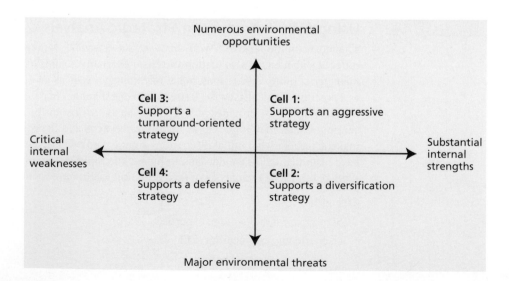

external situation. Cell 1 is the most favorable situation; the firm faces several environmental opportunities and has numerous strengths that encourage pursuit of those opportunities. This situation suggests growth-oriented strategies to exploit the favorable match. Our example of Apple Computer's intensive market development strategy in the online music services and the iPod is the result of a favorable match of its strong technical expertise, early entry, and reputation resources with an opportunity for impressive market growth as millions of people sought a legally viable, convenient way to obtain, download, store, and use their own customized music choices.

Recent efforts by Kodak to compete in the ink-jet printer market, highlighted later in this chapter in Exhibit 6.12, Strategy in Action (see page 164), offer another example of a firm in cell 1. Kodak views its expertise in ink pigments, and how to display them in an inexpensive yet impressive manner on all types of paper, as a unique strength from its photography roots that give it a basis for a competitive advantage in both costs and quality with traditional printer makers. Furthermore, it sees consumer frustration with the high costs of ink cartridge replacements in all ink-jet printers as a major external opportunity upon which it can capitalize by offering a printer solution that dramatically lowers a user's total printing costs over time.

Cell 4 is the least favorable situation, with the firm facing major environmental threats from a weak resource position. This situation clearly calls for strategies that reduce or redirect involvement in the products or markets examined by means of SWOT analysis. Texas Instruments (TI) offers a good example of a cell 4 firm. It was a sprawling maker of chips, calculators, laptop PCs, military electronics, and engineering software on a sickening slide toward oblivion just 10 years ago. Rich Templeton, current chairman and CEO, rose to this position based on his success in helping to define and execute TI's strategy to focus narrowly on semiconductors for signal processing. Templeton convinced his boss at the time, Tom Engibous, to divest TI of most of the products and businesses in which it had become involved in order to rebuild TI around its core semiconductor technology, even during the worst downturn in semiconductor history. These actions ultimately reinvigorated the ailing electronics giant and turned it into one of the hottest plays in signal semiconductors by betting the company on an emerging class of chips know as digital signal processors—DSPs. The chips crunch vast streams of data for an array of digital gadgets, phones, and other cellular devices. TI has experienced increasing market share every year since then, and now commands more than 60 percent of the global market for advanced DSPs, becoming the No. 1 chip supplier to the digital wireless phone industry.

In cell 2, a firm that has identified several key strengths faces an unfavorable environment. In this situation, strategies would seek to redeploy those strong resources and competencies to build long-term opportunities in more opportunistic product markets. IBM, a dominant manufacturer of mainframes, servers, and PCs worldwide, has nurtured many strengths in computer-related and software-related markets for many years. Increasingly, however, it has had to address major threats that include product commoditization, pricing pressures, accelerated pace of innovation, and the like. IBM's decision to sell its PC business to the Chinese firm Lenovo and focus instead on continued development of ISSC, better known now as IBM Global Services, has allowed IBM to build a long-term opportunity in the (hopefully) more profitable, growing markets of the next decade. In the past 10 years, Global Services has become the fastest-growing division of the company, its largest employer, and the keystone of IBM's strategic future. The group does everything from running a customer's IT (information technology) department to consulting on legacy system upgrades to building custom supply-chain management applications. As IBM's hardware divisions struggle against price wars and commoditization and its software units fight to gain share beyond mainframes, it is Global Services that drives the company's growth.

A firm in cell 3 faces impressive market opportunity but is constrained by weak internal resources. The focus of strategy for such a firm is eliminating the internal weaknesses so as to more effectively pursue the market opportunity. Microsoft has big problems with computer viruses. Alleviating such problems, or weaknesses, is driving massive changes in how Microsoft writes software—to make it more secure before it reaches the market rather than fix it later with patches. Microsoft is also shaking up the security software industry by acquiring several smaller companies to accelerate its own efforts to create specialized software that detects, finds, and removes malicious code.[2]

Limitations of SWOT Analysis

SWOT analysis has been a framework of choice among many managers for a long time because of its simplicity and its portrayal of the essence of sound strategy formulation—matching a firm's opportunities and threats with its strengths and weaknesses. But SWOT analysis is a broad conceptual approach, making it susceptible to some key limitations.

1. **A SWOT analysis can overemphasize internal strengths and downplay external threats.** Strategists in every company have to remain vigilant against building strategies around what the firm does well now (its strengths) without due consideration of the external environment's impact on those strengths. Apple's success with the iPod and its iTunes downloadable music Web site provides a good example of strategists who placed a major emphasis on external considerations—the legal requirements for downloading and subsequently using individual songs, what music to make available, and the evolution of the use of the Web to download music—as a guide to shaping Apple's eventual strategy. What would Apple's success have been like if its strategy had been built substantially with a focus on its technology in making the iPod device and offering it in the consumer marketplace—without bothering with the development and creation of iTunes?

2. **A SWOT analysis can be static and can risk ignoring changing circumstances.** A frequent admonition about the downfall of planning processes says that plans are one-time events to be completed, typed, and relegated to their spot on a manager's shelf while s/he goes about the actual work of the firm. So it is not surprising that critics of SWOT analysis, with good reason, warn that it is a one-time view of a changing, or moving, situation. Major U.S. airlines pursued strategies built around strengths that were suddenly much less important when airline deregulation took place. Likewise, those airlines built huge competitive advantages around "hub and spoke" systems for bringing small-town flyers to key hubs to be redistributed to flights elsewhere and yet allow for centralized maintenance and economies of scale. The change brought about by discount airlines that "cherry-picked" key routes, and eventual outsourcing of routine maintenance to Latin America and the Caribbean, did great harm to those strategies. Bottom line: SWOT analysis, along with most planning techniques, must avoid being static and ignoring change.

3. **A SWOT analysis can overemphasize a single strength or element of strategy.** Dell Computer's long-dominant strength based on a highly automated, Internet, or phone-based direct sales model gave Dell, according to chairman and founder Michael Dell, "a competitive advantage [strength] as wide as the Grand Canyon." He viewed it as being

---

[2] "Aiming to Fix Flaws, Microsoft Buys Another Antivirus Firm," *The Wall Street Journal,* February 9, 2005, p. B1.

prohibitively expensive for any rival to copy this source of strength. Unfortunately for Dell shareholders, Dell's reliance on that "key" strength proved to be an oversimplified basis around which to sustain the company's strategy for continued dominance and growth in the global PC industry. HP's size alone, with its reemphasis on printing and technical skills, and Lenovo's home base in the fast-growing Asian market have overcome Dell's dominance in the global PC industry.

4. A strength is not necessarily a source of competitive advantage. Cisco Systems Inc. has been a dominant player in providing switching equipment and other key networking infrastructure items around which the global computer communications system has been able to proliferate. It has substantial financial, technological, and branding expertise. Cisco Systems twice attempted to use its vast strengths in these areas as the basis to enter and remain in the market for home computer networks and wireless home-networking devices. It failed both times and lost hundreds of millions of dollars in the process. It possesses several compelling strengths, but none were sources of sustainable competitive advantage in the home-computer-networking industry. After leaving that industry for several years, it recently chose to reenter it by acquiring Linksys, an early pioneer in that industry. Cisco management acknowledged that it was doing so precisely because it did not possess those sources of competitive advantage and that, furthermore, it would avoid any interference with that business lest it disrupt the advantage around which Linksys success has been built.

In summary, SWOT analysis is a longtime, traditional approach to internal analysis among many strategists. It offers a generalized effort to examine internal capabilities in light of external factors, most notably key opportunities and threats. It has limitations that must be considered if SWOT analysis is to be the basis for any firm's strategic decision-making process. Another approach to internal analysis that emerged, in part, to add more rigor and depth in the identification of competitive advantages around which a firm might build a successful strategy is value chain analysis. We examine it next.

VALUE CHAIN ANALYSIS

value chain
A perspective in which business is seen as a chain of activities that transforms inputs into outputs that customers value.

The term **value chain** describes a way of looking at a business as a chain of activities that transform inputs into outputs that customers value. Customer value derives from three basic sources: activities that differentiate the product, activities that lower its cost, and activities that meet the customer's need quickly. **Value chain analysis** (VCA) attempts to understand how a business creates customer value by examining the contributions of different activities within the business to that value.

value chain analysis
An analysis that attempts to understand how a business creates customer value by examining the contributions of different activities within the business to that value.

VCA takes a process point of view: it divides (sometimes called disaggregates) the business into sets of activities that occur *within the business,* starting with the inputs a firm receives and finishing with the firm's products (or services) and after-sales service to customers. VCA attempts to look at its costs across the series of activities the business performs to determine where low-cost advantages or cost disadvantages exist. It looks at the attributes of each of these different activities to determine in what ways each activity that occurs between purchasing inputs and after-sales service helps differentiate the company's products and services. Proponents of VCA believe it allows managers to better identify their firm's competitive advantages by looking at the business as a process—a chain of activities—of what actually happens in the business rather than simply looking at it based on arbitrary organizational dividing lines or historical accounting protocol.

Exhibit 6.3 shows a typical value chain framework. It divides activities within the firm into two broad categories: primary activities and support activities. **Primary activities** (sometimes called *line functions*) are those involved in the physical creation of the product, marketing and transfer to the buyer, and after-sale support. **Support activities** (sometimes

EXHIBIT 6.3
The Value Chain

Source: Based on Michael Porter. *On Competition*, 1998. Harvard Business School Press.

The Value Chain

Support Activities	General administration					Margin
	Human resource management					
	Research, technology, and systems development					
	Procurement					
	Inbound logistics	Operations	Outbound logistics	Marketing and sales	Service	Margin

Primary Activities

primary activities
The activities in a firm of those involved in the physical creation of the product, marketing and transfer to the buyer, and after-sale support.

Primary Activities

- **Inbound logistics**—Activities, costs, and assets associated with obtaining fuel, energy, raw materials, parts components, merchandise, and consumable items from vendors; receiving, storing, and disseminating inputs from suppliers; inspection; and inventory management.
- **Operations**—Activities, costs, and assets associated with converting inputs into final product form (production, assembly, packaging, equipment maintenance, facilities, operations, quality assurance, environmental protection).
- **Outbound logistics**—Activities, costs, and assets dealing with physically distributing the product to buyers (finished goods warehousing, order processing, order picking and packing, shipping, delivery vehicle operations).
- **Marketing and sales**—Activities, costs, and assets related to sales force efforts, advertising and promotion, market research and planning, and dealer/distributor support.
- **Service**—Activities, costs, and assets associated with providing assistance to buyers, such as installation, spare parts delivery, maintenance and repair, technical assistance, buyer inquiries, and complaints.

support activities
The activities in a firm that assist the firm as a whole by providing infrastructure or inputs that allow the primary activities to take place on an ongoing basis.

Support Activities

- **General administration**—Activities, costs, and assets relating to general management, accounting and finance, legal and regulatory affairs, safety and security, management information systems, and other "overhead" functions.
- **Human resources management**—Activities, costs, and assets associated with the recruitment, hiring, training, development, and compensation of all types of personnel; labor relations activities; development of knowledge-based skills.
- **Research, technology, and systems development**—Activities, costs, and assets relating to product R&D, process R&D, process design improvement, equipment design, computer software development, telecommunications systems, computer-assisted design and engineering, new database capabilities, and development of computerized support systems.
- **Procurement**—Activities, costs, and assets associated with purchasing and providing raw materials, supplies, services, and outsourcing necessary to support the firm and its activities. Sometimes this activity is assigned as part of a firm's inbound logistic purchasing activities.

FedEx Uses Value Chain Analysis to Reinvent Itself

Stories of Fred Smith's early years creating Federal Express, like when he went to Las Vegas to gamble in order to [luckily] win $28,000 to use the next day to make payroll, are the stuff of legend. But the analysis and decision to reinvent FedEx into a logistics information company, rather than an overnight transportation company, has created a revolution in how companies around the world do business, allowing FedEx to maximize the value it adds in the process and the value it receives from doing so. FedEx becomes the logistical infrastructure for any client's business, handling everything from the customer order to the delivery, often including assembly and warehousing in the process.

"Moving an item from point A to point B is no longer a big deal," said James Barksdale, an early architect of the FedEx transformation. "Having the information about the item, where it is, what to connect it up with, and the best way to use that info . . . that is the value. The companies that maximize that step in their value chain will be the big winners." Fred Smith bought into that concept, envisioning a time when FedEx's value—long built on large planes and trucks—

would be build on information, computers, coordination, and the FedEx brand.

That day has arrived at FedEx. It is now the linchpin of a just-in-time revolution for companies worldwide. Its planes and trucks are mobile warehouses, sometimes stopping at FedEx-operated assembling centers serving clients, all the while significantly cutting costs and increasing productivity for clients worldwide, large and small.

FedEx's value chain has dramatically shrunk the area involved with planes and trucks, while the overall logistical value added now contributes more than 90 percent of FedEx annual revenues. And, this all started with an objective, careful analysis of the FedEx value chain 10 years ago. That was followed by a visionary commitment to build that chain around activities that contribute the most value to a customer, in the process seeking to make them the core competencies upon which FedEx reinvented itself and built its future success.

Source: Various FedEx Annual Reports and www.fedex.com.

called *staff* or *overhead functions*) assist the firm as a whole by providing infrastructure or inputs that allow the primary activities to take place on an ongoing basis. The value chain includes a profit margin because a markup above the cost of providing a firm's value-adding activities is normally part of the price paid by the buyer—creating value that exceeds cost so as to generate a return for the effort.[3]

Judgment is required across individual firms and different industries because what may be seen as a support activity in one firm or industry may be a primary activity in another. Computer operations might typically be seen as infrastructure support, for example, but may be seen as a primary activity in airlines, newspapers, or banks. Exhibit 6.4, Strategy in Action, describes how Federal Express reconceptualized its company using a value chain analysis that ultimately saw its information support become its primary activity and source of customer value.

Conducting a Value Chain Analysis

Identify Activities

The initial step in value chain analysis is to divide a company's operations into specific activities or business processes, usually grouping them similarly to the primary and support activity categories shown earlier in Exhibit 6.3. Within each category, a firm typically

---

[3] Different "value chain" or value activities may become the focus of value chain analysis. For example, companies using Hammer's *Reengineering the Corporation* might use (1) order procurement, (2) order fulfillment, (3) customer service, (4) product design, and (5) strategic planning plus support activities.

performs a number of discrete activities that may be key to the firm's success. Service activities, for example, may include such discrete activities as installation, repair, parts distribution, and upgrading—any of which could be a major source of competitive advantage or disadvantage. The manager's challenge at this point is to be very detailed attempting to "disaggregate" what actually goes on into numerous distinct, analyzable activities rather than settling for a broad, general categorization.

Allocate Costs

The next step is to attempt to attach costs to each discrete activity. Each activity in the value chain incurs costs and ties up time and assets. Value chain analysis requires managers to assign costs and assets to each activity, thereby providing a very different way of viewing costs than traditional cost accounting methods would produce. Exhibit 6.5 helps illustrate this distinction. Both approaches in Exhibit 6.5 tell us that the purchasing department (procurement activities) cost $320,075. The traditional method lets us see that payroll expenses are 73 percent [($175 + $57.5)/$320] of our costs with "other fixed charges" the second largest cost, 19 percent [$62/$320] of the total procurement costs. VCA proponents would argue that the benefit of this information is limited. Their argument might be the following:

> With this information we could compare our procurement costs to key competitors, budgets, or industry averages and conclude that we are better, worse, or equal. We could then ascertain that our "people" costs and "other fixed charges" cost are advantages, disadvantages, or "in line" with competitors. Managers could then argue to cut people, add people, or debate fixed overhead charges. However, they would get lost in what is really a budgetary debate without ever examining what it is those people do in accomplishing the procurement function, what value that provides, and how cost effective each activity is.

VCA proponents hold that the activity-based VCA approach would provide a more meaningful analysis of the procurement function's costs and consequent value added. The activity-based side of Exhibit 6.5 shows that approximately 21 percent of the procurement cost or value added involves evaluating supplier capabilities. A rather sizable cost, 20 percent, involves internal administration, with an additional 17 percent spent resolving problems and almost 15 percent spent on quality control efforts. VCA advocates see

EXHIBIT 6.5   The Difference between Traditional Cost Accounting and Activity-Based Cost Accounting

Traditional Cost Accounting in a Purchasing Department		Activity-Based Cost Accounting in the Same Purchasing Department for Its "Procurement" Activities	
Wages and salaries	$175,000	Evaluate supplier capabilities	$ 67,875
Employee benefits	57,500	Process purchase orders	41,050
Supplies	3,250	Expedite supplier deliveries	11,750
Travel	1,200	Expedite internal processing	7,920
Depreciation	8,500	Check quality of items purchased	47,150
Other fixed charges	62,000	Check incoming deliveries against	
Miscellaneous operating expenses	12,625	purchase orders	24,225
	$320,075	Resolve problems	55,000
		Internal administration	65,105
			$320,075

this information as being much more useful than traditional cost accounting information, especially when compared with the cost information of key competitors or other "benchmark" companies. VCA supporters assert the following argument that the benefit of this activity-based information is substantial:

> Rather than analyzing just "people" and "other charges," we are now looking at meaningful categorizations of the work that procurement actually does. We see, for example, that a key value-added activity (and cost) involves "evaluating supplier capabilities." The amount spent on "internal administration" and "resolving problems" seems high and may indicate a weakness or area for improvement if the other activities' costs are in line and outcomes favorable. The bottom line is that this approach lets us look at what we actually "do" in the business—the specific activities—to create customer value, and that in turn allows more specific internal analysis than traditional, accounting-based cost categories.

Recognizing the Difficulty in Activity-Based Cost Accounting

It is important to note that existing financial management and accounting systems in many firms are not set up to easily provide activity-based cost breakdowns. Likewise, in virtually all firms, the information requirements to support activity-based cost accounting can create redundant work because of the financial reporting requirements that may force firms to retain the traditional approach for financial statement purposes. The time and energy to change to an activity-based approach can be formidable and still typically involve arbitrary cost allocation decisions—trying to allocate selected asset or people costs across multiple activities in which they are involved. Challenges dealing with a cost-based use of VCA have not deterred use of the framework to identify sources of differentiation. Indeed, conducting a VCA to analyze competitive advantages that differentiate the firm is compatible with the resource-based view's examination of intangible assets and capabilities as sources of distinctive competence.

Identify the Activities That Differentiate the Firm

Scrutinizing a firm's value chain may not only reveal cost advantages or disadvantages, it may also bring attention to several sources of differentiation advantage relative to competitors. Google considers its Internet-based search algorithms (activities) to be far superior to any competitor's. Google knows it has a cost advantage because of the time and expense replicating this activity would take. But Google considers it an even more important source of value to the customer because of the importance customers place on this activity, which differentiates Google from many would-be competitors. Likewise, Federal Express, as we noted in Exhibit 6.4, considers its information management skills to have become the core competence and essence of the company because of the value these skills allow FedEx to provide its customers and the importance they in turn place on such skills. Exhibit 6.6 suggests some factors for assessing primary and support activities' differentiation and contribution.

Examine the Value Chain

Once the value chain has been documented, managers need to identify the activities that are critical to buyer satisfaction and market success. It is those activities that deserve major scrutiny in an internal analysis. Three considerations are essential at this stage in the value chain analysis. First, the company's basic mission needs to influence managers' choice of activities to be examined in detail. If the company is focused on being a low-cost provider, then management attention to lower costs should be very visible, and missions built around commitment to differentiation should find managers spending more on activities that

EXHIBIT 6.6 **Possible Factors for Assessing Sources of Differentiation in Primary and Support Activities**

General Administration				

- Capability to identify new-product market opportunities and potential environmental threats
- Quality of the strategic planning system to achieve corporate objectives
- Coordination and integration of all value chain activities among organizational subunits
- Ability to obtain relatively low-cost funds for capital expenditures and working capital
- Level of information systems support in making strategic and routine decisions
- Timely and accurate management information on general and competitive environments
- Relationships with public policymakers and interest groups
- Public image and corporate citizenship

Human Resource Management

- Effectiveness of procedures for recruiting, training, and promoting all levels of employees
- Appropriateness of reward systems for motivating and challenging employees
- A work environment that minimizes absenteeism and keeps turnover at desirable levels
- Relations with trade unions
- Active participation by managers and technical personnel in professional organizations
- Levels of employee motivation and job satisfaction

Technology Development

- Success of research and development activities in leading to product and process innovations
- Quality of working relationships between R&D personnel and other departments
- Timeliness of technology development activities in meeting critical deadlines
- Quality of laboratories and other facilities
- Qualification and experience of laboratory technicians and scientists
- Ability of work environment to encourage creativity and innovation

Procurement

- Development of alternate sources for inputs to minimize dependence on a single supplier
- Procurement of raw materials (1) on a timely basis, (2) at lowest possible cost, (3) at acceptable levels of quality
- Procedures for procurement of plant, machinery, and buildings
- Development of criteria for lease-versus-purchase decisions
- Good, long-term relationships with reliable suppliers

Support Activities / *Profit Margin*

Inbound Logistics	Operations	Outbound Logistics	Marketing and Sales	Service
■ Soundness of material and inventory control systems ■ Efficiency of raw material warehousing activities	■ Productivity of equipment compared to that of key competitors ■ Appropriate automation of production processes ■ Effectiveness of production control systems to improve quality and reduce costs ■ Efficiency of plant layout and work-flow design	■ Timeliness and efficiency of delivery of finished goods and services ■ Efficiency of finished goods warehousing activities	■ Effectiveness of market research to identify customer segments and needs ■ Innovation in sales promotion and advertising ■ Evaluation of alternate distribution channels ■ Motivation and competence of sales force ■ Development of an image of quality and a favorable reputation ■ Extent of brand loyalty among customers ■ Extent of market dominance within the market segment or overall market	■ Means to solicit customer input for product improvements ■ Promptness of attention to customer complaints ■ Appropriateness of warranty and guarantee policies ■ Quality of customer education and training ■ Ability to provide replacement parts and repair services

Profit Margin

Primary Activities

Source: Based on Michael Porter, *On Competition,* 1998, Harvard Business School Press.

are differentiation cornerstones. Retailer Wal-Mart focuses intensely on costs related to inbound logistics, advertising, and loyalty to build its competitive advantage, while Nordstrom builds its distinct position in retailing by emphasizing sales and support activities on which they spend twice the retail industry average.

Second, the nature of value chains and the relative importance of the activities within them vary by industry. Lodging firms like Holiday Inn have major costs and concerns that involve operational activities—it provides its service instantaneously at each location—and marketing activities, while having minimal concern for outbound logistics. Yet for a distributor, such as the food distributor PYA, inbound and outbound logistics are the most critical area. Major retailers like Wal-Mart have built value advantages focusing on purchasing and inbound logistics, while the most successful personal computer companies have built via sales, outbound logistics, and service through the mail-order process.

Third, the relative importance of value activities can vary by a company's position in a broader value system that includes the value chains of its upstream suppliers and downstream customers or partners involved in providing products or services to end users. A producer of roofing shingles depends heavily on the downstream activities of wholesale distributors and building supply retailers to reach roofing contractors and do-it-yourselfers. Maytag manufactures its own appliances, sells them through independent distributors, and provides warranty service to the buyer. Sears outsources the manufacture of its appliances while it promotes its brand name—Kenmore—and handles all sales and service.

As these examples suggest, it is important that managers take into account their level of vertical integration when comparing their cost structure for activities on their value chain to those of key competitors. Comparing a fully integrated rival with a partially integrated one requires adjusting for the scope of activities performed to achieve meaningful comparison. It also suggests the need for examining costs associated with activities provided by upstream or downstream companies; these activities ultimately determine comparable, final costs to end users. Said another way, one company's comparative cost disadvantage (or advantage) may emanate more from activities undertaken by upstream or downstream "partners" than from activities under the direct control of that company—therefore suggesting less of a relative advantage or disadvantage within the company's direct value chain.

COMPETITIVE ADVANTAGE VIA CUSTOMER VALUE: THREE CIRCLES ANALYSIS

three circles analysis
An internal analysis technique wherein strategists examine customers' needs, company offerings, and competitor's offerings to more clearly articulate what their company's competitive advantage is and how it differs from those of competitors.

There is considerable appeal and anecdotal evidence that a company must build a distinct value chain–based competitive advantage to grow and be profitable over the long term. However, in using the value chain approach just described or the resource-based approach (described in the next section), it can remain difficult for many strategists to clearly articulate what their company's competitive advantage is and how it differs from those of competitors while in the midst of strategic analysis activities. University of Notre Dame Professors Joel Urbany and James Davis have developed a clever, useful, and simple tool to help in this analysis that can also complement and help articulate the findings from a value chain analysis or the resource-based view.[4] In this section, we use their ideas and examples to describe their "three circle analysis."

To begin the **three circles analysis,** the strategizing team of executives should begin their analysis by thinking deeply about what customers of their type of product or service value and why. For example, they might value speedy service because they want to minimize

---

[4] Joel E. Urbany and James H. Davis, "Strategic Insight in Three Circles," *Harvard Business Review* 85, no. 11 (2007), pp. 28–30.

EXHIBIT 6.7

Three Circles Analysis

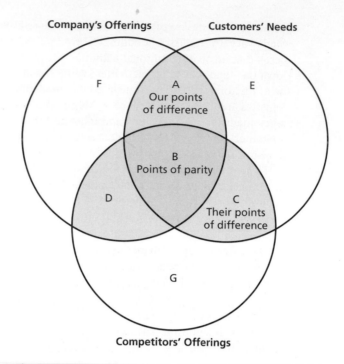

inventory costs with a just-in-time inventory system. Looking at findings from the value chain analysis, or from a resource-based view of the firm, but through the eyes of their key target customers, is a simple but often overlooked perspective from which to evaluate core competencies. It is a central part of this technique and logically hits the core of the reason for the firm's existence in the first place.

Next, the strategists should draw three circles as shown in Exhibit 6.7. The first circle (seen on the top right) is to represent the team's consensus of what the most important customers or customer segments need or want from the product or service.

Urbany and Davis observe that even in very mature industries, customers do not articulate all their wants in conversations with companies. For example, there was no consumer demand on Procter & Gamble to invent the Swiffer, whose category contributes significantly to the company's recent double-digit sales growth in home care products. Instead, the Swiffer emerged from P&G's careful observation of the challenges of household cleaning. Therefore, in conducting this initial phase of competitive advantage analysis, the consumers' unexpressed needs can often become growth opportunities.

The second circle represents the team's view of how customers perceive the company's offerings (seen on the top left). The extent to which the two circles overlap indicates how well the company's offerings are fulfilling customers' needs.

The third circle represents the strategists' view of how customers perceive the offerings of the company's competitors.

Each area within the circles is important, but areas A, B, and C are critical to identifying and building a real value-based competitive advantage. The planning team should ask questions about each:

- *Circle A:* How big and sustainable are our advantages? Are they based on distinctive capabilities?
- *Circle B:* Are we delivering effectively in the area of parity?
- *Circle C:* How can we counter our competitors' advantages?

As Urbany and Davis explain, the team should form hypotheses about the company's competitive advantages and test them by asking customers. The process can yield surprising insights, such as how much opportunity for growth exists in the white space (E). Another insight might be what value the company or its competitors create that customers do not need (D, F, or G). For example, Zeneca Ag Products discovered that one of its most important distributors would be willing to do more business with the firm only if Zeneca eliminated the time-consuming promotional programs that its managers thought were an essential part of their value proposition.

But the biggest surprise is often that area A, envisioned as huge by the company, turns out to be quite small in the eyes of the customer. One important contribution that the next internal analysis technique, the resource-based view of the firm, can make in this regard is to help provide an in-depth method to more thoroughly identify and examine a firm's existing or potential competitive advantages. Let's examine the resource-based view.

RESOURCE-BASED VIEW OF THE FIRM

Toyota versus Ford is a competitive situation virtually all of us recognize. Stock analysts look at the two and conclude that Toyota is the clear leader. They cite Toyota's superiority in tangible assets (newer factories worldwide, R&D facilities, computerization, cash, etc.) and intangible assets (reputation, brand name awareness, quality-control culture, global business system, etc.). They also mention that Toyota leads Ford in several capabilities to make use of these assets effectively—managing distribution globally, influencing labor and supplier relations, managing franchise relations, marketing savvy, and speed of decision making to take quick advantage of changing global conditions are just a few that are frequently mentioned. The combination of capabilities and assets, most analysts conclude, creates several competencies that give Toyota key competitive advantages over Ford that are durable and not easily imitated.

resource-based view
A method of analyzing and identifying a firm's strategic advantages based on examining its distinct combination of assets, skills, capabilities, and intangibles as an organization.

The Toyota–Ford situation provides a useful illustration for understanding several concepts central to the **resource-based view** (RBV) of the firm. The RBV is a method of analyzing and identifying a firm's strategic advantages based on examining its distinct combination of assets, skills, capabilities, and intangibles as an organization. The RBV's underlying premise is that firms differ in fundamental ways because each firm possesses a unique "bundle" of resources—tangible and intangible assets and organizational capabilities to make use of those assets. Each firm develops competencies from these resources, and, when developed especially well, these become the source of the firm's competitive advantages. Toyota's decision to enter global markets locally and regularly invest in or build newer factory locations in those global markets has given Toyota a competitive advantage analysts estimate Ford has lost and will take at least 20 years or longer, if ever, to match. Toyota's strategy for the past 15 years was based in part on the identification of these resources and the development of them into a distinctive competence—a sustained competitive advantage.

Core Competencies

core competence
A capability or skill that a firm emphasizes and excels in doing while in pursuit of its overall mission.

Executives charting the strategy of their business have more recently concentrated their thinking on the notion of a "core competence." A **core competence** is a capability or skill that a firm emphasizes and excels in doing while in pursuit of its overall mission. Core competencies that differ from those found in competing firms would be considered *distinctive competencies*. Apple's competencies in pulling together available technologies and others' software and combining this with their own product design skills and new-product introduction prowess result in an innovation competence that is different and distinct from any firm against which Apple competes. Toyota's pervasive organizationwide pursuit of quality; Wendy's systemwide emphasis on and ability to provide fresh meat daily; and the University of Phoenix's ability to provide comprehensive educational options for working adults worldwide are all examples of competencies that are unique to these firms and distinctive when compared to their competitors.

Distinctive competencies that are identified and nurtured throughout the firm, allowing it to execute effectively so as to provide products or services to customers that are superior to competitor's offerings, become the basis for a lasting *competitive advantage*. Executives, enthusiastic about the notion that their job as strategists was to identify and leverage core competencies into distinctive ones that create sustainable competitive advantage, encountered difficulty applying the concept because of the generality of its level of analysis. The RBV emerged as a way to make the core competency notion and thought process more focused and measurable—creating a very important, and more meaningful, tool for internal analysis. Let's look at the basic concepts underlying the RBV.

Three Basic Resources: Tangible Assets, Intangible Assets, and Organizational Capabilities

The RBV's ability to create a more focused, measurable approach to internal analysis starts with its delineation of three basic types of resources, some of which may become the building blocks for distinctive competencies. These resources are defined below and illustrated in Exhibit 6.8.

tangible assets
The most easily identified assets, often found on a firm's balance sheet. They include production facilities, raw materials, financial resources, real estate, and computers.

Tangible assets are the easiest "resources" to identify and are often found on a firm's balance sheet. They include production facilities, raw materials, financial resources, real estate, and computers. Tangible assets are the physical and financial means a company uses to provide value to its customers.

intangible assets
A firm's assets that you cannot touch or see but that are very often critical in creating competitive advantage: brand names, company reputation, organizational morale, technical knowledge, patents and trademarks, and accumulated experience within an organization.

Intangible assets are "resources" such as brand names, company reputation, organizational morale, technical knowledge, patents and trademarks, and accumulated experience within an organization. While they are not assets that you can touch or see, they are very often critical in creating competitive advantage.

organizational capabilities
Skills (the ability and ways of combining assets, people, and processes) that a company uses to transform inputs into outputs.

Organizational capabilities are not specific "inputs" like tangible or intangible assets; rather, they are the skills—the ability and ways of combining assets, people, and processes—that a company uses to transform inputs into outputs. Apple pioneered and has subsequently leveraged its iPod and iTunes success into a major leadership position in digitalized music, entertainment, and communication on a global basis for individual consumers. Microsoft and others have attempted to copy Apple, but remain far behind Apple's diverse organizational capabilities. Apple has subsequently revolutionized its own iPod, using it to automate and customize a whole new level of entertainment capability that combines assets, people, and processes throughout and beyond the Apple organization. Finely developed capabilities, such as Apple's Internet-based, customer-friendly iPod/iTunes system, can be a source of sustained competitive advantage. They enable a firm to take the same input factors as rivals (such as Microsoft, HP, or Dell) and convert them into products and services, either with greater efficiency in the process or greater quality in the output, or both.

What Makes a Resource Valuable?

Once managers identify their firm's tangible assets, intangible assets, and organizational capabilities, the RBV applies a set of guidelines to determine which of those resources represent strengths or weaknesses—which resources generate core competencies that are

EXHIBIT 6.8
Examples of Different "Resources"

Source: From R.M. Grant, *Contemporary Strategy Analysis,* Blackwell Publishing, 2001, p. 140. Reprinted with permission of Wiley-Blackwell.

Tangible Assets	Intangible Assets	Organizational Capabilities
Hampton Inn's reservation system	Budweiser's brand name	Travelocity's customer service P&G's management training program
Toyota Motor Company's cash reserves	Apple's reputation	Wal-Mart's purchasing and inbound logistics
Georgia Pacific's land holdings	Nike's advertising with LeBron James	Google's product-development processes
FedEx's plane fleet	Brain Williams as NBC's *Evening News* anchor	Coke's global distribution coordination
Coca-Cola's Coke formula	eBay's management team Goldman Sach's culture	3M's innovation process

Classifying and Assessing the Firm's Resources

Resource	Relevant Characteristics	Key Indicators
Tangible Resources		
Financial resources	The firm's borrowing capacity and its internal funds generation determine its resilience and capacity for investment.	• Debt/equity ratio • Operating cash flow/free cash flow • Credit rating
Physical resources	Physical resources constrain the firm's set of production possibilities and impact its cost position. Key characteristics include • The size, location, technical sophistication, and flexibility of plant and equipment • Location and alternative uses for land and buildings • Reserves of raw materials	• Market values of fixed assets • Vintage of capital equipment • Scale of plants • Flexibility of fixed assets
Intangible Resources		
Technological resources	Intellectual property: patent portfolio, copyright, trade secrets Resources for innovation: research facilities, technical and scientific employees	• Number and significance of patents • Revenue from licensing patents and copyrights • R&D staff as a percent of total employment • Number and location of research facilities
Reputation	Reputation with customers through the ownership of brands and trademarks; established relationships with customers; the reputation of the firm's products and services for quality and reliability. The reputation of the company with suppliers (including component suppliers, banks and financiers, employees and potential employees), with government and government agencies, and with the community.	• Brand recognition • Brand equity • Percent of repeat buying • Objective measures of comparative product performance (e.g., Consumers' Association ratings, J. D. Power ratings) • Surveys of corporate reputation (e.g., *BusinessWeek*)

sources of sustained competitive advantage. These RBV guidelines derive from the idea that resources are more valuable when they

1. Are *critical to* being able to *meet a customer's need* better than other alternatives.
2. Are *scarce*—few others if any possess that resource or skill to the degree you do.
3. *Drive* a key portion of overall *profits,* in a manner controlled by your firm.
4. Are *durable* or sustainable over time.

Before proceeding to explain each basis for making resources valuable, we suggest that you keep in mind a simple, useful idea: resources are most valuable when they meet all four of these guidelines. We return to this point after we explain each guideline more thoroughly.

RBV Guideline 1: Is the resource or skill critical to fulfilling a customer's need better than that of the firm's competitors?

Two restaurants offer similar food, at similar prices, but one has a location much more convenient to downtown offices than the other. The tangible asset, location, helps fulfill daytime workers' lunch-eating needs better than its competitor, resulting in greater profitability and sales volume for the conveniently located restaurant. Wal-Mart redefined discount retailing and outperformed the industry in profitability by 4.5 percent of sales—a 200 percent improvement. Four resources—store locations, brand recognition, employee loyalty, and sophisticated inbound logistics—allowed Wal-Mart to fulfill customer needs much better and more cost effectively than Kmart and other discount retailers. In both of these examples, *it is important to recognize that only resources that contributed to competitive superiority were valuable.* At the same time, other resources such as the restaurant's menu and specific products or parking space at Wal-Mart were essential to doing business but contributed little to competitive advantage because they did not help fulfill customer needs better than those of the firm's key competitors.

RBV Guideline 2: Is the resource scarce? Is it in short supply or not easily substituted for or imitated?

Short Supply   When a resource is scarce, it is more valuable. When a firm possesses a resource and few if any others do, and it is central to fulfilling customers' needs, then it can become the basis of a competitive advantage for the firm. Literal physical scarcity is perhaps the most obvious way a resource might meet this guideline. Very limited natural resources, a unique location, skills that are truly rare—all represent obvious types of scarce resource situations.

Availability of Substitutes   We discussed the threat of substitute products in Chapter 4 as part of the five forces model for examining industry profitability. This basic idea can be taken further and used to gauge the scarcity-based value of particular resources. Whole Foods has been an exciting growth company for several years, focused exclusively on selling wholesome, organic food. The basic idea was to offer food grown organically, without pesticides or manipulation, in a convenient grocery atmosphere. Investors were excited about this concept because of the processed, nonorganic foods offered by virtually every existing grocery chain. Unfortunately for their more recent investors, substitutes for Whole Foods's offerings are becoming easily available from several grocery chains and regional organic chains. Publix, Harris -Teeter, and even Wal-Mart are easily adapting their grocery operations to offer organic fare. With little change to their existing facilities and operational resources, these companies are quickly creating alternatives to Whole Foods's offerings if not offering some of the same items, cheaper. So some worry about the long-term impact on Whole Foods. Investors have seen the value of their Whole Foods's stock decline as substitute resources and capabilities are readily created by existing and new entrants into the organic grocery sectors.

Imitation   A resource that competitors can readily copy can only generate temporary value. It is "scarce" for only a short time. It cannot generate a long-term competitive advantage. When Wendy's first emerged, it was the only major hamburger chain with a drive-through window. This unique organizational capability was part of a "bundle" of resources that allowed Wendy's to provide unique value to its target customers: young adults seeking convenient food service. But once this resource, or organizational capability, proved valuable to fast-food customers, every fast-food chain copied the feature. Then Wendy's continued success was built on other resources that generated other distinctive competencies.

The scarcity that comes with an absence of imitation seldom lasts forever, as the Wendy's example illustrates. Competitors will match or better any resource as soon as they can. It should be obvious, then, that the firm's ability to forestall this eventuality is very important. So how does a firm create resource scarcity by making resources hard to imitate? The RBV identifies four characteristics, called **isolating mechanisms,** that make resources difficult to imitate:

isolating mechanisms
Characteristics that make resources difficult to imitate. In the RBV context these are physically unique resources, path-dependent resources, causal ambiguity, and economic deterrence.

• *Physically unique resources* are virtually impossible to imitate. A one-of-a-kind real estate location, mineral rights, and patents are examples of resources that cannot be imitated. Disney's Mickey Mouse copyright or Winter Park, Colorado's Iron Horse resort possess physical uniqueness. While many strategists claim that resources are physically unique, this is seldom true. Rather, other characteristics are typically what make most resources difficult to imitate.

• *"Path-dependent" resources* are very difficult to imitate because of the difficult "path" another firm must follow to create the resource. These are resources that cannot be instantaneously acquired but rather must be created over time in a manner that is frequently very expensive and always difficult to accelerate. Google's creation of proprietary search algorithms; interlocking and directly targeted online advertising; very easy to use, and also interwined, e-mail services; and an extraordinary environment to attract and retain the world's top talent have combined to create a combination of path-dependent resources that are very difficult for even the wealthiest software and Internet companies worldwide to easily emulate, acquire, or accelerate. It will take years for any competitor to develop the expertise, infrastructure, reputation, and capabilities to compete effectively with Google. Coca-Cola's brand name, Gerber Baby Food's reputation for quality, and Steinway's expertise in piano manufacture would take competitors many years and millions of dollars to match. Consumers' many years of experience drinking Coke or using Gerber or playing a Steinway would also need to be matched.

• *Causal ambiguity* is a third way resources can be very difficult to imitate. This refers to situations in which it is difficult for competitors to understand exactly how a firm has created the advantage it enjoys. Competitors can't figure out exactly what the uniquely valuable resource is or how resources are combined to create the competitive advantage. Causally ambiguous resources are often organizational capabilities that arise from subtle combinations of tangible and intangible assets and culture, processes, and organizational attributes the firm possesses. Southwest Airlines has regularly faced competition from major and regional airlines, with some like United and Continental eschewing their traditional approach and attempting to compete by using their own version of the Southwest approach—same planes, routes, gate procedures, number of attendants, and so on. They have yet to succeed. The most difficult thing to replicate is Southwest's "personality," or culture of fun, family, and frugal yet focused services and attitude. Just how that works is hard for United and Continental to figure out.

EXHIBIT 6.9
Degree to Which Resource Can Be Imitated

Source: © RCTrust LLC, 2010.

	Easily Imitated	Possibly Imitated	Hard to Imitate	Cannot be Imitated
Examples	Utilities	Skilled employees	Image/reputation	Unique location
	Cash	Additional capacity	Customer satisfaction	Patents
	Common raw materials	Economies of scale	Employee attitudes	Unique licenses/assets
Specific example: Google	Electricity Server farms	Smart people Larger server farms	Search leadership Brand image	Patented search algorithms "Google"

- *Economic deterrence* is a fourth source of inimitability. This usually involves large capital investments in capacity to provide products or services in a given market that are scale sensitive. It occurs when a competitor understands the resources that provide a competitive advantage and may even have the capacity to imitate, but chooses not to because of the limited market size that realistically would not support two players the size of the first mover.

While we may be inclined to think of the ability to imitate a resource as a yes-or-no situation, imitation is more accurately measured on a continuum that reflects difficulty and time. Exhibit 6.9 illustrates such a continuum. Some resources may have multiple imitation deterrents. For example, 3M's reputation for innovativeness may involve path dependencies and causal ambiguity.

RBV Guideline 3: Appropriability: Who actually gets the profit created by a resource?

Warren Buffett is known worldwide as one of the most successful investors of the last 25 years. One of his legendary investments was the Walt Disney Company, which he once said he liked "because the Mouse does not have an agent."[5] What he was really saying was that Disney owned the Mickey Mouse copyright, and all profits from that valuable resource went directly to Disney. Other competitors in the "entertainment" industry generated similar profits from their competing offerings, for example, movies, but they often "captured" substantially less of those profits because of the amounts that had to be paid to well-known actors or directors or other entertainment contributors seen as the real creators of the movie's value.

Disney's eventual acquisition of Pixar illustrates just the opposite situation for the home of the Mouse. Pixar's expertise in digital animation had proven key to the impressive success of several major animation films released by Disney in the past several years. While Disney apparently thought its name and distribution clout justified its sizable share of the profits this five-year joint venture generated, Steve Jobs and his Pixar team felt otherwise. Pixar's assessment was that their capabilities were key drivers of the huge profits by *Ants* and *Finding Nemo*, leading them not to renew their Disney partnership. Pixar's unmatched digitalization animation expertise quickly "appropriated" the profits generated by this key competitive advantage, and Disney Studios struggled to catch up. Disney eventually solved the dilemma by acquiring Pixar at a handsome premium. The movie *Cars* soon followed.[6]

Sports teams, investment services, and consulting businesses are other examples of companies that generate sizable profits based on resources (e.g., key people, skills, contacts) that are not inextricably linked to the company and therefore do not allow the company to easily capture the profits. Superstar sports players can move from one team to another or command excessively high salaries, and this circumstance could arise in other personal services business situations. It could also occur when one firm joint ventures with another, sharing resources and capabilities and the profits that result. Sometimes restaurants or lodging facilities that are

---

[5] *The Harbus,* March 25, 1996, p. 12.
[6] "Disney Buys Pixar," *Money.CNN.com,* January 1, 2006.

franchisees of a national organization are frustrated by the fees they pay the franchisor each month and decide to leave the organization and go "independent." They often find, to their dismay, that the business declines significantly. The value of the franchise name, reservation system, and brand recognition is critical in generating the profits of the business.

RBV Guideline 4: Durability: How rapidly will the resource depreciate?

The slower a resource depreciates, the more valuable it is. Tangible assets, such as commodities or capital, can have their depletion measured. Intangible resources, such as brand names or organizational capabilities, present a much more difficult depreciation challenge. The Coca-Cola brand has continued to appreciate, whereas technical know-how in various computer technologies depreciates rapidly. In the increasingly hypercompetitive global economy of the twenty-first century, distinctive competencies and competitive advantages can fade quickly, making the notion of durability a critical test of the value of key resources and capabilities. Some believe that this reality makes well-articulated visions and associated cultures within organizations potentially the most important contributor to long-term survival.[7]

Using the Resource-Based View in Internal Analysis

To use the RBV in internal analysis, a firm must first identify and evaluate its resources to find those that provide the basis for future competitive advantage. This process involves defining the various resources the firm possesses and examining them based on the preceding discussion to gauge which resources truly have strategic value. It is usually helpful in this undertaking to

- *Disaggregate resources*—break them down into more specific competencies—rather than stay with broad categorizations. Saying that Domino's Pizza has better marketing skills than Pizza Hut conveys little information. But dividing that into subcategories such as advertising that, in turn, can be divided into national advertising, local promotions, and coupons allows for a more measurable assessment. Exhibit 6.10 provides a useful illustration of this at the United Kingdom's largest full-service restaurant operator—Whitbread's Restaurant.
- *Utilize a functional perspective.* Looking at different functional areas of the firm, disaggregating tangible and intangible assets as well as organizational capabilities that are present, can begin to uncover important value-building resources and activities that deserve further analysis. Appendix 6A lists a variety of functional area resources and activities that deserve consideration.
- *Look at organizational processes* and combinations of resources and not only at isolated assets or capabilities. While disaggregation is critical, you must also take a creative, gestalt look at what competencies the firm possesses or has the potential to possess that might generate competitive advantage.
- *Use the value chain approach* to uncover organizational capabilities, activities, and processes that are valuable potential sources of competitive advantage.

Once the resources are identified, managers apply the four RBV guidelines for uncovering "valuable" resources. The objective for managers at this point is to identify resources and capabilities that are valuable for most if not all of the reasons our guidelines suggest a resource can be valuable.

If a resource creates the ability to meet a unique customer need, it has value. But if it is not scarce, or if it is easily imitated, it would be unwise to build a firm's strategy on that resource or capability unless that strategy included plans to build scarcity or inimitability into it. If a

---

[7] James C. Collins, *Good to Great: Why Some Companies Make the Leap . . . and Others Don't* (New York: HarperCollins, 2001).

EXHIBIT 6.10
Disaggregating Whitbread Restaurant's Customer Service Resource

Source: Andrew Campbell and Kathleen Sommers-Luchs, *Core Competency-Based Strategy* (London: International Thomson, 1997).

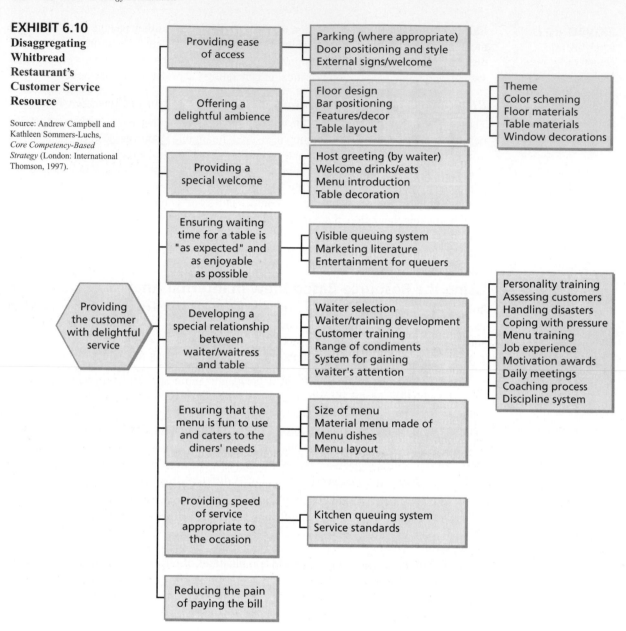

resource provided the basis for meeting a unique need, was scarce, was not easily imitated, and was easily sustainable over time, managers would be attracted to build a strategy on it more than likely. Our example of Pixar's relationship with Disney earlier in this chapter would seem to suggest this was Pixar's position early in its joint venture with Disney. Yet even with all of those sources confirming a very high value in its digital animation expertise and intellectual property resources, Pixar was not "appropriating" the share of the animation movie profits that were attributable to those resources. Pixar was fortunate: it had the choice not to renew its five-year contract with Disney, and so it did. That eventually led Disney to pay a premium price to acquire Pixar, to regain the strategic value of Pixar's unique resources.

The key point here is that applying RBV analysis should focus on identifying resources that contain all sources of value identified in our four guidelines. Consider the diagram in

EXHIBIT 6.11
Applying the Resource-Based View to Identify the Best Sources of Competitive Advantage

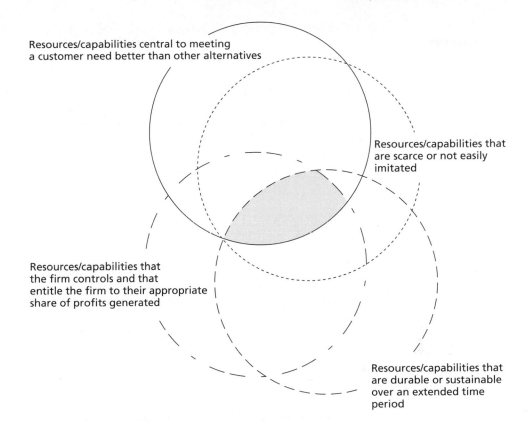

Resources/capabilities central to meeting a customer need better than other alternatives

Resources/capabilities that are scarce or not easily imitated

Resources/capabilities that the firm controls and that entitle the firm to their appropriate share of profits generated

Resources/capabilities that are durable or sustainable over an extended time period

Exhibit 6.11. Each circle in that diagram represents one way resources have value. The area where all circles intersect or overlap would represent resources that derive value in all four ways. Such resources are the ones managers applying the RBV should seek to identify. They are powerful sources around which to build competitive advantage and craft successful strategies. And resources that possess some but not all sources of value become points of emphasis by a management team able to identify ways to build the missing source of value into that resource over time much like Pixar did in its relationship with Disney.

By using RBV, value chain analysis, three circles analysis, and SWOT analysis, firms are virtually certain to improve the quality of internal analysis undertaken to help craft a company's competitive strategy. Central to the success of each technique is the strategists' ability to make meaningful comparisons. The next section examines how meaningful comparisons can be made.

INTERNAL ANALYSIS: MAKING MEANINGFUL COMPARISONS

Managers need objective standards to use when examining internal resources and value-building activities. Whether applying the SWOT approach, VCA, or the RBV, strategists rely on three basic perspectives to evaluate how their firms stack up on internal capabilities. These three perspectives are discussed in this section.

Comparison with Past Performance

Strategists use the firm's historical experience as a basis for evaluating internal factors. Managers are most familiar with the internal capabilities and problems of their firms because they have been immersed in the financial, marketing, production, and R&D activities. Not surprisingly, a manager's assessment of whether a certain internal factor—such as production facilities, sales organization, financial capacity, control systems, or key personnel—is a strength or a weakness will be strongly influenced by his or her experience in connection with that factor. In the capital-intensive package delivery industry, for example, operating margin is a strategic internal factor affecting a firm's flexibility to add capacity. A few years ago, UPS managers viewed its declining operating margins (down from 12 percent to 9 percent by mid-decade) as a troubling weakness, limiting their flexibility to aggressively continue to expand their overnight air fleet. FedEx managers viewed a similar operating margin around the same time as a growing strength because it was a steady improvement and almost double its 5 percent level five years earlier.

Although historical experience can provide a relevant evaluation framework, strategists must avoid tunnel vision in making use of it. NEC, Japan's HP, initially dominated Japan's PC market with a 70 percent market share by using a proprietary hardware system, much higher screen resolution, powerful distribution channels, and a large software library from third-party vendors. Far from worried, Hajime Ikeda, manager of NEC's planning division at the time, was quoted as saying, "We don't hear complaints from our users." Soon, IBM, Apple, and HP filled the shelves in Japan's famous consumer electronics district, Akihabara. Hiroki Kamata, president of a Japanese computer research firm, reported that Japan's PC market, worth more than $50 billion, saw Apple, Dell, IBM, and HP with more market share than NEC because of better technology, software, and the restrictions created by NEC's proprietary technology. As NEC learned, using only historical experience as a basis for identifying strengths and weaknesses can prove dangerously inaccurate.

Benchmarking: Comparison with Competitors

A major focus in determining a firm's resources and competencies is comparison with existing (and potential) competitors. Firms in the same industry often have different marketing skills, financial resources, operating facilities and locations, technical know-how, brand images, levels of integration, managerial talent, and so on. These different internal resources can become relative strengths (or weaknesses) depending on the strategy a firm chooses. In choosing a strategy, managers should compare the firm's key internal capabilities with those of its rivals, thereby isolating its key strengths and weaknesses.

In the global tech-services industry, New York–based IBM and India–based Tata Consultancy Services are major rivals. Tata has focused on large American and European companies providing lower-cost information technology (IT) services and business process simplification consulting. IBM has taken a different strategy, focusing in on helping U.S. clients cut costs while helping emerging market customers build out their technology infrastructure. Tata's strength has become its ability to offer low-cost outsourcing options to large U.S. and European firms for their information system operation needs. IBM, with a personnel cost structure that would put it at a disadvantage versus Tata in this regard, has emphasized systems design and optimization of the latest technology infrastructure to make that system perform well—building on its technical skills and computer technology expertise where it maintains a relative strength. Interestingly, this has led to a situation where Tata generates half of its revenue from U.S. clients, while IBM generates 65 percent of its revenue overseas and is the largest seller of tech services in India. Managers in both Tata and IBM have built successful strategies, yet those strategies are fundamentally different. Benchmarking each other, they have identified ways to build on relative strengths while avoiding dependence on capabilities at which the other firm excels.[8]

[8] Steve Hamm, "IBM vs. Tata: Who's More American:" *BusinessWeek.com,* April 23, 2008.

benchmarking
Evaluating the sustainability of advantages against key competitors. Comparing the way a company performs a specific activity with a competitor or other company doing the same thing.

Benchmarking, or comparing the way "our" company performs a specific activity with a competitor or other company doing the same thing, has become a central concern of managers in quality commitment companies worldwide. Particularly as the value chain framework has taken hold in structuring internal analysis, managers seek to systematically benchmark the costs and results of the smallest value activities against relevant competitors or other useful standards because it has proven to be an effective way to continuously improve that activity.

Exhibit 6.12 shows Kodak highlighting a value chain activity in which it believes it excels, low-cost/high-quality inks, and using it to differentiate its recently introduced printer. Kodak is seeking to not only highlight its internal managerial benchmarking versus other ink-jet printer makers, notably Hewlett-Packard, but it is also taking a page out of benchmarking to touch a long-held raw nerve they believe millions of customers share—the shock and awe they feel every time they go to a store and buy a new printer cartridge for their HP, Canon, or Epson printer. They want to identify with and inform the average consumer looking for a credible alternative when "benchmarking" different solutions to their printer needs.

The ultimate objective in benchmarking is to identify the "best practices" in performing a value chain activity and to learn how lower costs, fewer defects, or other outcomes linked to excellence can be achieved. Companies committed to benchmarking attempt to isolate and identify where their costs or outcomes are out of line with what they identify as the best practices of competitors or other companies or organizations that undertake similar tasks. Once identified and studied, this allows managers to change what they do or how they do these activities to achieve the new best practices "benchmarks." General Electric sends managers to benchmark FedEx's customer service practices, seeking to compare and improve on its own practices within a diverse set of businesses none of which compete directly with FedEx. It earlier did the same thing with Motorola, leading it to embrace Motorola's Six Sigma program for quality control and continuous improvement.

Comparison with Success Factors in the Industry

Industry analysis (see Chapter 4) involves identifying the factors associated with successful participation in a given industry. As was true for the evaluation methods discussed earlier, the key determinants of success in an industry may be used to identify a firm's internal strengths and weaknesses. By scrutinizing industry competitors as well as customer needs, vertical industry structure, channels of distribution, costs, barriers to entry, availability of substitutes, and suppliers, a strategist seeks to determine whether a firm's current internal capabilities represent strengths or weaknesses in new competitive arenas. The discussion in Chapter 4 provides a useful framework—five industry forces—against which to examine a firm's potential strengths and weaknesses. General Cinema Corporation, the largest U.S. movie theater operator, determined that its internal skills in marketing, site analysis, creative financing, and management of geographically dispersed operations were key strengths relative to major success factors in the soft-drink bottling industry. This assessment proved accurate. Within 10 years after it entered the soft-drink bottling industry, General Cinema became the largest franchised bottler of soft drinks in the United States, handling Pepsi, 7UP, Dr Pepper, and Sunkist. Or consider large-scale discount retailing, where two key success factors in that industry are same-store sales growth and steady updating of store facilities or new locations. During the last decade, once-mighty Wal-Mart saw itself begin to fall behind its key rivals in same-store sales growth and age/quality of 60 percent of its U.S. stores. These two critical success factors drive and indicate the relative health of large discount retail firms. Firms with solid same-store sales growth

The Ink Wars: Kodak Takes Benchmarking Public versus Hewlett-Packard

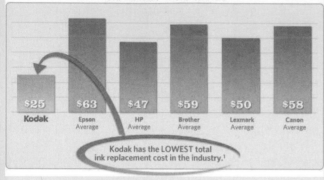

Save more every time you refill your printer with ink.
$9.99 black MSRP $14.99 color MSRP

| $25 Kodak | $63 Epson Average | $47 HP Average | $59 Brother Average | $50 Lexmark Average | $58 Canon Average |

Kodak has the LOWEST total ink replacement cost in the industry.[1]

Ink Value Comparison Chart

Kodak's promise to you is that you'll save up to 50% on everything you print compared to similar consumer inkjet printers[10]. View the information below for details on ink yield, as verified by third party test and quality assurance professionals.

What you get for every $5 (USD) spent on ink[6]

Black text documents[7]	Color graphics & text documents[7]	4 x 6 in. Color Photos[8]
Kodak 221 / Average of comparable consumer inkjet printers 76	Kodak 73 / Average of comparable consumer inkjet printers 35	Kodak 52 / Average of comparable consumer inkjet printers 16
2.3¢ per page / 6.6¢ per page	6.9¢ per page / 14.4¢ per page	9.6¢ per photo / 32.1¢ per photo

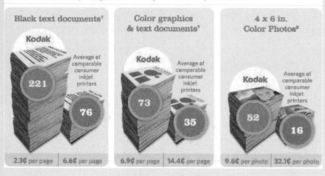

Look how much more you get a year for just $70.[5]

| Kodak | HP Average | Epson Average | Brother Average | Lexmark Average | Canon Average |
| 1500 photos & documents | 574 photos & documents | 541 photos & documents | 782 photos & documents | 308 photos & documents | 669 photos & documents |

— Select Printer Models Tested —

Kodak has long been a world leader in film processing, but it's a new player in the ink-jet printer industry, facing intense competition from entrenched players Hewlett-Packard, Epson, and Canon. Forgoing conventional wisdom based on the Gillette model to "give away" its printer and make money on consumables, the ink cartridges, Kodak seeks to differentiate itself and gain market share by tapping into consumer dissatisfaction with high ink prices by selling its printers for slightly more than the competition while selling its cartridges for less than half the price. Kodak is sharing its benchmarking results, suggesting its EasyShare printers have a lower total cost of ownership than competitors' models and that users will save substantially on consumables over the life of the printer.

Source: Reprinted with permission of Kodak, www.kodak.com.

indicate wise choices in location, attractiveness of their stores, and the merchandise inside them. Likewise, aging and probably substandard store facilities are typically not as efficient as newer ones, nor are they as inviting to shoppers. So Wal-Mart, Target, and other discount retailers conduct internal analyses in part by comparing themselves on these two

EXHIBIT 6.13
Illustration of the
Product Life Cycle

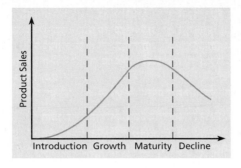

(and surely others) critical success factors to interpret their strength or weakness relative to factors that drive industry success.

Product Life Cycle

Product life cycle (PLC) is one way to identify success factors against which executives can evaluate their firm's competencies relative to its key product or products. The **product life cycle** is a concept that describes a product's sales, profitability, and competencies that are

product life cycle
A concept that describes a product's sales, profitability, and competencies that are key drivers of the success of that product as it moves through a sequence of stages from development, introduction to growth, maturity, decline, and eventual removal from a market.

key drivers of the success of that product as it moves through a sequence of stages from development, introduction to growth, maturity, decline, and eventual removal from a market. Exhibit 6.13 illustrates the "typical" product life cycle.

Core competencies associated with success are thought to vary across different stages of the product life cycle. Those competencies might include the following.

Introduction Stage

During this stage the firm needs competence in building product awareness and market development along with the resources to support initial losses:

- Ability to create product awareness.
- Good channel relationships in ways to get the product introduced quickly, gaining a first-mover advantage.
- Premium pricing to "skim" profitability if few competitors exist.
- Solid relationships with and access to trendsetting early adopters.
- Financial resources to absorb an initial cash drain and lack of profitability.

Growth

During this stage market growth accelerates rapidly, with the firm seeking to build brand awareness and establish/increase market share:

- Brand awareness and ability to build brand.
- Advertising skills and resources to back them.
- Product features that differentiate versus increased competitive offerings.
- Establishing and stabilizing market shares.
- Access to multiple distribution channels.
- Ability to add additional features.

Maturity

This stage sees growth in sales slow significantly, along with increased competition and similar product offerings leading the firm to need competencies that allow it to defend its market share while maximizing profit:

- Sustained brand awareness.
- Ability to differentiate products and features.
- Resources to initiate or sustain price wars.
- Operating advantages to improve slimming margins.
- Judgment to know whether to stay in or exit saturated market segments.

Decline

At this point the product and its competitors start to experience declining sales and increased pressure on margins. Competencies needed are:

- Ability to withstand intense price-cutting.
- Brand strength to allow reduced marketing.
- Cost cutting capacity and slack to allow it.
- Good supplier relationships to gain cost concessions.
- Innovation skills to create new products or "re-create" existing ones.

The PLC is an interesting concept or framework against which executives might gauge the strength of relevant competencies. Caution is necessary in its use beyond that purpose, however. In reality, very few products follow exactly the cycle portrayed in the PLC model. The length in each stage can vary, the length and nature of the PLC for any particular product can vary dramatically, and it is not easy to tell exactly what stage a product might be in at any given time. Not all products go through each stage. Some, for example, go from introduction to decline. And movement from one stage to the next can be accelerated by strategies or tactics executives emphasize. For example, price-cutting can accelerate the movement from maturity to decline.

Product life cycles can describe a single product, a category of products, or an industry segment. Applying the basic idea to an industry segment (category of products) rather than a specific product has been a more beneficial adaptation of the PLC concept, providing executives with a conceptual tool to aid them in strategic analysis and choice in the context of the evolution of an industry segment in which their firm competes. So we examine the concept of stages of evolution of an industry segment or category of products as a tool of strategic analysis and choice in Chapter 8.

Summary

This chapter looked at several ways managers achieve greater objectivity and rigor as they analyze their company's internal resources and capabilities. Managers often start their internal analysis with questions like, How well is the current strategy working? What is our current situation? What are our strengths and weaknesses? SWOT analysis is a traditional approach that has been in use for decades to help structure managers' pursuit of answers to these questions. A logical approach still used by many managers today, SWOT analysis has limitations linked to the depth of its analysis and the risk of overlooking key considerations.

Three techniques for internal analysis have emerged that overcome some of the limitations of SWOT analysis, offering more comprehensive approaches that can help managers identify and assess their firm's internal resources and capabilities in a more systematic, objective, and measurable manner. Value chain analysis has managers look at and disaggregate their business as a chain of activities that occur in a sequential manner to create the products or services they sell. The value chain approach breaks down the firm's activities into primary and support categories of activities, then breaks these down further into specific types of activities with the objective to disaggregate activity into as many meaningful subdivisions as possible. Once done, managers attempt to attribute costs to each. Doing this gives managers very distinct ways of isolating the things they do well and not so well, and it isolates activities that are truly key in meeting customer needs—true potential sources of competitive advantage. Three circles analysis provides an additional technique, simple yet insightful, for applying a customer needs perspective that should help improve the quality of a management team's internal analysis in understanding potential value-based sources of competitive advantage at the firm's disposal.

The third approach covered in this chapter was the resource-based view (RBV). RBV is based on the premise that firms build competitive advantage based on the unique resources, skills, and capabilities they control or develop, which can become the basis of unique, sustainable competitive advantages that allow them to craft successful competitive strategies. The RBV provides a useful conceptual frame to first inventory a firm's potential competitive advantages among its tangible assets, intangible assets, and its organizational capabilities. Once inventoried, the RBV provides four fundamental guidelines that managers can use to "value" these resources and capabilities. Those with major value, defined as ones that are valuable for several reasons, become the bases for building strategies linked to sustainable competitive advantages.

Finally, this chapter covered three ways objectivity and realism are enhanced when managers use meaningful standards for comparison regardless of the particular analytical framework they employ in internal analysis. This chapter is followed by two appendixes. The first provides a useful inventory of the types of activities in different functional areas of a firm that can be sources of competitive advantage. The second appendix covers traditional financial analysis to serve as a refresher and reminder about this basic internal analysis tool.

When matched with management's environmental analyses and mission priorities, the process of internal analysis provides the critical foundation for strategy formulation. Armed with an accurate, thorough, and timely internal analysis, managers are in a better position to formulate effective strategies. The next chapter describes basic strategy alternatives that any firm may consider.

Key Terms

benchmarking, *p. 163*
core competence, *p. 153*
intangible assets, *p. 154*
isolating mechanisms, *p. 157*
opportunity, *p. 140*
organizational capabilities, *p. 154*

primary activities, *p. 146*
product life cycle, *p. 165*
resource-based view, *p. 153*
strength, *p. 141*
SWOT analysis, *p. 140*
support activities, *p. 146*

tangible assets, *p. 154*
threat, *p. 140*
three circles analysis, *p. 151*
value chain, *p. 145*
value chain analysis, *p. 145*
weakness, *p. 141*

Questions for Discussion

1. Describe SWOT analysis as a way to guide internal analysis. How does this approach reflect the basic strategic management process?
2. What are potential weaknesses of SWOT analysis?
3. Describe the difference between primary and support activities using value chain analysis.
4. How is VCA different from SWOT analysis?
5. What is three circles analysis, and how might it help doing internal analysis?
6. What is the resource-based view? Give examples of three different types of resources.
7. What are three ways resources become more valuable? Provide an example of each.
8. Explain how you might use VCA, RBV, three circles analysis, and SWOT analysis to get a better sense of what might be a firm's key building blocks for a successful strategy.
9. Attempt to apply SWOT, VCA, RBV, and three circles analysis to yourself and your career aspirations. What are your major strengths and weaknesses? How might you use your knowledge of these strengths and weaknesses to develop your future career plans?

Chapter 6 Appendix A

Key Resources across Functional Areas

MARKETING

Firm's products-services: breadth of product line
Concentration of sales in a few products or to a few customers
Ability to gather needed information about markets
Market share or submarket shares
Product-service mix and expansion potential: life cycle of key products; profit-sales balance in product-service
Channels of distribution: number, coverage, and control
Effective sales organization: knowledge of customer needs
Internet usage; Web presence; e-commerce
Product-service image, reputation, and quality
Imaginativeness, efficiency, and effectiveness of sales promotion and advertising
Pricing strategy and pricing flexibility
Procedures for digesting market feedback and developing new products, services, or markets
After-sale service and follow-up
Goodwill—brand loyalty

FINANCIAL AND ACCOUNTING

Ability to raise short-term capital
Ability to raise long-term capital; debt-equity
Corporate-level resources (multibusiness firm)
Cost of capital relative to that of industry and competitors
Tax considerations
Relations with owners, investors, and stockholders
Leverage position; capacity to utilize alternative financial strategies, such as lease or sale and leaseback
Cost of entry and barriers to entry
Price-earnings ratio
Working capital; flexibility of capital structure
Effective cost control; ability to reduce cost
Financial size
Efficiency and effectiveness of accounting system for cost, budget, and profit planning

PRODUCTION, OPERATIONS, TECHNICAL

Raw materials' cost and availability, supplier relationships
Inventory control systems; inventory turnover
Location of facilities; layout and utilization of facilities
Economies of scale
Technical efficiency of facilities and utilization of capacity
Effectiveness of subcontracting use
Degree of vertical integration; value added and profit margin
Efficiency and cost-benefit of equipment

Effectiveness of operation control procedures: design, scheduling, purchasing, quality control, and efficiency
Costs and technological competencies relative to those of industry and competitors
Research and development—technology—innovation
Patents, trademarks, and similar legal protection

PERSONNEL

Management personnel
Employees' skill and morale
Labor relations costs compared with those of industry and competitors
Efficiency and effectiveness of personnel policies
Effectiveness of incentives used to motivate performance
Ability to level peaks and valleys of employment
Employee turnover and absenteeism
Specialized skills
Experience

QUALITY MANAGEMENT

Relationship with suppliers, customers
Internal practices to enhance quality of products and services
Procedures for monitoring quality

INFORMATION SYSTEMS

Timeliness and accuracy of information about sales, operations, cash, and suppliers
Relevance of information for tactical decisions
Information to manage quality issues: customer service
Ability of people to use the information that is provided
Linkages to suppliers and customers

ORGANIZATION AND GENERAL MANAGEMENT

Organizational structure
Firm's image and prestige
Firm's record in achieving objectives
Organization of communication system
Overall organizational control system (effectiveness and utilization)
Organizational climate; organizational culture
Use of systematic procedures and techniques in decision making
Top-management skill, capabilities, and interest
Strategic planning system
Intraorganizational synergy (multibusiness firms)

Using Financial Analysis

One of the most important tools for assessing the strength of an organization within its industry is financial analysis. Managers, investors, and creditors all employ some form of this analysis as the beginning point for their financial decision making. Investors use financial analyses in making decisions about whether to buy or sell stock, and creditors use them in deciding whether or not to lend. They provide managers with a measurement of how the company is doing in comparison with its performance in past years and with the performance of competitors in the industry.

Although financial analysis is useful for decision making, some weaknesses should be noted. Any picture that it provides of the company is based on past data. Although trends may be noteworthy, this picture should not automatically be assumed to be applicable to the future. In addition, the analysis is only as good as the accounting procedures that have provided the information. When making comparisons between companies, one should keep in mind the variability of accounting procedures from firm to firm.

There are four basic groups of financial ratios: liquidity, leverage, activity, and profitability.

Depicted in Exhibit 6.B1 are the specific ratios calculated for each of the basic groups. Liquidity and leverage ratios represent an assessment of the risk of the firm. Activity and profitability ratios are measures of the return generated by the assets of the firm. The interaction between certain groups of ratios is indicated by arrows.

Typically, two common financial statements are used in financial analyses: the balance sheet and the income statement. Exhibit 6.B2 is a balance sheet and Exhibit 6.B3 an income statement for the ABC Company. These statements will be used to illustrate the financial analyses.

LIQUIDITY RATIOS

Liquidity ratios are used as indicators of a firm's ability to meet its short-term obligations. These obligations include any current liabilities, including currently maturing long-term debt. Current assets move through a normal cash cycle of inventories—sales—accounts receivable—cash. The firm then uses cash to pay off or reduce its current liabilities. The best-known liquidity ratio is the current ratio: current assets divided by current liabilities. For the ABC Company, the current ratio is calculated as follows:

$$\frac{\text{Current assets}}{\text{Current liabilities}} = \frac{\$4,125,000}{\$2,512,500} = 1.64 \ (2012)$$

$$= \frac{\$3,618,000}{\$2,242,250} = 1.161 \ (2011)$$

Most analysts suggest a current ratio of 2 to 3. A large current ratio is not necessarily a good sign; it may mean that an organization is not making the most efficient use of its assets. The optimum current ratio will vary from industry to industry, with the more volatile industries requiring higher ratios.

Because slow-moving or obsolescent inventories could overstate a firm's ability to meet short-term demands, the quick ratio is sometimes preferred to assess a firm's liquidity. The quick ratio is current assets minus inventories, divided by current liabilities. The quick ratio for the ABC Company is calculated as follows:

$$\frac{\text{Current assets} - \text{Inventories}}{\text{Current liabilities}} = \frac{\$1,950,000}{\$2,512,500} = 0.78 \ (2012)$$

$$= \frac{\$1,618,000}{\$2,242,250} = 0.72 \ (2011)$$

A quick ratio of approximately 1 would be typical for American industries. Although there is less variability in the quick ratio than in the current ratio, stable industries would be able to operate safely with a lower ratio.

LEVERAGE RATIOS

Leverage ratios identify the source of a firm's capital—owners or outside creditors. The term *leverage* refers to the fact that using capital with a fixed interest charge will "amplify" either profits or losses in relation to the equity of holders of common stock. The most commonly used ratio is total debt divided by total assets. Total debt includes current liabilities and long-term liabilities. This ratio is a measure of the percentage of total funds provided by debt. A total debt–total assets ratio higher than 0.5 is usually considered safe only for firms in stable industries.

$$\frac{\text{Total debt}}{\text{Total assets}} = \frac{\$3,862,500}{\$7,105,000} = 0.54 \ (2012)$$

$$= \frac{\$3,667,250}{\$6,393,000} = 0.57 \ (2011)$$

The ratio of long-term debt to equity is a measure of the extent to which sources of long-term financing are provided by creditors. It is computed by dividing long-term debt by the stockholders' equity:

$$\frac{\text{Long-term debt}}{\text{Equity}} = \frac{\$1,350,000}{\$3,242,500} = 0.42 \ (2012)$$

$$= \frac{\$1,425,000}{\$2,725,750} = 0.52 \ (2011)$$

EXHIBIT 6.B1 **Financial Ratios**

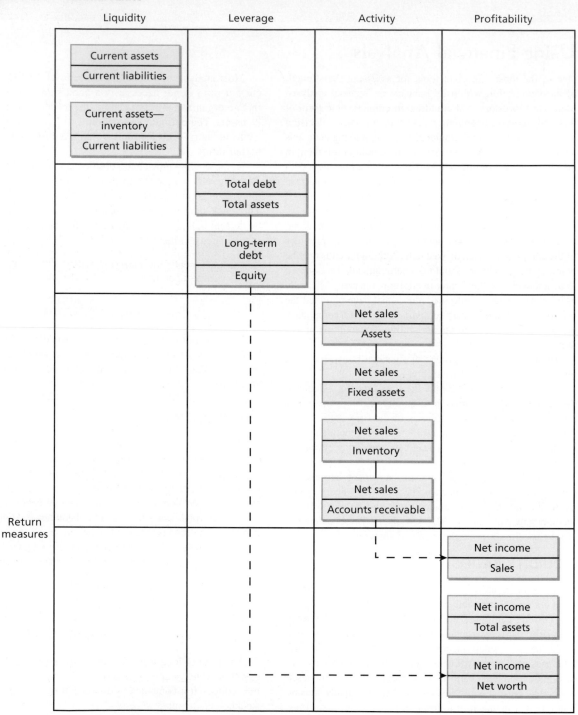

EXHIBIT 6.B2 ABC Company Balance Sheet as of December 31, 2011, and 2012

		2012		2011
Assets				
Current assets:				
Cash		$ 140,000		$ 115,000
Accounts receivable		1,760,000		1,440,000
Inventory		2,175,000		2,000,000
Prepaid expenses		50,000		63,000
Total current assets		4,125,000		3,618,000
Fixed assets:				
Long-term receivable		1,255,000		1,090,000
Property and plant	$2,037,000		$2,015,000	
Less: Accumulated depreciation	862,000		860,000	
Net property and plant		1,175,000		1,155,000
Other fixed assets		550,000		530,000
Total fixed assets		2,980,000		2,775,000
Total assets		$7,105,000		$6,393,000
Liabilities and Stockholders' Equity				
Current liabilities:				
Accounts payable		$1,325,000		$1,225,000
Bank loans payable		475,000		550,000
Accrued federal taxes		675,000		425,000
Current maturities (long-term debt)		17,500		26,000
Dividends payable		20,000		16,250
Total current liabilities		2,512,500		2,242,250
Long-term liabilities		1,350,000		1,425,000
Total liabilities		3,862,500		3,667,250
Stockholders' equity:				
Common stock				
(104,046 shares outstanding in 2012;				
101,204 shares outstanding in 2011)		44,500		43,300
Additional paid-in-capital		568,000		372,450
Retained earnings		2,630,000		2,310,000
Total stockholders' equity		3,242,500		2,725,750
Total liabilities and stockholders' equity		$7,105,000		$6,393,000

EXHIBIT 6.B3 ABC Company Income Statement for the years ending December 31, 2011, and 2012

		2012		2011
Net sales		$8,250,000		$8,000,000
Cost of goods sold	$5,100,000		$5,000,000	
Administrative expenses	1,750,000		1,680,000	
Other expenses	420,000		390,000	
Total		7,270,000		7,070,000
Earnings before interest and taxes		980,000		930,000
Less: Interest expense		210,000		210,000
Earnings before taxes		770,000		720,000
Less: Federal income taxes		360,000		325,000
Earnings after taxes (net income)		$ 410,000		$ 395,000
Common stock cash dividends		$ 90,000		$ 84,000
Addition to retained earnings		$ 320,000		$ 311,000
Earnings per common share		$ 3.940		$ 3.90
Dividends per common share		$ 0.865		$ 0.83

ACTIVITY RATIOS

Activity ratios indicate how effectively a firm is using its resources. By comparing revenues with the resources used to generate them, it is possible to establish an efficiency of operation. The asset turnover ratio indicates how efficiently management is employing total assets. Asset turnover is calculated by dividing sales by total assets. For the ABC Company, asset turnover is calculated as follows:

$$\text{Asset turnover} = \frac{\text{Sales}}{\text{Total assets}} = \frac{\$8,250,000}{\$7,105,000} = 1.16 \ (2012)$$

$$= \frac{\$8,000,0000}{\$6,393,000} = 1.25 \ (2011)$$

The ratio of sales to fixed assets is a measure of the turnover on plant and equipment. It is calculated by dividing sales by net fixed assets.

$$\frac{\text{Fixed asset}}{\text{turnover}} = \frac{\text{Sales}}{\text{Net fixed assets}} = \frac{\$8,250,000}{\$2,980,000} = 2.77 \ (2012)$$

$$= \frac{\$8,000,000}{\$2,775,000} = 2.88 \ (2011)$$

Industry figures for asset turnover will vary with capital-intensive industries, and those requiring large inventories will have much smaller ratios.

Another activity ratio is inventory turnover, estimated by dividing sales by average inventory. The norm for U.S. industries is 9, but whether the ratio for a particular firm is higher or lower normally depends on the product sold. Small, inexpensive items usually turn over at a much higher rate than larger, expensive ones. Because inventories normally are carried at cost, it would be more accurate to use the cost of goods sold in place of sales in the numerator of this ratio. Established compilers of industry ratios, such as Dun & Bradstreet, however, use the ratio of sales to inventory.

$$\frac{\text{Inventory}}{\text{turnover}} = \frac{\text{Sales}}{\text{Inventory}} = \frac{\$8,250,000}{\$2,175,000} = 3.79 \ (2012)$$

$$= \frac{\$8,000,000}{\$2,000,000} = 4.00 \ (2011)$$

The accounts receivable turnover is a measure of the average collection period on sales. If the average number of days varies widely from the industry norm, it may be an indication of poor management. A too-low ratio could indicate the loss of sales because of a too-restrictive credit policy. If the ratio is too high, too much capital is being tied up in accounts receivable, and management may be increasing the chance of bad debts. Because of varying industry credit policies, a comparison for the firm over time or within an industry is the only useful analysis. Because information on credit sales for other firms generally is unavailable, total sales must be used. Because not all firms have the same percentage of credit sales, there is only approximate comparability among firms:

$$\text{Accounts receivable turnover} = \frac{\text{Sales}}{\text{Accounts receivable}}$$

$$= \frac{\$8,250,000}{\$1,760,000} = 4.69 \ (2012)$$

$$= \frac{\$8,000,000}{\$1,440,000} = 5.56 \ (2011)$$

$$\text{Average collection period} = \frac{360}{\text{Accounts receivable turnover}}$$

$$= \frac{360}{4.69} = 77 \text{ days} \ (2012)$$

$$= \frac{360}{5.56} = 65 \text{ days} \ (2011)$$

PROFITABILITY RATIOS

Profitability is the net result of a large number of policies and decisions chosen by an organization's management. Profitability ratios indicate how effectively the total firm is being managed. The profit margin for a firm is calculated by dividing net earnings by sales. This ratio is often called *return on sales* (ROS). There is wide variation among industries, but the average for U.S. firms is approximately 5 percent.

$$\frac{\text{Net earnings}}{\text{Sales}} = \frac{\$410,000}{\$8,250,000} = 0.0497 \ (2012)$$

$$= \frac{\$395,000}{\$8,000,000} = 0.0494 \ (2011)$$

A second useful ratio for evaluating profitability is the *return on investment*—or ROI, as it is frequently called—found by dividing net earnings by total assets. The ABC Company's ROI is calculated as follows:

$$\frac{\text{Net earnings}}{\text{Total assets}} = \frac{\$410,000}{\$7,105,000} = 0.0577 \ (2012)$$

$$= \frac{\$395,000}{\$6,393,000} = 0.0618 \ (2011)$$

The ratio of net earnings to net worth is a measure of the rate of return or profitability of the stockholders' investment. It is calculated by dividing net earnings by net worth, the common stock equity and retained earnings account. ABC Company's *return on net worth or return on equity*, also called ROE, is calculated as follows:

$$\frac{\text{Net earnings}}{\text{Net worth}} = \frac{\$410,000}{\$3,242,500} = 0.1264 \ (2012)$$

$$= \frac{\$395,000}{\$2,725,750} = 0.1449 \ (2011)$$

It is often difficult to determine causes for lack of profitability. The Du Pont system of financial analysis provides management with clues to the lack of success of a firm. This financial tool brings together activity, profitability, and

EXHIBIT 6.B4 **Du Pont's Financial Analysis**

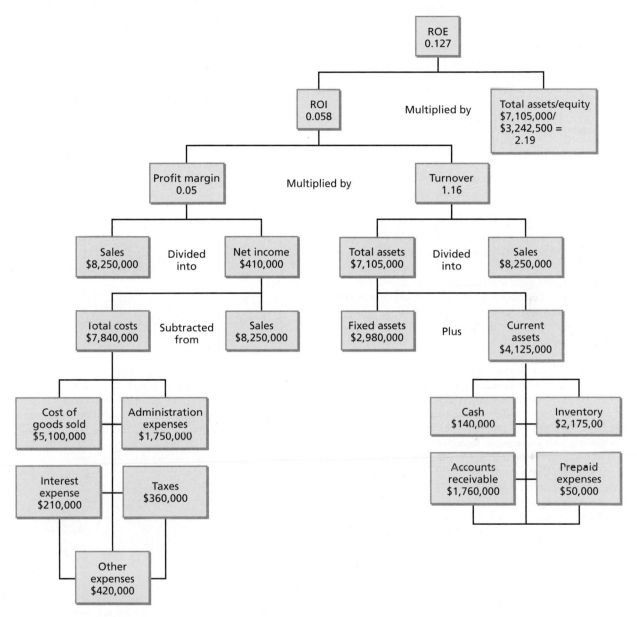

leverage measures and shows how these ratios interact to determine the overall profitability of the firm. A depiction of the system is set forth in Exhibit 6.B4.

The right side of the exhibit develops the turnover ratio. This section breaks down total assets into current assets (cash, marketable securities, accounts receivable, and inventories) and fixed assets. Sales divided by these total assets gives the turnover on assets.

The left side of the exhibit develops the profit margin on sales. The individual expense items plus income taxes are subtracted from sales to produce net profits after taxes. Net profits divided by sales gives the profit margin on sales. When the asset turnover ratio on the right side of Exhibit 6.B4 is multiplied by the profit margin on sales developed on the left side of the exhibit, the product is the return on assets (ROI) for the firm. This can be shown by the following formula:

$$\frac{\text{Sales}}{\text{Total assets}} \times \frac{\text{Net earnings}}{\text{Sales}} = \frac{\text{Net earnings}}{\text{Total assets}} = \text{ROI}$$

The last step in the Du Pont analysis is to multiply the rate of return on assets (ROI) by the equity multiplier, which is the ratio of assets to common equity, to obtain the rate of return on equity (ROE). This percentage rate of return, of course, could be calculated directly by dividing net income by common equity. However, the Du Pont analysis demonstrates how the return on assets and the use of debt interact to determine the return on equity.

The Du Pont system can be used to analyze and improve the performance of a firm. On the left, or profit, side of the exhibit, attempts to increase profits and sales could be investigated. The possibilities of raising prices to improve profits (or lowering prices to improve volume) or seeking new products or markets, for example, could be studied. Cost accountants and production engineers could investigate ways to reduce costs. On the right, or turnover, side, financial officers could analyze the effect of reducing investment in various assets as well as the effect of using alternative financial structures.

There are two basic approaches to using financial ratios. One approach is to evaluate the corporation's performance over several years. Financial ratios are computed for different years, and then an assessment is made about whether there has been an improvement or deterioration over time. Financial ratios also can be computed for projected, pro forma, statements and compared with present and past ratios.

The other approach is to evaluate a firm's financial condition and compare it with the financial conditions of similar firms or with industry averages in the same period. Such a comparison gives insight into the firm's relative financial condition and performance. Financial ratios for industries are provided by Robert Morris Associates, Dun & Bradstreet, Prentice Hall, and various trade association publications. (Associations and their addresses are listed in the *Encyclopedia of Associations* and in the *Directory of National Trade Associations.*) Information about individual firms is available through *Moody's Manual,* Standard & Poor's manuals and surveys, annual reports to stockholders, and the major brokerage houses.

To the extent possible, accounting data from different companies must be so standardized that companies can be compared or so a specific company can be compared with an industry average. It is important to read any footnotes of financial statements, because various accounting or management practices can have an effect on the financial picture of the company. For example, firms using sale-leaseback methods may have leverage pictures quite different from what is shown as debts or assets on the balance sheet.

ANALYSIS OF THE SOURCES AND USES OF FUNDS

The purpose of this analysis is to determine how the company is using its financial resources from year to year. By comparing balance sheets from one year to the next, we can determine how funds were obtained and how these funds were employed during the year.

To prepare a statement of the sources and uses of funds, it is necessary to (1) classify balance sheet changes that increase and decrease cash, (2) classify from the income statement those factors that increase or decrease cash, and (3) consolidate this information on a sources and uses of funds statement form.

Sources of Funds That Increase Cash

1. A net decrease in any other asset than a depreciable fixed asset.
2. A gross decrease in a depreciable fixed asset.
3. A net increase in any liability.
4. Proceeds from the sale of stock.
5. The operation of the company (net income, and depreciation if the company is profitable).

Uses of Funds

1. A net increase in any other asset than a depreciable fixed asset.
2. A gross increase in depreciable fixed assets.
3. A net decrease in any liability.
4. A retirement or purchase of stock.
5. Payment of cash dividends.

We compute gross changes to depreciable fixed assets by adding depreciation from the income statement for the period to net fixed assets at the end of the period and then subtracting from the total net fixed assets at the beginning of the period. The residual represents the change in depreciable fixed assets for the period.

For the ABC Company, the following change would be calculated:

Net property and plant (2012)	$1,175,000
Depreciation for 2012	+ 80,000
	$1,255,000
Net property and plant (2011)	−1,155,000
	$ 100,000

To avoid double counting, the change in retained earnings is not shown directly in the funds statement. When the funds statement is prepared, this account is replaced by the earnings after taxes, or net income, as a source of funds, and dividends paid during the year as a use of funds. The difference between net income and the change in the retained earnings account will equal the amount of dividends paid during the year. The accompanying sources and uses of funds statement was prepared for the ABC Company.

A funds analysis is useful for determining trends in working-capital positions and for demonstrating how the firm has acquired and employed its funds during some period.

ABC Company Sources and Uses of Funds Statement for 2012

Sources		Uses	
Prepaid expenses	$ 13,000	Cash	$ 25,000
Accounts payable	100,000	Accounts receivable	320,000
Accrued federal taxes	250,000	Inventory	175,000
Dividends payable	3,750	Long-term receivables	165,000
Common stock	1,200	Property and plant	100,000
Additional paid-in capital	195,550	Other fixed assets	20,000
Earnings after taxes (net income)	410,000	Bank loans payable	75,000
Depreciation	80,000	Current maturities of long-term debt	8,500
Total sources	$1,053,500	Long-term liabilities	75,000
		Dividends paid	90,000
		Total uses	$1,053,500

Conclusion

It is recommended that you prepare a chart, such as that shown in Exhibit 6.B5, so you can develop a useful portrayal of these financial analyses. The chart allows a display of the ratios over time. The "Trend" column could be used to indicate your evaluation of the ratios over time (e.g., "favorable," "neutral," or "unfavorable"). The "Industry Average" column could include recent industry averages on these ratios or those of key competitors. These would provide information to aid interpretation of the analyses. The "Interpretation" column could be used to describe your interpretation of the ratios for this firm. Overall, this chart gives a basic display of the ratios that provides a convenient format for examining the firm's financial condition.

Finally, Exhibit 6.B6 is included to provide a quick reference summary of the calculations and meanings of the ratios discussed earlier.

EXHIBIT 6.B5 A Summary of the Financial Position of a Firm

Ratios and Working Capital	2008	2009	2010	2011	2012	Trend	Industry Average	Interpretation
Liquidity: Current								
Quick								
Leverage: Debt-assets								
Debt-equity								
Activity: Asset turnover								
Fixed asset ratio								
Inventory turnover								
Accounts receivable turnover								
Average collection period								
Profitability: ROS								
ROI								
ROE								
Working-capital position								

EXHIBIT 6.B6 **A Summary of Key Financial Ratios**

Ratio	Calculation	Meaning
Liquidity Ratios:		
Current ratio	$\dfrac{\text{Current assets}}{\text{Current liabilities}}$	The extent to which a firm can meet its short-term obligations.
Quick ratio	$\dfrac{\text{Current assets–Inventory}}{\text{Current liabilities}}$	The extent to which a firm can meet its short-term obligations without relying on the sale of inventories.
Leverage Ratios:		
Debt-to-total-assets ratio	$\dfrac{\text{Total debt}}{\text{Total assets}}$	The percentage of total funds that are provided by creditors.
Debt-to-equity ratio	$\dfrac{\text{Total debt}}{\text{Total stockholders' equity}}$	The percentage of total funds provided by creditors versus the percentage provided by owners.
Long-term-debt-to-equity ratio	$\dfrac{\text{Long-term debt}}{\text{Total stockholders' equity}}$	The balance between debt and equity in a firm's long-term capital structure.
Times-interest-earned ratio	$\dfrac{\text{Profits before interest and taxes}}{\text{Total interest charges}}$	The extent to which earnings can decline without the firm becoming unable to meet its annual interest costs.
Activity Ratios:		
Inventory turnover	$\dfrac{\text{Sales}}{\text{Inventory of finished goods}}$	Whether a firm holds excessive stocks of inventories and whether a firm is selling its inventories slowly compared to the industry average.
Fixed assets turnover	$\dfrac{\text{Sales}}{\text{Fixed assets}}$	Sales productivity and plant equipment utilization.
Total assets turnover	$\dfrac{\text{Sales}}{\text{Total assets}}$	Whether a firm is generating a sufficient volume of business for the size of its assets investment.
Accounts receivable turnover	$\dfrac{\text{Annual credit sales}}{\text{Account receivable}}$	In percentage terms, the average length of time it takes a firm to collect on credit sales.
Average collection period	$\dfrac{\text{Account receivable}}{\text{Total sales/365 days}}$	In days, the average length of time it takes a firm to collect on credit sales.
Profitability Ratios:		
Gross profit margin	$\dfrac{\text{Sales – Cost of goods sold}}{\text{Sales}}$	The total margin available to cover operating expenses and yield a profit.
Operating profit margin	$\dfrac{\text{Earning before interest and taxes (EBIT)}}{\text{Sales}}$	Profitability without concern for taxes and interest.
Net profit margin	$\dfrac{\text{Net income}}{\text{Sales}}$	After-tax profits per dollar of sales.
Return on total assets (ROA)	$\dfrac{\text{Net income}}{\text{Total assets}}$	After-tax profits per dollar of assets; this ratio is also called *return on investment* (ROI).

EXHIBIT 6.B6 *(continued)*

Ratio	Calculation	Meaning
Return on stockholders' equity (ROE)	$\dfrac{\text{Net income}}{\text{Total stockholders' equity}}$	After-tax profits per dollar of stockholders investment in the firm.
Earnings per share (EPS)	$\dfrac{\text{Net income}}{\text{Number of shares of common stock outstanding}}$	Earnings available to the owners of common stock.
Growth Ratios:		
Sales	Annual percentage growth in total sales	Firm's growth rate in sales.
Income	Annual percentage growth in profits	Firm's growth rate in profits.
Earnings per share	Annual percentage growth in EPS	Firm's growth rate in EPS.
Dividends per share	Annual percentage growth in dividends per share	Firm's growth rate in dividends per share.
Price-earnings ratio	$\dfrac{\text{Market price per share}}{\text{Earnings per share}}$	Faster-growing and less risky firms tend to have higher price-earnings ratios.

Chapter **Seven**

Long-Term Objectives and Strategies

After reading and studying this chapter, you should be able to

1. Discuss seven different topics for long-term corporate objectives.

2. Describe the five qualities of long-term corporate objectives that make them especially useful to strategic managers.

3. Explain the generic strategies of low-cost leadership, differentiation, and focus.

4. Discuss the importance of the value disciplines.

5. List, describe, evaluate, and give examples of the 15 grand strategies that decision makers use as building blocks in forming their company's competitive plan.

6. Understand the creation of sets of long-term objectives and grand strategies options.

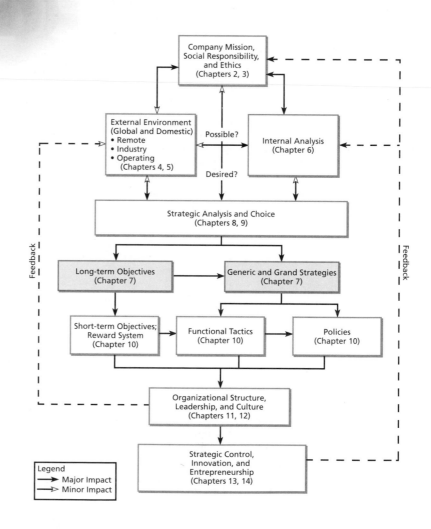

The company mission was described in Chapter 2 as encompassing the broad aims of the firm. The most specific statement of aims presented in that chapter appeared as the goals of the firm. However, these goals, which commonly dealt with profitability, growth, and survival, were stated without specific targets or time frames. They were always to be pursued but could never be fully attained. They gave a general sense of direction but were not intended to provide specific benchmarks for evaluating the firm's progress in achieving its aims. Providing such benchmarks is the function of objectives.[1]

The first part of this chapter will focus on long-term objectives. These are statements of the results a firm seeks to achieve over a specified period, typically three to five years. The second part will focus on the formulation of grand strategies. In combination, these two components of long-term planning provide a comprehensive general approach in guiding major actions designed to accomplish the firm's long-term objectives.

The chapter has two major aims: (1) to discuss in detail the concept of long-term objectives, the topics they cover, and the qualities they should exhibit; and (2) to discuss the concept of grand strategies and to describe the 15 principal grand strategy options that are available to firms singly or in combination, including three newly popularized options that are being used to provide the basis for global competitiveness.

LONG-TERM OBJECTIVES

Strategic managers recognize that short-run profit maximization is rarely the best approach to achieving sustained corporate growth and profitability. An often repeated adage states that if impoverished people are given food, they will eat it and remain impoverished; however, if they are given seeds and tools and shown how to grow crops, they will be able to improve their condition permanently. A parallel choice confronts strategic decision makers:

1. Should they eat the seeds to improve the near-term profit picture and make large dividend payments through cost-saving measures such as laying off workers during periods of slack demand, selling off inventories, or cutting back on research and development?
2. Or should they sow the seeds in the effort to reap long-term rewards by reinvesting profits in growth opportunities, committing resources to employee training, or increasing advertising expenditures?

For most strategic managers, the solution is clear—distribute a small amount of profit now but sow most of it to increase the likelihood of a long-term supply. This is the most frequently used rationale in selecting objectives.

To achieve long-term prosperity, strategic planners commonly establish long-term objectives in seven areas.

Profitability   The ability of any firm to operate in the long run depends on attaining an acceptable level of profits. Strategically managed firms characteristically have a profit objective, usually expressed in earnings per share or return on equity.

Productivity   Strategic managers constantly try to increase the productivity of their systems. Firms that can improve the input-output relationship normally increase profitability. Thus, firms almost always state an objective for productivity. Commonly used productivity objectives are the number of items produced or the number of services rendered per unit of input. However, productivity objectives sometimes are stated in terms of desired

---

[1] The terms *goals* and *objectives* are each used to convey a special meaning, with goals being the less specific and more encompassing concept.

cost decreases. For example, objectives may be set for reducing defective items, customer complaints leading to litigation, or overtime. Achieving such objectives increases profitability if unit output is maintained.

Competitive Position One measure of corporate success is relative dominance in the marketplace. Larger firms commonly establish an objective in terms of competitive position, often using total sales or market share as measures of their competitive position. An objective with regard to competitive position may indicate a firm's long-term priorities. For example, Gulf Oil set a five-year objective of moving from third to second place as a producer of high-density polypropylene. Total sales were the measure.

Employee Development Employees value education and training, in part because they lead to increased compensation and job security. Providing such opportunities often increases productivity and decreases turnover. Therefore, strategic decision makers frequently include an employee development objective in their long-range plans. For example, PPG has declared an objective of developing highly skilled and flexible employees and, thus, providing steady employment for a reduced number of workers.

Employee Relations Whether or not they are bound by union contracts, firms actively seek good employee relations. In fact, proactive steps in anticipation of employee needs and expectations are characteristic of strategic managers. Strategic managers believe that productivity is linked to employee loyalty and to appreciation of managers' interest in employee welfare. They, therefore, set objectives to improve employee relations. Among the outgrowths of such objectives are safety programs, worker representation on management committees, and employee stock option plans.

Technological Leadership Firms must decide whether to lead or follow in the marketplace. Either approach can be successful, but each requires a different strategic posture. Therefore, many firms state an objective with regard to technological leadership. For example, Caterpillar Tractor Company established its early reputation and dominant position in its industry by being in the forefront of technological innovation in the manufacture of large earthmovers. E-commerce technology officers will have more of a strategic role in the management hierarchy of the future, demonstrating that the Internet has become an integral aspect of corporate long-term objective setting. In offering an e-technology manager higher-level responsibilities, a firm is pursuing a leadership position in terms of innovation in computer networks and systems. Officers of e-commerce technology at GE and Delta Air Lines have shown their ability to increase profits by driving down transaction-related costs with Web-based technologies that seamlessly integrate their firms' supply chains. These technologies have the potential to "lock in" certain suppliers and customers and heighten competitive position through supply chain efficiency.

Public Responsibility Managers recognize their responsibilities to their customers and to society at large. In fact, many firms seek to exceed government requirements. They work not only to develop reputations for fairly priced products and services but also to establish themselves as responsible corporate citizens. For example, they may establish objectives for charitable and educational contributions, minority training, public or political activity, community welfare, or urban revitalization. In an attempt to exhibit their public responsibility in the United States, Japanese companies, such as Toyota, Hitachi, and Matsushita, contribute more than $500 million annually to American educational projects, charities, and nonprofit organizations.

Qualities of Long-Term Objectives

What distinguishes a good objective from a bad one? What qualities of an objective improve its chances of being attained? These questions are best answered in relation to five criteria that should be used in preparing long-term objectives: flexible, measurable over time, motivating, suitable, and understandable.

Flexible Objectives should be adaptable to unforeseen or extraordinary changes in the firm's competitive or environmental forecasts. Unfortunately, such flexibility usually is increased at the expense of specificity. One way of providing flexibility while minimizing its negative effects is to allow for adjustments in the level, rather than in the nature, of objectives. For example, the personnel department objective of providing managerial development training for 15 supervisors per year over the next five-year period might be adjusted by changing the number of people to be trained.

Measurable Objectives must clearly and concretely state what will be achieved and when it will be achieved. Thus, objectives should be measurable over time. For example, the objective of "substantially improving our return on investment" would be better stated as "increasing the return on investment on our line of paper products by a minimum of 1 percent a year and a total of 5 percent over the next three years." A great example is provided by IAG (Insurance Australia Group), which offers a wide range of commercial and personal insurance products. IAG stated its 2008 financial objective as a return on equity of 1.5 times the weighted average cost of capital.

Motivating People are most productive when objectives are set at a motivating level—one high enough to challenge but not so high as to frustrate or so low as to be easily attained. The problem is that individuals and groups differ in their perceptions of what is high enough. A broad objective that challenges one group frustrates another and minimally interests a third. One valuable recommendation is that objectives be tailored to specific groups. Developing such objectives requires time and effort, but objectives of this kind are more likely to motivate.

Objectives must also be achievable. This is easier said than done. Turbulence in the remote and operating environments affects a firm's internal operations, creating uncertainty and limiting the accuracy of the objectives set by strategic management. To illustrate, the rapidly declining U.S. economy in 2007–2009 made objective setting extremely difficult, particularly in such areas as sales projections.

Motorola provides a good example of well-constructed company objectives. Motorola saw its market share of the mobile telephone market shrink from 26 to 14 percent between 1996 and 2001, while its main rival Nokia captured all of Motorola's lost share and more. As a key part of a plan to recapture its market position, Motorola's CEO challenged his company with the following long-term objectives:

1. Cut sales, marketing, and administrative expenses from $2.4 billion to $1.6 billion within one year.
2. Increase gross margins from 20 to 27 percent within two years.
3. Reduce the number of Motorola telephone styles by 84 percent to 20 and the number of silicon components by 82 percent to 100 within three years.

Suitable Objectives must be suited to the broad aims of the firm, which are expressed in its mission statement. Each objective should be a step toward the attainment of overall goals. In fact, objectives that are inconsistent with the company mission can subvert the firm's aims. For example, if the mission is growth oriented, the objective of reducing the debt-to-equity ratio to 1.00 would probably be unsuitable and counterproductive.

Understandable Strategic managers at all levels must understand what is to be achieved. They also must understand the major criteria by which their performance will be evaluated. Thus, objectives must be so stated that they are as understandable to the recipient as they are to the giver. Consider the misunderstandings that might arise over the objective of "increasing the productivity of the credit card department by 20 percent within two years." What does this objective mean? Increase the number of outstanding cards? Increase the use of outstanding cards? Increase the employee workload? Make productivity gains each year? Or hope that the new computer-assisted system, which should improve productivity, is approved by year 2? As this simple example illustrates, objectives must be clear, meaningful, and unambiguous.

The Balanced Scorecard

balanced scorecard
A set of four measures directly linked to a company's strategy: financial performance, customer knowledge, internal business processes, and learning and growth.

The **balanced scorecard** is a set of measures that are directly linked to the company's strategy. It directs a company to link its own long-term strategy with tangible goals and actions. The scorecard allows managers to evaluate the company from four perspectives: financial performance, customer knowledge, internal business processes, and learning and growth.

The balanced scorecard, as shown in Exhibit 7.1, contains a concise definition of the company's vision and strategy. Surrounding the vision and strategy are four additional boxes; each box contains the objectives, measures, targets, and initiatives for one of the four perspectives:

- The box at the top of Exhibit 7.1 represents the financial perspective and answers the question "To succeed financially, how should we appear to our shareholders?"

Exhibit 7.1 **The Balanced Scorecard**

The balanced scorecard provides a framework to translate a strategy into operational terms

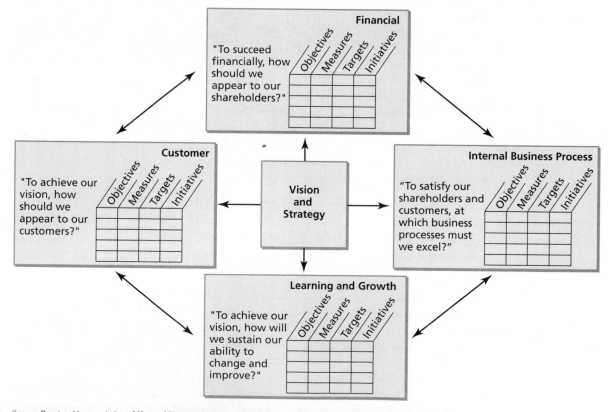

- The box to the right represents the internal business process perspective and addresses the question "To satisfy our shareholders and customers, what business processes must we excel at?"
- The learning and growth box at the bottom of Exhibit 7.1 answers the question "To achieve our vision, how will we sustain our ability to change and improve?"
- The box at the left reflects the customer perspective and responds to the question "To achieve our vision, how should we appear to our customers?"

All of the boxes are connected by arrows to illustrate that the objectives and measures of the four perspectives are linked by cause-and-effect relationships that lead to the successful implementation of the strategy. Achieving one perspective's targets should lead to desired improvements in the next perspective, and so on, until the company's performance increases overall.

A properly constructed scorecard is balanced between short- and long-term measures, financial and nonfinancial measures, and internal and external performance perspectives.

The balanced scorecard is a management system that can be used as the central organizing framework for key managerial processes. Chemical Bank, Mobil Corporation's US Marketing and Refining Division, and CIGNA Property and Casualty Insurance have used the balanced scorecard approach to assist in individual and team goal setting, compensation, resource allocation, budgeting and planning, and strategic feedback and learning.

GENERIC STRATEGIES

Many planning experts believe that the general philosophy of doing business declared by the firm in the mission statement must be translated into a holistic statement of the firm's strategic orientation before it can be further defined in terms of a specific long-term strategy. In other words, a long-term or grand strategy must be based on a core idea about how the firm can best compete in the marketplace.

generic strategy
A core idea about how a firm can best compete in the marketplace.

The popular term for this core idea is **generic strategy.** From a scheme developed by Michael Porter, many planners believe that any long-term strategy should derive from a firm's attempt to seek a competitive advantage based on one of three generic strategies:

1. Striving for overall *low-cost leadership* in the industry.
2. Striving to create and market unique products for varied customer groups through *differentiation*.
3. Striving to have special appeal to one or more groups of consumer or industrial buyers, *focusing* on their cost or differentiation concerns.

Advocates of generic strategies believe that each of these options can produce above average returns for a firm in an industry. However, they are successful for very different reasons.

Low-Cost Leadership

Low-cost leaders depend on some fairly unique capabilities to achieve and sustain their low-cost position. Examples of such capabilities are having secured suppliers of scarce raw materials, being in a dominant market share position, or having a high degree of capitalization. Low-cost producers usually excel at cost reductions and efficiencies. They maximize economies of scale, implement cost-cutting technologies, stress reductions in overhead and in administrative expenses, and use volume sales techniques to propel themselves up the earning curve.

A low-cost leader is able to use its cost advantage to charge lower prices or to enjoy higher profit margins. By so doing, the firm effectively can defend itself in price wars, attack competitors on price to gain market share, or, if already dominant in the industry, simply benefit from exceptional returns. As an extreme case, it has been argued that National Can Company, a corporation in an essentially stagnant industry, is able to generate attractive and improving profits by being the low-cost producer.

In the wake of the tremendous successes of such low-cost leaders as Wal-Mart and Target, only a rare few companies can ignore the mandate to reduce cost. Yet, doing so without compromising the key attributes of a company's products or services is a difficult challenge. One company that has succeeded in its efforts to become a low-cost leader while maintaining quality is IAG. The company's CEO Michael Wilkins expresses the principle of the company's focus on low costs in its mission statement by saying: "IAG's large scale allows us to manage costs across our brands through access to volume discounts throughout the supply chain, without sacrificing quality, thereby keeping costs per policy down."

Differentiation

Strategies dependent on differentiation are designed to appeal to customers with a special sensitivity for a particular product attribute. By stressing the attribute above other product qualities, the firm attempts to build customer loyalty. Often such loyalty translates into a firm's ability to charge a premium price for its product. Cross-brand pens, Brooks Brothers suits, Porsche automobiles, and Chivas Regal Scotch whiskey are all examples.

The product attribute also can be the marketing channels through which it is delivered, its image for excellence, the features it includes, and the service network that supports it. As a result of the importance of these attributes, competitors often face "perceptual" barriers to entry when customers of a successfully differentiated firm fail to see largely identical products as being interchangeable. For example, General Motors hopes that customers will accept "only genuine GM replacement parts."

Because advertising plays a major role in a company's development and differentiation of it brand, many strategists use celebrity spokespeople to represent their companies. These spokespeople, most often actors, models, and athletes, help give the company's products and services a popular, successful, trendy, modern, cachet.

Focus

A focus strategy, whether anchored in a low-cost base or a differentiation base, attempts to attend to the needs of a particular market segment. Likely segments are those that are ignored by marketing appeals to easily accessible markets, to the "typical" customer, or to customers with common applications for the product. A firm pursuing a focus strategy is willing to service isolated geographic areas; to satisfy the needs of customers with special financing, inventory, or servicing problems; or to tailor the product to the somewhat unique demands of the small- to medium-sized customer. The focusing firms profit from their willingness to serve otherwise ignored or underappreciated customer segments. The classic example is cable television. An entire industry was born because of a willingness of cable firms to serve isolated rural locations that were ignored by traditional television services. Brick producers that typically service a radius of less than 100 miles and commuter airlines that serve regional geographic areas are other examples of industries where a focus strategy frequently yields above-average industry profits.

While each of the generic strategies enables a firm to maximize certain competitive advantages, each one also exposes the firm to a number of competitive risks. For example, a low-cost leader fears a new low-cost technology that is being developed by a competitor;

a differentiating firm fears imitators; and a focused firm fears invasion by a firm that largely targets customers.

THE VALUE DISCIPLINES

International management consultants Michael Treacy and Fred Wiersema propose an alternative approach to generic strategy that they call the value disciplines.[2] They believe that strategies must center on delivering superior customer value through one of three value disciplines: operational excellence, customer intimacy, or product leadership.

Operational excellence refers to providing customers with convenient and reliable products or services at competitive prices. Customer intimacy involves offerings tailored to match the demands of identified niches. Product leadership, the third discipline, involves offering customers leading-edge products and services that make rivals' goods obsolete.

Companies that specialize in one of these disciplines, while simultaneously meeting industry standards in the other two, gain a sustainable lead in their markets. This lead is derived from the firm's focus on one discipline, aligning all aspects of operations with it. Having decided on the value that must be conveyed to customers, firms understand more clearly what must be done to attain the desired results. After transforming their organizations to focus on one discipline, companies can concentrate on smaller adjustments to produce incremental value. To match this advantage, less focused companies require larger changes than the tweaking that discipline leaders need.

Operational Excellence

Operational excellence is a specific strategic approach to the production and delivery of products and services. A company that follows this strategy attempts to lead its industry in price and convenience by pursuing a focus on lean and efficient operations. Companies that employ operational excellence work to minimize costs by reducing overhead, eliminating intermediate production steps, reducing transaction costs, and optimizing business processes across functional and organizational boundaries. The focus is on delivering products or services to customers at competitive prices with minimal inconvenience.

Operational excellence is also the strategic focus of General Electric's large appliance business. Historically, the distribution strategy for large appliances was based on requiring that dealers maintain large inventories. Price breaks for dealers were based on order quantities. However, as the marketplace became more competitive, principally as a result of competition multibrand dealers like Sears, GE recognized the need to adjust its production and distribution plans.

The GE system addresses the delivery of products. As a step toward organizational excellence, GE created a computer-based logistics system to replace its in-store inventories model. Retailers use this software to access a 24-hour online order processing system that guarantees GE's best price. This system allows dealers to better meet customer needs, with instantaneous access to a warehouse of goods and accurate shipping and production information. GE benefits from the deal as well. Efficiency is increased since manufacturing now occurs in response to customer sales. Additionally, warehousing and distribution systems have been streamlined to create the capability of delivering to 90 percent of destinations in the continental United States within one business day.

---

[2] The ideas and examples in this section are drawn from Michael Treacy and Fred Wiersema, "Customer Intimacy and Other Value Disciplines," *Harvard Business Review* 71, no. 1 (1993), pp. 84–94.

Firms that implement the strategy of operational excellence typically restructure their delivery processes to focus on efficiency and reliability, and use state-of-the art information systems that emphasize integration and low-cost transactions.

Customer Intimacy

Companies that implement a strategy of customer intimacy continually tailor and shape products and services to fit an increasingly refined definition of the customer. Companies excelling in customer intimacy combine detailed customer knowledge with operational flexibility. They respond quickly to almost any need, from customizing a product to fulfilling special requests to create customer loyalty.

Customer-intimate companies are willing to spend money now to build customer loyalty for the long term, considering each customer's lifetime value to the company, not the profit of any single transaction. Consequently, employees in customer-intimate companies go to great lengths to ensure customer satisfaction with low regard for initial cost.

Home Depot implements the discipline of customer intimacy. Home Depot clerks spend the necessary time with customers to determine the product that best suits their needs, because the company's business strategy is built around selling information and service in addition to home-repair and improvement items. Consequently, consumers concerned solely with price fall outside Home Depot's core market.

Companies engaged in customer intimacy understand the difference between the profitability of a single transaction and the profitability of a lifetime relationship with a single customer. The company's profitability depends in part on its maintaining a system that differentiates quickly and accurately the degree of service that customers require and the revenues their patronage is likely to generate. Firms using this approach recognize that not every customer is equally profitable. For example, a financial services company installed a telephone-computer system capable of recognizing individual clients by their telephone numbers when they call. The system routes customers with large accounts and frequent transactions to their own senior account representative. Other customers may be routed to a trainee or junior representative. In any case, the customer's file appears on the representative's screen before the phone is answered.

The new system allows the firm to segment its services with great efficiency. If the company has clients who are interested in trading in a particular financial instrument, it can group them under the one account representative who specializes in that instrument. This saves the firm the expense of training every representative in every facet of financial services. Additionally, the company can direct certain value-added services or products to a specific group of clients that would have interest in them.

Businesses that select a customer intimacy strategy have decided to stress flexibility and responsiveness. They collect and analyze data from many sources. Their organizational structure emphasizes empowerment of employees close to customers. Additionally, hiring and training programs stress the creative decision-making skills required to meet individual customer needs. Management systems recognize and utilize such concepts as customer lifetime value, and norms among employees are consistent with a "have it your way" mind set.

Product Leadership

Companies that pursue the discipline of product leadership strive to produce a continuous stream of state-of-the-art products and services. Three challenges must be met to attain that goal. Creativity is the first challenge. Creativity is recognizing and embracing ideas usually originating outside the company. Second, innovative companies must commercialize ideas quickly. Thus, their business and management processes need to be engineered for speed.

Product leaders relentlessly pursue new solutions to problems. Finally, firms utilizing this discipline prefer to release their own improvements rather than wait for competitors to enter. Consequently, product leaders do not stop for self-congratulation; they focus on continual improvement.

For example, Johnson & Johnson's organizational design brings good ideas in, develops them quickly, and looks for ways to improve them. In 1983, the president of J&J's Vistakon Inc., a maker of specialty contact lenses, received a tip concerning an ophthalmologist who had conceived of a method to manufacture disposable contact lenses inexpensively. Vistakon's president received this tip from a J&J employee from a different subsidiary whom he had never met. Rather than dismiss the tip, the executives purchased the rights to the technology, assembled a management team to oversee the product's development, and built a state-of-the-art facility in Florida to manufacture disposable contact lenses called Acuvue. Vistakon and its parent, J&J, were willing to incur high manufacturing and inventory costs before a single lens was sold. A high-speed production facility helped give Vistakon a six-month head start over the competition that, taken off guard, never caught up.

Like other product leaders, J&J creates and maintains an environment that encourages employees to share ideas. Additionally, product leaders continually scan the environment for new-product or service possibilities and rush to capitalize them. Product leaders also avoid bureaucracy because it slows commercialization of their ideas. In a product leadership company, a wrong decision often is less damaging than one made late. As a result, managers make decisions quickly, their companies encouraging them to decide today and implement tomorrow. Product leaders continually look for new methods to shorten their cycle times.

The strength of product leaders lies in reacting to situations as they occur. Shorter reaction times serve as an advantage in dealings with the unknown. For example, when competitors challenged the safety of Acuvue lenses, the firm responded quickly and distributed data combating the charges to eye care professionals. This reaction created goodwill in the marketplace.

Product leaders act as their own competition. These firms continually make the products and services they have created obsolete. Product leaders believe that if they do not develop a successor, a competitor will. So, although Acuvue is successful in the marketplace, Vistakon continues to investigate new material that will extend the wearability of contact lenses and technologies that will make current lenses obsolete. J&J and other innovators recognize that the long-run profitability of an existing product or service is less important to the company's future than maintaining its product leadership edge and momentum.

GRAND STRATEGIES

grand strategy
A master long-term plan that provides basic direction for major actions directed toward achieving long-term business objectives.

Grand strategies, sometimes called master or business strategies, provide basic direction for strategic actions. They are the basis of coordinated and sustained efforts directed toward achieving long-term business objectives.

The purpose of this section is twofold: (1) to list, describe, and discuss 15 grand strategies that strategic managers should consider and (2) to present approaches to the selection of an optimal grand strategy from the available alternatives.

Grand strategies indicate the time period over which long-range objectives are to be achieved. Thus, a grand strategy can be defined as a comprehensive general approach that guides a firm's major actions.

The 15 principal grand strategies are concentrated growth, market development, product development, innovation, horizontal integration, vertical integration, concentric diversification, conglomerate diversification, turnaround, divestiture, liquidation, bankruptcy, joint ventures, strategic alliances, and consortia. Any one of these strategies could serve as the basis for achieving the major long-term objectives of a single firm. But a firm involved with multiple industries, businesses, product lines, or customer groups—as many firms are—usually combines several grand strategies. For clarity, however, each of the principal grand strategies is described independently in this section, with examples to indicate some of its relative strengths and weaknesses.

1. Concentrated Growth

Many of the firms that fell victim to merger mania were once mistakenly convinced that the best way to achieve their objectives was to pursue unrelated diversification in the search for financial opportunity and synergy. By rejecting that "conventional wisdom," such firms as Martin-Marietta, KFC, Compaq, Avon, Hyatt Legal Services, and Tenant have demonstrated the advantages of what is increasingly proving to be sound business strategy.

These firms are just a few of the majority of businesses worldwide firms that pursue a concentrated growth strategy by focusing on a dominant product-and-market combination. **Concentrated growth** is the strategy of the firm that directs its resources to the profitable growth of a dominant product, in a dominant market, with a dominant technology. The main rationale for this approach, sometimes called a market penetration strategy, is that by thoroughly developing and exploiting its expertise in a narrowly defined competitive arena, the company achieves superiority over competitors that try to master a greater number of product and market combinations.

concentrated growth
A grand strategy in which a firm directs its resources to the profitable growth of a single product, in a single market, with a single dominant technology.

Rationale for Superior Performance

Concentrated growth strategies lead to enhanced performance. The ability to assess market needs, knowledge of buyer behavior, customer price sensitivity, and effectiveness of promotion are characteristics of a concentrated growth strategy. Such core capabilities are a more important determinant of competitive market success than are the environmental forces faced by the firm. The high success rates of new products also are tied to avoiding situations that require undeveloped skills, such as serving new customers and markets, acquiring new technology, building new channels, developing new promotional abilities, and facing new competition.

A major misconception about the concentrated growth strategy is that the firm practicing it will settle for little or no growth. This is certainly not true for a firm that correctly utilizes the strategy. A firm employing concentrated growth grows by building on its competencies, and it achieves a competitive edge by concentrating in the product-market segment it knows best. A firm employing this strategy is aiming for the growth that results from increased productivity, better coverage of its actual product-market segment, and more efficient use of its technology.

Conditions That Favor Concentrated Growth

Specific conditions in the firm's environment are favorable to the concentrated growth strategy. The first is a condition in which the firm's industry is resistant to major technological advancements. This is usually the case in the late growth and maturity stages of the product life cycle and in product markets where product demand is stable and industry barriers, such as capitalization, are high. Machinery for the paper manufacturing industry, in which the basic technology has not changed for more than a century, is a good example.

An especially favorable condition is one in which the firm's targeted markets are not product saturated. Markets with competitive gaps leave the firm with alternatives for growth, other than taking market share away from competitors. The successful introduction of traveler services by Allstate and Amoco demonstrates that even an organization as entrenched and powerful as the AAA could not build a defensible presence in all segments of the automobile club market.

A third condition that favors concentrated growth exists when the firm's product markets are sufficiently distinctive to dissuade competitors in adjacent product markets from trying to invade the firm's segment. John Deere scrapped its plans for growth in the construction machinery business when mighty Caterpillar threatened to enter Deere's mainstay, the farm machinery business, in retaliation. Rather than risk a costly price war on its own turf, Deere scrapped these plans.

A fourth favorable condition exists when the firm's inputs are stable in price and quantity and are available in the amounts and at the times needed. Maryland-based Giant Foods is able to concentrate in the grocery business largely due to its stable long-term arrangements with suppliers of its private-label products. Most of these suppliers are makers of the national brands that compete against the Giant labels. With a high market share and aggressive retail distribution, Giant controls the access of these brands to the consumer. Consequently, its suppliers have considerable incentive to honor verbal agreements, called bookings, in which they commit themselves for a one-year period with regard to the price, quality, and timing of their shipments to Giant.

The pursuit of concentrated growth also is favored by a stable market—a market without the seasonal or cyclical swings that would encourage a firm to diversify. Night Owl Security, the District of Columbia market leader in home security services, commits its customers to initial four-year contracts. In a city where affluent consumers tend to be quite transient, the length of this relationship is remarkable. Night Owl's concentrated growth strategy has been reinforced by its success in getting subsequent owners of its customers' homes to extend and renew the security service contracts. In a similar way, Lands' End reinforced its growth strategy by asking customers for names and addresses of friends and relatives living overseas who would like to receive Lands' End catalogs.

A firm also can grow while concentrating, if it enjoys competitive advantages based on efficient production or distribution channels. These advantages enable the firm to formulate advantageous pricing policies. More efficient production methods and better handling of distribution also enable the firm to achieve greater economies of scale or, in conjunction with marketing, result in a product that is differentiated in the mind of the consumer. Graniteville Company, a large South Carolina textile manufacturer, enjoyed decades of growth and profitability by adopting a "follower" tactic as part of its concentrated growth strategy. By producing fabrics only after market demand had been well established, and by featuring products that reflected its expertise in adopting manufacturing innovations and in maintaining highly efficient long production runs, Graniteville prospered through concentrated growth.

Finally, the success of market generalists creates conditions favorable to concentrated growth. When generalists succeed by using universal appeals, they avoid making special appeals to particular groups of customers. The net result is that many small pockets are left open in the markets dominated by generalists, and that specialists emerge and thrive in these pockets. For example, hardware store chains, such as Home Depot, focus primarily on routine household repair problems and offer solutions that can be easily sold on a self-service, do-it-yourself basis. This approach leaves gaps at both the "semi-professional" and "neophyte" ends of the market—in terms of the purchaser's skill at household repairs and the extent to which available merchandise matches the requirements of individual homeowners. To learn about the important success of BNSF with a concentrated growth strategy, read about CEO Matthew Rose's grand strategy in the railroad industry in Exhibit 7.2, Top Strategist.

Top Strategist
CEO Matthew Rose Focuses BNSF on Concentrated Growth

Exhibit
7.2

As CEO of BNSF, Matthew Rose's concentrated growth strategy relies on technology to improve operational efficiency in an increasingly congested rail network. Strategic planning in this industry is critical because rail tonnage was expected to increase by 88 percent between 2008 and 2035, and rail capacity was fully utilized in 2008. Missing the opportunity to increase capacity would lead to rail congestion, diminished safety, and an accelerated consumer shift to other channels of freight transportation.

BNSF's concentrated growth strategy required a tightly coordinated effort. A major component involved transferring ownership of railcars to third-party shippers. Divesting railcars improved customer service because third-party shippers were able to manage these assets more efficiently. By shifting focus away from railcar operations, BNSF was able to concentrate on improving its overall network utilization. Evidence of this strategic shift was the investment in a satellite-based computer program that optimized logistics and ensured that all trains are fully utilized. Additionally, BNSF used 10,000-foot trains to increase economies of scale and accommodate the growing West Coast shipping ports.

Maintaining quality through operational efficiency increased customer usage in this highly competitive industry. High-quality service also protected BNSF from pricing pressures and enabled investment in strategic positioning; as CEO Rose explained, "higher returns have allowed us to make the investments required to improve velocity and efficiency and to handle increased demand from our customers and the nation."*

Sources: Matthew K. Rose, "Executive Commentary," *The Journal of Commerce,* January 2008, p. 116; and Bill Mongelluzzo, "Long Hauls BNSF Breaks the 10,000-Foot Barrier with Intermodal Trains," *The Journal of Commerce,* October 6, 2008, p. 30.
*Matthew K. Rose, "Executive Commentary," *The Journal of Commerce,* January 2008, p. 116.

Risk and Rewards of Concentrated Growth

Under stable conditions, concentrated growth poses lower risk than any other grand strategy; but, in a changing environment, a firm committed to concentrated growth faces high risks. The greatest risk is that concentrating in a single product market makes a firm particularly vulnerable to changes in that segment. Slowed growth in the segment would jeopardize the firm because its investment, competitive edge, and technology are deeply entrenched in a specific offering. It is difficult for the firm to attempt sudden changes if its product is threatened by near-term obsolescence, a faltering market, new substitutes, or changes in technology or customer needs. For example, the manufacturers of IBM clones faced such a problem when IBM adopted the OS/2 operating system for its personal computer line. That change made existing clones out of date.

The concentrating firm's entrenchment in a specific industry makes it particularly susceptible to changes in the economic environment of that industry. For example, Mack Truck, the second-largest truck maker in America, lost $20 million as a result of an 18-month slump in the truck industry.

Entrenchment in a specific product market tends to make a concentrating firm more adept than competitors at detecting new trends. However, any failure of such a firm to properly forecast major changes in its industry can result in extraordinary losses. Numerous makers of inexpensive digital watches were forced to declare bankruptcy because they failed to anticipate the competition posed by Swatch, Guess, and other trendy watches that emerged from the fashion industry.

A firm pursuing a concentrated growth strategy is vulnerable also to the high opportunity costs that result from remaining in a specific product market and ignoring other options that could employ the firm's resources more profitably. Overcommitment to a specific technology and product market can hinder a firm's ability to enter a new or growing product market that offers more attractive cost-benefit trade-offs. Had Apple Computers maintained its policy of making equipment that did not interface with IBM equipment, it would have missed out on what have proved to be its most profitable strategic options.

Concentrated Growth Is Often the Most Viable Option

Examples abound of firms that have enjoyed exceptional returns on the concentrated growth strategy. Such firms as McDonald's, Goodyear, and Apple Computers have used firsthand knowledge and deep involvement with specific product segments to become powerful competitors in their markets. The strategy is associated even more often with successful smaller firms that have steadily and doggedly improved their market position.

The limited additional resources necessary to implement concentrated growth, coupled with the limited risk involved, also make this strategy desirable for a firm with limited funds. For example, through a carefully devised concentrated growth strategy, medium-sized John Deere & Company was able to become a major force in the agricultural machinery business even when competing with such firms as Ford Motor Company. While other firms were trying to exit or diversify from the farm machinery business, Deere spent $2 billion in upgrading its machinery, boosting its efficiency, and engaging in a program to strengthen its dealership system. This concentrated growth strategy enabled it to become the leader in the farm machinery business despite the fact that Ford was more than 10 times its size.

The firm that chooses a concentrated growth strategy directs its resources to the profitable growth of a narrowly defined product and market, focusing on a dominant technology. Firms that remain within their chosen product market are able to extract the most from their technology and market knowledge and, thus, are able to minimize the risk associated with unrelated diversification. The success of a concentration strategy is founded on the firm's use of superior insights into its technology, product, and customer to obtain a sustainable competitive advantage. Superior performance on these aspects of corporate strategy has been shown to have a substantial positive effect on market success.

A grand strategy of concentrated growth allows for a considerable range of action. Broadly speaking, the firm can attempt to capture a larger market share by increasing the usage rates of present customers, by attracting competitors' customers, or by selling to nonusers. In turn, each of these options suggests more specific options, some of which are listed in the top section of Exhibit 7.3.

When strategic managers forecast that their current products and their markets will not provide the basis for achieving the company mission, they have two options that involve moderate costs and risk: market development and product development.

2. Market Development

market development
A grand strategy of marketing present products, often with only cosmetic modification, to customers in related marketing areas.

Market development commonly ranks second only to concentration as the least costly and least risky of the 15 grand strategies. It consists of marketing present products, often with only cosmetic modifications, to customers in related market areas by adding channels of distribution or by changing the content of advertising or promotion. Several specific market development approaches are listed in Exhibit 7.3. Thus, as suggested by the exhibit, firms that open branch offices in new cities, states, or countries are practicing market

EXHIBIT 7.3
Specific Options under the Grand Strategies of Concentration, Market Development, and Product Development

Source: Adapted from Philip Kotler and Kevin Keller, *Marketing Management,* 12th Edition, 2006. Reprinted by permission of Pearson Education, Upper Saddle River, NJ.

Concentration (increasing use of present products in present markets):

1. Increasing present customers' rate of use:
   a. Increasing the size of purchase.
   b. Increasing the rate of product obsolescence.
   c. Advertising other uses.
   d. Giving price incentives for increased use.
2. Attracting competitors' customers:
   a. Establishing sharper brand differentiation.
   b. Increasing promotional effort.
   c. Initiating price cuts.
3. Attracting nonusers to buy the product:
   a. Inducing trial use through sampling, price incentives, and so on.
   b. Pricing up or down.
   c. Advertising new uses.

Market development (selling present products in new markets):

1. Opening additional geographic markets:
   a. Regional expansion.
   b. National expansion.
   c. International expansion.
2. Attracting other market segments:
   a. Developing product versions to appeal to other segments.
   b. Entering other channels of distribution.
   c. Advertising in other media.

Product development (developing new products for present markets):

1. Developing new-product features:
   a. Adapt (to other ideas, developments).
   b. Modify (change color, motion, sound, odor, form, shape).
   c. Magnify (stronger, longer, thicker, extra value).
   d. Minify (smaller, shorter, lighter).
   e. Substitute (other ingredients, process, power).
   f. Rearrange (other patterns, layout, sequence, components).
   g. Reverse (inside out).
   h. Combine (blend, alloy, assortment, ensemble; combine units, purposes, appeals, ideas).
2. Developing quality variations.
3. Developing additional models and sizes (product proliferation).

development. Likewise, firms are practicing market development if they switch from advertising in trade publications to advertising in newspapers or if they add jobbers to supplement their mail-order sales efforts.

Market development allows firms to leverage some of their traditional strengths by identifying new uses for existing products and new demographically, psychographically, or geographically defined markets. Frequently, changes in media selection, promotional appeals, and distribution signal the implementation of this strategy. Du Pont used market development when it found a new application for Kevlar, an organic material that police, security, and military personnel had used primarily for bulletproofing. Kevlar now is being used to refit and maintain wooden-hulled boats, since it is lighter and stronger than glass fibers and has 11 times the strength of steel. Coca-Cola provides another example, as described in Exhibit 7.4, Top Strategist. Under the leadership of CEO Muhtar Kent, Coca-Cola implemented advertising and public relations initiatives to develop its market share among the Hispanic population in North America.

The medical industry provides other examples of new markets for existing products. The National Institutes of Health's report of a study showing that the use of aspirin may lower the incidence of heart attacks was expected to boost sales in the $2.2 billion analgesic market. It was predicted that the expansion of this market would lower the market share of nonaspirin brands, such as industry leaders Tylenol and Advil. Product extensions currently planned include Bayer Calendar Pack, 28-day packaging to fit the once-a-day prescription for the prevention of a second heart attack.

Another example is Cheesebrough-Ponds, a major producer of health and beauty aids, which decided several years ago to expand its market by repacking its Vaseline Petroleum Jelly in pocket-size squeeze tubes as Vaseline "Lip Therapy." The corporation decided to place a strategic emphasis on market development, because it knew from market studies that its petroleum-jelly customers already were using the product to prevent chapped lips. Company leaders reasoned that their market could be expanded significantly if the product were repackaged to fit conveniently in consumers' pockets and purses.

3. Product Development

product development
A grand strategy that involves the substantial modification of existing products that can be marketed to current customers.

Product development involves the substantial modification of existing products or the creation of new but related products that can be marketed to current customers through established channels. The product development strategy often is adopted either to prolong the life cycle of current products or to take advantage of a favorite reputation or brand name. The idea is to attract satisfied customers to new products as a result of their positive experience with the firm's initial offering. The bottom section in Exhibit 7.3 lists some of the options available to firms undertaking product development. A revised edition of a college textbook, a new car style, and a second formula of shampoo for oily hair are examples of the product development strategy.

Similarly, Pepsi changed its strategy on beverage products by creating new products to follow the industry movement away from mass branding. This new movement was designed to attract a younger, hipper customer segment. Pepsi's new products include a version of Mountain Dew, called Code Red, and new Pepsi brands, called Pepsi Twist and Pepsi Blue.

The product development strategy is based on the penetration of existing markets by incorporating product modifications into existing items or by developing new products with a clear connection to the existing product line. The telecommunications industry provides an example of product extension based on product modification. To increase its estimated 8 to 10 percent share of the $5 to $6 billion corporate user market, MCI Communication Corporation extended its direct-dial service to 146 countries, the same as those serviced by AT&T, at lower average rates than those of AT&T. MCI's addition of 79 countries to its network underscores its belief in this market, which it expects to grow 15 to 20 percent annually. Another example of expansions linked to existing lines is Gerber's decision to engage in general merchandise marketing. Gerber's recent introduction included 52 items that ranged from feeding accessories to toys and children's wear. Likewise, Nabisco Brands seeks competitive advantage by placing its strategic emphasis on product development. With headquarters in Parsippany, New Jersey, the company is one of three operating units of RJR Nabisco. It is the leading producer of biscuits, confections, snacks, shredded cereals, and processed fruits and vegetables. To maintain its position as leader, Nabisco pursues a strategy of developing and introducing new products and expanding its existing product line. Spoon Size Shredded Wheat and Ritz Bits crackers are two examples of new products that are variations on existing products.

4. Innovation

innovation
A grand strategy that seeks to reap the premium margins associated with creation and customer acceptance of a new product or service.

In many industries, it has become increasingly risky not to innovate. Both consumer and industrial markets have come to expect periodic changes and improvements in the products offered. As a result, some firms find it profitable to make **innovation** their grand strategy. They seek to reap the initially high profits associated with customer acceptance of a new or greatly improved product. Then, rather than face stiffening competition as the basis of profitability shifts from innovation to production or marketing competence, they search for other original or novel ideas. The underlying rationale of the grand strategy of innovation is to create a new product life cycle and thereby make similar existing products obsolete. Thus, this strategy differs from the product development strategy of extending an existing product's life cycle. For example, Intel, a leader in the semiconductor industry, pursues expansion through a strategic emphasis on innovation. Companies under pressure to innovate often supplement their own R&D efforts by partnering with other firms in their industry that have complementary needs.

While most growth-oriented firms appreciate the need to be innovative, a few firms use it as their fundamental way of relating to their markets. An outstanding example is Polaroid, which heavily promoted each of its new cameras until competitors were able to match its technological innovation; by then, Polaroid normally was prepared to introduce a dramatically new or improved product. For example, it introduced consumers in quick succession to the Swinger, the SX-70, the One Step, and the Sun Camera 660.

Few innovative ideas prove profitable because the research, development, and premarketing costs of converting a promising idea into a profitable product are extremely high. A study by the Booz Allen Hamilton management research department provides some understanding of the risks. As shown in Exhibit 7.5, Booz Allen found that fewer than 2 percent of the innovative projects initially considered by 51 companies

Exhibit 7.5
Decay of New Product Ideas (51 Companies)

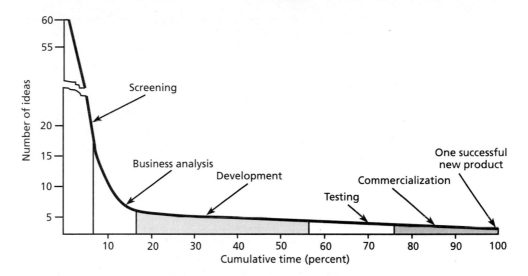

eventually reached the marketplace. Specifically, out of every 58 new product ideas, only 12 pass an initial screening test that finds them compatible with the firm's mission and long-term objectives, only 7 remain after an evaluation of their potential, and only 3 survive development attempts. Of the three survivors, two appear to have profit potential after test marketing and only one is commercially successful.

5. Horizontal Integration

horizontal integration

A grand strategy based on growth through the acquisition of similar firms operating at the same stage of the production-marketing chain.

When a firm's long-term strategy is based on growth through the acquisition of one or more similar firms operating at the same stage of the production-marketing chain, its grand strategy is called **horizontal integration.** Such acquisitions eliminate competitors and provide the acquiring firm with access to new markets. One example is Warner-Lambert's acquisition of Parke Davis, which reduced competition in the ethical drugs field for Chilcott Laboratories, a firm that Warner-Lambert previously had acquired. Another example is the long-range acquisition pattern of White Consolidated Industries, which expanded in the refrigerator and freezer market through a grand strategy of horizontal integration, by acquiring Kelvinator Appliance, the Refrigerator Products Division of Bendix Westinghouse Automotive Air Brake, and Frigidaire Appliance from General Motors. Nike's acquisition in the dress shoes business and N. V. Homes's purchase of Ryan Homes have vividly exemplified the success that horizontal integration strategies can bring.

The attractions of a horizontal acquisition strategy are many and varied.[3] However every benefit provides the parent firm with critical resources that it needs to improve overall profitability. For example, the acquiring firm that uses a horizontal acquisition can quickly expand its operations geographically, increase its market share, improve its production capabilities and economies of scale, gain control of knowledge-based resources, broaden its product line, and increase its efficient use of capital. An added attraction of horizontal acquisition is that these benefits are achieved with only moderately increased risk, because the success of the expansion is principally dependent on proven abilities.

[3] This section was drawn from John A. Pearce II and D. Keith Robbins, "Strategic Transformation as the Essential Last Step in the Process of Business Turnaround," *Business Horizons* 50, no. 5 (2008).

A horizontal merger can provide the firm with an opportunity to offer its customers a broader product line. This motivation has sparked a series of acquisitions in the security software industry. Because Entrust purchased Business Signatures, the consolidated company is able to offer banks a full suite of antifraud products. Similarly, Verisign's acquisitions of m-Qube and Snapcentric, enabled Verisign to expand its cross-marketing options by offering password-generating software, transaction monitoring software, and identity protection. RSA Security's horizontal acquisitions started with the purchase of PassMark, which reduced competitors in the authentication software space. RSA Security then acquired Cyota to provide its customers with both transaction monitoring and authentication software. As a final example, Symantec bought both Veritas Software and WholeSecurity to provide its customers of storage with additional features, such as antivirus software.

The motivation to gain market share has prompted the financial industry to feature horizontal merger strategies. The acquisition of First Coastal Bank by Citizens Business Bank provided new bases of operation in Los Angeles and Manhattan for Citizen Business Bank. The merger of Raincross Credit Union with Visterra Credit Union enabled these credit unions to achieve the size to justify the expansion of services their customers were demanding.

Some horizontal mergers are motivated by the opportunity to combine resources as a means to improve operational efficiency. In the energy industry, for example, there were eight announced horizontal acquisitions with a combined value of $64 billion between January 2004 and January 2007. In each case, increased operational efficiencies resulted from the elimination of duplicated costs. In 2005, Duke Energy acquired Cinergy Corp. for $14.1 billion. The friendly takeover worked well because Duke Energy's North America division was a great match with Cinergy's energy trading operation and provided economies of scale and scope. The combined company lowered costs by an estimated $400 million per year by using a broad platform to serve both electricity and natural gas customers.[4]

A second example of an efficiency-driven merger is one between Constellation and FPL, which saves between $1.5 and $2.1 billion by eliminating overlapping operations.[5] Another example is the acquisition of Green Mountain Power by Gaz Metro, a subsidiary of Northern New England Energy Power for $187 million. The merger was prompted by Green Mountain Power's expiring supplier contracts that threatened it with high costs of going to suppliers who were out of its geographic region—but within the region of Gaz Metro. The horizontal acquisition enabled Green Mountain Power to avail itself of Gaz Metro's suppliers.

Deutsche Telekom's growth strategy was horizontal acquisition. Deutsche Telekom was a dominant player in the European wireless services market, but without a presence in the fast-growing U.S. market in 2000. To correct this limitation, Deutsche Telekom horizontally integrated by purchasing the American firm VoiceStream Wireless, a company that was growing faster than most domestic rivals and that owned spectrum licenses providing access to 220 million potential customers.

Finally, through a horizontal integration designed to take advantage of the multiple strengths of the grand strategy, Aon acquired its top rival Benfield. The new company Aon Benfield promises to be the world leader in reinsurance brokerage and expects significant cost reductions, increased efficiencies, and stronger presence in the reinsurance market, as discussed in Exhibit 7.6, Strategy in Action.

---

[4] G. Terzo,"Duke and Cinergy Spur Utility M&A," *The Investment Dealer's Digest IDD,* January 16, 2006, p. 1.
[5] J. Fontana,"A New Wave of Consolidation in the Utility Industry," *Electric Light and Power* 84, no. 4 (July/August 2006), pp. 36–38.

Horizontal Integration of Aon and Benfield

In 2008, Aon acquired its top rival Benfield and immediately undertook a full horizontal integration. Aon could then deliver new solutions in expanded reinsurance markets under a new brand: Aon Benfield.

Aon and Benfield were ideal candidates for horizontal integration due to their shared focus on service excellence and creating value for clients through thought leadership. The firms also overlapped in their targeted developing markets, including those in Asia, central and eastern Europe, Africa, and Latin America.

Aon Benfield anticipated that once the integration was complete, shared services would lead to $122 million in annual cost savings. The acquisition also doubled the new combination's access to key major accounts, allowing Aon Benfield to serve most global insurance and reinsurance carriers. Importantly, Aon gained access to property-catastrophe markets in the southeastern United States, where it can leverage Benfield's unique risk analysis and modeling technologies.

Source: "Aon Completes Acquisition of Benfield Group Limited," *Marketwatch*, November 28, 2008.

6. Vertical Integration

vertical integration
A grand strategy based on the acquisition of firms that supply the acquiring firm with inputs or new customers for its outputs.

When a firm's grand strategy is to acquire firms that supply it with inputs (such as raw materials) or are customers for its outputs (such as warehousers for finished products), **vertical integration** is involved. To illustrate, if a shirt manufacturer acquires a textile producer—by purchasing its common stock, buying its assets, or exchanging ownership interests—the strategy is vertical integration. In this case, it is *backward* vertical integration, because the acquired firm operates at an earlier stage of the production-marketing process. If the shirt manufacturer had merged with a clothing store, it would have been *forward* vertical integration—the acquisition of a firm nearer to the ultimate consumer.

Amoco emerged as North America's leader in natural gas reserves and products as a result of its acquisition of Dome Petroleum. This backward integration by Amoco was made in support of its downstream businesses in refining and in gas stations, whose profits made the acquisition possible.

Exhibit 7.7 depicts both horizontal and vertical integration. The principal attractions of a horizontal integration grand strategy are readily apparent. The acquiring firm is able to

Exhibit 7.7
Vertical and Horizontal Integrations

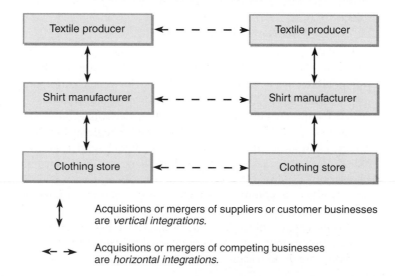

Acquisitions or mergers of suppliers or customer businesses are *vertical integrations.*

Acquisitions or mergers of competing businesses are *horizontal integrations.*

greatly expand its operations, thereby achieving greater market share, improving economies of scale, and increasing the efficiency of capital use. In addition, these benefits are achieved with only moderately increased risk, because the success of the expansion is principally dependent on proven abilities.

The reasons for choosing a vertical integration grand strategy are more varied and sometimes less obvious. The main reason for backward integration is the desire to increase the dependability of the supply or quality of the raw materials used as production inputs. That desire is particularly great when the number of suppliers is small and the number of competitors is large. In this situation, the vertically integrating firm can better control its costs and, thereby, improve the profit margin of the expanded production-marketing system. Forward integration is a preferred grand strategy if great advantages accrue to stable production. A firm can increase the predictability of demand for its output through forward integration; that is, through ownership of the next stage of its production-marketing chain.

Some increased risks are associated with both types of integration. For horizontally integrated firms, the risks stem from increased commitment to one type of business. For vertically integrated firms, the risks result from the firm's expansion into areas requiring strategic managers to broaden the base of their competencies and to assume additional responsibilities.

7. Concentric Diversification

concentric diversification

A grand strategy that involves the operation of a second business that benefits from access to the first firm's core competencies.

Concentric diversification involves the acquisition of businesses that are related to the acquiring firm in terms of technology, markets, or products. With this grand strategy, the selected new businesses possess a high degree of compatibility with the firm's current businesses. The ideal concentric diversification occurs when the combined company profits increase the strengths and opportunities and decrease the weaknesses and exposure to risk. Thus, the acquiring firm searches for new businesses whose products, markets, distribution channels, technologies, and resource requirements are similar to but not identical with its own, whose acquisition results in synergies but not complete interdependence.

Abbott Laboratories pursues an aggressive concentric growth strategy. Abbott seeks to acquire a wide range of businesses that have some important connection to its basic business. In recent years, this strategy has led the company to acquire pharmaceuticals, a diagnostic business, and a medical device manufacturer.

8. Conglomerate Diversification

conglomerate diversification

A grand strategy that involves the acquisition of a business because it presents the most promising investment opportunity available.

Occasionally a firm, particularly a very large one, plans to acquire a business because it represents the most promising investment opportunity available. This grand strategy is commonly known as **conglomerate diversification.** The principal concern, and often the sole concern, of the acquiring firm is the profit pattern of the venture. Unlike concentric diversification, conglomerate diversification gives little concern to creating product-market synergy with existing businesses. What such conglomerate diversifiers as ITT, Textron, American Brands, Litton, U.S. Industries, Fuqua, and I. C. Industries seek is financial synergy. For example, they may seek a balance in their portfolios between current businesses with cyclical sales and acquired businesses with countercyclical sales, between high-cash/low-opportunity and low-cash/high-opportunity businesses, or between debt-free and highly leveraged businesses.

The principal difference between the two types of diversification is that concentric diversification emphasizes some commonality in markets, products, or technology, whereas conglomerate diversification is based principally on profit considerations.

Several of the grand strategies discussed above, including concentric and conglomerate diversification and horizontal and vertical integration, often involve the purchase or acquisition of one firm by another.

Motivation for Diversification

Grand strategies involving either concentric or conglomerate diversification represent distinctive departures from a firm's existing base of operations, typically the acquisition or internal generation (spin-off) of a separate business with synergistic possibilities counterbalancing the strengths and weaknesses of the two businesses. For example, Head Ski sought to diversify into summer sporting goods and clothing to offset the seasonality of its "snow" business. Additionally, diversifications occasionally are undertaken as unrelated investments, because of their high profit potential and their otherwise minimal resource demands.

Regardless of the approach taken, the motivations of the acquiring firms are the same:

- Increase the firm's stock value. In the past, mergers often have led to increases in the stock price or the price-earnings ratio.
- Increase the growth rate of the firm.
- Make an investment that represents better use of funds than plowing them into internal growth.
- Improve the stability of earnings and sales by acquiring firms whose earnings and sales complement the firm's peaks and valleys.
- Balance or fill out the product line.
- Diversify the product line when the life cycle of current products has peaked.
- Acquire a needed resource quickly (e.g., high-quality technology or highly innovative management).
- Achieve tax savings by purchasing a firm whose tax losses will offset current or future earnings.
- Increase efficiency and profitability, especially if there is synergy between the acquiring firm and the acquired firm.[6]

9. Turnaround

For any one of a large number of reasons, a firm can find itself with declining profits. Among these reasons are economic recessions, production inefficiencies, and innovative breakthroughs by competitors. In many cases, strategic managers believe that such a firm can survive and eventually recover if a concerted effort is made over a period of a few years to fortify its distinctive competencies. This grand strategy is known as **turnaround.** It typically is begun through one of two forms of retrenchment, employed singly or in combination:

turnaround
A grand strategy of cost reduction and asset reduction by a company to survive and recover from declining profits.

1. *Cost reduction.* Examples include decreasing the workforce through employee attrition, leasing rather than purchasing equipment, extending the life of machinery, eliminating elaborate promotional activities, laying off employees, dropping items from a production line, and discontinuing low-margin customers.

2. *Asset reduction.* Examples include the sale of land, buildings, and equipment not essential to the basic activity of the firm and the elimination of "perks," such as the company airplane and executives' cars.

[6] Godfrey Devlin and Mark Bleackley, "Strategic Alliances—Guidelines for Success," *Long Range Planning*, October 1988, pp. 18–23.

A Model of the Turnaround Process

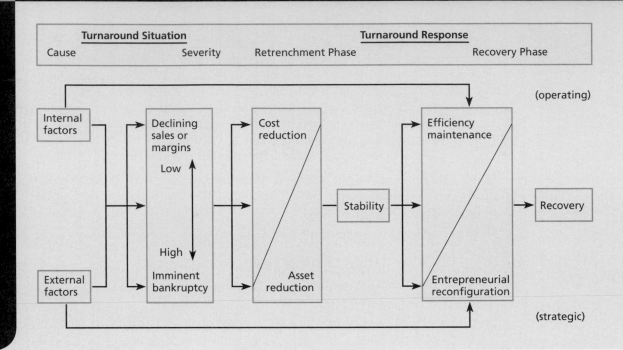

Turnaround Situation		Turnaround Response	
Cause	Severity	Retrenchment Phase	Recovery Phase

Interestingly, the turnaround most commonly associated with this approach is in management positions. In a study of 58 large firms, researchers Schendel, Patton, and Riggs found that turnaround almost always was associated with changes in top management.[7] Bringing in new managers was believed to introduce needed new perspectives on the firm's situation, to raise employee morale, and to facilitate drastic actions, such as deep budgetary cuts in established programs.

Strategic management research provides evidence that the firms that have used a *turnaround strategy* have successfully confronted decline. The research findings have been assimilated and used as the building blocks for a model of the turnaround process shown in Exhibit 7.8, Strategy in Action.

The model begins with a depiction of external and internal factors as causes of a firm's performance downturn. When these factors continue to detrimentally impact the firm, its financial health is threatened. Unchecked decline places the firm in a turnaround situation.

A *turnaround situation* represents absolute and relative-to-industry declining performance of a sufficient magnitude to warrant explicit turnaround actions. Turnaround situations may be the result of years of gradual slowdown or months of sharp decline. In either case, the recovery phase of the turnaround process is likely to be more successful in accomplishing turnaround when it is preceded by planned retrenchment that results in the

[7] D. Schendel, R. Patton, and J. Riggs, "Corporate Turnaround Strategies: A Study of Profit Decline and Recovery," *Journal of General Management* 3, no. 3 (1976), pp. 3–11.

achievement of near-term financial stabilization. For a declining firm, stabilizing operations and restoring profitability almost always entail strict cost reduction followed by a shrinking back to those segments of the business that have the best prospects of attractive profit margins. The need for retrenchment was reflected in unemployment figures during the 2000–2003 recession. More layoffs of American workers were announced in 2001 than in any of the previous eight years when U.S. companies announced nearly 2 million layoffs as the economy sunk into its first recession in a decade.

The immediacy of the resulting threat to company survival posed by the turnaround situation is known as *situation severity*. Severity is the governing factor in estimating the speed with which the retrenchment response will be formulated and activated. When severity is low, a firm has some financial cushion. Stability may be achieved through cost retrenchment alone. When turnaround situation severity is high, a firm must immediately stabilize the decline or bankruptcy is imminent. Cost reductions must be supplemented with more drastic asset reduction measures. Assets targeted for divestiture are those determined to be underproductive. In contrast, more productive resources are protected from cuts and represent critical elements of the future core business plan of the company (i.e., the intended recovery response).

Turnaround responses among successful firms typically include two stages of strategic activities: retrenchment and the recovery response. *Retrenchment* consists of cost-cutting and asset-reducing activities. The primary objective of the retrenchment phase is to stabilize the firm's financial condition. Situation severity has been associated with retrenchment responses among successful turnaround firms. Firms in danger of bankruptcy or failure (i.e., severe situations) attempt to halt decline through cost and asset reductions. Firms in less severe situations have achieved stability merely through cost retrenchment. However, in either case, for firms facing declining financial performance, the key to successful turnaround rests in the effective and efficient management of the retrenchment process.

The primary causes of the turnaround situation have been associated with the second phase of the turnaround process, the *recovery response*. During the first year of the recent recession, many firms cut costs sharply to avoid financial failure. For examples of firms that turned losses into profits in 2008 by cost-cutting, read Exhibit 7.9, Strategy in Action. For firms that declined primarily as a result of external problems, turnaround most often has been achieved through creative new entrepreneurial strategies. For firms that declined primarily as a result of internal problems, turnaround has been most frequently achieved through efficiency strategies. *Recovery* is achieved when economic measures indicate that the firm has regained its predownturn levels of performance.

10. Divestiture

divestiture strategy
A grand strategy that involves the sale of a firm or a major unit of a firm as a going concern.

A **divestiture strategy** involves the sale of a firm or a major component of a firm. Sara Lee Corp. (SLE) provides a good example. It sells everything from Wonderbras and Kiwi shoe polish to Endust furniture polish and Chock Full o'Nuts coffee. The company used a conglomerate diversification strategy to build Sara Lee into a huge portfolio of disparate brands. A new president, C. Steven McMillan, faced stagnant revenues and earnings. So he consolidated, streamlined, and focused the company on its core categories—food, underwear, and household products. He divested 15 businesses, including Coach leather goods, which together equaled more than 20 percent of the company's revenue, and laid off 13,200 employees, nearly 10 percent of the workforce. McMillan used the cash from asset sales to snap up brands that enhanced Sara Lee's clout in key categories, like the $2.8 billion purchase of St. Louis–based breadmaker Earthgrains Co. to quadruple Sara Lee's bakery operations. In another case of divestitures, Kraft Foods found that it could

Cutting Costs to Increase Profits

Because of successful cost-cutting at Gap, which boosted profits despite declining industry sales, shares of Gap increased 27 percent in the first three quarters of 2008, even as sales fell 8 percent for competitors Banana Republic and Old Navy. Gap's survival odds were aided by cost savings achieved through reduced inventory levels and the sell-off of noncore assets such as selected real estate holdings.

Similarly, in the face of sharply declining revenues, Dell undertook cost-cutting in 2008, including massive layoffs that totaled 11,000 employees for the year and an aggressive plan to sell its manufacturing facilities worldwide.

Although many firms find it possible to maintain some level of profit by cost-cutting for as long as one full year, aggressive cost-cutters must eventually find ways to increase their revenues. Circuit City and Radio Shack cut costs and increased profit margins in 2008 but were undone by sharp declines in their revenues. Circuit City filed for bankruptcy in November, the day after it announced that it would close 155 retail stores, and Radio Shack lost 50 percent of its market value for the year of 2008.

improve its overall operations by selling some of its best-known brands, including Cream of Wheat.

When retrenchment fails to accomplish the desired turnaround, or when a nonintegrated business activity achieves an unusually high market value, strategic managers often decide to sell the firm. However, because the intent is to find a buyer willing to pay a premium above the value of a going concern's fixed assets, the term *marketing for sale* is often more appropriate. Prospective buyers must be convinced that because of their skills and resources or because of the firm's synergy with their existing businesses, they will be able to profit from the acquisition.

Corning undertook a turnaround that followed retrenchment with divestitures. In 2001, Corning found itself in a declining market for its core product of fiber-optic cable. The company needed to develop a strategy that would allow it to turn around its falling sales and begin to grow once more. It began with retrenchment. Corning laid off 12,000 workers in 2001 and another 4,000 in 2002. Corning also began the divestiture of its noncore assets, such as its nontelecom businesses and its money-losing photonics operation, to stabilize its financial situation so that it could begin its recovery.

The reasons for divestiture vary. They often arise because of partial mismatches between the acquired firm and the parent corporation. Some of the mismatched parts cannot be integrated into the corporation's mainstream activities and, thus, must be spun off. A second reason is corporate financial needs. Sometimes the cash flow or financial stability of the corporation as a whole can be greatly improved if businesses with high market value can be sacrificed. The result can be a balancing of equity with long-term risks or of long-term debt payments to optimize the cost of capital. A third, less frequent reason for divestiture is government antitrust action when a firm is believed to monopolize or unfairly dominate a particular market.

Although examples of the divestiture grand strategy are numerous, CBS Inc. provides an outstanding example. In a two-year period, the once diverse entertainment and publishing giant sold its Records Division to Sony, its magazine publishing business to Diamandis Communications, its book publishing operations to Harcourt Brace Jovanovich, and its music publishing operations to SBK Entertainment World. Other firms that have pursued this type of grand strategy include Esmark, which divested Swift & Company, and White Motors, which divested White Farm.

The Ultimate Failure of Circuit City

On November 10, 2008, Circuit City filed for Chapter 11 bankruptcy, as a consequence of bad management in an industry where competition for market share is fierce among competitors such as Best Buy and Wal-Mart.

An article in *Time* magazine called the culprit in Circuit City's disastrous performance "good ole fashioned bad management." Specifically, Circuit City's failure is attributed to inconvenient store locations, eliminating appliances from the product line, languishing in the gaming market, utilizing an underpaid and undertrained workforce, and ignoring big-name cross-promotional opportunities. Such missteps suggested an underlying cause: marketplace complacency. In the fiercely competitive retail electronics industry, Circuit City faced, most notably, Best Buy and Wal-Mart and a myriad of lesser firms, including Amazon, Apple, Costco, Dell, Fry's Electronics, and Radio Shack.

Circuit City was the largest electronics retailer in the United States through the mid-1990s. During that time, the company signed leases on cheap, often out-of-the-way real estate, which made for some uninviting shopping experiences in too-big spaces. As sales decreased, Circuit City replaced its higher paid, more experienced workforce with lower paid, less experienced workers, resulting in a deteriorating reputation for bad customer service. In the meantime, competitors secured better real estate deals, offered better services, and adapted more quickly to the competitive marketplace. Circuit City lost its market share lead to Best Buy, which became known as a higher end, customer-centric retailer, as contrasted to Wal-Mart, the low-price provider.

On January 16, 2009, Circuit City announced that it could not resolve its financial problems and would close its remaining 567 U.S. stores (with 34,000 employees) and liquidate the business. It continued to negotiate the sale of its 765 retail stores and dealer outlets in Canada.

Hudson Capital Partners, the liquidator for Circuit City, estimated the retail value of the company's assets at $1.8 billion. These items were placed on sale at a 30 percent discount that increased until the liquidation was complete.

Sources: A. Hamilton, "Why Circuit City Busted, While Best Buy Boomed," *Time Online*, 2008, http://www.time.com/time/business/article/0,8599,1858079,00.html; and S. Rosenbloom, "Electronics Store Files for Bankruptcy," *The New York Times*, 2008, p. B1.

11. Liquidation

liquidation
A grand strategy that involves the sale of the assets of the business for their salvage value.

When **liquidation** is the grand strategy, the firm typically is sold in parts, only occasionally as a whole—but for its tangible asset value and not as a going concern. In selecting liquidation, the owners and strategic managers of a firm are admitting failure and recognize that this action is likely to result in great hardships to themselves and their employees. For these reasons, liquidation usually is seen as the least attractive of the grand strategies. As a long-term strategy, however, it minimizes the losses of all the firm's stockholders. Faced with bankruptcy, the liquidating firm usually tries to develop a planned and orderly system that will result in the greatest possible return and cash conversion as the firm slowly relinquishes its market share.

Planned liquidation can be worthwhile. For example, Columbia Corporation, a $130 million diversified firm, liquidated its assets for more cash per share than the market value of its stock. Much more commonly, liquidation goes hand-in-hand with bankruptcy, as shown in the Circuit City experience that is discussed in Exhibit 7.10, Strategy in Action.

12. Bankruptcy

bankruptcy
When a company is unable to pay its debts as they become due, or has more debts than assets.

Business failures are playing an increasingly important role in the American economy. In an average week, more than 300 companies fail and file for **bankruptcy.** More than 75 percent of these financially desperate firms file for a *liquidation bankruptcy*—they agree to a complete distribution of their assets to creditors, most of whom receive a small fraction of the amount they are owed. Liquidation is what the layperson views as bankruptcy: the business cannot pay its debts, so it must close its doors. Investors lose their money, employees lose their jobs, and managers lose their credibility. In owner-managed firms, company and personal bankruptcy commonly go hand in hand.

The other 25 percent of these firms refuse to surrender until one final option is exhausted. Choosing a strategy to recapture its viability, such a company asks the courts for a *reorganization bankruptcy*. The firm attempts to persuade its creditors to temporarily freeze their claims while it undertakes to reorganize and rebuild the company's operations more profitably. The appeal of a reorganization bankruptcy is based on the company's ability to convince creditors that it can succeed in the marketplace by implementing a new strategic plan, and that when the plan produces profits, the firm will be able to repay its creditors, perhaps in full. In other words, the company offers its creditors a carefully designed alternative to forcing an immediate, but fractional, repayment of its financial obligations. The option of reorganization bankruptcy offers maximum repayment of debt at some specified future time if a new strategic plan is successful.

The Bankruptcy Situation

Imagine that your firm's financial reports have shown an unabated decline in revenue for seven quarters. Expenses have increased rapidly, and it is becoming difficult, and at times not possible, to pay bills as they become due. Suppliers are concerned about shipping goods without first receiving payment, and some have refused to ship without advanced payment in cash. Customers are requiring assurances that future orders will be delivered and some are beginning to buy from competitors. Employees are listening seriously to rumors of financial problems and a higher than normal number have accepted other employment. What can be done? What strategy can be initiated to protect the company and resolve the financial problems in the short term?

Chapter 7: The Harshest Resolution

If the judgment of the owners of a business is that its decline cannot be reversed, and the business cannot be sold as a going concern, then the alternative that is in the best interest of all may be a liquidation bankruptcy, also known as Chapter 7 of the Bankruptcy Code. The court appoints a trustee, who collects the property of the company, reduces it to cash, and distributes the proceeds proportionally to creditors on a pro rata basis as expeditiously as possible. Because all assets are sold to pay outstanding debt, a liquidation bankruptcy terminates a business. This type of filing is critically important to sole proprietors or partnerships. Their owners are personally liable for all business debts not covered by the sale of the business assets unless they can secure a Chapter 7 bankruptcy, which will allow them to cancel any debt in excess of exempt assets. Although they will be left with little personal property, the liquidated debtor is discharged from paying the remaining debt.

The shareholders of corporations are not liable for corporate debt and any debt existing after corporate assets are liquidated is absorbed by creditors. Corporate shareholders may simply terminate operations and walk away without liability to remaining creditors. However, filing a Chapter 7 proceeding will provide for an orderly and fair distribution of assets to creditors and thereby may reduce the negative impact of the business failure.

Chapter 11: A Conditional Second Chance

A proactive alternative for the endangered company is reorganization bankruptcy. Chosen for the right reasons, and implemented in the right way, reorganization bankruptcy can provide a financially, strategically, and ethically sound basis on which to advance the interests of all of the firm's stakeholders.

A thorough and objective analysis of the company may support the idea of its continuing operations if excessive debt can be reduced and new strategic initiatives can be undertaken. If the realistic possibility of long-term survival exists, a reorganization under Chapter 11 of the Bankruptcy Code can provide the opportunity. Reorganization allows a business debtor to restructure its debts and, with the agreement of creditors and approval of the court, to continue as a viable business. Creditors involved in Chapter 11 actions often receive less than the total debt due to them but far more than would be available from liquidation.

A Chapter 11 bankruptcy can provide time and protection to the debtor firm (which we will call the *Company*) to reorganize and use future earnings to pay creditors. The Company may restructure debts, close unprofitable divisions or stores, renegotiate labor contracts, reduce its workforce, or propose other actions that could create a profitable business. If the plan is accepted by creditors, the Company will be given another chance to avoid liquidation and emerge from the bankruptcy proceedings rehabilitated.

Seeking Protection of the Bankruptcy Court

If creditors file lawsuits or schedule judicial sales to enforce liens, the Company will need to seek the protection of the Bankruptcy Court. Filing a bankruptcy petition will invoke the protection of the court to provide sufficient time to work out a reorganization that was not achievable voluntarily. If reorganization is not possible, a Chapter 7 proceeding will allow for the fair and orderly dissolution of the business.

If a Chapter 11 proceeding is the required course of action, the Company must determine what the reorganized business will look like, if such a structure can be achieved, and how it will be accomplished while maintaining operations during the bankruptcy proceeding. Will sufficient cash be available to pay for the proceedings and reorganization? Will customers continue to do business with the Company or seek other more secure businesses with which to deal? Will key personnel stay on or look for more secure employment? Which operations should be discontinued or reduced?

Emerging from Bankruptcy

Bankruptcy is only the first step toward recovery for a firm. Many questions should be answered: How did the business get to the point at which the extreme action of bankruptcy was necessary? Were warning signs overlooked? Was the competitive environment understood? Did pride or fear prevent objective analysis? Did the business have the people and resources to succeed? Was the strategic plan well designed and implemented? Did financial problems result from unforeseen and unforeseeable problems or from bad management decisions?

Commitments to "try harder," "listen more carefully to the customer," and "be more efficient" are important but insufficient grounds to inspire stakeholder confidence. A recovery strategy must be developed to delineate how the company will compete more successfully in the future.

An assessment of the bankruptcy situation requires executives to consider the causes of the Company's decline and the severity of the problem it now faces. Investors must decide whether the management team that governed the company's operations during the downturn can return the firm to a position of success. Creditors must believe that the company's managers have learned how to prevent a recurrence of the observed and similar problems. Alternatively, they must have faith that the company's competencies can be sufficiently augmented by key substitutions to the management team, with strong support in decision making from a board of directors and consultants, to restore the firm's competitive strength.

The 12 grand strategies just discussed, used singly and much more often in combinations, represent the traditional alternatives used by firms in the United States. Recently, three new grand types have gained in popularity (thus totaling the 15 grand strategies we said we would discuss); all fit under the broad category of corporate combinations. Although they do not fit the criterion by which executives retain a high degree of control over their operations, these grand strategies deserve special attention and consideration—especially by companies that operate in global, dynamic, and technologically driven industries. These three newly popularized grand strategies are joint ventures, strategic alliances, and consortia.

13. Joint Ventures

Occasionally two or more capable firms lack a necessary component for success in a particular competitive environment. For example, no single petroleum firm controlled sufficient resources to construct the Alaskan pipeline. Nor was any single firm capable of processing and marketing all of the oil that would flow through the pipeline. The solution was a set of **joint ventures,** which are commercial companies (children) created and operated for the benefit of the co-owners (parents). These cooperative arrangements provided both the funds needed to build the pipeline and the processing and marketing capacities needed to profitably handle the oil flow.

joint venture
A grand strategy in which companies create a co-owned business that operates for their mutual benefit.

The particular form of joint ventures discussed above is *joint ownership.* In recent years, it has become increasingly appealing for domestic firms to join foreign firms by means of this form. For example, Diamond-Star Motors was the result of a joint venture between a U.S. company, Chrysler Corporation, and Japan's Mitsubishi Motors Corporation. Located in Normal, Illinois, Diamond-Star was launched because it offered Chrysler and Mitsubishi a chance to expand on their long-standing relationship in which subcompact cars (as well as Mitsubishi engines and other automotive parts) were imported to the United States and sold under the Dodge and Plymouth names.

The joint venture extends the supplier-consumer relationship and has strategic advantages for both partners. For Chrysler, it presented an opportunity to produce a high-quality car using expertise brought to the venture by Mitsubishi. It also gave Chrysler the chance to try new production techniques and to realize efficiencies by using the workforce that was not included under Chrysler's collective bargaining agreement with the United Auto Workers. The agreement offered Mitsubishi the opportunity to produce cars for sale in the United States without being subjected to the tariffs and restrictions placed on Japanese imports.

As a second example, Bethlehem Steel acquired an interest in a Brazilian mining venture to secure a raw material source. The stimulus for this joint ownership venture was grand strategy, but such is not always the case. Certain countries virtually mandate that foreign firms entering their markets do so on a joint ownership basis. India and Mexico are good examples. The rationale of these countries is that joint ventures minimize the threat of foreign domination and enhance the skills, employment, growth, and profits of local firms.

It should be noted that strategic managers understandably are wary of joint ventures. Admittedly, joint ventures present new opportunities with risks that can be shared. On the other hand, joint ventures often limit the discretion, control, and profit potential of partners, while demanding managerial attention and other resources that might be directed toward the firm's mainstream activities. Nevertheless, increasing globalization in many industries may require greater consideration of the joint venture approach, if historically national firms are to remain viable.

Collaborative Growth in China through Joint Ventures[8]

A prime example of the value of joint ventures is seen in their use by foreign businesses that seek to do business in China. Until very recently, China enthusiastically invited foreign

---

[8] This section was drawn from Pearce II and Robbins, "Strategic Transformation as the Essential Last Step in the Process of Business Turnaround."

investment to help in the development of its economy. However, in the early 2000s, China increased its regulations on foreign investment to moderate its economic growth and to ensure that Chinese businesses would not be at a competitive disadvantage when competing for domestic markets. The new restrictions require local companies to retain control of Chinese trademarks and brands, prevent foreign investors from buying property that is not for their own use, limit the size of foreign-owned retail chains, and restrict foreign investment in selected industries.[9] With these increasing regulations, investment in China through joint ventures with Chinese companies has become a prominent strategy for foreign investors who hope to circumvent some of the limitations on their strategies, therefore more fully capitalizing on China's economic growth.

In China, a host country partner can greatly facilitate the acceptance of a foreign investor and help minimize the costs of doing business in an unknown nation. Typically, the foreign partner contributes financing and technology, while the Chinese partner provides the land, physical facilities, workers, local connections, and knowledge of the country.[10] In a wholly owned venture, the foreign company is forced to acquire the land, build the workspace, and hire and train the employees, all of which are especially expensive propositions in a country in which the foreign company lacks guanxi.[11] Additionally, because China restricts direct foreign investment in the life insurance, energy, construction of transportation facilities, higher education, and health care industries, asset or equity joint ventures are sometimes the only option for foreign firms.

Foreign partners in equity joint ventures benefit from speed of entry to the Chinese market, tax incentives, motivational and competitive advantages of a mutual long-term commitment, and access to the resources of its Chinese partner. Two large joint ventures in the media industry were created when Canada's AGA Resources partnered with Beijing Tangde International Film and Culture Co and when the United States' Sequoia Capital formed a joint venture with Hunan Greatdreams Cartoon Media.[12] Joint ventures in China's asset management industry include the 2006 partnerships between Italy's Banca Lombarda, the United States' Lord Abbett, and Chinese companies.

Similar opportunities exist for international joint ventures in the construction and operation of oil refineries, in the building of the nation's railroad transportation system, and in the development of specific geographic areas. In special economic zones, foreign firms operate businesses with Chinese joint venture partners. The foreign companies receive tax incentives in the form of rates that are lower than the standard 30 percent corporate tax rate. For example, in the Shanghai Pudong New Area, a 15 percent tax rate applies.[13]

The number of international joint ventures is increasing because of China's admission to the World Trade Organization (WTO). Under the conditions of its membership, China is expanding the list of industries that permit foreign investment.[14] As of 2007, for example, foreign investors that participate with Chinese partners in joint ventures are permitted to hold an increased share of JVs in several major industries: banks (up to 20 percent), investment funds (33 percent), life insurance (50 percent), and telecommunications (25 percent).

---

[9] E. Kurtenbach, "China Raising Stakes for Foreign Investment," *Philadelphia Inquirer,* September 24, 2006.

[10] Ying Qui, "Problems of Managing Joint Ventures in China's Interior: Evidence from Shaanxi," *Advanced Management Journal* 70, no. 3 (2005), pp. 46–57.

[11] J. A. Pearce II and R. B. Robinson Jr., "Cultivating Guanxi as a Corporate Foreign-Investor Strategy," *Business Horizons* 43, no. 1 (2000), pp. 31–38.

[12] Andrew Bagnell, "China Business," *China Business Review* 33, no. 5 (2006), pp. 88–92.

[13] N. P. Chopey, "China Still Beckons Petrochemical Investments," *Chemical Engineering* 133, no. 8 (2006) pp. 19–23.

[14] "China's WTO Scorecard: Selected Year-Three Service Commitments," *The US-China Business Council* (2005), pp. 1–2.

14. Strategic Alliances

strategic alliances
Contractual partnerships because the companies involved do not take an equity position in one another

Strategic alliances are distinguishable from joint ventures because the companies involved do not take an equity position in one another. In many instances, strategic alliances are *partnerships* that exist for a defined period during which partners contribute their skills and expertise to a cooperative project. For example, one partner provides manufacturing capabilities while a second partner provides marketing expertise. In other situations, a strategic alliance can enable similar companies to combine their capabilities to counter the threats of a much larger or new type of competitor.

Strategic alliances are sometimes undertaken because the partners want to develop in-house capabilities to supplant the partner when the contractual arrangement between them reaches its termination date. Such relationships are tricky because, in a sense, the partners are attempting to "steal" each other's know-how.

In other instances, strategic alliances are synonymous with *licensing agreements*. Licensing involves the transfer of some industrial property right from the U.S. licensor to a motivated licensee in a foreign country. Most tend to be patents, trademarks, or technical know-how that are granted to the licensee for a specified time in return for a royalty and for avoiding tariffs or import quotas. Bell South and U.S. West, with various marketing and service competitive advantages valuable to Europe, have extended a number of licenses to create personal computers networks in the United Kingdom. Another example of licensing is UTEK Corporation's successful strategy for licensing discoveries resulting from research efforts at universities.

Another licensing strategy is to contract the manufacturing of its product line to a foreign company to exploit local comparative advantages in technology, materials, or labor. MIPS Computer Systems licensed Digital Equipment Corporation, Texas Instruments, Cypress Semiconductor, and Bipolar Integrated Technology in the United States and Fujitsu, NEC, and Kubota in Japan to market computers based on its designs in the partner's country.

Service and franchise-based firms—including Anheuser-Busch, Avis, Coca-Cola, Hilton, Hyatt, Holiday Inns, Kentucky Fried Chicken, McDonald's, and Pepsi—have long engaged in licensing arrangements with foreign distributors as a way to enter new markets with standardized products that can benefit from marketing economies.

Outsourcing is a basic approach to strategic alliances that enables firms to gain a competitive advantage. Significant changes within many segments of American business continue to encourage the use of outsourcing practices. Within the health care arena, an industry survey recorded 67 percent of hospitals using provider outsourcing for at least one department within their organization. Services such as information systems, reimbursement, and risk and physician practice management are outsourced by 51 percent of the hospitals that use outsourcing.

consortia
Large interlocking relationships between businesses of an industry.

keiretsu
A Japanese consortia of businesses that is coordinated by a large trading company to gain a strategic advantage.

Another successful application of outsourcing is found in human resources. A survey of human resource executives revealed 85 percent have personal experience leading an outsourcing effort within their organization. In addition, it was found that two-thirds of pension departments have outsourced at least one human resource function. Within customer service and sales departments, outsourcing increases productivity in such areas as product information, sales and order taking, sample fulfillment, and complaint handling.

chaebol
A Korean consortia financed through government banking groups to gain a strategic advantage.

15. Consortia, *Keiretsus,* and *Chaebols*

Consortia are defined as large interlocking relationships between businesses of an industry. In Japan such consortia are known as **keiretsus;** in South Korea as **chaebols.**

In Europe, consortia projects are increasing in number and in success rates. Examples include the Junior Engineers' and Scientists' Summer Institute, which underwrites cooperative learning and research; the European Strategic Program for Research and Development in Information Technologies, which seeks to enhance European competitiveness in fields related to computer electronics and component manufacturing; and EUREKA, which is a joint program involving scientists and engineers from several European countries to coordinate joint research projects.

A Japanese *keiretsu* is an undertaking involving up to 50 different firms that are joined around a large trading company or bank and are coordinated through interlocking directories and stock exchanges. It is designed to use industry coordination to minimize risks of competition, in part through cost sharing and increased economies of scale. Examples include Sumitomo, Mitsubishi, Mitsui, and Sanwa.

A South Korean *chaebol* resembles a consortium or keiretsu except that it is typically financed through government banking groups and is largely run by professional managers trained by participating firms expressly for the job.

SELECTION OF LONG-TERM OBJECTIVES AND GRAND STRATEGY SETS

At first glance, the strategic management model, which provides the framework for study throughout this book, seems to suggest that strategic choice decision making leads to the sequential selection of long-term objectives and grand strategies. In fact, however, strategic choice is the simultaneous selection of long-range objectives and grand strategies. When strategic planners study their opportunities, they try to determine which are most likely to result in achieving various long-range objectives. Almost simultaneously, they try to forecast whether an available grand strategy can take advantage of preferred opportunities so the tentative objectives can be met. In essence, then, three distinct but highly interdependent choices are being made at one time. Several triads, or sets, of possible decisions are usually considered.

A simplified example of this process is shown in Exhibit 7.11, Strategy in Action. In this example, the firm has determined that six strategic choice options are available. These options stem from three interactive opportunities (e.g., West Coast markets that present little competition). Because each of these interactive opportunities can be approached through different grand strategies—for options 1 and 2, the grand strategies are horizontal integration and market development—each offers the potential for achieving long-range objectives to varying degrees. Thus, a firm rarely can make a strategic choice only on the basis of its preferred opportunities, long-range objectives, or grand strategy. Instead, these three elements must be considered simultaneously, because only in combination do they constitute a strategic choice.

In an actual decision situation, the strategic choice would be complicated by a wider variety of interactive opportunities, feasible company objectives, promising grand strategy options, and evaluative criteria. Nevertheless, Exhibit 7.11 does partially reflect the nature and complexity of the process by which long-term objectives and grand strategies are selected.

In the next chapter, the strategic choice process is fully explained. However, knowledge of long-term objectives and grand strategies is essential to understanding that process.

SEQUENCE OF OBJECTIVES AND STRATEGY SELECTION

The selection of long-range objectives and grand strategies involves simultaneous, rather than sequential, decisions. While it is true that objectives are needed to prevent the firm's direction and progress from being determined by random forces, it is equally true that objectives can be achieved only if strategies are implemented. In fact, long-term objectives

A Profile of Strategic Choice Options

| | Six Strategic Choice Options | | | | | |
Interactive opportunities	1	2	3	4	5	6
	West Coast markets present little competition		Current markets sensitive to price competition		Current industry product lines offer too narrow a range of markets	
Appropriate long-range objectives (limited sample):						
Average 5-year ROI.	15%	19%	13%	17%	23%	15%
Company sales by year 5.	+ 50%	+ 40%	+ 20%	+ 0%	+ 35%	+ 25%
Risk of negative profits.	.30	.25	.10	.15	.20	.05
Grand strategies	Horizontal integration	Market development	Concentration	Selective retrenchment	Product development	Concentration

and grand strategies are so interdependent that some business consultants do not distinguish between them. Long-term objectives and grand strategies are still combined under the heading of company strategy in most of the popular business literature and in the thinking of most practicing executives.

However, the distinction has merit. Objectives indicate what strategic managers want but provide few insights about how they will be achieved. Conversely, strategies indicate what types of actions will be taken but do not define what ends will be pursued or what criteria will serve as constraints in refining the strategic plan.

Does it matter whether strategic decisions are made to achieve objectives or to satisfy constraints? No, because constraints are themselves objectives. The constraint of increased inventory capacity is a desire (an objective), not a certainty. Likewise, the constraint of an increase in the sales force does not ensure that the increase will be achieved, given such factors as other company priorities, labor market conditions, and the firm's profit performance.

DESIGNING A PROFITABLE BUSINESS MODEL

business model
A clear understanding of how the firm will generate profits and the strategic actions it must take to succeed over the long term.

The process of combining long-term objectives and grand strategies produces a **business model.** Creating an effective model requires a clear understanding of how the firm will generate profits and the strategic action it must take to succeed over the long term.

Adrian Slywotzky, David Morrison, and Bob Andelman identified 22 business models—designs that generate profits in a unique way.[15] They present these models as examples,

[15] This section is excerpted from A. J. Slywotzky, D. J. Morrison, and B. Andelman, *The Profit Zone; How Strategic Business Design Will Lead You To Tomorrow's Profits* (New York: Times Books, 1997).

believing that others do or can exist. The authors also believe that in some instances profitability depends on the interplay of two or more business models. Their study demonstrates that the mechanisms of profitability can be very different but that a focus on the customer is the key to the effectiveness of each model.

Slywotzky, Morrison, and Andelman suggest that the two most productive questions asked of executives are these:

1. What is our business model?
2. How do we make a profit?

The classic strategy rule suggested: "Gain market share and profits will follow." This approach once worked for some industries. However, because of competitive turbulence caused by globalization and rapid technological advancements, the once-popular belief in a strong correlation between market share and profitability has collapsed in many industries.

How can businesses earn sustainable profits? The answer is found by analyzing the following questions: Where will the firm make a profit in this industry? How should the business model be designed so that the firm will be profitable? Slywotzky, Morrison, and Andelman describe the following profitability business models as ways to answer those questions.

1. *Customer development customer solutions profit model.* Companies that use this business model make money by finding ways to improve their customers' economics and investing in ways for customers to improve their processes.

2. *Product pyramid profit model.* This model is effective in markets where customers have strong preferences for product characteristics, including variety, style, color, and price. By offering a number of variations, companies can build so-called product pyramids. At the base are low-priced, high-volume products, and at the top are high-priced, low-volume products. Profit is concentrated at the top of the pyramid, but the base is the strategic firewall (i.e., a strong, low-priced brand that deters competitor entry), thereby protecting the margins at the top. Consumer goods companies and automobile companies use this model.

3. *Multicomponent system profit model.* Some businesses are characterized by a production/marketing system that consists of components that generate substantially different levels of profitability. In hotels, for example, there is a substantial difference between the profitability of room rentals and that of bar operations. In such instances, it often is useful to maximize the use of the highest-profit components to maximize the profitability of the whole system.

4. *Switchboard profit model.* Some markets function by connecting multiple sellers to multiple buyers. The switchboard profit model creates a high-value intermediary that concentrates these multiple communication pathways through one point or "switchboard" and thereby reduces costs for both parties in exchange for a fee. As volume increases, so too do profits.

5. *Time profit model.* Sometimes, speed is the key to profitability. This business model takes advantage of first-mover advantage. To sustain this model, constant innovation is essential.

6. *Blockbuster profit model.* In some industries, profitability is driven by a few great product successes. This business model is representative of movie studios, pharmaceutical firms, and software companies, which have high R&D and launch costs and finite product cycles. In this type of environment, it pays to concentrate resource investments in a few projects rather than to take positions in a variety of products.

7. *Profit multiplier model.* This business model reaps gains, repeatedly, from the same product, character, trademark capability, or service. Think of the value that Michael Jordan Inc. creates with the image of the great basketball legend. This model can be a powerful engine for businesses with strong consumer brands.

8. *Entrepreneurial profit model.* Small can be beautiful. This business model stresses that diseconomies of scale can exist in companies. They attack companies that have become comfortable with their profit levels with formal, bureaucratic systems that are remote from customers. As their expenses grow and customer relevance declines, such companies are vulnerable to entrepreneurs who are in direct contact with their customers.

9. *Specialization profit model.* This business model stresses growth through sequenced specialization. Consulting companies have used this design successfully.

10. *Installed base profit model.* A company that pursues this model profits because its established user base subsequently buys the company's brand of consumables or follow-on products. Installed base profits provide a protected annuity stream. Examples include razors and blades, software and upgrades, copiers and toner cartridges, and cameras and film.

11. *De facto standard profit model.* A variant of the installed base profit model, this model is appropriate when the installed base model becomes the de facto standard that governs competitive behavior in the industry.

Summary

Before we learn how strategic decisions are made, it is important to understand the two principal components of any strategic choice; namely, long-term objectives and the grand strategy. The purpose of this chapter was to convey that understanding.

Long-term objectives were defined as the results a firm seeks to achieve over a specified period, typically five years. Seven common long-term objectives were discussed: profitability, productivity, competitive position, employee development, employee relations, technological leadership, and public responsibility. These, or any other long-term objectives, should be flexible, measurable over time, motivating, suitable, and understandable.

Grand strategies were defined as comprehensive approaches guiding the major actions designed to achieve long-term objectives. Fifteen grand strategy options were discussed: concentrated growth, market development, product development, innovation, horizontal integration, vertical integration, concentric diversification, conglomerate diversification, turnaround, divestiture, liquidation, bankruptcy, joint ventures, strategic alliances, and consortia.

Key Terms

balanced scorecard, *p. 182*
bankruptcy, *p. 203*
business model, *p. 210*
chaebol, *p. 208*
concentrated growth, *p. 188*
concentric diversification, *p. 198*
conglomerate diversification, *p. 198*
consortia, *p. 208*
divestiture strategy, *p. 201*
generic strategy, *p. 183*
grand strategy, *p. 187*
horizontal integration, *p. 195*
innovation, *p. 194*
joint venture, *p. 206*
keiretsu, *p. 208*
liquidation, *p. 203*
market development, *p. 191*
product development, *p. 193*
strategic alliances, *p. 208*
turnaround, *p. 199*
vertical integration, *p. 197*

Questions for Discussion

1. Identify firms in the business community nearest to your college or university that you believe are using each of the 15 grand strategies discussed in this chapter.
2. Identify firms in your business community that appear to rely principally on 1 of the 15 grand strategies. What kind of information did you use to classify the firms?

3. Write a long-term objective for your school of business that exhibits the seven qualities of long-term objectives described in this chapter.

4. Distinguish between the following pairs of grand strategies:

   a. Horizontal and vertical integration.
   b. Conglomerate and concentric diversification.
   c. Product development and innovation.
   d. Joint venture and strategic alliance.

5. Rank each of the 15 grand strategy options discussed in this chapter on the following three scales:

High	Low
Cost	

High	Low
Risk of failure	

High	Low
Potential for exceptional growth	

6. Identify firms that use the eight specific options shown in Exhibit 7.3 under the grand strategies of concentration, market development, and product development.

Chapter Eight

Business Strategy

After reading and studying this chapter, you should be able to

1. Determine why a business would choose a low-cost, differentiation, or speed-based strategy.

2. Explain the nature and value of a market focus strategy.

3. Illustrate how a firm can pursue both low-cost and differentiation strategies.

4. Identify requirements for business success at different stages of industry evolution.

5. Determine good business strategies in fragmented and global industries.

6. Decide when a business should diversify.

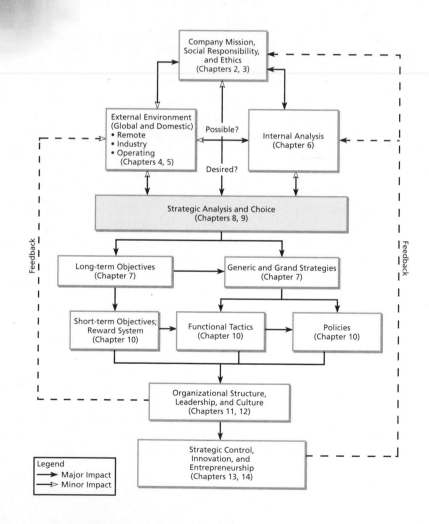

Strategic analysis and choice is the phase of the strategic management process in which business managers examine and choose a business strategy that allows their business to maintain or create a sustainable competitive advantage. Their starting point is to evaluate and determine which competitive advantages provide the basis for distinguishing the firm in the customer's mind from other reasonable alternatives. Businesses with a dominant product or service line must also choose among alternate grand strategies to guide the firm's activities, particularly when they are trying to decide about broadening the scope of the firm's activities beyond its core business. This chapter examines strategic analysis and choice in single- or dominant-product/service businesses by addressing two basic issues:

1. **What strategies are most effective at building sustainable competitive advantages for single business units?** What competitive strategy positions a business most effectively in its industry? For example, Scania, the most productive truck manufacturer in the world, joins its major rival Volvo as two anchors of Sweden's economy. Scania's return on sales of 9.9 percent far exceeds Mercedes (2.6 percent) and Volvo (2.5 percent), a level it has achieved most of the last 60 years. Scania has built a sustainable competitive advantage with a strategy of focusing solely on heavy transport vehicles in three geographic markets—Europe, Latin America, and Asia—by providing vehicles customized to specific tasks yet built using modularized components (20,000 components per vehicle versus 25,000 for Volvo and 40,000 for Mercedes). Scania is a low-cost producer of a differentiated heavy transport vehicle that can be custom-manufactured quickly and sold to a regionally focused market.

2. **Should dominant-product/service businesses diversify to build value and competitive advantage?** For example, Dell and Coca-Cola managers have examined the question of diversification and apparently concluded that continued concentration on their core products and services and development of new markets for those same core products and services are best. IBM and Pepsi examined the same question and concluded that concentric diversification and vertical integration were best. Why?

EVALUATING AND CHOOSING BUSINESS STRATEGIES: SEEKING SUSTAINED COMPETITIVE ADVANTAGE

Business managers evaluate and choose strategies that they think will make their business successful. Businesses become successful because they possess some advantage relative to their competitors. The two most prominent sources of competitive advantage can be found in the business's cost structure and its ability to differentiate the business from competitors. DisneyWorld in Orlando offers theme park patrons several unique, distinct features that differentiate it from other entertainment options. Costco offers retail customers the lowest prices on popular consumer items because they have created a low-cost structure that results in a competitive advantage over most competitors.

Businesses that create competitive advantages from one or both of these sources usually experience above-average profitability within their industry. Businesses that lack a cost or differentiation advantage usually experience average or below-average profitability. Two well-recognized studies found that businesses that do not have either form of competitive advantage perform the poorest among their peers, while businesses that possess both forms of competitive advantage enjoy the highest levels of profitability within their industry.[1]

[1] G. G. Dess and G. T. Lumpkin, "Emerging Issues in Strategy Process Research," in *Handbook of Strategic Management*, M. A. Hitt, R. E. Freeman, and J. S. Harrison (eds) (Oxford: Blackwell, 2001), pp. 3–34; and R. B. Robinson and J. A. Pearce, "Planned Patterns of Strategic Behavior and Their Relationship to Business Unit Performance," *Strategic Management Journal* 9, no. 1 (1988), pp. 43–60.

The average return on investment for more than 2,500 businesses across seven industries looked like this:

Differentiation Advantage	Cost Advantage	Overall Average ROI across Seven Industries
High	High	35.0%
Low	High	26.0
High	Low	22.0
Low	Low	9.5

Initially, managers were advised to evaluate and choose strategies that emphasized one type of competitive advantage. Often referred to as generic strategies, firms were encouraged to become either a differentiation-oriented or low-cost-oriented company. In so doing, it was logical that organizational members would develop a clear understanding of company priorities and, as these studies suggest, likely experience profitability superior to competitors without either a differentiation or low-cost orientation.

The studies mentioned here, and the experience of many other businesses, indicate that the highest profitability levels are found in businesses that possess both types of competitive advantage at the same time. In other words, businesses that have one or more resources/capabilities that truly differentiate them from key competitors and also have resources/capabilities that let them operate at a lower cost will consistently outperform their rivals that don't. So the challenge for today's business managers is to evaluate and choose business strategies based on core competencies and value chain activities that sustain both types of competitive advantage simultaneously. Exhibit 8.1, Top Strategist, describes how Facebook founder Mark Zuckerberg and COO Sheryl Sandberg are charting a Facebook course that is pursuing a strategy that includes both low-cost and differentiation elements, which they strongly feel will help Facebook achieve long-term success and viability in the Web-based business environment of 2030.

Evaluating Cost Leadership Opportunities

Business success built on cost leadership requires the business to be able to provide its product or service at a cost below what its competitors can achieve. And it must be a sustainable cost advantage. Through the skills and resources identified in Exhibit 8.2, a business must be able to accomplish one or more activities in its value chain activities—procuring materials, processing them into products, marketing the products, and distributing the products or support activities—in a more cost-effective manner than that of its competitors or it must be able to reconfigure its value chain so as to achieve a cost advantage. Exhibit 8.2 provides examples of such **low-cost strategies.**

Strategists examining their business's value chain for low-cost leadership advantages evaluate the sustainability of those advantages by benchmarking (refer to Chapter 6 for a discussion of this comparison technique) their business against key competitors and by considering the effect of any cost advantage on the five forces in their business's competitive environment. Low-cost activities that are sustainable and that provide one or more of these advantages relative to key industry forces should become a key basis for the business's competitive strategy:

Low-cost advantages that reduce the likelihood of pricing pressure from buyers   When key competitors cannot match prices from the low-cost leader, customers pressuring the leader risk establishing a price level that drives alternate sources out of business.

low-cost strategies
Business strategies that seek to establish long-term competitive advantages by emphasizing and perfecting value chain activities that can be achieved at costs substantially below what competitors are able to match on a sustained basis. This allows the firm, in turn, to compete primarily by charging a price lower than competitors can match and still stay in business.

Top Strategist
Zuckerberg and Sandberg Choose Differentiation and Long-Term Low Costs to Build Facebook's Long-Term Business Strategy

**Exhibit
8.1**

Mark Zuckerberg, CEO, Facebook Sheryl Sandberg, CEO, Facebook

A dramatic emphasis on cutting expenses and forgoing growth took place in 2009—even in Silicon Valley. Not at Facebook. Founder and CEO Mark Zuckerberg, along with COO Sheryl Sandberg, are emphasizing accelerated growth in their worldwide user base to build a site for the next 30 years while also creating a basis to significantly differentiate Facebook from current social networking business models.

LOW-COST LEADERSHIP

Facebook's emphasis on aggressively pursuing sustained user growth, even during a global depression, is—at its heart—a way to build economies of scale years out that will allow Facebook to be a cost leader among social networking sites in the value it can offer advertisers and other customers desiring to get the widest audience exposure per dollar spent within a social networking venue. Rather than being someone in social networking for a fast buck, says Sheryl Sandberg, "We're in this game for 20 to 30 years." So, in the face of a global economic depression, Facebook is not cutting costs, but rather taking developers off ad revenue generation and instead cooking up versions in languages

like French Canadian, Tagalog, Xhosa, and Arabic. Says Zuckerberg, "A social networking site that can connect people with friends in Saudi Arabia or the Phillipines or Tonga is simply more valuable than one that can't." So Facebook is also aggressively looking for acquisitions of sites in Brazil, Germany, India, and Japan as "a way for us to acquire a geography or a demographic," says CFO Gideon Yu. Ultimately, if it works, Facebook will have a size advantage that will allow it to offer advertisers an unparalleled cost advantage in reaching social network users on a broad global basis, or in narrower geographic or demographic settings.*

DIFFERENTIATION—FACEBOOK STYLE

Facebook is creating a business model designed to go beyond traditional online advertising. It seeks to have ad business, but also to create interactive ads that are more like digital bulletin boards than traditional banner ads. Called *engagement ads,* such advertising would seek comments on a *Tropic Thunder* movie trailer or thoughts about other advertisers linked to Facebook through individual connections and messages. A second leg of the "new" Facebook expects to differentiate itself by including e-commerce—selling digital items and virtual gifts, which sell for modest amounts like $1 a pop. Sending digital flowers, guitars, and other virtual gifts from one Facebook user to another via Facebook is rapidly growing as a revenue source and, more importantly, a way to differentiate the Facebook social network user experience, which in turn creates a different milieu for commercial advertisers. Third, Facebook has opened itself to software developers/entrepreneurs who can make applications to be used on Facebook with advertisers paying the developers (where relevant) and Facebook taking a cut.

*"Facebook Lures Advertisers at MySpace's Expense," *BusinessWeek,* July 9, 2009; "Zuckerberg on Facebook's Future," *BusinessWeek.com,* March 6, 2008; and "Facebook's Sheryl Sandberg," *BusinessWeek.com,* April 9, 2009.

Truly sustained low-cost advantages may push rivals into other areas, lessening price competition Intense, continued price competition may be ruinous for all rivals, as seen occasionally in the airline industry.

Exhibit 8.2
Evaluating a Business's Cost Leadership Opportunities

Source: Based on Michael Porter, *On Competition*, 1998, Harvard Business School Press.

A. Skills and Resources That Foster Cost Leadership

Sustained capital investment and access to capital
Process engineering skills
Intense supervision of labor or core technical operations
Products or services designed for ease of manufacture or delivery
Low-cost distribution system

B. Organizational Requirements to Support and Sustain Cost Leadership Activities

Tight cost control
Frequent, detailed control reports
Continuous improvement and benchmarking orientation
Structured organization and responsibilities
Incentives based on meeting strict, usually quantitative targets

C. Examples of Ways Businesses Achieve Competitive Advantage via Cost Leadership

Technology Development	Process innovations lower production costs		Product redesign reduces the number of components	
Human Resource Management	Safety training for all employees reduces absenteeism, downtime, and accidents			
General Administration	Reduced levels of management cut corporate overhead		Computerized, integrated information system reduces errors and administrative costs	
Procurement	Favorable long-term contracts; captive suppliers or key customer for supplier.			
Global, online suppliers provide automatic restocking of orders based on our sales.	Economy of scale in plant reduces equipment costs and depreciation.	Computerized routing lowers transportation expense.	Cooperative advertising with distributors creates local cost advantage in buying media space and time.	Subcontracted service technicians repair product correctly the first time or they bear all costs.
Inbound logistics	Operations	Outbound logistics	Marketing and Sales	Service

Profit Margin

New entrants competing on price must face an entrenched cost leader without the experience to replicate every cost advantage   EasyJet, a British start-up with a Southwest Airlines copycat strategy, entered the European airline market with much fanfare and low-priced, city-to-city, no-frills flights.

Analysts have cautioned for some time that British Airways, KLM's no-frills off-shoot (Buzz), and Virgin Express will simply match fares on easyJet's key routes and let high landing fees and flight delays take their toll on the British upstart. Yet first-mover easyJet has survived and solidified its leadership position in the European airline industry's low-cost segment.[2]

Low-cost advantages should lessen the attractiveness of substitute products   A serious concern of any business is the threat of a substitute product in which buyers can meet their original need. Low-cost advantages allow the holder to resist this happening because it allows them to remain competitive even against desirable substitutes, and it allows them to lessen concerns about price facing an inferior, lower-priced substitute.

[2] "EasyJet Expands as Profits Soar," *BBC News*, November 14, 2006; and "Demand Boost Cuts easyJet Losses," *BBC News*, May 9, 2007.

Higher margins allow low-cost producers to withstand supplier cost increases and often gain supplier loyalty over time   Sudden, particularly uncontrollable increases in the costs suppliers face can be more easily absorbed by low-cost, higher-margin producers. Severe droughts in California quadrupled the price of lettuce—a key restaurant demand. Some chains absorbed the cost; others had to confuse customers with a "lettuce tax." Furthermore, chains that worked well with produce suppliers gained a loyal, cooperative "partner" for possible assistance in a future, competitive situation.

Once managers identify opportunities to create cost advantage–based strategies, they must consider whether key risks inherent in cost leadership are present in a way that may mediate sustained success. The key risks with which they must be concerned are discussed next.

Many cost-saving activities are easily duplicated   Computerizing certain order entry functions among hazardous waste companies gave early adopters lower sales costs and better customer service for a brief time. Rivals quickly adapted, adding similar capabilities with similar effects on their costs.

Exclusive cost leadership can become a trap   Firms that emphasize lowest price and can offer it via cost advantages where product differentiation is increasingly not considered must truly be convinced of the sustainability of those advantages. Particularly with commodity-type products, the low-cost leader seeking to sustain a margin superior to lesser rivals may encounter increasing customer pressure for lower prices with great damage to both leader and lesser players.

Obsessive cost cutting can shrink other competitive advantages involving key product attributes   Intense cost scrutiny can build margin, but it can reduce opportunities for or investment in innovation, processes, and products. Similarly, such scrutiny can lead to the use of inferior raw materials, processes, or activities that were previously viewed by customers as a key attribute of the original products. Some mail-order computer companies that sought to maintain or enhance cost advantages found reductions in telephone service personnel and automation of that function backfiring with a drop in demand for their products even though their low prices were maintained.

Cost differences often decline over time   As products age, competitors learn how to match cost advantages. Absolute volumes sold often decline. Market channels and suppliers mature. Buyers become more knowledgeable. All of these factors present opportunities to lessen the value or presence of earlier cost advantages. Said another way, cost advantages that are not sustainable over a period of time are risky.

Once business managers have evaluated the cost structure of their value chain, determined activities that provide competitive cost advantages, and considered their inherent risks, they start choosing the business's strategy. Those managers concerned with differentiation-based strategies, or those seeking optimum performance incorporating both sources of competitive advantage, move to evaluating their business's sources of differentiation.

Evaluating Differentiation Opportunities

differentiation
A business strategy that seeks to build competitive advantage with its product or service by having it be "different" from other available competitive products based on features, performance, or other factors not directly related to cost and price. The difference would be one that would be hard to create and/or difficult to copy or imitate.

Differentiation requires that the business have sustainable advantages that allow it to provide buyers with something uniquely valuable to them. A successful differentiation strategy allows the business to provide a product or service of perceived higher value to buyers at a "differentiation cost" below the "value premium" to the buyers. In other words, the buyer feels the additional cost to buy the product or service is well below what the product or service is worth compared with other available alternatives.

Differentiation usually arises from one or more activities in the value chain that create a unique value important to buyers. Perrier's control of a carbonated water spring in France,

Exhibit 8.3
Evaluating a Business's Differentiation Opportunities

Source: Based on Michael Porter, *On Competition*, 1998, Harvard Business School Press.

A. Skills and Resources That Foster Differentiation

Strong marketing abilities
Product engineering
Creative talent and flair
Strong capabilities in basic research
Corporate reputation for quality or technical leadership
Long tradition in an industry or unique combination of skills drawn from other businesses
Strong cooperation from channels
Strong cooperation from suppliers of major components of the product or service

B. Organizational Requirements to Support and Sustain Differentiation Activities
Strong coordination among functions in R&D, product development, and marketing
Subjective measurement and incentives instead of quantitative measures
Amenities to attract highly skilled labor, scientists, and creative people
Tradition of closeness to key customers
Some personnel skilled in sales and operations—technical and marketing

C. Examples of Ways Businesses Achieve Competitive Advantage via Differentiation

Technology Development	Use cutting-edge production technology and product features to maintain a "distinct" image and actual product.
Human Resource Management	Develop programs to ensure technical competence of sales staff and a marketing orientation of service personnel.
General Administration	Develop comprehensive, personalized database to build knowledge of groups of customers and individual buyers to be used in "customizing" how products are sold, serviced, and replaced.
Procurement	Maintain quality control presence at key supplier facilities; work with suppliers' new-product development activities.

Inbound logistics	Operations	Outbound logistics	Marketing and Sales	Service
Purchase superior quality, well-known components, raising the quality and image of final products.	Carefully inspect products at each step in production to improve product performance and lower defect rate.	Coordinate JIT with buyers; use own or captive transportation service to ensure timeliness.	Build brand image with expensive, informative advertising and promotion.	Allow service personnel considerable discretion to credit customers for repairs.

Profit Margin

Stouffer's frozen food packaging and sauce technology, Apple's control of iTunes download software that worked solely with iPods at first, American Greeting Card's automated inventory system for retailers, and Federal Express's customer service capabilities are all examples of sustainable advantages around which successful differentiation strategies have been built. A business can achieve differentiation by performing its existing value activities or reconfiguring in some unique way. And the sustainability of that differentiation will depend on two things: a continuation of its high perceived value to buyers and a lack of imitation by competitors.

Exhibit 8.3 provides examples of the types of key skills and resources on which managers seeking to build differentiation-based strategies would base their underlying, sustainable competitive advantages. Examples of value chain activities that provide a differentiation advantage are also provided.

Strategists examining their business's resources and capabilities for differentiation advantages evaluate the sustainability of those advantages by benchmarking (refer to Chapter 6 for a discussion of this comparison technique) their business against key competitors and by considering the effect of any differentiation advantage on the five forces in their business's competitive environment. Sustainable activities that provide one or more of the following opportunities relative to key industry forces should become the basis for differentiation aspects of the business's competitive strategy:

Rivalry is reduced when a business successfully differentiates itself   BMW's Z4, made in Greer, South Carolina, does not compete with Saturns made in central Tennessee. A Harvard education does not compete with an education from a local technical school. Both situations involve the same basic needs—transportation or education. However, one rival has clearly differentiated itself from others in the minds of certain buyers. In so doing, they do not have to respond competitively to that competitor.

Buyers are less sensitive to prices for effectively differentiated products   The Highlands Inn in Carmel, California, and the Ventana Inn along the Big Sur charge a minimum of $750 and $1,000, respectively, per night for a room with a kitchen, fireplace, hot tub, and view. Other places are available along this beautiful stretch of California's spectacular coastline, but occupancy rates at these two locations remain over 90 percent. Why? You can't get a better view and a more relaxed, spectacular setting to spend a few days on the Pacific Coast. Similarly, buyers of differentiated products tolerate price increases low-cost-oriented buyers would not accept. The former become very loyal to certain brands. Harley-Davidson motorcycles continue to rise in price, and its buyer base continues to expand worldwide, even though many motorcycle alternatives more reasonably priced are easily available.

Brand loyalty is hard for new entrants to overcome   Many new beers are brought to market in the United States, but Budweiser continues to gain market share. Why? Brand loyalty is hard to overcome! And Anheuser-Busch has been clever to extend its brand loyalty from its core brand into newer niches, such as nonalcohol brews, that other potential entrants have pioneered.

Managers examining differentiation-based advantages must take potential risks into account as they commit their business to these advantages. Some of the more common ways risks arise are discussed next.

Imitation narrows perceived differentiation, rendering differentiation meaningless   AMC pioneered the Jeep passenger version of a truck 40 years ago. Ford created the Explorer, or luxury utility vehicle, in 1990. It took luxury car features and put them inside a jeep. Ford's payoff was substantial. The Explorer became Ford's most popular domestic vehicle. However, virtually every vehicle manufacturer offered a luxury utility a few years later, resulting in customers beginning to be hard pressed to identify clear distinctions between lead models. Ford's Explorer managers have sought to shape a new business strategy for the next decade that relies both on new sources of differentiation and placing greater emphasis on low-cost components in their value chain.

Technological changes that nullify past investments or learning   The Swiss controlled more than 95 percent of the world's watch market into the 1970s. The bulk of the craftspeople, technology, and infrastructure resided in Switzerland. U.S.-based Texas Instruments decided to experiment with the use of its digital technology in watches. Swiss producers were not interested, but Japan's SEIKO and others were. In 2010, the Swiss will make less than 2 percent of the world's watches.

The cost difference between low-cost competitors and the differentiated business becomes too great for differentiation to hold brand loyalty   Buyers may begin to choose to sacrifice some of the features, services, or image possessed by the differentiated business for large cost savings. The rising cost of a college education, particularly at several "premier" institutions, has caused many students to opt for lower-cost destinations that offer very similar courses without image, frills, and professors who seldom teach undergraduate students anyway.

Evaluating Speed as a Competitive Advantage

The cool design of the iPod is often cited as prima facie evidence of the product's greatness. But what you hear less about are the scores of little strategic decisions that were equally important in its speed-related tactics that ultimately made it a phenomenon. For instance, Apple licensed key technologies for the gadget's guts to accelerate its readiness for proto-type availability; it acquired, rather than wrote, the software that became iTunes for the same reason; and chief executive Steve Jobs set a demanding nine-month time line to get the first version done, which focused internal attention throughout the organization on the device and ensured speed to market. Altogether, those steps systematically "de-risked" the iPod launch by placing a key emphasis on *speed* and enabled the phenomenal success of Apple's $100 million bet.[3]

speed-based strategies
Business strategies built around functional capabilities and activities that allow the company to meet customer needs directly or indirectly more rapidly than its main competitors.

Speed-based strategies, or rapid responses to customer requests or market and technological changes, have become a major source of competitive advantage for numerous firms in today's intensely competitive global economy. Speed is certainly a form of differentiation, but it is more than that. Speed involves the *availability of a rapid response* to a customer by providing current products quicker, accelerating new-product development or improvement, quickly adjusting production processes, and making decisions quickly. While low cost and differentiation may provide important competitive advantages, managers in tomorrow's successful companies will base their strategies on creating speed-based competitive advantages. Exhibit 8.4, Strategy in Action, tells how Irishman Michael O 'Leary built Ryanair using a speed-based competitive strategy. Exhibit 8.5 describes and illustrates key skills and organizational requirements that are associated with speed-based competitive advantage. Jack Welch, the now-retired CEO who transformed General Electric from a fading company into one of Wall Street's best performers over the past 25 years, had this to say about speed:

> Speed is really the driving force that everyone is after. Faster products, faster product cycles to market. Better response time to customers. . . . Satisfying customers, getting faster communications, moving with more agility, all these things are easier when one is small. And these are all characteristics one needs in a fast-moving global environment.[4]

Speed-based competitive advantages can be created around several activities:

Customer Responsiveness   All consumers have encountered hassles, delays, and frustration dealing with various businesses from time to time. The same holds true when dealing business to business. Quick response with answers, information, and solutions to mistakes can become the basis for competitive advantage—one that builds customer loyalty quickly.

Product Development Cycles   Japanese automakers have focused intensely on the time it takes to create a new model because several experienced disappointing sales growth in the last decade in Europe and North America competing against new vehicles like Ford's Explorer and Renault's Megane. VW had recently conceived, prototyped, produced, and marketed a totally new 4-wheel-drive car in Europe within 12 months. Honda, Toyota, and Nissan lowered their product development cycle from 24 months to 9 months from conception to production. This capability is old hat to 3M Corporation, which is so successful at speedy product development that one-fourth of its sales and profits each year are from products that didn't exist five years earlier.

Product or Service Improvements   Like development time, companies that can rapidly adapt their products or services and do so in a way that benefits their customers or creates new customers have a major competitive advantage over rivals that cannot do this.

[3] "Don't Worry, Be Ready," *BusinessWeek,* May 28, 2007.
[4] "Jack Welch: A CEO Who Can't Be Cloned," *BusinessWeek,* September 17, 2001.

Building Ryanair with an Emphasis on SPEED

In 2009, Michael O'Leary was pushing the idea of a quick, low-cost, internal flight service from Europe to America . . . fly across the pond last minute for $55. Vintage O'Leary. Years earlier he drove a World War II tank to England's Luton airport demanding access to "attack" rival easyJet and liberate the public from easyJet's high fares. Behind it all is a strategy built around SPEED.

SPEED1: Ryanair uses small, secondary airports outside major cities. They allow Ryanair to fly into and out of an area quicker, turn around faster, and get customers on their way with far less time lost compared to regular airlines and airports. These airports also cost less to use, get people close to big city destinations, and get planes back in the air in 25 minutes—half the time competitors experience.

This allows Ryanair to provide more frequent flights, adding time-saving convenience for both leisure and business travelers.

SPEED2: Ryanair has made large bulk purchases of Boeing's newest 737 airplanes. These planes require less maintenance and are easy to handle in smaller airports—all leading to speedier operations on a daily basis and quicker in and out maintenance downtimes.

SPEED3: Ryanair sells more than 98 percent of its tickets on Ryanair.com—allowing for quicker, more accessible service for customers seeking simplicity, speed, and convenience. It also sells hotels, car rentals, and various other offerings at the same Web site, further simplifying and saving considerable time [think speed] for customers.

Speed in Delivery or Distribution Firms that can get you what you need when you need it, even when that is tomorrow, realize that buyers have come to expect that level of responsiveness. Federal Express's success reflects the importance customers place on speed in inbound and outbound logistics.

Information Sharing and Technology Speed in sharing information that becomes the basis for decisions, actions, or other important activities taken by a customer, supplier, or partner has become a major source of competitive advantage for many businesses. Telecommunications, the Internet, and networks are but a part of a vast infrastructure that is being used by knowledgeable managers to rebuild or create value in their businesses via information sharing.

These rapid response capabilities create competitive advantages in several ways. They create a way to lessen rivalry because they have *availability* of something that a rival may not have. It can allow the business to charge buyers more, engender loyalty, or otherwise enhance the business's position relative to its buyers. Particularly where impressive customer response is involved, businesses can generate supplier cooperation and concessions because their business ultimately benefits from increased revenue. Finally, substitute products and new entrants find themselves trying to keep up with the rapid changes rather than introducing them.

While the notion of speed-based competitive advantage is exciting, it has risks managers must consider. First, speeding up activities that haven't been conducted in a fashion that prioritizes rapid response should only be done after considerable attention to training, reorganization, and/or reengineering. Second, some industries—stable, mature ones that have very minimal levels of change—may not offer much advantage to the firm that introduces some forms of rapid response. Customers in such settings may prefer the slower pace or the lower costs currently available, or they may have long time frames in purchasing such that speed is not that important to them.

223

Exhibit 8.5   Evaluating a Business's Rapid Response (Speed) Opportunities

A. Skills and Resources That Foster Speed

Process engineering skills
Excellent inbound and outbound logistics
Technical people in sales and customer service
High levels of automation
Corporate reputation for quality or technical leadership
Flexible manufacturing capabilities
Strong downstream partners
Strong cooperation from suppliers of major components of the product or service

B. Organizational Requirements to Support and Sustain Rapid Response Activities

Strong coordination among functions in R&D, product development, and marketing.
Major emphasis on customer satisfaction in incentive programs
Strong delegation to operating personnel
Tradition of closeness to key customers
Some personnel skilled in sales and operations—technical and marketing
Empowered customer service personnel

C. Examples of Ways Businesses Achieve Competitive Advantage via Speed

Technology Development	Use companywide technology sharing activities and autonomous product development teams to speed new-product development.			
Human Resource Management	Develop self-managed work teams and decision making at the lowest levels to increase responsiveness.			
General Administration	Develop highly automated and integrated information processing system. Include major buyers in the "system" on a real-time basis.			
Procurement	Integrate preapproved online suppliers into production.			
	Work very closely with suppliers to include their choice of warehouse location to minimize delivery time.	Standardize dies, components, and production equipment to allow quick changeover to new or special orders.	Ensure very rapid delivery with JIT delivery plus partnering with express mail services.	Use of laptops linked directly to operations to speed the order process and shorten the sales cycle.	Locate service technicians at customer facilities that are geographically close.
	Inbound logistics	Operations	Outbound logistics	Marketing and Sales	Service

Profit Margin

Evaluating Market Focus as a Way to Competitive Advantage

Small companies, at least the better ones, usually thrive because they serve narrow market niches. This is usually called **market focus,** the extent to which a business concentrates on a narrowly defined market. Take the example of Soho Beverages, a business former Pepsi manager Tom Cox bought from Seagram after Seagram had acquired it and was unable to make it thrive. The tiny brand, once a healthy niche product in New York and a few other East Coast locations, languished within Seagrams because its sales force was unused to selling in delis. Cox was able to double sales in one year. He did this on a lean marketing budget that didn't include advertising or database marketing. He hired Korean- and Arabic-speaking college students and had his people walk into practically every deli in Manhattan in order

Top Strategist
Zhang Ruimin, Chairman, Haier Corporation

Exhibit 8.6

Zhang Ruimin has emphasized a focus strategy in first building Haier into a well-known maker of refrigerators in China and now a significant force in the U.S. market and beyond. The result has been a 40 percent annualized growth in sales so far this century.

It all started several years ago in China with a sledgehammer. Appointed to run a marginal state-owned refrigerator factory, Ruimin quickly saw that "the real problem was that workers had no faith in the company and didn't care. Quality didn't even enter into anybody's mind." So after a customer complained, Ruimin lined up 76 defective models on the factory floor. He picked up a sledgehammer and told those responsible to smash them. He included himself in the task. "The message got through that there's no A, B, C, and D quality," said Ruimin, "There's only acceptable and unacceptable."

Fast-forward to taking Haier into the United States. Instead of trying to compete in the market for large, high-end refrigerators as it does in China, Ruimin chose a market focus strategy, introducing a multipurpose mini-refrigerator designed for use in college dormitories and as a small wine cellar. Haier's niche products rapidly gained in popularity.

Combined with its legendary commitment to quality control that all started with sledgehammer-wielding Zhang Ruimin emphasizing the importance of quality to his employees, Ruimin's Haier has leveraged its FOCUS strategy to move into different product lines and grab market share in the United States. By choosing market focus, Haier delivered a clear and unique value proposition to American consumers.

market focus
This is a generic strategy that applies a differentiation strategy approach, or a low-cost strategy approach, or a combination—and does so solely in a narrow (or "focused") market niche rather than trying to do so across the broader market. The narrow focus may be geographically defined or defined by product type features, or target customer type, or some combination of these.

to reacquaint owners with the brand, spot consumption trends, and take orders. He provided rapid stocking services to all Manhattan-area delis, regardless of size. The business has continued sales growth at more than 50 percent per year. Why? Cox says, "It is attributable to focusing on a niche market, delis; differentiating the product and its sales force; achieving low costs in promotion and delivery; and making rapid, immediate response to any deli owner request its normal practice."[5]

Two things are important in this example. First, this business focused on a narrow niche market in which to build a strong competitive advantage. But focus alone was not enough to build competitive advantage. Rather, Cox created several capabilities, resources, and value chain activities that achieved differentiation, low-cost, and rapid response competitive advantages within this niche market that would be hard for other firms, particularly mass market—oriented firms, to replicate. Exhibit 8.6, Top Strategist, describes how China's Zhang Rumin used quality and a sledgehammer to evaluate and choose a market focus strategy that Haier subsequently used to enter the U.S. refrigerator market.

Market focus allows some businesses to compete on the basis of low cost, differentiation, and rapid response against much larger businesses with greater resources. Focus lets a business "learn" its target customers—their needs, special considerations they want accommodated—and establish personal relationships in ways that "differentiate" the smaller firm or make it more valuable to the target customer. Low costs can also be achieved, filling niche needs in a buyer's operations that larger rivals either do not want to bother with or cannot do as cost effectively. Cost advantage often centers around the high level of customized

[5] Michael Porter, *On Competition* (Boston: Harvard Business School Press, 1998), p. 57.

service the focused, smaller business can provide. And perhaps the greatest competitive weapon that can arise is rapid response. With enhanced knowledge of its customers and intricacies of their operations, the small, focused company builds up organizational knowledge about timing-sensitive ways to work with a customer. Often the needs of that narrow set of customers represent a large part of the small, focused business's revenues. Exhibit 8.6, Top Strategist, illustrates how China's Haier has become the global leader in small refrigerators via the focused application of low cost, differentiation, and quality.

The risk of focus is that you attract major competitors who have waited for your business to "prove" the market. Domino's proved that a huge market for pizza delivery existed and now faces serious challenges. Likewise, publicly traded companies built around focus strategies become takeover targets for large firms seeking to fill out a product portfolio. And perhaps the greatest risk of all is slipping into the illusion that it is focus itself, and not some special form of low cost, differentiation, or rapid response, that is creating the business's success.

Managers evaluating opportunities to build competitive advantage should link strategies to resources, capabilities, and value chain activities that exploit low cost, differentiation, and rapid response competitive advantages. When advantageous, they should consider ways to use focus to leverage these advantages. One way business managers can enhance their likelihood of identifying these opportunities is to consider several different "generic" industry environments from the perspective of the typical value chain activities most often linked to sustained competitive advantages in those unique industry situations. The next section discusses key generic industry environments and the value chain activities most associated with success.

Stages of Industry Evolution and Business Strategy Choices

The requirements for success in industry segments change over time. Strategists can use these changing requirements, which are associated with different stages of industry evolution, as a way to isolate key competitive advantages and shape strategic choices around them. Exhibit 8.7 depicts four stages of industry evolution and the typical functional capabilities that are often associated with business success at each of these stages.

Competitive Advantage and Strategic Choices in Emerging Industries

Emerging industries are newly formed or re-formed industries that typically are created by technological innovation, newly emerging customer needs, or other economic or sociological changes. **Emerging industries** of the last decade have been the Internet social networking, satellite radio, surgical robotics, and online services industries.

From the standpoint of strategy formulation, the essential characteristic of an emerging industry is that there are no "rules of the game." The absence of rules presents both a risk and an opportunity—a wise strategy positions the firm to favorably shape the emerging industry's rules.

Business strategies must be shaped to accommodate the following characteristics of markets in emerging industries:

* Technologies that are mostly proprietary to the pioneering firms and technological uncertainty about how product standardization will unfold.
* Competitor uncertainty because of inadequate information about competitors, buyers, and the timing of demand.
* High initial costs but steep cost declines as the experience curve takes effect.
* Few entry barriers, which often spurs the formation of many new firms.
* First-time buyers requiring initial inducement to purchase and customers confused by the availability of a number of nonstandard products.

emerging industry
An industry that has growing sales across all the companies in the industry based on growing demand for the relatively new products, technologies, and/or services made available by the firms participating in this industry.

- Inability to obtain raw materials and components until suppliers gear up to meet the industry's needs.
- Need for high-risk capital because of the industry's uncertainty prospects.

For success in this industry setting, business strategies require one or more of these features:

1. The ability to *shape the industry's structure* based on the timing of entry, reputation, success in related industries or technologies, and role in industry associations.
2. The ability to *rapidly improve product quality* and performance features.
3. *Advantageous relationships* with key suppliers and promising distribution channels.
4. The ability to *establish the firm's technology as the dominant one* before technological uncertainty decreases.
5. The early acquisition of *a core group of loyal customers* and then the expansion of that customer base through model changes, alternative pricing, and advertising.
6. The ability to *forecast future competitors* and the strategies they are likely to employ.

A firm that has had repeated successes with business in emerging industries is 3M Corporation. In each of the past 20 years, more than 25 percent of 3M's annual sales have come from products that did not exist five years earlier. Start-up companies enhance their success by having experienced entrepreneurs at the helm, a knowledgeable management team and board of directors, and patient sources of venture capital. Steven Jobs's dramatic unveiling of Apple's iPod came to be seen by many as the catalyst for the emergence of a new personalized digital music industry. Jobs and Apple certainly took advantage by building a strategy that shaped the industry's structure, established the firm's technology as a dominant one, endeared themselves to a core group of loyal customers, and rapidly improved the product quality and Internet-based music service.

Competitive Advantages and Strategic Choices in Growing Industries

growth industry strategies
Business strategies that may be more advantageous for firms participating in rapidly growing industries and markets.

Rapid growth brings new competitors into the industry. Oftentimes, those new entrants are large competitors with substantial resources who have waited for the market to "prove" itself before they committed significant resources. At this stage, **growth industry strategies** that emphasize brand recognition, product differentiation, and the financial resources to support both heavy marketing expenses and the effect of price competition on cash flow can be key strengths. Accelerating demand means scaling up production or service capacity to meet the growing demand. Doing so may place a premium on being able to adapt product design and production facilities to meet rapidly increasing demand effectively. Increased investment in plant and equipment, in research and development (R&D), and especially marketing efforts to target specific customer groups along with developing strong distribution capabilities place a demand on the firm's capital resources.

For success in this industry setting, business strategies require one or more of these features:

1. The ability to *establish strong brand recognition* through promotional resources and skills that increase selective demand.
2. The ability and resources to *scale up to meet increasing demand*, which may involve production facilities, service capabilities, and the training and logistics associated with that capacity.
3. *Strong product design skills* to be able to adapt products and services to scaled operations and emerging market niches.
4. The ability to *differentiate the firm's product[s]* from competitors entering the market.

EXHIBIT 8.7   **Sources of Distinctive Competence at Different Stages of Industry Evolution**

Functional Area	Introduction	Growth	Maturity	Decline
Marketing	Resources/skills to create widespread awareness and find acceptance from customers; advantageous access to distribution	Ability to establish brand recognition, find niche, reduce price, solidify strong distribution relations, and develop new channels	Skills in aggressively promoting products to new markets and holding existing markets; pricing flexibility; skills in differentiating products and holding customer loyalty	Cost-effective means of efficient access to selected channels and markets; strong customer loyalty or dependence; strong company image
Production operations	Ability to expand capacity effectively, limit number of designs, develop standards	Ability to add product variants, centralize production, or otherwise lower costs; ability to improve product quality; seasonal subcontracting capacity	Ability to improve product and reduce costs; ability to share or reduce capacity; advantageous supplier relationships; subcontracting	Ability to prune product line; cost advantage in production, location, or distribution; simplified inventory control; subcontracting or long production runs

Growth rate ≤ 0

Unit sales

Profit (dollars)

5. *R&D resources and skills* to create product variations and advantages.

6. The ability to *build repeat buying from established customers* and attract new customers.

7. Strong capabilities in *sales and marketing*.

IBM entered the personal computer market—which Apple pioneered in the growth stage—and was able to rapidly become the market leader with a strategy based on its key strengths in brand awareness and possession of the financial resources needed to support consumer advertising. Many large technology companies today prefer exactly this approach: to await proof of an industry or product market and then to acquire small pioneer firms with first-mover advantage as a means to obtain an increasingly known brand, or to acquire technical know-how and experience behind which the firms can put its resources and distribution strength to build brand identify and loyalty. In 2005 as the PC market matured, IBM sold its PC division to China's Lenovo and now outsources its PCs.

Competitive Advantages and Strategic Choices in Mature Industry Environments

As an industry evolves, its rate of growth eventually declines. This "transition to maturity" is accompanied by several changes in its competitive environment: Competition for market

EXHIBIT 8.7 *(continued)*

Functional Area	Introduction	Growth	Maturity	Decline
Finance	Resources to support high net cash overflow and initial losses; ability to use leverage effectively	Ability to finance rapid expansion, to have net cash outflows but increasing profits; resources to support product improvements	Ability to generate and redistribute increasing net cash inflows; effective cost control systems	Ability to reuse or liquidate unneeded equipment; advantage in cost of facilities; control system accuracy; stream-lined management control
Personnel	Flexibility in staffing and training new manage-ment; existence of employees with key skills in new products or markets	Existence of an ability to add skilled personnel; motivated and loyal workforce	Ability to cost effectively, reduce workforce, increase efficiency	Capacity to reduce and reallocate personnel; cost advantage
Engineering and research and development	Ability to make engi-neering changes, have technical bugs in product and process resolved	Skill in quality and new feature develop-ment; ability to start developing successor product	Ability to reduce costs, develop variants, differen-tiate products	Ability to support other grown areas or to apply product to unique customer needs
Key functional area and strategy focus	Engineering: market penetration	Sales: consumer loyalty; market share	Production effi-ciency; successor products	Finance; maximum investment recovery

share becomes more intense as firms in the industry are forced to achieve sales growth at one another's expense. Firms working with the **mature industry strategies** sell increasingly to experienced, repeat buyers who are now making choices among known alternatives. Competition becomes more oriented to cost and service as knowledgeable buyers expect similar price and product features. Industry capacity "tops out" as sales growth ceases to cover up poorly planned expansions. New products and new applications are harder to come by. International competition increases as cost pressures lead to overseas production advantages. Profitability falls, often permanently, as a result of pressure to lower prices and the increased costs of holding or building market share.

These changes necessitate a fundamental strategic reassessment. Strategy elements of successful firms in maturing industries often include the following:

1. *Product line* pruning, or dropping unprofitable product models, sizes, and options from the firm's product mix.
2. *Emphasis on process innovation* that permits low-cost product design, manufacturing methods, and distribution synergy.
3. *Emphasis on cost reduction* through exerting pressure on suppliers for lower prices, switching to cheaper components, introducing operational efficiencies, and lowering administrative and sales overhead.
4. *Careful buyer selection* to focus on buyers who are less aggressive, more closely tied to the firm, and able to buy more from the firm.

Strategy in Action

Exhibit 8.8

Milliken's Strategic Choice to Reduce Its Environmental Impact

Milliken personnel responsible for cost-control strategic choices related to waste and environmental impact management communicate the essence of those choices in the interesting triangular "Waste Management Pyramid" shown here. The least desirable option for Milliken facilities to handle manufacturing waste is to dispose of it in a secure, legal landfill. Milliken sees this as the most costly option, both directly and in liability terms. Reuse is the most desirable option—least liability and least costly. Shown also are the results Milliken achieved in 2008: a 6 percent reduction in waste over the previous year, with only 0.008 percent of its waste going to landfills, none incinerated, 26.6 percent converted to energy at Milliken facilities, 68.8 percent recycled, and 15.7 percent reused.

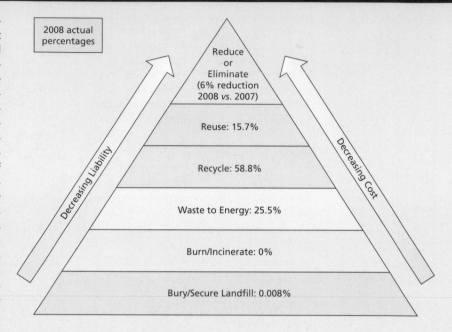

Source: Innoventure Sustainability Forum, Moore School of Business, University of South Carolina, presentation by Miliken Sustainability Team, February, 2009.

5. *Horizontal integration* to acquire rival firms whose weaknesses can be used to gain a bargain price and that are correctable by the acquiring firms.

6. *International expansion* to markets where attractive growth and limited competition still exist and the opportunity for lower-cost manufacturing can influence both domestic and international costs.

Milliken, the world's largest private textile company and a chemical company, offers a notable example of a company making solid strategic choices in what are often considered mature industries. Milliken's choice has been to emphasize technology and process innovation, integrate textiles capabilities and chemical capabilities, achieve international expansion, and promote careful buyer selection—thus serving major consumer and industrial industry buyers with significant fabric-related needs. Milliken also includes constant emphasis on cost reduction along with environmental impact reduction. Taken together, these strategic choices regularly result in Milliken being named one of the top global companies in many recognition forums, plus being named one of the world's most ethical companies by Ethisphere.com—all this in two "mature" industries that have seen numerous well-known companies exit or lose out to low-cost competitors in emerging economies. Exhibit 8.8, Strategy in Action, illustrates just one strategic choice at Milliken—minimizing its environmental impact while also endeavoring to save costs and limit future waste-related liability.

Business strategists in maturing industries must avoid several pitfalls. First, they must make a clear choice among the three generic strategies and avoid a middle-ground approach, which would confuse both knowledgeable buyers and the firm's personnel. Second, they must avoid sacrificing market share too quickly for short-term profit. Finally, they must avoid waiting too long to respond to price reductions, retaining unneeded excess capacity, engaging in sporadic or irrational efforts to boost sales, and placing their hopes on "new" products, rather than aggressively selling existing products.

Competitive Advantages and Strategic Choices in Declining Industries

declining industry
An industry in which the trend of total sales as an indicator of total demand for an industry's products or services among all the participants in the industry have started to drop from the last several years with the likelihood being that such a trend will continue indefinitely.

Declining industries are those that make products or services for which demand is growing slower than demand in the economy as a whole or is actually declining. This slow growth or decline in demand is caused by technological substitution (such as the substitution of electronic calculators for slide rules), demographic shifts (such as the increase in the number of older people and the decrease in the number of children), and shifts in needs (such as the decreased need for red meat).

Firms in a declining industry should choose strategies that emphasize one or more of the following themes:

1. *Focus* on segments within the industry that offer a chance for higher growth or a higher return.
2. *Emphasize product innovation and quality improvement,* where this can be done cost effectively, to differentiate the firm from rivals and to spur growth.
3. *Emphasize production and distribution efficiency* by streamlining production, closing marginal production facilities and costly distribution outlets, and adding effective new facilities and outlets.
4. *Gradually harvest the business*—generate cash by cutting down on maintenance, reducing models, and shrinking channels and make no new investment.

Strategists who incorporate one or more of these themes into the strategy of their business can anticipate relative success, particularly where the industry's decline is slow and smooth and some profitable niches remain. Penn Tennis, the nation's no. 1 maker of tennis balls, watched industrywide sales steadily decline over the last decade. In response it started marketing tennis balls as "dog toys" in the rapidly growing pet products industry. It secondly made Penn balls the official ball at major tournaments. Third, it created three different quality levels; then, as sales revived, Penn Sports sold its tennis ball business to Head Sports.

Competitive Advantage in Fragmented Industries

Fragmented industries are another setting in which identifiable types of competitive advantages and the strategic choices suggested by those advantages can be identified.

fragmented industry
An industry in which there are numerous competitors (providers of the same or similar products or services the industry involves) such that no single firm or small group of firms controls any significant share of the overall industry sales.

A **fragmented industry** is one in which no firm has a significant market share and can strongly influence industry outcomes. Fragmented industries are found in many areas of the economy and are common in such areas as professional services, retailing, distribution, wood and metal fabrication, and agricultural products. The funeral industry is an example of a highly fragmented industry. Business strategists in fragmented industries pursue low-cost or differentiation strategies or focus competitive advantages in one of five ways:

Tightly Managed Decentralization   Fragmented industries are characterized by a need for intense local coordination, a local management orientation, high personal service, and local autonomy. Recently, however, successful firms in such industries have introduced a high degree of professionalism into the operations of local managers.

"Formula" Facilities   This alternative, related to the previous one, introduces standardized, efficient, low-cost facilities at multiple locations. Thus, the firm gradually builds a low-cost advantage over localized competitors. Fast-food and motel chains have applied this approach with considerable success.

Increased Value Added   The products or services of some fragmented industries are difficult to differentiate. In this case, an effective strategy may be to add value by providing more service with the sale or by engaging in some product assembly that is of additional value to the customer.

Specialization Focus strategies that creatively segment the market can enable firms to cope with fragmentation. Specialization can be pursued by

1. *Product type.* The firm builds expertise focusing on a narrow range of products or services.
2. *Customer type.* The firm becomes intimately familiar with and serves the needs of a narrow customer segment.
3. *Type of order.* The firm handles only certain kinds of orders, such as small orders, custom orders, or quick turnaround orders.
4. *Geographic area.* The firm blankets or concentrates on a single area.

Although specialization in one or more of these ways can be the basis for a sound focus strategy in a fragmented industry, each of these types of specialization risks limiting the firm's potential sales volume.

Bare Bones/No Frills Given the intense competition and low margins in fragmented industries, a "bare bones" posture—low overhead, minimum wage employees, tight cost control—may build a sustainable cost advantage in such industries.

Competitive Advantage in Global Industries

Global industries present a final setting in which success is often associated with identifiable sources of competitive advantage. A **global industry** is one that comprises firms whose competitive positions in major geographic or national markets are fundamentally affected by their overall global competitive positions. To avoid strategic disadvantages, firms in global industries are virtually required to compete on a worldwide basis. Oil, steel, automobiles, apparel, motorcycles, televisions, and computers are examples of global industries.

Global industries have four unique strategy-shaping features:

- Differences in prices and costs from country to country due to currency exchange fluctuations, differences in wage and inflation rates, and other economic factors.
- Differences in buyer needs across different countries.
- Differences in competitors and ways of competing from country to country.
- Differences in trade rules and governmental regulations across different countries.

These unique features and the global competition of global industries require that two fundamental components be addressed in the business strategy: (1) the approach used to gain global market coverage and (2) the generic competitive strategy. Three basic options can be used to pursue global market coverage:

1. *License* foreign firms to produce and distribute the firm's products.
2. *Maintain a domestic production base* and export products to foreign countries.
3. *Establish foreign-based plants and distribution* to compete directly in the markets of one or more foreign countries.

Along with the market coverage decision, strategists must scrutinize the condition of the global industry features identified earlier to choose among four generic global competitive strategies:

1. *Broad-line global competition*—directed at competing worldwide in the full product line of the industry, often with plants in many countries, to achieve differentiation or an overall low-cost position.

global industry
Industry in which competition crosses national borders.

Nineteenth-Century French Steelmaker Crafts a Global Focus Strategy

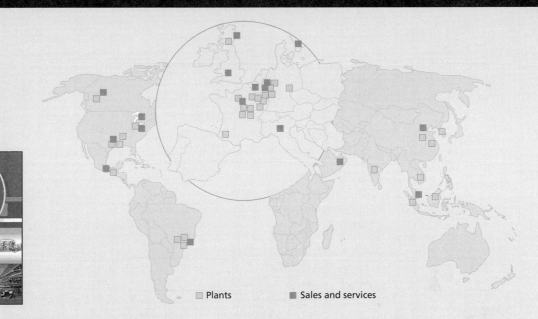

☐ Plants   ■ Sales and services

Vallourec's beginnings go back to the late 1800s in northern France with construction, engineering, metallurgy, and steelmaking. Early the next century, it began making welded and eventually seamless tubes (round pipe). As it prepared to enter the twenty-first century, with all of its plants in Europe, its management decided to sell off various parts of its businesses and commit instead to a global focus strategy providing seamless steel pipes, primarily to the oil and gas and electric power industries.

Vallourec acquired MSA in Brazil in 2000, and, by 2009, had moved almost half its manufacturing capacity outside Europe, shown in the accompanying world map.

It is the world leader in the global seamless steel tube market. Its global focus strategy is reinforced by a decentralized organizational structure, where regional subsidiaries enjoy considerable autonomy to work closely with clients in their target markets. The global focus strategy must be working well, as evidenced in 2009 by more than 12,000 employees—more than 68 percent of its workforce—choosing to buy 750,000 shares of Vallourec stock, in globally depressed equity and oil markets, at the current market price. At the ground level of a global focus strategy, that is a strong vote of confidence.

Source: www.vallourec.com

2. *Global focus* strategy—targeting a particular segment of the industry for competition on a worldwide basis.

3. *National focus* strategy—taking advantage of differences in national markets that give the firm an edge over global competitors on a nation-by-nation basis.

4. *Protected niche* strategy—seeking out countries in which governmental restraints exclude or inhibit global competitors or allow concessions, or both, that are advantageous to localized firms.

Competing in a global context has become a reality for most businesses in virtually every economy around the world. So most firms must consider among the global competitive strategies identified above. Exhibit 8.9, Strategy in Action, describes how an "Old World" French steelmaker did just this to craft a global focus strategy selling steel pipe worldwide and in the process become the world leader in seamless steel tubing.

DOMINANT PRODUCT/SERVICE BUSINESSES: EVALUATING AND CHOOSING TO DIVERSIFY TO BUILD VALUE

McDonald's has frequently looked at numerous opportunities to diversify into related businesses or to acquire key suppliers. Its decision has consistently been to focus on its core business using the grand strategies of concentration, market development, and product development. Rival Yum Brands, on the other hand, has chosen to diversify into related businesses and vertical integration as the best grand strategies for it to build long-term value. Both firms experienced unprecedented success during the last 20 years.

Many dominant product businesses face this question as their core business proves successful: What grand strategies are best suited to continue to build value? Under what circumstances should they choose an expanded focus (diversification, vertical integration); steady continued focus (concentration, market or product development); or a narrowed focus (turnaround or divestiture)? This section examines two ways you can analyze a dominant product company's situation and choose among 12 grand strategies identified in Chapter 7.

grand strategy selection matrix
A four-cell guide to strategies based upon whether the business is (1) operating from a position of strength or weakness and (2) rely on its own resources versus having to acquire resources via merger or acquisition.

Grand Strategy Selection Matrix

One valuable guide to the selection of a promising grand strategy is the **grand strategy selection matrix** shown in Exhibit 8.10. The basic idea underlying the matrix is that two variables are of central concern in the selection process: (1) the principal purpose of the grand strategy and (2) the choice of an internal or external emphasis for growth or profitability.

Exhibit 8.10 **Grand Strategy Selection Matrix**

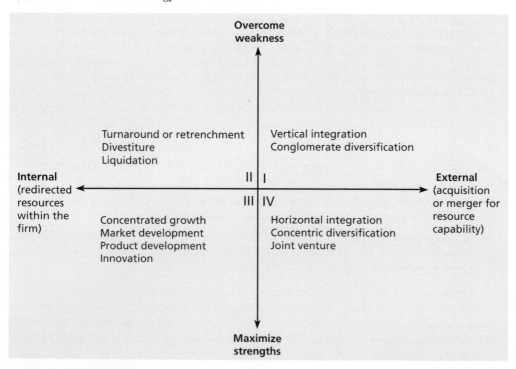

vertical integration
Acquisition of firms that supply inputs such as raw materials, or customers for its outputs, such as warehouses for finished products.

conglomerate diversification
Acquiring or entering businesses unrelated to a firm's current technologies, markets, or products.

retrenchment
Cutting back on products, markets, operations because the firm's overall competitive and financial situation cannot support commitments needed to sustain or build its operations.

divestiture
The sale of a firm or a major component.

liquidation
Closing down the operations of a business and selling its assets and operations to pay its debts and distribute any gains to stockholders.

concentrated growth
Aggressive market penetration where a firm's strong position and favorable market growth allow it to "control" resources and effort for focused growth.

market development
Selling present products, often with only cosmetic modification, to customers in related marketing areas by adding channels of distribution or by changing the content of advertising or promotion.

In the past, planners were advised to follow certain rules or prescriptions in their choice of strategies. Now, most experts agree that strategy selection is better guided by the conditions of the planning period and by the company strengths and weaknesses. It should be noted, however, that even the early approaches to strategy selection sought to match a concern over internal versus external growth with a desire to overcome weaknesses or maximize strengths.

The same considerations led to the development of the grand strategy selection matrix. A firm in quadrant I, with "all its eggs in one basket," often views itself as overcommitted to a particular business with limited growth opportunities or high risks. One reasonable solution is **vertical integration,** which enables the firm to reduce risk by reducing uncertainty about inputs or access to customers. Another is **conglomerate diversification,** which provides a profitable investment alternative with diverting management attention from the original business. However, the external approaches to overcoming weaknesses usually result in the most costly grand strategies. Acquiring a second business demands large investments of time and sizable financial resources. Thus, strategic managers considering these approaches must guard against exchanging one set of weaknesses for another.

More conservative approaches to overcoming weaknesses are found in quadrant II. Firms often choose to redirect resources from one internal business activity to another. This approach maintains the firm's commitment to its basic mission, rewards success, and enables further development of proven competitive advantages. The least disruptive of the quadrant II strategies is **retrenchment,** pruning the current activities of a business. If the weaknesses of the business arose from inefficiencies, retrenchment can actually serve as a *turnaround* strategy—that is, the business gains new strength from the streamlining of its operations and the elimination of waste. However, if those weaknesses are a major obstruction to success in the industry and the costs of overcoming them are unaffordable or are not justified by a cost-benefit analysis, then eliminating the business must be considered. **Divestiture** offers the best possibility for recouping the firm's investment, but even **liquidation** can be an attractive option if the alternatives are bankruptcy or an unwarranted drain on the firm's resources.

A common business adage states that a firm should build from strength. The premise of this adage is that growth and survival depend on an ability to capture a market share that is large enough for essential economies of scale. If a firm believes that this approach will be profitable and prefers an internal emphasis for maximizing strengths, four grand strategies hold considerable promise. As shown in quadrant III, the most common approach is **concentrated growth,** that is, market penetration. The firm that selects this strategy is strongly committed to its current products and markets. It strives to solidify its position by reinvesting resources to fortify its strengths.

Two alternative approaches are **market development** and **product development.** With these strategies, the firm attempts to broaden its operations. Market development is chosen if the firm's strategic managers feel that its existing products would be well received by new customer groups. Product development is chosen if they feel that the firm's existing customers would be interested in products related to its current lines. Product development also may be based on technological or other competitive advantages. The final alternative for quadrant III firms is **innovation.** When the firm's strengths are in creative product design or unique production technologies, sales can be stimulated by accelerating perceived obsolescence. This is the principle underlying the innovative grand strategy.

Maximizing a firm's strengths by aggressively expanding its base of operations usually requires an external emphasis. The preferred options in such cases are shown in quadrant IV. **Horizontal integration** is attractive because it makes possible a quick increase in output capability. Moreover, in horizontal integration, the skills of the managers of the original

product development
The substantial modification of existing products or the creation of new but related products that can be marketed to current customers through established channels.

innovation
A strategy that seeks to reap the initially high profits associated with customer acceptance of a new or greatly improved product.

business often are critical in converting newly acquired facilities into profitable contributors to the parent firm; this expands a fundamental competitive advantage of the firm—its management.

Concentric diversification is a good second choice for similar reasons. Because the original and newly acquired businesses are related, the distinctive competencies of the diversifying firm are likely to facilitate a smooth, synergistic, and profitable expansion.

The final alternative for increasing resource capability through external emphasis is a **joint venture** or **strategic alliance.** This alternative allows a firm to extend its strengths into competitive arenas that it would be hesitant to enter alone. A partner's production, technological, financial, or marketing capabilities can reduce the firm's financial investment significantly and increase its probability of success.

Model of Grand Strategy Clusters

A second guide to selecting a promising strategy is the **grand strategy cluster** shown in Exhibit 8.11. The figure is based on the idea that the situation of a business is defined

Exhibit 8.11   **Model of Grand Strategy Clusters**

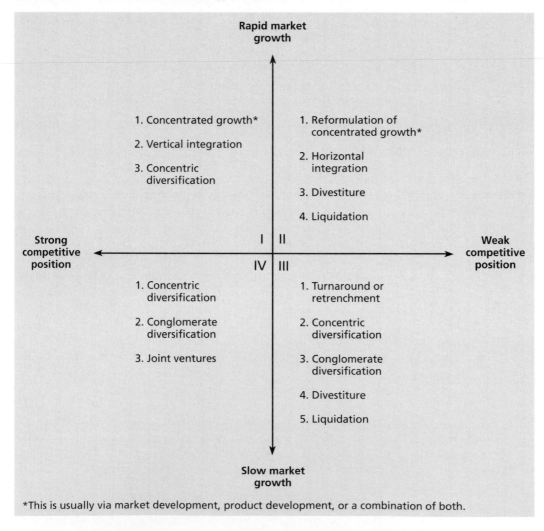

*This is usually via market development, product development, or a combination of both.

horizontal integration
Growth through the acquisition of one or more similar firms operating at the same stage of the production-marketing chain.

concentric diversification
Acquisition of businesses that are related to the acquiring firm in terms of technology, markets, or products.

joint ventures
Commercial companies created and operated for the benefit of the co-owners; usually two or more separate companies that form the venture.

strategic alliances
Partnerships that are distinguished from joint ventures because the companies involved do not take an equity position in one another.

grand strategy clusters
Strategies that may be more advantageous for firms to choose under one of four sets of conditions defined by market growth rate and the strength of the firm's competitive position.

in terms of the growth rate of the general market and the firm's competitive position in that market. When these factors are considered simultaneously, a business can be broadly categorized in one of four quadrants: (I) strong competitive position in a rapidly growing market, (II) weak position in a rapidly growing market, (III) weak position in a slow-growth market, or (IV) strong position in a slow-growth market. Each of these quadrants suggests a set of promising possibilities for the selection of a grand strategy.

Firms in quadrant I are in an excellent strategic position. One obvious grand strategy for such firms is continued concentration on their current business as it is currently defined. Because consumers seem satisfied with the firm's current strategy, shifting notably from it would endanger the firm's established competitive advantages. McDonald's Corporation has followed this approach for 25 years. However, if the firm has resources that exceed the demands of a concentrated growth strategy, it should consider vertical integration. Either forward or backward integration helps a firm protect its profit margins and market share by ensuring better access to consumers or material inputs. Finally, to diminish the risks associated with a narrow product or service line, a quadrant I firm might be wise to consider concentric diversification; with this strategy, the firm continues to invest heavily in its basic area of proven ability.

Firms in quadrant II must seriously evaluate their present approach to the marketplace. If a firm has competed long enough to accurately assess the merits of its current grand strategy, it must determine (1) why that strategy is ineffectual and (2) whether it is capable of competing effectively. Depending on the answers to these questions, the firm should choose one of four grand strategy options: formulation or reformulation of a concentrated growth strategy, horizontal integration, divestiture, or liquidation.

In a rapidly growing market, even a small or relatively weak business often is able to find a profitable niche. Thus, formulation or reformulation of a concentrated growth strategy is usually the first option that should be considered. However, if the firm lacks either a critical competitive element or sufficient economies of scale to achieve competitive cost efficiencies, then a grand strategy that directs its efforts toward horizontal integration is often a desirable alternative. A final pair of options involves deciding to stop competing in the market or product area of the business. A multiproduct firm may conclude that it is most likely to achieve the goals of its mission if the business is dropped through divestiture. This grand strategy not only eliminates a drain on resources but also may provide funds to promote other business activities. As an option of last resort, a firm may decide to liquidate the business. This means that the business cannot be sold as a going concern and is at best worth only the value of its tangible assets. The decision to liquidate is an undeniable admission of failure by a firm's strategic management and, thus, often is delayed—to the further detriment of the firm.

Strategic managers tend to resist divestiture because it is likely to jeopardize their control of the firm and perhaps even their jobs. Thus, by the time the desirability of divestiture is acknowledged, businesses often deteriorate to the point of failing to attract potential buyers. The consequences of such delays are financially disastrous for firm owners because the value of a going concern is many times greater than the value of its assets.

Strategic managers who have a business in quadrant III and expect a continuation of slow market growth and a relatively weak competitive position will usually attempt to decrease their resource commitment to that business. Minimal withdrawal is accomplished through retrenchment; this strategy has the side benefits of making resources available for other investments and of motivating employees to increase their operating efficiency. An alternative approach is to divert resources for expansion through investment in other businesses. This approach typically involves either concentric or conglomerate diversification because the firm usually wants to enter more promising arenas of competition than integration or concentrated growth strategies would allow. The final options for quadrant III businesses are divestiture, if an optimistic buyer can be found, and liquidation.

Quadrant IV businesses (strong competitive position in a slow-growth market) have a basis of strength from which to diversify into more promising growth areas. These businesses have characteristically high cash flow levels and limited internal growth needs. Thus, they are in an excellent position for concentric diversification into ventures that utilize their proven acumen. A previous example in this chapter described how the no. 1 tennis ball maker, Penn Racquet Sports, chose concentric diversification from humans to dogs as their best option. A second option is conglomerate diversification, which spreads investment risk and does not divert managerial attention from the present business. The final option is joint ventures, which are especially attractive to multinational firms. Through joint ventures, a domestic business can gain competitive advantages in promising new fields while exposing itself to limited risks.

Opportunities for Building Value as a Basis for Choosing Diversification or Integration

The grand strategy selection matrix and model of grand strategy clusters are useful tools to help dominant product company managers evaluate and narrow their choices among alternative grand strategies. When considering grand strategies that would broaden the scope of their company's business activities through integration, diversification, or joint venture strategies, managers must examine whether opportunities to build value are present. Opportunities to build value via diversification, integration, or joint venture strategies are usually found in market-related, operating-related, and management activities. Such opportunities center around reducing costs, improving margins, or providing access to new revenue sources more cost effectively than traditional internal growth options via concentration, market development, or product development. Major opportunities for sharing and value building as well as ways to capitalize on core competencies are outlined in the next chapter, which covers strategic analysis and choice in diversified companies.

Dominant product company managers who choose diversification or integration eventually create another management challenge. That challenge is charting the future of a company that becomes a collection of several distinct businesses. These distinct businesses often encounter different competitive environments, challenges, and opportunities. The next chapter examines ways managers of such diversified companies attempt to evaluate and choose corporate strategy. Central to their challenge is the continued desire to build value, particularly shareholder value.

Summary

This chapter examined how managers in businesses that have a single or dominant product or service evaluate and choose their company's strategy. Two critical areas deserve their attention: (1) their business's value chain, and (2) the appropriateness of 12 different grand strategies based on matching environmental factors with internal capabilities.

Managers in single-product-line business units examine their business's value chain to identify existing or potential activities around which they can create sustainable competitive advantages. As managers scrutinize their value chain activities, they are looking for three sources of competitive advantage: low cost, differentiation, and rapid response capabilities. They also examine whether focusing on a narrow market niche provides a more effective, sustainable way to build or leverage these three sources of competitive advantage.

Managers in single- or dominant-product/service businesses face two interrelated issues: (1) They must choose which grand strategies make best use of their competitive advantages. (2) They must ultimately decide whether to diversify their business activity. Twelve grand strategies were identified in this chapter along with three frameworks that aid managers in choosing which grand strategies should work best and when diversification or integration should be the best strategy for the business. The next chapter expands the coverage of diversification to look at how multibusiness companies evaluate continued diversification and how they construct corporate strategy.

Key Terms

concentrated growth, *p. 235*
concentric diversification, *p. 237*
conglomerate diversification, *p. 235*
declining industry, *p. 231*
differentiation, *p. 219*
divestiture, *p. 235*
emerging industry, *p. 226*
fragmented industry, *p. 231*

global industry, *p. 232*
grand strategy clusters, *p. 237*
grand strategy selection matrix, *p. 234*
growth industry strategies, *p. 227*
horizontal integration, *p. 237*
innovation, *p. 236*
joint ventures, *p. 237*
liquidation, *p. 235*

low-cost strategies, *p. 216*
market development, *p. 235*
market focus, *p. 225*
mature industry strategies, *p. 229*
product development, *p. 236*
retrenchment, *p. 235*
speed-based strategies, *p. 222*
strategic alliances, *p. 237*
vertical integration, *p. 235*

Questions for Discussion

1. What are three activities or capabilities a firm should possess to support a low-cost leadership strategy? Use Exhibit 8.2 to help you answer this question. Can you give an example of a company that has done this?

2. What are three activities or capabilities a firm should possess to support a differentiation-based strategy? Use Exhibit 8.3 to help you answer this question. Can you give an example of a company that has done this?

3. What are three ways a firm can incorporate the advantage of speed in its business? Use Exhibit 8.5 to help you answer this question. Can you give an example of a company that has done this?

4. Do you think it is better to concentrate on one source of competitive advantage (cost versus differentiation versus speed) or to nurture all three in a firm's operation?

5. How does market focus help a business create competitive advantage? What risks accompany such a posture?

6. Using Exhibits 8.10 and 8.11, describe situations or conditions under which horizontal integration and concentric diversification would be preferred strategic choices.

Chapter **Nine**

Multibusiness Strategy

After reading and studying this chapter, you should be able to

1. Understand the portfolio approach to strategic analysis and choice in multibusiness companies.

2. Understand and use three different portfolio approaches to conduct strategic analysis and choice in multibusiness companies.

3. Identify the limitations and weaknesses of the various portfolio approaches.

4. Understand the synergy approach to strategic analysis and choice in multibusiness companies.

5. Evaluate the parent company role in strategic analysis and choice to determine whether and how it adds tangible value in a multibusiness company.

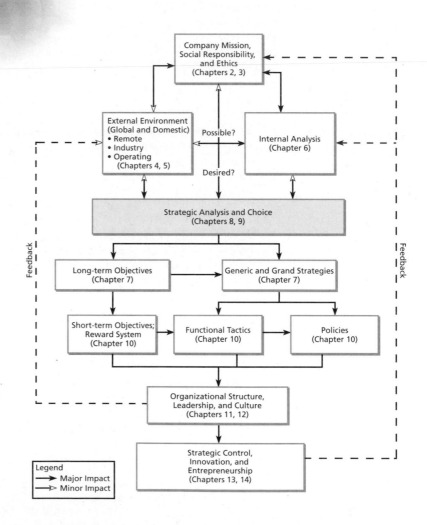

Company Mission, Social Responsibility, and Ethics (Chapters 2, 3)

External Environment (Global and Domestic)
• Remote
• Industry
• Operating
(Chapters 4, 5)

Possible?

Desired?

Internal Analysis (Chapter 6)

Strategic Analysis and Choice (Chapters 8, 9)

Long-term Objectives (Chapter 7)

Generic and Grand Strategies (Chapter 7)

Short-term Objectives; Reward System (Chapter 10)

Functional Tactics (Chapter 10)

Policies (Chapter 10)

Organizational Structure, Leadership, and Culture (Chapters 11, 12)

Strategic Control, Innovation, and Entrepreneurship (Chapters 13, 14)

Feedback

Feedback

Legend
→ Major Impact
⇢ Minor Impact

Jeff Immelt has faced two recessions and accelerated global competition in his first decade at General Electric's helm, personally selected for the job by his predecessor, the globally admired Jack Welch. The current global economic crisis, driven by a swift virtual collapse of the global financial system, has made Immelt's challenge even greater as it places in jeopardy GE Capital, one of five GE business groups and a usual key source of profit to finance its other businesses. GE remains—and has long been—one of the world's most admired companies, a bellwether of the global economy, even in the face of these unprecedented challenges in 2010. The job facing Immelt and his executive team, in addition to figuring out how to weather this unprecedented financial challenge, is to determine what businesses GE should remain in, and which it should exit, to survive and prosper in the twenty-first century. Should it continue with plans to sell its appliance business? Should it grow its energy infrastructure businesses, enter biomedicine, stay in movies and TV? Which businesses should receive the greatest investment of its currently limited resources, and which should it sell or otherwise reduce to generate resources and shift talent? Go to www.ge.com, and look over the description of its five core businesses; then consider what your recommendation to Immelt would be should he visit and ask your opinion on just this question.

Japan-based Sony Corporation, once the darling of the electronics world, is proving a major challenge to Welsh-born American CEO Howard Stringer. A slowing global economy, a rising yen, an organizational culture based on consensus decision making facing swiftly changing conditions—and conglomerate Sony being outfought by more focused, leaner companies: Nintendo in games, Apple in audio entertainment, Cannon in cameras, Samsung in TVs, and Microsoft in software. Five years into his tenure, Stringer is at a crossroads. Facing its first operating losses in 14 years, what should he do? Should he emphasize certain businesses? Sell others? Outsource and refocus the nature of each business?

Strategic analysis and choice is complicated for corporate-level managers because they must create a strategy to guide a company that contains numerous businesses. They must examine and choose which businesses to own and which ones to forgo or divest. They must consider business managers' plans to capture and exploit competitive advantage in each business, and then decide how to allocate resources among those businesses. This chapter covers ways managers in multibusiness companies analyze and choose what businesses to be in and how to allocate resources across those businesses.

The portfolio approach was one of the early approaches for charting strategy and allocating resources in multibusiness companies. This approach, with its appealing fundamental logic, was initially popularized by consulting groups like the Boston Consulting Group and McKinsey and Company as they helped corporate clients pursue and "rationalize" diversification strategies. Inevitably, some corporate managers, concerned with possible shortcomings in this type of approach, welcomed new options. Yet, while some companies moved on to other techniques, the portfolio approach remains a useful way of evaluating corporate strategy options. Interestingly, GE pioneered one form of the approach, which was subsequently abandoned under Jack Welch, only to now have successor Jeff Immelt bring it back as part of GE's corporate strategy vocabulary and decision making. Immelt's comments to GE stakeholders during his tenure to date that show this include:

> I would ask investors to think about the progress we have made with our portfolio [of businesses] . . . We have executed a disciplined portfolio strategy to aggressively reshaped GE . . . We have exited businesses with revenues of about $50 billion—the equivalent of a *Fortune* 50 company. We have exited all or most of our insurance, materials, equipment services, and slow-growth entertainment and industrial platforms . . . our mortgage origination business and our personal loan business in Japan . . . Over the same time period

we acquired $80 billion of new businesses—the equivalent of a *Fortune* 30 company . . . investing in Infrastructure, creating one of the largest renewable-energy businesses in the world . . . diversified our Healthcare and NBC Universal (NBCU) franchises by investing in fast-growth markets such as life sciences, healthcare IT, and cable programming . . . and created a new high-tech industrial business called Enterprise Solutions. We sold our Plastics business because of rampant inflation in raw material costs . . . used that capital to acquire Vetco Gray, adding a subsea platform in Oil & Gas; we acquired Smiths Aerospace to create an avionics platform; we built global cable content through the acquisition of Oxygen and Sparrowhawk; and we added several industrial service platforms.

Today we have six leadership businesses: Infrastructure, Healthcare, Commercial Finance, NBC Universal, Industrial, and GE Money. Each of these businesses can hit our financial goals while adding to the strategic value of GE. We like businesses where good management results in superior financial results. We like broadly diversified businesses with multiple ways to grow. We believe that our process skills create a competitive advantage. We like businesses where we can "retool" our strategies to capture new opportunities for profitable growth.[1]

Perhaps history repeats itself, or what goes around comes around in terms of using a portfolio approach. Some see GE and argue, particularly in recent economic times, that it is too big and complicated to achieve success compared to what could be achieved if its various businesses were separated. Others point out that it has produced impressive innovation and growth for most of its 130 years and that its individual businesses benefit from synergies gained across each other as they face common global themes. Both perspectives have legitimate points. Regardless, where managers in a company like GE, with multiple diverse businesses, need to examine and develop corporate level strategy, the need to look at the "whole" as a porfolio of different businesses appears one way to pursue that task.[2] Exhibit 9.1, Strategy in Action, shows eBay's view of its business portfolio's evolution and its current questioning about Skype.

Improvement on the portfolio approach focused on ways to broaden the rationale behind pursuit of diversification strategies. This approach centered on the idea that at the heart of effective diversification is the identification of core competencies in a business or set of businesses to then leverage as the basis for competitive advantage in the growth of those businesses and the entry in or divestiture of other businesses. This notion of leveraging core competencies as a basis for strategic choice in multibusiness companies has been a popular one for the past 20 years.

Recent evolution of strategic analysis and choice in this setting has expanded on the core competency notion to focus on a series of fundamental questions that multibusiness companies should address in order to make diversification work. With both the accelerated rates of change in most global markets and trying economic conditions, multibusiness companies have adapted the fundamental questions into an approach called "patching" to map and remap their business units swiftly against changing market opportunities. Finally, as companies have embraced lean organizational structures, strategic analysis in multibusiness companies has included careful assessment of the corporate parent, its role, and value or lack thereof in contributing to the stand-alone performance of their business units. This chapter will examine each of these approaches to shaping multibusiness corporate strategy.

---

[1] "Letter to Shareholders," 2006, 2007, 2008 *G.E. Annual Reports.*
[2] "GE's Immelt: An Ever Hotter Throne," *BusinessWeek,* November 8, 2008; and "In Grim Times, Hoping for 'Reset,'" *Fortune,* January 28, 2009.

eBay's Business Portfolio—Three Businesses . . . Does Skype Fit?

This map from eBay shows the evolution of its "3 Legged Stool" business portfolio. Many analysts and eBay sellers question the rationale of having Skype in the mix. Many see Skype as having snookered former CEO Meg Whitman into paying $3.1 billion in 2005 for "synergies" that have never materialized, thus the name "Whitman's Folly." eBay took a $1.4 billion write-down two years later, and Skype's fourth president since the acquisition, Josh Silverman, is trying to accelerate Skype's financial relevance to eBay and acquire some anticipated synergies by already selling a partial interest in Skype and, just maybe, even selling the whole thing.

Source: Fair Use per EBay

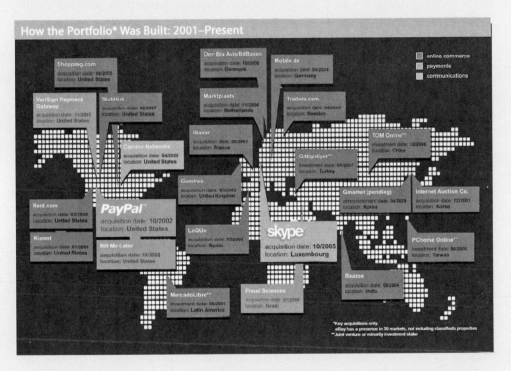

THE PORTFOLIO APPROACH: A HISTORICAL STARTING POINT

portfolio techniques
An approach pioneered by the Boston Consulting Group that attempted to help managers "balance" the flow of cash resources among their various businesses while also identifying their basic strategic purpose within the overall portfolio.

The past 30 years we have seen a virtual explosion in the extent to which single-business companies seek to acquire other businesses to grow and to diversify. There are many reasons for this emergence of multibusiness companies: companies can enter businesses with greater growth potential; enter businesses with different cyclical considerations; diversify inherent risks; increase vertical integration, and thereby reduce costs; capture value added; and instantly have a market presence rather than slower internal growth. As businesses jumped on the diversification bandwagon, their managers soon found a challenge in managing the resource needs of diverse businesses and their respective strategic missions, particularly in times of limited resources. Responding to this challenge, the Boston Consulting Group (BCG) pioneered an approach called **portfolio techniques** that attempted to help managers "balance" the flow of cash resources among their various businesses while also identifying their basic strategic purpose within the overall portfolio. Three of these techniques are reviewed here. Once reviewed, we will identify some of the problems with the portfolio approach that you should keep in mind when considering its use.

The BCG Growth-Share Matrix

market growth rate
The projected rate of sales growth for the market being served by a particular business.

relative competitive position
The market share of a business divided by the market share of its largest competitor.

stars
Businesses in rapidly growing markets with large market shares.

cash cows
Businesses with a high market share in low-growth markets or industries.

dogs
Low market share and low market growth businesses.

Managers using the BCG matrix plotted each of the company's businesses according to market growth rate and relative competitive position. **Market growth rate** is the projected rate of sales growth for the market being served by a particular business. Usually measured as the percentage increase in a market's sales or unit volume over the two most recent years, this rate serves as an indicator of the relative attractiveness of the markets served by each business in the firm's portfolio of businesses. **Relative competitive position** usually is expressed as the market share of a business divided by the market share of its largest competitor. Thus, relative competitive position provides a basis for comparing the relative strengths of the businesses in the firm's portfolio in terms of their positions in their respective markets. Exhibit 9.2 illustrates the growth-share matrix.

The **stars** are businesses in rapidly growing markets with large market shares. These businesses represent the best long-run opportunities (growth and profitability) in the firm's portfolio. They require substantial investment to maintain (and expand) their dominant position in a growing market. This investment requirement is often in excess of the funds that they can generate internally. Therefore, these businesses are often short-term, priority consumers of corporate resources.

Cash cows are businesses with a high market share in low-growth markets or industries. Because of their strong competitive positions and their minimal reinvestment requirements, these businesses often generate cash in excess of their needs. Therefore, they are selectively "milked" as a source of corporate resources for deployment elsewhere (to stars and question marks). Cash cows are yesterday's stars and the current foundation of corporate portfolios. They provide the cash needed to pay corporate overhead and dividends and provide debt capacity. They are managed to maintain their strong market share while generating excess resources for corporatewide use.

Low market share and low market growth businesses are the **dogs** in the firm's portfolio. Facing mature markets with intense competition and low profit margins, they are managed for short-term cash flow (e.g., through ruthless cost cutting) to supplement corporate-level resource needs. According to the original BCG prescription, they are divested or liquidated once this short-term harvesting has been maximized.

EXHIBIT 9.2
The BCG Growth-Share Matrix

Source: The growth-share matrix was originally developed by the Boston Consulting Group.

Description of Dimensions

Market share: Sales relative to those of other competitors in the market (dividing point is usually selected to have only the two to three largest competitors in any market fall into the high market share region)

Growth rate: Industry growth rate in constant dollars (dividing point is typically the GNP's growth rate)

Cash Generation (market share)

	High	Low
High (growth rate)	★ Star	? Problem Child
Low	$ Cash Cow	X Dog

Cash Use (growth rate)

Question marks are businesses whose high growth rate gives them considerable appeal but whose low market share makes their profit potential uncertain. Question marks are cash guzzlers because their rapid growth results in high cash needs, while their small market share results in low cash generation. At the corporate level, the concern is to identify the question marks that would increase their market share and move into the star group if extra corporate resources were devoted to them. Where this long-run shift from question mark to star is unlikely, the BCG matrix suggests divesting the question mark and repositioning its resources more effectively in the remainder of the corporate portfolio.

The Industry Attractiveness–Business Strength Matrix

Corporate strategists found the growth-share matrix's singular axes limiting in their ability to reflect the complexity of a business's situation. Therefore, some companies adopted a matrix with a much broader focus. This matrix, developed by McKinsey & Company at General Electric, is called the industry attractiveness–business strength matrix. This matrix uses multiple factors to assess industry attractiveness and business strength rather than the single measures (market share and market growth, respectively) employed in the BCG matrix. It also has nine cells as opposed to four—replacing the high/low axes with high/medium/low axes to make finer distinctions among business portfolio positions.

The company's businesses are rated on multiple strategic factors within each axis, such as the factors described in Exhibit 9.3. The position of a business is then calculated by "subjectively" quantifying its rating along the two dimensions of the matrix. Depending on the location of a business within the matrix as shown in Exhibit 9.4, one of the following strategic approaches is suggested: (1) invest to grow, (2) invest selectively and manage for earnings, or (3) harvest or divest for resources. The resource allocation decisions remain quite similar to those of the BCG approach.

Although the strategic recommendations generated by the industry attractiveness–business strength matrix are similar to those generated by the BCG matrix, the industry attractiveness–business strength matrix improves on the BCG matrix in three fundamental ways:

1. The terminology associated with the industry attractiveness–business strength matrix is preferable because it is less offensive and more understandable.
2. The multiple measures associated with each dimension of the business strength matrix tap many factors relevant to business strength and market attractiveness besides market share and market growth.
3. In turn, this makes for broader assessment during the planning process, bringing to light considerations of importance in both strategy formulation and strategy implementation.

BCG's Strategic Environments Matrix

BCG's latest matrix offering (see Exhibit 9.5) took a different approach, using the idea that it was the nature of competitive advantage in an industry that determined the strategies available to a company's businesses, which in turn determined the structure of the industry. Their idea was that such a framework could help ensure that individual businesses' strategies were consistent with strategies appropriate to their strategic environment. Furthermore, for corporate managers in multiple-business companies, this matrix offered one way to rationalize which businesses they are in—businesses that share core competencies and associated competitive advantages because of similar strategic environments.

The matrix has two dimensions. The number of sources of competitive advantage could be many with complex products and services (e.g., automobiles, financial services) and few with commodities (chemicals, microprocessors). Complex products offer multiple

EXHIBIT 9.3
Factors Considered
in Constructing
an Industry
Attractiveness–
Business Strength
Matrix

Industry Attractiveness	Business Strength
Nature of Competitive Rivalry	**Cost Position**
Number of competitors Size of competitors Strength of competitors' corporate parents Price wars Competition on multiple dimensions	Economies of scale Manufacturing costs Overhead scrap/waste/rework Experience effects Labor rates Proprietary processes
Bargaining Power of Suppliers/ Customers	**Level of Differentiation**
Relative size of typical players Numbers of each Importance of purchases from or sales to Ability to vertically integrate	Promotion effectiveness Product quality Company image Patented products Brand awareness
Threat of Substitute Products/ New Entrants	**Response Time**
Technological maturity/stability Diversity of the market Barriers to entry Flexibility of distribution system	Manufacturing flexibility Time needed to introduce new products Delivery times Organizational flexibility
Economic Factors	**Financial Strength**
Sales volatility Cyclicality of demand Market growth Capital intensity	Solvency Liquidity Break-even point Cash flows Profitability Growth in revenues
Financial Norms	**Human Assets**
Average profitability Typical leverage Credit practices	Turnover Skill level Relative wage/salary Morale Managerial commitment Unionization
Sociopolitical Considerations	**Public Approval**
Government regulation Community support Ethical standards	Goodwill Reputation Image

opportunities for differentiation as well as cost, while commodities must seek opportunities for cost advantages to survive.

The second dimension is size of competitive advantage. How big is the advantage available to the industry leader? The two dimensions then define four industry environments as follows:

volume businesses
Businesses that
have few sources of
advantage, but the size
is large—typically
the result of scale
economies.

- **Volume businesses** are those that have few sources of advantage, but the size is large—typically the result of scale economies. Advantages established in one such business may be transferable to another as Honda has done with its scale and expertise with small gasoline engines.

EXHIBIT 9.4   The Industry Attractiveness–Business Strength Matrix

		Business Strength		
		Strong	**Average**	**Weak**
Industry Attractiveness	**High**	**Premium—invest for growth:** • Provide maximum investment • Diversify worldwide • Consolidate position • Accept moderate near-term profits • Seek to dominate	**Selective—invest for growth** • Invest heavily in selected segments • Share ceiling • Seek attractive new segments to apply strengths	**Protect/refocus— selectively invest for earnings:** • Defend strengths • Refocus to attractive segments • Evaluate industry revitalization • Monitor for harvest or divestment timing • Consider acquisitions
	Medium	**Challenge—invest for growth:** • Build selectively on strengths • Define implications of leadership challenge • Avoid vulnerability—fill weaknesses	**Prime—selectively invest for earnings:** • Segment market • Make contingency plans for vulnerability	**Restructure—harvest or divest:** • Provide no unessential commitment • Position for divestment or • Shift to more attractive segment
	Low	**Opportunistic—selectively invest for earnings:** • Ride market and maintain overall position • Seek niches, specialization • Seek opportunity to increase strength (for example through acquisition) • Invest at maintenance levels	**Opportunistic—preserve for harvest:** • Act to preserve or boost cash flow • Seek opportunistic sale or • Seek opportunistic rationalization to increase strengths • Prune product lines • Minimize investment	**Harvest or divest:** • Exit from market or prune product line • Determine timing so as to maximize present value • Concentrate on competitor's cash generators

Source: Reprinted by permission of the publisher, from Strategic Market Planning by Bernard A. Rausch, AMACOM, division of American Management Association, New York, 1982, www.amanet.org.

EXHIBIT 9.5
BCG's Strategic Environments Matrix

Source: From R.M. Grant, *Contemporary Strategy Analysis,* Blackwell Publishing, 2001, p. 327. Reprinted with permission of Wiley-Blackwell.

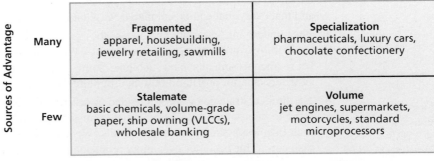

		Small	Big
Sources of Advantage	**Many**	**Fragmented** apparel, housebuilding, jewelry retailing, sawmills	**Specialization** pharmaceuticals, luxury cars, chocolate confectionery
	Few	**Stalemate** basic chemicals, volume-grade paper, ship owning (VLCCs), wholesale banking	**Volume** jet engines, supermarkets, motorcycles, standard microprocessors

Size of Advantage

- **Stalemate businesses** have few sources of advantage, with most of those small. This results in very competitive situations. Skills in operational efficiency, low overhead, and cost management are critical to profitability.

- **Fragmented businesses** have many sources of advantage, but they are all small. This typically involves differentiated products with low brand loyalty, easily replicated technology, and minimal scale economies. Skills in focused market segments, typically geographic, the ability to respond quickly to changes, and low costs are critical in this environment.

- **Specialization businesses** have many sources of advantage and find those advantages potentially sizable. Skills in achieving differentiation—product design, branding expertise, innovation, first-mover, and perhaps scale—characterize winners here.

BCG viewed this matrix as providing guidance to multibusiness managers to determine whether they possessed the sources and size of advantage associated with the type of industry facing each business and allowed them a framework to realistically explore the nature of the strategic environments in which they competed or were interested in entering.

Limitations of Portfolio Approaches

Portfolio approaches made several contributions to strategic analysis by corporate managers convinced of their ability to transfer the competitive advantage of professional management across a broad array of businesses. They helped convey large amounts of information about diverse business units and corporate plans in a greatly simplified format. They illuminated similarities and differences between business units and helped convey the logic behind corporate strategies for each business with a common vocabulary. They simplified priorities for sharing corporate resources across diverse business units that generated and used those resources. They provided a simple prescription that gave corporate managers a sense of what they should accomplish—a balanced portfolio of businesses—and a way to control and allocate resources among them. While these approaches offered meaningful contributions, they had several critical limitations and shortcomings:

- A key problem with the portfolio matrix was that it did not address how value was being created across business units—the only relationship between them was cash. Addressing each business unit as a stand-alone entity ignores common core competencies and internal synergies among operating units.

- Truly accurate measurement for matrix classification was not as easy as the matrices portrayed. Identifying individual businesses, or distinct markets, was not often as precise as underlying assumptions required. Comparing business units on only two fundamental dimensions can lead to the conclusion that these are the only factors that really matter and that every unit can be compared fairly on those bases.

- The underlying assumption about the relationship between market share and profitability—the experience curve effect—varied across different industries and market segments. Some have no such link. Some find that firms with low market share can generate superior profitability with differentiation advantages.

- The limited strategic options, intended to describe the flow of resources in a company, came to be seen more as basic strategic missions, which creates a false sense of what each business's strategy actually entails. What do we actually "do" if we're a star? A cash cow? This becomes even more problematic when attempting to use the matrices to conceive strategies for average businesses in average-growth markets.

- The portfolio approach portrayed the notion that firms needed to be self-sufficient in capital. This ignored capital raised in capital markets.

- The portfolio approach typically failed to compare the competitive advantage a business received from being owned by a particular company with the costs of owning it. The 1980s saw many companies build enormous corporate infrastructures that created only small gains at the business level. The reengineering and deconstruction of numerous global conglomerates in the past 10 years reflects this important omission. We will examine this consideration in greater detail later in this chapter.

- Recent research by well-known consulting firm Booz Allen Hamilton suggests that "conventional wisdom is wrong. Corporate managers often rely on accounting metrics [based on past performance] to make business decisions." They go on to argue that "past performance is a poor predictor of the future. When performance is assessed over time, greater shareholder value can be created by improving the operations of the company's worst-performing businesses." "The way to thrive," they say, "is to love your dogs." Their point, backed up by impressive research, is that a corporate manager can learn to identify "value assets," hold and nurture them, and produce superior performance ultimately leading to increased shareholder value more so than can be achieved by acquiring and trying to add value to an overvalued "star."[3]

Constructing business portfolio matrices must be undertaken with these limitations in mind. Perhaps it is best to say that they provide one form of input to corporate managers seeking to balance financial resources. While limitations have meant portfolio approaches are seen as mere historical concepts, others appear to find them useful in evaluating strategic options as we saw happening in the chapter introduction example about General Electric's current efforts to manage its diverse business portfolio in the rapidly changing global economy of the twenty-first century. Perhaps this foretells a continued use of the portfolio approach, recognizing its limitations, to provide a picture of the "balance" of resource generators and users, to test underlying assumptions about these issues in more involved corporate planning efforts, and to leverage core competencies to build sustained competitive advantages. The next major approach in the evolution of multibusiness strategic analysis is to leverage shared capabilities and core competencies.

THE SYNERGY APPROACH: LEVERAGING CORE COMPETENCIES

Opportunities to build value via diversification, integration, or joint venture strategies are usually found in market-related, operations-related, and management activities. Each business's basic value chain activities or infrastructure become a source of potential synergy and competitive advantage for another business in the corporate portfolio. Morrison's Cafeterias, once a mainstay of the food-service industry in malls across much of the United States, accelerated its diversification into other restaurant concepts such as Ruby Tuesday's, followed by L&N Seafood Grill, Silver Spoon Café, Mozzarella's, and Tia's Tex-Mex. It also acquired three other food-contract firms. Numerous opportunities for shared operating capabilities and management capabilities drove this decision and, upon repeated strategic analysis, accelerated corporate managers' decision to move Morrison's totally out of the cafeteria segment a few years later. Some of the more common opportunities to share value chain activities and build value are identified in Exhibit 9.6.

---

[3] A comprehensive discussion of these ideas to include their research examining the performance of "falling stars" and "rising dogs" can be found at Harry Quaris, Thomas Pernsteiner, and Kasturi Rangan, "Love your 'Dogs,'" *Strategy+Business Magazine*, Booz Allen Hamilton, www.strategy-business.com/ resiliencereport/resilience/rr00030, 2007.

EXHIBIT 9.6   **Value Building in Multibusiness Companies**

Opportunities to Build Value or Sharing	Potential Competitive Advantage	Impediments to Achieving Enhanced Value
Market-Related Opportunities		
Shared sales force activities, shared sales office, or both	Lower selling costs Better market coverage Stronger technical advice to buyers Enhanced convenience for buyers (can buy from single source) Improved access to buyers (have more products to sell)	• Buyers have different purchasing habits toward the products. • Different salespersons are more effective in representing the product. • Some products get more attention than others. • Buyers prefer to multiple-source rather than single-source their purchases.
Shared after-sale service and repair work	Lower servicing costs Better utilization of service personnel (less idle time) Faster servicing of customer calls	• Different equipment or different labor skills, or both, are needed to handle repairs. • Buyers may do some in-house repairs.
Shared brand name	Stronger brand image and company reputation Increased buyer confidence in the brand	• Company reputation is hurt if quality of one product is lower.
Shared advertising and promotional activities	Lower costs Greater clout in purchasing ads	• Appropriate forms of messages are different. • Appropriate timing of promotions is different.
Common distribution channels	Lower distribution costs Enhanced bargaining power with distributors and retailers to gain shelf space, shelf positioning, stronger push and more dealer attention, and better profit margins	• Dealers resist being dominated by a single supplier and turn to multiple sources and lines. • Heavy use of the shared channel erodes willingness of other channels to carry or push the firm's products.
Shared order processing	Lower order processing costs One-stop shopping for buyer to enhance service and, thus, differentiation	• Differences in ordering cycles disrupt order-processing economies.
Operating Opportunities		
Joint procurement of purchased inputs	Lower input costs Improved input quality Improved service from suppliers	• Input needs are different in terms of quality or other specifications. • Inputs are needed at different plant locations, and centralized purchasing is not responsive to separate needs of each plant.
Shared manufacturing and assembly facilities	Lower manufacturing/assembly costs Better capacity utilization, because peak demand for one product correlates with valley demand for the other Bigger scale of operation to improve access to better technology, resulting in better quality	• Higher changeover costs in shifting from one product to another. • High-cost special tooling or equipment is required to accommodate quality differences or design differences.

EXHIBIT 9.6   *(continued)*

Opportunities to Build Value or Sharing	Potential Competitive Advantage	Impediments to Achieving Enhanced Value
Operating Opportunities (cont.)		
Shared inbound or outbound shipping and materials handling	Lower freight and handling costs Better delivery reliability More frequent deliveries, such that inventory costs are reduced	• Input sources or plant locations, or both, are in different geographic areas. • Needs for frequency and reliability of inbound/outbound delivery differ among the business units.
Shared product and process technologies, technology development, or both	Lower product or process design costs, or both, because of shorter design times and transfers of knowledge from area to area More innovative ability, owing to scale of effort and attraction of better R&D personnel	• Technologies are the same, but the applications in different business units are different enough to prevent much sharing of real value.
Shared administrative support activities	Lower administrative and operating overhead costs	• Support activities are not a large proportion of cost, and sharing has little cost impact (and virtually no differentiation impact).
Management Opportunities		
Shared management know-how, operating skills, and proprietary information	Efficient transfer of a distinctive competence—can create cost savings or enhance differentiation More effective management as concerns strategy formulation, strategy implementation, and understanding of key success factors	• Actual transfer of know-how is costly or stretches the key skill personnel too thinly, or both. • Increased risks that proprietary information will leak out.

Source: Based on Michael Porter, *On Competition,* Harvard Business School Press.

Strategic analysis is concerned with whether or not the potential competitive advantages expected to arise from each value opportunity have materialized. Where advantage has not materialized, corporate strategists must take care to scrutinize possible impediments to achieving the synergy or competitive advantage. We have identified in Exhibit 9.6 several impediments associated with each opportunity, which strategists are well advised to examine. Good strategists assure themselves that their organization has ways to avoid or minimize the effects of any impediments, or they recommend against further integration or diversification and consider divestiture options.

Two elements are critical in meaningful shared opportunities:

1. The shared opportunities must be a significant portion of the value chain of the businesses involved. Returning to Morrison's Cafeteria, its purchasing and inbound logistics infrastructure gave Ruby Tuesday's operators an immediate cost-effective purchasing and inventory management capability that lowered its cost in a significant cost activity.

2. The businesses involved must truly have shared needs—need for the same activity—or there is no basis for synergy in the first place. Skype is a pioneering success story of the use of the Internet for telephone and video communication between any two computer locations worldwide. eBay acquired Skype, anticipating numerous synergies with its worldwide online auction business—but such synergies have yet to emerge. It appears clear, however, that eBay grossly overpaid for Skype, and it remains unclear what shared needs are common to both businesses that provide the basis for synergy. Indeed, eBay appears to have given up on synergies between the two, choosing instead to let Skype operate independently, and hopes it can one day sell Skype for close to the $2 billion value still remaining on eBay's books.[4]

Corporate strategies have repeatedly rushed into diversification only to find perceived opportunities for sharing were nonexistent because the businesses did not really have shared needs.

The most compelling reason companies should diversify can be found in situations where core competencies—key value-building skills—can be leveraged with other products or into markets that are not a part of where they were created. Where this works well, extraordinary value can be built. Managers undertaking diversification strategies should dedicate a significant portion of their strategic analysis to this question.

General Cinema was a company that grew from drive-in theaters to eventually dominate the multicinema, movie exhibition industry. Next, they entered soft-drink bottling and became the largest bottler of soft drinks (Pepsi) in North America. Their stock value rose 2,000 percent in 10 years. They found that core competencies in movie exhibition—managing many small, localized businesses; dealing with a few large suppliers; applying central marketing skills locally; and acquiring or crafting a "franchise"—were virtually the same in soft-drink bottling. IBM CEO Sam Palmisano and his management team have done an extraordinary job of creating a virtually new IBM by adapting a multibusiness strategy centered around finding, sharing, and leveraging core competencies across a seemingly diverse set of businesses and markets. Not only have they done so with existing competencies, but their organization has proven remarkably adept at leveraging newly found technologies and capabilities within each business across other businesses—enterprise focused business competencies deployed in consumer product offerings and vice versa as described in Exhibit 9.7, Top Strategist.

Each Core Competency Should Provide a Relevant Competitive Advantage to the Intended Businesses

The core competency must assist the intended business in creating strength relative to key competition. This could occur at any step in the business's value chain. But it must represent a major source of value to be a basis for competitive advantage—and the core competence must be transferable. Honda of Japan viewed itself as having a core competence in manufacturing small, internal combustion engines. It diversified into small garden tools, perceiving that traditional electric tools would be much more attractive if powered by a lightweight, mobile, gas combustion motor. Their core competency created a major competitive advantage in a market void of gas-driven hand tools. When Coca-Cola added bottled water to its portfolio of products, it expected its extraordinary core competencies in marketing and distribution to rapidly build value in this business. Ten years later, Coke

---

[4] Adam Lashinsky, "Is Skype on Sale at eBay?" *Fortune,* October 27, 2008.

Top Strategist
IBM's Sam Palmisano

Exhibit 9.7

Sam Palmisano, CEO at IBM, sets the stage for explaining IBM's global integrated enterprise product and service offerings by describing "the new global business" as a way of explaining what they can help clients do because they do it for themselves:

> Start with a simple jar of face cream. The jar's pump is a packaging innovation created by an independent inventor in Sweden. The jar itself is manufactured in China—an arrangement made by a global procurement center in Manila. The natural ingredients in the cream are sourced by a wholesaler in Italy. The finished product is assembled in the US. Customer service is provided by a call center in Nova Scotia. And all of these functions integrate seamlessly across a shared, standard global technology infrastructure, allowing the consumer-packaged goods company that owns the face-cream brand to sell its moisturizer in seven different scents and three sizes for $8.00 less than the competitor. Welcome to the Globally Integrated Enterprise.

IBM has spent the past several years becoming, in essence, a social networking organization, allowing it to identify internal expertise, capacity, and availability among its more that 175,000 employees and numerous production or operational facilities in 160 countries around the world. It then pulls needed people/capacity together in, most often, a virtual fashion to get work done for projects and clients worldwide in the most efficient, timely, and cost-effective manner possible. This "experiment" has been an extraordinary path toward identifying and leveraging core competencies both within IBM and then out to all types of businesses and industries from enterprise computing to consumer products.

IBM's internal Facebook, called BeeHive, contains a wide variety of personal and work-related information about every IBMer worldwide. A special search engine, SmallBlue, scans BeeHive, e-mails, reports, instant messages, personal calendars, and everything digital and makes determinations of skills, availability, cost, and proximity (think automated identification and leveraging of core competencies across people, operating units, and locations worldwide) to assemble teaming options to provide solutions, solve problems, and create products efficiently and effectively.

Recently, IBM introduced a commercial version of SmallBlue called IBM Atlas for sale to customers. And look out, Palmisano's avatar and serious IBMers have now spent several years in Second Life seeking to leverage this networked concept in reverse—IBM is learning from the consumer world's computerized virtual space to create new services and products to offer. It has rapidly learned that video gaming is perhaps the best format for managerial development in the globalized twenty-first century, which it is using to train IBM managers, and it will soon sell the ability to do so to other clients globally.

Source: www.ibm.com

sold its water assets, concluding that the product did not have enough margin to interest its franchised bottlers and that marketing was not a significant value-building activity among many small suppliers competing primarily on the cost of "producing" and shipping water. In the last few years, however, Coke has reversed its decision and added the Dasani water brand because a rapidly increasing consumer demand has made the value of its extensive distribution network a relevant competitive advantage to the Dasani water product line.

Businesses in the Portfolio Should Be Related in Ways That Make the Company's Core Competencies Beneficial

Related versus unrelated diversification is an important distinction to understand as you evaluate the diversification question. "Related" businesses are those that rely on the same or similar capabilities to be successful and attain competitive advantage in their respective product markets. Earlier, we described General Cinema's spectacular success in both movie exhibition and soft-drink bottling. Seemingly unrelated, they were actually very related businesses in terms of key core competencies that shaped success—managing a network of diverse business locations, localized competition, reliance on a few large suppliers, and centralized marketing advantages. Thus, the products of various businesses do not necessarily have to be similar to leverage core competencies. While their products may not be related, it is essential that some activities in their value chains require similar skills to create competitive advantage if the company is going to leverage its core competence(s) in a value-creating way. Exhibit 9.7 offered an example of IBM's remarkable effectiveness in doing just this the last five years. In fact, their CEO now even has an avatar on Second Life to build an understanding of ways IBM's core competencies could be related to and leveraged in the emerging virtual world which you can check out at www.ibm.com/3dworlds/businesscenter/us/en/.

Situations that involve "unrelated" diversification occur when no real overlapping capabilities or products exist other than financial resources. We refer to this as *conglomerate diversification* in Chapter 7. Recent research indicates that the most profitable firms are those that have diversified around a set of resources and capabilities that are specialized enough to confer a meaningful competitive advantage in an attractive industry, yet adaptable enough to be advantageously applied across several others. The least profitable are broadly diversified firms whose strategies are built around very general resources (e.g., money) that are applied in a wide variety of industries, but that are seldom instrumental to competitive advantage in those settings.[5]

Any Combination of Competencies Must Be Unique or Difficult to Recreate

Skills that corporate strategists expect to transfer from one business to another, or from corporate to various businesses, may be transferable. They may also be easily replicated by competitors. When this is the case, no sustainable competitive advantage is created. Sometimes strategists look for a combination of competencies, a package of various interrelated skills, as another way to create a situation where seemingly easily replicated competencies become unique, sustainable competitive advantages. 3M Corporation has the enviable record of having 25 percent of its earnings always coming from products introduced within the last five years. 3M has been able to "bundle" the skills necessary to accelerate the introduction of new products so that it consistently extracts early life-cycle value from adhesive-related products that hundreds of competitors with similar technical or marketing competencies cannot touch.

All too often companies envision a combination of competencies that make sense conceptually. This vision of synergy develops an energy of its own, leading CEOs to relentlessly push the merger of the firms involved. But what makes sense conceptually and is seen as difficult for competitors to recreate often proves difficult if not impossible to create in the first place.

[5] David J. Collis and Cynthia A. Montgomery, *Corporate Strategy* (New York: McGraw-Hill/Irwin, 2005), p. 88; "Why Mergers Fail," *McKinsey Quarterly Report,* 2001, vol. 4; and "Deals That Create Value," *McKinsey Quarterly Report,* 2001, vol. 1.

THE CORPORATE PARENT ROLE: CAN IT ADD TANGIBLE VALUE?

Realizing synergies from shared capabilities and core competencies is a key way value is added in multibusiness companies. Research suggests that figuring out if the synergies are real and, if so, how to capture those synergies is most effectively accomplished by business unit managers, not the corporate parent.[6] How then can the corporate parent add value to its businesses in a multibusiness company? We want to acquaint you with two perspectives to use in attempting to answer this question: the parenting framework and the patching approach.

The Parenting Framework

parenting framework

The perspective that the role of corporate head-quarters (the "parent") in multibusiness (the "children") companies is that of a parent sharing wisdom, insight, and guidance to help develop its various businesses to excel.

The **parenting framework** perspective sees multibusiness companies as creating value by influencing—or parenting—the businesses they own. The best parent companies create more value than any of their rivals do or would if they owned the same businesses. To add value, a parent must improve its businesses. Obviously there must be room for improvement. Advocates of this perspective call the potential for improvement within a business "a parenting opportunity." They identify 10 places to look for parenting opportunities, which then become the focus of strategic analysis and choice across multiple businesses and their interface with the parent organization.[7] Let's look at each briefly.

Size and Age

Old, large, successful businesses frequently engender entrenched bureaucracies and over-head structures that are hard to dismantle from inside the business. Doing so may add value, and getting it done may be best done by an external catalyst, the parent. Small, young businesses may lack some key functional skills, or outgrow their top managers' capabilities, or lack capital to deal with a temporary downturn or accelerated growth opportunity. Where these are relevant issues within one or more businesses, a parenting opportunity to add value may exist.

Management

Does the business employ managers superior in comparison with its competitors? Is the business's success dependent on attracting and keeping people with specialized skills? Are key managers focused on the right objectives? Ensuring that these issues are addressed and objectively assessed and assisting in any resolution may be a parenting opportunity that could add value.

Business Definition

Business unit managers may have a myopic or erroneous vision of what their business should be, which, in turn, has them targeting a market that is too narrow or broad. They may employ too much vertical integration or not enough. Accelerated trends toward outsourcing and strategic alliances are changing the definitions of many businesses. All of this creates a parenting opportunity to help redefine a business unit in a way that creates greater value.

[6] Michael Goold, Andrew Campbell, and Marcus Alexander, "The Quest for Parenting Advantage," *Harvard Business Review,* March–April 1995; Michael Goold, Andrew Campbell, and Marcus Alexander, "How Corporate Parents Add Value to the Stand-Alone Performance of Their Businesses," *Business Strategy Review,* Winter 1994.

[7] Ibid, p. 126. These 10 areas of opportunity are taken from an insert entitled "Ten Places to Look for Parenting Opportunities" on this page of the *Harvard Business Review* article.

Predictable Errors

The nature of a business and its unique situation can lead managers to make predictable mistakes. Managers responsible for previous strategic decisions are vested in the success of those decisions, which may prevent openness to new alternatives. Older, mature businesses often accumulate a variety of products and markets, which becomes excessive diversification within a particular business. Cyclical markets can lead to underinvestment during downturns and overinvestment during the upswing. Lengthy product life cycles can lead to overreliance on old products. All of these are predictable errors a parent can monitor and attempt to avoid, creating, in turn, added value.

Linkages

Business units may be able to improve market position or efficiency by linking with other businesses that are not readily apparent to the management of the business unit in question. Whether apparent or not, linkages among business units within or outside the parent company may be complex or difficult to establish without parent company help. In either case, an opportunity to add value may exist.

Common Capabilities

Fundamental to successful diversification, as we have discussed earlier, is the notion of sharing capabilities and competencies needed by multiple business units. Parenting opportunities to add value may arise from time to time through regular scrutiny of opportunities to share capabilities or add shared capabilities that would otherwise go unnoticed by business unit managers closer to daily business operations.

Specialized Expertise

There may be situations in which the parent company possesses specialized or rare expertise that may benefit a business unit and add value in the process. Unique legal, technical, or administrative expertise critical in a particular situation or decision point, which is quickly and easily available, can prove very valuable.

External Relations

Does the business have external stakeholders—governments, regulators, unions, suppliers, shareholders—the parent company could manage more effectively than individual business units? If so, a natural parenting opportunity exists that should add value.

Major Decisions

A business unit may face difficult decisions in areas for which it lacks expertise—for example, making an acquisition, entering China, a major capacity expansion, divesting and outsourcing a major part of the business's operations. Obtaining capital externally to fund a major investment may be much more difficult than doing so through the parent company—GE proved this could be a major parenting advantage in the way it developed GE Capital into a major source of capital for its other business units as well as to finance major capital purchases by customers of its own business units.

Major Changes

Sometimes a business needs to make major changes in ways critical to the business's future success yet which involve areas or considerations in which the business unit's management

Top Strategist
Indra Nooyi, CEO, PepsiCo

Exhibit
9.8

Indra Nooyi played lead guitar in an all-women Madras, India, rock band. She played cricket in college. She still sings karaoke at corporate gatherings, even while leading almost 200,000 PepsiCo employees in 200 countries and always calling her mom in India twice a day. She settled in the United States after an MBA at Yale, she has two daughters, and she joined PepsiCo as chief strategist 15 years ago. She has been engineering dramatic, profitable change at PepsiCo ever since.

Seeing a declining future in fast food, she quickly convinced PepsiCo leaders to sell off KFC, Pizza Hut, and Taco Bell. She bet on beverages and packaged food and engineered the acquisition of Tropicana and Quaker Oats, maker of Gatorade. In 2006, she was one of two finalists for CEO, and, after getting the nod, flew to personally visit the other contender and said, "Tell me what I need to do to keep you." Offering to pay him so as to nearly match her, he has served as her key executive.*

She is now trying to take PepsiCo from snack food to health food, from caffine drinks to fruit juices, and to emphasize a corporate commitment to sustainability. Creating the mantra "Performance with Purpose," she has set a goal for 2010 that half of PepsiCo's revenue will come from healthful products and that the company will move in favor of wind and solar energy sources while also campaigning against obesity. "It doesn't mean subtracting from the bottom line," she said, "that we bring together what is food for business with what is good for the world." Serious challenges exist to pull this off: rising commodity prices, a global recession, public aversion to bottled water like PepsiCo's Aquafina, and the ever-present potential cola wars with Coke.**

But Indra Nooyi has been a compasionate competitor all her life, and a 15-year catalyst for profitable change at PepsiCo. This major-change challenge will alter some lines of business and add others—all the while necessitating linkages and shared core competencies throughout PepsiCo's global organization to unfold successfully.

*"Indra Nooyi: Keeping Cool in Hot Water, " *BusinessWeek,* June 11, 2007.
**Ibid.

has little or no experience. A complete revamping of a business unit's information management process, outsourcing all that capability to India, or shifting all of a business unit's production operations to another business unit in another part of the world—these are just a few examples of major changes in which the parent may have extensive experience with what feels like unknown territory to the business's management team.

Overlap in some of these 10 sources of parenting opportunities may exist. For example, specialized expertise in China and a major decision to locate or outsource operations there may be the same source of added value. And that decision would involve a major change. The fact that overlap or redundancy may exist in classifying sources of parenting opportunity is a minor consideration, however, relative to the value of the parenting framework for strategic analysis in multibusiness companies. The portfolio approaches focus on how businesses' cash, profit, and growth potential create a balance within the portfolio. The core competence approach concentrates on how business units are related and can share technical and operating know-how and capacity. The parenting framework adds to these approaches and the strategic analysis in a multibusiness company because it focuses on competencies of the parent organization and on the value created from the relationship between the parent and its businesses. Exhibit 9.8, Top Strategist, shows how PepsiCo's chairwoman and CEO Indra Nooyi has created a significant corporate parenting role as she led dramatic changes in PepsiCo's business portfolio and their strategies by fostering innovations, acquiring new brands, divesting certain businesses—all the time building organizational linkages and sharing core competencies across several PepsiCo business units and brands, both domestically and globally.

The Patching Approach

patching
The process by which corporate executives routinely "remap" their businesses to match rapidly changing market opportunities—adding, splitting, transferring, exiting, or combining chunks of businesses.

Another approach that focuses on the role and ability of corporate managers to create value in the management of multibusiness companies is called "patching."[8] **Patching** is the process by which corporate executives routinely remap businesses to match rapidly changing market opportunities. It can take the form of adding, splitting, transferring, exiting, or combining chunks of businesses. Patching is not seen as critical in stable, unchanging markets. When markets are turbulent and rapidly changing, patching is seen as critical to the creation of economic value in a multibusiness company.

Proponents of this perspective on the strategic decision-making function of corporate executives say it is the critical, and arguably only, way corporate executives can add value beyond the sum of the businesses within the company. They view traditional corporate strategy as creating defensible strategic positions for business units by acquiring or building valuable assets, wisely allocating resources to them, and weaving synergies among them. In volatile markets, they argue, this traditional approach results in business units with strategies that are quickly outdated and competitive advantages rarely sustained beyond a few years.[9] As a result, they say, strategic analysis should center on **strategic processes** more than **strategic positioning.** In these volatile markets, patchers' strategic analysis focuses on making quick, small, frequent changes in parts of businesses and organizational processes that enable dynamic strategic repositioning rather than building long-term defensible positions. Exhibit 9.9 compares differences between traditional approaches to shaping corporate strategy with the patching approach.

strategic processes
Decision making, operational activities, and sales activities that are critical business processes.

strategic positioning
The way a business is designed and positioned to serve target markets.

To be successful with a patching approach to corporate strategic analysis and choice in turbulent markets, Eisenhardt and Sull suggest that managers should flexibly seize opportunities—as long as that flexibility is disciplined. Effective corporate strategists, they argue, focus on key processes and *simple rules.* The following example at Miramax helps illustrate the notion of strategy as simple rules:

> Miramax—well known for artistically innovative movies such as *The Crying Game, Life is Beautiful,* and *Pulp Fiction*—has boundary rules that guide the all-important movie-picking process: First, every movie must revolve around a central human condition, such as love *(The Crying Game)* or envy *(The Talented Mr. Ripley).* Second, a movie's main character must be appealing but deeply flawed—the hero of *Shakespeare in Love* is gifted and charming but steals ideas from friends and betrays his wife. Third, movies must have a very clear story line with a beginning, middle, and end (although in *Pulp Fiction* the end comes first). Finally, there is a firm cap on production costs. Within the rules, there is flexibility to move quickly when a writer or director shows up with a great script. The result is an enormously creative and even surprising flow of movies and enough discipline to produce superior, consistent financial results. *The English Patient,* for example, cost $27 million to make, grossed more than $200 million, and grabbed nine Oscars.[10]

---

[8] Kathleen M. Eisenhardt and Shona L. Brown, "Patching: Restitching Business Portfolios in Dynamic Markets," *Harvard Business Review,* May–June 1999, pp. 72–82.
[9] Ibid, p. 76; and K. M. Eisenhardt and D. N. Sull, "Strategy as Simple Rules," *Harvard Business Review,* January 2001.
[10] Ibid, Eisenhardt and Sull, p. 111.

EXHIBIT 9.9 **Three Approaches to Strategy**

Managers competing in business can choose among three distinct ways to fight. They can build a fortress and defend it; they can nurture and leverage unique resources; or they can flexibly pursue fleeting opportunities within simple rules. Each approach requires different skill sets and works best under different circumstances.

	Position	Resources	Patching [Simple Rules]
Strategic logic	Establish position	Leverage resources	Pursue opportunities
Strategic steps	Identify an attractive market	Establish a vision Build resources	Jump into the confusion Keep moving
	Locate a defensible position	Leverage across markets	Seize opportunities Finish strong
	Fortify and defend		
Strategic question	Where should we be?	What should we be?	How should we proceed?
Source of advantage	Unique, valuable position with tightly integrated activity system	Unique, valuable, inimitable resources	Key processes and unique simple rules
Works best in	Slowly changing, well-structured markets	Moderately changing, well-structured markets	Rapidly changing, ambiguous markets
Duration of advantage	Sustained	Sustained	Unpredictable
Risk	Too difficult to alter position as conditions change	Too slow to build new resources as conditions change	Too tentative in executing promising opportunities
Performance goal	Profitability	Long-term dominance	Growth

Source: Reprinted by permission of *Harvard Business Review.* Exhibit from "Strategy as Simple Rules," by Kathleen M. Eisenhardt and Donald M. Sull, January 2001. Copyright 2001 by the Harvard Business School Publishing Corporation; all rights reserved.

Different types of rules help managers and strategists manage different aspects of seizing opportunities. Exhibit 9.10 explains and illustrates five such types of rules. These rules are called "simple" rules because they need to be brief, be axiomatic, and convey fundamental guidelines to decisions or actions. They need to provide just enough structure to allow managers to move quickly to capture opportunities with confidence that the judgments and commitments they make are consistent with corporate intent. At the same time, while they set parameters on actions and decisions, they are not thick manuals or rules and policies that managers in turbulent environments may find paralyze any efforts to quickly capitalize on opportunities.

The patching approach then relies on simple rules unique to a particular parent company that exist to guide managers in the corporate organization and its business units in making rapid decisions about quickly reshaping parts of the company and allocating time as well as money to capitalize on rapidly shifting market opportunities. The fundamental argument of this approach is that no one can predict how long a competitive advantage will last, particularly in turbulent, rapidly changing markets. While managers in stable markets may be able to rely on complex strategies built on detailed predictions of future trends, managers in

EXHIBIT 9.10   **Simple Rules, Summarized**

In turbulent markets, managers should flexibly seize opportunities—but flexibility must be disciplined. Smart companies focus on key processes and simple rules. Different types of rules help executives manage different aspects of seizing opportunities.

Type	Purpose	Example
How-to rules	Spell out key features of how a process is executed—"What makes our process unique?"	Akami's rules for the customer service process: Staff must consist of technical gurus, every question must be answered on the first call or e-mail, and R&D staff must rotate through customer service.
Boundary rules	Focus on which opportunities can be pursued and which are outside the pale.	Cisco's early acquisitions rule: Companies to be acquired must have no more than 75 employees, 75 percent of whom are engineers.
Priority rules	Help managers rank the accepted opportunities.	Intel's rule for allocating manufacturing capacity: Allocation is based on a product's gross margin.
Timing rules	Synchronize managers with the pace of emerging opportunities and other parts of the company.	Nortel's rules for product development: Project teams must know when a product has to be delivered to the customer to win, and product development time must be less than 18 months.
Exit rules	Help managers decide when to pull out of yesterday's opportunities.	Oticon's rule for pulling the plug on projects in development: If a key team member—manager or not—chooses to leave the project for another within the company, the project is killed.

Source: Reprinted by permission of *Harvard Business Review*. Exhibit from "Strategy as Simple Rules," by Kathleen M. Eisenhardt and Donald M. Sull, January 2001. Copyright 2001 by the Harvard Business School Publishing Corporation; all rights reserved.

complex, fast-moving markets—where significant growth and wealth creation may occur—face constant unpredictability; hence, strategy must be simple, responsive, and dynamic to encourage success.

Summary

This chapter examined how managers make strategic decisions in multibusiness companies. One of the earliest approaches was to look at the company as a portfolio of businesses. This portfolio was then examined and evaluated based on each business's growth potential, market position, and need for and ability to generate cash. Corporate strategists then allocated resources, divested, and acquired businesses based on the balance across this portfolio of businesses or possible businesses.

The notion of synergy across business units—sharing capabilities and leveraging core competencies—has been another very widely adopted approach to making strategic decisions in multibusiness companies. Sharing capabilities allows for greater efficiencies, enhanced expertise, and competitive advantage. Core competencies that generate competitive advantage can often be leveraged across multiple businesses, thereby expanding the impact and value added from that competitive advantage.

Globalization, rapid change, outsourcing, and other major forces shaping today's economic landscape have ushered in multibusiness strategic decision making that also focuses on the role and value-added contributions, if any, of the parent company itself. Does the parent company add or could it add value beyond the sum of the businesses it owns? Two perspectives that have gained popularity in multibusiness companies' strategic decision making are the parenting framework and the patching approach. The parenting framework focuses on 10 areas of opportunity managers should carefully explore to find ways the parent organization might add value to one or more businesses and the overall company. The patching approach concentrates on multibusiness companies in turbulent markets of the twenty-first century, where managers need to make quick, small shifts and adjustments in processes, markets, and products, and offers five types of "simple rules" that managers use as guidelines to structure quick decisions throughout a multibusiness company on a continuous basis.

Key Terms

cash cows, *p. 244*
dogs, *p. 244*
fragmented businesses, *p. 248*
market growth rate, *p. 244*
parenting framework, *p. 255*
patching, *p. 258*

portfolio techniques, *p. 243*
question marks, *p. 245*
position, *p. 244*
relative competitive
specialization
businesses, *p. 248*

stalemate businesses, *p. 248*
stars, *p. 244*
strategic positioning, *p. 258*
strategic processes, *p. 258*
volume businesses, *p. 246*

Questions for Discussion

1. How does strategic analysis at the corporate level differ from strategic analysis at the business unit level? How are they related?
2. When would multibusiness companies find the portfolio approach to strategic analysis and choice useful?
3. What are three types of opportunities for sharing that form a sound basis for diversification or vertical integration? Give an example of each from companies you have read about.
4. Describe three types of opportunities through which a corporate parent could add value beyond the sum of its separate businesses.
5. What does "patching" refer to? Describe and illustrate two rules that might guide managers to build value in their businesses.

Part **Three**

Strategy Implementation, Control, and Innovation

The last section of this book examines what is often called the action phase of the strategic management process: implementation of the chosen strategy. Up to this point, three phases of that process have been covered—strategy formulation, analysis of alternative strategies, and strategic choice. Although important, these phases alone cannot ensure success.

To ensure success, the strategy must be translated into carefully implemented action. This means that

1. The strategy must be translated into guidelines for the daily activities of the firm's members.
2. The strategy and the firm must become one—that is, the strategy must be reflected in
   a. The way the firm organizes its activities.
   b. The key organization leaders.
   c. The culture of the organization.
3. The company's managers must put into place "steering" controls that provide strategic control and the ability to adjust strategies, commitments, and objectives in response to ever-changing future conditions.
4. Increasingly, organizations must make a serious commitment to be innovative and must consider bringing the entrepreneurship process into their company to survive, grow, and prosper in a vastly more competitive and rapidly changing global business arena.

Chapter 10 explains how organizational action is successfully initiated through four interrelated steps:

1. Creation of clear *short-term objectives* and *action plans*.
2. Development of specific *functional tactics*, to include *outsourcing*, that create competitive advantage.
3. Empowerment of operating personnel through *policies* to guide decisions.
4. Implementation of effective *reward systems*.

Short-term objectives and action plans guide implementation by converting long-term objectives into short-term actions and targets. Functional tactics, whether done internally or outsourced to other partners, translate the business strategy into activities that build advantage. Policies empower operating personnel by defining guidelines for making decisions. Reward systems encourage effective results.

Today's competitive environment requires careful analysis in designing the organizational structure most suitable to build and sustain competitive advantage. Chapter 11 examines traditional organizational structures—their pros and cons. It looks at the pervasive trend toward outsourcing, along with outsourcing's pros and cons. It concludes with examination of the latest developments in creating ambidextrous, virtual, boundaryless organizations designed to adapt in a highly interconnected, lightning-speed, global business environment.

There can be no doubt that effective organizational leadership and the consistency of a strong organizational culture reinforcing norms and behaviors best suited to the organization's mission are two central ingredients in enabling successful execution of a firm's strategies and objectives. Chapter 12 examines leadership, the critical things good leaders do, and how to nurture effective operating managers as they become outstanding future organizational leaders. Chapter 12 then examines the organizational culture, how it is shaped, and creative ways of managing the strategy-culture relationship.

Because the firm's strategy is implemented in a changing environment, successful implementation requires strategic control—an ability to "steer" the firm through an extended future time period when premises, sudden events, internal implementation efforts, and general economic and societal developments will be sources of change not anticipated or predicted when the strategy was conceived and initiated. Chapter 13 examines how to set up strategic controls to deal with the important steering function during the implementation process. The chapter also examines operational control functions and the balanced scorecard approach to integrating strategic and operational control.

The overriding concerns in executing strategies and leading a company are survival, growth, and prosperity. In a global economy that allows everyone everywhere instant information and instant connectivity, change often occurs at lightning speed. Thus, leaders are increasingly encouraging their firms to embrace innovation and entrepreneurship as key ways to respond to such overwhelming uncertainty. Chapter 14 examines innovation in general, different types of innovation, and the best ways to bring more innovative activity into a firm. It examines the entrepreneurship process as another way to build innovative responsiveness and opportunity recognition into a firm, both in new-venture settings and in large business organizations.

Implementation is "where the action is." It is the arena that most students enter at the start of their business careers. It is the strategic phase in which staying close to the customer, achieving competitive advantage, and pursuing excellence become realities. These five chapters in Part Three will help you understand how this is done and how to prepare to take your place as a future leader of successful, innovative business organizations.

Chapter **Ten**

Implementation

After reading and studying this chapter, you should be able to

1. Understand how short-term objectives are used in strategy implementation.

2. Identify and apply the qualities of good short-term objectives to your own experiences.

3. Illustrate what is meant by functional tactics and understand how they are used in strategy implementation.

4. Gain a general sense of what outsourcing is and how it becomes a choice in functional tactics decisions for strategy implementation.

5. Understand what policies are and how to use policies to empower operating personnel in implementing business strategies and functional tactics.

6. Understand the use of financial reward in executive compensation.

7. Identify different types of executive compensation and when to use each in strategy implementation.

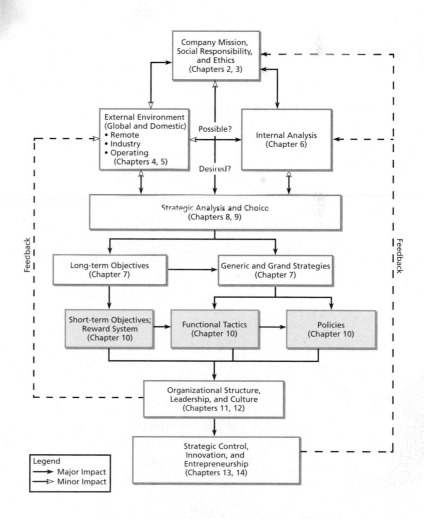

Xerox and Hewlett-Packard faced difficult times as this decade began. For Xerox, bankruptcy was a real possibility given its $14 billion debt and its serious problems with the U.S. Securities and Exchange Commission. Hewlett-Packard was falling behind in the computer business while living solely on profits from its printer division. Anne Mulcahy became Xerox CEO during this time. Carly Fiorina became HP's CEO. Five years later, Anne Mulcahy was celebrated for the success of her strategy at Xerox while Carly Fiorina was dismissed for the failure of the path she chose. Two legendary technology companies and two celebrated CEOs who shattered the "glass ceiling" in being selected to lead two legendary companies back to glory: why did one succeed and the other fail?

Analysts suggest that the "devil is in the detail." Fiorina's strategy was to acquire Compaq, build the size of HP's PC business, and use profits from HP's venerable printer business to sustain a reorganization of the combined companies. Mark Anderson, an investment analyst who has followed HP for more than 20 years, said this about Carly Fiorina's strategy:

> I would say it stinks, but it isn't even a strategy. A few bullet points don't make a strategy. Such an approach lacks the technical and market understanding necessary to drive HP.[1]

In other words, Carly Fiorina's strategy was a glitzy combination of two large computer companies, but it was less clear exactly what key actions and tactics would bring about a reinvented, "new," profitable HP.

Anne Mulcahy took a different approach, in part reflecting her 28 years inside Xerox. She set about to "reinvent" Xerox as well, but made four functional tactics and their respective short-term objectives very clear building blocks for reinventing Xerox: (1) She prioritized aggressive cost cutting—30 percent—throughout the company to restore profitability. (2) She emphasized a productivity increase in each Xerox division. (3) She quickly settled Xerox's SEC litigation about its accounting practices, and she refinanced Xerox's massive debt. (4) She made a major point of continued heavy R&D funding even as every other part of Xerox suffered through severe cost cutting. This, she felt, sent a message of belief in Xerox's future. It clearly established her priorities.

Mulcahy's articulation of specific tactical efforts, and the short-term objectives they were intended to achieve, turned Xerox around in three short years. As she proudly pointed out:

> Probably one of the hardest things was to continue investing in the future, in growth. One of the most controversial decisions we made was to continue our R&D investment. When you're drastically restructuring in other areas, that's a tough decision. It makes it harder for the other businesses to some extent. But it was important for the Xerox people to believe we were investing in the future. Now two-thirds of our revenue is coming from products and services introduced in the last two years.[2]

The reason Anne Mulcahy succeeded while Carly Fiorina did not, the focus of this chapter, involves translating strategic thought into organizational action. In the words of two well-worn phrases, they move from "planning their work" to "working their plan." Anne Mulcahy successfully made this shift at Xerox when she did these five things well:

1. Identify short-term objectives.
2. Initiate specific functional tactics.
3. Outsource nonessential functions.
4. Communicate policies that empower people in the organization.
5. Design effective rewards.

[1] "The Only HP Way Worth Trying," Viewpoint, *BusinessWeek,* March 9, 2005.

[2] "American Innovation: A Competitive Crisis," speech by Anne M. Mulcahy at The Chief Executive's Club of Boston, June 12, 2008; and "She Put the Bounce Back in Xerox," *BusinessWeek*, January 10, 2005.

Top Strategist
John Thompson, CEO, Symantec

Exhibit 10.1

John Thompson believes very strongly in the importance of short-term objectives to help managers guide strategy implementation. He views these objectives as "vectors" for how you are performing "now" and as indicators of how you will perform in the future.

"I am a little old-fashioned—I don't believe you can manage what you can't measure," Thompson has said. "The importance of objectives becomes more important as the company grows in size and scale. Objectives also serve as an indication for the 'team' about what you are paying attention to. If employees know you are measuring market growth and customer satisfaction, they will pay attention to those considerations and act based on indicators that you, as leader, emphasize within the company. Objectives help teams and focus on what's important for the company to succeed."*

Describing what makes a good objective into an effective management tool, Thompson said "the best objectives are simple to understand, simple to communicate, and relatively easy for everyone to get access to the data that represents the results. If you make your objectives hard to measure, manage, and communicate, they won't be effective. Simplicity is key." Thompson also believes in brevity, saying that "experience has proven to me the importance of picking the few objectives that are most critical for running the business or your unit. Stick with them—and communicate them to both internal and external audiences."**

*"The Key to Success? Go Figure," *BusinessWeek*, July 21, 2003.
**Ibid; and "Symantec's CEO Takes the Long View," *BusinessWeek*, February 8, 2007.

Short-term objectives translate long-range aspirations into this year's targets for action. If well developed, these objectives provide clarity, a powerful motivator and facilitator of effective strategy implementation. In Exhibit 10.1, Top Strategist, John Thompson, CEO of Symantec, summarizes how short-term objectives are critical to his success.

Functional tactics translate business strategy into daily activities people need to execute. Functional managers participate in the development of these tactics, and their participation, in turn, helps clarify what their units are expected to do in implementing the business's strategy.

Outsourcing nonessential functions normally performed in-house frees up resources and the time of key people to concentrate on leveraging the functions and activities critical to the core competitive advantages around which the firm's long-range strategy is built.

Policies are empowerment tools that simplify decision making by empowering operating managers and their subordinates. Policies can empower the "doers" in an organization by reducing the time required to decide and act.

Rewards that align manager and employee priorities with organizational objectives and shareholder value provide very effective direction in strategy implementation.

SHORT-TERM OBJECTIVES

Chapter 7 described business strategies, grand strategies, and long-term objectives that are critically important in crafting a successful future. To make them become a reality, however, the people in an organization who actually "do the work" of the business need guidance in

EXHIBIT 10.2
Potential Conflicting Objectives and Priorities

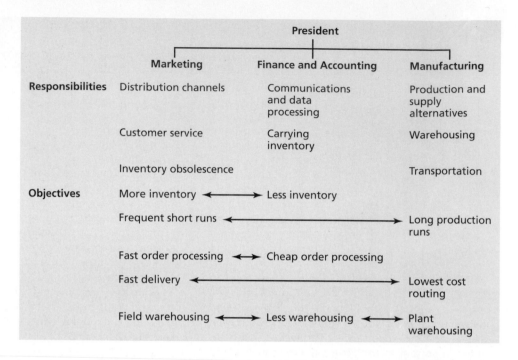

exactly what they need to do. Short-term objectives help do this. **Short-term objectives** are measurable outcomes achievable or intended to be achieved in one year or less. They are specific, usually quantitative, results operating managers set out to achieve in the immediate future.

Short-term objectives help implement strategy in at least three ways:

1. Short-term objectives "operationalize" long-term objectives. If we commit to a 20 percent gain in revenue over five years, what is our specific target or objective in revenue during the current year, month, or week to indicate we are making appropriate progress?

2. Discussion about and agreement on short-term objectives help raise issues and potential conflicts within an organization that usually require coordination to avoid otherwise dysfunctional consequences. Exhibit 10.2 illustrates how objectives within marketing, manufacturing, and accounting units within the same firm can be very different even when created to pursue the same firm objective (e.g., increased sales, lower costs).

3. Finally, short-term objectives assist strategy implementation by identifying measurable outcomes of action plans or functional activities, which can be used to make feedback, correction, and evaluation more relevant and acceptable.

Short-term objectives are usually accompanied by action plans, which enhance these objectives in three ways. First, action plans usually identify functional tactics and activities that will be undertaken in the next week, month, or quarter as part of the business's effort to build competitive advantage. The important point here is *specificity*—what exactly is to be done. We will examine functional tactics in a subsequent section of this chapter. The second element of an action plan is a clear *time frame for completion*—when the effort will begin and when its results will be accomplished. A third element action plans contain is identification of *who is responsible* for each action in the plan. This accountability is very important to ensure action plans are acted upon.

Qualities of Effective Short-Term Objectives
Measurable

Short-term objectives are more consistent when they clearly state *what* is to be accomplished, *when* it will be accomplished, and *how* its accomplishment will be *measured*. Such objectives can be used to monitor both the effectiveness of each activity and the collective progress across several interrelated activities. Exhibit 10.3 illustrates several effective and ineffective short-term objectives. Measurable objectives make misunderstanding less likely among interdependent managers who must implement action plans. It is far easier to quantify the objectives of *line* units (e.g., production) than of certain *staff* areas (e.g., personnel). Difficulties in quantifying objectives often can be overcome by initially focusing on *measurable activity* and then identifying *measurable outcomes*.

Priorities

Although all annual objectives are important, some deserve priority because of a timing consideration or their particular impact on a strategy's success. If such priorities are not established, conflicting assumptions about the relative importance of annual objectives may inhibit progress toward strategic effectiveness. Anne Mulcahy's turnaround of Xerox described at the beginning of this chapter emphasized several important short-term objectives. But it was clear throughout Xerox that her highest priority in the first two years was to dramatically lower overhead and production costs so as to satisfy the difficult challenge of continuing to invest heavily in R&D while also restoring profitability.

Priorities are established in various ways. A simple ranking may be based on discussion and negotiation during the planning process. However, this does not necessarily communicate the real difference in the importance of objectives, so such terms as primary, top, and secondary may be used to indicate priority. Some firms assign weights (e.g., 0 to 100 percent) to establish and communicate the relative priority of objectives. Whatever the

EXHIBIT 10.3
Creating Measurable Objectives

Examples of Deficient Objectives	Examples of Objectives with Measurable Criteria for Performance
To improve morale in the division (plant, department, etc.)	To reduce turnover (absenteeism, number of rejects, etc.) among sales managers by 10 percent by January 1, 2010. *Assumption:* Morale is related to measurable outcomes (i.e., high and low morale are associated with different results).
To improve support of the sales effort	To reduce the time lapse between order data and delivery by 8 percent (two days) by June 1, 2010. To reduce the cost of goods produced by 6 percent to support a product price decrease of 2 percent by December 1, 2010. To increase the rate of before- or on-schedule delivery by 5 percent by June 1, 2010.
To improve the firm's image	To conduct a public opinion poll using random samples in the five largest U.S. metropolitan markets to determine average scores on 10 dimensions of corporate responsibility by May 15, 2010. To increase our score on those dimensions by an average of 7.5 percent by May 1, 2010.

EXHIBIT 10.4
Milliken Global
Environmental
Objectives: 2009

Source: "Enhancing
Sustainability at Milliken,"
presentation at SwampFox 2009
Sustainability Forum, Moore
School of Business, University
of South Carolina, Columbia,
SC.

Strategic Priority	Functional Tactic	2009 Objectives (reductions 2009 vs 2008)
Complete compliance	Zero serious environmental incidents	Number of serious incidents: 0 20% fewer significant incidents
Zero waste to landfill	Reduce solid waste	Zero waste to landfill 5% less solid waste/pound Increase reuse/recycle 75% to 78%
Conserve national resources	Reduce energy use	10% less energy consumed per pound
Conserve national resources	Reduce water use	10% less water consumed per pound
Zero emissions to air	Zero net greenhouse gas emissions	5% reduction greenhouse gas emit per pound
Environmental education	100% plant coverage worldwide	100% plant coverage worldwide
Quality control	ISO-14001 registration	ISO regulations for St. George; Gillespie; Autotex; Brazil; Zhangliangang; China

method, recognizing priorities is an important dimension in the implementation value of short-term objectives.

Cascading: From Long-Term Objectives to Short-Term Objectives

The link between short-term and long-term objectives should resemble cascades through the firm from basic long-term objectives to specific short-term objectives in key operation areas. The cascading effect has the added advantage of providing a clear reference for communication and negotiation, which may be necessary to integrate and coordinate objectives and activities at the operating level.

Milliken, a U.S.–based global leader and innovator in the global textile industry, provides a good example of cascading objectives. One of Milliken's long-term priorities is sustainability—being an exemplary corporate steward of its global environment. That strategic commitment has been in existence almost 20 years—since Roger Milliken set forth four strategic principles and goals for all of Milliken's plants and facilities:

- Complete regulatory compliance.
- Strive for zero waste generation.
- Conserve natural resources.
- Continuously develop new environmental solutions.

Exhibit 10.4 shows how Milliken's Sustainability Team translates the four long-range goals into cascading and more specific, measurable short-term objectives for 2009. This cascading approach gives solid guidance to Milliken "associates" at all its plants and facilities worldwide—cascading downward in specificity and also, ultimately, cascading upward to consolidate and evaluate Miliken's overall improvement in global environmental stewardship.[3]

[3] "Enhancing Sustainability at Milliken," SwampFox 2009 Sustainability Forum, Moore School of Business, University of South Carolina, Columbia, SC.

FUNCTIONAL TACTICS THAT IMPLEMENT BUSINESS STRATEGIES

functional tactics
Detailed statements of the "means" or activities that will be used by a company to achieve short-term objectives and establish competetive advantage.

Functional tactics are the key, routine activities that must be undertaken in each functional area—marketing, finance, production/operations, R&D, and human resource management—to provide the business's products and services. In a sense, functional tactics translate thought (grand strategy) into action designed to accomplish specific short-term objectives. Every value chain activity in a company executes functional tactics that support the business's strategy and help accomplish strategic objectives.

Exhibit 10.6, Strategy in Action, illustrates the difference between functional tactics and business strategy. It also shows that functional tactics are essential to implement business strategy. It explains the situation at the leading U.K. restaurant company, where consultants were brought in to identify specific tactical things employees needed to do or deal with to implement an overall business strategy to differentiate the growing chain from many other restaurant competitors. The business strategy outlined the competitive posture of its operations in the restaurant industry. To increase the likelihood that these strategies would be successful, specific functional tactics were needed for the firm's operating components. These functional tactics clarified the business strategy, giving specific, short-term guidance to operating managers and employees in the areas of marketing, operations, and finance. Exhibit 10.5 summarizes key benefits that result from clearly stated functional tactics accompanied by measurable short-term objectives during the implementation process.

Differences between Business Strategies and Functional Tactics

Functional tactics are different from business or corporate strategies in three fundamental ways:

1. Specificity.
2. Time horizon.
3. Participants who develop them.

Specificity

Functional tactics are more specific than business strategies. Business strategies provide general direction. Functional tactics identify the specific activities that are to be undertaken in each functional area and thus allow operating managers to work out *how* their unit is expected to pursue short-term objectives. Exhibit 10.6, Strategy in Action, illustrates the nature and value of specificity in functional tactics versus business strategy at the United Kingdom's leading restaurant chain.

Specificity in functional tactics contributes to successful implementation by

- Helping ensure that functional managers know what needs to be done and can focus on accomplishing results.
- Clarifying for top management how functional managers intend to accomplish the business strategy, which increases top management's confidence in and sense of control over the business strategy.

EXHIBIT 10.5
The Value-Added Benefit of Short-Term Objectives and Specific Functional Tactics

- They give operating personnel a better understanding of their role in the firm's mission.
- The process of developing them becomes a forum for raising and resolving conflicts between strategic intent and operational reality.
- They provide a basis for developing budgets, schedules, trigger points, and other sources of strategic control.
- They can be powerful motivators, especially when connected to the reward system.

The Nature and Value of Specificity in Functional Tactics versus Business Strategy

A restaurant business was encountering problems. Although its management had agreed unanimously that it was committed to a business strategy to differentiate itself from other competitors based on concept and customer service rather than price, the multi-location business continued to encounter inconsistencies across different store locations in how well it did this. Consultants indicated that the customer experience varied greatly from store to store. The conclusion was that while the management understood the "business strategy," and the employees did too in general terms, the implementation was inadequate because of a lack of specificity in the functional tactics—what everyone should do every day in the restaurant—to make the vision a reality in terms of the customers' dining experience. The following breakdown of part of their business strategy into specific functional tactics just in the area of customer service helps illustrate the value specificity in functional tactics brings to strategy implementation.

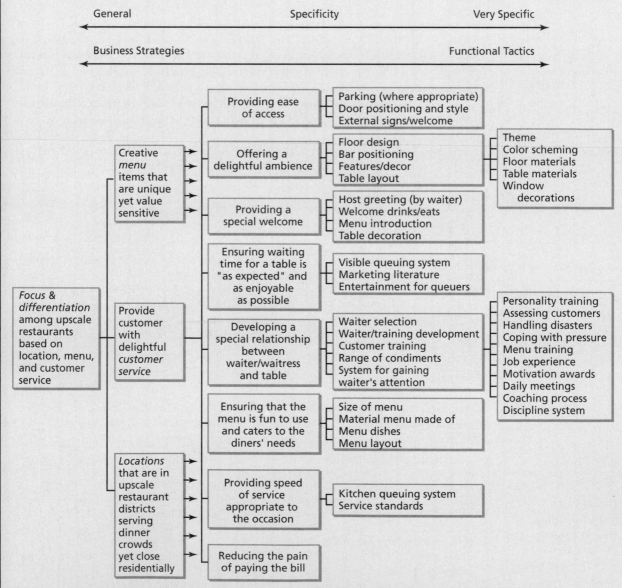

Source: Adapted from A. Campbell and K. Luchs, Eds., *Core Competency – Based Strategy* (London: Thompson, 1997).

Top Strategist
Tim Cook, Apple

Exhibit 10.7

Tim Cook, the little known heir apparent to Steve Jobs, is an intensely private Auburn University engineering grad (1982) and Apple workaholic passionate about cycling, outdoors, and Auburn football. His operational and tactical genius has been the behind-the-limelight reason for Apple's amazing success. A few examples of his tactics:

- When Apple introduced the Nano, which was revolutionary in its use of flash memory far superior to others on the market, Cook prepaid $1.25 billion to suppliers Samsung and Hynix, effectively cornering the market through 2010 on that specific kind of memory.

- Upon arriving at Apple, Cook closed factories and warehouses and instead established relationships with contract manufacturers, reducing Apple's days in inventory from months to days, equaling Dell's gold standard in computer manufacturing efficiency.

Yet Cook's tactics continually control a diverse supply chain and ensure a seamless orchestration of Apple's product introductions and delivery—unveiling revolutionary products kept completely secret until they magically appear in stores worldwide as promised.

Source: Adam Lashinsky, "The Genius Behind Steve Jobs," *CNNMoney.com*, January 15, 2009.

- Facilitating coordination among operating units within the firm by clarifying areas of interdependence and potential conflict.

Time Horizon

Functional tactics identify activities to be undertaken "now" or in the immediate future. Business strategies focus on the firm's posture three to five years out. Exhibit 10.7, Top Strategist, describes how Tim Cook, Apple's rising star, implemented immediate functional tactics to quickly turnaround that company's broken manufacturing operations shortly after Steve Jobs brought him on board specifically to help do just that.

The shorter time horizon of functional tactics is critical to the successful implementation of a business strategy for two reasons. First, it focuses the attention of functional managers on what needs to be done *now* to make the business strategy work. Second, it allows functional managers like those at 3M to adjust to changing current conditions.

Participants

Different people participate in strategy development at the functional and business levels. Business strategy is the responsibility of the general manager of a business unit. That manager typically delegates the development of functional tactics to subordinates charged with running the operating areas of the business. The manager of a business unit must establish long-term objectives and a strategy that corporate management feels contributes to corporate-level goals. Similarly, key operating managers must establish short-term objectives and operating strategies that contribute to business-level goals. Just as business strategies and objectives are approved through negotiation between corporate managers and business managers, so, too, are short-term objectives and functional tactics approved through negotiation between business managers and operating managers.

Involving operating managers in the development of functional tactics improves their understanding of what must be done to achieve long-term objectives and, thus, contributes to successful implementation. It also helps ensure that functional tactics reflect the reality of the day-to-day operating situation. And perhaps most important, it can increase the commitment of operating managers to the strategies developed.

OUTSOURCING FUNCTIONAL ACTIVITIES

outsourcing
Obtaining work previously done by employees inside the companies from sources outside the company.

A generation ago, it was conventional wisdom that a business has a better chance of success if it controls the doing of everything necessary to produce its products or services. Referring back to Chapter 6's value chain approach, the "wise" manager would have sought to maintain control of virtually all the "primary" activities and the "support" activities associated with the firm's work. Not any longer. Starting for most firms with the outsourcing of producing payroll each week, companies worldwide are embracing the idea that the best way to implement their strategies is to retain responsibility for executing some functions while seeking outside people and companies to do key support and key primary activities where they can do so more effectively and more inexpensively. **Outsourcing,** then, is acquiring an activity, service, or product necessary to provide a company's products or services from "outside" the people or operations controlled by that acquiring company.

DuPont Co. has always run corporate training and development out of its Wilmington (Delaware) head office. But these days, Boston-based Forum Corp. handles it instead. In Somers, New York, PepsiCo Inc. employees, long used to receiving personal financial planning from their employer, now get that service from KPMG Peat Marwick. Denver's TeleTech Holdings Inc. is taking customer-service calls from AT&T customers and books seat reservations for Continental Airlines.

Wyck Hay's first entrepreneurial effort was a smashing success: The co-founder of herbal tea maker Celestial Seasonings helped sell the company to Kraft Foods for $40 million in 1984. But Hay found managing 300 employees a headache. So when he launched Woodside (California)-based Kaboom Beverages a few years ago, he kept a decidedly small payroll: himself. In lieu of a workforce, Hay assembled a team of contractors to perform every task at his $2 million business—from label design to manufacturing of his "power juice" drinks. Hay said outsourcing saves him at least 30 percent, while minimizing his daily distractions. "I don't know that I ever plan to hire any employees," he mused.[4]

Relentless cost-cutting was an early driver behind the trend to outsource. When Tim Cook first came to Apple from Compaq Computer, he was a 16-year computer industry veteran with 12 years at IBM. His mandate at Apple was to clean up the atrocious state of Apple's manufacturing, distribution, and supply apparatus. He quickly closed factories and warehouses around the world and instead established relationships with contract manufacturers. By outsourcing almost all of its manufacturing and warehousing, Apple cut its inventory costs by a substantial amount (see Exhibit 10.7, Top Strategist, on page 273).

Outsourcing now occurs across every function in a business—marketing, product design, and computer operations are just a few functions other than typical rote functions that have been regularly outsourced by many companies. Infosys, the India–based bastion of early call center outsourcing followed by many types of outsourcing, is itself now outsourcing

---

[4] Dean Foust et al., "The Outsourcing Food Chain," *BusinessWeek Online*, March 11, 2004.

EXHIBIT 10.8
Outsourcing Is
Increasing

Source: Estimated based on
various articles in *BusinessWeek*
on outsourcing.

ORDERING OUT... Companies That Say They Outsource Some Functional Activity		
	Yes	**No**
2008	98%	2%
2000	75	25
1995	52	48
1990	23	77
. . . FOR EVERYTHING Functional Activities Most Frequently Outsourced		
Payroll		75%
Manufacturing		72
Maintenance		68
Warehousing/transportation/distribution		62
Information technology		52
Travel		48
Temporary service		48
HR activities (varied)		40
Product design		35
R&D		25
Marketing		22

back to the United States certain software engineering activities—the leading outsourcer outsourcing itself.[5] Exhibit 10.8 shows how rapidly outsourcing has become commonplace in today's global economy.

The embrace of outsourcing's benefits, however, can obscure the potential for numerous problems. Boeing's 787 Dreamliner was three years late before finally being delivered to the early customers in late 2010 because of repeated production and design mistakes from a large number of outsourced partners around the globe. Communication glitches, production delays, and routine design adjustments required in any major production effort can be a real problem when they occur with outsourced partners halfway around the globe, rather than when the project is all done under one roof. Southern Pacific Railroad suffered through numerous computer breakdowns, delays, and scheduling mistakes after outsourcing its internal computer network to IBM.

The important point to recognize at this point is that functional activities long associated with doing the work of any business organization are increasingly subject to be outsourced if they can be done more cost effectively by other providers. So it becomes critical for managers implementing strategic plans to focus company activities on functions deemed central to the company's competitive advantage and to seek others outside the firm's structure to provide the functions that are necessary, but not within the scope of the firm's core competencies. And, increasingly, this decision considers every organizational activity fair game—even marketing, product design, innovation. We will explore this in greater detail in Chapter 11.

---

[5] A. Giridharadas, "Outsourcing Works, So India Is Exporting Jobs," *NYTimes.com*, September 25, 2007.

EMPOWERING OPERATING PERSONNEL: THE ROLE OF POLICIES

Specific functional tactics provide guidance and initiate action implementing a business's strategy, but more is needed. Supervisors and personnel in the field have been charged in today's competitive environment with being responsible for customer value—for being the "front line" of the company's effort to truly meet customers' needs. Meeting customer needs is a buzzword regularly cited as a key priority by most business organizations. Efforts to do so often fail because employees that are the real contact point between the business and its customers are not empowered to make decisions or act to fulfill customer needs. One solution has been to empower operating personnel by pushing down decision making to their level. General Electric allows appliance repair personnel to decide about warranty credits on the spot, a decision that used to take several days and multiple organizational levels. American Air Lines allows customer service personnel and their supervisors wide range in resolving customer ticket pricing decisions. Federal Express couriers make decisions and handle package routing information that once involved five management levels in the U.S. Postal Service.

empowerment
The act of allowing an individual or team the right and flexibility to make decisions and initiate action.

Empowerment is the act of allowing an individual or team the right and flexibility to make decisions and initiate action. It is being expanded and widely advocated in many organizations today. Training, self-managed work groups, eliminating whole levels of management in organizations, and aggressive use of automation are some of the ways and ramifications of this fundamental change in the way business organizations function. At the heart of the effort is the need to ensure that decision making is consistent with the mission, strategy, and tactics of the business while at the same time allowing considerable latitude to operating personnel. One way operating managers do this is through the use of policies.

policies
Broad, precedent-setting decisions that guide or substitute for repetitive or time-sensitive managerial decision making.

Policies are directives designed to guide the thinking, decisions, and actions of managers and their subordinates in implementing a firm's strategy. Sometimes called *standard operating procedures,* policies increase managerial effectiveness by standardizing many routine decisions and clarifying the discretion managers and subordinates can exercise in implementing functional tactics. Logically, policies should be derived from functional tactics (and, in some instances, from corporate or business strategies) with the key purpose of aiding strategy execution.[6] Exhibit 10.9, Strategy in Action, illustrates selected policies of several well-known firms.

Creating Policies That Empower

Policies communicate guidelines to decisions. They are designed to control decisions while defining allowable discretion within which operational personnel can execute business activities. They do this in several ways:

1. *Policies establish indirect control over independent action* by clearly stating how things are to be done *now*. By defining discretion, policies in effect control decisions yet empower employees to conduct activities without direct intervention by top management.

---

[6] The term *policy* has various definitions in management literature. Some authors and practitioners equate policy with strategy. Others do this inadvertently by using "policy" as a synonym for company mission, purpose, or culture. Still other authors and practitioners differentiate policy in terms of "levels" associated, respectively, with purpose, mission, and strategy. "Our policy is to make a positive contribution to the communities and societies we live in" and "Our policy is not to diversify out of the hamburger business" are two examples of the breadth of what some call policies. This book defines *policy* much more narrowly as specific guides to managerial action and decisions in the implementation of strategy. This definition permits a sharper distinction between the formulation and implementation of functional strategies. And, of even greater importance, it focuses the tangible value of the policy concept where it can be most useful—as a key administrative tool to enhance effective implementation and execution of strategy.

Selected Policies That Aid Strategy Implementation

3M Corporation has a *personnel policy,* called the *15 percent rule,* that allows virtually any employee to spend up to 15 percent of the workweek on anything that he or she wants to, as long as it's product related. (This policy supports 3M's corporate strategy of being a highly innovative manufacturer, with each division required to have a quarter of its annual sales come from products introduced within the past five years.)

Wendy's has a *purchasing policy* that gives local store managers the authority to buy fresh meat and produce locally, rather than from regionally designated or company-owned sources. (This policy supports Wendy's functional strategy of having fresh, unfrozen hamburgers daily.)

General Cinema has a *financial policy* that requires annual capital investment in movie theaters not to exceed annual depreciation. (By seeing that capital investment is no greater than depreciation, this policy supports General Cinema's financial strategy of maximizing cash flow—in this case, all profit—to its growth areas. The policy also reinforces General Cinema's financial strategy of leasing as much as possible.)

Crown, Cork, and Seal Company has an *R&D policy* of not investing any financial or people resources in basic research. (This policy supports Crown, Cork, and Seal's functional strategy, which emphasizes customer services, not technical leadership.)

Bank of America has an *operating policy* that requires annual renewal of the financial statement of all personal borrowers. (This policy supports Bank of America's financial strategy, which seeks to maintain a loan-to-loss ratio below the industry norm.)

2. *Policies promote uniform handling of similar activities.* This facilitates the coordination of work tasks and helps reduce friction arising from favoritism, discrimination, and the disparate handling of common functions—something that often hampers operating personnel.

3. *Policies ensure quicker decisions* by standardizing answers to previously answered questions that otherwise would recur and be pushed up the management hierarchy again and again—something that requires unnecessary levels of management between senior decision makers and field personnel.

4. *Policies institutionalize basic aspects of organization behavior.* This minimizes conflicting practices and establishes consistent patterns of action in attempts to make the strategy work—again, freeing operating personnel to act.

5. *Policies reduce uncertainty in repetitive and day-to-day decision making,* thereby providing a necessary foundation for coordinated, efficient efforts and freeing operating personnel to act.

6. *Policies counteract resistance to or rejection of chosen strategies by organization members.* When major strategic change is undertaken, unambiguous operating policies clarify what is expected and facilitate acceptance, particularly when operating managers participate in policy development.

7. *Policies offer predetermined answers to routine problems.* This greatly expedites dealing with both ordinary and extraordinary problems—with the former, by referring to these answers; with the latter, by giving operating personnel more time to cope with them.

8. *Policies afford managers a mechanism for avoiding hasty and ill-conceived decisions in changing operations.* Prevailing policy can always be used as a reason for not yielding to emotion-based, expedient, or temporarily valid arguments for altering procedures and practices.

Make Sure Policies Aren't Used to Drive Away Customers

Every year *Inc.* magazine sponsors a conference for the 500 fastest growing companies in the United States to share ideas, hear speakers, and network. A recent conference included a talk by Martha Rogers, co-author of *The One to One Future*. Here is an interesting anecdote about policies she used in her talk:

> The story was about a distinguished-looking gentleman in blue jeans who walked into a bank and asked a teller to complete a transaction. The teller said she was sorry, but the person responsible was out for the day. The man would have to come back. He then asked to have his parking receipt validated. Again, she said she was sorry, but under bank policy she could not validate a parking receipt unless the customer completed a transaction. The man pressed her. She did not waver. "That's our policy," she said.
>
> So the man completed a transaction. He withdrew all $1.5 million from his account. It turned out he was John Akers, then chairman of IBM.
>
> The moral: Give employees information about the value of customers, not mindless policies.

Policies may be written and formal or unwritten and informal. Informal, unwritten policies are usually associated with a strategic need for competitive secrecy. Some policies of this kind, such as promotion from within, are widely known (or expected) by employees and implicitly sanctioned by management. Managers and employees often like the latitude granted by unwritten and informal policies. However, such policies may detract from the long-term success of a strategy. Formal, written policies have at least seven advantages:

1. They require managers to think through the policy's meaning, content, and intended use.
2. They reduce misunderstanding.
3. They make equitable and consistent treatment of problems more likely.
4. They ensure unalterable transmission of policies.
5. They communicate the authorization or sanction of policies more clearly.
6. They supply a convenient and authoritative reference.
7. They systematically enhance indirect control and organizationwide coordination of the key purposes of policies.

The strategic significance of policies can vary. At one extreme are such policies as travel reimbursement procedures, which are really work rules and may not have an obvious link to the implementation of a strategy. Exhibit 10.10, Strategy in Action, provides an interesting example of how the link between a simple policy and strategy implementation regarding customer service can have serious negative consequences when it is neither obvious to operating personnel nor well thought out by bank managers. At the other extreme are organizationwide policies that are virtually functional strategies, such as Wendy's requirement that every location invest 1 percent of its gross revenue in local advertising.

Policies can be externally imposed or internally derived. Policies regarding equal employment practices are often developed in compliance with external (government) requirements, and policies regarding leasing or depreciation may be strongly influenced by current tax regulations.

Regardless of the origin, formality, and nature of policies, the key point to bear in mind is that they can play an important role in strategy implementation. Communicating specific policies will help overcome resistance to strategic change, empower people to act, and foster commitment to successful strategy implementation.

Policies empower people to act. Compensation, at least theoretically, rewards their action. The last decade has seen many firms realize that the link between compensation, particularly executive management compensation, and value-building strategic outcomes within their firms was uncertain. The recognition of this uncertainty has brought about increased recognition of the need to link management compensation with the successful implementation of strategies that build long-term shareholder value. The next section examines this development and major types of executive bonus compensation plans.

BONUS COMPENSATION PLANS[7]

Major Plan Types

Company shareholders typically believe that the goal of a bonus compensation plan is to motivate executives and key employees to achieve maximization of shareholder wealth. Because shareholders are both owners and investors of the firm, they desire a reasonable return on their investment. Because they are absentee landlords, shareholders expect their board of directors to ensure that the decision-making logic of their firm's executives is concurrent with their own primary motivation.

However, the goal of shareholder wealth maximization is not the only goal that executives may pursue. Alternatively, executives may choose actions that increase their personal compensation, power, and control. Therefore, an executive compensation plan that contains a bonus component can be used to orient management's decision making toward the owners' goals. The success of bonus compensation as an incentive hinges on a proper match between an executive bonus plan and the firm's strategic objectives. As one author has written, "Companies can succeed by clarifying their business vision or strategy and aligning company pay programs with its strategic direction."[8] Exhibit 10.11 summarizes five types of executive compensation plans we will now explore in more detail.

Stock Options

Λ common measure of shareholder wealth creation is appreciation of company stock price. Therefore, a popular form of bonus compensation is stock options. Stock options have typically represented more than 50 percent of a chief executive officer's average pay package.[9] **Stock options** provide the executive with the right to purchase company stock at a fixed price in the future. The precise amount of compensation is based on the difference, or "spread," between the option's initial price and its selling, or exercised, price. As a result, the executive receives a bonus only if the firm's share price appreciates. If the share price drops below the option price, the options become worthless.

Stock options were the source of extraordinary wealth creation for executives, managers, and rank-and-file employees in the technology boom of the 1990s. Behind using options as compensation incentives was the notion that they were essentially free. Although they dilute shareholders' equity when they're exercised, taking the cost of stock options as an expense against earnings was not required. That, in turn, helped keep earnings higher than actual costs to the company and its shareholders. The bear market and corporate scandals of

stock options
The right, or "option," to purchase company stock at a fixed price at some future date.

---

[7] We wish to thank Roy Hossler for his assistance on this section.

[8] James E. Nelson, "Linking Compensation to Business Strategy," *The Journal of Business Strategy* 19, no. 2 (1998), pp. 25–27.

[9] Louis Lavelle, Frederick Jespersen, and Spencer Ante, "Executive Pay," *BusinessWeek*, April 21, 2003.

EXHIBIT 10.11   **Types of Executive Bonus Compensation**

Bonus Type	Description	Rationale	Shortcomings
Stock option grants	Right to purchase stock in the future at a price set now. Compensation is determined by "spread" between option price and exercise price.	Provides incentive for executive to create wealth for shareholders as measured by increase in firm's share price.	Movement in share price does not explain all dimensions of managerial performance.
Restricted stock plan	Shares given to executive who is prohibited from selling them for a specific time period. May also include performance restrictions.	Promotes longer executive tenure than other forms of compensation.	No downside risk to executive, who always profits unlike other shareholders.
Golden handcuffs	Bonus income deferred in a series of annual installments. Deferred amounts not yet paid are forfeited with executive resignation.	Offers an incentive for executive to remain with the firm.	May promote risk-averse decision making due to downside risk borne by executive.
Golden parachute	Executives have right to collect the bonus if they lose position due to takeover, firing, retirement, or resignation.	Offers an incentive for executive to remain with the firm.	Compensation is achieved whether or not wealth is created for shareholders. Rewards either success or failure.
Cash based on internal business performance using financial measures	Bonus compensation based on accounting performance measures such as return on equity.	Offsets the limitations of focusing on market-based measures of performance.	Weak correlation between earnings measures and shareholder wealth creation. Annual earnings do not capture future impact of current decisions.

the last few years brought increased scrutiny on the use of and accounting for stock options. Recent changes in SEC guidelines have encouraged expensing stock options to more accurately reflect company performance. The following table shows the effect expensing stocks options would have on the net earnings of Standard & Poor's (S&P) 500 firms between 1996 and 2005. "Stock options were a free resource, and because of that, they were used freely," said BankOne CEO James Dimon, who voluntarily began to expense stock options in 2003. "But now," he said, "when you have to expense options, you start to think, 'Is it an effective cost? Is there a better way?'" The Financial Accounting Standards Board issued a ruling in 2004 that required expensing of stock options beginning in 2006.[10]

[10] U.S. GAAP (generally accepted accounting principles) required expensing of stock options using one of two acceptable valuation methods starting in the first fiscal year after June 15, 2005. (www.wikipedia.org/wiki/employee_stock_options)

A Big Hit to Earnings

If options had been expensed between 1996 and 2005, earnings would have been whacked as their popularity grew as shown below:

Options Expense as a Percent of Net Earnings for S&P 500 Companies

1996	1998	2000	2002	2005
2%	5%	8%	23%	22%

Source: *The Analysis Accounting Observer,* R. G. Associates Inc.

Microsoft shocked the business world in 2003 by announcing it would discontinue stock options, eliminating a form of pay that made thousands of Microsoft employees millionaires and helped define the culture of the tech industry. Starting in September 2003, the company began paying its 54,000 employees with restricted stock, a move that will let employees make money even if the company's share price declines. Like options, the restricted stock will vest gradually over a five-year period, and grants of restricted stock are counted as expenses and charged against earnings. Said CEO Steven Ballmer, "We asked: Is there a smarter way to compensate our people, a way that would make them feel even more excited about their financial deal at Microsoft and at the same time be something that was at least as good for the shareholders as today's compensation package?" At the time of Ballmer's announcement, more than 20,000 employees who had joined Microsoft in the past three years held millions of stock options that were "under water," meaning the market value of Microsoft stock was far below the stock price of their stock options.

Restricted stock has the advantage of offering employees more certainty, even if there is less potential for a big win. It also means shareholders don't have to worry about massive dilution after employees exercise big stock gains, as happened in the 1990s. Another advantage is that grants of restricted stock are much easier to value than options because restricted stock is equivalent to a stock transfer at the market price. That improves the transparency of corporate accounting.[11]

Research suggests that stock option plans lack the benefits of plans that include true stock ownership. Stock option plans provide unlimited upside potential for executives, but limited downside risk because executives incur only opportunity costs. Because of the tremendous advantages to the executive of stock price appreciation, there is an incentive for the executive to take undue risk. Thus, supporters of stock ownership plans argue that direct ownership instills a much stronger behavioral commitment, even when the stock price falls, because it binds executives to their firms more than do options.[12] Additionally, "Executive stock options may be an efficient means to induce management to undertake more risky projects."[13]

---

[11] Many argue that stock options are critical to start-up firms as a way to motivate and retain talented employees with the promise of getting rich should the new venture succeed. Among them appear to be FASB chairman Robert Herz, who favors sentiment to make special exceptions in the expensing of options in pre-IPO firms.

[12] Jeffrey Pfeffer, "Seven Practices of Successful Organizations," *California Management Review,* Winter 1998.

[13] Richard A. DeFusco, Robert R. Johnson, and Thomas S. Zorn, "The Effect of Executive Stock Option Plans on Stockholders and Bondholders," *Journal of Finance* 45, no. 2 (1990), pp. 617–35.

Options may have been overused and indeed abused in the last two bull markets,[14] but evidence suggests that the smart use of options and other incentive compensation does boost performance. Companies that spread ownership throughout a large portion of their workforce deliver higher returns than similar companies with more concentrated ownership. If options seemed for a time to be the route that enriched CEOs, employees, and investors alike, it still appears they will be used, although with less emphasis than a mix of options, restricted stock, and cash bonuses. Whatever the exact mix, they are likely to be more closely tied to achieving specific operating goals. The next section examines restricted stock and cash bonuses in greater detail.

Restricted Stock

restricted stock

Stock given to an employee who is prohibited or "restricted" from selling the stock for a certain time period and not at all if they leave the company before that time period.

A **restricted stock** plan is designed to provide benefits of direct executive stock ownership. In a typical restricted stock plan, an executive is given a specific number of company stock shares. The executive is prohibited from selling the shares for a specified time period. Should the executive leave the firm voluntarily before the restricted period ends, the shares are forfeited. Therefore, restricted stock plans are a form of deferred compensation that promotes longer executive tenure than other types of plans.

In addition to being contingent on a vesting period, restricted stock plans may also require the achievement of predetermined performance goals. Price-vesting restricted stock plans tie vesting to the firm's stock price in comparison to an index or to reaching a predetermined goal or annual growth rate. If the executive falls short on some of the restrictions, a certain amount of shares are forfeited. The design of these plans motivates the executive to increase shareholder wealth while promoting a long-term commitment to stay with the firm.

If the restricted stock plan lacks performance goal provisions, the executive needs only to remain employed with the firm over the vesting period to cash in on the stock. Performance provisions make sure executives are not compensated without achieving some level of shareholder wealth creation. Like stock options, restricted stock plans offer no downside risk to executives because the shares were initially gifted to the executive. Unlike options, the stock retains value tied to its market value once ownership is fully vested. Shareholders, on the other hand, do suffer a loss in personal wealth resulting from a share price drop.

Golden Handcuffs

golden handcuffs

A form of executive compensation where compensation is deferred (either a restricted stock plan or bonus income deferred in a series of annual installments).

The rationale behind plans that defer compensation forms the basis for another type of executive compensation called golden handcuffs. **Golden handcuffs** refer to either a restricted stock plan, where the stock compensation is deferred until vesting time provisions are met, or to bonus income deferred in a series of annual installments. This type of plan may also involve compensating an executive a significant amount upon retirement or at some predetermined age. In most cases, compensation is forfeited if the executive voluntarily resigns or is discharged before certain time restrictions.

Many boards consider their executives' skills and talents to be their firm's most valuable assets. These "assets" create and sustain the professional relationships that generate revenue and control expenses for the firm. Research suggests that the departure of key executives is unsettling for companies and often disrupts long-range plans when new key executives

---

[14] Erik Lie and Randall A. Heron, "Does Backdating Explain the Stock Price Pattern Around Stock Option Grants," *Journal of Financial Economics* 83, (2007), pp. 271–95. Lie and Heron found 30 percent of all U.S. publicly traded firms apparently manipulated (backdated) stock option grants to increase the payoff to executives receiving the grants.

adopt a different management strategy.[15] Thus, the golden handcuffs approach to executive compensation is more congruent with long-term strategies than short-term performance plans, which offer little staying-power incentive.

Firms may turn to golden handcuffs if they believe stability of management is critical to sustained growth. Jupiter Asset Management recently tied 10 fund managers to the firm with golden handcuffs. The compensation scheme calls for a cash payment in addition to base salaries if the managers remain at the firm for five years. In the first year of the plan, the firm's pretax profits more than doubled, and their assets under management increased 85 percent. The firm's chairman has also signed a new incentive deal that will keep him at Jupiter for four years.

Deferred compensation is worrisome to some executives. In cases where the compensation is payable when the executives are retired and no longer in control, as when the firm is acquired by another firm or a new management hierarchy is installed, the golden handcuff plans are considerably less attractive to executives.

Golden handcuffs may promote risk averseness in executive decision making due to the huge downside risk borne by executives. This risk averseness could lead to mediocre performance results from executives' decisions. When executives lose deferred compensation if the firm discharges them voluntarily or involuntarily, the executive is less likely to make bold and aggressive decisions. Rather, the executive will choose safe, conservative decisions.

Golden Parachutes

golden parachute
A form of bonus compensation that guarantees a substantial cash payment if the executive quits, is fired, or simply retires.

Golden parachutes are a form of bonus compensation that guarantees a substantial cash payment to an executive if the executive quits, is fired, or simply retires. In addition, the golden parachute may also contain covenants that allow the executive to cash in on noninvested stock compensation.

The popularity of golden parachutes grew with the increased popularity of takeovers, which often led to the ouster of the acquired firm's top executives. In these cases, the golden parachutes encouraged executives to take an objective look at takeover offers. The executives could decide which move was in the best interests of the shareholders, having been personally protected in the event of a merger. The "parachute" helps soften the fall of the ousted executive. It is "golden" because the size of the cash payment often varies from several to tens of millions of dollars.

AMP Incorporated, the world's largest producer of electronic connectors, had golden parachutes for several executives. When Allied Signal proclaimed itself an unsolicited suitor for AMP, the action focused attention on the AMP parachutes for its three top executives. Robert Ripp became AMP's chief executive officer during this time. If Allied Signal ousted him, he stood to receive a cash payment of three times the amount of his salary as well as his highest annual bonus from the previous three years. His salary at the time was $600,000 and his previous year's bonus was $200,000. The cash payment to Ripp would therefore exceed $2 million. Parachutes would also open for the former chief executive officer and the former chairman who were slated to officially retire a year later. They stood to receive their parachutes if they were ousted before their respective retirement dates with each parachute valued at more than $1 million.

In addition to cash payments, these three executives' parachutes also protect existing blocks of restricted stock grants and nonvested stock options. The restricted stock grants were scheduled to become available within three years. Should the takeover come to fruition, the executives would receive the total value of the restricted stock even if it was not yet vested. The stock options would also become available immediately. Some of the restricted

---

[15] William E. Hall, Brian J. Lake, Charles T. Morse, and Charles T. Morse Jr., "More Than Golden Handcuffs," *Journal of Accountancy* 184, no. 5 (1997), pp. 37–42.

stock was performance restricted. Under normal conditions this stock would not be available without the firm reaching certain performance levels. However, the golden parachutes allow the executives to receive double the value of the performance-restricted stock.

Golden parachutes are designed in part to anticipate hostile takeovers like this. In AMP's case, Ripp's position is to lead the firm's board of directors in deciding if Allied Signal's offer is in the long-term interests of shareholders. Because Ripp is compensated heavily whether AMP is taken over or not, the golden parachute has helped remove the temptation that Ripp could have of not acting in the best interests of shareholders.

Cash

Executive bonus compensation plans that focus on accounting measures of performance are designed to offset the limitations of market-based measures of performance. This type of plan is most usually associated with the payment of periodic (quarterly or annual) cash bonuses. Market factors beyond the control of management, such as pending legislation, can keep a firm's share price repressed even though a top executive is exceeding the performance expectations of the board. In this situation, a highly performing executive loses bonus compensation due to the undervalued stock. However, accounting measures of performance correct for this problem by tying executive bonuses to improvements in internally measured performance.

Traditional accounting measures, such as net income, earnings per share, return on equity, and return on assets, are used because they are easily understood, are familiar to senior management, and are already tracked by firm data systems.[16] Sears bases annual bonus payments on such performance criteria, given an executive's business unit and level with the firm. The measures used by Sears include return on equity, revenue growth, net sales growth, and profit growth.

Critics argue that because of inherent flaws in accounting systems, basing compensation on these figures may not result in an accurate gauge of managerial performance. Return on equity estimates, for example, are skewed by inflation distortions and arbitrary cost allocations. Accounting measures are also subject to manipulation by firm personnel to artificially inflate key performance figures. Firm performance schemes, critics believe, need to be based on a financial measure that has a true link to shareholder value creation.[17] This issue led to the creation of the Balanced Scorecard, which emphasizes not only financial measures, but also such measures as new-product development, market share, and safety as discussed in Chapter 12.

Matching Bonus Plans and Corporate Goals

Exhibit 10.12 matches a company's strategic goal with the most likely compensation plan. On the vertical axis are common strategic goals. The horizontal axis lists the main compensation types that serve as incentives for executives to reach the firm's goals. A rationale is provided to explain the logic behind the connection between the firm's goal and the suggested method of executive compensation.

Researchers emphasize that fundamental to these relationships is the importance of incorporating the level of strategic risk of the firm into the design of the executive's compensation plan. Incorporating an appropriate level of executive risk can create a

[16] Francine C. McKenzie and Matthew D. Shilling, "Avoiding Performance Measurement Traps: Ensuring Effective Incentive Design and Implementation," *Compensation and Benefits Review,* July–August 1998, pp. 57–65.

[17] William Franklin, "Making the Fat Cats Earn Their Cream," *Accountancy,* July 1998, pp. 38–39.

EXHIBIT 10.12   **Compensation Plan Selection Matrix**

| | Type of Bonus Compensation | | | | | |
Strategic Goal	Cash	Golden Handcuffs	Golden Parachutes	Restricted Stock Plans	Stock Options	Rationale
Achieve corporate turnaround					X	Executive profits only if turnaround is successful in returning wealth to shareholders.
Create and support growth opportunities					X	Risk associated with growth strategies warrants the use of this high-reward incentive.
Defend against unfriendly takeover			X			Parachute helps takeover remove temptation for executive to evaluate takeover based on personal benefits.
Evaluate suitors objectively			X			Parachute compensates executive if job is lost due to a merger favorable to the firm.
Globalize operations					X	Risk of expanding overseas requires a plan that compensates only for achieved success.
Grow share price incrementally	X					Accounting measures can identify periodic performance benchmarks.
Improve operational efficiency	X					Accounting measures represent observable and agreed-upon measures of performance.
Increase assets under management				X		Executive profits proportionally as asset growth leads to long-term growth in share price.
Reduce executive turnover		X				Handcuffs provide executive tenure incentive.
Restructure organization					X	Risk associated with major change in firm's assets warrants the use of this high-reward incentive.
Streamline operations				X		Rewards long-term focus on efficiency and cost control.

desired behavioral change commensurate with the risk level of strategies shareholders and their firms want.[18] To help motivate an executive to pursue goals of a certain risk-return level, the compensation plan can quantify that risk-return level and reward the executive accordingly.

[18] Lavelle, Jespersen, and Ante, "Executive Pay."

Top Strategist
Carol Bartz, CEO, Yahoo!

**Exhibit
10.13**

Yahoo! stock was battered for several years, leading up to the crisis-laden replacement of CEO and co-founder Jerry Yang with Carol Bartz. Several poor competitive strategy decisions, compounded by Yang's spurning overtures and offers to buy Yahoo! from Microsoft, led Yahoo!'s board to "encourage" Yang to finally step down in early 2009 to be replaced by Bartz, Autodesk CEO at the time. Her compensation package upon taking the helm at Yahoo! was intended to focus her efforts on rebuilding the Yahoo! stock price. The seven elements of her initial Yahoo! compensation package were:

1. Annual base salary of $1,000,000.
2. Annual bonus with a target of 200% of base salary and a maximum of two times the target, to be determined by the Compensation Committee of the Board of Directors of Yahoo!

3. Stock options for 5,000,000 shares at the price on February 1, 2009.
4. Annual equity grants as generally made to senior executives, including a grant valued at $8 million in February 2009.
5. Health, life, disability insurance, an employee stock purchase plan, a 401k plan, and four weeks vacation per year.
6. $150,000 in advisory fees related to this agreement.
7. An equity grant valued at $10,000,000 to compensate Bartz for forfeiture of the value of equity grants and medical coverage with her previous employer, Autodesk.

What is your evaluation of this "deal?" Does it seem fair and appropriate to Bartz, Yahoo!, and its stockholders? If you want to see what other people thought about this arrangement, you can view comments from a wide variety of people at http://www.businessinsider.com/2009/1/carol-bartzs-pay-1-million-salary-2-million-bonus-yhoo.

Source: http://idea.sec.gov/Archives/edgar/data/1011006/000089161809000005/f51094e8vk.htm.

The links we show between bonus compensation plans and strategic goals were derived from the results of prior research. The basic principle underlying Exhibit 10.12 is that different types of bonus compensation plans are intended to accomplish different purposes; one element may serve to attract and retain executives; another may serve as an incentive to encourage behavior that accomplishes firm goals.[19] Although every strategy option has probably been linked to each compensation plan at some time, experience shows that there may be scenarios where a plan type best fits a strategy option. Exhibit 10.12 attempts to display the "best matches."

Once the firm has identified strategic goals that will best serve shareholders' interests, an executive bonus compensation plan can be structured in such a way as to provide the executive with an incentive to work toward achieving these goals. Exhibit 10.13, Top Strategist, summarizes the compensation plan Yahoo!'s board gave new CEO Carol Bartz, which sought to match her compensation with one key goal—increasing Yahoo!'s stock price after it had been steadily battered with the way co-founder and CEO Jerry Yang mishandled Microsoft's acquisition overtures and company strategy for several years.

[19] Nelson, "Linking Compensation to Business Strategy."

Summary

The first concern in the implementation of business strategy is to translate that strategy into action throughout the organization. This chapter discussed five considerations for accomplishing this.

Short-term objectives are derived from long-term objectives, which are then translated into current actions and targets. They differ from long-term objectives in time frame, specificity, and measurement. To be effective in strategy implementation, they must be integrated and coordinated. They also must be consistent, measurable, and prioritized.

Functional tactics are derived from the business strategy. They identify the specific, immediate actions that must be taken in key functional areas to implement the business strategy.

Outsourcing of selected functional activities has become a central tactical agenda for virtually every business firm in today's global economy. Can we get that activity done more effectively—and more inexpensively—outside our company? This question has become a regular one managers ask as they seek to make their business strategies work.

Employee empowerment through policies provides another means for guiding behavior, decisions, and actions at the firm's operating levels in a manner consistent with its business and functional strategies. Policies empower operating personnel to make decisions and take action quickly.

Compensation rewards action and results. Once the firm has identified strategic objectives that will best serve stockholder interests, there are five bonus compensation plans that can be structured to provide the executive with an incentive to work toward achieving those goals.

Objectives, functional tactics, policies, and compensation represent only the start of the strategy implementation. The strategy must be institutionalized—it must permeate the firm. The next chapter examines this phase of strategy implementation.

Key Terms

empowerment, *p. 276*
functional tactics, *p. 271*
golden handcuffs, *p. 282*

golden parachute, *p. 283*
outsourcing, *p. 274*
policies, *p. 276*

restricted stock, *p. 282*
short-term objective, *p. 268*
stock options, *p. 279*

Questions for Discussion

1. How does the concept "translate thought into action" bear on the relationship between business strategy and operating strategy? Between long-term and short-term objectives?
2. How do functional tactics differ from corporate and business strategies?
3. What key concerns must functional tactics address in marketing? finance? production/operations management? personnel?
4. What is "outsourcing?" Why has it become a key element in shaping functional tactics within most business firms today?
5. How do policies aid strategy implementation? Illustrate your answer.
6. Use Exhibits 10.11 and 10.12 to explain five executive bonus compensation plans.
7. Illustrate a policy, an objective, and a functional tactic in your personal career strategy.
8. Why are short-term objectives needed when long-term objectives are already available?

Chapter 10 Appendix

Functional Tactics

FUNCTIONAL TACTICS THAT IMPLEMENT BUSINESS STRATEGIES

Functional tactics are the key, routine activities that must be undertaken in each functional area—marketing, finance, production/operations, R&D, and human resource management—to provide the business's products and services. In a sense, functional tactics translate thought (grand strategy) into action designed to accomplish specific short-term objectives. Every value chain activity in a company executes functional tactics that support the business's strategy and help accomplish strategic objectives.

The next several sections will highlight key tactics around which managers can build competitive advantage and add value in each of the various functional areas.

FUNCTIONAL TACTICS IN PRODUCTION/OPERATIONS

Basic Issues

Production/operations management (POM) is the core function of any organization. That function converts inputs (raw materials, supplies, machines, and people) into value-enhanced

output. The POM function is most easily associated with manufacturing firms, but it also applies to all other types of businesses (e.g., service and retail firms). POM tactics must guide decisions regarding (1) the basic nature of the firm's POM system, seeking an optimum balance between investment input and production/operations output, and (2) location, facilities design, and process planning on a short-term basis. Exhibit 10.A1 highlights key decision areas in which the POM tactics should provide guidance to functional personnel.

POM facility and equipment tactics involve decisions regarding plant location, size, equipment replacement, and facilities utilization that should be consistent with grand strategy and other operating strategies. In the mobile home industry, for example, the facilities and equipment tactic of Winnebago was to locate one large centralized, highly integrated production center (in Iowa) near its raw materials. On the other extreme, Fleetwood Inc., a California-based competitor, located dispersed, decentralized production facilities near markets and emphasized maximum equipment life and less-integrated, labor-intensive production processes. Both firms are leaders in the mobile home industry, but have taken very different tactical approaches.

The interplay between computers and rapid technological advancement has made flexible manufacturing systems (FMS) a major consideration for today's POM tacticians.

EXHIBIT 10.A1   Key Functional Tactics in POM

Functional Tactic	Typical Questions That the Functional Tactic Should Answer
Facilities and equipment	How centralized should the facilities be? (One big facility or several small facilities?)
	How integrated should the separate processes be?
	To what extent should further mechanization or automation be pursued?
	Should size and capacity be oriented toward peak or normal operating levels?
Sourcing	How many sources are needed?
	How should suppliers be selected, and how should relationships with suppliers be managed over time?
	What level of forward buying (hedging) is appropriate?
Operations planning and control	Should work be scheduled to order or to stock?
	What level of inventory is appropriate?
	How should inventory be used, controlled, and replenished?
	What are the key foci for control efforts (quality, labor cost, downtime, product use, other)?
	Should maintenance efforts be oriented to prevention or to breakdown?
	What emphasis should be placed on job specialization? Plant safety? The use of standards?

FMS allows managers to automatically and rapidly shift production systems to retool for different products or other steps in a manufacturing process. Changes that previously took hours or days can be done in minutes. The result is decreased labor cost, greater efficiency, and increased quality associated with computer-based precision.

Sourcing has become an increasingly important component in the POM area. Many companies now accord sourcing a separate status like any other functional area. Sourcing tactics provide guidelines about questions such as: Are the cost advantages of using only a few suppliers outweighed by the risk of overdependence? What criteria (e.g., payment requirements) should be used in selecting vendors? Which vendors can provide "just in time" inventory, and how can the business provide it to our customers? How can operations be supported by the volume and delivery requirements of purchases?

POM planning and control tactics involve approaches to the management of ongoing production operations and are intended to match production/operations resources with longer-range, overall demand. These tactical decisions usually determine whether production/operations will be demand oriented, inventory oriented, or outsourcing oriented to seek a balance between the two extremes. Tactics in this component also address how issues such as maintenance, safety, and work organization are handled. Quality control procedures are yet another focus of tactical priorities in this area.

Just-in-time (JIT) delivery, outsourcing, and statistical process control (SPC) have become prominent aspects of the way today's POM managers create tactics that build greater value and quality in their POM system. JIT delivery was initially a way to coordinate with suppliers to reduce inventory carrying costs of items needed to make products. It also became a quality control tactic because smaller inventories made quality checking easier on smaller, frequent deliveries. It has become an important aspect of supplier-customer relationships in today's best businesses.

Outsourcing, or the use of a source other than internal capacity to accomplish some task or process, has become a major operational tactic in today's downsizing-oriented firms. Outsourcing is based on the notion that strategies should be built around the core competencies that add the most value in the value chain and that functions or activities that add little value or that cannot be done cost effectively should be done outside the firm—outsourced. When done well, the firm gains a supplier that provides superior quality at lower cost than it could provide itself. JIT and outsourcing have increased the strategic importance of the purchasing function. Outsourcing must include intense quality control by the buyer. ValuJet's tragic 1996 crash in the Everglades was caused by poor quality control over its outsourced maintenance providers.

The Internet and e-commerce have begun to revolutionize functional tactics in operations and marketing. How we sell, where we make things, how we logistically coordinate what we do—all of these basic business functions and questions have new perspectives and ways of being addressed because of the technological effect of the globally emerging ways we link together electronically, quickly, and accurately.

FUNCTIONAL TACTICS IN MARKETING

The role of the marketing function is to achieve the firm's objectives by bringing about the profitable sale of the business's products/services in target markets. Marketing tactics should guide sales and marketing managers in determining who will sell what, where, to whom, in what quantity, and how. Marketing tactics at a minimum should address four fundamental areas: products, price, place, and promotion. Exhibit 10.A2 highlights typical questions marketing tactics should address.

In addition to the basic issues raised in Exhibit 10.A2, marketing tactics today must guide managers addressing the effect of the communication revolution and the increased diversity among market niches worldwide. The Internet and the accelerating blend of computers and telecommunications has facilitated instantaneous access to several places around the world. A producer of plastic kayaks in Easley, South Carolina, receives orders from somewhere in the world about every 30 minutes over the Internet without any traditional distribution structure or global advertising. It fills the order within five days without any transportation capability. Speed linked to the ability to communicate instantaneously is causing marketing tacticians to radically rethink what they need to do to remain competitive and maximize value.

Diversity has accelerated because of communication technology, logistical capability worldwide, and advancements in flexible manufacturing systems. The diversity that has resulted is a virtual explosion of market niches—adaptations of products to serve hundreds of distinct and diverse customer segments that would previously have been served with more mass-market, generic products or services. Where firms used to rely on volume associated with mass markets to lower costs, they now encounter smaller niche players carving out subsegments they can serve more timely *and* more cost effectively. These new, smaller players lack the bureaucracy and committee approach that burdens the larger firms. They make decisions, outsource, incorporate product modifications, and make other agile adjustments to niche market needs before their larger competitors get through the first phase of committee-based decision making.

FUNCTIONAL TACTICS IN ACCOUNTING AND FINANCE

While most functional tactics guide implementation in the immediate future, the time frame for functional tactics in the area of finance varies because these tactics direct the use

EXHIBIT 10.A2 **Key Functional Tactics in Marketing**

Functional Tactic	Typical Questions That the Functional Tactic Should Answer
Product (or service)	Which products do we emphasize? Which products/services contribute most to profitability? What product/service image do we seek to project? What consumer needs does the product/service seek to meet? What changes should be influencing our customer orientation?
Price	Are we competing primarily on price? Can we offer discounts on other pricing modifications? Are our pricing policies standard nationally, or is there regional control? What price segments are we targeting (high, medium, low, and so on)? What is the gross profit margin? Do we emphasize cost/demand or competition-oriented pricing?
Place	What level of market coverage is necessary? Are there priority geographic areas? What are the key channels of distribution? What are the channel objectives, structure, and management? Should the marketing managers change their degree of reliance on distributors, sales reps, and direct selling? What sales organization do we want? Is the sales force organized around territory, market, or product?
Promotion	What are the key promotion priorities and approaches? Which advertising/communication priorities and approaches are linked to different products, markets, and territories? Which media would be most consistent with the total marketing strategy?

of financial resources in support of the business strategy, long-term goals, and annual objectives. Financial tactics with longer time perspectives guide financial managers in long-term capital investment, debt financing, dividend allocation, and leveraging. Financial tactics designed to manage working capital and short-term assets have a more immediate focus. Exhibit 10.A3 highlights some key questions that financial tactics must answer.

Accounting tactics increasingly emphasize more accurately identifying a meaningful basis from which managers can determine the relative value of different activities undertaken throughout the company contribute to the company's overall success. Traditional cost accounting approaches proved inadequate in doing this, as we discussed in Chapter 6. So, in addition to accounting tactics centered on positioning the company to accurately comply with securities, tax, and regulatory considerations, considerable accounting tactical attention centers on providing value-based accounting of the costs of creating and providing the business' products and services so that managers in different units—as well as company executives—can more truly understand the value of activities undertaken in, between, and among those units. See Exhibit 6.6 in Chapter 6 for a refresher explanation of activity-based versus traditional cost accounting tactics.

FUNCTIONAL TACTICS IN RESEARCH AND DEVELOPMENT

With the increasing rate of technological change in most competitive industries, research and development has assumed a key strategic role in many firms. In the technology-intensive computer and pharmaceutical industries, for example, firms typically spend between 4 and 6 percent, respectively, of their sales dollars on R&D. In other industries, such as the hotel/motel and construction industries, R&D spending is less than 1 percent of sales. Thus, functional R&D tactics may be more critical instruments of the business strategy in some industries than in others.

Exhibit 10.A4 illustrates the types of questions addressed by R&D tactics. First, R&D tactics should clarify whether basic research or product development research will be emphasized. Several major oil companies now have solar energy subsidiaries in which basic research is emphasized, while the smaller oil companies emphasize product development research.

The choice of emphasis between basic research and product development also involves the time horizon for R&D efforts. Should these efforts be focused on the near term or the long term? The solar energy subsidiaries of the major oil

EXHIBIT 10.A3   Key Functional Tactics in Finance and Accounting

Functional Tactic	Typical Questions That the Functional Tactics Should Answer
Acquiring capital	What is the optimal balance between external and internal funding? What proportion of debt should be long-term versus short-term? How should leasing be used? What levels of common versus preferred equity would be best? What ownership restrictions apply? What is a target cost of capital?
Using/allocating capital	What are priorities for allocating capital across different parts of the business and key projects? What approval processes and what levels should be allowed to make capital allocation decisions? How should competing demands for capital be resolved?
Working capital management	What levels of cash flow are needed? What are maximum/minimum cash flow requirements and balances? What should the credit policies be? How might client-specific changes be determined? What are payment terms, limits on credit, and what collection steps/procedures are needed? What are our payment policies, terms, and timing procedures?
Dividends	Are dividends important in support of the company's overall strategy? What portion of earnings, or range, should be used to set dividend payout levels? When can dividends be raised or lowered? How important is dividend stability? Should dividends be exclusively cash? What other things other than cash are appropriate?
Accounting	How can we best account for the costs of creating and providing our business's products and services? What is the "value" of each activity within different parts of our business versus traditional cost categories?

Source: © RC Trust, LLC, 2010.

EXHIBIT 10.A4   Key Functional Tactics in R&D

R&D Decision Area	Typical Questions That the Functional Tactics Should Answer
Basic research versus product and process development	To what extent should innovation and breakthrough research be emphasized? In relation to the emphasis on product development, refinement, and modification? What critical operating processes need R&D attention? What new projects are necessary to support growth?
Time horizon	Is the emphasis short term or long term? Which orientation best supports the business strategy? The marketing and production strategy?
Organizational fit	Should R&D be done in-house or contracted out? Should R&D be centralized or decentralized? What should be the relationship between the R&D units and product managers? Marketing managers? Production managers?
Basic R&D posture	Should the firm maintain an offensive posture, seeking to lead innovation in its industry? Should the firm adopt a defensive posture, responding to the innovations of its competitors?

companies have long-term perspectives, while the smaller oil companies focus on creating products now in order to establish a competitive niche in the growing solar industry.

R&D tactics also involve organization of the R&D function. For example, should R&D work be conducted solely within the firm, or should portions of that work be contracted out? A closely related issue is whether R&D should be centralized or decentralized. What emphasis should be placed on process R&D versus product R&D?

Decisions on all of these questions are influenced by the firm's R&D posture, which can be offensive or defensive, or both. If that posture is offensive, as is true for small high-technology firms, the firm will emphasize technological innovation and new-product development as the basis for its future success. This orientation entails high risks (and high payoffs) and demands considerable technological skill, forecasting expertise, and the ability to quickly transform innovations into commercial products.

A defensive R&D posture emphasizes product modification and the ability to copy or acquire new technology. Converse Shoes is a good example of a firm with such an R&D posture. Faced with the massive R&D budgets of Nike and Reebok, Converse placed R&D emphasis on bolstering the product life cycle of its prime products (particularly canvas shoes).

Large companies with some degree of technological leadership often use a combination of offensive and defensive R&D strategy. GE in the electrical industry, IBM in the computer industry, and Du Pont in the chemical industry all have a defensive R&D posture for currently available products *and* an offensive R&D posture in basic, long-term research.

FUNCTIONAL TACTICS IN HUMAN RESOURCE MANAGEMENT

The strategic importance of human resource management (HRM) tactics received widespread endorsement in the 1990s. HRM tactics aid long-term success in the development of managerial talent and competent employees, the creation of systems to manage compensation or regulatory concerns, and guiding the effective utilization of human resources to achieve both the firm's short-term objectives and employees' satisfaction and development. HRM tactics are helpful in the areas shown in Exhibit 10.A5. The recruitment, selection, and orientation should establish the basic parameters for bringing new people into a firm and adapting them to "the way things are done" in the firm. The career development and training component should guide the action that personnel take to meet the future human resources needs of the overall business strategy. Merrill Lynch, a major brokerage firm whose long-term corporate strategy is to become a diversified financial service institution, has moved into such areas as investment banking, consumer credit, and venture capital. In support of its long-term objectives, it has incorporated extensive early-career training and ongoing career development programs to meet its expanding need for personnel with multiple competencies. Larger organizations need HRM tactics that guide decisions regarding labor relations; Equal Employment Opportunity Commission requirements; and employee compensation, discipline, and control.

Current trends in HRM parallel the reorientation of managerial accounting by looking at their cost structure anew.

EXHIBIT 10.A5   **Key Functional Tactics in HRM**

Functional Tactic	Typical Questions That HRM Tactics Should Answer
Recruitment, selection, and orientation	What key human resources are needed to support the chosen strategy? How do we recruit these human resources? How sophisticated should our selection process be? How should we introduce new employees to the organization?
Career development and training	What are our future human resource needs? How can we prepare our people to meet these needs? How can we help our people develop?
Compensation	What levels of pay are appropriate for the tasks we require? How can we motivate and retain good people? How should we interpret our payment, incentive, benefit, and seniority policies?
Evaluation, discipline, and control	How often should we evaluate our people? Formally or informally? What disciplinary steps should we take to deal with poor performance or inappropriate behavior? In what ways should we "control" individual and group performance?
Labor relations and equal opportunity requirements	How can we maximize labor-management cooperation? How do our personnel practices affect women/minorities? Should we have hiring policies?

HRM's "paradigm shift" involves looking at people expense as an investment in human capital. This involves looking at the business's value chain and the "value" of human resource components along the various links in that chain. One of the results of this shift in perspective has been the downsizing and outsourcing phenomena of the last quarter century. While this has been traumatic for millions of employees in companies worldwide, its underlying basis involves an effort to examine the use of "human capital" to create value in ways that maximize the human contribution. This scrutiny continues to challenge the HRM area to include recent major trends to outsource some or all HRM activities not regarded as part of a firm's core competence. The emerging implications for human resource management tactics may be a value-oriented perspective on the role of human resources in a business's value chain as suggested here:

Traditional HRM Ideas	Emerging HRM Ideas
Emphasis solely on physical skills	Emphasis on total contribution to the firm
Expectation of predictable, repetitious behavior	Expectation of innovative and creative behavior
Comfort with stability and conformity	Tolerance of ambiguity and change
Avoidance of responsibility and decision making	Accepting responsibility for making decisions
Training covering only specific tasks	Open-ended commitment; broad continuous development
Emphasis placed on outcomes and results	Emphasis placed on processes and means
High concern for quantity and throughput	High concern for total customer value
Concern for individual efficiency	Concern for overall effectiveness
Functional and subfunctional specialization	Cross-functional integration
Labor force seen as unnecessary expense	Labor force seen as critical investment
Workforce is management's adversary	Management and workforce are partners

Source: From A. Miller and G. Dess, *Strategic Management,* 2002, p. 400. Reprinted with permission of The McGraw-Hill Companies, Inc.

To summarize, functional tactics reflect how each major activity of a firm contributes to the implementation of the business strategy. The specificity of functional tactics and the involvement of operating managers in their development help ensure understanding of and commitment to the chosen strategy. A related step in implementation is the development of policies that empower operating managers and their subordinates to make decisions and to act autonomously.

Chapter **Eleven**

Organizational Structure

After reading and studying this chapter, you should be able to

1. Identify five traditional organizational structures and the pros and cons of each.

2. Describe the product-team structure and explain why it is a prototype for a more open, agile organizational structure.

3. Explain five ways improvements have been sought in traditional organizational structures.

4. Describe what is meant by agile, virtual organizations.

5. Explain how outsourcing can create agile, virtual organizations, along with its pros and cons.

6. Describe boundaryless organizations and why they are important.

7. Explain why organizations of the future need to be ambidextrous learning organizations.

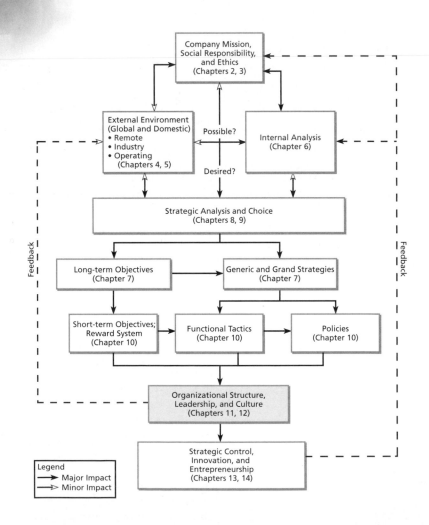

Company Mission, Social Responsibility, and Ethics (Chapters 2, 3)

External Environment (Global and Domestic)
• Remote
• Industry
• Operating
(Chapters 4, 5)

Possible?

Internal Analysis (Chapter 6)

Desired?

Strategic Analysis and Choice (Chapters 8, 9)

Long-term Objectives (Chapter 7)

Generic and Grand Strategies (Chapter 7)

Short-term Objectives; Reward System (Chapter 10)

Functional Tactics (Chapter 10)

Policies (Chapter 10)

Organizational Structure, Leadership, and Culture (Chapters 11, 12)

Strategic Control, Innovation, and Entrepreneurship (Chapters 13, 14)

Feedback

Feedback

Legend
→ Major Impact
⇢ Minor Impact

Until this point in the strategic management process, managers have maintained a decidedly market-oriented focus as they formulate strategies and begin implementation through action plans detailing the tactics and actions that will be taken in each functional activity. Now the process takes an organizational focus—getting the work of the business done efficiently and effectively so as to make the strategy work. What is the best way to organize people and tasks to execute the strategy effectively? What should be done "in-house" and what activities should be "outsourced" for others to do?

What has happened at Hewlett-Packard over the course of this decade? It began with new CEO Carly Fiorina taking over HP in the midst of a global recession. The unfortunate reality for her: HP's lumbering organization was losing touch with its global customers. Her response: as illustrated in Exhibit 11.1, Strategy in Action, Fiorina immediately dismantled the decentralized structure honed throughout HP's 64-year history. Pre-Fiorina, HP was a collection of 83 independently run units, each focused on a product such as scanners or security software. Fiorina collapsed those into four sprawling organizations. One so-called back-end unit developed and built computers; another focused on printers and imaging equipment. The back-end divisions were to hand products off to the two "front-end" sales and marketing groups to peddle the wares—one to consumers, the other to corporations. The theory: the new structure would boost collaboration, giving sales and marketing execs a direct pipeline to engineers so products were developed from the ground up to solve customer problems. This was the first time a company with thousands of product lines and scores of businesses attempted a front-back approach, a structure that requires laser focus and superb coordination.

Fiorina believed she had little choice lest the company experience a near-death experience like Xerox or, 10 years earlier, IBM. The conundrum: how could HP put the full force of the company behind winning in its immediate fiercely competitive technology business when they must also cook up brand-new megamarkets? It's a riddle Fiorina said she could solve only by sweeping structural change that would ready HP for the next stage of the technology revolution, when companies latch on to the Internet to transform their operations. At its core lay a conviction that HP must become "ambidextrous and boundaryless," excelling at short-term execution while pursuing long-term visions that create new markets.

Did it work? No. After five years, Fiorina was dismissed. The chairman of the HP board of directors, Patricia Dunn, said at that time that the board did not intend to change HP's strategy. She indicated that the board was confident in HP's overall strategy even though, she acknowledged, several analysts and stockholders disagreed with the board on this. Confident that the strategy was correct, she indicated that the HP board concluded it had been execution of that strategy, particularly with regard to the "new" HP organizational structure, that the board felt was a major contributor to the lack of success at HP. So, Dunn said, the board wanted a new CEO who would simply execute better. Two months later, Mark Hurd, a 25-year veteran of NCR's sprawling portfolio of businesses, became HP's new chief executive.

Hurd had distinguished himself turning around NCR over the previous two years by cutting costs and tightening marketing and increasing accountability. His NCR turnaround produced eight consecutive profitable quarters at NCR. His organizational structure preference—smaller independently run units, each with a narrow product focus—allowed a clear sense of responsibilities, measurable accountability, tight spending controls, and the ability to execute by controlling their units' production-to-sales activities.

The result: HP's return to smaller, semi-autonomous units led to exceptional success at HP culminating in it recently eclipsing Dell as the world's largest computer company, while remaining a global leader and highly profitable printer company. The HP saga is a useful one for you to keep in mind because it shows you a well-known, major, global technology company trying to find an organizational structure to help it be more competitive in the twenty-first century. And it highlights the need for more openness in an organizational structure—a "boundaryless"

Fiorina Gives Way to Hurd at Hewlett-Packard

When Carly Fiorina arrived at HP, the company was a confederation of 83 autonomous product units reporting through four groups. She radically revamped the structure into two "back-end" divisions—one developing printers, scanners, and the like, and the other computers. These report to "front-end" groups that market and sell HP's wares. Here's how the overhaul went:

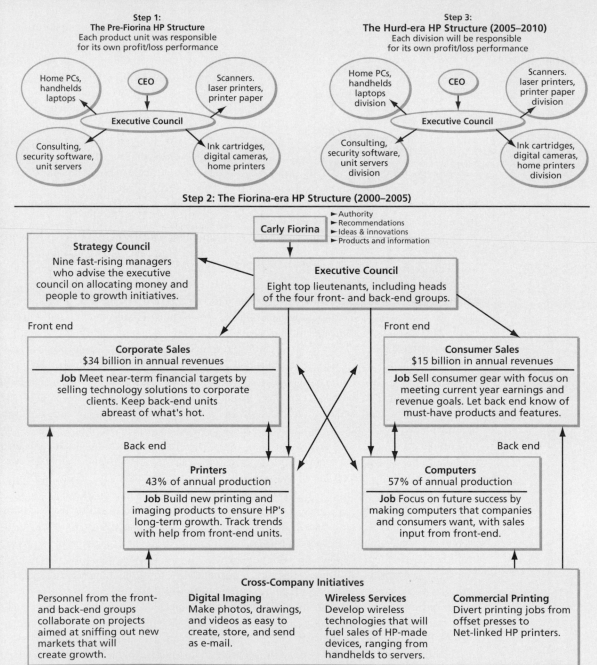

Step 1:
The Pre-Fiorina HP Structure
Each product unit was responsible for its own profit/loss performance

- Home PCs, handhelds laptops
- CEO
- Scanners. laser printers, printer paper
- Executive Council
- Consulting, security software, unit servers
- Ink cartridges, digital cameras, home printers

Step 3:
The Hurd-era HP Structure (2005–2010)
Each division will be responsible for its own profit/loss performance

- Home PCs, handhelds laptops division
- CEO
- Scanners. laser printers, printer paper division
- Executive Council
- Consulting, security software, unit servers division
- Ink cartridges, digital cameras, home printers division

Step 2: The Fiorina-era HP Structure (2000–2005)

Carly Fiorina
► Authority
► Recommendations
► Ideas & innovations
► Products and information

Strategy Council
Nine fast-rising managers who advise the executive council on allocating money and people to growth initiatives.

Executive Council
Eight top lieutenants, including heads of the four front- and back-end groups.

Front end

Corporate Sales
$34 billion in annual revenues

Job Meet near-term financial targets by selling technology solutions to corporate clients. Keep back-end units abreast of what's hot.

Front end

Consumer Sales
$15 billion in annual revenues

Job Sell consumer gear with focus on meeting current year earnings and revenue goals. Let back end know of must-have products and features.

Back end

Printers
43% of annual production

Job Build new printing and imaging products to ensure HP's long-term growth. Track trends with help from front-end units.

Back end

Computers
57% of annual production

Job Focus on future success by making computers that companies and consumers want, with sales input from front-end.

Cross-Company Initiatives

Personnel from the front- and back-end groups collaborate on projects aimed at sniffing out new markets that will create growth.

Digital Imaging
Make photos, drawings, and videos as easy to create, store, and send as e-mail.

Wireless Services
Develop wireless technologies that will fuel sales of HP-made devices, ranging from handhelds to servers.

Commercial Printing
Divert printing jobs from offset presses to Net-linked HP printers.

(continued)

Exhibit 11.1 cont.

Fiorina's Expectations The Assessment	What Actually Happened over Fiorina's 5 Years The Assessment
Happier Customers Clients should find HP easier to deal with, since they'll work with just one account team.	**Overwhelmed with Duties** With so many products being made and sold by just four units, HP execs have more on their plates and could miss the details that keep products competitive.
Sales Boost HP should maximize its selling opportunities because account reps will sell all HP products, not just those from one division.	**Poorer Execution** When product managers oversaw everything from manufacturing to sales, they could respond quickly to changes. That will be harder with front- and back-end groups synching their plans only every few weeks.
Real Solutions HP can sell its products in combination as "solutions"—instead of just PCs or printers—to companies facing e-business problems.	**Less Accountability** Profit-and-loss responsibility is shared between the front- and back-end groups so no one person is on the hot seat. Finger-pointing and foot-dragging could replace HP's collegial cooperation.
Financial Flexibility With all corporate sales under one roof, HP can measure the total value of a customer, allowing reps to discount some products and still maximize profits on the overall contract.	**Fewer Spending Controls** With powerful division chiefs keeping a tight rein on the purse strings, spending rarely got out of hand in the old HP. In the fourth quarter, expenses soared as those lines of command broke down.

organization, as management icon Jack Welch called his approach—but also the importance of coordination and control of the organization's performance and execution of strategy through its structure. In some ways Fiorina's structure more reflected the way twenty-first-century organizations are seeking to organize themselves, while Hurd's approach is a return to a more traditional organization. Hurd's approach has found success in part because it is an attempt to combine attributes of traditional organizational structures and those of newer, boundaryless or virtual organization approaches in an effort to balance a need for control, coordination, openness, and innovation in implementing a strategy best suited to HP's situation.

Today's fast-changing, global economy demands ever-increasing productivity, speed, and flexibility from companies that seek to survive, perhaps thrive. To do so, companies must change their organizational structures dramatically, retaining the best of their traditional (hierarchical) structures while embracing radically new structures that leverage the value of the people who generate ideas, collaborate with colleagues and customers, innovate and therein generate future value for the company. So this chapter seeks to familiarize you with both perspectives on organizational structure and the major trends in structuring business organizations today. Let's start by looking at what have been traditional ways to organize, along with the advantages and disadvantages of each organizational structure.

TRADITIONAL ORGANIZATIONAL STRUCTURES AND THEIR STRATEGY-RELATED PROS AND CONS

You may be one of several students who choose to start your own business rather than take a job with an established company when you finish your current degree program. Or perhaps you are currently in a full-time job position but soon plan to leave that job and start

organizational structure
Refers to the formalized arrangements of interaction between and responsibility for the tasks, people, and resources in an organization.

simple organizational structure
Structure in which there is an owner and a few employees and where the arrangement of tasks, responsibilities, and communication is highly informal and accomplished through direct supervision.

your own company. Like millions of others who have done or will soon do the same thing, usually with a few other "partners," your group will be faced with the question of how to organize your work and the activities and tasks necessary to do the work of your new company. What you are looking for is an organizational structure. We do not mean, here, the "legal" structure of your company such as a proprietorship, corporation, limited liability corporation, or limited partnership to mention a few. **Organizational structure** refers to the formalized arrangement of interaction between and responsibility for the tasks, people, and resources in an organization. It is most often seen as a chart, often a pyramidal chart, with positions or titles and roles in cascading fashion. The organizational structure you and your partners would have in this start-up of which you are a part would most likely be a "simple" organization.

Simple Organizational Structure

In the smallest business enterprise, a simple structure usually prevails. A **simple organizational structure** is one where there is an owner and, usually, a few employees and where the arrangement of tasks, responsibilities, and communication is highly informal and accomplished through direct supervision. All strategic and operating decisions are made by the owner, or a small owner-partner team. Because the scope of the firm's activities are modest, there is little need to formalize roles, communication, and procedures. With the strategic concern primarily being survival, and the likelihood that one bad decision could seriously threaten continued existence, this structure maximizes the owner's control. It can also allow rapid response to product/market shifts and the ability to accommodate unique customer demands without major coordination difficulties. This is in part because the owner is directly involved with customers on a regular basis. Simple structures encourage employees to multitask, and they are efficacious in businesses that serve a simple, local product/market or narrow niche.

The simple structure can be very demanding on the owner-manager. If it is successful, and starts to grow, this can cause the owner-manager to give increased attention to day-to-day concerns, which may come at the expense of time invested in stepping back and examining strategic questions about the company's future. At the same time, the company's reliance on the owner as the central point for all decisions can limit the development of future managers capable of assuming duties that allow the owner time to be a strategist. And, this structure usually requires a multitalented, resourceful owner, good at producing and selling a product or service—and at controlling scarce funds.

Most businesses in this country and around the world are of this type. Many survive for a period of time, then go out of business because of financial, owner, or market conditions. Some grow, having been built on an idea or capability that taps a great need for what the company does. As they grow, the need to "get organized" is increasingly heard among owners and a growing number of employees in the growing company. That fortunate circumstance historically led to the need for a functional organizational structure.

Functional Organizational Structure

Continuing our example, you and your partners, no doubt being among the successful ones, find increased demand for your product or service. Your sales have grown substantially—and so have the number of people you employ to do the work of your business. Once you reach 15 to 25 people in the organization, you will experience a need to have some people handle sales, some operations, a financial accounting person or two—that is, you will need to have different people focus on different functions within the business to become better organized and efficient, and to achieve control and coordination.

functional organizational structure
Structure in which the tasks, people, and technologies necessary to do the work of the business are divided into separate "functional" groups (e.g., marketing, operations, finance) with increasingly formal procedures for coordinating and integrating their activities to provide the business's products and services.

A **functional organizational structure** is one in which the tasks, people, and technologies necessary to do the work of the business are divided into separate "functional" groups (such as marketing, operations, finance) with increasingly formal procedures for coordinating and integrating their activities to provide the business's products and services.

Functional structures predominate in firms with a single or narrow product focus and that have experienced success in their marketplace, leading to increased sales and an increased number of people needed to do the work behind those sales. Such firms require well-defined skills and areas of specialization to build competitive advantages in providing their products or services. Dividing tasks into functional specialties enables the personnel of these firms to concentrate on only one aspect of the necessary work. This allows use of the latest technical skills and develops a high level of efficiency.

Product, customer, or technology considerations determine the identity of the parts in a functional structure. A hotel business might be organized around housekeeping (maids), the front desk, maintenance, restaurant operations, reservations and sales, accounting, and personnel. An equipment manufacturer might be organized around production, engineering/quality control, purchasing, marketing, personnel, and finance/accounting. Two examples of functional organizations are illustrated in Exhibit 11.2.

The strategic challenge presented by the functional structure is effective coordination of the functional units. The narrow technical expertise achieved through specialization can lead to limited perspectives and to differences in the priorities of the functional units. Specialists may see the firm's strategic issues primarily as "marketing" problems or "production" problems. The potential conflict among functional units makes the coordinating role of the chief executive critical. Integrating devices (such as project teams or planning committees) are frequently used in functionally organized firms to enhance coordination and to facilitate understanding across functional areas.

Divisional Structure

When a firm diversifies its product/service lines, covers broad geographic areas, utilizes unrelated market channels, or begins to serve heterogeneous customer groups, a functional

EXHIBIT 11.2
Functional Organization Structures

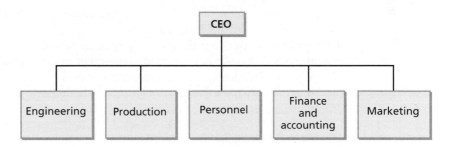

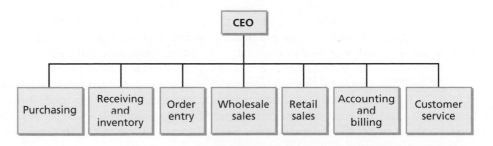

A process-oriented functional structure (an electronics distributor):

Strategic Advantages	Strategic Disadvantages
1. Achieves efficiency through specialization	1. Promotes narrow specialization and functional rivalry or conflict
2. Develops functional expertise	2. Creates difficulties in functional coordination and interfunctional decision making
3. Differentiates and delegates day-to-day operating decisions	3. Limits development of general managers
4. Retains centralized control of strategic decisions	4. Has a strong potential for interfunctional conflict—priority placed on functional areas, not the entire business
5. Tightly links structure to strategy by designating key activities as separate units	5. May cost more to do a function than it does "outside" the company, unless outsourced

structure rapidly becomes inadequate. If a functional structure is retained under these circumstances, production managers may have to oversee the production of numerous and varied products or services, marketing managers may have to create sales programs for vastly different products or sell through vastly different distribution channels, and top management may be confronted with excessive coordination demands. A new organizational structure is often necessary to meet the increased coordination and decision-making requirements that result from increased diversity and size, and the divisional structure is the form often chosen.

A **divisional organizational structure** is one in which a set of relatively autonomous units, or divisions, are governed by a central corporate office but where each operating division has its own functional specialists who provide products or services different from those of other divisions. For many years, global automobile companies have used divisional structures organized by product groups. Manufacturers often organize sales into divisions based on differences in distribution channels.

A divisional structure allows corporate management to delegate authority for the strategic management of distinct business entities—the division. This expedites decision making in response to varied competitive environments and enables corporate management to concentrate on corporate-level strategic decisions. The division usually is given profit responsibility, which facilitates accurate assessment of profit and loss. Exhibit 11.3 illustrates a divisional organizational structure and specifies the strategic advantages and disadvantages of such structures.

Strategic Business Unit

Some firms encounter difficulty in controlling their divisional operations as the diversity, size, and number of these units continues to increase. Corporate management may encounter difficulty in evaluating and controlling its numerous, often multi-industry divisions. Under these conditions, it may become necessary to add another layer of management in order to improve implementation, promote synergy, and gain greater control over the diverse business interests. The **strategic business unit** (SBU) is an adaptation of the divisional structure whereby various divisions or parts of divisions are grouped together based on some common strategic elements, usually linked to distinct product/market differences. General Foods, after originally organizing itself along product lines (which served overlapping markets), created an SBU organization along menu lines with SBUs for breakfast foods, beverages, main meals, desserts, and pet foods. This change allowed General Foods

divisional organizational structure
Structure in which a set of relatively autonomous units, or divisions, are governed by a central corporate office but where each operating division has its own functional specialists who provide products or services different from those of other divisions.

strategic business unit
An adaptation of the divisional structure in which various divisions or parts of divisions are grouped together based on some common strategic elements, usually linked to distinct product/market differences.

EXHIBIT 11.3
Divisional
Organization
Structure

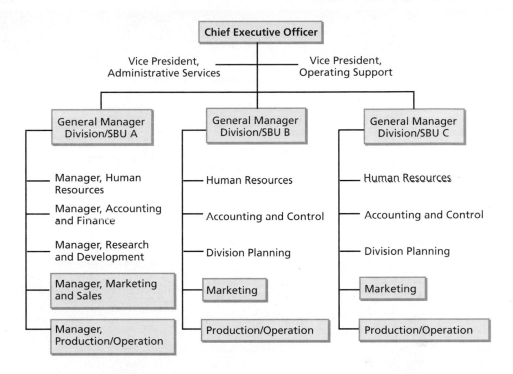

Strategic Advantages	Strategic Disadvantages
1. Forces coordination and necessary authority down to the appropriate level for rapid response	1. Fosters potentially dysfunctional competition for corporate-level resources
2. Places strategy development and implementation in closer proximity to the unique environments of the division	2. Presents the problem of determining how much authority should be given to division managers
3. Frees chief executive officer for broader strategic decision making	3. Creates a potential for policy inconsistencies among divisions
4. Sharply focuses accountability for performance	4. Presents the problem of distributing corporate overhead costs in a way that's acceptable to division managers with profit responsibility
5. Retains functional specialization within each division	5. Increases costs incurred through duplication functions
6. Provides good training ground for strategic managers	6. Creates difficulty maintaining overall corporate image
7. Increases focus on products, markets, and quick response to change	

to adapt a vast divisional organization into five strategic business areas with a distinct market focus for each unit and the divisions each contained.

The advantages and disadvantages of the SBU form are very similar to those identified for divisional structures in Exhibit 11.3. Added to its potential disadvantages would be the increased costs of coordination with another "pricy" level of management. Exhibit 11.4, Strategy in Action, describes how two companies you will easily recognize have recently made key

Changing Organizational Structures to Better Implement a Company's Strategy

Dell founder and CEO Michael Dell recently reorganized its divisions focused on selling to business customers, saying that "customer requirements are increasingly being defined by how they use technology rather than where they use it. That's why we won't let ourselves be limited by geographic boundaries in solving their needs."

So at Dell, instead of three business units focused geographically on the Far East, the Americas, and Europe (including Africa and Middle East), Dell's new business sales unit will be structured based on type of business customer, regardless of global location. Its new structure will have a large enterprise unit, a public unit, and a small and medium business unit. "We have laid the foundation for the transition from a global business that's run regionally to businesses that are really globally organized," said Michael Dell.

GE reduced its business units from six to four, centered around serving what it calls its three "core industries": infrastructure, finance, and media. This decision combines GE's commercial and consumer finance divisions into one unit; splits off its energy infrastructure businesses into a separate unit; and combines the enterprise solutions business with aviation, transportation, and health care. By elevating energy into a separate unit, GE is reflecting the strategic importance of this fast-growing area. Separating infrastructure into two divisions while combining financial services into one signals increased strategic importance on infrastructure while reducing its commitments in the troubled financial services industry.

Nortel CEO Mike Zafirovski recently blogged about the company's decision to abandon its matrix structure in favor of a strategic business unit structure, focusing on being able to make decisions with greater speed: "By having discrete business units and eliminating a complex matrix organization that we have historically operated within, the individual BUs can make quicker decisions, optimize their processes and structures, make strategic partnerships, and adjust technology and market strategy far faster than before . . . As Nortel transforms into this BU formation, we will be a company that has discrete and fully integrated focus on the enterprise evolved market and the next-generation carrier market. Each of those BUs will be lean, focused, and autonomous and with that posture will have an increased capability to make rapid decisions and execute in their markets."

Source: "Reflections on Dell's Latest Reorganization," *Supply Chain Matters,* Bob Ferrari's Blog, www.theferrairgroup.com; GE Reduces Divisions to Four as Immelt Sheds Slow-Growth Units," www.Bloomberg.com, July 26, 2008; and "Mike Z Letter to Nortel Employees," *Nortel BuzzBoard,* www.community.nortel.com, May 11, 2009.

changes in their divisional structures in order to improve their strategy execution. Dell changed from a geographically focused divisional structure to a customer-type divisional structure to be able to improve its sales response. GE collapsed six formerly autonomous, worldwide divisions into three SBUs to intensify its focus on three core areas—infrastructure, finance, and media.

Holding Company

holding company structure
Structure in which the corporate entity is a broad collection of often unrelated businesses and divisions such that it (the corporate entity) acts as financial overseer "holding" the ownership interest in the various parts of the company, but has little direct managerial involvement.

A final form of the divisional organization is the **holding company structure,** where the corporate entity is a broad collection of often unrelated businesses and divisions such that it (the corporate entity) acts as financial overseer "holding" the ownership interest in the various parts of the company but has little direct managerial involvement. Berkshire Hathaway owns a wide variety of businesses in full or in part. Essentially, at the corporate level, it provides financial support and manages each of these businesses, or divisions, through financial goals and annual review of performance, investment needs, and so forth. Otherwise, strategic and operating decisions are made in each separate company or division, which operates autonomously. The corporate office acts simply as a holding company.

This approach can provide a cost savings over the more active SBU approach since the additional level of "pricy" management is not that much. The negative, of course, becomes the degree to which the corporate office is dependent on each business unit's management team and the lack of control over the decisions those managers make in terms of being able to make timely adjustments or corrections.

Matrix Organizational Structure

matrix organizational structure

The matrix organization is a structure in which functional and staff personnel are assigned to both a basic functional area and to a project or product manager. It provides dual channels of authority, performance responsibility, evaluation, and control.

In large companies, increased diversity leads to numerous product and project efforts of major strategic significance. The result is a need for an organizational form that provides skills and resources where and when they are most vital. For example, a product development project needs a market research specialist for two months and a financial analyst one day per week. A customer site application needs a software engineer for one month and a customer service trainer one day per month for six weeks. Each of these situations is an example of a matrix organization that has been used to temporarily put people and resources where they are most needed. Citicorp, Matsushita, Microsoft, IBM, Procter & Gamble (P&G), and Accenture are just a few of many firms that now use some form of matrix organization.

The **matrix organizational structure** is one in which functional and staff personnel are assigned to both a basic functional area and to a project or product manager. It provides dual channels of authority, performance responsibility, evaluation, and control, as shown in Exhibit 11.5. The matrix form is intended to make the best use of talented people within a firm by combining the advantages of functional specialization and product-project specialization.

EXHIBIT 11.5
Matrix Organizational Structure

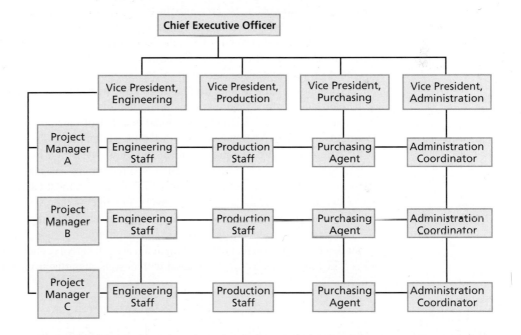

Strategic Advantages	Strategic Disadvantages
1. Accommodates a wide variety of project-oriented business activities	1. May result in confusion and contradictory policies
2. Provides good training ground for strategic managers	2. Necessitates tremendous horizontal and vertical coordination
3. Maximizes efficient use of functional managers	3. Can proliferate information logjams and excess reporting
4. Fosters creativity and multiple sources of diversity	4. Can trigger turf battles and loss of accountability
5. Gives middle management broader exposure to strategic issues	

The matrix structure also increases the number of middle managers who exercise general management responsibilities (through the project manager role) and, thus, broaden their exposure to organizationwide strategic concerns. In this way, the matrix structure overcomes a key deficiency of functional organizations while retaining the advantages of functional specialization.

Although the matrix structure is easy to design, it is difficult to implement. Dual chains of command challenge fundamental organizational orientations. Negotiating shared responsibilities, the use of resources, and priorities can create misunderstanding or confusion among subordinates. These problems are heightened in an international context with the complications introduced by distance, language, time, and culture. Exhibit 11.4, Strategy in Action, also describes how Nortel recently abandoned its matrix structure in favor of an SBU approach due to just these kinds of problems.

Product-Team Structure

product-team structure

Assigns functional managers and specialists to a new product, project, or process team that is empowered to make major decisions about their product. Team members are assigned permanently in most cases.

To avoid the deficiencies that might arise from a permanent matrix structure, some firms are accomplishing particular strategic tasks, by means of a "temporary" or "flexible" *overlay structure*. This approach, used recently by such firms as Motorola, Matsushita, Philips, and Unilever, is meant to take *temporary* advantage of a matrix-type team while preserving an underlying divisional structure. This adaptation of the matrix approach has become known as the "product-team structure." The **product-team structure** seeks to simplify and amplify the focus of resources on a narrow but strategically important product, project, market, customer, or innovation. Exhibit 11.6 illustrates how the product-team structure looks.

The product-team structure assigns functional managers and specialists (e.g., engineering, marketing, financial, R&D, operations) to a new product, project, or process team that is empowered to make major decisions about their product. The team is usually created at the inception of the new-product idea, and they stay with it indefinitely if it becomes a viable business. Instead of being assigned on a temporary basis, as in the matrix structure, team members are assigned permanently to that team in most cases. This results in much lower coordination costs and, because every function is represented, usually reduces the number of management levels above the team level needed to approve team decisions.

It appears that product teams formed at the beginning of product-development processes generate cross-functional understanding that irons out early product or process design problems. They also reduce costs associated with design, manufacturing, and marketing, while

EXHIBIT 11.6
The Product-Team Structure

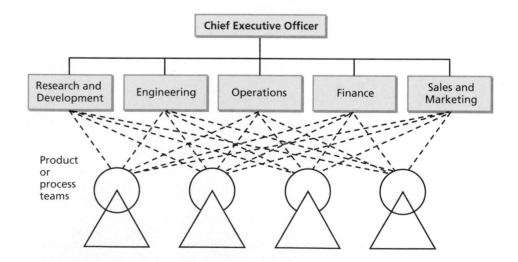

Cross-Functional Teams Add Value in Implementing a Company's Strategy

Monsanto CEO Hugh Grant took over Monsanto when it was a chemical conglomerate, selling for $10 per share. Five years later, it had become a global leading producer of biotech seeds. Within the first 100 days at Monsanto, Grant's management team made the decision to reduce staff and product lines in its chemicals businesses and redirect resources to the new but still unprofitable biotech seeds business. Furthermore, they decided to abandon wheat and focus on corn, soybeans, and cotton. All were very risky bets.

To help enable this transformation of Monsanto to more high-tech, fast-changing lines of business, Grant introduced the extensive use of cross-functional teams. These teams would draw on people from five or six different functional specialties within Monsanto and focus on a specific problem related to new seeds, markets, and or similar issues. That structure accelerated to an ability to commercialize the newest seed technologies, ultimately becoming a strategic advantage at Monsanto and credited with its 12-fold rise in market capitalization.

Bentley College business graduate turned **IBM** Workplace Domain Engineer Sally McSwiney is a prime example of IBM's extensive use of cross-functional teams to become more competitive in a global computer services marketplace. She said this about her role on a cross functional team: "As part of a cross-functional software product development team, I manage product requirements by working with clients, analysts, and experts to adapt the product and strengthen its position. I have regular meetings and discussions with my cross-functional team members located in North Carolina, Massachusetts, and China. And as external communicator for my team, I talk with customers, press, analysts—and provide product demos to audiences worldwide—regularly."[1]

Electronic Arts (EA) CEO Bing Gordon describes how it brings constant new video games to a worldwide customer audience: "At EA, innovative games come from small, cross-functional teams of programmers, designers, artists, development, and marketing people. We have found that the best way to avoide the usual "turf" conflict between development/programming [EA's "operations"] and marketing is to have a cross-functional team leader with experience in both camps."[2]

BMW's CEO Norbert Reithofer has used cross-functional teams to accelerate BMW's ability to create new 3 series cars in a quality, yet recording-setting, time frame. Drawing upon relationships he had built throughout the company in 20+ years from maintenance planner to head of production, he assembled a cross-functional team from R&D and production to design and build the newest 3 series offering in half the normal time necessary to do so. The result continues BMW's strategy of technical excellence and reinforced its competitive advantage in a globally stressed automobile industry.[3]

[1]"Always on the Go at Big Blue," *BusinessWeek,* May 17, 2007.
[2]"Bing Gordon's Game Revealed," *BusinessWeek,* June 26, 2007.
[3]"Managing a Brand: Concept to Product," *BusinessWeek,* October 16, 2006.
Source: www.monsanto.com/careers and www.monsanto.com/who_we_are.

typically speeding up innovation and customer responsiveness because authority rests with the team allowing decisions to be made more quickly. That ability to make speedier, cost-saving decisions has the added advantage of eliminating the need for one or more management layers above the team level, which would traditionally have been in place to review and control these types of decisions. While seemingly obvious, it has only recently become apparent that those additional management layers were also making these decisions with less firsthand understanding of the issues involved than the cross-functional team members brought to the product or process in the first place. Exhibit 11.7, Strategy in Action, gives examples of a product-team approach at several well-known companies and some of the advantages that appear to have accrued.

WHAT A DIFFERENCE A CENTURY MAKES

Exhibit 11.8 offers a useful perspective for designing effective organizational structures in tomorrow's global economy. In contrasting twentieth- and twenty-first-century corporations

EXHIBIT 11.8
What a Difference a Century Can Make

Source: From "21st Century Companies," *Business Week.* Reprinted from August 28, 2000 issue of *Business Week* by special permission. Copyright © 2000 by The McGraw-Hill Companies, Inc.

Contrasting Views of the Corporation		
Characteristic	**20th Century**	**21st Century**
Organization	The pyramid	The Web or network
Focus	Internal	External
Style	Structured	Flexible
Source of strength	Stability	Change
Structure	Self-sufficiency	Interdependencies
Resources	Atoms—physical assets	Bits—information
Operations	Vertical integration	Virtual integration
Products	Mass production	Mass customization
Reach	Domestic	Global
Financials	Quarterly	Real time
Inventories	Months	Hours
Strategy	Top-down	Bottom-up
Leadership	Dogmatic	Inspirational
Workers	Employees	Employees and free agents
Job expectations	Security	Personal growth
Motivation	To compete	To build
Improvements	Incremental	Revolutionary
Quality	Affordable best	No compromise

on different characteristics, it offers a historical or evolutionary perspective on organizational attributes associated with successful strategy execution today and just a few years ago. Successful organizations once required an internal focus, structured interaction, self-sufficiency, a top-down approach. Today and tomorrow, organizational structure reflects an external focus, flexible interaction, interdependency, and a bottom-up approach, just to mention a few characteristics associated with strategy execution and success. Three fundamental trends are driving decisions about effective organizational structures in the twenty-first century: globalization, the Internet, and speed of decision making.

Globalization

Pulitzer Prize–winning author Thomas Friedman[1] described the first 10 years of the twenty-first century as "Globalization 3.0." This, he says, is a whole new era in which the world is shrinking from a size "small" to a size "tiny" and flattening the global playing field for everyone at the same time. He describes it as follows:

> Globalization 1.0 was countries globalizing;
> Globalization 2.0 was companies globalizing;
> Globalization 3.0 is the newfound power for *individuals*
> To collaborate and compete globally, instantly;
> Individuals from every corner of the flat world are
> Being empowered to enter a wide open, global marketplace.[2]

[1] Thomas L. Friedman, *The World Is Flat* (New York: Farrar, Straus and Giroux, 2005).
[2] Ibid, p. 10.

This means that companies in virtually every industry either operate globally (e.g., computers, aerospace) or will soon do so. In the past 15 years, the percentage of sales from outside the home market for these five companies grew dramatically:

	1995	2000	2005	2010 est.
General Electric	16%	35%	41%	55%
Wal-Mart	0	18	32	43
McDonald's	46	65	71	79
Nokia	85	98	99	99+
Toyota	44	53	61	78

The need for global coordination and innovation is forcing constant experimentation and adjustment to get the right mix of local initiative, information flow, leadership, and corporate culture. At Swedish-based Ericsson, top managers scrutinize compensation schemes to make managers pay attention to global performance and avoid turf battles, while also attending to their local operations. Companies such as Dutch electronics giant Philips regularly move headquarters for different businesses to the hottest regions for new trends—the "high voltage" markets. Its digital set-top box is now in California; its audio business moved from Europe to Hong Kong.[3]

Global once meant selling goods in overseas markets. Next was locating operations in numerous countries. Today companies will call on talents and resources wherever they can be found around the globe, just as they now sell worldwide. Such companies may be based in the United States, do their software programming in New Delhi, their engineering in Germany, and their manufacturing in Indonesia. The ramifications for organizational structures are revolutionary.

The Internet

The Net gives everyone in the organization, or working with it—from the lowest clerk to the CEO to any supplier or customer—the ability to access a vast array of information instantaneously, from anywhere. Ideas, requests, and instructions zap around the globe in the blink of an eye. The Net allows the global enterprise with different functions, offices, and activities dispersed around the world to be seamlessly connected so that far-flung customers, employees, and suppliers can work together in real time. The result—coordination, communication, and decision-making functions are accomplished quickly and easily, making traditional organizational structures look slow, inefficient, and noncompetitive.

Speed

Technology, or digitization, means removing human minds and hands from an organization's most routine tasks and replacing them with computers and networks. Digitizing everything from employee benefits to accounts receivable to product design cuts cost, time, and payroll, resulting in cost savings and vast improvements in speed. "Combined with the Internet, the speed of actions, deliberations, and information will increase dramatically," says Intel's Andy Grove. "You are going to see unbelievable speed and efficiencies," says Cisco's John Chambers, "with many companies about to increase productivity 20 percent to 40 percent per year." Leading-edge technologies will enable employees throughout the

[3] Wendy Zellner, "See the World, Erase Its Borders," *BusinessWeek*, August 28, 2000.

organization to seize opportunity as it arises. These technologies will allow employees, suppliers, and freelancers anywhere in the world to converse in numerous languages online without need for a translator to develop markets, new products, new processes. Again, the ramifications for organizational structures are revolutionary.

Whether technology assisted or not, globalization of business activity creates a potential velocity of decision making that challenges traditional hierarchical organizational structures. A company like Cisco, for example, may be negotiating 50 to 60 alliances at one time due to the nature of its diverse operations. The speed at which these negotiations must be conducted and decisions made requires a simple and accommodating organizational structure lest the opportunities may be lost.

Faced with these and other major trends, what are managers doing to structure effective organizations? Let's examine this question two ways. First, we will summarize some key ways managers are changing traditional organizational structures to make them more responsive to this new reality. Second, we will examine current ideas for creating agile, virtual organizations.

INITIAL EFFORTS TO IMPROVE THE EFFECTIVENESS OF TRADITIONAL ORGANIZATIONAL STRUCTURES

Major efforts to improve traditional organizational structures seek to reduce unnecessary control and focus on enhancing core competencies, reducing costs, and opening organizations more fully to outside involvement and influence. One key emphasis in large organizations has been corporate headquarters.

Redefine the Role of Corporate Headquarters from Control to Support and Coordination

The role of corporate management in multibusiness and multinational companies increasingly face a common dilemma: how can the resource advantages of a large company be exploited, while ensuring the responsiveness and creativity found in the small companies against which each of their businesses compete? This dilemma constantly presents managers with conflicting priorities or adjustments as corporate managers:[4]

• Rigorous financial controls and reporting enable cost efficiency, resource deployment, and autonomy across different units; flexible controls are conducive to responsiveness, innovation and "boundary spanning."

• Multibusiness companies historically gain advantage by exploiting resources and capabilities across different businesses and markets, yet competitive advantage in the future increasingly depends on the creation of new resources and capabilities.

• Aggressive portfolio management seeking maximum shareholder value is often best achieved through independent businesses; the creation of competitive advantage increasingly requires the management—recognition and coordination—of business interdependencies.

Increasingly, globally engaged, multibusiness companies are changing the role of corporate headquarters from one of control, resource allocation, and performance monitoring to one of coordinator of linkages across multiple businesses, supporter, and enabler of innovation and synergy. One way this has been done is to create an executive council comprised of top managers from each business, usually including four to five of their key managers,

[4] Robert M. Grant, *Contemporary Strategy Analysis* (Oxford: Blackwell, 2001), p. 503.

with the council then serving as the critical forum for corporate decision, discussions, and analysis. IBM's Sam Palmisano uses this approach today at IBM to cross-fertilize ideas and opportunities across its software, enterprise services, chip design, and now virtual world business activities. These councils replace the traditional corporate staff function of overseeing and evaluating various business units, replacing it instead with a forum to share business unit plans, to discuss problems and issues, to seek assistance and expertise, and to foster cooperation and innovation.

John Chambers's experiment at Cisco provides a useful example. He realized that Cisco's hierarchical structure was precluding it from moving quickly into new markets, so he began to group executives like cross-functional teams. Chambers figured that putting together managers in sales and leaders in engineering would break down walls. It then expanded to be a means to replace corporate executives with "councils" or "boards" composed of three to seven managers from various Cisco businesses and functional areas to quickly find synergies, opportunities, and expedite decisions.[5]

Balance the Demands for Control/Differentiation with the Need for Coordination/Integration

Specialization of work and effort allows a unit to develop greater expertise, focus, and efficiency. So it is that some organizations adopt functional, or similar, structures. Their strategy depends on dividing different activities within the firm into logical, common groupings—sales, operations, administration, or geography—so that each set of activities can be done most efficiently. Control of sets of activities is at a premium. Dividing activities in this manner, sometimes called "differentiation," is an important structural decision. At the same time, these separate activities, however they are differentiated, need to be coordinated and integrated back together as a whole so the business functions effectively. Demands for control and the coordination needs differ across different types of businesses and strategic situations.

The rise of a consumer culture around the world has led brand marketers to realize they need to take a multidomestic approach to be more responsive to local preferences. Coca-Cola, for example, used to control its products rigidly from its Atlanta headquarters. But managers have found in some markets consumers thirst for more than Coke, Diet Coke, and Sprite. So Coke has altered its structure to reduce the need for control in favor of greater coordination/integration in local markets where local managers independently launch new flavored drinks. At the same time, GE, the paragon of new-age organization, had altered its GE Medical Systems organization structure to allow local product managers to handle everything from product design to marketing. This emphasis on local coordination and reduced central control of product design led managers obsessed with local rivalries to design and manufacture similar products for different markets—a costly and wasteful duplication of effort. So GE reintroduced centralized control of product design, with input from a worldwide base of global managers and their customers, resulting in the design of several single global products produced quite cost competitively to sell worldwide. GE's need for control of product design outweighed the coordination needs of locally focused product managers.[6] At the same time, GE obtained input from virtually every customer or potential customer worldwide before finalizing the product design of several initial products, suggesting that it rebalanced in favor of more control, but organizationally coordinated input from global managers and customers so as to ensure a better potential series of medical

---

[5] "Cisco Systems Layers It On," *Fortune*, December 3, 2008.

[6] Zellner, "See the World, Erase Its Borders."

scanner for hospitals worldwide. Virtually all companies serving global markets face a similar organizational puzzle—how does the company integrate itself with diverse markets yet ensure adequate control and differentiation of internal units so that it executes profitably and effectively? We will examine some ways to do so later in this chapter.

Restructure to Emphasize and Support Strategically Critical Activities

restructuring

Redesigning an organizational structure with the intent of emphasizing and enabling activities most critical to a firm's strategy to function at maximum effectiveness.

Restructuring is redesigning an organizational structure with the intent of emphasizing and enabling activities most critical to the firm's strategy to function at maximum effectiveness. At the heart of the restructuring trend is the notion that some activities within a business's value chain are more critical to the success of the business's strategy than others. Wal-Mart's organizational structure is designed to ensure that its impressive logistics and purchasing competitive advantages operate flawlessly. Coordinating daily logistical and purchasing efficiencies among separate stores lets Wal-Mart lead the industry in profitability yet sell retail for less than many competitors buy the same merchandise at wholesale. Motorola's organizational structure is designed to protect and nurture its legendary R&D and new-product development capabilities—spending over twice the industry average in R&D alone each year. Motorola's R&D emphasis continually spawns proprietary technologies that support its technology-based competitive advantage. Coca-Cola emphasizes the importance of distribution activities, advertising, and retail support to its bottlers in its organizational structure. All three of these companies emphasize very different parts of the value chain process, but they are extraordinarily successful in part because they have designed their organizational structures to emphasize and support strategically critical activities. Two developments that have become key ways many of these firms have sought to improve their emphasis and support of strategic activities are business process reengineering and downsizing/self-management.

business process reengineering

A customer-centric restructuring approach. It involves fundamental rethinking and radical redesigning of a business process so that a company can best create value for the customer by eliminating barriers that create distance between employees and customers.

Business process reengineering (BPR) was originally advocated by consultants Michael Hammer and James Champy[7] as a "customer-centric" restructuring approach. BPR is intended to place the decision-making authority that is most relevant to the customer closer to the customer, in order to make the firm more responsive to the needs of the customer. This is accomplished through a form of empowerment, facilitated by revamping organizational structure.

Business reengineering reduces fragmentation by crossing traditional departmental lines and reducing overhead to compress formerly separate steps and tasks that are strategically intertwined in the process of meeting customer needs. This "process orientation," rather than a traditional functional orientation, becomes the perspective around which various activities and tasks are then grouped to create the building blocks of the organization's structure. This is usually accomplished by assembling a multifunctional, multilevel team (the product-team approach discussed earlier) that begins by identifying customer needs and how the customer wants to deal with the firm. Customer focus must permeate all phases. Companies that have successfully reengineered their operations around strategically critical business processes have pursued the following steps:[8]

• Develop a flowchart of the total business process, including its interfaces with other value chain activities.

• Try to simplify the process first, eliminating tasks and steps where possible and analyzing how to streamline the performance of what remains.

[7] Michael Hammer, *The Agenda* (New York: Random House, 2001); and Michael Hammer and James Champy, *Reengineering the Corporation* (New York: HarperBusiness, 1993).

[8] Judy Wade, "How to Make Reengineering Really Work," *Harvard Business Review* 71, no. 6 (November–December 1993), pp. 119–31.

From Reengineering to Reinvention: The IBM Journey to Becoming an "On Demand Business"

Facing a challenge of sheer survival, IBM looked intensely at all of its business processes. Eventually, IBM leveraged the Internet and global connectivity to simplify access to information and enable simple, Web-based transactions. The company integrated processes both within the business and among a group of core clients, partners, and suppliers. For example, IBM created a master database, dubbed the "Blue Monster," of all its service employees—where they were, what they worked on, what their expertise and experiences were, etc. While IBM reaped enormous efficiency gains from these efforts, it saw opportunities to continuously reengineer and challenge long-accepted practices, processes, and organizational structures that limited its—and most other companies'—options in the face of globalization, industry consolidation, and disruptive technologies.

This became a real business opportunity at IBM. IBM chairman and CEO Sam Palmisano dubbed this "On Demand Business," and IBM committed itself to becoming not simply a case study, but a living laboratory for On Demand Business. The company identified key business characteristics—horizontally integrated, flexible, and responsive—and the IT infrastructure needed to produce its enterprise transformation—integrated, open, virtualized, and autonomic. IBM focused on tackling the complex issues surrounding significant changes to essential business processes, organizational culture, and IT infrastructure and worked to find new ways to access, deploy, and finance solutions.

Today, IBM is hitting a new stride. A powerful combination of innovation and value creation is driving top-line revenue growth. Client satisfaction is climbing. And the company continues to operate in a highly disciplined manner, focusing on increased productivity and IT optimization to drive bottom-line earnings. Because this is precisely the type of growth that tops the majority of CEOs' agendas, many will find IBM's story particularly timely and relevant. IBM has gone from doing this for its top 25 clients in seven countries to more than 750 global companies—and the number is only rising as IBM moves forward.

Source: http://www-03.ibm.com/industries/healthcare/doc/content/resource/insight/1591291105.html?g_type=rssfeed_leaf

- Determine which parts of the process can be automated (usually those that are repetitive, time-consuming, and require little thought or decision); consider introducing advanced technologies that can be upgraded to achieve next-generation capability and provide a basis for further productivity gains down the road.

- Evaluate each activity in the process to determine whether it is strategy-critical or not. Strategy-critical activities are candidates for benchmarking to achieve best-in-industry or best-in-world performance status—and ones to emphasize in reengineered organizational structures.

- Weigh the pros and cons of outsourcing activities that are noncritical or that contribute little to organizational capabilities and core competencies.

- Design a structure for performing the activities that remain; reorganize the personnel and groups who perform these activities into the new structure.

IBM provides a good example of reengineering. As globalization started to take hold in the world's economy, IBM was struggling to survive. To do so, it embraced reengineering—with efforts designed to simplify its enormous complexity associated with its highly decentralized organization. Said its CEO at the time, "It's called reengineering. It's called getting competitive. It's called reducing cycle time and cost, flattening organizations, increasing customer responsiveness. All of this requires close collaboration with the customer, with suppliers, and with vendors." The effort saved IBM, and continues to this day. CEO Sam Palmisano observed the following payoff as IBM gained efficiencies, and that has now led to IBM adopting its reengineering experiences into a new business service which IBM calls On Demand Business, as described in Exhibit 11.9, Strategy in Action.

Top Strategist
John Byrne, *BusinessWeek*

Exhibit
11.10

Delayering and empowering—what are some key questions, and answers?

Question	Answer
How many management layers between the CEO and the work level?	Many large companies had up to 12; most have cut that to 4 or 5; above 6 is seen as excess now.
What is the new span of control?	Many companies see up to 1 manager for 30 subordinates; 1:8 or less is seen as excess now.
How much work or how many tasks are cut when delayering and empowering?	Part of delayering is eliminating unnecessary or redundant work. Should see management tasks reduced by 25 percent to 50 percent in a successful effort.
What skills are key for remaining managers and work teams?	The skill to accept more responsibility and the ability to identify and eliminate unneeded work.
How large should your largest profit center be?	Some argue, even in the biggest firm, that breaking operating units into less than 500 people is wise . . . gaining entrepreneurial tendencies and loosing bureaucracy.
What should happen at corporate headquarters given fewer layers?	Surprisingly, to some, the largest reductions on a percentage basis should come at corporate headquarters. It is typically overstaffed, and far from customers.

Source: John Byrne, "The 21st Century Corporation," *BusinessWeek,* August 28, 2000.

downsizing
Eliminating the number of employees, particularly middle management, in a company.

self-management
Allowing work groups or work teams to supervise and administer their work as a group or team without a direct supervisor exercising the supervisory role. These teams set parameters of their work, make decisions about work-related matters, and perform most of the managerial functions previously done by their direct supervisor.

IBM has developed a system that lets it shift work to the areas with available skills at the lowest-available costs. The goal is to deliver higher-quality services at competitive prices. Clearly one opportunity associated with globalization is costs. You have access to expertise wherever it is in the world—if you have the infrastructure and the relationships to take advantage of it.[9]

Downsizing and self-management at operating levels are additional ways companies restructure critical activities. **Downsizing** is eliminating the number of employees, particularly middle management, in a company. The arrival of a global marketplace, information technology, and intense competition caused many companies to reevaluate middle management activities to determine just what value was really being added to the company's products and services. The result of this scrutiny, along with continuous improvements in information processing technology, has been widespread downsizing of the number of management personnel in thousands of companies worldwide. *BusinessWeek's* John Byrne has spent years observing downsizing, delayering, and self-management in leading global companies. A synthesis of his observations are shown in Exhibit 11.10, Top Strategist.

One of the outcomes of downsizing was increased **self-management** at operating levels of the company. Cutbacks in the number of management people left those who

[9] Steve Hamm, "Big Blue Wields the Knife Again," *BusinessWeek,* May 30, 2007.

remained with more work to do. The result was that remaining managers had to give up a good measure of control to operating personnel. Spans of control, traditionally thought to maximize at under 10 people, have become much larger due to information technology, running "lean and mean," and delegation to lower levels. Ameritech, for example, has seen its spans of control rise to as much as 30 to 1 in some divisions because most of the people who did staff work—financial analysts, assistant managers, and so on—have disappeared. This delegation, also known as *empowerment,* is accomplished through concepts such as self-managed work groups, reengineering, and automation. It is also seen through efforts to create distinct businesses within a business—conceiving a business as a confederation of many "small" businesses, rather than one large, interconnected business. Whatever the terminology, the idea is to push decision making down in the organization by allowing major management decisions to be made at operating levels. The result is often the elimination of up to half the levels of management previously existing in an organizational structure.

CREATING AGILE, VIRTUAL ORGANIZATIONS

virtual organization
A temporary network of independent companies—suppliers, customers, subcontractors, and even competitors—linked primarily by information technology to share skills, access to markets, and costs.

agile organization
A firm that identifies a set of business capabilities central to high-profitability operations and then builds a virtual organization around those capabilities.

outsourcing
Obtaining work previously done by employees inside the companies from sources outside the company.

Corporations today are increasingly seeing their "structure" become an elaborate network of external and internal relationships. This organizational phenomenon has been termed the **virtual organization,** which is defined as a temporary network of independent companies—suppliers, customers, subcontractors, even competitors—linked primarily by information technology to share skills, access to markets, and costs.[10] An **agile organization** is one that identifies a set of business capabilities central to high-profitability operations and then builds a virtual organization around those capabilities, allowing the agile firm to build its business around the core, high-profitability information, services, and products. Creating an agile, virtual organization structure involves outsourcing, strategic alliances, a boundaryless structure, an ambidextrous learning approach, and Web-based organization. Let's examine each of the approaches to creating a virtual organization in more detail.

Outsourcing—Creating a Modular Organization

Outsourcing was an early driving force for the virtual organization trend. Dell does not make PCs. Cisco doesn't make its world renowned routers. Motorola doesn't make cell phones. **Outsourcing** is simply obtaining work previously done by employees inside the companies from sources outside the company. Managers have found that as they attempt to restructure their organizations, particularly if they do so from a business process orientation, numerous activities can often be found in their company that are not "strategically critical activities." This has particularly been the case with numerous staff activities and administrative control processes previously the domain of various middle management levels in an organization. But it can also refer to primary activities that are steps in their business's value chain—purchasing, shipping, manufacturing, and so on. Further scrutiny has led managers to conclude that these activities either add little or no value to the product or services, or that they can be done much more cost effectively (and competently) by other businesses specializing in these activities. If this is so, then the business can enhance its competitive advantage by outsourcing the activities.

[10] W. H. Davidow and M. S. Malone, *The Virtual Corporation* (New York: Harper, 1992); and Steven Goldman, *Agile Competitors and Virtual Organizations* (New York: Van Nostrand Reinhold, 1995).

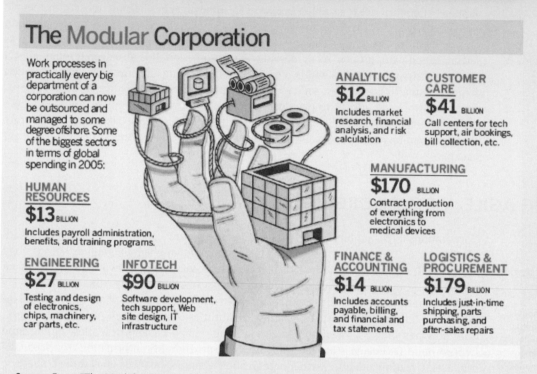

The Modular Corporation

Work processes in practically every big department of a corporation can now be outsourced and managed to some degree offshore. Some of the biggest sectors in terms of global spending in 2005:

HUMAN RESOURCES

$13 BILLION

Includes payroll administration, benefits, and training programs.

ENGINEERING

$27 BILLION

Testing and design of electronics, chips, machinery, car parts, etc.

INFOTECH

$90 BILLION

Software development, tech support, Web site design, IT infrastructure

ANALYTICS

$12 BILLION

Includes market research, financial analysis, and risk calculation

CUSTOMER CARE

$41 BILLION

Call centers for tech support, air bookings, bill collection, etc.

MANUFACTURING

$170 BILLION

Contract production of everything from electronics to medical devices

FINANCE & ACCOUNTING

$14 BILLION

Includes accounts payable, billing, and financial and tax statements

LOGISTICS & PROCUREMENT

$179 BILLION

Includes just-in-time shipping, parts purchasing, and after-sales repairs

Source: From "The Modular Corporation," *BusinessWeek*. Reprinted from January 30, 2006 issue of *BusinessWeek* by special permission. Copyright © 2006 by The McGraw-Hill Companies, Inc.

modular organization

An organization structured via outsourcing where the organization's final product or service is based on the combination of several companies' self-contained skills and business capabilities.

Choosing to outsource activities has been likened to creating a "modular" organization. A **modular organization** provides products or services using different, self-contained specialists or companies brought together—outsourced—to contribute their primary or support activity to result in a successful outcome. Dell is a "modular" organization because it uses outsourced manufacturers and assemblers to provide parts and assemble its computers. It also uses outsourced customer service providers in different parts of the world to provide most of its customer service and support activities. These outsourced providers are independent companies, many of which offer similar services to other companies including, in some cases, Dell's competitors. Dell remains the umbrella organization and controlling organization in fact and certainly in the customers' mind, yet it is able to do so based on putting together a variety of "modules" or parts because of its ability to provide computers and related services through extensive dependence on outsourcing.

Many organizations long ago started outsourcing functions like payroll and benefits administration—routine administrative functions more easily and cost effectively done by a firm specializing in that activity. But outsourcing today has moved into virtually every aspect of what a business does to provide the products and services it exists to provide. Exhibit 11.11, Top Strategist, shows the biggest sectors for outsourcing so far. And not only large companies are involved. Veteran entrepreneur and co-founder of Celestial

Seasonings, Wyck Hay, has returned from retirement to build a new company, Kaboom Beverages, in California. What is interesting is that Hay, like many entrepreneurs today, is building a totally modular organization. Every function in Kaboom Beverages is outsourced to a variety of specialists and specialized companies. Indeed, one of the drivers for outsourcing to create a modular organization is to be able to combine world-class talent, wherever it resides, into a company's ability to deliver the best product and service it can.

Boeing opened its own engineering center in Moscow, where it employs 1,100 skilled but relatively inexpensive aerospace engineers to design parts of the 787 Dreamliner. It also has Japanese, Korean, and European companies making various parts of that critical new plane. Chicago-based law firm Baker and Mckenzie has its own English-speaking team in Manila that drafts documents and does market research. Bank of America (BoA) has its own India subsidiary, but also teamed up with InfoSys and Tata Consultancies—BoA estimates that it has saved almost $200 million in IT work in their first two years, while improving product quality at the same time.

business process outsourcing

Having an outside company manage numerous routine business management activities previously done by employees inside the company such as HR, supply procurement, finance and accounting, customer care, supply-chain logistics, engineering, R&D, sales and marketing, facilities management, and management/ development.

Business process outsourcing (BPO) is the most rapidly growing segment of the outsourcing services industry worldwide. BPO includes a broad array of administrative functions—HR, supply procurement, finance and accounting, customer care, supply-chain logistics, engineering, research and development, sales and marketing, facilities management and even management training and development.[11] Earlier this decade, IBM strategist Bruce Harreld estimated that the world's companies spend about $19 trillion each year on sales, general, and administrative expenses. Only $14 trillion-worth of this, he estimated, has been outsourced to other firms. He further expected that many of the advantages in scale, wage rates, and productivity found when manufacturing was outsourced will quickly emerge driving a rapid increase in BPO over the next 10 years.[12] Many big companies estimate they could outsource half or more of this work currently done in-house. Similarly, banking services currently deliver less than 1 percent of their services remotely—a major global outsourcing opportunity.[13]

Perhaps the more controversial outsourcing trends involve product design and even innovation activities. Particularly in consumer electronics markets, companies such as Dell, Motorola, and Philips are buying complete designs of some digital devices from Asian developers, tweaking them to their own specifications, and just adding their brand name before selling or having a more effective sales channel sell the product for them. This trend seems to be spreading. Boeing works with an Indian software company to develop its software for landing gear, navigation systems, and cockpit controls in its newest planes. Procter & Gamble, the consummate innovator, wants half of its new-product ideas by 2010 to come from outside the company—outsourced R&D or innovation—versus 20 percent right now. Eli Lilly has outsourced selected biotech research for new drugs to an Asian biotech research firm. Consider this comment in a recent *BusinessWeek* article:

> The result is a rethinking of the structure of the modern corporation. What, specifically, has to be done in-house anymore? At a minimum, most leading Western companies are turning toward a new model of innovation, one that employs global networks of partners. These can include U.S. chipmakers, Taiwanese engineers, Indian software developers, and Chinese factories. IBM is even offering the smarts of its famed research labs and a new global

---

[11] Pete Engardio and Bruce Einhorn, "Outsourcing Innovation," *BusinessWeek,* March 21, 2005.

[12] "A World of Work," *The Economist,* November 11, 2004.

[13] "Time to Bring It Back," *The Economist,* March 3, 2005.

team of 1,200 engineers to help customers develop future products using next-generation technologies. When the whole chain works in sync, there can be a dramatic leap in the speed and efficiency of product development.[14]

Outsourcing as a means to create an agile, virtual organization has many potential advantages:

1. *It can lower costs incurred when the activity outsourced is done in-house.*

An accountant with a masters degree from UGA working for Ernst & Young in Atlanta, Georgia, costs E&Y $75,000 annually. Her colleague with the same education returning to her native Philippines to live, works on a similar E&Y audit team in Southeast Asia and via the Internet in the United States—$7,000 annual salary.

2. *It can reduce the amount of capital a firm must invest in production or service capacity.*

Lenovo will cover the capital expenditure for its new Chinese PC manufacturing facilities; IBM will not. IBM will sell Lenovo its existing PC manufacturing facilities around the world, freeing up that capital for investment in IBM's development of its own core competencies, and just buy PCs very cheaply from Lenovo as it needs them. It will include a markup in doing so to pass along to its IT management services clients.

3. *The firm's managers and personnel can concentrate on mission-critical activities.*

As noted in the preceding example, not only does IBM free up capital, but it frees up its people and remaining capital to focus more intensely on its new emphasis on IT systems, BPO, and consulting.

4. *This concentration and focus allow the firm to control and enhance the source of its core competitive advantage.*

Dell outsources the manufacture of its computers. It carefully controls and continuously improves its Web-based direct sales capability so that it increasingly distances itself from the closest competitors. It is able to build such a strong direct sales capability because that is virtually all it concentrates on, even though it is a computer company.

5. *Careful selection of outsourced partners allows the firm to potentially learn and develop its abilities through ideas and capabilities that emerge from the growing expertise and scope of work done by the outsource partner for several firms.*

Outsourced cell phone manufacturers in Korea and Taiwan have become large providers to several large, global cell phone companies. Their product design prototypes and improvements for one client quickly find their way to the attention of other clients. Their improvement in logistics with some firms becomes knowledge incorporated in their dealings with another client.

Outsourcing is not without its "cons," however. There are several:

1. *Outsourcing involves loss of some control and reliance on "outsiders."*

By definition, outsourcing places control of that function or activity "outside" the requesting firm. This loss of control can result in many future problems such as delays, quality issues, customer complaints, and loss of competitor-sensitive information. Recent thefts of personal ID information from U.S.–based bank clients using major information management outsourcing services from Indian companies have caused major problems for the banks obtaining these services.

---

[14] Engardio and Einhorn, "Outsourcing Innovation."

2. *Outsourcing can create future competitors.*

Companies that supply the firm with basic IT services or software programming assistance or product design services may one day move "up the chain" to undertake the higher level work the firm was attempting to reserve for itself. IBM has outsourced considerable work to Indian companies related to its "value-added" IT system management services—its strategic future. It now is experiencing competition from some of these former suppliers of programming support that have become multi-billion-dollar software and IT service providers in their own right.

3. *Skills important to a product or service are "lost."*

While things a company does may not be considered essential to its core competency, they still may be quite important. And as it continues over time to outsource that activity, it loses any capacity in the firm of being able to do it effectively. That, potentially, leaves the company vulnerable.

4. *Outsourcing may cause negative reaction from the public and investors.*

Outsourcing manufacturing, tech support, and back-office work may make sense to investors, but product design and innovation? Asking what value the company is providing and protecting will be an obvious potential reaction. Publicly, the loss of jobs from home country to low-cost alternative locations represents difficult job losses and transitions for people who bring political heat.

5. *Crafting good legal agreements, especially for services, is difficult.*

When outsourced manufacturers send product, you take delivery, inspect, and pay. When service providers supply a service, it is a continuous process. Bottom line: it takes considerable trust and cross-cultural understanding to work.

6. *The company may get locked into long-term contracts at costs that are no longer competitive.*

Multiyear IT management contracts can be both complex and based on costs that are soon noncompetitive because of other sources providing much more cost-effective solutions.

7. *Cost aren't everything: What if my supplier underbids?*

EDS (Dallas, Texas) has a multiyear contract as an outsource provider to the U.S. Navy to provide IT services and consolidate 70,000 different IT systems. Two years into the contract, in 2005, it was $1.5 billion in the red. It hopes to make that heavy loss up over the life of the contract. But what if it was a smaller company and couldn't afford to carry a loss for a contract it poorly bid?

8. *Outsourcing can lead to increasingly fragmented work cultures where low-paid workers get the work done with little initiative or enthusiasm.*

"A mercenary may shoot a gun the same as a soldier, but he will not create a revolution, build a new society, or die for the homeland," says a Silicon Valley manager who objects to his company's turning to contract workers for services.[15]

Its potential disadvantages not withstanding, outsourcing has become a key, standard means by which agile, virtual organization structures are built. It has become an essential building block; most firms in any market anywhere in the world structure some of their business activities to allow them to remain cost competitive, dynamic, and able to develop their future core competencies. As outsourcing moves from sourcing manufacturing and IT management to all business management processes, careful attention and efforts to

---

[15] "Time to Bring It Back," *The Economist,* March 3, 2005.

build trust and cross-cultural understanding will be important as will effective contractual arrangements to govern multiyear, ongoing relationships.

Strategic Alliances

strategic alliances
Alliances with suppliers, partners, contractors, and other providers that allow partners in the alliance to focus on what they do best, farm out everything else, and quickly provide value to the customer.

Strategic alliances are arrangements between two or more companies in which they both contribute capabilities, resources, or expertise to a joint undertaking, usually with an identity of its own, with each firm giving up overall control in return for the potential to participate in and benefit from the joint venture relationship. They are different from outsourcing relationships because the requesting company usually retains control when outsourcing, whereas strategic alliances involve firms giving up overall control to the joint entity, or alliance, in which they become a partner. Texas-based EDS was awaiting word at the time of this writing on whether the "Atlas Consortium" would be awarded a 10-year, $7.6 billion contract to manage 150,000 computers and networking software for British military personnel. The Atlas Consortium is a strategic alliance, formed by EDS as the "lead" firm with the Dutch firm LogicaCMG and a British subsidiary of the defense company, EADS, as full partners. While EDS is the "lead" member of the alliance, final control of the alliance rests not in EDS but in the governance that all three partners have the right to influence and shape.

This is a good example of a strategic alliance—three different firms all with other major business commitments and activities. They have joined together, investing time, analysis resources, and negotiations so as to be in a position to bid as a team (or alliance) on a major 10-year contract. In a few weeks they will know. If they get the contract, then their alliance will have a lengthy commitment to the British military and their firms to the Atlas Consortium. If they don't, then they may or may not work together to pursue other deals. But this relationship allowed each firm to seek work it could not have otherwise pursued independently because of restrictions imposed by the British government, the limitations of each firm individually, or both. It expanded the exposure of each firm to the other, to selected markets, to the building of relationships that may be usefully leveraged in each company's interests in the future.

Strategic alliances can be for long-term or for very short periods. Engaging in alliances, whether long-term or one time, lets each participant take advantage of fleeting opportunities quickly, usually without tying up vast amounts of capital. Strategic alliances allow companies with world-class capabilities to partner together in a way that combines different core competencies so that within the alliance each can focus on what they do best, but the alliance can pull together what is necessary to quickly provide superior value to the customer. FedEx and the U.S. Postal Service have formed an alliance—FedEx planes carry USPS next-day letters and USPS delivers FedEx ground packages—to allow both to challenge their common rival, UPS.

Strategic alliances have the following pros and cons for firms seeking agile, responsive organizational structures:

Advantages

1. *Leverages several firms' core competencies.*

This allows alliance members to be more competitive in seeking certain project work or input.

2. *Limits capital investment.*

One partner firm does not have to have all the resources necessary to do the work of the alliance.

3. *Is flexible.*

Alliances allow a firm to be involved yet continue to pursue its other, "regular" business opportunities.

4. *Leads to networking and relationship building.*

Alliances get companies together, sometimes even competitors. They allow key players to build relationships that are valuable, even if the present alliance doesn't "pan out." Alliance partners learn more about each others' capabilities and gain advantage or benefit from referrals and other similar behaviors, creating win–win situations.

Disadvantages

1. *Can result in loss of control.*

A firm in an alliance by definition cedes ultimate control to the broader alliance for the undertaking for which the alliance is formed. This can prove problematic if the alliance doesn't work out as planned—or is not well planned.

2. *Can be hard to establish good management control of the project—loss of operational control.*

Where multiple firms have interrelated responsibilities for a sizable joint project, it should not be difficult to imagine problems arising as the players go about implementing a major project as in the example of EDS and its Dutch and British partners in the Atlas Consortium. It requires good up-front planning and use of intercompany project team groups early on in the bidding process.

3. *Can distract a participating company's management and key players.*

One strategic alliance can consume the majority attention of key players essential to the overall success of the "home" company. Whether because of their technical skills, managerial skills, key roles, or all three, the potential for lost focus or time to devote to key responsibilities exists.

4. *Raises issues of control of proprietary information and intellectual property.*

Where technology development is the focus of the alliance, or maybe part of it, firms partnered together may also compete in other circumstances. Or they may have the potential to do so. So partnering together gives each the opportunity to learn much more about the other, their contacts, capabilities, and unique skills or trade secrets.

Strategic alliances have proven a very popular mechanism for many companies seeking to become more agile competitors in today's dynamic global economy. They have proven a major way for small companies to become involved with large players to the benefit of both—allowing the smaller player to grow in a way that builds its future survival possibilities and the larger player to tap expertise and knowledge it can no longer afford to retain or develop in-house.

Toward Boundaryless Structures

boundaryless organization

Organizational structure that allows people to interface with others throughout the organization without need to wait for a hierarchy to regulate that interface across functional, business, and geographic boundaries.

Management icon Jack Welch coined the term **boundaryless organization** to characterize his vision of what he wanted GE to become: to be able to generate knowledge, share knowledge, and get knowledge to the places it could be best used to provide superior value. A key component of this concept was erasing internal divisions so the people in GE could work across functional, business, and geographic boundaries to achieve an integrated diversity—the ability to transfer the best ideas, the most developed knowledge, and the most valuable people quickly, easily, and freely throughout GE. Here is his description:

> Boundaryless behavior is the soul of today's GE . . . Simply put, people seem compelled to build layers and walls between themselves and others, and that human tendency tends to be magnified in large, old institutions like ours. These walls cramp people, inhibit creativity, waste time, restrict vision, smother dreams and above all, slow things down . . . Boundaryless

behavior shows up in actions of a woman from our Appliances Business in Hong Kong helping NBC with contacts needed to develop satellite television service in Asia . . . And finally, boundaryless behavior means exploiting one of the unmatchable advantages a multibusiness GE has over almost any other company in the world. Boundaryless behavior combines 12 huge global businesses—each number one or number two in its markets—into a vast laboratory whose principal product is new ideas, coupled with a common commitment to spread them throughout the Company.

> —*Letter to Shareholders, Jack Welch,*
> *chairman, General Electric Company, 1981–2001*

horizontal boundaries
Rules of communication, access, and protocol for dealing with different departments or functions or processes within an organization.

Boundaries, or borders, arise in four "directions" based on the ways we traditionally structure and run organizations:

1. **Horizontal boundaries**—between different departments or functions in a firm. Salespeople are different from administrative people or operating people or engineering people. One division is separate from another.
2. **Vertical boundaries**—between operations and management, and levels of management; between "corporate" and "division," in virtually every organization.
3. **Geographic boundaries**—between different physical locations; between different countries or regions of the world (or even within a country) and between cultures.
4. **External interface boundaries**—between a company and its customers, suppliers, partners, regulators, and, indeed, its competitors.

vertical boundaries
Limitations on interaction, contact, and access between operations and management personnel; between different levels of management; and between different organizational parts like corporate versus divisional units.

geographic boundaries
Limitations on interaction and contact between people in a company based on being at different physical locations domestically and globally.

external interface boundaries
Formal and informal rules, locations, and protocol that separate and/or dictate the interaction between members of an organization and those outside the organization—customers, suppliers, partners, regulators, associations, and even competitors.

Outsourcing, strategic alliances, product-team structures, reengineering, restructuring—all are ways to move toward boundaryless organization. Culture and shared values across an organization that value boundaryless behavior and cooperation help enable these efforts to work.

As we noted at the beginning of this section, globalization has accelerated many changes in the way organizations are structured, and that is certainly driving the recognition by many organizations of their need to become more boundaryless, to become an agile, virtual organization. Technology, particularly driven by the Internet, has and will be a major driver of the boundaryless organization. Commenting on technology's effect on Cisco, John Chambers observed that with all its outsourcing and strategic alliances, roughly 90 percent of all orders come into Cisco without ever being touched by human hands. "To my customers, it looks like one big virtual plant where my suppliers and inventory systems are directly tied into our virtual organization," he said. "That will be the norm in the future. Everything will be completely connected, both within a company and between companies. We will become boundaryless. The people who get that will have a huge competitive advantage."[16]

The Web's contribution electronically has simultaneously become the best analogy in explaining the future boundaryless organization. And it is not just the Web as in the Internet, but a weblike shape of successful organizational structures in the future. If there are a pair of images that symbolize the vast changes at work, they are the pyramid and the web. The organizational chart of large-scale enterprise had long been defined as a pyramid of ever-shrinking layers leading to an omnipotent CEO at its apex. The twenty-first-century corporation, in contrast, is far more likely to look like a web: a flat, intricately woven form that links partners, employees, external contractors, suppliers, and customers in various collaborations. The players will grow more and more interdependent. Fewer companies will try to master all the disciplines necessary to produce and market their goods but will instead

---

[16] Peter Burrows, "Can Cisco Shift into Higher Gear?" *BusinessWeek Online,* October 4, 2004.

EXHIBIT 11.12
From Traditional Structure to B-Web Structure

Source: Reprinted by permission of Harvard Business School Publishing. Exhibit from *Digital Capital: Harnessing the Power of Business Webs,* by Don Tapscott, David Ticoll and Alex Lowy. Copyright 1993 by the Harvard Business School Publishing Corporation; all rights reserved.

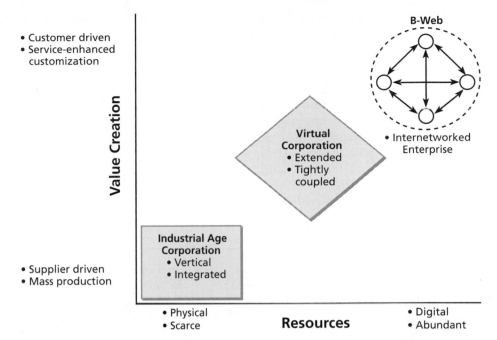

outsource skills—from research and development to manufacturing—to outsiders who can perform those functions with greater efficiency.[17]

Exhibit 11.12 illustrates this evolution in organization structure to what it calls the B-Web, a truly Internet-driven form of organization designed to deliver speedy, customized, service-enhanced products to savvy customers from an integrated boundaryless B-Web organization, pulling together abundant, world-class resources digitally. Take Colgate-Palmolive. The company needed a more efficient method for getting its toothpaste into the tube—a seemingly straightforward problem. When its internal R&D team came up empty-handed, the company posted the specs on InnoCentive, one of many new marketplaces that link problems with problem-solvers. A Canadian engineer named Ed Melcarek proposed putting a positive charge on fluoride powder, then grounding the tube. It was an effective application of elementary physics, but not one that Colgate-Palmolive's team of chemists had ever contemplated. Melcarek was duly rewarded with $25,000 for a few hours' work. Today, some 120,000 scientists like Melcarek have registered with InnoCentive and hundreds of companies pay annual fees of roughly $80,000 to tap the talents of a global scientific community. Launched as an e-business venture by U.S. pharmaceutical giant Eli Lilly, the company now provides on-demand solutions to innovation-hungry titans such as Boeing, Dow, DuPont, P&G, and Novartis.[18]

Managing this intricate network of partners, spin-off enterprises, contractors, and free-lancers will be as important as managing internal operations. Indeed, it will be hard to tell the difference. All of these constituents will be directly linked in ways that will make it nearly impossible for outsiders to know where an individual firm begins and where it ends. "Companies will be much more molecular and fluid," predicts Don Tapscott, co-author of *Digital Capital.* "They will be autonomous business units connected not necessarily by a

[17] John Byrne, "The 21st Century Organization," *BusinessWeek,* August 28, 2000.
[18] www.innocentive.com.

big building but across geographies all based on networks. The boundaries of the firm will be not only fluid or blurred but in some cases hard to define.[19]

Ambidextrous Learning Organizations

The evolution of the virtual organizational structure as an integral mechanism managers use to implement strategy has brought with it recognition of the central role knowledge plays in this process. *Knowledge* may be in terms of operating know-how, relationships with and knowledge of customer networks, technical knowledge upon which products or processes are based or will be, relationships with key people or a certain person that can get things done quickly, and so forth. Consulting firm McKinsey's organizational expert, Lowell Bryan, and co-author Claudia Joyce, describe the role of knowledge in effective organizational structures this way:

> We believe that the centerpiece of corporate strategy for most large companies should become the redesign of their organizations. We believe this for a very simple reason—it's where the money is.
>
> Let us explain. Most companies today were designed for the 20th century. By remaking them to mobilize the mind power of their 21st century workforces, these companies will be able to tap into the presently underutilized talents, knowledge, relationships, and skills of their employees, which will open up to them not only new opportunities but also vast sources of new wealth.[20]

Bryan and Joyce see this shaping future organizational structure with managers becoming knowledge "nodes" through which intricate networks of personal relationships—inside and outside the formal organization—are constantly coordinated to bring together relevant know-how and successful action.

A shift from what Subramanian Rangan calls *exploitation to exploration* indicates the growing importance of organizational structures that enable a **learning organization** to allow global companies the chance to build competitive advantage.[21] Rather than going to markets to exploit brands or for inexpensive resources, in Rangan's view, the smart ones are going global to learn. This shift in the intent of the structure, then, is to seek information, to create new competences. Demand in another part of the world could be a new-product trendsetter at home. So a firm's structure needs to be organized to enable learning, to share knowledge, to create opportunities to create it. Others look to companies like 3M or Procter & Gamble that allow slack time, new-product champions, manager mentors—all put in place in the structure to provide resources, support, and advocacy for cross-functional collaboration leading to innovation in new-product development, and the generation and use of new ideas. This perspective is similar to the boundaryless notion—accommodate the speed of change and therefore opportunity by freeing up historical constraints found in traditional organizational approaches. So having structures that emphasize coordination over control, that allow flexibility (are **ambidextrous**), that emphasize the value and importance of informal relationships and interaction over formal systems, techniques, and controls are all characteristics associated with what are seen as effective structures for the twenty-first century.

---

learning organization

Organization structured around the idea that it should be set up to enable learning, to share knowledge, to seek knowledge, and to create opportunities to create new knowledge. It would move into new markets to learn about those markets rather than simply to bring a brand to it, or find resources to exploit in it.

ambidextrous organization

Organization structure most notable for its lack of structure wherein knowledge and getting it to the right place quickly are the key reasons for organization. Managers become knowledge "nodes" through which intricate networks of personal relationships—inside and outside the formal organization—are constantly, and often informally, coordinated to bring together relevant know-how and successful action.

---

[19] Ibid.

[20] Lowell L. Bryan, and Claudia I. Joyce (McKinsey and Company), *Mobilizing Minds* (New York: McGraw-Hill, 2007), p. 1.

[21] Subramanian Rangan, *A Prism on Globalization* (Fountainebleau, France: INSEAD, 1999).

Summary

This chapter has examined ways organizations are structured and ways to make those structures most effective. It described five traditional organizational structures–simple organization, functional structure, divisional structure, matrix structure, and product-team structure. Simple structures are often found in small companies, where tight control is essential to survival. Functional structures take advantage of the specialization of work by structuring the organization into interconnected units like sales, operations, and accounting/finance. This approach generates more efficiency, enhances functional skills over time, and is perhaps the most pervasive organizational structure. Coordination and conflict across functional units are the perpetual challenge in functional structures.

As companies grow they add products, services, and geographic locations, which leads to the need for divisional structures which divide the organization into units along one or more of these three lines. This division of the business into units with common settings increases focus and allows each division to operate more like an independent business itself. That in turn can generate competition for corporate-level resources and potentially loose consistency and image corporatewide. Companies that work intensely with certain clients or projects created the matrix organization structure to temporarily assign functional specialists to those activities while having them remain accountable to their "home" functional unit. The product-team structure has evolved from the matrix approach, where functional specialists' assignments can be for an extended time and usually center around creating a functionally balanced team to take charge of a new-product idea from generation to production, sales, and market expansion. This approach has been found to create special synergy, teamwork, and cooperation because these specialists are together building a new revenue stream from its inception through its success and expansion.

The twenty-first century has seen an accelerating move away from traditional organizational structures toward hybrid adaptations that emphasize an external focus, flexible interaction, interdependency, and a bottom-up approach. Organizations have sought to adapt their traditional structures in this direction by redefining the role of corporate headquarters, rebalancing the need for control versus coordination, adjusting and reengineering the structure to emphasize strategic activities, downsizing, and moving toward self-managing operational activities.

More successful organizations are becoming agile, virtual organizations—temporary networks of independent companies linked by information technology to share skills, markets, and costs. Outsourcing has been a major way organizations have done this. They retain certain functions, while having other companies take full responsibility for accomplishing other functions necessary to provide the product or services of this host organization. Strategic alliances are arrangements between two or more companies who typically contribute resources or skills to a joint undertaking where the joint entity is a separate, distinct organization itself and usually created to seek a particular contract or activities that represent too great an undertaking for any one player in the alliance.

Twenty-first century leaders have increasingly spoken about making their organizations boundaryless, by which they mean the absence of internal and external "boundaries" between units, levels, and locations that lessen their company's ability to generate knowledge, share knowledge, and get knowledge to the places it can be best used to create value. Forward thinkers describe ambidextrous learning organizations as ones that innately share knowledge, enable learning within and across organizations, and nurture informal relationships within and outside organizations to foster opportunities to be at the forefront of creating new knowledge.

Key Terms

agile organization, *p. 313*

ambidextrous organization, *p. 322*

boundaryless organization, *p. 319*

business process outsourcing, *p. 315*

business process reengineering, *p. 310*

divisional organizational structure, *p. 300*

downsizing, *p. 312*

external interface boundaries, *p. 320*

functional organizational structure, *p. 299*

geographic boundaries, *p. 320*

holding company structure, *p. 302*

horizontal boundaries, *p. 320*

learning organization, *p. 322*

matrix organizational structure, *p. 303*

modular organization, *p. 314*

organizational structure, *p. 298*

outsourcing, *p. 313*

product-team structure, *p. 304*

restructuring, *p. 310*

self-management, *p. 312*

simple organizational structure, *p. 298*

strategic alliances, *p. 318*

strategic business unit, *p. 300*

vertical boundaries, *p. 320*

virtual organization, *p. 313*

Questions for Discussion

1. Explain each traditional organizational structure.
2. Select a company you have worked for or research one in the business press that uses one of these traditional structures. How well suited is the structure to the needs and strategy of the organization? What seems to work well, and what doesn't?
3. What organizations do you think are most likely to use product-team structures? Why?
4. Identify an organization that operated like a twentieth-century organization but has now adopted a structure that manifests twenty-first-century characteristics. Explain how you see or detect the differences.
5. How would you use one or more of the ways to improve traditional structures to improve the company you last worked in? Explain what might result.
6. What organization are you familiar with that you would consider the most agile, virtual organization? Why?
7. What situation have you personally seen outsourcing benefit?
8. What "boundary" would you first eliminate or change in an organization you are familiar with? Explain what you would do to eliminate it or change it and how that should make it more effective.

Chapter **Twelve**

Leadership and Culture

After reading and studying this chapter, you should be able to

1. Describe what good organizational leadership involves.
2. Explain how vision and performance help leaders clarify strategic intent.
3. Explain the value of passion and selection/development of new leaders in shaping an organization's culture.
4. Briefly explain seven sources of power and influence available to every manager.
5. Define and explain what is meant by organizational culture, and how it is created, influenced, and changed.
6. Describe four ways leaders influence culture.
7. Explain four strategy-culture situations.

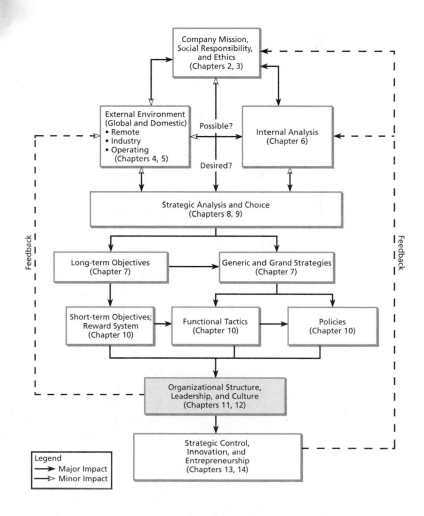

Company Mission, Social Responsibility, and Ethics (Chapters 2, 3)

External Environment (Global and Domestic)
- Remote
- Industry
- Operating
(Chapters 4, 5)

Possible?

Internal Analysis (Chapter 6)

Desired?

Strategic Analysis and Choice (Chapters 8, 9)

Long-term Objectives (Chapter 7)

Generic and Grand Strategies (Chapter 7)

Short-term Objectives; Reward System (Chapter 10)

Functional Tactics (Chapter 10)

Policies (Chapter 10)

Organizational Structure, Leadership, and Culture (Chapters 11, 12)

Strategic Control, Innovation, and Entrepreneurship (Chapters 13, 14)

Feedback

Feedback

Legend
→ Major Impact
⇾ Minor Impact

The job of leading a company has never been more demanding, and it will only get more challenging amidst the global dynamism businesses face today. The CEO will retain ultimate authority, but the corporation will depend increasingly on the skills of the CEO and a host of subordinate leaders to lead, coordinate, make decisions, and act quickly. The accelerated pace and complexity of business will continue to force corporations to push authority down through increasingly horizontal, flattened management structures. As we saw in the last chapter, these organizations will also need to be more and more open, agile, and boundaryless. This will require all the more emphasis on able leadership and a strong culture to shape decisions that must be made quickly, even when the stakes are big. In the future, every line manager will have to exercise leadership's prerogatives—and bear its burdens—to an extent unthinkable 20 years ago.[1]

John Kotter, a widely recognized leadership expert, predicted this evolving role of leadership in an organization when he distinguished between management and leadership:

> Management is about coping with complexity. Its practices and procedures are largely a response to one of the most significant developments of the twentieth century: the emergence of large organizations. Without good management, complex enterprises tend to become chaotic in ways that threaten their very existence. Good management brings a degree of order and consistency to key dimensions like the quality and profitability of products.
>
> Leadership, by contrast, is about coping with change. Part of the reason it has become so important in recent years is that the business world has become more competitive and more volatile.... The net result is that doing what was done yesterday, or doing it 5 percent better, is no longer a formula for success. Major changes are more and more necessary to survive and compete effectively in this new environment. More change always demands more leadership.[2]

organizational leadership
The process and practice by key executives of guiding and shepherding people in an organization toward a vision over time and developing that organization's future leadership and organization culture.

Organizational leadership, then, involves action on two fronts. The first is in guiding the organization to deal with constant change. This requires CEOs who embrace change, and who do so by clarifying strategic intent, who build their organization and shape their culture to fit with opportunities and challenges change affords. The second front is in providing the management skill to cope with the ramifications of constant change. This means identifying and supplying the organization with operating managers prepared to provide operational leadership and vision as never before. Thus, organizational leadership is guiding and shepherding toward a vision over time and developing that organization's future leadership and organizational culture.

Consider the challenge currently facing Ford Motor Company CEO Alan Mulally as he seeks to transform Ford's culture and return the company to profitability after years of accelerating decline and a severe economic downturn. He was brought in by CEO Bill Ford, great-grandson of the founder, who finally threw up his arms in frustration and concluded that an insider could no longer fix Ford. Mulally was not Bill Ford's first choice, but Ford concluded Mulally was someone who knows how to shake the company to its foundations.

Mulally inherited virtually all the managers he must work through. Ford was losing from $3,000 to $5,000 on most every car it sold. There is a legacy within the company of placing a premium on personal ties to the Ford family, sometimes trumping actual performance in promotion decisions. Mulally had no experience in the automobile industry and was viewed with suspicion as an outsider in a town that places a premium on lifelong association with

[1] Ram Charan, *Leadership in the Era of Economic Uncertainty* (New York: McGraw-Hill, 2008); Larry Bossidy, "What Your Leader Expects of You," *Harvard Business Review,* June 2007; and Anthony Bianco, "The New Leadership," *BusinessWeek,* August 28, 2000.
[2] John P. Kotter, "What Leaders Really Do," *Harvard Business Review* (May–June 1990), p. 104.

the industry. On Mulally's first meeting with his inherited management team, one manager asked early on: "How are you going to tackle something as complex and unfamiliar as the auto business when we are in such tough financial shape?"

Wall Street was skeptical early on. Of 15 analysts surveyed by Bloomberg.com, only two rated it a buy. The other 13's opinion: fixing Ford will require much more than simply whacking expenses and replacing a few key people. The company will have to figure out how to produce more vehicles consumers actually want. And doing that requires addressing the most fundamental problem of all: Ford's dysfunctional, often defeatist, culture. Once a model of efficiency, it has degenerated into a symbol of inefficiency, and its managers seem comfortable with the idea of losing money.

If you were Alan Mulally, how would you lead the dramatic change that appears to be needed at Ford Motor Company? How would you seek to move Ford's 300,000-plus employees and managers in a direction that abandons ingrained, and to some "sacred," cultural and leadership norms, quickly.

Consider another example. Jeff Immelt took the reins of leadership of GE from Jack Welch, recognized worldwide as one of the truly great business leaders of the twentieth century, and faced a leadership and organizational culture challenge quite different in some ways from what Alan Mulally is addressing. GE under Welch built more value for its stockholders than any other company in the history of global commerce. That legacy alone would be pressure enough on a new leader, wouldn't you think?

Fortunately, some would quickly answer, Immelt had trained for many years under and in Welch's shadow. He was Welch's choice as successor. He was deeply schooled in the GE way and the Jack Welch leadership approach, as were all the other 300,000 GE employees over the prior 20 years. That Welch/GE way valued, above all, executives who could cut costs, cut deals, and generate continuous improvement in their business units. They were evaluated personally by Welch on an annual basis, in front of each other at the GE School.

But a storm was brewing. Shortly after Immelt became CEO, the 9/11 tragedy unfolded. A major recession and stock market drop soon followed. The option to continue mega deal making was slowing down with fewer candidates. The ability to generate GE-caliber earnings growth via sales growth combined with relentless efficiency was slowing down. So Immelt concluded that he could not continue with the old strategy. Rather, he would have to embark on virtually a new direction at GE that would dramatically change what he needed GE executives as leaders to prioritize and become. Instead of being experts in deal making and continuous improvement, they needed, in Immelt's vision, to become creative, innovators of internal growth generated by identifying new markets and technologies and needs as yet unknown.

With a slower-growing domestic economy, less tolerance among investors for buying your way to growth, and more global competitors, Immelt, like many of his peers, is being forced to shift the emphasis from deals and cost-cutting to new products, services, and markets. "It's a different world," says Immelt, than the one Welch knew. And so, he inherited one of the world's greatest companies yet faced a situation he concluded required dramatic changes in the way GE would be led, in the nature of the culture it needed, and in the fundamental priorities its managers would build GE's future. The dramatic 2008–2010 financial services initiated global economic collapse further underscored the challenge Immelt faced.

If you were Jeff Immelt, how would you lead such a change? How would you seek to move GE's 300,000 people in a direction that abandons "sacred" cultural and leadership norms that were well used and entrenched under Welch's watch to make GE great? How would you quickly and convincingly lead those people to accept massive change throughout this special company and very quickly have that uncertain change produce the growth and profitability investors understandably expect?

The challenges Immelt and Mulally faced were different, but both were nothing short of a revolution. The bottom line is that Immelt and Mulally, as well as all good executives, focus intensely and aggressively on the organizational leadership and organizational culture elements we will now examine.

STRATEGIC LEADERSHIP: EMBRACING CHANGE

The blending of telecommunications, computers, the Internet, and one global marketplace has increased the pace of change exponentially during the past 10 years. All business organizations are affected. Change has become an integral part of what leaders and managers deal with daily. The opening example about Jeff Immelt shows a manager normally able to celebrate 20 years of historically unmatched accomplishment, only to face the need for dramatic change at a GE employees and investors had come to believe was infallible.

The leadership challenge is to galvanize commitment among people within an organization as well as stakeholders outside the organization to embrace change and implement strategies intended to position the organization to succeed in a vastly different future. Leaders galvanize commitment to embrace change through three interrelated activities: clarifying strategic intent, building an organization, and shaping organizational culture.

Clarifying Strategic Intent

strategic intent
Leaders' clear sense of where they want to lead their company and what results they expect to achieve.

Leaders help their company embrace change by setting forth their **strategic intent**—a clear sense of where they want to lead the company and what results they expect to achieve. They do this by concentrating simultaneously and very clearly on two very different issues: vision and performance.

Vision

leader's vision
An articulation of a simple criterion or characterization of what a leader sees the company must become in order to establish and sustain global leadership.

A leader needs to communicate clearly and directly a fundamental vision of what the business needs to become. Traditionally, the concept of vision has been a description or picture of what the company could be that accommodates the needs of all its stakeholders. The intensely competitive, rapidly changing global marketplace has refined this to be targeting a very narrowly defined **leader's vision**—an articulation of a simple criterion or characterization of what the leader sees the company must become to establish and sustain global leadership. Former IBM CEO Lou Gerstner is a good example of a leader in the middle of trying to shape strategic intent when he began to try to change IBM from a computer company to a business solutions management company. He said at the time: "One of the great things about this industry is that every decade or so, you get a chance to redefine the playing field." He further commented, "We're in that phase of redefinition right now, and winners or losers are going to emerge from it. We've got to become the leader in 'network-centric computing.' It's a shift brought about by telecommunications-based change that is changing IBM more than semiconductors did in the last decade." Said Gerstner, "I sensed there were too many people inside IBM who wanted to fight the war we lost," referring to PCs and PC software, so he aggressively instilled network-centric computing as the strategic intent for IBM in the next decade. It is a comment on his sense of vision that his successor, Sam Palmisano, sold IBM's PC business to China's Lenovo, creating the world's third-largest PC company, and is aggressively pushing his IBMers to concentrate on newer IBM businesses in IT services, software, and servers—and seriously examining IBM's future in the online digital world, the 3D Internet.

Keep the Vision Simple The late Sam Walton's vision for Wal-Mart, *value to the consumer,* lives on in that amazing global company, guiding its development in a vastly changed world. Meg Whitman's leadership of eBay has produced explosive growth, keeping everyone committed to a vision that eBay simply exists to help you buy or sell anything, anywhere, anytime. Coca-Cola's legendary former CEO and chairman Roberto Goizueta said, "Our company is a global business system for which we raise capital to make concentrate and sell it at an operating profit. Then we pay the cost of that capital. Shareholders pocket the difference." Coke averaged 27 percent annual return on stockholder equity for 18 years under his leadership. Exhibit 12.1, Top Strategist, shows how Mayor Michael Bloomberg articulated a radical yet simple vision of New York City that has resonated with New York's famously cynical citizenry, who give him a 75 percent approval rating. All four of these organizations are very different, but their leaders were each effective in shaping and communicating a vision that clarified strategic intent in a way that helped everyone understand, or at least have a sense of, where the organization needed to go and, as a result, created a better sense of the rationale behind any new, and often radically changing, strategy.

Performance

Clarifying strategic intent must also ensure the survival of the enterprise as it pursues a well-articulated vision, and after it reaches the vision. So a key element of good organizational leadership is to make clear the performance expectations a leader has for the organization, and managers in it, as they seek to move toward that vision.

Oftentimes this can create a bit of a paradox, because the vision is a future picture and performance is now and tomorrow and next quarter and this year. Steven Reinemund, former CEO of PepsiCo and responsible for its impressive performance the last several years, offered an insightful way to think about this role of a good leader in clarifying strategic intent. "As I am looking to select other leaders, it's important to remember that results count. If you can't get the results over the goal line, are you really a leader?" The job of a good leader, in clarifying strategic intent, is to do so by painting a picture of that intent in future terms, and in setting sound performance expectations while moving toward that vision and as the vision becomes a reality.[3]

Jim McNerney, Boeing CEO and GE alumnus, described how he handles this paradox at Boeing and 3M as a contrast between an encouraging style (visioning) and setting expectations (performance).

> I think the harder you push people, the more you have to encourage them. Some people feel you either have a demanding, command-and-control management style or you have a nurturing, encouraging management style. I believe you have to have both. If you're only demanding, without encouraging, eventually that runs out of gas. And if you're only encouraging, without setting high expectations, you're not getting as much out of people. It's not either/or. You can't have one without the other.[4]

A real challenge for Alan Mulally at Ford is changing managers' mindsets about being profitable. When he was reviewing Ford's 2008 product line as the new CEO, he was told that Ford loses close to $3,000 every time a customer buys a Focus compact. "Why haven't you figured out a way to make a profit?" he asked. Executives explained that Ford needed the high sales volume to maintain the company's CAFÉ, or corporate average fuel economy, rating and that the plant that makes the car is a high-cost UAW factory in Michigan. "That's not what I asked," he shot back. "I want to know why no one figured out a way to build

[3] Diane Brady, "The Six "Ps" of PepsiCo's Chief," *BusinessWeek Online,* January 10, 2005.
[4] Michael Arndt, "The Hard Work in Leadership," *BusinessWeek Online*, April 12, 2004.

Top Strategist
Mike Bloomberg, New York's CEO Leader

**Exhibit
12.1**

Michael Bloomberg, classic entrepreneurial success story, has proven to be an extraordinary leader as mayor of New York City. Sworn in as mayor shortly after 9/11, Bloomberg's leadership approach was based on a businesslike view of NYC—NYC is the company; its citizens are its customers; its public servants NYC's talent; and Bloomberg the CEO responsible for results. Here's his leadership approach.

BE BOLD AND TAKE RISKS

Bloomberg's first major decision was to raise property taxes to put NYC in a better financial condition. Overwhelmingly advised this was political suicide, Bloomberg saw only two choices, reduce services or increase taxes. The risk paid off. NYC's finances improved—and economic activity in the city improved in the process. At the same time, he sought to have NYC win the 2012 Winter Olympics. He lost to London. Bloomberg's reaction: "In business, you reward people for taking risks. When it doesn't work out, you promote them because of their willingness to try new things. If people come back and tell me they skied all day and never fell down, I tell them to try a different mountain."

BE OPEN ABOUT PERFORMANCE AND RESULTS

He insisted that employees, and customers, see decision making in action and regularly see results. So he first changed doors on key meeting rooms and offices from wood to glass, so people could look inside the city's administrative activities. Second, he made semi-annual reports in detail about NYC's revenues and expenses, so citizens and others can see in paper and online a detailed financial picture of what each agency of NYC government costs, is doing, and so forth.

COMMUNICATE WITH CUSTOMERS

Bloomberg has long been obsessed with maintaining constant customer contact and feedback. So as mayor, he immediately established a 311 telephone and Web-based system so that any citizen or guest of NYC could call, 24/7, to comment on any- and everything being done in NYC. And, Bloomberg personally reviewed weekly summaries of all calls to get a feeling for key citizen concerns. The number of calls reached 50 million within the first 16 months and has resulted in numerous improvements in services and actions solving problems or complaints. It has also reduced dramatically the number of 911 calls, by more than 1 million annually, meaning critical first-responders are used more for real emergencies, while nonemergency concerns get addressed in a more appropriate manner.

RECRUIT TOP OPERATIONAL TALENT

Most politicians fill top jobs with people owed political patronage. Not Bloomberg. He views as critical to his success as a leader, regardless of whether he is leading a business or a government, the priority of filling key operating positions with the best talent he can get. And he wants that talent to be able to identify targets for their units, and then lead their people in achieving them. He immediately sought to hire Katherine Oliver, a talented executive with Bloomberg—the business operation in London—to join NYC to build first-class film and TV operations in NYC. The targets she set were impressive, and the results have been even more so.

Bloomberg has maintained a very high approval rating in perhaps the world's most cynical city populace. He recently managed to change the rules to be allowed to run for an unprecedented third term as NYC mayor. His impressive, open, dedicated leadership style has won him not only the approval of his citizenry and NYC employees, it has won him admiration worldwide as a proven leader in both business and government settings.

Source: "The CEO Mayor," *BusinessWeek*, June 25, 2007.

this car at a profit, whether it has to be built in Michigan or China or India, if that's what it takes." Nobody had a good answer.[5]

Building an Organization

The previous chapter examined alternative structures to use in designing the organization necessary to implement strategy. Leaders spend considerable time shaping and refining their organizational structure and making it function effectively to accomplish strategic intent. Because leaders are attempting to embrace change, they are often rebuilding or remaking their organization to align it with the ever-changing environment and needs of a new strategy. And because embracing change often involves overcoming resistance to change, leaders find themselves addressing problems such as the following as they attempt to build or rebuild their organization:

- Ensuring a common understanding about organizational priorities.
- Clarifying responsibilities among managers and organizational units.
- Empowering newer managers and pushing authority lower in the organization.
- Uncovering and remedying problems in coordination and communication across the organization and across boundaries inside and outside the organization.
- Gaining the personal commitment to a shared vision from managers throughout the organization.
- Keeping closely connected with what's going on inside and outside the organization and with its customers.

There are three ways good leaders go about building the organization they want and dealing with problems and issues like those listed: education, perseverance, and principles.

leadership development

The effort to familiarize future leaders with the skills important to the company and to develop exceptional leaders among the managers employed.

Education and **leadership development** is the effort to familiarize future leaders with the skills important to the company and to develop exceptional leaders among the managers you employ. Jack Welch was legendary for the GE education center in Croton-on-Hudson, New York, and its role in allowing the GE leader to educate current and future GE managers on the ways of GE and the vision of its future. It allowed a leader to shape future leaders, thereby building an organization. His successor, Jeff Immelt, uses the same facility to interact with and discuss GE's future with a new crop of future leaders.

Leaders do this in many ways. Larry Bossidy, former chairman of Honeywell and coauthor of the best seller, *Execution,* spent 50 percent of his time each year flying to Allied Signal's various operations around the world, meeting with managers and discussing decisions, results, and progress. Bill Gates at Microsoft reportedly spent two hours each day reading and sending e-mail to any of Microsoft's 36,000 employees who want to contact him. All managers adapt structures, create teams, implement systems, and otherwise generate ways to coordinate, integrate, and share information about what their organization is doing and might do. Once again, here is what Jim McNerney had to say:

> It comes down to personal engagement. I spend a lot of time out with our people. I probably do 30 major events a year with 100 people or more, where I spend time debating things and pushing my ideas, telling them what I am thinking and soliciting feedback. Most CEOs are smart enough to figure out where to go with a company. The hard work is engaging everyone in doing it. That's the hard work in leadership.[6]

Others create customer advisory groups, supplier partnerships, R&D joint ventures, and other adjustments to build an adaptable, learning organization that buys into the leader's

---

[5] David Kiley, "New Heat on Ford," *BusinessWeek,* June 4, 2007.

[6] Ibid.

Top Strategist
Jeff Bezos, Founder and CEO, Amazon.com

**Exhibit
12.2**

Since starting Amazon.com, Jeff Bezos has often been in Wall Street's doghouse. The main reason is his insistence on building capacity to support new services his team has determined Amazon's customers need, even as their stock price steadily declines or fluctuates wildly. Asked about his seemingly consistent ability to ignore Wall Street's criticism, Bezos offered these thoughts: "We don't claim that our long-term approach is the right approach. We just claim it's ours. Our approach has been to be as clear as we can be about what kind of company we are and let investors choose." To his employees, Bezos repeatedly makes it clear that Amazon's vision is to find ways that make Amazon's operations more efficient and lower its costs so that it can make its customer experience more value-added while also less costly. And, Bezos notes, "I've taken repeated criticism about our stock price, but never about our customer experience." He goes on to describe that he has repeatedly sat with harsh critics discussing fluctuations in Amazon's stock price yet its insistence on innovation investments, and then, he notes, they would end the meeting saying "I am a huge [Amazon] customer."

Bezos also describes how he clarifies this simple vision to his employees—continuously improving on providing what Amazon customers need. "We have three all-hands meetings a year, and I'll tell people that if the stock is up 30%, please don't feel you are 30% smarter. Because when the stock is 30% down, it's not good to feel 30% dumber." The key is to continuously focus on ways to improve the ways we provide customers what they need. "Companies get skills-focused, instead of customer-needs-focused. When they look at growing their business into some new area, the first question is 'why should we do that—we don't have any skills in that area.' " That approach, Bezos believes, leads eventually to a company's decline because the world constantly changes and a company's current skills eventually become less important. So he leads Amazon by focusing on one simple question, "What do our customers need?" From there he urges his managers to determine if Amazon has the skills to meet the needs and, if not, to go out and hire the people that do. Bezos cites Amazon's Kindle, and electronic books, as a clear example of doing just that, hiring people who know how to build hardware devices, creating a whole new book-reading-related competency in the process. His principles and perseverance to stick with that simple question as Amazon's foundation have proven, over time, to provide solid leadership, ultimately allowing Amazon to emerge as a key Internet-based business model.

Source: "Bezos on Innovation," *BusinessWeek,* April 17, 2008.

**perseverance
(of a leader)**
The capacity to see a commitment through to completion long after most people would have stopped trying.

vision and strategic intent and the change driving the future opportunities facing the business. These, in addition to the fundamental structural guidelines described in the previous chapter for restructuring to support strategically critical activities, are key ways leaders constantly attempt to educate and build a supportive organization.

Perseverance is the capacity to see a commitment through to completion long after most people would have stopped trying. Exhibit 12.2, Top Strategist, describes how Jeff Bezos personifies perseverance in leading Amazon.com. The opening example about Jeff Immelt conjures up images of some people in GE being hesitant to follow him because of their longtime loyalty to Jack Welch and his ways. Immelt will need to have patience and perseverance to deal with these people, to help them gradually shift their loyalty and accept the new. The example also conjures up another image, one of people excited to embrace Immelt's effort to take GE in a new direction—just because of the excitement of the moment along with some sense that a change is needed. But imagine that the first signs are not good, that it is unclear whether the radical new approach will work or not. It is relatively easy to then imagine a significant negative shift in the enthusiasm and faith of this group—again, Immelt must call on considerable perseverance to simply continue to bring them along and build their commitment over the long term.

"When the going gets tough, the tough get going" is a mantra often heard in sports and in U.S. Marine Corps leadership training. The real point in this is perseverance. NYC Mayor Michael Bloomberg's perspective on risk described in Exhibit 12.1 reflects an emphasis on perseverance. The capacity to take a risk, to make a tough decision, to commit to a new vision, and then to stick with that decision even when it doesn't appear "right" early on is a scenario often found in the history of effective leadership that ultimately creates a favorable future. A broad panel of U.S. historians recently rated Abraham Lincoln the best American president—based in large part on his perseverance in preserving the union. Winston Churchill's perseverance was perhaps his most compelling trait as he successfully led England through World War II.

Principles (of a leader)

A leader's fundamental personal standards that guide her sense of honesty, integrity, and ethical behavior.

Principles are your fundamental personal standards that guide your sense of honesty, integrity, and ethical behavior. If you have a clear moral compass guiding your priorities and those you set for the company, you will be a more effective leader. This observation is repeatedly one of the first thing effective leaders interviewed by researchers, business writers, and students mention when they answer a question about what they think is most important in explaining their success as leaders and the success of leaders they admire. Steven Reinemund, PepsiCo's very successful (former) CEO, said it this way:

> It starts with basic beliefs and values. It's important to make clear to the people in the organization what those are, so you're transparent. They have to be consistent with the values of the organization, or there will be a problem. If you look at all the issues that have happened in the corporate world of the last few years, . . . it all boils down to a basic lack of a moral compass and checks and balances among leaders. We as leaders have to check each other. We're going to make mistakes. If we don't check each other on them, you get in trouble. Most of the companies that got into trouble had a set of stated principles, but the leaders didn't check each other on those principles.[7]

Principle boils down to a personal philosophy we all deal with at an individual level choices involving honesty, integrity, ethical behavior. Indeed Exhibit 12.3, Strategy in Action, gives you the chance to "test" *your* personal principles in comparison with the actions of some of your business school peers at Duke university's MBA program, and *BusinessWeek*'s thoughts too. The key thing to remember as a future leader is that your personal philosophies, or choices, manifest themselves exponentially for you or any key leaders of any organization. The people who do the work of any organization watch their leaders and what their leaders do, sanction, or stand for. So do people outside that organization who deal with it. These people then reflect those principles in what they do or come to believe is the way to do things in or with that organization. An effective organization is better built—is stronger—when its leaders show by example what they want their people to do and the principles they want their people to operate by on a day-to-day basis and in making decisions shaped by values and principles—a clear sense of right or wrong. "Values," "Lead by example," "Do as I say AND as I do"—these are very basic notions that good leaders find great strength in using. *BusinessWeek*'s "The Ethics Guy" says simply that principles should boil down to "five easy principles," which are:[8]

1. Do no harm.
2. Make things better.

[7] Brady, "The Six Ps."
[8] Bruce Weinstein, "Five Easy Principles," *BusinessWeek*, January 10, 2007.

Test *YOUR* Principles

Just a few years ago, the dean of Duke's Fuqua School of Business announced that 10 percent of its MBA class had been caught cheating on a take-home final exam and would be dismissed. These MBAs were "cream of the crop" students with six years of corporate experience and careers under way in the new "wiki" world of online collaboration and aggregation of other's knowledge via the Web as an emerging key source of competitive advantage. So they collaborated in crafting answers to the take-home final exam, sharing insights and ideas, and so forth. Their professors saw the similarity in answers, and, looking to evaluate individual performance, found the collaboration unethical, dishonest, lacking integrity, and fundamentally wrong. So they were dismissed for cheating.

A *BusinessWeek* Commentary took issue with the decision—and saw a different interpretation. Their point: the new world order is about teamwork, shared information. Social networking, a new culture of shared information, postmodern learning wiki style.

Text messaging, downloading essays, getting questions answered from others, often unknown, via the Web. All of these are the new ways we work today. We function in an interdependent world, where success often hinges on creative collaboration, networking, and "googling" to tap a literal world of information and expertise available at the click of a keyboard or a cell phone.

Others, starting with their Duke professors, viewed these students collaborating on a take-home exam as a conscious effort to break the rules, or at least, gain unauthorized advantage. And maybe, they apparently thought, this was a good situation about which to make an example in order to rein in an increasingly rudderless business culture.

What do you think? Is what these students did ethical, principled leadership? Is it "cheating," or simply collaborative learning?

Source: Michelle Conlin, "Commentary: Cheating—or Postmodern Learning?" *BusinessWeek,* May 14, 2007.

---

3. Respect others.
4. Be fair.
5. Be compassionate.

The value of that kind of clarity, and transparency, as PepsiCo's Reinemund described it, can become a major force by which a leader will shape and move his or her organization.

Shaping Organizational Culture

Leaders know well that the values and beliefs shared throughout their organization will shape how the work of the organization is done. And when attempting to embrace accelerated change, reshaping their organization's culture is an activity that occupies considerable time for most leaders. Elements of good leadership—vision, performance, perseverance, principles, which have just been described—are important ways leaders shape organizational culture as well. Leaders shape organizational culture through their passion for the enterprise and the selection/development of talented managers to be future leaders. We will examine these two ideas and then cover the notion of organizational culture in greater detail.

passion (of a leader)
A highly motivated sense of commitment to what you do and want to do.

Passion, in a leadership sense, is a highly motivated sense of commitment to what you do and want to do. PepsiCo's Reinemund described it this way:

I remember when I was a kid, Kennedy made the announcement that he wanted to put a man on the moon and bring him back safely to earth. That was so motivating and passionate. Nobody believed it could happen, but he inspired them to do it with his passion.[9]

Like many other traits of good leaders, passion is best seen through the leaders' intermittent behaviors while in the throws of the challenging times of the organizations they lead.

---

[9] Ibid.

They must use special moments to convey a sincere passion for and delight in the work of the company they lead. These observations by and about Ryanair CEO Michael O'Leary about competing in the increasingly competitive European airline industry and archrival easyJet provide a useful example:

> It was vintage Michael O'Leary. On May 13, the 42-year-old CEO of Dublin-based discount airline Ryanair outfitted his staff in full combat gear, drove an old World War II tank to England's Luton airport, an hour north of London, then demanded access to the base of archrival easyJet Airline Co. With the theme to the old television series *The A-Team* blaring, O'Leary declared he was "liberating the public from easyJet's high fares." When security—surprise!—refused to let the Ryanair armor roll in, O'Leary led the troops in his own rendition of a platoon march song: "I've been told and it's no lie. EasyJet's fares are way too high!" So it is that there are new rivals for O'Leary to conquer. "When we were a much smaller company, we compared ourselves to British Airways. But they are such a mess, most people just feel sorry for them," O'Leary says. "Now we're turning the guns on easyJet."[10]

It was readily apparent to anyone on this scene that O'Leary was passionate about Ryanair, and that example sent a clear message that he wanted an organizational culture that was aggressive, competitive, and somewhat freewheeling in order to take advantage of change in the European airline industry. He did this by passionate example, by expectations felt by his managers, and in the way decision making is approached within Ryanair.

Sam Walton used to lead cheers at every Wal-Mart store he visited each year before and long after Wal-Mart was an overwhelming success. Kathy Mulhany at Xerox, a 28-year company veteran when she assumed the presidency with Xerox close to bankruptcy, started and continues to travel to every Xerox location worldwide twice annually just to convey her passion for Xerox as a way of rallying veteran Xerox employees to continue to buy into her vision and continue its extraordinary turnaround. GE's Jeff Immelt is described by a board member as a natural salesman who still happily recounts the days when he drove around his territory in a Ford Taurus while at GE Plastics. "He knows the world looks to GE as a harbinger of future trends," says Ogilvy & Mather Worldwide CEO Rochelle Lazarus, who sits on the board. "He really feels GE has a responsibility to the world to get out in front and play a leadership role." Immelt, it would seem, is passionate about GE and its future opportunities. Indeed, at a recent gathering of GE's top 650 executives, amidst a situation where GE stock price is down more than 70 percent since he became CEO, Immelt insisted that "there's never been a better day, a better time, or a better place to be," meaning than GE. That's passion.

Leaders also use reward systems, symbols, and structure among other means to shape the organization's culture. Travelers' Insurance Co.'s notable turnaround was accomplished in part by changing its "hidebound" culture through a change in its agent reward system. Employees previously on salary with occasional bonuses were given rewards that involved substantial cash bonuses and stock options. A major Travelers' customer and risk management director at drug-maker Becton Dickinson said: "They're hungrier now. They want to make deals. They're different than the old, hidebound Travelers' culture." Jeff Immelt is doing something similar to reshape the ingrained GE culture—tying executive compensation to their ability to come up with new ideas that show improved customer service, generate cash growth, and boost sales instead of simply meeting bottom-line targets.[11]

As leaders clarify strategic intent, build an organization, and shape their organization's culture, they look to one key element to help—their management team throughout their

[10] "Ryanair Rising," *BusinessWeek,* June 2, 2003.
[11] "Jeff Immelt on Pay, His AAA Rating, and Taking the Train," *BusinessWeek,* February 1, 2009.

organization. As Honeywell's chairman Larry Bossidy candidly observed when asked about how after 42 years at General Electric, Allied Signal, and now Honeywell, with seemingly drab businesses, he could expect exciting growth: "There's no such thing as a mature market. What we need is mature executives who can find ways to grow."[12] Leaders look to managers they need to execute strategy as another source of leadership to accept risk and cope with the complexity that change brings about. So selection and development of key managers become major leadership roles.

Recruiting and Developing Talented Operational Leadership

Fundamental to a leader's responsibility in developing operational talent is to serve as a role model to younger managers. The purpose of doing so is to model behaviors and habits that become instinctive ways those younger managers address issues and make decisions. This has been particularly critical in the dramatic global economic downturn—which virtually every business has been dealing with the past few years. It has required leadership that is lean and focused at every level, and particularly at operating levels of the organization.

Modeling behavior and desired habits is particularly relevant in the depressed economic times most companies have been facing for the past few years and that many still face today. In many cases, their very survival may be at stake. Thus, modeling and ensuring these specific leadership habits can be absolutely critical.

As we noted at the beginning of this section on organizational leadership, the accelerated pace and complexity of business beyond the immediate economic contraction will also increase pressure on corporations to push authority down in their organizations, ultimately meaning that every line manager will have to exercise leadership's prerogatives to an extent unthinkable a generation earlier. We also defined one of the key roles of good organizational leadership as building the organization by educating and developing new leaders. They will each be global managers, change agents, strategists, motivators, strategic decision makers, innovators, and collaborators if the business is to survive and prosper. So we want to examine this more completely by looking at key competencies these future managers need to possess or develop. Exhibit 12.4, Strategy in Action provides an interesting interview with IBMer Helen Cheng about her introduction to the *World of Warcraft* online game and how it is now a key way IBM is using online multiplayer games to develop its young managers of global teams into better team leaders and future global leaders for the reality of today's fast-paced, global marketplace.

Today's need for fluid learning organizations capable of rapid response, sharing, and cross-cultural synergy place incredible demands on young managers to bring important competencies to the organization. Exhibit 12.5 describes the needs organizations look to managers to meet and then identifies the corresponding competencies managers would need to do so. Ruth Williams and Joseph Cothrel drew this conclusion in their research about competencies needed from managers in today's fast-changing business environment.

> Today's competitive environment requires a different set of management competencies than we traditionally associate with the role. The balance has clearly shifted from attributes traditionally thought of as masculine (strong decision making, leading the troops, driving strategy, waging competitive battle) to more feminine qualities (listening, relationship-building, and nurturing). The model today is not so much "take it on your shoulders" as it is to "create the environment that will enable others to carry part of the burden." The focus is on unlocking the organization's human asset potential.[13]

[12] Diane Brady, "The Immelt Revolution," *BusinessWeek Online,* October 18, 2005.
[13] Ruth Williams and Joseph Cothrel, *Current Trends in Strategic Management* (New York: Blackwell Publishing, 2007).

Helen Cheng and MMORPG—IBM's Setting for Twenty-First-Century New Leaders, Skill Development

MMORPGs (massively multiplayer online role-playing games) like *World of Warcraft* are perhaps the most realistic setting for leadership training and development in our new "wiki" world, according to IBM leadership development researchers. "Its not a stretch to think that résumés that include detailed gaming experience will be landing on the desks of *Fortune* 500 executives in the very near future. Those hiring managers would do well to look closely at that experience, and not disregard it as a mere hobby. After all, that gamer may just be your next CEO."* Reading the experience of Helen Cheng helps explain why IBM is moving aggressively into the use of MMORPGs as a basis for leadership selection and development at IBM, as well as at client businesses worldwide. Helen Cheng got her first taste of online gaming three years ago, when a friend got her to join up with *Star Wars Galaxies*™. "I was pretty skeptical," she recalled. "I mean, fighting dragons in a fantasy world? Sounds kinda nerdy." Three days later Cheng was hooked. She soon moved on to *World of Warcraft*™, an online game that counts more than 8 million members. She moved quickly up the ranks and spent six months as a level-60 guild leader, the highest level of leadership in the game. Here are some of her leadership lessons gleaned from the game:

Q: Do you consider yourself a natural leader?

A: I'm pretty quiet. The first time I thought I could be a leader was during a raid that involved 40 people. The raid went bad, and everybody died. The designated raid leader went silent. Everyone was waiting for instruction. I pushed my button to talk and rallied the troops. It was me, a girl, talking to 39 guys. To my surprise, everyone complied, and we got going. That was a defining moment for me, eventually leading to me becoming a guild leader.

Q: What was it about the environment that made it easy for you to try a leader role?

A: The speed at which things happens contributes to that. You don't have a lot of time, and decisions have to be made. Also, there are different forms of communication. You can send instant messages, use a chat channel, speak over VOIP [Voice Over Internet Protocol], even leave messages on the Web site. These different communications mediums affort opportunities to lead.

Q: What is it like managing people you never see in person?

A: Not that different from real life. I've had my share of personality conflicts that I had to mediate. In my last guild, we had a raid officer who was extremely capable. He was great leading 40-man raids in real time. But he was extremely practical and did not care about other guild members' feelings, or guild unity. On the other hand, we had a recruiting officer who was very friendly and gung ho about building relationships. They often went head-to-head on issues. I found it difficult to mediate between them. So eventually I left to go raid with another guild that was more advanced.

Q: Kind of like climbing the corporate ladder?

A: Something like that.

*"Virtual World, Real Leaders: Online Games Put the Future of Business Leadership on Display," IBM Corporation, http://domino.research.ibm.com/comm/www_innovate.nsf/images/gio-gaming/$FILE/ibm_gio_gaming_report.pdf, 2008.

EXHIBIT 12.5
What Competencies Should Managers Possess?

Source: From Ruth L. Williams and Joseph P. Cothrel, "Building Tomorrow's Leaders Today," *Strategy and Leadership* 26, October 1997. Reprinted with permission of Emerald Group Publishing Limited.

The Leadership Needs of Organizations

The ability to
- Build confidence
- Build enthusiasm
- Cooperate
- Deliver results
- Form networks
- Influence others
- Use information

The Required Competencies of Business Leaders

- Business literacy
- Creativity
- Cross-cultural effectiveness
- Empathy
- Flexibility
- Proactivity
- Problem solving
- Relation building
- Teamwork
- Vision

position power
The ability and right to influence and direct others based on the power associated with your formal position in the organization.

reward power
The ability to influence and direct others that comes from being able to confer rewards in return for desired actions or outcomes.

information power
The ability to influence others based on your access to information and your control of dissemination of information that is important to subordinates and others yet not otherwise easily obtained.

punitive power
Ability to direct and influence others based on your ability to coerce and deliver punishment for mistakes or undesired actions by others, particularly subordinates.

expert influence
The ability to direct and influence others because they defer to you based on your expertise or specialized knowledge that is related to the task, undertaking, or assignment in which they are involved.

referent influence
The ability to influence others derived from their strong desire to be associated with you, usually because they admire you, gain prestige or a sense of purpose by that association, or believe in your motivations.

Researcher David Goleman addressed the question of what types of personality attributes generate the type of competencies described in Exhibit 12.5. His research suggested that a set of four characteristics commonly referred to as emotional intelligence play a key role in bringing the competencies needed from today's desirable manager:[14]

- *Self-awareness* in terms of the ability to read and understand one's emotions and assess one's strengths and weaknesses, underlain by the confidence that stems from positive self-worth.
- *Self-management* in terms of control, integrity, conscientiousness, initiative, and achievement orientation.
- *Social awareness* in relation to sensing others' emotions (empathy), reading the organization (organizational awareness), and recognizing customers' needs (service orientation).
- *Social skills* in relation to influencing and inspiring others; communicating, collaborating, and building relationships with others; and managing change and conflict.

A key way these characteristics manifest themselves in a manager's routine activities is found in the way they seek to get the work of their unit or group done over time. How do they use power and influence to get others to get things done? Effective leaders seek to develop managers who understand they have many sources of power and influence, and that relying on the power associated with their position in an organization is often the least effective means to influence people to do what is needed. Managers have available seven sources of power and influence:

Organizational Power	Personal Influence
Position power	Expert influence
Reward power	Referent influence
Information power	Peer influence
Punitive power	

Organizational sources of power are derived from a manager's role in the organization. **Position power** is formally established based on the manager's position in the organization. By virtue of holding that position, certain decision-making authorities and responsibilities are conferred that the manager is entitled to use to get things done. It is the source of power many new managers expect to be able to rely on, but often the least useful. **Reward power** is available when the manager confers rewards in return for desired actions and outcomes. This is often a power source. **Information power** can be particularly effective and is derived from a manager's access to and control over the dissemination of information that is important to subordinates yet not easily available in the organization. **Punitive power** is the power exercised via coercion or fear of punishment for mistakes or undesired actions by a manager's subordinates.

Leaders today increasingly rely on their personal ability to influence others perhaps as much, if not more so, than organizational sources of power. Personal influence, a form of "power," comes mainly from three sources. **Expert influence** is derived from a leader's knowledge and expertise in a particular area or situation. This can be a very important source of power in influencing others. **Referent influence** comes from having others want

[14] D. Goleman "What Makes a Leader?" *Harvard Business Review* (November–December 1998), pp. 93–102.

EXHIBIT 12.6
Management Processes and Levels of Management

Sources: C. A. Bartlett and S. Ghoshal, "The Myth of the General Manager: New Personal Competencies for New Management Roles," *California Management Review* 40 (Fall, 1997); R. M. Grant, *Contemporary Strategy Analysis* (Oxford: Blackwell, 2001), p. 529.

Front-Line Management	Middle Management	Top Management
Attracting resources and capabilities and developing the business	**RENEWAL PROCESS** Developing operating managers and supporting their activities; maintaining organizational trust	Providing institutional leadership through shaping and embedding corporate purpose and challenging embedded assumptions
Managing operational interdependencies and personal networks	**INTEGRATION PROCESS** Linking skills, knowledge, and resources across units; reconciling short-term performance and long-term ambition	Creating corporate direction; developing and nurturing organizational values
Creating and pursuing opportunities; managing continuous performance improvement	**ENTREPRENEURIAL PROCESS** Reviewing, developing, and supporting initiatives	Establishing performance standards

peer influence
The ability to influence individual behavior among members of a group based on group norms, a group sense of what is the right thing or right way to do things, and the need to be valued and accepted by the group.

to identify with the leader. We have all seen or worked for leaders who have major influence over others based simply on their charisma, personality, empathy, and other personal attributes. And finally, **peer influence** can be a very effective way for leaders to influence the behavior of others. Most people in organizations and across an organization find themselves put in groups to solve problems, serve customers, develop innovations, and perform a host of other tasks. Leaders can use the assignment of team members and the charge to the team as a way to enable peer-based influence to work on key managers and the outcomes they produce.

Effective leaders make use of all seven sources of power and influence, very often in combination, to deal with the myriad situations they face and need others to handle. The exact best source(s) of power and influence are often shaped by the nature of the task, project, urgency of an assignment, or the unique characteristics of specific personnel, among myriad factors. Organizational leaders such as Jeff Immelt at GE draw on all these sources and, equally important, seek to develop their organizations around subordinate leaders and managers who insightfully and effectively make use of all their sources of power and influence.

One final perspective on the role of organizational leadership and management selection is found in the work of Bartlett and Ghoshal. Their study of several of the most successful global companies in the 1990s suggests that combining flexible responsiveness with integration and innovation requires rethinking the management role and the distribution of management roles within a twenty-first-century company. They see three critical management roles: the *entrepreneurial process* (decisions about opportunities to pursue and resource deployment), the *integration process* (building and deploying organizational capabilities), and the *renewal process* (shaping organizational purpose and enabling change). Traditionally viewed as the domain of top management, their research suggests that these functions need to be shared and distributed across three management levels as suggested in Exhibit 12.6.[15]

[15] C. A. Barlett and S. Ghoshal, "The Myth of the General Manager: New Personal Competencies for New Management Roles," *California Management Review* 40 (Fall 1997), pp. 92–116; "Beyond Structure to Process," *Harvard Business Review* (January–February 1995).

ORGANIZATIONAL CULTURE

organizational culture
The set of important assumptions and beliefs (often unstated) that members of an organization share in common.

Organizational culture is the set of important assumptions (often unstated) that members of an organization share in common. Every organization has its own culture. An organization's culture is similar to an individual's personality—an intangible yet ever-present theme that provides meaning, direction, and the basis for action. In much the same way as personality influences the behavior of an individual, the shared assumptions (beliefs and values) among a firm's members influence opinions and actions within that firm. Exhibit 12.7, Strategy in Action, shows the results of a *BusinessWeek* survey conducted by Staffing.org to identify how employees view their company's culture in the context of various TV shows or cartoon characters.

A member of an organization can simply be aware of the organization's beliefs and values without sharing them in a personally significant way. Those beliefs and values have more personal meaning if the member views them as a guide to appropriate behavior in the organization and, therefore, complies with them. The member becomes fundamentally committed to the beliefs and values when he or she internalizes them; that is, comes to hold them as personal beliefs and values. In this case, the corresponding behavior is *intrinsically rewarding* for the member—the member derives personal satisfaction from his or her actions in the organization because those actions are congruent with corresponding personal beliefs and values. *Assumptions become shared assumptions through internalization among an organization's individual members.* And those shared, internalized beliefs and values shape the content and account for the strength of an organization's culture.

The Role of the Organizational Leader in Organizational Culture

The previous section of this chapter covered organizational leadership in detail. Part of that coverage discussed the role of the organizational leader in shaping organizational culture. Several points in that discussion apply here. We will not repeat them, but it is important to emphasize that the leader and the culture of the organization s/he leads are inextricably intertwined. The leader is the standard bearer, the personification, the ongoing embodiment of the culture (Steve Jobs, Anne Mulcahy) or the new example (Alan Mulally, Mike Bloomberg) of what it should become. As such, several of the aspects of what a leader does or should do represent influences on the organization's culture, either to reinforce it or to exemplify the standards and nature of what it needs to become. How the leader behaves and emphasizes those aspects of being a leader become what all the organization sees are "the important things to do and value."

Build Time in the Organization

Some leaders have been with the organization for a long time. If they have been in the leader role for an extended time, then their association with the organization is usually strongly entrenched. They continue to reinforce the current culture, are empowered by it, and understandably go to considerable lengths to reinforce it as a key element in sustaining continued success. The problematic long-time leaders are those who have built a successful enterprise that also sustains a culture that appears unethical or worse. Either type of long-time leader is often a widely known figure in today's media-intense business world. And in their setting, while the culture may be exceptionally strong, their role in creating it usually means they seemingly hold sway over the culture rather than the other way around.

Many leaders in recent years, and inevitably in any organization, are new to the top post of the organization. Their relationship with the organization's culture is perhaps more

What Is Your Workplace Culture Most Like?

BusinessWeek

THE BIG PICTURE

THINK YOUR WORKPLACE is like a sitcom? In an online survey, Staffing.org, a performance research firm, asked 300 people to describe their company's culture using one of four fictional touchstones. The results:

| "A lot like *The Office*" 57% | "More like *Dilbert* than I'd like to admit" 24% | "*M*A*S*H*, on a good day" 14% | "Like *Leave It to Beaver*" 5% |

Source: From "The Big Picture," *BusinessWeek*. Reprinted from May 25, 2007 issue of *BusinessWeek* by special permission. Copyright © 2007 by The McGraw-Hill Companies, Inc.

complex. Those who built a management career within that culture—Jeff Immelt at GE, Anne Mulcahy at Xerox, Alan Lafley at P&G—have the benefit of knowledge of the culture and credibility as an "initiated" member of that culture. This may be quite useful in helping engender confidence as they take on the task of leader of that culture or, perhaps more difficult (as with these three), as change agent for parts of that culture as the company moves forward.

In the other situation, a new leader who is not an "initiated" member of the culture or tribe faces a much more challenging task. Quite logically, they must earn credibility with the "tribe," which is usually somewhat resistant to change. And, very often, they are being brought in with a board of directors desiring change in the strategy, company, and usually culture. That becomes a substantial challenge for these new leaders to face. Some make it happen, others find the strength of the organization's culture far more powerful than their ability to change it.

"Cultural awareness is one of the most neglected and yet most powerful predictors of executive success and it's also one of the things [incoming new] executives know the least about," says Kenneth Siegel, a managerial psychologist with Beverly Hills–based Impact Group, who works with boards and executive teams to improve performance.[16] And just because an executive worked in a high-performance company does not necessarily mean they are the right person to lead somewhere else. Siegel suggests that board members and

[16] "Culture Club," *BusinessWeek*, March 3, 2008.

others engaged in hiring senior management ask themselves a simple question before hiring their next executive: "Will this person enhance the culture we have here or be devoured by it?"[17] Why? Because a cultural mismatch could disrupt organizational performance for years to come as well as have a major impact on that executive's future career options. That makes the decision of bringing in an outsider, as a new leader, as important to the executive as it is to the hiring organization.[18]

Exhibit 12.8, Strategy in Action, provides an interesting example of these two perspectives as viewed through the experience of the same founder/CEO of successful companies with two very different cultures. It explains how Netflix founder and CEO Reed Hastings sought to dramatically change the culture and way of doing things at Netflix, his second company, after his experience with the nature of the culture that his first start-up, Pure Software, grew into as it became a part of IBM through a series of acquisitions and mergers. Hastings said of Pure, "We got more bureaucratic as we grew," and that it went from being a place that was fast-paced and the "where-everybody-wanted-to-be" place to a "dronish, when-does-the-day-end" software factory. After leaving Pure, Hastings spent about two years thinking about how to build a culture in his next start-up that would not have "big company creep."

At Netflix, Hastings has instilled a very unique "freedom and responsibility" culture that seeks to revolutionize both the way people rent movies and, perhaps more important to Hastings, how his managers work. In the face of Blockbuster, Wal-Mart, Amazon, the cable companies, and Apple, Hastings is attempting to create a culture so unique at Netflix that it is an "A" talent magnet, ensuring the best players in the business line up to help Netflix outsmart these very sizable competitors. And in doing so, Hastings is a "new" leader of a new company with a different business model that is trying to outlast and outcompete other, well established, major players in selling movie rentals. So in a sense, Hastings is a new leader, but with solid experience as a successful entrepreneur and innovator in similarly competitive, large, firmly entrenched, industry niches.

It may suggest that one way new leaders coming to established cultures can improve their chances of succeeding (where changing that culture is desired) is if they bring a similar background such that they establish credibility quicker, lower resistance easier, or simply have a better basis for understanding the situation. At the same time, examples such as former R. J. Reynolds executive Lou Gerstner, who took over and pulled a declining IBM from the ashes, suggest that it can also be done if you come from an entirely different industry. So it may be that the skills of the leader and other relevant experience in the strategic dynamics at previous assignments are both critical to new leaders facing established cultures they must change.

ethical standards
A person's basis for differentiating right from wrong.

Ethical standards are a person's basis for differentiating right from wrong. An earlier section of this chapter emphasized the importance of "principles" in defining what a leader needs to incorporate in his or her recipe to become an effective leader. We need not repeat those points in the context of being a leader, but it is critical to recognize that the culture of an organization, and particularly the link between the leader and the culture's very nature, is inextricably tied to the ethical standards of behavior, actions, decisions, and norms that leader personifies. Enron, Merrill Lynch, WorldCom, Ken Lay, Jeff Skilling, Bernie Ebbers, and Martha Stewart are companies, people, and situations we discussed in Chapter 3—they are all imprinted in each of our minds. They speak volumes about this very point: leaders, and their key associates, play a key role in shaping and defining the ethical standards that become absorbed into and shape the culture of the organizations

[17] Ibid.
[18] Ibid.

Hastings Builds a Revolutionary, Unique Culture

BusinessWeek

"I had the great fortune of doing a mediocre job at my first company," says Netflix Inc. founder Reed Hastings. He's talking about his 1990s start-up Pure Software, a wildly successful maker of debugging programs that, through a series of mergers, became part of IBM. Hastings says Pure, like many other outfits, went from being a heat-filled, everybody-wants-to-be-here place to a dronish, when-does-the-day-end sausage factory. "We got more bureaucratic as we grew," says Hastings.

After Pure, the Stanford-trained engineer spent two years thinking about how to ensure his next endeavor wouldn't suffer the same big-company creep.

The resulting sequel is Netflix, where Hastings is trying to revolutionize not only the way people rent movies but also how his managers work. Hastings pays his people lavishly, gives them unlimited vacations, and lets them structure their own compensation packages. In return, he expects ultra-high performance. His 400 salaried employees are expected to do the jobs of three or four people. Netflix is no frat party with beer bashes and foosball tables. Nor does the company want to play cruise director to its employees. Rather, Netflix is a tough, fulfilling, "fully formed adult" culture, says marketing manager Heather McIlhany. "There's no place to hide at Netflix."

Hastings calls his approach "freedom and responsibility." And as one might expect, employees get all cinematic when describing the vibe. Netflix is the workplace equivalent of *Ocean's 11,* says Todd S. Yellin, hired to perfect the site's movie-rating system. Hastings is Danny Ocean, the bright, charismatic leader who recruits the best in class, gives them a generous cut, and provides the flexibility to do what they *do best,* all while uniting them on a focused goal. The near-impossible mission, in this case, is trying to out-maneuver Blockbuster, Amazon, the cable companies, and Apple in the race to become the leading purveyor of online movies.

Today, Netflix is embroiled in an even tougher, two-front war: competing with Blockbuster for online supremacy in DVD rentals while also inaugurating a digital streaming service to compete with the likes of Apple. That's one mighty gang of entrenched competitors. "There's usually room in a marketplace for more than one," says Wedbush Morgan Securities analyst Michael Pachter. "But in this case there really isn't."

Hastings is betting on Netflix's *culture* to get the company out of this corner. The plan includes continuing to increase what Hastings calls "talent density." Most companies go to great scientific lengths to ensure they are paying just enough to attract talent but not a dollar more than they need to. Netflix, which hands out salaries that are typically much higher than what is customary in Silicon Valley, is unabashed in its we-pay-above-market swagger. "We're unafraid to pay high," says Hastings.

To ensure that the company is constantly nabbing A players, company talent hunters are told that money is no object. Each business group has what amounts to an internal boutique headhunting firm. Employees often recommend people they bonded with at work before (that *Ocean's 11* effect again).

Gibson Biddle, who runs the Web site, knew that Yellin, who had both deep tech and film expertise, was the perfect guy to help Netflix improve how it recommends movies to customers on its site. Yellin had worked for Biddle at a family entertainment site during the boom. The snag was that Yellin, also a film-maker, was finishing up his first feature film, *Brother's Shadow,* in Los Angeles. He also was allergic to anything corporate or publicly traded.

Impossible sell, right? But Netflix threw so much cash and flexibility at Yellin that he couldn't turn it down. During his first three months he flew back and forth between L.A. and San Francisco doing his Netflix job and finishing his movie. "This company is *über-*flexible," says Yellin. "I'm given the freedom to do what I do well without being micromanaged."

NO GOLDEN HANDCUFFS

Pay is not tied to performance reviews, nor to some predetermined raise pool, but to the job market. Netflix bosses are constantly gleaning market compensation data from new hires and then amping up salaries when needed. And what happens when someone doesn't live up to expectations? "At most companies, average performers get an average raise," says Hastings. "At Netflix, they get a generous severance package." Why? Because Hastings believes that otherwise managers feel too guilty to let someone go.

Source: From "Netflix Flees to the Max," *BusinessWeek.* Reprinted from September 24, 2007 issue of *BusinessWeek* by special permission. Copyright © 2007 by The McGraw-Hill Companies, Inc.

they lead. Those ethical standards then become powerful, informal guidelines for the behaviors, decisions, and dealings of members of that culture or tribe.

Leaders use every means available to them as an organizational leader to influence an organization's culture and their relationship with it. It bears repeating in this regard that reward systems, assignment of new managers from within versus outside the organization, composition of the firm's board of directors, reporting relationships, and organizational structure—each of these fundamental elements of executing a company's vision and strategy are also a leader's key "levers" for attempting to shape organizational culture in a direction she or he sees it needing to go. Because we have already discussed these levers, we move on to other ways leaders have sought to shape and reinforce their organization's culture.

Emphasize Key Themes or Dominant Values

Businesses build strategies around distinct competitive advantages they possess or seek. Quality, differentiation, cost advantages, and speed are four key sources of competitive advantage. Insightful leaders nurture key themes or dominant values within their organization that reinforce competitive advantages they seek to maintain or build. Key themes or dominant values may center around wording in an advertisement. They are often found in internal company communications. They are most often found as a new vocabulary used by company personnel to explain "who we are." At Xerox, the key themes include respect for the individual and services to the customer. At Procter & Gamble (P&G), the overarching value is product quality; McDonald's uncompromising emphasis on QSCV— quality, service, cleanliness, and value—through meticulous attention to detail is legendary; Southwest Airlines is driven by the "family feeling" theme, which builds a team spirit and nurtures each employee's cooperative attitude toward others, cheerful outlook toward life, and pride in a job well done. Du Pont's safety orientation—a report of every accident must be on the chairman's desk within 24 hours—has resulted in a safety record that was 27 times better than the chemical industry average and 68 times better than the all-manufacturing average.

Encourage Dissemination of Stories and Legends about Core Values

Companies with strong cultures are enthusiastic collectors and tellers of stories, anecdotes, and legends in support of basic beliefs. Frito-Lay's zealous emphasis on customer service is reflected in frequent stories about potato chip route salespeople who have slogged through sleet, mud, hail, snow, and rain to uphold the 99.5 percent service level to customers in which the entire company takes great pride. Milliken (a textile leader) holds "sharing" rallies once every quarter at which teams from all over the company swap success stories and ideas. Typically, more than 100 teams make five-minute presentations over a two-day period. Every rally is designed around a major theme, such as quality, cost reduction, or customer service. No criticisms are allowed, and awards are given to reinforce this institutionalized approach to storytelling. L.L.Bean tells customer service stories; 3M tells innovation stories; P&G, Johnson & Johnson, IBM, and Maytag tell quality and innovation stories. These stories are very important in developing an organizational culture, because organization members identify strongly with them and come to share the beliefs and values they support.

Institutionalize Practices That Systematically Reinforce Desired Beliefs and Values

Companies with strong cultures are clear on what their beliefs and values need to be and take the process of shaping those beliefs and values very seriously. Most important, the values espoused by these companies underlay the strategies they employ. For example, McDonald's has a yearly contest to determine the best hamburger cooker in its chain. First, there is a competition to determine the best hamburger cooker in each store; next, the store winners compete in regional championships; finally, the regional winners compete in the "All-American" contest. The winners, who are widely publicized throughout the company, get trophies and All-American patches to wear on their McDonald's uniforms.

Adapt Some Very Common Themes in Their Own Unique Ways

The most typical beliefs that shape organizational culture include (1) a belief in being the best (or, as at GE, "better than the best"); (2) a belief in superior quality and service; (3) a belief in the importance of people as individuals and a faith in their ability to make a strong contribution; (4) a belief in the importance of the details of execution, the nuts and bolts of doing the job well; (5) a belief that customers should reign supreme; (6) a belief in inspiring people to do their best, whatever their ability; (7) a belief in the importance of informal communication; and (8) a belief that growth and profits are essential to a company's well-being. Every company implements these beliefs differently (to fit its particular situation), and every company's values are the handiwork of one or two legendary figures in leadership positions. Accordingly, every company has a distinct culture that it believes no other company can copy successfully. And in companies with strong cultures, managers and workers either accept the norms of the culture or opt out from the culture and leave the company.

The stronger a company's culture and the more that culture is directed toward customers and markets, the less the company uses policy manuals, organization charts, and detailed rules and procedures to enforce discipline and norms. The reason is that the guiding values inherent in the culture convey in crystal-clear fashion what everybody is supposed to do in most situations. Poorly performing companies often have strong cultures. However, their cultures are dysfunctional, being focused on internal politics or operating by the numbers as opposed to emphasizing customers and the people who make and sell the product.

Manage Organizational Culture in a Global Organization[19]

The reality of today's global organizations is that organizational culture must recognize cultural diversity. *Social norms* create differences across national boundaries that influence how people interact, read personal cues, and otherwise interrelate socially. *Values* and *attitudes* about similar circumstances also vary from country to country. Where individualism is central to a North American's value structure, the needs of the group dominate the value structure of their Japanese counterparts. *Religion* is yet another source of cultural differences. Holidays, practices, and belief structures differ in very fundamental ways that must

---

[19] Differing backgrounds, often referred to as *cultural diversity,* is something that most managers will certainly see more of, both because of the growing cultural diversity domestically and the obvious diversification of cultural backgrounds that result from global acquisitions and mergers. For example, Harold Epps, manager of a computer keyboard plant in Boston, manages 350 employees representing 44 countries of origin and 19 languages.

EXHIBIT 12.9
**Managing the
Strategy-Culture
Relationship**

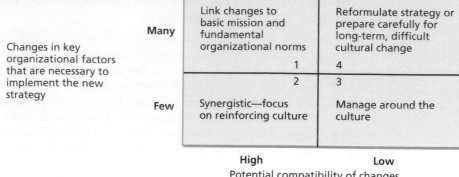

Changes in key
organizational factors
that are necessary to
implement the new
strategy

	High	**Low**
Many	Link changes to basic mission and fundamental organizational norms 1	Reformulate strategy or prepare carefully for long-term, difficult cultural change 4
Few	2 Synergistic—focus on reinforcing culture	3 Manage around the culture

Potential compatibility of changes
with existing culture

be taken into account as one attempts to shape organizational culture in a global setting. Finally, *education,* or ways people are accustomed to learning, differs across national borders. Formal classroom learning in the United States may teach things that are only learned via apprenticeship in other cultures. Because the process of shaping an organizational culture often involves considerable "education," leaders should be sensitive to global differences in approaches to education to make sure their cultural education efforts are effective. Henning Kagermann, former CEO of German-based global software company SAP, spoke to this issue when he said: "If you are a big company, you need to tap into the global talent pool. It's foolish to believe the smartest people are in one nation. In Germany, we now have this big public debate about there being a shortage of engineers in the country. Well, I don't care, or at least not as CEO of SAP. We are a collection of talented engineers in Germany, India, China, the U.S., Israel, Brazil, and the diversity therein represented enriches the culture, creativity, and market responsiveness of SAP."[20] Kagermann was seeking significant representation of cultures and communities worldwide so that SAP truly reflected the vast global settings in which it does business.

Manage the Strategy-Culture Relationship

Managers find it difficult to think through the relationship between a firm's culture and the critical factors on which strategy depends. They quickly recognize, however, that key components of the firm—structure, staff, systems, people, style—influence the ways in which key managerial tasks are executed and how critical management relationships are formed. And implementation of a new strategy is largely concerned with adjustments in these components to accommodate the perceived needs of the strategy. Consequently, managing the strategy-culture relationship requires sensitivity to the interaction between the changes necessary to implement the new strategy and the compatibility or "fit" between those changes and the firm's culture. Exhibit 12.9 provides a simple framework for managing the strategy-culture relationship by identifying four basic situations a firm might face.

Link to Mission

A firm in cell 1 is faced with a situation in which implementing a new strategy requires several changes in structure, systems, managerial assignments, operating procedures, or other fundamental aspects of the firm. However, most of the changes are potentially compatible with the existing organizational culture. Firms in this situation usually have a tradition of

[20] "Tapping Global Talent in Software," *BusinessWeek,* June 9, 2007.

effective performance and are either seeking to take advantage of a major opportunity or are attempting to redirect major product-market operations consistent with proven core capabilities. Such firms are in a very promising position: they can pursue a strategy requiring major changes but still benefit from the power of cultural reinforcement.

Four basic considerations should be emphasized by firms seeking to manage a strategy-culture relationship in this context:

1. *Key changes should be visibly linked to the basic company mission.* Because the company mission provides a broad official foundation for the organizational culture, top executives should use all available internal and external forums to reinforce the message that the changes are inextricably linked to it.

2. *Emphasis should be placed on the use of existing personnel* where possible to fill positions created to implement the new strategy. Existing personnel embody the shared values and norms that help ensure cultural compatibility as major changes are implemented.

3. *Care should be taken if adjustments in the reward system are needed.* These adjustments should be consistent with the current reward system. If, for example, a new product-market thrust requires significant changes in the way sales are made, and, therefore, in incentive compensation, common themes (e.g., incentive oriented) should be emphasized. In this way, current and future reward approaches are related, and the changes in the reward system are justified (encourage development of less familiar markets).

4. *Key attention should be paid to the changes that are least compatible with the current culture,* so current norms are not disrupted. For example, a firm may choose to subcontract an important step in a production process because that step would be incompatible with the current culture.

P&G's new innovation approach under Alan Lafley, described in Exhibit 12.10, Strategy in Action, offers an excellent example of a company in this situation. P&G's long-standing mission as a consumer products company had been one of innovative product design and development. Alan Lafley was very careful to push for a more open culture in terms of who would help P&G innovate more effectively, but he was also emphatic about linking these new efforts at changing how the "great innovator" innovated with the core notion that P&G people, and P&G's 100-year-old tradition or mission was still *THE* global consumer products innovator. He linked changes to the basic P&G mission. Lafley next emphasized speaking positively about P&G people and getting them to buy in to the changes he sought. He placed emphasis on existing personnel. Third, he included new rewards to encourage acceptance of the different way of doing things. And fourth, he made sure on changes that were "stretching people too much" to use what he called an accelerator and a throttle approach. He identified himself as the accelerator, pushing aggressively for change. And he assigned his managers as his throttle, to regularly meet and discuss and perhaps alter the pace of change, depending on their assessment of whether the changes were taking or whether people were being pushed to change too quickly. So in this way Lafley made sure to monitor changes least compatible with P&G's current culture.

Maximize Synergy

A firm in cell 2 needs only a few organizational changes to implement its new strategy, and those changes are potentially quite compatible with its current culture. A firm in this situation should emphasize two broad themes:

1. *Take advantage of the situation to reinforce and solidify the current culture.*
2. *Use this time of relative stability to remove organizational roadblocks to the desired culture.*

Recreating P&G and Its 170-Year-Old Culture

Alan Lafley has dramatically changed Procter & Gamble since he became CEO. Founded in 1837, it has long had a culture that emphasized internally focused, "invented-here" innovation; incremental innovation; and intense loyalty to its brands like Tide, Crest, and Pampers. Lafley, a P&G veteran, turned it upside down, much to others' surprise. He followed Durk Jager, an aggressive change agent who launched several new brands, openly criticized P&G's internally focused culture, and sought to dramatically change that culture. Jager's efforts at changing P&G failed to improve earnings, which, along with employee resistance, resulted in his departure. Lafley then replaced Jager.

Lafley, considered an insider, has opened up P&G far beyond what anyone expected. He has made innovation from folks outside P&G a key priority, started new product lines, and outsourced key functions like IT and soap manufacturing. He has made major acquisitions and moved P&G into the beauty care business. He personally spends considerable time with everyday consumers around the globe to understand their basic cleaning product needs and processes.

Lafley described his perspective in an interview with Jay Greene of *BusinessWeek*:

Q: When you started, you weren't perceived as a forceful change agent like your predecessor. Yet you're making more dramatic changes. Can you discuss that?

A: Durk and I had believed very strongly that the company had to change and make fundamental changes in a lot of the same directions. There are two simple differences: One is I'm very externally focused. I expressed the change in the context of how we're going to serve consumers better, how we're going to win with the retailer, and how we're going to defeat the competitor in the marketplace.

The most important thing—I didn't attack. I avoided saying P&G people are bad. I thought that was a big mistake [on Jager's part]. The difference is, I preserved the core of the culture and pulled people where I wanted to go. I enrolled them in change. I didn't tell them.

Q: Why did you both see a need for change?

A: We were looking at slow growth. An inability to move quickly, to commercialize on innovation and get full advantage out of it. We were looking at new technologies that were changing competition in our industry, retailers, and the supply base. We were looking at a world that all of a sudden was going to go 24/7, and we weren't ready for that kind of world.

Q: Are you concerned about the [trying to change P&G too fast]?

A: I'm worried that I will ask the organization to change ahead of its understanding, capability, and commitment, because that's a problem.

I have been a catalyst of change and encourager of change and a coach of change management.

And I've tried not to drive change for the sake of change.

Q: How do you pace change?

A: I have tremendous trust in my management team. I let them be the brake. I am the accelerator. I help with direction and let them make the business strategic choices.

Q: Did the fact that P&G was in crisis when you came in help you implement change?

A: It was easier. I was lucky. When you have a mess, you have a chance to make more changes.

Source: Jay Greene and Mike France, "P&G: New & Improved," *BusinessWeek*, July 7, 2003.

3M's current effort to reacquire its culture of innovation illustrates this situation. Earlier this decade, James McNerney became the first outsider to lead 3M in its 100-year history. He had barely stepped off the plane before he announced he would change the DNA of the place. His playbook was classic pursuit of efficiency: he axed 8,000 workers (about 11 percent of the workforce), intensified the performance-review process, tightened the purse strings, and implemented a Six Sigma program to decrease production defects and increase efficiency. Five years later, McNerney abruptly left for a bigger opportunity—Boeing. His successor, George Buckley, faced a challenging question: whether the relentless emphasis on efficiency had made 3M a less creative company. That's a vitally important issue for a company whose very identity is built on innovation—the company that has always prided itself on drawing at least one-third of sales from products released in the past five years; today that fraction has slipped to only one-quarter.

Those results are not coincidental. Efficiency programs such as Six Sigma are designed to identify problems in work processes—and then use rigorous measurement to reduce variation and eliminate defects. When these types of initiatives become ingrained in a company's culture, as they did at 3M, creativity can easily get squelched. After all, a breakthrough innovation is something that challenges existing procedures and norms. "Invention is by its very nature a disorderly process," says CEO Buckley, who has dialed down some key McNerney initiatives as he attempts to return 3M to its roots and its culture of innovation. "You can't put a Six Sigma process into that area and say, well, I'm getting behind on invention, so I'm going to schedule myself for three good ideas on Wednesday and two on Friday. That's not how creativity works." While process excellence demands precision, consistency, and repetition, innovation calls for variation, failure, and serendipity.[21] Buckley is taking advantage of this difficult situation to reinforce and solidify 3M's "re"-embrace of its former, innovation culture by bringing back flexible funding for innovative ideas among other traditions. At the same time, he is using the general embrace of a return to its old culture to make some key changes in manufacturing practices and plant locations outside the United States to make 3M more cost effective and competitive in a global economy.

Manage around the Culture

A firm in cell 3 must make a few major organizational changes to implement its new strategy, but these changes are potentially inconsistent with the firm's current organizational culture. The critical question for a firm in this situation is whether it can make the changes with a reasonable chance of success.

A firm can manage around the culture in various ways: create a separate firm or division; use task forces, teams, or program coordinators; subcontract; bring in an outsider; or sell out. These are a few of the available options, but the key idea is to create a method of achieving the change desired that avoids confronting the incompatible cultural norms. As cultural resistance diminishes, the change may be absorbed into the firm.

IBM's 2004 sale of its PC business to China's Lenovo, creating the third-largest global PC firm behind Dell and HP, was a strategic decision it took three years to conclude. IBM management became increasingly concerned with the problem that the PC business, and the culture surrounding it, were incompatible with the culture and direction IBM's core business had been taking for some time. The conflict, and the inability to reconcile different cultural needs, led IBM executives to explore the sale of the PC division to Lenovo. At the time IBM's PC division was in disarray and losing $400 million annually. Lenovo's reaction was to send IBM packing out of China with a sense they had tried to take Lenovo's executives for fools who would buy a "pig in a poke." But IBM executives, still desperately concerned about the fundamental and cultural difference between the PC business and the rest of IBM set about an intense 18-month effort to wring costs out of the PC's supply chain, bring it back to profitability, and then go to call on Lenovo again. They achieved both in 18 months and, in their next business, found a more receptive Lenovo management team—ultimately concluding the deal a few months later. In so doing, IBM worked feverishly even to include creating a profitable global PC business only to then sell it quickly and cheaply so that it could "manage around a culture" in the sense of allowing IBM to unify around a different

[21] "At 3M, a Struggle Between Efficiency and Creativity," *BusinessWeek*, June 11, 2007.

business model and remove the business it was most known for, the IBM-PC business, from its organization along with the cultural incompatibility it represented.

Reformulate the Strategy or Culture

A firm in cell 4 faces the most difficult challenge in managing the strategy-culture relationship. To implement its new strategy, such a firm must make organizational changes that are incompatible with its current, usually entrenched, values and norms. A firm in this situation faces the complex, expensive, and often long-term challenge of changing its culture; it is a challenge that borders on impossible.

When a strategy requires massive organizational change and engenders cultural resistance, a firm should determine whether reformulation of the strategy is appropriate. Are all of the organizational changes really necessary? Is there any real expectation that the changes will be acceptable and successful? If these answers are yes, then massive changes are often necessary. Alan Mulally's actions at Ford over the last few years saw him making major changes in an attempt to change Ford's culture to suit its new strategy: bringing outsiders in as top execs, changing long-standing executive compensation programs, emphasizing sales and marketing over the traditional, patronage-based culture as, sadly, Ford's most "prized" cultural element. These are elements through which Ford, under Mulally, is undergoing massive change as he tries to build a different culture compatible with a new vision and strategy.

The John Deere company faced a growing challenge in a globally competitive farm equipment industry as it moved into the twenty-first century. Its financial performance was marginal, and it retained a "family" culture borne out of its century-long roots in the land and farm setting it served. New CEO Bob Lane first developed a new strategy that placed straightforward emphasis on improving Deere's efficient use of its assets and clear profitability targets. Pursuing this strategy required several organizational changes at Deere, which were received relatively easily in a tradition-laden company. But Lane quickly found that a greater challenge needed confronting—and that was Deere's "family" culture, which manifests itself in what he called a "best efforts mentality." That mentality drove the culture that had many Deere managers often satisfied with making earnest efforts and doing "pretty good." Lane had to change that culture, or change his new results-driven strategy. He chose to change the culture, which meant moving from the commonly heard expression of "the John Deere family" to one that prioritized high-performance teams. As Lane described it, "We're changing from being a family to being a high-performance team. To use an American football analogy, some people prefer to play intramurals. That's okay, but they are no longer a good fit for John Deere. It was as if you could always count on Deere to move the ball at least six or seven yards. And when we got to that point, we could say 'good work, good enough'—even though we hadn't reached the first-down marker." Now, Deere people are expected to have exhausted every legitimate effort to move the ball farther and meet the goal, and then move the ball farther again. CEO Lane, and his management team, have decided to stick with the strategy and reformulate Deere's culture.[22]

[22] "Leading Change," *McKinsey on Organization,* McKinsey and Company, December 2006.

Summary

This chapter has examined organizational leadership and organization culture—two factors essential to the successful implementation and execution of a company's strategic plan. Organizational leadership is guiding and shepherding an organization over time and developing that organization's future leadership and its organization culture.

We saw that good organizational leadership involves three considerations: clarifying strategic intent, building an organization, and shaping the organization's culture. Strategic intent is clarified through the leader's vision, a broad picture of where he or she is leading the firm, and candid attention to and clear expectations about performance.

Leaders use education, principles, and perseverance to build their organization. Education involves familiarizing managers and future leaders with an effective understanding of the business and the skills they need to develop. Perseverance, the ability to stick to the challenge when most others falter, is an unquestionable tool for leaders to instill faith in the vision they seek when times are hard. Principles are the leader's personal standards that guide her or his sense of honesty, integrity and ethical behavior. They are more essential than ever in today's world as key building blocks for the type of organization for which a leader's principles reflect and are watched with great interest by every manager, employee, customer, and supplier of the organization.

Leaders start to shape organizational culture by the passion they bring to their role, and their choice and development of young managers and future leaders. Passion, a highly motivated sense of commitment to what you do and want to do, is a force that permeates attitudes throughout an organization and helps them buy into your cultural aspirations. Combining those with the skills, aspirations, and inclinations you seek to make the vision a reality—and then helping them develop—is a key way to build a culture over the long term. One of the key skills of these rising leaders is to learn how to motivate, lead, and get others to do what they need.

Understanding seven sources of power and influence, rather than just the power of position and punishment, is a critical skill for effective future leaders to grasp.

Organizational culture is the set of important assumptions, values, beliefs, and norms that members of an organization share in common. The organizational leader plays a critical role in developing, sustaining, and changing organizational culture. Ethical standards, the leader's basis for differentiating right from wrong, quickly spread as a centerpiece between the leader and the organization's culture. Leaders use many means to reinforce and develop their organization's culture—from rewards and appointments to storytelling and rituals. Managing the strategy-culture relationship requires different approaches, depending on the match between the demands of the new strategy and the compatibility of the culture with that strategy. This chapter examined four different scenarios.

Key Terms

ethical standards, *p. 342*
expert influence, *p. 338*
information power, *p. 338*
leadership development, *p. 331*
leader's vision, *p. 328*
organizational culture, *p. 340*

organizational leadership, *p. 326*
passion (of a leader), *p. 334*
peer influence, *p. 339*
perseverance (of a leader), *p. 332*
position power, *p. 338*
principles (of a leader), *p. 333*

punitive power, *p. 338*
referent influence, *p. 338*
reward power, *p. 338*
strategic intent, *p. 328*

Questions for Discussion

1. Think about any two leaders you have known, preferably one good and one weak. They can be businesspersons, coaches, someone you work(ed) with, and so forth. Make a list of five traits, practices, or characteristics that cause you to consider one good and the other weak. Compare the things you chose with the seven factors used to differentiate effective organizational leadership in the first half of this chapter.

2. This chapter describes seven attributes that enable good leadership—vision, performance, principles, education of subordinates, perseverance, passion, and leader selection/development. Which one have you found to be the most meaningful to you in the leaders you respond to the best?

3. Consider the following situation and determine whether the VC group is engaging in something that would violate your principles, or be totally acceptable to you. Explain why.

> Who likes those ubiquitous online pop-up ads planted by intrusive spyware? Technology Crossover Ventures is betting few do. The Silicon Valley venture-capital firm helped to finance the anti-spyware company Webroot Software. But it appears to hedge that bet with a sizable investment in Claria, a company vilified for spreading spyware.
>
> More than 40 million Web surfers viewed Claria ads. TCV pumped at least $13 million into Claria, but it has removed the company from a list of investments on its Web site.
>
> Critics wonder why TCV would make dual investments. "Users are rubbed the wrong way by even the suggestion that the same companies that made this mess are now profiting from helping to clean it up," says Harvard University researcher and spyware expert Ben Edelman. TCV declined to comment. There is a similar element in both ventures: the potential to make money.

4. Read Exhibit 12.3. What would you do if you were asked to serve as an Ethics Review Arbitrator and render a decision on what should happen to the Duke MBA students? Summarize the key reasons supporting your ruling.

5. Do you think Alan Lafley is a good organizational leader? What is his most important contribution to his organizational culture in your opinion?

6. What three sources of power and influence are best suited to you as a manager?

7. Describe two organizations you have been a part of based on differences in their organizational cultures.

8. What key things is Alan Mulally doing at Ford as an organizational leader to shape Ford's organizational culture? Do you think he will succeed? Why?

Chapter **Thirteen**

Strategic Control

After reading and studying this chapter, you should be able to

1. Describe and illustrate four types of strategic control.

2. Summarize the balanced scorecard approach and how it integrates strategic and operational control.

3. Illustrate the use of controls to guide and monitor strategy implementation.

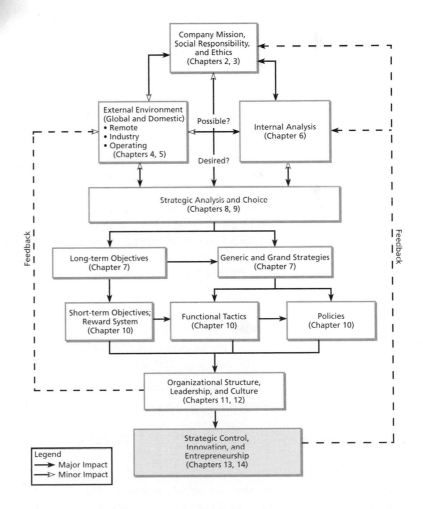

Company Mission, Social Responsibility, and Ethics (Chapters 2, 3)

External Environment (Global and Domestic)
- Remote
- Industry
- Operating
(Chapters 4, 5)

Possible?

Internal Analysis (Chapter 6)

Desired?

Strategic Analysis and Choice (Chapters 8, 9)

Long-term Objectives (Chapter 7)

Generic and Grand Strategies (Chapter 7)

Short-term Objectives; Reward System (Chapter 10)

Functional Tactics (Chapter 10)

Policies (Chapter 10)

Organizational Structure, Leadership, and Culture (Chapters 11, 12)

Strategic Control, Innovation, and Entrepreneurship (Chapters 13, 14)

Feedback

Legend
→ Major Impact
⇢ Minor Impact

STRATEGIC CONTROL

Strategies are forward looking, designed to be accomplished several years into the future. They are based on management assumptions about numerous events that have not yet occurred. How should executives "control" a strategy, and its execution?

Consider the recent experiences of Motorola and Dell Computer. Motorola's CEO Ed Zander looked like a genius in early 2007, executing his strategy of cranking out "wow" products like the Razr phone and delivering them via an even-more-efficient supply chain. Then, quickly, Motorola ran into a cell-phone price war, and its profit margins sank dramatically, revealing an outsourced manufacturing process that was much less efficient and more costly than rival Nokia's in-house operations were steadily delivering. Motorola's stock quickly dropped almost 50 percent in value, and CEO Zander faced some serious challenges to his leadership and the efficacy of the Motorola strategy.

Dell Computer saw its rival Hewlett-Packard struggle with a poorly integrated acquisition of Compaq and a confusing reorganization of HP a few years ago. IBM sold its PC business to China's Lenovo, admitting it couldn't compete with the Dell approach. Dell was a world leader in PCs and was broadening its offerings into printers and other electronic devices. But within two years, HP's new CEO Mark Hurd had HP much more focused, and it soon eclipsed Dell as the world's largest seller of PCs. Lenovo was gaining strength in the Asia-Pacific area. And Apple's renewal was putting pressure on, too, as more people saw the Mac as a viable and desirable option to PCs. Dell finds itself continuing to loose market share—experiencing declining profitability, excess inventory, and major problems with outsourced customer service. Founder Michael Dell's return as CEO to replace his handpicked successor Ken Rollins has had more than three years to work, but he still is yet to make major headway rebuilding Dell and any newly successful strategy.

So we see two great companies with seemingly solid strategies that deteriorated very quickly. What they have done or done better? How could Motorola and Dell have adjusted their strategies and actions when key premises, technology, competitors, or sudden events changed everything for them? How could they have established better "strategic control" and reduced the impact of negative events or taken advantage of new opportunities?

strategic control
Management efforts to track a strategy as it is being implemented, detect problems or changes in its underlying premises, and make necessary adjustments.

Strategic control is concerned with tracking a strategy as it is being implemented, detecting problems or changes in its underlying premises, and making necessary adjustments. In contrast to postaction control, strategic control is concerned with guiding action on behalf of the strategy as that action is taking place and when the end result is still several years off. Managers responsible for the success of a strategy typically are concerned with two sets of questions:

1. Are we moving in the proper direction? Are key things falling into place? Are our assumptions about major trends and changes correct? Are we doing the critical things that need to be done? Should we adjust or abort the strategy?
2. How are we performing? Are objectives and schedules being met? Are costs, revenues, and cash flows matching projections? Do we need to make operational changes?

The rapidly accelerating level of change in the global marketplace has made the need for strategic control key in managing a company. This chapter examines strategic control.

ESTABLISHING STRATEGIC CONTROLS

The control of strategy can be characterized as a form of "steering control." As time elapses between the initial implementation of a strategy and achievement of its intended results, investments are made and numerous projects and actions are undertaken to implement the strategy. Also, during that time, changes are taking place in both the environmental situation and the firm's internal situation. Strategic controls are necessary to steer the firm through these events. They must provide the basis for adapting the firm's strategic actions and directions in response to these developments and changes. The four basic types of strategic control summarized in Exhibit 13.1 are

1. Premise control.
2. Strategic surveillance.
3. Special alert control.
4. Implementation control.

Premise Control

premise control

Management process of systematically and continuously checking to determine whether premises upon which the strategy is based are still valid.

Every strategy is based on certain planning premises—assumptions or predictions. **Premise control** is the systematic recognition and analysis of assumptions upon which a strategic plan is based, to determine if those assumptions remain valid in changing circumstances and in light of new information. If a vital premise is no longer valid, the strategy may have to be changed. The sooner an invalid premise can be recognized and rejected, the better are the chances that an acceptable shift in the strategy can be devised. Planning premises are primarily concerned with environmental and industry factors.

Environmental Factors

Although a firm has little or no control over environmental factors, these factors exercise considerable influence over the success of its strategy, and strategies usually are based on key premises about them. Inflation, technology, interest rates, regulation, and demographic/social changes are examples of such factors.

The third-generation Internet, Web 3.0, with cloud computing, virtualization, and ultra mobility, is spawning an instantaneously connected global youth culture that presents both a challenge to the old ways of doing business and an opportunity to gain tremendous leverage via the right goods and services. "Flying blind" is how some executives describe their effort to adapt to it: the tens of millions of digital elite who are the vanguard of a fast emerging global culture based on smartphones, blogs, text messaging, social networks, YouTube, Facebook, iPhone apps, to mention a few. These highly influential young people are sharing ideas and information across borders that will drive products, employment, services, food, fashion, and ideas—rapidly. Savvy companies are recognizing this phenomenon as perhaps the most critical environmental factor/phenomenon they need to monitor and understand.[1]

Industry Factors

The performance of the firms in a given industry is affected by industry factors. Competitors, suppliers, product substitutes, and barriers to entry are a few of the industry factors about which strategic assumptions are made.

Rubbermaid has long been held up as a model of predictable growth, creative management, and rapid innovation in the plastic housewares and toy industry. Its premise in its most recent strategic plan was that large retail chains would continue to prefer its products over competitors' because of this core competence. This premise included continued receptivity to regular price increases when necessitated by raw materials costs. Retailers, most notably Wal-Mart, recently balked at Rubbermaid's attempt to raise prices to offset the rapid doubling of petroleum-based resin costs in 2008. Furthermore, traditionally overlooked

---

[1] Steve Hamm, "Children of the Web," *BusinessWeek*, July 2, 2007.

EXHIBIT 13.1
Four Types of
Strategic Control

Source: From *Academy of Management Review* by G. Schreyogg and H. Steinmann. Copyright © 1987 by Academy of Management. Reproduced with permission of Academy of Management via Copyright Clearance Center.

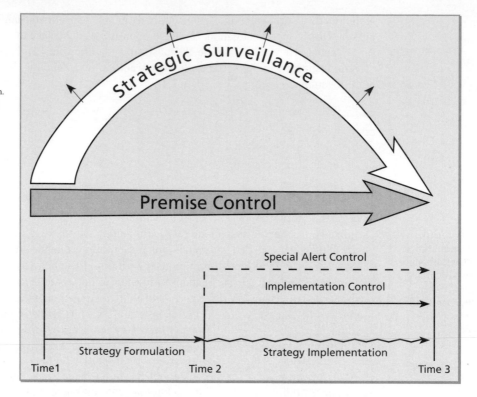

Characteristics of the Four Types of Strategic Control

	Types of Strategic Control			
Basic Characteristics	**Premise Control**	**Implementation Control**	**Strategic Surveillance**	**Special Alert Control**
Objects of control	Planning premises and projections	Key strategic thrusts and milestones	Potential threats and opportunities related to the strategy	Occurrence of recognizable but unlikely events
Degree of focusing	High	High	Low	High
Data acquisition:				
Formalization	Medium	High	Low	High
Centralization	Low	Medium	Low	High
Use with:				
Environmental factors	Yes	Seldom	Yes	Yes
Industry factors	Yes	Seldom	Yes	Yes
Strategy-specific factors	No	Yes	Seldom	Yes
Company-specific factors	No	Yes	Seldom	Seldom

Source: From *Academy of Management Review* by G. Schreyogg and H. Steinmann. Copyright © 1987 by Academy of Management. Reproduced with permission of Academy of Management via Copyright Clearance Center.

competitors have begun to make inroads with computerized stocking services. Rubbermaid is moving aggressively to adjust its strategy because of the response of Wal-Mart and other key retailers. And that adjustment required, paradoxically, an amazingly rapid readjustment as those same petroleum prices fell precipitously in 2009.

Strategies are often based on numerous premises, some major and some minor, about environmental and industry variables. Tracking all of these premises is unnecessarily expensive and time consuming. Managers must select premises whose change (1) is likely and (2) would have a major impact on the firm and its strategy.

Strategic Surveillance

strategic surveillance
Management efforts to monitor a broad range of events inside and more often outside the firm that are likely to affect the course of its strategy over time.

By their nature, premise controls are focused controls; strategic surveillance, however, is unfocused. **Strategic surveillance** is designed to monitor a broad range of events inside and outside the firm that are likely to affect the course of its strategy.[2] The basic idea behind strategic surveillance is that important yet unanticipated information may be uncovered by a general monitoring of multiple information sources.

Strategic surveillance must be kept as unfocused as possible. It should be a loose "environmental scanning" activity. Trade magazines, *The Wall Street Journal,* trade conferences, conversations, and intended and unintended observations are all subjects of strategic surveillance. Despite its looseness, strategic surveillance provides an ongoing, broad-based vigilance in all daily operations that may uncover information relevant to the firm's strategy. P&G's widely admired CEO Alan Lafley has long used "commercial anthropology," his way of describing strategic surveillance, to identify and monitor developments that are central to the success of its ongoing innovation strategy to provide products that meet basic needs better and do so repeatedly. In Exhibit 13.2, Top Strategist, Lafley talks about watching women wash clothes in rivers in China, watching others doing laundry in Mexico, and having European managers study consumer preferences in buying diapers from German and French discount retails—all examples of strategic surveillance, Alan Lafley style.

Special Alert Control

special alert control
Management actions undertaken to thoroughly, and often very rapidly, reconsider a firm's strategy because of a sudden, unexpected event.

Another type of strategic control, really a subset of the other three, is special alert control. A **special alert control** is the thorough, and often rapid, reconsideration of the firm's strategy because of a sudden, unexpected event. The tragic events of September 11, 2001; an outside firm's sudden acquisition of a leading competitor; an unexpected product difficulty, like the fingertip in a bowl of Wendy's chili—events of these kinds can drastically alter the firm's strategy.

Such an event should trigger an immediate and intense reassessment of the firm's strategy and its current strategic situation. In many firms, crisis teams handle the firm's initial response to unforeseen events that may have an immediate effect on its strategy. IBM's shock at the precipitous decline in the sales growth and profitability of its core IT services business resulted in a special alert and ongoing focus on this business's strategy to allow it to immediately adjust by cutting staff or changing services frequently each quarter.

The sudden release of a photo of Olympic Gold Medalist Michael Phelps at a South Carolina fraternity house party using a special pipe often associated with smoking marijuana in early 2009 caused an instant crisis for several companies paying Phelps as a celebrity sports endorser of their products after his unprecedented eight gold medals in the Olympics held months earlier in China. Kellogg chose to cancel his contract with their cereals, while

[2] G. Schreyogg and H. Steinmann, "Strategic Control: A New Perspective," *Academy of Management Review* 12, no. 1 (1987), p. 101.

Top Strategist
Alan Lafley, CEO, P&G

**Exhibit
13.2**

Alan Lafley turned P&G into a global juggernaut. Some 4 billion people, more than half the world's population, use a P&G product each day. Lafley's philosophy on how to do that is very simple: observe people going about their daily lives, identify their unmet needs, and come up with new products that meet them.

He tells the story of how he had managers in Mexico study the daily washing rituals of low-income women to help kick start P&G sales in that country. He once described another time doing this himself: "I have sat with my legs in the water of a rural village in China talking with an interpreter to an older woman and her daughter doing her laundry in the river. I have probably done laundry in 25 countries. It is like being a social anthropologist." He went on to say it is really "commercial" rather than social or academic anthropology, but clarifying that in saying, "We are observing because we believe that if we don't do anything to improve the life then we don't do anything to deserve to reap the commercial rewards."

Lafley's insistence on strategic surveillance, or commercial anthropology, takes place in many forums. P&G managers in Europe noticed the accelerated growth of private-label consumer products due to the rapid growth of discount retailers like Germany's Aldi and France's Leader Price. While other leading brands were hurt, P&G's manager had been following articles in European publications looking at consumer lifestyles. "We have studied this trend for some time, and concluded that discounters can be a real opportunity." Good strategic surveillance, or commercial anthropology? Lafley was no doubt very proud.

Source: Elizabeth Rigby, "I Normally Have Lunch in 10 Minutes," *Financial Times*, December 6, 2008, Life and Arts, p.3.

Speedo chose to continue their association with Phelps. While others pondered what to do, it showed vividly why a process of special alert controls has become a key for companies using celebrity endorsers as described in Exhibit 13.3, Strategy in Action. Around the same time, the fortunately successful landing of a USAir flight in New York's Hudson River, saving all 155 lives onboard—and a reminder of United Airlines on September 11, 2001—serves to show why firms have crisis teams and contingency plans ready to activate as part of their strategic alert control processes.

Implementation Control

Strategy implementation takes place as a series of steps, programs, investments, and moves that occur over an extended time. Special programs are undertaken. Functional areas initiate strategy-related activities. Key people are added or reassigned. Resources are mobilized. In other words, managers implement strategy by converting broad plans into the concrete, incremental actions and results of specific units and individuals.

Implementation control is the type of strategic control that must be exercised as those events unfold. **Implementation control** is designed to assess whether the overall strategy should be changed in light of the results associated with the incremental actions that implement the overall strategy. The two basic types of implementation control are (1) monitoring strategic thrusts and (2) milestone reviews.

implementation control
Management efforts designed to assess whether the overall strategy should be changed in light of results associated with the incremental actions that implement the overall strategy. These are usually associated with specific strategic thrusts or projects and with predetermined milestone reviews.

PREMISE CONTROL AT NEWSCRED.COM

NewsCred.com is a Web site–based business that seeks to build advertising and content success around global obsession with news coverage. As we sit here writing this chapter, NewsCred.com is a very cool news site with a variety of applications that will become more interesting and powerful as more people visit the site and participate in its applications.

The premise underlying NewsCred.com's strategy is that people around the world will visit its site to rank the credibility of a whole host of news sources, from mainstream to bloggers, with the result being that the most credible—accurate, believable, and honest— will rise to the top of the community rankings. Some observers argue that in a politically polarized society and world, some people will trash the publications they disagree with. So, for example, *The Wall Street Journal* or *The New York Times* will be relegated to mediocre status, while media outlets and blogs barely known will rise to the top. So NewsCred.com will have to carefully monitor and control its premise, or it may just lose out on what seems an interesting Net-based business opportunity.

IMPLEMENTATION CONTROL

Boeing was scheduled to be delivering its first 787 Dreamliners in 2008. It has not. Boeing has been forced to delay the 787 program four times due to problems with a shortage of parts, the need to redesign parts of the aircraft, and incomplete work by suppliers. For example, Boeing found out in early 2009 that tens of thousands of fasteners on several aircraft had apparently been incorrectly installed after mechanics at Boeing's Seattle plant misunderstood installation instructions. Boeing's ambitious worldwide outsourcing strategy—combined with the 787 being the largest, lightest, biggest plane in history—clearly necessitated careful, coordinated implementation planning and control to meet the milestones and deadline Boeing promised its many customers.

Virgin Atlantic is one typical example. Virgin committed to buy 15 of the new aircraft, at prices approaching $200 million each. This necessitated deposits of notable sums, plus plans and commitments on Virgin's part in working these planes into its fleet, its schedules, its decisions about existing aircraft and routes, and so forth. Virgin, as we write this, having expected delivery in April 2011, is "guessing" it will be mid-2013 at the earliest.

The consolation that Boeing will pay them some compensation for the impact of these delays offers Virgin little solace. What they want from Boeing is better control of the implementation of its Dreamliner strategy. That, and a safe aircraft, seem like reasonable expectations for a $200 million price tag each.

STRATEGIC SURVEILLANCE AT WELLS FARGO

Wells Fargo, and most other banks large and small via the American Bankers Association, aggressively fought and lobbied against Wal-Mart's application for a bank charter. They didn't like the idea of losing credit card processing fees. They won the lobbying battle and Wal-Mart withdrew its application to open a bank in the United States.

According to Wal-Mart's management at the time of their application, their primary motivation was to reduce the cost of allowing customers to buy on credit every time they used a Discover, MasterCard, or Visa branded charge card. Every time a customer uses one of these cards, Wal-Mart pays a small processing fee to the bank that processes the payment. And so, from Wal-Mart's perspective, why should they give that fee to Wells Fargo or others when they could just as easily handle the processing through their own bank? They could then pass that fee back to their customer, thereby saving them money.

Wells Fargo is now carefully engaging in strategic surveillance of Wal-Mart's activities related to banking because of this situation—and because Wal-Mart now has banking operations in 38 Mexican Wal-Marts with plans to increase that number 10-fold with new "banking booths" over the next few years. Wal-Mart has filed an application in Canada seeking to open a pocket bank for its Canadian subsidiary. So is Wal-Mart going to enter the U.S. bank market from its new foreign bases? You can bet Wells Fargo and others have ongoing strategic surveillance of Wal-Mart's Mexican and Canadian banking activities so as to be ready to act.

SPECIAL ALERT CONTROL FOR CELEBRITY ENDORSEMENT COMPANIES

Critical to the strategies, and the success of many companies is the use of celebrity endorsements to promote their products and the perception of that product in the buyer's mind. Tiger Woods is almost always believable as a user of everything he endorses. Nike and Michael Jordan, Bill Cosby and Jell-O, Dan Marino and NutriSystem. But Paris Hilton's ads for

(continued)

Exhibit 13.3 cont.

Carl's Jr. and Hardees? Peyton Manning for Oreo Cookies? Catherine Zeta Jones for T-Mobile? Jason Alexander for KFC? Or, Michael Phelps for Frosted Flakes? Or even Tiger Woods for Buick (recently dropped) or Tag Heuer?

Bottom line: any company that uses the celebrity endorsement approach to build its brand and image has committed to a part of "borrowed equity," meaning they define their product by borrowing the equity, image, and reputation of the celebrity as a user/endorser. In so doing, they are well advised to maintain a careful special alert control for changes that might immediately or gradually erode the connection with that celebrity.

Monitoring Strategic Thrusts or Projects

strategic thrusts or projects
Special efforts that are early steps in executing a broader strategy, usually involving significant resource commitments yet where predetermined feedback will help management determine whether continuing to pursue the strategy is appropriate or whether it needs adjustment or major change.

As a means of implementing broad strategies, narrow strategic projects often are undertaken—projects that represent part of what needs to be done if the overall strategy is to be accomplished. These **strategic thrusts** provide managers with information that helps them determine whether the overall strategy is progressing as planned or needs to be adjusted.

Although the utility of strategic thrusts seems readily apparent, it is not always easy to use them for control purposes. It may be difficult to interpret early experience or to evaluate the overall strategy in light of such experience. One approach is to agree early in the planning process on which thrusts or which phases of thrusts are critical factors in the success of the strategy. Managers responsible for these implementation controls will single them out from other activities and observe them frequently. Another approach is to use stop/go assessments that are linked to a series of meaningful thresholds (time, costs, research and development, success, and so forth) associated with particular thrusts. Exhibit 13.3 describes Boeing's challenge to do this as it coordinates globally diverse outsourcing partners' production of various parts of the revolutionary new 787 Dreamliner fuselage and its components.

Milestone Reviews

milestone reviews
Points in time, or at the completion of major parts of a bigger strategy, where managers have predetermined they will undertake a go–no go type of review regarding the underlying strategy associated with the bigger strategy.

Managers often attempt to identify significant milestones that will be reached during strategy implementation. These milestones may be critical events, major resource allocations, or simply the passage of a certain amount of time. The **milestone reviews** that then take place usually involve a full-scale reassessment of the strategy and of the advisability of continuing or refocusing the firm's direction.

A useful example of implementation control based on milestone review is offered by an earlier Boeing's product-development strategy of entering the supersonic transport (SST) airplane market. Boeing had invested millions of dollars and years of scarce engineering talent during the first phase of its SST venture, and competition from the British/French Concorde effort was intense. Because the next phase represented a billion-dollar decision, Boeing's management established the initiation of the phase as a milestone. The milestone reviews greatly increased the estimates of production costs; predicted relatively few passengers and rising fuel costs, thus raising the estimated operating costs; and noted that the Concorde, unlike Boeing, had the benefit of massive government subsidies. These factors led Boeing's management to scrap its SST strategy in spite of high sunk costs, pride, and patriotism. Only an objective, full-scale strategy reassessment could have led to such a decision. A similar decision by Boeing regarding its strategic "bet" on the new 787 Dreamliner is very unlikely as it nears final assembly and initial test flights of this revolutionary, next-generation, composite airplane (see Exhibit 13.3).

In the SST example, a milestone review occurred at a major resource allocation decision point. Milestone reviews may also occur concurrently when a major step in a strategy's implementation is being taken or when a key uncertainty is resolved. Managers even may set an arbitrary period, say, two years, as a milestone review point. Whatever the basis for selecting that point, the critical purpose of a milestone review is to thoroughly scrutinize the firm's strategy so as to control the strategy's future.

Implementation control is also enabled through operational control systems like budgets, schedules, and key success factors. While strategic controls attempt to steer the company over an extended period (usually five years or more), operational controls provide postaction evaluation and control over short periods—usually from one month to one year. To be effective, operational control systems must take four steps common to all postaction controls:

1. Set standards of performance.
2. Measure actual performance.
3. Identify deviations from standards set.
4. Initiate corrective action.

Exhibit 13.4 illustrates a typical operational control system. These indicators represent progress after two years of a five-year strategy intended to differentiate the firm as a customer-service–oriented provider of high-quality products. Management's concern is to compare *progress to date* with *expected progress*. The *current deviation* is of particular interest because it provides a basis for examining *suggested actions* (usually suggested by subordinate managers) and for finalizing decisions on changes or adjustments in the firm's operations.

From Exhibit 13.4, it appears that the firm is maintaining control of its cost structure. Indeed, it is ahead of schedule on reducing overhead. The firm is well ahead of its delivery cycle target, while slightly below its target service-to-sales personnel ratio. Its product returns look OK, although product performance versus specification is below standard. Sales per employee and expansion of the product line are ahead of schedule. The absenteeism rate in the service area is on target, but the turnover rate is higher than that targeted. Competitors appear to be introducing products more rapidly than expected.

After deviations and their causes have been identified, the implications of the deviations for the ultimate success of the strategy must be considered. For example, the rapid product-line expansion indicated in Exhibit 13.4 may have been a response to the increased rate of competitors' product expansion. At the same time, product performance is still low, and, while the installation cycle is slightly above standard (improving customer service), the ratio of service to sales personnel is below the targeted ratio. Contributing to this substandard ratio (and perhaps reflecting a lack of organizational commitment to customer service) is the exceptionally high turnover in customer service personnel. The rapid reduction in indirect overhead costs might mean that administrative integration of customer service and product development requirements have been cut back too quickly.

This information presents operations managers with several options. They may attribute the deviations primarily to internal discrepancies. In that case, they can scale priorities up or down. For example, they might place more emphasis on retaining customer service personnel and less emphasis on overhead reduction and new-product development. On the

EXHIBIT 13.4   **Monitoring and Evaluating Performance Deviations**

Key Success Factors	Objective, Assumption, or Budget	Forecast Performance at This Time	Current Performance	Current Deviation	Analysis
Cost control: Ratio of indirect overhead cost to direct field and labor costs	10%	15%	12%	+3 (ahead)	Are we moving too fast, or is there more unnecessary overhead than was originally thought?
Gross profit	39%	40%	40%	0%	
Customer service: Installation cycle in days	2.5 days	3.2 days	2.7 days	+0.5 (ahead)	Can this progress be maintained?
Ratio of service to sales personnel	3.2	2.7	2.1	−0.6 (behind)	Why are we behind here? How can we maintain the installation-cycle progress?
Product quality: Percentage of products returned	1.0%	2.0%	2.1%	−0.1% (behind)	Why are we behind here? What are the ramifications for other operations?
Product performance versus specification	100%	92%	80%	−12% (behind)	
Marketing: Monthly sales per employee	$12,500	$11,500	$12,100	+$600 (ahead)	Good progress. Is it creating any problems to support?
Expansion of product line	6	3	5	+2 products (ahead)	Are the products ready? Are the perfect standards met?
Employee morale in service area: Absenteeism rate	2.5%	3.0%	3.0%	(on target)	Looks like a problem!
Turnover rate	5%	10 %	15%	−8% (behind)	Why are we so far behind?
Competition: New-product introductions (average number)	6	3	6	−3 (behind)	Did we underestimate timing? What are the implications for our basic assumptions?

other hand, they might decide to continue as planned in the face of increasing competition and to accept or gradually improve the customer service situation. Another possibility is reformulating the strategy or a component of the strategy in the face of rapidly increasing competition. For example, the firm might decide to emphasize more standardized or lower-priced products to overcome customer service problems and take advantage of an apparently ambitious salesforce.

This is but one of many possible interpretations of Exhibit 13.4. The important point here is the critical need to monitor progress against standards and to give serious in-depth attention to both the causes of observed deviations and the most appropriate responses to them. After the deviations have been evaluated, slight adjustments may be made to keep progress, expenditure, or other factors in line with the strategy's programmed needs. In the unusual event of extreme deviations—generally because of unforeseen changes—management is alerted to the possible need for revising the budget, reconsidering certain functional plans related to budgeted expenditures, or examining the units concerned and the effectiveness of their managers.

The Balanced Scorecard Methodology

An alternative approach linking operational and strategic control, developed by Harvard Business School professors Robert Kaplan and David Norton, is a system they named the **balanced scorecard.** Recognizing some of the weaknesses and vagueness of previous implementation and control approaches, the balanced scorecard approach was intended to provide a clear prescription as to what companies should measure in order to "balance" the financial perspective in implementation and control of strategic plans.[3] The global consulting firm Bain and Company estimates that more than 60 percent of all large global companies are using the balanced scorecard.[4]

The balanced scorecard is a management system (not only a measurement system) that enables companies to clarify their strategies, translate them into action, and provide meaningful feedback. It provides feedback around both the internal business processes and external outcomes in order to continuously improve strategic performance and results. When fully deployed, the balanced scorecard is intended to transform strategic planning from a separate top management exercise into the nerve center of an enterprise. Kaplan and Norton describe the innovation of the balanced scorecard as follows:

> The balanced scorecard retains traditional financial measures. But financial measures tell the story of past events, an adequate story for industrial age companies for which investments in long-term capabilities and customer relationships were not critical for success. These financial measures are inadequate, however, for guiding and evaluating the journey that information age companies must make to create future value through investment in customers, suppliers, employees, processes, technology, and innovation.[5]

The balanced scorecard methodology adapts the total quality management (TQM) ideas of customer-defined quality, continuous improvement, employee empowerment, and measurement-based management/feedback into an expanded methodology that includes traditional financial data and results. The balanced scorecard incorporates feedback around

balanced scorecard
A management control system that enables companies to clarify their strategies, translate them into action, and provide quantitative feedback as to whether the strategy is creating value, leveraging core competencies, satisfying the company's customers, and generating a financial reward to its shareholders.

[3] This methodology is covered in great detail in a number of books and articles by R. S. Kaplan and D. P. Norton. It is also the subject of frequent special publications by the *Harvard Business Review,* providing updated treatment of uses and improvements in the balanced scorecard methodology. See, for example, "Harvard Business Review Balanced Scorecard Report," *Harvard Business Review,* monthly, 2002 to present; Robert S. Kaplan, and David P. Norton, "The Balanced Scorecard: Measures That Drive Performance," *Harvard Business Review,* July 2005, pp. 71–79; Robert S. Kaplan, and David P. Norton, *Alignment: Using the Balanced Scorecard to Create Corporate Synergies* (Boston: Harvard Business School Press, 2008); Paul R. Niven, *Balanced Scorecard Step-by-Step: Maximizing Performance and Maintaining Results,* 2nd ed. (New York: John Wiley & Sons, 2006). Numerous Web sites also exist such as www.bscol.com and www.balancedscorecard.org.

[4] Darrell Rigby, "Management Tools 2008: An Executive's Guide," Bain and Company, 2009.

[5] Another useful treatment of various aspects of the balanced scoreboard that includes further learning opportunities you may wish to explore, especially with regard to the use of this approach with governmental organizations, may be found at www.balancedscorecard.org. Chapter 7 in this book describes how the balanced scorecard approach is used to help create measurable objectives linked directly to the company's strategy.

EXHIBIT 13.5
Integrating
Shareholder Value
and Organizational
Activities across
Organizational Levels

Source: From R.M. Grant,
*Contemporary Strategy
Analysis,* Blackwell Publishing,
2001, p. 56. Reprinted with
permission of Wiley-Blackwell.

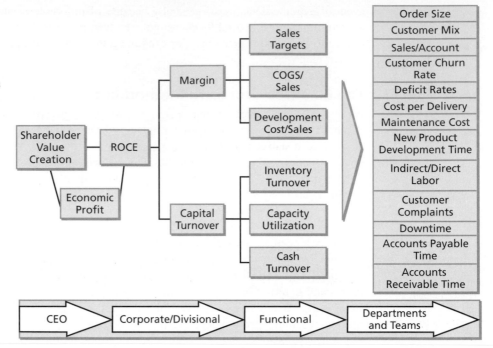

internal business process *outputs,* as in TQM, but also adds a feedback loop around the *outcomes* of business strategies. This creates a "double-loop feedback" process in the balanced scorecard. In doing so, it links together two areas of concern in strategy execution—quality operations and financial outcomes—that are typically addressed separately yet are obviously critically intertwined as any company executes its strategy. A system that links shareholder interests in return on capital with a system of performance management that is linked to ongoing, operational activities and processes within the company is what the balanced scorecard attempts to achieve.

Exhibit 13.5 illustrates the balanced scorecard approach drawing on the traditional Du Pont formula discussed in Chapter 6 and historically used to examine drivers of stockholder-related financial performance across different company activities. The balanced scorecard seeks to "balance" shareholder goals with customer goals and operational performance goals, and Exhibit 13.5 shows that they are interconnected: shareholder value creation is linked to divisional concerns for return on capital employed, which, in turn, is driven by functional outcomes in sales, inventory, capacity utilization, that, in turn, come about through the results of departments' and teams' daily activities throughout the company. The balanced scorecard suggests that we view the organization from four perspectives and to develop metrics, collect data, and analyze it relative to each of these perspectives:

1. *The learning and growth perspective: How well are we continuously improving and creating value?* The scorecard insists on measures related to innovation and organizational learning to gauge performance on this dimension—technological leadership, product development cycle times, operational process improvement, and so on.

2. *The business process perspective: What are our core competencies and areas of operational excellence?* Internal business processes and their effective execution as measured

by productivity, cycle time, quality measures, downtime, and various cost measures, among others, provide scorecard input here.

3. *The customer perspective: How satisfied are our customers?* A customer satisfaction perspective typically adds measures related to defect levels, on-time delivery, warranty support and product development, among others, that come from direct customer input and are linked to specific company activities.

4. *The financial perspective: How are we doing for our shareholders?* A financial perspective typically uses measures like cash flow, return on equity, sales, and income growth.

Through the integration of goals from each of these four perspectives, the balanced scorecard approach enables the strategy of the business to be linked with shareholder value creation while providing several measurable short-term outcomes that guide and monitor strategy implementation. The integrating power of the balanced scorecard can be seen at ExxonMobil Corporation's North American Marketing and Refining business (NAM&R). NAM&R's scorecard is shown in Exhibit 13.6. Assisted by Kaplan and Norton, an unprofitable NAM&R adopted the scorecard methodology to better link its strategy with financial objectives and to translate these into operating performance targets tailored to outcomes in each business unit, functional departments and operating process within them. They included measures developed with key customers from their perspective. The result was an integrated system in which scorecards provided measurable outcomes through which the performance of each department and operating unit, team, or activity within NAM&R was monitored, adjusted, and used to determine performance-related pay bonuses.[6]

Executives and CEOs are increasingly monitoring specific measurable outcomes related to the execution of their strategies. Now, thanks to the Internet and new Web-based software tools known as **dashboards,** accessing this type of specific information is as easy as clicking a mouse. Exhibit 13.7, Top Strategists, shows how a few well-known CEOs embrace the dashboard as a key management tool for timely strategic and operational control. So, for example, an executive at ExxonMobil Corporation might now use a dashboard to monitor updated information on where the company stands on some of the key measures generated through their balanced scorecard process as shown in Exhibit 13.6. The opportunity to react, take action, ask questions, and so forth approaches real time with the advent of the dashboard software options. That is, of course, when there is a high level of confidence in the reliability of the data that appear—both for the CEO and the managers who might expect a question or expression of concern. The variety of ways the four executives in Exhibit 13.7 report they use their dashboards gives an interesting look at the different ways they might use them, and the different types of information they would choose as key indicators about the unfolding success of their strategies.

Strategic controls and comprehensive control programs like the balanced scorecard bring the entire management task into focus. Organizational leaders can adjust or radically change their firm's strategy based on feedback from a balanced scorecard approach as well as other strategic controls. Other, similar approaches like Six Sigma, which is described in Chapter 14, can also be sources of information and specific measurable outcomes useful in strategic and operational control efforts. The overriding goal is to enable

dashboard
A user interface that organizes and presents information from multiple digital sources simultaneously in a user-designed format on the computer screen.

---

[6] "How ExxonMobil Became a Strategy-Focused Organization," Chapter 2 in R. Kaplan and D. Norton, *The Strategy-Focused Organization* (Boston: Harvard Business School Press, 2001). For an online version of the ExxonMobil NAM&R case study, see www.bscol.com.

EXHIBIT 13.6
Balanced Scorecard for ExxonMobil Corporation's NAM&R

Source: Reprinted by permission of Harvard Business School Publishing. Exhibit from *The Strategy Focused Organization*, by Robert Kaplan and David Norton. Copyright by the Harvard Business School Publishing Corporation; all rights reserved.

		Strategic Objectives	Strategic Measures
Financially Strong	Financial	F1 Return on Capital Employed F2 Cash Flow F3 Profitability F4 Lowest Cost F5 Profitable Growth F6 Manage Risk	• ROCE • Cash Flow • Net Margin • Full cost per gallon delivered to customer • Volume growth rate vs. industry • Risk index
Delight the Consumer **Win–Win Relationship**	Customer	C1 Continually delight the targeted consumer C2 Improve dealer/distributor profitability	• Share of segment in key markets • Mystery shopper rating • Dealer/distributor margin on gasoline • Dealer/distributor survey
Safe and Reliable **Competitive Supplier** **Good Neighbor** **On Spec On Time**	Internal	I1 Marketing 　1. Innovative products and services 　2. Dealer/distributor quality I2 Manufacturing 　1. Lower manufacturing costs 　2. Improve hardware and performance I3 Supply, Trading, Logistics 　1. Reducing delivered cost 　2. Trading organization 　3. Inventory management I4 Improve health, safety, and environmental performance I5 Quality	• Non-gasoline revenue and margin per square foot • Dealer/distributor acceptance rate of new programs • Dealer/distributor quality ratings • ROCE on refinery • Total expenses (per gallon) vs. competition • Profitability index • Yield index Delivered cost per gallon vs. competitors • Trading margin • Inventory level compared to plan and to output rate • Number of incidents • Days away from work • Quality index
Motivated and Prepared	Learning and growth	L1 Organization involvement L2 Core competencies and skills L3 Access to strategic information	• Employee survey • Strategic competitive availability • Strategic information availability

the survival and long-term success of the business. In addition to using controls, leaders are increasingly embracing innovation and entrepreneurship as a way to accomplish this overriding goal in rapidly changing environments. They look to young business graduates, like you, to bring a fresh sense of innovativeness and entrepreneurship with you as you join their companies. We will examine innovation and entrepreneurship in the next chapter.

Top Strategists
Using a Dashboard for Strategic Control

Exhibit
13.7

IVAN SEIDENBERG, VERIZON

Seidenberg and others can choose from more than 300 metrics to put on their dashboards, from broadband sales to wireless defections. Managers pick the metrics they want to track, and the dashboard flips the pages 24 hours a day.

LARRY ELLISON, ORACLE

A fan of dashboards, Ellison uses them to track sales activity at the end of a quarter, the ratio of sales divided by customer service requests, and the number of hours that technicians spend on the phone solving customer problems.

JAMES P. CAMPBELL, GENERAL ELECTRIC

Campbell looks at his dashboard first thing every morning to get a quick global view of sales and service levels across GE's Consumer and Industrial Division. "It's a key strategic control tool in our business," says Campbell. Fellow GE executives use them to follow production of everything from lightbulbs to jet engines, making sure production lines run smoothly.

JEFF RAIKES MICROSOFT AND, NOW, GATES FOUNDATION

Jeff Raikes, while president of Microsoft's Office Division, said that more than half of Microsoft Division's employees use dashboards. "Every time I go to see Balmer, or now Gates, it was an expectation that I bring my dashboard." Ballmer, he says, reviews the dashboards of his seven business heads in one-on-one meetings to focus on sales, customer satisfaction, and the status of key product development.

Summary

Strategies are forward looking, usually designed to be accomplished over several years into the future. They are often based in part on management assumptions about numerous events and factors that have not yet occurred. Strategic controls are intended to steer a company toward its long-term strategic goals under uncertain, often changing, circumstances.

Premise controls, strategic surveillance, special alert controls, and implementation controls are four types of strategic controls. All four types are designed to meet top management's needs to track a strategy as it is being implemented; to detect underlying problems, circumstances, or assumptions surrounding that strategy; and to make necessary adjustments. These strategic controls are linked to environmental assumptions and the key operating requirements necessary for successful strategy implementation. Ever-present forces of change fuel the need for and focus of strategic control.

Operational control systems require systematic evaluation of performance against predetermined standards and targets. A critical concern here is identification and evaluation of performance deviations, with careful attention paid to determining the underlying reasons for and strategic implications of observed deviations before management reacts. Approaches like the balanced scorecard and Six Sigma (discussed in the next chapter) have emerged as comprehensive control systems that integrate strategic goals, operating outcomes, customer satisfaction, and continuous improvement into an ongoing strategic management system.

The emergence of the Internet has led to innovative software that further assists executives in more closely and carefully monitoring outcomes in real time as a strategy is being implemented. This allows executives and managers to have *dashboards* on their computers, laptops, or mobile devices that further enhance their ability to control and adjust strategies as they are being executed.

A central goal with any strategy is the survival, growth, and improved competitive position of the company in the face of ever-accelerating rates of change. Executives, as they seek to control the execution of their strategy, are also increasingly aware of the need for innovation and entrepreneurial thinking as a companion to their emphasis on control as a means to accomplish these key goals in the face of rapid global change. The next chapter will examine innovation and entrepreneurship.

Key Terms

balanced scorecard, *p. 363*
dashboard, *p. 365*
implementation control, *p. 358*

milestone reviews, *p. 360*
premise control, *p. 355*
special alert control, *p. 357*

strategic control, *p. 354*
strategic surveillance, *p. 357*
strategic thrusts or projects, *p. 360*

Questions for Discussion

1. Distinguish between strategic control and operating control. Give an example of each.
2. Select a business whose strategy is familiar to you. Identify what you think are the key premises of the strategy. Then select the key indicators that you would use to monitor each of these premises.
3. Explain the differences between implementation controls, strategic surveillance, and special alert controls. Give an example of each.
4. Why are budgets, schedules, and key success factors essential to operations control and evaluation?
5. What are the key considerations in monitoring deviations from performance standards?
6. How is the balanced scorecard related to strategic and operational control?
7. What is a dashboard?

Chapter Fourteen

Innovation and Entrepreneurship

After reading and studying this chapter, you should be able to

1. Summarize the difference between incremental and breakthrough innovation.

2. Explain what is meant by continuous improvement and how it contributes to incremental innovation.

3. Summarize the risks associated with an incremental versus a breakthrough approach to innovation.

4. Describe the three key elements of the entrepreneurship process.

5. Explain intrapreneurship and how to enable it to thrive.

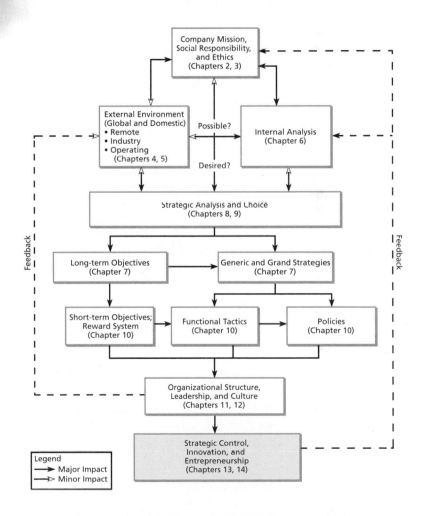

Company Mission, Social Responsibility, and Ethics (Chapters 2, 3)

External Environment (Global and Domestic)
• Remote
• Industry
• Operating
(Chapters 4, 5)

Possible?

Internal Analysis (Chapter 6)

Desired?

Strategic Analysis and Choice (Chapters 8, 9)

Long-term Objectives (Chapter 7)

Generic and Grand Strategies (Chapter 7)

Short-term Objectives; Reward System (Chapter 10)

Functional Tactics (Chapter 10)

Policies (Chapter 10)

Organizational Structure, Leadership, and Culture (Chapters 11, 12)

Strategic Control, Innovation, and Entrepreneurship (Chapters 13, 14)

Feedback

Feedback

Legend
→ Major Impact
⇢ Minor Impact

Survival and long-term success in a business enterprise eventually come down to two outcomes: sales growth or lower costs, and hopefully both. Rapid change, globalization, and connectivity in the global economy have led to impressive growth across many sectors of the global economy. Most companies have spent the last decade or two putting continuous pressure on their organizations to drive out excessive costs and inefficiencies so as to compete in this increasingly price sensitive global arena. Increasingly, executives in these same companies see growth, particularly growth via innovation, as the key priority to their firm's long-term survival and prosperity.

Recent studies by four prominent consulting organizations have documented the critical importance of innovation for CEOs of companies large and small around the globe as these CEOs seek to chart the destinies of their companies into the next decade. IBM's study of almost 800 CEOs found innovation in three ways to be the central focus among today's CEOs:—product/service/market innovation, business model innovation, and operational innovation.[1] Accenture and the Center for Strategy Research surveyed executives in the *Fortune* 1000 companies and found innovation to be very important to 95 percent of the firms represented, with innovation being most important when it results in improvements to existing products or services, decreases in costs, or improvements in meeting customer needs.[2] McKinsey and Company interviewed 2,000 executives and found accelerated embrace of innovation—and, specifically, open innovation—now deemed essential to the future growth and success of their companies. They report increasing use of customers, suppliers, independent inventors, and universities as active participants in their innovation efforts as the new-age approach to innovation.[3]

While executives logically embrace innovation, a Boston Consulting Group survey of senior executives in 500 companies headquartered across 47 countries found that fewer than half of these executives were satisfied with the returns on their investments to date in innovation. "Unless companies improve their approach to innovation," BCG Senior Vice President Jim Andrew said, "increased investment may in fact lead to increased disappointment." These executives indicated their three biggest problems with innovation were

1. Moving quickly from the idea generation to initial sales.
2. Leveraging suppliers for new ideas.
3. Appropriately balancing risks, time frames, and returns.

Yet these executives were anxious to become more innovative. After identifying Apple, 3M, GE, Microsoft, and Sony as the innovators they most admire—the "most innovative" companies worldwide, 80 percent of these executives indicated that they anticipated even higher innovation spending by 2007.[4]

WHAT IS INNOVATION?

invention
The creation of new products or processes through the development of new knowledge or from new combinations of knowledge.

Common to the vocabulary of most business executives is a distinction between *invention* and *innovation*. We define the two using this common perspective:

Invention is the creation of new products or processes through the development of new knowledge or from new combinations of existing knowledge. The jet engine was patented in 1930, yet the first commercial jet airplane did not fly until 1957. Computers were based on three different sets of knowledge created decades before the first computer.

[1] *IBM Global CEO Study,* IBM Global Business Services, www-935.ibm.com/services, 2007.
[2] Toni Langlinais and Bruce Bendix, "Moving from Strategy to Execution to High Performance," *Accenture Outlook,* No. 2, (October 2006).
[3] Jacques R. Bughin, Michael Chui, and Brad Johnson, "The Next Step in Open Innovation," *The McKinsey Quarterly* 4, (June 2008), pp. 113–23.
[4] "Global Firms Will Increase Their Spending on Innovation," *PRNewswire,* December 8, 2004.

innovation
The initial commercialization of invention by producing and selling a new product, service, or process.

Innovation is the initial commercialization of invention by producing and selling a new product, service, or process. As executives across each of the surveys summarized earlier typically put it, "Innovation is turning ideas into profits."[5]

Apple's iPod was a *product innovation* that applied Apple's chip storage technology with sleek device styling to create an innovation within six months in 2001 at Apple. Steven Jobs then worked intensely for almost two years negotiating digital music rights with a recalcitrant music industry, culminating in the launching of iTunes in 2003—a music download *service innovation* with an initial 200,000 digital songs to choose from for your iPod. In five short years, that became 3 million songs and more than $5 billion in annual revenue added to the business, allowing Apple in the process to replace Wal-Mart as the world's largest music retailer. Starbucks added the simple service of wireless access free to its customers at most of its 8,000 stores in what turned out to be a highly successful *service innovation* that resulted in customers using the service staying nine times longer than regular customers, and doing so during off-peak hours.

While these two leading innovators are creating profitable product and service innovations, Toyota is perhaps the most envied business *process innovator* worldwide due to its meticulous attention to business and operating processes. Several years ago, Toyota made one change to its production lines, using a single brace to hold auto frames together instead of the 50 it previously took. While a minute part of Toyota's overall production process, this "global body line" system slashed 75 percent off the cost of refitting a production line. It is the reason behind Toyota's ability to make different models on a single production line, estimated to save Toyota more than $3 billion annually.

To some business managers, "innovation seems as predictable as a rainbow and as manageable as a butterfly. Penicillin, Teflon, Post-it-notes—they sprang from such accidents as moldy Petri dishes, a failed coolant, and a mediocre glue." Not surprisingly, many managers forgo trying to harness innovation systematically. "Our approach has always been very simple, which is to try not to manage innovation," says Michael Moritz, a partner with world-renowned venture capital firm Sequoia Capital. "We prefer to just let the market manage it."[6] For those managers who try to manage innovation, it is important to distinguish two types of innovations: incremental innovation and breakthrough innovation.

Incremental Innovation

incremental innovation
Simple changes or adjustments in existing products, services, or processes.

continuous improvement
The process of relentlessly trying to find ways to improve and enhance a company's products and processes from design through assembly, sales, and service. It is called *kaizen* in Japanese. It is usually associated with incremental innovation.

Incremental innovation refers to simple changes or adjustments in existing products, services, or processes. There is growing evidence that companies seeking to increase the payoff from innovation investments best do so by focusing on incremental innovations. We will examine the payoff research more completely in a subsequent section on risks associated with innovation. First, however, we need to examine how companies are seeking incremental innovation. A major driver of incremental innovation in many companies the last several years has come from programs aimed at continuous improvement, cost reduction, and quality management.

Continuous improvement, what in Japanese is called *kaizen,* is the process of relentlessly trying to find ways to improve and enhance a company's products and processes from design through assembly, sales, and service. This approach, or really an operating philosophy, seeks to always find slight improvements or refinements in every aspect of what

[5] Ibid.
[6] Robert Hof, Steve Hamm, Diane Brady, and Ian Rowley, "Building an Idea Factory," *BusinessWeek*, October 11, 2004.

Top Strategist
Taiichi Ohno . . . Father of the Toyota Production System

Exhibit 14.1

All we are doing is looking at the time line, from the moment the customer gives us an order to the point when we collect the cash. And we are reducing the time line by reducing the non-value-adding wastes.

—*Taiichi Ohno*

Why not make the work easier and more interesting so that people do not have to sweat? The Toyota style is not to create results by working hard. It is a system that says there is no limit to people's creativity. People don't go to Toyota to "work" they go there to "think."

—*Taiichi Ohno*

Every 20-year-old factory worker, or designer, and every Toyota executive reveres the heritage bestowed upon them by Taiichi Ohno. Sixty years ago, after observing Henry Ford's work, and American grocery stores, he set about creating in-house precepts at Toyota's production facilities to eliminate waste while improving efficiency, which became JIT; continuous improvement (*kaizen*); mistake proofing (*pokayoke*); and regular brainstorming sessions among suppliers, designers, engineering, and sales personnel. The result has revolutionized car manufacturing.

Toyota's plants are high-tech marvels, building multiple car models on the same production line with parts descending on time from above and below via numerous conveyor belts like a manufacturing ballet. While sophisticated, Ohno's spirit is ever present, seeking creative frugality—reducing the use of Power-Point handouts in meetings to save on ink costs, or lessening heating during working hours at company dormitories, or pushing suppliers to reduce the number of side-view mirror sizes from 50 to 3 for all Toyota cars. All these actions and many, many more reflect Ohno's passion for continuous, simple innovation borne out of the minds of Toyota's employees going about their daily work, building the best cars and trucks in the world.

Source: http://www.kellogg.northwestern.edu/course/opns430/modules/lean_operations/ohno-tps.pdf; and quotes courtesy of www.matthrivnak.com

---

a company does so that it will result in lower costs, higher quality and speed, or more rapid response to customer needs.[7]

Toyota's extraordinary success in becoming the world's leading automobile company is one good example of a cost-oriented continuous improvement effort (see Exhibit 14.1, Top Strategist). Now called **CCC21** (Construction of Cost Competitiveness for the 21st Century), Toyota embarked on this intense scrutiny of every product it purchases or builds to include in the assembly of its automobiles in response to growing concern about the relative cost advantage to be derived from a surge in global automobile company mergers starting with Daimler-Chrysler. The result: a stunning $20 billion in cost savings over the last decade in the parts it buys, while also improving quality significantly. Taking the Japanese perspective, 1001 small innovations or improvements together have become something transformative. A good example would be Toyota engineers disassembling the horns made by a Japanese supplier and finding ways to eliminate 6 of 28 horn components, saving 40 percent in costs and improving quality. Or, interior assist grips above each door—once there were 35 different grips but now, across 90 different Toyota models, there are only 3.

CCC21
A world-famous, cost-oriented continuous improvement program at Toyota (Construction of Cost Competitiveness for the 21st Century).

---

[7] TQM, total quality management, is the initial continuous improvement philosophy used worldwide to focus managers and employees on customer defined quality since starting in Japan in the 1970s.

Toyota engineers call this process *kawaita zokin wo shiboru,* or "wringing drops from a dry towel," which means an excruciating, unending process essential to Toyota's continuous improvement success.

Six Sigma is another continuous improvement approach widely used by many companies worldwide to spur incremental innovation in their businesses. Six Sigma is a rigorous and analytical approach to quality and continuous improvement with an objective to improve profits through defect reduction, yield improvement, improved consumer satisfaction, and best-in-class performance. Six Sigma complements TQM philosophies such as management leadership, continuous education, and customer focus while deploying a disciplined and structured approach of hard-nosed statistics.[8]

Companies such as Honeywell, Motorola, BMW, GE, SAP, IBM, and Texas Instruments have adopted the Six Sigma discipline as a major business initiative. Many of these companies invested heavily in and pursued this model initially to create products and services that were of equal and higher quality than those of its competitors and to improve relationships with customers. A Six Sigma program at many organizations simply means a measure of quality that strives for near perfection in every facet of the business including every product, process, and transaction:

Six Sigma

A continuous improvement program adopted by many companies in the last two decades that takes a very rigorous and analytical approach to quality and continuous improvement with an objective to improve profits through defect reduction, yield improvement, improved customer satisfaction, and best-in-class performance.

How the Six Sigma Statistical Concept Works

Six Sigma means a failure rate of 3.4 parts per million or 99.9997 percent. At the sixth standard deviation from the mean under a normal distribution, 99.9996 percent of the population is under the curve with not more than 3.4 parts per million defective. The higher the sigma value, the less likely a process will produce defects as excellence is approached.

If you played 100 rounds of golf per year and played at:

2 Sigma: You'd miss 6 putts per round.
3 Sigma: You'd miss 1 putt per round.
4 Sigma: You'd miss 1 putt every 9 rounds.
5 Sigma: You'd miss 1 putt every 2.33 years.
6 Sigma: You'd miss 1 putt every 163 years!

Source: From John Petty, "When Near Enough Is Not Good Enough," *Australian CPA,* May 2000, pp. 34–35. Reprinted with permission of the author.

Many frameworks, management philosophies, and specific statistical tools exist for implementing the Six Sigma methodology and its objective to create a near-perfect process or service. One such method for improving a system for existing processes falling below specification while looking for incremental improvement is the DMAIC process (define, measure, analyze, improve, control) shown in Exhibit 14.2.

Incremental innovation via continuous improvement programs is viewed by most proponents as virtually a new organizational culture and way of thinking. It is built around an intense focus on customer satisfaction; on accurate measurement of every critical variable in a business's operation; on continuous improvement of products, services, and processes; and on work relationships based on trust and teamwork. One useful explanation of the continuous improvement philosophy suggests 10 essential elements that lead to meaningful incremental innovation:

1. *Define quality and customer value.* Rather than be left to individual interpretation, company personnel should have a clear definition of what *quality* means in the job,

---

[8] ISO certification, from the International Standards Organization, is another widely used means of encouraging rigorous and analytically based assessment and confirmation of meeting quality and building continuous improvement into the way the organization functions.

EXHIBIT 14.2 The DMAIC Six Sigma Approach

Define

- Project definition
- Project charter
- Gathering voice of the customer
- Translating customer needs into specific requirements

Measure

- Process mapping (as-is process)
- Data attributes (continuous vs. discrete)
- Measurement system analysis
- Gauge repeatability and reproducibility
- Measuring process capability
- Calculating process sigma level
- Visually displaying baseline performance

Analyze

- Visually displaying data (histogram, run chart, Pareto chart, scatter diagram)
- Value-added analysis

- Cause-and-effect analysis (a.k.a. Fishbone, Ishikawa)
- Verification of root causes
- Determining opportunity (defects and financial) for improvement
- Project charter review and revision

Improve

- Brainstorming
- Quality function deployment (house of quality)
- Failure modes and effects analysis (FMEA)
- Piloting your solution
- Implementation planning
- Culture modification planning for your organization

Control

- Statistical process control (SPC) overview
- Developing a process control plan
- Documenting the process

department, and throughout the company. It should be developed from your customer's perspective and communicated as a written policy. Thinking in terms of customer value broadens the definition of *quality* to include efficiency and responsiveness. Said another way, quality to your customer often means that the product performs well; that it is priced competitively (efficiency); and that you provide it quickly and adapt it when needed (responsiveness). Customer value is found in the combination of all three—quality, price, and speed.

2. *Develop a customer orientation*. Customer value is what the customer says it is. Don't rely on secondary information—talk to your customers directly. Also recognize your "internal" customers. Usually less than 20 percent of company employees come into contact with external customers, while the other 80 percent serve internal customers—other units with real performance expectations—in a process that looks like this:

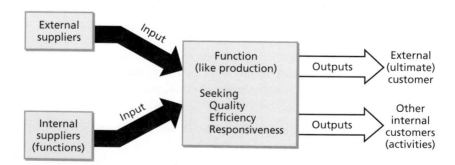

3. *Focus on the company's business processes*. Break down every minute step in the process of providing the company's product or service, and look at ways to improve it, rather

than focusing simply on the finished product or service. Each process contributes value in some way, which can be improved or adapted to help other processes (internal customers) improve. Here are several examples of ways customer value is enhanced across business processes in several functions:

	Quality	Efficiency	Responsiveness
Marketing	Provides accurate assessment of customer's product preferences to R&D	Targets advertising campaign at customers, using cost-effective medium	Quickly uncovers and reacts to changing market trends
Operations	Consistently produces goods matching engineering design	Minimizes scrap and rework through high-production yield	Quickly adapts to latest demands with production flexibility
Research and development	Designs products that combine customer demand and production capabilities	Uses computers to test feasibility of idea before going to more expensive full-scale prototype	Carries out parallel product/process designs to speed up overall innovation
Accounting	Provides the information that managers in other functions need to make decisions	Simplifies and computerizes to decrease the cost of gathering information	Provides information in "real time" (as the events described are still happening)
Purchasing	Selects vendors for their ability to join in an effective "partnership"	Given the required vendor quality, negotiates prices to provide good value	Schedules inbound deliveries efficiently, avoiding both extensive inventories and stock-outs
Personnel	Trains workforce to perform required tasks	Minimizes employee turnover, reducing hiring and training expenses	In response to strong growth in sales, finds large numbers of employees and quickly teaches needed skills

4. *Develop customer and supplier partnerships.* Organizations have a destructive tendency to view suppliers and even customers adversarily. It is better to understand the horizontal flow of a business—outside suppliers to internal suppliers/customers (a company's various departments) to external customers. This view suggests suppliers are partners in meeting customer needs, and customers are partners by providing input so the company and suppliers can meet and exceed those expectations.

Ford Motor Company's Dearborn, Michigan, plant is linked electronically with supplier Allied Signal's Kansas City, Missouri, plant. A Ford computer recently sent the design for a car's connecting rod to an Allied Signal factory computer, which transformed the design into instructions that it fed to a machine tool on the shop floor. The result: quality, efficiency, and responsiveness.

5. *Take a preventive approach.* Many organizations reward "fire fighters" not "fire preventers" and identify errors after the work is done. Management, instead, should be rewarded for being prevention oriented and seeking to eliminate non-value-added work as CCC21 does quite well at Toyota.

6. *Adopt an error-free attitude.* Instill an attitude that "good enough" is not good enough anymore. "Error free" should become each individual's performance standard, with

managers taking every opportunity to demonstrate and communicate the importance of this Six Sigma–type imperative.

7. *Get the facts first.* Continuous improvement–oriented companies make decisions based on facts, not on opinions. Accurate measurement, often using readily available statistical techniques, of every critical variable in a business's operation—and using those measurements to trace problems to their roots and eliminate their causes—is a better way.

8. *Encourage every manager and employee to participate.* Employee participation, empowerment, participative decision making, and extensive training in quality techniques, statistical techniques, and measurement tools are the ingredients continuous improvement companies employ to support and instill a commitment to customer value.

9. *Create an atmosphere of total involvement.* Quality management cannot be the job of a few managers or of one department. Maximum customer value cannot be achieved unless all areas of the organization apply quality concepts simultaneously.

10. *Strive for continuous improvement.* Stephen Yearout, director of Ernst & Young's Quality Management Center, recently observed that "Historically, meeting your customers' expectations would distinguish you from your competitors. The twenty-first century will require that you anticipate customer expectations and deliver quality service faster than the competition."

Quality, efficiency, and responsiveness are not one-time programs of competitive response because they create a new standard to measure up to. Organizations quickly find that continually improving quality, efficiency, and responsiveness in their processes, products, and services is not just good business; it's an excellent means to identify incremental innovations that become foundations for long-term survival.

Disciplines like Six Sigma are systematic ways to improve customer service and quality; the added benefit that emerged has been its effectiveness in cutting costs and improving profitability. That has made it a powerful tool, but the notion that Six Sigma is a survival cure-all is subsiding. Once a company has created incremental innovations that maximize profitability, some argue that "kick-starting the top line" becomes paramount, which in turn means acquisition or dramatic, revenue-generating product or service innovations. And that, they argue, calls less for Six Sigma's "define, measure, analyze, improve, control" regimen and more for a "fuzzier" front-end, creative-idea-generation type of orientation.[9] That calls for a more disruptive form of innovation, which we call *breakthrough innovation.*

Breakthrough Innovation

Clayton Christensen of Harvard Business School makes the distinction between "sustaining" technologies, which are incremental innovations that improve product or process performance, and "disruptive" technologies, which revolutionize industries and create new ones.[10] Rather than an innovation that reduces the cost of a mirror on a car by 40 percent, Christensen is focusing when speaking of disruptive technologies on the product idea that works 10 times better than existing ones or costs less than half what the existing ones do to make—a breakthrough innovation. A **breakthrough innovation,** then, is an innovation in a product, process, technology, or the cost associated with it that represents a quantum leap forward in one or more of these ways.

Apple's innovation with iPod and iTunes is a breakthrough innovation. It was not an incremental improvement in Apple's computer offerings. It was an application of the

breakthrough innovation

An innovation in a product, process, technology, or the cost associated with it that represents a quantum leap forward in one or more of these ways.

[9] Brian Hindo and Brian Grow, "Six Sigma: So Yesterday?" *BusinessWeek,* June 11, 2007.

[10] Clayton M. Christensen, *The Innovator's Dilemma* (New York: HarperCollins, 2003).

microprocessor technology associated with Apple's computers, applied in a totally different industry. Apple, which only has a 2 percent market share in the personal computer industry, now has positioned itself as a dominant force in the emerging digital music and entertainment industries based on this breakthrough innovation, becoming the top music retailer worldwide in five short years after it introduced iTunes.

Breakthrough innovations, which Christensen calls "disruptive," often shake up the industries with which they are associated, even though many times they may come from totally different origins or industry settings than the industry to start with. Apple seems to make a habit of creating new industries; Apple's original innovation 20 years earlier in Jobs's and Wozniak's garage that created the first Apple computer was viewed as a toy by most players in the computer industry at the time, but it quickly tore the mainstream computer industry apart and almost brought down the mighty IBM. Texas Instrument's digital watch resulted in the virtual destruction of the dominant Swiss watch industry. Breakthrough innovations can also be appreciated by some fringe (often new) customer group for features such as being cheap, simple, easy to use, or smaller, which is seen as underperforming the mainstream products. San Disk's memory stick, Wal-Mart's discount retailing, and health insurance industry HMOs are all examples of breakthrough innovations that ultimately caused the demise of or significant reduction in key industry participants. Former Digital Equipment Company CEO Ken Olsen, a leading industry figure and a leading computer manufacturer at the time, said of Apple and the idea of a personal computer in your home when the early Apple computers were being sold: "I can think of no reason why an individual should wish to have a computer in his own home."[11]

Breakthrough approaches to innovation are inherently more risky than incremental innovation approaches. The reason can be seen in Exhibit 14.3, which is provided by the Industrial Research Institute in Washington, D.C. Their conclusion is that firms committed to breakthrough innovation must first have the ability to explain clearly to all employees, at every level, just how critical the breakthrough project is to the company's future. The second is to set next-to-impossible goals for those involved. The third is to target only "rich domains" — areas of investigation where plenty of answers are still waiting to be found. The fourth, and maybe the most important, is to move people regularly between laboratories and business units, to ensure that researchers fully understand the needs of the marketplace. These thoughts, of course, apply more to larger firms and particularly ones where breakthrough efforts are concentrated in laboratories and other separate R&D units.

Smaller firms are often sources for breakthrough innovation because they have less invested in serving a large, established customer base and gradually improving on the products, services, or processes used to serve them. We will explore these differences more completely in the section on entrepreneurship. Regardless of the size of a firm, it is important to consider risks associated with incremental versus breakthrough innovation.

Risks Associated with Innovation[12]

Innovation involves creating something that doesn't now exist. It may be a minor creation or something monumental. In either case, there is risk associated with it. Exhibit 14.3 shows the conclusions of the Industrial Research Institute's examination of breakthrough innovation outcomes, which suggests that you need to start with 3,000 "bright" ideas,

---

[11] Robert M. Grant, *Contemporary Strategic Analysis* (Oxford: Blackwell, 2002), p. 330.

[12] See Morten Hansen and Julian Birkinshaw, "The Innovation Value Chain," *Harvard Business Review*, June 2007, for an interesting use of a value chain "breakdown" of innovation to use in assessing risks and sources of problems in innovation efforts.

EXHIBIT 14.3
**From Idea to
Profitable Reality**

Source: Industrial Research
Institute, Washington, D.C.

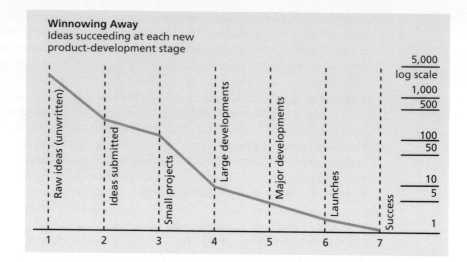

Winnowing Away
Ideas succeeding at each new
product-development stage

which are winnowed down to four product launches, then one major success emerges. Long odds for sure.

A study reported in *The Economist* of 197 product innovations, 111 of which were successes and 86 failures, sought to compare the two groups in order to see what might explain differences between innovation success and innovation failure. They first sought to examine what was common to successful innovations and what was common to failing innovations First, they found that successful innovations had some, or all, of the following five characteristics:[13]

- Moderately new to the marketplace.
- Based on tried and tested technology.
- Saved money for users of the innovation.
- Reportedly met customer needs.
- Supported existing practices.

In contrast, product innovations that failed were based on cutting-edge or untested technology, followed a "me-too" approach, or were created with no clearly defined problem or solution in mind.

The second set of findings from this study emerged from the researchers' examination of what they called "idea factors." Idea factors were concerned with how the idea for the innovation originated. They identified six idea factors:

- *Need spotting*—actively looking for an answer to a known problem.
- *Solution spotting*—finding a new way of using an existing technology.
- *Mental inventions*—things dreamed up in the head with little reference to the outside world.
- *Random events*—serendipitous moments when innovators stumbled on something they were not looking for but immediately recognized its significance.
- *Market research*—traditional market research techniques to find ideas.
- *Trend following*—following demographic and other broad trends and trying to develop ideas that may be relevant and useful.

[13] "Expect the Unexpected," *The Economist*, September 4, 2004.

The researchers then compared the "success-to-failure" ratio of these six idea factors to see which idea factors were more often associated with success or failure of the related innovation. The two most failure-prone idea factors were trend following and mental inventions, both producing three times as many failures as successes. Need spotting produced twice as many successes as failures. Market research produced four times as many, and solution spotting seven times more successes than failures. Taking advantage of random events was the clear winner, generating 13 times more successes than failures. Their conclusion: focus on eliminating bad ideas early in the process, emphasize market research and technology application/solution spotting efforts, while being open to serendipitous outcomes in the process.

Inherent in their analysis is the presence of two key risks associated with innovation—market risks and technology risks. Market risks come from uncertainty with regard to the presence of a market, its size, and its growth rate for the product or service in question: do customers exist and will they buy it? Technology risks derive from uncertainty about how the technology will evolve and the complexity through which technical standards and dominant designs or approaches emerge: will it work?

Research by Michael Treacy of GEN3 Partners reported in the *Harvard Business Review* suggests that incremental innovation is far more effective than breakthrough innovation in managing the market and technology risk associated with innovation. Exhibit 14.4 provides a visual portrayal of his research.[14] In it he suggests that technology risk is primary and marketplace risk secondary in product innovations; the reverse is true for business model or process innovations.

The point that emerges from this graph is that breakthrough innovation, while glamourous and exciting, is very risky compared with incremental innovation. Breakthrough innovations, according to Treacy's examination of much of the research to date on innovation, usually get beaten down or outperformed by the slow and steady approach of incremental innovation. He makes several useful points about managing the resulting risks:

- Remember, *the point of innovation is growth*. So ask the question, Can I increase revenue without innovation? Retain existing customers and improve targeted coverage of existing and similar new customers, where innovation isn't necessary to keep existing customers.

- *Get the most out of minimum innovation.* Tweaking a business process doesn't incur much technology risk. Incremental product or service innovation does not incur nearly the market risk that a radical one would. So emphasize an incremental approach to most innovation efforts.

- Incremental product innovations can be particularly good at *locking in existing customers*. Every saved customer is an additional source of revenue.

- Incremental business process innovations can *generate more revenue gain or cost savings with less risk* than radical ones. The earlier example about Toyota's single brace to hold auto frames is a dramatic example of the payoff—$2.6 billion annually—from one simple, incremental business process innovation.

- Radical innovations are often *too radical for existing markets,* and customers will balk at paying for that new approach, product, process, or technology. So it will fail with existing customers.

- The time to launch breakthrough innovations is not when they are necessary, important, or of interest to your business, but *when they are essential to the marketplace.* And that usually takes time, like the 10 years it has taken for car buyers to become interested in the electric/hybrid vehicles that have been available for more than 10 years.

[14] Michael Treacy, "Innovation As a Last Resort," *Harvard Business Review,* July 1, 2004.

EXHIBIT 14.4 **Risks Associated with Innovation**

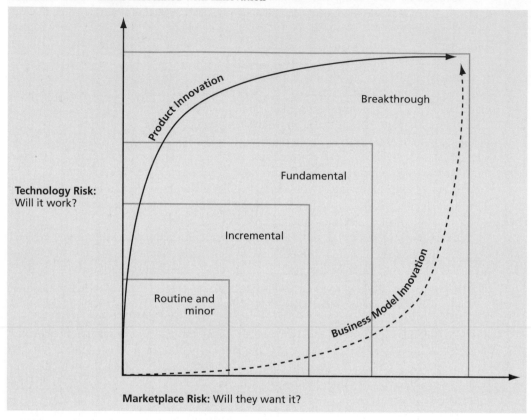

Source: Reprinted by permission of *Harvard Business Review.* Exhibit from "Innovation as a Last Resort," by Michael Treacy, July 1, 2004. Copyright 2004 by the Harvard Business School Publishing Corporation; all rights reserved.

disruptive innovation
A term to characterize breakthrough innovation popularized by Harvard Professor Clayton Christensen; usually shakes up or revolutionizes industries with which they are associated even though they often come from totally different origins or industry settings than the industry they "disrupt."

The case for incremental innovation as a less risky approach than breakthrough innovation is widely advocated. Clayton Christensen offers a word of caution in this regard, arguing that as important as incremental improvements are, steady improvements to a company's product do not conquer new markets. Nor do they guarantee survival. He argues that while **disruptive** (breakthrough) **innovations** may underperform established products in mainstream markets, they often offer features or capabilities appreciated by some fringe (usually new) customer group—like being easier to use, cheaper, smaller, or more versatile. Often, his research suggests, those fringe customers swell in numbers to become the mainstream market, absorbing the newly informed old mainstream in the process. And in so doing, they "disrupt" or bring about the downfall of leading existing industry players.

Not surprisingly, many companies are experimenting with new ways to lower risks and improve chances for failure regardless of the innovation approach they use. For years the idea of product teams and cross-functional groups within the company has played a major role in trying to improve the odds that innovations will succeed, or that bad ideas are eliminated much earlier in the innovation management process. This approach broadens to include several more:

• *Joint ventures* with other firms that have an interest in the possible innovation share the costs and risks associated with the effort. Toyota is now negotiating with General Motors to share its hybrid vehicle technology and jointly build a manufacturing facility in the United States to lower both companies' risk associated with this innovation.

• *Cooperation with lead users* is increasingly used in both types of innovation. Nike tests new shoes with inner-city street gangs; software companies beta-test their new software with loyal users; GE works with railroad companies to create a new, ecofriendly locomotive.

• *"Do it yourself"* innovation allows a company to work directly with key existing or expected customers, further allowing these customers to play a lead role in developing a product, service, or process—not just get a sense of their reaction to developments. This approach allows a company to go beyond the traditional market research model or simply cooperating with lead users. Instead, it has customers actually conceptualize or make design proposals which become the starting point for developing a new innovation. BMW sent 1,000 customers a "toolkit" that let them develop ideas, showing how the firm could take advantage of telematics and in-car online services. BMW chose 15 submissions, brought them to Germany from all over the world, and worked further with them to flesh out those ideas. Four ideas are now in prototype stage, and BMW anticipates several will emerge in new models along with an increased use of this new customer-innovation effort.

• *Acquiring innovation* has become a major way larger companies bring innovation into their firm while mitigating the risk/reward trade-off in the process. Cisco has built itself into a dominant player in the computer and networking equipment industries in large part by buying smaller companies that had developed and tentatively proven new market niches but who needed capital and distribution to rapidly exploit the new technological advantage. Cisco acquired these companies for a premium using stock, but it invested little or nothing in the early development of the technology. Thus, the smaller firm bore all the early risk of failure, and those that succeeded were rewarded in the price of the sale of their company, but Cisco got to avoid the losses associated with the majority of the innovations attempted but not successful. Exhibit 14.5, Strategy in Action, describes how Google does something similar in acquiring innovation and how the results are not always to the liking of the entrepreneur company founders they acquire in the process.

• *Outsourcing innovation*, particularly product design, has become a major part of the "modular" organizational structure of today's global technology companies. Nokia, Samsung, and Motorola—cell phone giants—get proposed new-product design prototypes from HTC, Flextronics, and Cellon—unknown global, billion-dollar-plus companies that create new designs and sell them to cell phone and other electronics brand-name companies annually at the biggest trade shows around the world. To Nokia and it competitors, this shifts the risk of product design innovation to these emerging technology outsourcing powerhouses.

ideagoras
Web-enabled, virtual marketplaces which connect people with unique ideas, talents, resources, or capabilities with companies seeking to address problems or potential innovations in a quick, competent manner.

Procter & Gamble, under Alan Lafley, has radically changed that company's culture so that it accepts as a matter of corporate strategy that 50 percent of its consumer product innovations will come from outside P&G. The resulting growth and profitability due to new-product innovations at P&G over the last five years have made it the new model of open source product/service/market innovation worldwide.[15]

Ideagoras, defined as places where millions of ideas and solutions change hands in something akin to an eBay for innovation, reflects one of the newest approaches to open innovation, which leverages the value of the Internet to access talent worldwide, instantly. Also referred to as "crowdsourcing" and "open innovation," companies seeking solutions

---

[15] "P&G: What's the Big Idea," *BusinessWeek*, May 4, 2007.

Google Acquires Dodgeball to Innovate, Then Has the Latitude to Drop the Ball

Dodgeball started life as a Manhattan company providing a cell phone service aimed at young barhoppers wanting to let their friends know where they were hanging out. Founders Dennis Crowley and Alex Rainert sold it to Google in 2005, providing a good payday for them and a potential basis for a social networking niche innovation for Google. Within two years, Crowley and Rainert left Google, frustrated by what they reported as minimal support from Google.* Crowley stayed in New York City to run the operation, but had trouble competing for attention of other Google engineers to expand the service. "If you're a product manager, you have to recruit people from their '20 percent time,' " said Crowley,[†] who then started building a new location-based service called FourSquare.

Google, for its part, found the concepts behind Dodgeball interesting and adapted those concepts to create *Latitude,* a more sophisticated add-on to Google Maps that lets people share their location with friends and family automatically, while including different privacy and communication options. Said Google's senior engineering vice president, "Maybe it worked in Manhatten. It didn't fly in Chicago, or St. Louis, or Denver, or the rest of the world."[‡] Still, Google appears to have found innovations worth adapting, as its new Latitude service seems to indicate.

* See their Flickr departure posting at http://www.flickr.com/photos/dpstyles/460987802/.

[†] Vindu Goel, "How Google Decides to Pull the Plug," *The New York Times,* February 15, 2009.

[‡] Ibid.

---

to seemingly insoluble problems can tap the insights of hundreds of thousands of enterprising scientists without having to employ any of them full time. Take, for example, Colgate-Palmolive, which needed a more efficient method for getting its toothpaste into the tube—a seemingly straightforward problem. When its internal R&D team came up empty-handed, the company posted the specs on InnoCentive, one of many ideagoras or marketplaces that link problems with problem solvers. A Canadian engineer named Ed Melcarek proposed putting a positive charge on fluoride powder, then grounding the tube. It was an effective solution, an application of elementary physics, but not one that Colgate-Palmolive's team of chemists had ever contemplated.[16] Melcarek earned $25,000 for a few hours work, and a timely innovation from outside the company accrued to another client company.

Today more than 160,000 scientists like Melcarek have registered with InnoCentive, and hundreds of companies pay annual fees of roughly $80,000 to tap the talents of this global scientific community. Launched as an e-business by Eli Lilly in 2001, InnoCentive was spun off in 2005, enabling it to expand its offerings and serve clients in a variety of industries. The company now provides solutions to some of the world's most well-known and innovation-hungry companies. The reason? Mature companies cannot keep up with the speed of innovation nor the demands for growth by relying on internal capabilities alone. This approach creates a much more flexible, free-market mechanism; secondly, it taps a vastly changing global landscape where the talent to generate disruptive or path-breaking innovation will increasingly reside in China, India, Brazil, Eastern Europe, or Russia. P&G figures that for every one of its 9,000 top-notch scientists, there are another 200 outside who are just as good. That's a total of 1.8 million talented people it could potentially tap,

[16] Don Tapscott and Anthony D. Williams, "Ideagora, a Marketplace for Minds," *BusinessWeek,* February 15, 2007.

using ideagoras to seek out ideas, innovations, and uniquely qualified minds on a global scale quickly, efficiently, and productively.[17]

Such openness in seeking new, key innovations that determine a company's future survival and growth—as opposed to doing innovation on a closely guarded, internal basis—is viewed with skepticism and as a risk that cuts at the very core of what a company essentially exists to do. Product design, major innovations, even incremental innovations, have long been viewed as key, secret core competencies and competitive advantages that generate the long-term success of the company that possesses them. Outsourcing these activities, or doing so via ideagoras, puts the whole firm at risk in the minds of observers opposed to this open type of innovation. That said, the impressive progress Dwayne Spratlin has engineered at InnoCentive, described in Exhibit 14.6, Top Strategist, seems to be reflective of a broadening embrace of Web-enabled, wide-open collaboration in breakthrough innovation.

Another way of looking at the notion of innovation, and an organization's ability to manage it effectively, is found in the argument that innovation is associated with entrepreneurial behavior. And so, to be more innovative, a firm has to become more entrepreneurial.

The examples of Cisco and Google, as they used the "acquiring innovation" approach illustrate the useful ways some companies deal with the reality that breakthrough innovation occurs very often in the smallest of firms, where focus, intensity, and total survival depend on that innovation succeeding. Advocates of this perspective make the point that many industry-creating and paradigm-changing breakthrough innovations (e.g., personal computers; digital file sharing), as well as seemingly obvious incremental innovations ignored by large industry players (e.g., Paychex serving small businesses), came from start-up or small companies—entrepreneurs—that have since become major industry leaders.

Taking this perspective has led some other forward-thinking large companies to seek ways to make themselves more entrepreneurial and to enable their "entrepreneurs within" to emerge and succeed in building new businesses around innovative ideas. Such people, termed "intrapreneurs" in the business and academic press, have proven to be effective champions of innovation-based growth in many companies that have sincerely encouraged their emergence. But whether it is through the entrepreneurs within, or becoming or teaming with independent entrepreneurs, ensuring the presence of entrepreneurship in an organization is central to innovation, long-term survival, and renewal.

WHAT IS ENTREPRENEURSHIP?

The Global Entrepreneurship Monitor estimates that 15 percent of all working adults are self-employed, a number they project is steadily growing.[18] New entrepreneurial ventures are recognized globally as key drivers of economic development, job creation, and innovation. So what is entrepreneurship? What does it involve?

---

[17] Ibid. See also www.innovate-ideagora.ning.com; "Innovation in the Age of Mass Collaboration," *BusinessWeek,* February 1, 2007; "The New Science of Sharing," *BusinessWeek,* March 2, 2007; *Wikinomics,* by Don Tapscott and Anthony Williams; and Satish Nambisan and M. Sawhney, "A Buyer's Guide to the Innovation Bazaar," *Harvard Business Review,* June 2007, p. 109.

[18] The Global Entrepreneurship Monitor is a not-for-profit research consortium that is the largest single study of entrepreneurial activity in the world. Initiated in 1999 by Babson College and London Business School, it now involves research teams at universities and other organizations worldwide. It provides annual and quarterly GEM updates at www.gemconsortium.org.

Top Strategist
Dwayne Spradlin, President and CEO, InnoCentive, www.innocentive.com

Exhibit 14.6

InnoCentive is the premier open-innovation marketplace in the world, where corporations and nonprofits ("seekers") post their toughest research problems and a global network of 160,000 "solvers" takes a crack at solving them for cash rewards. Dwayne Spradlin was a co-founder of InnoCentive, based on his passionate belief that crowdsourcing—allowing experts around the world to help solve problems and create innovation—would easily become a powerful tool for more efficient and speedy problem solving, allowing clients to develop new commercial solutions and allowing many opportunities for more effectively doing good. Spradlin says of this approach, "In this prize-based world, companies and organizations [those pursuing a crowdsourcing approach] are paying predominantly for success. Most innovation efforts fail. With the monolithic view of R&D and innovation, one of the main reasons it's insufficient is that you're paying for failure. In this [crowdsourcing, open-innovation] InnoCentive model, you're paying only for the winning solutions."

He offers a few recent examples: Oil Spill Recovery Institute out of Cordova, Alaska, needed to find a new and novel way to get oil off the bottom of Prince William Sound from the Exxon Valdez spill. For 15 years, that oil has been sitting down there at the bottom of the ocean. They could get the oil off the bottom and onto the barges, but the surface temperature drops so dramatically that the oil almost solidifies and they can't pump it through the barge system.

The solver ended up being an engineer out of the Midwest, and he recognized a way to solve that problem using technology that is fairly common in the construction industry. He recognized that was very similar to the problem of keeping cement liquid when pouring a foundation. They used commercial-grade vibrating equipment on the barges to keep the oil fluid enough so they could process it through the system.

Prize4Life, which is focused on ALS, also known as Lou Gehrig's disease, wanted to find a biomarker to help identify and treat Lou Gehrig's disease patients. They decided to run the challenge in multiple phases. The first phase was a prize to anyone on Earth who can come up with a new and novel way of identifying where a promising biomarker might be.

What's amazing about this was that solutions were coming not necessarily from the medical field—computer scientists; experts in bioinformatics, who were suggesting algorithmic approaches; and machine manufacturers, who knew enough about the disease to say the following kind of approach might provide a highly predictive model of who might be susceptible to this disease were all participating. They were getting solutions from outside the establishment that ended up generating some of the most innovative thinking in that field in recent years.

Crowdsourcing works in other settings too. Toronto-based Goldcorp, a gold mining company heavily in debt, facing labor strikes and high costs, was about to fold. In desperation, CEO Rob McEwen published all their proprietary geological data, a usually carefully guarded company secret in the mining industry, on the Web—400 megabytes of data about 55,000 acres. McEwen made $575,000 in prize money available to anyone who could propose the best methods of finding gold and estimating the likely find.

Within weeks, submissions came from around the world, ultimately resulting in several awards and, for Goldcorp, totally new ways to prospect. The company has now reached more than $6 billion in gold sales by applying the solutions "problem-solvers" from around the world helped them find: $100 invested in Goldcorp in 1993 is worth more than $4,000 today.

Swiss drugmaker Novartis has done something similar, again unheard of in the world of large pharmaceuticals. It decided to share online, after investing millions in secret proprietary research, all of its raw data regarding its efforts to unlock the genetic basis for type 2 diabetes. Among the most challenging and potentially lucrative areas of broad public health needs, Novartis and its partners at MIT decided that their groundbreaking research is still a first step, and the problem is still sufficiently complex that Novartis hopes to leverage the talents and training of a global scientific community to speed the development of gene-related interventions to help solve the type 2 diabetes challenge.

Source: www.innocentive.com.

EXHIBIT 14.7
Who Is the Entrepreneur?

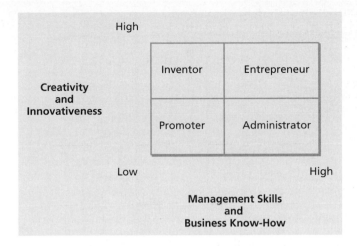

entrepreneurship
The process of bringing together the creative and innovative ideas and actions with the management and organizational skills necessary to mobilize the appropriate people, money, and operating resources to meet an identifiable need and create wealth in the process.

Entrepreneurship is the process of bringing together creative and innovative ideas and actions with the management and organizational skills necessary to mobilize the appropriate people, money, and operating resources to meet an identifiable need and create wealth in the process. Whether the process is undertaken by a single individual or a team of individuals, there is mounting evidence that growth-minded entrepreneurs possess not only a creative and innovative flair but also solid management skills and business know-how—or they ensure the presence of both in the fledgling organizations they start. Exhibit 14.7 illustrates the fundamental skills associated with being entrepreneurial versus those suitable for promoters, managers, and inventors.

Inventors are exceptional for their technical talents, insights, and creativity. But their creations and inventions often are unsuccessful in becoming commercial or organizational realities because their interests and skills are lacking in terms of reading a market and bringing products or services to creation and then marketing and selling them effectively. *Promoters* are in some way just the opposite—clever at devising schemes or programs to push a product or service, but aimed more at a quick payoff than a profitable, business-building endeavor for the longer term.

Administrators, the good ones, develop strong management skills, specific business know-how, and the ability to organize people. They usually take pride in overseeing the smooth, efficient functioning of operations largely as they are. Their administrative talents are focused on creating and maintaining efficient routines and organization—creative and innovative behavior may actually be counterproductive within the organizations they operate.

The ideal *entrepreneur* has that unusual combination of talent: strength in both creativity and management. In a new venture, these strengths enable the entrepreneur to conceive and launch a new business as well as make it grow and succeed. In a large organization, these talents enable strong players to emerge and build new ideas into impressive new revenue streams and profitability for a larger company. Because these strengths so rarely coexist in one individual, entrepreneurship is increasingly found to involve teams of people that combine their strengths to build the business they envision. Exhibit 14.8, Strategy in Action, tells the story of just such a rare entrepreneur, Fred Smith, founder and chairman of Federal Express.

New ventures and small, growth-oriented business entrepreneurs are able to achieve success from effectively managing three elements central to the entrepreneurial process in

Fred. W. Smith: Entrepreneur Extraordinaire

Frederick W. Smith, a Yale economics major, first laid out his idea for an express delivery service in what is now the most infamous term paper in business school settings. Legend has it he received a low C, though Smith is rather vague on that folklore. Whatever the professorial critique, he was undetered. After a stint with the Marines in Vietnam, he returned to hawk the idea to venture capitalists, ultimately getting a significant investment to which he added his family's holdings. He purchased a used aircraft company in Little Rock, Arkansas, and used it to start Federal Express in Memphis, Tennessee.[1]

Smith apparently had transportation in his blood. His grandfather was a steamboat captain; his father built a regional bus service from scratch, ultimately selling it to Greyhound Bus System. Smith learned to fly on weekends as a charter pilot while attending Yale. FedEx's first night's run involved just seven packages.

The postal monopoly was a big headache early in the effort to start FedEx. Smith became so desparate for cash at one point that he flew to Las Vegas, played blackjack, and won $27,000—which he wired back to Memphis to use to make payroll at one critical point in the company's survival. But by the late 1970s, FedEx started to take off as America came to rely on its overnight delivery. Merrill Lynch excutives came to find that employees even used it to deliver documents overnight between floors of its Manhattan headquarters because it was more reliable and faster than interoffice mail.[2]

Today, FedEx is a global supply chain linchpin for global companies worldwide. It carries more than 8 million shipments in 240 countries every day. All because a young college student first sensed a need for overnight delivery others couldn't or didn't see.

[1]"Frederick W. Smith: No Overnite Success," *BusinessWeek,* September 20, 2004.
[2]"ibid."

creating and sustaining new ventures. Those three elements are opportunity, the entrepreneurial team, and resources:

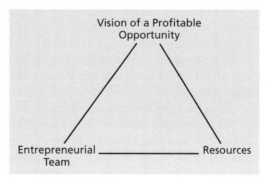

Source: RCTrust, LLC, © 2010.

Opportunity

The most frequent cause of failure of new ventures, as reported by Dun & Bradstreet (D&B) in its yearly failure record, is lack of sales; the second is competitive weakness. Both causes stem from the lack of appreciation of the necessity for a market orientation as the basis of any new venture. In other words, failure among new ventures, is heavily linked to ventures started because someone had the idea for such a business but did not identify a concrete market opportunity.

Entrepreneurs doomed to learn from their all too frequent failure conceive an idea for a product or service and immediately become enamored of it. They invest time, money, and energy in developing the idea into a commercial reality. And, tragically, they make only a minimum investment in identifying the customers, the customers' needs, and their willingness to buy the product or service as an answer to those needs. Such entrepreneurs are focused inward, perhaps satisfying their own personal ego needs. The result is often a product or service that few customers will buy. The customers are seeking to buy benefits, and the ineffective entrepreneur is consumed with selling his/her product.

The effective entrepreneur is more likely to assume a marketing orientation and look outward at a target market to identify or confirm the presence of a specific need or desired solution. Here the entrepreneur is focused on potential customers and on seeking to understand their need. The effective entrepreneur seeks to confirm an opportunity defined by what the customer wants and is willing to pay. It is interesting that the most effective approach in the way firms seek to innovate is to bring customers into the innovation process to help shape the solution they seek. In essence, customers define what they want. The design of an effective entrepreneur's product or service comes in response to an opportunity, not the other way around.

Another way to determine if an entrepreneur is focused on simply an idea or a good opportunity is to apply the same criteria venture capitalists use to evaluate new venture investment opportunities. It is important to recognize that these criteria are applied by investors interested primarily in high-growth ventures. The criteria for smaller ventures would be less demanding in scope (e.g., a minimum $250 million market) but similar in the types of concerns that should be addressed in an effort to determine whether the opportunity is a good one. Let's look at each criterion individually:

1. *The venture team can clearly identify its customers and the market segment(s) it plans to capture.* Exactly who are the target customers? Who makes the buying decision? Does the entrepreneur have evidence that these customers are enthusiastic about the product or service and will act favorably (e.g., pay in advance) on that enthusiasm? Firm purchase orders or other tangible purchase commitments help confirm the timing is right.

2. *A minimum market as large as $250 million.* A market this size suggests that the firms can achieve significant sales without having to attain a dominant share of its market. That, in turn, means the new venture can grow without attracting much competitive reaction. It is important to recognize that this threshold pertains to high-growth opportunities, not smaller, lifestyle ventures.

3. *A market growing at a rate of 30 to 50 percent.* This is another indicator that the timing is right to act on an opportunity; it means new entrants can enter the fray without evoking defensive reactions from established competitors. On the other hand, if the market is static or growing only marginally, then either the opportunity must offer a realistic chance of revolutionizing the industry—a rare occurrence—or the timing is bad.

4. *High gross margins (selling price less direct, variable costs) that are durable.* When entrepreneurs can sell their product or service at gross margins in the 50+ percent range, there is an attractive cushion built in that covers the mistakes they are likely to make while developing a new enterprise. When margins are small, the margin for error is too.

5. *There is no dominant competitor in the market segments representing the venture opportunity.* A market share of 40 to 60 percent usually translates into significant power over suppliers, customers, pricing, and costs. The absence of such a competitor means more room for the newcomer to maneuver, without fear of serious retaliation.

6. *A significant response time, or lead time, in terms of technical superiority, proprietary protection, distribution, or capacity.* When a new venture possesses this type of legitimate "unfair advantage," the new firm should be able to create barriers to entry or expansion by others who are aware of the profitable opportunity. When an entrepreneur can take advantage of this sort of proprietary edge, and the edge will last, the timing is right.

7. *An experienced entrepreneur or team capable of enthusiastically and professionally building a company to exploit the profitable opportunity.* Venture capitalists universally

identify this as an essential ingredient for the timing to be right to invest in a proposed venture. Aspiring entrepreneurs should likewise use it as a criterion for whether it is wise to pursue the new venture opportunity they are considering. Let's examine this last point more fully.

Entrepreneurial Teams

Successful entrepreneurs and entrepreneurial teams bring several competencies and characteristics to their new ventures. Let's examine both.

- *Technical competence.* The entrepreneur or team must possess the knowledge and skill necessary to create the products or services the new venture will provide. It may be that some of those competencies exist outside the entrepreneur or team, in which case meaningful arrangements to outsource them become part of the technical competence equation. But know-how and capability are essential to success.
- *Business management skills.* The survival and growth of a technically viable new venture depend on the ability of the entrepreneur to understand and manage the economics of the business. Financial and accounting know-how in areas of cash flow, liquidity, costs and contributions, record keeping, pricing, structuring debt, and asset acquisition are essential. People management skills, marketing, organizational skills, sales, computer literacy, and planning skills are just some of those essential to success.

Technical and business skills being critical, they alone are not enough. Observers identify several behavioral and psychological characteristics that are usually associated with successful entrepreneurs:

- *Endless commitment and determination.* Ask any number of entrepreneurs the secret of their success, and they inevitably cite this one. Entrepreneurs' level of commitment can usually be gauged by their willingness to jeopardize personal economic well-being, to tolerate a lower standard of living than they would otherwise enjoy early in the enterprise, and even to sacrifice time with their family.
- *A strong desire to achieve.* Need to achieve is a strong entrepreneurial motivator. Money is a way to keep score, but outdoing their own expectations is an almost universal driver.
- *Orientation toward opportunities and goals.* Good entrepreneurs always like to talk about their customers and their customers' needs. They can readily respond when asked what their goals are for this week, month, and year.
- *An internal locus of control.* Successful entrepreneurs are self-confident. They believe they control their own destiny. To use a sports analogy, they want the ball for the critical last-second shot.
- *Tolerance for ambiguity and stress.* Start-up entrepreneurs face the need to meet payroll when revenue has yet to be received, jobs are constantly changing, customers are ever new, and setbacks and surprises are inevitable.
- *Skills in taking calculated risks.* Entrepreneurs are like pilots: they take calculated risks. They do everything possible to reduce or share risks. They prepare or anticipate problems; confirm the opportunity and what is necessary for success; create ways to share risk with suppliers, investors, customers, and partners; and are typically obsessed with controlling key roles in the execution of the firm's operations.
- *Little need for status and power.* Power accrues to good entrepreneurs, but their focus is on opportunities, customers, markets, and competition. They may use that power in these settings, but they do not often seek status for the sake of having it.

- *Problem solvers.* Good entrepreneurs seek out problems that may affect their success and methodically go about overcoming them. Not intimidated by difficult situations, they are usually decisive and capable of enormous patience.

- *A high need for feedback.* "How are we doing?" The question is ever-present in an entrepreneur's mind. They seek feedback. They nurture mentors to learn from and expand their network of contacts.

- *Ability to deal with failure.* Entrepreneurs love to win, but they accept failure and aggressively learn from it as a way to better manage their next venture.

- *Boundless energy, good health, and emotional stability.* Their challenges are many, so good entrepreneurs seem to embrace their arena and pursue good health to build their stamina and emotional well-being.

- *Creativity and innovativeness.* New ways of looking at things, tinkering, staying late to talk with a customer or employee—all these are typical of entrepreneurs' obsession with doing things better, more efficiently, and so forth. They see an opportunity instead of a problem, a solution instead of a dilemma.

- *High intelligence and conceptual ability.* Good entrepreneurs have "street smarts," a special sense for business, and the ability to see the big picture. They are good strategic thinkers.

- *Vision and the capacity to inspire.* The capacity to shape and communicate a vision in a way that inspires others is a valuable skill entrepreneurs need in themselves or from someone in their core team.

Resources

The third element in new venture entrepreneurship involves *resources*—money and time. Let's summarize money first. A vital ingredient for any business venture is the capital necessary to acquire equipment, facilities, people, and capabilities to pursue the targeted opportunity. New ventures do this in two ways. **Debt financing** is money provided to the venture that must be repaid at some point in time. The obligation to pay is usually secured by property or equipment bought by the business, or by the entrepreneur's personal assets. **Equity financing** is money provided to the venture that entitles the provider to rights or ownership in the venture and which is not expected to be repaid. It entitles the source to some form of ownership in the venture, for which the source usually expects some future return or gain on that investment.

Debt financing is generally obtained from a commercial bank to pay for property, equipment, and maybe provide working capital—all available only after there is proven revenue coming into the business. Family and friends are debt sources, as are leasing companies, suppliers, and companies that lend against accounts receivable. Entrepreneurs benefit when using debt capital because they retain ownership and increase the return on their investment if things go as planned. If not, debt financing can be a real problem for new ventures because rapid growth requires steady cash flow (to pay salaries, bills, interest), which creates a real dilemma if interest rates rise and sales slow down. Most new ventures find early debt capital hard to get anyway, so gradually nurturing a relationship with a commercial lender, letting them get to know the entrepreneur and the business, is a wise approach for the new entrepreneur.

Equity financing is usually obtained from one or more of three sources: friendly sources, informal venture investors, or professional venture capitalists. In each case, it is often referred to as "patient money," meaning it does not have to be paid back immediately or on any particular schedule. *Friendly sources* are prevalent early in many new ventures—friends, family, wealthy individuals who know the entrepreneur. *Informal venture investors,*

debt financing
Money "loaned" to an entrepreneur or business venture that must be repaid at some point in time.

equity financing
Money provided to a business venture that entitles the provider to rights or ownership in the venture and which is not expected to be repaid.

usually wealthy individuals, or what are now called "angel" investors (for obvious reasons), are increasingly active and accessible as possible equity investors. *Professional venture capitalists* seek investment in the truly high-growth potential ventures. They have stringent criteria as we have seen, and expect a return of five times their money in three to five years! A fourth source of equity capital, *public stock offerings,* is available for a very select few new ventures. They are usually firms that have gone through the other three sources first.

Regardless of the source, equity capital is money that does not have to be repaid on an immediate, regular basis as debt capital requires. So when a firm is rapidly growing and needs to use all its cash flow to grow, not having to repay makes equity more attractive than debt. The unattractive aspect of equity financing for some people is that it constitutes selling part of the ownership of the business and, with it, a say in the decisions directing the venture.

The other resource is time—time of the entrepreneur(s) and key players in the business venture's chance for success. The entrepreneur is the catalyst, the glue that holds the fledgling business together and oftentimes the critical source of energy to make success happen. As we noted earlier, determination is a key characteristic of entrepreneurs. And time is the most critical resource, combined with determination, to virtually "will" the new venture's success at numerous junctures in its early development.

Successful entrepreneurs are impressive growth and value building innovators. Their success often comes at the expense of large firms with which they compete, do business, obtain supplies, and such. Their success in commercializing new ideas has drawn the attention of many larger companies leading to the question, Can a big firm be more entrepreneurial? The conclusion has been a tentative yes, that larger firms can increase their level of innovation and subsequent commercialization success if they encourage entrepreneurship and entrepreneurs within their organizations. Understanding and encouraging entrepreneurship in large organizations to improve future survival and growth has become a major agenda in thousands of large companies today. The ideas behind these efforts, which have been called *intrapreneurship,* are examined in the next section.

Intrapreneurship

Intrapreneurship, or entrepreneurship in large companies, is the process of attempting to identify, encourage, enable, and assist entrepreneurship within a large, established company so as to create new products, processes, or services that become major new revenue streams and sources of cost savings for the company. Gordon Pinchot, founder of a school for intrapreneurs and creator of the phrase itself, suggests 10 **freedom factors** that need to be present in large companies seeking to encourage intrapreneurship:

1. *Self-selection.* Companies should give innovators the opportunity to bring forth their ideas, rather than making the generation of new ideas the designated responsibility of a few individuals or groups.

2. *No hand-offs.* Once ideas surface, managers should allow the person generating the idea to pursue it rather than instructing him or her to turn it over ("hand it off") to someone else.

3. *The doer decides.* Giving the originator of an idea some freedom to make decisions about its further development and implementation, rather than relying on multiple levels of approval for even the most minor decision, enhances intrapreneurship.

4. *Corporate "slack."* Firms that set aside money and time ("slack") facilitate innovation.

5. *End the "home run" philosophy.* Some company cultures foster an interest in innovative ideas only when they represent major breakthroughs. Intrapreneurship is restricted in that type of culture.

intrapreneurship
A term associated with entrepreneurship in large, established companies; the process of attempting to identify, encourage, enable, and assist entrepreneurship within a large, established company so as to create new products, processes, services, or improvements that become major new revenue streams and/or sources of cost savings for the company.

intrapreneurship freedom factors
Ten characteristics identified by Dr. Gorden Pinchot and elaborated upon by others that need to be present in large companies seeking to encourage and increase the level of intrapreneurship within their company.

6. *Tolerance of risk, failure, and mistakes.* Where risks and failure are damaging to their careers, managers carefully avoid them. But innovations inherently involve risks, so calculated risks and some failures should be tolerated and chalked up to experience.

7. *Patient money.* The pressure for quarterly profits in many U.S. companies stifles innovative behavior. Investment in intrapreneurial activity may take time to bear fruit.

8. *Freedom from turfness.* In any organization, people stake out turf. Boundaries go up. Intrapreneurship is stifled by this phenomenon because cross-fertilization is often central to innovation and successful entrepreneurial teams.

9. *Cross-functional teams.* Organizations inhibit cross-functional interaction by insisting that communication flow upward. That inhibits sales from learning from operations and company people from interacting with relevant outsiders.

10. *Multiple options.* When an individual with an idea has only one person to consult or one channel to inquire into for developing the idea, innovation can be stifled. Intrapreneurship is encouraged when people have many options for discussing or pursuing innovative ideas.

When you read Pinchot's 10 freedom factors, they sound very much like characteristics associated with entrepreneurs or the nature of the types of resources—money and time—that we identified as being central to the entrepreneurship process. And that, obviously, is exactly what intrapreneurship is trying to do—replicate the presence of entrepreneurs (small undertakings) inside a large enterprise that offers the potential advantage of easier money, expertise, facilities, distribution, and so forth. Exhibit 14.9, Strategy in Action, describes a variety of intrapreneurial successes with companies you should readily recognize. Nine specific ways companies are attempting to enable intrapreneurs and intrapreneurship to flourish in their companies are given here:[19]

- *Designate intrapreneurship "sponsors."* Formally identify several people with credibility and influence in the company to serve as facilitators of new ideas. These "sponsors" usually have discretionary funds to allocate on the spot to help innovators develop their ideas.

- *Allow innovation time.* 3M was know for its "15 percent rule," which means that members of its engineering group can spend 15 percent of their time tinkering with whatever idea they think has market potential. Google gives employees one day a week to work on their own projects.

- *Accommodate intrapreneurial teams.* 3M calls it "tin cupping." American Cement calls it "innovation volunteers." P&G sets up teams across product divisions to intentionally cross-pollinate new business. The idea is for companies to give managers interdepartmental or unit flexibility to let informal idea-development teams (a marketing person, an engineer, and an operations person) interact about promising ideas and develop them as though they were an independent business.

- *Provide intrapreneurial forums.* Owens Corning calls them "skunkworks, innovation boards, and innovation fairs." 3M has "technical forums," annual "technical review fairs," and "sales clubs." P&G, eBay, and Amazon bring in outsiders, customers especially, to help form the basis for interaction about new ideas where ones that gain traction can quickly move to more serious pursuit using other specific ways described here.

- *Use intrapreneurial controls.* Quarterly profit contribution does not work with intrapreneurial ventures at their early stages. Milestone reviews like we discussed earlier in this chapter—key timetables, resource requirements—provide a type of control more suited to early, innovative activity.

[19] For elaboration on these and other ideas, see "Lessons from Apple," *The Economist,* June 7, 2007; "Remember to Forget, Borrow, and Learn," *BusinessWeek,* March 28, 2007; "Clayton Christensen's Innovation Brain," *BusinessWeek,* June 15, 2007; and www.Businessweek.com/innovation.

Intrapreneurs—They Are Everywhere! Just Give Them Time to Blossom

Google encourages all its employees to spend 20 percent of their time on ideas that they would like to develop or feel passionate about. This is the reason Google is constantly introducing new products such as Gmail, Google Earth, and Google Apps. Google Adsense and Adwords were created by an employee who was paid $10 million for his internal-entrepreneurial effort.

Arthur Fry, 53, a 3M chemical engineer, used to get annoyed at how pieces of paper that marked his church hymnal always fell out when he stood up to sing. He knew that Spencer Silver, a scientist at 3M, had accidentally discovered an adhesive that had very low sticking power. Normally that would be bad, but for Fry it was good. He figured that markers made with the adhesive might stick lightly to something and would come off easily. Since 3M allows employees to spend 15 percent of their office time on independent projects, he began working on the idea. Fry made samples and then distributed the small yellow pads to company secretaries. They were delighted. 3M eventually began selling it under the name **Post-it.** Sales last year were more than **$100 million.**

Ken Kutaragi was working in Sony's sound labs when he bought his daughter a Nintendo game console. Watching her play, he was dismayed by the system's primitive sound effects. With Sony's blessing, Kutaragi worked with Nintendo to develop a CD-ROM–based Nintendo. But Nintendo decided not to go forward with it, so Kutaragi helped Sony develop its own gaming system, which became the PlayStation. The first PlayStation made Sony a major player in the games market, but the PlayStation 2 did even better, becoming the best-selling game console of all time. Kutaragi founded Sony Computer Entertainment, one of the Sony's most profitable divisions.

W.L. Gore, known primarily as the maker of Gore-Tex rain gear, encourages employees to develop new ideas through its "dabble time" policy: 10 percent of a workday can be devoted to personal projects. A few years ago, the company was experimenting with ePTFE, a chemical cousin to Teflon, to coat push-pull cables for use in animatronics. Dave Myers, an associate in the company's medical unit, thought the coating might be good for guitar strings and recruited both marketing and manufacturing personnel to work on the project. Myers's team originally believed that the coating's appeal would be in making strings more comfortable to use. But extensive market research, piloted by John Spencer, and more than 15,000 guitar-player field tests led the team to realize their real selling point: better sound. The coated strings were only nominally more comfortable than noncoated strings, but they kept their tone longer than conventional guitar strings. W.L. Gore launched them under the brand name ELIXIR Strings, now the No. 1 seller of acoustic guitar strings and the overall No. 2 seller in the guitar string market.

There's an engineer in Dallas whose "wasteful" tinkering with a flow problem he had to deal with every day almost got him fired. Now his oil delivery spout invention is used by almost every major oil company in the world.

Caterpillar took its own internal logistics problem and created Caterpillar Logistics, which now spans 25 countries and six continents.

Alicia Ledlie, co-manager at a Wal-Mart store in Long Island, New York, attended a conference at the company's Arkansas headquarters and heard about a possible new venture: in-store health clinics. It was Ledlie's idea to include drug-testing services for Wal-Mart job applicants in the clinics' scope of services. Ledlie knew that all new hires had to have a drug test within 24 hours of receiving a job offer. "Working in the stores, I'd seen how this requirement created a challenge for recruits who relied on public transportation," she says. "Adding this service to the clinics' roster was a quick win. Store managers raved about the effect it had on helping them keep new recruits." Wal-Mart plans to add as many as 2,000 sites in the next five to seven years.

Jim Lynch's big idea came out of the most ordinary of activities—cleaning the gutters on his suburban Massachusetts home. "It occurred to me that this was a perfect job for a robot," Lynch says, "because it fit into our company's three criteria: dumb, dirty, and dangerous." A senior electrical engineer at Burlington, Massachusetts–based iRobot, Lynch began tinkering with different models and built a prototype using a spaghetti ladle and an electric screwdriver. His chance to present it came in September 2006, when the company held its first-ever "idea bake-off," where employees got 10 minutes each to pitch an idea for a new product. Lynch's project was green-lighted by the company brass, and the new gutter-cleaning robot, named "Looj" (after the Olympic sport), launched on schedule last year.

Source: www.bnet.com/2403-1313070_23-196888.htm, and 23-196890.htm.

- *Provide intrapreneurial rewards.* Recognition for success, financial bonuses if successful, and most importantly the opportunity to "do it again," with even greater freedom in developing and implementing the next idea are extremely important to this type of venture.

- *Articulate specific innovation objectives.* Clearly setting forth organizational objectives that legitimize and indeed call for intrapreneurship and innovation helps encourage an organizational culture to support this activity. 3M is the "granddaddy" of this approach, having long held to a corporate objective, which they have hit every year since 1970, that "25 percent of annual sales each year will come from products introduced within the last five years." P&G has a corporate goal that 50 percent of its innovations originate outside the company to encourage collaborative, "open," innovative behavior.

- *Create a culture of intrapreneurship.* Jeff Bezos of Amazon.com calls it a "culture of divine discontent," in which everyone itches to improve things. P&G calls it letting outsiders into P&G to innovate, and CEO Lafley is working to ensure that more than half of P&G new products will come from outsiders teamed with inside intrapreneurs. GE's Immelt hires successful intrapreneurs from other companies to become leaders in a usually insider-promoted organization, both to get the intrapreneur involved and even more importantly to send a message of fundamental cultural change toward intrapreneurship. Other firms create internal "banks" to invest in new internal start-ups. Intel has its own venture capital arm investing aggressively in entrepreneurial ventures inside and outside the company, often spinning them off.

- *Encourage innovation from without as well as within.* Apple is widely assumed to be an innovator "within." In fact, its real skill lies in stitching together its own ideas with technologies from outside and then wrapping the results in elegant software and simple, stylish designs.

Innovation and entrepreneurship are intertwined phenomena and processes. Organizations seeking to control their destiny, which most all seek to do, increasingly "get it" that even having a destiny may be the issue. And to have that opportunity or chance, organizations need leaders who embrace the importance of being innovative and entrepreneurial to give their companies the chance to find ways to adapt, be relevant, to position themselves in a future that, to use a trite phrase, has but one real constant—change.

Summary

A central goal with any strategy is the survival, growth, and improved competitive position of the company in the future. Executives seek ways to make their organizations innovative and entrepreneurial because these are increasingly seen as essential capabilities for survival, growth, and relevance. Incremental innovation—where companies increasingly, in concert with their customers, seek to steadily refine and improve their products, services, and processes—has proven to be a very effective approach to innovation. The continuous improvement philosophy, and programs such as CCC21 and Six Sigma, are key ways firms make incremental innovation a central part of their organization's ongoing work activities.

Breakthrough innovation involves far more risk than the incremental approach yet brings high reward when successful. Firms with this approach need a total commitment and are often going against mainstream markets in the process. Large, well-known global companies are increasingly embracing "open" approaches to innovation, including breakthrough innovation, in ways that would have been unthinkable 20 years ago. They have embraced the outsourcing of much product design innovation in recent years and are rapidly adopting Web-enabled forums for tapping expertise located around the globe to gain assistance and collaboration in generating breakthrough innovation. They also increasingly look to innovate by acquiring small, entrepreneurial firms that often generate breakthrough innovations because they have a narrow focus, tolerate risks, have a passion for what they are doing, and benefit greatly if they succeed.

Entrepreneurship is central to making businesses innovative and fresh. New-venture entrepreneurship is the source of much innovation, and it is really a process involving opportunity, resources, and key people. Opportunity is focusing intensely on solving problems and benefits to customers rather than product or service ideas someone just dreams up. Resources involve money and time. Key people, the entrepreneurial team, need to bring technical skill, business skill, and key characteristics to the new venture endeavor for it to succeed.

Intrapreneurship is entrepreneurship in large organizations. Many firms now claim that they seek to encourage intrapreneurship. For intrapreneurship to work, individual intrapreneurs need freedom and support to pursue perceived opportunities, be allowed to fail, and do more of the same more easily if they succeed.

Key Terms

breakthrough innovation, *p. 376*
CCC21, *p. 372*
continuous improvement, *p. 371*
debt financing, *p. 389*
disruptive innovation, *p. 380*

entrepreneurship, *p. 385*
equity financing, *p. 389*
ideagoras, *p. 381*
incremental innovation, *p. 371*
innovation, *p. 371*

intrapreneurship, *p. 390*
intrapreneurship freedom
factors, *p. 390*
invention, *p. 370*
Six Sigma, *p. 373*

Questions for Discussion

1. What is the difference between incremental and breakthrough innovation? What risks are associated with each approach?
2. Why is continuous improvement, and programs such as CCC21 and Six Sigma, a good way to develop incremental innovation?
3. What is an ideagora?
4. How are big, global companies looking "outward" to accelerate their innovativeness and breakthrough innovations?
5. Why do most breakthrough innovations occur in smaller firms?
6. What are the three key elements in the entrepreneurship process in new ventures?
7. What is intrapreneurship, and how is it best enabled?

Part **Four**

Cases

Guide to Strategic Management Case Analysis

THE CASE METHOD

Case analysis is a proven educational method that is especially effective in a strategic management course. The case method complements and enhances the text material and your professor's lectures by focusing attention on what a firm has done or should do in an actual business situation. Use of the case method in a strategic management course offers you an opportunity to develop and refine analytical skills. It also can provide exciting experience by allowing you to assume the role of the key decision maker for the organizations you will study.

When assuming the role of the general manager of the organization being studied, you will need to consider all aspects of the business. In addition to drawing on your knowledge of marketing, finance, management, production, and economics, you will be applying the strategic management concepts taught in this course.

The cases in this book are accounts of real business situations involving a variety of firms in a variety of industries. To make these opportunities as realistic as possible, the cases include a variety of quantitative and qualitative information in both the presentation of the situation and the exhibits. As the key decision maker, you will need to determine which information is important, given the circumstances described in the case. Keep in mind that the results of analyzing one firm will not necessarily be appropriate for another since every firm is faced with a different set of circumstances.

PREPARING FOR CASE DISCUSSION

The case method requires an approach to class preparation that differs from the typical lecture course. In the typical lecture course, you can still benefit from each class session even if you did not prepare, by listening carefully to the professor's lecture. This approach will not work in a course using the case method. For a case course, proper preparation is essential.

Suggestions for Effective Preparation

1. *Allow adequate time in preparing a case.* Many of the cases in this text involve complex issues that are often not apparent without careful reading and purposeful reflection on the information in the cases.

2. *Read each case twice.* Because many of these cases involve complex decision making, you should read each case at least twice. Your first reading should give you an overview of the firm's unique circumstances and the issues confronting the firm. Your second reading allows you to concentrate on what you feel are the most critical issues and to understand what information in the case is most important. Make limited notes identifying key points during your first reading. During your second reading, you can add details to your original notes and revise them as necessary.

3. *Focus on the key strategic issue in each case.* Each time you read a case you should concentrate on identifying the key issue. In some cases, the key issue will be identified by the case writer in the introduction. In other cases, you might not grasp the key strategic issue until you have read the case several times. (Remember that not every piece of information in a case is equally important.)

4. *Do not overlook exhibits.* The exhibits in these cases should be considered an integral part of the information for the case. They are not just "window dressing." In fact, for many cases you will need to analyze financial statements, evaluate organizational charts, and understand the firm's products, all of which are presented in the form of exhibits.

5. *Adopt the appropriate time frame.* It is critical that you assume the appropriate time frame for each case you read. If the case ends in 2009, that year should become the present for you as you work on that case. Making a decision for a case that ends in 2009 by using data you could not have had until 2011 defeats the purpose of the case method. For the same reason, although it is recommended that you do outside reading on each firm and industry, you should not read material written after the case ended unless your professor instructs you to do so.

6. *Draw on all of your knowledge of business.* As the key decision maker for the organization being studied, you will need to consider all aspects of the business and industry. Do not confine yourself to strategic management concepts presented in this course. You will need to determine if the key strategic issue revolves around a theory you have learned in a functional area, such as marketing, production, finance, or economics, or in the strategic management course.

USING THE INTERNET IN CASE RESEARCH

The proliferation of information available on the Internet has direct implications for business research. The Internet has become a viable source of company and industry data to assist those involved in case study analysis. Principal sources of useful data include company Web sites, U.S. government Web sites, search engines, investment research sites, and online data services. This section will describe the principal Internet sources of case study data and offer means of retrieving that data.

Company Web Sites

Virtually every public and private firm has a Web site that any Internet user can visit. Accessing a firm's Web site is easy. Many firms advertise their Web address through both TV and print advertisements. To access a site when the address is known, enter the address into the address line on any Internet service provider's homepage. When the address is not known, use of a search engine will be necessary. The use of a search engine will be described later. Often, but not always, a firm's Web address is identical to its name, or is at least an abbreviated form of its name.

Company Web sites contain data that are helpful in case study analysis. A firm's Web site may contain descriptions of company products and services, recent company accomplishments and press releases, financial and stock performance highlights, and an overview of a firm's history and strategic objectives. A company's Web site may also contain links to relevant industry Web sites that contain industry statistics as well as current and future industry trends. The breadth of data available on a particular firm's Web site will vary but in general larger, global corporations tend to have more complete and sophisticated Web sites than do smaller, regional firms.

U.S. Government Web Sites

The U.S. government allows the public to access virtually all of the information that it collects. Most of this information is available online to Internet users. The government collects a great range of data types, from firm-specific data the government mandates all publicly traded firms to supply to highly regarded economic indicators. The usefulness of many U.S. government Web sites depends on the fit between the case you are studying and the data located on the Web site. For example, a study of an accounting firm may be supplemented with data supplied by the Internal Revenue Service Web site, but not the Environmental Protection Agency Web site. A sampling of prominent government Web sites and their addresses is shown here:

Environmental Protection Agency: www.epa.gov

General Printing Office: www.gpo.gov

Internal Revenue Service: www.irs.ustreas.gov

Libraries of Congress: www.loc.gov

National Aeronautics and Space Administration: www.hq.nasa.gov

SEC's Edgar Database: www.sec.gov/edgarhp.htm

Small Business Administration: www.sba.gov

STAT-USA: www.stat-usa.gov

U.S. Department of Commerce: www.doc.gov

U.S. Patent and Trademark Office: uspto.gov

U.S. Department of Treasury: www.ustreas.gov

One of the most useful sites for company case study analysis is the Securities and Exchange Commission's EDGAR database. The EDGAR database contains the documents that the government mandates all publicly traded firms to file including 10-Ks and 8-Ks. A Form 10-K is the annual report that provides a comprehensive overview of a firm's financials in addition to discussions regarding industry and product background. Form 8-K reports the occurrence of any material events or corporate changes that may be of importance to investors. Examples of reported occurrences include key management personnel changes, corporate restructures, and new debt or equity issuance. This site is very user friendly and requires the researcher to provide only the company name in order to produce a listing of all available reports.

Search Engines

Search engines allow a researcher to locate information on a company or industry without prior knowledge of a specific Internet address. Generally, to execute a search the search engine requires the entering of a keyword, for example, a company name. However, each search engine differs slightly in its search capabilities. For example, to narrow a search on one search engine may be accomplished differently than narrowing a search on another.

The information retrieved by search engines typically includes articles and other information that contain the entered keyword or words. Because the search engine has retrieved data that contain keywords does not necessarily mean that the information is useful. Internet data are unfiltered, meaning they may not be checked for accuracy before the data are posted online. However, data copyrighted or published by a reputable source may greatly increase the chance that the data are indeed accurate. Popular search options like google.com, bing.com, yahoo.com, and ask.com should work just fine to allow you to do basic research on the companies and industries discussed in the cases.

Investment Research Sites

Investment research sites provide company stock performance data including key financial ratios, competitor identification, industry data, and links to research reports and SEC filings. These sites provide support for the financial analysis portion of a case study, but only for publicly traded businesses. Most investment research sites also contain macro market data that may not be company specific, but may still affect many investors of equities.

Investment research sites usually contain a search mechanism if a desired stock's ticker symbol is not known. In this case, the company name is entered to enable the site to find the corresponding equity. Because these sites are geared toward traders who want recent stock prices and data, searching for data relevant to a case may require more elaborate investigations at multiple sites. The following list includes many popular investment research sites:

American Stock Exchange: www.amex.com

CBS Market Watch: cbsmarketwatch.com

CNN FinancialNews: money.cnn.com

DBC Online: www.esignal.com

Hoover's Online: www.hoovers.com

InvestorGuide: www.investorguide.com

Wall Street Research Net: www.wsrn.com

Market Guide: www.marketguide.com

Money Search: www.moneysearch.com

MSN Money: moneycentral.msn.com

NASDAQ: www.nasdaq.com

New York Stock Exchange: www.nyse.com

PC Financial Network: www.csfbdirect.com

Quote.Com: finance.lycos.com

Stock Smart: www.stocksmart.com

Yahoo.com/finance

Wright Investors' Service on the World Wide Web: www.wisi.com

The Wall Street Journal Online: online.wsj.com/public/us

Zacks Investment Research: my.zacks.com

One site that conveniently contains firm, industry, and competitor data is Hoover's Online. Hoover's also provides financials, stock charts, current and archived news stories, and links to research reports and SEC filings. Yahoo!'s "Finance" option is another excellent resource for company-related research. Some of these data, most notably the lengthy research reports produced by analysts, are fee-based and must be ordered.

Online Data Sources

Online data sources provide wide access to a huge volume of business reference material. Information retrieved from these sites typically includes descriptive profiles, stock price performance, SEC filings, and newspaper, magazine, and journal articles related to a particular company, industry, or product. Online data services are popular with educational and financial institutions. While some services are free to all users, to utilize the entire array of these sites' services, a fee-based subscription is usually necessary.

Accessing these sites requires only the source's address, or the use of a search engine to find the address. The source's homepage will clearly indicate the nature of the information available and describe how to search for and access the data. Most sites have help screens to assist in locating the desired information.

One of the most useful online sources for business research is the Lexis-Nexis Universe. This source provides a wide array of news, business, legal, and reference information. The information is categorized into dozens of topics including general news; company and industry news; company financials that include SEC filings; government and political news; accounting, auditing, and tax data; and legal research. One particularly impressive service is a search mechanism that allows a user to locate a particular article when the specific citation is known. A list of several notable online data sources is shown here:

ABI/Inform (Proquest Direct): www.il.proquest.com/proquest

American Express: americanexpress.com

Bloomberg Financial News Services: www.bloomberg.com

BusinessWeek Online: businessweek.com

Dow Jones News Retrieval: http://bis.dowjones.com

EconLit: www.econlit.org

Lexis-Nexis Universe: www.lexis-nexis.com

PARTICIPATING IN CLASS

Because the strategic management course uses the case method, the success and value of the course depend on class discussion. The success and value of the class discussion, in turn, rely on the roles both you and your professor perform. Following are aspects of your role and your professor's that, if kept in mind, will enhance the value and excitement of this course.

Students as Active Learners

The case method requires your active participation. This means your role is no longer one of sitting and listening.

1. *Attend class regularly.* Not only is your grade likely to depend on your involvement in class discussions, but the benefit you derive from this course is directly related to your involvement in and understanding of the discussions.

2. *Be prepared for class.* The need for adequate preparation already has been discussed. You will benefit more from the discussions, will understand and participate in the exchange of ideas, and will avoid the embarrassment of being called on when not prepared. By all means, bring your book to class. Not only is there a good chance you will need to refer to a

specific exhibit or passage from the case, you may need to refresh your memory of the case (particularly if you made notes in the margins while reading).

3. *Participate in the discussion.* Attending class and being prepared are not enough; you need to express your views in class. You can participate in a number of ways: by addressing a question asked by your professor, by disagreeing with your professor or your classmates (by all means, be tactful), by building on an idea expressed by a classmate, or by simply asking a relevant question.

4. *Participate wisely.* Although you do not want to be one of those students who never raises his or her hand, you also should be sensitive to the fact that others in your class will want to express themselves. You have probably already had experience with a student who attempts to dominate each class discussion. A student who invariably tries to dominate the class discussion breeds resentment.

5. *Keep a broad perspective.* By definition, the strategic management course deals with the issues facing general managers or business owners. As already mentioned, you need to consider all aspects of the business, not just one particular functional area.

6. *Pay attention to the topic being discussed.* Focus your attention on the topic being discussed. When a new topic is introduced, do not attempt to immediately introduce another topic for discussion. Do not feel you have to have something to say on every topic covered.

Your Professor as Discussion Leader

Your professor is a discussion leader. As such, he or she will attempt to stimulate the class as a whole to share insights, observations, and thoughts about the case. Your professor will not necessarily respond to every comment you or your classmates make. Part of the value of the case method is to get you and your classmates to assume this role as the course progresses.

The professor in a strategic management case course performs several roles:

1. *Maintaining focus.* Because multiple complex issues need to be explored, your professor may want to maintain the focus of the class discussion on one issue at a time. He or she may ask you to hold your comment on another issue until a previous issue is exhausted. Do not interpret this response to mean your point is unimportant; your professor is simply indicating there will be a more appropriate time to pursue that particular comment.

2. *Getting students involved.* Do not be surprised if your professor asks for input from volunteers and nonvolunteers alike. The value of the class discussion increases as more people share their comments.

3. *Facilitating comprehension of strategic management concepts.* Some professors prefer to lecture on strategic management concepts on a "need-to-know" basis. In this scenario, a lecture on a particular topic will be followed by an assignment to work on a case that deals with that particular topic. Other professors will have the class work through a case or two before lecturing on a topic to give the class a feel for the value of the topic being covered and for the type of information needed to work on cases. Still other professors prefer to cover all of the theory in the beginning of the course, thereby allowing uninterrupted case discussion in the remaining weeks of the term. All three of these approaches are valued.

4. *Playing devil's advocate.* At times your professor may appear to be contradicting many of the comments or observations being made. At other times your professor may adopt a position that does not immediately make sense, given the circumstances of the case. At other times your professor may seem to be equivocating. These are all examples

of how your professor might be playing devil's advocate. Sometimes the professor's goal is to expose alternative viewpoints. Sometimes he or she may be testing your resolve on a particular point. Be prepared to support your position with evidence from the case.

ASSIGNMENTS

Written Assignments

Written analyses are a critical part of most strategic management courses. Each professor has a preferred format for these written analyses, but a number of general guidelines will prove helpful to you in your written assignments.

1. *Analyze.* Avoid merely repeating the facts presented in the case. Analyze the issues involved in the case and build logically toward your recommendations.

2. *Use headings or labels.* Using headings or labels throughout your written analysis will help your reader follow your analysis and recommendations. For example, when you are analyzing the weaknesses of the firm in the case, include the heading Weaknesses. Note the headings in the cases that follow.

3. *Discuss alternatives.* Follow the proper strategic management sequence by (a) identifying alternatives, (b) evaluating each alternative, and (c) recommending the alternative you think is best.

4. *Use topic sentences.* You can help your reader more easily evaluate your analysis by putting the topic sentence first in each paragraph and following with statements directly supporting the topic sentence.

5. *Be specific in your recommendations.* Develop specific recommendations logically and be sure your recommendations are well defended by your analysis. Avoid using generalizations, clichés, and ambiguous statements. Remember that any number of answers are possible and so your professor is most concerned about how your reasoning led to your recommendations and how well you develop and support your ideas.

6. *Do not overlook implementation.* Many good analyses receive poor evaluations because they do not include a discussion of implementation. Your analysis will be much stronger when you discuss how your recommendation can be implemented. Include some of the specific actions needed to achieve the objectives you are proposing.

7. *Specifically state your assumptions.* Cases, like all real business situations, involve incomplete information. Therefore, it is important that you clearly state any assumptions you make in your analysis. Do not assume your professor will be able to fill in the missing points.

Oral Presentations

Your professor is likely to ask you and your classmates to make oral presentations on a particular case. Oral presentations usually are done by groups of students. In these groups, each member will typically be responsible for one aspect of the overall case. Keep the following suggestions in mind when you are faced with an oral presentation:

1. *Use your own words.* Avoid memorizing a presentation. The best approach is to prepare an outline of the key points you want to cover. Do not be afraid to have the outline in front of you during your presentation, but do not just read the outline.

2. *Rehearse your presentation.* Do not assume you can simply read the outline you have prepared or that the right words will come to you when you are in front of the class making

your presentation. Take the time to practice your speech, and be sure to rehearse the entire presentation with your group.

3. *Use visual aids.* The adage "a picture is worth a thousand words" contains quite a bit of truth. The people in your audience will more quickly and thoroughly understand your key points—and will retain them longer—if you use visual aids. Think of ways you and your team members can use the blackboard in the classroom; a graph, chart, or exhibit on a large posterboard; or, if you will have a number of these visual aids, a flip chart.

4. *Be prepared to handle questions.* You probably will be asked questions by your classmates. If questions are asked during your presentation, try to address those that require clarification. Tactfully postpone more elaborate questions until you have completed the formal phase of your presentation. During your rehearsal, try to anticipate the types of questions that you might be asked.

Working as a Team Member

Many professors assign students to groups or teams for analyzing cases. This adds more realism to the course, since most strategic decisions in business are addressed by a group of key managers. If you are a member of a group assigned to analyze a case, keep in mind that your performance is tied to the performance of the other group members, and vice versa. The following are some suggestions to help you be an effective team member:

1. *Be sure the division of labor is equitable.* It is not always easy to decide how the workload can be divided equitably, since it is not always obvious how much work needs to be done. Try breaking down the case into the distinct parts that need to be analyzed to determine if having a different person assume responsibility for each part is equitable. All team members should read and analyze the entire case, but different team members can be assigned primary responsibility for each major aspect of the analysis. Each team member with primary responsibility for a major aspect of the analysis also will be the logical choice to write that portion of the written analysis or to present it orally in class.

2. *Communicate with other team members.* This is particularly important if you encounter problems with your portion of the analysis. Because, by definition, the team members are dependent on each other, it is critical that you communicate openly and honestly with each other. Therefore, it is essential that your team members discuss problems, such as some members not doing their fair share of work or members insisting that their point of view dominate the team's report.

3. *Work as a team.* A group's output should reflect a combined effort, so the whole group should be involved in each part of the analysis, even if different individuals assume primary responsibility for different parts of the analysis. Avoid having the marketing major do the marketing portion of the analysis, the production major handle the production issues, and so forth. This will both hamper the group's aggregate analysis and do all of the team members a disservice by not giving each member exposure to decision making involving the other functional areas. The strategic management course provides an opportunity to look at all aspects of the business situation, to develop the ability to see the big picture, and to integrate the various functional areas.

4. *Plan and structure team meetings.* When you are working with a group on case analysis, it is impossible to achieve the team's goals and objectives without meeting outside of class. As soon as the team is formed, establish mutually convenient times for regular meetings, and be sure to keep this time available each week. Be punctual in going to the meetings, and manage the meetings so they end at a predetermined time. Plan several

shorter meetings, as opposed to one longer session right before the case is due. (This, by the way, is another way realism is introduced in the strategic management course. Planning and managing your time is essential in business, and working with others to achieve a common set of goals is a critical part of life in the business world.)

SUMMARY

The strategic management course is your opportunity to assume the role of a key decision maker in a business organization. The case method is an excellent way to add excitement and realism to the course. To get the most out of the course and the case method, you need to be an active participant in the entire process.

The case method offers you the opportunity to develop your analytical skills and to understand the interrelationships of the various functional areas of business; it also enables you to develop valuable skills in time management, group problem solving, creativity, organization of thoughts and ideas, and human interaction.

Short Cases

Case 1

Facebook vs. Twitter: *The Coming Facebook-Twitter Collision*

1   Every time monthly Web traffic numbers are released, you can expect at least a half-dozen blogs to run a graph showing Facebook gaining on MySpace in some made-up social media war. And as more "adults" join Facebook,[1] the more likely you are to hear about Facebook threatening LinkedIn.[2] Forget about rivalries with MySpace and LinkedIn. Facebook's real competition is coming from upstart microblogging site Twitter.

2   I have long argued that such comparisons are invalid since these are three very different sites. They all aim to connect people, but they go about it in sharply contrasting ways.[3] There is one company that's on a collision course with Facebook,[4] however. It's called Twitter.[5] Heard of it?

3   Signals of the potential rivalry abound, most recently in Facebook's redesign, details of which were unveiled on Mar. 4. One change will let public figures communicate with fans and followers on Facebook in much the same way they do on Twitter. Another lets individual users get more regular updates of what their friends are doing and thinking—similar to the way it's done on, you guessed it, Twitter. Some industry watchers called the moves a desperate attempt to mimic Twitter.

4   I call it preemptive. I had a recent exchange in San Francisco with a group of Boston College undergrads that illustrates why. No question these kids like technology; they gave up their spring break to hang out with Silicon Valley tech types. And yet, a good number of them just didn't get Twitter. It was one of the only times I recall where the old person in the room—me—was explaining the relevance of a new Web technology to younger people. It's not that they didn't get the point of staying connected (cue Old Man Stewart shaking his fist).[6] They get it just fine. That's what they use Facebook for. Facebook's redesign gives them fewer reasons to try Twitter.

AN EVENTUAL THREAT?

5   Sure, Facebook investor and board member Peter Thiel can try to damp enthusiasm for Twitter by saying Facebook is eyeing lots of acquisitions.[7] But there's a reason Facebook

---

[1] "[Old] Fogeys Flock to Facebook," *BusinessWeek,* August 6, 2007, http://www.businessweek.com/technology/content/aug2007/tc2007085_051788.htm.

[2] www.linkedin.com.

[3] "What MySpace Facebook Rivalry?" *BusinessWeek,* October 19, 2007, http://www.businessweek.com/technology/content/oct2007/tc20071019_750615.htm.

[4] www.facebook.com.

[5] www.twitter.com.

[6] "Twitter Frenzy," *The Daily Show,* March 2, 2009, http://www.thedailyshow.com/video/index.jhtml?videold=219519&title=twitter-frenzy.

[7] "Facebook's Thiel Explains Failed Twitter Takeover," *BusinessWeek,* March 1, 2009, http://www.businessweek.com/technology/content/mar2009/tc2009031_743025.html.

was hungry enough for Twitter that it offered $500 million in stock and cash to a company with a small staff and no revenue—in the middle of a recession.

6   And there's a reason Twitter didn't take it. Twitter knows it's just getting started, and it is the closest thing to an eventual threat. It would have been like Facebook taking Viacom up on its $750 million offer or accepting $1 billion from Yahoo! back in 2006.

7   When I last spoke to Twitter founder and CEO Evan Williams, he coyly told me he was nowhere near done building out Twitter as a service or a business and that he has a clear vision for both. He's not going into a lot of detail, but I can tell you it has a lot to do with the real-time news feed that Twitter has become; there's also a lot of potential in the way Twitter lets you search for information on the Web in real time—not at some fixed point in the Web's recent past. With a fresh round of capital in the bank, and all the hype in the world at his back, why would he sell now? Remember, Williams already went down that road with Blogger, and quickly left the acquirer Google as soon as his lockup expired. He's not someone who likes working for other people, and he made enough from preinitial public offering options in Google that he doesn't have to.

ADVANTAGES TO EACH

8   There are some key differences between the sites. It's far easier to find people on Facebook. Most of the time you can tell if it's actually them. Facebook also has more capacity for sharing videos and photos without forcing you to link out to other applications.

9   One of Twitter's greatest advantages lies in its so-called asynchronous nature. Relationships with others go one-way on Twitter. Someone can choose to "follow" you to get your updates, but you don't have to follow them. That simple distinction allows for a range of possibilities in what people can do on the site. For instance, a celebrity can broadcast to fans[8] but only follow the people he or she really knows. Facebook's recent changes make it easier for a celebrity or company or organization to build this kind of one-way communication, but if I want to be friends with an individual, that person still needs to accept my friend request. So Twitter still holds an advantage as far as individuals are concerned.

10   Another important Twitter feature lies in its stellar search technology—bought from Summize, a small company in Washington, D.C.—that allows you to track real-time coversations outside your network.

11   To be fair, Twitter and Facebook are on a slow collision course. This is not a zero-sum game. A lot of people will use both sites, and there are a good many people in the world who still aren't on either. Facebook has about 150 million users, compared with Twitter's 6 million. Both companies are wise to focus on their own products and markets and less on competing with each other. Indeed, they complement each other in key ways. You can update your Facebook status from Twitter, and arguably Twitter gets a marketing platform every time someone's Twitter stream spills over onto their Facebook News Feed.

12   In the near term, it's Google that should be more worried about both. If the last round of the Web was about organizing information, Web 2.0 is about organizing people. The Google-backed OpenSocial initiative that creates a common coding language for social media sites and their developers isn't going to cut it. Neither did Jaiku, a Twitter clone Google bought and recently shut down.[9] Maybe the possible threat explains why Google CEO Eric Schmidt on Mar. 3 called Twitter "poor man's e-mail."

---

[8] "Finally, a Use for Twitter," February 19, 2009, http://sesquipedalis.blogspot.com/2009/02/finally-use-for-twitter.html.

[9] "Google Axes Dodgeball, Jaiku, Video and More," www.techcrunch.com, January 14, 2009, http://www.techcrunch.com/2009/01/14/google-axes-dodgeball-jaiku-video-and-more/.

13   I see that coming back to haunt him. My hunch is Twitter represents a lot more than that. And if anyone wants a shot at beating Facebook at its own game, Twitter is the property to get you there.

Case 2

Microsoft Defends Its Empire

1   Microsoft is under siege from rivals offering cheap or free software on the Web. So it's revamping its Office suite and shifting into online services.

2   When a Microsoft salesman dropped by IT consultant Westcon Group's Tarrytown (N.Y.) headquarters for a round of negotiations in late 2008, Westcon's chief information officer, William Hurley, decided he had enough. "I'm sick of this," he said to the sales rep, complaining of the high costs of buying and maintaining Microsoft's broad portfolio of business software. "I don't want to do this anymore."

3   Much to Hurley's surprise, the rep offered alternatives. Within weeks, Hurley agreed to receive a new version of Exchange—the back-office software that makes corporate e-mail systems run—for a monthly fee, with Microsoft maintaining the bulky program and data on its own servers. The deal promised to save the company hundreds of thousands of dollars a year in hardware, software, and IT personnel costs. "This is a very different Microsoft than it was two or three years ago," says Hurley.

4   That's for sure. The Internet has thrown even the mighty Microsoft back on its heels. No longer able to impose its will on the computing world, the Redmond (Wash.) software giant is scrambling to catch up with all the changes the Web is unleashing. Over the past few years, CEO Steve Ballmer has come to two conclusions about the future of his business. First, Microsoft needs to move away from selling software and toward renting it out, in order to compete with cheap or free Web alternatives. Second, it must revamp its programs to satisfy customers' desire for more Internet-based collaboration. Now, Microsoft is putting those ideas into action, overhauling not only what it makes but how to deliver and change for it.

5   The front line of the new Microsoft is its highly profitable business division. The group includes the Office suite if applications (Word, Excel, PowerPoint, and the Outlook program, which lets users read and compose e-mails), as well as its SharePoint collaboration software and its Exchange e-mail server program. Microsoft in November [2008] began offering Exchange and SharePoint as a Web service for a monthly fee. For customers tired of maintaining these unwieldy programs on their own servers, the change is welcome: They usually end up paying less to subscribe to the software than they spent buying the program and paying for the staff and hardware to run it.

6   What's more, Microsoft has dramatically upgraded its Office applications. Microsoft Office 2010, scheduled to be released by the middle of next year, represents a radical departure from the past. For the first time, Microsoft will offer a free version of Office with limited functionality to customers who don't want to pay up for the whole shebang. Among other things, the free version, which will be supported in part by online advertising, will let users access any Word or Excel document remotely, via cell phone or a Web site.

7   The paid version is much heftier. It will allow teams of workers to create documents, spreadsheets, and presentations as a group in real time and track down other people with a click and invite them to join in. It also boasts a broader array of fonts and formatting options and much more number-crunching power than the free version. By focusing less on the PC and more on the people who use them across organizations, "We're trying to redefine our notion of productivity," says 14-year Microsoft vet Ayca Yuksel, who demonstrated the software for *BusinessWeek* in June.

8   As of now, Microsoft hasn't committed to offering Office 2010 as a monthly subscription service like it does for Exchange and SharePoint. Instead it'll charge its normal up-front

price, and companies will maintain the programs on their own servers. But company insiders say sooner or later Office is likely to go the subscription route as well.

9   Microsoft is betting that the subscription model will generate fatter revenues—and, indeed, it should. Microsoft can charge big corporate customers significantly more to rent software and contract for service than it charges them just to buy the programs. The wild card is on the expense side: Microsoft doesn't know for sure how costly it will be to assume the maintenance load. The answer will determine whether the company can afford to make Office or other programs available via subscription anytime soon. Hanging in the balance is one of the great profit machines of all time.

10   Risky though the subscription gambit may be, Microsoft has few alternatives. The era of PC dominance is passing, as consumers and workers shift their computing to a dizzying array of devices, such as iPhones, BlackBerrys, netbooks, and Kindles. Intrepid customers can get software much like Office on the Web for free via Google Apps and IBM's Symphony. As customers weigh the merits of those alternatives, Microsoft has had to slash the price of its Windows operating system and Office suite to compete. "The big danger for Microsoft is that its software will be commoditized," says Michael A. Cusumano, a professor at the Massachusetts Institute of Technology. "It's happening as we speak." Analysts expect that when Microsoft reports fiscal 2009 results in late July, annual revenue will have declined for the first time since the company went public in 1986.

11   To be sure, Microsoft remains one of the world's most profitable companies, with estimated earnings of $15.2 billion for the fiscal year ending June 30 on revenue of $59.9 billion. And it has generated plenty of buzz for its new Bing search engine, introduced in May, and its upcoming Windows 7 operating system.

12   But neither has lifted the company's languid stock, which, despite a jump since March, trades at the same price it fetched in 1998—even though the company has almost four times the profit. Analysts are no longer whispering that Microsoft's glory days may have passed—they're saying it openly. "The Roman Empire remained a pretty nice place to live for 400 years after Rome peaked," says longtime PC analyst Roger L. Kay. "But there's no doubt that the Microsoft empire is in decline."

13   Ballmer, naturally, disagrees. He exudes nothing but confidence in the upcoming Office rollout: "I think people are just going to say, 'Wow, they did it again.'"

A MESSY COURTSHIP

14   A key player in the new Microsoft is Stephen Elop, an outsider from Silicon Valley brought in last year by Ballmer to overhaul the business division. Elop, a veteran of Adobe Systems and Juniper Networks, has been pushing the makeover aggressively. A native Canadian, the 45-year-old father of five is known for his buzz cut and workaholic tendencies. He commuted to Silicon Valley from Toronto for six years and still pulls the occasional all-nighter.

15   While well-regarded for his operations and sales expertise, Elop was a controversial choice. Before arriving in Redmond, the biggest company he had run was Internet software maker Macromedia, whose $440 million in sales at the time was less than 3% of the size of Microsoft's business division.

16   Elop's messy courtship raised more doubts. In late 2007, Elop held the No. 2 post at router maker Juniper, having joined the company less than a year earlier with a personal assurance from then-CEO Scott Kriens that he was next in line for the CEO job. As the year drew to a close, Ballmer flew to Toronto and spent hours at Elop's home discussing the Office job with him and singing Seattle's praises to Elop's wife, Nancy. With the press

release announcing Elop as Juniper's new CEO already written, Elop told Kriens a few days after Christmas that he was going to Microsoft instead. Elop says the 10-minute phone call was "very tough" and that the move was "unquestionably the hardest decision I've ever had to make." (Kriens ended up recruiting Microsoft's Internet chief, Kevin Johnson, as CEO and says in an e-mail, "It all worked out for the best.")

17   Elop joined Microsoft in January 2008 with a mandate to overhaul the business group. Tops on the priority list: to use the Internet more aggressively as a way to deliver and improve Office's capabilities.

A "LOOKING-GLASS WALL"

18   Ballmer had started the process in 2004 after returning from a sales trip in which customers complained about the overhead and headaches associated with running Microsoft's software. He asked Ron Markezich, the vice-president responsible for Microsoft's own tech systems, to see if Markezich could figure out how to run Microsoft's Exchange e-mail software and SharePoint collaboration program for a few trial customers to use over the Net. Markezich found that Microsoft could do so—and save customers money.

19   Elop's job is to put that and other big ideas into action. Shortly after he arrived in Redmond, he began showing off a flashy video with futuristic visions of how Office could enhance people's productivity. One idea: a "looking-glass wall" that lets people on different continents communicate as though they were together—with real-time translation if they speak different languages and a display of the full history of e-mails and related documents. Elop also doubled the size of the staff at Office Labs, the team that made the video and is charged with dreaming up new ideas for the group.

20   This was a huge change for a division that had a reputation as Microsoft's no-nonsense boy scouts—never missing deadlines or releasing bug-filled code like their brethren in the Windows group. Rather than lavish global bashes featuring big-name rock stars, the team's idea of celebration after a product release is a 10-minute romp in a fountain outside Building 36 on the Redmond campus. Beer is available, but in moderation. "We're not the most colorful group," admits Jeff Teper, founder of SharePoint. "We'd rather let the results speak for themselves."

21   Elop is also changing the way the division prioritizes its investments. "We're going to make fewer, bigger bets," he says. One example: He more than doubled Microsoft's investment in SharePoint, which companies use to let employees share documents and collaborate on "wikis." Elop says he made the call after visiting customers around the world. "When something is hot, you pour gasoline on it," he says. The nine-year-old SharePoint business is one of Microsoft's fastest-growing, with sales climbing by double digits even in the weak economy.

22   Perhaps most important, Elop has championed the move to the "cloud," meaning customers can get Microsoft software from its giant data centers rather than from their own servers. He sped up the rollout of the Exchange and SharePoint subscription services and other online programs, which are now available in 19 countries. Hundreds of companies, from Westcon and GlaxoSmithKline to Coca-Cola Enterprises, have signed up for what Microsoft calls the Business Productivity Online Standard Suite.

23   Ingo Elfering, vice-president for IT strategy at drugmaker GlaxoSmithKline, says his tech staff can now focus on more important projects than computer maintenance. "[Maintenance] has no more value to our business than paying the electric bill or serving food in the cafeteria," he says. "I really don't need to be buying groceries for my employees. I'm not very good at it."

24 But while Microsoft is tinkering with delivery mechanisms, what matters most is whether customers are willing to pay up for its wares in the era of cheap Web alternatives. Its hope is that Office 2010 will persuade customers to dig deep into their wallets. On July 13, Elop is expected to reveal the details of the program, which was designed very much with the Twitter generation in mind. One major change is something called "co-authoring." Rather than have one person create a document or PowerPoint presentation and then e-mail it around to others, teams will be able to work on the project simultaneously. One group member could grab a particular paragraph or slide and fiddle with it. Once they save the changes, others can see and weigh in on that bit of content.

ARRIVING VIA THE WEB

25 Another feature of Office 2010 is called "unified communications." When a user moves the cursor over the name of a colleague, up pops a box that shows whether that person is online—and offers the option of e-mailing, calling, or setting up a meeting. The program will also offer new social networking capabilities and ways to track down co-workers with specific skills.

26 Some corporate customers see big potential in blending Microsoft's software with the reach of the Internet. Elfering of GlaxoSmithKline says he wants Microsoft to make the paid version of Office 2010 available as a Web service now. He envisions a day when millions of companies share access to some of their knowledge. "If there were a collaboration platform out there with 60 million people, imagine the insights one could glean," says Elfering.

27 But first things first. Before Microsoft can roll out the Office subscription service, it needs to learn how to deliver Exchange and SharePoint profitably. It'll have to beef up its call centers, reduce the number of bugs in its programs, and in all ways bend over backward to keep customers happy. After all, if the software doesn't work, Microsoft won't get paid. At least not for long.

28 Such radical moves haven't come naturally. Given the company's enormous success over the years, Ballmer concedes it took him a while to get comfortable with Microsoft's new path. Now, though, he says he is convinced the shift will pay off down the road. "It's not that I'm in love with the past," Ballmer explains. "But we needed to think really hard before we embraced the future."

Microsoft's Key Revenue Streams

MICROSOFT'S BUSINESS DIVISION
Revenues: $19.4 billion
Likely the most profitable unit in 2009, it will offer free Web versions of Word and Excel to drum up interest for Office 2010. And it's selling more of its programs as online services—trading up-front payments for monthly fees. The bet: that such "cloud"-based sales will rise more than profit margins fall.

MICROSOFT'S WINDOWS
Revenues: $14.6 billion
On Oct. 22, Microsoft will replace its beleaguered Vista version of Windows with Windows 7, which is winning unfamiliar raves for reliability. And to compete in a post-PC world, the new operating system is designed to work with smartphones—particularly those running the company's Windows Mobile code.

MICROSOFT'S SERVER SOFTWARE
Revenues: $14.2 billion
Microsoft's fastest-growing business makes the software used by companies to run their computer networks. The outlook is bright. Low-cost servers that use Windows continue to displace pricier IBM mainframes, and they hold their own against models that run on the free Linux operating system.

MICROSOFT'S INTERNET
Revenues: $3.1 billion
In going after Google, Microsoft has lost $3.5 billion in its Internet business over the past three years. Analysts think the Net operation will need to be subsidized by profits from the Windows and Office units for years to come, even though Microsoft's new Bing search engine is off to a strong start.

MICROSOFT'S ENTERTAINMENT & DEVICES
Revenues: $8.1 billion
Cell phones that use Windows Mobile software have lost ground to Apple's iPhone and Research In Motion's BlackBerry. Microsoft's Zune MP3 player continues to struggle, and its Xbox isn't the phenomenon Nintendo's Wii is. Still, improved sales of the game console have put the division into the black after years of losses.

Source: "Microsoft Defends Its Empire," *BusinessWeek*. Reprinted from the June 24, 2009, issue of *BusinessWeek* by special permission. Copyright © 2009 by The McGraw-Hill Companies, Inc.

Case 3

Mozilla's Crowdsourcing Mystique[1]

1   There's a cool new video player in the Firefox Web browser that Mozilla released in 2009. But the onscreen buttons used to control it are too small for some visually impaired users to see. So Ken Saunders, a 41-year-old, legally blind volunteer for Mozilla, took it upon himself to create a tool that makes the player easier to use for people with vision problems. As the maker of the Firefox Web browser relies on volunteer developers, such for-profit companies as Google, Microsoft, and LinkedIn strain to copy the Mozilla model in some profitable fashion.

2   Saunders is among hundreds of people who donate time and skills to *Mozilla,* the Mountain View (Calif.) company that releases Firefox and other open-source software. Even as Mozilla's internal staff has grown to 250, from 15 in 2005, an army of volunteers still contributes about 40% of the company's work, which ranges from tweaks to the programming code to designing the Firefox logo.

3   How Mozilla channels those efforts is a model for a growing number of companies trying to tap into the collective talents of large pools of software developers and other enthusiasts of a product, brand, or idea. "There's structure in it," says Mike Beltzner, who runs Firefox. "But at the same time you allow people to innovate and to explore and [give them] the freedom to do what they want along those edges—that's where innovation tends to happen in startling and unexpected ways."

4   At Firefox, Beltzer calls it "leading from behind." His team makes only the highest, direction-setting decisions, such as the date each new version of Firefox has to ship. It's up to Mozilla staff and volunteers to meet those deadlines through a process of identifying specific tasks that need to be done and accomplishing them. A system of recognition has formed among volunteers, who can be designated as "module owners" and given authority over certain areas, such as the layout.

LINKEDIN QUERY VEXED A LOT OF USERS

5   Companies would like to follow the examples of Mozilla and online encyclopedia Wikipedia, which relies on unpaid contributors, as well as Linux, the open-source operating system developed by programmers who work for no pay. "There's no easy way to copy Mozilla," says Clay Shirky, author of *Here Comes Everybody: The Power of Organizing Without Organizations.* "But I do think that companies are increasingly going to look for ways to motivate their users to be participants."

6   Not all of these efforts go smoothly. In June, business networking site LinkedIn[2] polled 12,000 of its users who had identified themselves as translators to find out what would motivate them to help translate the site's content into other languages. While 18% said they would do it "for fun" and about half of the respondents wanted some form of recognition, many took umbrage at the request.[3] The American Translators Association[4] even sent a letter

---

[1] "Mozilla's Crowdsourcing Mystique," by Douglas McMillian, *BusinessWeek,* July 1, 2009. © 2009 McGraw-Hill Companies, Reprinted by Permission.

[2] www.Linkedin.com.

[3] http://www.businessweek.com/the_thread/blogspotting/archives/2009/06/everything_migh.html.

[4] www.atanet.org.

to LinkedIn's CEO calling the aim of the survey "misguided" and "troubling." Company spokeswoman Kay Luo says LinkedIn wasn't trying to solicit free labor. "Our intention was to survey our members to see what level of interest there was," she says.

7   Google recently came under comparable criticism from artists after issuing an open call to use their work as decorative skins for the company's Web browser. Google wasn't willing to pay, but emphasized the opportunity for exposure. "We believe these projects provide a unique and exciting opportunity for artists to display their work in front of millions of people," the company said in a statement.

A VOLUNTEER HELPS BOOST PRIVACY

8   Getting people to donate labor may be easier for Mozilla, which operates under a nonprofit umbrella foundation. Still, the Mozilla model holds lessons for a broad range of companies. "The profit motive wouldn't matter if the company is committed to fostering community and openness," says Kevin Gerich, a Web development manager at International Data Group who has contributed to Mozilla on and off since 2002.

9   One of the biggest breakthroughs in the newest version, Firefox 3.5, came from an outside contributor. The organization wanted to include a feature to let users surf the Web without recording their history in the browser, but abandoned the idea when its developers couldn't get it to work. With the deadline approaching, a volunteer came up with a plan for such a feature that Beltzer describes as "absolutely perfect." A private browsing mode made it into the release.

10   The leader in Web browsers, Microsoft's Internet Explorer, also has a privacy mode, but it doesn't include certain functions that Firefox thought up, such as the ability to retroactively erase browsing history from a particular site. Analysts say ingenuity like that is helping Mozilla get an edge in the browser wars.[5] "Right now Mozilla definitely has some momentum," says Sheri McLeish, an analyst at Forrester. "They're not in it for profit, but their notion of what they're providing resonates with a lot of people." In May, Firefox's share of the browser market rose to 22.5%, from 19% a year earlier, according to data tracker Net Applications.[6] Internet Explorer's share slid more than 7%, to 65.5%.

11   Shirky, who has spent several years researching collaboration in technology, says people tend to contribute to organizations or causes like Mozilla for three reasons: It aligns with their interests, they can get recognition, and they can meet other people doing it. While just about anyone can find an activity that accomplishes the first two, the Internet has played a key role in providing the third by helping people volunteer while widening their network. "If you talk to people about these collaborative communities, over and over you hear: 'I found all these other people who are interested in what I'm interested in,' " Shirky says.

12   That's true of Mozilla volunteer Saunders, a resident of Acushnet, Mass. In the past four years, as he's contributed to features that make Firefox more accessible to people with disabilities, Saunders has interacted daily with like-minded volunteers from Australia, Estonia, and Michigan. He notes, "We're co-workers, so to speak."

[5] http://www.businessweek.com/technology/content/apr2007/tc20070405_395663.htm.
[6] http://www.businessweek.com/technology/content/mar2009/tc20090311_813488.htm; and www.netapplications.com.

Case 4

The Pet Economy: *Americans Spend an Astonishing $41 Billion a Year on Their Furry Friends*

1   If there's still any doubt whether the pampering of pets is getting out of hand, the debate should be settled once and for all by Neuticles, a patented testicular implant that sells for up to $919 a pair. The idea, says inventor Gregg A. Miller, is to "let people restore their pets to anatomical preciseness" after neutering, thereby allowing them to retain their natural look and self-esteem. "People thought I was crazy when I started 13 years ago," says the Oak Grove (Mo.) entrepreneur. But he has since sold more than 240,000 pairs (a few of which went on prairie dogs, water buffalo, and monkeys). "Neutering is creepy. But with Neuticles, it's like nothing has changed." Nothing, except there's a fake body part where a real one used to be.

2   Americans now spend $41 billion a year on their pets—more than the gross domestic product of all but 64 countries in the world. That's double the amount shelled out on pets a decade ago, with annual spending expected to hit $52 billion in the next two years, according to Packaged Facts, a consumer research company based in Rockville, Md. That puts the yearly cost of buying, feeding, and caring for pets in excess of what Americans spend on the movies ($10.8 billion), playing video games ($11.6 billion), and listening to recorded music ($10.6 billion) combined. "People are no longer satisfied to reward their pet in pet terms," argues Bob Vetere, president of the American Pet Products Manufacturers Assn. (APPMA). "They want to reward their pet in human terms." That means hotels instead of kennels, braces to fix crooked teeth, and frilly canine ball gowns. Pet owners are becoming increasingly demanding consumers who won't put up with substandard products, unstimulating environments, or shoddy service for their animals. But the escalating volume and cost of services, especially in the realm of animal medicine, raises ethical issues about how far all this loving should go.

Reigning Cats and Dogs: Where the Money Goes

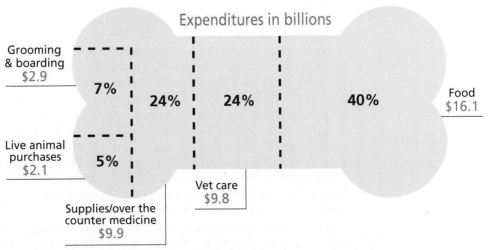

Source: American Pet Products Manufacturers Association.

3   It wasn't so very long ago that the phrase "a dog's life" meant sleeping outside, enduring the elements, living with aches, and sitting by the dinner table, waiting for a few scraps to land on the floor. Today's dog has it much better. APPMA reports that 42% of dogs now sleep in the same bed as their owners, up from 34% in 1998. Their menu reflects every fad in human food—from locally sourced organic meat and vegan snacks to gourmet meals bolstered by, say, glucosamine to ward off stiff joints. Half of all dog owners say they consider their pet's comfort when buying a car, and almost a third buy gifts for their dogs' birthdays. Richard G. Wolford, chairman and CEO of Del Monte Foods Co., refuses even to use the word "owner." "Anyone who has a pet understands who owns whom," says Wolford, who is owned by two Jack Russell terriers. His company's pet business has gone from nothing to 40% of overall sales through acquisitions of brands such as Meow Mix and Milk-Bone in the past five years.

4   The rising status of pets has started an unprecedented wave of entrepreneurship in an industry once epitomized by felt mice and rubber balls. There are now $430 indoor potties, $30-an-ounce perfume, and $225 trench coats aimed solely at four-footed consumers and their wallet-toting companions. Even those who shun animal couture are increasingly willing to spend thousands on drugs for depression or anxiety in pets, as well as psychotherapy, high-tech cancer surgery, cosmetic procedures, and end-of-life care. About 77% of dogs and 52% of cats have been medicated in the past year, according to APPMA, an increase of about 20 percentage points from 1996. Some spending can be spurred by vets who find such services more lucrative than giving shots or ending a pet's life when it contracts a painful or terminal disease.

GRAVY TRAIN

5   Once acquired as sidekicks for kids, animal companions are more popular now with empty-nesters, single professionals, and couples who delay having children. What unites these disparate demographic groups is a tendency to have time and resources to spare. With more people working from home or living away from their families, pets also play a bigger role in allaying the isolation of modern life. About 63% of U.S. households, or 71 million homes, now own at least one pet, up from 64 million just five years ago. And science is starting to validate all those warm feelings with research that documents the depth of the human-animal bond.

6   It doesn't take a scientist to figure out that there's money to be made in this environment. Companies from Procter & Gamble and Nestlé to fashion brands including Polo Ralph Lauren and thousands of small entrepreneurs are sniffing around for new opportunities in the pet sector. After consumer electronics, pet care is the fastest-growing category in retail, expanding about 6% a year. More new pet products were launched in the first six months of last year than in all of 2005. And that doesn't account for the ways existing products are being recast to woo pet lovers. Del Monte has refocused staples to look more like human snacks—from Snausages breakfast treats shaped like bacon and eggs to Pup-Peroni rib snacks so appetizing that Wolford had to stop a TV anchor from popping one into his mouth on air. Even Meow Mix now comes in plastic cups rather than cans.

7   The typical target of such products is a pet lover like Graham Gemoets, a caterer in Houston, who showers luxuries on his beloved "chi weenie" (Chihuahua/dachshund mix), Bradford. "He's my best friend and my best-accessorized friend," says Gemoets, whose splurges for Bradford include a $1,200 Hermès collar and leash, as well as $500 Chanel pearls for parties. "I know it's crazy, but I've had him for five years, and if you priced it out per month, it's like a phone bill."

8   Thanks to passionate consumers like that, the quality gap between two-legged and four-legged mammals is rapidly disappearing in such industries as food, clothing, health care, and services. The race now is to provide animals with products and services more closely modeled after the ones sold to humans. Most of the pet business world's attention is directed at the country's 88 million cats and 75 million dogs. The reason is simple. As Philip L. Francis, CEO of PetSmart Inc., the world's largest pet specialty retailer, explains: "You can't train a fish or groom a snake."

9   PetSmart, for one, has shifted its mission from being the top seller of pet food to helping consumers become better "pet parents." Along with making his 928 retail locations homier and hosting pet parties, Francis is rolling out blue-shingled "pet hotels" (kennels) in his stores. They feature private suites with raised platform beds and TVs airing shows from Animal Planet for $31 a night, as well as "bone booths," where pets can take calls from their owners, and porous pebble floors where dogs can pee. Cats get live fish tanks to watch in their rooms and separate air filtration systems so their scents don't drive the dogs crazy. The hotels, along with services such as grooming, training, and in-store hospitals, have helped PetSmart expand its service business from essentially nothing in 2000 to $450 million, or 10% of overall sales, this year. Pet owners are now less driven by price than "emotion and passion," says Francis, who shares a bed with his wife and their mutt, Bit o' Honey.

10   Those are the same primal urges that drive the fashion world. Mario DiFante, who staged New York's first Pet Fashion Week last August, has an elevated view of the place of dogs and cats in the family hierarchy. As he puts it: "Many of us consider pets as the new babies." That means clothing furry little ones in an ever-expanding range of sweaters, raincoats, leather jackets, and dresses. For Lara Alameddine, co-founder of Little Lily, a better word might be "babes." Her four-year-old company clears $1 million a year selling products including doggie slippers, bikinis, and even canine versions of Oscar-night gowns. It's popular with celebrity dog owners such as Paris Hilton, who often dresses up her Chihuahua, Tinkerbell. "We're catering to the owner's sense of style," says Alameddine. "There are no bones on our clothes."

11   Pet products now aim to make people feel they're being extra good to their little ones—much as toymakers have long encouraged parents to spoil kids. Along with doggie spas, there are mobile pet-grooming vans, pedicure services, professional dog walkers, and massage therapy for animals. Trainers like Cesar Millan—better known to millions as the Dog Whisperer—find that their expertise is suddenly in greater demand. Along with having the No. 1 series on the National Geographic Channel, Millan boasts best-selling books, DVDs, a line of products, and his famous Dog Psychology Center of Los Angeles that's a favorite with Hollywood clientele.

12   The growing willingness of owners to spare no expense for their animals has also made the outsourcing of the yucky aspects a burgeoning business. More than 350 service agencies with names such as Doody Duty, Scoopy-Poo, and Pooper Trooper have sprung up solely to relieve owners of the need even to pick up a pet's waste in their yard by doing it for them. With annual growth nearing 50%, "the pooper scooper industry is now experiencing a lot of consolidation," says Jacob D'Aniello of DoodyCalls, which has 20 locations nationwide.

13   But few parts of the business have seen as much diversification and expansion as the pet food business. As with humans, there's a growing concern about the nutrition, taste, and even ethical standards of what goes into a pet's stomach. Owners increasingly mirror their own preferences—for vegetarian cuisine, kosher meals, and even locally sourced food—in feeding their pets. And when things go wrong, the reaction is as explosive as if the victims were children. Consumers were outraged by a massive recall of melamine-contaminated pet food that killed or sickened thousands of U.S. cats and dogs. Because pets are now such valued members of the family, says Duane Ekedahl, president of the Pet Food Institute, "it had a higher impact than maybe it would have had 10 years ago."

14   As food becomes a more emotionally charged issue for people, owners are more inclined to get emotional about what's on their pets' menu. Witness the growth of what one industry executive calls the "Godiva-ization" of food, with a demand for meats fit for human consumption, visible vegetables, and nutritional supplements. It has become common to reach for a canine or cat equivalent of ketchup, such as Iams Co.'s popular "savory sauce" for dogs that comes in Country Chicken, Savory Bacon, and Roasted Beef flavor—descriptions that are, needless to say, lost on the actual consumer.

THOROUGHLY VETTED

15   Fancy food products are easy targets for critics of indulgent pet owners. But a far more controversial issue is animal medicine, especially at a time of urgent national debate about human health care. Americans now spend $9.8 billion a year on vet services. That doesn't include the over-the-counter drugs and other supplies, which add $9.9 billion in costs.

16   The annual compound growth rate for core veterinary services alone has been about 10% over the past decade, and the menu of services is becoming more elaborate by the month. Much of the inflation in pet care is due to medical advances that have people digging deep for everything from root canals for aging cats to cancer surgery for rabbits. "There has been an evolution of the entire profession," says Tom Carpenter, president of the American Animal Hospital Assn. "Pocket pets and animals who wouldn't even have been taken to vets now go for regular visits."

17   Suzanne Kramer of Chicago spent close to $380 on vet visits and drugs to treat a tumor in her hamster, Biffy, before he died last year. "Some might say: 'Well, he's just a hamster,' but I loved him," says Kramer. Barbara Miers of Rochester, N.Y., also took her son's hamster, Henry, to a vet and bought antibiotics for a tumor, even though the animal was nearing the end of his life span and died shortly after the final treatment. For Miers, the issue had parallels to human health. As she puts it: "Do you not give old people health care because they're old?"

18   No wonder "it's a good time to be in our profession," as Carpenter says. A vet's job has become more wide-ranging and thus more lucrative. There are even animal grief counselors to help families cope with the demise of beloved pets. Not only is state-of-the-art technology such as magnetic resonance imaging, with costs that range around $1,500 a scan, now available in small-town labs, but consumers' expectations of medical care have been transformed. They want the same best-in-class care for their pets that they want for themselves.

19   That's creating a market for new products like Pfizer Inc.'s dog-obesity drug Slentrol, which will cost $1 to $2 a day. Reconcile, a new drug from Eli Lilly & Co, for "canine separation anxiety," is based on the active ingredients in Prozac. Lilly has not suggested a retail price for Reconcile, and vets have a lot of latitude in deciding how much to charge for it. Overall, sales of pet health products have grown at a compound annual growth rate of 8.8% in recent years, more than double the rate in the late 1990s.

20   There's little doubt that human-quality care has helped to extend radically the life span of pets. Dogs routinely live 12 to 14 years now, a big jump from the average a few decades ago. John Payne, acting CEO of Banfield, the Pet Hospital, likes to boast that his cat, Gizmo, stayed perky until he died last November at the advanced age of 23½. More than 60% of new customers of his chain, which has more than 600 locations nationwide, enroll their pets in wellness plans. One reason is that standard pet insurance often doesn't cover preventive care. While pet insurance is still in its infancy, with 1% of owners having coverage, the number of clients is growing by double digits each year. Jamie Ward invested in a $25.77-a-month plan with Veterinary Pet Insurance (VPI) for her American Staffordshire terrier, Loki, only to discover that it didn't cover any of the $2,000 in expenses for a kneecap injury (VPI says it abided by the terms of the contract.)

21   The ever-expanding roster of drugs and treatment can run into tens of thousands of dollars in expenses, creating a dilemma for owners. Steve Zane of Hoboken, N.J., choked slightly when a veterinarian presented him and his wife, Lily, an estimate of $3,700 to help cure liver failure in their cat, Koogle, over Christmas. "We looked at each other and said: 'Well, he's family,'" recalls Zane, a graphic designer who's still paying off the final bill for the recovered cat. "If it had been $15,000, I think we would almost have had to say no."

22   The anthropomorphization of pets has also created the perception that they have human problems such as separation anxiety and depression. While a number of vets say such issues are real, especially just after the death of a dog's four-footed chum or the removal of puppies, others say it simply creates yet more opportunities for new products. Americans are expected to spend 52% more on medicines to treat their pets this year than they spent five years ago. Drugmakers love the category because, compared with human drugs, there's less risk of liability, less competition, and less pressure to switch to generics because so few consumers carry pet insurance. Even so, Dawn M. Boothe, a professor of clinical physiology and pharmacology in the Auburn University College of Veterinary Medicine, argues that "the recovery of costs" for drug companies may take a long time as people may scoff at pricey treatments for pets.

23   Much of the attention is going to the growing problem of pet obesity. As many as 40% of dogs are estimated to be overweight or obese, with similarly high rates among cats, thanks to the indulgent habits of their owners. Being plied with carob bonbons all day while getting rolled around in an all-terrain stroller (retail price: about $210) is not an ideal lifestyle for any animal. People who overeat or don't get enough exercise tend to draw their pets into the same behavior, vets say, and the growing inclination to regale pets with treats has come at a cost to their waistline. Along with creating interest in new anti-obesity drugs, it's prompting interest in diet pet food. It has also created a market for procedures including pet liposuction, which is becoming more common in cities like Los Angeles where owners are used to getting nips and tucks for themselves.

24   And for some pet lovers, no medical procedure is too extreme. Plastic surgeons offer rhinoplasty, eye lifts, and other cosmetic procedures to help tone down certain doggy features, from droopy eyes to puggish noses. Root canals, braces, and even crowns for chipped teeth are also becoming more popular.

25   Some might question whether all this primping and pampering of pets has the makings of a bubble that could have owners telling Fido to get his own damn bone once the economy takes a turn. After all, Paola Freccero admits that when she grew up in Massachusetts, "Pets were pets. You didn't dress them, you didn't feed them special food, you didn't take them to play dates." But thanks to the advice of her vet and what she read on the Internet, she wouldn't serve up anything but the best for her puggle (pug/beagle mix), Lucy, including treats at $2 apiece. And from the moment Eric Olander paid $500 for a plane ticket to get a stray chow chow mix from Atlanta to his home in Los Angeles, the dog has been a focal point of his life. "I call him my 401(k) with paws," he says, "because that's where all my money goes."

Case 5

The Battle to Be Top Dog—PetSmart vs. Petco: *PetSmart and Petco Have Adopted Different Strategies as Each Seeks the Dominant Position in the Animal Care Industry*

1   The news hit the Phoenix offices of PetSmart on a Friday afternoon: The U.S. Food & Drug Administration was recalling tainted pet food manufactured in China. PetSmart's Chief Executive Philip Francis told his team to pounce. The company ripped recalled products from shelves, put up informational signs at stores, staffed up at its customer-service call centers, and gave refunds to folks returning tainted products. In some cases, PetSmart paid vet bills for sick animals.

2   Francis didn't stop there. He had the company mine its customer database and send warning notices to folks who'd recently bought recalled products. The move prompted grateful letters and e-mails from customers. "For the first time in my life, a company has sent me something of value," one wrote. Says Francis: "I'd prefer the recall hadn't happened, but from a customer loyalty standpoint, you just can't spend enough on advertising to accomplish what it did for us."

3   Francis has to move quickly these days because he has someone nipping at his heels: His San Diego-based archrival, Petco Animal Supplies. PetSmart and Petco are the two top dogs in the $41 billion animal care industry. Petco is the older of the two, founded in 1965. It was the first retail chain to take the pet food businesses out of dark, smelly mom-and-pop stores and into a modern category-killer format. Today, both companies operate in about as many locations: 908 for PetSmart, 850 for Petco. But they often have different approaches.

4   Petco's stores tend to be smaller and more ubiquitous, almost replacing the neighborhood pet store. They're located in strip malls. PetSmart stores are bigger and tend to be in the larger "power centers," alongside other discount chains. According to a recent analysis from JPMorgan retail analyst Nancy Hoch, PetSmart's prices were on average 8% higher than those of Wal-Mart Stores but 11% below Petco's.

SHIFTING STOCK AND SERVICES

5   A former supermarket executive, Francis joined PetSmart when the company was suffering a crisis in 1998. In much the way Toys 'R' Us and Tower Records struggled in their niches, PetSmart's stock-'em-high warehouse format was no longer working as discounters such as Walmart and Target loaded up on pet supplies, particularly the higher-end products such as Iams dog food that only vets and pet stores had sold previously. Francis shrunk the stores, cutting the typical store size from 28,000 sq. ft. to 20,000 sq. ft. He kept the same assortment of product but stocked less on shelves, sending trucks from central warehouses more frequently to restock and thus avoiding the warehouse look.

6   Most important, he added services: adoption, training, veterinary, grooming, day care, and pet hotels. Last year the company groomed 7.5 million dogs, a 16% increase over the year before. It provided 378,000 training classes, another 16% increase. Overall, services are expected to generate $450 million in sales this year, about 10% of the company's $4.5 billion total, but representing 26% annual growth since the strategy was hatched in 2000.

ROOM AND BOARD

7   Today, the inside of the store looks a lot homier, with a little blue shingled area inside with brick and siding that houses the hotel and day care area. Inside the hotel section, visitors are greeted to slate tiles and wooden reception desk. In the dog area, owners can choose between regular boarding, where dogs congregate in a big room and then sleep alone in kennels, or private suites with raised platform beds and televisions airing the Animal Planet cable network and other pet programming. Since the stores are in strip malls, the company developed a porous pebble floor where the dogs could urinate. There's also a "bone phone" that allows owners to call in and talk to their pets. Cats have quarters with separate air filtration systems so their smell doesn't drive the dogs crazy. The cats also get to watch a live fish tank.

8   Francis says he can add a pet hotel to an existing location for less than half the cost of building a similar standalone location. Plus, the hotel shares the cost of the heating and air conditioning system, parking lot, employee break area, armor car pickups, and other overhead. Overnight stays start at $21 a night, $31 for a suite. Day care starts at $14 a day. After five years the hotels can help boost a store's sales by 29% and double its profitability, both because the hotels are a high-margin business and because customers come more frequently and buy other things when they do. A typical PetSmart store with a hotel earns $879,000 on sales of $7.1 million.

9   Even with numbers such as those, Francis says he's rolling out the hotel concepts slowly. They're in just 62 of the stores today, although Francis says they could ultimately be in 435 stores, or 40% of the chain, by 2010. He's taking it slow because "people get angrier about bad service than a bad product. It's more personal. We have to make sure we get it right."

GROSS-OUT PETS

10   Petco has a different approach. The $2.2 billion company still does two-thirds of its business in dog and cat products, but Petco features a broader selection of goods for other animals, everything from hamsters to tarantulas. The company recently featured a "Reptile Rendezvous" at 200 stores. The events included "in the terrarium" photo contests and demonstrations for products such as a new clay that reptile owners can mold into small hills and caves. Snakes, iguanas, and turtles remain very popular with teenage boys, says Petco's CEO James Myers: "Anything that grosses your parents out."

11   Petco has not embraced the services strategy quite as aggressively as PetSmart. Its stores do prominently feature grooming services, and the company provides doggie day care at some locations. But Petco stores, at about 14,000 sq. ft., aren't as large as PetSmarts and for now Myers is holding back on overnight pet-sitting. "I'm not sure that plays everywhere in America," he says.

12   There is another difference: Petco is privately held. It was bought last year by private equity firms Texas Pacific Group and Leonard Green & Partners. Ironically, it was the second time Los Angeles-based Leonard Green had taken the company private. PetSmart's Francis says he gets calls from time to time from people interested in a buyout. So far he's been against the idea. "I've got all the money I need," he says. "Our goal is to keep our stock price up so nobody can afford to take us private."

Case 6

American Public Education, Inc.

1   For active duty soldiers, the price can't be beat. American Public Education's courses are free to military personnel, thanks to government tuition benefits. But the government doesn't pay that much, just $750 per three-credit course. That forced the for-profit educator to keep its expenses low.

2   But those low prices, often half what some competitors charge, could give APE a leg up on the civilian side. "Convenience and cost, that's what working adults are looking for," said Harry T. Wilkens, APE's executive vice president and chief financial officer. The school saw revenue climb 55% in 2008. It has grown by double-digits in each quarter since APE went public in 2007. Enrollment jumped 50% in 2008 to 45,200 students.

CIVILIAN SURGE

3   More than two-thirds of them are military personnel. But the civilian side is growing fast. Wilkens thinks teachers, police officers and other civilians could make up half or more of the student body in three or four years. The recession that started in 2008 has given the entire for-profit education sector a boost as workers scramble to update their skills and burnish resumes.

4   But the military side has legs, too. It grew faster than expected in the fourth quarter of 2008 in part due to an expanded partnership with the U.S. Navy. The number of active duty and reserve personnel in the U.S. services has held relatively constant for decades at a little above 2.1 million. But there's a churn of about 300,000 new soldiers a year replacing retiring ones.

5   The DoD's [Department of Defense's] tuition program has become a key Pentagon recruiting and retention tool. More soldiers are applying that tuition credit to online schools, APE thinks. It calculates that it now has about 12% of the military education market, up from 10% a year earlier. Wilkens says the school is committed to keeping the course free to military personnel.

6   A typical three-credit undergraduate course costs about $750. A graduate-level course costs $850. The company throws in the books to make sure there are no out-of-pocket expenses for military personnel. But with its DNA firmly rooted in that military cost structure, it can deliver that same cheap education to the civilian sector.

7   A full four-year degree totals about $30,000, far less than a brick-and-mortar university. And a masters in business administration costs about $10,000 total, vs. $20,000 to $25,000 at other online institutions, such as Capella Education, Apollo Group's University of Phoenix, and Strayer Education.

8   Those institutions instead push the quality of their education, support programs they offer, and their longer histories. "But in the end of the day, if consumers are unwilling to take on more debt looking for a post-secondary education, then American Public wins," Barrington Research's Alexander Paris Jr. said. Barrington has done banking business with APE.

Source: This mini-case is developed from "Commercial Online School Keeps Costs Low for Military Personnel," *Investors Business Daily,* March 24, 2009. © Investor's Business Daily, Inc. 2009. Reprinted by permission of *Investor's Business Daily*.

9   West Virginia-based American Public was formed in 1991 by retired Marine Corps Major Jim Etter. He had taught at the Corps' Amphibious Warfare School and wanted to help service personnel continue their educations. The school, then known as American Military University, enrolled its first students in January 1993. Over the years, it built up its course offerings and earned the accreditations necessary to grant degrees.

10   In 2002, it formed a second university, American Public University, to better appeal to the civilian market. It created American Public Education as the parent over the two institutions. With shared faculty and administration, the two universities have a combined 74 degree and 51 certificate programs in areas such as national security, military studies, criminal justice, technology, business administration, education, and liberal arts. American Public Education, Inc., went public in 2005 [symbol APEI].

11   Now, it's actively reaching out to police, teachers and other civilian-sector groups, where education can bolster careers, but costs are still a concern. The programs became eligible for federal Title IV loans in late 2006, opening the doors wider to the civilian students.

12   But to keep costs under the DoD reimbursement rate, American Public Education has had to watch costs. It pays its professors based on the number of students enrolling, for instance. So if enrollment dips, so do expenses.

WORD OF MOUTH

13   APE is also very modest in its market expenses. It relies instead on word-of-mouth marketing. About 55% of students heard about the school from another student, which analysts say is tops in the industry. One "strategic" challenge will be keeping that cost of acquiring students down as it expands beyond the civilian market. So far, APE has been able to do so. And, the DoD hasn't raised its tuition reimbursement rate in years. Should it do so, which should happen with the new GI bill, that would allow APE to raise tuitions.

PROFITABILITY

14   APE [earnings] per share [was] 86 cents in 2008, up from 64 cents in 2007. The company projected 2009 EPS to come in between $1.16 and $1.20. Stock market analysts were even more optimistic, expecting a minimum of $1.21 per share.

15   American Public's low-cost model could give it traction against its civilian-focused competitors, analysts think. "It's pretty interesting and potentially disruptive in that marketplace," said Trace Urdan, an analyst with Signal Hill. "But we haven't really seen it take off yet. I guess it's still in the category of promising."

Learn—That's an Order

American Public Education has grown by providing online education to U.S. military personnel. But its ability to live within the government's tuition reimbursement rates means it can offer those same degrees to civilians at less cost than competitiors.

Total registration

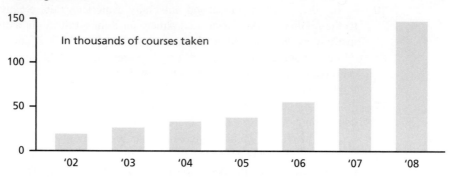

Enrollment, as of Dec. 31

Students, as of Dec. 31

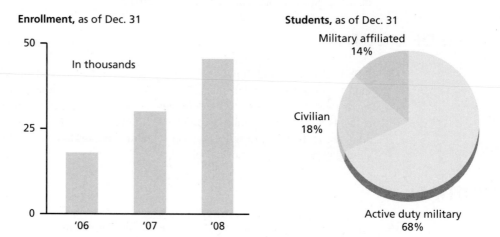

Source: © Investor's Business Daily, Inc. 2008. All Rights Reserved.

	Year Ended December 31,				
	2004	**2005**	**2006**	**2007**	**2008**
	(In thousands, except per share and net registration data)				
Statement of Operations Data:					
Revenues:	$23,119	$28,178	$40,045	$69,095	$107,147
Cost and expenses:					
Instructional costs and services	10,944	13,247	17,959	29,479	43,561
Selling and promotional	2,206	4,043	4,895	6,765	12,361
General and administrative	5,737	7,364	9,150	15,335	21,302
Write-off of software development project[1]	—	—	3,148	—	—
Depreciation and amortization	674	1,300	1,953	2,825	4,235
Total costs and expenses	19,561	25,954	37,105	54,404	81,459
Income from continuing operations before interest income and income taxes	3,558	2,224	2,940	14,691	25,688
Interest income, net	56	225	289	888	706
Income from continuing operations before income taxes	3,614	2,449	3,229	15,579	26,394
Income tax expense	1,327	1,061	771	6,829	10,207
Income from continuing operations	2,287	1,388	2,458	8,750	16,187
Preferred stock charge and accretion	(1,085)	(12,985)	—	—	—
Income (loss) from continuing operations attributable to common stockholders	1,202	(11,597)	2,458	8,750	16,187
Loss from discontinued operations, net of income tax benefit	—	(303)	(660)	—	—
Net income (loss) attributable to common stockholders	$ 1,202	$(11,900)	$ 1,798	$ 8,750	$ 16,187
Income (loss) from continuing operations per common share:					
Basic	$ 0.22	$ (1.44)	$ 0.21	$ 0.69	$ 0.91
Diluted	$ 0.22	$ (1.44)	$ 0.20	$ 0.64	$ 0.86
Net income (loss) attributable to common stockholders per common share:					
Basic	$ 0.22	$ (1.48)	$ 0.15	$ 0.69	$ 0.91
Diluted	$ 0.22	$ (1.48)	$ 0.15	$ 0.64	$ 0.86
Weighted average number of shares outstanding:					
Basic	5,386	8,055	11,741	12,759	17,840
Diluted	5,407	8,055	12,178	13,601	18,822
Other Data:					
Net cash provided by operating activities	$ 4,546	$ 3,660	$ 8,929	$17,517	$ 29,757
Capital expenditures	$ 2,612	$ 4,613	$ 4,475	$ 6,827	$ 10,009
Stock-bases compensation[2]	$ 0	$ 1,198	$ 284	$ 1,033	$ 1,674
Net course registrations[3]	32,558	37,506	54,828	94,846	147,124

	As of December 31,				
	2004	**2005**	**2006**	**2007**	**2008**
			(In thousands)		
Consolidated Balance Sheet Data:					
Cash and cash equivalents	$ 7,250	$ 5,511	$11,678	$26,951	$47,714
Working capital[4]	$ 7,197	$ 5,741	$10,412	$21,433	$36,357
Total assets	$18,223	$22,444	$28,750	$48,980	$78,813
Total redeemable preferred stock	$11,339	$ —	$ —	$ —	$ —
Stockholders' equity	$ 738	$14,539	$16,821	$33,507	$53,475

	As of December 31,				
	2004	**2005**	**2006**	**2007**	**2008**
			(In thousands)		
Income from continuing operations	$2,287	$1,388	$2,458	$ 8,750	$16,187
Interest (income), net	(56)	(225)	(289)	(888)	(706)
Income tax expense	1,327	1,061	771	6,829	10,207
Depreciation and amortization	674	1,300	1,953	2,825	4,235
EBITDA from continuing operations	$4,232	$3,524	$4,893	$17,516	$29,923

(1) During 2006, $3.1 million of capitalized software development costs were written off when management determined that the asset related to these costs was impaired because we are no longer pursuing the related project.

(2) Effective January 1, 2006, we adopted Statement of Financial Accounting Standards No. 123(R)-Share-Based Payment, or SFAS 123R, which requires companies to expense share-based compensation based on fair value. Prior to January 1, 2006, we accounted for share-based payment in accordance with Accounting Principles Board Opinion No. 25-Accounting for Stock Issued to Employees, and provided the disclosure required in SFAS 123-Accounting for Stock-Based Compensation, as amended by SFAS No.148-Accounting for Stock-Based Compensation-Transition and Disclosure-An Amendment of FASB Statement No. 123. Stock-based compensation expense for the year ended December 31, 2005, resulted from the repurchase of shares of common stock acquired upon exercise of employee stock options.

(3) Net course registrations represent the total number of course registrations for students that have attended a portion of a course.

(4) Working capital is calculated by subtracting total current liabilities from total current assets.

Case 7

The Apollo Group, Inc. [University of Phoenix]   Richard B. Robinson

1   John G. Sperling was a late bloomer as an entrepreneur. A Cambridge University PhD who had spent most of his career teaching at San Jose State University after brief stints at Maryland, Ohio State and Northern Illinois, he didn't launch Apollo Group Inc.—parent of the University of Phoenix—until 1976, when he was 55. But what Sperling lacked in precociousness he more than made up for in ambition: His goal was nothing less than to turn conventional higher education on its head.

2   Rather than catering to 18- to 22-year-olds looking to find themselves, Sperling focused on the then-neglected market of working adults. And he recruited working professionals as teachers, rather than tenured professors. Although UOP and its online campus, University of Phoenix Online, have more than 18,000 faculties, only about 450 are full-time. Most radical of all, while nearly all other universities are nonprofits, Sperling ran his university to make money. Those ideas sparked overwhelming resistance from the education establishment, which branded UOP a "diploma mill." The result? "We faced failure every day for the first 10 years," said Founder Sperling, who turned 88 in 2009.

3   From an IPO adjusted price of $0.76 to a mid-2005 high of $98, Apollo's stock reflected a company *BusinessWeek* considered among the top 50 performing companies on Wall Street. The Phoenix-based company, whose day-to-day operations were still generating average annual revenue growth exceeding 30% over that time, saw its revenues reach $2.5 billion in 2006 with net income exceeding $414 million. With a price-earnings ratio of 76, Apollo had one of the richest price-earnings multiples on Wall Street at the time.

4   Tuition at Apollo averages only $10,000 a year, 55% of what a typical private college charges. A key factor, says Sperling, is that universities for the young require student unions, sports teams, student societies, and so on. The average age of a UOP student is 35, so UOP doesn't have those expenses. It also saves by holding classes in leased office spaces around the country. By 2005, over 135,000 of its 275,000 students studied at University of Phoenix Online.

5   By 2006, Phoenix Online had become the dominant player in the online education market that still has lots of potential for growth. The bricks-and-mortar University of Phoenix was one of the first institutions to identify and serve the burgeoning market for educating working adults. In the late 1980s, long before the Web debuted, the school began to experiment with offering its classes online. It got off to a slow start, "and we lost money for a number of years," recalled Brian Mueller, Apollo's president.

6   As a result of this head start, however, Phoenix Online was ready to capitalize on an online-education market that began exploding in the mid-1990s. Today, about 15% of the 600,000 or so U.S. students earning a degree via the Net are enrolled at Phoenix Online.

Phoenix Online also garners an outsize share of the industry's revenues—about one-third of the total. That's because as the market leader, it can charge higher tuition than most rivals. Undergraduates pay a little more than $10,000 a year at Phoenix Online, while students seeking a master's degree pay nearly $12,500. "They're by far the giant in this industry," says Eduventure market analyst Sean Gallagher. Appendix A at the end of this case lists some of the other key players or "competitors."

7   Is the best yet to come? Both Phoenix Online and the broader industry are still in their infancy. "There are 70 million working adults in this country who don't have a college degree," says Gallagher. Increasingly, they realize that they need a degree to get ahead. But because they often have a family as well as a job, studying online is the most convenient solution. Howard Block, an analyst at Banc of America Securities, predicts "dramatic enrollment growth" for Phoenix Online. He expects that half of the students in post-secondary education will one day make at least some use of the Internet to earn their degrees.

GLOBAL OUTREACH

8   Phoenix Online began to tap the international market in 2005, initially "bringing in about 500 students a month," said Mueller. "But that's just the tip of the iceberg." Though Phoenix Online started offering classes only in English, it has begun to offer courses in Spanish and plans to introduce Mandarin soon as well. Ironically, one of the hottest tech stocks of recent years has done all this with plain-vanilla technology. While other companies charged into online education with dazzling digital content, Phoenix Online offers a text-heavy format that can easily be accessed with dial-up modems.

9   This might sound like a recipe for failure. But Phoenix Online realized that interaction with humans—the professor and other students in the class—was far more important to success than interaction with the digital content. Thus, Phoenix Online keeps its classes small, averaging just 12 students. And to combat the Achilles heel of distance education—a high dropout rate—it offers its students plenty of hand-holding, including round-the-clock tech support. The result: 65% of its students go on to graduate.

10   Some see plain technology as a potential negative for the virtual college. "At some point, Phoenix Online will need to upgrade the sophistication of its platform," warns Trace Urdan, an analyst with ThinkEquity Partners, a boutique investment bank. That will require more spending on research and development and information technology, he warns, which could crimp margins. Still, any extra spending could be easily offset if Phoenix Online bumped up its class size to 15 students, argues Block. Even with today's small classes, operating profit margins now top 30%.

THE ONLINE TREND

11   The dot-com bubble may have burst in the world of commerce, but the promise of harnessing the Internet for paradigm-changing growth—and even profits—still thrives in the halls of academia. At the University of Maryland University College, enrollment in classes offered over the Net soared to 63,000 in the past academic year, up 50% from the year before. UMUC students can now earn some 70 degrees and certificates entirely online. The University of Phoenix Online saw revenues jump some 76% in the fiscal year ended Aug. 31, to $181 million, while profits grew 82%, to $32 million.

12   Since the U.S. Army began rolling out an e-learning program in 2001, annually more than 10,400 soldiers are taking classes and earning degrees online from 24 participating colleges. Students at eArmyU, as it's known, receive a free laptop and printer and 100% of their tuition. The Army enrollment hit 80,000 after it took the program Army-wide in 2006.

13 Nearly seven years after the dot-com fizzle began, e-learning has emerged from the wreckage as one of the Internet's most useful applications. Nearly 75% of the 4,000 major colleges and universities in the U.S. now offer classes over the Internet or use the Web to enhance campus classes, according to market researcher International Data Corp. About 6 million students take online classes from U.S. higher-ed institutions in 2007 according to John G. Flores, head of the U.S. Distance Learning Assn., a nonprofit trade group outside Boston. And it's not just a U.S. phenomenon: students from developing countries are jumping online, too.

FIGURE 1
Corporations Are Charging into E-Learning

Data: International Data Corp.

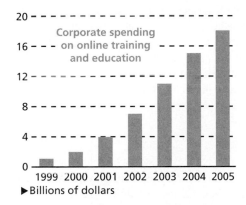

FIGURE 2
The E-Learning Explosion

Data International Data Corp., Eduventures.com. IDC. U.S. Distance Learning Assn.

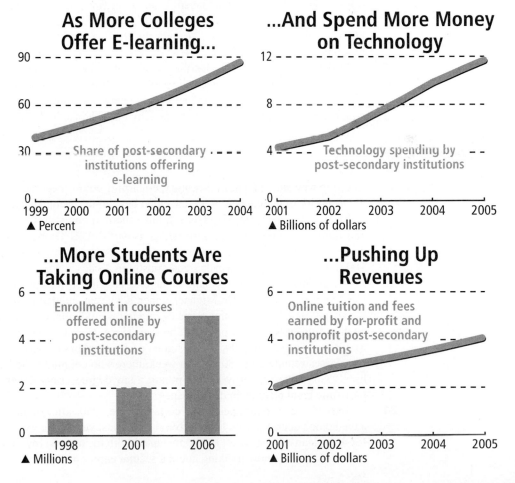

14   These classes are opening new horizons for the fastest-growing segment of higher education: working adults, who often find it difficult to juggle conventional classes with jobs and families. Adults over 25 now represent nearly half of higher-ed students; most are employed and want more education to advance their careers.

15   E-learning is an influence in the traditional college class as well. Online classes won't replace the college experience for most 18- to 24-year-olds. But from the Massachusetts Institute of Technology to Wake Forest University in North Carolina, colleges are using the Web in on-campus classes to augment textbooks and boost communication.

16   There are still plenty of hurdles to clear before the e-learning world can take off. For one thing, most of the success is with established universities, like UMUC, which can leverage their brand names to reach out to working adults. The for-profit start-ups, by contrast, have struggled with accreditation and poor name recognition. Many have fallen by the wayside, including BigWords.com, an Amazon-like purveyor of textbooks, while only a handful make money, like UOP Online.

MASS MARKET?

17   Quality is a problem, which is a key reason why many online students drop out. That will force a further shakeout, eliminating mediocre players. Many colleges grapple with such issues as how much time their faculty should devote to e-teaching. And long-established rules make it difficult for online students to get financial aid. Even as these problems are resolved, "online learning will never be as good as face-to-face instruction," argues Andy DiPaolo, director of the Stanford Center for Professional Development, which offers online graduate classes to engineers.

18   Ultimately, the greatest e-learning market may lie in the developing world, where the population of college-age students is exploding. Just as cell phones leapfrogged land-based telephones in many developing countries, so may e-learning help to educate the masses in countries that lack the colleges to meet demand—and can't afford to build them.

ROAD WORK

19   Looking way out, as far as mid-century, e-learning could "become the environment in which the majority of human beings are educated beyond the secondary level," asserts University of Melbourne President Alan Gilbert. His school, along with Canada's McGill University and more than a dozen other universities, is part of U21 Global, a virtual university being created through a joint venture with textbook giant Thomson Learning. It aims to enroll 100,000 students by the decade's end, mostly in Asia.

20   Meanwhile, e-learning demand in the U.S. is rising, driven by higher education's changing demographics. Take Dr. Michael Kaner, a 43-year-old dentist in suburban Philadelphia who's halfway through adding a law degree to his credentials. Attending a night program at an area law school wasn't practical, he says, since it would have required 12 hours of commuting a week. So in 1999, Kaner signed up for Kaplan's Concord law program. Although the classes require 25 to 30 hours a week, there's no commute and he studies when it suits him. "This is the only way I could pursue a law degree," says Kaner, who hopes to build a part-time legal practice in dental issues.

21   Judy Rowe, who dropped out of college in the 1960s after running out of money, earned a bachelor's degree in psychology from UMUC last year while working as a flight attendant for American Airlines Inc. "I took my laptop with me and did my assignments on the road," says Rowe, who's now thinking about a second career in psychology.

COST-EFFECTIVE

22 E-learning is a good fit with the military, where frequent transfers complicate pursuing a degree. The U.S. Army awarded PWC Consulting a $453 million, five-year contract to create an electronic university that allows soldiers to be anywhere and study at Kansas State University or any of the 24 colleges involved in the program.

23 eArmyU already has changed the perspective of soldiers like Sergeant Jeremy Dellinger, 22, who had been planning to leave the Army to go back to school when his basic enlistment ends. Then he enrolled in eArmyU to earn his bachelor's degree from Troy State University in Alabama. "Now I can get my degree and still do the work I love" as a supply sergeant, says the Fort Benning (Ga.)-based soldier. Like Dellinger, about 15% of those who have signed up so far have reenlisted or extended their commitment. By cutting turnover, "eArmyU could almost pay for itself," says program director Lee Harvey, since it costs nearly $70,000 to train green recruits.

24 Corporations, too, see e-learning as a cost-effective way to get better-educated employees. Indeed, corporate spending on e-learning is expected to more than quadruple by 2005, to $18 billion, estimates IDC. At IBM, some 200,000 employees received education or training online last year, and 75% of the company's Basic Blue class for new managers is online. The move cut IBM's training bill by $350 million last year, because online classes don't require travel.

25 Even as online higher-ed catches on, however, few private-sector providers are turning a profit. During the boom years, venture capitalists pumped some $5 billion into e-learning companies, says Adam Newman, a senior analyst at Eduventures.com. Roughly $1 billion went to companies that have already flamed out, he says. Beyond Phoenix, probably only half a dozen companies are making money now. Lack of name recognition is the biggest problem for companies like Capella, Jones International, and Cardean, UNext's virtual campus. And winning accreditation—crucial for attracting students—is tough going, too. It took Capella five years to make the grade; Jones waited four years. Concord's grads can sit for the California Bar Exam, but the American Bar Assn. still hasn't granted it accreditation.

CAUTIOUS ELITES

26 Phoenix Online aside, the big e-learning winners so far are the traditional nonprofit universities. They have captured nearly 95% of online enrollments, figures A. Frank Mayadas, head of e-learning grants at the Alfred P. Sloan Foundation. Most active are state and community colleges that started with strong brand names, a faculty, and accreditation, says Mayadas, as well as a tradition of extension programs.

27 By contrast, many elite universities have been far more cautious about diluting the value of their name. Harvard Business School believes it would be impossible to replicate its classroom education online. "We will never offer a Harvard MBA online," vows professor W. Earl Sasser, chairman of HBS Interactive, which instead develops e-learning programs for companies. MIT faculty nixed teaching classes online, fearing "it would detract from the residential experience," says former faculty chair Steven Lerman.

28 That didn't stop MIT from embracing the Internet in a different way. Over the next five years, MIT plans to post lecture notes and reading assignments for most of its 2,000 classes on the Web for free, calling the effort "OpenClassWare." Lerman says "it's a service to the world," but he says it's no substitute for actual teaching, so faculty aren't worried about a threat to classroom learning.

29 A few other top schools see profit-making opportunities. Since 1996, Duke University's Fuqua School of Business has been offering MBAs for working executives. In these blended

programs, some 65% of the work is done online and just 35% in classes held during required residencies that consume 9 to 11 weeks over two years. Duke charges up to $90,000 for these programs—vs. $60,000 for its traditional residential MBA. Yet they have been so popular that by next year, "we'll have more students in nontraditional programs than the daytime program," says Fuqua Dean Douglas T. Breeden. The extra revenues are helping Fuqua to double its faculty.

The Adult Education Market

30   The adult education market is a significant and growing component of the post-secondary education market, which is estimated by the U.S. Department of Education to be a more than $275 billion industry. According to the U.S. Department of Education, over 6 million, or 40% of all students enrolled in higher education programs are over the age of 24. This number is projected to reach 6.7 million in 2011. The market for adult education in the U.S. is expected to increase as working adults seek additional education and training to update and improve their skills, to enhance their earnings potential, and to keep pace with the rapidly expanding knowledge-based economy.

31   Many working adults are seeking accredited degree programs that provide flexibility to accommodate the fixed schedules and time commitments associated with their professional and personal obligations. UOP's format since its inception has focused on working adult students by providing an accredited collegiate education that enables them to attend classes and complete classwork in a schedule and manner more convenient to the constraints their work life imposes on their ability to obtain a college or advanced degree. UOP has long felt that most colleges and universities as well as newer emerging technology-based education and training companies do not effectively address the unique requirements of working adult students. They often cite the following attributes of the traditional, not-for-profit education industry:

- Traditional universities and colleges were designed to fulfill the educational needs of conventional, full-time students aged 18 to 24, who remain the primary focus of these universities and colleges.
- This focus has resulted in a capital-intensive teaching/learning model in typical state and private colleges and universities that may be characterized by:
  - a high percentage of full-time tenured faculty with doctoral degrees;
  - fully-configured library facilities and related full-time staff;
  - dormitories, student unions, and other significant plant assets to support the needs of younger students;
  - often major investment in and commitment to comprehensive sports programs;
  - major administrative overhead for all the various university functions;
  - politically-based funding;
  - major resistance to change in any academic programs, even in the face of rapid global change across disciplines and professions;
  - an emphasis on research and the related staff and facilities; and
  - faculty with PhDs and a research focus but limited practical experience, even in key programs like business and other working-related professions.
- The majority of accredited colleges and universities continue to provide the bulk of their educational programming from September to mid-December and from mid-January to May. As a result, most full-time faculty members only teach during that limited period of time.
- While this structure serves the needs of the full-time 18- to 24-year-old student, it limits the educational opportunity for working adults who must delay their education for up to five months during these spring, summer, and winter breaks.

- Traditional universities and colleges are also limited in their ability to market to or provide the necessary customer service for working adult students because it requires the development of additional administrative and enrollment infrastructure.

THE APOLLO GROUP, INC.

32   The Apollo Group, Inc. [AGI] has provided higher education to working adults for over 30 years through its four subsidiaries listed below. They enrolled and served slightly over 275,000 students enrolled in 2005.

- **The University of Phoenix [UOP]**—the largest private university in the U.S. and source of the majority of the Apollo Group's revenue.
- **Institute for Professional Development**—provides adult-education program development and management consulting services to 23 regionally accredited private colleges and universities.
- **The College for Financial Planning Institutes**—one of the nation's leading providers of financial services education for individuals and corporations in the financial services industry.
- **Western International University**—adapts the Apollo model with younger professionals that seek individualized instruction through campuses in Arizona, and more recently China, India and the Netherlands.

33   Revenue during the last five fiscal years for the UOP versus the other three parts of The Apollo Group have almost tripled with combined revenues up 140% companywide. They were as follows the last five years [in $millions]:

	FY2006	FY2005	FY2004	FY2003	FY2002
Univ. of Phx	$2,075	$2,014	$1,697	$1,251	$ 931
Other 3 Schs	$ 402	$ 235	$ 97	$ 87	$ 78
Corporate	$ 1	$ 1	$ 4	$ 1	$ 0.2
	$2,478	$2,251	$1,798	$1,339	$ 1,009.2

34   The Apollo Group network spanned 101 campuses and 165 learning centers in 39 states and five other countries in 2007. UOP locations identified on its website were as follows in mid-2007:

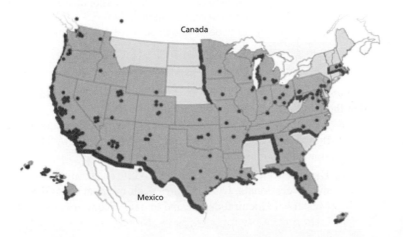

The University of Phoenix Strategy

35 The University of Phoenix [UOP] strategy includes six key elements.

1. **Establish New University of Phoenix campuses and Learning Centers.** The University of Phoenix [UOP] plans to continue the addition of campuses and learning centers throughout the United States and Canada. New locations are selected based on an analysis of various factors, including the population of working adults in the area, the number of local employers and their educational reimbursement policies, and the availability of similar programs offered by other institutions. Chairman Todd Nelson offered this comment relative to establishing new locations:

   Even after 30 years we are still in only 35 states. So we still have 15 states to go, including New York and Connecticut. And in many states there are multiple markets. So we probably easily have another 35 to 40 new markets to expand into in the U.S. Over the next ten years our plan is to have a physical campus not only in every state but also in every major U.S. metropolitan area.

2. **International Expansion.** The UOP believes that the international market for UOP's services is a major growth opportunity. The U.S. is the most common destination for international students studying abroad. They believe that more working adult students would opt for a U.S. education that does not involve living in the U.S. because they could do so without leaving their employment and incurring the high travel and living costs and stringent visa requirements associated with studying abroad. UOP's belief is supported by the fact that University of Phoenix Online has students located in approximately 75 countries despite having used only limited advertising. In addition, many U.S. residents live and work in foreign countries and would benefit from the opportunity to continue their education while abroad. UOP plans to offer the University of Phoenix educational model at physical campuses in international markets. The UOP now has a location in Juarez, Mexico, and expects a Mexico City campus soon. Its Western University operation has a location in China, India, Dubai, and the Netherlands from which AGI expects to expand into a UOP presence.

3. **Enhance Existing Educational Programs.** UOP's current enrollment by college is spread across eight core programs:

College of Undergraduate Business	41%
College of Graduate Business	18
College of Info Systems & Technology	11
College of Social & Behavioral Sciences	8
College of General & Professional Studies	8
College of Education	7
College of Health Sciences and Nursing	6
School of Advanced Studies	1
	100%

President Mueller notes several strengths he believes are underpinnings of these programs that the UOP works continuously to improve:

   3a. **Accredited Degree Programs.** UOP currently offers 15 degree programs across these eight core program areas that are accredited by The Higher Learning Commission or the regional accrediting associations.

   3b. **Experienced Faculty Resources.** While substantially all of UOP's faculty are working professionals, UOP requires each member of AGI's faculty to possess either a Masters or Doctoral degree and to have five years of recent professional experience in a field related to the subject they teach. UOP's classes are designed to be small, with an average of one instructor for every fifteen students. Faculty members are also required to be accessible to students by maintaining office hours. The UOP now claims to have over 17,500 instructors available on a regular basis with advanced degrees and currently working in relevant professional positions as well as having completed rigorous instructor training and evaluation programs to ensure the quality of their instruction content and approach.

3c. **Current and Relevant Standardized Programs.** UOP uses content experts selected from AGI's approximately 17,600 faculty to design UOP's curriculum. This enables UOP to offer current and relevant standardized programs to UOP's students.

3d. **Emphasize Input from Employers of UOP Students.** The employers of UOP's students often provide input to faculty members in designing curriculum, and class projects are typically based on issues relevant to the companies that employ AGI's students. AGI's classes are taught by a practitioner faculty that emphasizes the skills desired by employers. In addition, the time flexibility provided by AGI's classes further benefits employers since it avoids conflict with their employees' work schedules. A recent survey by University of Phoenix showed that approximately 60% of its students receive some level of tuition assistance from their employers. Two pedagogical innovations described below were developed at the UOP based on input from several major global companies and employers of UOP students seeking improvements on the realism in business course materials and greater options for incorporating both online and in-person learning. Pres. Mueller offered this comment:

We consider the employers that provide tuition assistance to their employees through tuition reimbursement plans or direct bill arrangements UOP's secondary customers.

3c. **Pedagogical Innovations.** FlexNet® is one example of UOP adapting its means of delivering course material to accommodate different learner needs. FlexNet® combines online and face-to-face instruction allowing any UOP student to choose among three approaches to receive course instruction and interaction. Virtual Organizations represent another innovation—six composite businesses, schools, health care and government organizations that have been developed as learning tools by subject matter experts and professionals in those fields. These virtual organizations allow UOP students and their instructors to immerse themselves inside virtual real-world settings to include Internet and intranet sites to provide a more realistic form of experiential learning than case studies and simulations while also fostering critical thinking and resourcefulness as the students engage the virtual organization learning experience.

3f. **Small class-size with quality instructor contact.** The UOP has long sought to overcome the "diploma mill" perception long associated with non-traditional collegiate education by structuring quality instruction into its daily approach. One way this has steadily paid off and separated UOP from that perception has been through having every class remain small. The UOP has recently allowed its average online course to increase in size from 10 to 12 students. The average on-ground class has gone from 14 students to 15 students. President Mueller offered these recent observations on this cornerstone aspect of the UOP strategy:

Yes, we've taken the average class size from 10 to 12 online, and 14 to 15 on-ground. That has actually reduced instructional costs because of our overall size. We will never have large classes compared to other universities. A classroom environment with

20 students or less, like we offer, is better than a strategy class with 50 students or a lecture class with 200 students like most public universities offer. At the UOP we know that a good education means students need access to their faculty, easily.

And he went on to suggest that the acid test for quality of UOP instruction versus other non-traditional universities or even traditional universities can be measured by students' employers willingness to reimburse for taking UOP classes:

This is a free-market economy. If we don't provide value, the companies that are reimbursing students [to take UOP courses] are not going to pay. We are not seeing any deterioration in this area. Rather, we are seeing just the opposite.

3g. **Offer a Low Cost Advantage.** UOP's tuition is running about $10,000 annually, for a full load. It is increasing at an average 4%–5% annually. The average traditional university tuition is running about $15–$20,000 annually, and increasing approximately 10% annually. The variance is even more pronounced for graduate programs, where an MBA, for example, costs slightly over $12,500 at UOP versus an average $28,000 nationwide.

4. **Expand Educational Programs.** UOP regularly evaluates and responds to the changing educational needs of working adults and their employers by introducing new undergraduate and graduate degree programs as well as training programs. To its degree offerings, University of Phoenix recently added the Master of Business Administration in Health Care Management and specializations in Marketing and Human Resources Management to its Master of Business Administration; specializations in Elementary and Secondary Education and Adult Education and Distance Learning to its Master of Arts in Education; and a specialization in Educational Counseling to its Master of Counseling. To its certificate programs, University of Phoenix has recently added graduate certificates in e-Business, Technology Management, and Global Management, as well as a certificate in Operations and Supply Chain Management. UOP believes that expanding its program offerings will help it improve UOP's market position as a provider of higher education and training for working adults.

President Mueller made this observation regarding new courses and degrees UOP may add soon:

We always have new programs being developed. Criminal justice is a big area of growth. Engineering is a possibility. And some new nursing programs—for registered nurses and licensed practical nurses—are a possibility in 2007.

5. **Serve a Broader Student Age Group.** The UOP has built tremendous success focusing on the working adult student population in the U.S. Based on recent surveys of incoming students, the average age of University of Phoenix's students is in the midthirties, approximately 54% are women and 46% are men. Approximately 67% of University of Phoenix's students have been employed on a full-time basis for nine years or more. The approximate age percentage distribution of incoming UOP students is:

Age	Percentage of Students
25 and under	16.5%
26 to 33	38.0%
34 to 45	34.7%
46 and over	10.8%
	100.0%

Recently, the UOP has adapted this focus and initiated a conscious effort to direct more attention to younger students, to include targeting high school students as they make decisions to consider college. President Mueller offered these comments about this new emphasis at UOP on the traditional collegiate market of 18- to 22-year-old students:

> If you look at the higher education market, at least half your students are in this [18- to 22-year-old] age group, and over the next decade, this will be the fastest area of growth. Also, we've had literally tens of thousands of 18- to 22-year-olds who have shown interest. We're not going to add dormitories. We're not after the traditional younger student [who goes off to live at college]. We're going after the younger student who is working. And they have similar needs to [our working adult students], including the flexibility of classes that can start any time of the day, evening or weekend.

6. **Market Aggressively.** The Apollo Group spent $545 million in the last fiscal year marketing its academic programs, mostly the UOP. This is a staggering amount when you consider that few traditional universities spend even close to $10 million in direct marketing expenditures. Yet Apollo's earnings almost doubled since 2003 and revenue grew by over 90% during the same period.

Barmak Nasirian, associate director of the American Association of Collegiate Registrars and Admissions Officers, warns: "This rate of growth may not be sustainable." His group represent traditional colleges, many of which are critical of Apollo and the UOP. President Mueller at the Apollo Group offered this observation:

> We had enrollment growth, so you would have expected marketing costs to rise comparably. Two things are behind the increase. First, the cost of leads are more expensive. And second, because we were having a good year financially, we felt it was wise to spend aggressively in the marketing area.

The Apollo Group Looks to the Future

36   The Apollo Group's reputation was sullied in late 2005 with the release of a U.S. Education Dept. report depicting a high-pressure sales culture at the UOP that resembled a telemarketing boiler room more than a university admissions office. "Phoenix recruiters soon find out that UOP bases their salaries solely on the number of students they recruit," the report charged. That's prohibited by federal law. One recruiter who started at $28,000, for instance, was bumped to $85,000 after recruiting 151 students in six months. But another who started at $28,000 got just a $4,000 raise after signing up 79 students. Websites like www.uopsucks.com have emerged as blog-like forums for former students and employees unhappy with or distrustful of the UOP's offerings.

37   Ultimately, such violations could have led the government to bar Phoenix from the federal student loan program, crippling the university. Former CEO Nelson called the report "very misleading and full of inaccuracies." But he says he decided to settle rather than wage a protracted legal fight. The Apollo Group agreed to change its compensation system and pay a $9.8 million fine without admitting guilt. Still, Apollo's defenders note that the point of the law is to prevent for-profits from luring unqualified students. If the UOP is doing that, it hasn't showed up in student-loan default rates, which remain a low 6%—below the average for traditional colleges and universities.

38   With the regulators off its back, and with tuition growth surging 30% during the quarter following the release of the report, the UOP once again focused on growth. The online program, with approximately 150,000 students, was seen as far from saturated. And for the first time the UOP started targeting high school graduates, who are expected to hit a record later this decade as a "baby boomer echo" factor. Similarly, the UOP has barely

begun to scratch the international market, where experts see huge demand for U.S.-style education. Phoenix opened its first Mexican campus in 2005, and has big hopes for China, where Apollo's Western International University now has just 50 students, and India.

39   But the UOP will have to fill acres of classroom seats to keep up its pace—and it is paying an ever-increasing cost to do so. The company already has over 270,000 students. Some 90% of those are enrolled at the University of Phoenix, making it by far the nation's largest private university. Given that size, it had to add nearly 57,000 students—the equivalent of another University of Texas at Austin—in 12 months just to make its growth target. And that has proven very difficult to accomplish at Apollo since it experienced successively lower enrollment growth for nine straight quarters through Q1, 2007. Adding to these problems has been an SEC investigation of stock option grant irregularities in late 2006 that have resulted in a restatement of financial statements to be completed in 2007.

40   "Since early 2007 we have focused on making significant changes in two major areas of our business: marketing and retention," said President Mueller. "Much of the work required to launch our marketing and branding efforts is complete and we are already seeing evidence of its effectiveness." Mueller added that retention and academic strategies take longer to implement, but that he's confident that investments in such improvements will benefit students and stockholders in the long run.

Acquisition Activity

41   Mueller and the Apollo Group may see other ways to grow student counts. In early 2007 Apollo announced the acquisition of Insight Schools, a company that runs online charter schools in Washington state, for $15 million. Competitor Kaplan followed several months later with the acquisition of Sagemont Virtual, a company that runs the University of Miami Online High School. Apollo's entry into high schools began in 2005 when it formed a partnership with Orange Lutheran High School in California. It converted many of the school's courses so they could be delivered in an online format, a move that was embraced by the school's students and faculty, according to Mueller. "We became convinced we could provide that service to high school students, and it would have the same kind of value educationally—if not greater—at the high school level than even at the higher educational level," said Mueller. That sounds quite familiar to the start founder John Sperling engineered over thirty years ago.

42   About 700,000 public pre-collegiate students were enrolled in at least one online or blended course in 2007. Online high school courses are becoming popular with states with large rural areas and those seeking to expand both high level offerings as well as special course offerings. Some analysts think an educational setting with 50 million high school students might well be attractive as a growth vector when compared to a mature higher education market, domestically, with about 15 million students.

43   And, when you consider the number of high school aged students worldwide, and the special delivery needs in needy areas that online options may assist, you have to wonder if this may be a major new trend. Then, too, if a high schooler gets comfortable with an online approach, that may well feed directly into an online higher educational choice. Meanwhile, Barbara Stein, manager of 21st century education at the National Education Assn., is concerned that students who attend virtual high schools may be loosing out on the benefits of a traditional high school experience. "We think those are not a great idea. Most students do not do that well when they have no face-to-face interactions," says Stein. "There may be extreme situations where that is the appropriate recourse, but for most students it is not."

APPENDIX A   Guide to Online Universities
As e-learning has exploded, here is a brief look at the range of providers:

1. University of Maryland University College

The largest state university provider of online classes, it moved online in the mid-90s, building on its long heritage of offering extension classes. Last year, enrollments in its online classes hit 63,000, up 50% in one year. Students can now earn 70 different degrees and certificates online. In addition to classes, UMUC provides a comprehensive array of online student services, from applications to academic advising and financial aid consulting.

COST: Same as for UMUC's traditional classroom classes. That means Maryland residents are charged just $197 per semester hour for undergrad classes, and $301 per semester for graduate classes. But out-of-state residents must pay over 50% more.

2. University of Phoenix Online

The nation's largest for-profit virtual university, offering the same kind of business, education and technical classes for working adults that have made its bricks-and-mortar counterpart, the University of Phoenix, such a success. In business, students may earn everything from undergraduate degrees in accounting, management and marketing to an MBA and even a Doctor of Management in Organizational Leadership. Phoenix Online provides lots of attention to its students. Classes are kept small, and instructors insist on participation.

COST: $400 to $500 per credit; an MBA degree costs about $23,000.

3. eArmyU (The U.S. Army's Virtual University)

Since January, eArmyU has allowed enlisted soldiers to take classes and earn degrees from 24 different institutions, ranging from Central Texas College to Utah State. So far, 10,400 soldiers have signed up on the three Army bases where it's offered. The plan is to offer it Army-wide.

COST: Free to soldiers, who receive a laptop, printer, Internet connection and 100% of tuition. Civilians are not eligible for eArmy.

4. Western Governors University

Virtual university founded by 19 western states in 1997. A pioneer in "competency-based degrees," which require students to demonstrate mastery of a subject, rather than complete a certain number of credit hours. In practice, this means students are assessed when they enter a program. An individual class of study is then developed for each student to fill the gaps in their knowledge. The result is that the length of time needed to complete a degree varies widely, and is dependent on what the student knows. While it may sound radical, WGU is backed by some two-dozen corporate sponsors, including IBM, AOL and Microsoft.

COST: WGU charges about $4,500 for the assessment and mentoring needed for a two-year degree. Students must pay separately for classes, which are offered by some 40 different institutions.

5. Concord Law School

Launched by Kaplan Inc., a unit of the Washington Post Co, Concord has grown to become the nation's largest virtual law school, with 800 students at present. Kaplan argues that the law is ideally suited to online learning, because it facilitates communication (via e-mail) among students and professors. While the program is not yet accredited by the American Bar Association, students may sit for the California Bar Exam.

COST: $6,000 per year, or $24,000 for four-year law degree.

6. Duke's Fuqua School of Business

"Blended" MBA programs for working executives, in which 65% of the work is done over the Net, and 35% in classes that meet for 9 or 11 weeks during 20-month programs. There are two blended programs. The "Global Executive" program is designed for executives who manage a large international business unit or a global staff. The average global student has 14 years of professional experience. In contrast, the "Cross Continent" program is aimed at more junior managers—with an average of six years of experience—who have already demonstrated success at the department level.

COST: Up to $90,000 for "Global Executive" program, versus $60,000 for normal daytime MBA. The extra costs cover the residential program, which in the case of Global Executive is held in various spots around the world, including Europe, Asia and the Duke campus.

APPENDIX A   Guide to Online Universities—Continued
As e-learning has exploded, here is a brief look at the range of providers:

7. Cardean University

The virtual university founded by UNext.com, one of the highest profile e-learning start-ups. UNext partnered with some of the world's best known universities—including Stanford, the University of Chicago and Columbia—to develop its cutting-edge business curriculum. It is now offering classes to employees of General Motors and a number of other companies, and will shortly begin marketing its business classes to consumers.

COST: About $25,000 for MBA.

8. Jones International University

The virtual university founded in 1993 by cable pioneer Glenn R. Jones, who earlier offered distance classes via cable TV through his Mind Extension University. Jones offers more than 40 executive and professional education programs. Students may earn a bachelor's degree in business, an MBA, as well as various masters' degrees in education.

COST: 3-credit class runs $925; MBA costs about $12,000.

9. Capella University

A for-profit virtual university that offers some 500 online classes every quarter. Students may choose from 15 different degree programs, and some 80 different specializations. Most of the 4,000 students study business, education or information technology.

COST: Classes (which offer 3 to 5 credits) tend to cost from $1150 to $1600. A master's degree runs about $20,000, and a PhD about $34,000.

10. Walden University

Originally founded in 1970 to offer graduate degrees, Walden moved online in the mid-1990s. Walden is 41% owned by Sylvan Learning Systems, which has other online education programs as well. Walden specializes in graduate programs in business, education, psychology, public health and human services.

COST: An MBA runs about $20,000, while a PhD can cost $47,000.

11. The Electronic Campus of the Southern Regional Education Board

A sweeping smorgasbord of online classes organized by the Southern Regional Education Board, an organization formed to promote education reform in 16 southern states. The electronic campus offers over 5,000 online classes from 325 different schools, ranging from Auburn University to West Virginia University.

COST: Tuition varies widely, since it is set by the college that actually offers a given class. As one example, a class on American History since 1865 offered by Oklahoma State costs $365.

12. Harvard Extension School

Your best chance to take an online class from Harvard, these classes are offered by Harvard's extension school. While the Harvard Extension School currently offers over 500 classes in the traditional classroom setting, only about three dozen are currently available online. However, the plan is to expand the number of online offerings. Most of the classes available this year are computer science classes, on topics like website development and algorithms.

COST: Same as for attending a class at the extension school. The cost ranges from $275 for a class on American Constitutional History taken without credit, to $1,750 for the class on website development.

13. UT TelecampUS

An excellent example of the expanding e-learning programs offered by state university systems, the UT TelecampUS was launched in 1998 by the University of Texas system. Students may earn an MBA, Masters in Computer Science, and various other online degrees from a school within the UT system. Students who wish to earn a degree must first apply and be admitted to one of the universities in the UT system. That campus will then serve as the student's "home" campus, and ultimately award the degree.

COST: Texas residents pay about $300 for a 3-credit undergraduate class, and $500 for a 3-credit graduate class. Non-residents are charged roughly twice as much.

APPENDIX A   Guide to Online Universities—Continued
As e-learning has exploded, here is a brief look at the range of providers:

14. Stanford Center for Professional Development

One of the most challenging and prestigious online programs. The Stanford Center offers both online degrees and non-degree classes from Stanford's School of Engineering and affiliated departments. The center now provides over 250 online credit classes in electrical engineering, mechanical engineering, computer science, etc. These are not watered-down classes. They are taught by the Stanford faculty, and students must be admitted, just like on-campus students. The online classes are designed strictly for employed engineers and scientists. The attraction is that they may keep working, while furthering their education.

COST: About $3,000 for a credit class, 40% more than it would cost to take a similar class on campus. Typically, the companies employing the students pick up the tab.

APPENDIX B   Apollo Group Financial Information

	August 31,				
	2006	2005	2004 Restated(1)	2003	2002
Revenues:					
Tuition and other, net	$2,477,533	$2,251,114	$1,800,047	$1,338,982	$1,007,936
Costs and expenses:					
Instructional costs and services	1,112,660	956,631	781,437	630,556	531,332
Selling and promotional	544,706	485,451	383,800	272,348	198,889
General and administrative	149,928	94,485	84,326	61,314	54,388
Goodwill impairment	20,205	—	—	—	—
Share based compensation(2)	—	16,895	100,283	—	—
Total costs and expenses	1,827,499	1,553,462	1,349,846	964,228	784,609
Income from operations	650,034	697,652	450,201	374,754	223,327
Interest income and other, net	18,054	16,787	16,305	14,238	11,181
Income before income taxes	668,088	714,439	466,506	388,992	234,508
Provision for income taxes	253,255	286,506	186,421	153,109	99,107
Net income	$ 414,833	$ 427,933	$ 280,085	$ 235,883	$ 135,401

(1) See Note 3, "Restatement of Consolidated Financial Statements" included in Item 8 of this Form 10-K.
(2) Share-based compensation in 2005 and 2004 is related to the 2004 conversion of the UPX Online stock options into Apollo Group Class A stock options. Share-based compensation expense resulting from the revised measurement dates is included in instructional costs and services, selling and promotional, and general and administrative expenses.

	August 31,				
	2006	**2005**	**2004**	**2003**	**2002**
			Restated(1)		
Total cash, cash equivalents, restricted cash and securities, and marketable securities	$ 646,995	$ 685,748	$ 993,875	$1,045,802	$ 688,656
Total assets	$1,283,005	$1,281,548	$1,487,750	$1,417,388	$1,018,659
Current liabilities	$ 595,756	$ 566,745	$ 525,239	$ 384,520	$ 297,632
Long-term liabilities	82,876	80,583	67,546	48,072	44,562
Total shareholders' equity	604,373	634,220	894,965	984,796	676,465
Total liabilities and shareholders' equity	$1,283,005	$1,281,548	$1,487,750	$1,417,388	$1,018,659
Operating Statistics:					
Degreed enrollments at end of year(2)	282,300	271,400	238,400	189,800	144,400
Number of locations at end of year:					
Campuses	99	90	82	71	65
Learning centers	163	154	137	121	111
Total number of locations	262	244	219	192	176

(1) See Note 3, "Restatement of Consolidated Financial Statements" included in Item 8 of this Form 10-K.
(2) Restated Degreed Enrollments includes only UPX and Axia College and represent individual students enrolled in our degree programs that attended a course during the quarter and did not graduate as of the end of the quarter (including Axia students enrolled in UPX and WIU). Previously, the Company used a different definition of enrollment. Previously reported enrollment numbers are restated above.

The following table presents the most significant components as percentages of total tuition and other, net revenue for the years ended August 31, 2006, 2005, and 2004:

	Year Ended August 31,					
	2006		**2005**		**2004**	
			Restated(1)		**Restated(1)**	
($ in millions)						
Tuition revenue	$2,304.3	93.0%	$2,114.1	93.9%	$1,679,0	93.3%
IPD services revenue	74.4	3.0%	69.5	3.1%	62.6	3.5%
Application and related fees	33.8	1.4%	36.4	1.6%	28.7	1.6%
Online course material revenue	138.7	5.6%	104.5	4.6%	69.1	3.8%
Other revenue	31.7	1.3%	33.8	1.5%	23.0	1.3%
Tuition and other revenue, gross	2,582.9	104.3%	2,358.3	104.7%	1,862.4	103.5%
Less: Discounts	(105.4)	(4.3)%	(107.2)	(4.7)%	(62.4)	(3.5)%
Tuition and other revenue, net	$2,477.5	100.0%	$2,251.1	100.0%	$1,800.0	100.0%

Information about our tuition and other net revenues by reportable segment on a percentage basis is as follows:

	Year Ended August 31,		
	2006	**2005**	**2004**
UPX	83.7%	89.5%	94.4%
Other Schools	16.2%	10.4%	5.4%
Corporate	0.1%	0.1%	0.2%
Tuition and other, net	100.0%	100.0%	100.0%

Instructional costs and services increased by 16.3% in 2006 versus 2005, and 22.4% in 2005 versus 2004. The following table sets forth the increases in significant components of instructional costs and services:

	Year Ended August 31,			% of Revenues Year Ended August 31,			% Change 2006 vs. 2005	% Change 2005 vs. 2004
	2006	**2005**	**2004**	**2006**	**2005**	**2004**	**2005**	**2004**
			Restated (1)		Restated (1)			Restated (1)
($ in millions)								
Employee compensation and related expenses	$ 382.3	$343.9	$282.5	15.4%	15.3%	15.7%	11.2%	21.7%
Faculty compensation	212.3	195.1	154.2	8.6%	8.7%	8.6%	8.8%	26.5%
Classroom lease expenses and depreciation	193.4	171.3	145.1	7.8%	7.6%	8.1%	12.9%	18.1%
Other instructional costs and services	158.2	142.0	122.3	6.4%	6.3%	6.8%	11.4%	16.1%
Bad debt expenses	101.6	57.2	31.1	4.1%	2.5%	1.7%	77.6%	83.9%
Financial aid processing costs	52.5	43.3	32.4	2.1%	1.9%	1.8%	21.2%	33.6%
Share based compensation	12.4	3.8	4.0	0.5%	0.2%	0.2%	226.3%	(5.0)%
U.S. Department of Education settlement	—	—	9.8	N/A	N/A	0.5%	N/A	N/A
Instructional costs and services	$1,112.7	$956.6	$781.4	44.9%	42.5%	43.4%	16.3%	22.4%

(1) See Note 3, "Retatement of Consolidated Financial Statements," included in Item 8 of this Form 10-K.

Selling and promotional expenses increased by 12.2% in 2006 versus 2005, and 26.5% in 2005 versus 2004. The following table sets forth the increases in significant components of selling and promotional expenses:

	Year Ended August 31,			% of Revenues Year Ended August 31,			% Change 2006 vs.	% Change 2005 vs.
	2006	2005	2004	2006	2005	2004	2005	2004
		Restated (1)			Restated (1)			Restated (1)
($ in millions)								
Enrollment advisors' compensation and related expenses	$ 254.3	$204.6	$155.6	10.3%	9.1%	8.6%	24.3%	31.5%
Advertising	231.6	224.0	174.6	9.3%	10.0%	9.7%	3.4%	28.3%
Other selling and promotional expenses	56.5	56.2	52.9	2.3%	2.5%	2.9%	0.5%	6.2%
Share based compensation	2.3	0.6	0.7	0.1%	0.0%	0.1%	283.3%	(14.3)%
Selling and promotional expenses	$544.7	$485.4	$383.8	22.0%	21.6%	21.3%	12.2%	26.5%

(1) See Note 3, "Retatement of Consolidated Financial Statement," included in Item 8 of this Form 10-K.

Summary financial information by reportable segment is as follows:

	Year Ended August 31,		
	2006	2005	2004
		Restated	Restated
($ in thousands)			
Tuition and other revenue, net			
UPX	$2,074,443	$2,014,124	$1,699,005
Other Schools	402,051	235,183	96,982
Corporate	1,039	1,807	4,060
Total tuition and other revenue, net	2,477,533	$2,251,114	$1,800,047
Income from operations:			
UPX	605,708	$ 636,463	$ 478,639
Other Schools	65,790	70,417	15,665
Corporate/Eliminations	(21,464)	(9,228)	(44,103)
	650,034	697,652	450,201
Reconciling items:			
Interest income and other, net	18,054	16,787	16,305
Income before income taxes	$ 668,088	$ 714,439	$ 466,506

Case 8

McDonald's and Its Critics, 1973–2009   Isaac Cohen

1   As the McDonald's Corporation entered the 21st century, its corporate practices had become more vulnerable than ever before. A large variety of public interest groups made McDonald's the target of their attacks. McDonald's critics contended that the world's largest fast-food company paid its employees low wages, hired part-time workers—often teenagers—to avoid paying overtime premiums, and enforced an aggressive anti-union policy throughout its fast-food empire. More damaging to McDonald's reputation were charges made by consumer advocates, health officials, and educators that McDonald's exploited children, cultivating in them a taste for fat at an early age and thereby contributing to child obesity. Similarly, public interest groups accused McDonald's of selling unhealthy, fatty foods to grownups, hence being responsible, at least in part, for the increasing rates of adult obesity. Among McDonald's critics, perhaps the most influential was Eric Schlosser, author of the 2001 [book], *Fast Food Nation: The Dark Side of the All-American Meal*, a longstanding best-seller read by millions worldwide, and turned into a major motion picture. In 1999, at the meeting of the World Trade Organization (WTO), anti-globalization protesters attacked McDonald's outlets in Seattle. In 2002, French protesters lead by Jose Bove, a sheep farmer, demolished a McDonald's restaurant under construction in France, and subsequently, Bove gained worldwide fame and a jail sentence. Between 1997 and 2000, several fast-food outlets around the world were damaged by bombs, among them McDonald's restaurants in St. Petersburg, Athens, Rio de Janeiro, Antwerp, London, and Cali, Columbia.[1]

2   These attacks played a considerable role in the company's financial results. In 1998, McDonald's announced its first job cut since it had gone public in 1965, and for the first time, the company recorded a decline in net income. Despite several initiatives promoted by the company's CEO [chief executive officer], Jack Greenberg, business failed to improve and McDonald's performance continued to deteriorate. In 2002, McDonald's closed nearly 200 underperforming units, and at the end of the year, the fast-food giant posted the first quarterly loss in its history. McDonald's financial crisis, in turn, forced Greenberg to resign and the company appointed a new CEO at the beginning of 2003.[2]

WOULD McDONALD'S RECOVER?

3   To assess the ways in which the company responded to the crisis of 1998–2003, the case looks back historically at McDonald's and its critics, exploring the evolution of the company over time. The case begins with the company's foundations laid out by its founder Ray Kroc, and moves on to the food consolidation of the food service network under Fred Turner's direction (1973–1987). The case proceeds with McDonald's global expansion

This case was presented in the June 2009 Meeting of the World Association of Case Method Research and Application at Vancouver, Canada. Copyright Isaac Cohen. I am grateful for the San Jose State University College of Business for its support.

[1] Eric Schlosser, *Fast Food Nation* (New York: Harper, 2005), pp. 244–246; "McDonald's Corporation," *International Directory of Company Histories* (New York: St. James, 204), vol. 63, p. 285.

[2] "McDonald's," *International Directory of Company Histories*, pp. 284–285, "McDonald's," *Hoover's Handbook of American Business*, 2008, p. 557.

under Michael Quinlan's leadership (1987–1998), pays close attention to the growing public criticism of the company, and examines Jack Greenberg's (1998–2003) attempts to address the issues raised by McDonald's critics. Following a brief account of Greenberg's failed leadership, the case moves on to the present, showing how, under Jim Skinner's stewardship (2004–), McDonald's managed to answer its critics, launch successful reforms, and come back strongly as a highly profitable, globally-competitive growth company.

FOUNDATIONS: RAY KROC, 1955–1973

4   The McDonald brothers, Richard and Maurice (Dick & Mac), had operated a carhop drive-in restaurant in San Bernardino, California, since the 1930s. By the early 1950s, the brothers had replaced the carhop service with self service, simplified the menu to offer just hamburgers, cheeseburgers, French fries, milkshakes, soft drinks, and apple pie, and ran the restaurant like an assembly line operation.[3] "[T]he brothers' concept of a limited menu allowed them to break down food preparation into simple, repetitive tasks that could be learned quickly even by those stepping into the commercial kitchen for the first time," McDonald's historian, John Love wrote in 1986. "Typically, there were three 'grill men,' who did nothing but grill hamburgers, two 'shake men,' who did nothing but make milkshakes, two 'fries men,' who specialized in making French fries, two 'dressers,' who dressed and wrapped the hamburgers, and three 'countermen' who did nothing but fill orders at the two customers windows."[4] The resulting labor cost savings, combined with the increased volume of sales, allowed the McDonald brothers to cut the price of a hamburger from 30 to 15 cents.

5   Such was the mode at operation of the San Bernardino restaurant in 1954, when Ray Kroc, a salesman who supplied the McDonald brothers with multi-mixer milkshake machines, decided to travel to California and observe the brothers at work.

6   Inspecting carefully the brothers' operation, Kroc realized that the McDonalds' formula of self service, paper service, and quick service was something radically different from anything hitherto known in the food service industry. He believed the formula was a ticket to business success, and bought from the brothers the rights to set up McDonald's restaurant franchises across the country. Kroc opened his first McDonald's restaurant in Des Plaines, Illinois, near Chicago in 1955, incorporating his company as the McDonald's Corporation. Under Kroc's ownership, McDonald's grew rapidly from 14 restaurants in 1958, to 38 in 1958, 100 in 1959, and 1,000 by 1968. In 1962, McDonald's introduced the world famous Golden Arches logo ("now more widely recognized than the Christian cross," according to 2001 study of McDonald's), and in 1965 the company went public. Twenty years later, in 1985, the McDonald's Corporation joined the 30 companies that made up together the Dow Jones Industrial Average.[5]

7   Kroc's sales background convinced him that the key to successful franchising was uniformity. Uniformity was a revolutionary concept in the food service industry in the 1950s; at the time, franchisers paid little attention to training franchisees, setting quality standards, and supervising purchasing. In a stark contrast to the prevailing practice, Kroc sought to develop standards of operation, to train licensees to meet them, and to monitor restaurants to make sure franchisees followed the standards. From the outset, the

---

[3] "McDonald's," *International Directory of Company Histories,* p. 280.

[4] John Love, *McDonald's Behind the Arches* (New York: Bantam Books, 1986, 1995), pp. 17–18.

[5] "McDonald's," *International Directory of Company Histories,* pp. 280–281. The quotation is from Schlosser, *Fast Food Nation,* p. 5.

hallmark of Kroc's franchise system was commitment to quality, service, and cleanliness (QSC).[6]

8　　Although Kroc managed to obtain strict operating uniformity among franchisees, his centralized system did not stifle individual creativity. On the contrary, franchisees were often innovators. The introduction of the Big Mac menu item was a case in point.

9　　The Big Mac was a double-decker hamburger sold for more than twice the price of a McDonald's regular hamburger. It was developed, tested, and introduced by a Kroc's franchisee from the Pittsburgh, Pennsylvania, area who ran about 12 local McDonald's outlets. To compete successfully with rival brands, the Pittsburgh franchisee asked McDonald's for permission to test a large sandwich he called the "Big Mac." Persuading the chain's top management to broaden the menu was not easy; only after several delays did the franchisee receive corporate permission to test the Big Mac hamburger. The permission was restricted to a single restaurant. Once introduced, the Big Mac increased the restaurant's sales by 10%–12% in a few months. This success soon attracted the attention of McDonald's corporate management. Following repeated visits to the Pittsburgh area restaurants, McDonald's corporate managers tested the Big Mac item in other markets, scoring a 10% gain in sales. McDonald's Corporation finally put the new item into nationwide distribution in 1968, and within less than a year, accounted for nearly 20% of all McDonald's sales. Over time, the Big Mac became McDonald's most recognizable item.[7]

CONSOLIDATION: FRED TURNER, 1973–1987

10　　A year after opening McDonald's first restaurant in Illinois, Ray Kroc hired Fred Turner, a 23-year-old college dropout, to manage one of his restaurants. An ambitious fast learner who paid close attention to details, Turner mastered the task of overseeing restaurant operations at a remarkable speed. In 1957, Kroc asked Turner to train new franchisees, and develop standard operating procedures for all franchised restaurants. Leading McDonald's operation division during the late 1950s and 1960s, Turner laid the foundation for a successful franchise system that lasted well into the 21st century.

Management Science

11　　From the outset, Turner attempted to turn the task of running a restaurant from an art to a science. Shortly after joining McDonald's, Turner drafted a 15-page training manual, which expanded to 75 pages two years later, and 360 pages by 1974. Turner's training manual converted the systematic knowledge the McDonald's corporation gained from operating its franchises into a "management science."[8]

12　　In part, the manual was a time and motion study that defined operating techniques in minute details. It instructed operators how to grill hamburgers, fry potatoes, and prepare milkshakes. It specified cooking times for all food items, the precise temperature setting for each cooking equipment, and the standard portions of all products. It established quality control measures unknown in the food service industry at the time (for example, meat and potatoes items held in a serving bin for over 10 minutes needed to be discarded). And describing food service as an assembly line operation, the manual told franchisees how to staff each "station," and the optimal size of crew members needed for each shift of operation.

---

[6] Love, *McDonald's Behind the Arches,* pp. 114–116.

[7] Love, *McDonald's Behind the Arches,* pp. 293–295.

[8] Max Boas and Steve Chain, *Big Mac: The Unauthorized Story of McDonald's* (New York: New American Library, 1976), p. 72; Love, *McDonald's Behind the Arches,* p. 140.

13 Turner's manual, in addition, showed operators how to prepare work schedules, financial reports, and sales projections. To calculate operating costs, franchisees were told to break down expenses for labor, food, and non-food supplies. To better plan future purchasing, the manual instructed operators to break down sales by food items. Such information helped franchisees track down inventories, control costs, detect quality problems, and forecast demand.[9]

Training

14 McDonald's operations manual was the main text used in classes taught at the "Hamburger University" (HU), a training center set up under Turner's supervision. Conferring a degree in "Hamburgerology," the university expanded from a one classroom school in 1961 to a $500,000 facility in 1968, and a $40 million campus in 1983. In 1973, the year Turner succeeded Kroc as McDonald's CEO, the HU turned out 150 graduates each month, offering several classes simultaneously. Altogether, about 7,000 trainees graduated from the University between 1961 and 1973. Classes were taught in three areas—food, equipment, and management techniques—and course titles included "Buns," "Shortening," "Hot Apple Pie," "Basic Refrigeration," "Frozen Products Care," "Management Decision Skills," and "Competition." By 1983, the university employed 30 faculty members and had an overall capacity to train 750 students in seven auditorium classrooms. It was the only school in the fast-food industry accredited by the American Council of Education.[10]

Supervising Franchisees

15 Beginning in 1957 Kroc asked Turner to visit franchisees and to evaluate the performance of their restaurants. Early on, Turner drafted a seven page "field service report," and soon thereafter, he developed a more detailed report that evaluated franchisees' performance in four areas—service, quality, cleanliness, and overall performance—and assigned them a summary grade (A, B, C, D, or F). The McDonald's Corporation, in turn, created a new position of "Field Consultant," and by the mid 1960s, it employed several full-time consultants whose specialty was visiting stores and inspecting their compliance with McDonald's operating standards. The field service report played a key role in the decision to grant or deny existing franchisees permission to operate additional restaurants. Under Turner's leadership, furthermore, the consultant position had become a prerequisite for promotion; managers wishing to climb up the corporate ladder were required to have experience working as field consultants.

16 Over time, the McDonald's Corporation invested heavily in expanding its field service operation. By 1992, McDonald's spent $27 million to employ more than 300 full-time field consultants. Each consultant was expected to visit and grade 21 restaurants several times a year. The grade a restaurant received determined its "expandability" as well as its future prospects; a B grade was now necessary for getting a license to operate additional stores.[11]

Management Style

17 As Turner became president in 1968, he began decentralizing McDonald's organizational structure. He first increased the number of regional offices from five in 1967 to 12 in 1975, and then expanded the authority of regional managers. Under Turner's revamped structure, decisions on both granting franchises and selecting new restaurant sites were made by

---

[9] Love, *McDonald's Behind the Arches,* pp. 140–141.

[10] Boas and Chain, *Big Mac,* Chapter 5; Love, *McDonald's Behind the Arches,* pp. 147–149.

[11] Love, *McDonald's Behind the Arches,* pp. 144–146.

regional managers, not corporate officers. In the food service industry, Turner observed, "the closer decision making is to the stores and the marketplace, the better the decision that managers make," and accordingly, McDonald's growth decisions in each region were narrowly tailored to local conditions. The result was rapid expansion. During Turner's first five years as president (1968–1973), annual sales per restaurant almost doubled, and the total number of McDonald's outlets tripled.[12]

Advertising

18 One of McDonald's most successful advertising projects involved its corporate mascot "Ronald McDonald." The ad project was launched in the early 1960s when a team of company marketers created a clown character named Ronald, and featured it on local TV. Soon becoming the national spokesperson for the chain, Ronald McDonald had a magic touch with children, and gave the company an important advantage over its competitors in the children's market. By the mid 1960s, most of McDonald's advertising budget was spent on promoting Ronald McDonald on national TV, and spending on its ads rose precipitously. In 1967, McDonald's national advertising budget totaled $5 million, in 1969 $15 million, and by 1974 it climbed to $60 million, placing McDonald's among the nation's top 30 advertisers. Under Turner's direction, Ronald McDonald's role expanded beyond TV ads. In the mid 1970s, some 50 Ronald McDonald "greeting" and "performing" clowns were employed by the corporation, and live Ronald McDonald clowns attended birthday parties held for children in restaurants. A variety of Ronald items that included Ronald dolls, wristwatches, and wall clocks were sold in the stores.[13]

19 McDonald's appeal to children had remained powerful long after Turner stepped down. In 1992, McDonald's delivered 40% of the fast food sold to children under seven, a figure widely exceeding its 33% total share in the fast-food market. A 1996 survey of American school children found that fully 96% of all children could identify Ronald McDonald; the only fictional character more recognizable to American children was Santa Claus. A Ronald McDonald Web site operating since the late 1990s encouraged children to send Ronald an e-mail listing their favorite menu items at the chain.[14]

McDonald's Under Attack: Franchisees' Rights

20 During Turner's tenure as president and CEO, McDonald's faced two major problems, one pertaining to franchisee relations, the other to employee relations.

21 From the start, not all franchisees were willing to accept McDonald's tight control over their store operations. In the mid 1970s, a group of about 50 franchisees staged an open rebellion against McDonald's, establishing their own organization, the McDonald's Operators Association (MOA). The dissident group had two major complaints. First, franchisees resented McDonald's prerogative to revoke their initial franchise at the end of a 20-year contract. Second, franchisees complained about the loss of sales at existing McDonald's restaurants caused by the opening of new McDonald's outlets nearby.

22 To diffuse this threat of dissention, Turner promptly embarked on reform. He established the National Operators Advisory Board (NOAB), a representative body composed of two elected franchisees from each region, which dealt with policy issues pertaining to McDonald's relationships with its franchisees. In addition, Turner appointed an ombudsman who heard franchisees' complaints and issued advisory judgments.

---

[12] Love, *McDonald's Behind the Arches,* pp. 280–281, but see also p. 385.

[13] Boas and Chain, *Big Mac,* Chapter 7; but see also Love, *McDonald's Behind the Arches,* pp. 220–221.

[14] Love, *McDonald's Behind the Arches,* p. 222; Schlosser, *Fast Food Nation,* pp. 4, 45, 294.

23   Turner's reform measures eroded the foundations of the MOA. Losing members and sympathizers, the dissident group of franchisees survived for just two years, 1975–1977.[15]

McDonald's Under Attack: Union Rights

24   Turner was the architect of McDonald's longstanding labor policy of keeping unions out. In the late 1960s, he commissioned a study of McDonald's labor relations from a management consulting firm in Chicago, finding out that the chain's outlets were all vulnerable to union organizing. Turner then hired John Cooke, a labor management consultant who was a former union organizer. Overseeing McDonald's labor relations in the late 1960s and 1970s, Cooke trained store managers to detect union threats; he organized "flying squads" of experienced managers who quickly arrived at any restaurant suspected of becoming a target for union organizing and held "rap sessions" with the employees to defeat the organizing drive. Altogether, Turner and Cooke managed to turn back more than 400 organizing drives at McDonald's outlets.

25   Using flying squads, closing down restaurants threatened by union organizing, and hiring anti-union labor lawyers were among the tactics used successfully by McDonald's to remain union free for the next three decades. In 2006, McDonald's operated nearly 14,000 restaurants in the United States, none of which were unionized.[16]

EXPANSION: MICHAEL QUINLAN, 1987–1998

26   Michael Quinlan succeeded Fred Turner as president in 1982 and CEO in 1987. Quinlan began his career at McDonald's mailroom in 1963 and steadily worked his way up. A low profile, reserved manager who, unlike his two predecessors, did not seek the limelight, Quinlan was the first McDonald's CEO to hold an MBA degree. A shrewd competitor who combined street smarts with boardroom skills, Quinlan's reputation for informality combined with his hands-off management style helped him gain popularity among McDonald's employees. Leading the company through the late 1980s and 1990s, Quinlan transformed McDonald's into a global empire, extending the chain's reach to over 100 national markets.[17]

Customer Service

27   Launched by Quinlan early on, McDonald's Service Enhancement Program was a customer care initiative. Implemented throughout McDonald's 12,000 restaurants, the program sought to empower employees at all levels to do "whatever it takes" to satisfy customers' requests. To improve customer service, the company conducted face-to-face orientation with each crew member employed at any of the chain's outlets. Using consumer focus groups, employee "rap sessions," complaint tracking systems, and other service enhancement techniques, the program differentiated customer service at McDonald's from service at competing chains. McDonald's employees were encouraged to solve problems on the spot, were empowered to settle disputes with customers without calling the manager, and were rewarded for exemplary customer care. Store managers, similarly, were instructed to spend more time with customers, listening to their concerns.[18]

[15] Boas and Chain, *Big Mac,* Chapter 9; Love, *McDonald's Behind the Arches,* Chapter 16.

[16] Love, *McDonald's Behind the Arches,* pp. 394–395; Boas and Chain, *Big Mac,* Chapter 10; Schlosser, *Fast Food Nation,* pp. 76–78.

[17] "McDonald's Names Quinlan as Chief, Succeeding Turner," *Wall Street Journal,* October 21, 1986; "McDonald's," *International Directory of Company Histories,* pp. 280–281.

[18] Michel Quinlan, "How Does Service Drive the Service Company?" *Harvard Business Review,* November–December 1991, p. 146; Love, *McDonald's Behind the Arches,* pp. 459–460.

Cost Cutting

28   Another initiative introduced by Quinlan was cost cutting. Under Quinlan's direction, McDonald's lowered its restaurants' construction costs by three means; first, redesigning restaurant buildings; second, using more efficient construction methods; and third, substituting pricy materials with cheaper alternatives. As a result, the average restaurant's construction cost fell by 27% between 1990 and 1993. Next, McDonald's reduced the insurance costs of U.S. restaurants by giving franchisees the opportunity to choose among eight competing insurance companies rather than offering them a single company-approved insurance program. The flexibility of selecting an insurer through competitive bidding resulted in cost savings of about $50 million annually across 9,300 U.S. outlets in the mid-1990s (or $4,000 per restaurant).

29   In addition, the company introduced its newly designed "mini McDonald's" in the early 1990s—an outlet which occupied half the floor space of the standard restaurant but was capable of handling an equal volume of sales. Building a mini McDonald's was 30% cheaper than the construction costs of "full sized" restaurants, and as a consequence, the break-even point of the smaller units was considerably lower than that of the larger ones. Low cost mini McDonald's made up 60% of all restaurant openings in 1992 and 80% in 1993.

30   Finally, in the early and mid-1990s, McDonald's expanded aggressively into small-size non-traditional sites, thereby lowering its operating and construction costs in still another way. McDonald's opened restaurants in hospitals, military bases, gas stations, shopping malls, recreation sites, sport stadiums, and big box retail stores like Wal-Mart.[19]

International Expansion

31   McDonald's international presence dates back to the mid-1960s. Historically, McDonald's entered most foreign markets by means of joint ventures with local partners. To ensure uniform standards, the McDonald's Corporation sought a greater degree of control over foreign than domestic operations. In most cases, McDonald's formed partnerships with local entrepreneurs acting as franchisees and owning 50% of the business. If successful, the foreign entrepreneur might buy McDonald's 50% share in the business, and become a full fledged franchisee.

32   During Quinlan's first five years at the helm, McDonald's international sales nearly tripled from $3 to $8.6 billion, and the share of its overseas sales grew from 27% to nearly 40%. In 1992, one in three McDonald's outlets was located overseas, McDonald's operated in 65 countries, and its leading foreign markets were Japan (865 stores), Canada (642 stores), and the UK (445 stores). By 1994, the "Big Six" foreign markets—Japan, Canada, UK, Australia, France, and Germany—accounted for 80% of McDonald's foreign income.[20]

33   Two milestones in McDonald's international expansion were its entry into the Russian and Chinese markets. Following some 20 years of negotiations with the Soviet authorities, McDonald's opened its first restaurant in Moscow in 1990—its largest single unit employing a crew of 1,200, and serving 50,000 customers a day. Two years later, McDonald's opened its first restaurant in Beijing, drawing some 40,000 customers a day. Working closely with the Chinese government to establish a web of suppliers who would deliver 95% of its products (beef, chicken, fish, potatoes, lettuce, and beverages), McDonald's opened 100 additional outlets in Beijing and other Chinese cities by 1996.[21]

---

[19] Love, *McDonald's Behind the Arches,* pp. 461–462.

[20] Love, *McDonald's Behind the Arches,* pp. 416, 462–463.

[21] Tony Royle, *Working in McDonald's in Europe* (London: Routledge, 2000), pp. 24–25; Love, *McDonald's Behind the Arches,* pp. 464–466.

34   During the late 1990s, the pace of international expansion accelerated further. Between 1994 and 1998, McDonald's opened 5,800 new restaurants abroad, more than the total number added by its five largest competitors combined. In 1997, 85% of McDonald's new restaurant openings took place abroad, and McDonald's replaced Coca-Cola as the world's best known brand. Altogether, during Quinlan's 10-year tenure, McDonald's foreign sales were growing at a rate of 18.2%; the corresponding figure for its domestic sales was 5.6%. "We are light years ahead of where we were five years ago," Quinlan said in 1994, adding "our international potential is boundless." With restaurants operating in 109 countries in 1998, McDonald's was serving less than 1% of the world population, according to a company spokesperson.[22]

McDonald's in Crisis

35   While McDonald's expanded rapidly into foreign markets, domestic sales languished. First, a variety of new products introduced by Quinlan in the 1990s—vegetable burgers, pasta, fried chicken, fajitas, and pizza—did not catch on and were later withdrawn (McDonald's last successful [new] product was the Chicken Nugget launched in 1983).[23]

36   Second, McDonald's again faced a growing revolt among some 300 embittered franchisees. A San Diego-based group of franchisees called "Consortium" claimed that many of the new restaurants opened recently by McDonald's were cannibalizing the business of existing restaurants and driving operators out of business. Under Quinlan's direction, McDonald's embarked on a major U.S. expansion just as domestic sales were slowing down. "They built a whole bunch of new stores in the wrong places," the dissident group's leader told *BusinessWeek* in 1998. During the 1990s, franchisees' per store profits declined by 30%, and a 1997 survey among McDonald's domestic operators revealed that only 28% of the franchisees believed McDonald's was on the right track.[24]

37   Third, McDonald's was losing market share. A 1998 Harris poll showed that fast-food consumers preferred Wendy's and Burger King's offerings over McDonald's. Altogether, McDonald's share in the domestic fast-food market dropped from 18% to 16% between 1987 and 1998, and its per share profits in the United States fell by 20% (or 40% after inflation) in the decade ending March 1998. During Quinlan's last two years at the top (March 1996 to March 1998), the company's share price inched up 3% while the Standard and Poor's stock index climbed 63%.[25]

CRISIS: JACK GREENBERG, 1998–2003

38   As Quinlan stepped down in May 1998, McDonald's board of directors selected Jack Greenberg to lead the company. On the day the board announced the new CEO, Greenberg called each of McDonald's 20 largest shareholders, including Warren Buffett, telling them "I'm a different person, I'll have a different style." Wall Street responded enthusiastically; McDonald's stock gained 4% on the day of the announcement.[26]

---

[22] J. P. Donlon, "Quinlan Fries Harder," *Chief Executive,* January/February 1998, online ABI database, Start Page 4. The quotation is from Love, *McDonald's Behind the Arches,* p. 463.

[23] "McDonald's," *International Directory of Company Histories,* pp. 280–281; David Leonhardt, "McDonald's: Can It Regain Its Golden Touch?" *BusinessWeek,* March 9, 1998, online ABI database, Start Page 70.

[24] *BusinessWeek,* March 9, 1998.

[25] *BusinessWeek,* March 9, 1998.

[26] Patricia Sellers, "McDonald's Starts Over," *Fortune,* June 22, 1998, online, ABI database, Start Page 122.

39   Unlike Quinlan and Turner, Greenberg was the first senior manager at McDonald's recruited from outside the firm. A former partner in the accounting firm of Arthur Young, he joined McDonald's in 1982 as the company's chief financial officer (CFO). Ambitious, he undertook training in operations and later became a regional manager of hundreds of stores while still serving as CFO. After running McDonald's U.S. unit between 1996 and 1998, he was named CEO.[27]

40   Widely described as an "agent of change," Greenberg launched a strategy aimed at "recasting the image of McDonald's from a stodgy consumer products company to a dynamic global brand [in the words of one industry analyst]." Impressed by his initial efforts to reinvent McDonald's, editors of *Restaurants and Institutions* named Greenberg the magazine's 1999 Executive of the Year.[28]

41   Greenberg broke with tradition in three different ways. First, he departed from Kroc's decades-long practice of relying almost exclusively on homegrown talent, and instead hired outside executives from other firms.[29] Second, Greenberg did not conform to Kroc's model of offering a uniform, unchanging menu of a few standardized items but rather changed McDonald's menu to an extent previously unknown. And third, Greenberg sought growth through mergers, a policy violating Kroc's unbroken rule of focusing on the McDonald's brand, and the McDonald's brand only.

New Menu

42   The idea of expanding McDonald's limited menu dated back to the mid-1990s. As McDonald's marketers found out that customers preferred Wendy's and Burger King's products, Quinlan sought to improve the chain's competitive position by offering a new menu. The new expanded menu developed under Greenberg's supervision at the time he ran McDonald's domestic operation. Once promoted to CEO in 1998, Greenberg moved aggressively to implement the new project.

43   The expanded menu required a new food preparation system based on the "just in time" principle of product customization. To accommodate customers' preferences, McDonald's offered customers a variety of new items—for example, a chicken sandwich—made to order, a choice readily available in menus offered by Burger King and Wendy's. Dubbed "Made For You," the new food preparation system was intended to improve the quality of the food served as well as facilitate the development of additional food innovations.

44   Greenberg implemented the "Made For You" project at a remarkable speed. By the spring of 2000, the new system was fully installed in the company's 12,500 domestic restaurants. Yet the changeover was not cheap. Installing the new kitchen cost about $25,000 per restaurant, and many franchisees were reluctant to cover the installation cost. To provide franchisees with an incentive, McDonald's paid up to 50% of the unit's installation cost.[30]

Acquisitions

45   Greenberg moved quickly towards the acquisition of additional brands. He sought to broaden "the view of the brand," transforming McDonald's single-line brand into a multiple

[27] *Fortune,* June 22, 1998.

[28] The quotations, in order, are from *Fortune,* June 22, 1998, and Scott Hume, "Jack Greenberg's New Populism," *Restaurants and Institutions,* July 1, 1999, online, ABI database, Start Page 109.

[29] Dayan Machan, "Polishing the Golden Arches," *Forbes,* June 15, 1998, online, ABI database, Start Page 42.

[30] Amy Zuber, "Jack Greenberg: Bringing New Luster to the Golden Arches," *Nation's Restaurants News,* January 2000, online, ABI database, Start Page 90; *Fortune,* June 22, 1998; *Restaurants and Institutions,* July 1, 1999.

line of different brands. "[We are] selling hamburgers and chicken under the McDonald's brand, pizza under the Donatos brand . . . and burritos under the Chipotle brand," he told the *Foreign Policy* journal in 2001, listing two of his recent acquisitions.[31]

46   McDonald's had never before taken control of another food chain. In early 1998, as Quinlan was getting ready to step down, McDonald's made its first acquisition, purchasing a minority interest in the Colorado-based Chipotle Mexican Grill chain. Greenberg followed up with other acquisitions. He first bought Aroma Café, a London chain of 23 coffee and sandwich shops and next purchased the 150-unit Midwestern chain Donatos Pizza, both in 1999. A year later, in 2000, Greenberg completed his largest acquisition, buying Boston Market, a network of some 850 restaurants specializing in serving home style meals (with rotisserie chicken as the chain's best selling item). Greenberg, in addition, bought a 33% stake in Pret A Manger, an upscale chain of 110 stores selling fresh sandwiches in the United Kingdom. And lastly, he increased McDonald's controlling interest at Chipotle to more than 50%.[32]

The Attacks on McDonald's

47   While Greenberg was busy purchasing regional chains, a worldwide campaign against the fast-food industry—launched by public interest groups, environmentalists, and consumer advocates—was in full swing. A major event that galvanized the campaign was the publication in 2001 of Eric Schlosser's *Fast Food Nation*. Translated to many languages, the best-selling book focused, among other things, on the recent increase in child obesity, and placed the responsibility for such a development on strategies undertaken by the global fast-food chains. It singled out McDonald's as the principal culprit, generating unfavorable publicity, and damaging McDonald's reputation. "Schlosser has done for the fast-food industry what Upton Sinclair did nearly a century ago [for] . . . the meatpacking industry in *The Jungle*," one writer reviewing the book commented.[33]

48   Another event generating negative publicity directed at McDonald's was the 2000 trial of Jose Bove, a farmer and social activist. Leading a group of protesters, Bove destroyed a half-built McDonald's outlet in Millau, France, published a French best-seller targeting McDonald's "lousy food" *(The World Is Not for Sale—and Nor Am I!)*, and was briefly imprisoned. Blaming McDonald's for undermining traditional farming methods with agribusiness practices, Bove became a hero in France, and was invited to meet France's president as well as its prime minister. French President Jacques Chirac expressed his sympathy with Bove when he declared: "I am in complete solidarity with Frances's farm workers, and I detest McDonald's," and French Prime Minister Lionel Jospin agreed: "I am personally not very pro McDonald's." Similarly, in Britain, the Duke of Edinburgh, Prince Philip commented: "[McDonald's is] destroying the rainforests of the world . . . cutting down trees to graze [its] cheap cattle to sell [its] hamburgers."[34]

49   Even more damaging to McDonald's reputation was the so called "McLibel Trial." The famous libel trial was the focus of a longstanding and tenacious campaign launched by Greenpeace activists in London against McDonald's.

50   In 1986, several members of Greenpeace in London distributed a six-page leaflet accusing McDonald's of selling unhealthy food, exploiting children, mistreating workers,

---

[31] Moises Haim, "McAtlas Shrugged," *Foreign Policy,* May/June 2001, online ABI database, Start Page 124.

[32] "McDonald's," *International Directory of Company Histories,* p. 284; *Nation's Restaurants News,* January 2000.

[33] Reprinted in Eric Schlosser, *Fast Food Nation,* under "Praise for Fast Food Nation."

[34] Eric Schlosser, *Fast Food Nation,* p. 244. The quotation is from *Foreign Policy,* May/June 2001.

destroying rain forests, and torturing animals. A series of slogans—"McDollars," "McGreedy," "McCancer," "McMurder," "McProfits," "McGarbage," —sprinkled with the golden arches was printed along the top edge of the leaflet. The activist group distributed the leaflet for four years until the McDonald's Corporation decided to sue five group members for libel in 1990, claiming the entire content of the leaflet was false. Soon thereafter, three of the accused settled, apologizing to McDonald's. The two remaining activists were determined to fight back in court, and fight to the end.

51   The libel trial turned into a public spectacle. It produced 18,000 pages of transcript and 40,000 pages of documents and witness statements. It began in 1994 and ended in 1997 with an 800-page judgment. The judge found the two Greenpeace defendants guilty of libeling McDonald's, imposed a combined fine of 60,000 Sterling on both, and ruled nontheless that some allegations were true: McDonald's did indeed "exploit children" through advertising, paid workers lower wages, and served an unhealthy diet (increasing "the risk of cancer of the bowel and of the breast to some extent"). These allegations were widely publicized.[35]

52   Next, the two Greenpeace defendants appealed the verdict to the UK's Court of Appeal. In 1999, one year into the Greenberg tenure, a three justice Court of Appeal heard the case, overturned parts of the original verdict (supporting, for example, the allegation that eating food served by McDonald's may increase the risk of heart disease), and reduced the fine to 40,000 Sterling. In the meantime, the activists' campaign against McDonald's intensified. The McDonald's corporation wanted the case to go away and announced that it would no longer try to stop Greenpeace members from distributing the leaflet.

53   Still, the two Greenpeace defendants were not done. They appealed the Court of Appeal's ruling to the British House of Lords. When the Lords refused to hear the case, the defendants filed an appeal with the European Court of Human Rights. As of 2002—Greenberg's last year at McDonald's—the appeal to the European Court was still pending.[36]

Financial Results

54   Under Greenberg's leadership, McDonald's financial performance had remained lackluster. The introduction of the expanded menu failed to increase sales, the new acquisitions produced disappointing results, and the global attack on McDonald's public image turned customers away.

55   To begin with, the "Made For You" system was too labor intensive, and as such, increased both implementation costs and service times. A company internal document obtained by *Fortune* magazine in 2002 cited "alarming research" showing serious problems with customer service. "Mystery shoppers" hired by the company to visit restaurants found that operators met their "speed-to-service" standards only 46% of the time. It also cited complaints about "rude service, slow service, unprofessional service, and inaccurate service." The *Strategy Direction* journal, similarly, reported in 2003 that in recent years waiting time at McDonald's restaurants doubled, commenting: "[t]aking some of the "fast" away from fast food has not proven especially popular with customers." Additionally, surveys published in the American Customer Survey Index showed that customer satisfaction at McDonald's fell well below the levels at Wendy's and Burger King, its two direct competitors.[37]

56   Nor did the regional chains bought by Greenberg perform as expected. Underperforming, the newly acquired chains were sold one after another during the six-year period

[35] The quotations, in order, are from Eric Schlosser, *Fast Food Nation,* pp. 245–247, and John Vidal, *McLibel: Burger Culture on Trial* (New York: New Press, 1997), p. 306.

[36] Eric Schlosser, *Fast Food Nation,* p. 249.

[37] David Stired, "Fast Food, Slow Service," *Fortune,* September 30, 2002, online ABI database, Start Page 38; "Has McDonald's Lost Its Plot?" *Strategic Direction,* April 2003, online ABI database, Start Page 14.

2001–2006. In 2001, McDonald's sold off the Aroma Café chain, and in 2003, shortly after Greenberg had stepped down, McDonald's announced that it would henceforth focus on its core hamburger business and sell off other ventures. In 2003, McDonald's sold Donatos Pizza back to its founder, and disposed of all Boston Market outlets outside the U.S. In 2006, McDonald's sold off the Chipotle chain, and in 2007 it divested itself completely of Boston Market, selling the chain to a private equity firm for $250 million.[38]

57   The global criticism of McDonald's hurt the company's financial performance as well. In the United States, the image of McDonald's as a seller of unhealthy, fatty food triggered an increasing number of lawsuits filed against the company by consumers alleging that eating regularly at McDonald's made them overweight. Overseas, the "McLibel Trial" turned into a public relations disaster as it gained worldwide publicity—the Greenpeace leaflet alone was translated to 27 languages. One likely result of the global attack on McDonald's public image was the company's decision to pull out of several countries, including Bolivia and two Middle Eastern nations.[39]

58   The decline in McDonald's performance under Greenberg's direction was evident across several key financial indices. During both 2000 and 2001, same store sales—sales at restaurants opened more than a year—fell and McDonald's U.S. market share was growing at a slower rate (2.2%) than that of Burger King (2.7%) and Wendy's (2.5%). In 2002, McDonald's stock price was trading at a seven-year low, and during seven of the eight quarters ending summer 2002, McDonald's earnings declined. As McDonald's disclosed its third quarter results in December 2002—showing no improvement—Greenberg announced his resignation.[40]

COMEBACK: JIM SKINNER, 2004–

59   McDonald's board elected James Cantalupo, a former head of the company's international operations, to succeed Greenberg, and added two other senior executives to a newly formed turnaround team: Charles Bell and Jim Skinner. A year later Cantalupo died of a heart attack, and Bell, in turn, assumed the company's leadership. Stepping down a few months later to fight a battle against terminal cancer, Bell himself was succeeded by Skinner in November 2004.[41]

60   Unlike Greenberg, Skinner was a McDonald's insider, as were both Quinlan and Turner. The son of a bricklayer, Skinner started his career at McDonald's flipping hamburgers at an Iowa restaurant in 1962. Never graduating from college, he steadily made his way up the corporate ladder, and eventually took charge of McDonald's Europe operation. In 2003, McDonald's board promoted Skinner to vice chairman, and a year later to CEO.[42]

[38] "McDonald's," *International Directory of Company Histories,* pp. 284–285; McDonald's Corporation, "History," Hoovers.Com, retrieved May 27, 2008.

[39] Eric Schlosser, *Fast Food Nation,* p. 249; "McDonald's," *International Directory of Company Histories,* pp. 284–285.

[40] "McDonald's," *International Directory of Company Histories,* pp. 284–285; Kate MacArthur, "McD's Boss Blasts Chain 'Naysayers,' " *Advertising Age,* March 18, 2002, online ABI database, Start Page 11; Shirley Leung, "McDonald's Chief Plans to Leave," *Wall Street Journal,* December 6, 2002.

[41] Dale Buss, "McDonald's Salad Days," *Chief Executive,* November 2005, online ABI database, Start Page 16.

[42] Carolyn Walkup, "2006 Golden Chain: Jim Skinner," *Nation's Restaurant News,* October 16, 2006, online ABI database, Start Page 88; Andrew Martin, "The Happiest Meal," *New York Times,* January 11, 2009; Lauren Foster and Jeremy Grant, "McDonald's Woos Its 'Burger Flippers,' " *Financial Times,* April 15, 2005.

61   Skinner was a congenial, low-profile chief executive who ate daily at McDonald's, stopping regularly at restaurants to mingle with employees, often jumping in to help the kitchen crew at the back end of the restaurant ("I don't touch the cash register. I don't know anything about [it]"). "He's very down-to-earth, rooted and very approachable," a McDonald's supplier described Skinner. "He's extremely witty and has a great way of putting people at ease." Popular with both subordinates and peers, Skinner was a good listener and a skilled consensus builder; he routinely brought managers with different viewpoints together soliciting their advice before undertaking important decisions.[43]

62   Working together with Cantalupo and Bell to turn McDonald's performance around, Skinner helped forge a new strategic initiative called "Plan to Win." Implemented company-wide during Skinner's first four years at the helm (2004–2008), the plan prescribed two principal goals: first, the upgrading of customer service in order to improve financial performance of existing restaurants (rather than open new ones), and second, the introduction of nutritional, healthful, and higher quality food choices coupled with the promotion of a "balanced life style."

Improving Stores' Operations

63   Under the leadership of both Quinlan and Greenberg, McDonald's expanded aggressively, building an excessive number of new restaurants, many of which were cutting into the profits of existing ones. In addition, customer service at McDonald's had steadily deteriorated, reaching its lowest level during Greenberg's last two years in office, as noted.

64   Skinner's "Plan to Win" was designed to address both problems. First, McDonald's expanded internally, investing in existing stores instead of adding new locations. Most existing stores were redecorated, and thousands were completely remodeled. Aided by the company, franchisees replaced crumbling plastic booths with large comfortable chairs, installed soft lights in place of bright ones, repainted the walls, and added Internet access. Selected McDonald's outlets went further, displaying wide-screen televisions, installing video games, and placing stationary bicycles with video screens in a new play area within the restaurant.[44]

65   To bring in new customers as well as attract old ones, store hours were extended. Opening earlier and closing late, restaurants could now serve both early risers and late night diners. By 2009, fully 34% of McDonald's stores in the United States were open 24 hours.[45]

66   Another initiative undertaken by Skinner was diversification into premium coffee drinks. Competing head-to-head with the Starbucks Corporation, McDonald's began installing coffee bars ("McCafés") with "baristas" preparing espressos, cappuccinos, and lattes in its McDonald's U.S. restaurants. To begin with, McDonald's marketing department conducted a large scale study of Starbucks' customers. Interviewing and videotaping respondents talking about their coffee drinking experiences, and offering them espresso drinks at McDonald's, the study found that a large number of Starbucks' customers were sitting "on the fence" ready to experiment with McDonald's choices of espresso drinks—all of which were sold at a price lower than Starbucks'. Encouraged by its findings, the McDonald's Corporation implemented the program promptly, and by 2007, 800 McDonald's U.S. restaurants were serving espresso drinks. McDonald's installed 5,700 additional "McCafés" in

---

[43] The quotations, in order, are from *New York Times,* January 11, 2009, and *Nation's Restaurant News,* October 16, 2006.

[44] Janet Adamy, "Boss Talk: How Jim Skinner Flipped McDonald's?" *Wall Street Journal,* January 5, 2007; "McDonald's Takes on a Weakened Starbucks," *Wall Street Journal,* January 7, 2008; *New York Times,* January 11, 2009.

[45] *New York Times,* January 11, 2009.

its U.S. restaurants in 2008, bringing the total to 6,500 out of some 14,000 outlets operating nationwide at the end of the year. In the meantime, the Starbucks Corporation was struggling, closing down stores and laying off employees for the first time in its history.[46]

Answering Its Critics

67 Fast food nutritional critics continued to target McDonald's long after Greenberg stepped down. In 2004, as Skinner assumed the company's leadership, a documentary film entitled "Super Size Me" was released and played in movie theaters around the world. The film depicted a man getting increasingly sick as he consumed an all-McDonald's diet and nothing else for a whole month.[47]

68   The renewed attack on McDonald's required a speedy response. Skinner, accordingly, discontinued the chain's Super Size menu and substituted healthier food choices; in 2004, McDonald's promoted fruit and milk as substitutes for French fries and soda drinks in kids' meals, and, for a limited period, added a bottle of water and a pedometer to adults' "Happy Meals." In addition, McDonald's offered customers deli sandwiches, served on either French or rye rolls, a new line of premium salads, and apple slices. Milk was no longer sold in large size cartons but in small bottles.[48]

69   In 2005–2006, McDonald's launched a Balanced Lifestyle (smart eating) and Fitness program, and re-focused its marketing strategy on exercising. In a typical ad released in 2006, Ronald McDonald is featured as an "ambassador of balanced lifestyle," and is depicted in a running position.[49]

70   McDonald's promotion of healthier food choices was not confined to the U.S. but extended to Europe. In Britain, in the mid-2000s, McDonald's reduced the salt added to French fries and chicken nuggets by 25%–30%, and in Ireland by 50%. McDonald's also provided consumers with nutritional information, labeling all its products, and listing the products' fat and salt contents on signposts placed in stores. In both the United States and Europe, McDonald's phased out completely trans-fats in 2008, using a newly developed blend of canola, corn, and soybean oils to cook French fries, hash browns, chicken, and fish filet.[50]

71   Still, the most far-reaching change in McDonald's food offerings under Skinner was the shift from beef to chicken products. In 2009, McDonald's menu included four chicken choices: grilled chicken sandwich, Southern-style chicken sandwich, wrap chicken sandwich, and chicken for breakfast. Between 2002 and 2009, chicken sales at McDonald's doubled while beef sales remained flat, and by 2009, the McDonald's Corporation was purchasing annually more chicken than beef worldwide.[51]

72   McDonald's nutritional efforts did not go unnoticed by its critics. Kelly Brownell, director of the Rudd Center of Food Policy and Obesity at Yale University, pointed out that McDonald's was more responsive to critics than its competitors. "As fast food restaurants go, McDonald's has been pretty progressive," Brownell told the *New York Times* in 2009. "If

[46] *Wall Street Journal,* January 7, 2008; *New York Times,* January 11, 2009; Janet Adamy, "McDonald's to Expand, Posting Strong Results," *Wall Street Journal,* January 27, 2009.

[47] Steven Gray and Janet Adamy, "McDonald's Gets Healthier," *Wall Street Journal,* February 23, 2005.

[48] Amy Garber, "New McD Chief," *Nation's Restaurant News,* December 13, 2004, online ABI database, Start Page 50; *Chief Executive,* November 2005.

[49] Janet Adamy and Richard Gibson, "McDonald's Readies Strategy to Deflect Critics' Next Barrage," *Wall Street Journal,* April 12, 2006.

[50] Joanne Bowery, "McDonald's Gets Back to Basics," *Marketing,* October 25, 2006, online ABI database, Start Page 16; Janet Adamy, "McDonald's Loses Its Trans Fats," *Wall Street Journal,* May 23, 2008.

[51] *New York Times,* January 11, 2009.

you look at the last five years, McDonald's has introduced some better foods and resisted the urge to offer bigger burgers."[52]

Financial Results

73　Skinner's turnaround efforts resulted in a resounding success: during Skinner's first four years at the helm, McDonald's posted its best financial results ever.

74　As Skinner completed his first year as CEO, same-store sales in the United States rose by nearly 10%, the largest increase in 30 years. During Skinner's first two years, McDonald's market value doubled, and during the deepening recession of 2008, McDonald's surprised analysts—month after month—with stronger than expected results. Throughout 2008—a year in which the stock market lost more than a third of its value in the worst performance since the Great Depression—McDonald's stock gained 6%, and the McDonald's Corporation emerged as one of the only two companies (together with Wal-Mart) listed in the Dow Jones Industrial Average to post a stock price increase. In 2008, McDonald's global revenues rose by 5%, and its net income tripled, producing a rate of return on sales of 18%. McDonald's served 58 million customers a day globally in January 2009, eight million more than two years earlier.[53]

75　Finally, under Skinner's leadership, McDonald's planned further expansion in 2009. At that time an increasing number of restaurants, both in the United States and Europe, were struggling to remain in business, McDonald's announced its plan to open 650 additional outlets within a year (2009), 240 of them in Europe, and to spend more than $2 billion on this effort.[54] Asked whether McDonald's was "recession proof," Skinner replied: "No, we are recession-resistant. I don't know if we are depression-resistant," though.[55]

[52] Cited in the *New York Times,* January 11, 2009.

[53] *Chief Executive,* November 2005; *New York Times,* January 11, 2009; "McDonald's Press Release October 22, 2008," online, McDonalds.com; *Wall Street Journal,* January 5, 2007 and January 27, 2009.

[54] *Wall Street Journal,* January 27, 2009; Jonathan Brichall and Jenny Wiggins, "McDonald's Bucks Trend by Creating Jobs," *Financial Times,* January 24, 2009.

[55] Quoted in the *New York Times,* January 11, 2009.

Case 9

Fiji Water and Corporate Social Responsibility—Green Makeover or "Greenwashing"?[1]

James McMaster and Jan Nowak

"Bottled water is a disaster, for several reasons. First there's the issue of the sustainability of underground aquifers, from where much of the bottled water is drawn. And then there's the carbon footprint. Water is heavy, and transporting it around the world uses a lot of energy."

Jeff Angel, Total Environment Centre, Sydney, Australia[2]

"We survived before we had water in bottles. It is unnecessary. When you see water imported from Fiji in plastic bottles, you know it's bad for the environment all round."

Lee Rhiannon, Australia's Greens MP[3]

"I think the world is slowly going insane. No thanks but I prefer water in bottles, that way you know it's clean and you know, healthy. Not a sacrifice people should make when plastic bags are still rampant. Those Greens are extremists and I don't see this 'tap water alternative' ever being viable."

Anthony L, N.S.W.[4]

"Consumers who choose FIJI Water will actually be helping the environment by taking carbon out of the atmosphere with every purchase."

Thomas Mooney, senior vice-president, sustainable growth,
FIJI Water, Los Angeles, California[5]

James McMaster and Jan Nowak wrote this case solely to provide material for class discussion. The authors do not intend to illustrate either effective or ineffective handling of a managerial situation. The authors may have disguised certain names and other identifying information to protect confidentiality. James McMaster is a professor at the Graduate School of Business. The University of the South Pacific, and Jan Nowak is a professor at the Central European University Business School.

Ivey

Richard Ivey School of Business
The University of Western Ontario

Version: (A) 2009-15-14

[1] This case has been written on the basis of published sources only. Consequently, the interpretation and perspectives presented in this case are not necessarily those of FIJI Water LLC. or any of its employees.

[2] "Disaster in a bottle," *Sydney Morning Herald,* April 24, 2007.

[3] Kelly Fedor, "Greens call for ban on bottled water," *Livenews.com,* March 22, 2008.

[4] A reader's comment posted on Livenews.com on March 22, 2008.

[5] "FIJI Water Becomes First Bottled Water Company to Release Carbon Footprint of its Products," Press Release from FIJI Water, April 9, 2008, www.bevnet.com.

1 2008 was a trying year for FIJI Water LLC., a U.S.-based company that marketed its famous brand in more than a dozen countries out of its bottling plant located in the Fiji Islands. The company was facing some complex challenges to achieve its goal of a carbon negative outcome at its production plant and in the transportation of its products, and to convince its consumers and other stakeholders that it was leading the industry in carbon footprint disclosure and offset. The environmental protest against bottled water in general, and FIJI brand in particular, in the United States, United Kingdom and other developed countries was gathering steam as the message on the carbon impact of bottled water was more and more widely publicized to consumers. FIJI Water was singled out as a primary example of "water insanity" due to the fact that the product was shipped from a remote island in the South Pacific to its main markets thousands of miles away. In response to this protest, the company launched a new promotion campaign under a slogan "every drop is green," only to be immediately accused by environmentalist groups of engaging in greenwashing activities. The claim was also challenged by government watchdogs in some countries where FIJI Water was sold.

2 At the same time, the company's relationships with the Fiji government were at the lowest point. The government accused FIJI Water of transfer price manipulations and seized hundreds of containers carrying FIJI brand. After assessing the company's contribution to the Fiji economy, the government tried to impose a hefty tax on exported water and the company took the drastic action of laying off its employees in Fiji to pressure the government to repeal the initial 20-cents-a-litre tax that would have greatly reduced FIJI Water's profitability by increasing its tax bill by about FJ$50 million per year. The company intensified its PR activities, focusing on its contributions to the local communities, to show how good a corporate citizen it was in Fiji.

THE PRODUCT CONCEPT AND COMPANY BACKGROUND

3 The product concept was developed in the early nineties by David Gilmour, the Canadian-born owner and founder of Fiji's renowned Wakaya Island Resort. Simply put, the concept was to bottle Fiji natural artesian water and market it both locally and internationally as a unique and exotic product. An important aspect of the product concept was to bottle the water straight from the source—the source being an old artesian aquifer containing tropical rainwater, filtered for 450 years through layers of volcanic rock. The aquifer was found in the Yaqara Range of the Nakauvadra Mountains. Being separated by 1,500 kilometres of ocean, far away from major polluting sources, and being formed before any industrial activity could contaminate it, the water could only be of the purest quality and of distinct taste. Moreover, this silica-rich water was attributed anti-aging and immunity-boosting properties. The product was expected to appeal to health-conscious and image-oriented consumers.[6]

4 To extract and bottle Fiji's artesian water, in 1993 Gilmour founded a company under the name Nature's Best. In 1995, the company's name was changed to Natural Waters of Viti Ltd. The first bottling plant was built in 1996 at the cost of FJ$48 million at Yaqara in Ra, on land sub-leased from the Yaqara Pastoral Company. The plant was built where the source of artesian water had been found.[7] The site was in a remote and underdeveloped rural area of the island of Viti Levu that was poorly served with public infrastructure. The unpolluted,

---

[6] James McMaster and Jan Nowak, "Natural Waters of Viti Limited—Pioneering a New Industry in the Fiji Islands." *Journal of the Australian and New Zealand Academy of Management,* 9:2, 2003 (Special Edition on Management Cases).

[7] Reserve Bank of Fiji, "Natural Waters of Viti Limited." Briefing Paper, August 2001, p. 1; and Ed Dinger, "Fiji Water LLC," *International Directory of Company Histories,* 74, 2003.

pristine location of the water source and factory guaranteed that the artesian water was of the highest purity. However, the site's remoteness from the capital city of Suva, where Fiji's main port is located, entailed higher road transport costs compared to other alternative mineral water sources. In 1996, FIJI Water LLC corporate headquarters was established in Basalt, Colorado, to handle the product distribution in the United States, which was intended to be the main market for FIJI Water.

5   The production process began with the extraction of the water from a bore-hole. The water was then channelled through a pipe into the factory, treated and bottled in four bottle sizes: 0.33, 0.5, 1.0 and 1.5 litres. Using imported bottle caps, PET resin and labels, the bottles were manufactured by the company on its premises and were filled with water during the same production cycle. Bottles were packed into cartons for shipment to domestic and international markets. The cartons were made in Fiji by Golden Manufacturers.[8]

6   Rising demand for FIJI Water led to the construction of a new 110,000-square-foot, state-of-the-art bottling plant, completed in 2000. Demand continued to build in the 2000s, leading to the airlifting of a new bottling line in 2004 to help increase capacity to more than 50 million cases a year. The design and construction of the factory was regarded as among the best in the world, with high-quality and high-speed production capability.

7   In 2004, the company was sold by its main shareholder, David Gilmour, to Roll International Corporation for an undisclosed price. Roll International was controlled by one of Hollywood's richest couples, Stewart and Lynda Resnik.[9] Following this acquisition, FIJI Water's corporate headquarters was moved to Los Angeles. While the Fiji Islands-based operation focused on mineral water extraction, bottling and transportation within Fiji, the corporate headquarters handled marketing and logistics functions worldwide. The new owner expanded the Fiji plant's production capacity by adding a new (third) bottling line in 2006. In 2007, the state-of-the-art factory could churn more than a million bottles of FIJI Water a day.[10]

8   As of 2008, FIJI Water marketed its bottled mineral water in about a dozen countries in North America (including Mexico and the Caribbean), Asia-Pacific, Europe and the Middle East. It was marketed as FIJI Natural Mineral Water in Europe and as FIJI Natural Spring Water in Australia. The two main markets for the product were the United States and Australia.

9   In the latter part of 2008, the bottling plant at Yaqara had about 400 employees. Of the total number of employees, only about 10 per cent were employed with the administration, finance and management sections; the rest were factory-floor workers. The company employed only a handful of expatriates and placed an emphasis on the hiring, training and advancement of the inhabitants of nearby villages, most of whom had little or no employment opportunities prior to Natural Waters of Viti Ltd. locating its factory at Yaqara. The company claimed to be one of the highest paying employers in Fiji.[11]

THE GLOBAL MARKET FOR BOTTLED WATER—CONSUMPTION TRENDS

10   Sales of FIJI Water in the domestic market were relatively very small. More than 90 per cent of all production was exported. Therefore, for FIJI Water global trends in bottled water consumption and demand were of paramount importance.

[8] Ibid.

[9] Roll International also owned such companies as POM Wonderful, which produced and marketed juices and fresh pomegranates; Teleflora, the largest online flower shop in the world; Paramount Farms, the largest grower and producer of pistachios and almonds in the world; and Paramount Citrus, a leader in the California orange and lemon markets (www.roll.com).

[10] Charles Fishman, "Message in a Bottle," *Fast Company,* 117, July/August 2007, p. 110.

[11] Company website: www.fijiwater.com.

EXHIBIT 1 Global Bottled Water Market
Leading Countries' Consumption and Compound Annual Growth Rates, 2002–2007

Rank, 2007	Countries	Consumption in Millions of Gallons		CAGR*
		2002	**2007**	**2002/07**
1	United States	5,795.6	8,823.0	8.8%
2	Mexico	3,898.6	5,885.2	8.6%
3	China	2,138.4	4,787.8	17.5%
4	Brazil	2,541.8	3,621.1	7.3%
5	Italy	2,558.2	3,100.9	3.9%
6	Germany	2,291.5	2,743.2	3.7%
7	Indonesia	1,622.5	2,400.6	8.2%
8	France	2,225.6	2,283.2	0.5%
9	Thailand	1,277.0	1,533.1	3.7%
10	Spain	1,191.4	1,284.0	1.5%
	Top 10 Subtotal	**25,540.7**	**36,462.2**	**7.4%**
	All Others	9,054.2	13,407.3	8.2%
	WORLD TOTAL	**34,594.9**	**49,869.6**	**7.6%**

*Compound annual growth rate.
Source: "The Global Bottled Water Market Report 2007," Beverage Marketing Corporation, January 2008.

11   Since the beginning of the last decade, the beverage product category had been shaken by rapidly changing consumer preferences that had led to a radical shift away from traditional beverages and toward "New Age" products, like bottled water. In fact, bottled water had been the fastest growing segment of the entire beverage business. As Exhibit 1 shows, between 2002 and 2007 the world's bottled water consumption was increasing by 7.6 per cent annually and by 2007 reached close to 50 billion gallons (approximately 185 billion litres). As a result, by 2007 bottled water had become the second largest beverage category, after soft drinks.

12   As Exhibit 1 also indicates, the United States was the world's leading consumer of bottled water in 2007. Americans drank 8.8 billion gallons of bottled water, as compared to 5.9 billion consumed by Mexicans and 4.8 billion consumed by Chinese. Altogether, the top 10 consuming nations accounted for 73 per cent of the world's bottled water consumption in 2007. However, it should be pointed out that China's consumption grew the fastest among the top three consumers in the world between 2002 and 2007, at the compound annual rate of 17.5 per cent, which was twice the world's average. Therefore, China was expected to become the largest consumer of bottled water in the world in the next decade. Another emerging big consumer of bottled water was India. Although not among the leading bottled water consuming nations in 2007, India had experienced one of the fastest growth rates in the world during the period shown in Exhibit 1, even faster than China.[12]

13   When per capita consumption was taken into account, the nation's ranking looked different (see Exhibit 2). In 2007, the United Arab Emirates, Mexico and Italy showed the highest consumption per person in the world, and the United States was ranked ninth, with only a slightly higher consumption per capita than Hungary and Switzerland. It is noteworthy that

[12] "The Global Bottled Water Market. Report 2007," Beverage Marketing Corporation, January 2008.

EXHIBIT 2   Global Bottled Water Market
Per Capita Consumption by Leading Countries, 2002–2007

Rank, 2007	Countries	Consumption in Gallons Per Capita	
		2002	2007
1	United Arab Emirates	35.2	68.6
2	Mexico	37.7	54.1
3	Italy	44.2	53.3
4	Belgium-Luxembourg	32.7	39.5
5	France	37.1	35.8
6	Germany	27.8	33.3
7	Spain	29.7	31.7
8	Lebanon	24.9	29.3
9	United States	20.1	29.3
10	Hungary	13.5	28.5
11	Switzerland	24.2	28.2
12	Slovenia	18.8	25.2
13	Austria	20.9	25.0
14	Czech Republic	21.1	24.6
15	Croatia	14.9	24.3
16	Saudi Arabia	23.8	24.1
17	Cyprus	21.4	24.0
18	Thailand	20.1	23.6
19	Israel	12.4	23.2
20	Portugal	19.9	22.4
	GLOBAL AVERAGE	**5.6**	**7.6**

Source: "The Global Bottled Water Market Report 2007," Beverage Marketing Corporation, January 2008.

Australia and the United Kingdom, two markets of interest to FIJI Water, were not among the biggest consumers of bottled water in the world, neither in terms of total consumption nor per capita.

14   In 2007, Europe and North America were the biggest regional markets for bottled water, accounting for 30.9 and 30.7 per cent of the world's sales volume, respectively. Asia accounted for 24.3 per cent and the rest of the world accounted for 14.1 per cent.[13]

FIJI WATER'S INTERNATIONAL MARKET EXPANSION

15   While responding to those world market trends, FIJI Water had made its strategy revolve around capturing international market opportunities and strongly positioning the brand in large and growing markets for bottled water, but markets that were not overly price competitive, as FIJI Water, right from the beginning, was designed to be a premium brand. The first, and critical, international market to conquer was the United States.

[13] Ibid.

EXHIBIT 3   U.S. Bottled Water Market Per Capita Consumption, 1997–2007

Year	Gallons Per Capita	Annual % Change
1997	13.5	—
1998	14.7	8.3%
1999	16.2	10.2%
2000	16.7	3.5%
2001	18.2	8.6%
2002	20.1	10.6%
2003	21.6	7.2%
2004	23.2	7.5%
2005	25.4	9.7%
2006	27.6	8.4%
2007	29.3	6.4%

Source: "The Global Bottled Water Market. Report 2007," Beverage Marketing Corporation, January 2008.

Conquering the U.S. Market

16   To begin its international market expansion, FIJI Water was first launched in California in 1997, using Los Angeles and Palm Beach as a beachhead for a subsequent and gradual roll-out of the product across the United States. In 1998, the company entered the sophisticated New York market, firmly positioning itself on the East Coast. At the same time, FIJI Water was also introduced to the Canadian market, starting with the country's West Coast. The North American market provided the company with tremendous growth opportunities. The U.S. market in particular was so embracing that after about five years of the product's presence there, FIJI Water had achieved the second selling position in the U.S. market among imported still water brands, and in 2008 it had climbed to the number one position among imported bottled waters in the United States.[14] Such a strong market position had been achieved in the market where competition was fierce and which was characterized by industry consolidation and the increasing dominance of major soft drink companies in bottled water marketing, such as Coca-Cola and PepsiCo, which had entered the market with their own proprietary brands, Dasani and Aquafina, respectively. At the same time, FIJI Water had benefited from the overall beverage market trend that had shown a major shift in beverage consumption preferences in the United States.

17   As Exhibit 3 shows, the per capita consumption of bottled water in the United States increased from 13.5 gallons in 1997, when the FIJI Water brand was introduced to the U.S. market, to 29.3 gallons in 2007, thus more than doubling. This was part of the exponential growth trend in bottled water consumption over a longer period, although growth clearly accelerated after 1990.[15]

18   The above shifts in the consumption of beverages could be linked to changing lifestyles and growing concerns of the effects of sweetened carbonated drinks on people's health. The baby boom generation, which constituted about a third of the total population in North

[14] "FIJI Water Becomes First Bottled Water Company to Release Carbon Footprint of Its Products," Press Release from FIJI Water, April 9, 2008, www.bevnet.com.

[15] "The Global Bottled Water Market. Report 2007." Beverage Marketing Corporation, January 2008.

EXHIBIT 4   U.S. Bottled Water Market Volume and Growth by Segment, 2000–2007

Year	Non-sparkling		Domestic Sparkling		Imports		Total	
	Volume*	Change	Volume*	Change	Volume*	Change	Volume*	Change
2000	4,443.0	—	144.2	—	137.9	—	4,725.1	—
2001	4,917.3	10.7%	144.0	−0.1%	123.9	−10.1%	5,185.3	9.7%
2002	5,487.5	11.6%	149.5	3.8%	158.7	28.0%	5,795.7	11.8%
2003	5,923.9	8.0%	152.6	2.1%	193.3	21.8%	6,269.8	8.2%
2004	6,411.3	8.2%	166.8	9.3%	228.6	18.2%	6,806.7	8.6%
2005	7,171.4	11.9%	185.0	10.9%	182.2	−20.2%	7,538.9	10.8%
2006	7,899.9	10.2%	189.3	2.3%	164.3	−10.0%	8,253.5	9.5%
2007	8,435.7	6.8%	201.2	6.3%	186.0	13.2%	8,823.0	6.9%

* Millions of gallons.
Source: "The Global Bottled Water Market. Report 2007," Beverage Marketing Corporation, January 2008.

America, had become obsessively health-conscious and fitness-oriented. Bottled water had become popular among the younger generation as well. Over the last decade, bottled water had gained a reputation of not only being healthy but also a fashionable, elegant and "trendy" drink.

19   In 2007, total U.S. bottled water sales surpassed 8.8 billion gallons, a 6.9 per cent advance over 2006's volume level. That translated into more than 29 gallons per person, which meant U.S. residents drank more bottled water annually than any other beverage, other than carbonated soft drinks (CSDs). While CSDs still had volume and average intake levels more than twice as high as those of bottled water, the soft drink market had been struggling because of competition from bottled water. Per capita consumption of bottled water had been growing by at least one gallon annually, thereby more than doubling between 1997 and 2007. In 2007, U.S. consumers spent $15 billion on bottled water, more than on iPods or movie tickets.[16]

20   As Exhibit 4 shows, sales of non-sparkling bottled water by far exceeded sales of its sparkling counterpart. Also, between 2000 and 2007, non-sparkling water's sales grew faster than those of sparkling water. At the same time, it is noteworthy that imported bottled water constituted only a little more than two per cent of the total sales of this product category, and imports tended to fluctuate widely from one year to another. The biggest sellers in the U.S. market were local brands, such as Arrowhead, Poland Spring, Zephyrhills, Ozarka, Deer Park, and Ice Mountain. The market was dominated by four large companies: Nestlé, Coca-Cola, PepsiCo and Danone. Nestlé had the largest market share of all—in 2007 the company's brands of bottled water accounted for 26 per cent of total sales of the product category.[17]

21   During the product's introduction into the U.S. market, FIJI Water LLC was responsible for the marketing and logistics of FIJI brand. The company had two senior VPs, in charge of the East Coast and the West Coast, respectively, reporting to the company's CEO, Mr. Doug Carlson.[18]

[16] Fishman, "Message in a Bottle." July/August 2007. p. 110.
[17] Ibid., p. 115.
[18] McMaster and Nowak. "Natural Waters of Viti Limited—Pioneering a New Industry in the Fiji Islands," 2003, p. 42.

22   The successful launch of FIJI Water in the United States was attributed to a skilful marketing strategy and the high quality of the people who drove the initial marketing campaign.[19] FIJI Water LLC's marketing personnel were able to differentiate the FIJI brand in a crowded market where about 400 brands of bottled water competed with each other. This was mainly achieved through unique product positioning, innovative packaging, premium-product pricing, effective distribution, and image-creating publicity. The latter had elevated this otherwise mundane commodity to celebrity status.

23   Due to its light mineralization, FIJI Water was characterized by a smooth taste and no aftertaste. The light mineralization also gave the water a clean, pure taste. Many U.S. consumers instantly liked the taste of the water and, having tried it, repurchased the product in preference to the more mineralized waters. FIJI Water had been top-rated in taste tests sponsored by such influential magazines and guides as Chicago Magazine, Cook's Illustrated Buying Guides, and Men's Health. Taste therefore was one of FIJI Water's main advantages over other bottled water brands. The company continued to educate the consumer about the difference between purified, spring and artesian bottled water.[20] In addition to superb taste, the water had a high level of silica, the ingredient that was believed to promote rejuvenation and anti-aging. Another distinct aspect of the product was its purity, stemming from the fact that the source of the water was a virgin, unpolluted ecosystem, located 1,500 kilometres away from any metropolitan and industrial area, and the fact that the water was 450 years old, thus formed before industrial pollution could affect its purity. All this added to the mystique that the product seemed to be surrounded by in the minds of consumers. Due to FIJI Water's superb taste, purity and mystique, a premium-product positioning had been followed right from the beginning.

24   Although of paramount importance, the product content was only part of the successful marketing equation. Another important element was packaging. For many years, all bottles containing natural water were the same—round, with paper labels. Packaging, one of the most fundamental ways to differentiate a product, was not used as such a tool in bottled water markets. Over the last decade, both companies and consumers had discovered the power of packaging in bottled water brand positioning and imagery. FIJI Water had utilized the power of packaging to its benefit. Natural Waters of Viti Ltd. was the first company in the industry to use a square bottle and this had become the product's signature trait. Furthermore, since FIJI was the only brand that came from a tropical paradise—not a cold, mountainous region—the packaging reflected that in an artful and compelling way: consumers could see that immediately when they looked at the unique square bottle bearing bright, three-dimensional graphics.[21]

25   FIJI Water's packaging was initially designed by a New York-based advertising agency and had been refined several times since its original design. When the brand was introduced to the U.S. market, its square-shaped bottle was unique and had great appeal to consumers. The gold border on the label gave an image of quality. The blue cap was colour-coordinated with the blue waterfall and the blue-green colours in the see-through labels. Consumers had reported favourably on the attractive label with the Pacific image and see-through waterfall. Later on, the company had redesigned the labelling and added new features to the bottle's front and back labels. The front label, in addition to the brand name, featured a pink hibiscus flower, a national flower of the Fiji Islands. In a new version of the bottle design, the inside

[19] Paul Yavala, "Fiji Water Travels." *The Fiji Times,* November 2000, p. 4.

[20] www. fijiwater.com.

[21] Nancy Christy, "Age of enlightenment," *Beverage Aisle,* August 2001.

of the back label, instead of a waterfall, displayed a large palm frond, which was amplified when the bottle was filled with water, and the outside of that label explained the water's distinct characteristics, such as its remote and pristine source and its unique mineral composition. In fact, in 2008 FIJI Water had four different outside back labels, each of which illustrated a unique image and communicated a different part of the FIJI Water story; they included: "bottled in Fiji," "what ecosystem is your water from," "what is artesian water," and "untouched by man."

26   Similarly to packaging, a premium-price policy reinforced the product's high-quality image. Anyway, high freight costs between Fiji and the United States would have made a low- or even medium-price policy impossible. FIJI Water's price was higher than that of most brands offered to U.S. consumers. For example, in the Californian market, FIJI Water was positioned slightly below Perrier but above Evian.

27   Another important factor that had contributed to FIJI Water's success in the U.S. market was its distribution. Having good distributors was important in that it enabled the brand to be well-placed in and readily available to the market. While in Fiji the company used exclusively Coca-Cola Amatil to distribute its product, in the U.S. market the product was sold by numerous distributors, including wholesalers, retail chains and individual retailers. In addition to stores, the product was sold on the premises of many highend restaurants and hotels. The product was also available online in the continental United States. To support the brand's continued growth, FIJI Water LLC had expanded distribution beyond exclusive retailers to include mass merchandisers, convenience stores, drug stores, and even gas stations.[22] This intensification of distribution might sound like a contradiction of the product's exclusive positioning, but the company representatives claimed that it was all part of "the affordable luxury" strategy.

28   Destined for the U.S. market, FIJI Water was shipped from the ports of Suva or Lautoka on Viti Levu to three major distribution centres in the United States—Los Angeles, New Jersey and Miami. It was then distributed throughout most of the United States. Initially, the physical distribution to and within the United States was contracted out to specialized logistics firms, which delivered the product to a variety of distributors who then carried it through their distribution channels. Occasionally, these logistics firms delivered the product directly to consumers. In 2000, FIJI Water entered into an exclusive distributorship agreement with Cadbury Schweppes. This partnership was crucial to FIJI Water's aggressive expansion and success in the U.S. market, where the FIJI brand was available at tens of thousands of outlets. Canadian shipments were sent to Vancouver, the only location where the product was initially available. In 1999, FIJI Water appointed Brio Industries Inc. as Canada-Wide Master Distributor of the FIJI brand.[23] In 2008, the U.S.-market distributorship agreement with Cadbury Schweppes was extended to cover Canada also. Since February of that year, FIJI Water had been exclusively distributed by Cadbury across Canada among grocery, convenience, drug and most other retail stores.[24]

29   Building an image of the high quality, uniqueness and class of the product was another aspect of this successful marketing campaign. At the beginning, FIJI Water did very little "formal" or paid advertising, which included only some printed advertisements placed in

---

[22] Heather Landi, "Paradise in a Bottle," *Beverage World*, November 2007, p. 24.

[23] "Brio Industries Inc. Appointed Canada-Wide Master Distributor of Fiji Water," *Business Wire*, Vancouver, British Columbia, April 15, 1999, http://findarticles.com/p/articles/mi_m0EIN/is_1999_April_15/ai_54381790.

[24] "Canadians Have a Taste for FIJI Water," FIJI Water Press Release, Toronto, Ontario, March 10, 2008. www.nkpr.net/pressreleases/FW_Cadbury_Schweppes_Release.pdf.

in-flight magazines, such as those of Air Pacific. The brand achieved an explosive growth early on, mostly through word-of-mouth advertising, free product placement and targeted sampling. According to Thomas Mooney, senior vice-president of sustainable growth, the company continued its focus on introducing new customers to the brand and converting them to "brand evangelists." While doing so, FIJI Water targeted locations and venues that resonated with the brand's premium image. Said Mooney: "It's different to get a bottle of water after walking off the subway than it is to get a bottle at an after-party following the Oscars."[25] In fact, the product had received a lot of publicity through movies, as Hollywood celebrities, such as Tom Cruise, Pierce Brosnan, Whoopi Goldberg and Vin Diesel, and popular singers, such as Michael Bolton, Tina Turner and Jessica Simpson, had eagerly endorsed the product. FIJI Water had also become a favourite at the dining tables of some of New York's better restaurants and hotels, including Jean Georges, Four Seasons Restaurant, Pierre Hotel, Trump International Hotels & Towers, and the Carlyle and the Paramount. And there were celebrity chefs using FIJI Water as a cooking ingredient in their kitchens, such as "Sam the Cooking Guy," an Emmy-Award winning TV show.

30   In 2007, the company launched a new marketing campaign, aiming at communicating the core benefits of FIJI Water. Revolving around the theme "untouched," the campaign followed an integrated marketing communication approach, combining advertising, PR, direct marketing, product placements and event marketing. The advertising part of the campaign used a striking blue-colour creative copy that brought out the pristine nature, magical allure and mystery that the Fiji Islands embodied. The advertising campaign was developed by FIJI Water's in-house creative agency and used both out-of-home (OOH) and print media.[26]

31   In sum, the secret of FIJI Water's success in the United States seemed to lie in its marketers' ability to elevate the world's simplest drink to celebrity status. FIJI Water was much more than just pure, good-tasting liquid. It was a promise of good health, refinement, status, and exclusivity. It evoked images of unspoiled natural beauty and purity. It was a tropical paradise captured in a bottle!

Expanding into the Australian Market

32   With the tremendous success achieved by FIJI Water in the United States, the firm entered the Australian market in 2003 from a position of strength. As shown earlier, Australia was not among the leading bottled water consuming countries. However, the country's relatively large market and, more importantly, its proximity to Fiji made it an attractive market to enter. Moreover, before the product was launched in Australia, many Australians visiting Fiji had a chance to develop a taste for FIJI Water. It was common to see Australian vacationers returning from Fiji carrying cartons of FIJI water with them back home. This created awareness of, and even pent-up demand for, the product before it was officially launched.

33   The product was initially introduced to select hotels and restaurants, before becoming available in gourmet, deli and independent convenience stores. In 2005, FIJI Water gained national distribution in more than 400 Coles supermarkets, and in 2007 FIJI Water's Australian subsidiary signed a national distribution agreement with Cadbury Schweppes Australia.[27] At that time, Cadbury Schweppes had a national market share of about eight per cent, with its Cool Ridge, Spring Valley Twist and FIJI Water brands.

---

[25] Heather Landi, "Paradise in a Bottle," *Beverage World,* November 2007, p. 24.

[26] FIJI Water Press Releases, www.fijiwater.com, accessed July 23, 2008.

[27] "National Packaging Covenant," FIJI Water (Australia) Pty Ltd., Annual Report, July 2006–June 2007, South Yara, Victoria, Australia.

34   The Australian bottled water market had sustained a high growth rate in the past decade and was predicted to continue to grow strongly in the next one. FIJI Water was emerging as a major brand in the premium market segment and was facing stiff competition. The Australian bottled water market was very competitive, and it was also less consolidated than the U.S. market. In Australia, about one thousand brands of bottled water competed for market share. Coca-Cola Amatil's Mount Franklin was Australia's leading water brand and was sourced from select Australian springs.

35   According to the Australasian Bottled Water Institute (ABWI) website, consumer research suggested that although bottled water was consumed in Australia by people of varying age groups and occupations, a large majority of them tended to be young singles and couples, in particular females, aged between 14 and 35 years. In terms of psychographics, bottled water consumers could be described as being more health-conscious, progressive and socially aware.[28]

36   Another Fiji company, whose brand name was Island Chill, with a very similar bottle design to FIJI Water, successfully entered the Australian market a few years after FIJI Water's launch there. Island Chill also contained silica and had been well-received in the Melbourne market. Although Melbourne was initially Island Chill's primary sales focus area, the brand was expanding to other Australian cities. The noticeable similarities in bottle shape and label design between the FIJI Water and Island Chill brands had led to a trademark dispute between the two companies in both Australia and the United States. According to the Island Chill website's press centre, in February of 2007 the Federal Court of Australia ruled in favour of Island Chill, dismissing FIJI Water's complaint against Island Chill.[29] In the United States, the dispute was settled outside of court in June of 2008, when Island Chill agreed to remove the hibiscus flower from its bottle's label.[30]

Experiencing a Backlash in the U.K. Market

37   One year after FIJI Water entered the Australian market, it made an attempt to crack the U.K. market. The company launched FIJI brand through the supermarket chains Waitrose and Selfridge's, department stores Harvey Nichols and Harrods, and a number of specialty stores carrying whole-food products.

38   Soon after the brand had arrived in Britain, FIJI Water gained the reputation as the best-travelled bottled water in the country.[31] The fact that the product had to travel 10,000 miles to reach the British consumer could not escape the attention of environmentalist and conservation groups, in a country where quality of tap water was among the highest in the world. In a newspaper article published in 2004, an official from the Food Commission was reported to have said that "it was ludicrous to bring water from the other side of the world when essentially the same product was available out of the tap."[32] At the same time, it was noted that the most popular French bottled water brands—Evian and Vittel—travelled "only" between 400 and 460 miles to reach Britain. As a result of this backlash, FIJI Water had so far been largely unsuccessful in penetrating the U.K. market. Moreover, FIJI Water's appearance in the United Kingdom had fuelled the debate around the environmental impact of bottled water.

[28] www.bottledwater.org.au.

[29] www.islandchill.com/press.html.

[30] "Island Chill and Fiji Water end trademark dispute," *FOODBEV.COM,* June 24, 2008.

[31] "Bottle of water that has travelled the world," *The Daily Telegraph,* November 3, 2004.

[32] Ibid., p. 3.

39   In 2008, British environmentalists and conservationists took up the war against bottled water. They were joined by some political leaders and government officials as well. For example, the mayor of London and the CEO of Thames Water Authority launched a campaign called "London on Tap" to encourage consumers to order tap water in restaurants.[33] Their message to consumers was that using less bottled water would help tackle climate change by cutting carbon emissions with its production, storage, transport and disposal. Campaign partners included London Remade, the Crafts Council and WaterAid, and the supporters included Friends of the Earth and London Sustainability Exchange.

40   On January 18, 2008, the BBC broadcast a TV documentary that featured FIJI Water in a Panorama documentary called "Bottled Water—Who Needs It?" It gave a critical analysis of the negative impact the success of the U.K. bottled water industry was having on the environment.[34] It pointed out that, "In the UK last year we spent nearly £2 billion buying bottled water, yet a billion people around the world don't have access to safe drinking water" and that, "Sales of bottled water have boomed in recent decades, growing 200-fold from the 1970s. But a litre of one of the UK's most popular French mineral waters generates up to 600 times more CO2 equivalent than a litre of Thames tap water."[35] The programme travelled to Fiji, where they visited the FIJI Water bottling plant, Fijian villages and hospitals, noting that one in three Fijians did not have access to safe tap water. The documentary was wrapped up with the following statement: "Indeed Fiji Water would make the case that if you really care about the plight of Fijians, you should buy Fiji water as it provides jobs and income for the islands. But tell people here on the street that we buy bottled water from Fiji and most will still roll their eyes and ask: Why?"[36] The 2008 BBC Panorama story focusing on FIJI Water had 3.5 million viewers!

41   Growing concerns about bottled water's harmful effects on the environment might have caused a reversal of a growing trend in bottled water consumption in the United Kingdom. For the first time in years, a nine per cent drop of retail sales of bottled water was reported in the first quarter of 2008.[37] This was largely attributed to an Evening Standard campaign to get Londoners to turn to tap water instead of buying expensive and environmentally harmful bottled water. A fifth of diners in London restaurants were reported to opt for tap water. The government's Food Standards Agency banned bottled water from its offices. This move was followed by a growing number of Whitehall departments doing the same, including Downing Street. Food and health lobby group "Sustain" launched a campaign for government departments and official bodies to turn to tap water. The campaign's director, Richard Watts, believed it had worked. He said: "This looks to be the first ever recorded fall in bottled water sales. It is a significant development. The message about bottled water being unnecessary, expensive and damaging to the environment is finally getting through."[38]

---

[33] Hannah Marriott, "Bottled water under fire: how industry responded," *PRWeek(UK)*, February 21, 2008.

[34] The documentary can be accessed from http://news.bbc.co.uk/2/hi/programmes/panorama/7247130.stm.

[35] Ibid.

[36] Ibid.

[37] Lucy Hanbury, "Bottled water sales dry up as London turns to tap," *Evening Standard*, April 14, 2008.

[38] Ibid.

WORLDWIDE CONTROVERSIES OVER BOTTLED WATER'S IMPACT ON THE ENVIRONMENT

42   In the last 10 years, the high sustained global growth rate of bottled water sales of about eight per cent per annum had been a triumph of modern marketing and a dynamic, profitable segment of the beverage market for the growing number of producers. FIJI Water had been very successful in gaining market share in this rapidly growing industry. Advertising campaigns had promoted bottled water as a healthy alternative to high-calorie CSDs and purer alternative to tap water. The advertisements focused on its pristine pureness, safeness and better taste compared to tap water. However, conservationists pointed out that the price of bottled water was about 500 to 1000 times higher than that of tap water. Since the launch of FIJI Water in the United Kingdom, the bottled water industry had been under attack in the media and FIJI brand had been singled out for criticism by environmental groups and by a BBC documentary that had been widely broadcast.

43   The Swiss-based conservation group World Wide Fund for Nature had published a research study it funded, which found that bottled water was often no healthier or safer to drink than tap water and it had used the findings to argue strongly that bottled water was not only environmentally unfriendly but also a waste of money. [39] Another watchdog, Corporate Accountability International, had mounted a campaign called "Think Outside the Bottle."[40] The group advocated ending state contracts with bottled water suppliers, promoting water systems and improving the quality of water infrastructure.

44   According to Janet Larsen's article "Bottled Water Boycotts," in 2007 city governments, high-class restaurants, schools, and religious groups from San Francisco to New York to Paris were ditching bottled water in favour of tap water.[41] The U.S. Conference of Mayors, which represented some 1,100 American cities, discussed at its June 2007 meeting the mayors' role in promoting the consumption of municipal tap water and many city councils were banning the purchase of bottled water for their employees. In the same year, New York City launched a campaign to persuade people to cut back on bottled water and return to tap water. San Francisco's mayor banned city employees from using public money to buy imported water, while Chicago's mayor imposed a five-cents-a-bottle tax on plastic bottles to compensate for the financial burden bottled water caused for municipal waste disposal systems.[42] It was somewhat ironic that in the United States, more than a quarter of bottled water was just purified tap water, including Pepsi's top-selling Aquafina and Coca-Cola's Dasani.

FIJI WATER'S "CARBON NEGATIVE" CAMPAIGN

45   In response to the environmentalists' criticism, in 2008 FIJI Water LLC launched a "carbon negative" PR campaign, claiming that it was the first bottled water company to release carbon footprint of its products.[43] It had also joined the Carbon Disclosure Project Supply

---

[39] Catherine Ferrier, "Bottled Water: Understanding a Social Phenomenon," Discussion Paper commissioned by WWF, April 2001.

[40] "Corporate Accountability International: Challenging Abuse, Protecting People," www.stopcorporateabuse.org.

[41] Janet Larsen, "Bottled Water Boycotts," Earth Policy Institute, 2007.

[42] Lucy Siegle, "It's just water, right? Wrong. Bottled water is set to be the latest battleground in the eco war," *The observer* February 10, 2008, p.30.

[43] "FIJI Water Becomes First Bottled Water Company to Release Carbon Footprint of Its Products," April 9, 2008, www.bevnet.com.

Chain Leadership Collaboration and had started working with the Carbon Disclosure Project (CDP), the world's largest investor coalition on climate change, to disclose its own and its suppliers' carbon emissions. As measurement is the first step to managing and reducing carbon emissions, FIJI Water Company estimated its total annual carbon footprint at 85,396 metric tons of CO2eq. This was for the base year ending June 30, 2007.[44]

46   While measuring its carbon footprint, FIJI Water calculated its carbon emissions across every stage in the product lifecycle: starting from producing raw materials for packaging, through transporting raw materials and equipment to the plant, manufacturing and filling bottles, shipping the product from Fiji to markets worldwide, distributing the product, refrigerating the product in stores, restaurants, and other outlets, to disposing/recycling the packaging waste. It estimated that about 75 per cent of its carbon emissions resulted from the operations of supply chain partners. The company also looked at carbon emissions from its administrative and marketing activities. At the same time, the company launched a product-specific emissions disclosure via a website (www.fijigreen.com). The website provided consumers with access to product lifecycle emissions data and analysis for each of the company's products. The company's senior VP for sustainable growth, Mooney, argued that "the only way consumers can turn their good environmental intentions into good decisions is to give them the information they need regarding the emissions associated with the products they buy."[45]

47   As part of its "carbon negative" campaign, FIJI Water was planning to offset its total carbon footprint by 120 per cent, by removing from the earth's atmosphere not only all the emissions its activities produced, but also an additional 20 per cent. In that sense, the company's impact on carbon emissions would be negative. To achieve this goal, FIJI Water had undertaken a number of steps towards sustainable growth. These steps included:

- reducing packaging by 20 per cent,
- supplying at least 50 per cent of the energy used at its bottling plant with renewable energy,
- optimizing logistics and using more carbon-efficient transportation modes,
- restoring degraded grasslands in the Yaqara Valley by planting native tree species,
- supporting recycling programs for plastic PET bottles.

48   According to a company press conference held in April 2008, FIJI Water had already implemented several measures to reduce its carbon emissions. By optimizing its logistics, the company had reduced trucking miles by 26 per cent on average. FIJI Water's 1.5-litre bottle had been redesigned to reduce the packaging by seven per cent. The company had also managed to reduce motor fuel consumption in Fiji by 50 per cent by using more fuel-efficient trucks in transporting its products from the plant to ports.[46]

49   All in all, the above sustainable growth commitment provided FIJI Water with an opportunity to use that commitment as a PR pitch: a sale of every bottle of FIJI Water would result in a net reduction of carbon in the atmosphere! In other words—"every drop is green," as the company's website emphasized.

[44] Ibid.

[45] Ibid.

[46] "FIJI Water Becomes First Bottled Water Company to Release Carbon Footprint of Its Products," FIJI Water Press Release, Los Angeles, April 9, 2008, www.bevnet.com.

CONSERVATIONISTS' ATTACKS ON FIJI WATER'S GREEN MAKE-OVER

50   Conservation groups had not been impressed by FIJI Water's claim that it was going carbon negative. It was perceived as pure greenwashing at its best. The 10th Edition of the Concise Oxford English Dictionary recognizes the word "greenwash," defining it as "Disinformation disseminated by an organisation so as to present an environmentally responsible public image." Greenwashing was defined in law in Australia by the Competition and Consumer Commission that ensured compliance with the Commonwealth Trade Practices Act 1974. The Act contains a general prohibition on "conduct that is misleading or deceptive or is likely to mislead or deceive." Section 53 of the Act prohibits a corporation from representing that "goods or services have sponsorship, approval, performance characteristics, accessories, uses or benefits they do not have."

51   Conservation groups argued that the new website launched by FIJI Water in 2008 to sell its carbon negative message failed to provide a detailed description of the actual calculation of its carbon footprint and its reduction by the measures that were promised to be implemented in the future. At the same time, the groups pointed to the basic carbon footprint advantages of consuming local tap water. They argued that the new slogan "every drop is green" was straightforward greenwashing pushed to its limits.

52   The Food and Water Watch website posted a blog, entitled "Greenwashed: Fiji Water Bottles the Myth of Sustainability," about FIJI Water's carbon negative claim that summarized the response of the environmental watchdogs.[47] The website stated: "Corporate attempts to label their products as 'green' for the sake of turning a fast buck are nothing new. Corporations exist, after all, in order to make money, and capitalizing on whatever is capturing the public's collective imagination is often the best way of doing so. But *Fiji* Artisanal *Water*'s entree into the green movement strikes us as particularly suspect. The company has recently launched *fiji*green.com, a website outlining the ways in which their *water* is 'good for the environment.' If you're anything like us, you are probably wondering how this claim could be true. It can't."[48]

53   The Greenwash Brigade (part of the Public Insight Network), a U.S. organization of environmental professionals that are dedicated to exposing "greenwash" as they examine eco-friendly claims by companies, was quick to respond to FIJI Water's claim that it was going carbon negative. In an article by Heidi Siegelbaum on June 6, 2008, titled "Fiji Water by the numbers," she summarized FIJI Water's environmental impact by the following numbers:

- 5,500 miles per trip from Fiji to Los Angeles;
- 46 million gallons of fossil fuel;
- 1.3 billion gallons of water;
- 216,000,000 pounds of greenhouse gases.[49]

54   And she commented: "Fiji is using staggering amounts of energy, water, and fossil fuels to take a naturally occurring product (which is not regulated like drinking water here in the US), put it in an inherently problematic container and then have that forever-container tossed into landfills or incinerators all over America (and Asia, where we have a healthy export market for plastics)."[50]

[47] www.foodandwaterwatch.org/blog/archive/2008/05/02/greenwashed-fiji-water-bottles-the-myth-of-sustainability.

[48] Ibid.

[49] Heidi Siegelbaum, "Fiji Water by the numbers," June 6, 2008.

[50] Ibid.

55   Tony Azios summarized the reaction in the United States to the response of bottled water companies to the environmental protests, as follows: "Even as bottled water companies continue to see increased sales, the recent raft of negative media coverage and activist campaigns against the industry has caused a product once seen as fundamentally green and healthy to lose some of its luster. Now, brand-name bottlers are scrambling to reposition their products by upping their green credentials to fend off further consumer backlash fermenting in churches, college campuses, and city halls across the country."[51]

56   Rob Knox, in his article titled "Green or Greenwashing? Fiji Water," was also not convinced that "every drop is green."[52] His evaluation of the green makeover was that it was greenwashing. Knox reported: "[. . .] In March they took out a massive booth at the Natural Products Expo, part of a larger 'hey we're green now' campaign by the company. The booth featured a gigantic banner proclaiming 'every drop is green.' "

57   He continued: "Allow me free reign to mock Fiji for a moment. Let's discuss what every drop of Fiji water is—and here's a hint, it's not green. Every drop of Fiji water is imported from Fiji. That's right, the Fiji that is an island in the middle of the Pacific Ocean, thousands of miles from the mainland United States. This company takes water, which can be found in rather large quantities in the US, all the way from Fiji to your neighborhood. Every drop of Fiji water represents thousands of miles in completely unnecessary transportation and hundreds of gallons of fuel, all so you can drink expensive water from a pretty bottle."[53]

58   In 2007, Pablo Päster, an engineer and MBA, claimed to have undertaken a thorough and exhaustive study of the cost of bringing a litre of FIJI Water to America that was reported about on the Treehugger website in an article by Lloyd Alter entitled "Pablo Calculates the True Cost of Bottled Water." His study found that, "In summary, the manufacture and transport of that one kilogram bottle of Fiji water consumed 26.88 kilograms of water (7.1 gallons), .849 kilograms of fossil fuel (one litre or .26 gallons) and emitted 562 grams of Greenhouse Gases (1.2 pounds)."[54]

RELATIONS WITH THE FIJI GOVERNMENT

59   Natural Waters of Fiji Ltd., the Fiji Islands-based production subsidiary of FIJI Water LLC, played an important role in the Fiji economy, particularly as a source of export earnings. While in 1998 FIJI Water brand exports ranked 14th among product categories exported from Fiji,[55] its position among exports had climbed to number two in 2007, bringing FJ$105 million in export earnings.[56] Only sugar, whose exports in 2007 stood at FJ$185 million, brought more export revenues than bottled water, which was virtually all accounted for by FIJI Water. Since export revenues from sugar had been on the decline since 2000, there was a possibility that bottled water would soon become the number one export earner for Fiji, provided the Fiji government did not do any harm to the rapidly growing bottled water industry. The stand-off between Fiji's bottled water companies and the government over the

[51] Ibid.

[52] Robert Knox, "Green or Greenwashing? Fiji Water," www.greenopia.com/USA/news/15063/7-16-2008/Green-or-Greenwashing?-Fiji-Water.

[53] Ibid.

[54] www.treehugger.com/files/2007/02/pablo_calculate.php.

[55] McMaster and Nowak, "Natural Waters of Viti Limited—Pioneering a New Industry in the Fiji Islands," 2003.

[56] Fiji Islands Bureau of Statistics, "Key Statistics: Overseas Merchandise Trade," March 2008, p. 71.

20-cents-per-litre export duty and excise in 2008 might put a brake on this industry's growth and erode a substantial part of Fiji's export earnings. In 2007, bottled water accounted for almost 10 per cent of Fiji's total export revenues.[57]

Taxation Issues

60   Over the last decade, the Fiji government had observed the rapid growth of a new export industry led by FIJI Water.[58] When Natural Waters of Viti Ltd. was established, it applied to the government for financial incentives under the Tax Free Factory Scheme and was granted a thirteen-year tax holiday from the government. Also, it was granted approval to import the plant and equipment for its factory free of import duty.[59]

61   The success of FIJI Water was very evident to all citizens of Fiji as they observed the large number of trucks transporting containers of bottled water to the ports of Lautoka and Suva using the Queens highway. FIJI Water received positive media reports and was a sponsor of the Fiji Exporter of the Year Awards. A film was made about the company's past growth and plans for the future, and was broadcast several times on the local TV station Fiji One.

62   It was not until 2008 that the government started to review the potential tax contribution that could be levied on the bottled water industry. FIJI Water appeared to provide little direct benefits to government revenue because of the tax-free status granted by earlier governments. One could argue that the damage caused to the national roads and bridges by the huge number of heavily laden trucks carrying FIJI Water might have exceeded the road and fuel tax, and that the citizens of Fiji were subsidizing FIJI Water. The bottling plant of FIJI Water was fully automated with state-of-the-art equipment and featured a highly capital-intensive production process employing a relatively small workforce given the volume of exports.

63   On July 4, 2008, without any prior consultation with the industry, the Fiji government imposed a 20-cents-per-litre export duty on all mineral water exports and the same level of excise duty on mineral water sold for domestic consumption.[60] This new tax was put into effect by amending the Customs Tariff Act (Amendment) (No 3) Promulgation 2008 And Excise Act (Amendment) (No 1) Promulgation 2008.[61]

64   The local media reported that the interim finance minister, Mahendra Chaudhry, said, "The main purpose of this new duty was to stimulate conservation of our scarce natural resources."[62]

65   These new taxes came into effect on July 1, 2008. In a press statement released on July 20 by Fiji Islands Revenue and Customs Authority chief executive officer, Jitoko Tikolevu, it was announced that: "Should there be a change in the rates in the future as decided by government, the Authority will refund any excess revenue collected from these taxes."[63]

66   Based on FIJI Water's export levels, the new export tax would result in the company paying many millions to the government coffers. In 2006, FIJI Water exported 119,000,000

---

[57] Ibid.

[58] According to Fiji Times (August 12, 2008, p. 2), FIJI Water accounts for 98 per cent of bottled water exports from Fiji.

[59] McMaster and Nowak, "Natural Waters of Viti Limited—Pioneering a New Industry in the Fiji Islands, 2003."

[60] "Cabinet Approves Tariff, Excise Act," *Fiji Times*, July 4, 2008.

[61] Ibid.

[62] Ibid.

[63] "Duty on Bottled Water Remains," *Fiji Times*, July 20, 2008.

litres of bottled water to the United States. Applying a tax of 20-cents-per-litre to this level of export to the United States would result in a tax bill of FJ$24 million to FIJI Water just for its exports to one market. It was likely that FIJI Water could end up paying as much as FJ$50 million for the new tax.[64]

67   FIJI Water and the nine other companies immediately mounted a campaign against the new tax. They first threatened to cease production and to lay workers off. They issued press releases that argued the new tax would destroy the whole industry and greatly undermine foreign investor confidence, which was already at a low level. The 10 bottled water companies formed an industry association and appointed a spokesperson to lead the media campaign. They argued that this sudden decision by the Cabinet was made without thorough analysis of the economic costs and benefits. They stated that the government did not have detailed information on company costs and profitability and that the firms could not absorb the ill-conceived new tax that would have a major negative impact on the whole economy. It would be the death knell of this new export industry and would greatly reduce export earnings and foreign exchange earnings, and lead to job losses and slower economic growth. They pointed out that it would undermine the government's economic development strategy that was based on increasing the level of investment and export-oriented growth.

68   The new industry association comprising 10 firms—Warwick Pleass, FIJI Water, VTY, Mr Pure, Island Chill, Aqua Pacific, Diamond Aqua, Tappoos Beverage, Fresh Spring Limited and Minerals Water of Fiji—lobbied the members of the Military Council and the media and gained strong support of the local newspapers. The main local newspaper, The Fiji Times, published an editorial in July 2008 calling for the sacking of the interim minister of finance, who was seen as the architect of this new tax. The bottled water industry was required to make its submissions to the Finance Ministry on the new tax.

69   A critical issue was the likely impact of this new tax on both foreign and local investment. It was seen as moving the goalposts after the start of the game. Foreign investor confidence was already at a very low level because of the military takeover of the democratically elected government in December 2006. Investors are not attracted to a country where the taxation environment can alter dramatically overnight without consultation.

70   On July 23, 2008, Natural Waters of Viti Limited laid off about 400 workers and shut down operations along with five other major exporting companies. The following day, the Fiji Times, the leading local newspaper, published an editorial comment on the so-called "Water Debacle."[65] The editorial stated that: "the closure of Fiji Water's operations yesterday shows what happens when governments take draconian measures to impose unrealistic taxes on large corporate entities. This major contributor to the national economy has closed its doors, sent staff home and deprived the nation of $3 million in export revenue per week." The editorial continued, stressing out the importance of FIJI Water operations for the livelihood of workers and their families, for tax revenues, as well as for retail revenues in the nearby towns of Rakiraki and Tavua. It also pointed out the impact of the plant closure on dockworkers and drivers."[66]

71   Also the following day, a spokesperson for the bottlers, Jay Dayal, said they had decided to take legal action, as their patience had been exhausted. The bottlers had filed for a judicial review over the government decision to impose the 20-cents-per-litre tax.[67] On the

[64] FIRCA Press Release, July 21, 2008, www.frca.org.fj/docs/firca/press_releases/Press Release 21.07.pdf

[65] "Water Debacle," *Fiji Times,* July 24, 2008.

[66] Ibid.

[67] "FIJI Water bottlers file suit against government, Association says 20-cent tax will kill industry." Radio New Zealand International, www.rnzi.com.

same day, FIJI Water released a statement saying that the lawsuit was caused by the lack of movement by the interim government on the imposition of tax by Fiji Islands Revenue and Customs Authority (FIRCA), pending a final decision by the interim Cabinet. "Unfortunately, FIJI Water must take this action because we have now reached a critical juncture where we can no longer effectively operate our business," the statement said. "We have neither sold nor exported any product since July 1, forcing us to cancel multiple port calls from various shipping lines. As long as the crisis continues, the nation of Fiji will continue to lose approximately FJ$3 million in export revenue each week (more than FJ$150 million annually)."[68]

72   Behind the scenes, the bottlers were very active in seeking the support of the media and key decision makers, trade unions, village leaders and local chiefs as well as lobbying interim ministers and members of the Military Council. One of the bottlers described the tax-induced crisis as "like a war had broken out or a bomb had exploded." There were tens of millions of dollars at stake that could be collected from the bottlers.

73   On July 25, 2008, the Fiji government made an announcement that it had decided to drop the new tax. This decision by interim Prime Minister Commodore Voreqe Bainimarama was praised by the proprietors of water bottling companies.[69] Immediately after the announcement of the repeal of the tax, the major bottled water-exporting companies resumed production and re-employed the hundreds of workers who had been laid off.[70]

74   FIJI Water had for a number of years been a sponsor of the Fiji Exporter of the Year Awards, an annual event to celebrate successful exporters. On August 3, 2008, FIJI Water's local CEO, David Roth, announced the company's decision to withdraw its sponsorship of the Awards because of the lack of support of FTIB during the taxation dispute.[71] David Roth said: "Fiji Islands Trade and Investment Bureau (FTIB) did not provide any support or assistance towards the bottled water industry during this struggle, and in fact FTIB's chairman publicly supported the imposition of the unreasonable and draconian excise and export duties, in spite of many of us trying to explain to him that his assumptions about our businesses were simply incorrect." Roth added that the company's decision to withdraw had nothing to do with its attitude toward others in government.[72]

75   In November 2008, the Fiji government re-introduced the disputed water tax as part of the 2009 budget in a different form. It was called "water resource tax" and was progressive depending on the amount of water extracted. For extractions up to 4,999,999 litres it was set at 0.11 cents per litre; for extractions between 5,000,000 and 9,999,999 litres it was 0.22 cents per litre; and an extraction volume of 10,000,000 litres or more would attract a tax of 0.33 cents per litre.[73] The tax was to be imposed only on extracted (artesian) water; companies engaged in the bottling of rainwater or purified tap water would be exempt from the tax. The tax was supposed to be collected from January 2009. It was expected that the Fiji government would collect FJ$1.5 million through the water extraction tax.[74]

[68] "Fiji Water Shuts down Operations," *Fiji Daily Post,* July 24, 2008.

[69] Margaret Wise, "Sigh of Relief as State Drops Tax," *Fiji Times,* July 25, 2008.

[70] " Bottled Water Back in Action," Fiji Live website, July 24, 2008.

[71] "Fiji Bottlers Reconsider Boycott Decision," Fiji Live website, August 3, 2008.

[72] Ibid.

[73] PriceWaterhouseCoopers, 2009 Fiji Islands Budget Summary, November 21, 2008.

[74] "$1.5 million expected from water tax," Fiji Live website, November 21, 2008.

Transfer Pricing

76 In January 2008, the government became concerned that FIJI Water was engaging in transfer price manipulations, selling the water shipments produced in Fiji at a very low price to the company headquarters in Los Angeles. It was feared that very little of the wealth generated by the company was coming into Fiji as foreign reserves from export earnings, which Fiji badly needed to fund its imports. Seemingly, FIJI Water was funnelling most of its cash to the United States.

77 As a result of these concerns, FIRCA decided to take action against FIJI Water and it halted exports in January 2008 at the ports by putting 200 containers loaded with FIJI Water bottles under armed guard, and issued a statement accusing FIJI Water of transfer price manipulations. FIRCA's chief executive, Jitoko Tikolevu, said, "The wholly US-owned Fijian subsidiary sold its water exclusively to its US parent at the declared rate, in Fiji, of US$4 (NZ$5) a carton. In the US, though, the same company then sold it for up to US$50 a carton."[75]

78 Natural Waters of Viti Ltd. immediately filed a lawsuit against FIRCA with the High Court of Fiji. The High Court issued an interim order, allowing the company to resume shipment of the embargoed containers upon payment of an FJ$5 million bond to the Court.[76]

79 The U.S. ambassador to Fiji, Larry Dinger, issued a barely veiled threat to Fiji. "The example [the authority] and the interim government set regarding fair and impartial treatment in this case will surely have a major impact on global perceptions of Fiji's investment climate. American companies have to receive fair and impartial treatment around the world. That applies in Fiji, too. 'Rule of law' and a 'level playing field' are critically important factors when there are commercial disputes, and those elements have a major impact in decisions by foreign investors, including American investors, on where they will direct their funds," he stated.[77]

80 A press release by FIRCA, issued in January 2008, noted that FIJI Water had received advice from international law firm Baker & McKenzie, which conducted an economic study on transfer pricing and declared what the company was doing in Fiji was fair. FIRCA rejected the claim by stating that: "FIRCA will not passively accept the verdict of Baker & McKenzie without itself having access to the information on which same is based, and to the instructions on which same is based, and without the opportunity to conduct its own transfer pricing study based on such matters and upon the profitability of Natural Waters of Viti Limited."[78]

81 The FIJI Water dispute with the government over transfer pricing attracted the attention of the University of the South Pacific economist Sukhdev Shah, who published an article on "The true cost of water" in the Fiji Times on January 24, 2008, to give the general public a lecture on the complexities of transfer pricing. He stated that: "Multinational companies as represented by FIJI Water are capable of spreading their risks across countries where they do business. They do this by shifting most of their profits and asset holdings to their affiliates in low-tax countries that are also considered safe. Given a choice between US and Fiji, FIJI Water would definitely take a bet on US—partly for the reason of lower tax obligation but mostly because it can be a safe-haven."[79]

[75] Michael Field, "Fiji-US row brews over water exports." *The Dominion Post,* January 21, 2008.

[76] "High Court set to rule in Fiji Water case," *Fiji Times,* February 8, 2008.

[77] Field, "Fiji-US row brews over water exports," January 21, 2008.

[78] "Press Release," Fiji Islands Revenue & Customs Authority, January 11, 2008, p. 3.

[79] Sukhdev Shah, "The true cost of water." *Fiji Times,* January 24, 2008

RELATIONS WITH THE LOCAL COMMUNITY

82   The company had recognized the importance of establishing and maintaining good relations with the five neighbouring Fijian villages that were the traditional landowners of the Yaqara basin, where the bottling plant was located. These villages were: Draunivi, Togovere, Naseyani, Nananu and Rabulu. FIJI Water's bottling plant drew most of its workforce from these villages. It employed a young workforce and most of the workers had not previously had a wage job but had been engaged in subsistence farming and fishing activities. The company provided its staff with on-the-job training in operating the sophisticated production line. In return, its workers showed a lot of enthusiasm, loyalty, and pride in working for the company. Through strong leadership, FIJI Water had established an excellent work environment with good interpersonal relationships among the workforce. The company supported children's education. To assist the children in getting an early start, it had constructed a kindergarten classroom in each village to provide early childhood education. The company had also provided the pre-schools with equipment, educational material, teacher training and other support.

83   In March 2002, the company voluntarily established an independently administrated community development trust fund and allocated FJ$275,000 to it. The trust fund was established after a series of negotiations with the members of the community. It was designed to support village projects to improve the hygiene and sanitation of the community. Through this fund, the company intended to finance projects to supply potable water to the villages and reticulate it to the households. It also aimed at supporting projects to reduce pollution and improve hygiene. Through improving the quality of hygiene and sanitation, it was hoped to improve the health of the villagers and of the workforce of the company.[80]

84   As a result of the above-described trust fund, Draunivi and Togovere were first provided with clean, safe drinking water. The water supply project was then extended in 2008 to cover three other villages in the vicinity of the bottling plant—Naseyani, Nananu and Rabulu.[81] Moreover, in the same year, FIJI Water teamed with the Rotary Club in Suva to fund the Pacific Water for Life Trust. The Trust provided funds for developing the infrastructure, expertise and skills needed to supply clean, safe and sustainable water to more than 100 communities, schools, health centres and nursing stations throughout Fiji.[82]

85   Natural Waters of Viti Ltd. was a strong believer in contracting out. It had contracted out services to a local company that employed tens of people in the following functions: transport of workers to and from work; security office to guard the factory; the preparation of food for workers in the canteen; ground maintenance; and laundry.

86   In recognition of FIJI Water's involvement in local community development in Fiji, in 2004 the U.S. State Department honoured the company with the Award for Corporate Excellence for Outstanding Corporate Citizenship, Innovation and Exemplary International Business Practice. The award was presented to FIJI Water founder David Gilmour by Secretary of State Colin Powell in October 2004, who remarked, "Fijians take special pride in their island's tranquil beauty and Fiji Water has matched their passion with action . . . More than a good corporate citizen, Fiji Water is a good neighbour to all the people of Fiji."[83] Ironically, two months later FIJI Water was sold by Gilmour to Roll International.

---

[80] McMaster and Nowak, "Natural Waters of Viti Limited—Pioneering a New Industry in the Fiji Islands."
[81] www.fijiwater.com.
[82] Ibid.
[83] "Here's to you: Fiji Water." *Beverage World,* March 8, 2007.

WHAT NEXT?

87　In 2009 and beyond, FIJI Water will continue facing complex CRS challenges. It will have to live up to its promise of becoming a carbon negative company. Any attempt to engage in greenwashing will be quickly identified and protested by environmental groups. Keeping true to its slogan "every drop is green" will require substantial new investment in a renewable energy plant and equipment and in tree-planting offset activities.

88　FIJI Water's tax-free concession granted by the Fiji government for 13 years in 1995 came to an end in October 2008 and the company will be required to pay corporate tax in Fiji. The new water resource tax, although much lower than the draconian 20-cents-a-litre excise, is nevertheless likely to erode the company's profitability by adding about FJ$1 million to its costs every year. This is expected to coincide with a slow-down of growth or even stagnation of FIJI Water sales in its main markets due to the global recession.

89　Maintaining good relations with the Fiji government will be vital. A series of ads sponsored by FIJI Water, placed in the popular daily Fiji Times in late 2008 and early 2009, was focused on letting the public (and the government!) know how good a corporate citizen the company is. The ads highlighted FIJI Water's contribution to creating new jobs, improving education and raising standards of living in Fiji. In January 2009, FIJI Water donated US$0.5 million to Fiji's National Disaster, Relief and Rehabilitation Fund, which was created by the prime minister's office in the aftermath of devastating floods.[84] Clearly, FIJI Water was making efforts to live up to its good corporate citizenship claim. But is it enough to dispel government officials' and ordinary citizens' doubts about FIJI Water's positive contribution to the local economy and community?

90　Designing and implementing a sustainable growth strategy and a socially and environmentally responsible marketing plan will require dealing effectively with the promise to go carbon negative as well as meeting the demanding needs of customers, clients and other stakeholders. Will FIJI Water be able to successfully navigate through these rough waters of corporate social responsibility? What should it do to breathe new life into this otherwise clever marketing strategy?

[84] "Fiji Water donates to PM's Relief Fund," Press Release, Fiji Government On-line, January 27, 2009.

Case 10

Southwest Airlines 2008 Andrew C. Inkpen

"You are now free to move about the country."™

1   In 2008, Southwest Airlines (Southwest), the once scrappy underdog in the U.S. airline industry, carried more domestic passengers than any other U.S. airline. The company, unlike all of its major competitors, had been consistently profitable for decades and had weathered recessions, energy crises, and the September 11 terrorist attacks. In the first quarter of 2008, the company was profitable and experienced record first quarter revenue and a record passenger load factor (percentage of available seats sold). However, the earnings release made it clear that the "threat of volatile and unprecedented jet fuel prices" was a major issue that threatened future growth. Operating expenses were rising, and Southwest announced that it would cut 2009 growth in available seats to less than 3%. Over the previous decade, growth had been about 5–10% a year. This cut in planned growth was consistent with previous responses to difficult environments. An insight into Southwest's operating philosophy can be found in the company's 2001 Annual Report:

> Southwest was well poised, financially, to withstand the potentially devastating hammer blow of September 11. Why? Because for several decades our leadership philosophy has been: We manage in good times so that our Company and our People can be job secure and prosper through bad times. . . . Once again, after September 11, our philosophy of managing in good times so as to do well in bad times proved a marvelous prophylactic for our Employees and our Shareholders.

THE U.S. AIRLINE INDUSTRY

2   The U.S. commercial airline industry was permanently altered in October 1978 when President Carter signed the Airline Deregulation Act. Before deregulation, the Civil Aeronautics Board regulated airline route entry and exit, passenger fares, mergers and acquisitions, and airline rates of return. Typically, two or three carriers provided service in a given market, although there were routes covered by only one carrier. Cost increases were passed along to customers and price competition was almost nonexistent. The airlines operated as if there were only two market segments: those who could afford to fly, and those who couldn't.

3   Deregulation sent airline fares tumbling and allowed many new firms to enter the market. The financial impact on both established and new airlines was enormous. The fuel crisis of 1979 and the air traffic controllers' strike in 1981 contributed to the industry's difficulties, as did the severe recession that hit the U.S. during the early 1980s. During the first decade of deregulation, more than 150 carriers, many of them start-up airlines, collapsed into bankruptcy. Eight of the 11 major airlines dominating the industry in 1978 ended up filing for bankruptcy, merging with other carriers, or simply disappearing from the radar

screen. Collectively, the industry made enough money during this period to buy two Boeing 747s.[1] The three major carriers that survived intact—Delta, United, and American—ended up with 80% of all domestic U.S. air traffic and 67% of trans-Atlantic business.[2]

4   Competition and lower fares led to greatly expanded demand for airline travel. Controlling for inflation, the average price to fly one domestic mile dropped by more than 50% since deregulation. By the mid-1990s, the airlines were having trouble meeting this demand. Travel increased from 200 million travelers in 1974 to 700 million in 2007, with increases in runway and airport capacity lagging far behind. Exhibits 1A–E provide industry financial and operating data.

5   Despite the financial problems experienced by many airlines started after deregulation, new firms continued to enter the market. Between 1994 and 2004, 66 new airlines were certified by the FAA. By 2007, 43 had shut down. Most of the new airlines competed with limited route structures and lower fares than the major airlines. The new airlines created a second tier of service providers that saved consumers billions of dollars annually, and provided service in markets abandoned or ignored by major carriers.

6   Although deregulation fostered competition and the growth of new airlines, it also created a regional disparity in ticket prices and adversely affected service to small and remote communities. Airline workers generally suffered, with inflation-adjusted average employee wages falling from $42,928 in 1978 to much lower levels over the subsequent decades. About 20,000 airline industry employees were laid off in the early 1980s, while productivity of the remaining employees rose 43% during the same period. In a variety of cases, bankruptcy filings were used to diminish the role of unions and reduce unionized wages. In the most recent round of bankruptcies, airline workers at United, Delta, and other major airlines were forced to accept pay cuts of up to 35%.

Industry Economics

7   About 80% of airline operating costs were fixed or semi-variable. The only true variable costs were travel agency commissions, food costs, and ticketing fees. The operating costs of an airline flight depended primarily on the distance traveled, not the number of passengers on board. For example, the crew and ground staff sizes were determined by the type of aircraft, not the passenger load. Therefore, once an airline established its route structure, most of its operating costs were fixed.

8   Because of this high fixed-cost structure, the airlines developed sophisticated software tools to maximize capacity utilization, known as load factor. Load factor was calculated by dividing RPM (revenue passenger miles—the number of passengers carried multiplied by the distance flown) by ASM (available seat miles—the number of seats available for sale multiplied by the distance flown).

9   On each flight by one of the major airlines (excluding Southwest and a few other carriers), there were typically a dozen categories of fares. The airlines analyzed historical travel patterns on individual routes to determine how many seats to sell at each fare level. All of the major airlines used this type of analysis and flexible pricing practice, known as a "yield management" system. These systems enabled the airlines to manage their seat inventories and the prices paid for those seats. The objective was to sell more seats on each flight at higher yields (total passenger yield was passenger revenue from scheduled operations divided by scheduled RPMs). The higher the ticket price, the better the yield.

---

[1] P. S. Dempsey, "Transportation Deregulation: On a Collision Course," *Transportation Law Journal*, 13, 1984, p. 329.

[2] W. Goralski, "Deregulation Deja Vu," *Telephony*, June 17, 1996, pp. 32–36.

EXHIBIT 1A Revenue Passenger-Miles (RPM)* 1989–2007 (in billions)

	American	America West	Continental	Delta	Northwest	Southwest	TransWorld	United	US Airways	Total
2007	138.4	17.7	81.4	103.3	72.9	72.3		117.4	43.5	646.9
2006	139.4	23.5	76.3	98.8	72.6	67.7		117.2	37.4	632.9
2005	138.4	24.3	68.4	103.7	75.9	60.3		114.3	40.2	625.5
2004	130.2	23.3	63.4	98.3	73.4	53.5		115.2	40.5	597.8
2003	120.3	21.3	57.6	89.4	68.8	48		104.4	37.8	547.6
2002	121.7	19.9	57.3	95.3	72.1	45.5		109.4	40	561.2
2001	106.2	19.1	58.8	97.7	73.3	44.7	20.8	116.6	46	583.2
2000	116.6	19.1	62.4	107.8	79.2	42.4	27.3	126.9	46.9	628.6
1999	110.2	17.7	58	104.8	74.2	36.8	26.1	125.5	41.5	594.8
1998	108.9	16.4	51	102	66.8	31.6	24.5	124.6	41.4	567.2
1997	107	16.2	44.3	99.7	72.1	26.4	25.2	121.4	41.7	554
1996	104.6	15.3	37.6	93.9	68.7	27.3	27.3	116.7	39.2	530.6
1995	102.7	13.3	35.8	85.2	62.6	23.5	25.1	111.8	38.1	498.1
1994	98.8	12.2	38.1	86.4	58.5	19.9	24.8	108.2	38.4	485.3
1993	97.1	11.2	40.1	82.9	58.7	16.9	22.8	101.3	35.5	466.5
1992	97.1	11.8	43.5	80.6	58.7	13.9	29.2	92.7	35.4	462.9

*Revenue Passenger-Miles, or RPM, is a measure of the volume of air passenger transportation. A revenue passenger-mile is equal to one paying passenger carried one mile.
Source: Bureau of Transportation Statistics, *Table T1: U.S. Air Carrier Traffic and Capacity Summary by Service Class.*

EXHIBIT 1B   **Passenger Revenue per RPM* 1992–2007 (in cents)**

	American	America West	Continental	Delta	Northwest	Southwest	TransWorld	United	US Airways
2007	10	11	10	9	10	9		10	9
2006	13	12	12	12	12	13		12	14
2005	12	10	12	11	12	12		11	13
2004	12	10	11	11	13	11		11	13
2003	12	10	12	12	11	11		10	13
2002	12	10	12	12	11	12		10	13
2001	13	10	12	12	11	12	11	12	14
2000	14	11	13	13	12	13	12	13	16
1999	13	11	12	13	12	12	11	12	17
1998	15	12	13	14	13	13	13	14	21
1997	15	12	15	14	14	13	13	14	20
1996	14	11	15	14	14	13	13	14	20
1995	15	12	15	14	15	12	13	13	20
1994	13	11	12	14	14	12	13	12	16
1993	14	11	12	15	13	12	13	12	18
1992	12	10	11	14	12	12	11	12	17

*Passenger Revenue per Revenue Passenger Mile, also known as Passenger Yield, is computed by dividing passenger revenues by revenue passenger-miles. Computed from Bureau of Transportation Statistics, *Air Carrier Financial Statistics Schedule P-12*, and *Table T1: U.S. Air Carrier Traffic and Capacity Summary by Service Class.*

EXHIBIT 1C   Load Factors 1992–1997

	American	America West	Continental	Delta	Northwest	Southwest	TransWorld	United	US Airways*
2007	82	83	83	81	85	73		83	80
2006	80	80	82	79	85	73		82	78
2005	79	80	80	78	82	71		82	75
2004	75	77	77	75	80	70		78	75
2003	74	79	77	76	76	70		77	75
2002	70	73	71	66	74	63		72	68
2001	69	72	73	69	74	68	66	71	69
2000	72	71	75	73	77	71	72	72	70
1999	70	68	74	72	75	69	73	71	70
1998	70	67	72	73	73	66	71	72	73
1997	70	69	71	72	74	64	69	72	71
1996	69	71	68	70	73	67	67	72	69
1995	66	69	66	66	71	64	66	71	65
1994	63	68	62	65	65	67	63	70	62
1993	59	66	62	62	64	68	62	64	59
1992	63	62	63	61	62	65	63	66	59

*US Airways merged with American beginning in 2005. Data reported under US Airways is for both companies starting 10/2007. Previously, data was reported seperately.
Source: Department of Transportation, Bureau of Transportation Statistics, *Table T-100 All Carriers.*

EXHIBIT 1D Operating Revenues (in millions of dollars) 1992–2007

	American	America West	Continental	Delta	Northwest	Southwest	TransWorld	United	US Airways	Total
2007	17,177	2,737	10,615	14,515	9,545	7,369		15,075	6,463	83,496
2006	22,493	3,770	13,010	17,339	12,555	9,086		19,334	8,076	105,663
2005	20,657	3,397	11,108	16,112	12,316	7,584		17,304	7,212	95,690
2004	18,608	2,482	9,851	15,154	11,266	6,530		15,701	7,073	86,665
2003	17,403	2,223	7,333	14,203	9,184	5,937		13,398	6,762	76,443
2002	15,871	2,021	7,353	12,410	9,152	5,522		13,916	6,915	73,160
2001	15,639	2,035	7,972	13,211	9,592	5,555	2,633	16,087	8,253	80,977
2000	18,117	2,309	9,129	15,321	10,957	5,650	3,585	19,331	9,181	93,580
1999	16,090	2,164	8,027	14,901	9,868	4,736	3,309	17,967	8,460	85,522
1998	16,299	1,983	7,299	14,630	8,707	4,164	3,259	17,518	8,556	82,415
1997	15,856	1,887	6,361	14,204	9,984	3,817	3,330	17,335	8,501	81,275
1996	15,136	1,752	5,487	13,318	9,751	3,407	3,554	16,317	7,704	76,426
1995	15,610	1,562	4,919	12,557	8,909	2,873	3,281	14,895	6,985	71,591
1994	14,951	1,414	4,734	12,346	8,929	2,417	3,350	13,887	6,579	68,607
1993	14,737	1,332	5,086	12,376	8,448	2,067	3,094	14,354	6,623	68,117
1992	13,581	1,303	5,210	11,639	7,964	1,685	3,570	12,725	6,236	63,913

Source: Bureau of Transportation Statistics, *Air Carrier Financial Reports Table P-12.*

EXHIBIT 1E Operating Profits, U.S. Majors, 1992–2007, in millions of dollars

	American	America West	Continental	Delta	Northwest	Southwest	TransWorld	United	US Airways	Total
2007	842	–19	552	1,040	1,028	664		1,072	646	5,825
2006	816	–35	410	31	782	934		451	592	3,981
2005	–351	–121	–94	–1,198	–895	820		–241	–213	–2,293
2004	–421	–4	–290	–1,613	–434	554		–1,166	–348	–3,722
2003	–1,444	24	30	–1,157	–277	482		–1,554	–421	–4,317
2002	–3,313	–164	–481	–1,035	–783	418		–3,022	–919	–9,299
2001	–2,558	–423	–342	–972	–797	631	–645	–3,743	–1,181	–10,030
2000	1,243	–13	587	1,459	664	1,021	–233	741	–44	5,425
1999	1,004	198	480	1,730	769	782	–343	1,358	202	6,180
1998	1,748	198	660	1,793	–129	684	–65	1,435	990	7,314
1997	1,447	163	645	1,621	1,203	524	–27	1,226	586	7,388
1996	1,331	69	394	571	1,108	350	–199	1,130	369	5,123
1995	968	155	238	1,038	910	309	37	832	235	4,722
1994	912	146	–84	–215	876	290	–238	513	–505	1,695
1993	564	121	–46	–275	331	281	–248	295	–129	894
1992	–77	–75	–195	–826	–309	182	–369	–496	–376	–2,541

Source: Bureau of Transportation Statistics, *Air Carrier Financial Reports Table P-12.*

10   Although reducing operating costs was a high priority for the airlines, the nature of the cost structure limited cost reduction opportunities. Fuel costs (17% of total operating costs at Southwest in 2004; 31% in 2008) were largely beyond the control of the airlines, and many of the larger airlines' restrictive union agreements limited labor flexibility. The airline industry's extremely high fixed costs made it one of the worst net profit margin performers when measured against other industries. Airlines were far outpaced in profitability by industries such as banks, health care, automobile manufacturing, consumer products, and publishing.

11   To manage their route structures, the major airlines (except Southwest) maintained their operations around a "hub-and-spoke" network. The spokes fed passengers from outlying points into a central airport—the hub—where passengers could travel to additional hubs or their final destination. For example, to fly from Phoenix to Boston on Northwest Airlines, a typical route would involve a flight from Phoenix to Northwest's Detroit hub. The passenger would then take a second flight from Detroit to Boston.

12   Establishing a major hub in a city like Chicago or Atlanta required a huge investment for gate acquisition and terminal construction. JetBlue's new facility at JFK in New York was expected to cost $800 million. Although hubs created inconveniences for travelers, hub systems were an efficient means of distributing services across a wide network. The major airlines were very protective of their so-called "fortress" hubs, and used the hubs to control various local markets. For example, Northwest handled about 80% of Detroit's passengers and occupied nearly the entire new Detroit terminal that opened in 2002. And, Northwest's deal with the local government assured that it would be the only airline that could have a hub in Detroit. When Southwest entered the Detroit market, the only available gates were already leased by Northwest. Northwest subleased gates to Southwest at rates 18 times higher than Northwest's costs. Southwest eventually withdrew from Detroit, and then reentered, one of only four markets Southwest had abandoned in its history (San Francisco, Denver, and Beaumont, Texas, were the other three).

Recent U.S. Airline Industry Performance

13   Despite steadily growing customer demand, the airline industry was in crisis. In 2002, United Airlines filed for Chapter 11 bankruptcy protection, citing liquidity problems. US Airways, after emerging out of bankruptcy in March 2003, filed for bankruptcy protection in 2004. Delta and Northwest both filed for and entered . . . bankruptcy in 2005. ATA Airlines, the tenth largest carrier in the United States, filed for bankruptcy in 2004 and shut down completely in 2008 as did Aloha Airlines and Skybus. Airline labor unions were reeling in the face of wage reductions, pension cutbacks, and job uncertainty. Exhibits 1, 2, and 3 provide comparative data for the major airlines.

14   After the September 11, 2001, terrorist attacks, domestic airlines lost about $30 billion. The specter of terrorism cast a long shadow on the global airline industry, exacerbated by the ongoing war in Iraq and the 2003 SARS epidemic. In 2008, fuel costs were rapidly rising, putting a damper on the industry's return to profitability. For example, Delta paid an average of $1.16 per gallon in 2004 and $2.61 a gallon in the 4th quarter 2007 (despite a fuel hedging program that generated $40 million in gains for the quarter).

Other Pressures on the Industry

15   In addition to the difficult profit environment for airlines in 2008, the industry was faced with other pressures:

1. **Customer Dissatisfaction with Airline Service.** Service problems were leading to calls for new regulation of airline competitive practices.

EXHIBIT 2   Airline Performance 2007

Airline	Load Factor (%)	Domestic Passengers Carried
American	82	76,581,414
America West	83	14,674,045
Continental	83	37,117,030
Delta	81	61,599,411
Northwest	85	43,812,180
Southwest	**73**	**101,947,800**
United	83	56,420,151
US Airways	80	37,220,911

Source: Bureau of Transportation Statistics, *Air Carriers: T-100 Domestic Market (U.S. Carriers)*.

EXHIBIT 3   Domestic Costs and Revenues per Available Seat Mile Data (in cents)

Airline	Cost/ASM 2007
American	11.4
America West	11.3
Continental	10.8
Delta	11.9
JetBlue	8.4
Northwest	10.8
Southwest	**9.1**
United	13.9
US Airways	11.3

Source: Company financial statements.

2. **Aircraft Safety Maintenance.** The aging of the general aircraft population meant higher maintenance costs and eventual aircraft replacement. The introduction of stricter government regulations for older planes placed new burdens on operators of older aircraft. For example, in April 2008 American was forced to ground its fleet of MD-11s for several days for FAA mandated inspections.

3. **Debt servicing.** The airline industry's debt load greatly exceeded U.S. industry averages.

4. **Air-Traffic Delays.** Increased air-traffic-control delays caused by higher travel demand and related airport congestion were expected to negatively influence airlines' profitability.

5. **Mergers.** Although most U.S. airline mergers had not delivered on their promises, financial pressures were pushing airlines into new merger discussions.

6. **Open Skies Agreement.** 2007 legislation allowing greater access to U.S. markets by European carriers was expected to increase competitive pressure.

SOUTHWEST AIRLINES BACKGROUND

16 In 1966, Herb Kelleher was practicing law in San Antonio when a client named Rollin King proposed starting a short-haul airline similar to California-based Pacific Southwest Airlines. The airline would fly the Golden Triangle of Houston, Dallas, and San Antonio and, by staying within Texas, avoid federal regulations. Kelleher and King incorporated a company, raised initial capital, and filed for regulatory approval from the Texas Aeronautics Commission. Unfortunately, the other Texas-based airlines, namely Braniff, Continental, and Trans Texas (later called Texas International), opposed the idea and waged a battle to prohibit Southwest from flying. Kelleher argued the company's case before the Texas Supreme Court, which ruled in Southwest's favor. The U.S. Supreme Court refused to hear an appeal filed by the other airlines. In late 1970, it looked as if the company could begin flying.

17 Southwest began building a management team, and the purchase of three surplus Boeing 737s was negotiated. Meanwhile, Braniff and Texas International continued their efforts to prevent Southwest from flying. The underwriters of Southwest's initial public stock offering withdrew, and a restraining order against the company was obtained two days before its scheduled inaugural flight. Kelleher again argued his company's case before the Texas Supreme Court, which ruled in Southwest's favor a second time, lifting the restraining order. Southwest Airlines began flying the next day, June 18, 1971.[3]

18 When Southwest began flying to three Texas cities, the firm had three aircraft and 25 employees. Initial flights were out of Dallas' older Love Field airport and Houston's Hobby Airport, both of which were closer to downtown than the major international airports. Flamboyant from the beginning, original flights were staffed by flight attendants in hot pants. By 1996, the flight attendant uniform had evolved to khakis and polo shirts. The "Luv" theme was a staple of the airline from the outset and became the company's ticker symbol on Wall Street.

19 Southwest management quickly discovered that there were two types of travelers: convenience, time-oriented business travelers, and price-sensitive leisure travelers. To cater to both groups, Southwest developed a two-tiered pricing structure. In 1972, Southwest was charging $20 to fly between Houston, Dallas, and San Antonio, undercutting the $28 fares of the other carriers. After an experiment with $10 fares, Southwest decided to sell seats on weekdays until 7:00 p.m. for $26 and after 7:00 p.m. and on weekends for $13.[4] In response, in January 1973, Braniff Airlines began charging $13 for its Dallas–Houston Hobby flights. This resulted in one of Southwest's most famous ads, which had the caption, "Nobody's going to shoot Southwest out of the sky for a lousy $13." Southwest offered travelers the opportunity to pay $13 or $26 and receive a free bottle of liquor. More than 75% of the passengers chose the $26 fare, and Southwest became the largest distributor of Chivas Regal scotch whiskey in Texas. In 1975, Braniff abandoned the Dallas–Houston Hobby route. When Southwest entered the Cleveland market, the unrestricted one-way fare between Cleveland and Chicago was $310 on other carriers; Southwest's fare was $59.[5] One of Southwest's problems was convincing passengers that its low fares were not just introductory promotions but regular fares.

---

[3]K. Freiberg & J. Freiberg, *Nuts: Southwest Airlines' Crazy Recipe for Business and Personal Success* (Austin, TX: Bard Press, 1996), pp. 14–21.
[4]Ibid., p.31.
[5]Ibid., p.55.

SOUTHWEST OPERATIONS

20   Although Southwest became one of the largest airlines in the United States, the firm did not deviate from its initial focus: primarily short-haul (less than 500 miles), point-to-point flights, a fleet consisting only of Boeing 737s, high frequency flights, low fares, and no international flights. In 2007, the average Southwest one-way fare was $105.37.

21   Southwest was the only large airline to operate without major hubs, although cities such as Phoenix, Houston, Chicago, Dallas, and Las Vegas were increasingly becoming important transit points for Southwest trips. For example, daily departures from Chicago, Southwest's second busiest airport, increased to 227 in 2007. Point-to-point service provided maximum convenience for passengers who wanted to fly between two cities, but insufficient demand could make such nonstop flights economically unfeasible. For that reason, the hub-and-spoke approach was generally assumed to generate cost savings for airlines through operational efficiencies. However, Southwest saw it another way: hub-and-spoke arrangements resulted in planes spending more time on the ground waiting for customers to arrive from connecting points.

22   Turnaround time—the time it takes to unload a waiting plane and load it for the next flight—was about 15 minutes for Southwest, compared with the industry average of 45 minutes. This time savings was accomplished with a gate crew 50% smaller than other airlines. Pilots sometimes helped unload bags when schedules were tight. Flight attendants regularly assisted in the cleanup of airplanes between flights.

23   Relative to the other major airlines, Southwest had a "no frills" approach to services: no reserved seating or meals were offered. Seating was first come, first served. As to why the airline did not have assigned seating, Kelleher explained: "It used to be we only had about four people on the whole plane, so the idea of assigned seats just made people laugh. Now the reason is you can turn the airplanes quicker at the gate. And if you can turn an airplane quicker, you can have it fly more routes each day. That generates more revenue, so you can offer lower fares."[6]

24   Unlike some of the major carriers, Southwest rarely offered delayed customers a hotel room or long distance telephone calls. Southwest had only a limited participation in computerized reservation systems, preferring to have travel agents and customers book flights through its reservation center. Southwest was the first national carrier to sell seats from an Internet site, and was the first airline to create a home page on the Internet. In 2007, 74% of Southwest tickets were booked online. The company estimated that the online ticketing cost was $1 per booking and $6–8 with a travel agent. Southwest was also one of the first airlines to use ticketless travel, first offering the service in 1995. Southwest was the only major airline with a frequent flyer program based on the number of flights taken by a passenger, not miles flown.

25   Over the years, Southwest's choice of markets resulted in significant growth in air travel at those locations. In Texas, traffic between the Rio Grande Valley (Harlingen) and the Golden Triangle grew from 123,000 to 325,000 within 11 months of Southwest entering the market.[7] Within a year of Southwest's arrival, the Oakland–Burbank route became the 25th largest passenger market, up from 179th. The Chicago–Louisville market tripled in size 30 days after Southwest began flying that route. Southwest was the dominant carrier in

---

[6]Herb Kelleher, @www.iflyswa.com/cgi-bin/imagemap/swagate 530.85.
[7]Freiberg & Freiberg, p. 29.

EXHIBIT 4   **Southwest 37-Year Comparison**

	1971	1999	2007
Size of fleet (end of year)	4	306	515
Number of employees	195	29,005	34,378
Number of passengers carried	108,554	52,600,000	101,947,800
Number of cities served	3	55	64
Number of trips flown	6,051	602,578	1,160,699
Total operating revenues (millions $)	2.33	4,736	7,369
Net income (millions $)	−3.8	433	645

Sources: Company press releases, and Southwest Airlines Fact Sheet at http://www.southwest.com/about_swa/press/factssheet.html

a number of cities, ranking first in market share in more than 50% of the largest U.S. city-pair markets. Exhibit 4 shows a comparison of Southwest in 1971 and 2007.

Service Changes in 2007

26   In 2007, Southwest made several changes to its service offering:

- Signed deals to participate in the Galileo and Worldspan reservations systems.
- Added three new fare categories, including higher-tier fares for business travelers.
- Began revamping gate areas that eventually will include television monitors, power ports, and new tables and seats.
- Established new boarding processes; for example, travelers could pay extra to board first.
- Modified the frequent flyer program to allow high status customers to board first.
- Increased emphasis on corporate sales.

27   The rationale for the changes is explained by CEO Gary Kelly:

> We've always been a business traveler's airline. At the same time, over 37 years we hadn't done much to try to customize the travel experience for the varieties of customer needs that we had. It was one-size-fits-all, and in today's competitive environment, we felt that was not the best way to remain on top. We had the desire to improve our overall customer experience for the business traveler.[8]

Southwest's Performance

28   Southwest bucked the airline industry trend by earning a profit in 36 consecutive years (Exhibit 1E shows Southwest recent operating profits). Since 1987, Southwest ranked first in fewest overall customer complaints as published in the Department of Transportation's Air Travel Consumer Report. *Fortune* magazine recognized Southwest as the 5th most admired company in 2007. In its latest global survey of Top Performing Airlines, *Aviation Week & Space Technology* ranked Southwest second behind Singapore Airlines. Unfortunately for shareholders, the stock performance over the past few years lagged far behind the performance of the 1980s and 90s.

[8]"The 25 Most Influential Executives of 2007," *Business Travel News,* February 4, 2008.

29   The average Southwest aircraft trip was 633 miles with an average duration of about one hour and 48 minutes. This was up from 462 miles in 1999 and 394 in 1996. Southwest had 3,300 flights per day, serving 64 cities. Each plane flew about seven flights daily, almost twice the industry average. Planes were used an average of 13 hours a day, about 40% more than major carriers like Delta and Northwest. Southwest's cost per available seat mile was the lowest in the industry for the major carriers (Exhibit 3), and the average age of its fleet was nine years, the lowest for the major carriers. Employee cost per available seat mile was much lower than major competitors.

30   Southwest accomplished its enviable record by challenging accepted norms and setting competitive thresholds for other airlines to emulate. The company established numerous new industry standards. Southwest flew more passengers per employee than any other major airline, while at the same time it had the fewest number of employees per aircraft. Southwest maintained a debt-to-equity ratio much lower than the industry average, and was one of the few airlines in the world with an investment grade credit rating. The company had never curtailed service because of a union strike, and no passenger had ever died because of a safety incident.

31   Southwest had a fleet of 520 737s, up from 417 in 2005, 106 in 1990, and 75 in 1987. Of the total fleet, 425 aircraft were owned and the remainder leased.

HERB KELLEHER

32   Herb Kelleher was CEO of Southwest from 1981 to 2001. In 2001, at age 71, Kelleher stepped down as CEO but remained chairman until 2008 when he resigned from the board of directors. Kelleher's leadership style combined flamboyance, fun, and a fresh, unique perspective. Kelleher played Big Daddy-O in one of the company videos, appeared as Elvis Presley in in-flight magazine advertisements, and earned the nickname "High Priest of Ha-Ha" from *Fortune*.[9] Although Kelleher was unconventional and a maverick in his field, he led his company to consistently new standards for itself and for the industry. Sincerely committed to his employees, Kelleher generated intense loyalty to himself and the company. His ability to remember employees' names and to ask after their families was just one way he earned respect and trust. At one point, Kelleher froze his salary for five years in response to the pilots agreeing to do the same. Often when he flew, Kelleher would help the ground crew unload bags or help the flight crew serve drinks. His humor was legendary and served as an example for his employees to join in the fun of working for Southwest. He was called "a visionary who leads by example—you have to work harder than anybody else to show them you are devoted to the business."[10]

33   Although Kelleher tried to downplay his personal significance to the company, especially when he gave up the CEO position in 2001, many analysts following Southwest credited the airline's success to Kelleher's unorthodox personality and engaging management style. As one analyst wrote, "The old-fashioned bond of loyalty between employees and company may have vanished elsewhere in corporate America, but it is stronger than ever at Southwest."[11] From October 1 to December 2001, Kelleher, CEO James Parker, and COO Colleen Barrett voluntarily relinquished their salaries. Gary Kelly, Southwest's former CFO, became CEO in 2004.

[9] K. Labich, "Is Herb Kelleher America's Best CEO?" *Fortune,* May 2, 1994, p. 45.
[10] "24th Annual CEO Survey: Herb Kelleher, Flying His Own Course," *IW,* November 20, 1995, p. 23.
[11] Labich, p. 46.

THE SOUTHWEST SPIRIT

34   Customer service far beyond the norm in the airline industry was not unexpected at Southwest and had its own name—Positively Outrageous Service. Some examples of this service included: a gate agent volunteering to watch a dog (a Chihuahua) for two weeks when an Acapulco-bound passenger showed up at the last minute without the required dog crate; an Austin passenger who missed a connection to Houston, where he was to have a kidney transplant operation, was flown there by a Southwest pilot in his private plane. Another passenger, an elderly woman flying to Phoenix for cancer treatment, began crying because she had no family or friends at her destination. The ticket agent invited her into her home and escorted her around Phoenix for two weeks.[12]

35   Southwest Airlines customers were often surprised by Southwest Spirit. On some flights, magazine pictures of gourmet meals were offered for dinner on an evening flight. Flight attendants were encouraged to have fun; songs, jokes, and humorous flight announcements were common. One flight attendant had a habit of popping out of overhead luggage compartments as passengers attempted to stow their belongings, until the day she frightened an elderly passenger who called for oxygen.[13] Herb Kelleher once served in-flight snacks dressed as the Easter Bunny.

36   Intense company communication and camaraderie was highly valued and essential to maintaining the *esprit de corps* found throughout the firm. The Southwest Spirit, as exhibited by enthusiasm and extroverted personalities, was an important element in employee screening conducted by Southwest's People Department. Employment at Southwest was highly desired. In 2006, 3,363 employees were hired and 284,827 applications were received. Once landed, a job was fairly secure. The airline had not laid off an employee since 1971. Historically, employee turnover hovered around 7%, the lowest rate in the industry. In 2008, Southwest had more than 33,000 employees; in 1990, Southwest had 8,600 employees and less than 6,000 in 1987.

37   During initial training periods, efforts were made to share and instill Southwest's unique culture. New-employee orientation, known as the new-hire celebration, have in the past included Southwest's version of the Wheel of Fortune game show, scavenger hunts, and company videos including the "Southwest Airlines Shuffle" in which each department introduced itself, rap style, and in which Kelleher appeared as Big Daddy-O. To join the People Department (i.e. Human Resources), employees required frontline customer experience.

38   Advanced employee training regularly occurred at the University of People at Love Field in Dallas. Various classes were offered, including team building, leadership, and cultural diversity. Newly promoted supervisors and managers attended a three-day class called "Leading with Integrity." Each department also had its own training division focusing on technical aspects of the work. "Walk-a-Mile Day" encouraged employees from different departments to experience firsthand the day-to-day activities of their co-workers. The goal of this program was to promote respect for fellow workers while increasing awareness of the company.[14]

39   Employee initiative was supported by management and encouraged at all levels. For example, pilots looked for ways to conserve fuel during flights, employees proposed designs for ice storage equipment that reduced time and costs, and baggage handlers learned to place luggage with the handles facing outward to reduce unloading time.

---

[12]*IW*, p. 23.

[13]B. O'Brian, "Flying on the Cheap," *Wall Street Journal*, October 26, 1992, p. A1.

[14]A. Malloy, "Counting the Intangibles," *Computerworld*, June 1996, pp. 32–33.

40   Red hearts and "Luv" were central parts of the internal corporate culture, appearing throughout company literature. A mentoring program for new hires was called CoHearts. "Heroes of the Heart Awards" were given annually to one behind-the-scenes group of workers, whose department name was painted on a specially designed plane for a year. Other awards honored an employee's big mistake through the "Boner of the Year Award." When employees had a story about exceptional service to share, they were encouraged to fill out a "LUV Report."

41   Southwest placed great emphasis on maintaining cooperative labor relations: 87% of all employees were unionized. Southwest pilots belonged to an independent union and not the Airline Pilots Association, the union that represented more than 60,000 pilots. The company encouraged the unions and their negotiators to conduct employee surveys and to research their most important issues prior to each contract negotiation. At its 1994 contract discussion, the pilots proposed a 10-year contract with stock options in lieu of guaranteed pay increases over the first five years of the contract. In 1974, Southwest was the first airline to introduce employee profit sharing. Through the plan, employees owned about 10% of the company's stock.

42   Herb Kelleher summed up the Southwest culture and commitment to employees:

> We don't use things like TQM. It's just a lot of people taking pride in what they're doing. . . . You have to recognize that people are still the most important. How you treat them determines how they treat people on the outside. . . I give people the license to be themselves and motivate others in that way. We give people the opportunity to be a maverick. You don't have to fit in a constraining mold at work—you can have a good time. People respond to that.[15]

SOUTHWEST IMITATORS

43   Southwest's strategy spawned numerous imitators, most of which failed. Two of the more successful start-up firms, Midwest Express and America West, both went through Chapter 11 bankruptcy proceedings. ValuJet was grounded after its May 1996 crash in the Florida Everglades, reemerging a year later as AirTran.

44   The major airlines tried to compete directly with Southwest. The Shuttle by United, a so-called "airline within an airline," was started in October 1994. United's objective was to create a new airline owned by United with many of the same operational elements as Southwest: a fleet of 737s, low fares, short-haul flights, and less restrictive union rules. United saturated the West Coast corridor with short-haul flights on routes such as Oakland–Seattle, San Francisco–San Diego, and Sacramento–San Diego. The Shuttle was unable to achieve the same level of productivity as Southwest and, in 2001, United discontinued Shuttle service and folded the remaining flights into its regular service. US Airways did the same with its Metrojet discount service. In 2003 United started a new discount carrier called TED.

45   Some of the attempts to imitate Southwest were almost comical. Continental Lite (CALite) was an effort by Continental Airlines to develop a low-cost service and revive the company's fortunes after coming out of bankruptcy in April 1993. In March 1994, Continental increased CALite service to 875 daily flights. Continental soon encountered major operational problems with its new strategy.[16] With its fleet of 16 different planes,

---

[15]H. Lancaster, "Herb Kelleher Has One Main Strategy: Treat Employees Well," *Wall Street Journal,* August 31, 1999, pp. B1.

[16]B. O'Brian, "Heavy Going: Continental's CALite Hits Some Turbulence in Battling Southwest," *Wall Street Journal,* January 10, 1995, pp. A1, A16.

mechanical delays disrupted turnaround times. Various pricing strategies were unsuccessful. The company was ranked last among the major carriers for on-time service, and complaints soared by 40%. In January 1995, Continental announced that it would reduce its capacity by 10% and eliminate 4,000 jobs. By mid-1995, Continental's CALite service had been largely discontinued. In October 1995, Continental's CEO was ousted.

A Successful Start-up: JetBlue Airways

46   Morris Air, patterned after Southwest, was the only airline Southwest had acquired and integrated into its own operations. Prior to the acquisition, Morris Air flew Boeing 737s on point-to-point routes, operated in a different part of the U.S. than Southwest, and was profitable. When Morris Air was acquired by Southwest in December 1993, seven new markets were added to Southwest's system. In 1999, Morris Air's former president, David Neeleman, announced plans for JetBlue Airways, a new airline based at New York's JFK Airport. JetBlue had a successful IPO in April 2002, with the stock rising 70% on the first day of trading. JetBlue had a geographically diversified flight schedule that included both short-haul and long-haul routes. Although JetBlue was viewed as a low-fare carrier, the airline emphasized various service attributes, such as leather seats, free LiveTV (a 24-channel satellite TV service with programming provided by DirecTV), and preassigned seating.

47   In 2008, JetBlue served 55 cities in the domestic United States, Mexico, and the Caribbean. JetBlue had a fleet of 194 Airbus A320 aircraft and 30 Embraer 190 regional jet aircraft. JetBlue revenue in 2007 was $2.6 billion, one-quarter the size of Southwest. The company had a net loss in 2005 and 2006 but returned to profitability in 2007. A major ice storm that hit New York in early 2007 severely tested the company. More than 1,200 flights were cancelled over a six-day period. Not long after, David Neeleman was asked by the board to step down as CEO. He remained as chairman.

SOUTHWEST EXPANSION

48   Southwest grew steadily over the years prior to 2008, but the growth was highly controlled. New airports were carefully selected, and only a few new cities were added each year. As Kelleher wrote to his employees in 1993, "Southwest has had more opportunities for growth than it has airplanes. Yet, unlike other airlines, it has avoided the trap of growing beyond its means. Whether you are talking with an officer or a ramp agent, employees just don't seem to be enamored of the idea that bigger is better."[17]

49   In October 1996, with the initiation of flights to Providence, Rhode Island, Southwest entered the northeast market. The entry into the northeast region of the U.S. was, in many respects, a logical move for Southwest. The northeast was the most densely populated area of the country and the only major region where Southwest did not compete. New England could provide a valuable source of passengers to Florida's warmer winter climates. Southwest's entry into Florida was exceeding initial estimates.

50   Despite the large potential market, the northeast offered a new set of challenges for Southwest. Airport congestion and air-traffic control delays could prevent efficient operations, lengthening turnaround time at airport gates, and wreaking havoc on frequent flight scheduling. Inclement weather posed additional challenges for both air service and car travel to airports. Nevertheless, Southwest continued to add new northeast cities. A few years later, Southwest was flying to various northeast airports, including Long Island, New

[17]Freiberg & Freiberg, p. 61.

Hampshire, and Hartford. In 2004, Southwest began flying to Philadelphia, which was the first major northeast market entry. As of 2008, Southwest had not entered any markets outside the domestic United States.

FUTURE CHALLENGES

51   With the airline industry in turmoil in 2008, Southwest was in an interesting and unique position. Although the company had a strong financial position, major carriers like Delta and Northwest had come out of bankruptcy protection with lower costs and more efficient operations. While Southwest's employee productivity remained high, its operating costs were rising. The company had the highest salaries for pilots of narrow-body jets.

52   Clearly, 2008 and the years following would result in dramatic changes to airline industry structure. Would Southwest be able to maintain its position as America's most prosperous airline? Could Southwest quickly expand share in the northeast and still ensure that customer service and company performance were satisfactory? Should Southwest look at internationalization options? Would the major airlines finally learn how to compete on cost with companies like Southwest and JetBlue?

53   In anticipation of tough times, the Chairman's message in the 2007 Annual Report ended with:

> While our near-term outlook is cautious, we are prepared for bad times, and our long-term outlook is enthusiastic. Our People have Warrior Spirits, Servants' Hearts, and Fun LUVing Attitudes.

Case 11

Koots Green Tea
Armand Gilinsky, Wakako Kusumoto, and Carl Kay

Photo courtesy of Wakako Kusumoto

1   "Is now the right time for me to take the leap, leave my job here in Japan as President of FoodxGlobe, and move to the United States to continue to test market my new tea drink retail chain, Koots Green Tea (Koots)? I have a sister who is married and lives in Los Angeles. You know, when I first met my wife in college I brainwashed her into believing that I wanted to start my own business in the future. She thought I was crazy then, but now, sixteen years later, she is not so sure," said Kouta Matsuda (Kouta), a 37-year-old entrepreneur to his companions Hitoshi Suga (who preferred to be called Suga-san), and the case writers. On a blustery grey day in mid-December 2006, we were discussing Kouta's options for the U.S. expansion of his Koots retail beverage chain over lunch at the inaugural Koots store, located in the Kamiyacho district of Tokyo, Japan.

2   Three years earlier, Kouta had founded Koots, which subsequently grew to encompass nine retail locations in Japan—six wholly owned stores in and around Tokyo, including Narita International Airport, and three other stores in other regions of Japan. Earlier in 2006, Matsuda also opened Koots' first United States (U.S.) store in an office park complex near Seattle, Washington. He planned to open a second store in Seattle in early 2007. The Koots chain, together with the Tully's Coffee Japan specialty coffee retail chain business, comprised FoodxGlobe, the *mochikabu* or holding company over which Kouta presided. Just two months earlier, in October 2006, Kouta had completed the sale of a majority stake in FoodxGlobe to Ito-en. Ito-en was Japan's largest tea company. Ito-en reportedly paid ¥6.7 billion (about $57.3 million) for its 51 percent stake in FoodxGlobe, of which Kouta

This case was prepared by Professor Armand Gilinsky, Sonoma State University, Dr. Wakako Kusumoto, and Carl Kay, as a basis for class discussion, not to illustrate either effective or ineffective handling of an administrative situation. All events and individuals are real. The host organization has released this case for review purposes only. Do not copy or distribute without permission of the authors. Draft dated August 20, 2008.

EXHIBIT 1   FoodxGlobe Japan Consolidated Statements of Operations
FY 2004–2006 *(in thousands of US dollars)*

	31-Mar-04	31-Mar-05	31-Mar-06
Coffeehouse sales	$81,190.0	$100,207.4	$108,805.9
Other sales incl. Koots Green Tea		1,582.6	2,304.1
Total net sales	81,190.0	101,790.0	111,110.0
Cost of sales and related occupancy costs	37,130.9	45,825.2	49,626.6
Operating expenses	30,131.6	40,608.6	44,914.5
Store opening and closing expenses	330.4	676.3	830.1
Depreciation and amortization of goodwill	5,588.5	8,598.7	9,242.4
General and administrative expenses	8,517.4	11,169.3	11,802.7
Operating income (loss)	(508.8)	(5,088.2)	(5,306.2)
Other income (expense):			
Interest income	21.9	7.3	3.9
Interest expense	(81.2)	(101.8)	(111.1)
Income (loss) before provision for income taxes	(568.1)	(5,182.6)	(5,413.5)
Provision for income tax	(125.0)	(1,140.2)	(1,191.0)
Net income after tax	($693.1)	($6,322.8)	($6,604.4)

Source: Case writers' estimates. Numbers are disguised by a common factor, but representative of actual relationships. Some quantities have been rounded up to the nearest whole integer using US$1.00 = J¥117.70.

had held an approximate 20 percent stake, now valued at about $10 million.[1] Under the terms of the acquisition, he was expected to remain at least temporarily as President of Tully's Coffee Japan, and retained 100 percent ownership of Koots Green Tea's fledgling operation outside Japan. Shortly afterwards, Ito-en had publicly stated its intention to expand the Tully's coffee brand but wind down the Koots store operations in Japan. Exhibits 1 and 2 show fiscal 2004–2006 income statements and fiscal 2004–2005 balance sheets for Foodx-Globe, prior to its sale in October 2006 to Ito-en. As shown in Exhibit 1, FoodxGlobe was unprofitable, primarily due to the write-down of goodwill from the acquisition of licensing rights to Tully's Coffee in Japan, but remained cash flow positive.

3   When asked about Kouta's dilemma about whether to stay in Japan to oversee his current business or move to America to expand his new venture, Suga-san, Matsuda's partner and vice-president of FoodxGlobe, told us:

> You must understand that Kouta represents a new breed of entrepreneurs in Japan. He is a hero. He is extremely committed. Before I met him, most of the Japanese entrepreneurs I had known were "drop-outs" of the traditional business culture. Their ethics were somewhat suspect, in that they tried to cheat or bypass the system. Kouta is different. He is well educated, persistent, and has a business background. When I first met him back in 1997, he was sweeping the street outside of his first [Tully's] coffee store on the Ginza, and I asked him one question then: "Do you want to grow or not?" He answered, "Yes, but I need help."

[1] Currency conversions from Japanese yen (¥) to U.S. dollars ($) were made at the rate of $1.00 = ¥117.70, as of December 2006.

EXHIBIT 2   **FoodxGlobe Japan Consolidated Balance Sheets**
FY 2005–2006 *(in thousands of US dollars)*

ASSETS	31-Mar-05	31-Mar-06
Current assets:		
Cash and cash equivalents	$7,863.3	$10,523.8
Accounts receivable	899.7	1,184.8
Other receivables	2,289.8	1,510.8
Income tax receivable	164.5	623.2
Inventories	6,863.5	7,879.9
Prepaid expenses and other current assets	1,288.8	609.2
Total current assets	19,369.6	22,331.7
Property and equipment, net of accumulated depreciation and amortization	74,033.7	85,025.6
Notes receivable	159.1	111.4
Restricted cash	888.4	745.9
Other assets	25,410.5	19,181.9
Total assets	$119,861.3	$127,396.6
LIABILITIES AND SHAREHOLDERS EQUITY		
Current liabilities:		
Accounts payable	$11,937.8	$13,574.1
Accrued compensation	9,051.3	12,029.4
Accrued expenses	12,089.7	13,978.5
Deferred revenue	11,318.0	13,566.5
Current portion of deferred compensation	545.5	545.5
Current portion of note payable and revolving credit facility	2,361.0	2,361.0
Total current liabilities	47,303.3	56,055.0
Note payable and revolving credit facility, less current maturities	67,569.4	65,208.4
Deferred rent liability	770.8	847.9
Deferred revenue	0.0	0.0
Minority interests in affiliates	194.6	150.0
Total long-term liabilities	68,534.8	66,206.3
Shareholders equity:		
Common stock	18.9	21.2
Additional paid-in capital	11,020.2	18,734.4
Accumulated deficit	(7,015.9)	(13,620.3)
Total shareholders equity	4,023.3	5,135.3
Total liabilities and shareholders equity	$119,861.3	$127,396.6

Source: Case writers' estimates. Numbers are disguised by a common factor, but representative of actual relationships. Some quantities have been rounded up to the nearest whole integer using US$1.00 = J¥117.70.

4   Suga-san continued his reflection,

> So you might say that Kouta's idea of building an empire in green tea—a "Starbucks" of
> green tea—is not only unusual, but also would require him to overcome overwhelming odds.
> Japanese entrepreneurs here face numerous challenges, including a very small domestic
> angel investment and venture capital community relative to the U.S., a society that prefers the
> job security of elite government ministries or large corporations to risk-taking, and a culture
> characterized by "rigid corporate norms" that lead to the imposition of severe penalties for
> failure. Since the early 1990s, you understand, the number of business start-ups in Japan has
> been lower than that of business closures.

5   As Suga-san was speaking, wintry wind gusts suddenly blew over the trashcan and signage
outside the store. Kouta politely excused himself to go outside and bring the wind-blown
items inside, while store staff patiently served tea latté drinks and small *bento* lunch boxes to
customers. Customers at this store were mostly fashionably dressed young Japanese women
and office workers.

6   Returning to our luncheon table, Kouta reflected on his opportunity as he saw it in
December 2006:

> Japanese entrepreneurs are like "frogs inside a well." No Japanese food retail chain has ever
> made it outside of Japan, with the possible exception of Rocky Aoki's "Benihana of Tokyo."
> No one knows how to do it. No one else has the passion. I was a novice when I first started in
> the coffee retail business with my first Tully's franchise store in Tokyo. My vision since then
> has evolved: I want to bridge the gap between Japanese and American food culture and do it
> by growing the green tea business. My goal is to open 300–400 Koots shops in the U.S. in the
> next few years. One question in my mind is how much do Americans like green tea or can be
> educated to do so. Another is what my future role running both Tully's Coffee Japan and Koots
> Green Tea for Ito-en might involve. Those details have not yet been fully worked out.

Ito-en

7   Ito-en was Japan's largest green tea beverage manufacturer. It had a 40-year history in the
tea market, starting in Japan where the brand established itself as a trendsetter. In addition to
bagged teas, Ito-en marketed a line of ready-to-drink (RTD) tea beverages, called Teas' Tea.

8   In the early 2000s, Ito-en had begun its diversification into other beverages. Green tea
beverages at that time accounted for about half of Ito-en's total sales. Ito-en began exporting
its green tea products overseas, including to the U.S. In June 2006, Ito-en acquired a Florida
supplement maker and sales company, Mason Distributors, which would enable Ito-en to
sell its bottled green tea drinks in more than 5,000 U.S. retail locations. In October 2006,
Ito-en announced it was buying a majority of the Japanese operator of Seattle-based Tully's
Coffee Co., the No. 3 coffee chain in Japan. Ito-en also predicted its green-tea sales in the
U.S. would grow more than fourfold in 2007, to $50 million.

9   Like many of its large Japanese rivals, Ito-en was primarily seeking growth via entry into
emerging markets such as Singapore, India, and China, rather than the domestic Japanese
market or in U.S. markets. To maintain growth momentum, the company planned to focus
on the dual policies of developing new brands while accelerating bids for mergers and
acquisitions. Hachiro Honjo, Ito-en's president, remarked in November 2006:

> We will continue to press ahead with M&As [mergers and acquisitions]. We need to
> strengthen our coffee business to avoid relying excessively on the market for green tea and
> related drinks. Though the domestic [Japanese] coffee market is mature, it is still valued at
> ¥1.4 trillion ($12 billion), including sales of coffee beans. Our coffee business is worth less
> than ¥20 billion ($171 million). We have been operating our own coffee roasting plant for
> 20 years, so we are familiar with the technology and cost. We believe we can improve the
> quality of products offered by Tully's and reduce expenses as well. FoodxGlobe's unprofitable
> operations, such as Koots Green Tea Japan Co., will be shut down in order to let the firm

EXHIBIT 3 Growth of Rival Specialty Coffee Chains in Japan, Fiscal years ending (FYE) 2003–2009 *(estimates) (# of stores)*

Fiscal Year Ended 31 March	Starbucks Japan	Tully's Coffee Japan	Doutor/ Excelsior	Other Specialty	Total Specialty Coffee Stores, Japan	Koots Green Tea Stores, Japan
2003	462	110	97	376	1,045	1
2004	514	186	115	426	1,241	3
2005	551	245	130	476	1,402	6
2006	591	330	145	526	1,592	9
2007	*631*	*415*	*160*	*576*	*1,782*	*25*
2008	*671*	*500*	*175*	*626*	*1,972*	*45*
2009	*711*	*585*	*175*	*676*	*2,147*	*75*

Note: Numbers in italics are based on estimates supplied by Kouta Matsuda and Hitoshi Suga.
Source: FoodxGlobe

focus its management resources on the Tully's chain. To this end, Ito-en and FoodxGlobe have set up a joint team to work out a business plan. I believe FoodxGlobe can be made profitable on an operating basis in the business year through March 2008.

10   Although Ito-en had spent about ¥10 billion (about $85.5 million) for the acquisitions of Mason Distributors and FoodxGlobe in 2006, it held ¥26.8 billion (about $229 million) in cash and deposits as of October 31, 2006. Exhibit 3 presents comparative half-year (six month) operating highlights for Ito-en in 2005 and 2006, and preliminary company estimates for fiscal 2007, ending on April 30, 2007. Ito-en's strong cash position would provide further support for its retail diversification strategy, one stock market analyst from Nikkei Securities commented.

Tully's Coffee U.S.

11   From its headquarters in Seattle, Washington, Tully's Coffee U.S. operated and franchised a chain of nearly 130 coffeehouses offering a variety of specialty blend coffees along with baked goods, espresso, and related supplies, mostly in Washington, California, and a handful of other western states. About 90 U.S. locations were company-owned; the rest were franchised. Tully's also sold branded coffee and related products to supermarkets and food service operators through its wholesale division, which distributed to some 4,000 grocery stores, including Safeway, Kroger, and Albertsons. Chairman Tom O'Keefe founded Tully's in 1992; he owned 27.5% of the company. The estate of Keith McCaw owned approximately 18% of the company. The late McCaw, a billionaire philanthropist and cell-phone magnate, was a longtime friend of O'Keefe.

12   Between 1992 and 2001, Tully's expanded to 114 company-operated stores. During this period, it financed retail expansion by raising over $60 million in equity securities and through licensing fees paid by foreign licensees of over $17 million. Between fiscal years 2001 and 2003, its financial performance was negatively impacted by the economic downturn that affected Seattle and San Francisco, Tully's two principal retail markets. During the same period, the market for new equity issues deteriorated significantly. To manage through this period and these challenges, management chose to reduce normal operating expenses by closing certain under-performing stores and slowing new store development plans to preserve capital. Between fiscal years 2002 and 2006, Tully's streamlined aspects of its operations and emphasized less capital-intensive business opportunities such as wholesale and franchising.

13   In 2004, Tully's had talked with FoodxGlobe about "integrating" the two businesses, but Tully's broke off negotiations. The failed merger talks cost Tully's $550,000 in fees and expenses. The company incurred operating losses from its inception through fiscal year 2005, though Tully's reported a profit in 2006 due in part to the sale of Japanese development rights to Tully's Coffee Japan in September 2005. Tully's Japan had developed about 280 owned and franchised Tully's locations before paying about $17.5 million for the rights to the brand in Japan. O'Keefe said in September 2005:

> We are thrilled to announce the evolution of our partnership with FOODX. I am confident that FOODX will continue to honor and protect the Tully's brand. Also, the proceeds from this transaction will immediately generate operating and growth capital without diluting shareholder value or adding interest costs. This allows Tully's to strengthen our wholesale and specialty segments, and to enhance retail—all key management objectives for sustaining the company's recent sales growth.

14   According to a statement filed with the U.S. Securities and Exchange Commission, Tully's net sales in fiscal year 2006 were $58.2 million (over $54.0 million in fiscal year 2005); fiscal year 2006 operating losses before interest and taxes were $1.3 million (versus $3.7 million in fiscal year 2005); and fiscal 2006 net income was $15.4 million (versus a net loss of $4.6 million in fiscal year 2005). Tully's had already filed to go public in early 2007. Proceeds from Tully's planned Initial Public Offering (IPO) were critical to achieve plans to open between 30 and 40 company-operated retail stores in 2007 and 2008, and a comparable or greater number the following year. The company also continued to develop new products, such as its single serve Tully's K-Cups and its Bellaccino bottled beverages; it was further investing in its wholesale business by adding more grocery stores to its distribution channel; and it planned to expand into emerging markets through opening more franchised stores.

THE SPECIALTY COFFEE AND TEA INDUSTRY

15   Perhaps no other word expressed the dynamism of the specialty coffee and tea industry better than Starbucks. Seattle-based Starbucks Corp. had more than 10,500 locations world-wide as of early 2006, of which over 600 were located in Japan, and posted fiscal 2006 revenues of $7.8 billion.[2] Exhibit 3 shows the growth in the number of Starbucks retail outlets in Japan compared with rival coffeehouse chains. The specialty coffee and tea retail industry in Japan in 2006 nevertheless could be described as highly fragmented, that is, primarily characterized by small chains and regional brands.

16   According to the Specialty Coffee Association of America (SCAA), a prominent industry trade group, several major trends were expected to drive continuing growth in the global coffee and teashop industry in the decade to 2010:

- *Consumers opting for gourmet beverages.* This trend reflected overall greater consumer awareness of specialty coffee and tea's perceived superior quality and taste. Consumers were becoming more educated, and understand and differentiate coffee and teas by origin and bean or leaf type. Discerning consumers generally demanded a wide selection of specialty coffee and tea beverages such as lattés, mochas, and blended drinks. This trend did

---

[2] Starbucks Japan, a joint venture with Sazaby, a Japanese manufacturer of apparel accessories (like handbags), finally achieved breakeven in the first quarter of 2006. This was largely due to its introduction of customized food items such as sandwiches and pastries. Japan was Starbucks' largest international market outside North America; the company planned to have 1,000 stores in operation in Japan by 2010 and eventually meet its goal of 2,000 outlets in Japan. The majority of the new stores were to be drive-through shops and roadside locations outside major cities.

not go unnoticed by Starbucks and other major coffee retail chains, which began to introduce new product lines of specialty latté drinks made with green teas and other teas.

- *Coffee and tea consumption as a lifestyle.* Consumers were pursuing coffee and tea consumption as a regular facet of their everyday lifestyles, in part due to the growing appeal of the coffeehouse as a gathering place outside of work and home, providing an inviting atmosphere for people to congregate and socialize. A 2006 Deutsche Bank research study indicated that 33 percent of non-coffee drinkers visited chain coffeehouses for the atmosphere and to socialize.

- *Widening demographics of coffee drinkers.* Young adults (18–24 years old) contributed to the increased penetration, as 31 percent of young adults consumed coffee or tea away from home daily in 2006, compared to 26 percent in 2005.

- *Increased food expenditures made away from home.* Food expenditures away from home rose as a percentage of total food expenditures, from 32 percent in 1980 to 41.4 percent in 2005.

17   *Datamonitor* reported that coffee drinks sales dominated the global hot drinks market, generating $37.7 billion in 2005 for a 67.9 percent share of worldwide hot drinks consumption. The tea segment, by comparison, generated $13.9 billion in revenues, representing a 25 percent share. From 2005–2010, *Datamonitor* forecasted that, combined together, coffee and tea drinks sales would grow at a 2.3 percent compound annual rate.

18   Tea, after all, was the second most popular beverage in the world to bottled water. Legend had it that the Chinese Emperor Shen Nung discovered tea around 2737 B.C., when a leaf from a wild Camellia *sinensis* tree blew into his cup of boiling water. All tea came from the Camellia, a now-cultivated shrub that thrived in high altitudes. (Herbal "teas" such as chamomile or mint technically were not tea.) The Camellia spawned more than 1,200 varieties, which fell roughly into four major categories: black, green, white, and oolong. Although the Boston Tea Party (during which green tea was reportedly thrown into Boston Harbor) convinced Americans to stop drinking tea for political reasons, tea was consumed alongside coffee for many years afterward. By the 20th century, strife within China, World War II, and the breakup of the British Empire disrupted tea supplies, and Americans began to drink more coffee and soda. From the end of World War II to the early 1980s, most tea drinkers favored tea-bag tea and iced tea, although British-style tearooms and some Chinatown/Japantown shops maintained a modest presence in the U.S.

19   In the mid to late 1970s, manufacturers and marketers of packaged herbal and medicinal teas, such as Celestial Seasonings in Boulder, Colorado; Traditional Medicinals in Sebastopol, California; and the Republic of Tea, in Novato, California, began offering green, wulong, black, herbal and flavored teas—although still in tea bags. The growing interest in premium tea, and teahouses, became part of the growing mainstream appreciation of tea, which began in the early 1980s as Baby Boomers searched for a low- or non-caffeinated alternative to coffee. Reports about tea's possible health benefits also fueled the boom. In the 1990s, international tea companies, including the Japanese giant Lupicia, began branding loose-leaf, premium teas with their names and labels, and selling them in shopping malls. Premium tea packagers such as Republic of Tea, Mighty Leaf Tea Company, Numi, Leaves, and Silk Road all began in the San Francisco Bay Area, and by 2006 commanded a national market. The world of artisan or varietal teas in many ways came to parallel the world of fine wines. The *cognoscenti* resembled wine connoisseurs, developing discriminating palates to appreciate the teas, and using a language that paralleled wine appreciation—vintages, single estates, harvest time and method, not to mention all the descriptors for the taste of tea, such as acid, tannins, weight, fruit, earth aromas and mineral characteristics.

20   The major types of tea included:

- Black tea, such as Ceylon and Darjeeling, was fully fermented, producing black leaves. Lapsang Souchong was a scented variety, deriving its flavor from the pinewood smoke used to dry its leaves.
- Green tea leaves were picked, left to wither, and then steamed or pan-heated to prevent oxidation, maintaining their color. The minimal processing also preserved disease-fighting catechins, a type of antioxidant, which were lost in fermentation.
- White tea, a relative newcomer to U.S. palates, was unfermented and made from the youngest shoots. Up to 80,000 buds were needed for a pound of white tea, one reason it could cost more than $10 an ounce. The leaves were steamed and gently dried, preserving antioxidants and a subtle flavor.
- Oolong, a partly fermented tea, had a full-bodied flavor that fell between black and green tea. One example was Pu-erh, which lowered triglycerides and reduced hunger—hence its nickname, "diet tea."
- Red "tea," known as *rooibos,* was made from leaves of the rooibos "red bush" native to South Africa. It was technically not a tea. But it was fermented like a black tea and produced a deliciously rich brew. It also packed 500% more antioxidants than white, green, or black tea, and was thought to be particularly beneficial for pregnant women and colicky babies. Since it was herbal, it was caffeine-free.
- Yerba maté was herbal tea made from the leaves of a holly-like plant found in South America.

21   According to *Datamonitor,* the purported health benefits of green tea, which provoked wide debate in the medical community, included the following:

- Boosts your immune system
- Lowers blood sugar
- Contains fluoride so helps prevent cavities and tooth decay
- Slows the ageing process
- Helps reduce the risk of cancer
- Lowers cholesterol and aids digestion
- Aids weight loss
- Reduces high blood pressure
- Prevents arthritis
- Reduces the risk of heart disease
- Reduces the risk of stroke
- Lowers the risk of blood clots
- A cup of green tea contains more antioxidants than a serving of broccoli, spinach, carrots or strawberries
- It is rich in vitamin C, an important detox vitamin

Japanese Tea Market

22   According to a survey of 6,500 Japanese consumers conducted by the Website Japan-Online in 2001, the most popular beverage in that country was green tea: 54 percent of the respondents drank green tea on a daily basis, while only 8 percent did not drink green tea at all. The survey also found that green tea—and tea in general—tended to be more popular among women (59 percent) than men (49 percent), while the opposite was true for the second most popular drink, coffee, which was consumed daily by 59 percent of men but only 46 percent of women, according to Just-Drinks.com.

23   From 2000–2005, Japan's ¥400 billion ($3.46 billion) green tea market became crowded with competitors. Green tea drinks, as opposed to black and herb teas, dominated the tea market in Japan. Companies including Coca-Cola Japan and Kirin Brewery launched a slew of tea drinks. The 7-Eleven convenience-store chain also introduced its own low-cost brand of green-tea drinks, priced at ¥98 (about 90 cents) for a 500-milliliter (17 fl. oz.) bottle, compared with ¥120 (about $1.00) or more for other brands, according to *Beverage World*. However, in the first nine months of 2006, demand for green tea drinks began to shrink—dropping about 6 percent from the same period a year earlier.

United States Tea Market

24   Industry observers estimated that tea was consumed in almost 80 percent of all U.S. households and every day, more than 127 million Americans drank a cup of tea. In 2005, Americans consumed well over 50 billion servings of tea, or over 2.25 billion gallons. About 87 percent of all tea consumed was black tea—primarily in the form of iced tea. Green tea held a 12.5 percent share of 2005 consumption, and the remaining 0.5 percent comprised oolong tea along with other herbal teas. Tea sales reached $6.2 billion in 2005, more than four times the level in the early 1990s. While tea sales still lagged far behind coffee, health-conscious Americans increasingly embraced new tea offerings—such as chai, barley, and green tea. Manufacturers of ready-to-drink (RTD) teas, by far the largest category in the U.S., promoted their products as being healthier than black tea or coffee, which led to a dramatic increase in sales of these niche tea products.

25   From 1994–2004, sales of RTD tea beverages in U.S. supermarkets grew nearly tenfold. By 2004, RTD tea sales in the U.S. were estimated at $2.1 billion, according to the U.S. Tea Council. That year was the 13th consecutive year of increased U.S. consumer purchases of tea.

26   Of the 220 million pounds of tea imported to the U.S. in 2005, green tea accounted for 15 percent of total imports. Teas imported from Japan accounted for just .53 percent of U.S. tea imports. Many U.S. RTD tea manufacturers blended imported green tea with other flavors to compensate for green tea's mild flavor and to appeal to Western tastes. Starbucks-owned Tazo Tea, for instance, sold a line of RTD green tea beverages, such as Plum Delicious (a selection of green teas brewed and blended with pomegranate and plum juices) and Passion Potion (green teas, mint and lemongrass blended with pear and apple juices.)

New Retail Entrants

27   By 2005, nearly 13,900 cafés in America served primarily coffee-type products, but tea drinks were beginning to make inroads into coffee drink sales. In the early 2000s the tea industry's focus began to widen from manufacturing for retailers to include small "artisan" teahouse chains, which hoped to capitalize on the rapid growth of RTD teas by serving made-to-order tea drinks. Exhibit 4 highlights comparisons among leading U.S. competitors in the tea shop industry segment. The United States Tea Association (USTA) reported in 2006 that tea shops, which served and sold specialty teas, grew in popularity from 1995–2005, from 200 to 2,000 locations nationwide. The USTA forecast that sales in the tea shop retail chain industry segment would grow at an average annual compound growth rate of 20% between 2005–2010. New entrants into this growing industry segment included privately held companies such as Argo Tea, based in Chicago, Illinois, with 150 employees; Far Leaves; Imperial Tea Court; Lupicia (560 employees); Teance; and Teavana. Of these teashop chains, Atlanta-based Teavana was the largest as of 2006, and it had venture capital backing to fund growth up to a planned initial public offering for 2008. American teashop chains offered fine teas as well as tea service, with the attendant cultural ambiance, utensils and education, moving tea culture into the 21st century, beyond the traditional Chinatown establishments to urban storefronts, suburban neighborhoods, and even to kiosks in suburban shopping malls.

EXHIBIT 4   Profiles of U.S. Specialty Tea Shop Chains

Company Name	Date Founded	Headquarters	Locations	Tea Products
Specialty Tea Chains				
Argo Tea Privately held	2003	Chicago, IL	6 Chicago area	Tea bar with tea smoothies, milky bubble tea, and tea lattés; light snacks (sandwiches, baked goods)
Cha for Tea Privately held—U.S. sales FY 2005: $8.5 billion	1999 (Taiwan parent company founded in 1953)	Taiwan (Ten Ren Tea)	2 Southern California (120 Ten Ren Tea stores globally)	Tea bar and light snacks
Chado Tea Room Privately held	1998	Los Angeles, CA	2 Southern California (Pasadena and Irvine)	300 blends sold at retail and Internet via mail order; in stores light snacks (sandwiches, baked goods)
Lupicia Privately held—¥200 million capital investment from three Japanese banks	1994	Tokyo	2 in San Francisco; 1 in Los Angeles (51 in Japan, 25 franchised; 5 in Australia, Taiwan, and South Korea)	Over 400 varieties of tea, primarily Japanese green tea; sold at retail and Internet via mail order; light snacks (sandwiches, baked goods)
Tea Geschwender Privately held	1978	Germany	3 Chicago area (130 locations in Europe, Middle East, and Brazil)	300 blends and tea accessories at retail and Internet via mail order
Tealuxe Privately held	1996	Franklin, MA	3 (Boston, Cambridge, Providence—planned stores in Florida, Arizona, and New York)	300 blends and tea accessories at retail and Internet via mail order
Teavana Privately held—U.S. sales 2006: est. $10 million+	1997	Atlanta, GA	50	100 blends and tea accessories sold at retail and Internet via mail order
TeazMeTea Privately held	2004	Chico, CA	4 Northern California (Chico, Roseville, San Francisco, Vacaville)	Tea bar with tea smoothies, milky bubble tea, and tea lattés
Specialty Coffee and Tea Chains				
Caribou Coffee Public—U.S. sales 2006: $236 million	1992	Minneapolis, MN	475 (33 franchised)	Introduced chai tea latté in April 2007
Coffee Bean and Tea Leaf Privately held—U.S. sales 2006: $179.5 million	1963	Los Angeles, CA	520 (275 company-owned and 245 franchised) in western U.S., Asia/Pacific, and Middle East	22 tea drinks at retail and packaged teas via mail order
Starbucks Public—Global sales 2006: $7.8 billion	1971 1996 (first international store in Tokyo)	Seattle, WA	13,000+ in 39 countries (7,521 company-owned, 5,647 licensed or joint ventures), 600+ in Japan	Introduced Green Tea Lattés in its U.S. stores, April 2006, replacing premixed Green Tea Frappuccino drinks introduced in 2005

Sources: Company websites

KOUTA'S EARLY ENTREPRENEURIAL EXPERIENCES

28   When Kouta was five, his family moved from Japan to Senegal, where his father worked for a fish importer. Three years later, they moved to a Boston suburb, Lexington, Massachusetts, where Kouta subsequently played goalie on a high school soccer team. Kouta's immersion into American culture over his ten years residency in Lexington, from 1976–1986, set the stage for his later entrepreneurial experiences. Kouta recounted:

> When I lived in Lexington, I worked as a newspaper boy delivering the *Boston Globe* for two years, starting in the final year of elementary school. I delivered the paper to 60 or 70 households by bike. Getting up at 5 every morning was hard, especially in the middle of winter. I remember going to work in a heavy snowstorm and even the truck that was supposed to bring all the bundles of papers for us to deliver couldn't make it in time. The job not only made me physically stronger but also taught me how to keep up with a demanding schedule. I also made a little money as a kid by mowing neighbors' lawns, selling lemonade, holding a garage sale, and so on. If kids growing up in Japan tried to do that, parents or schools would probably stop them and tell them off, but it wasn't unusual in the U.S. I think I owe my entrepreneurship partly to those early experiences.

29   As they persisted in mangling his Japanese name, Kouta's high school soccer teammates eventually nicknamed him "Koots." Matsuda remembered his American high school classmates told jokes that he ate "weird food" like raw fish. But instead of growing bitter, he later recounted, he dreamed of opening restaurants to hook Americans on sushi. While he was too late to catch the sushi boom that swept American cities in the late 1980s, from the start of his entrepreneurial career, he had his eye on the American food consumer.

30   After graduating from high school in America in 1986, Kouta returned to Japan to study international relations at Tsukuba University in Tokyo. During his undergraduate years, Kouta worked part-time in Japanese restaurants. He dreamed of starting a chain of restaurants that had sushi floating in boats on a conveyor belt, similar to the Genroku Zushi chain that had its origins in his mother's hometown, Miyagi, a district in northern Japan.[3] To obtain some business experience after graduating from Tsukuba University in 1990, Kouta went to work for Sanwa Bank, where he spent his first two years as a loan officer, analyzing financial statements, and his final four years in marketing, developing new corporate accounts. In his book, *Short Latté, Tall Cappuccino, and Grande Passion,* Matusda recounted that after his six-year banking career ended, he wanted to see how successful he could be at selling without the brand name of Sanwa Bank behind him. Kouta sold a range of items such as PC peripherals (mice, monitors) to friends and acquaintances, as well as chocolate-covered crickets from Louisiana, confections which were re-sold as novelties by Japanese toy stores.

31   In 1994 when he was 26 years old, Kouta received a letter from a former classmate and teammate on his high school soccer team, Jeff Farris. Farris was excited about the emerging food trends in the U.S. and advised Kouta to start a gourmet specialty coffee business in Japan, in order to capitalize on what was becoming known as the "Starbucks phenomenon." On a subsequent visit to Boston in 1995, to attend Farris's wedding, Kouta observed that the specialty coffee business was a big business: he saw lines out the door of a coffee store in Boston's Quincy Market—and also noticed the mini-board outside the store advertising coffee for $2.00–$3.50. In 1996, Kouta decided to take his holiday in Seattle to see the birthplace of the specialty coffee phenomenon first-hand. Once there, he observed that Starbucks was only one of many competitors in the specialty coffee retail business. "There were many bamboo shoots sprouting out of the ground." Kouta recalled, "I fell in love with Tully's—I felt it was the best."

[3] Kouta also noted that in 2004, the owner of Genroko Zushi approached him with a proposition to sell the 150-store chain to FoodxGlobe, but the FoodxGlobe board of directors rejected the proposal at the time.

TULLY'S COFFEE JAPAN

32   At age 28, Kouta finally took the leap and negotiated with Tully's Coffee, a Seattle-based chain, to open its first store in Japan. While still working at Sanwa Bank, Kouta had begun writing to Tom Tully O'Keefe, founder of Seattle's Tully's Coffee, for an initial meeting. Repeatedly rebuffed, when he heard that Tom O'Keefe, Tully's founder and chairman, was in Tokyo for business talks on selling wholesale coffee beans to Japanese cafés, in September 1996, Kouta rushed to his hotel and knocked on O'Keefe's door without an appointment. In his two-hour presentation in English, Kouta argued that Tully's should have its own cafés to penetrate the Japanese market, because Japanese consumers liked high-quality brands. In January 1997, O'Keefe finally gave Kouta approval and the first outlet opened in Japan that August. Kouta was thus able to secure the right to the Tully's name, and in just two months opened Japan's first Tully's coffee shop. Kouta told us that he had raised about ¥70 million ($564,000), of which $30,000 came from personal savings, $30,000 borrowed from friends and relatives, and the remainder from a guaranteed bank loan:

> After I made a three million yen ($25,000) initial payment for a place I found in Hiroo [a district in Tokyo], another place became available in Ginza. Ginza was the district I first had in mind when I came up with the plan to open Tully's here. But if I wanted to apply for the new place, I had to give up the three million yen I had paid for the other place. I was already in debt after raising the capital to start this business, and it wasn't 100 percent certain that the Ginza place would be mine if I applied. There was a risk of losing both. Ginza's rent was higher but it had more potential, as the area was more vibrant than Hiroo. In the end, I went for the bigger challenge and chose Ginza.

33   At our luncheon, Kouta recalled how he secured the Ginza store location:

> I was "green" when I first started in the coffee business. I had worked part-time at a McDonald's in high school and actually hated coffee! I had no track record as small business owner. The first Ginza store was near the existing Pronto Coffee and Starbucks stores. For several weeks, in front of another building just across the street from those two coffee stores, I stood outside with a counter, observing and counting the customers who went in to buy coffee from 7 a.m. to 9 p.m. Finally, I met the building owner one day when he was outside refilling the vending machines outside. He also ran a standalone coffee store in that building. He asked me what I was doing. I begged him, "Give me a chance to do a new-style coffee store."

34   Kouta had succeeded in winning the inital overseas exclusive licensing and franchise rights for coffee shops from Tully's, for a reported total cost of $4.2 million payable by October 1, 2001, according to a filing with the Securities and Exchange Commission made by Tully's on April 26, 2001.[4]

A Venture Capital Partner Enters the Picture

35   Kouta and Japanese-born but American-trained venture capitalist Hitoshi Suga first crossed paths in 1997, shortly after Suga-san became responsible for scouting up new businesses as President & CEO of MVC, the venture capital unit of a major Japanese trading company, Mitsui & Co., Ltd. (Mitsui Bussan). In 1996, Mitsui Bussan and other Mitsui group companies invested ¥450 million (approximately $4 million) to create a new venture capital business and appointed Suga-san to run it. Armed with a newly raised venture fund

---

[4] See www.secinfo.com/dRqWm.3543.d.htm, accessed April 9, 2008.

(MVC Global Japan Fund I) of $17 million, and a Harvard MBA, Suga-san felt confident that he could pick out the winners from the pack. Like Kouta, Suga-san had some education and experience in America. But day after day of being shown PowerPoint presentations, the sales pitches began to wear on him.

36   Then, almost by chance, Suga-san happened upon a little coffee shop in Ginza, Tokyo's fancy shopping district. He had just read about three young and very successful companies in the U.S. seeking to secure a foothold in Japan; Tully's Coffee was one of them. Suga-san's assistant at Mitsui Bussan urged him to go see Tully's, so he decided to pay a visit. His first impression upon entering the shop was the aroma—"it smelled good." His second impression was the amicable directness of the young man who served up his coffee order. When Suga-san asked to speak with the proprietor and after realizing the young man, Kouta, was indeed the shop's owner, Suga-san was asked to sit outside with him despite the chilly weather—to make the coffee shop look as though the business was "blooming."

37   In the short time that the two men drank coffee and talked about business prospects, Suga learned more about the shop's proprietor, Kouta, who had been born into a middle-class Japanese family, and whose approach to business appeared to Suga to be both very optimistic and persistent. Kouta was also a very hard worker: he basically lived in his shop in order to cut down on commuting time and increase his working time. When the conversation ended two hours later, Suga-san was convinced he had a winner with Kouta's vision and commitment. Suga-san offered to back his Tully's Coffee Japan venture, an offer that the young entrepreneur readily accepted.[5]

38   At the December 2006 luncheon at Koots Green Tea, Suga-san recalled why he had initially decided to back Kouta:

> People are by far the most important element in any investment decision. In Japan, investors often have to be fortune-tellers as to whether a person is going to be successful. If you're an entrepreneur looking for funding outside, you really have to develop a personal chemistry or synergy between yourself and the investor. This is more important than business plans and business models.

39   On behalf of MVC, Suga-san in late 1997 invested seed money of ¥30 million (about $260,000) into Kouta's venture, and researched future prospects for coffee shops in Japan. At that time, "mom-and-pop" style stores dominated the Japanese coffee shop market. However, the new foreign-style coffee shops represented a relatively new concept in Japan: they were smoke-free and brighter, they allowed freedom of movement (customers could walk around with their coffee mugs), and they were aimed at a younger and coed crowd. As cash-rich competitors Starbucks and Japanese-owned Doutor/Excelsior were already present in the coffee shop market, Tully's had its work cut out, but Suga-san felt that Tully's would "fly" because he was convinced that Kouta had the personality and the drive to make the new style of coffee shop in Japan succeed.[6]

---

[5] According to both Kouta and Suga-san, this indeed did happen, and was also reported by Yim, H. (2006), *op. cit.*, and by Fuyuno, I. (2003, September 11). Creative locations. *Far Eastern Economic Review, 166*(36): 66.

[6] According to Yamada & Yamashita (2006), ". . . it is extremely difficult for a single individual [in Japan] to establish inimitable competitive advantages through building a new business system. He or she may need to secure the advantages of a pioneer by continuous investment or constantly devising new business models. Innovation by entrepreneurs . . . in most cases is realized through actual business operation with partners after a process of trial and error . . . it is virtually impossible for a single outstanding entrepreneur to realize innovation on his or her own." Yamada, J. & Yamashita, M. (2006) Entrepreneurs' intentions and partnership towards innovation: evidence from the Japanese film industry. *Creativity and Innovation Management, 15*(3), 266.

40   In 2001, just two and a half years after the initial Tully's Coffee Japan store opening on Ginza, Kouta and Suga-san took Tully's Coffee Japan public, raising ¥1.2 billion ($10 million), which over the next five years would enable the company to expand to approximately 300 shops throughout Japan, on its way to a target of 330 shops by the end of calendar year 2006. Kouta's stake in the venture was valued at the time of the initial public offering at about $2 million. Business expansion was, according to Suga:

> . . . steady and very carefully planned, always with an eye on spending money in the most effective way possible. Tully's Coffee Japan did not have the kind of capital that [local] competitors Doutor/Excelsior and Starbucks had, and we desperately wanted to avoid the same fate that befell another famous U.S. coffee chain, Peet's Coffee of San Francisco, which exited Japan after only six months because of the extremely competitive business conditions.

41   Under Suga's financial leadership, Tully's Coffee Japan stretched capital investments by minimizing the costs of leasing space—which in Japan included "key money," a sticker shock for any new entrant into the retail business—while maximizing brand exposure.[7] "Whenever I found a good place to open a store, Starbucks and Doutor/Excelsior had already looked at it ahead of me," Kouta recalled. "We'd have lost out if we had fought directly with them."[8] One solution was to open kiosks in high traffic office buildings and car dealerships, which proved immensely successful, beginning with the first kiosk in the Otemachi office building of Mitsui Bussan, the venture capital's parent company. Rent for the kiosk was ¥250,000 per month (about $2,100) for only 16 square meters of space, but sales soon grew to ¥8–9 million ($70,000–$80,000) per month.

42   By late 2006, Tully's Coffee Japan operated more than 300 stores, becoming the most visible challenger to Starbucks in Japan, compared with more than 600 Starbucks outlets in Japan.

DIVERSIFICATION INTO KOOTS GREEN TEA

43   Kouta's strategy also began to evolve in the early 2000s. He decided to compete in a niche that Starbucks and Doutor/Excelsior had not yet entered by diversifying into an entirely new market segment: the green tea shop. Kouta thought that the green tea shop would appeal to an emerging consumer segment in Japan that was coming to be known as the "cultural creatives," that is, individuals who scored high on the LOHAS scale. LOHAS was an acronym for Lifestyles of Health and Sustainability. Kouta told us:

> Simply trying to sell more products is no longer the solution. Connecting with customers is increasingly important. To this end, public concern about health may be one of the key terms. Fair trade may be another. It may not be realistic to use organic ingredients for everything

---

[7] Commercial rent in Japan is expensive and typically four to six months' rent must be paid in advance. One month's rent is a fee for the realtor, another is 'thank you' money to the owner, another is for a security deposit, and finally three months' rent is paid in advance. A guarantor is required to sign for the borrower's lease. Complex labor laws make employing others quite a responsibility and firing people is not easy. Many Japanese are image conscious and working for a small company is still not as prestigious as working for a big company . . . many [Japanese] customers see an entrepreneurial business as unstable or risky, according to Helms, M. (2003), "The challenge of entrepreneurship in a developed economy: the problematic case of Japan," *Journal of Developmental Entrepreneurship, 8*(3), December, 252.

[8] To avoid going head-to-head with entrenched rivals like Starbucks and Doutor's, Matsuda's strategy was to be "really creative about location." One of the most successful Tully's stores opened in a Nissan Motor car showroom.

on the menu, but being more health conscious allows us to share the same concerns as our customers. Growing up, most of us think what our parents cook for us is the best, because they are the people we trust the most. Being in the food business, I'm hoping to replicate that kind of trust.

44 LOHAS consumers were said by industry observers to be passionate about preserving the natural environment, sustainability, social issues, and health. These consumers were variously referred to as "solution seekers" or "environmentally conscious consumers," and represented a sizable group in the U.S. By 2005, LOHAS had become a $227 billion market segment in the U.S., representing 17 percent of adults, or 36 million consumers. The Japan Economic Foundation in a 2006 survey identified nearly 29 percent of all adult Japanese consumers as LOHAS consumers.

45 Kouta believed that the key to sustainable future growth in the retail specialty food and drinks business was not in the Tully's coffee shops, but instead for a different café concept based on the traditional Japanese *kissaten* (tea shop). As it turned out, his idea for a green tea shop was hatched within close proximity to the Ginza Starbucks store. Suga-san recounted, "Kouta said to me 'Why open a Tully's next to a Starbucks shop? Sell green tea instead and also offer *onigiri* rice balls and Japanese desserts.'" One evening while operating the espresso machine at one of his Tully's stores, Kouta reportedly tried putting *matcha,* or green tea powder, into an espresso filter. The concoction exploded, covering him and the counter with hot green goo! Undaunted, he finally modified an espresso machine for matcha, which had a finer grind than espresso and did not need filters. Kouta sketched out a logo and decided to name the green tea shop Koots, after the nickname his American soccer buddies had given him back in high school. In 2003, Kouta opened the first Koots Green Tea Store in central Tokyo.

46 By mid-December 2006, crowds of office workers, predominantly young women, lined up at Koots' Tokyo stores to purchase drinks and rice balls wrapped in dried seaweed, a popular light lunch in Japan. Kouta said at that time that he did not intend to sell the rice balls in the U.S. for fear of bewildering Americans with too many unfamiliar items. Just bringing in *matcha* green tea, he insisted, would be sufficient to fulfill his dream of introducing traditional Japanese cuisine to Americans. "I always wanted to do this in the U.S., from day 1," Kouta said in December 2006, "I know that once Americans get familiar with the taste of quality tea, they'll pay $3 for a cup just like they pay $3 for a cup of coffee."

Koots' Store Operations

47 Koots' Azabu-juban store was located in a three-story building that had formerly been a Japanese retailer of loose-leaf teas, but which was now remodeled to convey post-industrial modernity. The store was located across the street from a McDonald's franchise. The Azabu-juban store had been designed from the beginning as a prototype for Koots' future U.S. stores. This store featured bamboo seats and tables, recessed spotlights in the ceilings and hanging orange tubes with accent lighting, and a seasonal Ikebana flower arrangement located in a mini *tokonoma* (an alcove, found in traditional Japanese homes, that featured decorations depicting the change of the seasons). Stores also featured a *tatami* mat seating area. A separate enclosed section for smokers was upstairs on the third floor. Big-band era music played in the background. Latté-style drinks were prepared by store staff with the aid of an electronic timer to assure the proper infusion of tea, and served in paper cups sporting Koots' blue-on-white lotus flower logo (derived from Kouta's family crest). Customers who wished to purchase freshly brewed premium green tea drinks in the traditional style, that is, without added flavors or soymilk, prepared their own infusions of green teas such as *sencha, genmaicha,* and *gyokuro* in china pots and drank out of china cups.[9] Self-prepared infusions of tea generally required about twice the time—about 5 minutes—compared with the average time it took for store staff to prepared the tea latté drinks. Kouta was aware of the need to reduce customer "wait states" for drinks.

48   In addition to offering plastic travel mugs in lime green or grey, Koots sold slim stainless-steel tea canisters, ideal for storing the loose organic Japanese teas retailing anywhere between ¥900 and ¥2200 (about $7.95 and $19.95) per 50-gram bag. Yet Koots' showpiece remained green-tea based drinks prepared by store staff, such as *matcha* choco-late (white-chocolate chips whisked in green-tea powder with steamed milk and organic whipped cream) and a *kuromitsu* latté (made with green-tea powder and enhanced by Japa-nese molasses.)[10]

Financial Issues

49   Kouta estimated that breakeven sales for each Koots store was approximately ¥150,000 (about $1,300) per day (about ¥4.5 million or $38,500 per month), but actual sales at Koots' busiest store in Tokyo had reached a peak of at about ¥100,000 per day (about $855) at that time.

50   Naoya Yamakoshi, Azabu-juban store manager and the Training Manager for all of Koots' Japan locations, commented on the challenge to achieving breakeven sales:

> Our biggest concern is to make more profit. Although Japanese consumers are now ready to pay a premium for green tea, as convenience stores sell ready-to-drink green tea successfully, our special teas are more labor intensive and require longer customer waiting time than convenience store teas or coffees from Starbucks and Tully's. Ingredients in the drinks we prepare—tea leaves—are of such high quality and cost that it reduces our margins.

51   Yamakoshi-san continued:

> I came over here after working at Tully's Coffee. I am involved in most new Koots store openings. This Azabu-juban store is our most successful store to date. We are still learning how to deal with clientele and improve hospitality. We use customer comment cards and also communicate with our 'regular customers' face to face. Most of our customers say they are here because they want to learn about Japanese tea culture.

Human Resources

52   In a late 2006 interview with the *Asian Wall Street Journal,* Kouta told the reporter that the key to successfully attracting and retaining people to work at Koots Green Tea was:

> First, you need to have a clear vision. You set specific targets based on it. Second, you have to be able to communicate the vision to the people you work with. Just sharing the vision isn't

---

[9] Japan is a collectivist and high context society. Japanese people value the feeling of *amae,* which means looking out for others in the group. This is reflected in the depiction of features like online clubs, family themes, and links to local companies . . . Japan also ranks high on the masculinity dimension, and Japanese web sites prominently exhibited clear gender roles. For example, men dominate all the important positions in the company, and women hold most of the customer service positions. . . [M]ost Japanese web sites are rich in colors, esthetics, elements of soft sell approach, and display a general feel of humbleness. Japanese love for beauty and esthetics is captured in two words, *shibui,* which refers to the quality of the beauty, and *mono-no-aware,* which symbolizes a merging of one's consciousness with an object's beauty, according to Singh, N., Zhao, H., & Hu, X. (2005), "Analyzing the cultural content of web sites: a cross-national comparison of China, India, Japan, and US, *International Marketing Review, 22*(2), 129–147.

[10] Many of Koots' beverages used *matcha,* a frothy green-tea powder perhaps too bitter for some Western palates, whereas the green tea served in Japanese restaurants tended to be *sencha,* a mild, boiled green tea made from young leaves.

enough. Within the organization all the minds have to resonate with one another. To this end, frequent dialogue is essential. I find it particularly effective to talk with employees outside official settings, having dinners or drinks with them. It is on those occasions that they really speak their minds. Third, you have to be passionate about your project. Even if there are people more skilled and talented than you working under you, if they know that you are more passionate than anyone about the business, they will support and follow you.

53   One young staff person at Koots' Azabu-juban store in Tokyo told us: "I'm working here because I like green tea and also want to help preserve Japanese tea culture," she said. She was completing her on-the-job training at the Azabu-juban store before moving over to work at the new Roppongi Midtown store, scheduled to open in the lobby of the tallest skyscraper in Tokyo in late January 2007. Typical of most of Koots' employees, she was a college student working part-time.

54   Yamakoshi-san said that staff turnover was high—about 50% per year—and that it was increasingly difficult to recruit experienced store personnel.[11] He conducted hiring interviews via cell phone. Staff were paid about ¥850/hour (about $7.25). Koots' store staff (regardless of gender) were called "fellows," wore blue aprons with the Koots lotus flower logo emblazoned in white on the front, and handed out business cards describing his or her favorite drink.[12]

FUTURE PLANS

55   As the December 2006 luncheon with us at Koots in Tokyo neared its end, Kouta affirmed that he still had much to learn:

> I started off owning only 20 percent of my company. When a company grows larger and larger, you see, the shareholders have other agendas. So, the lesson I learned is that, at the beginning, if you really want to be successful, try to own at least 50 percent.

56   Kouta reflected on the future expansion of Koots. Plans were already in motion to open a seventh Koots store in Tokyo and a second store in Seattle, both in January 2007, but as the chain was not yet successful in Japan from a breakeven standpoint, he remained unsure if green tea was a viable concept for a chain business and even if so, whether or not to focus his efforts on the Japanese stores or on building out the chain in the U.S. He said:

> It's not true that Ito-en will close all the Koots Tea stores, although they want me to focus on operating the Tully's Coffee Japan chain right now. I have given some thought about using the $10 million proceeds from the sale of FoodxGlobe [to Ito-en] to retire and pursue non-business interests, or maybe invest it into rapidly developing and promoting Koots as an upscale "brand" in the U.S. Our cost structures for raw materials and ingredients are substantially higher for the U.S. operation due to the fact that such items need to be imported, for example, *yame* from the Murozono tea farm.

57   Kouta added that he would need to "reconcile his vision for expanding the Koots chain with his needs to be responsive to the goals of Ito-en, his new corporate 'parent,' not to mention the challenges posed by an increasingly dynamic and uncertain competitive

---

[11] Difficulty of recruiting experienced personnel is said to be one major impediment to entrepreneurship in Japan: experienced managers appear risk-averse and reluctant to leave the security of large, established firms to join start-up firms, according to Lynskey, M. (2004), "Knowledge, finance and human capital: the role of social institutional variables on entrepreneurship in Japan," *Industry and Innovation, 11(4)*, December, 398.

[12] Kouta's business card read "Double Tall Latté," and Suga-san's read, "Grande Americano."

environment for tearooms." Yet well before Ito-en had entered the picture and gained control over FoodxGlobe, Kouta had found a capable financial backer, Suga-san, who continued to act as his financial mentor. Kouta said:

> Suga and I have discussed seeking additional venture capital in the U.S. for Koots. We might decide to create Koots franchises and sell them to U.S. franchisees. Other possibilities are to find a U.S. joint venture partner already in the foodservice industry, or maybe even attempt an initial public offering in the U.S. We could hire a CEO with U.S. foodservice chain experience to help position the company for sale someday to an existing U.S. specialty drinks or food chain.

58   According to Suga-san, business was said to be thriving, to the extent that, whenever he gave a presentation, he always needed to "double-check the number of shops" with Kouta. Suga-san continued, "Just having a [business] concept is very easy but you've got to substantiate that concept with your experience and track record. If Kouta's vision and strategy are correct, America will one day become a full-fledged Japanese green-tea-drinking nation, one that clamors for *matcha* Americanos, Genmaicha tea, and black-sesame smoothies."

59   "I'm looking at this venture long-term," Kouta replied as the luncheon ended. "[The] Japanese and Chinese have been drinking teas for 4,000 years. Look at how healthy we are."

Case 12

IMAX: Larger Than Life[1]

Anil Nair

FLASHBACK 2004

1 In Daytona, Florida, John watched a racecar going at more than 100 miles per hour crash into a concrete barrier. John ducked to escape the debris that appeared to be flying straight at him. A few moments later John was virtually within a racecar, next to the driver, zooming at more than 120 miles per hour around the racetrack. For the next half an hour, John experienced in three dimensions and on a larger-than-life scale crashing cars, dizzying turns, efficient pit crews, shining metal, burning rubber, swirling gas fumes and screaming fans. Finally, as the overhead lights at the theater gradually lit up, the audience sitting around John started applauding. John had just witnessed a screening of the IMAX movie *NASCAR.*

2 *NASCAR* set a box-office record as an original IMAX 3D film with the highest grossing opening weekend and the highest per-screen average. At $21,579, *NASCAR*'s per-screen average was higher than that of the weekend's top 10 films.[2] Reports of *NASCAR*'s box-office success would have surely pleased Richard Gelfond and Bradley Wechsler, the co-CEOs of IMAX Corporation.

INTRODUCTION

3 Gelfond and Wechsler had bought IMAX along with Wasserstein Perella Partners from the original owners in 1994 for $80 million. They took it public the same year to raise capital to fund IMAX's growth. For investors in IMAX, the years since then had been like a ride on a rollercoaster in the IMAX film *Thrill Ride:* exciting peaks when movies achieved commercial and critical acclaim, and scary drops when analysts questioned whether a niche player such as IMAX would be able to achieve consistent growth or even survive.

4 *NASCAR*'s success at the box office was evidence that the co-CEOs' efforts to reach a new audience—distinct from those typically attracted to IMAX's educational documentaries—might work. Another movie that was indicative of IMAX's emerging strategy was *The*

Anil Nair wrote this case solely to provide material for class discussion. The author does not intend to illustrate either effective or ineffective handling of a managerial situation. The author may have disguised certain names and other identifying information to protect confidentiality. The author would like to thank Professors Barbara Bartkus, Alan Eisner, Jim Key, participants at a case writing workshop organized by the Society for Case Research, and students at Old Dominion University for comments on earlier versions of the case. Thanks also to Lee-Hsien Pan for his research assistance.

Richard Ivey School of Business
The University of Western Ontario

[1] This case has been written on the basis of published sources only. Consequently, the interpretation and perspectives presented in this case are not necessarily those of IMAX or any of its employees.
[2] IMAX press release, March 14, 2004.

Polar Express. The Polar Express was the first time a Hollywood movie would be released simultaneously in commercial multiplexes and IMAX theaters. *NASCAR* and *The Polar Express* were symbolic of the direction in which Gelfond and Wechsler had pushed the company to achieve faster growth and higher margins. The two-pronged strategy involved expanding the reach of IMAX by (a) going beyond its cloistered museum environments into multiplexes and (b) presenting Hollywood films in IMAX format.

5   Despite the success of *NASCAR* and *The Polar Express,* IMAX faced several questions about its future:

- Could IMAX thrive as a niche player that made large format films and systems?
- Would increasing the number of Hollywood movies released in IMAX format save the firm or dilute the IMAX brand?
- Should Hollywood movies be released simultaneously in regular and large format?

THE BACKGROUND SCORE

6   Since the first moving images flickered in a dark theater, movies have captivated audiences around the world. About the time that people were getting familiar with programming their VCRs and learning to enjoy movies on the small television screen, a small group of people was developing a technology to project movies on giant screens. The idea for IMAX originated in 1967 when the success of a multi-screen theater system at the Montreal Expo led filmmakers Graeme Ferguson, Robert Kerr and Roman Kroitor to create a large format movie system. IMAX was founded as the only company in the world that was involved in all aspects of large format films. The first IMAX film premiered in 1970 at the Fuji Pavilion in Osaka, Japan.

7   IMAX was listed in the NASDAQ exchange in 1994 and achieved a market capitalization of $196 million in the first year itself.[3] As of December 12, 2008, market capitalization was down to $125 million. There were about 295 theaters showing IMAX movies in 40 countries, with almost 60 per cent of the theaters in North America.[4] Almost 50 per cent of the theaters were located in museums, aquariums, zoos and other institutions, and about the same percentage had the IMAX 3D technology. The IMAX movie library at the end of 2007 stood at 226 films; some produced by IMAX, many others produced by independent filmmakers or studios such as Time-Warner. In 2007/2008, some of the well-known films to be released in IMAX included *Harry Potter and the Order of the Phoenix, Shine a Light*—a film about the Rolling Stones by the famous film director Martin Scorcese—and *The Spiderwick Chronicles.*

THE IMAX STORY

Scope of IMAX

8   The company's main sources of revenues were long-term theater system lease and maintenance agreements, film production and distribution, and theater operations. Given its scope of operations, IMAX could be considered a part of three different industries: Photographic Equipment and Supplies (SIC code 3861), Motion Picture and Video Tape Production (SIC code 7812), and Motion Picture and Video Distribution (SIC code 7822). IMAX was a relatively small firm compared to a rival studio such as Disney/Pixar or a theater chain such as Regal Entertainment.

[3] S. N. Chakravarty, "A really big show," *Institutional Investor,* 35:10, October 2002, p. 20.
[4] Hoover's, www.Hoovers.com.

9   In 2007, it generated $59.12 million (51.04 per cent of total revenue) from IMAX systems sales, $36.57 million (31.57 per cent of total revenue) from films and $16.58 million (14.31 per cent of total revenue) from theater operations.[5] Order trends suggested that newer agreements were for 3D systems. The theater leases were generally for 10 to 20 years and renewable by the customer. As part of the lease, IMAX advised customers on theater design, supervised the installation of the system, trained theater staff and maintained the system.[6]

Inside IMAX

Hardware: The Film Technology

10   IMAX films were printed on films that were 10 times larger than the 35 mm films that were used in traditional multiplexes and were projected on screens that were (on average) eight stories high (approximately 88 feet) and 120-feet-wide, or in domes that were 81 feet in diameter. Please see Exhibit 1 for a comparison of 35 mm and IMAX film sizes.

11   IMAX theaters were designed so that projected images stretched up to the peripheral vision of the viewer, thus the viewer was completely immersed in the scene. Each frame of an IMAX film had 15 sprocket holes to guide it through projectors (compared to four in each frame of a 35 mm film). The films were projected to screens by IMAX-designed projectors that had special features—a higher shutter speed, rolling loop motion and vacuum to hold the film to the lens.[7] IMAX projectors used 15,000-watt bulbs, whereas the regular 35 mm projectors used bulbs between 3,000–4,000 watts. The projectors were cooled by circulating more than 50,000 cubic feet of air and nine gallons of distilled water per minute. These features of the IMAX projection system produced images on-screen that were brighter and sharper than those found in conventional movie theaters.

12   IMAX had developed the skills, knowledge and capabilities to design and assemble the critical elements involved in its projector and camera systems, though most of the components were purchased from vendors with whom it maintained long-term relationships. Strict quality control of components and end products had ensured an average service time of 99.9 per cent for its equipments installed in theaters. Company personnel visited each theater for servicing the systems; the projection systems were serviced every three months and the audio systems were serviced once a year.

13   In 2007, IMAX spent almost five per cent of its sales revenue on Research and Development, and 50 of its 318 employees were involved in it. The company had spent about $12.6 million in R & D in the past three years.[8] It had also received grants from Ontario Technology Fund for its R & D, and held 46 patents and had seven patents pending in the United States.[9] IMAX had successfully developed 3D cameras and projection systems to produce realistic 3D images. The audience used polarized or electronic glasses that split the images for the left and right eye by using liquid crystal shutter lenses that were controlled by an infrared signal and opened and shut 48 times per second in coordination with the projector to create a 3D effect. Another example of the firm's technological capabilities was a lightweight 3D camera that it had developed to shoot a movie about the International Space Station in space. IMAX worked with MSM Design, a small firm owned by Marty and Barbara Mueller, and developed a camera that weighed only 90 pounds, compared to

[5] Annual Report, 2007.

[6] Annual Reports.

[7] *Computer-Aided Engineering,* 15:8, 1996, pp. 8–9.

[8] Annual Report, 2007.

[9] Annual Report, 2007.

EXHIBIT 1 IMAX Film Size

Film Frames Actual Size

© 1994 Smithsonian Institution/Lockheed Martin Corporation

15/70mm

Standard 70mm

Standard 35mm

Source: IMAX, with permission.

the traditional IMAX 3D cameras that weighed 228 pounds.[10] IMAX 3D projectors were also capable of projecting 2D images. The visuals were supported by six-channel digital audio that typically produced 12,000 watts of realistic, distortion-free sound. The sound systems were developed by Sonics Associates Inc., a subsidiary in which IMAX had 51 per cent ownership. The company had even developed a 3D directional sound technology that offered location and depth to the audio. A testament to IMAX's technological prowess was the 1997 Oscar Award it received for Scientific and Technical Achievement.[11]

14 Because of its larger size, printing and distributing IMAX films was costlier than 35 mm films. IMAX had developed digital cameras and projectors that it planned to install in theaters starting in 2008 so that it could produce and distribute its movies in digital format. While the conversion to digital format required substantial upfront investment, it was expected that this shift would allow IMAX to lower its operational costs (of film production and distribution) significantly.

Software: IMAX Films

15 The motion picture industry produced several types of movies: horror, adventure, comedy, romantic comedy, family, drama and documentaries. Of these, the documentary segment was considered so significant that the Motion Picture Association of America (MPAA) in its annual Oscar Award ceremony gave out separate awards for these films. While the large-format film itself was a unique feature of IMAX, it had also differentiated itself by its library of films and locations. IMAX films were often educational and entertaining, and involved documentaries of natural and scientific wonders such as the Grand Canyon, space stations, etc. An IMAX film, *Fires of Kuwait,* was nominated for an Academy Award in 1993.

16 By locating itself in prestigious venues such as the Smithsonian Institution in Washington, Liberty Science Center in New Jersey, Museum of Science and Industry in Chicago, and Port Vell in Barcelona, Spain, the firm had created a unique brand image. In an interview with CNN, co-CEO Gelfond noted IMAX's advantage: "IMAX is also a brand, so we don't have to pay the same kind of talent that Hollywood has to pay, which is really a huge percentage of the costs. Once you take those costs down and you look at just making the film with the world around you as the talent, you get into much more manageable budget ranges. A typical two-dimensional film at IMAX is about $5 million; a typical 3D film at IMAX is about $10 million."[12] Hollywood studios would have to pay a major star (such as Tom Cruise or Eddie Murphy) more than $10 million for a movie. While top movie stars were celebrities and drew huge compensation, many others involved in the production, distribution and marketing of a film were neither well known nor highly paid. In 2007, according to the Bureau of Labor Statistics (BLS), the median salary for an actor in the motion picture and video industry was about $17 per hour.[13] Some of these talents had formed unions, such as the Screen Artists Guild, to negotiate higher wages for their labor. The disruption of TV programming in spring 2008 caused by the brief Writers Guild strike was suggestive of the power such groups had on studios.

17 Besides stars, the other major cost of movie-making was the marketing. It was estimated that a studio spent almost 30–50 per cent of the total cost of production and distribution of

---

[10] "Cam programming helps design 3d IMAX movie camera for NASA," *Computer Aided Engineering,* 19:3, March 2000, p. 10.

[11] W. C. Symonds, "Now showing in IMAX: Money!; The giant-screen technology will even bag an Oscar," *BusinessWeek,* 3520, March 31, 1997, p. 80.

[12] D. Michael, "Bigger is better: IMAX knocking competition down to size," *CNN,* November 6, 1998, www.cnn.com/SHOWBIZ/Movies/9811/06/imax/index.html?iref=newssearch, accessed March 23, 2008.

[13] www.bls.gov/oes/current/naics4_711500.htm, accessed December 23, 2008.

EXHIBIT 2 Average Marketing Spending on Various Media, 2007

Newspapers	12.9%
Network TV	16.1%
Spot TV	13.7%
Internet	5.3%
Trailers	4.9%
Other Media (cable TV, radio, magazines, billboards)	24.5%
Other Non-media (production/creative services, exhibitor services, promotion & publicity, market research)	22.6%

Source: www.mpaa.com.

a movie in its marketing. According to the Motion Picture Association of America (MPAA), the average cost of making and marketing a movie rose to more than $106 million in 2007, with marketing budgets averaging $36 million.[14] The marketing of the movie was done through several channels such as TV, the press, theaters, websites and promotions with retailers. Please see Exhibit 2 for average spending in each media. For example, most kids' movies released by studios such as Disney and SKG Dreamworks were promoted through tie-ups with restaurants such as McDonald's and Burger King, and also toy manufactures and other retailers. The Hollywood business model used the awareness created by the presence of stars and substantial marketing budgets to draw large audiences into theaters in the opening weekend itself.[15] To achieve high ticket sales on opening weekends, large numbers of prints of the movie were distributed. In contrast, traditionally, IMAX had not marketed its films aggressively. The company did have a sales force and marketing staff at its offices in Canada, the United States, Europe, Japan and China to market its theater systems. The movies were sold to theaters separately; as such, there was no national marketing or advertising.[16] Unlike Hollywood movies that had short lifespans in the theater circuit and were then withdrawn for release on DVD and pay-per-view format, IMAX films were often shown in theaters for years after their release. In recent years, IMAX films had received some marketing support. For example, for IMAX movie *Everest,* producer Greg MacGillivray spent $2 million in marketing and reportedly saw a 20–45 per cent increase in box-office revenues at each theater. Moreover, IMAX's alliances were helping in cross-promoting its movies. For example, for its *T-Rex: Back to the Cretaceous* 3D movie, it had a month-long promo on Showtime that was also shown in Imaginarium stores in malls across the United States.[17] The increasing number of Hollywood movies that were released in IMAX format allowed IMAX to ride on the coat-tails of marketing campaigns launched by the studios.

18   IMAX films were often produced by the firm or partially or fully financed by other parties. The firm hired the talent for the film on a project-by-project basis. Most of the post-production work was performed at David Keighley Production, a wholly-owned subsidiary of IMAX. IMAX (and any investors or sponsors) shared the ownership rights for a film, while usually IMAX controlled the distribution rights. As a result, IMAX had the distribution rights to the largest number of large format films. The distributor received a percentage

[14] M. Marr, "Now playing: Expensive movies; Average cost of a film tops $100 million for first time; Valenti set to leave MPAA," *The Wall Street Journal,* March 24, 2004, p. B. 4, www.mpaa.org/researchStatistics.asp, accessed December 23, 2008.

[15] Adam Leipzig, "How to Sell a Movie (or Fail) in Four Hours," *The New York Times,* November 13, 2005.

[16] D. Oestricher, "IMAX hopes for big run with Matrix," *The Wall Street Journal,* June 18, 2003, p. b5c.

[17] T. L. Stanley, "IMAX lands Showtime, GTE for 1st X-Promo," *Brandweek,* July 13, 1998, 39:28, p. 5.

EXHIBIT 3   Box Office Revenues for IMAX Movies (in Millions of $)

Rank	Title	Studio	Gross-to-date	Year
1	Everest	MFF	$87.18	1998
2	Space Station 3-D	IMAX	$77.10	2002
3	T-Rex: Back to the Cretaceous	IMAX	$53.14	1998
4	Fantasia 2000	BV	$52.26	2000
5	Mysteries of Egypt	IMAX	$40.59	1998
6	Deep Sea 3-D	WB	$37.09	2006
7	Magnificant Desolation	IMAX	$26.67	2005
8	Beauty and the Beast	BV	$25.49	2002
9	NASCAR 3D: The IMAX Experience	WB	$21.58	2004
10	Sea Monsters: A Prehistoric Adventure	NGC	$20.05	2007

Source: www.boxofficemojo.com. IMAX box office receipts have only recently started being tracked.

of the theater box office revenues. IMAX films often remained in distribution for four or five years. (Please see Exhibit 3 for box office revenues for IMAX films.)

Generating Growth

19   IMAX used a two-pronged strategy to maintain its growth. First, it had sought to expand beyond its institutional environment by opening IMAX theaters within multiplexes or converting existing multiplexes' screens to IMAX format. Second, it had launched Hollywood films in IMAX format.

An IMAX Near You

20   While early IMAX theaters were mostly located in institutional settings such as museums and aquariums, to reach a wider audience IMAX had engaged in alliances with commercial movie theater owners.[18] It grew rapidly during the late 1990s as theater owners such as AMC, Cinemark and Regal went on a building spree and bought IMAX systems to install in their multiplexes. According to Wechsler, this strategy backfired when IMAX could not escape the crisis that hit the theater industry in the late 1990s because of the overbuilding during that decade. As many theater-owners filed for bankruptcy, IMAX had to engage in belt-tightening of its own because of its receivable problems. Moody's downgraded IMAX's debt of $200 million senior notes from Ba2 to B2 and a $100 million note from B1 to Caa1 because of the risk of default by customers. In response, IMAX cut $14 million in overhead, laid off 200 employees and bought back $90 million of its debt.[19] Debt remained a critical problem for IMAX (please see Exhibits 4, 5 and 6 for IMAX financials).

21   In recent years, IMAX entered into partnerships with AMC and Regal Cinemas to screen IMAX films in multiplexes using its MPX technology. MPX technology allowed IMAX and theater-owners to convert traditional theaters to IMAX format.[20] It was estimated that

[18] L. Gubernick, "Hollywood Journal: Hollywood think bigger—your favorites, only taller: Can re-released movies breathe life into IMAX." *The Wall Street Journal,* February 15, 2002, p. W. 5.

[19] Z. Olijnyk, "One giant leap," *Canadian Business,* 75:17, September 16, 2002, pp. 46–48.

[20] D. Oestricher, "IMAX hopes for big run with Matrix," *The Wall Street Journal,* June 18, 2003, p. b5c.

EXHIBIT 4 IMAX Corporation Annual Balance Sheet (in thousands of dollars)

Period Ending	31-Dec-07	31-Dec-06	31-Dec-05	31-Dec-04
Assets				
Current Assets				
Cash and Cash Equivalents	16,901	25,123	24,324	28,964
Short-Term Investments	—	2,115	8,171	—
Net Receivables	25,505	26,017	89,171	19,899
Inventory	22,050	26,913	28,294	29,001
Other Current Assets	2,187	3,432	3,825	2,279
Total Current Assets	**66,643**	**83,600**	**153,785**	**80,143**
Long-Term Investments	59,092	65,878	—	59,492
Property Plant and Equipment	23,708	24,639	26,780	28,712
Goodwill	39,027	39,027	39,027	39,027
Intangible Assets	4,419	3,782	6,030	3,931
Accumulated Amortization	—	—	—	—
Other Assets	10,928	6,646	9,756	7,532
Deferred Long-Term Asset Charges	4,165	3,719	10,806	12,016
Total Assets	**207,982**	**227,291**	**246,184**	**230,853**
Liabilities				
Current Liabilities				
Accounts Payable	74,267	69,720	62,057	62,724
Short / Current Long-Term Debt	—	—	—	—
Other Current Liabilities	—	—	—	—
Total Current Liabilities	**74,267**	**69,720**	**62,057**	**62,724**
Long-Term Debt	160,000	160,000	160,000	160,000
Other Liabilities	—	—	—	—
Deferred Long-Term Liability				
Charges	59,085	55,803	44,397	50,505
Minority Interest	—	—	—	—
Negative Goodwill	—	—	—	—
Total Liabilities	**293,352**	**285,523**	**266,454**	**273,229**
Stockholders' Equity				
Common Stock	122,455	122,024	121,674	116,281
Retained Earnings	(213,407)	(184,375)	(144,347)	(160,945)
Other Stockholder Equity	5,582	4,119	2,403	2,288
Total Stockholder Equity	**(85,370)**	**(58,232)**	**(20,270)**	**(42,376)**

Source: Annual Reports.

EXHIBIT 5 IMAX Corporation Annual Income Statement (in thousands of dollars)

Period Ending	31-Dec-07	31-Dec-06	31-Dec-05	31-Dec-04
Total Revenue	115,832	129,452	144,930	135,980
Cost of Revenue	74,673	76,902	73,005	70,062
Gross Profit	41,159	52,550	71,925	65,918
Operating Expenses				
Research & Development	5,789	3,615	3,264	3,995
Selling General and Administrative	44,705	42,527	39,503	36,066
Non-recurring	562	1,073	−859	−639
Others	547	1,668	911	719
Total Operating Expenses	51,603	48,883	42,819	40,141
Operating Income or Loss	(10,444)	3,667	29,106	25,777
Income from Continuing				
Operations				
Total Other Income/Expenses Net	(933)	1,036	1,004	265
Earnings Before Interest and Taxes	(11,377)	4,703	30,110	26,042
Interest Expense	17,093	16,759	16,773	16,853
Income Before Taxes	(28,470)	(12,056)	13,337	9,189
Income Tax Expense	472	6,218	934	(255)
Minority Interest	0	0	0	0
Net Income from Continuing Ops	(28,942)	(18,274)	(12,403)	9,444
Non-recurring Events				
Discontinued Operations	2,002	1,425	1,979	800
Extraordinary Items	0	0	0	0
Effect of Accounting Changes	0	0	0	0
Other Items	0	0	0	0
Net Income	(26,940)	(16,849)	14,382	10,244

Source: Annual Reports.

it now cost only $175,000 to retrofit a multiplex and another $500,000 to install the IMAX system.[21] Regal Cinemas had built IMAX theaters in several markets and waited to see how they performed before adding more.[22] In March 2008, it signed another agreement with IMAX for 38 more theaters, bringing the total number of Regal IMAX theaters to 52 by 2010. Regal theaters would charge $2.50–5.00 more than their regular feature admission for IMAX films.[23] In December 2007, IMAX signed a deal with AMC to install 100 IMAX

[21] Katy Marquardt, "Imax Parlays a Huge Screen and 3-D Tech into an Experience You Can't Duplicate at Home. Coming soon to a multiplex near you," *US News and World Report,* Feb. 6, 2008, www.usnews.com/articles/business/2008/02/06/imax-parlays-3-d-tech-into-an-experience-you-cant-duplicate-at-home.html, accessed December 23, 2008.

[22] *The Wall Street Journal,* 2000.

[23] B. Pulley, "The really big screen," *Forbes,* 172:13, December 22, 2003, p. 222; *The Wall Street Journal,* 2003.

EXHIBIT 6   IMAX Corporation Cash Flow Statement (in thousands of dollars)

Period Ending	31-Dec-07	31-Dec-06	31-Dec-05	31-Dec-04
Net Income	(26,940)	(16,849)	14,382	10,244
Cash Flows Provided By or Used In Operating Activities				
Depreciation	17,738	16,872	15,867	14,947
Adjustments to Net Income	(3,520)	10,349	(8,678)	(4,577)
Changes in Accounts Receivables	675	(11,106)	(8,324)	(6,673)
Changes in Liabilities	4,781	4,399	(11,749)	(6,830)
Changes in Inventories	(1,603)	57	(383)	(283)
Changes in Other Operating Activities	2,648	(9,659)	(1,545)	4,583
Total Cash Flow from Operating Activities	(6,221)	(5,937)	1,786	11,411
Cash Flows Provided By or Used In Investing Activities				
Capital Expenditures	(2,150)	(1,985)	(1,597)	(320)
Investments	2,115	6,396	(7,818)	393
Other Cashflows from Investing Activities	(702)	2,105	(1,301)	(1,435)
Total Cash Flows from Investing Activities	(737)	6,516	(10,716)	(1,362)
Cash Flows Provided By or Used In Financing Activities				
Dividends Paid	—	—	—	—
Sale Purchase of Stock	420	286	3,633	558
Net Borrowings	(1,714)	—	—	(29,769)
Other Cash Flows from Financing Activities	—	—	786	800
Total Cash Flows from Financing Activities	(1,294)	286	4,419	(28,411)
Effect of Exchange Rate Changes	30	(66)	(129)	44
Change in Cash and Cash Equivalents	($8,222)	$799	($4,640)	($18,318)

Source: Annual Reports.

digital theaters systems in 33 markets, thereby substantially increasing its presence in the U.S. market. IMAX had identified 655 multiplexes without an IMAX nearby.[24] However, IMAX co-CEO Wechsler had stated that he did not expect IMAX theaters to be ubiquitous but exclusive, like flying first-class; while co-CEO Gelfond had suggested that the IMAX experience would be so unique that it could not be replicated at home. Consistent with this vision, the theater agreement that it recently signed gave AMC territorial exclusivity.[25]

[24] D. Oestricher, "IMAX hopes for big run with Matrix," *The Wall Street Journal,* June 18, 2003, p. b5c.
[25] Katy Marquardt, "Imax Parlays a Huge Screen and 3-D Tech Into an Experience You Can't Duplicate at Home. Coming soon to a multiplex near you," *US News and World Report,* February 6, 2008, www.usnews.com/articles/business/2008/02/06/imax-parlays-3-d-tech-into-an-experience-you-cant-duplicate-at-home.html, accessed December 23, 2008.

Unlike past agreements where theater chains bought the system from IMAX, the newer agreements required the partner theater chain to make the investment for retrofitting the theater, while IMAX paid for the system installation in return for revenue-sharing on future ticket sales. Analysts expected that such agreements (and digital conversion) would lower IMAX's capital requirements and help it pay off its debt.[26]

Go West IMAX!

22   Another strategic move by IMAX to ensure its growth was the conversion of Hollywood movies into IMAX format. IMAX had developed a patented digital re-mastering (DMR) technology that allowed it to convert traditional 35 mm films such as *Harry Potter, Spider-man, Antz* and *The Simpsons* into the large-screen format and even develop 3D versions of such movies. The development of this technology was critical because merely projecting a 35 mm film on the large IMAX screen would have produced a grainy picture. According to co-CEO Gelfond, the firm invested millions of dollars to sharpen the resolution of the converted pictures and it took more than five years to develop the technology.[27] The re-mastering of *Apollo 13* took 16 weeks, while *The Matrix Revolutions* was re-mastered as it was being produced, allowing for near-simultaneous theater and IMAX releases. As IMAX had worked out the teething problems with this technology, the costs of conversion had come down. For each print, it now cost $22,500 to convert a standard two-dimensional film and $45,000 to convert a 3D film. It was expected that moving to a digital format would further lower the conversion costs. If the conversion succeeded at the box office, more studios might be willing to spend the extra money to convert their standard 35 mm films to IMAX format.[28] This would also attract theater chains to open new IMAX screens. Though IMAX made only seven per cent of the box office revenue from reformatted films by other studios, compared to the nearly 30 per cent that it made on its own movies,[29] the conversion of Hollywood movies might allow IMAX to survive, according to co-CEO Gelfond.[30] An announcement to launch the *Harry Potter* movie on IMAX resulted in an almost 11 per cent surge in its stock price that day. Gelfond noted that IMAX could continue making educational films that could be screened in theaters during daytime for families, students and tourists, while its reformatted Hollywood movies could be screened in the evening. In an interview with Amusement Business, co-CEO Wechsler noted that the IMAX strategy of moving into the commercial movie business would hopefully expand the core audience.[31] "Our research tells us that a lot of people will pay that extra $3 to $5," Gelfond said in an interview with USA Today.[32]

23   The first full-length Hollywood movie released on IMAX was *Fantasia 2000* in January 2000.[33] The classic *Beauty and the Beast,* which had a 20-week show on 67 IMAX screens in 2002, generated $32 million in revenue.[34] The first live action commercial movie to be

[26] Ibid.

[27] S. N. Chakravarty, "A really big show," *Institutional Investor,* 35:10, October 2002, p. 20.

[28] *The Wall Street Journal,* 2000; *Institutional Investor,* 2002.

[29] D. Lieberman, "IMAX supersizes its plans for future flicks," *USA Today,* December 16, 2002, www.usatoday.com/tech/news/techinnovations/2002-12-16-IMAX_x.htm, accessed December 23, 2008.

[30] Z. Olijnyk, "One giant leap," *Canadian Business,* 75:17, September 16, 2002, pp. 46–48.

[31] N. Emmons, "IMAX may turn toward mainstream," *Amusement Business,* 112:49, December 4, 2000, p. 1, pp. 20–21.

[32] D. Lieberman, "IMAX supersizes its plans for future flicks," *USA Today,* December 16, 2002, www.usatoday.com/tech/news/techinnovations/2002-12-16-IMAX_x.htm, accessed December 23, 2008.

[33] R. Ricklefs, "IMAX hopes to take cast screen into mainstream—a new 'fantasia' tests film strategy of Canadian firm," *The Wall Street Journal,* December 10, 1999, p. 1.

[34] D. Oestricher, "IMAX hopes for big run with Matrix," *The Wall Street Journal,* June 18, 2003, p. B5c.

launched in IMAX format was *Apollo 13,* which generated an additional $2 million in revenue. Later, *Star Wars* was released on IMAX followed by *The Matrix Reloaded,* which generated $11.7 million.[35] These movies were released in IMAX after their theatrical release.[36]

24   As more Hollywood movies were converted to IMAX format, the studios had to decide whether these should be released simultaneously in theaters and IMAX format. Could the expansion into IMAX theaters cannibalize the traditional theatrical revenues? It was found that almost 90 per cent of *The Matrix Reloaded* IMAX viewers had seen the movie in theaters earlier. *The Polar Express,* which was released simultaneously in IMAX and traditional theaters during the 2004 Christmas season, was a big hit with $45 million in revenues in the IMAX format.[37] On December 12, 2008, the movie *The Day the Earth Stood Still* was released simultaneously on IMAX and multiplex screens. At $31 million, the movie had the highest box office gross over a weekend. More than $3.8 million (about 12 per cent) of the total revenue came from IMAX theaters. Notably, the average revenue per IMAX theater was $30,800, compared to the national average theater revenues of $8,100.[38] Such track records should give more studios the confidence to release their movies simultaneously in commercial and IMAX theaters.

INDUSTRY DYNAMICS

25   Motion picture production and distribution was part of the service sector of the economy and included firms such as Disney/Pixar, MGM, Regal Entertainment, Lions Gate and Carmike. Many of the production and distribution companies were now part of other, larger, diversified firms. For example, Columbia Pictures was now part of Sony, Warner Brothers was a subsidiary of Time-Warner, Paramount Studios was part of Viacom and Pixar and Miramax were part of Disney. Over the years, media firms had sought to vertically integrate their operations by owning not only the production facilities but also distribution networks.

26   Film production remained a risky business. Only one in 10 films ever recovered its investment from domestic theater release; and only six out of 10 movies ever recouped the original investment. Competition among movies within the same genre was so high that studios scheduled releases carefully to avoid direct competition. Thus, release dates were announced several years in advance and production was designed around preferred holiday release dates such as Thanksgiving, July 4th, Memorial Day weekends or the first weekend of May.

27   IMAX films faced competition from other films produced by studios such as Pixar/Disney that were targeted for families or children. Within the large format film segment, Iwerks was the only rival to IMAX.[39] Iwerks was founded in 1986 and continued to be involved in all aspects of large format films and simulation rides. It produced films in the 15/70 and 8/70 formats; however, the focus of the firm was more on ride simulation

[35] T. Lowry, "Now playing at IMAX: Hit movies" *BusinessWeek,* 3807, November 11, 2002, p. 46.; N. Sperling, "IMAX executives hoping Warner's 'The Matrix' is 'the one'," *Amusement Business,* 115:46, 2003, pp. 24–25.

[36] T. King, "Hollywood Journal: When a 'Sure thing' Isn't—Even the $20 million stars can't guarantee a hit; trying to ignore 'Pluto'," *The Wall Street Journal,* October 11, 2002, p. w11.

[37] W. D. Crotty, "IMAX's screen gets bigger," The Motley Fool, September 15, 2005, www.fool.com/investing/general/2005/09/15/imaxs-screen-gets-bigger.aspx?terms=Imax+screen+gets+bigger&vstest=search_042607_linkdefault, accessed December 23, 2008.

[38] "Imax rises as consumers embrace large screens," *Associated Press,* December 16, 2008, http://biz.yahoo.com/ap/081216/imax_mover.html?.v=1, accessed December 23, 2008.

[39] C. Booth, "IMAX gets bigger (by getting smaller)," *Time,* June 29, 1998, 151:25, pp. 48–49.

EXHIBIT 7   **Substitute Activities to Movies in 2007**

	Activity	Attendance (in millions)	Average Ticket Price (in $)
1	Movies	1400	6.88
2	Theme Parks	341	35.30
3	Ice Hockey/NHL	21	44.60
4	Basketball/NBA	22	46.75
5	Football/NFL	17	65.25
6	Baseball/MLB	77	23.50

Source: MPAA, www.mpaa.com.

packages located in theme parks, zoos, museums and other destinations. Iwerks had received two Academy Awards for Scientific and Technical Achievement. In 2002, Iwerks merged with SimEx (a firm founded in 1991), which was involved in ride simulation and animation production. Another firm, Megasystems, which was involved in the development of large format projection systems, production and consulting in marketing, operations and technical services, had discontinued its projection system production and was renamed Pollavision. Pollavision was now only involved in consulting (and maintenance) services for large format film theaters.[40]

Technology Trends

28   Potential IMAX viewers could consume many alternative sources of entertainment such as live plays, sport events, TV programs, the Internet, etc. Please see Exhibits 7 and 8 for admissions, prices and time spent on alternative entertainment sources. Viewers might choose to watch a movie on DVD, pay-per-view or video on demand rather than at the theater. The development of high-definition DVD recording, big-screen TVs and cheaper home theater projection and sound systems posed an even bigger threat to box office ticket sales. Please see Exhibit 9 for DVD sales trends in the United States. According to one estimate, almost 85 per cent of a film's revenue now came from home viewing through various channels such as DVD/VHS, cable and TV.[41] Yet, it had been found that the success of secondary sources such as DVD sales and rentals was a function of the movie's box office success.[42] According to Jack Valenti, former president of MPAA, 50 per cent of DVD viewers and almost 38 per cent of VCR movie-users were frequent moviegoers. He said, "People who love movies are eager to watch them again in different environments."[43]

29   The development of new technologies, such as cheaper high definition camcorders, as well as the proliferation of new distribution channels such as cable, satellite and the Internet, had also created opportunities for new independent firms to enter the industry. One such firm that leveraged its knowledge of computer technology to develop blockbuster animated films was Pixar. New firms might enter one or more parts of the film industry value chain—talent management, production, post-production, distribution, etc. Specialists in post-production processes had emerged who were responsible for editing, special effects,

---

[40] www.pollavision.com, accessed December 23, 2008.

[41] E. J. Epstein, "Hollywood's death spiral," *Slate,* July 25, 2005.

[42] Bruce Orwall, "A Dud at Theaters Will Be a Dud DVD," *The Wall Street Journal,* November 26, 2005, p. A2.

[43] J. Valenti, MPAA Press Release, 2002.

EXHIBIT 8   Media Consumption Based on Hours Per Person Per Year

Filmed Entertainment	2003	2004	2005	2006	2007
Cable & Satellite TV	886	909	980	997	1,010
Broadcast TV	729	711	679	676	676
Consumer Internet	153	164	169	177	181
Home Video (DVD & VHS)	60	67	63	62	64
Box Office	13	13	12	12	13
In-flight Entertainment & Mobile Content	5	8	10	13	18
Subtotal	1,846	1,872	1,913	1,937	1,962
Other Entertainment					
Broadcast & Satellite Radio	831	821	805	778	769
Recorded Music	187	196	195	186	171
Newspapers	195	192	188	178	172
Consumer Magazines	122	125	124	121	119
Consumer Books	108	108	107	108	108
Video Games	76	78	73	76	82
Subtotal	1,522	1,520	1,492	1,447	1,421

Source: MPAA, www.mpaa.com.

EXHIBIT 9   DVD Consumption in The United States (in millions of units)

	Rental DVDs	Sell-through DVDs	Total DVDs	Avg. Price of DVD
2007	171.2	1,084.6	1,255.8	22.11
2006	180.2	1,129.0	1,309.2	22.29
2005	179.0	1,114.5	1,293.6	21.20
2004	149.3	1,063.3	1,212.6	20.32
2003	105.4	768.3	873.6	20.15

Source: MPAA, www.mpaa.com.

media transfers, subtitling, etc. However, entry into all aspects of the value chain simultaneously had been rare. A recent example of such an entry was SKG Dreamworks, a studio that was started by film industry veterans Spielberg, Katzenberg and Geffen.

30   Such technological changes had also increased the potential for piracy. According to the Motion Picture Association of America, the U.S. film industry lost more than $3 billion annually because of piracy. Section 8, Article 1 of the U.S. Constitution offers Congress the power to offer copyright protection. The Copyright Act of 1976 that was amended in 1982 offers strong penalties for copyright violations. Please see www.copyright.gov/title17 for recent developments in copyright law. Violations were considered felonies and were subject to federal criminal charges and civil lawsuits. The Motion Picture Association was working closely with the U.S. Congress to enforce sentencing guidelines and improve copyright protection as newer technologies emerged and posed fresher challenges. According to Karen Randall of Vivendi, whose production *The Hulk* was released on the Internet

by pirates before its theatrical release, the FBI was very cooperative and aggressive in pursuing the case.[44]

Other Trends

31 IMAX had to cease screening its movie *Volcanoes of the Deep Sea* in some parts of the United States, as certain religious groups were offended by its position on, and depiction of, evolution.[45] Concerns about violence and sex in movies had generated considerable efforts to organize and lobby political action to regulate the industry. For example, Tipper Gore and Lynn Cheney (spouses of former vice-presidents Al Gore and Dick Cheney, respectively) had worked hard to curtail the levels of violence, sex and vulgar language found in popular media.[46]

32 Another trend that might help firms such as IMAX was the increased consumption of educational entertainment. Ever since Sesame Street succeeded in educating and entertaining kids simultaneously, the "edutainment" market had grown as parents increasingly sought out play activities for their children that were educational. This trend had been attributed to increasing belief among parents that in a knowledge economy, their kids' success might depend on education. The widespread popularity among parents of the concept of the "Mozart effect"—a finding that babies that listened to Mozart recordings in the womb or at early stages of birth had richer cognitive development—was seen as evidence of their desire to produce smart kids.[47] Other trends that were driving this growth could include higher education levels of parents and overscheduled kids and parents.[48] As a result, zoos, museums, software, TV shows and toys were all redesigning their products to entertain and educate.

33 According to IMAX, more than 20 per cent of IMAX audiences were school groups. About 70 per cent of IMAX viewers were between 19 and 65 years of age, and the majority were college- or university-educated, with an average household income of more than $70,000, and with 33 per cent earning more than $100,000.[49] MPAA offered a more fine-grained analysis of demographic data on movie attendance. It reported that 12–24 year olds (38 per cent of admissions) had the largest attendance for feature films in theaters in 2007, followed by the 25- to 39-year-olds group (29 per cent of admissions).[50] The 12–24-year-olds were also frequent moviegoers (at least one movie per month), representing 41 per cent of frequent moviegoers. IMAX needed to figure out a way to attract this demographic.

U.S. and Global Market

34 In 2007, 603 movies were released in the United States and collected revenues of $9.6 billion.[51] According to the MPAA, there were 1.4 billion movie theater attendances

---

[44] S. McBride and B. Orwall, "Movie industry steps up drive against pirates," *The Wall Street Journal,* January 27, 2004, p. B1.

[45] Cornelia Dean, "A new test for IMAX: The Bible vs. the volcano," March 19, 2005.

[46] Richard Goldstein, "Scary Move: When Both Parties Team Up to Target Hollywood, Be Afraid. Be Very Afraid!" *Village Voice,* October 3, 2000, p.20.

[47] Jeffrey Kluger and Alice Park, "The Quest For A Superkid," *Time,* April 22, 2001 www.time.com/time/nation/article/0,8599,107265-1,00.html, accessed December 23, 2008.

[48] R. White, "That's Edutainment," White Hutchinson Leisure & Learning Group, 2003.

[49] www.IMAX.com.

[50] J. Valenti, MPAA Press Release, 2002.

[51] US Entertainment Industry: 2007 MPAA statistics. See also, M. Marr, "Now playing: Expensive movies; Average cost of a film tops $100 million for first time; Valenti set to leave MPAA," *The Wall Street Journal,* March 24, 2004, p. B. 4.

EXHIBIT 10   Theater Box Office Revenues, Average U.S. Attendance, Price and Economy

Year	Revenue (in billions $)	Ticket price (in $)	Attendance (in billions)	GDP Growth (in %)	CPI Inflation (in %)
1990	5.02	4.22	1.19	1.9	5.4
1991	4.8	4.21	1.14	−0.2	4.2
1992	4.56	4.15	1.1	3.3	3.0
1993	4.89	4.14	1.18	2.7	3.0
1994	5.18	4.08	1.24	4.0	2.6
1995	5.27	4.35	1.21	2.5	2.8
1996	5.81	4.42	1.32	3.7	3.0
1997	6.21	4.59	1.35	4.5	2.3
1998	6.76	4.69	1.44	4.2	1.6
1999	7.31	5.06	1.44	4.5	2.2
2000	7.46	5.39	1.38	3.7	3.4
2001	8.12	5.65	1.44	0.8	2.8
2002	9.27	5.8	1.60	1.6	1.6
2003	9.16	6.03	1.52	2.5	2.3
2004	9.21	6.21	1.48	3.6	2.7
2005	8.83	6.41	1.38	2.9	3.4
2006	9.14	6.55	1.39	2.8	3.2
2007	9.63	6.88	1.40	2.0	2.8

Source: National Association of Theater Owners (NATO), www. natoonline.org; Bureau of Economic Analysis, www.bea.gov; and Bureau of Labor Statistics, www.bls.gov.

in the United States in 2007.[52] Jack Valenti, former president of the MPAA, noted that Americans had the highest per capita movie attendance in the world at 5.3 films a year. By excluding those who did not see at least one movie a year, the per capita attendance rose to 8.6 films per year.[53] Exhibit 10 displays theater revenues, average U.S. ticket prices, attendance annual growth rate, consumer price index (CPI) and growth of the U.S. economy. Theater-owners realized that ticket prices could not go up forever, as this might drive away more viewers; so they tried to generate revenue by screening more commercials before showing the feature film. According to some experts, release of big budget franchise movies or sequels of popular movies attenuated the adverse impact of the economy on theater attendance.

35   Movies were now increasingly becoming a global industry. More than 5000 films were released worldwide in 2007, with seven billion attendances and annual global box office revenues estimated at $26.7 billion.[54] The Asia-Pacific region had the largest share of the global market. While Hollywood movies had always enjoyed an international audience,

[52] James Jaeger, The Movie Industry, www.mecfilms.com/moviepubs/memos/moviein.htm, accessed December 23, 2008.

[53] 2007 movie attendance study, MPAA.

[54] 2007 International Theatrical Snapshot, MPAA, www.mpaa.org/International%20Theatrical%20 Snapshot.pdf, accessed March 4, 2009.

EXHIBIT 11   **Domestic and Overseas Revenues for 2007 (in millions of dollars)**

Rank	Title	Domestic	Overseas	World
1	Pirates of the Caribbean: At World's End	309.4	649.0	958.4
2	Harry Potter and the Order of the Phoenix	292.0	645.0	937.0
3	Spider-Man 3	336.5	548.9	885.4
4	Shrek the Third	321.0	470.4	791.4
5	Transformers	319.1	382.0	701.1
6	Ratatouille	206.4	409.5	615.9
7	I am Legend	256.4	327.6	584.0
8	Simpsons Movie, The	183.1	342.4	525.5
9	300	210.6	246.0	456.6
10	National Treasure: Book of Secrets	220.0	234.0	454.0

Source: www.worldwideboxoffice.com.

with globalization and the increased movement of people across national borders movies from other regions such as Hong Kong and India were also finding an international audience. For Hollywood movies, a significant part of the revenues now came from outside the United States. Please see Exhibit 11 on domestic and foreign sources for the top 10 films in 2007.

THE LARGER ISSUES

36   At this point in its evolution, IMAX faced two critical questions. Would IMAX lose its differentiation if it exhibited too many Hollywood movies? Greg MacGillvray, who had made several films in the IMAX format, including the highly successful *Everest,* argued that IMAX ran the risk of losing its brand identity as it moved into non-educational entertainment films. He said: "There's also been a slight brand erosion given that these films have not been really educational experiences, but more entertainment experiences." According to MacGillvra, IMAX's own research showed that the brand's trustworthiness was rooted in the fact that IMAX grew up in institutional settings.[55]

37   Another question that the present co-CEOs had faced for several years was: Should IMAX be sold to a larger studio such as Sony, Disney or Time-Warner? That is, was it too small to survive on its own? Some analysts had speculated that IMAX was ripe for acquisition. Co-CEO Gelfond had once stated, "Someday it will make sense for IMAX to be part of a studio." [56]

[55] P. Waal, "Call in the barbarians," *Canadian Business,* 73:17, September 18, 2000, pp. 85–87.

[56] P. Waal, "The plot quickens," *Canadian Business,* 71:11, June 26–July 10, 1998, pp. 51–57.

Case 13

MTV Networks: *The Arabian Challenge*   Dr. Deba Purkayastha

> *"[. . .] MTV has a penchant for airing controversial material and making a mockery of convention. And of course, it's an American brand . . . The challenge, therefore, is transforming a notoriously risqué channel into a Middle Eastern–friendly platform for music and creativity without stripping MTV of its edge. It isn't without some irony that a channel known for angering religious, political, and conservative communities is operating in and catering to a region renowned for reacting (and sometimes overreacting) negatively to controversial content."[1]*

> —Dana El Baltaji, Special Projects Manager, Trends magazine in Dubai, in 2008

> *"In many ways (MTV Arabia) is the epitome of our localization strategy. It's a different audience (in the Middle East) but this is what we do—we reflect culture and we respect culture. The programming mix on this one is going to be a little more local than normal."[2]*

> —William H. Roedy, Vice Chairman for MTV Networks and President MTVI Network International, in 2007

A LITMUS TEST FOR MTV'S LOCALIZATION STRATEGY

1   MTV Networks (MTVN) launched MTV Arabia on November 17, 2007, in partnership with Arabian Television Network[3] (ATN) as part of its global expansion strategy. According to analysts, MTV's presence in the Middle East would provide the region with an international music brand, which till then, did not have an international music brand though it had clusters of local music channels. On its part, the region promised to offer tremendous growth opportunities to MTVN.

2   Analysts felt that MTV Arabia was MTVN's most ambitious and challenging venture. The Middle East offered huge growth potential to MTVN given its huge youth populace. However, according to analysts, MTV's success in the Middle East was contingent upon a tactical balancing between delivery of international quality music and the culturally sensitive environment prevalent in the region. Some analysts felt that the channel was well equipped to achieve this considering MTVN's extensive experience in the global market and its ability to provide localized content without diluting what MTV stood for.

3   To ensure that its programs won over the hearts of the Arabs and adhered to the local taste and culture without diluting MTV's global brand, MTV Arabia designed a much localized Arabic version of its international music and reality shows. In this connection, Patrick Samaha (Samaha), General Manager of MTV Arabia, said, "We've created programs that

Center for Management Research, Hyderabad, India

[1] Dana El Baltaji, "I Want My MTV," www.arabmediasociety.com, May 11, 2008.

[2] Lynne Roberts, "MTV Set for Middle East Launch," www.arabianbusiness.com, October 17, 2007.

[3] Arabian Television Network (ATN) is a Dubai, United Arab Emirates based broadcast media company, part of the Arab Media Group's Arabian Broadcasting Network (ABN). ABN is a part of the Arab Media Group (AMG). As of 2007, AMG was the largest media group in the UAE, with approximately 1,500 employees. It was an unit of TECOM Investments that was controlled by Dubai's ruler.

are an Arabic version of MTV programs. It is the first time that programs like this will really reflect the youth culture here, but we've been mindful all the way about respecting the local culture."[4]

4   According to the company, the launch of MTV Arabia was also expected to act as a culturally unifying force by propelling Arabic Music to the global forefront and vice versa. While launching MTV Arabia, William H. Roedy (Roedy), Vice Chairman for MTV Networks and President of MTVI, said, "Tonight's [November 16, 2007] MTV Arabia launch show celebrates one of the most important landmarks in MTV's 25-year history. MTV Arabia will reach the largest potential audience of any MTV channel outside the United States. MTV is proud to celebrate the voice of the Arab youth and through our global network we can showcase what this rich and diverse culture is all about to new audiences around the world."[5]

BACKGROUND NOTE

5   MTV (short for Music Television), which pioneered the concept of a cable music channel, was launched on August 1, 1981, and marked the commencement of the cable TV revolution. It was promoted by Warner Amex Satellite Entertainment Company, a joint venture between Warner Communications and American Express. In 1984, the company was renamed MTV Networks (MTVN) with its operations confined to the US.

6   At the time of its launch, the MTV channel primarily catered to those in the 12 to 24 age group, airing heavy-metal and rap music. However, over the years, it also launched many sister channels such as VH-1(short for video hits one) which was formed in 1985 to play light popular music; Rhythm and Blues (R&B, for jazz, country music, and classics targeted at the 18 to 35 age group; and Nickelodeon,[6] which was launched in 1977 keeping children as its target segment. While these sister channels of MTVN continued playing different varieties of music, the core channel MTV began to diversify in 1990. Besides playing music, it also started airing non-music, reality shows. "The Real World" and "MTV Fear" were some of the popular reality shows aired. Animated cartoon series were also introduced, the most popular of them being "Beavis and Butthead."

7   In 1986, MTVN was acquired by Viacom Inc. (Viacom) (Refer to Exhibit I for a note on Viacom). Thereafter, in 1987, MTVN launched its first overseas channel in Europe and this marked the beginning of MTV's global expansion. The international arm of MTVN was known as MTVI. In addition to MTV, MTVI managed a bouquet of channels like VH-1 and Nickelodeon.

8   By the mid-1990s MTVI realized that to become a successful brand globally, it had to adapt to local conditions. Hence it adopted a strategy of "Think Globally, Act Locally." Thereafter, MTVI became the first international TV network to offer channels like MTV Australia, MTV Asia, MTV India, MTV China, MTV Germany, etc. in local languages with localized content.[7] To penetrate any new market, MTVI initially tied up with a local music channel and in course of time, it acquired the local company in that region. For instance, in

---

[4] Jolanta Chudy, "MTV's Arab Net Thinking Locally," www.hollywoodreporter.com, November 6, 2007.

[5] "Akon and Ludacris Dazzle the Desert in their Middle East Debuts to Celebrate the Launch of MTV Arabia," www.dubaicityguide.com, November 16, 2007.

[6] Nickelodeon's primarily caters to children in age group 7–11, but along with this it also airs weekend programmes in TEENick catering to children in age group 12–17 and also weekday morning programs aimed at children in age group 2–6 and a late-night segment known as Nick at Nite aimed at general audiences.

[7] Dirk Smillie, "Tuning in First Global TV Generation," *The Christian Science Monitor,* June 4, 1997.

EXHIBIT I   A Note on Viacom Inc.

Viacom was established as a public company in 1971. In 1985, it acquired a 65 percent stake in MTV Networks, which included MTV, VH-1, and Nickelodeon, and purchased the remaining interest in 1986. In 1991, Viacom completed its purchase of MTV Europe by acquiring a 50 percent stake from British Telecommunications and other parties. In 1994, the Viacom Entertainment Group was formed through a merger with Paramount Communications Inc. In 2000, CBS Corporation, a major media network in the US, merged with Viacom, as a result of which TNN (re-named as Spike TV in 2003) and CMT (Country Music Television) joined the MTV Networks. The BET (Black Entertainment Television) channel was acquired by Viacom in 2001. In the early 2000s, Viacom launched many channels worldwide under MTV Networks and BET.

In 2005, Viacom Corporation split into Viacom Inc. and CBS Corporation. In 2006, Viacom Inc. was one of the world's leading media companies operating in the Cable and Satellite Television Networks (C&S) and film production divisions.

VIACOM INC. BRANDS*

Cable Networks & Digital Media

- MTV Networks (Comedy Central, CMT, LOGO, MTV, MTV 2, MTV U, MTV Networks Digital Suite, **MTV International,** MTV Networks online, Nickelodeon, Nick @ Nite, The N, Noggin, Spike, TV Land, VH-1)
- BET Networks presents the best in Black media and entertainment featuring traditional and digital platforms. Brands including BET, BET J, BET Gospel, BET Hip Hop, BET.com, BET Mobile, BET Event Productions, and BET International deliver relevant and insightful content to consumers of Black culture in more than 84 million households.

Entertainment (Film & Music Publishing)

- Paramount Pictures
- Paramount Home Entertainment
- DreamWorks SKG
- Famous Music

* The list is not exhaustive
Source: www.viacom.com

the early 2000s, MTVI entered the Australian market by setting up a joint venture between Austereo (a national commercial radio network in the country) and MTVN. Later on, it acquired Austereo to become MTV Australia.

9   Initially, some analysts were doubtful as to how far MTVN's global expansion would be successful, given the latent and overt anti-American sentiments in various parts of the world. However, the channel did not face too many difficulties. Commenting on this, Roedy said, "We've had very little resistance once we explain that we're not in the business of exporting American culture."[8] According to some analysts, Roedy was instrumental in taking MTVI across many countries worldwide. To gain an entry into difficult markets such as China, Israel, and Cuba, Roedy even met the political leaders of those countries to explain the network's initiatives to them.

10   Overall, despite the initial hiccups, the channel's global expansion strategy proved successful. Thus, by following a policy of having a global presence with a local outlook, by mid-2006, MTVI catered to an audience of more than 1 billion and expanded its presence in 179 countries across Europe, Asia, Latin America, and Australia.[9] It operated more than 130 channels in over 25 languages and it comprised MTV Networks Europe (MTVN Europe),

[8] Kerry Capell, Catherine Belton, Tom Lowry, Manjeet Kripalani, Brian Bremner, and Dexter Roberts, "MTV's World," *BusinessWeek,* February 18, 2002.
[9] www.viacom.com/cable.jhtml.

MTV Networks Asia-Pacific (MTVN Asia-Pacific), and MTV Networks Latin America (MTVN Latin America). In addition to this, it operated some broadband services and more than 130 websites.[10]

11   According to analysts, a noteworthy reason behind MTV's global success was that the channel adopted a decentralized structure and gave commercial and creative autonomy to the local staff. This policy of minimal interference in local operations led to innovation and rapid expansion. Commenting on this, Roedy said, "Something we decided early on was to not export just one product for the world but to generate a very different experience for our brands depending on the local cultures."[11]

12   MTV's impressive growth globally contributed significantly to the revenues of its holding company Viacom over the years and it also became Viacom's core network. As of end 2007, MTVI had more than 140 channels around the world catering to a potential 1.5 billion viewers globally.[12] In the US alone, it reached 87.6 million homes.[13] Its Emerging Markets group was the network's fastest growing business segment.[14] For the year ending 2008, Viacom's total revenues (including cable network and entertainment divisions) were US$14,625 million. Out of this, the revenue from Media Network channels (which includes MTVN) was US$8,756 million (Refer to Exhibit II for selected financials of Viacom).

EXHIBIT II   Selected Financials of Viacom (US$, millions)

	2008	2007	2006
Revenues	14,625	13,423	11,361
Operating Income	2,523	2,936	2,767
Net Earnings	1,251	1,838	1,592
From Media Networks			
Revenue	8,756	8,101	7,241
Operating Income	2,729	3,048	2,904

Source: Adapted from http://www.viacom.com/news/News_Docs/78157ACL.PDF

PREPARING FOR THE LAUNCH

13   With the growing popularity of MTV, there was a mushrooming of many similar channels across the world. Though the Arab media was late in adopting this concept, some European and US channels had started offering such programs in this region, analysts pointed out. In the mid-1990s, some Arab music channels too entered the fray. Some of these channels were influenced by MTV. By the mid-2000s, there were a number of Arab music channels (Refer to Exhibit III for a note on major music channel in Saudi Arabia). These channels relied heavily on Arab artists but also aired international numbers by entering into agreements with production houses and other TV networks. MTV was available in the region through a

[10] MTVI operated more than 130 websites of its international channels while MTVN, totally, operated more than 150 websites, which included online representations of channels broadcast in the US.

[11] Brad Nemer, "How MTV Channels Innovation," *BusinessWeek,* November 6, 2006.

[12] Tamara Walid, "Finally Got My MTV," www.arabianbusiness.com, November 22, 2007.

[13] "MTV to Launch Music TV Channels in Three Baltic States," www.eubusiness.com, March 6, 2006.

[14] "Arab Media Group and MTV Networks International to Launch Nickelodeon Arabia in 2008," www.media.ameinfo.com, October 20, 2007.

EXHIBIT III   Music and Entertainment Channels in Saudi Arabia

As of early-2008, there are 370 Arabic satellite TV networks broadcasting in the Middle East. This is an increase of 270 percent since 2004.* Among these, 56 belong to private companies, 54 are music channels, and 38 are state owned. Most of these are headquartered in United Arab Emirates (22 percent), Saudi Arabia (15 percent), and Egypt (11 percent).

In Saudi Arabia alone, there are more than 200 free-to-air satcasters and 50 music channels in the region. Some of the important music and entertainment channels are:†

Mazzika, which offers a variety of music and light entertainment programs.

Melody Hits, which is a music channel airing Arabic and international music videos.

MBC, headquartered in Dubai, which is a pan-Arab news and entertainment television channel. MBC 2 is a non-stop premium movie channel. MBC 3 is a childrens' channel and it broadcasts famous animated kids' shows, including exclusive translated titles and live action and animated feature films. It also airs family shows and family movies for younger audiences as well as the adult audience. MBC 4 broadcasts specifically American programs.

Nojoom, which is a music channel airing Arabic and international music videos.

Rotana TV network, which broadcasts Arabic music and films. It has six channels under its wings—Mousica, Rotana Clip, Rotana Tarab, Rotana Khalijiyya, Rotana Cinema, and Rotana Zaman. The channels are dedicated to Arabic pop music, Arabic classical music, interactive games, Gulf music, cinema, featuring the biggest and latest blockbuster releases, and old classical movies.

Saudi Arabian TV, which features live coverage of Ramadan, Hajj, and Eid prayers. It also shows popular movies and news programs.

Shada channel—a part of the Al Majd Group—which is a channel totally devoted to Islamic songs (Anasheed).

Wanasah TV channel, which broadcasts music videos and some variety programs. All its programs are in Arabic.

Panorama FM, which is a music radio channel in Arabic.

Radio Rotana FM, which broadcasts customized programs and the latest Arabic hits fifteen days ahead of any of its competitors due to an exclusive deal with Rotana Music.

Radio Fann FM, which broadcasts a mix of the latest Arabic, English, and International music hits, along with hourly news broadcasts and various customized programs.

Al-Ikhbariya channel, which broadcasts news and current affairs.

* "Arab Satellite TV channels Rapidly Expanding," www.xrdarabia.org, November 14, 2007.
† The list is not exhaustive
Source: Compiled from various sources.

special deal with Showtime Arabia[15] (Showtime). As part of the deal, Showtime aired Nickelodeon and MTV in English with Arabic subtitles.[16] The channel catered to the middle and upper classes, who had been exposed to the West and had an interest in Western entertainment. Analysts felt that MTV was popular with a section of the audience in the region who were waiting eagerly for its launch there.

14   The first announcement that MTVI was preparing to launch MTV Arabia came in August 2006. During MTV's 25th anniversary of its first US channel, the company said that it was on the lookout for local partners in the Middle East and would provide the audience in the region content that would be very different from that offered by popular Arab music

[15] Showtime Arabia is one of the leading subscription-based television networks in the Middle East. It is partly owned by Viacom.

[16] Zeid Nasser, "Showtime Braces for Impact of Free-to-air MTV Arabia & Arabic Nickelodeon," http://mediame.com, October 16, 2007.

channels. Dean Possenniskie, Vice President and General Manager for Emerging Markets, MTVI, said, "[MTV is] very interested in the [Arab satellite channel] market and realizes how important it is . . . Hopefully [we] will be in the market in the next 24 months . . . it all depends on finding the right local partners."[17] By the end of the year, it was announced that MTVI would launch the channel in the region in partnership with Arabian Television Network (ATN), which was a part of the Arabian Broadcasting Network (ABN).[18]

15   MTVI's venturing into the Middle East was a result of the combined efforts of innovative and enthusiastic personalities such as Roedy, Bhavneet Singh[19] (Singh), Senior Vice President and Managing Director of MTVNI Emerging Markets group, and Abdullatif Al Sayegh (Sayegh), CEO and Chairman of ABN.

16   Analysts felt that it would have been very difficult for a western company like MTVI to venture into the highly regulated and complex business arena of the Middle East on its own. In this regard, Singh said, "A market such as the Middle East, however, also brings a level of complexity in the way business is done and regulatory challenges which mean it takes a Western media company a long time to get its head around it."[20] Hence, it entered the Middle East by tying up with a local partner, the Arab Media Group (AMG), an established player in the Arab media industry with eight radio stations and three daily newspapers. The channel MTV Arabia was formed as a result of a licensing arrangement between MTV and AMG. MTV would earn an estimated US$10 million annually in licensing fees from AMG for 10 years.[21]

17   On the other hand, an alliance with MTV was a winning deal for AMG too as it could access the former's world-class resources to enhance its visibility in the Arab media as well as across the globe. "We found it very good to start our TV business with MTV Arabia because it's a great name to start with. Great team, great people; they provided us with a lot of resources. We believe that MTV is the beginning of a new era in television in this part of the world,"[22] said Sayegh.

18   However, the tie-up with a local partner was not enough to guarantee the success of MTV's launch in the Middle East given the conflict between the hip-hop explicit music culture portrayed by MTV and the conservative social culture prevalent in the Middle East. Hence, before launching the channel, Samaha conducted an extensive survey of the region to understand what people wanted. The survey team targeted people in the age group 18–24 and travelled around the region to schools and universities canvassing opinions. They also spoke to the elderly and figures of authority to assure them that they were there to entertain people within the limits of Arab traditions and had no intention of showing disrespect to the local culture. On this Samaha commented, "We also spoke to the governments, leaders, and parents and said, 'Don't worry, it will be nice,' so they know what's going on,"[23] said Samaha.

19   Accordingly, MTV Arabia's programming team decided to air MTVN's globally successful music shows but with a local flavor that would suit the Arab mindset and this laid

[17] Faisal Abbas, "MTV Eyes Middle East Market," www.asharq-e.com, August 8, 2006.

[18] "Arabian Television Network Partners with MTV to Launch MTV Arabiya," http://mediame.com, December 27, 2006.

[19] On April 23, 2007, Bhavneet Singh was promoted to Senior Vice President and Managing Director of MTVNI's Emerging Markets group.

[20] Andrew Edgecliffe-Johnson, "MTV Tunes in to a Local Audience," www.us.ft.com, October 26, 2007.

[21] Sarah Raper Larenaudie, "MTV's Arab Prizefight," www.time.com, November 2, 2007.

[22] Tamara Walid, "Finally Got My MTV," www.arabianbusiness.com, November 22, 2007.

[23] Matt Pomroy, "The Revolution Will be Televised," www.arabianbusiness.com, November 15, 2007.

the foundation for a planned launch of MTV in Arabia. The launch team comprised a mix of Saudis, Palestinians, Emiratis, Iraqis, and Lebanese.[24] "MTV first launched in 1981 when cable television was in its infancy. Since then we've grown into the world's largest TV network by becoming part of the fabric of youth culture, and by respecting audience diversity and different cultures. We're delighted to be launching MTV Arabiya and looking forward to working with our partners to provide the best youth programming,"[25] said Singh.

20   MTV commissioned ad agencies TBWA\Raad and Fortune Promoseven to handle the launch of the channel in the Middle East.[26] "We're targeting normal Arabs. We're not targeting educated, private school people. Those are Arab society's niche. They are not more than 10 percent of the population. We are trying to appeal to the masses,"[27] said Samer Al Marzouqi, channel manager, MTV Arabia.

MTV ENTERS THE MIDDLE EAST

21   MTV Arabia was considered by experts as the biggest launch in MTVI's history in terms of potential audience at launch.[28] An exclusive, star-studded preview event marked the launch of MTV in the Middle East. The launch featured performances by eminent stars such as Akon, Ludacris, and Karl Wolf along with local hip hop group Desert Heat. The channel was formally launched on November 17, 2007, as a 24-hour, free-to-air television channel, having a target audience in Saudi Arabia, Egypt, United Arab Emirates, Lebanon, Bahrain, Jordan, Kuwait, Oman, Qatar, Yemen, Palestine, and Syria. MTVa.com, an Arabic and English language website, complemented the channel and provided users with a wide range of online community and interactive elements.

22   In line with its mixed-content strategy, MTV Arabia was to showcase 60 percent international music and 40 percent Arabic music, along with the local version of the channel's popular international non-music shows. About 45 percent of MTV Arabia's content was to be produced locally, with the rest translated. In this regard, Roedy commented, "The key is that the packaging, attitude, and obviously the language, should reflect the country. There is already great music there."[29] The channel's programming was to have a mix of music videos, music-based programming, general lifestyle and animated programs, reality shows, comedy and dramatic series, news specials, interviews, and documentaries. Besides international MTV shows, MTV Arabia was also to design new shows in Arabic to cater to pan-Arab youth audiences.

23   The company also said that the channel could act as a cultural unifying force in a region known for its political tensions. "The launch of MTV's 60th channel is a chance to correct misconceptions of the region . . . This part of the world has been associated with stresses and tensions . . . the one thing music can do is act as a unifying cultural force across regions,"[30] Roedy said.

[24] Sarah Raper Larenaudie, "MTV's Arab Prizefight," www.time.com, November 2, 2007.

[25] "Arabian Television Network Partners with MTV to Launch MTV Arabia," www.mediame.com, December 27, 2006.

[26] Iain Akerman, "MTV Hires Two Agencies for Launch of MTV Arabiya," www.brandrepublic.com, May 23, 2007.

[27] Dana El Baltaji, "I Want My MTV," www.arabmediasociety.com, May 2008.

[28] Irene Lew, "MTVNI Ups Singh," www.worldscreen.com, April 30, 2008.

[29] Lynne Roberts, "MTV Set for Middle East Launch," www.arabianbusiness.com, October 17, 2007.

[30] Simeon Kerr and Peter Aspden, "MTV Arabia Beams 'Bling' to Gulf," www.ft.com, November 17, 2007.

RATIONALE BEHIND THE VENTURE

24 Favorable demographics had been one of the key rationales behind MTV's commercial launch in the Middle East. About 65 percent of the Arab population consisted of youth under the age of 25 and the launch of MTV Arabia would provide MTV an opportunity to cater to a 190 million audience.[31] Further, though the Arab market was crowded with more than 50 channels, none of them provided a global platform to export the musical talent of the local youth. In this regard, Sayegh said, "Through our network, we now have more platforms to talk to our youth and in ways that have never been done before in the Middle East." Since young people "represent 65% of the population in the Middle East, it's time they were heard . . . Understanding the next generation is a key priority."[32] MTV being an international brand, had global reach and this became its key selling proposition for gaining critical mass in the Arab music world. Singh commented, "The fact that there has been no real youth platform, no real brand out there for the kids, makes us [feel] there is an opportunity for us."[33]

25 Moreover, the Middle East had the potential to offer MTV not only lucrative ad revenues but also numerous media like mobiles and the Internet to reach its end consumers. Singh said, "There are 37 million mobile subscribers in the wider Middle East, which is phenomenal and the average revenue per user is comparable to Western Europe. We believe that's where the future is—the ability to watch content wherever and however you want. We want to provide Middle East youth with the opportunity to watch MTV on mobile, on broadband, and on television. We're in discussions with mobile operators in the UAE, Kuwait, and Egypt, to look at how to distribute MTV content. There's been a huge amount of interest in that."[34] Products such as MTV Overdrive in which the user could download the video at broadband speed, and MTV Flux in which the online users could create their own TV channel were expected to help in luring the various Internet service providers in the region to MTV and to become major sources of its revenue.

26 The existence of various communication media with mass reach was expected to act as a catalyst in augmenting the channel's penetration rate in the Arabic region. In times to come if the channel validated its success in the Middle East, it would become a major revenue contributor to the MTV group.

KEY CHALLENGES AND SUCCESS STRATEGY

27 MTV was known for airing sexually explicit and provocative programmes. In other words, it carried with it an image of open Western culture. This explicit Western culture projected by MTV went contrary to the socially conservative culture of the Middle East and could be a key bottleneck to the channel's acceptance in the Arab region, according to analysts. "As a brand, one would think that MTV is the ultimate example of what the religious, conservative cultures of the Middle East would most revile about Western pop culture,"[35] according to leading brand portal brandchannel.com. Adapting content to suit local tastes too could prove challenging because of many different countries comprising the region. What was acceptable in Dubai may not be acceptable in other parts of Saudi Arabia; what

[31] "MTV Arabia to launch November 17," www.mediame.com, October 28, 2007.

[32] Ali Jaafar, "MTV Arabia Announces Lineup," www.variety.com, October 28, 2007.

[33] Von Andrew Edgecliffe Johnson, "MTV Tunes in to a Local Audience," www.ftd.de, October 26, 2007.

[34] "MTV Arabia to be Launched Soon," www.oceancreep.com, October 8, 2007.

[35] "Will the MTV Brand Change the Middle East?" www.brandchannel.com, December 3, 2007.

was acceptable in Egypt may not be acceptable in Jeddah (in Saudi Arabia). Analysts felt that the company also had to maintain what it stood for and too much localization could dilute its brand. And to complicate matters, there were strong anti-American sentiments prevalent among a large section of the population. Issues such as the US invasion of Iraq and its support to arch enemy Isreal had left many Arabs angry.

28   However the channel seemed well prepared to overcome such impediments to its growth plans in the Arab market. Though MTV Arabia would air its popular international programs, the network said that music videos and reality shows like "HIP Hop Na" and "Pimp My Ride" would be appropriately edited to ensure their alignment with the cultural ethos prevailing in the Middle East. Commenting on this, Sayegh said, "when we come to people's homes, we want to earn their respect."[36] He explained that there would be "culturally sensitive editors going through content of the programming."[37] In short, the channel expected to respect the local culture without diluting its brand. The channel aimed to prove that despite being a global brand, it would be a channel for the Arabs and made by Arabs—by people just like them.

29   Analysts said that MTVN's entry into the Middle East, which already had more than 50 local music channels operating, would be marked by stiff competition. In other words, unlike its past forays into India and Europe, MTV would not be entering a virgin music industry when it came to the Middle East. If on the one hand, the existence of a youth population was a business opportunity for MTVN, the same favorable demographic factor had also led to the explosion of dozens of local music channels which had a better understanding of the local audience's taste and could pose a formidable threat to MTVN's growth in the Middle East.

30   Also channels such as Rotana and Melody, which had already created a niche for themselves in the region, could pose a big competitive threat to MTVN. These channels had been functioning taking into account the tastes of the youth and had been able to attract a huge chunk of their target segment by offering creative concepts like games that allowed viewers to be part of the action from home along with interesting programs, music videos, and various artist albums and concerts. Moreover, some popular Arab music stars had already signed exclusive deals with some local channels. The challenge for MTV would be to not only find the right content but also ways to connect and captivate the Arabian youth, who were habituated to log on to any number of sites and enjoy music channels and videos according to their whims and fancies.

31   However, MTV Arabia was confident of scoring over its competitors and posting an impressive growth in the years to come. To overcome competition, the channel planned to project itself as unique and different from the existing lot. It proposed to establish itself as a platform wherefrom the Arab youth could voice their local concerns as well as advertise their music talent. For instance, MTV Arabia's flagship show "HIP Hop Na" would audition the best local hip-hop acts in seven different Middle Eastern cities. Thereafter, the winner from each city would get a chance to record a track for a compilation CD produced by Fred Wrecks.[38]

32   In a nutshell, MTV Arabia would not only provide entertainment but would also leverage on its global reach to advertise the musical talent of Arab youths. In this connection,

[36] "MTV Aims to Win over Middle East," www.cnn.com, November 19, 2007.

[37] Ibid.

[38] Fred Wrecks is a Palestinian-born hip-hop producer who has worked under some of the eminent record label such as Dogghouse Records, Virgin Records, etc. He has also worked with many distinguished rap stars like 50 Cent and Snoop Dogg.

Samaha said, "We are not only a music channel, we are an entertainment channel where young Arabs will get a voice."[39] He added, "MTV Arabia is a fresh take on MTV the brand, made by Arabs for Arab youth, and is dedicated to their self-expression. We've done extensive research to listen to our audiences, and MTV Arabia will be the first free-to-air channel to celebrate young people and their lives and talents from across this dynamic, vibrant region. We'll also offer audiences a window to the world of global youth culture, bringing top international entertainment to the region and showcasing the Arab region in the context of what's happening around the world. Through MTV's global network, we'll also be able to export Arabic music and culture to the international stage."[40]

33 Also, the programming line-up would feature more local content (Refer to Exhibit IV for a note on local production program to be aired on MTV Arabia) in comparison to other localized MTV ventures. There would be a localized version of popular shows such as "MADE" (al Helm) and "Boiling Point" (Akher Takka), which would constitute 40 percent of the content to be aired on MTV Arabia (Refer to Exhibit V for a list of some shows subsequently aired on MTV Arabia).

34 The company also said it did not expect anti-American sentiments to affect its chances in the region. MTV said that it expected to win over the target segment with content relevant to them. Moreover, it said that its research before the launch had shown that the majority of respondents thought that MTV was a European or Indian brand.[41]

EXHIBIT IV Local Productions to be Aired on MTV Arabia

The flagship local show:

Hip Hop Na, a twelve-episode series which follows auditions to uncover the best local hip hop acts in four different Middle Eastern cities

Music Related Show:

Waslati, viewers with webcams become VJs and introduce three of their favorite videos.

Baqbeeq is a music trivia show with a twist, where interesting and hilarious bits of trivia pop up through the most popular videos in the world.

Introducing Block goes behind the scenes in the music industry, with exclusive interviews and performances by the biggest international and Arab stars.

Other Programs:

Al Helm, based on MTV's *MADE* format, follows the journey of aspiring teenagers looking to fulfill their dreams with the help of an MTV Arabia-supplied 'coach.'

Al Hara tours the Middle East's street scene, and features previously unknown artists displaying innovative talent in skills like beat-boxing, break-dancing, or magic acts. The show is based on MTV's international program format, *Barrio 19.*

In *Akher Takka,* based on MTV's hit format, *Boiling Point,* actors antagonize stressed-out "victims" who can win a cash prize if they manage to keep their cool in extremely annoying situations.

Source: Compiled from various sources.

[39] "MTV Looks to Conquer Middle East Market," www.aol.in, November 18, 2007.

[40] "MTV Arabia to Launch November 17," www.middleeastevents.com, October 27, 2007.

[41] Adam Sherwin, "MTV Arabia to Feature Regional Talent and Tone Down Network's Risque Content," www.business.timesonline.co.uk, November 16, 2007.

EXHIBIT V   Some Shows Aired on MTV Arabia

MTV Arabia Shows	Other MTV shows aired in MTV Arabia
• Hip Hop Na	• Celebrity Deathmatch
• Introducing	• Made
• Baqabeeq	• Pimp My Ride
• Banat	• My Own
• Rewes	• Life of Ryan
• Waslity	• Why Can't I Be You
• Amour	• True Life
• Cimena	• Two-A-Days
• MTV Weyakom	• Cribs
• Na3na3	• Teen Cribs
	• Punk'd
	• The Ashlee Simpson Show
	• Making the Band
	• Taquita & Kaui
	• The Trip
	• The Shop
	• Wrestling Society X
	• Adventures in Hollyhood
	• Diary
	• Total Request Live
	• Rob & Big
	• Room 401
	• Hogan Knows Best
	• Miss Seventeen
	• My Super Sweet 16
	• Headbangers Ball
	• The Hills
	• Boiling Points

* Data as of 2009.
* The list is not exhaustive
Source: http://mtv_arabia.totally explained.com and other sources.

THE ROAD AHEAD

35   MTVN catered to a huge market segment of nearly 2 billion people worldwide and was expected to provide a global platform for Arabic music and culture. It had influenced young people all over the world and given them a voice and it would try to do the same in the Middle East. An Arabic category was already added in MTV Europe Music Awards 2007, giving Arabic music the much needed global platform.

36   The MTV-AMG combine would not only provide entertainment to the region but would also take up social issues and try to contribute to Arab society, according to the network. In this regard, Sayegh commented, "We are going to encourage education and look for solutions to problems such as unemployment. These are all causes on our agenda."[42]

[42] Simeon Kerr and Peter Aspden, "MTV Arabia Beams 'Bling' to Gulf," www.ft.com, November 17, 2007.

37   MTVN along with AMG, planned to expand its operations in the Middle East. It had already announced the launch of Nickelodeon Arabia in 2008. It would be the first free-to-air channel for children in Arabic. Roedy commented, "Adding the voices of Arab children to our worldwide Nickelodeon family is a significant milestone in our history, and advances our ambitious strategy to build a portfolio of integrated kids businesses across the region. The Middle East is a dynamic, thriving market with vast growth opportunities, and we look forward to launching even more MTVNI brands and businesses through our successful partnership with AMG."[43] Singh added, "The launch of Nickelodeon Arabia is a part of our wider, ongoing multi-platform strategy encompassing consumer products, digital media, hotels and theme parks, which we hope will establish Nickelodeon as the premier destination for kids in the region."[44]

38   Thus far, MTVN's model of entering a market in partnership with a local partner and following a localization strategy had worked well for the company. Analysts felt that only time would tell whether the company would succeed in the Middle East. But Singh had a rather philosophical take on what success meant. To him, the venture would be a success when people in the smallest cities of the Middle East came up to him and professed their love for MTV. "After all, it's not about how many eyeballs you reach, it's about how many people relate to you," he said.[45]

REFERENCES & SUGGESTED READINGS

1. Dirk Smillie, "Tuning in First Global TV Generation," *The Christian Science Monitor,* June 4, 1997.
2. Kerry Capell, Catherine Belton, Tom Lowry, Manjeet Kripalani, Brian Bremner, and Dexter Roberts, "MTV's World," *BusinessWeek,* February 18, 2002.
3. "MTV to Launch Music TV Channels in Three Baltic States," www.eubusiness.com, March 6, 2006.
4. Faisal Abbas, "Q&A with Showtime Arabia's CEO Peter Einstein," www.asharq-e.com, June 29, 2006.
5. Faisal Abbas, "MTV Eyes Middle East Market," www.asharq-e.com, August 8, 2006.
6. Brad Nemer, "How MTV Channels Innovation," *BusinessWeek,* November 6, 2006.
7. "Arabian Television Network Partners with MTV to Launch MTV Arabiya," www.mediame.com, December 27, 2006.
8. Michael Learmonth, "MTV Maps Mideast Move," www.variety.com, December 27, 2006.
9. Iain Akerman, "MTV Hires Two Agencies for Launch of MTV Arabiya," www.brandrepublic.com, May 23, 2007.
10. Salman Dossari, "A Talk With MTV Vice Chairman Bill Roedy," www.asharq-e.com, July 23, 2007.
11. Ali Jaafar, "MTV Arabia Ready to Rock Middle East," www.variety.com, September 25, 2007.

[43] "Arab Media Group and MTV Networks International to Launch Nickelodeon Arabia in 2008," www.ameinfo.com, October 20, 2007.

[44] Stuart Kemp, "MTV, Arab Media to Launch Nickelodeon Arabia," www.hollywoodreporter.com, October 17, 2007.

[45] Tamara Walid, "Finally Got My MTV," www.arabianbusiness.com, November 22, 2007.

12. "MTV Arabia to be Launched Soon," www.oceancreep.com, October 8, 2007.

13. Kerry Capell, "The Arab World Wants Its MTV," www.businessweek.com, October 11, 2007.

14. Lynne Roberts, "MTV Set for Middle East launch," www.arabianbusiness.com, October 17, 2007.

15. Stuart Kemp, "MTV, Arab Media to Launch Nickelodeon Arabia," www.hollywood-reporter.com, October 17, 2007.

16. Andrew Edgecliffe Johnson, "MTV Targets Muslim Countries as it Tunes in to Local Audiences," www.theaustralian.news.com, October 18, 2007.

17. "Arab Media Group and MTV Networks International to Launch Nickelodeon Arabia in 2008," www.ameinfo.com, October 20, 2007.

18. Von Andrew Edgecliffe Johnson, "MTV Tunes in to a Local Audience," www.ftd.de, October 26, 2007.

19. "MTV Arabia to Launch November 17," www.middleeastevents.com, October 27, 2007.

20. Ali Jaafar, "MTV Arabia Announces Lineup," www.variety.com, October 28, 2007.

21. "MTV Arabia to Launch November 17," www.mediame.com, October 28, 2007.

22. Irene Lew, "MTV Arabia to Launch in November," www.worldscreen.com, October 29, 2007.

23. Sarah Raper Larenaudie, "MTV's Arab Prizefight," www.time.com, November 2, 2007.

24. Jolanta Chudy, "MTV's Arab Net Thinking Locally," www.hollywoodreporter.com, November 6, 2007.

25. Matt Pomroy, "The Revolution Will Be Televised," www.arabianbusiness.com, November 15, 2007.

26. "Akon and Ludacris Dazzle the Desert in Their Middle East Debuts to Celebrate the Launch of MTV Arabia," www.dubaicityguide.com, November 16, 2007.

27. Adam Sherwin, "MTV Arabia to Feature Regional Talent and Tone Down Network's Risque Content," www.timesonline.co.uk, November 16, 2007.

28. Simeon Kerr and Peter Aspden, "MTV Arabia Beams 'Bling' to Gulf," www.ft.com, November 17, 2007.

29. "MTV Launches New Arabic Service," www.news.bbc.co.uk, November 18, 2007.

30. "MTV Looks to Conquer Middle East Market," www.aol.in, November 18, 2007.

31. "'MTV Arabia,': Will It Work?" www.scopical.com, November 19, 2007.

32. "MTV Aims to Win over Middle East," www.cnn.com, November 19, 2007.

33. "Muslim Hip-hop Turban Wrote, That's Good," www.reuters.donga.com, November 19, 2007.

34. Barbara Surk, "MTV for Young Arab Is Less Naughty," www.cincinnati.com, November 21, 2007.

35. Barbara Surk, "MTV Launches Arab Music Video Channel," www.theeagle.com, November 22, 2007.

36. Tamara Walid, "Finally Got My MTV," www.arabianbusiness.com, November 22, 2007.

37. "Will the MTV Brand Change the Middle East?" www.brandchannel.com, December 2, 2007.

38. Irene Lew, "MTVNI Ups Singh," www.worldscreen.com, April 30, 2008.

39. Dana El Baltaji, "I Want My MTV," www.arabmediasociety.com, May 11, 2008.

40. www.topfive.com

41. www.en.wikipedia.org

42. www.mtva.com

43. www.viacom.com

Case 14

The Oil and Gas Industry
Andrew Inkpen

Keeping America competitive requires affordable energy. And here we have a serious problem: America is addicted to oil, which is often imported from unstable parts of the world. The best way to break this addiction is through technology.

President George W. Bush
State of the Union Address
January 31, 2006

I propose that California be the first in the world to develop a low-carbon fuel standard that leads us away from fossil fuels. And let us use the freedom and the flexibility of the market to accomplish it. Let us blaze the way, for the U.S. and for China and for the rest of the world. . . . Our country has been dependent on foreign oil for too long. So, I ask you to set to motion the means to free ourselves from oil and from OPEC.

Governor Arnold Schwarzenegger
California State of the State Address
January 9, 2007

In the past two years, he [Chávez] has raised foreign oil companies' corporate income tax to 50 percent from 30 percent, and increased royalties payable to the government from as low as 1 percent to 33 percent. . . . For Chávez, it's a matter of national pride—and political bragging points. Around the country, the government has put up posters and billboards showing Chávez extending his arms in a victory salute, accompanied by the slogan, "Full oil sovereignty: Joint ventures—more benefits for the people!"[1]

Nowadays, "Big Oil" reigns supreme in only a relatively small niche: the most technologically challenging and expensive project. Unfortunately, these investments bring higher risks and lower rewards. Such trends should be worrying all oil bosses.[2]

1   The year 2007 marked another tumultuous year in the oil and gas industry, that included continued efforts from oil-producing countries like Kazakhstan, Russia, and Venezuela to exert greater control over their resources (i.e., economic nationalism), major technological advances in offshore drilling, Chinese firms acquiring exploration rights at record high prices, ongoing strife in Sudan, Nigeria, Chad, and other major oil exporting nations, continued heated discussion about global warming and nonhydrocarbon sources of energy, and near $100 per barrel crude prices. All of this came amid predictions that the global demand for energy would increase by 40 percent by 2030, which many experts believed was not sustainable.

[1] Robert Collier, "Chávez Drives a Hard Bargain, But Big Oil's Options are Limited," *San Francisco Chronicle*, 2006, September 24, www.sfgate.com.

[2] "Big Oil: Browne Out," *The Economist*, 2007, January 20, p. 17.

BACKGROUND

2 When Colonel Edwin Drake struck oil in northwestern Pennsylvania in 1859, the first phase of the oil industry began. John D. Rockefeller emerged in those early days as a pioneer in industrial organization. When Rockefeller combined Standard Oil and 39 affiliated companies to create Standard Oil Trust in 1882, his goal was not to form a monopoly, because these companies already controlled 90 percent of the kerosene market. His real goal was economies of scale, which was achieved by combining all the refining operations under a single management structure. In doing so, Rockefeller set the stage for what historian Alfred Chandler calls the "dynamic logic of growth and competition that drives modern capitalism."[3]

3 With the Spindletop discovery of oil in East Texas in 1901, a new phase of the industry began. Before Spindletop, oil was used mainly for lamps and lubrication. After Spindletop, petroleum would be used as a major fuel for new inventions, such as the airplane and automobile. Ships and trains that had previously run on coal began to switch to oil. For the next century, oil, and then natural gas, would be the world's most important sources of energy.

4 Since the beginning of the oil industry, there have been fears from petroleum producers and consumers that eventually the oil would run out. In 1950, the U.S. Geological Survey estimated that the world's conventional recoverable resource base was about one trillion barrels. Fifty years later, that estimate had tripled to three trillion barrels. In recent years, the concept of peak oil has been much debated. The peak oil theory is based on the fact that the amount of oil is finite.

5 After peak oil, according to the Hubbert Peak Theory, the rate of oil production on earth will enter a terminal decline. In the U.S., oil production peaked in 1971, and some analysts have argued that on a global basis the peak has also occurred. Others argue that peak oil is a myth. An article in *Science* argued:

> Although hydrocarbon resources are irrefutably finite, no one knows just how finite. Oil is trapped in porous subsurface rocks, which makes it difficult to estimate how much oil there is and how much can be effectively extracted. Some areas are still relatively unexplored or have been poorly analyzed. Moreover, knowledge of in-ground oil resources increases dramatically as an oil reservoir is exploited. To "cry wolf" over the availability of oil has the sole effect of perpetuating a misguided obsession with oil security and control that is already rooted in Western public opinion—an obsession that historically has invariably led to bad political decisions.[4]

6 Regardless of whether the peak has or has not been reached, oil and natural gas are an indispensable source of the world's energy and petrochemical feedstocks, and will be for many years to come. The difficulty in determining oil and gas reserves is that technology is always changing and prices are not stable. As prices rise, reserves once considered noneconomic to develop may become feasible. Crude oil prices ranged between $2.50 and $3.00 from 1948 through the end of the 1960s. The Arab oil embargo of 1974 resulted in a large price increase. Events in Iran and Iraq led to another round of crude oil price increases in 1979 and 1980. The 1990s saw another spike in prices that ended with the 1997 Asian financial crisis. Prices then started back up, only to fall after September 11, 2001. Since 9/11, prices have generally been on the upswing[5] (see Exhibit 1).

---

[3] Alfred D. Chandler, "The Enduring Logic of Industrial Success," *Harvard Business Review*, 1990, March–April, 68 Issue 2, pp. 130–140.

[4] Leonardo Maugeri, "Oil: Never Cry Wolf—Why the Petroleum Age Is Far from Over," *Science*, 2004, 304, pp. 1114–1115.

[5] WTRG Economics, www.wtrg.com/prices.htm.

EXHIBIT 1
Crude Oil Prices

Source: WTRG Economics,
www.wtrg.com.

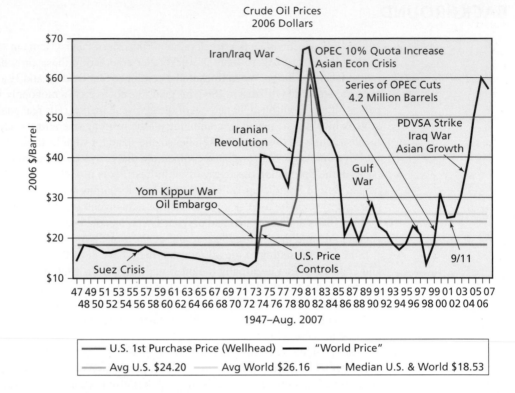

Crude Oil Prices
2006 Dollars

1947–Aug. 2007

——— U.S. 1st Purchase Price (Wellhead) ——— "World Price"

——— Avg U.S. $24.20 ——— Avg World $26.16 ——— Median U.S. & World $18.53

7 The oil sands of Alberta, Canada, are a good illustration of how difficult it is to accurately measure oil and gas reserves. Oil sands are deposits of bitumen, a molasses-like viscous oil that will not flow unless heated or diluted with lighter hydrocarbons. Although the oil sands in Alberta are now considered second only to the Saudi Arabia reserves in the potential amount of recoverable oil, for many years these were not viewed as real reserves because they were non-economical to develop. In 2008, the main town in the oil sands region, Athabasca, was in the midst of a boom not unlike the gold rush booms of the 1800s. Housing and labor were scarce and the infrastructure was struggling to keep pace with the influx of people, companies, and capital. The development of the oil sands occurred because of a combination of rising oil prices and technological innovation. It was estimated that oil sands production could reach three million barrels per day (b/d) by 2020, and possibly even five million b/d by 2030.

Oil and Gas and the Global Economy

8 Oil and gas played a vital role in the global economy. ExxonMobil's analysis predicted that energy demand would rise by an average of 1.6 percent each year through 2030, reaching close to 325 million barrels per day of oil-equivalent (MBDOE). Demand in 2030 will be 60 percent higher than in 2000. Demand in the non-OECD nations will account for approximately 80 percent of the global increase. Most of the world's growing energy needs through 2030 will continue to be met by oil, gas, and coal. With increased energy efficiency, energy as a percentage of total GDP has fallen and is expected to continue to fall. If the world were to remain at 2005 energy intensity levels, global demand by 2030 could be 40 percent higher than predicted demand.[6]

[6] http://www.exxonmobil.com/Corporate/Citizenship/Imports/EnergyOutlook06/index.html.

EXHIBIT 2
Top Oil Producers:
Percentage Change
in Production
1996–2006

Source: BP Statistical Review
of World Energy 2007

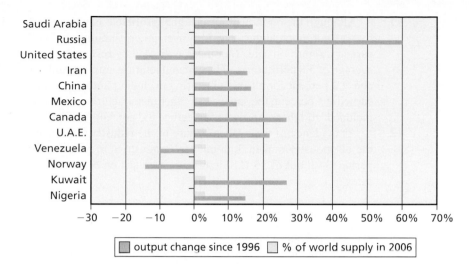

EXHIBIT 3
Top Natural
Gas Producers:
Percentage Change
in Production
1996–2006

Source: BP Statistical Review
of World Energy 2007

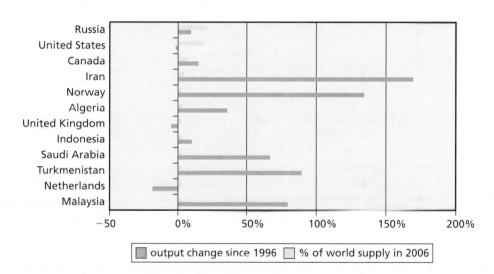

Oil and Gas Supply

9 Exhibits 2 and 3 show the major oil- and gas-producing nations.

Industry Financial Performance

10 The oil and gas industry has been widely criticized by politicians and the media for its high profits of recent years. In the U.S., there has been talk of an excess profits tax, prompting Lee Raymond, former ExxonMobil CEO, to comment in 2005: "I can't remember any of these people seven years ago, when the price was $10 a barrel, coming forward and saying, are you guys going to have enough money to be able to continue to invest in this business? I don't recall my phone ringing and anybody asking me that question."[7]

---

[7] Fox News, Transcript: Exxonmobil's Lee Raymond, Monday, 2005, October 17, http://www.foxnews.com.

11 Although the oil industry was highly profitable in some years, its long-term profitability was not much higher than U.S. average profitability. In 2007, the oil and gas industry earned a return on sales (net income divided by revenue) of 7.6 percent, compared to an average of 5.8 percent for all U.S. manufacturing, mining, and wholesale trade corporations and 9.2 percent for all manufacturing excluding autos. In 2006, the oil and gas industry earned 9.5 percent, the same as all other manufacturing excluding autos. When autos were included, all other manufacturing earned 8.2 percent in 2006.[8]

12 As evidence of the cyclical nature of the industry, a decade ago *Fortune* reported that the oil industry ranked 30th out of 36 industries in return to investors over the 1985–95 period, 34th out of 36 U.S. industries in return on equity in 1995, and 32nd in return on sales.[9]

The Role of OPEC

13 The oil and gas industry has seen a remarkable bevy of government regulations and interventions over the past century, from heavy taxation of gasoline in Europe to U.S. price controls on domestic production. The creation of the Organization of the Petroleum Exporting Countries (OPEC) represents government intervention on a global scale. OPEC was founded in 1960 with the objective of shifting bargaining power to the producing countries and away from the large oil companies. In 2006, Angola became the 12th member of OPEC, and there was speculation that Sudan might be next. OPEC's mission is "to coordinate and unify the petroleum policies of Member Countries and ensure the stabilization of oil prices in order to secure an efficient, economic, and regular supply of petroleum to consumers; a steady income to producers; and a fair return on capital to those investing in the petroleum industry."[10] Despite being a cartel, OPEC's ability to control prices was questionable. Surging oil prices in the 1980s resulted in energy conservation and increased exploration outside OPEC. Maintaining discipline among OPEC members has been a major problem (as is typical in cartels). Massive cheating was blamed for the oil price crash of 1986, and in the 1990s Venezuela was considered one of the bigger OPEC cheats in regularly producing more than its quota.

14 Exhibit 4 shows the relationship between OPEC production and crude oil prices.

The Resource Curse

15 One of the anomalies of the oil and gas industry, termed the resource curse, is that despite high resource prices, the economies of many of the large oil-producing countries struggle. This condition has led to the inability of countries rich in natural resources to use that wealth to strengthen their economies and, counter-intuitively, to have lower economic growth than countries without an abundance of natural resources.[11] When times are good and oil prices are high, oil-rich countries may prosper. When oil prices fall, as they inevitably do, an overreliance on the oil sector can leave a country in a perilous situation. Moreover, the oil industries of the petroleum-nationalistic countries often suffer from a lack of investment and heavily subsidized domestic petroleum products. For example, although Iran

---

[8] API, "Putting Earnings Into Perspective," http://www.api.org/statistics/earnings/upload/010908_EarningsPaper.pdf.

[9] The *Fortune* 500 Medians. *Fortune*, 1996, April 29, pp. 23–25.

[10] www.opec.org.

[11] Richard Auty, *Sustaining Development in Mineral Economies: The Resource Curse Thesis*. 1993, London: Routledge.

EXHIBIT 4
Crude Oil Production and Price

Source: WTRG Economics, www.wtrg.com

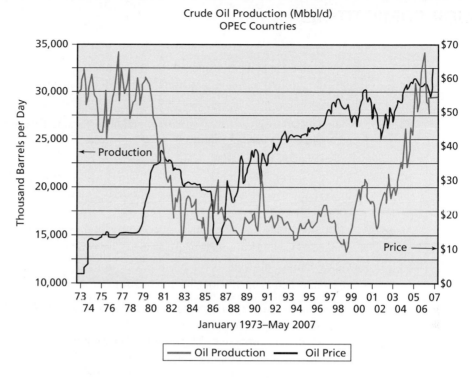

Crude Oil Production (Mbbl/d)
OPEC Countries

January 1973–May 2007

—— Oil Production —— Oil Price

was second to Saudi Arabia in the size of its reserves, the country's oil industry was in a shambles. Iran's 2007 production was only about two-thirds of the level reached under the government of the former Shah of Iran in 1979. In mid-2007, Iran was importing about 40 percent of its gasoline and was unable to produce sufficient crude to meet its OPEC quota. In June 2007, Iran introduced gasoline rationing, which reduced imports and resulted in widespread black marketeering. Some experts predicted that without huge foreign direct investment in the industry, Iran's oil production would decline precipitously over the next few decades. According to one analyst:

> Iran burns its candle at both ends, producing less and less [oil] while consuming more and more. Absent some change in Iranian policy, a rapid decline in exports seems likely. Policy gridlock and a Soviet-style command economy make practical problem-solving almost impossible.[12]

16   Mexico also had declining production and significant imports of refined products. The Mexican constitution does not allow foreign direct investment in the oil and gas industry. After many years of underinvestment and of Mexican governments using the oil industry as their primary source of revenue, the industry was in dire straits. Without major investment and new technology, Mexico's oil production was poised to fall. For example, production at the Cantarell oil field, one of the largest fields in the world, fell from more than 2 million b/d in 2004 to 1.46 million b/d in 2007.[13]

[12] Roger Stern, "Iran Actually is Short of Oil: Muddled Mullahs," *International Herald Tribune*, 2007, January 8, www.iht.com.

[13] Marla Dickerson, "Woes Mount for Mexico's State Oil Titan," *Los Angeles Times*, 2008, January 2, www.latimes.com.

MAJOR COMPETITORS

IOCs

17   The term integrated oil companies (IOCs) refers to companies that are vertically integrated from exploration to refining, marketing, and retail. For many years, the largest IOCs (also known as oil majors) were the "Seven Sisters" and included:

- Standard Oil of New Jersey (Esso), which later became Exxon and then merged with Mobil to create ExxonMobil.
- Royal Dutch Shell
- Anglo-Persian Oil Company, which became British Petroleum, then BP Amoco following a merger with Amoco (which was formerly Standard Oil of Indiana). The company is now known as BP.
- Standard Oil of New York (Socony) became Mobil, which merged with Exxon
- Standard Oil of California (Socal) became Chevron
- Gulf Oil, most of which became part of Chevron
- Texaco, which merged with Chevron in 2001

18   By 2008, the list of the major IOCs looked very different (Exhibit 5) and was evidence of two factors: mergers and acquisitions, and the extent to which the industry had globalized in production and ownership. Based on market capitalization, the top 10 publicly traded (and in some cases government controlled) companies now included Petrochina (China), Gazprom (Russia), Sinopec (China), Petrobras (Brazil), Total (France), and Eni (Italy). Just beyond the top 10 were Rosneft (Russia), StatoilHydro (Norway), and Lukoil (Russia). ONGC of India, primarily an upstream company, had made public its commitment to participate in the entire hydrocarbon value chain (i.e., become vertically integrated). According to the former chairman of ONGC:

> We have to be an integrated oil company. Every major global oil company is an integrated player. I'm not being arrogant, but oil and gas is big business where the big boys play. You can survive in this business only if you are integrated; otherwise, you will be out.[14]

19   Given the long product lifecycles and the huge capital investment required in the oil industry, the large IOCs were regularly described as stodgy and conservative. Before bankruptcy, Enron executives regularly derided the oil majors as dinosaurs that were too slow moving and that would eventually become extinct. The reality, of course, is very different. Oil majors like BP, Shell, ExxonMobil, and their predecessor companies have been around for more than a century. Through experience that is occasionally painful, the IOCs have learned how to deal with the enormous financial and political risks of the oil and gas industry. The IOCs take a long-term view and recognize that cycles and uncertainty are an inherent part of the industry. As Lee Raymond, former ExxonMobil CEO said, "We're in a commodity [business]. We go through peaks and valleys, but our business is to level out the peaks and valleys, so that, over the cycle, our shareholders see an adequate return on their investment."[15]

---

[14] "We Have to Be An Integrated Oil Company," *Hindu Business Line*, 2003, August 10, www.thehindubusinessline.com.

[15] Fox News, Transcript.

EXHIBIT 5 Top 15 Integrated Oil and Gas Companies with Publicly Trade Shares Based on 2007 Year-End Market Capitalization*

Rank	Company	Market Cap (billions USD)
1	Petrochina	723.2
2	ExxonMobil	511.9
3	Gazprom**	332.0
4	Royal Dutch Shell	264.6
5	Sinopec	249.5
6	Petrobras	241.7
7	BP	230.7
8	Total	198.5
9	Chevron	197.1
10	Eni	146.3
11	ConocoPhillips	141.2
12	Rosneft	101.4
13	StatoilHydro	99.6
14	BG	76.6
15	Lukoil	74.0

*Eni, Gazprom, Petrochina, Petrobras, Sinopec, Rosneft, and Statoil have both publicly traded shares and government-owned shares. The government ownership ranges from 90% for Petrochina to 32% for Petrobras.

**Gazprom is an integrated natural gas company. The other companies on the list are involved in oil and/or natural gas.

Source: PFC Energy

20   On the surface, the IOCs looked similar in terms of the activities they performed. All appeared to be vertically integrated from exploration to retail distribution. However, there were fundamental organizational and financial differences among the firms. The IOCs used various organizational designs to deal with vertical integration. ExxonMobil, for example, was organized around global businesses and global functions, with common global operating processes, global enterprise back-office systems, such as SAP, and integrated operating structures at major sites. BP announced in 2007 that it would adopt a global structure organized around different businesses. The other IOCs tended to use more regional processes and regional management structures.

21   On the performance side, ExxonMobil consistently generated more profit per barrel of oil than its competitors. Shell, on the other hand, "remains well behind the rest of the international integrated oil group [in upstream results]."[16] As well, the ability to develop projects on time and on budget differed among companies. For ExxonMobil, of its $1 billion-plus projects developed from 2001–2006, less than 20 percent were more than 15 percent over budget. For Shell, only about a third came in within 15 percent of budget, and about half were more than 40 percent over budget.[17]

22   Exhibit 6 provides comparative financial data for several of the IOCs. Exhibit 7 provides a snapshot view of the origins of a few of the companies and their distinctive capabilities.

[16] Integrated Oils, Upstream Matrix Performance Analysis (1996–2005); Tenth Edition, A.G. Edwards, 2006, June 1.

[17] Ed Crooks, "Project Costs: Hostile Lands Empty Coffers," *Financial Times*, 2006, December 5, Special Report Gas, p. 5.

EXHIBIT 6   **2007 Comparative Data for the Integrated Oil & Gas Companies (millions USD and euro)**

	ExxonMobil	Shell	BP	Chevron	Total SA(€)[a]	Total SA ($)
Revenues	$365,457	$318,845	$265,906	$204,892	€132,689	$167,188
Operating Income	$ 67,402	$ 44,628	$ 35,568	$ 17,138	€ 24,130	$ 30,404
Net Income	$ 39,500	$ 26,311	$ 22,626	$ 17,138	€ 11,400	$ 14,364
Net Income by industry segment						
Exploration and Production	$ 26,230	$ 15,195	$ 29,629	$ 13,142	€ 8,754	$ 11,030
Refining and Marketing	$ 8,454	$ 7,125	$ 5,541	$ 3,973	€ 2,631	$ 3,315
Petrochemicals	$ 4,382	$ 1,064	nr	$ 539	€ 507	$ 639
Gas, Power, and Renewables	nr	$ 2,650	$ 1,321	nr	nr	nr
Corporate and other	$ 434	$ 277	-$ 13,865	-$ 584	nr	nr
Cash Flow From Operations	$ 49,286	$ 31,696	$ 28,172	$ 24,323	€ 16,061	$ 20,237
Capital Expenditures and Acquisitions	$ 19,855	$ 23,096	$ 16,910	$ 16,611	€ 11,852	$ 14,934
Exploration and Production	$ 16,231	$ 16,638	$ 13,075	$ 12,819	€ 9,011	$ 11,354
Refining and Marketing	$ 2,729	$ 3,363	$ 3,122	$ 3,175	€ 1,775	$ 2,237
Petrochemicals	$ 756	$ 821	nr	$ 200	€ 995	$ 1,254
Gas, power, and renewables	nr	$ 1,977	$ 432	nr	nr	nr
Corporate and other	$ 139	$ 297	$ 281	$ 417	€ 81	$ 102
Plant, property and equipment	$113,687	$100,988	$182,984	$135,988		
Exploration and Production	$ 68,410	ncd	ncd	$ 54,436	ncd	ncd
Refining and Marketing	$ 28,918	ncd	ncd	$ 11,974	ncd	ncd
Petrochemicals	$ 9,319	ncd	ncd	$ 720	ncd	ncd
Gas, power, and renewables	nr	ncd	ncd	nr	ncd	ncd
Corporate and other	$ 7,040	ncd	ncd	$ 68,858	ncd	ncd
Capital employed	$116,961	ncd	ncd	ncd	€ 54,368	$ 71,766
Exploration and Production	$ 57,871	ncd	ncd	ncd	€ 25,544	$ 33,718
Refining and Marketing	23,628	ncd	ncd	ncd	€ 15,172	$ 20,027
Petrochemicals	$ 13,183	ncd	ncd	ncd	€ 6,675	$ 8,811
Gas, power, and renewables	nr	ncd	ncd	ncd	nr	nr
Corporate and other	$ 27,891	ncd	ncd	ncd	€ 7,415	$ 9,788
Assets	$219,015	$235,276	$217,601	$132,628	€105,223	$138,894
Current Assets	$ 75,777	$ 91,885	$ 74,261	$ 36,304	€ 42,787	$ 56,479
Fixed and non-current assets	$143,238	$143,391	$142,262	$ 96,324	€ 62,436	$ 82,416
Liabilities	$219,015	$235,276	$217,601	$132,628	€105,223	$138,894
Current Liabilities	$ 48,817	$ 76,748	$ 75,298	$ 28,409	€ 33,522	$ 44,249
Long Term Liabilities	$ 52,550	$ 43,583	$ 56,784	$ 34,715	€ 29,118	$ 38,436
Minority interest & preferred stock	$ 3,804	$ 9,219	$ 841	$ 209	€ 2,262	$ 2,986
Shareholders equity (excluding minority interest)	$113,844	$105,726	$ 84,624	$ 68,935	€ 40,321	$ 53,224
Debt-to-equity ratio (%)	6.0	11.3	28.4	13.9	29.5	29.5
Operating margin (%)	17.1	14	13.4	8.4	18.2	18.2
Return on sales (%)	10.8	8.3	8.5	8.4	8.6	8.6
Return on assets (%)	18.0	11.2	10.4	12.9	10.8	10.8
Return on average capital employed (%)	32.2	23.4	22	22.6	26	26
Return on equity (%)	34.7	24.9	26.7	24.9	28.3	28.3
Production						
Oil (thousand barrels per day)	2,681	1,948	1,351	1,732	1,506	1,506
Natural Gas (million cubic fees per day)	9,334	8,368	7,412	4,956	4,674	4,674
Total estimated reserves						
Oil (million barrels)	11,568	3,270	5,893	5,294	6,471	6,471
Natural Gas (billions cubic fees)	67,560	30,058	42,168	19,910	25,539	25,539
Reserves replacement ratio (RRR, %)	129	nr	34	nr	nr	nr
Production costs ($/boe)	$ 6.04	$ 6.95	nr	$ 6.76	nr	nr
Average oil realization ($/bbl)	$ 58.34	$ 60.13	$ 61.91	$ 56.66	nr	nr
Average natural gas realization ($/kcl)	$ 6.08	$ 5.08	$ 4.72	$ 6.29	nr	nr
Number of employees	82,100	108,000	97,000	55,882	95,070	95,070

ncd = no comparable data available; nr = not reported

[a] Total SA figures were originally reported in euros. They were converted by applying the 2007 average exchange rate of 1.26 USD per euro to income statement items and the year end exchange rate of 1.18 USD per euro to balance sheet items.

[b] Sum of developed and estimated undeveloped reserves.

Source: Annual reports to shareholders, and Forms 10-K and 20-F.

EXHIBIT 7   **Distinctive Capabilities as a Consequence of Childhood Experiences: The Oil Majors**

Company	Distinctive Capability	Historical Origin
Exxon	Financial management	Exxon's predecessor, Standard Oil (NJ), was the holding company for Rockefeller's Standard Oil Trust
Royal Dutch/Shell Group	Coordinating a decentralized global network of 200+ operating companies	Shell Transport & Trading headquartered in London and founded to sell Russian oil in China and the Far East
BP	"Elephant hunting"	Discovered huge Persian reserves, went on to find the Forties field (North Sea) and Prudhoe Bay (Alaska)
Eni	Deal-making in politicized environments	The Enrico Mattei legacy; the challenge of managing government relations in post-war Italy
Mobil	Lubricants	Vacuum Oil Co. founded in 1866 to supply patented petroleum lubricants

Source: Grant, Robert M. *Contemporary Strategy Analysis.* Oxford: Blackwell Publishing, 2005, p. 166.

NOCs

23   One of the most important trends of the new century has been the growing importance of the national oil companies (NOCs). Although ExxonMobil, BP, and Shell are among the largest publicly traded companies in the world, they do not rank in the top ten of the world's largest oil and gas firms measured by reserves. The largest oil and gas firms are, by a large margin, national oil companies (NOCs), which are partially or wholly state-owned firms. Exhibit 8 shows an estimate of the market value for the largest nonpublicly traded oil and gas companies. The NOCs control about 90 percent of the world's oil and gas, and most new oil was expected to be found in their territories.

EXHIBIT 8   **Market Value of Non-Public Oil and Gas Companies**

Rank	Company	Industry	Country	Est. Market Value ($B)	Ownership
1	Saudi Aramco	Oil & gas	Saudi Arabia	781	State
2	Pemex	Oil & gas	Mexico	415	State
3	Petroleos de Venezuela	Oil & gas	Venezuela	388	State
4	Kuwait Petroleum	Oil & gas	Kuwait	378	State
5	Petronas	Oil & gas	Malaysia	232	State
6	Sonatrach	Oil & gas	Algeria	224	State
7	National Iranian Oil Company	Oil & gas	Iran	220	State
9	Pertamina	Oil & gas	Indonesia	140	State
10	Nigerian National Petroleum Corporation	Oil & gas	Nigeria	120	State
11	Adnoc	Oil & gas	UAE	103	State
12	INOC	Oil & gas	Iraq	102	State
13	Libya National Oil Company	Oil & gas	Libya	99	State
18	Qatar Petroleum	Oil & gas	Qatar	78	State

Source: McKinsey & Co., as reported in the *Financial Times,* December 15, 2006, p. 11. Analysis assumes restructuring of firms to create capital structures similar to that of publicly traded peers.

24   Viewed from an economic and business perspective, the NOCs had a mixed reputation. The national oil company of Indonesia, Pertamina, was described a few years ago as a bloated and inefficient bureaucracy:

> . . . [Pertamina] operated almost as a sovereignty unto itself, ignoring transparent business practices, often acting independently of any ministry, and increasingly taking on the role of a cash cow for then-President Suharto and his cronies. During the 32-year tenure of President Suharto, Pertamina awarded 159 contracts to companies linked to his family and cronies. These contracts were awarded without formal bidding or negotiation processes. . . Indonesian petroleum law dictated that every aspect of operation in the country was subject to approval by Pertamina's foreign contractor management body, Bppka. Dealing with the incomprehensible Bppka bureaucracy on simple matters, such as acquiring work permits for expatriate personnel, can take hours of filling in applications and months of waiting.[18]

25   Venezuela nationalized its oil industry in the 1970s and created Petróleos de Venezuela (PDVSA). PDVSA developed a reputation for professionalism and competence and was relatively free from the corruption and cronyism that pervaded, and continues to pervade, so many of the NOCs.[19] By 1998, 36 foreign oil firms were operating in Venezuela and PDVSA had ambitious expansion plans. In 1999 Hugo Chávez became president and almost immediately began to question the management and autonomy of PDVSA. After a bitter strike in 2002, PDVSA lost about two-thirds of its managerial and technical staff. From a peak of 2.9 million b/d in 1998, output fell to an estimated 1.6 million b/d in 2006. In 2007, Venezuela's oil industry shrank by 5.3% according to the Venezuelan Central Bank. As a company, PDVSA was indistinguishable from the government. Its CEO, Rafael Ramírez, was also Minister of Energy. The company was required to spend a tenth of its investment budget on social programs, which included sending low-cost heating oil to poor Americans. Company hiring policy was based on social and political goals; e.g., candidates from larger families were given priority. In 2006, the Venezuelan Congress approved new guidelines to turn 32 privately run oil fields over to state-controlled joint ventures. ExxonMobil, alone among the foreign oil companies, rejected the new joint venture agreements, and sold its stake in the 15,000 b/d Quiamare-La Ceiba field to its partner Repsol YPF. ExxonMobil subsequently filed an arbitration claim.

26   According to *The Economist,* nationalization has failed to live up to expectations almost everywhere. All NOCs suffered to some extent from government intervention. Many NOCs operated as the *de facto* treasury for the country. In Nigeria, for example, oil revenues represented more than 90 percent of hard currency earnings and about 60 percent of GDP. Nigeria's economic and financial crimes commission estimated that more than $380 billion of government revenues had been stolen or misused since 1960.[20] Some of the Middle Eastern NOCs were required to hire large numbers of locals, leaving them heavily overstaffed.[21] Others, for example in India and Russia, had to sell their products at subsidized prices. Underinvestment was a chronic problem for many NOCs, resulting in countries like Indonesia and Iran, with huge reserves, having to import petroleum. Monopoly positions held by many NOCs contributed to underinvestment. In Russia, Gazprom controlled the pipeline network making it difficult for other Russian gas producers, such as TNK-BP, to expand their production. Russia increasingly was using its NOCs as agents of foreign policy. A dispute between

---

[18] "Indonesia Considers Legislation that Would End Pertamina's 30-Year Petroleum Monopoly, *Oil & Gas Journal,* 1999, July 26, pp. 27–32.

[19] "Special Report, National Oil Companies," *The Economist,* 2006, August 12, pp. 55–57.

[20] Dino Mahtani, "Nigeria Struggles to Eliminate Corruption from Its Oil Industry," *Financial Times,* 2007, January 11, p. 8.

[21] "Special Report, National Oil Companies," *The Economist,* 2006.

Belarus and Russia in early 2007 resulted in disruption of oil shipments to Western Europe. This prompted speculation in Germany that the government might rethink its decision to phase out nuclear power because of uncertainty about oil supplied from Russia.

27   Some NOCs were well-run and profitable enterprises. Statoil of Norway was considered to be among the best of the NOCs. In 2007, Statoil acquired Norsk Hydro in a $30 billion deal. According to analysts, the motivation for the deal was that a larger company would make it easier for expansion outside Norway. The NOCs of Brazil and Malaysia were also viewed as reasonably well-run companies.

28   The role that NOCs would play in the future was not clear. Some analysts viewed many of the NOCs as inefficient and corrupt arms of government that could never compete in a true economic sense. Other analysts raised different issues, suggesting that the NOCs were in a period of transition and would become competitive forces to be reckoned with. Regardless of what would happen, the NOCs and their sovereign owners controlled most of the world's oil and gas reserves.

29   As Paolo Scaroni, the chairman of ENI, the Italian IOC, commented:

> Big Western oil firms are like addicts in denial. . . . The oil giants are trying to do business as usual as if nothing was wrong. Yet they are, in fact, having trouble laying their hands on their own basic product. State-owned national or state-controlled oil companies are sitting on as much as 90 percent of the world's oil and gas and are restricting outsiders' access to it. Worse, the best NOCs are beginning to expand beyond their own frontiers and to compete with the oil majors for control over the remaining 10 percent of resources. The first step in overcoming this predicament is admitting that it is a problem.[22]

Independents

30   The term independents described the nongovernment-owned companies that tended to focus on either the upstream or the downstream. Many of these companies were sizable players and ranked in the top 50 of all nongovernment-owned oil and gas companies. The large independents in the upstream included EnCana and Talisman (Canada), Devon Energy, Apache, Anadarko (United States), and Woodside (Australia) (see Exhibit 9). In the downstream refining and marketing area, the largest independents were scattered around the world's largest energy-consuming countries (see Exhibit 10). The downstream independents had lower market capitalizations than the upstream independents.

Other Firms

31   In addition to the IOCs, NOCs, and independents, the oil and gas industry included a huge number of other firms that performed important functions across the industry value chain. The oilfield services firms, the three largest of which were Schlumberger (80,000 employees), Halliburton (106,000 employees), and Baker Hughes (30,000 employees), played a critical role throughout the exploration, development, and production phases. These firms provide both products and services that, according to Baker Hughes' Web site, help oil and gas producers "find, develop, produce, and manage oil and gas reservoirs." Because the oil field service firms did not seek ownership rights to oil and gas reserves, many analysts predicted that their role would become increasingly important in the future as partners to the NOCs. The major gas utilities, such as Gaz de France and Tokyo Gas, were enormous customers for the gas producers. Pipeline companies distributed gas, crude oil, and petroleum products. The firms involved in drilling and seismic services provided drilling rigs and

---

[22] "Face Value: Thinking Small," *Economist*, 2006, July 22, p. 64.

EXHIBIT 9   Top 15 Independent E&P Oil and Gas Companies Based on 2007 Year-End Market CAP

Rank	Company	Market CAP (billions USD)
1	CNOOC	75.4
2	ONGC	67.1
3	Occidental	63.8
4	Encana	51.2
5	Devon Energy	39.6
6	Canadian Nat'l Resources	39.5
7	Apache	35.8
8	BHP Billiton	*
9	Anadarko	30.6
10	Woodside	30.4
11	INPEX	25.3
12	XTO Energy	24.8
13	Novatek	22.8
14	EOG Resources	22.0
15	Chesapeake	20.0

*BHP Billiton is a diversified company primarily focused on minerals. The value of its oil and gas E&P business was estimated by PFC to be $30-35 billion.

Source: PFC Energy

EXHIBIT 10   Top 15 Independent R&M Oil and Gas Companies Based on 2007 Year-End Market CAP

Rank	Company	Market CAP (billions USD)
1	Reliance*	106.3
2	Valero	38.5
3	Formosa Petrochemical	27.7
4	Indian Oil	24
5	SK Energy	17.7
6	Nippon Oil	11.8
7	Slavneft	10.5
8	S-Oil	9.5
9	Essar Oil	9.4
10	Neste Oil	9.1
11	PKN Orlen	9.1
12	Sunoco	8.5
13	Tupras	7.3
14	Tesoro	6.5
15	Mangalore Refining	4.2

*Besides refining, Reliance is also involved in exploration and production, chemicals, and textiles.

Source: PFC Energy

expertise for onshore and offshore wells. In 2007, the drilling services firms were busier than ever. A global shortage of offshore drilling rigs was driving up lease rates to more than $500,000 a day and slowing down development for some projects. The diamond-crusted bits used in drilling cost about $50,000 apiece, and one well in deep water could use a dozen.

BUSINESS SEGMENTS

Upstream: Exploration and Production

32   The term *upstream* refers to the exploration, production, and transport of oil prior to the refining process. Production is the process of drilling and extracting the crude oil from the ground. Many factors have an impact on the cost of exploration and production. Offshore wells are the most expensive, with deepwater wells in the Gulf of Mexico costing more than $100 million each.

33   A reality of the upstream sector is that exploration and development of oil resources must take place where the resources are located. Since virtually all oil ownership regimes are based on state sovereignty, companies have to deal with government policies and regulations in more detail than they would in most other industries. Most countries grant oil and gas development rights to private companies through a process of either negotiation or bidding. The main aim of the private company is profit maximization, whereas the host country government is interested in maximizing revenue. Not surprisingly, these two aims often result in conflict. Most agreements between oil companies and governments come under the term production-sharing agreements (see Appendix 1 for an overview of production-sharing agreements).

34   The method used to bid for, grant, and then renew or extend oil and gas rights varies from country to country (see Appendix 2 for some summary information on how different countries manage oil leases). Once the rights to explore are acquired, a well is drilled. A financial analysis is a determining factor in the classification of a well as an oil well, natural gas well, or dry hole. If the well can produce enough oil or gas to cover the cost of completion and production, it will be put into production. Otherwise, it is classified as a dry hole even if oil or gas is found. The percentage of wells completed is used as a measure of success. Immediately after World War II, 65 percent of the wells drilled were completed as oil or gas wells. This percentage declined to about 57 percent by the end of the 1960s. It then rose steadily during the 1970s to reach 70 percent at the end of that decade, primarily because of the rise in oil prices. This was followed by a plateau or modest decline through most of the 1980s. Beginning in 1990, completion rates increased dramatically to 77 percent. The increases of the 1990s had more to do with new technology than higher prices.[23]

35   Most upstream projects were done in some type of partnership structure. For example, a production-sharing agreement for the Azeri, Chirag, and Gunashli development in Azerbaijan was signed in September 1994. BP was the operator with a 34.1 percent stake; the partners were Chevron with 10.3 percent, Socar 10 percent, Inpex 10 percent, Statoil 8.56 percent, ExxonMobil 8 percent, TPAO 6.8 percent, Devon 5.6 percent, Itochu 3.9 percent, and Hess 2.7 percent.

Reservoir Management

36   For companies involved in the upstream, reservoir management was an essential skill. Reservoir management involved ensuring that reserves were replaced and that existing oil and gas fields were efficiently managed. Asset acquisition, divestiture, and partnering were a key aspect of reservoir management. Upstream companies generally sought to replace more than 100 percent of the oil and gas produced. Determining the level of proved reserves (the amount of oil and gas the firm is reasonably certain to recover under existing economic

---

[23] Oil Price History and Analysis, WTRG Economics, http://www.wtrg.com/prices.htm.

and operating conditions) was a complex process. Consider the following comment on the auditing of reserves:

> Though the word "audit" is customarily used for these evaluations, oil and gas reserves cannot be "audited" in the conventional sense of a warehouse inventory or a company's cash balances. Rather, "proved reserves" are an approximation about formations thousands and even tens of thousands of feet below ground. Their size, shape, content, and production potential are estimated in a complex combination of direct evidence and expert interpretation from a variety of scientific disciplines and methodologies. Added to the science is economics; if it costs more to produce oil from a reservoir than one can sell it for profitably, then one cannot "book it" as a reserve. Reserves are "proved" if there is a 90 percent chance that ultimate recovery will exceed that level. . . . As perverse as it may sound, under the "production-sharing agreements" that are common in many oil-producing countries, when the price goes up, proved reserves go down.[24]

37　　Matthew Simmons, founder of the energy-focused investment bank Simmons and Company, recently commented that "95 percent of world 'proven reserves' are in-house guesses"; "most reserve appreciation is exaggerated"; and "95 percent of the world's 'proven reserves' are unaudited."[25] The pressure to replace reserves has on occasion resulted in some unintended behaviors. In 2004, Shell's CEO left earlier than anticipated after revelations that the company had overstated its reserves by nearly 25 percent.

Upstream Profitability

38　　Profitability was a function of costs and commodity prices. According to Simmons and Company, Saudi Arabia oil producers could make a profit if the price of crude oil fell to $10/barrel, the Canadian oil sands company Suncor could be profitable at $25/barrel with existing facilities, North Sea oil producers could be profitable at $25/barrel with existing facilities, Venezuelan heavy oil required a price of $25–30/barrel for profitability, new facilities in the Canadian oil sands would need a price of at least $50/barrel to make a profit, and for U.S. ethanol production to be competitive, the price of crude had to be at least $50/barrel.[26]

Downstream: Oil Refining and Marketing

39　　The refining of crude oil produced a variety of products, including gasoline, diesel fuel, jet fuel, home heating oil, and chemical feedstocks. In the U.S., about 60 percent of refinery product volume was gasoline. Products were sold directly to end users though retail locations; directly to large users, such as utilities and commercial customers; and through wholesale networks. A merchant refinery referred to a refinery that was stand-alone and not part of an integrated distribution system. For example, Hess and PDVSA jointly operated a merchant refinery in St. Croix, U.S. Virgin Islands, with a crude oil processing capacity of 495,000 b/d, one of the largest in the world. Increasingly, NOCs such as Saudi Aramco were jumping into the merchant refining business as a means of capturing additional value added from their crude production. Although it is much more economical to transport crude oil versus refinery products such as gasoline, in 2006 the United States imported about 13 percent of its gasoline supply. The volume of imported refinery products was a function of regional arbitrage opportunities due to short-term swings in local supply and demand balances.

[24] Daniel Yergin, "How Much Oil Is Really Down There?" *Wall Street Journal*, 2006, April 27, p. A.18.

[25] http://www.simmonsco-intl.com/files/HBS%20Energy%20Forum.pdf.

[26] http://www.simmonsco-intl.com.

EXHIBIT 11
Return on Investment for U.S. Refining and Marketing and All Other Lines of Business 1977–2006

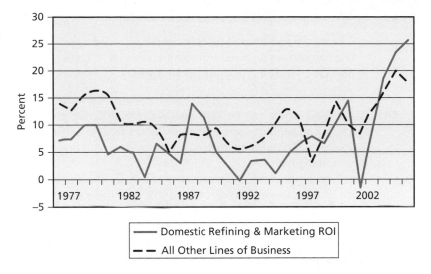

40   The financial performance of the refining industry has always been volatile. The primary measure of industry profitability is the refining margin, which is the difference between the price of crude oil and that of the refined products. Crude prices can fluctuate for many reasons. Weather in the Gulf Coast states, political instability in oil-producing countries, or OPEC actions, for example, all influence the price of crude oil. These fluctuations were not always accompanied by matching changes in the price of finished products, leading to large expansions or contractions of the margin. Exhibit 11 shows that profits on refining are usually lower than profits in other lines of business for petroleum companies. To put the downstream business in perspective, Lee Raymond, former ExxonMobil CEO, said in 1997, "I've been pessimistic on refining for 30 years, and I've run the damn places."[27] In 1999, BP CEO John Browne announced a bold plan for improving returns at BP that included a strategic decision to sharply reduce global refining capacity in the expectation of persistently weak profit margins.

41   Shell's head of downstream operations described the business as, "Grubbing [i.e., begging] for pennies in a street . . . If this industry, and especially the downstream, were to let its cost base slip, then we're going to have difficulty getting through those down-low cycles."[28]

42   There are several reasons why the price of finished products does not track that of the crude inputs. According to the New York Mercantile Exchange:

> A petroleum refiner, like most manufacturers, is caught between two markets: the raw materials he needs to purchase, and the finished products he offers for sale. The prices of crude oil and its principal refined products, heating oil and unleaded gasoline, are often independently subject to variables of supply, demand, production economics, environmental regulations, and other factors. As such, refiners and nonintegrated marketers can be at enormous risk when the prices of crude oil rise while the prices of the finished products remain static or even decline. Such a situation can severely narrow the crack spread, the margin a refiner realizes when he procures crude oil while simultaneously selling the products into an increasingly competitive market. Because refiners are on both sides of the market at once, their exposure to market risk can be greater than that incurred by companies who simply sell crude oil at the wellhead, or sell products to the wholesale and retail markets.[29]

[27] Richard Teitelbaum, "Exxon: Pumping up Profits," *Fortune*, 1997, April 28.

[28] Ed Crooks, "Interview: Rob Routs: You Have to Keep Changing," *Financial Times*, 2006, October 20, Special Report Energy, p. 10.

[29] New York Mercantile Exchange, *Crack Spread Handbook*, 2000, p. 4.

43   What this means is that profitability of refining is set by a combination of:

1. The supply and demand for refinery products (i.e., if refining capacity is tight, the refining margins are high and refineries make a lot of money), and

2. Refinery product prices, which are set by a combination of the supply and demand of refinery products and crude oil prices.

44   Gasoline prices can be high because of high crude prices, but refining margins and refining profitability can be weak if the demand for refinery products is also weak. In 2005–2006, U.S. refining experienced an unusual situation with both high crude prices and high refining margins.

45   According to the U.S. Department of Energy, the number of operating U.S. refineries dropped from 195 in 1987 to 149 in 2007, but during that period U.S. production capacity increased from just under 15 million b/d to more than 17 million b/d. The increased refining capacity came from debottlenecking (expanding) existing refineries, which was much cheaper than building new ones. Refineries operated at nearly 90 percent capacity in 2007 versus approximately 70 percent in the 1980s.[30] At the same time, demand for refined products was steadily increasing, leading to an ever-widening profit margin.

46   In contrast to the situation in the United States and Europe, there was plenty of new refinery construction activity in other countries, primarily because of increasing local demand. In 2008, Reliance Industries was building the world's largest refinery complex on the northwest coast of India. The refinery complex would have a capacity of 1.2 million b/d, and the number of construction workers at the site was expected to reach 150,000. Reliance planned to ship about 40 percent of the gasoline output to the U.S because R&M margins were sufficiently high to justify the 9,000 mile shipping cost.[31] In early 2008, the Canadian company Irving Oil was planning a 300,000 b/d refinery in Eastern Canada near the U.S. border, primarily to serve U.S. demand. Irving, in partnership with Repsol YPF of Spain, was also planning a liquefied natural gas (LNG) import and regassification terminal to export gas to the U.S.

Gasoline Retailing

47   In the gasoline retail sector, competition was intense and margins had eroded over the past 10–15 years. For the IOCs, returns on capital employed were much lower in retail than in other business areas. The entry of supermarkets into retail gasoline sales in Western Europe had displaced small dealer networks, and national players found they could make good money from convenience store sales. That said, Shell's head of downstream dismissed the notion that convenience store sales should be the focus for the fuels marketing business:

> The industry thought it could save itself with Coke. . . . we found out that maybe the fuels game is more our game than the convenience store game. . . . It's not a saviour for our industry. The important thing in retail is that you need to keep on changing things: that you keep different customer value propositions and you keep changing them all the time.[32]

48   In the U.S., supermarket and "petropreneur" entry into gasoline sales was also occurring, although not with the same speed as in Europe. In most countries, gasoline was seen as a commodity product, which meant spending money on brand development would have questionable results. The weakness of brands favored the entry of supermarkets because they

[30] Council of Economic Advisors. *Economic Report of the President*, 2006, February, p. 235.

[31] Steve Levine & Patrick Barta, "Giant New Oil Refinery in India Shows Forces Roiling Industry," *Wall Street Journal*, 2006, August 29, p. A1.

[32] Ed Crooks, *Financial Times*.

could compete on price and proximity and sell fuel as a loss leader. Competitive pressure meant that the largest retailers had downsized in recent years. For example, ExxonMobil's global retail network went from almost 43,000 retail sites in 2001 to about 34,000 in 2008. In the U.S., several recent industry entrants, such as Tosco (subsequently part of ConocoPhilips) and Valero, were able to buy refinery and retail assets and knit together profitable retail networks that were integrated with their refinery acquisitions. In doing so Valero became one of the largest retailers, with more than 5,000 outlets in the U.S., Canada, and the Caribbean.

Natural Gas

49   Natural gas, an important global energy source, is a naturally occurring fossil fuel found by itself or near crude oil deposits in deep underground pockets. Like oil, the largest gas reserves are found in countries such as Russia, Venezuela, Iran, and throughout the Middle East. In the U.S., gas accounts for approximately a quarter of the energy consumed, and the OECD average is 22 percent. Natural gas represented less than 3 percent of China's energy consumption in 2005, but demand is rising by more than 20 percent per year.

50   Historically, natural gas was a niche product because, unlike crude oil, natural gas is not easily transported. Without a pipeline infrastructure, gas cannot be transported far from its source. In some parts of the world, such as Canada, the U.S., and Western Europe, a network of pipelines allows gas to be distributed efficiently. In the U.S., there are 160 gas pipeline companies operating more than 285,000 miles of pipe. In other parts of the world, such as offshore Africa or Aceh province in Indonesia, pipelines to customers are not feasible. To transport the "stranded" gas, it must be converted to LNG. To liquefy natural gas, impurities such as water, carbon dioxide, sulfur, and some of the heavier hydrocarbons are removed. The gas is then cooled to about –259 degrees F (–162 degrees C) at atmospheric pressure to condense the gas to liquid form. LNG is transported by specially designed cryogenic sea vessels and road tankers.

51   Historically, the costs of LNG treatment and transportation were so huge that development of gas reserves was slow. In recent years, LNG has moved from being a niche product to a vital part of the global energy business. As more players take part in investment, both in upstream and downstream, and as new technologies are adopted, the prices for construction of LNG plants, receiving terminals, and ships have fallen, making LNG a more competitive energy source. LNG ships are also getting much larger. In 2008, a Korean shipyard is expected to deliver a ship with a capacity of about 265,000 cubic meters, almost double the size of existing ships. The larger ships, plus larger LNG trains (i.e., plants to convert the gas to LNG), are expected to result in a 25 percent reduction in delivery cost relative to the cost in 2000. In addition, natural gas to liquid technology provides an alternative to LNG, and converts gas to liquid products, such as fuels and lubricants, that can be easily transported.

52   In 2008 the gas industry was undergoing major structural change. A short-term LNG market was virtually nonexistent a decade ago. Traditionally, long-term contracts were sought to ensure security of supply for the buyer and security of revenue for the producer. Recent changes in the LNG market and in LNG shipping were leading to increased flexibility overall and to contracts negotiated for shorter periods of time.[33] The agreement to develop the huge Qatargas 2 project, jointly owned by ExxonMobil and Qatar Petroleum, was finalized in 2002 without contracts for gas sales in place. An LNG ship can deliver its gas anywhere there is an LNG terminal, making LNG almost as flexible in delivery as crude oil (although a shortage of LNG terminals and a reluctance of many communities to allow them to be developed has been a growth constraint).

---

[33] http://www.eia.doe.gov/oiaf/analysispaper/global/lngmarket.html.

53   There was also speculation that the rapid growth in Middle East LNG supply could lead to a global convergence in gas pricing and markets, with LNG someday becoming a true commodity. As well, buyers and sellers have been taking on new roles. Buyers have been investing in the upstream, including liquefaction plants (e.g., Tokyo Gas and the Tokyo Electric Power Company have invested in the Darwin liquefaction plant in Australia). Producers, such as BP and Shell, have leased capacity at terminals and are extending their role into trading. New buyers have been emerging, including independent power producers.

Petrochemicals

54   Although all of the major IOCs were involved in chemicals to some degree, they employed different strategic approaches. ExxonMobil Chemical, one of the world's largest chemical businesses, included both cyclical commodity-type products, such as olefins and polyethylene, as well as a range of less-cyclical specialty businesses. Many of ExxonMobil's refineries and chemical plants were co-located, providing opportunities for shared knowledge and support services and the creation of product-based synergies. Historically, BP and Shell had chemical businesses that were among the largest in the world.[34] In 2005, BP decided that its chemical business was non-core and divested the majority of the business. BP's remaining chemicals businesses became part of the refining and marketing division and were no longer considered a separate corporate division. Shell also downsized its chemicals business. The rising players in chemicals were in the Middle East and Asia and included NOCs, such as Sabic (Saudi Arabia) and Sinopec (China), and nonstate-owned companies, such as Reliance (India). An industry concern was that excess capacity was being created in Asia, and especially in commodity products in China.

EVOLUTION OF THE INDUSTRY

Innovation and Technology

55   Innovation plays a key role in all parts of the oil and gas industry. Innovations in areas such as deep water drilling and LNG shipping were discussed earlier. In the upstream, several key technological improvements have been developed in the past few decades, including increased use of 3-D seismic data to reduce drilling risk, and directional and horizontal drilling to improve production in reservoirs.[35] Innovations in financial instruments were used to limit exposure to resource price movements. In oilfield management, wireless technologies allowed for faster and cheaper communication than the traditional wired underground infrastructure. In refining, nanotechnology has enabled refiners to tailor refining catalysts to accelerate reactions, increase product volumes, and remove impurities, which has led to increased refining capacity. In retailing, innovations like ExxonMobil's *Speedpass* have made retail transactions fast and simple.

Mergers and Acquisitions

56   Mergers and acquisitions have been an important element in the oil and gas industry since its inception. Although the megamergers, such as BP-Amoco, Total-PetroFina, Chevron-Texaco, and Exxon-Mobil, received most of the press, there were also many smaller deals. 2007 was a relatively low year for M&As. In the U.S. exploration sector, M&A activity was at its lowest level in four years. Some of the biggest deals were in oilfield services and included the biggest global deal of the year, the $17.3 billion merger of GlobalSantaFe and Transocean (Exhibit 12).

---

[34] Peter Partheymuller, Chemicals, Hoover's, http://premium.hoovers.com.
[35] WTRG Economics, http://www.wtrg.com/prices.htm.

EXHIBIT 12   Largest Deals in Oil and Gas in 2007

Target	Target Country	Acquiror	Acquiror Country	Form	Deal* Value
GlobalSantaFe	United States	TransOcean	United States	Merger	17.3
SK	South Korea	Shareholders	South Korea	Divestiture	17.0
Yukossibneft Oil	Russian Federation	LLC Neft-Aktiv	Russian Federation	Acq. of Assets	6.8
Yukossibneft Oil	Russian Federation	LLC Neft-Aktiv	Russian Federation	Acq. of Assets	6.4
Western Oil Sands	Canada	Marathon Oil	United States	Acquisition	6.2
Gazprom Neft	Russian Federation	EniNeftegaz	Italy	Acq. Part. Int.	5.8
Dominion Resources	United States	ENI SpA	Italy	Acq. of Assets	4.8
Canetic Resources Trust	Canada	Penn West Energy Trust	Canada	Merger	3.7
Pogo Producing	United States	Plains Exploration and Production	United States	Acquisition	3.5
Halliburton	United States	Halliburton	United States	Divestiture	3.1
Amoruso Field	United States	Encana	Canada	Acq. of Assets	2.6
Dominion Resources	United States	XTO Energy	United States	Acq. of Assets	2.5
TODCO	United States	Hercules Offshore	United States	Acquisition	2.4
OAO Mosenergo	Russian Federation	OAO Gazprom	Russian Federation	Acq. Part. Int.	2.3

* In billions of US dollars, including net debt of target company.
Source: Thomson Financial

57   In looking at the large M&A deals done over the past few decades, one might conclude that eventually there will only be a handful of oil companies in the world. The reality is different. Research shows that the oil industry is much less concentrated today than it was 50 years ago.[36] There are opportunities for new entrants despite the huge size of the largest IOCs and NOCs. In the downstream in the 1990s, new entrants, such as Tosco, Premcor, and Petroplus, had a significant impact on industry structure. In chemicals, Ineos, the privately held British company, grew through a series of related acquisitions to become the world's third largest chemical company with sales of about $33 billion. In the upstream, the huge financial scale of projects such as Sakhalin I and II or Qatargas 2 made it unlikely that a new entrant could challenge the IOCs. However, if NOCs in China and India continued to do acquisitions, they might develop the technological and financial skills to compete for the largest and most complex upstream projects.

China and India

58   In 1998, China became a net importer of oil for the first time. In 2006, China overtook Japan to become the world's second largest importer. By 2030, it was predicted that China might have to import 80 percent of its oil. Clearly, China and Chinese companies were going to be major players in the oil and gas industry. In 2008, China had about 90,000 gas stations, almost all owned by Chinese companies. BP, Chevron (Caltex), ExxonMobil, and Shell had joint ventures in fuels marketing in China in 2008. Retail prices were regulated, which resulted in some unintended consequences. If the government increased prices, especially

[36] Pankaj Ghemawat & Fariborz Ghadar, "The Dubious Logic of Global Megamergers," *Harvard Business Review,* 2000, July–August, 78 Issue 4, pp. 65–72.

for diesel, there could be social unrest. Because refiners were losing money on diesel, they cut back on diesel production, leading to widespread diesel shortages in 2007 and significant increases in diesel imports. Refiners had little capital available for upgrades and modernization, and purchased low-quality crudes high in sulfur content. China had much-less-stringent environmental regulations than the developed world; and more stringent regulations would mean higher fuel costs. As a comparison, the United States allowed maximum sulfur concentrations of 15 parts per million for most diesel fuels, while China allowed up to 2,000 parts per million.[37] China's cities were among the most polluted in the world.

59   India had about 35,000 gas stations, up from 17,000 in 1999. With recent liberalization of the industry, new entrants, such as Reliance, aggressively entered the retail market. Reliance rapidly built a network of 1,200 service stations, but then slowed its expansion after losing money due to government control over retail prices. In 2008, Shell, with 35 stations in southern India, was the only oil major to have a retail presence in India.

60   In 2005, CNOOC (Chinese National Offshore Oil Company) made an unsuccessful bid to acquire Unocal. In 2006, CNOOC paid $2.7 billion for a Nigerian oil block stake, its largest overseas acquisition to date. Also, in 2006, a bid for exploration rights in offshore Angola from a consortium led by China's Sinopec was the highest ever offered for exploration acreage anywhere in the world (ExxonMobil and BP chose not to bid).[38] Chinese companies, many with no historical connection to the oil industry, were aggressively searching for oil in countries around the world. For example, *The Wall Street Journal* cited Ni Zhaoxing, a 50-year-old Chinese real estate developer who, in 2005, began prospecting for oil in Western Canada because, he said, "We have a responsibility to increase the world's resources either by conserving energy or finding more." In 2006, his company, ZhongRong, struck oil in Saskatchewan.[39]

Alternative Fuels

61   The role and future of nonhydrocarbon-based fuels and energy sources has become a critical issue for policymakers and the oil and gas companies. Various factors are contributing to a large investment flow into alternative fuel projects, including the rapid rise in oil and gas prices in recent years, concerns about global climate change, perceived competitive opportunities by energy companies (new entrants and entrenched players), and government subsidies. Some analysts saw 2006 as the beginning of a real shift to biofuels, leading to flat growth in demand for petroleum products over the next few years. Forecasts by the International Energy Agency suggested biofuels output could rise to the equivalent of more than five million barrels of crude oil a day by 2011, close to triple the output of 2005. Global oil demand in 2007 was 85.7 million b/d.

WHAT NEXT?

62   In 2008, a few predictions seemed fairly safe: the demand for oil and gas will continue to rise over the next few decades; the NOCs will continue to expand beyond their home markets; finding new sources of oil and gas will get harder and require innovative new technologies; the pressure to develop nonhydrocarbon energy sources will continue; and, despite the high prices of recent years, the industry will continue to go though up and down cycles.

[37] Keith Bradsher, "Trucks Power China's Economy, at a Suffocating Cost," *New York Times*, 2007, December 8, www.nytimes.com.

[38] Stanley Reed, "A Bidding Frenzy for Angola's Oil: Record Bids for Drilling Rights Demonstrate the Big Bets Oil Companies are Making to Secure Reserves of Black Gold," *BusinessWeek Online*, 2006, June 8.

[39] Shai Oster, "Feeding China's Oil Thirst," *Wall Street Journal*, 2007, January 2, p. A10.

63   ExxonMobil's 2006 annual report stated that rapidly expanding personal ownership of vehicles, especially in non-OECD countries, will drive demand for liquid energy. "The world is endowed with huge oil resources," stated the report. "However, access to these resources, huge investments, and the ongoing development and application of new technology are essential." In December 2006, Anadarko and Devon Energy announced an oil discovery in the Gulf of Mexico in a well drilled to a depth of about 25,000 feet, including 7,300 feet of water. A few weeks later, *The Wall Street Journal* reported on this activity, stating: "Anadarko's rig strategy [in the Gulf] shows off the company's entrepreneurial culture at a time when other energy-industry companies are getting stodgier."[40] Anadarko was placing a huge bet on deep water in the Gulf, and in 2007 had more time leased with drilling rigs in the Gulf of Mexico than any other firm, and more than twice as much as BP, the number two firm. In doing so, Anadarko was operating the way the oil and gas industry has always operated: committing huge sums of money to risky investments that, if they paid off, would generate sizeable returns to the capital owners.

APPENDIX 1   Production-Sharing Agreements

Production-Sharing Agreements (PSAs) are contractual arrangements for petroleum exploration and development.[41] Under a PSA, the state or one of its agencies, such as an NOC, engages a foreign oil company (FOC) as a contractor to provide technical and financial services. The FOC (usually a consortium or joint venture) acquires an entitlement to a share of the oil produced as a reward for the risk taken and services rendered. The state remains the owner of the petroleum produced, subject to the contractor's entitlement to its share of production. The government, or its NOC, usually has the option to participate in different aspects of the exploration and development process. In addition, PSAs frequently provide for the establishment of a joint monitoring committee involving all parties.

PSAs were first introduced in Indonesia in 1966 in response to increasing criticism and hostility towards the existing concession system that had started at the turn of the century in the Middle East. Under a concession agreement, all crude oil produced belonged to the FOC, which then paid a royalty, based on production, to the state. FOC profit varied significantly depending on the region and state involved in the PSA. Between 1966 and 1998, the highest maximum profit oil for FOCS was in Central America, with 65 percent, and by far the lowest was in the Middle East.[42]

PSAs have several key elements:

- The FOC carries the entire exploration risk. If no oil is found, the FOC receives no compensation.

- The government owns both the resource and the installations.

- The FOC partner pays a royalty on gross production to the government. After the royalty is deducted, the FOC is entitled to a prespecified share of production for cost recovery. The remainder of the production, so-called profit oil, is then shared between the government and FOC at a stipulated share (e.g., 65 percent for the government and 35 percent for the FOC). The contractor then has to pay income tax on its share of profit oil.

Under PSAs, the risk-return nature of the upstream oil business changed. PSAs do not divide profits out of market proceeds, but instead divide the physical production after allowing a portion of output to be retained by the FOC for the recovery of preproduction and production costs. Costs can only be recovered once oil is produced, which means the definition of costs can be a source of considerable dispute. Over time, PSAs have changed substantially, and today they take many different forms. PSAs have many variables beyond royalty rates and profit sharing, including duration of exploration and exploitation, bonuses, duties, state participation in the operation, tax holidays, pricing, marketing, associated gas, compensation, and arbitration. Contracts may be negotiated between the FOC and the national oil company or directly with the government.

continued

[40] Russell Gold, "The Rig Stock: Anadarko's Bet It Snaps Up Hard-to-Get 'Deep Water' Structures to Win Business, but Will Its Shares Benefit?" *Wall Street Journal*, 2006, December 27, p. C1.

[41] Bindemann, 1999.

[42] Bindemann, 1999.

APPENDIX 1   Production-Sharing Agreements (Continued)

The Sakhalin II project, a joint venture involving Gazprom, Shell, Mitsui, and Mitsubishi has three main elements in its PSA:[43]

1. Under the PSA, the Russian Federation government retains its rights and ownership of the oil and gas resources. The company invests all the capital needed to develop the fields, and pays bonuses to the Russian Federation at key milestones during the project development.

2. Sakhalin Energy pays a royalty of 6 percent of the oil and gas produced to the Russian government throughout the lifetime of the project. The balance of revenues, less operating expenses from production sales in the early years, is used to repay capital investment. The remaining production, after payback of investments, is shared between the Russian Federation, the Sakhalin Oblast (regional government), and Sakhalin Energy.

3. The Russian Federation government will receive an increasing proportion of revenues from production as the project progresses. If profitability exceeds certain specified levels, then the Russian Federation government receives an increasingly bigger share of the extra revenues, which can be as high as 70 percent. In addition, Sakhalin Energy pays tax on any profit that the company earns.

APPENDIX 2   Summary Information on Oil Leases

Angola

Exploration and production activities are governed by production-sharing agreements with an initial exploration term of four years and an optional second phase of two to three years. The production period is for 25 years, and agreements generally provide for a negotiated extension.

Canada

Exploration permits are granted for varying periods of time, with renewals possible. Production leases are held as long as there is production on the lease. The majority of Cold Lake leases were taken for an initial 21-year term in 1968–1969 and renewed for a second 21-year term in 1989–1990. The exploration acreage in eastern Canada is currently held by work commitments of various amounts.

Chad

Exploration permits are issued for a period of five years, and are renewable for one or two further five-year periods. The terms and conditions of the permits, including relinquishment obligations, are specified in a negotiated convention. The production term is for 30 years, and may be extended at the discretion of the government.

Nigeria

Exploration and production activities in the deepwater offshore areas are typically governed by productionsharing contracts (PSCs) with the national oil company, the Nigerian National Petroleum Corporation (NNPC). NNPC holds the underlying Oil Prospecting License (OPL) and any resulting Oil Mining Lease (OML). The terms of the PSCs are generally 30 years, including a 10-year exploration period (an initial exploration phase plus one or two optional periods) covered by an OPL.

Norway

Licenses issued prior to 1972 were for an initial period of six years and an extension period of 40 years, with relinquishment of at least one-fourth of the original area required at the end of the sixth year.

Russia

Terms for ExxonMobil's acreage are fixed by the production sharing agreement (PSA) that became effective in 1996 between the Russian government and the Sakhalin-1 consortium, of which ExxonMobil is the operator. The term of the PSA is 20 years from the Declaration of Commerciality, which would be 2021. The term may be extended thereafter in 10-year increments as specified in the PSA.

[43] http://www.sakhalinenergy.com.

APPENDIX 2   Summary Information on Oil Leases (Continued)

United Kingdom

Acreage terms are fixed by the government and are periodically changed. For example, many of the early licenses issued under the first four licensing rounds provided for an initial term of six years with relinquishment of at least one-half of the original area at the end of the initial term, subject to extension for an additional 40 years.

United States

Oil and gas leases have an exploration period ranging from one to ten years, and a production period that normally remains in effect until production ceases. In some instances, a "fee interest" is acquired where both the surface and the underlying mineral interests are owned outright.

Source: ExxonMobil 10K, 2005

Case 15

Western Union in 2008: *Send Me The Money!*   Armand Gilinsky, Jr.

1   When Jorge Ochoa, Vice President of Finance, and Raul Duany, Director of Corporate Communications joined The Western Union Company (WU) in November 2008, both were cautiously optimistic about the company's future prospects in the global money transfer market. The primary customers for global money transfers, immigrants, flowed from poorer to wealthier countries, seeking better opportunities. When immigrants left their home countries, they often left behind family members who depended upon them for financial support. To send money back home, immigrants most often used money transmitters like WU.

2   Founded in 1851, WU had formerly enjoyed a long history as a telegraph and wire services company, but by 2006 it had discontinued its telegraph services to focus exclusively on money transfers. Its money transfer business had grown 13 percent during the third quarter of 2008, despite slowing growth in certain areas of the world. Declining growth in China, parts of Europe, and the critical U.S.-Mexico corridor offset rising transaction volumes in India and the Philippines.

3   On November 10, 2008, Ochoa and Duany were summoned to WU company headquarters in Englewood, Colorado, for a breakfast meeting with CEO Christina Gold. Her new executives' first assignment was to help develop a strategy for WU that would mitigate any impact of further erosion of its primary money transfer business, while remaining mindful of the need to address the company's critics regarding its commitment to social responsibility. Before joining WU, Ochoa and Duany were well aware that government regulators and shareholder activists were actively scrutinizing the operations and fee-charging practices of money transfer businesses. A shareholder initiative calling on WU to become a better corporate citizen and donor was released to the press on April 25, 2008, prior to Western Union's annual shareholder meeting in June (see Exhibit 1 for the transcript of the shareholder initiative). From summer 2007 to summer 2008, a consumer activist organization known as the *Transnational Institute for Grassroots Research and Action* (TIGRA) coordinated boycotts against WU in order to compel the company to decrease fees. TIGRA, based in Oakland, California, also called upon WU and other global money transfer companies to reinvest more into local communities, at the tune of $1 dollar per every $100 in money transfer transaction revenues.

A STORIED PAST

4   Prior to the boycotts in 2007 and 2008, WU had a chequered history. Fourteen years after its founders set out to build the first U.S. telegraph giant, WU's shares began trading on the New York Stock Exchange (NYSE) in 1865. In 1884, WU became one of the original 11 companies included in the Dow Jones Industrial Average. Over the years WU was

This case was prepared by Armand Gilinsky, Jr., Professor of Business at Sonoma State University, from published sources, as a basis for class discussion, not to illustrate either effective or ineffective handling of an administrative situation. An earlier version of this case was presented at the March 2009 Western Casewriters' Association conference in Midway, UT.

EXHIBIT 1   **Western Union Shareholder Resolution, 2008**

The federal law known as the Community Reinvestment Act (CRA) obligates federally insured banks and depository institutions to help meet the needs of communities in which they operate. No such law exists for money transfer agencies like Western Union.

In March 2007, Federal Reserve Chairman Ben Bernanke stated, "the CRA reaffirmed the long-standing principle that financial institutions must serve the convenience and needs . . . of the communities in which they are chartered."[1]

Western Union serves many of the financial needs of immigrant populations, as a bank might, with a major presence in poor and racially diverse neighborhoods.[2]

Western Union's customers are mostly urban and poor. The typical user of its remittance services is a low-wage immigrant worker who lives in urban America, makes $15,600 annually and sends home $293 a month, almost 30% of his or her net monthly income.[3] These remitters spend up to $300 a year on costly transaction fees and disadvantageous exchange rates, which equals one week's salary for the remitter or at least sixty days' salary for their kin in cities such as San Salvador, Mexico City, and Manila.[4]

Remittances contribute about 80% to a recipient household's total income.

Almost half of Philippine households who receive remittances depend solely on this source of income. The highest monthly allocations for expenses from remittances are for food, rent, and education.[5]

We believe onerous charges in the multi-billion dollar money transfer industry place an undue economic burden on low-income immigrant families in the United States and in their communities of origin while creating an increased reputational risk for our Company.

Western Union has faced numerous lawsuits based on predatory fees and unfair exchange rates. These suits have resulted in millions of shareholder dollars being spent on settlements. These practices, along with our Company's relatively low degree of community reinvestment, increase the risk our Company faces in the competitive consumer market.

BE IT RESOLVED THAT: the Company develop and implement a written policy for community reinvestment.

SUPORTING STATEMENT: In our view, community investment goes beyond charitable donations and corporate volunteering. We believe a policy and strategy to build social capital in communities is essential. Such a policy is best created by engaging community organizers to identify community needs to develop long-term programs that reflect those needs.

(1) The Community Reinvestment Act: Its Evolution and New Challenges, Federal Reserve Chairman Ben S. Bernanke, 3/30/07.
(2) Analysis of Alternative Financial Service Providers, Urban Institute, 2004.
(3) Distributing Prepaid Cards through Worker Centers: A Gateway to Asset Building for Low-Income Households, The Center for Financial Services Innovation, October 2006.
(4) Transnational Institute for Grassroots Research and Action Research, April 2007.
(5) Enhancing the Efficiency of Overseas Workers Remittance, Asian Development Bank, July 2004.
Source: Responsible Wealth, Boston, MA, http://www.faireconomy.org/news/western_union_shareholder_resolution_2008, accessed June 14, 2009.

featured in a Zane Grey novel and a movie depicting the company's creation of an inaugural U.S. transcontinental telecommunications link. Innovation was WU's hallmark: it had created the universal stock ticker, introduced the first consumer-to-consumer money transfer service, and launched the first U.S. commercial communications satellite service. However in 1992, WU went bankrupt, as telegraphs reached obsolescence, a victim of airmail and faxes, and the company was delisted from the NYSE.

5   WU re-emerged in 1994 solely as a money transfer company. Owing to a surge in migration, money transfers were at that time growing at 20 percent per year. In 1998, Chicago lawyer Matthew Piers represented plaintiffs in a class-action suit against WU and rival money transfer company MoneyGram, alleging that these firms had deceived customers with advertisements like, "Send $300 to Mexico for $15," when, in fact, the companies derived even higher profits (about 80% more) from settling foreign exchange rates from money transfers into local currencies to their advantage. The case was settled without either company admitting any wrongdoing.

6   After settling its share of the lawsuit for $375 million, a portion of which included the creation of a fund for immigrants' organizations, WU set out to recast its image. An internal marketing memo asserted that that WU appeared "money-oriented" and "cold," so the goal was modified to capture a "share of mind" and a "share of heart" in addition to a "share of wallet."[1] WU spent more than $1 billion on marketing, selectively dropped money transfer fees, donated to immigrants' rights groups and advocated a path to legalization for illegal immigrants. In sum, WU sought to portray itself as the migrants' "trusted friend."[2] Matthew Piers, the lawyer who had brought the suit against WU later told a *New York Times* reporter: "Western Union has become a company that values and protects its customers. No one was more surprised at the change than me, as I was Western Union critic Numero Uno."[3]

7   First Financial Management Corporation purchased WU in 1994, and a year later the combined entity merged with First Data Corporation in Colorado. In the ensuing ten years, WU grew its leading share of the consumer money transfer services market from 10 to over 17 percent, with an average transaction size of $350. By then, WU far exceeded other franchise businesses in terms of number of outlets worldwide—over 300,000—compared with McDonald's at 31,000 outlets, and processed nearly five times as many transactions as its closest rival, MoneyGram. WU offered services through a network of agents in more than 200 countries and territories, under the "Western Union" as well as its subsidiary brands, Orlandi Valuta (acquired in 1999 and based in Los Angeles, California) and Vigo Remittance Company (acquired in 2005 and based in Florida).

8   WU was again listed on the NYSE on January 26, 2006. In fiscal year 2007, WU continued to derive the majority of its $4.9 billion revenues from fees that consumers paid when they sent money. WU's primary segments included consumer-to-consumer (C2C: 83 percent of 2007 revenues) and consumer-to-business (C2B: 15 percent).

9   Led by the same core group of executives that had managed it under First Data, in 2008 WU continued to carry $3.5 billion in residual debt on its balance sheet as a result of the spin-off from First Data. CEO Christina Gold, who had joined WU in September 2006, after serving as executive vice president of global development at Avon Products, was seen by many industry observers to have been primarily responsible for WU's makeover. In 2007, Gold reflected upon her role to a reporter in Singapore:

> I look at running a company as stewardship for a period of time. . . I'm not the company—
> I try to keep that perspective because I think the brand stands for Western Union [and] I'm
> not the brand. I'm just a representative of the company and my organization and all of the
> people who work for it. As part of my stamp I hope to develop a positioning to be really
> recognized as a brand that stands for its consumers and it gives back to the community and it

---

[1] DeParle, J. (2007, November 22) "A Western Union Empire Moves Migrant Cash Home," *The New York Times*, A1.

[2] Ibid.

[3] Ibid.

EXHIBIT 2 **WESTERN UNION CO—Income Statements, 2005–2007** (*$ Millions except per share amounts*)

	12/31/05	12/31/06	12/31/07
Transaction Fees	$3,354.8	$3,696.6	$3,989.8
Foreign Exchange Revenue	531.0	653.9	771.3
Commission & Other Revenues	102.1	119.7	139.1
Total Revenues	$3,987.9	$4,470.2	$4,900.2
Cost of Services	2,118.9	2,430.5	2,808.4
Selling, General & Administrative Expense	599.8	728.3	769.8
Total Expenses	2,718.7	3,158.8	3,578.2
Operating Income	1,269.2	1,311.4	1,322.0
Interest Income	0.0	40.1	79.4
Interest Expense	0.0	(53.4)	(189.0)
Other Income (Expenses), net	74.9	37.0	10.0
Income before Income Taxes—Domestic	801.9	707.1	529.3
Income before Income Taxes—Foreign	542.2	628.0	693.1
Income before Taxes	1,344.1	1,335.1	1,222.4
Provision for Income Taxes	416.7	421.1	365.1
Net Income	$ 927.4	$ 914.0	$ 857.3
Weighted average shares outstanding-basic (millions of shares)		764.5	760.2
Weighted average shares outstanding-diluted (millions of shares)		768.6	772.9
Year end shares outstanding (millions of shares)		771.1	749.8
Earnings per share - basic		$1.20	$1.13
Earnings per share - diluted		$1.19	$1.11
Total number of employees		5,900	6,100
Number of stockholders		4,513	4,542

Sources: Mergent Online, accessed November 14, 2008, and company SEC filings.

does things that are meaningful and make a difference. However, when I do leave, I want to leave behind a company that is more diverse in its revenue streams and has a human face.[4]

10 Jack Greenberg, former Chairman and CEO of McDonald's and a member of First Data's board of directors, had also moved over in 2006 to become chairman of WU. Together, Gold and Greenberg pursued growth of the WU brand through international expansion. WU's revenues increased at a compound annual growth rate (CAGR) of 11.4 percent from 2004 to 2007, driven by foreign exchange revenues that increased at a 19.7 percent CAGR, comprising 13 to 16 percent of total revenues during that period. See Exhibits 2–4 for WU's 2005–2007 financial statements.

[4] Choudhury, A.R. (2007, November 24). "Christina Gold, the high-flying head of remittance firm Western Union, has her feet firmly planted on the ground," *Business Times Singapore*.

EXHIBIT 3   WESTERN UNION CO—Balance Sheets, 2005–2007 *($ Millions)*

	12/31/05	12/31/06	12/31/07
ASSETS			
Cash & Cash Equivalents	$ 510.2	$1,421.7	$1,793.1
Accounts Receivable		24.3	22.5
Other Current Assets	2,215.4	1,763.3	1,794.7
Total Current Assets	2,725.6	3,209.3	3,610.3
Property, Plant & Equipment, net	82.4	176.1	200.3
Goodwill and Other Intangible Assets, net	1,798.4	1,935.7	1,973.6
TOTAL ASSETS	$4,606.4	$5,321.1	$5,784.2
LIABILITIES AND SHAREHOLDERS' EQUITY			
Accounts Payable & Accrued Liabilities	$ 238.6	$ 554.8	$ 350.1
Other Current Liabilities	5,054.8	2,085.2	2,883.6
Total Current Liabilities	5,293.4	2,640.0	3,233.7
Long Term Debt		2,995.9	2,499.8
Borrowings		3,323.5	3,338.0
Stockholders' Equity	(687.0)	(314.8)	50.7
TOTAL LIABILITIES AND STOCKHOLDERS' EQUITY	$4,606.4	$5,321.1	$5,784.2

Sources: Mergent Online, accessed November 14, 2008, and company SEC filings.

CUSTOMERS AND MARKETS

11   According to *Morningstar*, about 200 million people lived outside their country of origin in 2008.[5] The ongoing growth in the worldwide immigration population was concomitantly driving growth in the money transfer business. See Exhibit 5 for data on worldwide money transfers from 1990–2007.

12   Most money transmitters had relationships with networks of agents that could collect and distribute cash across the globe—for a fee (see Exhibit 6 for estimated industry profits per transaction). Money transfers sent by immigrants back to their home countries typically were not discretionary, but covered the subsistence needs of their families. For instance, money transfers sent to El Salvador equaled more than 15% of that country's GDP, according to *Morningstar.*

COMPETITION

13   WU competed with Global Payments Inc., Euromet Worldwide, and MoneyGram International. Exhibit 7 presents comparative financial information on these three direct competitors. However, indirect competitors in the money transfer industry included financial

[5] "Western Union," (October 13, 2008). *Morningstar Reports.*

EXHIBIT 4   **WESTERN UNION CO—Statements of Cash Flow, 2005–2007** *($ Millions)*

	12/31/05	12/31/06	12/31/07
Net Income	$ 927.4	$ 914.0	$ 857.3
Depreciation & Amortization	79.5	103.5	123.9
Other Assets, net	42.4	(4.3)	85.2
Other Liabilities, net	(46.5)	95.7	37.1
Net Cash Flows from Operating Activities	$1,002.8	$1,108.9	$1,103.5
Capitalization of Contract Costs	(22.5)	(124.1)	(80.9)
Capitalization of Purchased & Developed Software			(27.7)
Capitalization of Software Development Costs	(7.7)	(14.4)	
Purchases of Property & Equipment	(34.8)	(63.8)	(83.5)
Notes Receivable Issued to Agents	(8.4)	(140.0)	(6.1)
Repayments of Notes Receivable Issued to Agents		20.0	32.0
Acquisition of Businesses, Net of Cash Acquired, & Contingent Purchase Consideration Paid	(349.1)	(66.5)	
Cash Received (Paid) on Maturity of Foreign Currency Forwards	(0.5)	4.1	
Purchase of Equity Method Investments	(5.4)	0.0	(35.8)
Net Cash Flows from Investing Activities	($ 428.4)	($ 384.7)	($ 202.0)
Net Proceeds from Commercial Paper	0.0	324.6	13.6
Net Proceeds from/(Repayments of) Net Borrowings under Credit Facilities	0.0	3.0	(3.0)
Proceeds from Exercise of Options	0.0	80.8	216.1
Cash Dividends to Public Stockholders	0.0	(7.7)	(30.0)
Common Stock Repurchased	0.0	0.0	(726.8)
Advances From/(To) Affiliates of First Data	(153.2)	160.2	
Capital Contributed by First Data in Connection with Acquisitions	369.2		
Notes Payable Issued to First Data	400.1		
Repayments of Notes Payable to First Data	(246.5)	(154.5)	
Additions to Notes Receivable from First Data	(504.7)	(7.5)	
Proceeds from Repayments of Notes Receivable from First Data	18.4	776.2	
Dividends to First Data	(417.2)	(2,953.9)	
Proceeds from Issuance of Debt		4,386.0	
Principal Payments on Borrowings		(2,400.0)	
Purchase of Treasury Shares	0.0	(19.9)	0.0
Net Cash Flows from Financing Activities	($ 533.9)	$ 187.3	($ 530.1)
Net Change in Cash & Cash Equivalents	$40.5	$ 911.5	$ 371.4
Cash & Cash Equivalents at Beginning of Year	469.7	510.2	1,421.7
Cash & Cash Equivalents at End of Year	$ 510.2	$1,421.7	$1,793.1

Sources: Mergent Online, accessed November 14, 2008, and company SEC filings.

EXHIBIT 5 Global Remittances (total $billions sent home by migrants around the world), 1990–2007

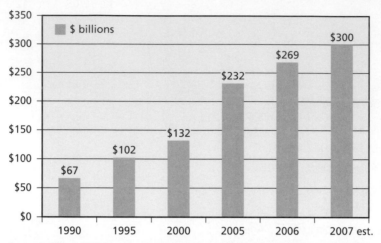

Sources: DeParle, J. (2007, November 22) "A Western Union Empire Moves Migrant Cash Home," *The New York Times*, A1; Transnational Institute for Grassroots Research and Action (TIGRA) http://www.boycottwesternunion.net/En/about.htm; Khakimov, S. (2008, February 29), "Can One Build a House Without A Base?" Results from The UN Forum on Remittances, http://www.scribd.com/doc/12911117/Results-from-the-UN-International-Forum-on-Remittances-20071.

services businesses such as: credit unions, ATM operators, card associations, card-based payment providers, informal remittance systems, Web-based services, telephone payment systems, postal organizations, retailers, check cashing services, and currency exchange providers. Banks, mass retailers like Wal-Mart, and cell phones also emerged as alternative channels for immigrants seeking money transfers. By the year 2013, 100 millions of cell

EXHIBIT 6 Estimated Industry Profit per Transaction ($), 2007

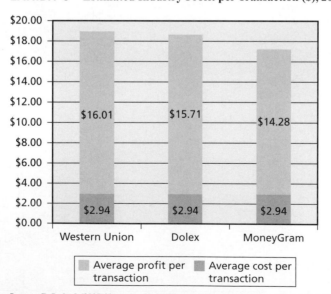

Sources: DeParle, J. (2007, November 22) "A Western Union Empire Moves Migrant Cash Home," *The New York Times*, A1; Transnational Institute for Grassroots Research and Action (TIGRA) http://www.boycottwesternunion.net/En/about.htm.

EXHIBIT 7 Comparative Financial Data—Payment Processing and Services (as of November 1, 2008)

Company	Stock Symbol	Market Cap. $ million	TTM Sales $ million	TTM Operating Income $ million	TTM Net Income $ million	Beta	Dividend Yield %	52 Week Price Range 11/1/07 – 11/1/08		P/E Ratio (x)
								High	Low	
Western Union	WU	$11,084.0	$5,179.0	$1,340.0	$ 898.0	1.00	0.30%	$28.62	$12.28	10.97
Global Payments	EEFT	3,294.0	1,369.0	278.0	177.0	0.74	0.02%	$49.87	$35.05	16.81
Euronet Worldwide	GPN	487.0	1,026.0	81.0	37.0	1.59	nil	$33.25	$ 7.79	16.69
MoneyGram International	MGI	81.0	470.0	nil	(1,480.0)	1.94	20.83%	$19.21	$ 0.80	NMF

TTM = Trailing Twelve Months
NMF = Not Meaningful Figure
Sources: Standard & Poor's *Stock Report: Western Union Co*, November 8, 2008; Google Finance, accessed November 14, 2008.

phone users were expected to transfer money via their mobile phones, according to Juniper Research.[6]

14   Many of these rivals were specialists in their industries or regions. Among the factors that gave certain rivals competitive advantages were local brand reputation, convenience, speed, varying payments, reliability, and price points. Pricing remained competitive in the money transfer business. Increasing price competition and regulatory burdens were driving out smaller rivals, leading to higher market shares for the remaining industry leaders.

CORPORATE STRATEGY OR ECONOMIC JUSTICE?

15   As increasing numbers of money transfer companies and banks moved into the field, WU felt increasing pressure to lower prices and compete for customers. Some critics, like TIGRA, advocated that WU heighten its commitment to community development.[7] Others, such as Efrain Jimenez, a community organizer in California who was spearheading a joint venture with WU for a Mexican community development project, were not so certain: "Yes, Western Union has a social responsibility, but they have the right as a company to make money too. They aren't a charity."[8] WU officials proclaimed that about $40 million in aid had been donated by the company's foundation to groups in 70 countries since 2000. These officials also maintained that the company had been aggressive in its philanthropy, while acknowledging that theirs was a corporate strategy also aimed at defending its business against the emergence of banks and other rivals in wire transfers.[9] In late spring 2008, WU publicly committed $50 million in donations to charitable organizations for the next five years.[10]

16   In July 2008, the Arizona Court of Appeals overturned a trial court's ruling in WU's favor regarding the authority of the Arizona Attorney General to seize money transfers originating in states other than Arizona and intended for payment in Mexico. WU subsequently asked the Arizona Supreme Court to reconsider this matter. Meanwhile, Arizona's Attorney General did not attempt to resume the type of seizures at issue in this litigation, and WU did not experience any immediate measurable impact to its Americas money transfer business as a result of this decision. The legal situation in Arizona remained unresolved as of November 2008.

FUTURE PROSPECTS

17   By late autumn of 2008, several forces had converged that could severely dampen WU's future prospects. A weak global employment market had prompted many money transfer customers—immigrants—to remain in their home countries. The global financial services industry was in free-fall after the failures of Bear Stearns, Lehman Brothers, and AIG, among other large financial services providers. Steep declines in the U.S. construction industry as well as the ongoing immigration debate in various state legislatures and the U.S. Congress slowed money transfer growth in the U.S.-Mexico corridor, WU's most profitable segment.

[6] Juniper Research (Oct 7, 2008) "100 Million Mobile Users to Make International Money Transfers by 2013." *Wireless News*.

[7] Thompson, G. (2007, May 11). "Immigrants push Western Union to Share the Wealth," *The Nation*, http://www.thenation.com/doc/2070528/thompson/print.

[8] Avila, O. and Olivo, A. (2007, October 21). "Western Union Boycott Divides," *Chicago Tribune*.

[9] Ibid.

[10] See http://www.transnationalaction.org/research/index.html#more, accessed December 12, 2008.

EXHIBIT 8 Operating Segment Data for Western Union, First Nine Months of FY 2008 v. FY 2007

Operating Segment	Three mos. ended 9/30/08	Three mos. ended 9/30/07	Three mos. revenue growth %	Three mos. transaction growth %	Nine mos. ended 9/30/08	Nine mos. ended 9/30/07	Nine mos. revenue growth %	Nine mos. transaction growth %
Consumer-to-Consumer Revenue								
EMEASA [A]	45%	41%	20%	27%	44%	40%	22%	26%
APAC [B]	33%	36%	0%	1%	34%	37%	0%	3%
AMERICAS [C]	7%	7%	23%	30%	7%	6%	28%	26%
Total Consumer-to-Consumer [D]	85%	84%			85%	83%		
Consumer-to-Business	13%	14%			14%	15%		
Other	2%	2%			1%	2%		
TOTAL	**100%**	**100%**			**100%**	**100%**		

[A]EMEASA = Europe, Middle East, Africa and South Asia.

[B]APAC = Asia/Pacific

[C]AMERICAS = North America, Latin America, the Caribbean, and South America.

[D]The geographic split was determined based upon the region where the money transfer was initiated and the region where the money transfer was paid, with each transaction and the related revenue split 50% between the two regions. For those money transfer transactions that were initiated and paid in the same region, 100% of the revenue and transactions were attributed to that region.

Source: Western Union *Form 10-Q, Quarterly Report*, SEC filing November 3, 2008, 34–37.

18   *Standard & Poor's* analysts at that time nevertheless remained bullish on WU's prospects, targeting compound annual revenue growth at 8 percent out to 2012.[11] A reason for analysts' optimism was that WU had generated $800 million of free cash flow during the first nine months of 2008, that is, for the first three fiscal quarters ending September 30, 2008. Exhibit 8 presents operating segment data for third quarter 2008 and for the first nine months of fiscal 2008. WU repurchased 17 million shares (at a total cost of $385 million) in the second quarter, and another 20 million shares (at a total cost of $523 million) in the third quarter of fiscal 2008.

19   CEO Gold had recently stated WU's intention to devote free cash to stock repurchases and acquisitions of rival money transfer firms.[12] Yet at the November 10, 2008, meeting with executives Ochoa and Duany, among the competing options on the table were: development of innovative financial services products that could be sold through the growing network of 335,000 WU agents worldwide, or perhaps even the creation of a micro-lending or small business development grant program for customers in developing nations.

---

[11] "Western Union," (November 8, 2008), *Standard & Poor's.*

[12] See July 22, 2008 Bloomberg TV interview with CEO Christina Gold at: http://www.clipsyndicate.com/publish/video/649933/spotlight_western_union.

Case 16

ChoicePoint Inc. and the Personal Data Industry

Cynthia Clark Williams

"We strive to create a safer and more secure society through the responsible use of information."[1]

—Derek V. Smith

1 In November 2005, Derek Smith, CEO of the embattled ChoicePoint, Inc. and staunch advocate of personal data collection, was facing some tough decisions. The company, the largest in its industry, had become the focal point for the negative publicity surrounding the personal data industry. Major news stories about data security breaches focused on improper use of sensitive data, such as social security numbers and consumers' privacy rights. Much of the turmoil stemmed from the company's September 2004 data breach involving the sale of personal data to fraudulent parties, allowing the thieves to resell the data from some 160 thousand personal records, including social security numbers and dates of birth. The breach resulted from a failure by ChoicePoint to properly authenticate the thieves who posed as legitimate business subscribers.

2 Data breaches were on the rise. According to one estimate, some 250 data breaches occurred in 2005 compromising the personal information of nearly 55 million individuals.[2] Yet, ChoicePoint remained the primary target of criticism, earning the "Lifetime Menace Award" from Privacy International and the "Worst Company in America" from Consumerist.com.

3 Although Smith had made some changes to the procedures for selling such data to small business clients since the breach, the political, legal, and social tension had not abated. Legislators were pressing for the elimination of the use of social security numbers across the board while privacy rights organizations questioned the very practice of profiting from another's personal information. At the same time, television and print outlets ran high profile news stories on how to protect against identity theft. In addition, some of Choice-Point's competitors had decided to limit access to social security numbers and other key information.[3]

[1] Company vision statement. Accessed January 9, 2007. http://www.choicepoint.com/about/vision.html.

[2] Equifax Corporation, Data Breach Solutions. http://www.equifax.com/biz/solutions/data_breach.shtml.

[3] In early 2005, the ABC television network aired a primetime special with Peter Jennings called *No Place to Hide,* and although Smith conveyed his commitment to creating a safer society, the exposé focused on inaccurate data and the vast amounts of personal information that the government had access to through private sector firms. Although errors in personal data were a concern for ChoicePoint, the company estimated that its error rate was less than one-tenth of a percent. In March 2005, the *Wall Street Journal* ran an article in its Personal Journal section outlining how consumers could protect their data. Testimony of Steve Buege, SVP of Business and Information News and Public Records before the House Energy and Commerce Committee (May 11, 2005); see also M. Ferris, "I.B.M. Asks Providers to Drop Social Security Numbers," *New York Times* (February 23, 2003): 3.

4   In the short term, Smith needed a plan to face the burgeoning issue of how and when ChoicePoint would use social security numbers. Yet, also weighing heavily on his mind was the strategic direction of the firm in an industry that was struggling to legitimize itself following an ever-increasing number of security breaches.

COMPANY BACKGROUND

5   Smith founded ChoicePoint in 1997. He grew up in the small town of Sayville, New York. After attending Penn State and playing wide receiver for the school's famous coach, Joe Paterno, Smith went to work for the credit-reporting agency, Equifax Inc. There, he ran a unit that was responsible for helping insurers and banks identify a customer's creditworthiness. Smith soon realized the power of combining personal information with publicly available data. By compiling it in a database, he learned he could package it and then broker it for a fee to governments, businesses, and other parties looking for ways to qualify people for various services. Equifax allowed Smith to pursue this expansion, which resulted in Smith buying access to some 16 hundred databases.

6   Equifax spun off the unit in 1997 with Smith as its CEO. Smith renamed the company ChoicePoint to indicate that the data would allow businesses to make smarter decisions when they faced a "choice point." By 2005, ChoicePoint had become one of the largest repositories of personal information in the United States—about 19 billion data files.[4] ChoicePoint had an extensive DNA lab that was instrumental in the identification of some of the September 11, 2001, terrorist attack victims. The company also helped to screen out violent offenders who applied for youth volunteer positions and to locate missing children.

7   In 2004, the company underwent a major reorganization to simplify its operations and reduce overhead as competitors began to enter the field. The result was four business segments: Insurance Services, Business Services, Marketing Services, and Government Services. ChoicePoint sold software and technology platforms to the government and other business clients and provided software tools and credentialing services to insurance and financial companies. It also conducted information searches of law enforcement records, business-to-business information, and government documents for a fee. ChoicePoint's Insurance Services segment, the largest by revenue, catered to businesses that needed their services in order to set appropriate premiums for home, commercial, auto, life, or health insurance. In 2005, about 75 percent of ChoicePoint's sales came from their Insurance and Business Services segments.

8   Most of ChoicePoint's revenue came from organizations seeking to qualify consumers for one reason or another. ChoicePoint's revenues were largely transaction-based because the company earned revenue each time its prescreened clients accessed its databases, generating cash flow and promoting the scalability of it products. For example, banks, real estate brokers, and other employers required information from various sources as part of their routine application processes and background checks. ChoicePoint's databases offered one-stop shopping for such information by using a network of subcontractors to gather dispersed public and non-public information. However, the data reports ChoicePoint sold routinely contained the four crucial ingredients for identity theft: name, address, date of birth (DOB), and social security number (SSN).[5]

[4] E. Perez and R. Brooks. "File Sharing: For Big Vendor of Personal Data, a Theft Lays Bare the Downside," *Wall Street Journal* (May 3, 2005): A1.

[5] T. Zeller. "How Millions of Pieces of Information are Bought and Sold," *New York Times* (March 17, 2005): C8.

EXHIBIT 1 **ChoicePoint Stock Price**

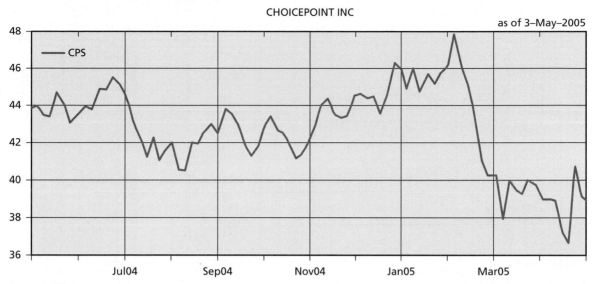

CHOICEPOINT INC

as of 3–May–2005

Source: http://finance.yahoo.com/

Impact of the Breach

9 Both ChoicePoint and those whose information was, unknowingly, in the hands of the company felt the impact of the breach. Since 1998, ChoicePoint's stock price had steadily increased. Yet, the breach had caused serious damage to its financial outlook. Exhibit 1 shows the stock performance in the months prior to the breach, July 2004, and the breach's negative effect by March 2005.

10 During 2005, ChoicePoint had significant cash flow, allowing financial flexibility to invest internally in the business and continue making acquisitions. In August 2005, the company's board approved a stock repurchase plan of $250 million over a two-year period to signal credibility and confidence following the breach. The company directed some 40 percent of its capital toward these buybacks.[6] ChoicePoint had increased its long-term debt by 72 percent since the quarter ending September 2005. At the end of the third quarter, ChoicePoint had $5.4 million in cash. The company employed approximately 5 thousand people. See Exhibit 2 for financial data.

11 For certain individual consumers, the breach had caused considerable damage. Elizabeth Rosen received a letter from ChoicePoint in February 2005 informing her that it had inadvertently disclosed her information to a group of criminals. Making the matter worse, Rosen learned, for the first time, what ChoicePoint did with her personal information. In Rosen's words, ChoicePoint "was profiting by collecting and selling confidential information about me without my knowledge or consent."[7]

12 As with most identity theft cases, it took time for Rosen to feel the full effects of the breach. Some months after the letter from ChoicePoint, she began to receive calls from bill collectors asking to speak to people whose names she did not know. According to identity theft experts, this was an indication that thieves had possibly set up accounts using her social security number under other names and addresses, a growing trend in identity fraud.

[6] ChoicePoint Annual Reports 2005, 2006.

[7] Anonymous. "Your Privacy for Sale," *Consumer Reports* 71 (10) (October 2006): 41–45.

EXHIBIT 2   ChoicePoint Inc. Operating Results

(dollars in thousands)			
Revenue By Segment	**Total 2003**	**Total 2004**	**Total 2005**
Insurance Services Revenue	$ 309,124	$352,368	$ 402,853
Screening and Authentication Services Revenue	—	212,706	242,054
Financial and Professional Services Revenue	—	113,768	117,510
Government Services Revenue*	339,483	70,523	129,358
Marketing Services Revenue	96,642	93,389	91,529
Royalty Revenue	5,102	4,504	2,398
Core Revenue (b)	$ 750,351	$847,258	$ 985,702
Revenue from Divested & Discontinued Lines (a)	—	—	—
Service Revenue	$ 750,351	$847,258	$ 985,702
Reimbursable Expenses per EITF 01-14 (f)	45,395	34,280	28,056
Total Revenue	$ 795,746	$881,538	$1,013,758
Insurance Services Operating Income	$ 172,158	$195,851	$ 221,670
Screening and Authentication Services			
Operating Income	—	43,715	58,980
Financial and Professional Services			
Operating Income	—	26,338	22,738
Government Services Operating Income	71,080	18,020	19,326
Marketing Services Operating Income	21,849	18,651	15,899
Royalty Operating Income	2,068	2,062	1,722
Divested & Discontinued Operating Income (a)	—	—	—
Corporate & Shared Expenses	(58,013)	(69,552)	(76,223)
Operating Income before other charges	$ 209,502	$235,085	$ 264,112
Other charges (c):			
Accelerated depreciation	—	—	—
Stock option expense	—	—	—
Other operating charges (d)	(30,942)	—	(28,773)
Operating Income (Loss)—Continuing Operations	$ 178,560	$ 235,085	$ 235,339

*For 2003, government services includes business services, as these units were combined prior to 2004.

13   During the past decade, critics had argued that companies in the personal data industry also made identity theft easier through lax authentication procedures and by maintaining files with errors in them. For example, in 1989, a *BusinessWeek* reporter misrepresented himself to a data broker, obtained an account and accessed the credit report of Dan Quayle. He used the information to write a cover story entitled, "Is Nothing Private?" *Consumer Reports,* a magazine that tested products and services, ran a report in October 2005 detailing its reporters' experiences with obtaining data from ChoicePoint and other large competitors in the personal data industry. Each of the reports contained errors, including incorrect addresses, names, and an incorrect social security number. One report contained 31 errors. Although errors in personal data were a concern for ChoicePoint, the company estimated that its error rate was less than one-tenth of a percent.[8] Still, such errors could cause permanent damage to the people involved, and they were costly to the company. According to the Data Warehouse Institute, the aggregate cost of such errors to the industry and to persons involved was $600 billion yearly in 2005.[9]

14   Although the personal data industry did not sell data to or obtain data from consumers, its practices had a direct impact on their lives. Typically, data providers collected the information from various record providers without any contact with an individual consumer, who had no say in the subsequent use of their information. Privacy advocates had argued that when consumers shared personal information, such as on a mortgage application or an insurance claims report, they rightly expected that the information they shared would remain private rather than being resold to a data provider.[10]

15   ChoicePoint believed the responsibility for maintaining accurate records was in the hands of the record provider (e.g., insurance companies, public records, motor vehicle departments, and credit agencies) and not with ChoicePoint itself. Similarly, LexisNexis stated in a cover letter accompanying its reports that, "We do not examine or verify our data."[11]

THE PERSONAL DATA INDUSTRY

16   Technology breakthroughs in the last decade and the compilation of large amounts of customer data allowed personal data sellers to experience considerable growth. Revenue estimates for the data brokerage industry were approximately $5 billion in 2005.[12]

17   Likewise, recent trends increased the need to screen job candidates due to the potential security, legal, and financial risks that had grown since the September 11 terrorist attacks. In addition, new markets were opening and companies were beginning to prequalify their vendors. Similarly, the personal data industry was looking to the insurance industry as it estimated that claims fraud would cost tens of billions of dollars per year. Lastly, many U.S.–based companies continued to create new operations overseas and hire foreign workers domestically, increasing the need overseas for screening services. Although there were many companies providing background-screening services in the U.S., only a handful were in the international screening business.[13]

Industry Structure

18   The personal data industry was very fragmented in 2005. Many firms were included in the "information retrieval services" industry classification, but this category also included

---

[8] M. H. Bosworth. "ChoicePoint gets a makeover," ConsumerAffairs.com. Accessed March 23, 2007. http://www.consumeraffairs.com/news04/2006/07/choicepoint_makeover.html

[9] Ibid.

[10] See S. Petronio, *Boundaries of Privacy: Dialectics of Disclosure*. (Albany: State University of New York Press, 2002).

[11] Ibid.

[12] B. Rigby and T. Kolker. "Continuing and Growing Consumer Fraud," *TBR News* (April 12, 2005).

[13] Mark Larson, "U.S. Employers' International Expansion Raising Demand for Overseas Background Checks," *Workforce Management* 85 (11) (June 12, 2006): 44–43, 2p, 1c.

companies such as Reuters, Bloomberg, and Yahoo, which did not sell personal information. In addition, many personal data companies specialized in one or two types of information, such as legal or medical. Consequently, the target market and product scope differed widely among competitors, making the exact industry concentration of the major competitors difficult to determine. For example, Acxiom, one of the largest companies by revenue, catered to the financial services, insurance, telecommunications, and publishing industries. Another big competitor, LexisNexis Group, served the legal, media, academic, and government arenas.

Suppliers

19   ChoicePoint and its competitors obtained information from a wide variety of third-party sources such as insurance companies' claims data, courts' deeds records, criminal dockets, and other court documents as well as motor vehicle records and data already ompiled by the three major reporting agencies (e.g., Equifax, Experion, and TransUnion). Although much of the information came from easily accessed public records, a great deal came from consumers themselves. When consumers made purchases (especially through catalogues), provided donations, ordered magazines, joined associations, or filled out warranty cards, they provided much information.

20   Some of this data were proprietary and non-public, such as recent purchase and travel data as well as name, address, DOB, and sometimes SSNs.[14] Personal data companies could buy such information on a short-term contract basis. Equifax and Trans-Union not only supplied the industry with some of this information but competed in the industry as well. A company's ability to obtain this key information, compile, and package it for easy use determined its ability to compete in the market for personal information.

Operations/Pricing

21   Operating in this industry required extensive human and technological investment and coordination in order to collect and prepare the vast array of data. However, insurance companies and financial services companies, two of the largest customer groups, began offering automated quotes, and their business customers typically requested multiple quotes to compare policies. Therefore, personal data companies used the personal data again, for multiple quotes, once they collected an individual's profile. For example, an auto insurance provider would use ChoicePoint's services to obtain the driving record of a customer seeking to renew a policy. Typically, that same customer would have contacted other auto insurance providers for comparison, which would use ChoicePoint's report again.

22   As a result, ChoicePoint charged multiple providers for the same report, spreading its up-front cost of preparing the report over the multiple quotes. ChoicePoint offered low-cost, on-line access to information about individuals and linked its searches together to provide information on relatives and neighbors. For new searches, the company typically charged for each step in the process of data retrieval from phone calling to faxing to photocopying. See Exhibit 3 on the rates for obtaining court documents.

Buyers

23   The personal data industry did not sell data directly to consumers. Instead, businesses seeking these services purchased access to the data compiled by companies like ChoicePoint by

---

[14] T. Zeller. "How Millions of Pieces of Information are Bought and Sold," *New York Times* (March 17, 2005): C8.

EXHIBIT 3 **ChoicePoint Rate Sheet**

Effective November 1, 2002

Court Document Retrieval

Research	$18.75 per quarter-hour (research is the time spent on the order)
Administrative Fee	(capped at $17.50 per order) $8.75 per quarter-hour
Photocopying	(or amount charged by court, if higher) $.65 per page
Telephone	(long-distance calls only) $2.00 per call
Local Fax	$0.50 per page
Long-Distance Fax	$1.50 per page
Transportation	$10.00
F.O.I.A. Requests	$35.00

SEC Filings

Forms 3, 4 & 5	$90.00 first five forms
	$10.00 each additional form after five forms

Source: http://www.choicepoint.com/products/wds.html?l2=credentialing_research&bc=bbcr&sb=b
Note: ChoicePoint provided on-site, same-day research capabilities at every court, legislature, and agency in the country.

submitting an application to become a subscriber and paying a fee. The application required the business to provide information and documentation that established it as a legitimate business and verified that its intended use was lawful. ChoicePoint accepted faxed copies of business licenses and other supporting documents. By 2005, ChoicePoint had some 50 thousand subscribers.[15]

24   A variety of organizations used the information that personal data companies sold, from insurance companies, to law enforcement, to crime labs, to private investigators working on behalf of parents choosing nannies for their children. See Figure 1 for a list of information users.

Major Competitors in 2005

25   One or two large firms dominated each market segment. For instance, LexisNexis (owned by Reed Elsevier Group) and Westlaw dominated the market for legal information. Companies that established a presence early in a specific market segment were often difficult to displace because they had already acquired ongoing access to essential nonpublic information by building a solid subcontractor network. Firms in the industry typically grew through mergers, acquisitions, or joint ventures with other companies. ChoicePoint had made some twenty-five acquisitions since 2000.

26   The industry's main competitors were Reed Elsevier, TransUnion, Equifax and Acxiom, with each vying for a particular segment of the personal data industry. Other potential competitors included a variety of general information services companies such as Moody's, Harte-Hanks, Laboratory Corp. of America, First Data Corporation, and First Advantage, as they were already home to large databases.[16] First Advantage was

[15] Federal Trade Commission Civil Action document (January 30, 2006). No. 1-06-CV-0198, p. 4.
[16] ChoicePoint report. Accessed March 13, 2007. http://global.factiva.com.

FIGURE 1 Users of Information

Information Control

The information industry has become an integral part of the U.S. economy and increasingly a contractor in the war on terror. An industry leader is Georgia-based ChoicePoint. With fifty-eight acquisitions over the past several years, ChoicePoint has become a one-stop for private and government organizations seeking people's personal information. An overview of the kinds of services that are available and the clients seeking them:

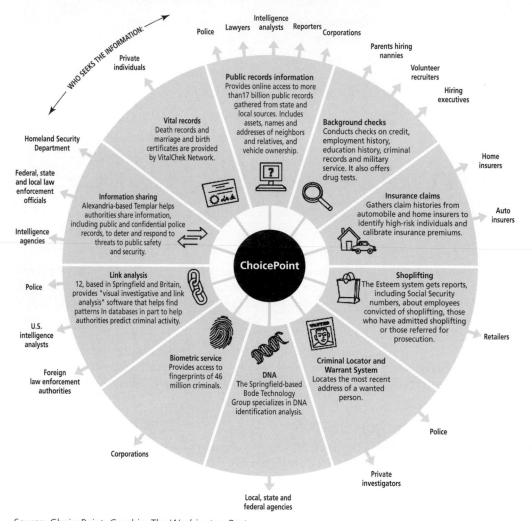

Source: ChoicePoint. Graphic: *The Washington Post.*

one of the few overseas companies, and it expected to double its international business prospects in 2006.[17]

Reed Elsevier Group

27 Reed Elsevier was involved in four distinct areas in 2005: legal, education, business, and science/medical. The company was a global supplier of information for research purposes and was home of the LexisNexis search engine.

[17] Mark Larson, "U.S. Employers' International Expansion Raising Demand for Overseas Background Checks," *Workforce Management* 85 (11) (June 12, 2006): 44–43, 2p, 1c.

28   LexisNexis provided information to lawyers, but more importantly its products targeted the risk management market that was ChoicePoint's main segment. Law enforcement, the government, and various corporations also used this service. LexisNexis Risk Management Solutions provided access to 1.6 billion public records and allowed users to compile the information into a report on a particular person. Reed Elsevier entered into the risk management market in 2004 by acquiring Seisnt for $775 million. The company's ability to search and compile large amounts of information made it an important ChoicePoint competitor. Revenue in 2005 was $8.8 billion and the company employed approximately 36 thousand people worldwide.

TransUnion, LLC

29   TransUnion, founded in 1968 as a holding company for the Union Tank Car Company, a business that leased railroad cars, entered the personal data industry in 1969 when it acquired the Credit Bureau of Cook County. The company held approximately 500 million consumer credit histories.

30   The company had recently acquired TrueCredit.com, which allowed consumers to track their credit ratings in the hopes of improving their credit scores and identifying errors in personal credit reports. For business customers, TransUnion offered identity verification and analysis tools that predicted the risk of customer fraud. In 2005, TransUnion remained a private company with revenue of approximately $1.14 billion.

Equifax, Inc.

31   Equifax, established in 1913, used its large database for identity verification and client decision making through its business unit, similar to ChoicePoint. However, Equifax began providing a new service directly aimed toward a common industry threat: data breaches. Its data breach service had provided data breach response plans for nearly 200 organizations over an eighteen-month period. The company posted revenue of $361 million in 2005, and employed more than 4,000 in thirteen countries.

Acxiom Corporation

32   Acxiom, founded under the name Demographics in 1969, offered products that used information to track down suspects and witnesses for law enforcement and corporate fraud departments while providing screening and identity tools. It focused on the financial services, insurance, direct marketing, publishing, retail, and telecommunication industries. The company's revenues in 2005 were $1.2 billion, up 21 percent from 2004, and it employed approximately 6,600 employees.

INCREASING REGULATORY OVERSIGHT

33   Although a number of different regulations governed personal data companies, no one law or government authority oversaw the commercial collection or distribution of the diverse information used by the personal data industry. Generally, though, any information revealed in these types of commercial transactions belonged to the company and, in the U.S., this meant an "opt in" policy for selling personal information whereby consumers were responsible for taking the necessary steps to "opt out." In contrast, the European Union took the opposite approach. Each individual could decide whether his/her information was used in such sales. In either case, however, the right to use this data to harm someone did not belong to the company, a bottom line ethical standard often referred to as the "moral minimum."[18]

---

[18] For an ethical discussion see R. T. DeGeorge, "Information, Computers, the Internet and Business," in *Business Ethics,* Chapter 18, p. 478 (2006).

34   Since the terrorist attacks of September 11, 2001, and the 2004 data breach, more people were becoming concerned about privacy. In response, critics began calling for changes to the two major existing privacy acts: the Privacy Act of 1974 and the Fair Credit Reporting Act.

35   In 1974, the U.S. government passed the Privacy Act, which required that all government agencies adopt a set of fair practices when handling data. For example, agencies had to allow people access to their own data and had to destroy it after a certain period, making any corrections to erroneous data. Under FRCA, companies were also restricted from sharing the data (e.g., issuing a consumer's report) with parties who did not have a "permissible purpose" for obtaining the data. Likewise, companies were required to maintain reasonable procedures for verifying the identity of a prospective user of the data. ChoicePoint was required to follow this legislation for activities such as pre-employment screening, auto and home insurance underwriting, tenant screening, and delivery of vital records, which comprised nearly 60 percent of its business.[19]

36   The Gramm-Leach-Bliley Act of 1999 (GLB), which allowed financial institutions and banks to enter into similar business activities, included two rules that pertained to privacy: the Safeguard Rule and the Financial Privacy Rule. The Safeguard Rule called for all financial institutions to design, implement, and maintain safeguards to protect customer information and give their customers privacy notices that explained the company's information collection and sharing practices. These two rules applied only to financial institutions, which included banks, securities firms, and insurance companies.

37   The privacy rule notice to financial companies applied only to "nonpublic personal information," which did not generally include SSNs. Section 502 of the GLB Act prohibited a financial institution from disclosing nonpublic personal information about a consumer to nonaffiliated third parties. In effect, the GLB permitted the dissemination of SSNs as long as the company using it had reason to believe it was "lawfully public" (e.g., a customer had provided it on an application or it was obtained from credit bureau documents).[20] However, calls for SSNs to become nonpublic personal information and to be disclosed only to government agencies had increased since the breach.[21] In May 2005, Steve Buege, senior vice president of Business and Information News and Public Records, and publisher of Westlaw's on-line legal database, testified that his company had voluntarily limited the distribution of SSNs to specific government agencies only.

38   Pending legislation also threatened the data ChoicePoint sold as well. The Data Accountability and Trust Act (DATA), if it became law, would extend the protection of the privacy acts to include all companies in possession of computerized individual data. Its aim was to require all companies, not simply credit reporting agencies as outlined by the FCRA, to put into place policies and procedures to protect consumer data and to rovide notification to consumers nationwide if a security breach occurred.[22] In 2005, only the state of California required such notification.

[19] Testimony of Don McGuffey before the House Committee on Financial Services. (May 4, 2005).

[20] See "Federal Trade Commission Privacy of Consumer Information," Sec 502 of the GLB Act (http://www.ftc.gov/os/2000/05/glb000512.pdf) and "In Brief: The Financial Privacy requirements of the Gramm-Leach-Bliley Act" (http://www.ftc. gov/bcp/conline/pubs/buspubs/glbshort.shtm). Accessed August 24, 2007.

[21] See "Federal Trade Commission Privacy of Consumer Information," Sec 502 of the GLB Act (http://www.ftc.gov/os/2000/05/glb000512.pdf) and "Testimony of Steve Buege, SVP of Business and Information News and Public Records before the House Energy and Commerce Committee" (May 11, 2005).

[22] United States Congress. Union Calendar No. 270. 109th Cong., 2d sess. HR4127 RH.

39   Also, in response to growing public concern, the House Committee on Energy and Commerce held a public hearing March 15, 2005, to learn more about protecting consumers' data. In this hearing, Representative Joe Barton (R-TX), the chairman of the committee, summed up the controversy concerning the sale of information, specifically SSNs, this way:

> I just think that's wrong. If I want somebody to have my Social Security number, I will give it to them. . . . but it's routinely given without my permission, and I just think that's fundamentally unfair.[23]

40   In response to the hearing, Representative Edward Markey (D-MA) introduced a second bill, the Social Security Number Protection Act, in an attempt to create only certain conditions under which SSNs could be sold, such as for law enforcement, national security, and public health purposes. This law would allow consumers to seek financial penalties of up to $5 million for each violation and to provide consent for certain uses.

41   Yet another bill resulted from the breach. In October 2005, the Notification of Risk to Personal Data Act outlined how and when individuals should be notified if a security breach occurred. Its language was more inclusive than the DATA Act, encompassing the outsourcing of data to private sector firms such as ChoicePoint.

42   According to one estimate, more than a dozen bills were introduced in 2005 following the ChoicePoint security breach.[24] Many came in response to criticism that the existing laws were often conflicting, differed from state to state, and were too market segment specific (e.g., the GLB applied to financial institutions only). Some critics suggested that this confusion allowed ChoicePoint to keep the controversy quiet by only notifying the 35 thousand Californians affected, per that state's law.[25] However, other states voluntarily notified the remaining consumers despite ChoicePoint's actions. As Jay Hoofnagle, associate director of the Electronic Privacy Information Center, a public interest research center in Washington, D.C., noted, ChoicePoint was just the beginning of the problem: "We're going to see this over and over again. This is not about a rotten apple. It's about a rotten barrel."[26]

43   Beth Givens, director of the Privacy Rights Clearinghouse, and Ed Mierzwinski, director of the U.S. Public Interest Research Group, also believed that more regulation of the personal data industry was essential.[27] However, Marc Rotenberg, president of EPIC pointed his organization's concerns directly at ChoicePoint:

> ChoicePoint has become the true invisible hand of the information economy. Its ability to determine the opportunities for American workers, consumers, and voters is without parallel.[28]

44   Smith believed these characterizations were unfair and stated that "this attack on our systems was far more sophisticated than we've seen before."[29]

---

[23] B. Sullivan, "ChoicePoint CEO Grilled by Congress: Data Broker Backs Some New Regulations, Smith says," MSNBC (March 15, 2005) from http://www.msnbc. msn.com/id/7189143/.

[24] T. Zeller. "Data Security Laws Seem Likely, so Consumers and Businesses Vie to Shape Them," *New York Times* (November 1, 2005): C3.

[25] T. Zeller. "Breach Points Up Flaws in Privacy Laws," *New York Times* (February 24, 2005): C1.

[26] Ibid.

[27] M. H. Bosworth. "ChoicePoint Gets a Makeover," ConsumerAffairs.com. Accessed March 23, 2007. http://www.consumeraffairs.com/news04/2006/07/choicepoint_makeover.html.

[28] Testimony of Marc Rotenberg before the House Energy and Commerce Committee (March 15, 2005).

[29] T. Zeller. "Data Security Laws Seem Likely, so Consumers and Businesses Vie to Shape Them," *New York Times* (November 1, 2005): C3.

ChoicePoint's Policies and Procedures

45   Prior to the breach, ChoicePoint documented its privacy principles and procedures for safe-guarding and maintaining personal data in its agreement for service as follows:

> [ChoicePoint] . . . uses administrative, technical, personnel, and physical safeguards to protect the confidentiality and security of personally identifiable consumer information in our possession. These safeguards are designed to ensure a level of security appropriate to the nature of the data being processed and the risks of confidentiality violations involved.[30]

46   In 2005, ChoicePoint also posted information on its Web site designed to address the concerns of consumers regarding privacy and the correct usage of the information it collected:

> Because ChoicePoint's ChoiceTrust understands its responsibility to treat consumers fairly and to protect their privacy, we have developed Fair Information Practices. These practices are derived from the Federal Fair Credit Reporting Act, but go beyond the equirements of that law. ChoicePoint allows access to your consumer reports only by those authorized under FCRA. In addition, each ChoicePoint customer must verify that he/she has a "permissible purpose" before receiving a consumer report.[31]

> Every ChoicePoint customer must successfully complete a rigorous credentialing process. ChoicePoint does not distribute information to the general public and monitors the use of its public record information to ensure appropriate use.[32]

47   However, in March 2005, Smith's comments at the Congressional hearing indicated minimal personal involvement both prior to and during the first months of the breach investigation. He testified that:

> On September 27, 2004, an employee became suspicious while credentialing a prospective small business customer based in the Los Angeles area. This employee brought his concerns regarding the application to our Security Services Department. After a preliminary review, the manager of the Security Services Department alerted the Los Angeles County Sheriff's Department. They decided to initiate an official police investigation and asked for our assistance.[33]

48   Smith did not find out about the breach until January 2005.[34]

49   Just prior to his testimony at the hearing, Smith spoke of the company's recent changes. Smith realized that tightening the credentialing process was a paramount concern in order for the company to regain its credibility. Accordingly, he decided that the company would no longer accept faxed versions of business licenses.

50   He explained that the company would discontinue the use of SSNs and other sensitive data except when the transaction was consumer-driven, or would benefit the consumer, and in cases where the inquiry supported the federal or a state or local government and for criminal justice purposes. According to the company's March 4, 2005, news release:

> . . . these actions will have an impact on the scope of products offered to some customers and the availability of information products in certain market segments, particularly small businesses.[35]

---

[30] Federal Trade Commission Civil Action document (January 30, 2006). No. 1-06-CV-0198, p. 33.

[31] Ibid. p. 10.

[32] Ibid. p. 10. Quoted material is from a Frequently Asked Questions letter sent to consumers who requested a copy of their public records file from ChoicePoint in 2005 (cited in FTC ruling).

[33] Testimony of Derek Smith before the House Energy and Commerce Committee (March 15, 2005).

[34] Interview with Derek Smith on MSNBC, March 4, 2005.

[35] Company news release, March 4, 2005. "ChoicePoint to Exit Non-FRCA, Consumer Sensitive Markets." Accessed July 30, 2007 from http://www.choice point. com/choicepoint/news.nsf/IDNumber/TXK2005-5381565?OpenDocument.

51   Small businesses accounted for about 3–5 percent of ChoicePoint's clientele.[36] Discontinuing the use of SSNs for these customers would cost the company $15–20 million in revenue.[37] EPIC's Marc Rotenberg was unimpressed by these changes, stating:

> Even their recent proposal to withdraw the sale of this information is not reassuring. They have left a significant loophole that will allow them to sell the data if they believe there is a consumer benefit.[38]

SMITH'S BELIEFS

52   Despite the mounting legal, social, and political tension, Smith believed that collecting details about individuals such as criminal histories, property ownership documents, and drivers' and marital license applications reduced crime and made the economy more efficient.[39] He also held strong views about the power of technology viewing it as capable of rekindling society's sense of community, security, and safety.[40]

53   Smith's beliefs led him to join other sellers of private consumer information in a $2.4 million lobbying effort aimed at Congress and a variety of federal agencies with his message of self-regulation. Although Smith and other personal data providers knew that Congress could rewrite certain laws, he was concerned that regulators might enact far-reaching laws that went beyond his suggestion that the government create a national notification system.[41] Other executives, such as Kurt Sanford of LexisNexis, also cautioned that overarching legislation could be harmful:

> Legislation must strike the right balance between security, protecting privacy and ensuring continued access to critically important information [provided by the personal data industry].[42]

54   Smith advocated a mandatory notification system as well as stiffer penalties for those who committed identity theft.[43] He believed this oversight should extend to all entities: public, private or academic.

55   Smith had mixed feelings about the prospect of eliminating SSNs. The personal data industry used SSNs because they provided the only truly unique identifier. Smith maintained that SSNs were necessary in order to differentiate between similar or even identical names. For example, there were some 23 thousand William Smiths.[44] ChoicePoint used

---

[36] T. Zeller. "Release of Consumer's Data Spurs ChoicePoint Inquiries," *New York Times* (March 5, 2005): A2.

[37] Company news release, "ChoicePoint to Exit Non-FCRA, Consumer Sensitive Markets" (March 4, 2005).

[38] Testimony of Marc Rotenberg before the House Energy and Commerce Committee (March 15, 2005).

[39] E. Perez and R. Brooks. "File Sharing: For Big Vendor of Personal Data, a Theft Lays Bare the Downside" *Wall Street Journal* (May 3, 2005): A1.

[40] Derek V. Smith. *Risk Revolution: The Threats Facing America and Technology's Promise for a Safer Tomorrow.* (Atlanta: Longstreet Press, 2004).

[41] See testimony of Derek Smith before the House Energy and Commerce Committee (March 15, 2005); testimony of Don McGuffey before the House Committee on Financial Services (May 4, 2005); and Penn State Public Broadcasting, speech and interview with Derek Smith recorded September 1, 2006, aired September 10, 2006. See also T. Zeller, "Data Broker Executives Agree Security Laws May Be Needed," *New York Times* (March 16, 2005): C3.

[42] T. Zeller, C3.

[43] Testimony of Derek Smith before the House Energy and Commerce Committee (March 15, 2005). See also T. Zeller. "Breach Points Up Flaws in Privacy Laws," *New York Times* (February 24, 2005): C1.

[44] Testimony of Derek Smith before the House Energy and Commerce Committee (March 15, 2005).

SSNs in most of the data reports it sold. If the calls for using SSNs for only government clients continued to move forward, ChoicePoint's revenue would suffer because it derived only 14 percent of its revenue from the government services sector.

56   During the March 2005 hearing, Rep. Ed Markey tried to clarify Smith's position on SSNs:

> [Markey:] Would you support a ban on the sale of Social Security numbers?

> [Smith:] Again, I would have to better understand the definition of "sale" and how it would be done, but I don't support. . . .

> [Markey:] But this is your field. You're an expert in this field; this is what I'm talking about, plain and simple—the sale of Social Security numbers.

> [Smith:] There are certain circumstances where the sale of those numbers are, in fact, in the consumer's best interest.

LOOKING TO THE FUTURE: CHOICES FOR CHOICEPOINT

57   Beyond the decisions he faced regarding the SSN issue, however, Smith had begun to wonder how his company could mitigate the growing legitimacy concerns in personal data brokerage without compromising the power of information.[45] He felt so strongly on the subject that he authored the book *Risk Revolution: The Threats Facing America and Technology's Promise for a Safer Tomorrow* in 2004. He believed that the recent problems with personal data related to human behavior and were not due to the technology itself. As Smith stated in an interview, "Technology is neither good nor bad, it's what humans do with it."[46]

58   Smith also recognized that in a democratic society individual citizens had a responsibility to protect themselves against identity theft and misuse. The privacy debate, he thought, was not about the logical but about the emotional.[47] He had argued for the security that such information provided and often countered the privacy advocates by stating, "It's not Big Brother who wants to destroy us. Big Brother didn't kill innocent people on September 11th."[48] Still, he believed that although consumers had a right to privacy, they did not have a right to anonymity.

59   For Derek Smith, the battle for anonymity came down to one thing: the "bone room" at Ground Zero in New York where the only identifiers were the victims' bones.[49] While he felt strongly that personal information was powerful and could help society, as in the case of the bone room, he also knew that the breach had stirred up important issues for his company and for the industry. In the short term, he wondered about a full elimination of SSNs: How would it affect competitiveness? Was it simply the right thing to do? In the longer term, he faced decisions about the best way to protect consumers' information and the role that regulation played in such protections. With these thoughts, Smith considered whether he should make further changes to his company, his industry, or both.

[45] Interview with Derek Smith on MSNBC (March 4, 2005).

[46] Penn State Public Broadcasting, speech and interview with Derek Smith recorded September 1, 2006, aired September 10, 2006.

[47] Interview with Derek Smith on MSNBC (March 4, 2005).

[48] *Risk Revolution,* p, 24.

[49] Penn State Public Broadcasting, speech and interview with Derek Smith recorded September 1, 2006, aired September 10, 2006.

Case 17

Intuitive Surgical, Inc.: *How Long Can Their Monopoly Last?*

Alan N. Hoffman

COMPANY HISTORY

1   Intuitive Surgical, Inc. (ISRG) is the global technology leader in robotic assisted minimally-invasive surgery (MIS). Founded in 1995, ISRG began with an initiative by the Defense Advanced Research Projects Agency (DARPA) to develop a technology called "SRI Green Telepresence Surgery." DARPA wanted to develop technology that would allow surgeons to operate remotely on soldiers wounded on the battlefield. Intuitive Surgical shifted the scope of their research away from the focus on remote surgery toward more commercial applications for use in hospitals. ISRG developed a highly accurate technology known as robotic-assisted minimally-invasive surgery. MIS is surgery typically performed through small incisions, rather than large, which results in shorter recovery times, fewer complications, reduced hospitalization costs and overall improved patient well-being.

2   The flagship product for Intuitive Surgical is the *da Vinci* Surgical System, which the company designs, manufactures, and markets. The system includes a "surgeon's console, a patient-side cart and a high performance vision system," as well as "proprietary 'wristed' instruments and surgical accessories." The system serves to seamlessly relay actual movement of the surgeon's hands from the controls of the console to the instruments positioned inside the patient through small incisions. The actual hand movements are scaled down to "micro-movements" carried out by the *da Vinci* instruments for improved agility and accuracy.[1]

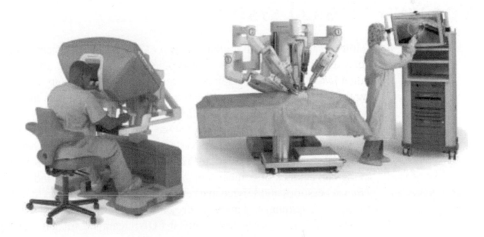

The author would like to thank Scott Coligan, Melanie Dunn, Amanda Genesky, Joe Lopatosky, and Dan Ryan for their research. Please address all correspondence to Dr. Alan N. Hoffman, MBA Program Director, LaCava 295, Bentley University, 175 Forest Street, Waltham, MA 02452; ahoffman@bentley.edu. Printed by permission of Dr. Alan N. Hoffman.

3   Surgeons had the first opportunity to use an early version of the *da Vinci* system for surgery on humans in 1997. During the second quarter of 1999, Intuitive Surgical was able to begin selling the system in Europe. The year 2000 was an important year in the company's annals. In the same year that it was able to raise $46 million in an initial public offering, the Food and Drug Administration (FDA) approved use of the *da Vinci* Surgical System for general laparoscopic surgery. The following year, it was approved for use in prostate surgery, and has continued to be approved for further uses since. The growth of Intuitive Surgical relies upon the continued adoption and FDA clearance for an increasing number of surgical procedures. Since receiving FDA approval for laparoscopic surgery in 2000, Intuitive Surgical has been approved for uses in the following procedures:[2]

- March 2001   —Non-cardiac thoracoscopic procedures
- May 2001   —Prostatectomy procedures
- November 2002   —Cardiotomy procedures
- July 2004   —Cardiac revascularization procedures
- March 2005   —Urologic surgical procedures
- June 2005   —Pediatric surgical procedures

4   Shortly before going public in 2000, the company was sued for patent infringement by Computer Motion, Inc., its chief rival at that time. Computer Motion had gotten into the robotic surgery field with its ZEUS Robotic Surgical System. In 2000, ISRG's *da Vinci* system had only been approved for use in Europe, they had not yet received FDA approval for use in the US. After years of litigation, Computer Motion agreed to a merger in 2003.[3] The newly merged company favored the *da Vinci* system, and ZEUS was phased out.

5   Headquartered in Sunnyvale, CA, Intuitive Surgical has approximately 850 employees and serves hospitals and academic institutions throughout the world. The company markets its products through sales representatives in the United States and through a combination of sales representatives and distributors in international markets.[4] Retailing for approximately $700,000 to $2.3 million, there have been 1,171 unit shipments worldwide as of March 31, 2009 with sales of 863 in North America, 211 in Europe, and 97 elsewhere (Ref 5).

THE *DA VINCI* SURGICAL SYSTEM

6   Intuitive Surgical's main product is the *da Vinci* Surgical System—a robotic surgical system designed to perform urologic, gynecologic, cardiothoracic, and general surgeries that are much less invasive than traditional surgery. The *da Vinci* Surgical System represents a disruptive technology in the healthcare market. Intuitive Surgical has pursued a "razor blade" product marketing strategy by offering a variety of proprietary surgical instruments and accessories for use in performing *da Vinci* surgeries as well as service and training contracts for institutions that purchase the system. This product strategy has essentially created dual monopolies for Intuitive Surgical. The first is the monopoly on robotic surgical systems due to the current lack of competition in the industry and the second is a monopoly over the *da Vinci* accessories and service market as customers are locked in to utilizing Intuitive Surgical for service, training, and maintenance once they have purchased a *da Vinci* Surgical System.

7   The *da Vinci* system has received FDA clearance for general laparoscopic, thoracoscopic, and thoracoscopically-assisted cardiotomy procedures. Intuitive Surgical is required to maintain accurate and detailed records of its servicing and parts repair process in order to meet FDA regulations. There are 3,000 different parts on a *da Vinci* Surgical System, many very sophisticated. Thus, the repair and reuse of parts is both complex and an important function of cost control.[6] Due to the complexity of the *da Vinci* system, quality must never be shortsighted. Patients' lives depend on the accuracy of the instruments. One slight error in calibration could result in a fatality which would be detrimental to the company. Legal implications would likely follow.

8   "At Intuitive Surgical, our priority is to achieve optimal customer satisfaction through superior product design, reliability and quality."[7] Intuitive Surgical offers an array of training programs including on-site *da Vinci* Surgical System training and off-site *da Vinci* surgical skills training. There are currently 19 active training centers in the United States and 2 in Europe. A list of the training centers is provided in Exhibit A. The off-site training consists of Live Procedure Observation and Surgeon Led Training. Live Procedure Observation training provides a novice *da Vinci* surgeon with the opportunity to observe an experienced *da Vinci* surgeon. The topics covered include: patient indications and selection, robotic-assisted surgical technique, anatomical reference, patient preparation, surgical positioning, port placement and instrumentation applications.[8] The complexity of the instrument creates a long learning curve for the surgeons. Therefore, the surgeons must be willing to commit their time to learning the functionalities of the system. They would be away from work and most often away from home during training.

EXHIBIT A   **Intuitive Surgical Training Centers**

US Training Centers
Boston Children's Hospital—Boston, MA
Clarian North—Carmel, IN
East Carolina Univ. Hospital—Greenville, NC
Ethicon Endosurgery Institute—Cincinnati, OH
Florida Hospital, Celebration—Orlando, FL
Good Samaritan Hospital—Cincinnati, OH
Hackensack Univ. Med. Center—Hackensack, NJ
Hospital, Univ. Pennsylvania—Philadelphia, PA
Intuitive Surgical Headquarters—Sunnyvale, CA
Johns Hopkins Univ. Hospital—Baltimore, MD
Memorial Hermann Med. Center—Houston, TX
Methodist Hospital—Houston, TX
Newark Beth Israel Medical Center—Newark, NJ
Ochsner Hospital—New Orleans, LA
Ohio State University Hospital—Columbus, OH
Uniformed Service University—Bethesda, MD
Univ. California, Irvine—Irvine, CA
Univ. California, San Diego—San Diego, CA
Univ. Illinois, Chicago—Chicago, IL
European Training Centers
IRCAD—Strasbourg, France
Prince of Wales Hospital, Chinese Univ. of Hong Kong

Source: IntuitiveSurgical.com

9   The *da Vinci* equipment is highly complex and sophisticated, therefore providing excellent service and maintenance is a challenge. Intuitive Surgical must be able to provide customers with fast, efficient and high-quality assistance for servicing the *da Vinci* Surgical System and must provide the appropriate add-on equipment. In order to achieve these metrics, Intuitive Surgical utilizes Amdocs CRM. This application provides Intuitive Surgical with a single view of its customers which has improved both customer service and how the company manages its complex inventory supply and repair processes. Since implementation, Intuitive Surgical has been able to reduce costs while continuing to grow its staff of field engineers in order to deliver faster service with less administration. Amdocs CRM has also enabled Intuitive Surgical to streamline its inventory by reducing the likelihood of overstocking, which is costly, and under-stocking, which could lead to delays in supplying critical parts to hospitals.[9] These results were noted earlier, as Intuitive Surgical has maintained consistent inventory levels amid strong growth. Despite these positive results, depending on technology can pose as a weakness in the chance that the systems utilized become obsolete and require upgrades and re-installations, which can be costly and time consuming.

STRATEGIC DIRECTION

10   Intuitive Surgical is in the business of offering minimally invasive robotic technology to improve surgical procedures. At the time of its debut in 1997, the technology for robotic-assisted MIS was a disruptive technology, pushing the limitations of surgery to vastly improve results for patients. The company's *da Vinci* Surgical System is currently the most widely used robotic surgical system in this emerging industry. As a first-mover for this technology, Intuitive Surgical enjoys the majority of market share and has had the benefit of establishing its brand before competitors enter the market. Continued investment in the development and marketing of this technology will allow the firm to maintain its dominant position well into the future.[10,11]

11   In its 2008 Annual Report Letter to the Shareholders, Intuitive Surgical emphasizes its goal to "take surgery beyond the limits of the human hand."[12] Intuitive Surgical's vision is "to extend the benefits of minimally invasive surgery to the broadest possible range of patients, while providing extraordinary value for its customers, investors and employees."[13] By introducing advanced technology into the surgical arena, the company seeks to increase what it refers to as "Patient Value."[14] Patient Value is measured by Intuitive Surgical as the ratio of procedure efficacy to invasiveness of the procedure:

$$\text{Patient} = \frac{\text{Efficacy of the Procedure}}{\text{Invasiveness}^2}$$

12   Robotic assistance makes the human elements of surgery more constant and accurate. More stable visual feedback and agile movement on the part of the robotic hands allow the surgeon to perform more effectively. At the same time, invasiveness is reduced by the insertion of small surgical instruments and an endoscope through significantly smaller incisions than would be used for open surgery. In this way, invasiveness is reduced and effectiveness increased simultaneously for each procedure, exponentially increasing Patient Value.[15]

13   Intuitive Surgical's primary objective is profitable growth. Its strategic objectives—which in turn help to meet financial objectives for shareholders—are the following:[16]

- **Focus on Key Procedures.** The procedures on which Intuitive Surgical are primarily focused (in order of size of business) are urologic surgery (prostatectomy, nephrectomy, cystectomy, pyeloplasty), gynecologic surgery (hysterectomy, myomectomy, sacral colpopexy), cardiothoracic surgery (mitral valve repair, revascularization), and general surgery (gastric bypass). Upon FDA approval, Intuitive Surgical is able to proceed into more intricate procedures, generating continued growth for shareholders.

- *Focus on Key Institutions.* The firm focuses on academic and community hospitals. When a hospital purchases one of the robotic systems, Intuitive Surgical helps educate surgeons and patients about the benefits of the machine. Maximum use of the systems and customer satisfaction will stimulate the purchase of more instruments and whole systems.

- *Focus on Leading Surgeons to Drive Rapid and Broad Adoption.* By focusing on the "thought leaders" in each medical field, Intuitive Surgical can utilize a superior word-of-mouth channel of system adoption. The surgeons targeted for system adoption are well-respected and their published experiences are relied on by peers in their fields. Trust in the systems for current procedures helps build confidence for use of the system on procedures that do not yet utilize robotic assistance.

- *Maintain Market Leadership.* Intuitive Surgical suggests that it will maintain its dominance in this new market "by continuing to develop and enhance [its] technology." Software developments, hardware developments, and new surgical instruments enhance the usefulness of the existing systems and pave the way for future developments in robotic surgery.

- *Develop Industry Alliances.* Intuitive Surgical will "continue to establish strategic alliances with leading medical device companies . . . in the areas of product development, training, and procedure development and marketing activities, [with such companies as] Gyrus ACMI, Johnson & Johnson, Johns Hopkins University, Novadaq Technologies, Inc., Olympus Corporation, Power Medical Inc., SurgiQuest, Inc. and USGI Medical, Inc."

- *Increase Patient Awareness.* More than ever before, patients and their family members are using the Internet as a resource for educating themselves to make healthcare decisions, including those related to surgical treatment options. Intuitive Surgical will take advantage of Internet opportunities to educate potential patients and healthcare providers on the benefits of robotic surgery via the *da Vinci* system.

14   Intuitive Surgical is the first-mover in the robotic-assisted surgical console market. The physical benefits of the new technology for patients have been widely communicated through statistical studies, surgeon support, and patient testimonies. Gradually, evidence of the cost-benefit value of the equipment is also persuading hospitals worldwide to make a rather large investment in the *da Vinci* Surgical System. The potential for industry growth is immense, and improvements in existing technology will only speed up robotic technology adoption rates in medical facilities.

15   ISRG is dedicated to providing a unique, differentiated product that changes the surgical process. Not only does the system increase Patient Value by decreasing invasiveness and increasing effectiveness, the *da Vinci* system also decreases hospital costs by reducing time spent in recovery (see Exhibit B). With faster patient turnover, hospitals will gain capacity

EXHIBIT B   Length of Hospital Stay after Hysterectomy

| Surgery | Length of Hospital Stay | | | | |
	da Vinci	Open	Difference	Laparascopic	Difference
Cancer	1.45	7.75	**6.3**	2.67	**1.22**
Benign	1.19	6.04	**4.85**	2.45	**1.26**

Source: Letter to the Shareholders, 2008 Annual Report. Page 3 to perform more procedures. With improved surgery results, fewer patients will have complications and thus will not require admittance or further surgery.[17] With its compounding benefits for hospitals that adopt it, the *da Vinci* Surgical System is well positioned to sell at high margins, and with rapid growth in sales, as the medical community converts to robotic-assisted MIS for many surgical procedures.

ISRG's BUSINESS MODEL

16   Intuitive Surgical implements a "razor blade" business model, generating revenue from both the initial capital sales of *da Vinci* Surgical Systems as well as recurring revenue, comprised of instrument, accessory, and service revenue. The *da Vinci* Surgical System generally sells for approximately $0.7 million to $2.3 million, depending on the selected configuration, includes one year of service, and represents a significant capital equipment investment for customers. Recurring revenue is generated as Intuitive Surgical's customers purchase their EndoWrist instruments and accessory products for use in performing procedures with the *da Vinci* Surgical System. EndoWrist instruments and accessories will either expire or wear out as they are used in surgery and will need to be replaced as they are consumed. They generate additional recurring revenue from ongoing system service, with customers typically entering into service contracts at the time the system is sold. These service contracts have been generally renewable at the end of the service period, typically with annual rates of approximately $100,000 to $180,000 per year, depending on the configuration of the underlying system.[18]

17   The services required to keep this robotic technology fully updated and optimally functioning create an opportunity for steady revenues. The *da Vinci* Surgical System sales price includes one year of service. Intuitive Surgical then contracts out annual service agreements on the devices at a cost of $100,000 to $180,000, creating a revolving revenue stream after the initial sale. As with the systems themselves, Intuitive Surgical also holds a monopoly over the market for associated services on its systems. An added opportunity for revenue flows exists with relation to the need for additional instruments and accessories for the devices.

POTENTIAL COMPETITION ON THE HORIZON

18   The overall industry attractiveness in medical robotics is strong. This is a new industry where profit margins and growth potential are high. As the industry attracts competition, there will be great pressure to add value for customers by maximizing equipment functionality and minimizing the cost. The current threat of existing competitors is weak, but increasing. Intuitive Surgical has a monopoly in robotic surgical systems. Today, Intuitive Surgical does not have any true competitors that would have a detrimental effect on their business. The possibility of a new competitor entering the market with its own technology exists, but such a company would face a growing competitive disadvantage. Intuitive Surgical is currently experiencing the benefits stemming from having the first-mover advantage in medical robotic surgery. Would-be competitors Hansen Medical and Stereotaxis both sell surgical robots, but for a different range of surgeries focused on catheter-based methods within the cardiac anatomy.[19] Another potential competitor is a robot that was developed in Korea, which features an internet-based interface, and may prove to be useful for remote surgery on the battlefield. However, in a hospital setting, most surgeons prefer to be in the same room as the patient.[20]

19   Although they do not compete directly against Intuitive Surgical now, companies such as Hitachi and Toshiba have the knowledge and resources necessary to develop competing robotic surgical systems.

Potential New Entrants: Hitachi, LTD. and Toshiba

20   Hitachi, Ltd., founded in 1910 and incorporated in 1920, with headquarters located in Tokyo, has a diversified portfolio with annual revenue of approximately $113 billion as reported for December 31, 2008. Hitachi operates in seven segments: Information & Telecommunication Systems, Electronic Devices, Power & Industrial Systems, Digital Media & Consumer Products, High Functional Materials & Components, Logistics, Services & Others and Financial Services. The company's Electronic Devices segment offers liquid crystal displays (LCD); semiconductor manufacturing, test and measurement, and medical electronics equipment; and semiconductors. Hitachi serves industrial companies, financial institutions, utilities, governments, and individual customers primarily in Japan, Asia, North America, and Europe.[21] As seen in Hitachi's portfolio, the company is not afraid to branch off into new businesses. Creating many strategic partnerships and collaborative relationships with large corporations such as General Electric, Matsushita, and Clarion, Hitachi will remain a strong competitor in the medical device industry.

21   Toshiba Corporation resulted from the merging of Tokyo Electric Company and Shibaura Engineering Works Co., Ltd. in 1939.[22] Headquartered in Tokyo, with annual revenues of approximately $80 billion, the company produces an array of products that provide the consumer with the capability of computing, controlling, powering, communicating, transporting, cooking, playing, or elevating. The products include personal and professional computers (notebook PCs, servers), telecommunications and medical equipment (mobile phones, X-ray machines), industrial machinery (power plant reactors, elevators), consumer appliances (microwaves, DVD players), electronic components (electron tubes, batteries), and semiconductors. Toshiba also provides equipment used in air traffic control and railway transportation systems.[23] The company continues to develop innovative technologies centering on the fields of Electronics and Energy. It strives to create products and services that will enhance human life and ultimately lead to a thriving, healthy society.[24] Toshiba also maintains many strategic partnerships with companies such as Fujitsu and Vital Images. The partnerships and continuous effort towards implementing innovative products will continue to add to the company's competitive advantage.

22   Intuitive Surgical also competes against the hospitals and physicians who prefer to conduct traditional open surgeries by hand, rather than using robotics. For a medical facility currently facing challenging economic times, the cost of a *da Vinci* Surgical System, the training of specialists, and the upkeep of the equipment are expensive.

23   The company is faced with the challenge of taking market share away from these traditional methods. Though it is not an easy task to overcome aversion to new technology, Intuitive Surgical is making great strides in providing value to patients and hospitals. "The *da Vinci* is expensive, but at the end of the day it's allowing the hospital to do better surgery," said Tao Levy of Deutsche Bank North America. "Also, hospitals without the device run the risk of losing business to those who have it."[25]

24   Intuitive Surgical now has a large and globally growing installed base of equipment. One competitive edge helping Intuitive Surgical is that it has "the deepest and broadest intellectual property portfolio of all the surgical robot companies," according to an Oppenheimer research report on September 2, 2008.[26] As the company continues to expand its presence in surgical procedures, the threat of traditional surgery as a competing method is shrinking. Additionally, the growing global base of *da Vinci* Surgical Systems will prove invaluable as

competitors attempt to enter the market in ten to fifteen years when Intuitive Surgical's key technology patents begin to expire.

Barriers to Entry

25   Barriers to entry in the robotic surgery industry are moderate but increasing. Intuitive Surgical expects new entrants to attempt to enter the robotic-assisted surgery industry in the near term due in part to the dramatic success of the *da Vinci* Surgical System. As previously mentioned, the most likely new entrants are established technology or medical supply companies that have the necessary capital, R&D [research and development] capabilities, and healthcare contacts. Intuitive Surgical can construct barriers to entry by accelerating growth and capturing a larger proportion of the potential market before competition has a chance to enter—diminishing the likely ROI [return on investment] for new entrants and making entry to the industry less attractive. Intuitive Surgical is aggressively taking full advantage of patent and trademark protections while locking up relationships with key healthcare institutions and physicians to deter future market entrants.

26   Intuitive Surgical CEO [chief executive officer] Lonnie Smith discussed the company's strategy to protect their leadership position in an interview with the Motley Fool:

> We are building a very attractive surgical category that will certainly invite competition . . . but we can and will continue to build barriers to entry, such as superior product offerings, intellectual property protection, multiple regulatory clearances, a large installation base, worldwide training centers, strong customer relationships, and an excellent balance sheet.[27]

27   Intuitive Surgical holds a number of valuable patents. New competitors entering the industry cannot legally copy the majority of technology Intuitive Surgical produces. Under the protection of these patents, the company has a monopoly in the robotic-assisted MIS market.

28   The company has *da Vinci* Surgical Systems installed in many hospitals already, and continues to grow its customer base. Many surgeons have acquired the knowledge necessary to perform a procedure using the *da Vinci*. As competitors enter the market when Intuitive Surgical's patents expire, the switching costs for a hospital will be high, requiring both time and capital investment.[28]

29   Since they are the industry first-mover, Intuitive Surgical has had the opportunity to work with many universities around the world, providing them an opportunity to network with future surgeons. Such networks are a resource that will be difficult for competitors to break into in future years.

30   Intuitive Surgical is in a strong financial position with an abundance of cash and minimal liabilities. This position allows the company flexibility and discretion while making capital investments.

31   While the *da Vinci* is FDA-approved, regulations in other nations are often less stringent and the opportunity exists for rapid development in international markets among more complex procedures. Although the less rigid regulations abroad allow faster introduction of technological breakthroughs, Intuitive Surgical must be careful not to soil its reputation by failing to ensure a safe product before taking it to market. A balance must be struck between the opportunity for quicker procedure adoption and the threat of damage to reputation should the technology cause any problems with its new procedures.

32   FDA approval for each procedure can consume significant time and resources on the part of innovators. A competitor may gain approval first, with the right legal team and political connections, gaining a brand marketing advantage by being the first to offer support for a given procedure.

33   Product recalls can pose a significant threat. If the robotic technology is later found to have potential problems, strict FDA regulation can impede development and even prevent

the use of existing systems. Even for component recalls, replacing parts of the systems that are already distributed to customers will be costly to companies such as Intuitive Surgical.

34 Lawsuits over system malfunctions are another threat to the robotic surgery industry. New technology can carry major legal risks in the sense that glitches can cause harm to consumers. Because robotic surgery puts people's lives in the robot's "hands," errors can be fatal. Injured patients or their families would be quick to blame the new technology. Strong controls must be in place to verify the machinery's accuracy in the instance of malpractice. If it is not abundantly clear that the machine was well-calibrated, and appropriately maintained [,] the likelihood of being sued for malpractice is inevitable.

35 Because of this increased statistical evidence, as well as the general acceptance stemming from more familiarity, patient demand for the availability of surgical robotics is increasing exponentially. This is pushing healthcare providers to wide-scale adoption, and thus providing Intuitive Surgical with ever-increasing demand.

THE 2009 RECESSION

36 The current recession is an opportunity for Intuitive Surgical because of its strong financial position. Intuitive Surgical carries no long-term debt, positioning the organization well under difficult market conditions when lending is tight. Where other firms may lose the opportunity to invest in entering this market, Intuitive Surgical is able to keep investing in R&D to maintain its hold on the new industry.

37 In an effort to stimulate the economy, the Obama Administration plans to invest significant funds in infrastructure and industries that support American jobs.[29] Potential increases in government spending on healthcare initiatives would leave hospitals with more resources to make large capital purchases, such as the *da Vinci* Surgical System.

38 The current economic recession poses a major threat to growth in the robotic surgical systems industry. The *da Vinci* Surgical System is quite expensive, ranging from $0.7 million to $2.3 million. This is a major capital expenditure for healthcare providers. Even with increased government funding, medical institutions, as with most companies, are faced with the need to reduce costs as much as possible. Market conditions are especially difficult right now, leading a greater number of healthcare providers to avoid or postpone making major capital purchases. For many healthcare providers, the cost is simply too great to make the purchase. Intuitive Surgical may be in a strong financial position, but if customers lack the funds to buy its products, growth and earnings will be negatively impacted.

39 As wars wage overseas, potential competitors of Intuitive Surgical have been investing in smaller, more portable robotics that will facilitate remote surgery. In other words, they envision the possibility of surgeons away from the field being available on demand to perform necessary surgery to save soldiers' lives when they otherwise face the threat of death en route to surgery. An investment in the reduction of size and weight of its existing technology may provide future opportunities for military applications.

40 In civilian medicine, if size, initial costs, and maintenance expenses can be reduced, this product has the potential to become a common tool at local hospitals. From a remote location, the best doctors in the world could perform surgeries. There are obvious obstacles to realizing this opportunity (training assistants, getting doctors comfortable with remote surgery, etc.), and it may be years off, but this seemingly impossible market might be the next blue ocean opportunity in robotic surgery. High quality surgical procedures would be more readily available, thus granting patients the ability to schedule sooner, have the procedure done closer to home, and, of course, to recover faster and go home earlier.

41　　An opportunity for the industry is the increasing age of the population, as baby boomers reach ages at which surgical procedures become a more probable requirement. The increasing need for surgery for the elderly, especially for safer, less invasive surgery, lends itself to high demand for more effective, less invasive, robotic-assisted surgery. Surgery in the elderly is associated with much higher risks than that for younger patients. Major open surgery can have a negative impact on brain functionality for older patients. The likelihood of complications could be minimized through the use of robotic-assisted MIS (Ref 30).

42　　Medical advances such as robotic surgery continue to extend life expectancy around the world. Extended life could mean a higher number of surgeries per person during a lifetime. Compounding this opportunity, each successful robotic surgery that saves a life potentially opens the opportunity for a future robotic-assisted surgical procedure. Though individuals are becoming healthier and surgical procedures are more effective, significantly increased life spans allow for more surgical procedures.

43　　With the advancement of safety through robotic technology, more healthcare providers and patients will feel secure in accepting the robotic-assisted surgical procedures. In surgery, safety is the primary concern. Thus, the safer this technology proves to be, the more widely it will be used.

44　　By increasing the tactile feedback capabilities of the system, Intuitive Surgical will appeal to surgeons who currently list this as a primary reason not to adopt.[31] The "feel" of the system for the surgeon is extremely important. The more this element of the technology evolves, the more surgeons will be willing to adopt it. An added benefit of increased tactile feedback can take place in the form of decreased training time for new users.

45　　This leads to another technological opportunity in training capabilities. As the training for these systems becomes stronger and faster, the barriers to implementation will continue to decline. This will favorably influence adoption of the systems.

2016: PATENTS EXPIRATION

46　　There are many technological threats that Intuitive Surgical faces in this marketplace. One of the most important is the impending expiration of existing patents. ISRG's last patent is due to expire in 2016. Intuitive Surgical has done a good job of protecting its IP and patenting technologies when possible. Once these patents are up, however, competitors will be able to utilize those technologies in the marketplace and that particular competitive advantage will be lost.

47　　As the technology used by Intuitive Surgical becomes more widely understood, it could become easier to copy or mimic. Through access to patent information (at expiration) and reverse engineering, competitors could enter the market with the same technological solutions found at Intuitive Surgical.

48　　Once in the market, competitors could make advances in the industry ahead of Intuitive Surgical to gain market share. Because Intuitive Surgical is primarily focused on its *da Vinci* Surgical Systems, the company could miss opportunities in new emerging robotic technologies. If competitors are able to patent these types of technologies, Intuitive Surgical may find itself on the outside looking in.

49　　The robotic surgery industry is an attractive one for competitors due to high margins, high growth opportunity, and a lack of existing competition. The barriers to entry involving technology, however, are still high. The cost of developing robotic surgical systems is high and therefore makes it difficult to enter the market. As the cost of robotic technology development decreases, Intuitive Surgical will face significant competition and could lose some of its market share.

50   With technology, there is always something new and improved on the horizon. It is possible that there could be a new, revolutionary technology not yet conceived which pulls the industry away from robotics. For now, however, robotics appear to be the future of surgical procedures.

51   Global markets are a major opportunity because they increase overall market potential. For robotic MIS, the market potential is as large as the number of hospitals in the world. At first, hospitals in developed nations will be the primary market as those hospitals are more likely to have the funding to purchase this new, expensive technology. As prices are reduced and the technology becomes more affordable, less-developed nations may seek this technology for their hospitals. Finally, as the technology proves its value, placement of the systems in severely underdeveloped nations may be supported by NPOs or various government powers.

52   Differing regulations abroad can create opportunities for faster technological developments. As products are released in other nations, a marketing opportunity can be generated where a brand can become well-known globally even while the product is still held up in the processes for FDA approval.

53   International operations can also mean an expanded resource pool. Rather than limiting researchers and other employees to only Americans, Intuitive Surgical has the opportunity to hire on a global basis, seeking only the most talented individuals available worldwide.

FINANCIAL OPERATIONS

54   In the past decade, Intuitive Surgical has experienced consistently improving revenues. As seen in Exhibit C, the company has not failed to achieve double-digit growth since it ended its litigation and acquired Computer Motion. As revenue has increased, Intuitive Surgical has managed to maintain high operating margins, averaging upwards of 35%. This is evidence of the company's ability to control operating costs and utilize resources effectively as the size of business has multiplied (see Exhibit D).

55   During this period of growth, the product mix has remained consistent. As was mentioned previously, Intuitive Surgical generates revenue through sales of the *da Vinci* units

EXHIBIT C
Intuitive Surgical Year-Over-Year Revenue Growth 2004 to 2008

Source of Data for Analysis: MorningStar "ISRG"

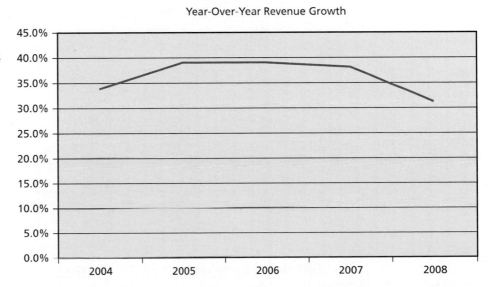

Year-Over-Year Revenue Growth

EXHIBIT D
Intuitive Surgical
Operating Margins
2004 to 2008

Source of Data for Analysis:
MorningStar "ISRG"

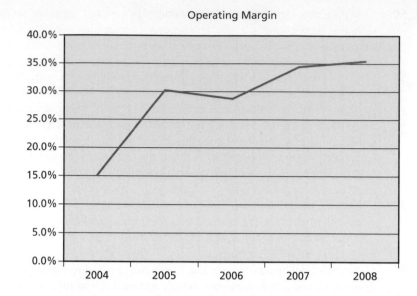

Operating Margin

themselves, the instruments and accessories that are necessary for the procedures themselves, and the corresponding service agreements. The mix has remained consistent, as noted in (see Exhibit E), with unit sales comprising more than half of gross sales. However, instruments and accessories sales have increased over the last several years as the adoption of increased procedures has opened the door for greater revenue growth in this area.

56   Quarterly results have been consistent with annual results. In Exhibits F and G, we can see that Intuitive Surgical has improved on quarterly results in both revenue and operating income. During this period of consistent growth, the company exceeded Wall Street's expectations. However, as the economy as a whole declined in 2008, so did the expectations from Wall Street. Since the equipment is capital intensive, there are expectations that Intuitive Surgical's results will decline in accordance with tighter budgetary restrictions set

EXHIBIT E
Intuitive Surgical
Product Mix

Source of Data for Analysis:
MorningStar "ISRG"

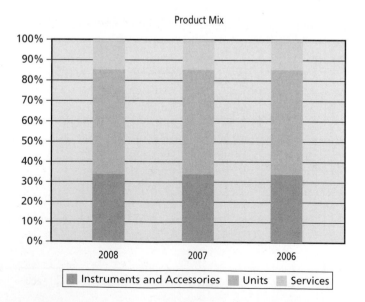

Product Mix

EXHIBIT F
Intuitive Surgical
Quarterly Revenue
Q1-07 to Q1-09

Source of Data for Analysis:
MorningStar "ISRG"

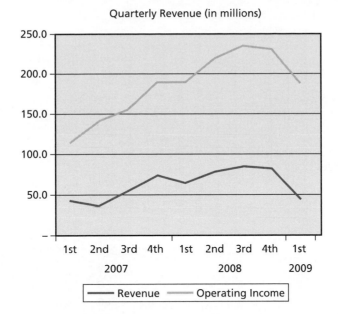

Quarterly Revenue (in millions)

forth by many hospitals and university institutions. Exhibit H shows the market price during this period and the ride it has taken. Of note are the first quarter 2009 results. This revenue has remained flat compared to the same period in 2008, but exceeded expectations for the quarter. When this was announced in April 2009, the stock price increased accordingly in response.

57   Of significant note is the lack of any long-term debt on the balance sheet (see Exhibit I). After financing capital expenditures in its infancy, the company has essentially been debt-free since 2004. The lack of the burden of debt payments has lead to increasing cash (and investment) reserves. From Exhibit J, we can see that the percentage of cash and investments has increased significantly, to 60% of total assets (approximately $900 million at December 31, 2008). This has provided the company with added security during the current recession, as they have reserves to fall and rely on if necessary.

58   This advantageous cash position has allowed Intuitive Surgical to explore a stock buy-back program. In March 2009, the Board of Directors authorized the repurchase of up to $300 million of the company's outstanding shares through a variety of means. Through the end of the First Quarter of 2009, Intuitive Surgical repurchased $150 million worth of shares.[32] The number of shares they are ultimately able to repurchase will depend on the activity of the market itself. As mentioned in the previous section, the stock price has fluctuated greatly over the past year. Accelerating the program now to take further advantage of the current climate is a way for management to capitalize on Wall Street's lowered expectations during a recessionary market.

59   The current economic climate has affected this company as well as most of the economy, and despite these reserves the company is playing a cautious hand. It has bought more land where it is headquartered, but has delayed construction of new facilities until 2010 as it awaits what the market will be like then. Although the company is holding off on some of its capital investment, it intends to keep research and development spending at its current levels, which for years 2006, 2007, and 2008 have been (as a percentage of revenue) 8%, 8%, and 9%, respectively. In order to secure its future, Intuitive Surgical cannot afford to cut back on the technology that will make a successful future a reality.

EXHIBIT G   ISRG Income Statement

	2008 12/31/08	2007 12/31/07	2006 12/31/06	2005 12/31/05
NET SALES OR REVENUES	874,919	600,828	372,682	227,338
Cost of Goods Sold (Excl Depreciation)	229,058	173,515	114,837	67,042
Depreciation, Depletion And Amortization	25,084	13,027	10,009	6,727
Depreciation	14,633	11,011	8,269	4,859
Amortization of Intangibles	10,451	2,016	1,740	1,868
Amortization of Deferred Charges	0	0	0	0
GROSS INCOME	620,777	414,286	247,836	153,569
Selling, General & Admin Expenses	309,942	207,544	140,481	84,797
Other Operating Expenses	0	0	0	0
Research and Development Expense	79,372	48,859	29,778	17,354
OPERATING INCOME	310,835	206,742	107,355	68,772
Extraordinary Credit—Pretax	11,600	0	0	0
Extraordinary Charge—Pretax	0	0	0	0
Non-Operating Interest Income	14,268	23,300	11,400	5,569
Other Income/Expenses—Net	(1,500)	7,192	1,383	(517)
Interest Expense On Debt	0	0	—	17
Interest Capitalized	0	0	0	0
PRETAX INCOME	335,203	237,234	120,138	73,807
Income Taxes	(130,888)	(92,697)	(48,094)	20,327
Current Domestic Income Tax	150,859	91,379	36,446	(60)
Current Foreign Income Tax	600	590	216	248
Deferred Domestic Income Tax	(20,834)	728	11,432	(22,227)
Deferred Foreign Income Tax	263	0	0	0
Income Tax Credits	0	0	0	(1,712)
Minority Interest	0	0	0	0
Equity in Earnings	0	0	0	0
After Tax Other Income/Expense	0	0	0	0
Discontinued Operations	0	0	0	0
NET INCOME BEFORE EXTRA ITEMS/PREFERRED DIVIDENDS	204,315	144,537	72,044	94,134
Extra Items & Gain/Loss Sale of Assets	0	0	0	0
Preferred Dividend Requirements	0	0	0	0
NET INCOME USED TO CALCULATE BASIC EARNINGS PER SHARE	204,315	144,537	72,044	94,134
Shares used in computing earnings per share—Basic	—	—	—	—
Shares used in computing earnings per share—Fully Diluted	39,943	39,021	38,093	37,488
Earning per Common Share—Basic	5.26	3.82	1.96	2.68
Earning per Common Share—Fully Diluted	5.12	3.70	1.89	2.51

() = Negative Values

Values are displayed in Thousands except for earnings per share Resources.

EXHIBIT H
Stock Prices April 22, 2007 to April 22, 2009

Source: Yahoo! Finance, "ISRG"

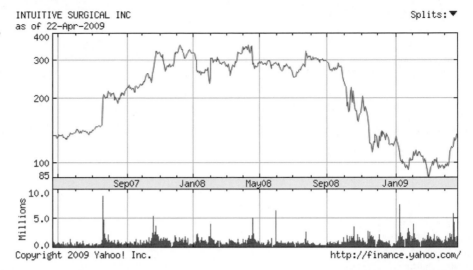

INTUITIVE SURGICAL INC
as of 22-Apr-2009

Splits: ▼

Copyright 2009 Yahoo! Inc.   http://finance.yahoo.com/

60   In the first quarter of 2009, efforts from the company's research and development investment came to fruition with the release of the *da Vinci Si*. This introduced three significant innovations from the previous model. First, it introduced a dual surgeons' console for use during surgery and for training. This hopes to open the door for further procedures being utilized through use of the equipment. Secondly, the imaging system was updated to incorporate a high definition picture to increase surgeon precision. Lastly, the interface was improved to make it more user-friendly. Through the introduction of the new model, the expectation is to get existing customers to upgrade to the system, along with the instruments and accessories that are needed.[33]

MARKETING

61   Intuitive Surgical's marketing tactics focus on communicating the value of the *da Vinci* Surgical System to patients, physicians, and hospitals. Marketing collateral targeted at patients touts the benefits of shorter hospital stays, faster recovery, and decreased pain. The following paragraph from an Intuitive Surgical marketing brochure illustrates their message strategy of comparing the benefits of *da Vinci* minimally invasive surgery to traditional surgeries:

> For most patients, dVP offers substantially less pain and a much shorter recovery than traditional prostatectomy. Other advantages include reduced need for blood transfusions; less scaring and less risk of infection. Moreover, studies suggest that dVP may offer improved cancer control and lower incidence of impotence and urinary incontinence.

62   This messaging seems to be designed to scare patients about the risks of traditional surgery while communicating the *da Vinci* Surgical System's ability to mitigate those risks—with the hope that patients will ask their physicians about *da Vinci* surgery or schedule their surgery at a facility that already has a *da Vinci* Surgical System.

63   A similar tactic is utilized in marketing materials directed at physicians and hospitals as Intuitive Surgical explains the cost savings, improved quality of care, and increased revenue that can result from purchasing a *da Vinci* Surgical System—while simultaneously hinting at the risk of becoming obsolete if they continue to only offer traditional surgeries.

EXHIBIT I   ISRG Balance Sheet

	2008 12/31/08	2007 12/31/07	2006 12/31/06
Cash	195	123	34
Short-Term Investments	257	305	205
ASSETS			
Cash & Short-Term Investments	**451**	**427**	**240**
Receivables—Net	**170**	**130**	**95**
Raw Materials	20	13	9
Work-in-Progress	4	3	2
Finished Goods	39	16	13
Inventories—Total	**63**	**32**	**24**
Prepaid Expenses	**—**	**—**	**—**
Other Current Assets	**19**	**19**	**16**
CURRENT ASSETS—TOTAL	**704**	**610**	**374**
Land	34	16	16
Buildings	38	23	23
Machinery & Equipment	32	26	20
Other Property, Plant & Equipment	—	13	10
Property, Plant, & Equipment under Capitalized Leases	—	—	—
Property, Plant and Equipment—Gross	164	102	85
Accumulated Depreciation	(47)	(34)	(25)
Property, Plant and Equipment—Net	**117**	**68**	**60**
Other Investments	451	208	91
Other Tangible Assets	346K	1	521K
Total Intangible Other Assets—Net	167	134	124
Other Assets—Total	**203**	**154**	**147**
TOTAL ASSETS	**1,439**	**1,021**	**650**
LIABILITIES			
Accounts Payable	21	30	11
Accrued Payroll	37	30	21
Other Current Liabilities	107	72	48
CURRENT LIABILITIES—TOTAL	**165**	**132**	**81**
Long Term Debt	**0**	**0**	**0**
Deferred Income	**1**	**875K**	**—**
Deferred Taxes—Debit	36	19	22
DEFERRED TAXES	**(36)**	**(19)**	**(22)**
Other Liabilities	**42**	**19**	**1**
TOTAL LIABILITIES	**172**	**133**	**60**
EQUITY			
Non-Equity Reserves	**0**	**0**	**0**
Minority Interest	**0**	**0**	**0**
Preferred Stock	**0**	**0**	**0**
Common Stock	39K	38K	37K
Capital Surplus	872	695	538
Retained Earnings	398	194	51

EXHIBIT I ISRG Balance Sheet (*Continued*)

	2008 12/31/08	2007 12/31/07	2006 12/31/06
Unrealized Foreign Exchange Gain/Loss	227K	118K	106K
Unrealized Gain/Loss on Marketable Securities	(3)	412K	599K
COMMON EQUITY	**1,267**	**889**	**590**
TOTAL LIABILITIES & SHAREHOLDERS' EQUITY	**1,439**	**1,021**	**650**
SHARE INFORMATION			
Common Shares Outstanding	39	38	37

() = Negative Values
Values are displayed in Millions except for earnings per share and where noted XI.

EXHIBIT J
**Intuitive Surgical
Cash Position**

Source of Data for Analysis:
MorningStar "ISRG"

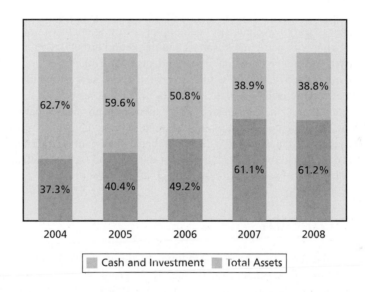

OPERATIONS

64 Intuitive Surgical has more than 500 patents globally, covering various technologies related to its robotics systems. These patents would make it difficult for a competitor to enter the market and design an equally effective product.[34] At the end of fiscal year 2007, Intuitive Surgical held exclusive field-of-use as well as non-exclusive licenses for over 200 U.S. patents and over 90 foreign patents, and owned outright over 140 U.S. patents and over 60 foreign patents.[35] Creating patents requires a great deal of time and is costly to the company. Another weakness related to having many patents is with the rapid improvements in technology, the patents in existence may become obsolete if a better, more efficient, more cost effective product is discovered.

AREAS OF CONCERN

65 One major concern tied to the robotic surgery industry is the possible displacement of surgeons and nurses at client facilities. Intuitive Surgical's marketing materials include a focus on cost savings from reduced surgical nursing staff in hospitals. Hospital workers and unions will no doubt find this a major concern and could create problems with system adoption in their hospitals.

66   Another major concern is the safety of the devices, or the potential flaws therein. A mechanical error with the devices could lead to major reputation and financial impacts. One bad incident could sway public perception of the devices, so Intuitive Surgical must be tirelessly diligent about quality and testing at all times.

67   There are relatively high training costs associated with the devices. It takes qualified people to lead the training and a fair amount of time for users to be trained. If Intuitive Surgical is responsible for the training, they must make sure that all training procedures and checkpoints have been met, and that it is all properly documented to avoid future lawsuits from incorrect use.

68   With a steep learning curve for the new robotic devices, established medical professionals may be hesitant to convert away from existing surgical procedures. As a younger, more technology savvy generation of doctors emerges, this resistance will likely fade. Intuitive Surgical is working to increase the number of young doctors familiar with its products by networking with academic hospitals and marketing directly to them in the expectation that they will buy the product, train their students on the machines, and that those students will come out of medical school with an expectation that surgery should be done with the assistance of robotic technology.

69   With the *da Vinci* Surgical System, there is a physical separation of the doctor and patient, from the console at which the doctor sits to the actual operating table. One could assume that this may lead to a decline in bedside manner as well. Doctors and nurses must be vigilant in making sure that this is not the case and that the patient is receiving the same high-quality care and attention before and after procedures.

ISRG: THE NEXT POLAROID?

70   One of the most successful monopolies of the post–World War II period was Polaroid Corporation of Massachusetts. For nearly 40 years, Polaroid had a monopoly in the area of instant photography. However, in the mid-1990s, Polaroid's monopoly ended with the advent of digital photography. Polaroid squandered its record profits by paying large executive bonuses and dividends to shareholders. They failed to invest in research and development nor did they make strategic acquisitions. This lack of respect for new competition and innovation led to Polaroid's eventual demise and bankruptcy.

71   ISRG needs to heed the lessons of Polaroid Corporation and formulate strategies to keep themselves competitive. ISRG should continue to invest in R&D and must be careful not to underestimate new competitors and new innovative technologies, as the surgical robotic market gains acceptance and grows worldwide.

REFERENCES

1. "Company Background." 2008 Annual Report (10-K), February 6, 2009. Pg 1-2.

2. Intuitive Surgical, Inc. Q1-2009 10-Q. "Regulatory Clearances." Intuitive Surgical, Inc. 10-Q, April 17, 2009. Pg 20. http://investor.intuitivesurgical.com/phoenix.zhtml?c=122359&p=irol-sec

3. Business Wire. "Intuitive Surgical and Computer Motion Close Merger; Intuitive Surgical Completes Reverse Stock Split." 30-Jun-2003. Intuitive Surgical

Press Release. IntuitiveSurgical.com. http://investor.intuitivesurgical.com/phoenix. zhtml?c=122359&p=irol-newsArticle&ID=427228&highlight

4. "Investor FAQs" section of the website http://intuitivesurgical.com/products/faq/index.aspx#20

5. Intuitive Surgical, Inc. Q1-2009 10-Q. "First Quarter 2009 Financial Highlights." Intuitive Surgical, Inc. 10-Q, April 17, 2009. Pg 21. http://investor.intuitivesurgical.com/phoenix.zhtml?c=122359&p=irol-sec

6. "Intuitive Surgical" www.amdocs.com

7. www.intuitivesurgical.com

8. See Reference #7.

9. See Reference #6.

10. "Company" section of the website: http://intuitivesurgical.com/corporate/index.aspx

11. "Patient Value" Pg 2- Letter to the Shareholders 2008. Annual Report (10-K), February 6, 2009.

12. See Reference #11.

13. See Reference #10.

14. "Looking Forward" Pg 5- Letter to the Shareholders 2008. Annual Report (10-K), February 6, 2009.

15. See Reference #14.

16. "Our Strategy." 2008 Annual Report (10-K), February 6, 2009. Pg 8.

17. "Length of Hospital Stay" Pg 3- Letter to the Shareholders 2008. Annual Report (10-K), February 6, 2009.

18. See Reference #5.

19. Maranjian, Selena. "Best Stock for 2008: Intuitive Surgical." http://www.fool.com/investing/high-growth/2007/12/31/best-stock-for-2008-intuitive-surgical.aspx?terms=Best+Stock+for+2008%3A+Intuitive+Surgical&vstest=search_042607_linkdefault December 31, 2007.

20. "Scientists Reveal Korea's First Internet Surgery Robot." www.kdcstaffs.com November 5, 2007.

21. Yahoo! Finance. "ISRG." http://finance.yahoo.com/q?s=isrg

22. www.toshiba.co.jp

23. AOL Finance. "ISRG." http://finance.aol.com/quotes/intuitive-surgical-inc/isrg/nas

24. See Reference #22.

25. Smith, Aaron. "Robots Grab Chunk of Prostate Surgery Biz." http://money.cnn.com/2007/03/23/news/companies/intuitive_surgical/index.htm March 23, 2007.

26. Savitz, Ryan. "Robotic Surgery: Meet Intuitive Surgical" http://www.bullishbankers.com/index.php?s=Robotic+Surgery%3A+Meet+Intuitive+Surgical September 18, 2008.

27. Smith, Rich. "The Intuitive Future of Medicine." The Motley Fool. 22-Nov-2006. http://www.fool.com/investing/high-growth/2006/11/22/the-intuitive-future-of-medicine.aspx

28. See Reference #19.

29. Stolberg, Sheryl Gay. "Obama Calls on Congress to Offset Spending Hikes with Budget Cuts." *The New York Times*. 25-Apr-2009. http://www.nytimes.com/2009/04/26/us/politics/26address.html?ref=global-home

30. Haddock, Vicki. "Elderly Face Special Surgery Risks." CNN.com. 10-Aug-2000. http://archives.cnn.com/2000/HEALTH/aging/08/10/surgery.risk.wmd/

31. Tasker, Fred. "Robot Surgery Finding New Uses." *The Miami Herald.* April 7, 2009. http://www.miamiherald.com/living/health/story/986753.html. 13 Apr 2009.

32. Intuitive Surgical, Inc. Q1-2009 10-Q. "Share Repurchase Program." Intuitive Surgical, Inc. 10-Q, April 17, 2009. Pg 16. http://investor.intuitivesurgical.com/phoenix.zhtml?c=122359&p=irol-sec

33. See Reference #5.

34. See Reference #7.

35. See Reference #7.

Case 18

Cardinal Health Inc. (A)   Mary B. Teagarden

INTRODUCTION

1 Bob Walter belted himself into his bright-red BMW two-seater and reflected on the pep talk that he was about to give to his top managers at the Embassy Suites, a five-minute drive away. Cardinal Health, the health care products-distribution industry merger and acquisition juggernaut, had hit an earnings speed bump. Cardinal was one of a handful of large U.S. companies that had achieved earnings-per-share growth in excess of 20 percent for 15 years straight. Nevertheless, Wall Street was questioning whether Cardinal Health, an empire that had grown through acquisition, could continue to grow at this remarkable rate using this approach. This doubt, coupled with recent questionable "stock crushing" accounting practices among wholesalers (including one of their own suppliers, Pfizer), was weighing down Cardinal's stock price despite their continued and healthy earnings growth.

2   Walter believed that recent blowups at major U.S. companies had occurred because of ultra-fast growth, high debt, and unfocused strategies, with Tyco serving as a prime example. Cardinal, by contrast, had grown gradually, had low debt (16 percent of total capital), and followed an acquisition program that never strayed from selling to pharmacies, hospitals, and pharmaceutical makers. Walter's fans, such as Peter Lynch, a Fidelity vice chairman, commented, "He's one of the best managers I've ever seen—and I've seen thousands" (Lashinsky). In 32 years, Walter had weathered other storms, and believed that this current speed bump was little more than the latest in a long line of "*crises du jour*" that included the Clinton health care plan of the early 1990s that had been expected to drive down drug prices, and the Internet threat of the late 1990s that had been expected to eliminate distributors altogether. Each time, Cardinal's stock rebounded. Walter believed the stock would rebound again as he repositioned Cardinal to compete beyond distribution into higher-margin services and pharmaceutical manufacturing.

THE HEALTH CARE INDUSTRY

3 Health care is a vital, dynamic industry with exciting prospects for future growth in the U.S. In 2006, health care expenditures totaled $2.5.trillion, which was 16.3 percent of the U.S. gross domestic product, and growing at a rate faster than the GDP. The U.S. population age 65 and over was expected to double in the next 25 years. By 2030, almost one out of five Americans (some 72 million people) would be 65 years or older. The age group 85 and older was the fastest growing segment of the U.S. population. They represented 27 percent of the U.S. population in 2002, and forecasts were that their numbers would increase 13 percent, totaling 85 million by 2007. This consumer segment spent $610 billion on health care, utilized 74 percent of all pharmaceuticals, represented 65 percent of hospital bed days, accounted for 42 percent of physician visits in 2002, and grew as forecasted. Europe and Asia showed similar trends (Summary Annual Report, 2001).

4   The health care industry was under tremendous pressure to cut costs while increasing service and functionality to several demanding sets of customers. They had been constantly asked to do more with less to combat labor shortages in nursing and pharmacy and eroding reimbursement rates from third-party payers. In addition, they faced stringent regulations and significant regulatory oversight, which limited their degree of freedom to conduct business in the most effective and profitable manner possible. Health care organizations rose to the challenge by undertaking ambitious programs to improve customer service and streamline business processes, often in partnership with companies like Cardinal. Without a single exception, these companies used state-of-the-art technology to achieve their goals. As an industry trade group research director observed, "That's impressive when you consider that health care has traditionally skimped on technology."[1]

5   Within the health care industry, pharmaceutical companies merged to become larger, truly global entities, and their habits of capital investment showed it. Free to ship their high-value, low-volume products worldwide with minimal impact on the bottom line, they turned unusual locations into hotbeds of pharmaceutical production. The U.S. and Europe saw their share of new construction, particularly in the biopharmaceutical sector. Puerto Rico, long a model for using tax incentives to attract high-tech industry, experienced resurgent interest. Ireland developed a very strong tax incentive program in the mid-1970s, and Singapore followed suit with a focus on pharmaceuticals (and electronics) in the mid-1990s, reaping a windfall of investment. It is no surprise that in 2000, Cardinal Health announced that it would build a $100 million facility in Ireland to gain better access to European customers, according to a publication of the Health Care Distribution Management Association (HDMA). In 2003, they acquired the Intercare Group PLC to expand pharmaceutical manufacturing and distribution capabilities in Europe.

6   The number of customers—hospitals, surgery centers, nursing homes, and drugstores—increased dramatically as baby-boomers aged. Most of these customers lacked warehousing facilities. Instead, they depended on health care distribution and service wholesalers with high service levels, like Cardinal, to make daily, precise deliveries of pharmaceuticals. "In a supermarket, if you're out of Heinz, Campbell is okay," observed Walter. In the pharmaceutical industry, where drugs were not good substitutes for each other, the opposite was true—accuracy and specificity mattered. When a physician prescribed a specific branded drug, the prescription had to be filled precisely according to the physician's directive. Just as the number of customers had grown steadily, the number of drugs had grown from 650 in the 1960s to in excess of 10,000 in forty-plus years. With another 10,000 new product targets in development by pharmaceutical research companies, the health care distributor's role became pivotal in the health care industry.

THE HEALTH CARE DISTRIBUTION AND SERVICES INDUSTRY SECTOR

7   While health care distributors may be relatively unknown to patients, they are vitally important to pharmaceutical manufacturers and those who need medicines or medical supplies. Health care distributors assure that products needed to diagnose, prevent, and treat health care ills are distributed to the many locations where they are used. To guarantee the accurate, efficient, and timely delivery of products, health care distributors expanded their services to provide the products themselves, and the information and other benefits

---

[1] *Information Week,* September 2000, p. 251. Gartner Group's research director for health care says the $1.4 trillion health care sector accounts for technology spending of $20 billion.

designed to make their customers—hospitals, surgery centers, nursing homes, and drug-stores—more efficient and effective. Cardinal had taken a leadership position in this shift. As government-licensed entities, health care distributors manage distribution and assure product safety, quality, integrity, and availability in the health care marketplace. They are integral partners in the health care industry, serving patients and reducing the cost of care. The Health Care Distribution Management Association identified 21 discrete services provided by health care distributors, ranging from price sticker and shelf labels to third-party reimbursement services (HDMA).

8   Industry experts argued that by 2002, health care distributors saved the health care system more than $146 billion each year by maximizing economies of scale, creating efficiencies, lowering expenses, and simplifying distribution. Through a fairly aggressive use of information technology (another area Cardinal had pioneered), health care distributors lowered their own operating cost and most passed these savings through to their customers. The Health Care Distribution Management Association estimated that without distributors there would be 4.393 billion transactions between pharmacies and pharmaceutical manufacturers. Pharmaceutical distributors reduced this number to 35.18 million transactions per year. The average distribution center held more than 28,000 different health care items. Distributors, however, did not set the price of the products they handled—this was done by pharmaceutical companies and manufacturers (HDMA).

DISINTERMEDIATION AND e-BUSINESS IN THE HEALTH CARE SERVICES SECTOR

9   The health care distribution and services industry was threatened by disintermediation—elimination of the middle man. Internet-facilitated disintermediation was a major environmental threat for health care service providers. Cardinal Health responded with a technology budget of $250 million in 2000, including $20 million allocated to a single effort—the ambitious cardinal.com project. The increased funding and emphasis on technology was a natural move for Cardinal Health as it absorbed its 1998 purchase of the medical-surgical product manufacturing and distribution company, Allegiance Corp. (*Information Week*).

10   Cardinal Health launched perhaps the most ambitious Web-based project in the industry. Designed to service the company's entire customer base of health care facilities and physicians' offices, cardinal.com was a procurement portal that offered more than 500,000 items for purchase. It was an aggressive move for the company, which had been transacting most business with customers via electronic data interchange for years since it was not evident that customers would accept new Web-based approaches. "We're thinking that many of our customers will move to the Web with us," Cardinal's CIO Kathy White said expectantly (*Information Week*).

11   Marketing guru Roger Blackwell observed, "Cardinal Health [was] able to use IT to manage a very complicated problem of many items in the pharmaceutical industry. Pharmaceutical products have to be carefully controlled. So firms like Cardinal Health [were] in the vanguard of using computerized control of those products. It doesn't necessarily mean they [had] pioneered applications, but they [had] certainly been on the forefront of development and increased efficiency from the very beginning" (Weston).

12   White had hoped that cardinal.com would increase the company's customer base. Because the system was online, White said, . . . "we can reach areas where we had very low penetration because it wasn't financially feasible for our sales representatives to call on physicians' offices and rural hospitals." White's predictions were on target. By 2002, twenty percent of cardinal.com's customers were new.

13   Walter had discounted the impact of disintermediation by the Internet on Cardinal. He commented, "We firmly put to rest the notion that upstart dotcoms would replace a company that has the scale and resources of Cardinal. We do believe that the Internet is a valuable efficiency tool, and will continue to invest in the technology to realize those benefits" (Summary Annual Report, 2001). Blackwell admired Walter's ability to turn a potential threat into an advantage. He commented, "That's what makes Walter, at Cardinal Health, and Sam Walton different from other people. They are able to conceptualize rather than just do. Most businesses are run by people who have tunnel data and tunnel vision. They accumulate data to tell them what has happened. The great leaders are those who understand what's at the end of the tunnel" (Weston). Walter would tell you he was simply meeting the needs of his customers and suppliers.

COMPANY BACKGROUND

14   Robert D. Walter, called "Bob the Builder" by *Forbes*, built Cardinal Health into the most valuable company in the U.S. health care services industry and the world's largest distributor of health care products like pharmaceuticals and surgical instruments (Tanzer (a)). Cardinal Health had revenues of $81 billion in 2006, was ranked Number 19 on the Fortune 500, and owned about 30 percent of the pharmaceutical distribution business. Regardless, most people had never heard of Cardinal Health, its founder Bob Walter, or the company's 32-year journey from a regional wholesale food distributor to an international health care distributor and service giant.

Cardinal Foods, Inc.

15   Walter used his undergraduate degree in mechanical engineering from Ohio University in his first job working on missile technology at North American Rockwell. He hated the bureaucracy he encountered and went back to graduate school to study business. In 1971, at 26 and fresh out of Harvard Business School, Walter borrowed $1.3 million to purchase Cardinal Foods, a wholesale food distributor in Dublin, Ohio, that served small retailers. Walter spent the early years at Cardinal Foods growing the business, and the company eventually became a strong regional food wholesaler. However, Walter realized that Cardinal Foods would never be a big player in the food business. He recognized that the food industry was rapidly consolidating and that it was dominated by a few large national competitors that would limit his company's growth potential. He also found that the barriers to national expansion were significant in food wholesaling, so he and his partners began looking for additional acquisition opportunities that would enable growth (Tanzer (b)). Walter put his MBA skills to work and found that the pharmaceutical distribution industry was highly fragmented, with 354 independently owned distributors, but only three public companies (Lashinsky). In addition, the pharmaceutical business was growing faster than the economy as a whole, and when a physician prescribed a drug, typically another drug could not be substituted.

Cardinal Distribution, Inc.

16   In 1979, Walter undertook the migration to pharmaceutical distribution; he took the distribution skills he learned in food wholesaling and applied them to pharmaceuticals through the acquisition of a local pharmaceutical distributor. Cardinal Foods evolved into Cardinal Distribution with the addition of two pharmaceutical distributors and a pharmaceutical and food distributor. Walter decided to take Cardinal into pharmaceutical wholesaling at a time when this industry sector was highly fragmented, offered strong growth prospects, was noncyclical, and already mature. For the next 15 years, Cardinal bought smaller distributors

that specialized in moving pharmaceuticals from one place to another. In the next five years, the pharmaceutical segment of Cardinal's business had grown to nearly twice the size of the food distribution business.

Cardinal Health: The Early Years

17. Cardinal Distribution went public in 1983 to raise capital for its fast-growing pharmaceutical business, and was renamed Cardinal Health Inc. to reflect its new positioning. By the end of 1988, the Cardinal Health name remained, but the company had exited the food business entirely (cardinal.com (a)). By 2000, Cardinal had a well-ingrained philosophy that focused on obvious things like customers and adding value, as indicated in their mission statement in Exhibit 1. "Quality service" was the vow Cardinal made to its customers. Just as important, Cardinal also focused on developing management talent for the future and achieving operational excellence by driving costs down and using advanced information technology. If you were lucky enough to have invested $10,000 into Cardinal stock in 1983, you would have been sitting on $700,000 in 2000. Shareholders and customers were not the only constituents Cardinal served; in 2002, management and employees owned about 10 percent of Cardinal (Gallagher).

18 Walter had grown Cardinal into the world's largest distributor of health care products such as pharmaceuticals and surgical instruments and, in the process, built Cardinal to a market value of $31 billion in 2000, the largest in the U.S. health care services industry. Cardinal's core pharmaceutical distribution business represented 75 percent of the firm's operating revenues and 22 percent of its growth in 2000. Industry analysts praised Cardinal as one of the best-managed health care companies and lauded their clear vision on direction of growth and how to capitalize the growth prospects. Between 1990 and 2000, Cardinal's stock price had compounded at an average 26 percent a year, and analysts believed that Cardinal was going to continue this pattern. (*Plain Dealer*). Cardinal consistently met or exceeded market expectations. On Wall Street, they called Cardinal Health the GE of

EXHIBIT 1   Cardinal Health Mission

Our Purpose

The people of Cardinal Health are driven by a common purpose: To help customers across the health care industry—from manufacturers to providers of patient care—find answers to the challenges they face.

Our success is dependent on helping our customers succeed.
Our approach is to be:

A Partner

We believe the best ideas come from creative collaboration with our customers and each other.

Applying Unparalleled Resources

We create powerful solutions with our customers by applying leading products and services to their needs in new and innovative ways.

With a Passion for Performance

We achieve the greatest results for our customers when we actively identify and capitalize on the opportunities created by the advancement of health care

Source: Cardinal Health, Annual Report, 2000.

the health care services industry. Cardinal's depth and breadth of management, its consistency, and its love affair with shareholders brought to mind GE under Jack Welch (Tanzer; cardinal.com (b)).

19   In 2001, Cardinal employed more than 49,000 associates—in 110 facilities in 22 countries on five continents—who spoke 12 languages. "However, we speak a universal language of high quality and commitment to our customer" (Summary Annual Report, 2001). Slightly more than 42 percent of Cardinal's associates were employed outside the U.S. Among Cardinal's employees were 1,800 pharmacists and 550 clinical, productivity, and logistics consultants. Cardinal's clinical consultants used a proprietary database of best-demonstrated practices identified in more than 1,600 studies of some 200 medical procedures. Cardinal also had 2,900 sales and service associates serving hospitals and other clinical-care providers, retail pharmacies, and pharmaceutical manufacturers (Slywotzky).

20   From their position in the middle of the value-added chain, Cardinal made life easier for companies at both ends of the pharmaceutical distribution chain—suppliers and customers. Essentially, Cardinal linked customers to solutions. An industry observer commented:

> Cardinal Health performs many of the functions that were once performed by retailers and manufacturers in the demand chain. For example, it provides sales and credit functions for the large pharmaceutical companies whose expertise lies more with the development of products than their distribution. For drug retailers and hospitals, a wholesaler such as Cardinal stores, warehouses, and controls inventory more efficiently than the retailers and hospitals can. This is especially true for highly specialized pharmaceutical products which carry a myriad of technical and regulatory concerns.
>
> Cardinal achieved its success . . . by monitoring consumer purchasing data while at the same time maintaining superior product knowledge for both itself and other channel members. The company also develops logistics systems required for shipping and inventory replenishment based on this information. (*HDMA*)

21   Between 1970 and 1980, the once-tranquil field of pharmaceutical distributors shrank by a mere five from 144 to 139 according to the National Wholesale Druggists' Association. By 1990, only 84 pharmaceutical distributors survived, and by 1996 that number shrank to 63. The top five controlled three-quarters of the market (*Columbus Business First*). Exhibit 2 identifies the top 10 North American pharmaceutical wholesalers in 2001.

EXHIBIT 2   Top 10 North American Wholesalers—2001

Wholesaler	Total Sales (000,000)	% Change	Stores
Cardinal Health	$47,948	60.5%	15,000
McKesson Corp.	$42,010	14.5%	18,000
AmerisourceBergen	$36,000	16.1%	25,000
Supervalu	$23,194	14.0%	6,800+
Fleming Co.	$14,444	1.2%	3,500+
Loblaw Cos	$13,425	5.5%	10,800
Sobey's	$7,374	3.7%	1,371
C&S Wholesale Grocers	$7,100	6.6%	4,000+
Wakefern Food	$5,800	5.5%	154
Giant Eagle	$4,221	3.2%	400

Source: *Private Label,* November 2001, pp. 82–84.

22   Pharmaceutical distributors joined the rest of the pharmaceutical industry in a rush toward consolidation in the 1990s, and competition within the pharmaceutical industry evolved at an exponential rate, making differentiation increasingly critical. By 2002, Cardinal recognized that in such a highly competitive market, its success could be derailed in a nanosecond. Larger firms, such as Cardinal Health and DSM Pharmaceuticals, began integrating services to include drug discovery and development, production for clinical trials, final dose formulation, and commercial production in an effort to provide "cradle-to-grave" outsourcing. Although not embraced by every industry player, an industry trend among the larger competitors was consolidation to provide one-stop-shopping for contract services (Mullen).

Cardinal Health Today

23   By 2006, three companies—Cardinal, Amerisource, and McKesson—controlled 90 percent of the sales in the health care distribution and services industry. All three were roughly the same size and offered the same basic products and services, as shown in Exhibit 3. Cardinal was one of the largest pharmaceutical distribution companies in the U.S. and, unlike their nearest competitors, a larger percentage of their overall operating income came from nondistribution activities. Their diversified operating income streams included distributing pharmaceuticals, packaging them, providing devices to hospitals that automate pharmaceutical dispensing through their Pyxis subsidiary, and providing pharmacy services through outlets like Medicine Shoppe. These diversified businesses all provided higher operating margins than the traditional pharmaceutical distribution business did.

24   By 2006, Cardinal depended heavily on several key customers and suppliers: CVS and Walgreens accounted for 35 percent of Cardinal's total revenue, growing to 40 percent by 2007. Fifteen percent of Cardinal's 2006 revenue was from group purchasing organizations (GPOs). Pfizer, Cardinal's largest supplier, accounted for nine percent of total suppliers, and their top five suppliers accounted for about 33 percent of total revenue. By 2007, according to company sources, 90 percent of all hospitals and 50 percent of all surgeries in the United States used Cardinal Health products or services. Each day, 50,000 deliveries were made to 40,000 customer sites, including hospitals, pharmacies, and other points of care. One-third of all pharmaceutical, laboratory, and medical products passed through Cardinal Health's logistics system. As important, Cardinal Health held 2,765 patents and patent applications on proprietary medical products, manufacturing processes, and medication management solutions. By 2007, Cardinal Health was an $87 billion diversified global health care products and services company, and its primary market was the United States.

EXHIBIT 3   Relative Share of Wholesalers in Health Care Products and Services Distribution 2006

Company	Pharmaceutical Distribution	Medical & Surgical Supplies	IT Provider	Automation Services	Long-Term Care Pharmacy
AmerisourceBergen	97%	n/a	n/a	n/a	3%
Cardinal Health	80%	13%	4%	3%	n/a
McKesson	94%	4%	2%	n/a	n/a

Source: www.wikinvest.com/stock/Cardinal_Health_(CAH), downloaded 12-18-08.

CARDINAL'S POSITION IN THE VALUE CHAIN

25   Cardinal Health, a multinational and a leading provider in the health care industry, applied vast resources, knowledge, and expertise to help customers—from health care manufacturers to providers of patient care. Cardinal's operations were extensive—it developed, manufactured, packaged, and marketed products for patient care; developed drug-delivery technologies; distributed pharmaceuticals, medical-surgical and laboratory supplies; and provided consulting and other services that improve quality and efficiency in health care.

26   Cardinal Health was a vital intermediary between manufacturers and providers of patient care. Upstream in the value chain, they served key suppliers—health care manufacturers—by offering product development, manufacturing and packaging services, distribution services, and marketing and sales services. Cardinal worked in partnership with pharmaceutical and biotechnology companies to develop unique dosage forms of drugs. Distribution services to these suppliers included warehousing and distribution of drugs, medical-surgical and laboratory products to hospitals, retail pharmacies, surgery centers, physician practices, and other points of care. Cardinal's marketing and sales services included specialized information systems, consulting, and promotional programs with community pharmacies and acute-care providers (Slywotzky).

27   At the other end of the value chain, Cardinal, one of the largest distributors of pharmaceuticals and other medical products, served key customers—health care providers—with similar services and an array of products and services that helped health care providers improve operational and clinical performance. They developed and manufactured a broad range of leading medical and surgical products, as well as automated supply and pharmaceutical dispensing systems. Cardinal also repackaged bulk pharmaceuticals into smaller volumes for more efficient use by hospitals and retail pharmacies. They provided systems to help customers streamline purchasing and inventory management. Cardinal helped retail pharmacies market themselves locally through Internet-based programs, patient education activities, and systems to maximize reimbursement from third-party payers. In addition, Cardinal's operations and clinical improvement services included consulting and information systems to help health care providers reduce supply costs, improve operational efficiencies, and enhance clinical outcomes.

28   Cardinal competed in four business segments: pharmaceutical distribution and provider sales, medical-surgical products and services, pharmaceutical technologies and services, and automation and information services. Exhibit 4 identifies the companies in each of these segments.

29   Cardinal was considered a master at cross-selling, bundling products and services, and making itself an indispensable partner of drug makers and health care providers. Essentially, the distributor leveraged its position in the middle to capture more of the dollars in the health care continuum though backward and forward vertical integration. For example, Cardinal-packaged drugs for pharmaceutical producers—a $1.5 billion market—provided contract manufacturing services and alternative drug-delivery formulations, such as softgel capsules and rapid-dissolving tablets, a $3 billion market (Tanzer (b)). They also consulted with health care providers on the other end of the value chain.

30   In 2006, Cardinal considered reorganization into two operating units: Health Care Supply Chain, providing prescription pharmaceuticals and medical products, and Clinical and Medical Products, to manufacture medical equipment and technologies, including infusion and medication dispensing, respiratory care, and infection prevention products used in hospitals and other primary care facilities. These were to be complemented by a third unit, Cardinal Pharmacy Services and Medicine Shoppe.

EXHIBIT 4   **Cardinal Health Inc. Companies by Business Segments 2006**

Pharmaceutical Distribution and Provider Service	Medical Products and Services	Clinical Technologies and Services	Pharmaceutical Technologies and Services
Cardinal Distribution	Allegiance—a Cardinal Health company	Cardinal Health Information Companies	ALP (Automated Liquid Packaging)—a Cardinal Health company
Cardinal Health Provider Pharmacy Services	Cardinal Health Consulting Services	Pyxis—a Cardinal Health company	Cardinal Health Manufacturing Services
Cardinal Health Staffing Network		Vistant—a Cardinal Health company	Cardinal Health Sales and Marketing Services
Central Pharmacy Services			IPC (International Processing)—a Cardinal Health company
CORD Logistics			PCI Services
Medicine Shoppe International—a Cardinal Health company			R.P. Scherer—a Cardinal Health company
Cardinal Health National PharmPak			SP Pharmaceutical—a Cardinal Health company
Cardinal NSS—National Specialty Services			

Source: cardinal.com (c).

CARDINAL BRAND EQUITY AND VALUE CREATION

31   In 2002, Walter maintained that the strengths Cardinal had built during the past three decades were the basis of future competitiveness. He commented, "The rich tradition and culture that exist within Cardinal give me particular comfort as I face the future. Our tradition is one of winning, playing fairly, acting ethically, continually raising our standards of performance, moving aggressively, taking appropriate risks to see the resulting rewards, and, finally, acting like owners. After all, our associates are owners. Our officers, directors, and associates have an equity stake in the company of more than $3 billion, making us collectively the second largest owner of Cardinal. We all know that the creation of economic value for ourselves and other shareholders depends on focused efforts to create value for our customers and the associates around us" (Tanzer (b)).

32   The creation of value for Cardinal's customers was accomplished through concentration on four operational drivers: "A relentless pursuit of *growth*, a total *focus on customer needs*, a continual push toward *operational excellence* in everything they do, and, finally, recognition that *leadership development* is critical to Cardinal's future success" (Cone). Cardinal had established and reinforced a position of leadership in providing proprietary products and services to health care providers and manufacturers worldwide. Superior scale, market leadership. and proprietary offerings were the foundation of Cardinal's strategy. For Cardinal, growth was an objective, not a by-product. Its focus on growth was purposefully intense (Summary Annual Report, 2001).

33   Cardinal used co-branding selectively. "Cardinal's corporate branding image and value are as a problem solver," said public affairs Vice President Geoffrey Fenton, who oversaw Cardinal's branding efforts. For example, they partnered with Home Diagnostics, Inc., to

provide *The Prestige Smart System* for diabetes monitoring (prestigesmartsystem.com). Walter observed, "Our strategy of focusing on health care, while building scale, leadership positions, and proprietary solutions, is working. Our ability to cross-sell our products and services accelerated our growth rate. . ." (*Columbus Business First*).

34   To reinforce the Cardinal brand, the company used training to align its employees with its mission, emphasizing "standards to make sure you are speaking, acting, behaving, representing yourself in a way that is consistent with the company's corporate brand image," said Fenton. Brand image rules also covered use of logos and graphics. The Cardinal Bird had size and color specs (branding-report.com). Nevertheless, Gary Dowdy, vice president of Cardinal's e-business, observed, "We're a complex business that is an amalgamation of many companies, and we have two different groups of customers—health care providers and pharmaceutical manufacturers. We want to have one Cardinal approach to present one Cardinal to all of our customers, but to do that, we need to first do things like extending adequate security to our heterogeneous software environment" (Cone). Information technology infrastructure development lagged Cardinal's brand strategy.

35   Cardinal Health leveraged its value chain position to capitalize on the expertise, systems, and information gained in its once-restrictive middleman role. Once one of several large players in a notoriously low-margin business—essentially delivering pills from Point A to Point B—they leveraged their unique vantage point to take advantage of their powerful insights into the rapidly changing pharmaceutical marketplace. Cardinal's executives realized that they could create offerings built on their unique position as a market knowledge and information expert that would meet the evolving needs of both customers and suppliers (Slywotzky).

36   Downstream hospitals and independent pharmacies experienced growing cost pressures while trying to maintain quality care. They also faced challenges, including the management of an increasingly complex body of patient and financial information. Cardinal addressed these problems. By using their distribution experience in inventory management and procurement, they began to host information systems for hospitals and pharmacies. Cardinal developed automated technology for ordering and dispensing medications and distributing them to hospital patients, thereby reducing loss and theft, improving accuracy, and maximizing data capture. This in turn led to the development of a range of hospital pharmacy management services from staffing to consulting to complete outsourcing of the pharmaceutical function. Cardinal also introduced a franchise option to independent retail pharmacists, offering them information systems, marketing resources, and purchasing power that were once beyond their reach (Slywotzky).

37   Upstream, Cardinal created specialized services for pharmaceutical makers in which Cardinal would design and produce customized packaging for pharmaceuticals. This again leveraged the intimate market knowledge Cardinal had derived from their position in the value chain. The company reduced its overall manufacturing and distribution costs by linking the two functions, which enabled just-in-time replenishment and smaller inventories. Cardinal was able to aggregate demand for less-common dosage forms, such as freeze-dried tablets, from multiple pharmaceutical companies to achieve scale production advantages. And it was able to profitably meet hospitals' needs for customized packaging of certain pharmaceuticals—something most pharmaceutical companies, with their "siloed" manufacturing operations, did poorly, if at all (Slywotzky).

38   These strategic moves in both directions on the value chain led Cardinal to expand its economic horizons beyond the pharmaceutical distribution market. By 2002, Cardinal was a major player in a dramatically larger market—one that encompassed consulting, information technology, pharmaceutical-packaging design and manufacture, pharmacy management, and other health care services. Cardinal managed more pharmacies than all of its

competitors combined. It handled prescription benefits for nearly three million individuals and provided automated pharmaceutical deliveries to four million patients a day. These new businesses generated a huge revenue stream with profit margins far greater than those in Cardinal's core business, but they also reinforced and bolstered the core business and gave Cardinal the best distribution margins in the industry. Between 1992 and 2002, Cardinal's revenues, operating profits, and market value grew at double-digit rates, far outpacing its closest competitor.

ACQUISITION HISTORY: BUILDING LAYERS OF COMPETENCE

39   Cardinal's history is one of aggressive growth through acquisitions. They grew primarily through acquisition and absorbed fifty-plus companies beginning in 1980, more than half of these between 1998 and 2002. Exhibit 5 shows Cardinal's acquisition history. During 2000 and 2001, Cardinal averaged an acquisition once every six weeks. Cardinal's strategy had been the acquisition of well-run companies in adjacent markets. The first venture into the pharmaceutical industry began with the acquisition of a local pharmaceutical distributor, Zanesville, in 1980, and a name change to Cardinal Distribution, Inc. Cardinal soon expanded nationwide by swallowing other distributors, including two pharmaceutical distributors headquartered in New York and a Massachusetts-based pharmaceutical and food distributor. Given the extensive consolidation in the food industry, Cardinal executives decided to narrow the focus of their business exclusively to distribution of pharmaceuticals. By 1988, Cardinal had sold its food group, including Midland Grocery Company and Mr. Moneysworth, Inc., to Roundy's (hoovers.com).

40   Drug distributors joined the rest of the pharmaceutical industry in the rush toward consolidation during the 1990s. Cardinal's acquisitions in those years included Ohio Valley-Clarksburg in the mid-Atlantic region, Chapman Drug in Tennessee, PRN Services in Michigan, Solomons Co. in Georgia, Humiston-Keeling in Illinois, and Behrens in Texas. One of Cardinal's most important acquisitions during this period was its cash purchase of Whitmire Distribution in 1994. Whitmire was the U.S.'s sixth largest pharmaceutical wholesaler; the purchase bumped Cardinal into the position of third largest. At that time, the company changed its name to Cardinal Health, and Melburn Whitmire, Whitmire's former president, became Cardinal's vice chairman. Cardinal Health had become the primary wholesaler for top drugstore chains, such as industry leaders CVC, Walgreen's, Kroger, and Kmart.

41   While the traditional pharmaceutical distribution business would remain their core, Cardinal then began incremental geographic expansion and growth into the larger health care industry, of which pharmaceutical distribution is a part. In 1995, Cardinal made its biggest acquisition up to that time when it purchased St. Louis-based Medicine Shoppe International, the largest franchiser of independent retail pharmacies. At the time of the purchase, Medicine Shoppe had 987 U.S. outlets and 107 abroad. A 1996 stock swap brought the company Pyxis, which provided hospitals with machines that automatically distributed pills to patients. Pyxis also provided pharmacy management services to hospital pharmacies. More than 90 percent of the hospitals in the U.S. used Pyxis' point-of-use systems to dispense more than four million prescriptions a day. This was an example of Cardinal's focus on higher-margin services when compared to its closest rival, McKesson. Cardinal was also the largest manager of hospital pharmacies in the U.S. (Gallagher). Later that year, Cardinal bought PCI Services, a pharmaceutical packaging company. In 1997, Cardinal acquired Owen Health Care, a provider of pharmacy management services. They tried to acquire Bergen Brunswig—later acquired by competitor Amerisouce—but the deal was blocked by the Federal Trade Commission (hoovers.com).

EXHIBIT 5   Cardinal Acquisition History 1980–2007

Acquisition Date	Company Name	Operating Sector
05/12/80	The Bailey Drug Company	Rx Distribution[1]
09/14/84	Ellicott Drug Company	Rx Distribution
01/20/86	John L. Thompson Sons & Co.	Rx Distribution
04/30/86	James W. Daly, Inc.	Rx Distribution
01/20/88	Marmac Distributors, Inc.	Rx Distribution
06/18/90	Ohio Valley-Clarksburg, Inc.	Rx Distribution
10/15/91	Chapman Drug Company	Rx Distribution
04/01/92	Medical Strategies, Inc.	Rx Distribution
05/04/93	Solomons Company	Rx Distribution
12/17/93	PRN Services, Inc.	Rx Distribution
02/07/94	Whitmire Distribution	Rx Distribution
07/01/94	Humiston-Keeling, Inc.	Rx Distribution
07/18/94	Behrens, Inc.	Rx Distribution
11/13/95	Medicine Shoppe International, Inc.	Rx Distribution
05/07/96	Pyxis Corporation	Automation[2]
10/11/96	PCI Services, Inc.	PTS[3]
03/18/97	Owen Health care, Inc.	Rx Distribution
02/18/98	MediQual Systems, Inc.	Automation
05/15/98	Comprehensive Reimbursements Consultants, Inc.	PTS
08/07/98	R.P. Scherer Corporation	PTS
02/03/99	Allegiance Corporation	Medical-Surgical P&S[4]
04/01/99	Surgical Instrument Repair Services	Medical-Surgical P&S
05/20/99	PHARMACISTS: PRN, Inc.	Rx Distribution
05/21/99	Pacific Surgical Innovations, Inc.	Medical-Surgical P&S
06/04/99	The Enright Group, Inc.	Medical-Surgical P&S
06/25/99	Pharmaceutical Packaging Specialties	PTS
06/30/99	AutoValet Systems Intl—product line purchase	Automation
07/12/99	MedSurg Industries, Inc.	Medical-Surgical P&S
08/25/99	Herd Mundy Richardson Holdings Ltd.	PTS
09/10/99	Automatic Liquid Packaging, Inc.	PTS
11/18/99	Trimaras Printing Company	PTS
12/30/99	HelpMate Robotics, Inc.	Automation
01/21/00	Contract Health Professionals and Pharmacists-Ance, Inc.	Rx Distribution
07/19/00	Rexam Cartons, Inc.	PTS
07/26/00	Dermatology division from Advanced Polymer Systems, Inc. (Enhanced Derm Technologies Inc.)	PTS

EXHIBIT 5   **Cardinal Acquisition History 1980–2007 (*Continued*)**

Acquisition Date	Company Name	Operating Sector
08/16/00	Bergen Brunswig Medical Corp.	Medical-Surgical P&S
09/01/00	ENDOlap, Inc.	Medical-Surgical P&S
11/01/00	Ni-Med kit manufacturing (from Oak Medical Inventories LLC)	Medical-Surgical P&S
11/01/00	CurranCare, LLC	Medical-Surgical P&S
12/15/00	Manufacturing facility in Humacao, Puerto Rico from Alcon (Puerto Rico) Inc.	PTS
12/22/00	VegiCaps from American Home Products Corp.	PTS
01/02/01	International Processing Corporation	PTS
02/14/01	Bindley Western Industries, Inc.	RxDistribution
02/26/01	Astra-Zeneca Plant in Corby, UK	PTS
03/16/01	Critical Care Concepts	Medical-Surgical P&S
03/23/01	American Threshold	Medical-Surgical P&S
03/28/01	FutureCare	Medical-Surgical P&S
06/29/01	SP Pharmaceuticals, LLC	PTS
10/23/01	Purchase of Manufacturing facility in Raleigh, NC from Schering-Plough Animal Health Corp.	PTS
11/15/01	Professional Health-Care Resources	Medical-Surgical P&S
01/07/02	Eon Media, Inc.	Automation
04/15/02	Megellan Laboratories	PTS
06/26/02	Boron, LePore & Associates, Inc.	PTS
8/15/02	Atlantes Services	PTS
11/05/02	KVM Technologies	PTS
1/01/03	Syncor International Corporation	PTS
10/01/03	Gala Biotech	Biopharmaceuticals
10/29/03	The Intercare Group	Pharmaceutical Mfg.
12/02/03	Medicap Pharmacies	RxDistribution
02/17/04	Beckloff Associates	Biopharmaceuticals
07/07/04	ALARIS Medical Systems	Medical-Surgical P&S
05/23/06	Denver Biomedical	Medical-Surgical P&S
06/01/06	The F. Dohmen Company	RxDistribution
07/18/06	MedMinded, Inc.	PTS
06/28/07	VIASYS Health care	PTS

[1]Pharmaceutical Distribution and Provider Service
[2]Automation and Information Services
[3]Pharmaceutical Technologies and Services
[4]Medical-Surgical Products and Services

42   Cardinal continued to expand beyond marketing and distribution when it acquired R. P. Scherer, the world's largest maker of softgels. They also bought an idle Schering-Plough plant in hopes of attracting biotechnology firms needing product development assistance and clinical supplies production and large pharmaceutical companies looking to outsource their product manufacturing business. Geoffrey Fenton, Cardinal's public affairs vice president, commented, "We're not in the business of pharmaceutical research, but we see the contract manufacturing of biologics as a rapidly growing area, and the purchase will certainly make Cardinal a better upstream partner" (West).

43   In 1999, Cardinal bought Baxter's Allegiance division, the largest manufacturer and distributor of medical, surgical, and lab supplies such as instruments, disposable surgical gloves, and gowns. This acquisition made Cardinal the leading distributor of surgical devices (with a market share of more than 30 percent) and increased its value as a one-stop shop for health providers. As a result, Walter—who demanded that his businesses must be number one or number two in the marketplace and the low-cost producer—commented, "When we go to a hospital, we can offer a broader array of services than our competition, and each is a market leader." Cardinal also announced plans to buy Automatic Liquid Packaging (ALP), which packaged liquid pharmaceuticals for companies such as Pfizer. ALP was successfully acquired. Then, in 2000, Cardinal announced plans to start an online health products marketplace called newhealthexchange.com with McKesson, AmerisourceBergen, Fischer Scientific, Owens, and Mino (West). A key rival was taken out of commission in February 2001 when Cardinal acquired Bindley Western Industries, one of the bigger regional firms that had rivaled the Big Three.

44   Walter outlined his core strategy and vision for the future in the 2001 Annual Report. "Strong internal growth combined with meaningful acquisitions and significant partnerships all contributed to the strong growth of last year. Every manager at Cardinal understands that opportunities are found in all three areas. First, we expect our businesses to outgrow its respective market by 50 percent each year. . . Second, we spent nearly $3.0 billion on 13 acquisitions. Each acquired company met our standard of being outstanding by itself, fitting closely into our strategy, and making Cardinal collectively stronger for the future. And third, we created long-term partnerships with providers and manufacturers and created incremental value for both partners."

45   The June 2002 acquisition of Syncor made Cardinal Health the largest pharmaceutical wholesaler in the U.S. The Syncor acquisition gave Cardinal Health a leading position in the nuclear pharmacy business, which was growing as radiopharmaceutical techniques were used more frequently in diagnosing diseases. Syncor had more than half of the nuclear pharmacy services market and also had medical imaging, manufacturing, and radiotherapeutics operations. In addition, they compounded and dispensed nuclear medicines used in diagnostic and therapeutic uses for heart diseases and cancer. Syncor had a network of more than 120 U.S. and 20 overseas nuclear pharmacy service centers (Tanzer; hoovers.com).

46   The Syncor acquisition came on the heels of the acquisition of Magellan Laboratories, a pharmaceutical research and analytical firm, in a string of acquisitions that were integrated into an outsourcing services business covering all steps in dosage formulation, from early analytical stages through commercial-scale manufacturing for oral and sterile systems (Mullen; Morse). Richard Shaw, a health care industry analyst at A. M. Best Company, commented, "They're doing the same thing that managed care did several years ago. They're accumulating critical mass and leverage over all the other players they deal with" (Mullen).

47   Cardinal's pattern of growth through acquisition had not been haphazard—their acquisitions had been guided by Walter's clear vision of future possibilities and uncanny ability to recognize strategic inflection points. First, Cardinal built wholesale distribution competency in the food industry. This was followed by incremental expansion of the

distribution competency into the pharmaceutical industry. Cardinal built critical mass as a wholesale distributor of pharmaceuticals in the U.S. and then expanded internationally. They also gradually expanded their value chain position in both directions, partnering with both suppliers and customers to incrementally add value for both. Cardinal had anticipated the *tsunami* of change in the health care industry and positioned itself to meet health care customer and supplier needs at the higher-margin end of the business. The company had changed so dramatically since it first came into Walter's hands that when he looked around for someone from the early days to toast the firm's 25th anniversary, there was no one left. Walter, a press-shy, modest fellow, commented, "I had a beer by myself to celebrate" (Morse).

CARDINAL'S FUTURE

48 Walter knew that the long-term future for the company he had built was far from certain. There were many unanswered questions. What could cause Cardinal's incredible growth to slow? Would customers or suppliers migrate into their market niches? What obstacles would Cardinal encounter as they continued to pursue international expansion? Would their business model work in other countries? Would they have collaboration opportunities with suppliers from low-cost countries? Would India—with low-cost suppliers and world-class IT services—pose a threat? Would their business model continue to be sustainable in the face of global competition? Was their "even better future" within grasp, or was it elusive? Walter wondered if Cardinal would have to reinvent itself one more time, and if he would stay around to guide the transformation. As he took the podium, Bob Walter told his managers, "We are builders, and we aren't done yet" (Speer).

REFERENCES

branding-report.com, http://branding-report.com/corporatebranding.html, downloaded 12-18-08.

Cardinal Health, Annual Report, 2000.

Cardinal Health, Summary Annual Report, 2001.

"Cardinal Health Climbs to the Top," *Plain Dealer*, June 23, downloaded 4-09-06.

"Cardinal Health Profit Up 23% in 4Q," *Columbus Business First*, July 31, 2001, http://columbus.bizjournals.com/columbus/stories/2001/07/30/daily9.html, downloaded 12-18-08.

cardinal.com (a), www.cardinal.com/us/en/aboutus/history/index.asp, 12-18-08.

cardinal.com (b), www.cardinal.com/content/about/ourhistory.asp, downloaded 12-18-08.

cardinal.com (c), www.cardinal.com/content/companies/cardcosopseg.asp, downloaded 04-09-06.

Cone, Edward, "Customercentric Model Is Top Priority," *Interactive Week*, 2001, p. 54.

Gallagher, Kathleen, "Cardinal Health Seen as Being a High-Flyer as Population Ages," *JS Online: Milwaukee Journal Sentinel*, 2002.

"HDMA, Health Care Product Distribution: A Primer," Health Care Distribution Management Association, 2002.

hoovers.com, www.hoovers.com/premium/profile/4/0.2147.12894.00.html, downloaded 12-18-08.

Information Week, September 2000, p. 251.

Lashinsky, Adam, "Big Man in the Middle," *Fortune*, 147 (7), 2003, pp. 160–162.

Morse, Andrew, "Cardinal Health Care Strikes Again," *The Daily Deal*, June 15, 2002.

Mullen, Rick, "Formulators Offer 'Cradle to Grave' Outsourcing," *Chemical Week*, April 24, 2002, p. 28.

prestigesmartsystem.com, www.prestigesmartsystem.com/3about/2enews.html, downloaded 12-18-08.

Slywotzky, Adrian, and Richard Wise, "The Growth Crisis—And How to Escape It," *Harvard Business Review*, 80 (7), 2002.

Speer, Tibbett, "Just Say Grow," *Hospitals & Health Networks*, 70 (15), 1996, pp. 34–35.

Tanzer, Andrew, "Bob the Builder," forbes.com, 2002a, www.forbes.com/global/2002/0415/072_print.html, downloaded 12-18-08.

Tanzer, Andrew, "I Can Get It for You Wholesale," *Forbes*, 169 (9), 2002b, pp. 74–79.

West, Diane, "Cardinal Health Ramps Up Drug Manufacturing Capabilities," *Drug Store News*, 23 (17), 2001, p. 35.

Weston, Randy, "Reinventing the Supply Chain," *Computerworld*, 2002, http://comptuerworld.com/news/1997/story/0,11280,10291,00.html, downloaded 12-18-08.

Case 19

Respironics, Incorporated: *Take a Deep Breath*

Janet L. Rovenpor
Armand Gilinsky Jr.

I ask people at parties, "If we could come up with an elegant way to eliminate snoring, would you pay $100 so your bed partner doesn't snore anymore?" So far I have gotten 100 percent "yes" on that question.[1]

—*John Miclot, CEO, Respironics, Inc.*

1   On August 30, 2006, John Miclot, President and CEO of Respironics, rang the opening bell at the NASDAQ in Times Square to commemorate the thirtieth anniversary of the company's founding. Standing next to him was Gerald McGinnis, the entrepreneur who had started Respironics with $13 thousand in capital raised from angel investors. From a small, one-product company that made surgical masks for the delivery of anesthesia, Respironics had evolved into a designer, manufacturer and marketer of medical devices for the treatment of sleep and respiratory disorders. Headquartered in Murrysville, Pennsylvania, Respironics manufactured and marketed continuous positive airway pressure systems (CPAPs) and masks to treat obstructive sleep apnea (OSA) to customers in over 131 countries.

2   Besides passing an important milestone in its history, Respironics had exceeded the $1 billion mark in revenues for the first time for the fiscal year that ended on June 30. The company had nearly $260 million in cash and marketable securities on hand to pursue new market opportunities. Yet, as Miclot celebrated this anniversary and pondered future avenues for growth, many challenges lay ahead. Respironics' stock price had fluctuated, reaching a high of $42.95 per share on October 4, 2005, sinking to a low of $32.66 per share on May 24, 2006, and standing at $36.67 per share on August 30, 2006. In the past fiscal year, it had recalled 172 thousand humidifiers at a cost of $5 million. Respironics' share of the domestic sleep therapy equipment market was slipping too, from 51.8 percent in 2004, to 48.5 percent in 2005, and to 45.4 percent in 2006. In the global sleep therapy equipment market, Respironics was locked in a tight two-way battle for market share with a formidable rival, ResMed, Incorporated (Exhibit 1, Exhibit 2, and Exhibit 3).

3   Becky Quick, a CNBC anchor, had asked John Miclot about ResMed just before the opening bell at the NASDAQ: "You know, you are not the only player in this area. ResMed (RMD) is also one of your competitors. They have seen even stronger revenue growth. How are you fighting off the competition here?" Miclot replied: "Well, our company has continued to innovate this therapy. Recently we introduced some new technology called C-Flex which reduces pressure on exhalation and makes a patient more comfortable. You know, we broke the billion dollar mark and have forecasted to grow mid teens top line and our earnings per share of 17 to 18 percent in FY '07. So we feel like we have got a very, very bright future."[2]

This case was developed for the sole purpose of providing material for class discussion. It is not intended to illustrate either effective or ineffective handling of a managerial situation.

The authors wish to thank Dr. Lew G. Brown, editor, and three anonymous reviewers for their helpful comments and suggestions in the refinement of this case.

[1] From interviews with John Miclot, in R. Grillot, "Tapping into the Problem Sleeper Market," *HomeCare Magazine* 28 (7) (July 2005): 30.

[2] "Respironics—Pres. & CEO Interview," CNBC/Dow Jones Business Video Transcripts (August 30, 2006).

EXHIBIT 1   Global Sleep Therapy Equipment Market Share Chart

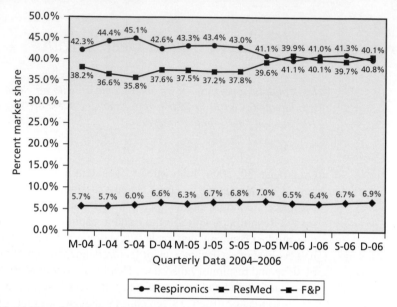

Source: Michael S. Matson, Senior Analyst, Medical Device Equity Research, *Sleep FQ307 Review & Medtrade Summary* (April 30, 2007), Wachovia Capital Markets, LLC.
Note: Other industry competitors, together, held between 12.0–13.9 percent market share across the same quarters.

EXHIBIT 2   Domestic Sleep Therapy Equipment Market Share Chart

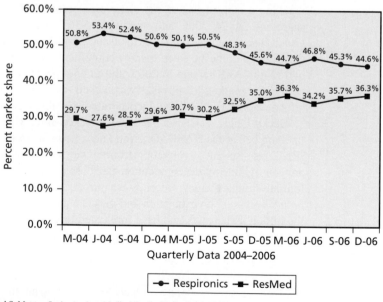

Source: Michael S. Matson, Senior Analyst, Medical Device Equity Research, *Sleep FQ307 Review & Medtrade Summary* (April 30, 2007), Wachovia Capital Markets, LLC.

4   Meanwhile, unknown to the public, another drama was unfolding. John Miclot had received a message from his office. Ivo Lurvink, the chief executive of Philips Consumer Healthcare Solutions, a unit of Royal Philips Electronics NV (Philips), wanted to arrange a

EXHIBIT 3 **International Sleep Therapy Equipment Market Share Chart**

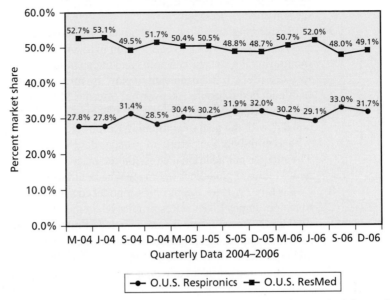

Source: Michael S. Matson, Senior Analyst, Medical Device Equity Research, *Sleep FQ307 Review & Medtrade Summary* (April 30, 2007), Wachovia Capital Markets, LLC.
Note: O.U.S.: Outside of the U.S.

meeting "to discuss matters of mutual business interest between Philips and Respironics."[3] Miclot knew what that meant. Philips, a Dutch conglomerate, had been rumored for some time to be seeking to purchase selected U.S.-based medical equipment manufacturers to bolster market expansion of its Medical Systems division. Philips group sales in fiscal year 2006 had been 27.0 million. Its medical systems division, which comprised both professional and consumer healthcare products, posted fiscal year 2006 sales of 6.7 million, having grown from 21 percent of Philips' portfolio in 2005 to 27 percent in 2006.

5   Perhaps Philips' interest in Respironics was friendly; perhaps it was not. During the past two years, Miclot had been approached by third parties on several occasions and his answer had always been the same—Respironics wanted to remain an independent company and was not interested in a business combination or acquisition.[4] Miclot wondered how he should respond now. He would need to discuss this development with his management team, and in the event of a bid, convene Respironics' board of directors.

COMPANY HISTORY

6   Gerald McGinnis, an inventor, founded Respironics in 1976. When a fire destroyed Respironics' sole manufacturing facility in western Pennsylvania, McGinnis, who had business associates in Hong Kong, moved manufacturing offshore to China. McGinnis was replaced as CEO of Respironics by Dennis Meteney in 1994. McGinnis continued as the company's chairman of the board and advanced technology officer. Apria Healthcare

---

[3] "Offer to Purchase," (January 3, 2008), Exhibit (a) (1) (A), Form SC TO-T. Retrieved from EDGAR.

[4] "Solicitation/Recommendation Statement under Section 14(d) (4) of the Securities Exchange Act of 1934," (January 3, 2008), Form SC 14D9. Retrieved from EDGAR.

demoted Respironics' status from primary to secondary supplier in 1996, resulting in a loss of sales in fiscal 1997. In that year, Respironics became mired in a patent infringement lawsuit filed by ResMed.

7   Respironics acquired Healthdyne Technologies, Incorporated for approximately $337 million in stock and $38 million in assumed debt in 1998. Healthdyne manufactured monitoring devices for newborns and therapeutic devices for sleep apnea and other respiratory disorders. It had been "put in play" by Invacare (a manufacturer of wheelchairs) which had launched a hostile takeover bid offering $15 a share. Respironics viewed Healthdyne as an excellent strategic fit, so it stepped in as a "white knight." The result was a "merger of equals" with the goal of combining Respironics' internal product development capabilities with Healthdyne's expertise in product development, licensing and product acquisition.[5] The merger put additional stress on the business, whose revenues were declining because new Medicare guidelines restricted who could use certain types of ventilators.

8   On July 29, 1999, Respironics announced a major restructuring. CEO Meteny was asked to resign. James Liken, a Respironics board member and health care consultant, became the new CEO. Board members had concluded that the company needed a leader with strong sales and marketing skills who could better relate to healthcare professionals, salespeople, and customers.[6] John Miclot, a senior vice president of sales and marketing at Healthdyne, was appointed president of Respironics' largest division, the Homecare Group. He was soon promoted into a newly created position, Chief Strategic Officer. Craig Reynolds, the CEO of Healthdyne at the time of the acquisition, was appointed to the newly created position of chief operating officer.

9   Liken inherited a company that, in his words, was "mentally flat" and "very bureaucratic."[7] He believed that Respironics had excellent engineering talent but had lost touch with its customers. Liken launched educational programs for customers and physicians. He held motivational talks with employees and delineated behavioral expectations. He gave managers the autonomy to implement strategies on their own. He also set up systems to evaluate progress on a continual basis, allocated resources to maximize shareholder value, and hired and retained the best employees.[8]

10   Forty-four-year-old John Miclot succeeded Liken as CEO in October 2003. Miclot believed that Respironics had the ability to extend its core competencies beyond the diagnosis and treatment of OSA to discover cures for insomnia, restless leg syndrome and circadian rhythm disorders. It could develop medical devices to treat asthma and end-of-life diseases (e.g., emphysema and chronic bronchitis). Miclot was concerned that too much of the company's business relied on sales of sleep therapy devices. If the fundamental market dynamics changed, the entire company would be at risk.[9]

11   On April 22, 2006, Respironics named Harvard Medical School professor of sleep medicine, Dr. David P. White, as its chief medical officer. At the age of fifty-six, White felt he had ten years or so of "kick" left in him to redefine the sleep industry.[10] As he commented,

---

[5] "Respironics to acquire Healthdyne technologies for 2.2 times revenue," *Weekly Corporate Growth Report* 970 (November 17, 1997): 9332.

[6] J. E. Robinet, "'Positive step for company and me,' says ousted CEO," *Pittsburgh Business Times* 19 (5) (August 27, 1999): 1.

[7] P. Gaynor, "Murrysville, Pa., Firm prospers making products to help people sleep better," *Knight Ridder Tribune Business News* (December 18, 2003): 1.

[8] T. Carbasho, "Manufacturer of the year award: Large-size category—Respironics, putting customers first," *Pittsburgh Business Times,* 23 (20) (December 5, 2003): S10.

[9] M. Moran, "Meet HME's new billion dollar baby," *HME News* 12 (9) (September, 2006): 1.

[10] J. Andrews, "The doctor is in, David White, M.D., assumes clinical controls at Respironics," *HME News* 12 (7) (July, 2006): 1.

"CPAPs have gotten better, quieter and smaller, but it's basically the same therapy. I think it would be exciting to change the paradigm and do something that ends up changing how we address breathing abnormalities."[11]

12   In fiscal year 2006, Respironics reported revenues of $1.046 billion, making it the fifth straight year that sales had grown by at least 15 percent.[12] Its fiscal 2006 net income was $99.9 million (or $1.36 a share) compared to fiscal 2005 net income of $84.4 million (or $1.17 a share). Frost & Sullivan, a global growth consulting company, gave Respironics two awards for market leadership—one in the sleep diagnostic device market and one in the positive airway pressure devices market. Respironics' Alice sleep diagnostic platform was described as being "by far one of the most popular and reliable sleep diagnostic systems ever introduced."[13] A research analyst at Frost & Sullivan praised Respironics' Flow Generator for OSA patients as representing the "gold standard in respiratory care."[14]

ORGANIZATIONAL STRUCTURE AND CULTURE

13   Respironics' basic organizational structure consisted of three groups, each with its own separate business units (see Exhibit 4). Two groups, the Sleep and Home Respiratory Group and the Hospital Group, reflected the location of a patient's diagnosis and treatment—in a sleep center or at home on the one hand, or in a hospital, on the other hand. Both groups had their own domestic sales forces. Sleep area sales representatives called on operators of sleep clinics (to sell sleep diagnostics equipment and services) and on durable medical equipment (DME) distributors (to sell CPAPs, surgical masks, ventilators, and oxygen concentrators). Hospital Group sales forces visited pulmonologists,[15] who managed intensive care units in hospitals, and marketed ventilators. The International Group was organized into three distinct geographic regions: Asia and the Pacific; Europe, the Middle East and Africa; the Americas (e.g., Canada and South America). Sales associates sold sleep and ventilator products in over twenty-five different countries.

14   Miclot spoke about Respironics' organizational structure: ". . . we've really created a bunch of little businesses underneath the broader organization, and that allows you to create entrepreneurship around the organization, even when you're performing well."[16]

15   Respironics' vision was "to be the worldwide leader at anticipating needs and providing valued solutions to the sleep and respiratory markets." It developed a set of core competencies to support its vision and organizational structure (see Exhibit 5). The three competencies were: "teaming," "market foresight" and "learning agility."

16   Respironics employed 47 hundred employees worldwide in 2006. It provided employees with medical and dental benefits, wellness programs and fitness centers, educational reimbursement, savings bonds, stock options, and shares and access to a credit union. Some employees were allowed to telecommute from home.[17] The company cared about the health and well-being of its employees. A walk in the hallways of its Murrysville headquarters revealed an informational flyer, part of a series, about the health benefits of herbs and

[11] Ibid.

[12] C. Snowbeck, "Respironics revenues top $1 billion," *Knight Ridder Tribune Business News* (July 28, 2006): 1.

[13] "Frost & Sullivan recognizes Respironics' leadership in the highly demanding sleep diagnostic devices market," *PR Newswire US* (June 6, 2006).

[14] "Frost & Sullivan lauds Respironics' market leadership in the U.S. positive airway pressure therapy devices markets," *PR Newswire US* (August, 2006).

[15] A pulmonologist is a physician who specializes in the lungs.

[16] R. Marano, "Market maker," *Smart Business Pittsburgh* 12 (9) (January 1, 2006): 25.

[17] "Respironics, Inc.," *Plunkett's Health Care Industry Almanac* (2004).

EXHIBIT 4   Respironics' Overall Structure

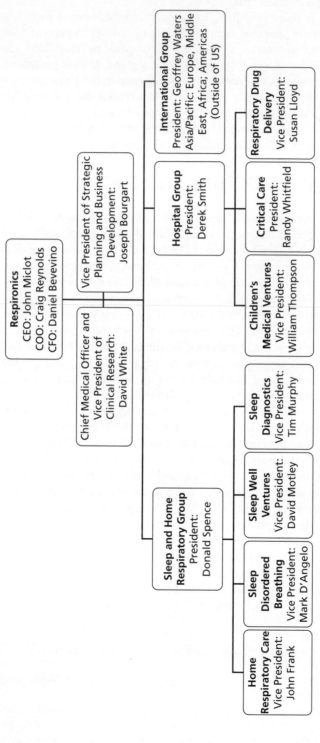

Source: Interview with Joseph Bourgart, vice president of strategic planning and business development (December 2006).

EXHIBIT 5
Respironics' Vision, Key Competencies and Core Practices

Source: Company documents.

Vision:
To be the worldwide leader at anticipating needs and providing valued solutions to the sleep and respiratory markets.

Key Competencies:

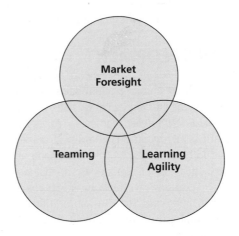

Core Practices:

- Focus on driving the success of our customers.
- Innovate valued solutions around the needs of our customers and the markets we serve; if in doubt, ask our customers.
- Drive quality, cost and speed as a competitive advantage.
- Hire the best people; retain the best people; accept no less.
- Lead, energize and empower everyone to make decisions, accept responsibility and get things done.
- Create clear simple methods to accomplish objectives; eliminate bureaucracy.
- Evaluate plans and progress continuously; enhance what is working and change what is not.
- Allocate resources relentlessly to achieve our objectives, maximize shareholder value and assure social responsibility.

spices. Ginger, for example, was good for nausea, vomiting and headaches. The flyer suggested that employees take advantage of the nice spring weather and walk outside during breaks to soak up vitamin D from the sun. It reminded employees to drink one-half of their body weight in ounces of water every day.

FINANCE AND ACCOUNTING

17   Whereas the functions of sales/marketing and research/development were decentralized and managed by the heads of the different business units and groups, all finance-related functions (i.e., billing and payments), were centralized at Respironics' Murrysville headquarters. Information management was totally integrated for Respironics' global operations, with SAP enterprise business software. The CFO received daily, monthly and quarterly reports so that he could react quickly to an aberration.

18   Daniel Bevevino, the CFO, oversaw three activities: (a) conducting financial audits and ensuring compliance with different laws and regulations, including Sarbanes-Oxley and the tax code; (b) completing transaction-oriented processes, including billing clients, collecting payments and handling cash receipts; (c) supporting value-added business processes that could involve investments in new projects and acquisitions of other businesses.

19   Bevevino described Respironics' acquisition screening processes as follows: "An acquisition candidate must first represent a strategic fit for the company. The target company also has to demonstrate financial fit. We would calculate net present value, years to pay back, dilution and accretion. Case studies featuring acquisitions and other contemporary business issues are used to provide our managers with relevant leadership training."

RESEARCH AND DEVELOPMENT

20   As a rule of thumb, new products, including major enhancements to existing ones, were to account for 40–50 percent of sales in every two-year period. An internal company Web site enabled design team members, consisting of engineers, manufacturing people, clinical staff, quality staff, document control staff, marketing employees and purchasing agents, to communicate with one another. All the documents associated with a project were posted as PDF files and were updated on a regular basis so that teams could identify and solve problems early on.[18]

21   Respironics invested approximately 6 percent of its annual revenues in R&D ($60 million in 2005 and $65 million in 2006). Joseph Bourgart, vice president of strategic planning and business development, believed these R&D investments were appropriate and that companies making respiratory devices should target the 5–7 percent range. Companies with high-tech products (e.g., pacemakers and pharmaceutical products) required higher R&D spends as a percentage of sales, while companies with low-tech products (e.g., band-aids and surgical gowns) had correspondingly lower R&D requirements.

22   Respironics also supported other types of research activities. In 2006, it gave $1.5 million to its foundation, formed for scientific, educational and charitable purposes and used to promote awareness of and research into the medical consequences of sleep and respiratory problems.[19] Respironics sponsored empirical articles and reviews for a 2005 special issue, "Behavioral Issues in Adherence to CPAP Therapy," in *Behavioral Sleep Medicine*.

MANUFACTURING AND ASSEMBLY

23   Respironics' manufacturing facilities were located in Murrysville, Pennsylvania; Atlanta, Georgia; Carlsbad, California; Wallingford, Connecticut; Shenzhen and Hong Kong, China; and Subic Bay, the Philippines. The company was in the process of establishing centers of excellence in manufacturing at each of its locations. Depending on the type of product being made, different facility layouts, material storage and handling processes, and manufacturing techniques were required. It made sense, therefore, to set up facilities to handle homogenous processes. They would be highly specialized and employees would gain experience with one type of process. Respironics planned, for example, to move the assembling of its high volume, disposable products (i.e., masks) to the Asian-Pacific [facility]. It would continue to make its high volume, electro-mechanical devices in Murrysville.

24   The facility in Murrysville used demand flow technology (DFT) to assemble electromechanical devices (e.g., CPAPs, hospital ventilators and life support equipment) and patient interface/Children's Medical Venture products (e.g., masks). Sleep devices were assembled in three, eight-hour hour shifts; the evening shift was added in 2005 to enable additional testing. The other products were assembled in two, eight-hour hour shifts.[20]

---

[18] P. E. Teague, "Hone-Grown websites," *Design News* 60 (6) (April 18, 2005): 12.

[19] Respironics, 10–K.

[20] Special thanks are given to Mr. Steve Buccilli, After Market Support Team Leader, who contributed to this section and gave one of the case authors a guided tour of the Murrysville manufacturing facility on May 24, 2007.

25   DFT meant that employees made products only based on orders received. They stored necessary components in a few bins near the line of workstations. Suppliers, who were alerted when one of the bins was depleted, replenished them. Line operators were trained in the jobs on either side of their own station so that they could "flex" to assist their neighbors when required to keep the production moving. Lines were designed so that multiple products could pass along them.[21] After Respironics implemented DFT in 1998, unit volume increased by 400 percent and component inventory was reduced by 60 to 70 percent.[22]

QUALITY ASSURANCE

26   If the on/off button on a vacuum cleaner malfunctioned, the worst that could happen was that the carpet did not get cleaned. If a respirator or ventilator failed, a patient's life could be at risk. Respironics worked to ensure that its products were of the highest quality. It, for example, improved the process in which adhesives were used in the manufacture of a manual resuscitator. In 1995, it used a system from EFD, Inc. to apply the adhesive in precise, repeated amounts; to use fixtures to hold parts during gluing and assembly; to alert assembly workers that the adhesive was in place. The adhesive was clear so a powdered colorant visible under UV light was added and a black light was mounted at the dispensing station. A soft purple tint assured assemblers that the adhesive had been applied as each cycle was completed.[23] Similar solutions were implemented as part of the imbedded quality assurance steps integrated into the company's current production lines. Customized test fixtures were put into use to assure quality levels were achieved and to minimize the number of units that ultimately were rejected upon inspection.

27   Quality assurance inspectors met across product lines to discuss quality issues. Assemblers were given training in QCDSM (quality, cost, delivery, safety, and morale)—each of which held equal importance to a job well done. Assemblers were able to rotate to different stations during the week. This reduced carpal tunnel injuries, enhanced quality, improved cross functionality and developed different skills among operators.

28   Respironics voluntarily recalled several of its products in recent years. In 2006, for example, it recalled 172 thousand humidifiers that had been in use for three to five years at a cost of $5 million. Respironics hired a firm to handle the collection and replacement of the units. The third party was responsible for contacting the patients and collecting the humidifiers. The process had to be handled with sensitivity since the medical equipment distributors wanted to maintain control over their rosters of customers.

SUPPLY CHAIN MANAGEMENT

29   Respironics bought components from many different suppliers. In 2004, Electronic Product Integration Company (EPIC) used a *kanban* system to deliver printed circuit boards (PCBs) to Respironics' Murrysville assembly facility on an as-needed basis. Respironics had three bins for PCBs, each of which held 1,672 boards. As soon as it depleted a bin, it faxed EPIC to start filling another one. EPIC kept two full bins. When it received notice, EPIC shipped a bin and started to fill a new one. Between them, they never had more than five days' worth of PCB inventory.[24]

[21] P. Baker, "The future is flow," *Works Management* (1999): 52–54.

[22] "Respironics. Breathe Easy," *Manufacturing in Action* (February, 2003). Retrieved May 25, 2007 from http://www.themanufacturer.com/us/profile/944/Respironics? PHPSESSID=1b8093.

[23] "Built-in quality," *Appliance Manufacturer* 43 (12) (December, 1995): 20.

[24] B. Roberts, "Just-in-time just makes sense," *Electronic Business* 30 (6) (June, 2004): 12.

30   Sometimes, it was hard to purchase certain items—especially relays, IR components and flow sensors—needed for medical devices. These were much in demand by firms in other industries, especially toy manufacturers. When quantities were low, suppliers might have preferred to sell their components to toy and electronics manufacturers. Respironics' procurement agents were quick to step in, explain the importance of its medical devices for patients and thereby appeal to the supplier's sense of social responsibility.

SLEEP AND RESPIRATORY MARKETS

31   Sleep, or the lack of it, had become an important issue by the beginning of the third millennium. According to the popular press, the two most brilliant inventions of 2006 were: sleep-inducing toothpaste and a head-nodding alarm to avert sleep while driving.[25] Individuals slept when they shouldn't (e.g., when driving a truck, operating equipment, or participating in military action) and couldn't sleep when they should (e.g., at night or after traveling across time zones). A poll conducted for the National Sleep Foundation revealed that three-quarters of adults said that they frequently had a sleep problem (e.g., snoring or waking during the night).[26] According to the U.S. Surgeon General, sleep deprivation and related disorders cost the nation $16 billion in annual health care expenses and $50 billion in lost productivity.[27]

32   There was a growing perception among the public that oxygen concentrators and ventilators were not used solely to treat a patient who was critically ill or in a coma. They were available to people of all ages, from premature infants to adults who were unable to breathe normally.[28] If Christopher Reeve, the actor who played Superman, needed a portable ventilator, then anyone might need one at some point in their lives. According to Medtech Insight, over $1.3 billion was spent on ventilators, oxygen therapy systems, and airway management accessories in 2004 in the U.S.; sales were expected to reach more than $1.9 billion by the year 2010 (a compound annual rate of 6.3 percent).[29]

Diagnosis and Treatment of Sleep-Related Disorders

33   The International Classification of Diseases (ICD) provided descriptions of over eighty recognized sleep disorders.[30] Individuals commonly reported that they suffered from minor problems, such as jet lag and snoring, to more severe problems, such as insomnia and sleep apnea.

Sleep Apnea

34   Individuals with narrow upper airways or poor muscle tone were prone to temporary collapses of the upper airway during sleep, called "apneas," and to near closures of the upper airway, called "hypopneas." These breathing irregularities resulted in a lowering of blood oxygen concentration, causing the central nervous system to react to the lack of oxygen

---

[25] D. Eatock and A. Horowitz, "Endpaper," *The New York Times Magazine* (December 10, 2006): 108.

[26] "Mergers & acquisitions; Sleep and respiratory company acquires Mini-Mitter," *World Disease Weekly* (May 3, 2005): 1118.

[27] D. Lazarus, "Sleep: Can't get enough of it," *San Francisco Chronicle* (March 1, 2006). Retrieved January 2, 2007 from http://www.sfgate.com/cgi-bin/article.cgi?file=/chronicle/archive/2006/03/01/BUGLTHFG8O50.DTL.

[28] P. Kurtzweil, "When machines do the breathing," *FDA Consumer* 33 (5) (September/October, 1999): 22–25.

[29] "U.S. Markets for Ventilators, Oxygen Therapy Systems, and Airway Management Accessories," (October, 2005). Retrieved December 29, 2006 from http://www.medtechinsight.com/ReportA366.html.

[30] "Managing sleep disorders," *Practitioner* (April 25, 2006): 226.

or increased carbon dioxide and signaling the body to respond. Typically, the individual subconsciously was aroused from sleep, causing the throat muscles to contract, opening the airway. After a few gasping breaths, or snores, blood oxygen levels increased and the individual resumed a deeper sleep until the cycle repeated itself. Sufferers of OSA typically experienced ten or more such cycles per hour. While these awakenings greatly impaired the quality of sleep, the individual was not normally aware of these disruptions. They could, however, lead to excessive daytime sleepiness, reduced cognitive functioning, depression and irritability.[31]

35 Sleep apnea could be a contributing factor in an individual's death. The disorder received public attention when retired NFL football player Reggie White died in 2004 at the age of forty-three. He suffered from respiratory diseases that included OSA. A study by ResMed and SleepTech found that football players were almost five times more likely to test positive for OSA than similarly aged adults; sleep apnea was associated with large body masses.[32] A strong association was also discovered between OSA and a number of cardiovascular diseases.[33] A recent study found that OSA increased an individual's risk of having a heart attack or dying by 30 percent over a period of four to five years.[34] Another study found that patients with OSA were twice as likely as people without OSA to have a car crash and three to five times as likely to have a serious crash involving personal injury.[35]

36 To receive a diagnosis of OSA, a patient might visit a general practitioner who would refer the patient to a clinical sleep lab. The patient would participate in an overnight sleep study in which he/she was connected through electrodes placed on the head, chin, alongside the eyes, nostrils and legs to equipment that measured brain waves, eye movements, muscle relaxation, airflow, and leg twitching. Other devices monitored the level of oxygen in the blood and air movement in the chest. A polysomnography recorded the number of abnormal respiratory episodes that occurred during the night.

37 To treat severe cases of OSA, sufferers could undergo uvulopalatopharyngoplasty (UPPP) surgery to remove excess tissue from the upper airway, to streamline the shape of the airway, or to implant a device to support the soft palate. In mandibular advancement surgery, a patient's lower jaw was moved forward to widen his or her airway. UPPP was expensive, painful and had less than a 50 percent success rate, Bourgart noted.

38 A non-invasive alternative, involving the use of continuous positive airway pressure devices (CPAP), was also available. An individual slept with a nasal interface connected to a small portable airflow generator that delivered room air at a positive pressure. He or she breathed in air from the flow generator and breathed out through an exhaust port in the interface. Continuous air pressure applied in this manner acted as a "pneumatic splint" to keep the upper airway open and unobstructed (See Exhibit 6 for photographs of masks and CPAPs). CPAP was not a cure for OSA, and needed to be used on a nightly basis. Patient compliance in using these devices on a regular, uninterrupted basis proved to be a major factor in the efficacy of CPAP treatment.[36]

[31] F. N. Kjelsberg, E. A. Ruud, and K. Stavem, "Predictors of symptoms of anxiety and depression in obstructive sleep apnea," *Sleep Medicine* 6 (4) (July, 2005): 341–346.

[32] J. Gundersen, "OSA linked to death of NFL veteran," *HME News* 11 (2) (February, 2005): 43–44.

[33] A. Quershi, R. D. Ballard, and H. S. Nelson, "Obstructive sleep apnea," *Journal of Allergy and Clinical Immunology* 112 (4) (October, 2003): 643–651.

[34] "Heart disease; Sleep apnea increases risk of heart attack or death by 30 percent," *Cardiovascular Business Week* (June 5, 2007): 114.

[35] "Sleep apnea; Sleep apnea patients have greatly increased risk of severe car crashes," *Biotech Week* (June 6, 2007): 153.

[36] H. Engleman, and M. R. Wild, "Improving CPAP use by patients with the sleep apnoea/hypopnoea syndrome (SAHS)," *Sleep Medicine Reviews* 7 (1) (February, 2003): 81–99.

EXHIBIT 6 Photographs of Masks and CPAP Machines for Sleep Apnea

  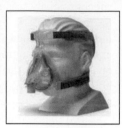 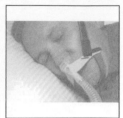

Source: www.respironics.com

Simple Snoring

39 Snoring occurred when the airway at the back of the throat constricted and caused air to be inhaled at increased velocity and pressure. The tissue at the back of the mouth vibrated, creating noise.[37] There were over 800 patented anti-snoring devices.[38] They ranged from nasal strips, special pillows, and dental appliances to a therapeutic ring that applied acupressure points and an electrical device that produced unpleasant stimuli when the patient snored. Surgery could be performed to correct a deviated nasal septum or to remove nasal polyps, enlarged adenoids and/or tonsils. That solved the problem for some patients. For others, snoring could be a symptom of OSA. They would go through the same diagnostic and treatment process as for sleep apnea. Chronic snorers could elect UPPP surgery or CPAP therapy.

Insomnia

40 Insomnia referred to the difficulty in initiating and maintaining sleep.[39] Short-term insomnia was attributed to stress, jet lag, drugs, or an unfamiliar sleep environment; long-term insomnia was related to hereditary factors and resulted from an underlying psychiatric or medical condition (e.g., post-traumatic stress disorder, chemical imbalances in the brain, or anatomical differences in the nervous system).[40]

41 Stimulus control therapy encouraged insomniacs to go to bed only when sleepy and wake up at the same set time every morning. Cognitive behavioral therapy encouraged individuals to talk with a trained psychologist; relaxation techniques taught individuals yoga and meditation; and light therapy suggested that individuals avoid bright lights at night. Finally, some insomniacs were prescribed sleeping pills.

Diagnosis and Treatment of Respiratory Disorders

42 As the baby boomers (those persons born between 1946 and 1964) aged and were eager to maintain active lifestyles, breathing devices needed to be portable and highly reliable. Ventilators had become substantially more sophisticated than the iron lungs that were first introduced in the 1920s. Noninvasive, positive pressure ventilators enabled an exchange of gases through facial or nasal masks that were attached to an oxygen concentrator. Bilevel positive airway pressure (bilevel PAP) ventilators responded to a patient's own airflow rates and cycles; they were designed to deliver two different levels of positive pressure: the

---

[37] "Device available to control snoring," *Journal Record* (February 17, 1993).
[38] J. M. Farrell, "Pinkie ring claims to relieve snoring," *Chicago Tribune* (May 23, 2006): 7.
[39] "Managing sleep disorders" (2006), op. cit.
[40] "Managing sleep disorders" (2006), op. cit.

amount of pressure during inspiration was set higher and the amount of pressure delivered to keep the airway open during expiration was set lower.[41]

43   The advantages of BiPAP ventilators were that the patient could talk, swallow and move around. The disadvantages were pressure sores, nasal dryness, eye irritation and air leaks.[42] Other ways of delivering ventilation were through volume ventilators, pressure-controlled ventilators or continuous positive airway pressure (CPAP) devices.[43]

44   Ventilators were used when patients suffered from neuromuscular disorders (e.g., Lou Gehrig's disease and spinal muscular atrophy), respiratory diseases (e.g., chronic obstructive pulmonary disease or COPD, cystic fibrosis and severe pneumonia), and bone disorders (severe curvature of the spine and deformities of the chest wall).[44]

COMPETITION

45   Respironics' primary competitors in the sleep disorder market were California-based ResMed, Inc. and New Zealand-based Fisher & Paykel Healthcare Corp. Ltd (see Exhibit 7, Exhibit 8, and Exhibit 9 for comparative financial data).

46   Joseph Bourgart, vice president of strategic planning, said, "Respironics is committed to finding solutions to all sleep and respiratory disorders. It will pursue any type of effective treatment—including medical devices, surgical procedures, pharmaceutical products, or some optimal combination of one or more of these therapies. It will provide the best possible products through any means possible—organic growth, licensing arrangements, strategic alliances, or by acquiring existing companies with unique technologies." As Bourgart believed, "continued diversification into the diagnosis and treatment of sleep disorders beyond OSA will have a profound effect on the value of the company in the long run."

47   At the same time, Bourgart acknowledged that Respironics' primary competitors had viable strategic plans and that only time would tell which approach would lead to ultimate success. ResMed, an early entrant in the market for medical devices to treat OSA, had taken a clinical perspective and was committed to extending its solid CPAP technology platform to treat different diseases and different stages of disease. Fisher & Paykel, which had been part of a large New Zealand-based appliance manufacturer before it was spun off in 2001, had built a solid foundation in humidification. To this, it added infant care products (e.g., warmers) and lower end, lower cost CPAP devices.

48   In the respiratory market, Respironics competed with Tyco Healthcare Group (a division of Tyco International Ltd.) and Invacare Corp.

ResMed

49   ResMed was founded as ResCare in 1989 after Peter Farrell led a management buyout of Baxter Healthcare's respiratory technology unit. Farrell, 63, was ResMed's CEO from its inception to 2007. ResCare initially developed the SULLIVAN nasal CPAP systems (named after inventor Colin Sullivan) in Australia. In 1991 it introduced the Bubble Mask and the APD2 portable CPAP device. Three years later, ResCare began marketing its first VPAP, which applied different air pressures for inhalation and exhalation, in the U.S. In 1995, the

---

[41] L. M. Tamburri, Assisting your patient's breathing with noninvasive ventilation, *Nursing* 28 (10) (October, 1998): 1–3.

[42] N. O'Neill, "Improving ventilation in children using bilevel positive airway pressure," *Pediatric Nursing* 24 (4) (July/August, 1998): 377–382.

[43] R. E. Hillberg, and D. C. Johnson, "Noninvasive ventilation," *The New England Journal of Medicine* 337 (24) (December 11, 1997): 1746–1752.

[44] Kurtzweil (1999), op. cit.

EXHIBIT 7   Comparative Income Statements, Fiscal Years 2003–2006

(all amounts in U.S. $000 except per share amounts)	F&P Healthcare				ResMed				Respironics			
	2003	2004	2005	2006	2003	2004	2005	2006	2003	2004	2005	2006
Income Statements												
Net Revenues from Cont. Ops.	103,063	132,056	162,599	199,556	273,570	339,338	425,505	606,996	629,817	759,550	911,497	1,046,141
Cost of Sales	33,412	38,468	66,324	83,645	100,483	122,602	150,645	230,101	310,385	356,625	413,215	473,263
Gross Profit	69,651	93,588	96,275	115,911	173,087	216,736	274,860	376,895	319,432	402,925	498,282	572,878
Operating Expenses												
Selling, General and Admin.	27,411	36,350	45,543	56,293	85,313	104,706	135,703	200,168	200,031	247,972	305,836	355,918
Research and Development	5,704	8,675	10,947	11,956	20,534	26,169	35,282	37,216	24,047	29,478	45,625	58,966
Donations to Foundations	0	0	0	0	0	500	500	760	0	2,844	3,000	1,500
Restructuring and/or Acquisition-Related Expenses	0	0	0	0	0	0	5,152	1,124	19,825	19,475	9,908	6,888
Amortization of Acquired Intangible Assets	0	0	0	0	0	0	870	6,327	0	0	0	0
Total Operating Expenses	33,115	45,025	56,490	68,249	105,847	131,375	177,507	245,595	243,903	299,769	364,369	423,272
Operating Profit	36,536	48,563	39,785	47,662	67,240	85,861	97,353	131,300	75,529	103,156	133,913	149,606
Interest and Other Net Income (loss)	18,458	1,180	22,102	24,301	(133)	(693)	(727)	2,094	(639)	2,078	1,806	9,616
Income (loss) before Tax	54,994	49,743	61,887	71,963	67,127	84,668	96,626	133,394	74,890	105,234	135,719	159,222
Less: Provision for Income Tax	18,941	16,125	20,383	23,743	21,398	27,384	31,841	45,183	28,309	40,214	51,363	59,329
Net Income	36,053	33,618	41,504	48,220	45,729	57,284	64,785	88,211	46,581	65,020	84,356	99,893
Weighted Avg. Shs. Out.-Basic (000)	511,837	512,120	508,687	508,382	66,108	67,388	68,644	72,307	67,170	68,754	70,896	72,311
Weighted Avg. Shs. Out.-Diluted (000)	519,802	524,113	523,841	524,847	68,878	70,250	74,942	77,162	68,688	70,619	72,255	73,570
Year End Shares Outstanding (000)	512,184	511,285	508,635	509,332	66,742	67,717	70,001	75,670	67,914	69,967	71,699	72,740
Net Income per Share-Basic	$0.07	$0.07	$0.08	$0.09	$0.69	$0.85	$0.94	$1.22	$0.69	$0.95	$1.19	$1.38
Net Income per Share-Diluted	$0.07	$0.06	$0.08	$0.09	$0.66	$0.82	$0.86	$1.14	$0.68	$0.92	$1.17	$1.36
Total Number of Employees	767	900	1,096	1,276	1,464	1,520	1,927	2,500	2,700	3,000	3,900	4,700

Sources: Fisher & Paykel Healthcare *Annual Reports, 2002–2006*; data for ResMed and Respironics from *Mergent Online,* accessed April 26, 2007.
Notes: (1) Fisher & Paykel Healthcare (F&P), fiscal year ending March 31; (2) ResMed (RMD) and Respironics (RESP) fiscal years ending June 30.

EXHIBIT 8   Comparative Balance Sheets, Fiscal Years 2003–2006 (All amounts in U.S. $000 For the year ending)

	F&P Healthcare March 31				ResMed June 30				Respironics June 30			
	2003	2004	2005	2006	2003	2004	2005	2006	2003	2004	2005	2006
Assets												
Cash and Marketable Securities	26,623	30,993	23,405	18,035	121,024	140,928	142,185	219,544	95,900	192,446	234,632	259,513
Short-term Investment												
Accounts Receivable, Net of Doubtful Accounts	32,495	32,012	34,480	34,746	56,694	67,242	103,951	138,147	128,127	140,634	153,479	187,502
Inventories	12,036	15,683	19,520	22,858	49,386	55,797	89,107	116,194	83,986	85,539	96,315	124,149
Prepaid Expenses and Other	198	206	316	224	6,500	6,821	9,737	9,763	7,890	8,621	11,931	19,197
Deferred income Tax	2,330	917	2,907	3,302	8,301	7,041	15,230	26,636	24,112	25,373	39,767	45,893
Total Current Assets	73,682	79,811	80,528	79,164	241,905	277,829	360,210	510,284	340,015	452,613	536,124	642,092
Property, Plant and Equipment, Net	39,354	46,604	52,359	81,032	104,687	147,268	174,168	245,376	98,680	111,057	127,376	137,943
Other Assets	10,786	16,984	10,079	6,664	7,098	8,173	58,662	55,949	34,592	37,466	48,319	55,981
Patents, Net	972	1,454	1,504	1,424	3,745	4,814						
Goodwill	1,203	1,173	894	651	102,160	106,075	181,106	195,612	108,909	110,003	166,627	181,362
Total Assets	125,997	146,026	145,464	168,934	459,595	544,159	774,146	1,007,221	582,196	711,139	878,446	1,017,378
Liabilities and Shareholders' Equity												
Accounts Payable, Trade	4,779	7,042	9,521	12,110	19,368	18,574	34,416	45,045	40,531	52,789	57,474	70,667
Accrued Expenses and Other Current Liabilities	13,268	12,782	12,921	15,686	31,215	42,017	68,700	79,086	68,389	88,255	126,242	122,173
Current Portion of Long-Term Debt	1,102	—	1,152	11,580	—	—	115,435	4,869	18,308	10,536	17,411	18,201
Total Current Liabilities	19,149	19,824	23,594	39,375	50,583	60,591	218,551	129,000	127,229	151,581	201,128	211,041
Long-Term Debt	209	1,471	340	336			58,934	116,212	16,513	26,897	29,241	26,756
Other Non-Current Liabilities	435	167	243	381	122,579	122,069	22,596	23,861	11,585	13,608	20,432	15,131
Total Liabilities	19,793	21,462	24,177	40,092	173,162	182,660	300,081	269,073	155,327	192,086	250,801	252,928
Shareholders' Equity												
Common Stock	134	135	140	303	375	385	787	797				
Additional Paid-In Capital	107,317	127,138	123,555	128,997	107,432	132,875	180,005	353,464	226,885	249,595	278,765	315,857
Retained Earnings					160,372	217,656	282,441	370,652	241,474	310,510	389,534	489,233
Less: Treasury Stock	-1,113	-2,574	-2,268	-155	-11,415	-30,440	-41,405	-41,405	-41,864	-41,437	-41,440	-41,439
Foreign Currency Translation Adjust.					29,901	41,267	52,884	55,134				
Unrealized Gains (Loss) on Securities	—	—	—	—	9	6	0	0	—			—
Total Shareholders' Equity	106,204	124,564	121,287	128,842	286,433	361,499	474,065	738,148	426,869	519,053	627,646	764,448
Total Liabilities and Shareholders' Equity	125,997	146,026	168,934		459,595	544,159	774,146	1,007,221	582,196	711,139	878,446	1,017,378

Sources: Fisher & Paykel Healthcare *Annual Reports*, 2002–2006; data for ResMed and Respironics from *Mergent Online*, accessed April 26, 2007.
Notes: (1) Fisher & Paykel Healthcare (F&P), fiscal year ending March 31; (2) ResMed (RMD) and Respironics (RESP) fiscal years ending June 30.

EXHIBIT 9   Revenues by Region, Fiscal Years 2003–2006

	2003	2004	2005	2006
ResMed				
Geographic Analysis ($000)				
USA	$124,375	$159,283	$210,495	$320,941
Germany	51,992	67,253	72,824	96,436
Australia	6,972	10,293	14,160	18,709
France	27,745	34,629	47,537	59,402
Rest of World	62,486	67,880	80,489	111,508
Total	$273,570	$339,338	$425,505	$606,996
Fisher & Paykel Healthcare				
Geographic Analysis ($000)				
North America	$50,071	$57,722	$70,522	$93,997
Europe	28,938	39,594	50,826	57,548
Asia Pacific	20,402	29,294	33,914	37,847
Rest of World	3,652	5,446	7,337	10,164
Total	$103,063	$132,056	$162,599	$199,556
Respironics				
Geographic Analysis ($000)				
USA	$467,943	$547,224	$625,211	$724,781
Europe, Africa and Middle East	74,441	95,001	143,375	163,292
Americas	9,272	31,309	37,425	44,544
Far East/Asia Pacific	78,161	86,016	105,486	113,524
Total	$629,817	$759,550	$911,497	$1,046,141

Sources: Fisher & Paykel Healthcare *Annual Reports*, 2002–2006; data for ResMed and Respironics from *Mergent Online*, accessed April 26, 2007.
Notes: (1) Fisher & Paykel Healthcare (F&P), fiscal year ending 3/31; (2) ResMed (RMD) and Respironics (RESP) fiscal years ending 6/30; (3) Respironics 2003 revenues for the Americas included only Latin America.

company went public, changing its name to ResMed (its former name was already taken by another medical company).

50   Farrell believed that the SDB market would continue to grow in the future due to increasing awareness of OSA; improved understanding of the role of SDB treatment in the management of cardiac, neurological, metabolic and related disorders; and an increase in home-based diagnosis. Even in the U.S., market penetration had reached only 10–12 percent; the company was simply "lacing" its "shoes before the marathon."[45] Tremendous opportunities were to be found in selling medical devices to the 83 percent of hypertension patients who also had SDB, to the 80 percent of type two diabetics who also had SDB, and to the 80 percent of long haul truckers who suffered from OSA.

51   In the words of Farrell:

> If you took a poll of people that use our products and competitors' products, you would find that we are the number-one choice. . . . If you look at what the signs and symptoms of sleep-disordered breathing are, it covers every medical silo. We know it does cause heart disease and it causes stroke. We know it causes gastroesophageal reflux, and we know it causes cognitive dysfunction, morning headaches, nocturia, (getting up a lot at night to take a pee) and so forth. I agree that there are other products in the marketplace, but branding is important. Respironics' base is bigger in the U.S. than ours. Outside, we are twice as big as they are in the sleep business: our growth rate was twice their growth rate in the U.S. That's a huge difference. They've got a big chunk of their business in Japan. We go through

[45] "ResMed Inc. at Wachovia Securities CEO Summit-Final," *Fair Disclosure Wire* (June 28, 2007).

a distributor there; they are direct. That [also] has a big impact. We will have opportunities in Canada and Latin America and India and China. But again, we have got to take care of business in Europe before we start pushing the boat too far out, too quickly. We think that there are plenty of opportunities because of our position in the sleep and breathing marketplace.[46]

52   ResMed relied on clinical literature to tell it where the market was headed. In the case, for example, of type two diabetes, early data suggested that CPAPs could help patients control their glucose levels. If diabetics did not get a good night's sleep, their leptin and ghrelin levels[47] were thrown off, they lost control over their appetites, their energy levels were low and, therefore, they overate. CPAPs could help diabetics sleep better at night so this cycle of events did not occur. ResMed's strategy was to work with endocrinologists and officers of the International Diabetes Federation, invite them to Sydney, show them the clinical literature, and let them draw their own conclusions. If the data were convincing, the endocrinologists would recommend sleep therapy to their patients. ResMed could then go to diabetes educators "to drive volume into the marketplace and help treat these disorders."[48]

53   ResMed's R&D and manufacturing facilities were located in Sydney, Australia. A $43.8 million expansion was underway at the Sydney plant, and its completion was expected in the second half of 2006.[49] About 13 percent of its workforce was devoted to research and development activities. In fiscal year 2006, ResMed invested $37.2 million, or 6.1 percent of revenues, in R&D. ResMed's innovation and worldwide distribution prowess set it apart from rivals, according to one industry analyst.[50] As of 2006, ResMed employed 25 hundred people and sold products in sixty-eight countries through a combination of wholly owned subsidiaries and independent distributors.

Fisher & Paykel Healthcare

54   Across the globe in New Zealand, Fisher & Paykel Healthcare (F&P) designed, manufactured, and marketed heated humidification products and systems for use in respiratory care and the treatment of OSA. It invested 5.4 percent of revenues (almost $12 million) in research and development in 2006. F&P also manufactured and marketed patient warming and neonatal care products, infant resuscitators, and infant CPAP systems, designed to improve infant respiratory function. Five new respiratory mask products were added to its OSA therapy line in 2005.[51] The company's products were sold in more than ninety countries, exposing the company to considerable exchange rate risk.

55   Fisher & Paykel employed 1,276 people as of March 31, 2006. The company was engaged in an NZ$60 million project (about US$38.5 million based on exchange rates as of May 4, 2006) to double the size of its factory in East Tamaki, Auckland, New Zealand, in order to bolster its position as a low-cost producer and provide more space for OSA product manufacturing and R&D.[52]

56   In 2003, severe acute respiratory syndrome (SARS) had boosted F&P's profits by millions. On November 17, 2005, Fisher & Paykel announced that it stood to make another

---

[46] "Q4 2005 ResMed Inc. earnings conference call," *Fair Disclosure Wire* (August 22, 2005).

[47] Leptin and ghrelin are two hormones that affect food intake and energy balance.

[48] "ResMed Inc. at Wachovia" (2007), op. cit.

[49] T. Somers, "Poway, Calif.-based maker of sleep apnea expects to continue growth trend," *Knight Ridder Tribune Business News* (December 30, 2005): 1.

[50] J. Stralow, "ResMed," Morningstar Ratings (April 18, 2006).

[51] G. Bond, "F&P adds to its range of masks," *New Zealand Herald* (September 26, 2005).

[52] G. Bond, "Good night's sleep boosts F&P health," *New Zealand Herald* (November 18, 2005).

windfall should avian (bird) flu become a human-to-human pandemic. Chief executive Michael Daniell said, "We are increasing inventory and putting measures in place to ensure we can help out."[53] One analyst, who declined to be identified, quipped, "It could be good for the [company's] stock [price] and bad for the world."[54]

Tyco Healthcare Group

57 Tyco Healthcare Group was one of the world's largest manufacturers of disposable medical devices and the largest producer of generic Acetaminophen. It generated over $9 billion in sales for its parent (one fourth of Tyco's total revenues). Tyco Healthcare had three divisions: medical devices and supplies, pharmaceutical, and retail products. The medical devices and supplies division manufactured wound care dressings, needles, medical imaging equipment, life support systems, and ventilators.

58 In August 2006, Tyco Healthcare acquired an equity interest in Airox, a French company that manufactured and marketed home respiratory ventilation systems. It announced plans to acquire the entire company for a total purchase price of approximately $108 million.[55] Tyco Healthcare was thus poised to strengthen its position in the respiratory market, though at the same time, its parent company, Tyco International, had already made plans to spin it off (along with two other business units) by the end of 2007.

Invacare

59 Invacare was the leading manufacturer of wheelchairs worldwide. It also made respiratory devices and other medical equipment products for the home and the extended care markets. Based on an estimated $177 million in revenues from sales of respiratory products worldwide in 2005, Invacare had achieved considerable market share for oxygen therapy products. Its line of HomeFill oxygen systems became very popular. Invacare had a presence in the sleep therapy market as well. Invacare had been particularly troublesome for Respironics going back to the days when it launched its unsuccessful, hostile takeover for Healthdyne Technologies.

60 In 1999, Invacare introduced a CPAP device called Polaris, using licensed ResMed technology. In 2004, Invacare received FDA approval to sell the Polaris EX with SoftX technology and announced its intention to capture 10 percent of the sleep market in three years.[56] That same year, Respironics filed a patent infringement lawsuit against Invacare, claiming that the SoftX technology was a copy of its C-Flex technology that Respironics had introduced in 2003. Invacare countersued, complaining that Respironics engaged in monopolistic behaviors. A federal trial court dismissed Invacare's anti-trust lawsuit in November 2006.

61 Invacare wasn't about to give up on the sleep apnea market. In September 2006, it had become the exclusive distributor for AEIOMed's products (which included a modular, lightweight CPAP and a nasal pillow interface).[57]

---

[53] S. Louisson, "F&P Healthcare poised to make windfall if birdflu hits humans," *New Zealand Press Association* (November 17, 2005).

[54] Ibid.

[55] "Mergers and acquisitions: Tyco Healthcare to acquire interest in ventilator maker Airox, expand respiratory products," *Managed Care Weekly Digest* (August 28, 2006): 81.

[56] J. Sullivan, "Invacare stirs and issues a wake-up call," *HME News* 10 (6) (June, 2004): 45–46.

[57] M. Moran, "Invacare jumps in 'with both feet,'" *HME News* 12 (9) (September, 2006): 97–98.

RESPIRONICS' STRATEGIES

Sleep and Respiratory Products

62   Respironics made progress in developing diagnostic tools and solutions for other sleep disorders. Market research had helped it identify different types of "problem sleepers."[58] "Pill dislikers" refused to take medication because they did not want to become dependent on a drug for sleep or they were taking an antibiotic or antidepressant and were afraid of dangerous drug interactions. For them, a mechanical device would work. "Pill likers" would get a prescription for Ambien or Sonata. "Solution seekers" tried to self-treat—using devices that blocked out noises, taking herbal remedies and experimenting with special positioning cushions (sleeping on one's side could alleviate snoring).[59] They would do anything to get a good night's sleep, except see a doctor. "Solution avoiders" did not seek treatment for their sleep disorders and accepted the fact that they were just poor sleepers.

63   Respironics' Sleep Well Ventures business unit was started in 2004 with six employees and with the goal of selling products directly to consumers without a doctor's prescription. It introduced its first product, a dental appliance to help people with mild to moderate OSA stop snoring, in 2005. In the same year, Respironics acquired the Mini Mitter Company for $10.5 million in cash, with future payments based on operating performance over the following two-year period. This acquisition resulted in the addition of two new products to Respironics' portfolio: (1) an Actiwatch, worn on a patient's wrist, and used by sleep researchers and sleep lab technicians to monitor insomnia; and (2) VitalSense, used to measure core and dermal body temperatures that, in turn, affected sleep-wake cycles.[60]

64   Respironics also made ventilator-related products. Its global hospital ventilation sales were $130 million in 2006 (up 15 percent from 2005). It made the Vision Ventilator to provide noninvasive ventilation to patients for use in hospitals and sub-acute care facilities. It developed a Cadence Self-Breathing technology, in which a tracheostomy tube attached to a catheter was inserted into a patient's carina (located in between the bronchial tubes of the lungs), instead of his/her trachea. The tube was then connected to an oxygen concentrator. This "minimally invasive" technique enabled a COPD patient to speak.

65   In 2006, Respironics acquired the OxyTec Medical Corporation (OxyTec) for $10.4 million in cash (including transaction costs), with provisions for up to $30 million of additional payments to be made based on its operating performance in future years. OxyTec had developed an innovative portable oxygen concentrator, the Oxy Tec 900, which could provide ambulatory oxygen patients with greater mobility. The Oxy Tec 900, renamed the EverGo, weighed nine pounds and could pump oxygen for eight hours. Respironics hoped that the new product would help it increase its market share in the oxygen business. Historically, its five-liter Millenium concentrator had lower market share than rival products from Invacare and AirSep.[61]

Respiratory Drug Delivery

66   Respironics began to acquire technologies and form partnerships so that it could offer medication, not just oxygen, to patients through their respiratory systems. Delivery of drugs through a patient's airways was effective because it improved the speed at which medications worked and decreased the doses needed.

---

[58] "Respironics, Inc. at Bank of America Health Care Conference—Final," Fair Disclosure Wire (May 30, 2007).

[59] R. Grilliot, "Tapping into the problem sleeper market," *HomeCare Magazine* 28 (7) (July, 2005): 30.

[60] "Mergers & acquisitions, Sleep and respiratory company acquires Mini-Mitter," *Medical Devices & Surgical Technology Week* (May 8, 2005): 305.

[61] J. Sullivan, "They're no one-trick pony: Respironics expands O2 biz," *HME News* 12 (7) (July, 2006): 39–40.

67   In 2004, Respironics acquired Profile Therapeutics for approximately $44.6 million. Profile used adaptive aerosol delivery (AAD) technology to deliver the antibiotic, Promixin, to patients suffering from cystic fibrosis. Respironics also was granted the right to market and distribute Aerogen's aerosolized delivery of therapies via its ventilators (for critical care) on a non-exclusive basis. In 2006, Respironics entered a licensing agreement with CoTherix Inc. so that its portable, battery-operated, third-generation AAD device, the I-neb system, could be used to deliver Ventavis to patients with pulmonary arterial hypertension.

Children's Medical Products

68   Respironics' Children's Medical Ventures (ChMV) provided products and services for premature infants in neonatal intensive care units. The lungs were the last organ that developed in human beings. Infants had special needs when they were born before their lungs were fully mature. Respironics expertise in products for infants dated back to its 1998 acquisition of Healthdyne Technologies. Before starting Healthdyne, Parker Petit, an engineer, had suffered a personal tragedy. His infant son had died of sudden infant death syndrome (SIDs) in June 1970. Working with three other engineers during his spare time, he developed a machine that monitored the breathing and heartbeat of an infant at risk for SIDs. Petit left his job at an aerospace company and founded Healthdyne.[62] Respironics continued to manufacture devices that monitored vital signs. Its Smart Monitor sounded an alarm when an infant stopped breathing and recorded the episodes so that physicians could study them further.

69   Through a series of acquisitions, Respironics expanded its infant care product line. In 2002, it acquired Novametrix, which had operated ChMV for two years (Novametrix acquired ChMV in 1999). Novametrix made such products as the Soothie pacifier and diapers for preemies. Respironics opted to retain the ChMV name. In 2006, Respironics acquired Omni Therm Inc., which made a line of warming products.[63] Respironics offered a simulation program for hospital workers—Preemie for a Day—so that they could experience what it was like to live in a neonatal intensive care unit. Administrators and nurses became aware of inappropriate behaviors. When, for example, they placed a clipboard on top of an incubator it "vibrated and disturbed its tiny occupant," Bourgart said. For older children with asthma, Respironics introduced a bilingual coloring and activity book, "Tucker Tackles Asthma," to teach them how to use a nebulizer.

International Markets

70   The incidence of sleep disorders and respiratory diseases were similar, if not sometimes higher, in countries across the world. Each country stood on its own and offered unique opportunities and challenges.[64] Despite its large population, electro-mechanical devices (e.g., CPAPs) were not very popular in China because only a fraction of homes could accommodate them. So, instead, Respironics sold its non-invasive ventilators with masks to hospitals in China. There were 12,500 hospitals in China and 70 percent of them did not even have a single ventilator.[65]

71   In France, Respironics successfully sold its portable sleep diagnostic tool, Stardust. Worn on the chest, the device recorded physiological data while the patient slept in the comfort of his/her own home. There was no channel to market this product in the U.S.

[62] M. E. Kanell, "Home-grown firm born of tragedy," *The Atlanta Constitution* (March 28, 1997): H2.

[63] C. Snowbeck, "Products for babies help Respironics keep growing," *Knight Ridder Tribune Business News* (June 29, 2006): 1.

[64] Personal interviews with Joseph Bourgart and Daniel Bevevino, May 24, 2007.

[65] "Respironics, Inc. Analyst Meeting-Final," *Fair Disclosure Wire* (February 1, 2007).

because patients and clinicians could not get medical reimbursement. It was argued that unattended home studies did not provide valid information for the diagnosis of a patient's conditions. Logistically, there were concerns regarding whether or not the patients would return the units to the distributors. Approval of home studies by the Centers for Medicare and Medicaid Services (CMS), however, could result in faster diagnosis and treatment of OSA sufferers; the wait for clinical sleep lab studies could be long. Respironics' strategy was to be prepared in case reimbursement policies changed in the future.

72 Until the early 2000s, the Japanese government did not recognize sleep apnea as a medical condition for health insurance reimbursement. To prepare the groundwork for future sales, Respironics established a school for sleep, home and respiratory therapy in Tokyo. It trained physicians in how to diagnose and treat sleep apnea; it also helped them start up their own sleep labs.[66] Respironics had to make sure its products met strict regulatory requirements regarding noise, power consumption and size (since homes were small). It faced competition from many homegrown manufacturers of airflow generators and oxygen concentrators. Tanita Corporation, a Japanese electronic scale maker, for example, recently announced that it had developed an SPL Monitor, placed under a mattress or futon, which recorded a person's pulse, breathing rate, number of tosses and turns during sleep, how long it took to fall asleep and how frequently the person woke up after sleep. At the same time, there were only a handful of medical equipment distributors. Respironics responded by acquiring Fuji RC Co. Ltd, a provider of home care and hospital products and services for respiratory impaired patients in Japan.

73 In 2006, Respironics acquired Normed AS in Norway and Spiropharma AS in Denmark in order to establish a direct presence in Scandinavian markets. It also expanded vertically by acquiring distributors in the UK, Italy, Switzerland, Finland, and Australia.

THE FUTURE

74 After the anniversary celebration in Times Square and already two months into fiscal year 2007, John Miclot was worried about the future of the company and his management team. Towards the end of the 2006 fiscal year, he had asked his team to identify opportunities for Respironics. Among the options on the table at that time were purchasing intellectual property, taking equity positions in related businesses, or seeking companies to acquire outright.

75 Based on Respironics' rising cash balances, perhaps as many as two to three new investments could be identified for fiscal 2007. On the short list might be RespCare, Inc., a startup, which had just introduced an inexpensive hybrid CPAP mask system, and Restore Medical, another startup, which had invented an implant procedure to reduce vibrations that caused snoring. Aspire Medical, a small, privately held medical device company, was conducting clinical trials of an implantable device to treat tongue-based breathing obstructions.

76 Yet now, Respironics was perhaps itself on the short list of Royal Philips Electronics! Maybe that was what Respironics needed, help from a larger company, so that it could retain its position as the global market share leader for OSA treatments. Or, perhaps, Respironics should fight to remain independent and make a bold move—such as borrowing sufficient additional funds—to acquire a major competitor in the sleep therapy equipment market. That could be either ResMed or F&P. In any event, it was time for John Miclot to meet Ivo Lurvink from Philips Consumer Healthcare Solutions to see exactly what he wanted.

---

[66] Ibid.

Case 20

Research In Motion—Entering a New Era   Sofy Carayannopoulos

1   In the summer of 2007, as Jim Balsillie, co-CEO of Research In Motion (RIM), sat down at his desk in the Waterloo, Ontario, headquarters, a news headline caught his eye: "Apple's iPhone to hit stores, jolt mobile industry."[1] Other coverage described it as a "BlackBerry killer" that would challenge RIM's primacy in the **enterprise**[*] market.

2   Balsillie believed the iPhone was "one more entrant into an already very busy space," but the launch of this product had analysts debating RIM's choices and its future. The technology was converging, competition was intensifying, and large competitors were starting to target RIM's enterprise market. Balsillie viewed developing a strategy in these conditions as being similar to white-water rafting. His objective was to get "every last dollar [he could] possibly get" in sales, but he had to constantly watch for "rocks" in the water ahead, and position the company to avoid them.

3   In order to grow, RIM had expanded its focus from the enterprise market to the mainstream consumer market with two new products—the BlackBerry "Pearl," and the BlackBerry "Curve." Although some analysts thought this was a wise move because RIM would otherwise be a "dominant player in the relatively small enterprise market,"[2] others believed that RIM should continue to place primary emphasis on the enterprise market.[3] Entering the consumer market exposed RIM to strong pricing pressure, as it would be competing against large companies such as Nokia and Motorola.

4   Balsillie allowed his gaze to wander to the autographed Aerosmith guitar that hung on his wall—a souvenir of a company party celebrating RIM's 20th anniversary. The analysts were right about the competitive and technological environment changing. Balsillie thought about what RIM had to do to maximize sales, avoid "rocks," and make sure it was well-positioned for the future.

RIM'S EXTERNAL ENVIRONMENT

Market

5   The global wireless market had approximately 2.7 billion wireless subscribers in 2006 and analysts expected it to surpass 3 billion by the end of 2007, with China, India, Japan, Russia, and the United States showing the fastest subscriber growth.[4]

Copyright © 2007 by the *Case Research Journal* and Sofy Carayannopoulos. The author gratefully acknowledges the support and guidance provided by the editor, Dr. Lew Brown, and the helpful suggestions of three anonymous reviewers. This case was prepared solely to provide material for discussion. Certain names and other identifying information may have been disguised to protect confidentiality. Research In Motion does not necessarily confirm the accuracy or endorse the opinions expressed by the author in this case.

[1] Scott Hillis, "Apple's iPhone to Hit Stores, Jolt Mobile Industry," *Reuters* (June 27, 2007), http://www.canada.com/.

[2] Simon Avery, "With Pearl, the World's RIM's Oyster," *Globe and Mail Update* (October 13, 2006), http://www.theglobeandmail.com.

[3] Jonathan Richards, "RIM: iPhone Is No Threat to BlackBerry," *Times Online* (March 5, 2007), http://business.timesonline.co.uk.

[4] Chetan Sharma, "Global Wireless Data Market Update 2006," http://www.chetansharma.com/worlddatatrends2006.htm.

[*] See the glossary on page 20-23 for definitions of all words in bold print.

EXHIBIT 1   **Relative Importance Score for Different Functions to Be Included in Most Frequently Used Mobile Device**

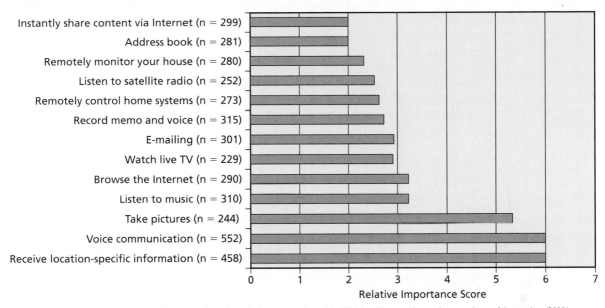

Source: Yuanzhe Cai. "Mobile Entertainment Platforms and Services," Parks and Associates, July 2005, http://www.parksassociates.com/research/reports/tocs/2005/multi-mobile_entertainment.htm.

n = number of respondents out of 1,919 owners of mobile devices surveyed that indicated interest in or use of a particular function Relative Importance Score = how important a function is to the user on a scale of 0–7 (0 = not important, 7 = extremely important)

6   Users of mobile communication devices consisted of the mainstream consumer who purchased the device for personal use, the prosumer who used the device for business and some personal use, and the enterprise, which purchased the product for employees' business use.

7   In order of declining preference, mainstream consumers used their devices for voice communication, listening to music, browsing the Internet, and e-mail (see Exhibit 1 for a detailed breakdown). Among non-business consumers in Japan and Korea, text messaging accounted for 30 percent of the data revenue collected by service providers. The remainder was from multimedia applications, browser traffic, and other infotainment applications. The opposite was true in Europe with approximately 70–80 percent of the data revenue coming from messaging. For North America, the data revenue from nonmessaging applications was approximately 20 percent.[5] A U.S. Census report published in the second quarter of 2006 showed that 34.6 million subscribers had accessed the Internet through their wireless devices in June 2006, most frequently accessing e-mail and weather sites.[6]

8   The mainstream consumer valued attractive devices that were easy to use, graphical, and small.[7] It was the most price sensitive of the three segments, sometimes causing device price drops of six to seven percent per quarter.[8] A survey of American consumers in 2007 found that, on average, they were willing to pay US$99 for a regular cellphone and US$199 for a

[5] Chetan Sharma, "Worldwide Wireless Data Trends—Mid-Year Update 2006," http://www.chetansharma.com/midyearupdateww06.htm.

[6] Telephia, "Mobile Internet Population Jumps to 34.6 Million, with E-mail, Weather, and Sports Websites Securing the Highest Reach, According to Telephia" (August 16, 2006), http://www.telephia.com/html/insights.html.

[7] Matt Walcoff, "BlackBerry Ripe for Change?" *Kitchener Waterloo Save & Sell* (September 1, 2006): 1, 5.

[8] Richards, "RIM: iPhone is No Threat."

smartphone with a two-year contract,[9] although they tended to seek out cellular telephones that could support the additional functions desired. An important subset of the consumer segment was the group that wanted phones with the lowest price and functionality. This segment was particularly prominent in the world's emerging phone markets such as India and China, and it would be a major driver behind future handset market growth.[10]

9   In the enterprise segment, the purchase decision involved the information technology (IT) department, which researched, approved, paid for, and supported devices for the enterprise's employees. In some cases, the user had no choice but to use a device chosen by IT. Employees used the devices primarily for e-mail and data communication, access to the enterprise network and data, personal organizer functions, and voice communication. IT departments' primary considerations in product selection were security, reliability, and data integration between the mobile device and the enterprise. The ability of the IT department to control the device to ensure the security of confidential enterprise information was also very important. Consequently, this segment tended to prefer personal digital assistant (PDA)-type devices, although with the changing technology, it was moving toward converged mobile devices that provided all but entertainment-oriented features.

10   The prosumer segment was difficult to distinguish from the other two as it used the product for both business and personal use. A prosumer could be an enterprise employee who had either purchased the device independently to increase his/her productivity, or had purchased a device approved, supported, and subsidized by the employer. The prosumer could also be an independent entrepreneur such as the Argentinean milk farmers who used their BlackBerrys to coordinate pick-up and delivery of produce. This segment was most likely to use the devices for voice communications, personal organizer functions, and data storage and access, but also wanted the flexibility of using some entertainment applications. Prosumers valued reliability, the availability of business applications, and multi-functionality so that they needed fewer devices. This segment was consequently very likely to purchase a converged mobile device. Prosumers were somewhat more sensitive to the price and appearance of the device than those in the enterprise segment, but not as much as mainstream consumers.

11   Although the three market segments had different priorities with respect to the devices, the technology of these devices was converging. Cellular telephones could now act as personal organizers, receive e-mail, and access the Internet, and PDAs could do the same. The most recent generation of products was "smartphones," or converged mobile devices. These were cellular telephones with **multimedia** and computer functionality. Smartphone features tended to include, but were not limited to, Internet access, e-mail access, personal organizer, music, television and/or video, and camera. The price of handheld devices depended upon the features offered and performance. Consumers could purchase cellular telephones with simple organizer and text-messaging features for under $100. Smartphones could cost as much as $600. Manufacturers believed that they would be able to maintain higher prices and margins on smartphones due to their features and functions, but recognized that low-cost devices would generate more sales volume.

12   As demand for multiple functions on all types of devices was increasing, manufacturers were focusing on enhancing their products' software capabilities, in addition to hardware features, in order to differentiate them. They were placing a stronger emphasis on adding

---

[9] Kurt Scherf, Michael Cai, and John Barret, "The iPhone: A Consumer Perspective," Parks Associates (2007): 1.

[10] ABI Research, "High Growth Handset Market Faces Low-Cost Dilemma" (June 8, 2006), http://linuxdevices.com/new/NS5105024528.html.

EXHIBIT 2A   **Worldwide Market for PDAs and Smartphones**

Unit Sales (millions)	2000	2003	2005	2006	2008	2010	2011
PDA Sales	11.43	12.75	13.51	13.88	14.82	15.97	16.60
Smartphone Sales	0.31	7.40	46.55	69.23	114.60	163.80	190.00

Source: "Smartphones to Outsell PDAs by 5:1 in 2006," *eTForecasts,* March 28, 2006, http://www .etforecasts.com/pr/pr0306.htm.

EXHIBIT 2B   **Worldwide PDA Market by Vendor, 2004–2006 (Thousands of Units)**

Company	Market Share (percent)		
	2006	2005	2004
Research In Motion	20.0	21.4	17.4
Palm	11.1	18.6	29.8
Hewlett-Packard	9.7	15.2	21.3
Nokia	Not applicable	6.8	2.0
T-Mobile	8.0	5.5	1.5
Others	Not applicable	32.5	28.0

Note: Totals do not include smartphones, but include wireless PDAs, such as the iPAQ 6315 and Nokia 9300.
Source: Gartner Dataquest February 14, 2006; October 9, 2006

EXHIBIT 2C   **Top Five Converged Mobile Device Vendors, 2005–2006 (Units)**

Vendor	Market Share (percent)		
	2006	2005	Share Growth
Nokia	48.1	50.3	35.8%
Research In Motion	7.5	7.2	46.3%
Panasonic	6.2	9.7	−9.1%
Motorola	6.1	4.2	104.2%
NEC	6.0	9.7	−12.7%
Others	26.2	18.9	97.2%
Total	**100.0**	**100.0**	**42.0**

Source: IDC Worldwide Quarterly Mobile Phone Tracker, February 2007

more support for software development tools for outside software developers and convincing third-party software suppliers to develop specialized applications for their devices.

13   Demand for products in all segments was high and growing (see Exhibit 2). The PDA market was 13.88 million units in 2006 and analysts predicted it would reach 16.6 million units by 2011. Analysts also predicted the annual worldwide demand for cellular telephones would reach 1.24 billion units by 2008. Although the smartphone segment represented a small portion of the cellular telephone market, analysts estimated that the smartphone segment of the handset market would grow from worldwide sales of 46.55 million units in 2005 to 164 million units in 2010 with global shipments reaching 1 billion by 2012.[11] Many organizations were implementing enterprise applications, especially in North America.[12]

[11] Symbian, "Fast Facts" (2007), http://www.symbian.com/about/fastfacts/fastfacts.html.
[12] Sharma, "Global Wireless Data."

EXHIBIT 2D   Mobile Phone Forecast, 2005–2008

Market Overview	2005	2006	2007	2008
Market demand (million units)	856.9	1,019.6	1,149.5	1,240.0
Replacement units (million units)	420.4	580.3	711.5	823.9
Replacement % of annual sales	49.0%	57.0%	62.0%	66.0%
Global subscriptions (million)	2,172.6	2,611.9	3,049.9	3,466.0
Net new subscriptions (million)	436.5	439.3	438.0	416.1
Handsets by Region (million units)				
North America	137.3	152.6	165.7	153.8
Latin America	109.3	120.9	138.8	147.0
Western Europe	162.6	184.7	192.8	201.2
EMEA	183.9	211.6	268.5	299.2
Asia Pacific	252.6	359.0	398.7	421.6
Total Unit Sell-in	845.8	1,028.7	1,164.6	1,222.8
Handsets (million units) and Market Share (%) by Vendor				
Nokia	264.8	347.5	431.7	445.2
	31.3%	33.8%	37.1%	36.4%
Motorola	146.0	217.4	204.0	226.4
	17.3%	21.1%	17.5%	18.5%
Samsung	102.1	118.0	131.0	140.2
	12.1%	11.5%	11.2%	11.5%
Sony Ericsson	51.1	74.8	96.8	99.8
	6.0%	7.3%	8.3%	8.2%
LG	55.6	64.6	68.9	72.3
	6.6%	6.3%	5.9%	5.9%
BenQ-Siemens	36.8	23.0	6.5	0.0
	4.4%	2.2%	0.6%	0.0%
Others	189.4	183.5	225.8	238.8
	22.4%	17.8%	19.4%	19.5%
Total	845.8	1,028.7	1,164.6	1,222.8

Source: M. Hoffman, J. Baxter. "Wireless Equipment—Mobile Phone Industry Still Seeking Balance," *Cowan and Company,* April 13, 2007.

Analysts predicted that by 2010 North American businesses would be spending over $10 billion annually on wireless enterprise data services,[13] and shipments of enterprise converged mobile devices would reach 63 million units.[14]

Network Providers (also known as Carriers or Operators)

14   Analysts ranked network providers based on the number of subscribers, and revenues. However, the two metrics did not always agree, partly because revenues were a function of both frequency of use and the nature of the use. Data transmission generated greater revenues per use than voice communications. See Exhibit 3 for details on the data revenues and subscribers of the largest network providers.

[13] StrategyAnalytics, "Mobile Email Revenues Set to Surpass SMS in $10 Billion North American Wireless Enterprise Market" (October 3, 2006), http://www.strategyanalytics.net/default.aspx?mod=PressRelease Viewer&a0=3088.
[14] Sharma, "Global Wireless Data."

EXHIBIT 3 **Top Wireless Carrier Revenues and Subscribers**

Carrier	Revenues FY 2006 (US$ billions)
NTT DoCoMo	10.75
China Mobile	6.90
KDDI	6.50
Verizon Wireless	4.30
AT&T Wireless	4.10
Sprint Nextel	4.00
SK Telecom	2.90
Vodafone Japan	2.70
02 UK	2.10
China Unicom	2.10

Carrier	Subscribers (millions)
China Mobile	301.0
Vodafone (Verizon in U.S.)	200.0
China Unicom	142.0
America Movil	125.0
Telefonica	102.0
SingTel	100.0
T-Mobile	106.0
Orange (France Telecom)	97.6

Source: Chetan Sharma, "Global Wireless Data Market Update 2006," http://www.chetansharma.com/worlddatatrends2006.htm.

15   The relationship between device manufacturers and network providers was one of mutual dependence. Device manufacturers needed networks on which their products could function—the better the networks, the more likely that products would perform well and satisfy consumers. The network providers also promoted and distributed their devices. The network providers needed the devices to attract subscribers to their networks and encourage network usage. Providers attracted subscribers by signing agreements with device manufacturers to promote mobile devices that could run on their networks—the more appealing and better performing the devices and the larger the coverage of the network, the more likely it was that customers would subscribe to a particular network.

16   To attract and "lock in" subscribers, most providers offered multi-year contracts that had high early cancellation fees, often packaged with reduced prices on mobile devices. One of the key areas of concern for providers was commoditization and the loss of subscribers who were attracted to other providers offering better performing or more interesting devices. The item of interest and value to the consumer was the device rather than the carrier or the network. One significant barrier to switching providers was that the subscriber would not be able to keep the same cellphone number (known as "number portability"). This was a particularly significant deterrent to switching providers for prosumers because their cellphone number was often a business contact. However, starting in 2001, countries around the world began enacting legislation requiring providers to allow number portability.

17   Network technology was continuing to evolve—networks allowed voice and data transmission, but providers were investing in new networks that would support multimedia messaging (MMS) such as pictures or video clips and would allow faster and better access to data and Internet resources. Given the sizable investments that providers were making for upgraded networks, they were eager for new devices that would attract subscribers and encourage consumers to use data.

Competition

18   The competitive landscape was crowded, with multiple companies fully committed to usurping RIM's leading position in the wireless handheld market (see Exhibit 4 for an overview of hardware and software competitors, and Exhibit 2 for worldwide market shares of some of these companies).

19   Cellphone manufacturers such as Nokia and Motorola had entered the wireless data market by leveraging their dominant positions in the cellphone industry. These companies had global brand equity, strong financial resources, experience in wireless communications, and network carrier partnerships around the world. They were already offering "cost-optimized" handsets (basic cellphones offered at very low prices) in emerging regions to increase their market share. Nokia and Motorola had 37.1 percent and 17.5 percent market shares, respectively, of the worldwide handset market. Motorola had the reputation as a leader in launching "must-have" handsets. However, these cellphone manufacturers still had limited experience in data transmission, and some, like Nokia, had chosen to partner with other firms to embed e-mail functionality in their products. Traditional computer/notebook manufacturers, including Hewlett-Packard (HP) and Dell, had also turned their attention to this market. These manufacturers had very limited experience in mobile telephones, but significant experience in computing.

20   In late 2006 and early 2007, Samsung and Apple had entered the PDA/smartphone market with competing devices. Samsung's "BlackJack" was a device that included a complete **QWERTY** keyboard, camera, **push** e-mail enabled by Good Technology, organization functions, Web-browsing, and viewing of video content. The BlackJack was wider and longer than the BlackBerry Pearl, and only 1 mm thinner. AT&T offered it at US$499.99. Some users, however, had criticized its keyboard as being too small and poorly designed.

21   Apple's iPhone dimensions were 4.5 by 2.4 by .46 inches, and users controlled it entirely through a large touch-screen. It had e-mail, camera, could play music and videos, and browse the Internet. Analysts described it as an attractive and user-friendly device that put multimedia first and productivity second. Early reviews were mixed. Although many users loved the sleek appearance, some were disappointed that, although the iPhone allowed users to view entire Web pages as they would on a computer screen, downloading was slow due to the slow speed of AT&T's network. It also did not have some important business features such as Microsoft Office/Exchange or third-generation capabilities, which would enable both voice and non-voice data exchange and downloading over the Internet. The iPhone offered limited security for e-mail and other data.[15] Its price was US$500–600, depending on memory capacity, and required a two-year contract from AT&T priced between $60 and $100 per month.

22   Like RIM, Apple had negotiated a portion of monthly network subscriber fees in addition to hardware sales. However, unlike almost all other mobile device producers, Apple was selling the iPhone directly to end users in Apple stores as well as through AT&T. Furthermore, subscribers had to go to Apple's iTunes music store to activate their phones rather than the network carrier. Balsillie believed this was a dangerous strategy as it exposed network providers to the risk of becoming even more of a commodity, and they might react

---

[15] Arik Hesseldahl, "Not Everyone Wants an iPhone," *BusinessWeek Online* (June 29, 2007), http://www.businessweek.com/print/technology/content/jun2007 /tc20070628_831343.htm.

EXHIBIT 4 Competitive Analysis, Hardware and Software Companies

Hardware Companies

Company	Device	Partnerships	Advantages	Limitations	Financials* (US$ millions)
Nokia	Nokia E61	• RIM: BlackBerry Connect Licensing Program • 48 percent ownership of Symbian OS • Visto and Good Technology for software	• World's largest cellphone maker • Financial strength and stability • Strong brand equity • In-house manufacturing and design • Competing device is slimmer with higher resolution and more easily customized software	• Less experience and knowledge of wireless data devices • Competing device: —Relatively new product —Inferior keyboard ergonomics	Rev. = 41,590 EBITDA = 6,420 56,896 employees
Motorola	Moto Q	• RIM: BlackBerry Connect Licensing Program • Microsoft for software, Kodak for mobile imaging	• World's second largest cellphone maker • Financial strength and stability • Competing device: —Thinnest and lightest handset —QWERTY keyboard	• Reputation for inferior design and execution • Less experience and knowledge of wireless data devices • Competing device is unproven, with "glitchy" software	Rev. = 36,840 EBITDA = 4,890 69,000 employees
Palm	Treo 650	• RIM: BlackBerry Connect Licensing Program • Microsoft for software • Acquired Handspring	• Recognized brand for PDA-type devices • Competing device: —Touch screen with higher resolution —MP3 player and camera —More customizable, e.g., loading memory cards	• Company has undergone tumultuous restructuring, with name changes and spin-offs • Founders left company • Competing device is heavier and larger, has reliability issues (missed messages)	Rev. = 1,410 EBITDA = 107 1,103 employees
HP	iPAQ hw6515	• Powered by Samsung	• World's leader in notebooks, with strategic shift in focus to grow handheld devices business • Global company with significant financial resources • Competing device has GPS and camera	• Relatively unknown wireless data devices with reputation for poor performance and reliability • Small customer base for handheld devices • Competing device has poor audio quality	Rev. = 87,900 EBITDA = 7,640 150,000 employees

(Continued)

Company	Product	Technology/Partners	Strengths	Weaknesses	Financials
Samsung	BlackJack	• Good Technology e-mail capabilities	• Global company with recognized brand for audio/video equipment and home appliances • Wide array of cellular telephone models	• Inferior keyboard ergonomics • Bulkier than Pearl	Rev. = 56,720 NIBT = 8,757 123,000 employees
Apple	iPhone	• HP • Intel	• Recognized brand for innovative and interesting computer designs and multimedia devices • Global company with strong innovative and marketing capabilities	• Less experience and knowledge of communication and business communication devices • Not 3G capable • Doesn't have Microsoft Exchange capabilities • Concerns regarding e-mail security	Rev. = 19,300 EBITDA = 2,424 17,787 employees
Dell	Axim X51v	• Powered by Good Technology	• Global presence • Financial strength and stability • Competing device has a touch screen	• Relatively unknown wireless data device • Small customer base for handheld devices • Competing device lacks QWERTY keyboard and has poor battery life	Rev. = 55,910 EBITDA = 4,840 65,200 employees
Software Companies					
Good Technology	GoodLink Enterprise	• Supports Dell, HP, Nokia, Motorola, Palm, and Symbol	• Software sits on virtually all smartphone platforms except Blackberry's operating system • Supports industry standards: Windows Mobile platforms	• Compatible only with servers running Microsoft's Exchange software, compared to RIM which can also handle Lotus Notes • Outstanding lawsuits with Visto	Privately held corporation Estimated revenue in 2003 = $25 160 employees (2003)
Microsoft Corp.	Microsoft Exchange Server, and Windows Mobile	• Supports Motorola and Palm	• World leader in software applications • Financial strength and stability	• Lacks interest and experience in wireless data communication	Revenue = 39,800 EBITDA = 15,400 71,000 employees

EXHIBIT 4 *(continued)*

Software Companies *(continued)*

Company	Platform	Partnerships	Advantages	Limitations	Financials* (US$ millions)
Danger Inc.	The Hiptop	• Support manufacturer Sharp Corp. and smaller technology providers	• Provides end-to-end platform including backend infrastructure	• Small customer base	Privately held corporation Estimated revenue in 2003 = $24 110 employees (2004)
Visto Corp.	Visto Mobile 5.5	• Supports Nokia, Motorola, SonyEricsson, Sony, Microsoft, Palm, Symbian, Sony, and Kyocera	• Unlike RIM, mobile e-mail service does not require specialized hardware • Partnerships with several technology companies • Holds twenty-five patents, fifty-seven pending	• Compatible only with servers running Microsoft's Exchange software	Privately heldcorporation Estimated revenue in 2002 = $10 80 employees (2003)
PalmSource (Palm)	Palm OS	• Supports Aceeca, Fossil, Garmin, Kyocera, Lenovo, Palm, Samsung, Song, and Symbol • Partnership with RIM 　—Jointly developing a software solution that enables BlackBerry connectivity to the Palm OS 　—Technology distribution agreement allowing RIM to license a BlackBerry Connect offering to Palm Powered licensees	• Leading operating system powering next-generation mobile devices 　—65 percent share in U.S., and 51 percent market share worldwide 　—Customer base: more than thirty-nine million mobile phones, handhelds, and other mobil devices	• Company has undergone tumultuous re-structuring, with multiple name changes, spin-offs, and acquisitions	Revenue = 17.9 EBITDA = 4.0 1,103 employees

Source: Case writer analysis based on information found in Tom Astle's "Competitive Update," *Merrill Lynch Global Securities Research,* January 13, 2003, company Web sites, Mergent Online, and sources listed in the footnotes.

*Financials reflect most recent year-end data available unless otherwise indicated.

by promoting competing products to reduce Apple's power. Nevertheless, the consumer enthusiasm for the iPhone and speculation that up to 25 percent of cellphone users who bought the iPhone on its release would be switching from another network provider had caused other providers including Orange, T-Mobile, and Vodafone to aggressively bid for European iPhone rights.[16]

23   Because RIM's product offering also comprised software licensing, its competitive environment included software companies such as Good Technologies, Microsoft, and Danger, Inc. The software these companies produced functioned on virtually any device, thereby increasing an enterprise's flexibility in selecting its own providers, handheld devices, networks, and platforms. Some analysts considered Microsoft one of the greatest competitive threats on the software horizon, if it decided to dedicate resources to the wireless communication market. However, Microsoft Mobile was one of the weak points in Motorola's Moto Q, and Palm's Treo 650 devices due to "glitchy" operation and reliability issues.

24   Palm, Inc., offered both the handheld device and accompanying software. Despite its recognized brand and product, internal restructuring had negatively affected Palm's growth. Between 2001 and 2005, there had been a series of spin-offs, acquisitions, and name changes. In late 2001/early 2002 the company split into two operational businesses—one focusing on developing and marketing the Palm Operating System (Palm OS), which it licensed to other PDA and device manufacturers, and one focused on its PDAs, which it sold to consumers. The restructuring aimed to improve Palm's ability to cater to its many licensees and developers and to address the complex and sometimes contradictory demands of its businesses. In its fourth-quarter fiscal 2007 results, its revenues were down in comparison to fiscal 2006. It also expected to see sales of its Treo smartphone stall due to the launch of the iPhone.[17]

RESEARCH IN MOTION

History

25   Mike Lazaridis and Douglas Fregin founded RIM in 1984. In 1992, Jim Balsillie sank a substantial portion of his savings into RIM and joined the company as co-CEO. Fregin became a director and vice-president of operations, and Lazaridis became president and co-CEO. Balsillie and Lazaridis worked as a team with Lazaridis concentrating on the technology and Balsillie focusing on expanding the business. From its inception, RIM focused on developing hardware and software for wireless data communication. It developed a capability in producing wireless two-way data communication devices that were small, lightweight, and energy-efficient.

The BlackBerry Bursts onto the Market

26   In January 1999, RIM launched BlackBerry—a product that combined hardware, software, and service to provide wireless e-mail messaging. Messages sent to a user's e-mail address were automatically forwarded ("**pushed**") to the BlackBerry handheld (see Exhibit 5). The user was notified of their arrival and could read and reply to them quickly. This represented a significant performance improvement, because with all other e-mail systems the user had to connect with a network to see if he/she had an e-mail and "pull" or retrieve the e-mail to his/her device.

[16] Philip Elmer-DeWitt, "Apple iPhone: It Stoppeth One of Four," *Apple 2.0* (July 13, 2007), http://blogs. business2.com/apple/2007/07/apple-iphone-it.html.

[17] Hillis, "Apple's iPhone to Hit Stores."

EXHIBIT 5 **How the BlackBerry Works**

1. Someone sends an e-mail to your e-mail address.
2. E-mail arrives at your desktop PC.
3. BlackBerry Enterprise Server (or desktop version) encrypts and forwards the message.
4. E-mail is forwarded to the handheld via the Internet to BlackBerry Operations Centre—Centre then forwards onto designated wireless network.
5. The handheld receives and decrypts the e-mail. User responds to e-mail using the keyboard on the BlackBerry handheld.

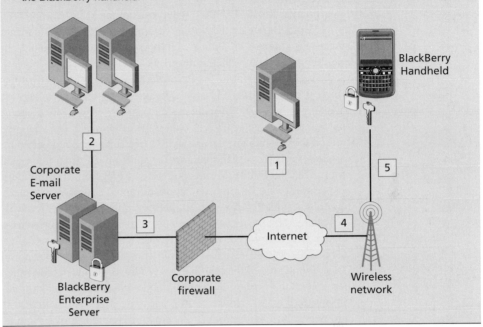

Source: Research In Motion

27   The BlackBerry hardware and software were easy to use, even by those unaccustomed to handling their own e-mails. The product was roughly the size of a pager, and had a small **QWERTY** keyboard that the user would type on using his/her thumbs. Extensive testing confirmed its ease of use. It ran on one AA battery that required replacement approximately once every two weeks. All of these elements represented significant technological and functional improvements over all other wireless products. Lazaridis also incorporated advanced **encryption software** in the BlackBerry that met Intel's security benchmark. Intel was RIM's chip supplier, but more importantly, meeting its security needs represented a significant source of product differentiation.

28   The BlackBerry solution enabled mobile users to manage e-mail while away from the office just as e-mail was increasing in popularity and wireless products were achieving wider acceptance. The only substitutes for the product at the time were laptops and a bulkier, slower device made by Motorola. Although Nokia and Motorola were both making advances in wireless communication, they focused on voice rather than data because it represented a larger market at the time. Personal digital assistants, such as the PalmPilot, focused on increasing functionality and memory, but did not have the technological capabilities for wireless communication. RIM targeted corporations and their employees, particularly those handling time-sensitive information such as financial services. It believed that corporations were more likely to find value in its product and more likely than individual consumers to purchase it.

29   RIM offered two versions of the product—a BlackBerry Enterprise Server (BES) and a non-server version of the BlackBerry. The non-server version routed the e-mails from the user's desktop computer to the BlackBerry handheld. The BES version worked with the corporation's e-mail system to redirect e-mail through the **corporate mail server**. This software allowed centralized administration of the BlackBerry by IT departments, and increased the e-mail security. The BES was designed to work with the most popular e-mail systems, which at the time were Microsoft Exchange and Lotus Domino.

30   RIM launched the non-server version first so that it could provide free trials to CEOs such as Jack Welsh, CEO of GE, without needing the approval or cooperation of the IT departments. Most IT departments resisted the idea of implementing new products, such as the BlackBerry, as they often complicated an already complex environment. It was a successful strategy, as almost everyone who tried the product chose to keep it, and many adopted it throughout their enterprises.

31   A final component of the BlackBerry solution was its own Operations Centre, through which it routed all wireless data to and from wireless networks. The Operations Centre involved a significant investment in hardware and software but helped ensure e-mail security and reliable and efficient data transmission. The efficiency and performance created by the Operations Centre meant RIM's users experienced better and more secure data transmission with a data plan that cost the same or less than that of other vendors. It also gave enterprises the ability to run their BlackBerrys on multiple networks without additional costs or software. It represented an additional source of revenue for RIM, as it charged a monthly service fee for each BlackBerry subscriber. The fee was included in the monthly fees charged by the network operators and paid by the operators to RIM. Similar operations centers were employed by Motorola and Visto.

32   By 2002, BlackBerry had become a proprietary brand that companies asked for by name. Users found it so addictive that Andy Grove of Intel coined the nickname "Crackberry." BlackBerry had become a popular and sometimes indispensable solution in such organizations as the U.S. House of Representatives and the military. It had even made its way into pop culture with product placement in popular movies and television shows. Analysts estimated that by fourth quarter of 2006, BlackBerry devices accounted for roughly 20 percent of all sales of personal digital assistants, and handled 59 percent of corporate wireless e-mail traffic.[18]

33   In May 2006, RIM initiated a trade-up program for the BlackBerry, which allowed existing customers to upgrade an older device to the newest BlackBerry model at a discount. The company did this to retain customers by encouraging them to upgrade to newer BlackBerry models rather than switching to a competitor's device. Balsillie believed this program also provided a strong signal to consumers that RIM was committed to innovation and to keeping pace with technological advances.

RESEARCH IN MOTION IN 2007

Financial Performance

34   Revenue for fiscal 2007 was US$3.04 billion, up 50 percent from US$2.07 billion the year before (see Exhibit 6 for financial statements). RIM's handhelds accounted for approximately 73 percent of revenue. OEM radios and other sources accounted for 3 percent, while service and software licenses and development accounted for 18.4 percent and 5.7 percent

---

[18] Ian Austen, "RIM Is Counting on Customers," *clnet NEWS.com* (September 18, 2006), http://news.com.

EXHIBIT 6   **Research In Motion Financial Results**

CONSOLIDATED STATEMENTS OF OPERATIONS (US$, THOUSANDS)

	For the Year Ended			
	March 3 2007	March 4 2006	February 6 2005	February 28 2004
Revenue	$3,037,103	$2,065,845	$1,350,447	$594,616
Cost of sales	1,378,301	925,215	635,914	323,365
Gross margin	1,657,802	1,140,630	714,533	271,251
Expenses				
R&D, net of government funding	236,173	157,629	101,180	62,638
Selling and administration	537,922	311,420	190,730	108,492
Amortization	76,879	49,951	35,941	27,911
Litigation and related expenses		201,791	352,628	35,187
Total expenses	850,974	720,791	680,479	234,228
Income from operations	806,828	419,839	34,054	37,023
Investment income	52,117	66,218	37,107	10,606
Provision for income taxes	227,373	103,979	−142,226	−4,200
Net income	**631,572**	**382,078**	**213,387**	**51,839**

REVENUE BREAKDOWN

	Fiscal 2007		Fiscal 2006		Fiscal 2005		Fiscal 2004	
Devices sold	6,400,000		4,043,000		2,444,000		920,000	
Average selling price	$336		$356		$382		$373	
Revenues								
Devices	$2,215,951	73.0%	$1,439,674	69.7%	$ 933,989	69.2%	$343,200	57.7%
Service*	560,116	18.4%	383,021	18.5%	235,015	17.4%	171,200	28.8%
Software	173,187	5.7%	156,556	7.6%	131,811	9.8%	47,400	8.0%
Other	87,849	2.9%	86,594	4.2%	49,632	3.6%	32,816	5.5%
Total	**$3,037,103**		**$2,065,845**		**$1,350,447**		**$594,616**	

*Service refers to one of the three RIM components in its BlackBerry solution (hardware and software being the other two). Service revenue is a charge of approximately US$8 per user per month charged to network operators for handling e-mail through the Operations Centre. The service charge for the "Pearl" was approximately $3.

of revenue, respectively. The approximate contribution margin[19] for each category was hardware—43 percent, and service and software—90 percent. Service revenues from enterprise subscribers were approximately $7 to $10 per month per subscriber, and $3 to $5 per consumer or prosumer subscriber.

[19] These margins are provided to further the case and enable analysis. They are based on industry averages and conversations with RIM employees, and may not reflect RIM's actual contribution margins.

EXHIBIT 6   *(continued)*

RESEARCH IN MOTION LIMITED CONSOLIDATED BALANCE SHEETS (US$, THOUSANDS) (AUDITED)

	March 3 2007	March 4 2006	February 6 2005	February 28 2004
ASSETS				
Current				
Cash and cash equivalents	$ 677,144	$ 459,540	$ 610,354	$1,156,419
Short-term investments	310,082	175,553	315,495	—
Trade receivables	572,637	315,278	227,750	95,213
Other receivables	40,174	31,861	13,125	12,149
Inventory	255,907	134,523	92,489	42,836
Restricted cash	—	—	111,987	36,261
Other current assets	41,697	45,035	22,857	12,527
Deferred tax asset	21,624	94,789	150,200	—
	1,919,265	1,256,579	1,544,248	1,355,405
Long-term portfolio investments	425,652	614,309	753,868	339,285
Capital assets	487,579	326,313	210,112	147,709
Goodwill and other intangible assets	256,453	114,955	112,766	94,378
Total assets	$3,088,949	$2,312,156	$2,620,994	$1,936,777
LIABILITIES				
Current				
Accounts payable and accrued liabilities	$ 417,899	$ 239,866	$ 155,597	$ 106,108
Accrued litigation and related expenses	—	—	455,610	84,392
Income taxes payable	99,958	17,584	3,149	1,684
Deferred revenue	28,447	20,968	16,235	16,498
Current portion of long-term debt	271	262	223	193
	546,575	278,680	630,814	208,875
Long-term debt	6,342	6,851	6,504	6,240
Deferred income tax liability	52,532	27,858	—	—
	605,449	313,389	637,318	215,115
Shareholders' equity				
Capital stock	2,099,696	1,852,713	1,892,266	1,829,388
Retained earnings	359,227	148,028	94,181	(119,206)
Paid-in capital	36,093	—	—	—
Acc. other comprehensive income	(11,516)	(1,974)	(2,771)	(11,480)
Total shareholders' equity	2,483,500	1,998,767	1,983,676	1,721,662
Total liabilities and shareholders' equity	$3,088,949	$2,312,156	$2,620,994	$1,936,777

EXHIBIT 7 Financial Comparison of RIM and Competitors (as of most recent annual financials at July, 2007. US$, millions.)

	Current Ratio	Debt/Equity	Cash	Revenues/Growth over Previous two years	ROE	Gross Margin	ROA and Asset Turnover	Marketing, Selling, and Admin. (% of revenue)	R&D (% of revenue)
RIM	3.51	.20	$677	$3,037 47.0% $(t_0 - t_{-1})$ 53.0% $(t_{-1} - t_{-2})$	32.60%	$1,658 54.60%	20.44% 0.98	$538 17.70%	$236 7.80%
Apple	2.24	.72	$6,392	$19,315 38.6% $(t_0 - t_{-1})$ 68.2% $(t_{-1} - t_{-2})$	19.90%	$5,598 29.00%	11.56% 1.12	$2,433 12.60%	$712 3.70%
Motorola	2.01	.23	$3,212	$42,879 16.4% $(t_0 - t_{-1})$ 17.6% $(t_{-1} - t_{-2})$	19.00%	$12,727 29.70%	8.45% 1.11	$4,504 10.50%	$3,680 10.00%
Nokia	1.83	.01	$2,024	$56,262 20.3% $(t_0 - t_{-1})$ 16.4% $(t_{-1} - t_{-2})$	36.20%	$19,019 33.80%	19.04% 1.82	$5,757 10.23%	$5,332 9.50%
Palm	1.95	.46	$65	$1,561 −1.0% $(t_0 - t_{-1})$ 24.0% $(t_{-1} - t_{-2})$	5.31%	$575 36.86%	3.64% 1.01	$308 19.70%	$136 9.00%

Source: Mergent Online

35   Gross margin for the year was 54.6 percent, down slightly from the previous years due to the increased percentage of revenue coming from smartphones such as their "Pearl." These consumer-oriented products had lower average selling prices than the devices targeting enterprise users. Nevertheless, the gross margin improved from fiscal 2005 and fiscal 2004 due to economies of scale and reductions in material costs. Service margins had also improved due to cost efficiencies caused by the increase in the BlackBerry subscriber account base. Operating expenses as a percentage of revenue increased slightly from the previous year due to increased investments in hardware and software development; new marketing programs associated with the launch of the consumer-oriented products; and higher administrative expenses in the second half of the year (see Exhibit 6 for detailed financials). RIM's cash and marketable securities were approximately US$635 million—a relatively strong cash position compared to such rivals as Palm (see Exhibit 7 for a financial comparison of RIM and some of its competitors).

Products

BlackBerry Wireless Devices

36   Each year RIM launched new BlackBerry models with a range of features, services, and prices, targeting enterprise users. Generally, basic features included e-mail, wireless Internet browsing, organizer applications, short message servicing (SMS), instant messaging, corporate data access, and paging. Recent models had added telephone capabilities and

EXHIBIT 8 Current Products

BLACKBERRY PEARL
8100

Size:
width: 5 cm/1.97"
height: 10.7 cm/4.2"
depth: 1.4 cm/.57"
weight: 87.88 grams/
3.1 ounces

BLACKBERRY CURVE
8300

Size:
width: 6 cm/2.4"
height: 10.7 cm/4.2"
depth: 1.52 cm/.6"
weight: 110.6 grams/
3.9 ounces

cameras, although RIM still offered some models without cameras. One of RIM's most recent innovations was its SureType keyboard technology. This technology allowed RIM to fit a full **QWERTY** keyboard on a smaller device by putting two letters on some of the keys. Users could "double tap" to select the letter of their choice, or allow the SureType technology to predict the word being typed by referencing its expandable 35,000-word vocabulary. This innovation addressed the concern of customers who resisted using the BlackBerry device as a phone because they felt its size made its use look awkward.

37 Two of RIM's most recent products were the BlackBerry "Pearl" (BlackBerry 8100), introduced in September 2006, and the BlackBerry "Curve" (BlackBerry 8300), launched in May 2007 (see Exhibit 8). Lazaridis stated that these products were responses to consumers who wanted other features, such as multimedia. The "Curve" measured 4.2 by 2.4 by 0.6 inches, weighed approximately 3.9 ounces, and was RIM's smallest and lightest full-QWERTY keyboard smartphone. It extended previous BlackBerry offerings by offering a two megapixel camera and software and Internet features such as TeleNav maps that would allow a user to find addresses and obtain directions. It was available for US$200 through AT&T with a two-year calling plan that began at US$30 per month.

38 The Pearl smartphone targeted mainstream consumers and prosumers. It weighed 3.1 ounces, and was roughly the size of a large cellular telephone (4.2 by 1.97 by .57 inches). It incorporated e-mail, messaging, Web browsing, and a 1.3 megapixel camera with three zoom levels and built-in flash. It also served as a multimedia player with stereo headset for MP3 and AAC music files, and it had expandable memory. It was sleek, available in three colors (black, white, and red) and used RIM's SureType technology. Upon launch the BlackBerry Pearl was available from T-Mobile in the United States at US$200, and Rogers Wireless Communications Inc. in Canada for CDN$250. AT&T and other providers in North America, as well as Europe, Asia and Latin America, launched the product by the end of 2006.

39 The Pearl had taken three years to bring to market. In 2003, RIM had recognized that many BlackBerry owners avoided using their devices as cellphones because they appeared awkward, and some resisted them because they were bulky. Although adding features such as a camera and MP3 player was easy, creating a small, attractive product that did not compromise the BlackBerry reputation for simple and reliable e-mail required significant research and design efforts. Furthermore, Lazaridis insisted that the BlackBerry Pearl was

not built as a budget version of the corporate devices—it was designed using the full Black-Berry platform. Balsillie described it as follows:

> It's the "Triple Crown"—it's the no-compromise smartphone for features, it's the no-compromise style phone for style purposes, and it's the no-compromise BlackBerry. So many of these things in the world have been addressed with fundamental compromises—people want more features, but don't want to give up the features they already have.

40   There was a great deal of speculation about how the BlackBerry Pearl would affect RIM. According to national retailers of cellphones and other wireless devices, the Pearl was selling well, and was attracting non-enterprise buyers between the ages of nineteen and thirty-seven who had never before shown any interest in owning a BlackBerry device.[20] Some analysts believed the move into the consumer market would boost RIM's revenue growth and sales volume.[21] Others were concerned that RIM's presence in the consumer market, where it had less than a one percent market share, would put it in direct competition with large multinationals such as Nokia and Motorola.

41   Furthermore, there was speculation that the new products would diminish RIM's image as an enterprise device manufacturer, which was one reason RIM had consciously avoided the consumer market. The inclusion of cameras and multimedia could also pose security issues for IT managers who would then be reluctant to adopt the BlackBerrys. RIM responded by assuring IT managers that they could disable cameras and multimedia features. There was also concern because other companies' attempts to market similar devices had resulted in limited success due to performance challenges and the cost of wireless Internet access, which was approximately US$40 per month.

42   Mainstream consumers who were users of the BlackBerry made comments like, "I used to change devices once a month because nothing worked well enough. Now I wouldn't consider changing my BlackBerry—its phone works great, and it perfectly synchronizes all of my information with my computer wirelessly and immediately." On the other hand, early purchasers of the iPhone commented, "I love my iPhone. When I show it to my friends at work who have BlackBerrys, the jealousy and interest are tangible."

43   BlackBerry products were sold through supply agreements with network operators. These operators marketed the products, bundled with voice and data packages, to subscribers. By the end of fiscal 2007, RIM had agreements with over 270 network operators in 110 countries, including those with some of the highest wireless data revenues in the world: NTT DoCoMo, Verizon, Vodafone, and Cingular. RIM signed over 100 new carrier agreements with operators in fiscal 2006, which further increased its geographic reach in Europe, Asia-Pacific, Africa, and Latin America. RIM had signed an agreement in May 2006 with China Mobile to offer service to BlackBerry devices and to make the devices themselves available at a later date.

44   However, reports showed that a growing gap existed between the number of devices shipped and the number of new wireless accounts. For example, in the quarter ending March 4, 2006, RIM reported shipping 1.12 million BlackBerry devices, while only 625,000 BlackBerry subscribers signed up for service, representing a difference of about 495,000. In the previous three quarters, the differences were 475,000, 335,000 and 248,000 respectively. These gaps indicated that RIM's BlackBerry shipments weren't selling through to end users as rapidly as they had previously. Some analysts were saying that they believed the market for business subscribers was approaching saturation.

[20] Avery, "With Pearl."
[21] Austen, "RIM Is Counting."

BlackBerry Subscribers

45   RIM had approximately nine million subscribers by June 2007, having added approximately one million subscribers since end of fiscal 2007 on March 3, 2007.[22] RIM had been doubling its subscriber base each year over the previous four years. It had 4.9 million subscribers at the end of fiscal 2006, as compared with 2.4 million (2005), one million (2004) and 500,000 (2003). More than 100,000 organizations had installed the BlackBerry Enterprise Server, and RIM had successfully expanded its target market to include the prosumer and individual consumer. At the end of fiscal 2007, over 27 percent of BlackBerry subscribers were non-enterprise users.

46   Although North America represented RIM's largest market, its subscriber account base had expanded to over 110 countries by end of fiscal year 2007. International customers outside North America accounted for approximately 28 percent of BlackBerry subscribers and 35 percent of overall revenues. Most of the company's international growth was in major European markets and Asia. Outside Europe, RIM's geographic expansion into the Pacific Rim included a plan to continue market penetration in Australia, India, Singapore, and Hong Kong.

Software

47   All BlackBerry models emphasized security. RIM had been awarded the FIPS 140-2 Validation by the U.S. National Institute of Standards and Technology for its encryption technology and was seeking similar types of validation in Europe, Australia, and New Zealand. This certification validated the high level of security that the BlackBerry products offered and was an important and often mandatory purchasing criterion for many organizations, including the government sector and the military. Lazaridis also insisted that new versions of the BES continued to provide IT departments with features that increased manageability, security, and centralized control of BlackBerry wireless handheld devices, such as the ability to remotely shut off devices that were lost, and the ability to disable multimedia features.

48   RIM's latest version of its BES software allowed the BlackBerry to be integrated with Microsoft Exchange, Lotus Domino and Novell GroupWise, ensuring its compatibility with the most popular e-mail programs and making it easier for users of these e-mail programs to use the BlackBerry.

Software Development Tools

49   RIM continued to offer the BlackBerry Developer Zone, software development kits, and other tools for creating applications for BlackBerry wireless handhelds. RIM recognized that independent software developers were constantly looking for opportunities to modify their existing programs to run on popular devices, as well as developing new and unique applications. RIM BlackBerry Developer Zone allowed developers to create specialized wireless applications that would increase the value of the BlackBerry for users through programs specifically designed for their needs. Enterprise customers and Independent Software Vendors (ISVs) could easily and quickly develop applications that leveraged the unique features of BlackBerry.

50   The BlackBerry Java Development Environment was a fully integrated development environment and simulation tool for creating applications for BlackBerry handhelds. Java, and its subset of programs known as J2ME, was the most popular software development environment. It enabled the development of new applications for space-constrained devices such as cellphones. By implementing Java as the application development software, RIM

---

[22] Subscribers included users of BlackBerry handheld devices as well as BlackBerry-enabled devices such as some Nokia cellular telephones.

was making its devices available as platforms for new applications reated by a large and growing developer community that included over three million software developers. One example of a specialized application that increased the BlackBerry's value in the healthcare industry was software that allowed diabetic patients and caregivers to automatically monitor a diabetic patient's activities and health conditions.

Licensing

51   In addition to its integrated solutions and service, RIM had begun licensing individual components of its products in 2002. The BlackBerry Connect Licensing Program enabled mobile devices from a variety of leading manufacturers to take advantage of BlackBerry "push" technology by allowing them to equip their devices with BlackBerry built-in e-mail and organizer applications. RIM's management believed this would allow consumers to benefit from RIM's technology on a device they were already familiar with and would provide the market with a broader choice of devices. It would also mean providers and corporations would not be forced to choose between their existing or strategic devices and BlackBerry.

52   Through this program, RIM licensed its **push** technology to mobile phone manufacturers such as Nokia in 2002, and Sony Ericsson in 2004. More recently, RIM licensed its "push" technology to Palm's Treo 650 in October 2005, and signed agreements with Motorola and Samsung in 2006. By end of fiscal 2007, there were 50 BlackBerry enabled devices. In addition to licensing revenue, this program also generated service revenue for RIM as the e-mail for the BlackBerry devices was routed through RIM's Operations Centre.

Manufacturing

53   RIM originally manufactured all of its products in-house because it wanted to ensure tight control over quality, and believed it benefited from the integration of manufacturing with research and development. However, in 2005 with demand growing globally, RIM began an outsourcing relationship with Elcoteq Network Corporation for the manufacture of certain devices in Europe and Mexico. At end of fiscal 2006, RIM began expansion of its manufacturing facility in Waterloo, which had a production capacity of five million devices per year, with the goal of doubling its existing 122,000 square foot facility. It would use the expanded facility for incremental production, materials storage, and co-location of some dispersed manufacturing operations.

Organization

Research and Development

54   RIM was continuing to focus on the development of next-generation handhelds, along with ongoing development of the BlackBerry platform/solution. The company had made notable increases in R&D expenditures over the years, increasing spending from US$62.6 million in 2004 to almost US$235 million in 2007. Approximately 2,100 employees (34 percent of RIM's employees) focused on research and development activities. To encourage innovation, RIM had created an Inventor's Banquet to honor those employees who had applied for patents, and rewarded the creators of key patents with substantial cash awards. By end of fiscal 2006, RIM held over 650 patents.

55   Lazaridis also insisted on a strong focus on quality testing. RIM tested its products extensively before releasing them. He commented, "We have a saying here at RIM. It is 'doing your math.' Our culture is to double-check, check twice, and ask customers before we undertake changes."

56   In fiscal 2007, RIM acquired Ascendent Systems, a San Jose, California, company which was a provider of enterprise voice mobility solutions. It purchased Ascendent because its

expertise would enable RIM to enhance the voice capabilities and features of its products. The intention was to provide enterprises with the same integration between desk and mobile telephones that RIM already provided with e-mail. For example, the user's BlackBerry could become a secure extension of a user's desk phone so that the user could be reached through one telephone number whether in the office or not, consolidation and access to a single voice mail-box, conference-calling capabilities, and even four- or five-digit extension dialing. Corporations with multiple locations, or large numbers of employees who spent a significant time away from their desks but needed to be accessible by telephone would find these features valuable.

57   RIM was also leveraging the expertise of SlipStream, a sixty-person company based in Waterloo that it acquired in 2006. SlipStream's expertise in efficiently transferring data through the Internet would increase the performance of Internet browsing on BlackBerry devices. SlipStream's capabilities could also potentially enable other multimedia functions on BlackBerry devices such as on-the-go video conferencing.

Culture, Control, and Human Resources

58   Management described RIM as a creative, energetic workplace that was fun but focused on success. The company had an employee turnover rate of less than one percent, and a reputation among the local universities as a coveted employer. Some examples of corporate events that RIM organized to keep its young image and culture were the celebration of achievements with concert performances by Barenaked Ladies and Aerosmith and the shutdown of the company for half days for each release of the *Star Wars* movies. Even meeting rooms were identified by names based on themes such as *Lord of the Rings* ("Frodo Room," "Samwise Room") or famous Canadian hockey players ("Wayne Gretzky Room," "Bobby Orr Room") rather than numbers.

59   Although RIM had grown from 1,850 employees in 2003 and 4,700 in 2006 to approximately 6,250 employees in 2007, Balsillie did not believe becoming bureaucratic and rigid was inevitable.

> If you value what's important and invest in culture, then the natural rigor mortis can be counteracted. With the go-to-market activities, we've evolved into business units that still give you projects that you can sink your teeth into. Two hundred go-to-market people meet once a week, and everyone will take a minute to talk about what they're doing. They see how they're interdependent and how each part is trusting the other and counting on it. Other parts of the organization like engineering naturally are project oriented. Mike does similar meetings with engineers, and there are lots of interdisciplinary meetings. There's ownership, latitude, and creativity, but it's still a synthesized and integrated experience so people still care and commit to it but recognize it's part of a bigger system.

60   With respect to control and structure, Balsillie believed organization charts were anachronistic and only useful insofar as outlining basic authority and reporting relationships (see Exhibit 9 for an organization chart). He described RIM's internal communications more fluid than hierarchical. He also rejected the idea of formal controls as necessary to monitor work efforts.

> Formal controls create a way to hide because you can hide in the system—there are teams and groups and the transparency and collaboration makes it pretty hard to be a renegade. . . . If you play a team sport you can't have five people doing their own thing—there is a system and an element of structure but a good system has lots of decision-making and creativity on the court. . . . These are smart people—you don't want to tell them what to do—as long as it resonates with their belief system, they will do it.

61   He did admit, however, that although visibility, transparency, and collaboration were important elements in the organization's success, his own visibility had declined and he was seeing less of everything due to the company's increased size and his responsibilities.

EXHIBIT 9 Organization Chart

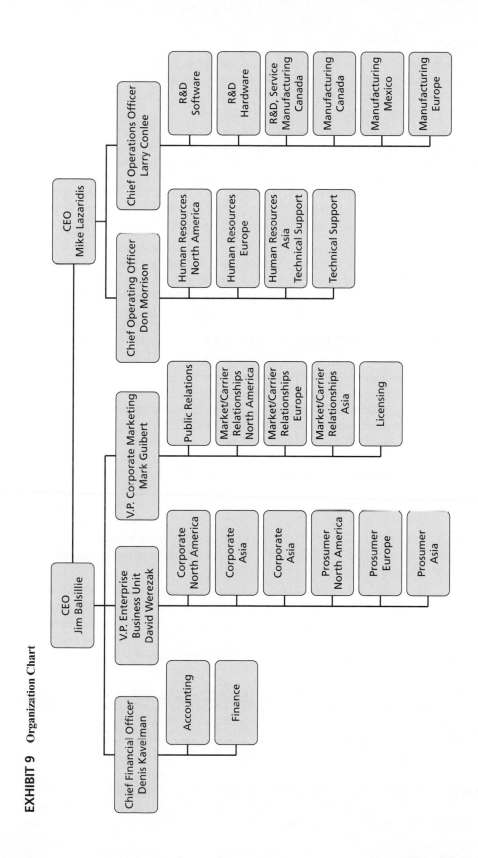

Strategy

62   Balsillie described RIM's approach to strategy as similar to white-water rafting. He and Lazaridis both believed that focusing on the fundamentals and identifying imperatives rather than setting specific expectations for the future was the right approach to ensuring success. Balsillie described their approach to strategy as follows:

> The way you become a good white-water rafter is fundamentally managing well what is in front of you now, and positioning for the next step—to go beyond that is useless and it takes you away from doing what you have before you now because there are too many contingent events and too much uncertainty to predict. If you focus on the fundamentals, the totality is better—if you look at it and say "I want 10 percent more sales, what do I have to do?" I think you're coming at it backwards. How many sales do I want? Every last dollar I can possibly get.

63   Balsillie described the strategic decision-making process as, "anything but ad hoc—it was deliberate, specific, and highly integrative." It involved consultation and collaboration with top management and relevant areas of the organization. He stated that this was important to him and Lazaridis not only so that they were making the best decision possible, but also so that all areas of the organization could understand what was being done and why, recognize the importance of their role in it, and ensure that they could be more adaptive to changing conditions.

EXAMINING CHOICES AS COMPETITION CHANGES

64   Balsillie smiled when he thought how flattering it was that a new product like the iPhone was described as a "BlackBerry killer." It signaled that RIM's products were the ones to beat. However, he recognized that the industry was changing—competitors were increasing and moving into RIM's enterprise market, and the technology was converging. His objective was to get every last sales dollar he could for RIM, and be well positioned to avoid "rocks" down the road. The analysts' debate about which market RIM should emphasize was in the back of his mind as he considered RIM's situation.

GLOSSARY

corporate mail server   A corporate mail server is a software application on a dedicated corporate computer that receives incoming e-mails and forwards outgoing e-mails for delivery. It is similar to a virtual mailroom in a company.

encryption   Encryption software translates data into a secret code that is unreadable until it is "decrypted." Encryption is the most effective way to achieve data security.

enterprise   A business—the enterprise market refers to the market segment where the entire company adopts a product. The devices are approved and installed by the organization; installation, support, and control is managed by the organization's information technology (IT) department.

multimedia   A combination of media such as text, audio, video, graphics, and interactive features that can be used to inform or entertain the user (i.e., a video game or a television program).

push   Push e-mail means that an e-mail message is automatically redirected to the user's handheld device, and the user is notified of its arrival. This is in contrast to "pull" e-mail systems where the user must connect with and retrieve e-mail manually.

QWERTY   The QWERTY keyboard is the standard keyboard letter configuration that allows users to benefit from the familiarity of letter locations and type faster and with less frustration than on a telephone touchpad.

Case 21

General Electric's Corporate Strategy

Andrew C. Inkpen

Like the premature obituary of writer Mark Twain, reports of the death of the conglomerate are often exaggerated. Diversified companies, straddling multiple industries or even just different parts of one large sector, remain a dominant, if not always fashionable, feature of stock markets from the U.S. to continental Europe and Asia. But a new backlash against conglomerates suggests a more lasting shift in investor preferences may be taking place— driven in part by the growing influence of hedge funds and private equity houses. In public markets, big has rarely appeared less beautiful.[1]

1 Through the 1980s and 1990s, large diversified firms, often called conglomerates, largely fell out of favor with investors. Arguments against conglomerates ranged from complexity in management to the difficulties that analysts and investors had in understanding their operations. More recently, conglomerates regained some respect. As the largest of the U.S. diversified multinational firms, General Electric Company (GE) generated a variety of opinions, such as:

Increasingly restive General Electric Co. shareholders, frustrated with six years of meager returns, are pressuring Chairman Jeffrey Immelt to break up the conglomerate. But some shareholders and analysts argue that GE's sprawling businesses are better off together than apart. GE's big umbrella, these investors say, can balance differing product and economic cycles, while helping all its businesses financially. And that would boost the stock price over the longer term.

"The main appeal of GE is its diversification," says Mark Demos, portfolio manager at Fifth Third Asset Management, which owns 12.6 million GE shares. He says this isn't the time to break up the company, because global economic trends and investor sentiment are moving toward bigger, more international companies such as GE.[2]

GE BACKGROUND

2 GE's roots go back to 1890 when Thomas Edison established Edison General Electric Company. In 1892, Edison General Electric Company merged with Thomson-Houston Company. The new company was called General Electric Company. Several of Edison's early products were still part of GE in 2008, including lighting, transportation, industrial products, power transmission, and medical equipment. GE is the only company listed in the Dow Jones Industrial Index today that was also included in the original index in 1896.

3 Over the century after its founding, GE made hundreds of acquisitions, and expanded far beyond its original businesses. By 1980, GE products ranged from plastics and consumer electronics to nuclear reactors and jet engines. In 1981, Jack Welch became CEO, and radically restructured the company. Welch urged his employees to be "better than the best," and

[1] Dan Roberts and John Authers, "The Harder They Fall," www.ft.com, October 27, 2005.
[2] Kathryn Kranhold, "For GE, No Lack of Ideas; As Frustrated Investors Identify Units to Sell, Others Back Status Quo," *Wall Street Journal,* May 9, 2007, p. C1.

challenged each of the diverse GE businesses to be the number 1 or number 2 competitor, or disengage. Between 1981 and 1990, GE divested more than 200 businesses, and made more than 370 acquisitions. Businesses sold included small appliances, consumer electronics, RCA Records, outdoor lawn equipment, oil exploration and refining, car auctions, and mining. Acquisitions included NBC, Kidder, Peabody & Company, Thomson/CGR medical equipment, Borg-Warner Chemicals, Penske Leasing, Tungsram light bulbs, and Polaris aircraft leasing. Welch also slashed layers of management, and began a series of internal initiatives, many of which set the standard for business practice around the world, such as Six Sigma. In 1980, the year before Welch became CEO, GE recorded revenue of $26.8 billion; in 2000, the year before Welch retired, revenue was nearly $130 billion.

4   In 2001, Jeff Immelt became CEO. Among his early goals were to strengthen GE's global presence and create a more collaborative culture. Under Immelt, GE sold its insurance and plastics businesses, and strengthened its presence in health care, financial services, and entertainment. In 2003, GE acquired 80 percent of Universal from the French company Vivendi.

GE'S STRATEGY

5   GE organized its many operations in six main businesses: infrastructure, industrial, commercial finance, healthcare, consumer finance, and NBC Universal. Exhibit 1 provides a summary of each of the businesses, and shows that each of the businesses employed tens of thousands of employees, and was a highly diversified business in its own right. If spun off from GE, the businesses would be among the largest and most profitable companies in their respective sectors.

6   Given the diversity of businesses, what was the strategic logic that held the company together? The CEO's letter to the shareholders in the 2003 Annual Report stated:

We are another year along with our five-initiative strategy to create high-margin, capital-efficient growth:

- **Technical Leadership**: Technology and innovation are at the heart of our initiatives. Technical leadership produces high-margin products, wins competitive battles, and creates new markets.
- **Services**: Technical leadership has created a massive installed base of more than 100,000 long-lived GE jet engines, power turbines, locomotives, and medical devices for which we can provide high-margin services for decades.
- **Customer Focus**: One of our successes is in "vertical selling," the practice of aligning our offerings in four industries that are critical to GE: healthcare, energy, transportation, and retail. They represent $47 billion of industrial revenues and $169 billion of financial services assets. GE brings a unique array of capabilities to these industries, including products, services, information, and financing. On this broad foundation, we can build deeper partnerships with our customers.
- **Globalization**: We can take every growth idea and multiply its effectiveness through globalization. Globalization is a GE core competency. We have made and sold products outside the U.S. for 100 years, and one-third of our leadership team is global. Our global revenues were almost $61 billion in 2003, up 14 percent, and should grow 15 percent in 2004. We succeed because we recognize one central fact: global growth requires more than simply shipping products. You must be equally committed to developing capabilities and relationships in the markets where you want to succeed.
- **Growth Platforms**: A key GE strength is our ability to conceptualize the future, identify "unstoppable" trends, and develop new ways to grow . . . We follow a disciplined process for growth. First, we segment broad markets and launch with a small platform acquisition. Then we transform the business model using our growth initiatives, such as services and globalization. Finally, we apply our financial strength to invest in organic growth or acquisitions. We can get big quickly while generating solid returns.

EXHIBIT 1   Summary of GE Businesses in 2008

GE Commercial Finance

2007 Revenue: $34.3 billion; **2007 Profit:** 14%; **Number of Employees:** 28,500
Products: Asset financing; Cash flow programs; Equipment leasing; Financing programs; Growth capital; Lending products; Operating leases; Revolving lines of credit

GE Healthcare

2006 Revenue: $17 billion; **2007 Profit:** −3%; **Number of Employees:** 47,000
Products: Drug discovery and biopharmaceutical manufacturing technologies; Imaging contrast agents and molecular diagnostics; Integrated healthcare IT systems; Medical diagnostic imaging equipment (X-ray, CT, MRI, ultrasound, PET scanners); Patient monitoring and anesthetics systems

GE Industrial

2006 Revenue: $17.7 billion; **2007 Profit:** 9%; **Number of Employees:** 72,000
Automation hardware and software solutions; Consumer appliances, lighting, and electrical equipment and products; Embedded computing systems, high speed networking and computer numeric controls; Innovative technology, service and support to the power quality industry; Protection, metering, control and automation systems; Security and life safety technologies; Sensors and nondestructive testing technology-driven inspection solutions

GE Infrastructure

2006 Revenue: $57.9 billion; **2007 Profit:** 22%; **Number of Employees:** 85,000
Advanced technology equipment and services for all segments of the global oil and gas industry; Broad-based commercial financial solutions, including structured equity, leveraged leasing, partnerships and project finance for aviation and energy industries; Diesel engines for marine and stationary power applications, motorized systems for mining trucks, and signaling and communications systems for the rail industry; Freight and passenger locomotives, locomotive parts, and locomotive services; Gear units for wind power; Jet engines; Power generation and energy delivery systems; Water treatment and purification, water reuse, water recovery, wastewater, mobile water, water services, and process filtration and purification

GE Money

2006 Revenue: $25.0 billion; **2007 Profit:** 31%; **Number of Employees:** 50,000
Corporate travel and purchasing cards; Credit cards; Debt consolidation; Home equity loans; Mortgage and motor solutions; Personal loans

NBC Universal

2006 Revenue: $15.4 billion; **2007 Profit:** 6%; **Number of Employees:** 15,000
Entertainment, news, and sports television programs; Movies; Online content; Vacation resorts and theme parks

7   The CEO's letter to the shareholders in the 2006 Annual Report included:

Our strategies create strengths and capabilities, which, in turn, drive competitive advantage. The consistent execution of the same strategic principles, year after year, provides the foundation to invest and deliver.

We expect them (the businesses) to be industry leaders in market share, value, and profitability. We want businesses where we can bring the totality of the company—products, services, information, and financing—to capitalize on the growth trends I mentioned earlier. We run these businesses with common finance and human resource processes. We have one leadership development foundation and one global research infrastructure to achieve excellent results with a common culture. We have a few company-wide councils, like Services, so we can share ideas with minimum bureaucracy . . . When we find that a business cannot meet our financial goals or could be run better outside GE, we will exit that business rather than erode shareowner value.

Our "average hold" of a business is measured in decades. We do not "flip" assets. We are builders of businesses. This takes people who believe in teamwork and have pride in workmanship. We have a team that is focused on building a company that has enduring value and makes the world a better place. Our culture matches the expectations of long-term investors.

8   In 2008, GE described itself as a reliable growth company. At GE's Annual Leadership Meeting in early 2008, Jeff Immelt described four strategic principles to achieve growth:

Invest in Leadership Businesses: We have spent the last six years assembling a portfolio to drive growth in today's more interconnected global economy. We will continue to refine the mix to capture market opportunities that ensure our portfolio keeps generating faster growth, has more balance, and creates a stronger competitive advantage. In 2008, we will continue to drive results from our Growth as a Process initiative by:

- Sustaining technical leadership
- Accelerating globalization
- Driving services growth
- Bringing lean and enterprise to customers
- Building adjacencies to the installed base

Execution and Financial Discipline: This year we are formalizing a process around operational excellence that will help us to grow margins and returns in a tough environment. Our process is being led by a new Operating Council and shared metrics to measure results.

Growth as a Process: Our focus on Growth as a Process continues to enable us to deliver organic revenue growth of 2–3x GDP. Our process is accelerating, it's visible, and it creates high confidence for investors. In 2006 and 2007, we achieved 9 percent organic revenue growth, and in 2008 we expect to maintain this level of growth.

Great People: GE has always attracted great talent. Converting talent into a strategic advantage means developing and retaining that talent so that we have the best leadership team. In 2008, we will do this by focusing on core capabilities of LIG (Leadership Innovation and Growth), accessing local knowledge for global growth, and leveraging our deep expertise.

9   In recent years, GE also talked more about organic growth. According to Jeff Immelt:

The focus on organic growth is also going to require people to stay in the same jobs longer. You can't plant a tree and see it grow in a year. This is very countercultural in an organization, where building a career has always meant packing your bags every 18 months. Going forward, you're still going to have some 18-month jobs, but over the course of 30 years, you're going to have more jobs that last five years.[3]

GE'S ACQUISITION STRATEGY

10   Acquisitions and divestitures played a key role in GE's corporate strategy. Exhibits 2 and 3 show GE's main acquisitions and divestitures over the past few decades. Exhibit 4 shows the stock price. Since 2002, GE exited businesses with revenues of about $50 billion, the equivalent of a Fortune 50 company. GE exited all or most of its insurance, materials,

[3] T. A. Stewart, "Growth as a Process: An Interview with Jeffrey R. Immelt," *Harvard Business Review,* June 2006, pp. 60–70.

EXHIBIT 2   Select GE Divestitures 1969–2007

Date	Business Sold	Value (where available)
1969	Aparatebau A.G. Goldach	
1969	Monogram Electric Housewares	
1983	KOA-AM and KOAQ-FM	$22M
1984	Utah International and Utah-Marcona	
1984	Houseware operations	$300M
1984	Electro-Chemical Energy Conversion Programs	$4.7M
1985	Simplex-GE	
1986	Coronet	
1987	RCA Global Communications	$160M
1987	NBC radio network operations and stations	
1987	Nuclear waste services assets	$5.5M
1987	Software International Corporation	$24M
1989	Instrument products operations	$110M
1990	Ladd Petroleum	$542M
1998	Domestic compressor motor business	$120M
1999	Ruffin Village	$3.5M
2002	Disaster Recovery Services Unit	
2003	Edison Life Insurance plus home and auto insurance businesses	$2.15B
2004	Water Technologies' transportation coolant aftermarket business	
2004	Nuovo Pignone and retail fueling business	$203.8M
2004	Commercial AC motor unit	$72.5M
2004	Dione PLC	$113M
2004	Storage USA	$2.3B
2006	GE Life	$910M
2007	Plastics business	$11.6B
2007	U.S. mortgage business	$117M

equipment services, and entertainment and industrial platforms. GE also exited its U.S. mortgage origination business, and announced plans to sell its personal loan business in Japan. In 2007, GE sold its plastics business because of "rampant inflation in raw material costs." (The plastics business is one that Jack Welch once ran.) Over the same time period, GE acquired $80 billion of new businesses. GE investments resulted in one of the largest renewable-energy businesses in the world. GE diversified its Healthcare and NBC Universal franchises by investing in markets such as life sciences, healthcare IT, and cable programming. GE created a new high-tech industrial business called Enterprise Solutions, and made several investments in financial services businesses in global markets. GE acquired Vetco Gray, a company that made products for the upstream oil and gas industry.

EXHIBIT 3   Select GE Acquisitions 1968–2007

Date	Company Acquired	Industry	Value
1968	Metropolitan Television	TV Broadcasting	
1969	Benerson	Manufacturing	
1981	Intersil	Integrated Circuits	$235M
1984	Employers Reinsurance	Insurance	$1.1B
1986	RCA	Consumer Electronics	$6.4B
1986	Kidder, Peabody, & Co.	Investment Banking	$600,000
1987	Gelco Payment Systems	Payment Processing	$414M
1987	D&K Financial	Financial Services	
1990	MNC Financial	Banking	
1990	Burton Group	IT Consulting	$329M
1990	Travelers Mortgage Services	Mortgage	
1990	ELLCO Leasing Corporation	Equipment Leasing	
1990	Tungsram	Lighting	$150M
1991	Businessland Rents	Rental/leasing	
1993	GNA Corporation	Annuity Sales	$577M
1993	United Pacific Life Insurance	Life Insurance	$550M
1997	Lockheed Martin Medical Imaging Systems	Medical Imaging	
1997	Imp Leas	Automobile Leasing	
1998	Unilec Corporation	Electrical Distribution	
1999	Syprotec	Substation Monitoring	
1999	Energy and Environmental Research	Nitrogen Oxide Control	
2000	Harmon Industries	Train Crossing Signals	$386M
2000	Young Generators	Electrical Generators	
2000	Smallworld Plc.	GIS/Mapping Software	$210M
2001	sofion AG	IT Services	
2001	Heller Financial	Commercial Banking	$5.3B
2002	Unison Industries	Aircraft Engines	
2002	Time Retail Finance	Consumer Credit	$210M
2002	Interlogix	Security Systems	$777M
2002	Druck Holdings	Sensor Technology	$335M
2002	Bravo (through NBC)	Cable Channel	$1.25B
2002	Enron Wind	Wind Power	$325M
2002	PII	Pipeline Inspection	$446M
2003	International Fiber Systems	Fiber Optics	
2003	Universal	Entertainment	$14B
2003	Transamerica Finance	Commercial Lending	$5.4B
2003	Mountain Systems	Manufacturing Systems	

EXHIBIT 3   Select GE Acquisitions 1968–2007 (*Continued*)

Date	Company Acquired	Industry	Value
2003	Monitoring Automation Systems	Security Systems	
2003	OSi Specialties	Chemicals	
2003	M.J. Harden Associates	GIS/mapping	$72M
2003	Triple G Systems Group	Medical Info Systems	$78M
2003	CitiCapital Fleet Services	Fleet Management	$1.2B
2003	Instrumentarium	Medical Equipment	$2.3B
2004	HPSC	Medical Financing	$72.4M
2004	Benchmark Group	Real Estate	$502M
2004	BHA Group	Air Pollution Control	$239M
2004	Dillard National Bank	Commercial Banking	$700M
2004	DeltaBank (Russia)	Commercial Banking	
2004	Ionics	Water Treatment	$1B
2004	Invision Technologies	Airport Screening	$885M
2005	IDX	Medical Info Systems	$1.4B
2005	Edwards Systems Technology	Fire Detection	$1.4B
2005	Recreational Vehicle and Marine Financing (from E-trade)	Online Brokerage	$60M
2006	Arden Realty	Real Estate	$4.8B
2006	SBS Technologies	Embedded Computing	$260M
2006	Biacore International AB	Life Sciences	$439M
2006	Trustreet Properties	Financial Services	$1.2B

EXHIBIT 4   Stock Price

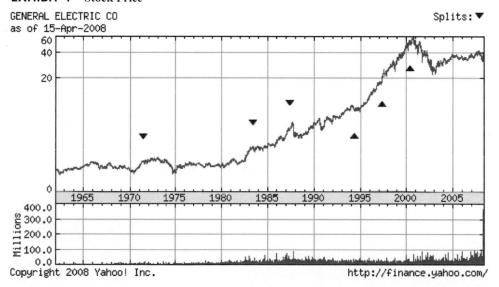

GENERAL ELECTRIC CO
as of 15-Apr-2008   Splits: ▼

Copyright 2008 Yahoo! Inc.   http://finance.yahoo.com/

11   Not all of GE's acquisitions were successful. It was widely acknowledged that the acquisition of brokerage firm Kidder, Peabody in the mid-1980s was a huge failure. The system of individual risk-taking and incentive compensation at Kidder, Peabody never meshed with GE's culture and values. Many questions were also raised when GE created NBC Universal in 2003 via the 80 percent acquisition of Vivendi's film and television unit, which included Universal Studios and theme parks. Universal had gone through several M&A deals before the GE acquisition. In 1990, the large Japanese electronics company Matsushita acquired MCA, Universal's parent, for $6.59 billion. In 1995, the Canadian spirits company, Seagram, acquired 80 percent of MCA from Matsushita for $5.7 billion. In 2000, the Vivendi Group acquired Seagram. The *Wall Street Journal* said the following about the GE-Universal deal:

> The strategic elements of the deal are harder for GE to justify. The media business is far more competitive than other industries in which GE can use its financial heft and strong brand name to squash the competition. GE executives have said they had no interest in owning a movie studio, with its unpredictable earnings and difficult personalities. GE acknowledged it "has previously chosen not to pursue the acquisition of theatrical movie studio assets because of the inherent volatility and unpredictability of the business." But, it quickly added, this deal is different because Universal is so good, because the studio's film library will help mellow the swings in revenue, and, if all else fails, the studio would make up only about 10 percent of the new entity's revenues, a manageable element . . . The assets of NBC and VUE (Vivendi Universal Entertainment) are extremely complementary, and the combination of VUE's rich content library, superior television production facility, and attractive cable brands with NBC's industry-leading broadcast network and well-established cable properties could benefit shareholders for years to come.[4]

12   Jack Welch commented on GE's success with acquisitions:

> Every acquisition GE makes has a perfect plan, but we know 20 or 30 percent will blow up in our face. A small company can only afford to make one or two bets or they go out of business. But we can afford to make lots more mistakes, and, in fact, we have to throw more things at the walls. The big companies that get into trouble are those that try to manage their size instead of experiment with it.[5]

GE CULTURE AND VALUES

13   GE's corporate values can be found in corporate statements that identify the traits that leaders should embody. For an example of a GE value statement during Jack Welch's tenure as CEO, see Table 1.

14   Table 2 shows a more recent statement of values and actions.

15   GE evaluated its leaders based on various traits. According to Jeff Immelt:

> By the end of 2004, we came up with five growth traits. The first is external focus. Then there's imagination and creativity. And a growth leader must be especially decisive and capable of clear thinking. Inclusiveness is also vital. Finally, leaders in these high-growth companies tend to have deep domain expertise.[6]

[4] K. Brown, "Will GE Be Enjoying the Movie? As It Jumps into the Vivendi Deal, Conglomerate Is Buying Low, But Investors Question the Fit," *Wall Street Journal,* September 3, 2003, p. C.1.

[5] R. Foster, "Manager's Journal: The Welch Legacy: Creative Destruction," *Wall Street Journal,* September 10, 2001, p. A.18.

TABLE 1 **GE Value Statement**

GE Leaders—always with unyielding integrity:

- Have a passion for excellence and hate bureaucracy
- Are open to ideas from anywhere, and committed to work out
- Live quality, and drive cost and speed for competitive advantage
- Have the self-confidence to involve everyone, and behave in a boundaryless fashion
- Create a clear, simple, reality-based vision, and communicate it to all constituencies
- Have enormous energy and the ability to energize others
- Stretch, set aggressive goals, and reward progress, yet understand accountability and commitment
- See change as opportunity, not threat
- Have global brains, and build diverse and global teams

TABLE 2 **GE Values Card**

VALUES	ACTIONS
CURIOUS PASSIONATE RESOURCEFUL ACCOUNTABLE TEAMWORK COMMITTED OPEN ENERGIZING	**imagine** We put imagination to work for our customers, people and communities **solve** We help solve some of the world's toughest problems **build** We are a performance culture that builds markets, people and shareholder value **lead** We are a meritocracy that leads through learning, inclusiveness and change
 Imagination at work	ALWAYS WITH UNYIELDING INTEGRITY

16 Table 3 provides more detail on the growth traits. For each growth trait, there were behaviors that represented "outstanding" and "needs improvement." For example, for clear thinking, "Confident in stand-up skills . . . without the PowerPoint" was an outstanding behavior. "Getting bogged down in details" was evidence of a need for improvement.

---

[6] Stewart, "Growth as a Process."

TABLE 3 GE Individual Growth Traits

External Focus

- Defines success in market/industry terms . . . understands customer needs, marketplace dynamics, industry trends, and the competitive landscape in your industry or function
- Considers the external impact of business activities and decisions on customers, market/industry, investors, media, government, and communities
- Anticipates customer needs and ensures that they are met . . . measures processes and performance through the customer's eyes
- Stays current with industry trends, including market intelligence and competitive analysis, and takes an active role in shaping their industry and/or function
- Takes action to enhance GE's reputation among all stakeholders . . . represents the Company well

Clear Thinking

- Simplifies strategy into specific actions, makes decisions, and communicates priorities
- Has strategic capacity to sift through complex information and focus on the critical few priorities
- Communicates messages clearly and concisely
- Able to translate strategy into business objectives with clear accountability
- Decisive . . . able to make decisions with speed and accuracy . . . based on best available information
- Is accountable for organic growth, and frees up resources to fund innovation
- Reality . . . ability to bring reality to situations to identify gaps between perception and facts

Imagination

- Has the imagination to take risks on both people and ideas . . . bold thinking to imagine a better way, and the courage to make it a reality
- Generates new and unique ideas . . . makes fresh connections . . . an original thinker
- Courage to take action on ideas . . . fights for growth, both internally and externally
- Supports an environment in which people can take risks, consistent with integrity, and experiment
- Brings creative ideas to fruition . . . good instincts about which ideas will work, and when
- Viewed as an advocate of innovation . . . pushes for "big bets" to accelerate our competitive advantage

Inclusiveness

- Can energize teams through inclusiveness and connection with people . . . builds loyalty and commitment
- Creates an engaging work environment . . . appeals to the unique interests of each team member
- Builds a connection with the team through personal involvement and trust . . . inspires people to want to perform at a higher level
- Promotes an environment that recognizes and celebrates individual and cultural differences
- Develops others . . . provides others with feedback and coaching . . . encourages personal growth

Expertise

- Has the confidence and perspective that comes through depth in industry/function to impact growth
- Learns from living with the impact of their decisions and actions
- Has demonstrated leadership throughout different business cycles
- Gains perspective through varied experiences and build-up of skills
- Continually strives to increase knowledge with up-to-date information

COMMENTS ON GE CULTURE

17   Dennis Dammerman, former GE Vice Chairman and CFO, made the following comments about how the GE culture evolved during Jack Welch's tenure:[7]

> Eventually, the businesses began to get flatter and flatter, with some interesting phenomena as by-products. For one, a whole new type of leader became necessary. One could no longer be a colorless, impersonal autocrat—a technician who could manipulate the management structure to produce results. The structure was gone. The leader now had to emerge from the corner office and excite teams—energize them, lead them rather than manage them. Not everyone was capable of doing that. Many stumbled for awhile and retired or otherwise departed. Some adapted amazingly well, and became excited and younger in their new role. The bureaucrats, many at significant pay levels, had a bad time of it. The kitchen light came on, and suddenly there were no longer the pipes and cabinets of bureaucracy to hide under. They left by the battalions.
>
> The phenomenon that best captures the sharing, learning, cooperative atmosphere at the new GE is what we call the CEC, our Corporate Executive Council meeting, which takes place quarterly. The leaders of our 12 big businesses—the senior corporate leadership and a few others, about 25 of us in all—assemble from around the world for two days and meet in a small room at our management center, downstate from here at Crotonville, to share insights, best practices, market intelligence, warnings, technology, anything of value, in an atmosphere I can only describe as approximating a coed frat house. The CEC is a family meeting with a lot of laughing, argument, shouting, good-natured insults, usually initiated by Welch, and incessant sharing. Someone who once sat in on this CEC meeting remarked with some amazement that "these guys sound like they actually like each other." A political remark, a "puffy" chart, a self-serving presentation are now so culturally alien that a pall of embarrassed silence descends over the room on the infrequent occasion one slips in.
>
> Our business leaders go away from these meetings refreshed, enlightened, renewed. They go back to the competitive wars knowing that every resource and every brain in this $100 billion global enterprise is instantly at their disposal, and whatever they need will be willingly given if they just pick up the phone. Those who persist in lumping GE with the classic conglomerates would need less than 10 minutes in that Crotonville meeting room to arrive at a new view.
>
> If there is a simple but profoundly important lesson we learned from those days, it is this: you must have a vision that, like "number one or number two in every business," is so clean and so clear that everyone from a trainee on a drill press to a Vice Chairman can understand it, and repeat it until you wake up at night saying it, then say it again the next day. And even more important, you must reinforce that vision with every action you take and, by proxy, every action your management team takes, because culture change can be smothered in its cradle by a very small number of visible contradictory actions.

18   Other comments on the culture from a former executive:

> I was proud to be a GE employee. GE always had a good reputation. I could go to my airline customers and say I was from GE—that gave me some respect.
>
> It was a tough place to work. There were always financial measures. You had to embrace the culture. You could have fun, be challenged, be rewarded.
>
> Working at GE is rewarding, intense, and unforgiving. It is results-driven and measurement-driven; it is unforgiving about integrity and business practices, unforgiving with regard to values, and unforgiving if you do not embrace the business measurements and initiatives.
>
> We used to say they would throw you in the swamp and then tell you it was full of alligators.
>
> GE was recognized for its training. I felt I could do battle with the best of them. I started from humble beginnings.

[7] D. D. Dammerman, *Executive Speeches,* October/November 1998, 13, No. 2; pp. 1–6.

TABLE 4   **GE Initiatives in Place When Jeff Immelt Became CEO**

Best Practices Sharing: Identifies particularly effective approaches, and spreads them across GE's businesses.

Change Acceleration Process: Equips leaders with a proven method of managing change, and prepares them to succeed as change agents.

Crotonville Customer Programs: Deploys the resources of GE's renowned internal training facility for the benefit of customers.

Multigenerational Product Development Plan: Ensures that new products are not simply optimized for the near term, but have the ability to evolve with customer needs.

Process Mapping: Creates visual representations of business processes to facilitate understanding and simplification.

Quick Market Intelligence: Builds on Wal-Mart's innovation of tapping into real-time data about customer and competitor behavior, and disseminating that insight rapidly throughout the organization.

Simplification: Drives out extraneous costs incurred by overcomplicated processes and proliferation of options in sourcing and other areas.

Six Sigma: Employs Motorola-pioneered methods to bring defect levels below 3.4 defects per million opportunities. Intensive quality training yields "green belts," "black belts," and "master black belts."

Work-Out: Uses cross-functional teams and town hall meetings to find ways to take unproductive work out of the system, like meetings, reports, and approval levels that add no value.

Source: T. A. Stewart, "Growth as a Process: An Interview with Jeffrey R. Immelt," *Harvard Business Review,* June 2006, pp. 60-70.

TABLE 5   **New GE Initiatives Since Jeff Immelt Became CEO**

Acquisition Integration Framework: Outlines a detailed process for ensuring that acquired entities are effectively assimilated into GE.

At the Customer, For the Customer: Brings GE's internal best practices, management tools, and training programs to customers facing their own managerial challenges.

CECOR Marketing Framework: Connects innovation and other growth efforts with market opportunities and customer needs by asking questions to *calibrate, explore, create, organize,* and *realize* strategic growth.

Customer Dreaming Sessions: Assembles a group of the most influential and creative people in an industry to envision its future and provoke the kind of interchange that can inspire new plans.

Growth Traits and Assessments: Outlines and enforces the expectation that GE's next generation of leaders will display five strengths: external focus, clear thinking, imagination, inclusiveness, and domain expertise.

Imagination Breakthroughs: Focuses top management's attention and resources on promising ideas for new revenue streams percolating up from anywhere in the organization.

Source: Stewart, 2006.

GROWTH AND CHANGE

24   The culture at GE revolved around change. The Change Acceleration Process (Table 4) was an initiative introduced specifically to help GE managers manage the change process. Jack Welch described change at GE:[9]

[9] S. Stratford, "A Master Class in Radical Change," *Fortune,* December 13, 1993. pp. 82–86.

You've got to be on the cutting edge of change. You can't simply maintain the status quo, because somebody's always coming from another country with another product, or consumer tastes change, or the cost structure does, or there's a technology breakthrough. If you're not fast and adaptable, you're vulnerable. This is true for every segment of every business in every country in the world.

People always ask, "Is the change over? Can we stop now?" You've got to tell them, "No, it's just begun." They must come to understand that it is never ending. Leaders must create an atmosphere where people understand that change is a continuing process, not an event.

The changes are always bigger than you initially sense. In the beginning of something like the defense industry downsizing, people are in denial—they can't get themselves to believe how big the change will be.

How do you bring people into the change process? Start with reality. Get all the facts out. Give people the rationale for change, laying it out in the clearest, most dramatic terms. When everybody gets the same facts, they'll generally come to the same conclusion. Only after everyone agrees on the reality and resistance is lowered can you begin to get buy-in to the needed change.

GE recognized that to drive change, you need to stick with it. You drive everyone by using the tools. You need to get scale so that the tool gets better. You don't allow for variation on the tools and initiatives because you need to build scale.

25   Another executive stated:

Change is in the GE DNA. The initiatives were always changing. Session C was a bit different every year. We were always hearing from Jack Welch about the need for change. If you are not comfortable with change, GE is not the place to be.

We were always looking for new ideas, and we wanted to share ideas with each other. We looked outside our business—Jack used to say don't look at competitors, they probably have the same challenges. We looked outside the business for ideas we could use. People were encouraged to look at best practices at other companies.

CONCLUSION

26   To conclude, some comments by Jeff Immelt from the 2007 GE Annual Report:

Investors often ask how we can execute in a company with such diverse businesses. We do it by running the company with common initiatives around growth and financial discipline . . . I want investors to see that GE is truly more than the "sum of the parts." The strength of GE is in the "totality." It is the ability to deliver in good times and bad. We do this because we invest and deliver. We are winning in the essential themes; we have built leadership businesses; we are a high-performance company; and we develop great leaders.

We have always believed that building strong leaders is a strategic imperative. When times are easy, leadership can be taken for granted. When the world is turbulent, you appreciate great people. Ultimately, we want to develop people who are guardians of GE's culture, champions of our legacy, and protectors of our reputation. They must perform with integrity, be disciplined and aggressive—and, at the same time, able to solve problems with global ingenuity.

Case 22

Wynn Resorts, Ltd.

Victoria Page
Alan N. Hoffman

ROAD TO GOLD TIMELINE

October 25, 2002	October 31, 2002	April 28, 2005	September 6, 2006	December 15, 2007	2009	Future
• IPO NASDAQ WYNN	• Ground-breaking of Wynn Las Vegas	• Doors Open at the Wynn Las Vegas	• Doors Open at the Wynn Macau	• 2nd Phase of Wynn Macau is Complete	• Expected Completion of the Encore Las Vegas Diamond Suites	• Wynn Resorts on the Cotai Strip

"KNOW WHEN TO HOLD'EM KNOW WHEN TO FOLD'EM"

1   Millions of people travel to Las Vegas each year with big dreams of hitting the jackpot; most of them leave Las Vegas empty-handed, heartbroken, and even further in debt. Very few people win big, and even fewer make their life's fortune in "Sin City"; Steve Wynn is one of the lucky few who has. From humble beginnings with a family run bingo parlor in Maryland, to Chief Executive Officer and Chairman of Wynn Resorts LTD, premium destination, world-class Casinos and Resorts. Seen by many in the entertainment industry as a visionary, Steve Wynn has revolutionized the City of Las Vegas one Casino at a time.[1]

2   From small stakes in the Frontier Hotel in 1967 as a newcomer to Vegas; to upping the ante with a complete renovation of the Golden Nugget from a dingy Downtown Vegas Casino to a four-star resort and gaming facility, Mr. Wynn was not satisfied with his accomplishment of attracting high net worth clientele to Downtown Vegas; he had dreams of expanding his Casino Empire, starting with a twin Golden Nugget Resort in Atlantic City, a rival gambling destination. Also on his repertoire of great successes are the magnificent Mirage (1989), Treasure Island (1993), and the breathtaking Bellagio (1998). After what was considered the largest merger in the gaming industry's history, the Mirage became a part of MGM, Inc. for $6.4 billion. Steve Wynn stepped down as Chairman and CEO and set his sights on developing his largest Casino Resort yet, the Five Diamond Wynn Las Vegas.

The authors would like to thank Khalifa Al Jalahma, Erin Cavanaugh, Sevgi Eason, Gary Held, Kelley Henry, John Kinnecome, Deb Lahteine, Antoinette Paone, and Farah Syed and Will Hoffman for their research. Please address all correspondence to Dr. Alan N. Hoffman, MBA Program Director, LaCava 295, Bentley College, 175 Forest Street, Waltham, MA 02452; ahoffman@bentley.edu. Printed by permission of Dr. Alan N. Hoffman.

[1] http://www.investingvalue.com/investment-leaders/steve-wynn/index.htm

3   Wynn Resorts LTD owns and operates the Wynn Las Vegas, NV, and the Wynn Macau, a casino resort located in the Macau Special Administrative Region of the People's Republic of China. The company is in the process of developing an expansion to the Wynn Las Vegas, called The Encore Diamond Suites. In addition, the company continues to explore opportunities to develop additional gaming or related businesses in other markets, both domestic and international.

4   The officers of the company include the following:

- Stephen A. Wynn
  Chairman of the Board and Chief Executive Officer
- Marc D. Schorr
  Chief Operating Officer
- John Strzemp
  Executive Vice President and Chief Administrative Officer
- Matt Maddox
  Chief Financial Officer and Treasurer

5   As mentioned, Mr. Wynn was previously the Chairman of the Board, President, and CEO of Mirage Resorts. In 1997 under his leadership, Mirage Resorts was ranked by Fortune magazine as the second most admired company among American companies; it was also rated in the top three for innovativeness and quality for their product and services. Steven Wynn is a man who is obsessed with details and continuously strives for perfection.

6   The Wynn Las Vegas Resort & Casino opened on April 28, 2005. The property, which encompasses 217 acres of land, is located at the intersection of the Las Vegas Strip and Sands Avenue. The resort not only features an 111,000 square foot casino with 137 table games, but also luxury hotel accommodations in 2,674 hotel rooms and suites, 36 fairway villas, and 6 private entry villas. The property offers its guests 18 restaurants, a Ferrari and Maserati car dealership, 76,000 square feet of high-end retail shops, recreational facilities including an 18-hole golf course, five swimming pools, full cabanas, a full service spa and salon, and lavish nightlife (nightclubs and lounge entertainment). The Wynn Las Vegas has been described on the strip as "intimate," since it is significantly smaller than some of its competitors' structures. Because of the demand for the services provided by Wynn Las Vegas, The Encore Diamond Suites are currently in development. Encore will be located on the Strip, adjacent to Wynn Las Vegas and is expected to be completed in 2009.

7   Wynn Resorts is constantly looking for additional locations and opportunities to expand both domestically and internationally. In addition, Wynn is currently looking at opportunities for possible resorts in the Philippines as well as expanding into new markets, such as horseracing.

WHO IS THE PIT BOSS?

8   The greatest operational strength Wynn Resorts LTD is the founder himself, Steve Wynn. With over 30 years experience in Las Vegas, this man has contacts, alliances and knowledge that could not be easily replaced. As told by a bartender at Wynn Las Vegas, Mr. Wynn continues to be a very hands-on CEO. He can be seen regularly on the casino floor talking with customers and employees. His passion for perfection can be seen throughout Las Vegas, from the Golden Nugget on Fremont Street to the Bellagio, and including the Wynn Casino, which shares his name. When talking about the Wynn Macau and its scale in comparison to some of the other casinos, Mr. Wynn stated "Bigger ain't better. Better is better." This is the idea that lays the foundation in which Wynn Resorts relies to differentiate their Resorts from those in direct competition.

9 Many of the other senior executives joined Mr. Wynn when he left The Mirage. The management team at Wynn Resorts has a tremendous amount of experience with building quality resort casinos. As Wynn Resorts continues its growth, the combined experience of these individuals will ensure the Resort continues to build world-class operations.

10 If Steve Wynn left the company for any reason other than death or a severe disability, the resort would lose all lines of credit. Although Mr. Wynn is an operational strength, the company's complete dependence on him is a significant weakness. "*Our ability to maintain our competitive position is dependent to a large degree on the efforts and skills of Stephen A. Wynn, the Chairman of the Board, Chief Executive Officer, and one of the principal stockholders of Wynn Resorts.*"[2]

ACES WILD

11 "The US tourism industry is the third largest retail industry after automotive and food stores, according to the TIA. Travel and tourism is also one of the nations largest services export industry."[3]

12 The hotel/tourism industry has changed in the recent years, due to possible threats of terrorism and cutbacks in consumer spending on travel. Post September 11th the US was forced to introduce more strict visa requirements as well as more meticulous passport requirements. These requirements started on January 1, 2007. Recent escalating airline fuel costs have also brought airfare increases. These changes impact the number of people who choose to travel and vacation farther away from home, thus affecting the overall industry.

13 There are many opportunities in the gaming industry from a social and demographic vantage point. As the legalization of gambling is spreading in the US, the social acceptance of the pastime is beginning to spread as rapidly. In the past, gambling has been negatively tied to addiction and corruption, but today gambling is being seen more and more as a socially acceptable and fun recreational activity, especially among the elderly.

14 In 2006, the Las Vegas strip had 38.9 million visitors, and Wynn Las Vegas enjoyed 94.4% occupancy at its 2,716-room hotel, far exceeding the area's average.[4] Wynn Resort's brand is synonymous with luxury in the casino market, and it capitalizes on this reputation, appealing to the high-end market.

15 Based on demographic trends in the US, Wynn Las Vegas is in the right industry at the right time. In a report provided by *Mintel Research* on Casino and Casino-Style Gambling, they note, that the population is aging which is good news for the industry; as people get older it is believed that they are more likely to gamble. "Overall, the US population is growing older . . . Casino gambling is very much a sport of a graying generation. Retirees and empty nesters typically enter casinos with a disposable income, financial security, and free time."[5] Currently in the US, the baby boomers are in the process of retiring, they are healthier and wealthier than earlier generations, and have greater spending power. As the boomers retire, they are spending more money on leisure and recreation, and they are piling

---

[2] Schuman, Michael, "Egos Bigger than China," *Time,* Vol. 168, Issue 7, October 23, 2006.

[3] "The North America Hospitality and Tourism Sectors." *Mergent Industry Report*. October, 2006.

[4] "Wynn Resorts, Limited: Form 10-K" United States Securities and Exchange Commission. Filed 31 December 2006. Available Online. Thompson Research.

[5] "Casino and Casino-style Gambling- US-November 2006." Available Online. http://academic.mintel.com .ezp.bentley.edu/sinatra/oxygen_academic/search_results/show&/display/id=177167/display/id=247080

into the casinos. This growing market segment represents an opportunity for the gaming industry and for Wynn Resorts more specifically.

16 There are a few social and demographic threats that Wynn Resorts must watch and take into account. First, the social norms in the United States differ from those practiced in Macau and should not be universally applied. The occupancy rate at the Wynn Macau resorts is 80%, which is significantly less than that of the Las Vegas resort.[6]

17 Of those that visit Macau, only 25% actually stayed overnight. Those that did stay overnight tended to stay for a short period of time (1–2 nights). This is significantly different than the average visitor in Las Vegas. While Wynn is investing in expansion of the Macau facility, it is important to bear in mind this distinction. While Macau visitor behavior may change, analysts agree that it will not happen overnight. Investing in the hotel arena may not be a safe bet for Wynn and other casinos.[7] Wynn's ideal client is what is referred to as a "whale" aka the risk-friendly, deep-pocketed, high-roller gambler. With increased global competition, it will be imperative for Wynn Resorts to maintain its social status and high brand image to attract and retain the "whale" customers. If they go elsewhere, it will be a substantial loss for the company.

PUT ON YOUR POKER FACE

18 Within the gaming and resort entertainment industry there are many competing properties, including The Mirage, Las Vegas Sands, The Venetian, Paris, and The Bellagio, to name a few. Each casino has their own theme, which attracts a significant number of visitors and directly competes with the Wynn Las Vegas.

- *Ameristar Casino* has casinos in St. Charles, Kansas City, Iowa, Blackhawk, Vicksburg, Cactus Petes and Horeshu. They have established themselves as the premier gaming and entertainment facility in these areas.
- *MGM Mirage* owns featured resorts such as The Mirage, Bellagio, Mandalay Bay, and Luxor just to name a few.
- *Las Vegas Sands Corporation* is one of the leading international developers of multi-use integrated resorts. The company owns The Venetian Resort Hotel Casino, the Sands Expo and Convention Center in Las Vegas and The Sands Macau in the People's Republic of China (PRC) Special Administrative Region of Macau. The company has recently opened 2 new resorts in 2007, The Palazzo Resort Hotel Casino in Las Vegas and The Venetian Macau Resort Hotel Casino in Macau. They are also developing the Cotai Strip, a development of resort casino properties in Macau, and were selected by the Singapore government to build The Marina Bay Sands, an integrated resort scheduled to open in Singapore by the end of 2009.
- *Boyd Gaming Corporation* is one of the premier casino entertainment companies in the United States. They have operations in Illinois, Indiana, Louisiana, Mississippi, New Jersey and Nevada.
- *Harrah's* owns, operates, and/or manages about 50 casinos, Bally's, Caesars, Harrah's, Horseshoe, and Rio just to name a few. The majority of the casinos are based primarily in the US and the UK. Operations include casino hotels, dockside and riverboat casinos, and Native American gaming establishments.

[6] "Wynn Resorts, Limited: Form 10-K" United States Securities and Exchange Commission. Filed 31 December 2006. Available Online. Thompson Research.

[7] Cohen, Muhammad. "No Sure Thing". *Macau Business*. December 2006. Available Online. http://www.macaubusiness.com/index.php?id=634

19   Steve Wynn feels unaffected by competition, as he believes his casinos cater to travelers who have higher demands. Wynn's main focus is to target high-end players with fancy new suites and baccarat tables. Wynn focuses on differentiating itself by concentrating on the atmosphere and design of the resorts and by enhancing customer service and luxury as a full-service provider.

20   The timing could not be better for Steve Wynn to start something new. The $9.4 billion merger between Harrah's and Caesar's Entertainment along with MGM and Mandalay Bay coming together give Wynn several top managers to choose from when developing his casinos. In addition, due to such mergers, it could be expected that casinos like Harrah's, which traditionally target middle-market gamblers, will reduce their focus away from the Caesars Palace high-end customer to target the middle-class gambler. Such a move could result in additional revenues for Wynn as such gamblers will look to Wynn Resort for higher-class amenities.

21   In general, rival casino operators say that new properties are good for Vegas because they create more reasons for people to come to town. Behind the scenes, however, they compete for the kind of gamblers who feel comfortable betting $10,000 or more per hand. MGM may already have launched its counteroffensive. "They're throwing tons of events, shopping sprees, baccarat tournaments, fishing trips," says Steve Conigliaro, an independent businessperson who hosts high rollers at various casinos. "Steve Wynn is going to take some business away. He knows what people like." "The idea of this building was to create extended spaces, to bring the outdoors inside, and to transport the guest into another realm," said spokesperson Denise Randazzo. "The real difference here is that we save all the really amazing features for the resort guests."[8]

LUCK OF THE DRAW

22   In the resort casino industry, the ability to find land and licenses in legal areas is very difficult as many countries have strict regulations around gaming resorts. Gaming licenses are difficult to obtain due to government regulations and limited availability. It is arguably more difficult to find a location that not only can support the size but also meets the legal requirements of that location. Today, Wynn Resorts LTD has a premier spot on the Las Vegas strip that is also home of the strip's only golf course. Wynn is also the holder of one of only four licenses in Macau. Having such scarce resources provides the company with a remarkable advantage.

23   Regulations regarding expansion in China remains questionable and could potentially be a barrier to entry. In Wynn Resorts' 10-K, they note certain risk factors for the company including the fact that their concession in Macau effectively expires in June 2017, at which time the government in Macau has the right to take over their operation. The company also notes that there are currently only three gaming concessions granted until 2009; if the government in Macau were to revise this situation by granting more concessions they would in essence alleviate this particular barrier to entry for other casinos and Wynn could potentially see more competition in the area.

24   Macau, an island located 37 miles southwest of Hong Kong and an hour ferry ride away, has become a popular gaming destination. At this time, there are 24 operating casinos in Macau with several others in the construction and development phase. Sociedade de Jogos de Macau (SJM) owns and operates 17 of these 24 casinos. "Most are relatively small facilities" and not on the high-end like The Wynn. However, they control three of

[8] Freiss, Steve. "In Las Vegas, a $2.7b haven for high rollers." *Boston Globe.* April 29, 2005

the largest casinos in Macau: the Hotel Lisboa, The Greek Mythology Casino and the Jai Alai.[9]

25   Currently, Wynn Macau is charged a 35% tax on gross gaming revenue, and they are forced to contribute up to 4% of gross gaming revenue for the promotion of public interests, social security, infrastructure, and tourism in Macau.[10] If regulations were to change and taxes were lowered, Wynn Resorts would be able to retain more of its earnings.

26   Currently, the Chinese government does not allow casinos on its mainland, only Macau,[11] so the breaking of the casino monopoly in Macau has provided to be an enormous growth opportunity for Wynn Resorts.[12] The government of Macau is trying to turn Macau into the "tourist destination of choice" in Asia.[13] In 2002, the "government-sanctioned" casino monopoly in Macau ended when the government granted concessions to three outside companies to operate casinos in Macau. Each of the three was allowed, with the approval of the government, to grant one sub-concession to another gaming operator.[14] If this legal situation were to occur in other areas of the globe, it could provide additional global growth opportunity for Wynn Resorts. Under the concession granted to Wynn Resorts, Wynn is able to develop an unlimited number of casino resorts in Macau with the government of Macau's approval.[15] This legal opportunity provides significant value for Wynn Resorts since they are one of a select few with such a right. In addition, since a limited number of companies have casino operating rights in Macau, Wynn is operating in a somewhat restricted competitive environment because they hold one of those six gaming licenses.[16]

27   Recently, Wynn Resorts was granted concession for its land application for 52 acres in Macau's Coati Strip. This legal right is essential for Wynn Resorts future expansion plans. Stephen Wynn stated in Wynn Resorts third quarter 2007 conference call that he plans to build "the most beautiful hotel on the earth in Coati." Currently, the designs include a 1,500 to 2,000 all suite hotel to occupy all 52 acres, and Stephen Wynn stated this hotel will have things that have never been seen before; it will be expensive but "it will be an experience."

28   The Chinese government has and is expected to continue to relax restrictions on travel and currency movements between China and Macau. Thus far, by relaxing its currency and travel restrictions, Chinese citizens from certain urban and economically developed areas are able to visit Macau without a tour group, and they are now allowed to bring an increased amount of money into Macau; this will possibly boost the profit potential for Wynn Macau.[17]

[9] "Wynn Resorts, Limited: Form 10-K" United States Securities and Exchange Commission. Filed 31 December 2006. Available Online. Thompson Research.

[10] "Wynn Resorts, Limited: Form 10-K" United States Securities and Exchange Commission. Filed 31 December 2006. Available Online. Thompson Research.

[11] Tan, Kopin. "Gambling on LVS, Wynn in Macau." 25 November 2007. Available Online. http://online.wsj.com/article/SB119594535268803103.html?mod=googlenews_wsj.

[12] "Macau Wow." *Economist*. 1 September 2007. Vol. 384, Issue 8544, Pg 62. Available Online. Business Sources Premier.

[13] "Wynn Resorts, Limited: Form 10-K" United States Securities and Exchange Commission. Filed 31 December 2006. Available Online. Thompson Research.

[14] "Wynn Resorts, Limited: Form 10-K" United States Securities and Exchange Commission. Filed 31 December 2006. Available Online. Thompson Research.

[15] "Wynn Resorts, Limited: Form 10-K" United States Securities and Exchange Commission. Filed 31 December 2006. Available Online. Thompson Research.

[16] "Wynn Resorts Ltd: Stock Report." Standard & Poor's. 22 September 2007. Available Online. www.etrade.com.

[17] "Wynn Resorts, Limited: Form 10-K" United States Securities and Exchange Commission. Filed 31 December 2006. Available Online. Thompson Research.

If the Chinese government continues to loosen its restriction on travel and currency, tourism to Macau will grow and the profit potential for Wynn Resorts will increase.

29   In 1999, Portugal retuned Macau to Chinese control after 450 years of Portuguese control. Macau's legislative, regulatory, and legal institutions are still in a phase of transition since this change in control occurred less than eight years ago.[18] The long-term success of Wynn Macau will depend on the successful development of the political, economic and regulatory framework in Macau. Wynn Resorts could be affected if an unfavorable environment develops in Macau.

30   By doing business in an emerging market, there are significant political, economic and social risks for Wynn Macau.[19] For example, domestic or international unrest, health epidemics such as the bird flu, terrorism or military conflicts in China or Macau will drastically affect Wynn Macau by not only reducing the inflow of customers from a decrease in tourism, but also, by decreasing discretionary consumer spending and by increasing the risk of higher taxes and government controls over gaming operations.

31   Furthermore, under Wynn Resorts' agreement with the government of Macau, the government has the right at any time to "assume temporary custody and control over the operation of a casino in certain circumstances."[20] The ability of the government to take control of the casino at any time it deems appropriate is a significant threat to the success of Wynn Resorts since it could lose control of its operations in Macau.

32   Additionally, Wynn Macau is subject to the strict regulatory controls by the government, which limits their freedom of operations and creativity. For example, one of the regulations requires them to have an executive director who is a permanent resident of Macau and holds at least 10% of the company's capital stock.[21] The Macau government must approve this executive director and any successor, and they have to approve all contracts for the management of the casino's operation in Macau. This is just one example of the type of restrictions and the level of control the government holds over Wynn Macau.

33   The Macau land concession poses additional threats to Wynn Resorts. Under the agreement, Wynn Macau is leasing the 16 acres from the government of Macau for 25 years. The government of Macau may redeem the concession beginning June 24, 2017, and Wynn Macau will be entitled to fair compensation based on the amount of revenue generated during the previous tax year.[22] If the government takes back the land, the long-term plans of Wynn Resorts would be derailed, possibly leaving them with high debt and no means to repay. However, if the government does not take back the land, the concession may be renewed but the semi-annual payments to use the land could substantially increase, taking away from Wynn's bottom line.

34   After April 1, 2009, the government of Macau has the right to offer additional concessions for the operation of casinos in Macau.[23] If additional concessions are granted, Wynn

[18] "Wynn Resorts, Limited: Form 10-K" United States Securities and Exchange Commission. Filed 31 December 2006. Available Online. Thompson Research.

[19] "Wynn Resorts, Limited: Form 10-K" United States Securities and Exchange Commission. Filed 31 December 2006. Available Online. Thompson Research.

[20] "Wynn Resorts, Limited: Form 10-K" United States Securities and Exchange Commission. Filed 31 December 2006. Available Online. Thompson Research.

[21] "Wynn Resorts, Limited: Form 10-K" United States Securities and Exchange Commission. Filed 31 December 2006. Available Online. Thompson Research.

[22] "Wynn Resorts, Limited: Form 10-K" United States Securities and Exchange Commission. Filed 31 December 2006. Available Online. Thompson Research.

[23] "Wynn Resorts, Limited: Form 10-K" United States Securities and Exchange Commission. Filed 31 December 2006. Available Online. Thompson Research.

Macau will face further competition since these competitors already own land in Macau but do not have concession to build yet. In addition, if the efforts to legalize gaming in Thailand or Taiwan are successful, Wynn will face additional competition from the surrounding area.[24] This competition will draw away customers, it will reduce the level of potential profits, and Wynn Macau could lose key employees to more attractive employment opportunities elsewhere in Asia.

35   Another threat exists in the possibility of Wynn Resorts being unable to collect on its gaming debts. This could have a significant negative impact on Wynn Macau's operating results if the company cannot collect their earnings. In Macau, taxes are due on gross gaming revenue regardless of whether revenue was actually collected. In essence, Wynn Macau would have to pay taxes on money it never received if it was unable to collect on the debt.[25]

36   As the competitive environment in Macau increases, the available employee talent pool will decrease which could hamper future expansion plans in Macau. Wynn Resorts will need to petition the government to allow visas for more immigrant workers, and if they are unable to do so, they run the risk of having employees who cannot run the facilities. If Wynn is successful, the strict immigration laws will take time to change that could threaten Wynn's future in Macau.

37   Wynn Resorts has positioned itself well in the growing gaming markets, particularly in Macau. The development of a casino in this area is a strategic opportunity. From an economic standpoint, Macau's GDP has grown nearly 30% in the first two quarters of 2007. The growth in gambling has also resulted in increased foreign investment in the area. US exports to Macau have seen a tremendous increase as well.[26]

38   Macau's GDP growth is not likely to be sustainable. With increased competition in the region, Wynn's first-mover advantage will be diminished. Also, the company only has two casinos producing revenue, and with development efforts underway on their next projects, cash flow is undoubtedly going to be an issue.

PUT YOUR MONEY WHERE YOUR MOUTH IS

39   One of Wynn Resorts Ltd's greatest marketing strengths is strategic development of its product. The product that Wynn sells is a luxury destination experience that makes the customers feel pampered and valued through high-quality amenities and customer service. This lavish experience allows consumers to justify spending significant amounts of money gambling, dining, drinking, shopping, and at the spas. The company strategically developed the Wynn brand name to be synonymous with high-quality goods and services. Continuous promotion of the brand is part of Wynn's overall company strategy.[27]

40   Steve Wynn is known for raising the luxury bar in Las Vegas. The packaging of Wynn's product is the glitz and glamour of its hotels, casinos, restaurants and shops (such as a Ferrari and Maserati dealership). As a customer enters the lobby of a Wynn hotel, they are

[24] "Wynn Resorts, Limited: Form 10-K" United States Securities and Exchange Commission. Filed 31 December 2006. Available Online. Thompson Research.

[25] "Wynn Resorts, Limited: Form 10-K" United States Securities and Exchange Commission. Filed 31 December 2006. Available Online. Thompson Research.

[26] "Macau." BuyUsa.Gov. 18 September 2007. Available Online. www.buyusa.gov/hongkong/en/macau.html

[27] Wynn 10k.

instantly struck with grandiose decor. This feel extends throughout the hotel in the hallways, hotel rooms, suites, villas and private-entry villas. The casino takes flash and glitz to another level, and a mere glimpse of the lights and sounds would make any customer excited to gamble. The casino floor is designed specifically for the high-end customer and contains many private VIP areas and high-roller tables. These special areas and tables further contribute to the high-end customer experience.

41 The resort is able to charge a premium price due to the clout of the Wynn name, the high-income base of its customers and the high quality of its products and services. In 2006, Wynn generated the highest room rate on the Las Vegas Strip. The average room rate for the quarter ending December 31, 2006, was $291, with the next highest being the Bellagio at $260 and then the Venetian at $243.[28]

42 Wynn is further segmenting the high-income customer market with the introduction of Encore at Wynn Las Vegas, an all-suite hotel with its own casino, restaurants, nightclub, pool and spa. This product layering allows Wynn to capitalize on the "celebrity" obsession with Las Vegas. Encore at Wynn Las Vegas will be superior to Wynn Las Vegas in luxury, amenities, and of course, price. This will serve to keep out people that cannot afford the price and will be attractive to elite customers who seek privacy as well as luxury.

43 Steve Wynn is by no means a newcomer to Las Vegas and he knows the importance of strategic placement on the Vegas Strip. Wynn owns 235 acres on the strip, which houses hotels, casinos and a golf course, the "only" golf course on the strip. Wynn was also strategic in its purchase of land in Macau and Cotai obtaining significant portions of land in the middle of all the excitement.

44 Wynn has been successful in the past with direct marketing to its high-end target customer. This past year, it has expanded its promotion to include various media channels such as print media, radio and television.[29] Wynn Macau provides the opportunity for cross-marketing with Wynn Las Vegas. Since the target market segment in both Wynn Las Vegas and Wynn Macau is high income, its customers have the resources to travel and vacation in other parts of the world, which can make cross-marketing very effective. Wynn is the only gaming operator to target high-end customers in both Las Vegas and Macau.[30] Wynn Las Vegas already has a strong client base of Asian customers and Macau provides the opportunity to increase this customer segment. Wynn recognizes that the Chinese economy is on the rise and that the population is becoming increasingly educated and wealthy. The "premium customer" in China, those in the top income brackets, will increase to approximately 180–200 million over the next 10 years.[31]

45 Since Wynn has the highest rates on the strip, it would be tough to extend its customer base beyond high-end clients. In addition, the already high prices may cause Wynn to increase rates at a slower percentage per year than other hotels on the strip. For the quarter ended December 31, 2006, Wynn's average room rate increased 4.4% from 2005 to 2006 while competitors' rates increased from 5.0% to 9.5%.[32]

46 Wynn faces the challenge of understanding the customer in Macau and other global markets. In order to accomplish this, Wynn has marketing executives located in offices around

[28] Kramer, Ron. *Wynn Resorts,* Bear Stearns Retail, Restaurants and Consumer Conference, March 1, 2007.
[29] Wynn 10k.
[30] Kramer, Ron. *Wynn Resorts,* Bear Stearns Retail, Restaurants and Consumer Conference, March 1, 2007.
[31] Ibid.
[32] Kramer, Ron. *Wynn Resorts,* Bear Stearns Retail, Restaurants and Consumer Conference, March 1, 2007.

the world. However, a sole marketing executive in strategic global locations may not be sufficient to conduct thorough market research and adjust the product as necessary. Lastly, focusing solely on the high-end market can be a marketing weakness in that Wynn is missing a large customer base of middle-income clients. This segment includes vacationers and younger people looking for a relatively inexpensive place to stay with the understanding that most of their budget will go to dining and entertainment.

47   When a customer pulls into the Wynn entrance off the Las Vegas or Macau strip, the feel is that of just being removed from a busy crowded city street and dropped into a tropical paradise. As you enter the casino, you are surrounded by beautiful flower gardens, and soothing sounds of water. Though close in the distance are the sounds of the casino floor, a gaming atmosphere is not the first to strike you. Wynn resorts makes their customers feel at ease by inviting them to relax and enjoy the serene surroundings. In the restaurants, specifically the Mediterranean themed Bartolotta's, the renowned chef comes out and interacts with the diners. Every moment in the casino and each interaction with staff are designed to be the ultimate customer experience. The staff is focused on giving the customer a luxury experience and quality customer service.

48   Wynn Resorts goal is to attract high-end gaming customers. In August of 2006, Wynn Resorts, Ltd. changed its tip pooling policy to include pit bosses and table supervisors. Operationally, this move made it feasible for experienced dealers to take positions as supervisors, who up until that point generally earned less than the dealers. The return on this new policy that the company expects is simply that as high-rollers gamble more, the pit bosses, or "table supervisors" will have more at stake in making sure the customers are happy. They will give comps more, and in return, customers will stay longer and return more often. This tip pooling policy is an example of the kind of moves Wynn has made to further the luxury experience the customer receives.

SMALL BLIND–BIG BLIND

49   It is clear that Mr. Steve Wynn was successful at building and operating a Casino Resort Empire that turned his personal worth into $1.6 billion. This feat was accomplished with his personal ambition, business savvy, and vision for what entertainment really means to the world. Although Steve Wynn appears to be the epitome of Casino Resort Gurus, this label does not hold the key for guaranteed future success of the Wynn Resorts Ltd, there are many challenges that Wynn will have to face, and the future may throw some curveballs along the way. As it stands now there are three major challenges the firm will need to address in the future; the first being that they need to secure a way to maintain their competitive advantage as increased competition will be introduced both domestically and abroad into the gaming industry. Secondly, the Macau Government reserves the right to take control of the Wynn Casino in 2017 [;] as mentioned above this would be detrimental to the profits for the Company Wynn Resorts Ltd, [so] some solutions will need to be devised to ensure that the survival of the company is not majorly dependent on the revenues generated by the Wynn Macau resort and casino. Moreover, a third concern about future success, but certainly not the final concern, is the loss of Mr. Steve Wynn himself. If this loss was to occur, someone else with his expertise, passion and governmental ties (concessions & licenses) are a scarce resource [;] in the most likely scenario a loss of Steve Wynn may result in the sale of the firm to a competing company such as MGM, Inc. The Wynn Resorts although is not guaranteed future success, it is certainly on the right track, and quite the remarkable company.

FINANCIAL STATEMENTS (February 22, 2008 10-K Edgar Online)

WYNN RESORTS, LIMITED AND SUBSIDIARIES
CONSOLIDATED STATEMENTS OF OPERATIONS
(amounts in thousands, except per share data)

	Year Ended December 31,		
	2007	2006	2005
Operating revenues:			
Casino	$1,949,870	$ 800,591	$ 353,663
Rooms	339,391	283,084	170,315
Food and beverage	353,983	309,771	173,700
Entertainment, retail and other	245,201	205,213	125,230
Gross revenues	2,888,445	$1,598,659	822,908
Less: promotional allowances	(200,926)	(166,402)	(100,927)
Net revenues	2,687,519	1,432,257	721,981
Operating costs and expenses:			
Casino	1,168,119	439,902	155,075
Rooms	83,237	73,878	44,171
Food and beverage	212,622	194,403	118,670
Entertainment, retail and other	161,087	134,530	80,185
General and administrative	310,820	231,515	118,980
Provision for doubtful accounts	36,109	21,163	16,206
Pre-opening costs	7,063	62,726	96,940
Depreciation and amortization	219,923	175,464	103,344
Contract termination fee	—	5,000	—
Property charges and other	60,857	25,060	14,297
Total operating costs and expenses	2,259,837	1,363,641	747,868
Equity in income from unconsolidated affiliates	1,721	2,283	1,331
Operating income (loss)	429,403	70,899	(24,556)
Other income (expense):			
Interest and other income	47,765	46,752	28,267
Interest expense, net of capitalized interest	(143,777)	(148,017)	(102,699)
Distribution to convertible debenture holders	—	(58,477)	—
Increase (decrease) in swap fair value	(6,001)	1,196	8,152
Gain on sale of subconcession right, net	—	899,409	—
Loss from extinguishment of debt	(157)	(12,533)	—
Other income (expense), net	(102,170)	728,330	(66,280)
Income (loss) before income taxes	327,233	799,229	(90,836)
Provision for income taxes	(69,085)	(170,501)	—
Net income (loss)	$258,148	$ 628,728	$(90,836)
Basic and diluted income (loss) per common share:			
Net income (loss):			
Basic	$2.43	$6.29	$(0.92)
Diluted	$2.34	$6.24	$(0.92)
Weighted average common shares outstanding:			
Basic	106,030	99,998	98,308
Diluted	112,685	111,627	98,308

WYNN RESORTS, LIMITED AND SUBSIDIARIES
CONSOLIDATED BALANCE SHEETS
(amounts in thousands, except per share data)

	December 31,	
	2007	**2006**
ASSETS		
Current assets:		
Cash and cash equivalents	$1,275,1,20	$ 789,407
Restricted cash and investments	—	58,598
Receivables, net	179,059	140,232
Inventories	73,291	64,368
Deferred income taxes	24,746	13,727
Prepaid expenses and other	29,775	30,659
Total current assets	1,581,991	1,096,991
Restricted cash and investments	531,120	178,788
Property and equipment, net	3,939,979	3,157,622
Intangibles, net	60,074	65,135
Deferred financing costs	83,087	74,871
Deposits and other assets	97,531	80,792
Investment in unconsolidated affiliates	5,500	5,981
Total assets	$ 6,299,282	$4,660,180
LIABILITIES AND STOCKHOLDERS' EQUITY		
Current liabilities:		
Accounts and construction payable	$ 182,718	$ 123,061
Current portion of long-term debt	3,273	6,115
Current portion of land concession obligation	5,738	7,433
Income taxes payable	138	87,164
Accrued interest	12,478	15,495
Accrued compensation and benefits	93,097	71,223
Gaming taxes payable	75,014	46,403
Other accrued expenses	18,367	10,742
Customer deposits and other related liabilities	177,605	127,751
Construction retention	16,755	15,700
Total current liabilities	585,183	511,087
Long-term debt	3,533,339	2,380,537
Other long-term liabilities	39,335	5,214
Long-term land concession obligation	6,029	11,809
Deferred income taxes	152,953	97,064
Construction retention	34,284	8,884
Total liabilities	4,351,123	3,014,595
Commitments and contingencies (Note 18)		
Stockholders' equity:		
Preferred stock, par value $0.0 1; 40,000,000 shares authorized; zero shares issued and outstanding	—	—
Common stock. par value $0.0 1; 400.000,000 shares authorized; 116,259,411 and 101,887,031 shares issued; 114,370,090 and 101,887,031 shares outstanding	1,162	1,018
Treasury stock, at cost; 1,889,321 shares	(179,277	—
Additional paid-in capital	2,273,078	2,022,408
Accumulated other comprehensive loss	(2,905)	(94)
Accumulated deficit	(143,899)	(377,747)
Total stockholders' equity	1,948,159	1,645,585
Total liabilities and stockholders' equity	$ 6,299,282	$4,660,180

WYNN RESORTS, LIMITED AND SUBSIDIARIES
CONSOLIDATED STATEMENTS OF CASH FLOWS
(amounts in thousands)

	Year Ended December 31,		
	2007	2006	2005
Cash flows from operating activities:			
Net income (loss)	$ 258,148	$628,728	$(90,836)
Adjustments to reconcile net income (loss) to net cash provided by operating activities:			
Depreciation and amortization	219,923	175,464	103,344
Deferred income taxes	68,152	170,321	—
Stock-based compensation	18,527	16,712	4,676
Amortization and writeoffs of deferred financing costs, and other	19,318	23,419	14,045
Loss on extinguishment of debt	157	11,316	—
Provision for doubtful accounts	36,109	21,163	16,206
Property charges and other	60,857	25,060	14,297
Equity in income of unconsolidated affiliates, net of distributions	481	(911)	(1,331)
Decrease (increase) in swap fair value	6,001	(1,196)	(8,152)
Gain on sale of subconcession right	—	(899,409)	—
Increase (decrease) in cash from changes in:			
Receivables, net	(75,029)	(72,927)	(104,418)
Inventories and prepaid expenses and other	(7,565)	(21,261)	(58,934)
Accounts payable and accrued expenses	54,093	164,287	159,578
Net cash provided by operating activities	659,172	240,766	48,475
Cash flows from investing activities:			
Capital expenditures, net of construction payables and retention	(1,007,370)	(643,360)	(877,074)
Restricted cash and investments	(293,734)	205,216	499,765
Investment in unconsolidated affiliates	—	—	(3,739)
Purchase of intangibles and other assets	(43,216)	(59,456)	(40,181)
Proceeds from sale of subconcession right, net	—	899,409	—
Proceeds from sale of equipment	21,581	—	109
Net cash provided by (used in) investing activities	(1,322,739)	401,809	(421,120)
Cash flows from financing activities:			
Proceeds from exercise of stock options	9,180	21,790	1,404
Proceeds from issuance of common stock	664,125	—	—
Cash distributions	(683,299)	(608,299)	—
Proceeds from issuance of long-term debt	1,672,987	746,948	—
Principal payments on long-term debt	(297,321)	(440,929)	(121,933)
Proceeds from termination of interest rate swap	—	6,605	—
Purchase of treasury stock	(179,277)	—	—
Payments on long-term land concession obligation	(7,411)	(9,000)	(8,921)
Payment of deferred financing costs and other	(27,045)	(4,572)	(21,008)
Net cash provided by (used in) financing activities	1,151,939	(287,457)	476,673
Effect of exchange rate on cash	(2,659)	—	—
Cash and cash equivalents:			
Increase in cash and cash equivalents	485,713	355,118	104,028
Balance, beginning of period	789,407	434,289	330,261
Balance, end of period	$1,275,120	$789,407	$434,289
Supplemental cash flow disclosures:			
Cash paid for interest, net of amounts capitalized	$ 178,072	$133,850	$95,839
Cash distributions to convertible debenture holders	—	58,477	—
Cash paid for income taxes	79,168	180	—
Equipment purchases financed by debt and accrued assets	—	—	860
Stock-based compensation capitalized into construction	809	1,353	2,651

Board of Directors (http://phx.corporate-ir.net/phoenix.zhtml?c=132059&p=irol-govboard)

Stephen A. Wynn
Chairman of the Board and Chief Executive Officer

Kazuo Okada
Vice Chairman of the Board

Linda Chen
Director

Dr. Ray R. Irani
Director

Robert J. Miller
Director

John A. Moran
Director

Alvin V. Shoemaker
Director

D. Boone Wayson
Director

Elaine P. Wynn
Director

Allan Zeman
Director

Case 23

Strategic Leadership and Innovation at Apple Inc.[1]

Loizos Heracleous

Angeliki Papachroni

"Stop and look at Apple for a second, since it's an odd company . . . While most high-tech firms focus on one or two sectors, Apple does all of them at once . . . Apple is essentially operating its own closed miniature techno-economy . . . If you follow conventional wisdom, Apple is doing it all wrong. And yet . . . this is the company that gave us three of the signature technological innovations of the past 30 years: the Apple II, the Macintosh and the iPod." (Grossman, 2005)

APPLE'S FALL AND RISE

1   Voted as the most innovative company for three consecutive years during 2006–2008 and as America's number 1 most Admired Company (McGregor, 2008), Apple seemed to have it all: innovative products that have redefined their markets (such as the iMac and the iPod), a consumer base as loyal as a fan club, and a business model characterized by vertical integration and synergies that no competitor could easily imitate. The Apple brand had transcended the barriers of the computer industry to traverse the consumer electronics, record, movie, and the video and music production industries (see Figure 1 for an outline of Apple's product and service portfolio). In 2008 the Apple brand was listed as the 24th most valuable global brand (up from 33rd place the previous year), valued at $13.7 billion (Interbrand, 2008).

2   After a lackluster period during 1989–1997 when Apple was nearly written off, its dynamic comeback was impressive. Between 2003 and 2008 Apple's sales tripled to $24 billion and profits increased to $3.5 billion, up from a mere $24 million (See Table 1 for an outline of Apple's financial performance during 2006–8). Apple topped Fortune 500 companies for total return to shareholders both over 2003–2008 (94% return) as well as over 1998–2008 (51% return) (Morris, 2008: 68), a remarkable achievement.

3   But things haven't always been that rosy for the company once known as the underdog of the computer industry. During the time when Steve Jobs was not part of the organization (1985–1997) Apple progressively degenerated to the point of struggling for survival. Apple charged premium prices and operated through a closed proprietary system, at a time when

[1] This case was prepared by Professor Loizos Heracleous and Angeliki Papachroni for the purposes of class discussion and is not meant to illustrate effective or ineffective handling of administrative situations. Warwick Business School, loizos.heracleous@wbs.ac.uk, January 2009.

FIGURE 1 Apple Inc. Product and Service Portfolio

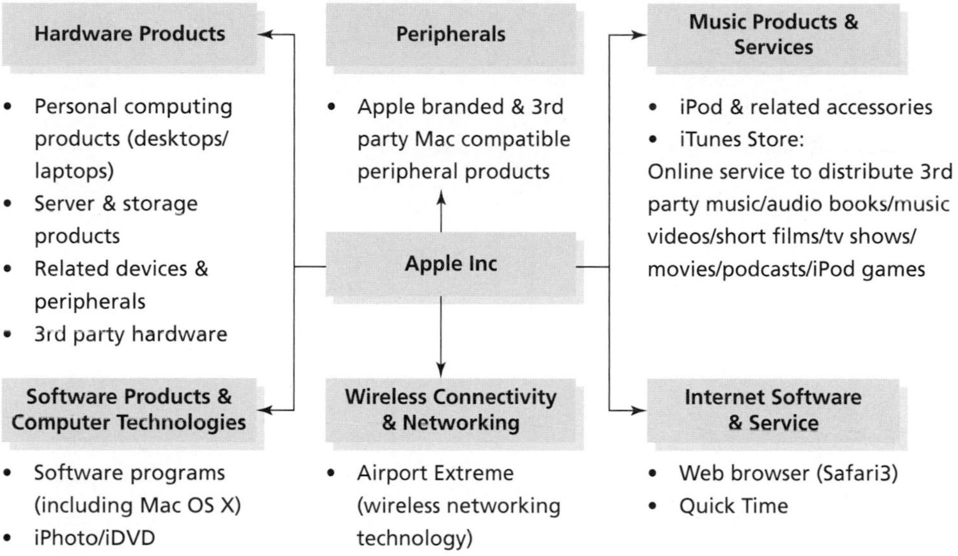

Hardware Products	Peripherals	Music Products & Services
• Personal computing products (desktops/laptops) • Server & storage products • Related devices & peripherals • 3rd party hardware	• Apple branded & 3rd party Mac compatible peripheral products **Apple Inc**	• iPod & related accessories • iTunes Store: Online service to distribute 3rd party music/audio books/music videos/short films/tv shows/movies/podcasts/iPod games
Software Products & Computer Technologies	**Wireless Connectivity & Networking**	**Internet Software & Service**
• Software programs (including Mac OS X) • iPhoto/iDVD	• Airport Extreme (wireless networking technology)	• Web browser (Safari3) • Quick Time

Source: Authors

more economical, IBM-compatible PCs gained mass appeal. Its cost base was high compared with its major competitors. This combination of factors led to shrinking market share and lower profitability. Apple lost momentum in the PC industry, despite the effort of three different CEOs to reverse the downfall (see Table 2 for a timeline of Apple's CEO tenures).

4   John Sculley attempted to gain market share (at the time around 7%) by introducing lower-priced products that still had a technological edge, forged alliances with IBM to work on a joint operating system and multimedia applications, and outsourced much of manufacturing to subcontractors to cut costs. A joint alliance was also formed with Novell and Intel to reconfigure Apple's OS to run on Intel chips. By the end of Sculley's tenure in 1993 however, market share was at around 8%, and Apple's gross profits reduced from around 50% to 34% (Yoffie & Slind, 2008).

5   During Spindler's tenure, the alliances with Intel and Novell, as well as with IBM, were exited, and a decision was taken to license Apple's OS to companies that would make Mac clones (a decision reversed by Jobs in 1997). There was focus on international growth, and more cost-cutting efforts. With performance remaining flat, Spindler was replaced by Gil Amelio. In 1996, under Amelio, Apple went through three successive restructurings and further cost cutting. At the same time, Amelio aimed to return Apple to its premium price, differentiation strategy (Yoffie & Slind, 2008). The biggest challenge at the time was the release of Apple's new generation operating system in response to the release of Microsoft's Windows 95, which had received great attention upon its release one year earlier. Apple's OS system named Copland, on the other hand, was so behind schedule that the company decided to turn to external help. Ironically, Apple turned to NeXT, a software company founded by Steve Jobs after his departure from Apple in 1985. Meanwhile, Apple's market share fell to 3% and Amelio was forced out by the board of directors.

6   After NeXT's help with the new version of Apple's operating system, Apple's executive board resolved to buy the company. A year later, in July 1997, Jobs was offered the title of Apple's CEO, after spending a few months as a consultant at Apple. This was a crucial

TABLE 1   Selected Apple Financial Data

	2008	Change	2007	Change	2006
Net Sales by Operating Segment:					
Americas net sales	$14,573	26%	$11,596	23%	$9,415
Europe net sales	7,622	40%	5,460	33%	4,096
Japan net sales	1,509	39%	1,082	(11)%	1,211
Retail net sales	6,315	53%	4,115	27%	3,246
Other Segments net sales (a)	2,460	40%	1,753	30%	1,347
Total net sales	$32,479	35%	$24,006	24%	$19,315
Unit Sales by Operating Segment:					
Americas Mac unit sales	3,980	32%	3,019	24%	2,432
Europe Mac unit sales	2,519	39%	1,816	35%	1,346
Japan Mac unit sales	389	29%	302	(1)%	304
Retail Mac unit sales	2,034	47%	1,386	56%	886
Other Segments Mac unit sales (a)	793	50%	528	58%	335
Total Mac unit sales	9,715	38%	7,051	33%	5,303
Net Sales by Product:					
Desktops (b)	$5,603	39%	$4,020	21%	$3,319
Portables (c)	8,673	38%	6,294	55%	4,056
Total Mac net sales	14,276	38%	10,314	40%	7,375
iPod	9,153	10%	8,305	8%	7,676
Other music related products and services (d)	3,340	34%	2,496	32%	1,885
iPhone and related products and services (e)	1,844	NM	123	NM	—
Peripherals and other hardware (f)	1,659	32%	1,260	15%	1,100
Software, service, and other sales (g)	2,207	46%	1,508	18%	1,279
Total net sales	$32,479	35%	$24,006	24%	$19,315
Unit Sales by Product:					
Desktops (b)	3,712	37%	2,714	12%	2,434
Portables (c)	6,003	38%	4,337	51%	2,869
Total Mac unit sales	9,715	38%	7,051	33%	5,303
Net sales per Mac unit sold (h)	$1,469	—%	$1,463	5%	$1,391
iPod unit sales	54,828	6%	51,630	31%	39,409
Net sales per iPod unit sold (i)	$167	4%	$161	(17)%	$195
iPhone unit sales	11,627	NM	1,389	NM	—

Source: Apple Inc. Annual Report, 2008.

(a) Other Segments include Asia Pacific and FileMaker.
(b) Includes iMac. Mac mini. Mac Pro, Power Mac, and Xserve product lines.
(c) Includes MacBook, iBook, MacBook Air, MacBook Pro, and PowerBook product lines.
(d) Consists of iTunes Store sales, iPod services, and Apple-branded and third-party iPod accessories.
(e) Derived from handset sales, carrier agreements, and Apple-branded and third-party iPhone accessories.
(f) Includes sales of Apple-branded and third-party displays, wireless connectivity and networking solutions, and other hardware accessories.
(g) Includes sales of Apple-branded operating system and application software, third-party software, AppleCare, and Internet services.
(h) Derived by dividing total Mac net sales by total Mac unit sales.
(i) Derived by dividing total iPod net sales by total iPod unit sales.
NM = Not Meaningful

TABLE 2
Timeline of Apple's Chief Executive Officers

(Source: Authors)

1977–1981	Michael Scott
1981–1985	Mike Markkula
1985–1993	John Sculley
1993–1996	Michael Spindler
1996–1997	Gil Amelio
1997–2000	Steve Jobs (Interim CEO)
2000–2009	Steve Jobs

time in the company's history. Apple's stock had sunk to $3.30 and the company reported a net loss of $708 million in its second quarter that year, flirting with bankruptcy. At the same time competitors like Dell and Microsoft were thriving, following the tech boom of the late 1990's. Jobs took on the role of Interim CEO in 1997 and then became CEO during 2000.

THE COMPETITIVE LANDSCAPE

The Giants: IBM and Microsoft

7   By 2009, the computer technology industry had undergone some profound changes that shaped the competitive context within which Apple operated. IBM, the once undisputed leader in PC manufacturing, has moved away from its traditional territory of computer hardware and with a focus on computer technology, research and service consulting became a very different company from what it used to be in the 1990s. In 2009 IBM was the world's second largest software company after Microsoft, and its acquisition of PwC Consulting in 2002 marked IBM's serious entry to the business services sector (Doz & Kosonen, 2008: 38). After selling its PC and laptop business to Chinese company Lenovo in 2005 (a segment it had itself created) to allow more strategic focus on services, and higher-end servers, IBM's strategy also moved to encompass open business approaches. IBM was a significant contributor to open source movements such as Linux by investing in the program's development, growth and distribution (Linux is supported on all modern IBM Systems) and in 2005 the company gave away approximately 500 software patents (valued over $10 million) so as to enhance global innovation and profit from newly created business opportunities. Through these actions, IBM aimed to enlarge the global market for IT products and services and to benefit by responding to this demand. IBM made over 50 acquisitions during 2002–2007, building a portfolio around "networked, modularized and embedded technologies, including service-oriented architecture (SOA), information on demand, virtualization and open, modular systems for businesses of all sizes" (IBM Annual Report, 2007: 2). With IBM exiting the PC manufacturing industry the competitive environment in this front included HP, Dell, Acer and Lenovo, which together accounted for more than 50% of worldwide PC shipments in 2007 (Yoffie & Slind, 2008).

8   Following the launch of the IBM PC, Microsoft dominated the PC operating system market mostly because it offered an open standard that multiple PC makers could incorporate into their products. Windows OS became the standard operating system in the industry with more than 85% of all PCs in the world running on some Windows version (Yoffie & Slind, 2008). Microsoft's revenue reached $60.4 billion in fiscal year 2008, an increase of 18 percent over the previous year (Microsoft Annual Report, 2008). By 2009 Microsoft faced increased competition in the software front from Apple, HP, IBM and Sun

Microsystems, as well as Linux OS derived from UNIX. Microsoft's portfolio also included the online search and advertising business (MSN portals, Live Search, etc.) in which the company sought to invest further. This was indicated by Microsoft's interest in acquiring Yahoo, a deal which by the end of 2008 had not reached agreement. The failing of initial talks led to calls for the resignation of Yahoo's CEO, who indicated that he would resign as soon as a successor was found. In late 2008 Microsoft's interest in Yahoo was rekindled, but only in its search business. Microsoft's position in the entertainment industry was holding strong with the Xbox 360 console selling more than 19 million units and Xbox Live having more than 12 million members (Microsoft Annual Report, 2008).

The Computer Vendors: Hewlett-Packard and Dell

9   After the acquisition of Compaq in 2002 that brought significant scale in its desktop and laptop product lines, HP became the world's largest PC vendor, surpassing rival Dell in 2007 with a 3.9% market share lead. In 2007 the company's reported revenue was $104 billion, making it the first IT company in history to exceed revenues of $100 billion, and the world's largest technology company in terms of sales after IBM. HP's portfolio included personal computing, imaging and printing-related products and services, and enterprise information technology infrastructure, including enterprise storage and servers, technology support and maintenance, consulting and integration and outsourcing services (HP Annual Report, 2007).

10   Dell Inc. offered a range of product categories including desktop personal computers, servers and networking products, storage, mobility products, software and peripherals, and services. It was the first computer company to sell customized PCs directly to consumers without using intermediaries. Once the leading PC vendor in terms of both profitability and market share, Dell faced increased competition in the desktop and notebook business that made it difficult to sustain its earlier growth and profitability rates. Although Dell had based its success in its distinctive business model of direct sales and built to order manufacturing, in 2007 the company initiated a strategic change program that included investment in the design and release of consumer friendly products through retail distribution.

11   Gaining scale from significant acquisitions, Acer became the 3rd largest PC vendor in the world. Acer focused on the consumer market and in particular in the production of notebook PCs. Lastly, China–based Lenovo became the 4th biggest PC vendor after acquiring IBM's PC business for $1.75 billion. Lenovo had a strong position in the Chinese market where it held 35% market share.

Microprocessors: Intel

12   In the microprocessors front Intel was the undisputed leader accounting for more than 80% share in the market of PC Central Processing Units. AMD was Intel's closest competitor in terms of market share. Intel's portfolio additionally included wired and wireless Internet connectivity products and communications infrastructure products. The company was effective in guiding the co-evolution of its offerings with those of its customers, and had relentlessly driven the evolution of computing power down a predictable trajectory of semiconductor density increase, cost reduction and performance improvement (Doz & Kosonen, 2008). As a result the 2007 fiscal year ended with an 8% revenue increase, at $38.3 billion, with net income of $7 billion, up by 38% over 2006. By 2007 Intel was investing in new product areas such as mobile internet devices and ultra-mobile PCs that leveraged on its microprocessor architecture and manufacturing technology (Intel Annual Report, 2007).

APPLE 1997–2009: TURNAROUND AND REBUILDING AN INNOVATIVE ORGANIZATION

Jobs' Turnaround

13 The return of Steve Jobs to Apple in 1997 marked the beginning of a new era for the company. Jobs worked for a salary of $1 per year for 30 months, leading Apple's successful turnaround. His priority was to revitalize Apple's innovation capability. "*Apple had forgotten who Apple was,*" as he noted in an interview (Burrows, 2004), stressing that it was time for Apple to return to its core values and build on them. At the time, Michael Dell was asked at an investor conference what Jobs should do with Apple. He replied "I'd shut it down and give the money back to the shareholders" (Burrows & Grover, 2006).

14 According to a former Apple executive who participated in Jobs' first meeting with the top brass on his return to Apple, Jobs went in with shorts, sneakers, and a few days' of beard, sat on a swivel chair, spun slowly, and asked them what was wrong with Apple. Jobs then exclaimed that it was the products, and that there was no sex in them anymore (Burrows & Grover, 2006). Upon taking charge, Jobs announced that Microsoft would invest $150 million in Apple, reaffirming its commitment to producing Microsoft Office and other products for the Mac, and soon scrapped the Mac OS licensing program, that he believed was cannibalizing Mac sales (Yoffie & Slind, 2008). He axed 70% of new products in development, kept 30% that he believed were "gems," and added some new projects that could offer breakthrough potential. He also revamped the marketing message to take advantage of the maverick, creative Apple brand, and repriced stock options to retain talent (and pushed for the resignation of board members who did not agree with the repricing) (Booth, 1997).

15 In January 2000, when Apple became profitable with a healthy share price, Apple announced that it would buy Jobs a Gulfstream V jet, at a cost of $88 million, fulfilling Jobs' request for an aeroplane so he could take his family on vacation to Hawaii and fly to the East coast. Larry Ellison, Oracle CEO and a board member at Apple, said at the time, "with what he's done, we ought to give him five airplanes!" (Elkind, 2008).

Innovation at Apple

16 Long before it was voted as the world's most innovative company, Apple had placed its trademark on a long list of technological breakthroughs including the mouse, the graphical user interface, color graphics, built-in sound, networking and wireless LAN, FireWire and many more. Apple's approach over the years had been to make use of a personal computer as easy and intuitive as possible through developing a highly responsive operating system, establishing standard specifications to which all applications software packages were expected to conform, strict control of outside developers, and delivering computers that did what they promised (Cruikshank, 2006).

17 Apple's innovations enhanced the consistency across applications, which translated to ease of use, an attribute that helped to explain to some extent Apple's loyal consumer base. Another significant characteristic of Apple's approach to innovation was the diffusion of innovation across the value chain (Cruikshank, 2006) with both high-end and low-end products that appealed to a much wider audience ranging from amateurs to professionals (see Figure 2 for an outline of Apple's key product innovations). According to Jobs, "*Apple's DNA has always been to try to democratize technology. If you make something great then everybody will want to use it*" (quoted in Morris, 2008: 69).

18 Many of the disruptive innovations Apple has introduced are based on what employees call "*deep collaboration,*" "*cross pollination*" or "*concurrent engineering.*" This refers

FIGURE 2 Timeline of Apple's Innovations

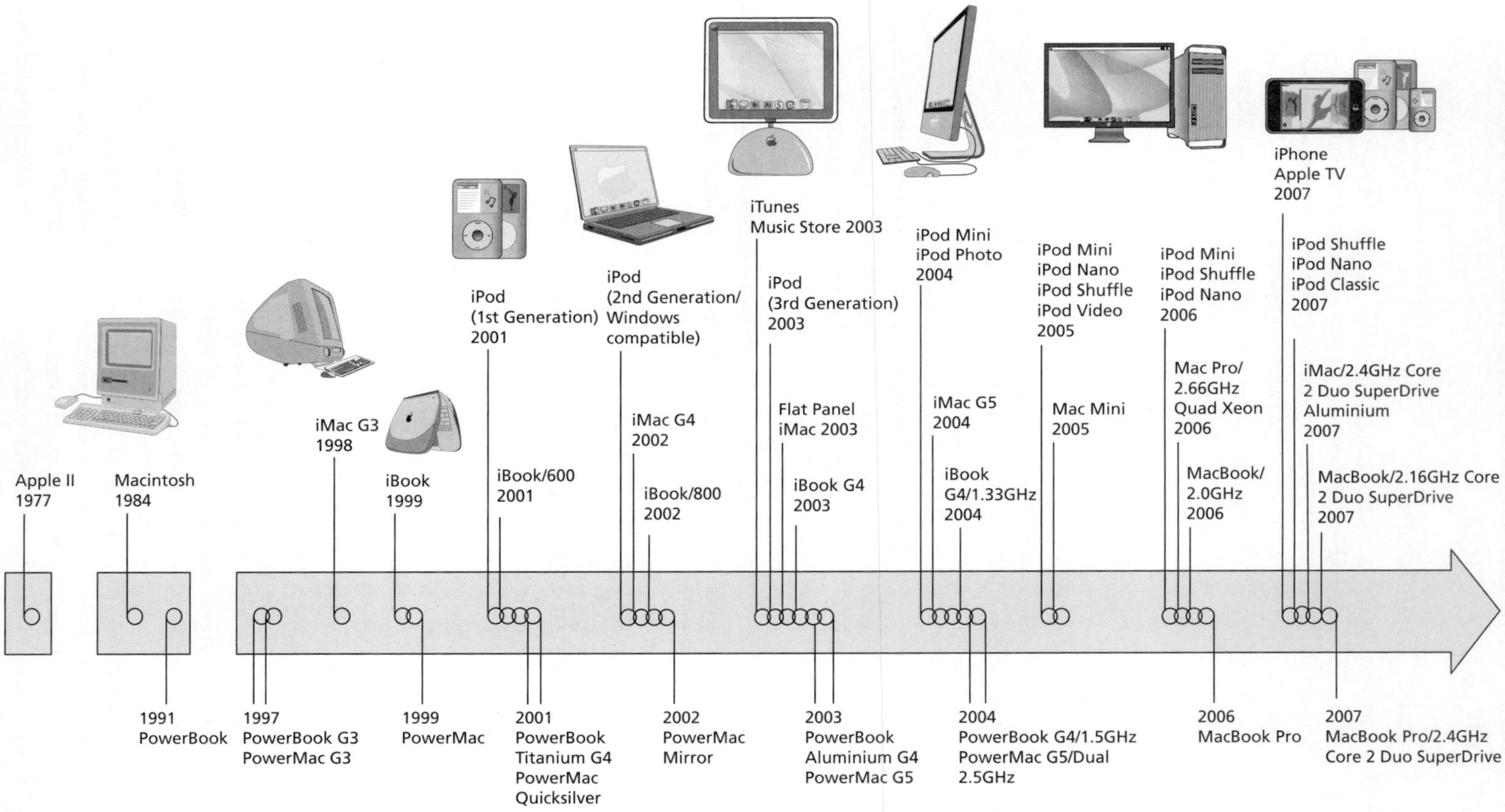

Apple II
1977

Macintosh
1984

1991
PowerBook

1997
PowerBook G3
PowerMac G3

iMac G3
1998

1999
PowerMac

iBook
1999

iPod
(1st Generation)
2001

iBook/600
2001

2001
PowerBook
Titanium G4
PowerMac
Quicksilver

iPod
(2nd Generation)
Windows
compatible)

iMac G4
2002

iBook/800
2002

2002
PowerMac
Mirror

iTunes
Music Store 2003

iPod
(3rd Generation)
2003

Flat Panel
iMac 2003

iBook G4
2003

2003
PowerBook
Aluminium G4
PowerMac G5

iPod Mini
iPod Photo
2004

iMac G5
2004

iBook
G4/1.33GHz
2004

2004
PowerBook G4/1.5GHz
PowerMac G5/Dual
2.5GHz

iPod Mini
iPod Nano
iPod Shuffle
iPod Video
2005

Mac Mini
2005

PowerBook G4/1.5GHz
PowerMac G5/Dual
2.5GHz

iPod Mini
iPod Shuffle
iPod Nano
2006

Mac Pro/
2.66GHz
Quad Xeon
2006

MacBook/
2.0GHz
2006

2006
MacBook Pro

iPhone
Apple TV
2007

iPod Shuffle
iPod Nano
iPod Classic
2007

iMac/2.4GHz Core
2 Duo SuperDrive
Aluminium
2007

MacBook/2.16GHz Core
2 Duo SuperDrive
2007

2007
MacBook Pro/2.4GHz
Core 2 Duo SuperDrive
2007

Notes: Figure shows selected product offerings that are indicative of their categories. Consumer segment products are shown above the timeline, and professional segment products are shown *below* the timeline.
Source: Authors

to products not developed in discrete stages but by "*all departments at once—design, hardware, software—in endless rounds of interdisciplinary design reviews*" (Grossman, 2005). In an interview about how innovation is fostered in the company, Jobs noted that the system for innovation is that there is no system: "*The reason a lot of us are at Apple is to make the best computers in the world and make the best software in the world. We know that we've got some stuff that (is) the best right now. But it can be so much better . . . That's what's driving us . . . And we'll sleep well when we do that*" (quoted in Cruikshank, 2006: 25.)

19   Although Apple has been envied for its ability to catch the wave in new technology fronts earlier than competitors (such as in the case of iTunes and the iPhone) Jobs describes it as a rather slow process: "*Things happen fairly slowly, you know. They do. These waves of technology, you can see them way before they happen, and you just have to choose wisely which ones you are going to surf. If you choose unwisely, then you can waste a lot of energy, but if you choose wisely, it actually unfolds fairly slowly*" (Jobs, quoted in Morris, 2008: 70)

Redefining the PC Industry

20   Loyal to the value of user friendliness, Steve Jobs led the launch of the first iMac in 1998, his first project after his return to the company. The iMac, or "*the computer for the rest of us*," its slogan when it was launched, revolutionized desktop computing by combining technological advancements and unique design. The combination of a CPU, a CD ROM drive and a modem all packed in a translucent case, that could support all "plug and play" peripherals that were designed for Windows–based machines, for the compelling price of $1,299, marked Apple's dynamic comeback.

21   Even though the iMac was the fastest selling Macintosh model ever, Apple refused to rest on its laurels, continually updating its hardware and operating system, and launching updated models and software almost every 4 months. Most importantly the iMac was the first Apple product with wide consumer acceptance, since 70% of sales where adding to the Macs already in use, helping Apple double its worldwide market share to 6% by the end of 1998 (Linzmayer, 2004).

22   In parallel Steve Jobs proceeded to simplify Apple's product mix in terms of four lines of desktop and portable computers designed for both the professional and consumer markets. Following the iMac's success, the iBook was launched in 1999. This consumer portable computer featured an optional AirPort wireless networking hub that allowed up to ten Macs to share an Internet connection. Just six weeks after the iBook's unveiling, Apple had received more than 140,000 advance orders, making it a success equal to the iMac (Linzmayer, 2004).

23   After the introduction of the iMac and the iBook, Apple's figures looked a lot healthier. In October 1999 Apple announced its eighth consecutive profitable quarter and closed that fiscal year with revenues of $6.1 billion and net earnings of $601 million. Whereas most of Apple's innovations led to an even more closed Apple archipelagos (software and hardware integration), at the same time Jobs decided to loosen control in other areas, for example the use of standard interfaces, such as the USB port. This change made the Mac a more open system since users of a Mac Mini for example could use a non-Mac keyboard (Yoffie & Slind, 2008). In the years to follow, a variety of innovative proprietary applications, developed in-house, supported the Macintosh product lines. These include programs such as those in the iLife package (iDVD, iMovie, iPhoto,) that offered editing and creative opportunities to users as well as Apple's own Web browser, Safari, developed in 2003.

Breakthrough Innovation in Consumer Electronics and Entertainment Industries

24 In 2001 Apple introduced its first iPod, launching a new era for the company as it entered the consumer electronics industry. Capitalizing on the emerging trend of MP3 music, Apple introduced a breakthrough product that soon became synonymous with the MP3 music player category. With impeccable design and easy to use menu, the iPod could load 1000 songs in just 10 minutes and play music for 10 hours. The integration with the iTunes 2.0 software also made synchronizing music libraries a matter of a few seconds. A year later, in 2002 Apple released more capacious iPods that could also work with Windows, a move that helped to skyrocket iPod sales. By the end of 2003 more than one million iPods were sold marking the first substantial stream of revenues apart from the Macintosh. Since then the iPod product range has been renewed every 3 to 5 months and the company announced in 2007 that it sold the 100 millionth iPod. These numbers made the iPod the fastest selling music player in history (Apple, 2007).

25 Arguably, one the most important innovations for Apple has been the launch of the iTunes Music store in 2003, a revolutionary service through which consumers could access and purchase online music for only $0.99 per song. The iTunes Music Store was compatible with all iPods (running both in Macs as well as Windows–based computers) and served as Apple's Trojan horse to what Jobs has envisioned as the digital hub where digital content and Apple devices would be seamlessly interconnected. The downloaded songs had royalty protection and could only be played by iPods, bringing the interoperability between Apple's hardware, software and content to a new level and creating higher barriers to entry in this ecosystem.

26 Apple's next big innovation was the iPhone, a device combining a phone, a music player and a personal computer that was expected to redefine the mobile phone industry in the same way iPod and iTunes revolutionized the music industry. According to Jobs, "*It was a great challenge: Let's make a great phone that we fall in love with. Nobody had thought about putting operating systems as sophisticated as an OS X inside a phone, so that was a real question*" (quoted in Morris, 2008: 69). iPhone's success is attributed not only to its technological capacity but also to its design: "*We had a different enclosure design for this iPhone until way too close to the introduction to ever change it. And it came one Monday morning and I said: I just don't love it. And we pushed the reset button. That happens more than you think because it is not just engineering and science. There is art too.*" (Jobs quoted in Morris, 2008: 70). According to Burrows & Grover (2006), "Jobs' true secret weapon is his ability to meld technical vision with a gut feel of what regular consumers want and then market it in ways that make regular consumers want to be part of tech's cool club."

PLAYING BY DIFFERENT RULES: STICKING WITH A PROPRIETARY ECOSYSTEM

27 Apple's innovations have redefined existing product categories such as music players, and helped the company successfully enter hotly contested new markets such as the entertainment industry. Key to these achievements have been the focus on design, the consumer experience, and the seamless integration of hardware and software (such as in the case of the iPod and iTunes).

28 The tight integration of its own operating system, hardware and applications, has been a strategy followed diligently by Apple. As Steve Jobs says: "*One of our biggest insights* *[years ago] was that we didn't want to get into any business we didn't own or control the primary technology, because you'll get your head handed to you. We realized that for almost all future consumer electronics, the primary technology was going to be software. And we were pretty good at software."* (Morris, 2008: 70)

29   Apple is nearly unique among contemporary technology companies in doing all of its own design in-house, at its Cupertino campus. Other companies have outsourced most or all of their product design function, relying on outsourced design manufacturers (ODMs) to develop the products that with minor adaptations will fit into their product lines. Apple however believes that having all the experts in one place—the mechanical, electrical, software, and industrial engineers, as well as the product designers, leads to a more holistic perspective on product development; and that a critical mass of talent makes existing products better and opens the door to entirely new products. According to Jobs, "*. . . you can't do what you can do at Apple anywhere else. The engineering is long gone in the PC companies. In the consumer electronics companies they don't understand the software parts of it. There's no other company that could make a MacBook Air and the reason is that not only do we control the hardware, but we control the operating system. And it is the intimate interaction between the operating system and the hardware that allows us to do that. There is no intimate interaction between Windows and a Dell computer*" (quoted in Morris, 2008).

30   The company's tightly knit proprietary system has been frequently seen as the reason for Apple's loss of initial momentum in the PC industry and increasing isolation until the mid 90's. According to Kahney, "*When Jobs returned to Apple in 1997, he ignored everyone's advice and tied his company's proprietary software to its proprietary hardware*" (Kahney, 2008: 142). He has persisted in following this strategy over the years even when all other Silicon Valley firms turned towards openness and interoperability. Tony Fadell, Vice President of engineering in the iPod division, notes that Apple aims to develop a self-reinforcing, synergistic system of products rather than a series of individual products: "*The product now is the iTunes Music Store and iTunes and the iPod and the software that goes on the iPod. A lot of companies don't really have control, or they can't really work in a collaborative way to truly make a system. We're really about a system*" (quoted in Grossman, 2005).

31   Over the years, there have been some notable exceptions to this proprietary approach. In order to reach a broader consumer base, in late 2003 Apple offered a Windows compatible version of iTunes allowing not only Windows users to use the iPod but more importantly to familiarize them with Apple products. Another milestone came with the company's switch from PowerPC processors made by IBM to Intel chips, a decision announced in mid-2005. This decision allowed Macs to run Windows software, implied lower switching costs for new Mac consumers and also allowed software developers to adapt more easily their programs for Apple. A previous alliance with Microsoft occurred in 1997 when Microsoft agreed to invest $150 million in Apple, reaffirming its commitment to develop core products such as Microsoft Office for the Mac.

32   Apple has developed a series of strategic alliances in the course of its efforts to become the center of the digital hub, where digital content would be easily created and transferred to any Apple device. Development of the iPod, iTunes and iPhone have necessitated these alliances, since entry in the entertainment and consumer electronics markets would not have been possible without some key strategic partners (for example the big record labels for iTunes such as EMI, Sony BMG, Universal and Warner Brothers, or YouTube for the iPhone). In this process of building systems, Apple has been very selective about its partners. Rather than aiming for the most partners, Apple focuses on engaging with the best companies for a specific purpose (for example Apple has partnered with Google, in developing mapping and video applications for the iPhone).

33   At the same time Apple has proceeded with a number of acquisitions intended to strengthen its core competencies. For example, in 2002 Apple acquired the German specialist in music software, Emagic, as well as Prismo Graphics, Silicon Grail and Nothing Real, three small companies involved in professional-level video creation and production. In April 2008 Apple also announced the acquisition of the boutique microprocessor company PA Semi, known for its highly sophisticated and low-priced chips. With that acquisition Apple is said to be moving towards bringing its chip design in-house, building an ever more tightly knit ecosystem that helps to prevent copycat designs from rivals and to design chips for supporting specific new products or applications. According to COO Tim Cook: "*One traditional management philosophy that's taught in many business schools is diversification. Well, that's not us. We are the antibusiness school*" (Burrows, 2007).

34   In 2001, Apple created a retail division to enable it to sell its products directly to the public. By mid-2008 there were 215 retail stores, most of them in the US, accounting for almost 20% of total revenues. In 2006 Apple entered into an alliance with Best Buy, and by the end of 2007 Apple products could be purchased in over 270 Best Buy stores (Yoffie & Slind, 2008).

CORPORATE CULTURE AND HUMAN CAPITAL

35   According to Apple's COO Tim Cook, Apple "*is not for the faint of heart*" (Morris, 2008: 69). Apple's culture is all about intense work and perfectionism but in a casual environment. Jobs stimulates thinking out of the box and encourages his employees to experiment and share with others "the coolest new thing" they have thought of. It may not be accidental that Apple's emblem of corporate culture is a pirate flag with an Apple rainbow colored eye patch, designed after a famous Jobs quote: "*It's better to be a pirate than join the navy.*" This flag was hanging over the Macintosh building as Apple's team was working on the first iMac, to act as a reminder of their mission. "*Processes lead according to Jobs to efficiency, not innovation nor new ideas. These come from people meeting up in the hallways, calling each other in the middle of the night to share a new idea or the solution to a long thought as unsolved problem*" (Grossman, 2005).

36   Along with the rebel spirit that Jobs wants to maintain, Apple has a tradition of long working hours and relentless pursuit of perfection. Each manufacturing and software detail is worked and reworked until a product is considered perfect, thus providing a seamless integration of software and hardware. Apple's engineers spend so much time on each and every product that they are able to foresee and respond to any possible difficulties a consumer might encounter when using it. "*It's because when you buy our products, and three months later you get stuck on something, you quickly figure out [how to get past it]. And you think, "Wow, someone over there at Apple actually thought of this!" And then six months later it happens again. There's almost no product in the world that you have that experience with, but you have it with a Mac. And you have it with an iPod*" (Jobs, quoted in Burrows, 2004).

37   Apple's employees are not paid astronomically. They are not pampered, nor do they enjoy unique privileges beyond what most large companies offer. They are talented people with passion for excellence, proud to be part of the Apple community. Moreover they want to be part of a company that believes that the best way to predict the future is to invent it. This pride stems from a corporate culture that fosters innovation and a sense of Apple's superiority against competitors. Apple recruits talent of the highest caliber, and Jobs is known for approaching people who are known as the best in what they do and recruiting them to Apple. According to Gus Mueller, founder of a software development firm that develops software for Apple, "*Apple only hires top-notch folks. I know a number of people there, and* *they are all super smart and creative. I don't know a single person who shouldn't be there*" (Guardian, 2008). As Steve Jobs said: "*We may not be the richest guy in the graveyard at the end of the day, but we're the best at what we do. And Apple is doing the best work in its history*" (quoted in Burrows, 2004).

STEVE JOBS' LEADERSHIP

38 When Jobs returned to Apple in 1997 after an absence of 12 years, he arrived with much historical baggage. He was Apple's co-founder at the age of 21, and was worth $200 million by the age of 25. He was then forced to resign by the age of 30, in 1985, after a battle over control with CEO John Sculley which ended in Jobs losing all operational responsibilities. Jobs (who had been executive VP and General Manager of the Macintosh division) was considered a threat to the company, accused of trying to "play manager" and control areas over which he had no jurisdiction. He was considered "a temperamental micromanager whose insistence on total control and stylish innovation had doomed his company to irrelevance" (Burrows & Grover, 2006).

39 Twenty-two years later however Jobs was voted as one of the greatest entrepreneurs of all time by *BusinessWeek* (Tozzi, 2007). His personality left a mark on Apple in a way that only a few leaders had achieved, making his name synonymous with the company and its remarkable turnaround. Described by his colleagues as brilliant, powerful and charismatic, he could also be a demanding and impulsive perfectionist. As Jobs puts it: "*My job is not to be easy on people. My job is to take these great people we have and to push them and make them even better. How? Just by coming up with more aggressive visions of how it could be*" (quoted in Morris, 2008: 70).

40 Many believe that Jobs' achievement of being regarded as one of the greatest technology entrepreneurs is not based so much on his knowledge of technology (he is not an engineer or a programmer, neither does he have an MBA or college degree) but on his innate instinct for design, the ability to choose the most talented team and "*the willingness to be a pain in the neck for what matters for him most*" (Grossman, 2005).

41 With regard to the iMac, for example, a product concept he and Jonathan Ive, head of design had envisioned, the engineers were initially sceptical: "*Sure enough, when we took it to the engineers, they said, 'Oh.' And they came up with 38 reasons. And I said, 'No, no, we're doing this.' And they said, 'Well, why?' And I said, 'Because I'm the CEO, and I think it can be done.' And so they kind of begrudgingly did it. But then it was a big hit*" (Grossman, 2005). Jobs has cited himself as "co-inventor" on 103 separate Apple patents (Elkind, 2008).

42 Jobs could be both inspirational but also experienced as scary. According to Guy Kawasaki, former head of developers, "*Working for Steve was a terrifying and addictive experience. He would tell you that your work, your ideas, and sometimes your existence were worthless right to your face, right in front of everyone. Watching him crucify someone scared you into working incredibly long hours . . . Working for Steve was also ecstasy. Once in a while he would tell you that you were great and that made it all worth it*" (Cruikshank, 2006: 147). Apart from displaying such behaviors as parking his car in handicapped places and publicly losing his temper, Jobs often made his employees burst into tears through direct and personal criticism. Robert Sutton, management professor at Stanford, discussed Steve Jobs in his book "The no asshole rule" in the chapter on the virtues of assholes (Sutton, 2007). Sutton then reflected further on his discussion of Steve Jobs in his blog, suggesting that Jobs may be mellowing as he gets older (Sutton, 2008). Yet, according to Palo Alto venture capitalist Jean-Louis Gasse, a former Apple executive who once worked with Jobs, "*Democracies don't make great products. You need a competent tyrant*" (Gasse, quoted in Elkind, 2008).

43   The high praise as well as high criticism made people try harder, jump higher and work later into the night. Jobs is credited with imposing discipline on Apple, a quality that the company had lacked for years. The company that used to be known as the "ship that leaks from the top" (Linzmayer, 2004) due to its relaxed management style and corporate culture was soon transformed into a tightly controlled and integrated machine after Jobs' arrival. At Pixar, things were seen differently than at Apple however. Reportedly Jobs spent less than a day per week there, and was hands-off, particularly on the creative front. According to a Pixar employee, "Steve doesn't tell us what to do . . . Steve's our benevolent benefactor" (quoted in Burrows & Grover, 2006).

44   Jobs' charisma is depicted in the way he briefed his team concerning a new product: "*Even though Steve didn't draw any of the lines, his ideas and inspiration made the design what it is. To be honest, we didn't know what it meant for a computer to be 'friendly' until Jobs told us*" (Terry Oyama, quoted in Cruikshank, 2006, p. 30). As author Scott Kelby put it: "*There is one thing I am certain of: Steve's the right man to lead Apple. There's never been anyone at Apple who has had the impact that Steve has since his return. He may be a tyrant, demanding, unforgiving and the worst boss ever. But he is also a visionary. A genius. A man who gets things done. And the man who kept Apple afloat when a host of other nice guys couldn't*" (Cruikshank, 2006, p. 175).

45   Jobs brought his own brand of strategic thinking to Apple: "*The clearest example was when we were pressured for years to do a PDA, and I realized one day that 90% of the people who use a PDA only take information out of it on the road. Pretty soon cell phones are going to do that so the PDA market's going to get reduced to a fraction of its current size. So we decided not to get into it. If we had gotten into it we wouldn't have the resources to do the iPod*" (quoted in Morris, 2008: 69). Jobs has often said "I'm as proud of what we don't do as I am of what we do" (quoted in Burrows & Grover, 2006).

Challenges on Steve Jobs' Watch

46   In October 2003 Jobs was diagnosed with pancreatic cancer. Whereas this disease is fatal, his case was a rare but treatable form, if operated on. Jobs, a vegetarian and Buddhist, decided not to get [an operation] but to follow a special diet and to seek alternative medical approaches that he believed would cure him. Apple's board of directors was aware of his condition, but a decision was made to not disclose it to investors. The board of Pixar, the other public company where Jobs was CEO, was not aware of his condition. In July 2004, after a scan revealed a growth in the tumor, Jobs finally had the surgery. The next day his employees and the media found out about his situation, through an email he sent his employees that was released to the press. On the day of the announcement Apple's shares dropped by 2.4%, a relatively low figure, bearing in mind the severity of the situation. Assuring everyone that he was cured, Jobs returned to his duties a few months later (Elkind, 2008).

47   Jobs' recent tenure has also been marred by other issues. In 2006, after a series of articles in the *Wall Street Journal* about options backdating, Apple set up a board committee to examine whether it had engaged in this practice, and the committee concluded that it had done so between 1997 and 2001 with regard to 6,428 option grants (around a sixth of the total). There were no backdating issues before Jobs took over as CEO. Disney also investigated option grants at Pixar during Jobs' CEO tenure and found irregularities as well. However, Steve Jobs did not personally benefit from the options backdating, and Apple has been extremely co-operative with the SEC investigation on the issue. The SEC filed charges against Apple's former general counsel and CFO for organising the backdated option grants and falsifying relevant documentation. In a public statement, the CFO said that he had made Jobs aware of the accounting implications of the backdated options (Elkind, 2008).

48   When Jobs took over at Apple in 1997, he restructured the board of directors to create a new board with six members, two of which remained from the earlier board. The new members included Oracle CEO Larry Ellison, a close friend of Jobs, as well as Intuit CEO Bill Campbell, a former employee of Apple and Jobs' neighbour. Former SEC chairman Arthur Levitt was surprised to be first invited by Jobs to join the new board, and then "dis-invited," after Jobs had read one of Levitt's speeches on corporate governance and concluded that the issues Levitt mentioned in that speech were not applicable to Apple.

49   This tight relationship between Jobs and Apple along with his health status that some perceive as fragile, have given room for speculation about his replacement, should that be necessary. Fortune magazine named Tim Cook, Apple's COO as the most probable candidate for the position (Lashinsky, 2008). Cook's role in Apple's operations since 1998 has given him a prominent position next to Jobs, as he is the only person to have a vast area of responsibility apart from Jobs himself and the one who replaced him while he was recovering from his pancreatic operation. In any case Jobs' plans regarding his future successor remain veiled. Jobs' immense influence on Apple has given pause for scepticism regarding Apple's future without him. As Fortune's editor Elkind notes: "*In the 26 years that Fortune has been ranking America's Most Admired Companies never has the corporation at the head of the list so closely resembled a one-man show*" (Elkind, 2008).

LOOKING TO THE FUTURE

50   In January 2007, Apple Computer changed its name to Apple Inc. (Yahoo Finance, 2008), signifying a shift away from its computer vendor roots. Since 2006, revenues from desktop and portable computers were accounting for less than half of Apple's total revenues. By early 2009, Apple had come a long away: it had produced the world's fastest personal computer, introduced a series of attractive new Macintosh models with a reliable, competitive operating system known for its astonishing backward compatibility, created a cult following of iPod users, and begun its inroads into the mobile phone industry with the iPhone.

51   Despite Apple's impressive comeback, its share in the worldwide PC industry hovered below 3%, and the growth prospects of the iPod and iPhone were far from guaranteed. The company was faced with the threat of commoditization as the iPod market in developed countries showed some signs of maturity and music over mobile phones was becoming increasingly popular. Apple's competitors were introducing alternative products and some were attempting to copy Apple's approach to doing business. Sony for example, hired one of Apple's former executives, Tim Schaaff, as the company's new senior vice president for software development, and set the goal of imitating Apple's interoperability amongst products (Edwards, Hall & Grover, 2008). In September 2008 T-Mobile, a mobile operator owned by Germany's Deutsche Telekom, presented its new phone, the G1, made by HTC, a Taiwanese manufacturer. The device was the first to be based on the Android software (Google's open-source operating system), while Samsung, HTC, LG Electronics, and Motorola were among the companies that said they would also produce phones that ran on Android.

52   E-giant Amazon set up its own online music store in September 2007 to provide music compatible with both Windows Media Player, iTunes and any MP3 player device. Half of the tracks available through Amazon MP3 store were priced at $0.89 compared to Apple iTunes' price at the time of $1.29 (Amazon, 2007). Finally MySpace, the world's largest social network, announced in April 2008 its cooperation with Sony, Universal and Warner to form MySpace Music, a one-stop shop where visitors could communicate, share and buy music (WMG press release, 2008).

53   Some analysts believed that Apple's closed system might once again hold the company back from its potential mass appeal (as in the 80s with the Mac OS) and recommended that Apple's future should be more based on openness and partnerships (Guardian, 2008).

54   In January 2009, Jobs announced that he was taking leave of absence from Apple until June, due to health issues relating to a "hormone imbalance." COO Tim Cook would handle day-to-day operations, and Jobs would stay involved in major strategic decisions. Commentators disagreed on the degree of impact Jobs' absence would have. Some said that the new products Apple would introduce over the following 18 months had already been developed under Jobs' leadership, and that Cook would manage Apple effectively in Jobs' absence. Others, however, believed that Jobs' motivational role, negotiation skills and creative vision were crucial for Apple (Macworld, 2009).

55   Meanwhile, a week later Apple announced that its performance for the last quarter of 2008 beat expectations, with a net profit of $1.61 billion. By that time, it also emerged that the Securities and Exchange Commission was carrying out an investigation to ensure that Jobs' health-related disclosures did not mislead investors (BBC, 2009; Bloomberg, 2009).

56   By early 2009, Apple was faced with some critical decisions regarding its strategy for the future. Was its competitive advantage becoming eroded through product imitation, and attempts by other companies to duplicate Apple's key competencies? Should Apple focus more on the consumer electronics or the computer markets? Was it time for Apple to rethink its closed proprietary ecosystem? What would happen to Apple if it lost Steve Jobs for good? Was Apple still on the rollercoaster that characterized its history, at risk of heading downwards, after its upward climb?

REFERENCES

Amazon, 2007. Amazon.com launches public beta of Amazon MP3, 25 September, http://phx.corporate-ir.net/phoenix.zhtml?c=176060&p=irolnewsArticle& ID=1055054&highlight=Amazon.com%20Launches%20Public%20Beta%20 of%20Amazon%20MP3, press release accessed on 1 December 2008.

Apple Inc. Annual Report, 2007–8, 95 pp.

Apple Inc. 2008. Apple reports first quarter results, 22 January, http://www.apple.com/pr/library/2008/01/22results.html, accessed on 1 December 2008.

Apple Inc. 2007. 100 million ipods sold. http://www.apple.com/pr/library/2007/04/09ipod.html, accessed on 23 December 2008.

BBC, 2009. Apple posts best quarterly profit. January 21. http://news.bbc.co.uk/1/hi/business/7843769.stm, accessed on 24 January 2009.

Bloomberg, 2009. Apple soars as record sales ease concerns about Jobs. http://www.bloomberg.com/apps/news?pid=20601087&sid=alPjQDdwDFnc&refer=home, accessed on 24 January 2009.

Booth, C. 1997. Steve's job: Restart Apple. *Time*, 18 August, http://www.time.com/time/magazine/article/0,9171,986849,00.html, accessed on 23 December 2008.

Burrows, P. 2004. The seed of Apple's innovation, Interview with Steve Jobs, *BusinessWeek*, 12 October, http://www.businessweek.com/bwdaily/dnflash/oct2004/nf20041012_4018_db083.htm, accessed on 1 December 2008.

Burrows, P. & Grover, R. 2006. Steve Jobs' magic kingdom. *BusinessWeek*, 6 February. http://www.businessweek.com/magazine/content/06_06/b3970001.htm, accessed on 23 December 2008.

Cruikshank, J. 2006. *The Apple Way*, McGraw Hill: New York.

Dell Annual Report, 2007, 105 pp.

Doz, Y. & Kosonen, M. 2008. *Fast Strategy*, Wharton School Publishing, Pearson Education, Harlow.

Edwards, C., Hall, K. & Grover, R. 2008. Sony chases Apple's magic, *BusinessWeek*, October 30, http://www.businessweek.com/magazine/content/08_45/b4107048234222.htm, accessed on 1 December 2008.

Elkind, P. 2008. The trouble with Steve Jobs, *Fortune*, March 5, http://money.cnn.com/2008/03/02/news/companies/elkind_jobs.fortune/index.htm, accessed on 1 December 2008.

Grossman, L., 2005. How Apple does it, *Time*, October 16, http://www.time.com/time/magazine/article/0,9171,1118384,00.html, accessed on 1 December 2008.

Guardian, 2008. Reading the runes for Apple, January 10, http://www.guardian.co.uk/technology/2008/jan/10/apple.steve.jobs, accessed on 11 December 2008.

HP Annual Report, 2007, 162 pp.

IBM Annual Report, 2007, 124 pp.

Intel Annual Report, 2007, 115 pp.

Interbrand, 2008, Best Global Brands Rankings, http://www.interbrand.com/best_global_brands.aspx , accessed on 23 December 2008.

Kahney, L. 2008. How Apple got everything right by doing everything wrong, *Wired Magazine*, April, pp. 137–142

Linzmayer, O. W. 2004. *Apple Confidential 2.0: The Definitive History of the World's Most Colorful Company*. San Francisco: No Starch Press.

Macworld, 2009. Jobs to take leave of absence until June. January 14. http://www.macworld.com/article/138215/2009/01/jobs.html?t=201, accessed on 24 January 2009.

Microsoft Annual Report, 2008, 71 pp.

McGregor, J. 2008. The world's most innovative companies. *BusinessWeek*, April 17. http://www.businessweek.com/magazine/content/08_17/b4081061866744.htm?chan=ma gazine+channel_special+report, accessed on 23 December 2008.

Morris, B. What Makes Apple Golden, *Fortune*, March 17, 2008, 157(5), pp. 68–71.

Sutton, R. I. 2008. Fortune story on the trouble with Steve Jobs: Asshole, genius, or both? March 6. http://bobsutton.typepad.com/my_weblog/2008/03/fortune-story-o.html, accessed on 23 December 2008.

Sutton, R. I. 2007. *The no asshole rule: Building a civilized workplace and surviving one that isn't*. Business Plus.

Tozzi, J. The Greatest Entrepreneurs of All Time, *BusinessWeek*, June 27 2007, http://www.businessweek.com/smallbiz/content/jun2007/sb20070627_564139.htm, accessed on 1/12/2008.

WMG Press Release, 2008. MySpace, Sony BMG Music Entertainment, Universal Music Group and Warner Music Group partner in landmark joint venture: 'MySpace Music. April 3rd, http://www.wmg.com/news/article/?id=8a0af81218f1a369011914f426661bb4, accessed on 1 December 2008.

Yahoo Finance, 2008. Apple Inc. profile. http://finance.yahoo.com/q/pr?s=AAPL, accessed on 23 December 2008.

Yoffie, D. B. & Slind, M. 2008. *Apple Inc.*, 2008. Harvard Business School Case 9-708-480, 32 pp.

Case 24

Unauthorized Disclosure: Hewlett-Packard's Secret Surveillance of Directors and Journalists

Anne T. Lawrence, Randall D. Harris, and Sally Baack

1 On September 28, 2006, members of Congress, their staffs, reporters, prospective witnesses, and the curious public packed the wood-paneled hearing room of the U.S. House Committee on Energy and Commerce. The subject of the day's hearing, called by the Subcommittee on Oversight and Investigations, was "Hewlett-Packard's Pretexting Scandal."[1] At issue were methods the technology firm had used to investigate the unauthorized disclosure of non-public information to the press by members of its board of directors. Hewlett-Packard (HP) apparently had hired investigators who had used a technique known as pretexting—calling the phone company and posing as someone else in order to obtain that person's records. *Newsweek* had summed up the situation in a cover story published ten days earlier: "Lying, spying, name-calling, finger-pointing—all of it is a tragicomedy that Shakespeare might've penned if he had gotten an MBA."[2]

2 Hewlett-Packard and its board chairman, Patricia Dunn, had initially defended the company's investigation of directors and journalists, saying aggressive efforts to ferret out the source of leaks were fully justified. But in the past few weeks, the situation had begun to spin out of control as the Securities and Exchange Commission and the California Attorney General had opened probes into the company's actions.[3] Now, nearly two dozen of HP's top executives, directors, lawyers, and investigators—including the company's CEO Mark Hurd—had been called before Congress to account for their firm's alleged out-of-bounds behavior and to explain what they intended to do about it. Shortly before the September hearing, Dunn had agreed to resign from the board, and HP's general counsel, Ann Baskins—who had supervised the investigation—had left the firm. Now, Dunn faced the daunting challenge of defending her actions, and Hurd, as CEO and newly appointed board chairman, had to chart a way forward for the company.

CORPORATE GOVERNANCE AT HEWLETT-PACKARD

3 Hewlett-Packard described itself as a "technology solutions provider to consumers, businesses and institutions globally."[4] Founded in 1939 in a garage near the Stanford University campus by David Packard and Bill Hewlett to make test and measurement instruments, the

[1] "Probing the Pretexters: Congress Grills Hewlett-Packard Executives Over 'Sleaze' Investigative Tactics," *Wall Street Journal* (September 29, 2006): B1.

[2] David A. Kaplan, "HP Scandal: The Boss Who Spied on Her Board," *Newsweek* (September 18, 2006).

[3] "HP Faces Probe over Its Inquiry into Board Leaks," *Wall Street Journal* (September 7, 2006): A1.

[4] http://www.hp.com/hpinfo.

company had grown to become a leader in the information technology industry. HP had four main business units, focusing on information technology infrastructure, imaging and printing, business services, and personal computers and devices. Headquartered in Palo Alto, California, the company in 2005 earned $3.5 billion on revenues of $86.7 billion.[5] It employed around 150,000 people and had a presence in more than 170 countries. (The company's credo, known as the "HP Way," is shown in Exhibit A.)

4   In 2006, an eleven-person board of directors had overall responsibility for HP's strategy and policies. Patricia Dunn, who had joined the board in 1998, served as chairman from February 2005 until her resignation in September 2006. Dunn, who held a degree in journalism, had begun her career as a secretarial assistant. She had risen rapidly to become, at age forty-two, CEO of Barclays Global Investors, a firm that managed more than $1 trillion in assets, primarily for institutions. At Barclays, Dunn was known for her customer focus and adherence to strict ethical standards in the stewardship of others' money. In 2002,

EXHIBIT A   The HP Way

We have trust and respect for individuals.

We approach each situation with the belief that people want to do a good job and will do so, given the proper tools and support. We attract highly capable, diverse, innovative people and recognize their efforts and contributions to the company. HP people contribute enthusiastically and share in the success that they make possible.

We focus on a high level of achievement and contribution.

Our customers expect HP products and services to be of the highest quality and to provide lasting value. To achieve this, all HP people, especially managers, must be leaders who generate enthusiasm and respond with extra effort to meet customer needs. Techniques and management practices which are effective today may be outdated in the future. For us to remain at the forefront in all our activities, people should always be looking for new and better ways to do their work.

We conduct our business with uncompromising integrity.

We expect HP people to be open and honest in their dealings to earn the trust and loyalty of others. People at every level are expected to adhere to the highest standards of business ethics and must understand that anything less is unacceptable. As a practical matter, ethical conduct cannot be assured by written HP policies and codes; it must be an integral part of the organization, a deeply ingrained tradition that is passed from one generation of employees to another.

We achieve our common objectives through teamwork.

We recognize that it is only through effective cooperation within and among organizations that we can achieve our goals. Our commitment is to work as a worldwide team to fulfill the expectations of our customers, shareholders and others who depend upon us. The benefits and obligations of doing business are shared among all HP people.

We encourage flexibility and innovation.

We create an inclusive work environment which supports the diversity of our people and stimulates innovation. We strive for overall objectives which are clearly stated and agreed upon, and allow people flexibility in working toward goals in ways that they help determine are best for the organization. HP people should personally accept responsibility and be encouraged to upgrade their skills and capabilities through ongoing training and development. This is especially important in a technical business where the rate of progress is rapid and where people are expected to adapt to change.

[5] *Hewlett-Packard Form 10-K for the fiscal year ending October 31, 2005*, p. 71.

Dunn stepped down as Barclays' CEO after being diagnosed with both breast cancer and melanoma; in 2004, she was diagnosed with stage IV ovarian cancer. Another prominent member of HP's board was Thomas Perkins, a partner in the powerful Silicon Valley venture capital firm Kleiner Perkins Caufield & Byers. Perkins had a long association with HP, having headed the company's research labs and later its computer division. George (Jay) Keyworth II, the board's longest-serving member, was a nuclear physicist and chair of the Progress & Freedom Foundation. (Exhibit B presents members of the board from 1999 to 2006 and indicates which board members were insiders.)

EXHIBIT B   Hewlett-Packard Board of Directors, 1999–2006

	1999	2000	2001	2002	2003	2004	2005	2006
Richard A. Hackborn	A	A	A	A	A	A	A	A
George A. Keyworth	A	A	A	A	A	A	A	A
Robert P. Wayman*	A	A	A	A			A	A
Sam Ginn	A	A	A	A	A			
Walter B. Hewlett**	A	A	A	A				
Susan Packard Orr**	A	A						
Thomas E. Everett	A							
John B. Fery	A							
Jean-Paul G. Gimon	A							
David M. Lawrence	A							
David W. Packard**	A							
Lewis E. Platt*	A							
Paul F. Miller								
Phillip M. Condit	A	A	A	A	A			
Patricia C. Dunn	A	A	A	A	A	A	A	A
Robert E. Knowling		A	A	A	A	A	A	
Carleton S. Fiorina*		A	A	A	A	A		
Lawrence T. Babbio					A	A	A	A
Lucille S. Salhany					A	A	A	A
Sanford M. Litvack					A	A		
Thomas J. Perkins					A		A	A
Robert L. Ryan						A	A	A
Sari M. Baldauf								A
John H. Hammergren								A
Mark V. Hurd*								A
Total Directors	14	10	9	9	11	9	9	11

Source: HP Proxy Statements

Notes:

A = Active board membership at the time of annual meeting. Board membership changed between meetings during this time period.

Lewis E. Platt completed his term as chairman in 1999. Carly Fiorina served as chairman from 1999–2005. Patricia Dunn served as chairman from February 2005 to September 2006. Mark Hurd became chairman in September 2006.

* Inside director (i.e., HP employee at the time of board service). Richard Hackborn and Thomas Perkins were former HP employees at the time of board service.

** Member of one of the founding families (Hewletts and Packards).

5   HP's board had four standing committees: the audit committee, which oversaw financial reporting to shareholders; the finance and investment committee, which oversaw HP's own investments; the HR and compensation committee, which oversaw its compensation structure; and the nominating and governance committee, which recommended candidates for directorships and oversaw the board's own processes. The board met several times throughout the year, culminating in a multi-day, off-site retreat generally held in January, where the board reviewed plans for the coming year.

6   HP's board had had a recent history of turmoil and turnover. In 2002, Carly Fiorina, CEO since 1999, had initiated a merger with computer-maker Compaq. Although most of the board supported the move, Walter Hewlett—a son of company founder Bill Hewlett and a long-time director—opposed it, saying the merger would destroy the egalitarian culture that was a core element of his father's legacy. Hewlett and his allies led a bruising proxy fight in which they worked to mobilize institutional investors to vote against the acquisition. Despite opposition from both the Hewlett and Packard families, stockholders ultimately approved the merger in a close vote, and Hewlett subsequently left the board.[6]

7   Shortly after the merger, Perkins rejoined the HP board (on which he had earlier served briefly), moving over from Compaq's board. One of Perkins' first actions as a director was to help organize a new technology committee "to make recommendations to the board as to scope, direction, quality, investment levels and execution of HP's technology strategies."[7] Initial members of the committee included Keyworth; Lawrence Babbio, the president of Verizon; and Richard Hackborn, HP's former executive vice president of computer products. According to James B. Stewart, writing in the *New Yorker,* the technology committee soon came to function as a virtual "board-within-the-board," taking up key strategic issues, including market entry and exit, mergers and acquisitions, and competitor and partner relationships.[8]

8   In their focus on strategy, members of the technology committee may have differed from other directors who were more concerned with governance processes. In an editorial that appeared on the day of the Congressional hearing, the *Wall Street Journal* offered the following observation about conflict on HP's board:

> The board's internal disagreements seem to have been about the role of directors. Mr. Keyworth, who was Ronald Reagan's science adviser and whose twenty-one years on the board go back to the era of founder David Packard, was part of a faction who believe directors need to be conversant enough with technology to appreciate the company's main business risks . . . Ms. Dunn, by contrast, is a former financier with little knowledge of the computer industry. She believed HP's board should focus more on supervisory process—for example, fulfilling its obligations under Sarbanes-Oxley.[9]

A LEAK OF CONFIDENTIAL BOARD DELIBERATIONS

9   The original unauthorized disclosure—leak of confidential board deliberations—that initiated the chain of events leading to the September 28 hearings had occurred twenty months earlier, before Dunn had become chairman. On January 21, 2005, Fiorina received an urgent

[6] The story of the merger proxy vote is told in Peter Burrows, *Back-Fire: Carly Fiorina's High-Stakes Battle for the Soul of Hewlett-Packard* (Hoboken, NJ: John Wiley & Sons, 2003) and George Anders, *Perfect Enough: Carly Fiorina and the Reinvention of Hewlett-Packard* (New York: Penguin, 2004).

[7] "Hewlett-Packard Company Board of Directors Technology Committee Charter," http://www.hp.com/hpinfo/investor/technology.pdf.

[8] James B. Stewart, "The Kona Files," *The New Yorker* (February 19 and 26, 2007): 155.

[9] "Dunn and Dumber" (editorial), *Wall Street Journal* (September 28, 2006): A16. The Sarbanes-Oxley Act, also known as the Public Company Accounting Reform and Investor Protection Act of 2002, set strict new standards for public companies, including rules governing the structure, operation, and performance of their boards.

e-mail from HP's press office, saying that the *Wall Street Journal* was planning to run a story about an off-site strategic planning meeting of the board that had taken place several days earlier. The reporter had apparently talked with several directors about the board's discussions. Did Fiorina wish to comment?

> [FIORINA:] It is hard to convey how violated I felt. Until a Board makes a decision, its deliberations are confidential . . . Trust is a business imperative. No Board or management team can operate effectively without it . . . I sent an e-mail message to the Board. I informed them of the leak. I said this was completely unacceptable behavior by a Board member. I convened a conference call for Saturday morning. I was as cold as ice during the call. I said the Board could not operate in this way and I would not . . . Jay [Keyworth], Dick [Hackborn] and Tom [Perkins] all acknowledged that the reporter had contacted them. They all denied they had spoken with her.[10]

10   On Monday morning, the *Wall Street Journal* ran an article on page A1.

> Directors of Hewlett-Packard Co., unhappy with the uneven performance of the giant printer and computer maker, are considering a reorganization that would distribute some key day-to-day responsibilities of Chairman and Chief Executive Carly Fiorina among other executives, said people familiar with the situation. At its annual planning meeting between Jan. 12 and Jan. 15, HP's Board discussed giving three senior executives more authority and autonomy over key operating units, according to people familiar with the matter . . . The Board's concerns, according to these people, include the mediocre performance of the PC business, which ekes out thin profits, and the perception that HP holds weak market positions against IBM and Dell . . . (Pui-Wing Tam, "Hewlett-Packard Considers a Reorganization; Management Move Stems from Performance Concerns; Helping Fiorina 'Succeed,'" *Wall Street Journal*, January 24, 2005.)

11   The board agreed to ask the company's outside counsel to conduct an investigation of possible leaks. Over the next several days, the attorney interviewed all members of the board. He reported his results to the board in a conference call on January 27.

> [FIORINA:] [The attorney] informed us that two, possibly three, Board members had leaked confidential Board conversations. His report named only one member, because only Tom Perkins was honest enough to admit that he'd spoken to the press, although he was adamant that he had been a "second source." Although I appreciated Tom's candor, I was deeply disturbed when no one else spoke up. As the call progressed, all but one Board member [Keyworth] asked questions or made comments . . .[11]

> [FIORINA:] Everyone on that call knew that both Tom and Jay were the sources. They were allies. They were the ones pushing for the reorganization described in the article. I was clear and unequivocal that this was unacceptable behavior. They didn't like that.[12]

12   The next meeting of the board was held on February 7 at the Chicago Airport, an off-site location chosen to avoid further press speculation. After some brief preliminaries, Dunn asked Fiorina if she had anything to say. Fiorina spoke to the group about her views on strategy and other matters. Dunn then asked her to leave the room. When Fiorina was called back three hours later, Dunn and Robert Knowling informed her she had been fired. Explaining the decision to the press afterwards, Dunn praised Fiorina for doing an "outstanding" job, but stated that "a new set of capabilities is called for."[13] (Fiorina herself wrote in her memoir

---

[10] Carly Fiorina, *Tough Choices: A Memoir* (New York: Penguin, 2006), 290–92.

[11] Ibid., 293.

[12] Quoted in Stewart, op. cit., 155.

[13] "Fallen Star, HP's Board Ousts Fiorina as CEO," *Wall Street Journal* (February 10, 2005): A1.

that the board "did not explain their decision or their reasoning."[14]) At their meeting, the board had also decided to name Dunn non-executive chairman and Robert Wayman, HP's chief financial officer, as interim chief executive while they conducted a search for a new CEO.

"SOMETHING HAD TO BE DONE"

[DUNN:] Not surprisingly, given [the] breakdown of boardroom sanctity and continued disclosures of Board-level information making their way into print over the ensuing week, many directors expressed to me their strong opinion that something had to be done to determine their source and bring them to an end. In fact, the majority of directors told me during my first few weeks as Chairman that, next to leading the board's CEO search, coming to grips with HP's famously leaky Board should be my top priority.[15]

13   Dunn thought that a vigorous leak investigation was imperative.

[DUNN:] The most fundamental duties of a director—the duties of deliberation and candor—rely entirely upon the absolute trust that each director must have in one another's confidentiality. This is true for trivial as well as important matters, because even trivial information that finds its way from the boardroom to the press corrodes trust among directors . . . The most sensitive aspects of a company's business come before its Board: strategy; executive succession; acquisitions; business plans; product development; and key supplier relations. That is exactly the type of information a company's competitors and those who trade in its stock would love to have before that information becomes public. Boards have an unquestionable obligation to take appropriate steps to prevent this happening.[16]

14   Dunn sought the advice of Wayman, who referred her to HP's chief of global security. He, in turn, referred her to Ron DeLia, whose firm, Security Outsourcing Solutions (SOS), based in Massachusetts, had done contract investigative work for HP for several years. Dunn later referred to DeLia's firm as a "captive subsidiary."[17] In April, Dunn and DeLia exchanged several phone calls and e-mails, putting in motion an investigation to identify the source of the leaks.[18] Dunn proposed to refer to the investigation by the code name Project Kona, after the location of her vacation home in Hawaii. By this time, the focus of the investigation had expanded to include several other journalists who had published articles in *BusinessWeek* and the *New York Times*. These articles had included information that had possibly been leaked following a board meeting in March, at which the board had discussed the selection of Mark Hurd as Fiorina's successor.

15   DeLia subcontracted part of the investigative work for Project Kona to the Action Research Group (ARG) of Melbourne, Florida. DeLia had known and worked with ARG for more two decades and had often used the firm to obtain phone and fax records for persons of interest. ARG, in turn, sometimes subcontracted work to other individuals. In

---

[14] Fiorina, op. cit., 302.

[15] Patricia C. Dunn, "My Role in the Hewlett-Packard Leak Investigation," written testimony provided to the Sub-Committee on Investigations of the House Energy and Commerce Committee, p. 2.

[16] Ibid, 3–4.

[17] "Interviews of Ron DeLia—DRAFT," August 21, 2006, by attorneys conducting an investigation of the investigation, Hearing Documents, p. 630; Dunn, "My Role," p. 9. DeLia's background is further described in "HP Investigator Has Contentious Past; Forays Into Other Ventures Have Sparked Disputes Over Business, Finance," *Wall Street Journal* (September 14, 2006): A18.

[18] DeLia to Dunn, e-mail, April 19, 2005, Hearing Documents, p. 237.

addition to analyzing phone records, DeLia reviewed articles written by the journalists and researched patterns of "potential affiliation" among the journalists and HP directors. On June 14, Security Outsourcing Solutions delivered its preliminary findings to Dunn. The report described the firm's methods, and indicated it had not found the source of the leaks. Although the investigation had not succeeded, Dunn was hopeful that the investigation itself had had a dampening effect.

> [DUNN:] By this time [August, 2005], no significant leaks from the boardroom had occurred for several months, and I hoped that simply the knowledge of an investigation had brought them to a halt.[19]

A NEW "MAJOR LEAK"

16   From January 19 to 21, 2006, the board met again for its annual off-site strategic planning meeting. Soon after, Dunn received an e-mail from the head of HP's public relations department, saying there had been a "major leak." The article in question had appeared on *CNET,* an online technology publication.

> Hewlett-Packard executives are mulling plans to improve over the next eighteen months the technology the company uses to manage its direct sales, while it continues with commercial printing efforts and acquisitions of software companies.
>
> . . . HP CEO Mark Hurd, the company's board of directors and senior executives gathered at the computer giant's annual management retreat to discuss long-term strategies . . .
>
> According to the source, HP is considering making more acquisitions in the infrastructure software arena. Those acquisitions would include security software companies, storage software makers and software companies that serve the blade server market . . . (Dawn Kawamoto and Tom Krazit, "HP Outlines Long-Term Strategy," *CNET,* January 23, 2006.)

17   Dunn circulated the *CNET* article to the board. To Perkins, she sent an e-mail:

> Tom, this will disturb you as much as it disturbs me. For our discussion. Break out the lie detectors. Regards, Pattie.[20]

18   Perkins responded:

> This is incredible! I can't believe that this has happened again. But, in reading it, I don't think it damages the company too much—it's just that the news should come from us when we want it to, and not when it is leaked. I doubt if this came from a board member. Frankly, I don't think a board member would have remembered this much detail . . . I think Mark [Hurd] must put the fear of God (i.e. Mark Hurd) . . . to stop this.[21]

19   This time, Dunn consulted Ann Baskins, HP's general counsel. Baskins recommended that the investigation be turned over to Kevin Hunsaker, a senior attorney in HP's legal department who had responsibility for overseeing investigations into violations of standards of business conduct, including employee wrongdoing.[22]

---

[19] Dunn, "My Role," 15.

[20] Stewart, op. cit., 152.

[21] Ibid., 154. Perkins apparently provided these e-mails to Stewart, who does not give their exact dates.

[22] Susan Beck, "Where Will the Troubles End for Sonsini and HP?" *Law.com,* December 6, 2006, at http://www.law.com

"ALL INVESTIGATIVE ALTERNATIVES"

20 On Monday, January 23—the day the article appeared—Hunsaker assembled a team to carry out the second leak investigation, which became known as Kona II. (Exhibit C shows the composition of the investigative team.)

21 The Kona II team went to work immediately. They assigned undercover operatives to Keyworth (whom they suspected from the beginning), following him to Boulder, Colorado, from January 30 to February 1, where he was giving a lecture at the University of Colorado. Surveillance teams later followed Keyworth's wife and also Dawn Kawamoto, the *CNET* journalist. These activities turned up nothing of relevance—the operatives observed Mrs. Keyworth playing bingo at a local community center and Kawamoto picking up her child after school.

22 Fred Adler, a member of HP's IT security team, examined the company's internal telephone and Internet records for evidence of contact with Kawamoto and her associates at *CNET*. This effort turned up nothing other than some routine contacts between *CNET* and HP's public relations department.

23 The Kona II team also came up with a plan to open a dialogue with Kawamoto, impersonating a fictional executive, "Jacob," with some purported inside information. On Wednesday, February 1, the team sent Kawamoto a message from a hotmail account that could not be traced to HP, offering "some information that I would be interested in passing along." Kawamoto responded, suggesting that Jacob call her at her office.

24 The following day, Thursday, February 2, the team provided an initial briefing to Dunn in HP's Palo Alto offices. The presentation slides reported that the team was considering "all investigative alternatives." It also noted, "While time is of the essence, the investigation must be comprehensive, accurate, and in compliance with all laws and accepted investigative principles."[23]

[DUNN to HUNSAKER, February 3, 2006:] Kevin, I came away with a good sense of what you and the team are doing, and encouraged that this effort is on the right track. As discussed, this is an unusually sensitive matter and we need to tap into the necessary expertise wherever it resides. I will count on you and the team to continue to do so.

EXHIBIT C **Project Kona II Investigation Team**

Kevin Hunsaker: Attorney, HP Legal Department, Global Standards of Business Conduct Team
Jim Fairbaugh: Director of Global Security, Real Estate and Workplace Services
Kevin Huska: Manager, Global Employee Protection Program
Anthony R. Gentilucci: Manager, Global Security Investigations
Vince Nye: Senior Investigator, Global Security Investigations
Tim O'Neill: Manager, IT Security Investigations
Fred Adler: Information Security Investigator, IT Security Investigations
Denis Lynch: HP Global Security, Global Employee Protection Program
Ron DeLia: Security Outsourcing Solutions [external]
Other security consulting firms [external]

Note: This list includes "individuals who participated in or were otherwise connected with the Kona II investigation."

[23] "Project Kona II," presentation slides, Hearings Documents, 315.

"SUBJECT: PHONE RECORDS"

25 As the team in California proceeded with their work, DeLia—working from Massachusetts—once again mobilized the Action Research Group. He instructed the Florida investigators to obtain the home phone, office phone, cell phone, and fax records of Kawamoto, as well as those of seven current and former board members (including Keyworth and Perkins), two HP employees, eight other journalists, and in some cases, those of their family members. ARG quickly began producing results, sending DeLia detailed logs of phone records, showing numbers called and the time and duration of the calls.

> [HUNSAKER to GENTILUCCI, January 30, 2006. Subject: Phone Records:] Hi Tony, How does Ron [DeLia] get cell and home phone records? Is it all above board?
>
> [GENTILUCCI:] The methodology used is social engineering. He has investigators call operators under some ruse, to obtain the cell phone records over the phone. It's verbally communicated to the investigator, who has to write it down. In essence the Operator shouldn't give it out, and that person is liable in some sense. Ron can describe the operation obviously better, as well as the fact that this technique since he, and others, have been using it, has not been challenged. I think it's on the edge, but above board. We use pretext interviews on a number of investigations to extract information and/or make covert purchases of stolen property, in a sense, all undercover operations.
>
> [HUNSAKER:] I shouldn't have asked. . . . [ellipses in original]

26 DeLia later told attorneys hired by HP to investigate the Kona II activities that he subscribed to proprietary databases, available only to licensed investigators and law enforcement officials, which provided Social Security numbers along with other information about individuals. The interview summary stated:

> DeLia supplied ARG with Social Security Numbers for all subjects of pretexting. DeLia thought that ARG used the last four digits of the numbers as required.

27 Perkins later asked AT&T, his phone service provider, whether or not his phone records had been pretexted during this period. AT&T responded:

> [T]he third-party pretexter who got details about Perkins's local home-telephone usage was able to provide the last four digits of Perkins's Social Security number and that was sufficient identification for AT&T. The impersonator convinced an AT&T customer-service representative to send the details electronically to an e-mail account at yahoo.com that on its face had nothing to do with Perkins.[24]

28 By February 10, DeLia's operatives had obtained information for more than 240 telephone, cell phone, and fax numbers.

"A KEY PIECE OF THE PUZZLE"

29 On Monday evening, February 6, DeLia provided the team with an apparently critical piece of evidence: telephone logs supplied by his investigator that showed several calls from Kawamoto to Keyworth's home shortly before her article came out. Even though it was after hours, some members of the team were apparently checking their e-mails and seemed immediately to recognize the information's importance.

---

[24] David A. Kaplan, "Intrigue in High Places," *Newsweek* (September 18, 2006), paraphrasing a letter from AT&T to Perkins and provided by Perkins to the SEC and to *Newsweek*.

[GENTILUCCI to HUNSAKER, DeLIA, NYE, and ADLER, 9:33 p.m.:] . . . appears to be a "key" piece of the puzzle, "worth" a lot of weight in this case. Sorry, I couldn't help myself. Lets keep on moving forward with the plan. Good work team.

[HUNSAKER to DeLIA, GENTILUCCI, NYE, and ADLER, 9:36 p.m.:] Do we have the outbound calls from Keyworth's home from that date, so we can confirm that he and/or his wife . . . were at home? . . . Do you know what time of day the call went from Kawamoto to the Keyworth residence? . . . I'm starting to get excited . . .

30   The next morning, a junior member of the investigation team, Vince Nye, contacted two of his superiors.

[NYE to GENTILUCCI, cc to HUNSAKER, February 7, 2006, 9:32 a.m.:] Tony: I have serious reservations about what we are doing. As I understand Ron's methodology in obtaining the phone record information it leaves me with the opinion that it is very unethical at the least and probably illegal. If it is not totally illegal, then it is leaving HP in a position that could damage our reputation or worse. I am requesting that we cease this phone number gathering method immediately and discount any of its information. I think we need to re-focus our strategy and proceed on the high ground course.

31   He also wrote Fred Adler, a fellow investigator.

[NYE to ADLER, February 7, 2006, 1:30 p.m.:] Fred: This information is too detailed to obtain via voice over the phone by a pretense operative . . .

32   He wrote again a few minutes later.

[NYE to ADLER, February 7, 2006, 1:46 p.m.:] Its clear from the earlier call, that this is "Don't ask Don't tell" with regard to Ron's role . . . Kevin Thinks . . . He doesn't want to go make sure she knows . . . This is the guy who is suppose to keep us above the board!!!!!!!

[ADLER to NYE, February 7, 2006, 2:42 p.m.:] Agreed, I am VERY concerned about the legality of this information.[25]

"IN COMPLIANCE WITH THE LAW"

33   Sometime that day the investigation team met to review their progress. Adler later testified before Congress:

[ADLER:] [A]t that meeting . . . both myself and Mr. Nye . . . started questioning Mr. Gentilucci and Mr. DeLia and Mr. Hunsaker about the pretext calling and how the information was being obtained and whether it was in compliance with the law.

34   Hunsaker apparently followed up on his team members' concerns about the legality of the methods used by DeLia's contractors, because he received the following e-mail from DeLia:

[DeLIA to HUNSAKER, February 7, 2006, 2:12 p.m.:] Kevin: I sent an email to my source in FL and asked them if there were any state laws prohibiting pretexting telephone companies for call records. Following is their response. We are comfortable there are no Federal laws prohibiting the practice. Note: The Federal Trade Commission has jurisdiction. The firm has been in business for over 20 years and is properly licensed in FL and other states. I have been utilizing their services for approximately 8 to 10 years. Ron. "As of right now there are no laws against pretexting. We are on top of everything going on regarding this issue and if any law were to pass we will be the first to let you know." [underlining in original]

---

[25] From the context, the "she" in Nye's e-mail appears to be Ann Baskins.

35   An attorney conducting an internal probe for HP later reported on an interview with Hunsaker about his research on the legality of pretexting:

> . . . after Nye and Adler expressed concern about the legality of pretexting . . . [Hunsaker] asked DeLia . . . to confirm the method's legality with the Florida investigators . . . Asked about the scope of his [own] research, Hunsaker said he did about an hour's worth of online research on the legality of pretexting . . .

36   Ann Baskins, HP's general counsel, later recalled that during a meeting with Hunsaker in or around early March she had specifically asked him to consult a legal expert to confirm the legality of pretexting. Hunsaker delegated this task to Gentilucci, who contacted an attorney he knew in Boston. This attorney advised the team that pretexting of financial institutions was prohibited by statute, but that no law specifically banned the pretexting of phone records.

37   Despite the apparent break in the case, the team moved forward with the "Jacob" operation. On February 9, the group sent another e-mail to Kawamoto with some genuine inside information, after seeking approval for this disclosure from Mark Hurd. A tracking device was attached to the e-mail in the hope that Kawamoto would forward it to her source for confirmation, thus revealing his or her identity. DeLia made a pretext call to confirm that Kawamoto was in her office, and the group posted a surveillance team to watch her movements. "This is like waiting for the Apollo 13 spacecraft to emerge from the dark side of the moon," Gentilucci e-mailed the team. *CNET's* firewall may have blocked the message; in any case, Kawamoto never responded or forwarded it.

"THE OVERWHELMING WEIGHT OF EVIDENCE"

38   On March 10, 2006, Hunsaker issued an eighteen-page draft report of the investigation, addressed to Dunn, Hurd, and Baskins. The executive summary concluded that the investigation had likely found the source of the leaks:

> [T]he overwhelming weight of evidence reviewed by the Investigation Team indicates that the source of the leak is HP Board member George Keyworth II. Specifically, the content of each of the articles citing a "source" written by Kawamoto in the past 4 years, the numerous connections made by the Investigation Team tying Keyworth to the leaks, and the telephonic contact between Kawamoto and Keyworth in January and February of 2006, all clearly identify and establish Keyworth as the only feasible source of the leaks.

39   The report concluded by posing—but not answering—the question "whether Keyworth should be interviewed in conjunction with the investigation" and, if so, by whom and to what purpose.

40   The following week, HP's directors and many top executives gathered in Los Angeles for the annual shareholders meeting. On the evening of March 18, Hurd, Dunn, and Baskins were in the lounge of the Park Hyatt Hotel when they noticed Keyworth, the board member they suspected, sitting at the bar. Hurd told his companions, "I'll take care of this."[26]

> [DUNN:] Mr. Hurd . . . has related many times to me and to others that he tried in every way he could to get Mr. Keyworth to come forward and admit his culpability. Ms. Baskins and I were sitting near them during this meeting, which occurred over cocktails in the hotel lobby, and I could see that Mr. Hurd was intensely engaged with Mr. Keyworth. Mr. Hurd subsequently described to me . . . that, although he gave Mr. Keyworth several chances to come forward, Mr. Keyworth declined to acknowledge his culpability.[27]

[26] Stewart, op. cit., 162.
[27] Dunn, "My Role," 21.

"BUT ONE BOARD SEAT FROM WHICH TO RESIGN"

41   On May 18, the board gathered in Palo Alto for its regular meeting. Ten directors were present. Immediately prior to the meeting, Robert Ryan, chairman of the audit committee, met with Keyworth privately to inform him about the findings of the investigation.

> [DUNN:] Mr. Ryan reported [to Hurd, Dunn, Baskins, and HP's outside counsel] after his interview with Mr. Keyworth that Mr. Keyworth's immediate response to hearing the investigation's results was to admit he was the leaker, followed by the question, "Why didn't you just ask me?" All of us were flummoxed by this response, as it was clear to all of us that for the prior 15 months Mr. Keyworth could have come forward at any time to acknowledge his culpability.[28]

42   According to the minutes of the May 18 meeting, the first item on the agenda was the findings of the leak investigation. Dunn reported that the investigation had been conclusive and then turned to Ryan, who summarized the report for the board and stated that Keyworth had been identified as the leaker and had, that morning, acknowledged being the source for the *CNET* article. After some further discussion, Keyworth addressed the group. The minutes of the meeting summarized his statement:

> [Keyworth] described the circumstances under which he became acquainted with Dawn Kawamoto, explaining that he initially established contact with Kawamoto at the request of former CEO Carly Fiorina, who asked Keyworth to speak with certain members of the media in support of the Compaq merger. He added that Kawamoto emerged as an influential reporter who reported favorably on HP. He said that his intent in describing the January Board meeting to Kawamoto was to help the Company and in particular to convey that HP and its CEO were addressing key growth opportunities and other important strategies rather than narrowly focused on cost-cutting efforts. Dr. Keyworth assured the Board that he had not been a source for other stories by different reporters, including articles written by Pui-Wing Tam of the Wall Street Journal. He indicated that he would not make unauthorized disclosures to the media in the future.

43   Keyworth then left the room. After a discussion that lasted about ninety minutes, the board voted by secret ballot, six to three, to ask for Keyworth's resignation. Dunn later recalled this discussion and its aftermath:

> [DUNN:] Mr. Perkins became very agitated when it became clear that a majority of the Board did not think Mr. Keyworth had handled his response to the Board appropriately and thus were strongly leaning toward asking for his resignation. A secret ballot, suggested by another director, was taken, in which a strong majority of the Board voted to ask Mr. Keyworth to resign, which later in the meeting he refused to do. At that point Mr. Perkins erupted in great anger. Mr. Perkins' anger was directed entirely at me, and centered on the "betrayal" he alleged at my not having abided by an agreement that he said we had to cover-up the name of the leaker. I had little opportunity to respond to this outburst except to say, "Tom, we had no such agreement." . . . At no point during Mr. Perkins' outburst did he make any statements whatsoever about the leak investigation—including its justification and methods. Mr. Perkins told the Board he resigned and he left the room, at which point a director put a motion on the table to accept his resignation, which was then seconded and carried unanimously.[29]

44   Several days later, Perkins wrote a confidential memo to the members of the board of the News Corporation, on which he served, to explain his actions, in which he stated:

---

[28] Dunn, "My Role," 23.
[29] Dunn, "My Role," 24–25.

I was very angry at the time, but now that over a week has passed, I think that I did the right thing, and to paraphrase the Revolutionary War hero, Nathan Hale ("I regret that I have but one life to give to my country"), I regret that I have but one HP Board seat from which to resign.

45   On May 22, HP filed a Form 8-K with the SEC reporting Perkins' resignation, as required by law, giving no reason for his action.

"UNTOWARD AND ILLEGAL PRACTICES"

46   On July 28, Perkins wrote Baskins, with a copy to Hurd and HP's outside counsel, saying he could not accept the minutes of the May 18 board meeting as written. One of his main points was that the minutes did not convey his concerns about the legality of the leak investigation.

> An essential point, which I explicitly made, questioned the legality of the surveillance of director's communications by the Chairman's outside experts. I specifically questioned this at the time of the meeting and question it still. As written the minutes state that I concurred in the nature of the investigation—this is not true. I was under the impression that the investigation involved examining calendars, travel schedules and such. I had no idea that personal communications were involved, and had I known that this was the case I would have brought the matter (of the intrusive nature of the investigation) to the board, for full examination, well in advance of the May 18th meeting.

47   On August 16, after an exchange of correspondence with AT&T, his telephone service provider, Perkins wrote again, this time asking that HP provide a copy of his letter to the SEC.

> I have direct proof of these untoward and illegal practices. My personal phone records were "hacked."

48   Baskins wrote back, indicating that the board had decided it would not amend the minutes or the filings with the SEC noting Perkins' resignation, because they were accurate. Perkins' attorney responded, threatening to "take appropriate action."[30] Shortly thereafter, the SEC, the FBI, and the California Attorney General began investigations.

49   In early September, the story broke wide open in the media. On September 18, *Newsweek* ran a cover story, "Intrigue in High Places: To Catch a Leaker, Hewlett-Packard's Chairwoman Spied on the Home-Phone Records of Its Board of Directors." The author, who was writing a book about Perkins' yacht, had interviewed Perkins extensively for the piece. Articles in *BusinessWeek,* the *Wall Street Journal,* and other leading publications also appeared around this time, and congressional staffers contacted the company about a possible House of Representatives inquiry.

"THE FINAL STORY"

50   When facing members of Congress, the press, and the public, only four of the potential witnesses called to the hearing—Dunn, Adler, Hurd, and HP's outside counsel—agreed to testify. The others—Baskins, Gentilucci, Hunsaker, DeLia, and various investigators from Florida, Colorado, Texas, and Georgia—all pleaded their Fifth Amendment rights against self-incrimination.

[30] Stewart, op cit., 165.

51   Dunn vigorously defended her actions and stated, "I do not take personal responsibility for what happened."

> [DUNN:] I am neither a lawyer nor an investigator, and in this matter, I relied on the expertise of people in whom I had full confidence based upon their positions with the company and my years of experience working with them. I deeply regret that so many people, including me, were badly let down by this reliance . . .

52   In her written testimony, she offered this reflection:

> When the final story is written on what happened at HP, I believe that its roots will be understood as emanating from a clash between the old and the new cultures of the Boardroom, driven importantly by Sarbanes-Oxley and related regulatory changes. The clash is perhaps particularly poignant in Silicon Valley, where the culture of innovation, freedom of maneuver and creativity are seen as essential to value creation.[31]

53   The final witness of the day was Mark Hurd, HP's CEO. He testified:

> HP is a company that has consistently earned recognition for our adherence to standards of ethics, privacy and corporate responsibility, and yet these practices that we have taken such pride in have recently been violated by people inside the company and by people outside the company with whom we contracted. This committee rightfully wonders what happened.
>
> What began as a proper and serious inquiry into leaks to the press of sensitive company information became a rogue investigation that violated our own principles and values. There is no excuse for this aberration. It happened; it will never happen again . . .
>
> The question remains: how did such abuse of privacy occur in a company renowned for its commitment to privacy? It is an age-old story. The ends came to justify the means. The investigation team became so focused on finding the source of the leaks that they lost sight of the values that this company has always represented.

---

[31] Dunn, "My Role," 29.

Case 25

Mattel's China Experience: *A Crisis in Toyland*

Mary B. Teagarden

Mattel realized very early that they were always going to be in the crosshairs of sensitivities about child labor and product safety, and they knew they had to really play it straight . . . Mattel was in China before China was cool, and they learned to do business there in a good way. They understood the importance of protecting their brand, and they invested.[1]

M. Eric Johnson
Professor, Dartmouth

1   Bob Eckert, Mattel's CEO, was concerned but not alarmed when Jim Walter, senior vice president of worldwide quality assurance, walked into his office on Friday, July 13, 2007, and announced, "We have an issue."[2] The Mattel executive had received confirmation that one of their European customers, Auchan, had found problems in a routine audit. The paint on the Sarge die-cast toy cars they produced in China contained lead levels in excess of U.S. federal toy safety regulations.[3] Mattel, a company known as an industry leader in corporate responsibility, was being pulled into a recall vortex that had seen a variety of products produced in and exported from China, including dog food, toothpaste, tires, and seafood, recalled in recent weeks. The Sarge recall would be the tip of the iceberg in which Mattel would face a major crisis. In the next several months, Mattel would recall 967,000 Chinese-made toys, which featured characters such as Batman, Sarge, Polly Pockets, and various Barbie accessory toys, for violation of lead safety standards or magnets detaching. Bob and his team moved into action to implement the recall process for Sarge cars and other toys that might contain excess levels of lead. More importantly, they had to identify an approach to the recalls that would protect the valuable Mattel brand and their sterling corporate reputation while not undermining their intent to be the "World's Premier Toy Brand—Today and Tomorrow."[4]

THE TOY INDUSTRY

2   Toys are serious business. The global toy market was estimated to be a $71 billion business in 2007, an increase of about six percent over the previous year.[5] North America was the largest regional market with about $24 billion in sales, or 36 percent of the global market.

[1] David Barboza and Louise Story, "Toymaking in China, Mattel's Way," *The New York Times*, July 26. 2007.

[2] http:cnnmoney.printthis.clickabilty.com/pt/cpt?action+cpt?action=cpt&title+Mattel+CEO+Bob+Eckert.

[3] Mattel communication to the Subcommittee on Commerce, Trade and Consumer Protection, September 5, 2007.

[4] mattel.com (http://www.mattel.com/about_us/default.asp).

[5] http://www.toy-icti.org/resources/wtf_2006_files/frame.htm.

EXHIBIT 1
2007 U.S. Toy Sales by Segment

Source: www.RetailingToday.com, June 9, 2008.

Infant and Preschool Toys	14.0%
Outdoor and Sports Toys	12.2%
Arts and Crafts	11.8%
Dolls	11.3%
Games and Puzzles	10.9%
Vehicles	10.4%
Action Figures and Accessories	6.3%
Plush Toys	5.9%
Youth Electronics	6.3%
Building Sets	3.2%
All Other Toys	9.5%

However, annual sales in the North American market were slower than in other global markets, about one percent per year. Europe was the next largest regional market with about $19 billion in sales, or 28 percent of the global market. The European market was growing at about five percent per year. The Asian region followed with slightly more than $16 billion in sales, or 25 percent of the global market. Asia was a bright spot for the industry, and sales were forecasted to grow at 25 percent per year, given the economic growth and growing middle class in both China and India. Latin America represented about seven percent of the global market and had sales of $4.5 billion per year. Latin America was also forecasted to have aggressive growth in countries like Brazil and Mexico, given the growth of the middle class and the large number of children.

3   The United States had about two percent of the world's children, yet they purchased about half of the world's toys. The dollars spent in the toy industry in the United States dipped about two percent in 2007 to $22.1 billion in sales.[6] Segments like action figures and accessories showed strong growth with sales increasing eight percent to $1.4 billion, while sales of dolls, at $2.5 billion, decreased by eight percent. Other segments and industry share are listed in Exhibit 1.

4   In this dynamic industry, children's preferences were shifting from traditional toys like dolls, games, and puzzles to movies, electronics, and video games. The percentage of children under 12, the primary toy industry target customer segment, was the smallest it had been in 20 years, and, to make matters worse, children were playing with toys for fewer years than their parents did.[7] Anita Frazier, a toy industry researcher observed, "Young kids really are the sweet spot for the toy industry, because they're not yet distracted by other entertainment choices as older kids might be."[8] The toy industry had evolved from one with simple, physical toys that emulated adult life (e.g., Tinker Toys, Lincoln Logs, Barbie) to one based on hardware and software technology platforms, and rich, interactive content which supported fantasy (e.g., Lego Mindstorms NXT, X-Box, Nintendo Wii).[9]

5   The industry had about 900 companies engaged in the manufacture of toys. The top 50 companies controlled 75 percent of the market. Mattel and Hasbro dominated with

[6] www.RetailingToday.com, June 9, 2008.
[7] Eric Clark, *The Real Toy Story*, 2007.
[8] ___, "U.S. Consumers Buying More Toys," *SCTWeek,* 13 (24), 2008, p. 2.
[9] Steve Babitch, Enric Gili Fort, Andy Kim, Pam Nyberg, and Albert Wang, "The Future of Play," Institute of Design, Illinois Institute of Technology, 2006.

EXHIBIT 2   Global Toy Manufacturers Ranked by Sales

Manufacturer	2007 Revenue	Headquarter Location
Mattel	$5,970.1 m	United States
Hasbro	$3,837.6 m	United States
Namco Bandai	$3,833.8 m	Japan
LEGO	$1,383.9 m	Denmark
Sammy Corporation	N/A	Japan
Sanrio	$940 m	Japan
JAKKS Pacific	$857.1 m	United States
LeapFrog	$442.3 m	United States
RC2	$489 m	United States
Ty	N/A	United States

Source: http://premium.hoovers.com.ezproxy.t-bird.edu/subscribe/ind/overview.xhtml?HICID=1207.

control of more than one-third of the toy market in the United States, and the majority of the world's largest competitors were headquartered in the United States. Mattel's most direct competitors were Hasbro, JAKKS Pacific, and LeapFrog. Exhibit 2 shows the top ten global toy manufacturers ranked by sales.

6   Competition in the toy industry intensified as a relentless focus on profit and brand redefined an industry once known for creativity. Industry giants like Mattel and Hasbro did not have to depend on product innovation to compete. Rather, they depended on television shows and movies and the creation of new toys, based on brands they had already developed or acquired, by doing such things as putting electronics in Playmobil characters, for example. These industry giants also exploited economies of scale and offshore manufacturing. Smaller industry competitors had to rely on innovation more than the big competitors with the hope of developing a successful breakthrough, like the Trivial Pursuit board game or Beanie Babies.[10] A big hit for the small players made the difference between struggle and success.

7   There was a symbiotic relationship between the toy and the entertainment industries. Industry expert Eric Clark contended that, "Toys and the entertainment industry have become two sides of the same coin—children's television programs and some movies exist only because of product tie-in and are structured to maximize sales of those products."[11] Indeed, many of the toys recalled in 2007 were based on Sesame and Disney characters. Increasingly, the toy industry was integrating into the entertainment business. Clark observed that, increasingly, toy companies viewed "their toys as entertainment or lifestyle properties—the books, TV series, and movies are not purely to sell more toys, but rather to enhance and reinforce the brand."[12]

8   Five large retailers—Wal-Mart, Target, Toys"R"Us, Kmart, and KB Toys—sold more than half of all toys in the United States.[13] Three retailers—Wal-Mart, Toys "R"Us, and Target—accounted for 43 percent of Mattel's consolidated worldwide sales in 2007. Wal-Mart,

[10] Clark, *The Real Toy Story*.
[11] Ibid.
[12] Ibid.
[13] U.S. Department of Commerce Industry Outlook: Dolls, Toys, Games, and Children's Vehicles, NAICS Code 33993.

the world's largest retailer and largest toy retailer, sold about 20 percent of Mattel's toys, Toys "R"Us sold about 14 percent, and Target sold about nine percent. These large retailers also sold competitors' toys and their own private-brand toys that they sourced directly, often from China.

TOY PRODUCTION IN CHINA

9   Companies seeking ever-lower prices have benefited from what *BusinessWeek* called the "China price," a price that was 30 to 50 percent cheaper than what it would cost a company to make the equivalent product in the U.S.[14] Companies manufacturing in China were able to produce at the "China price" for a variety of reasons, including lower business costs: labor, facilities, plant and equipment, and raw materials were all cheaper in part because of differences in absolute costs of labor, for example, and differences in regulatory oversight between China and many other countries, including the U.S. For example, the U.S banned lead in toys in 1978, whereas China only signed an agreement to do so in September of 2007.[15] Nevertheless, Chinese officials estimated that 50 percent of their exported products did not comply with Chinese law.[16] At the same time that the Chinese government agreed to ban lead, it also agreed to increase inspections and meet more regularly on export-related issues.[17] Skeptics believed that this was a public relations ploy to protect the reputation of "China, Inc." Analysts, while noting the incredible economic growth in China, identified the parallel pressure on the physical, technical, and human resource infrastructure that this growth had brought.[18]

10   Manufacturing in China is not going away. In 2007, China's manufacturing sector ranked fourth in the world after the U.S., Japan, and Germany. China's exports to the United States had grown by approximately 1,600 percent over the previous 15 years. According to the U.S.–China Business Council, the dollar value of imports from China was US$287.8 billion in total, and toys, games, and apparel as industrial segments represented 40.8 percent of this volume.[19] The North American toy industry was a US$24 billion dollar industry, and 80 percent of these toys were manufactured in China through company-owned plants and an extensive network of contractor and supplier relationships.[20] China toy imports to the United States accounted for 86 percent of total toy imports in 2006. This was up from 41 percent 14 years earlier. The rise in toy imports from China came at the expense of other toy-exporting countries like Mexico, Japan, Taiwan, and Hong Kong.

11   Toys were one of the first consumer products to be produced in China in significant volume, and Mattel was a pioneer in taking the manufacture of toys offshore. The importance of China in this industry could not be underestimated. Most of the toys produced in the world were produced in China, and most of these were produced in second- and third-tier and smaller cities surrounding Guangzhou and outside of Shanghai or Hong Kong. The supply networks for toys and their components were extensive, increasingly complex, and sometimes underscrutinized by the companies who branded and imported the toys. Mattel's

[14] Pete Engardio and Dexter Roberts, "The China Price," *BusinessWeek*, December 6, 2004.

[15] www.msnbc.msn.com/id/20726149/.

[16] http://energycommerce.house.gov/cmte_mtgs/110-ctcp-hrg.092007.Teagarden-testimony.pdf.

[17] Ibid.

[18] Paul Beamish, "The High Cost of Cheap Chinese Labor," *Harvard Business Review*, 2006.

[19] www.uschina.org/statistics/tradetable.html.

[20] Renae Merle, "Recalls of Toys Pressure Agency: CPSC Resources Called Inadequate," WashingtonPost.com, August 3, 2007.

network exemplified this complexity with more than 3,000 partners in China alone.[21] By moving their manufacturing overseas, toy companies shifted their focus to research and development, product design, marketing, and other core business activities of strategic importance.

12   Companies knew how to take advantage of the benefits of manufacturing in China while maintaining product quality and obeying U.S. laws for the products they imported. Many companies produced world-class quality products that were high-tech and difficult and complex to manufacture in Chinese plants. Companies also knew how to produce safe, quality products in China, whether in their own plants or through contracting relationships with Chinese suppliers. Indeed, Mattel, one of the high-profile companies involved in the toy recalls, had been manufacturing toys in China for 20 years. If we look at the recall statistics, Mattel had done a fairly good job of manufacturing safe toys in China. But the large number of highly visible product recalls in 2007 was eroding customer confidence in products made in China. This was a big problem for China, where the focus was to move away from simple toy assembly to high value-added manufacturing and knowledge work. The 2007 China product recall timeline is shown in Exhibit 3.

13   Given the global shift of toy manufacture to China, it was not surprising that the number of China toy recalls rose from one product category, or three percent of the total annual recall in 1988, to three product categories, or 79 percent of the total annual recall in 2006.[22] Of the 550 toy recalls by the Consumer Products Safety Commission (CPSC) since 1988, ". . . only about ten percent (or 54) of recalls were historically attributable to manufacturing defects such as poor craftsmanship, overheating of batteries, toxic paint, and inappropriate raw materials."[23] A history of the CPSC appears in Exhibit 4.

14   Lead paint on toys is a recognized danger to young children who tend to chew on toys, and thus its use in toy manufacture raises serious alarms. Exposure to this heavy metal poses a risk because even low levels of lead are dangerous for young children, as it can lead to lower IQ scores according to the Centers for Disease Control and Prevention.[24] Higher levels of lead can damage children's brains and nervous systems, slow growth, create hearing or behavior and learning problems because their growing bodies absorb more lead. Children's brains and nervous systems are more sensitive to the damaging effects of lead than are adults' brains.[25] As a result, lead use is banned or restricted in most developed countries, but the same is not true for developing countries.[26]

15   Environmental and occupational health experts found that India, China, and Malaysia still produced and sold paints with levels of lead that exceeded U.S. safety levels, even for products intended for use by children.[27] About 50 percent of the paint sold in these three countries had lead levels 30 times higher than U.S. regulations.[28] This heavy metal is used to improve the durability and color luster of paint. One of these experts, Scott Clark, commented, "There is a clear discrepancy in product safety outside the United States and in today's global economy; it would be irresponsible for us to ignore the public

[21] www.timesonline.co.uk/tol/news/world/article2259492.ece?print+yes&random=119.

[22] Hari Bapuji and Paul Beamish, "Toy Recalls: Is China Really the Problem?" Asia Pacific Foundation of Canada: Vancouver, Canada. http://www.asiapacific.ca/analysis/pubs/pdfs/2007/toyrecalls.pdf, November 2007.

[23] Ibid, p. 4.

[24] http://toys.about.com/od/healthandsafety/f/leadpoisoning.htm.

[25] http://www.epa.gov/lead/pubs/leadinfo.htm.

[26] http://www.ens-newswire.com/ens/aug2006/2006-08-24-02.asp.

[27] Ibid.

[28] Ibid.

EXHIBIT 3 **2007 Timeline of China Export Recalls**

March 15:	After consumer complaints prompted lab testing, Canada-based Menu Foods Inc. informed the FDA that it was recalling cat and dog food made with tainted wheat gluten. The recall included food sold under the Iams and Eukanuba labels.
April 30:	USDA and FDA officials said chickens on at least 30 Indiana poultry farms in February were fed remnants of pet food that was contaminated by poisoned wheat gluten imported from China. The officials said the farms had since processed the chickens, but added that the risk to humans is "very low." Officials earlier had revealed that the contaminated pet food was fed to hogs in at least six states. At least 6,000 hogs were quarantined and euthanized.
May 7:	An invoice offered evidence that two Chinese corporations, Xuzhou Anying Biologic Technology Development Co. and Binzhou Futian Biology Technology Co., were linked to tainted wheat gluten found in the recalled pet food.
May 10:	The Chinese cabinet vowed to crack down on the food industry, saying it will promote organic agriculture, beef up inspections of farms and butchers, and blacklist companies that make tainted products.
May 24:	Responding to reports that diethylene glycol was found in toothpaste made in China, the FDA announced it will block Chinese imports of toothpaste until they can be tested. The action followed reports that authorities have found the chemical in toothpaste in Panama, the Dominican Republic, and Australia.
May 30:	Beijing announced it will set up a food-recall system.
June 14:	Colgate-Palmolive Co. said counterfeit toothpaste falsely packaged as "Colgate" and possibly containing diethylene glycol was found in several discount stores in New York, New Jersey, Pennsylvania, and Maryland.
June 25:	About 450,000 Chinese-made tires sold in the U.S. were recalled after federal regulators and the U.S. tire distributor said the tires may lack an important safety feature designed to make them more durable.
June 27:	The Chinese government said it closed 180 food manufacturers found to have used industrial chemicals and additives in food products.
June 28:	The FDA announced it would detain all Chinese shipments of shrimp, catfish, basa, dace, and eel unless it is proven free of residues of illegal antibiotics and chemicals. An agency test of 89 samples from October 2006 to May 2007 showed 25 percent of the farm-raised seafood contained such residues.
June 29:	The European Union said it will follow the lead of the U.S. Food and Drug Administration, which is stepping up scrutiny of Chinese farm-raised seafood.
July 2–5:	American consumer-protection authorities recalled Chinese-made children's necklaces and earrings that were found to contain dangerously high levels of lead.
July 4:	China's quality-control watchdog said that nearly one-fifth of the products sold in China that it studied failed to meet the country's quality standards.
July 10:	Zheng Xiaoyu, the former head of China's State Food and Drug Administration, was executed for dereliction of duty and taking bribes from drug companies.
July 19:	The U.S. House Agriculture Committee agreed to require country-of-origin labels on meats beginning next year, but it softened penalties and record-keeping requirements that had concerned many food retailers and meatpackers who opposed the law.
July 20:	China said it had shut down several firms at the heart of food and drug safety scares. The country's quality supervision agency pulled the business license of Taixing Glycerin Factory, which has been accused of exporting diethylene glycol—a thickening agent used in antifreeze—and fraudulently passing it off as 99.5 percent pure glycerin. The mix of 15 percent diethylene glycol and other substances ended up in Panamanian medicines that killed at least 51 people. Also, two companies linked to melamine-tainted wheat gluten blamed for the deaths of 16 dogs and cats in North America had their licenses revoked.

EXHIBIT 3   2007 Timeline of China Export Recalls (*Continued*)

July 23:	The European Union's top product safety cop, on her first official trip to China, said she has an "ambitious" agenda and is prepared to send a tough message to the Chinese government that it needs to crack down on producers of defective goods sold in the 27-nation bloc.
July 31:	The U.S. Department of Health and Human Services sent a senior official to China to try to reach agreements aimed at improving the country's food and drug safety by the end of the year.
Aug. 2:	The U.S. Consumer Product Safety Commission said Mattel Inc.'s Fisher-Price unit will recall 967,000 toys that may contain hazardous levels of lead paint, including items featuring popular characters such as Elmo and Big Bird. The company said it would adjust second-quarter results by about $30 million to reflect the impact of the recall.
Aug. 7:	Mattel Inc. identified the Chinese factory involved in the company's recall of 1.5 million Chinese-made toys believed to contain lead paint. Mattel said the plant is Lee Der Industrial Co., located in Guangdong province.
Aug. 13:	A Chinese public security official said an owner of Lee Der Industrial Co., the toy factory at the center of a major recall by Mattel Inc. earlier this month, killed himself at his factory's warehouse in China's southern Guangdong province.
Aug. 14:	Mattel Inc. issued recalls for millions of Chinese-made toys that contain magnets that can be swallowed by children or could have lead paint. The recall involves 7.3 million play sets, including Polly Pocket dolls and Batman action figures, and 253,000 die-cast cars that contain lead paint. Also recalled were 345,000 Batman and "One Piece" action figures, 683,000 Barbie and Tanner play sets, and one million Doggie Day Care play sets.
Aug. 22:	China claims quality issues associated with imports of U.S. soybeans, and calls for the U.S. to investigate the situation. Analysts say the soybean complaint is simply a retaliatory gesture following the recent criticism of Chinese products.
Sept. 12:	U.S. and Chinese regulators move to ban the use of lead paint in toys, and promised changes to the way Chinese imports to the U.S. are scrutinized for safety compliance after public uproar surrounding product recalls.
Sept. 14:	Under immense international pressure, China's chief inspector of exported food said he is working to strengthen oversight of Chinese products. He also suggested that China's food exports had been unfairly targeted by the public furor over U.S. recalls of Chinese-made toys and animal feed.
Sept. 18:	China restricts the exportation of garlic and ginger to the U.S., ordering numerous facilities in Shandong province, a hub for the nation's agricultural exports, to stop shipping the foods until they can abide by tougher safety standards.
Sept. 21:	Mattel issued an apology to China over the recall of Chinese-made toys, saying most of the items were defective because of Mattel's design flaws rather than faulty manufacturing. The company also said it had recalled more lead-tainted Chinese toys than was justified.
Sept. 21:	U.S. regulators recalled about one million Chinese-made baby cribs, branded Simplicity and Graco, after the cribs were linked to at least two infant deaths. In both deaths, the cribs were assembled incorrectly by consumers.

Source: Adopted from *Wall Street Journal*, October 21, 2007.

health threat for the citizens [children or workers] in the offending countries, as well as the countries they do business with."[29] This health hazard has led to calls for global lead safety standards.

16   Merle A. Heinrichs, Chairman and CEO of Global Sources, an Asia-based corporation that serves as a platform for international trade connecting buyers and suppliers online,

[29] Ibid.

EXHIBIT 4   **History of the Consumer Product Safety Commission**

Toy Safety and the Consumer Product Safety Commission

Toy safety is regulated by the Consumer Product Safety Commission (CPSC) in the United States. The CPSC was authorized by Congress through the Consumer Product Safety Act of 1972. The CPSC, an independent governmental agency, was charged with "protecting the public from unreasonable risks of serious injury or death from more than 15,000 types of consumer products. . ." Deaths, injuries, and damage to property from consumer product injuries cost the United States more than $800 billion annually. The efforts of the CPSC had contributed significantly to the 30 percent decline in the rate of deaths and injuries associated with consumer products over some 30 years following its authorization, according to government reports. The CPSC reported 22 toy-related deaths and an estimated 220,500 toy-related injuries in 2006. Some potential toy hazards scrutinized by the CPSC included lead-tainted paint on toys, and other major hazards like small parts or small magnets that came loose from the toy and were swallowed.

The CPSC has many responsibilities, including the development of voluntary standards in collaboration with industry. They inform and educate consumers through media, state and local governments, private organizations, and by responding to consumer inquiries. In addition, they conduct research on potential product hazards, and obtain the recall of products or arrange for their repair. The CPSC does not certify or test products for safety prior to sale nor do they recommend the safest products or brands. The agency, with a budget of $66 million in 2006, employed 420 people who were responsible for monitoring the safety of more than 15,000 kinds of consumer products. Janell Mayo Duncan of the Consumers Union observed that the Consumer Product Safety Commission had only about 100 field investigators and compliance personnel nationwide to conduct inspections at ports, warehouses, and stores of US$24 billion worth of toys and other consumer products sold in the U.S. each day. She concluded that they needed more money and resources to perform more checks.

The CPSC relies on the voluntary compliance of companies who are required by law to report product safety hazards for products they have sold as soon as the manufacturer or importer becomes aware of the problem. The CPSC collects information from a variety of sources, including hospitals, physicians, consumer complaints, industry reports, investigations by the CPSC staff, and company self-reports. Once the CPSC is notified of a hazard, they work with the company to initiate and manage a recall.

Sources: http://www.cpsc.gov/about/about.html; Eric Lipton and David Barbosa, "As More Toys Are Recalled, Trail Ends in China," *The New York Times*, June 19, 2007.

face-to-face, and in print, observed that offshore manufacturers produce for a variety of markets, and that, "These markets, whether they are developed markets similar to Germany or the U.S., or developing markets such as India and Nigeria, will all have a variety of product standards and specifications. The importer of record is ultimately responsible to ensure that the offshore manufacturer he/she has selected, regardless of country, must understand the appropriate importing country's standards, and that the importer must take responsibility for the inspection prior to distribution."[30]

MATTEL OVERVIEW

17   California-based toy giant Mattel was founded in 1944 with a vision of capturing the post–World War II baby boom toy market. And capture they did. Founders Elliot and Ruth Handler began building Mattel's brand image in the mid-1950s by advertising on the very popular daily *Mickey Mouse Club* television program, a bold move because, at the time, toy advertising was seasonal. Mattel's iconic core product, Barbie, now pushing 50, was introduced in 1959. The company rolled out the equally iconic product, Hot Wheels, a decade later. Mattel, a true toy industry offshoring pioneer, began manufacturing toys in offshore

---

[30] Merle Heinrichs, Commentary, *Thunderbird International Business Review*, forthcoming, 2009.

locations to take advantage of lower manufacturing costs and to focus corporate resources and attention on building brand.

18   Mattel's Fisher-Price division was instrumental in developing the first toy safety standards in the industry as an extension of their focus on brand. Beginning in 1971, Fisher-Price worked with a team of experts from the American Academy of Pediatrics, the U.S. Consumer Product Safety Commission (CPSC), as well as toy industry designers and engineers, consumers, consultants, and retailers, to develop the very first voluntary toy safety standards. Eventually, these were adopted by the industry, as were Mattel's international testing standards developed to ensure compliance with safety standards. Almost 40 years later, many of the tests established by this group were still being used.[31]

19   Mattel endeavored to maintain supply network integrity as they executed an offshore manufacturing strategy in China and other locations. Roger Rambeau, a long-time Mattel employee who worked his way up from the production line to vice president of manufacturing, believed that the company was the leader in protecting the integrity of their supply network and a toy safety champion at the forefront of their industry. Rambeau cited Mattel's early voluntary collaboration with the U.S. Consumer Product Safety Commission and contributions to the development of the American Society for Testing and Materials (ASTM), an international product standards organization, as strong evidence of significant early efforts by Mattel to maintain supply network and product integrity.[32]

TROUBLE IN TOYLAND

20   In 1973, Mattel had a major change in leadership. After thirty years at the helm, Elliot and Ruth Handler left the company as Mattel's growth stalled due to operational problems in Mexico and Asia, and the SEC charged that Mattel had issued misleading financial reports. Arthur Spear, a former Revlon executive with extensive manufacturing experience, inherited a company in financial distress, characterized as ". . . the most incredible mess you have ever seen."[33]

21   In an endeavor to improve profitability and maintain consistent revenue streams, Mattel's new management team implemented a focus strategy for maximizing the value of core brands like Barbie and Hot Wheels. Mattel continued offshore manufacturing to take advantage of cost savings from labor arbitrage. By 1979, Spear had cut Mattel's debt to $20 million from $118 million, and diversified its product offering to include Intellivision, an electronic game system that was ahead of its time.[34] Spear grew Mattel's annual sales from $281 million in 1973 to $1 billion when he retired in 1986.

22   John Amerman followed Arthur Spear as chairman and CEO, and promised to slash costs and reinvigorate product design and development. Amerman, who came from Warner-Lambert Company's American Chicle division before joining Mattel in 1980, took the helm of a company that was losing money and had very little diversity in its product line, despite strong brand names like Barbie and equally strong marketing skills. He continued the practice of manufacturing the majority of Mattel's products in company-owned facilities around the world, a practice that was contrary to the industry norm of contracting manufacturing, usually to the lowest cost source.[35] In the 1990s, on Amerman's watch, Mattel came under

---

[31] http://www.mattel.com/about_us/Corp_Responsibility/CSR_FINAL.pdf.

[32] http://productglobal.typepad.com/gss/2007/07/mattel-a-model-.html.

[33] David Cay Johnson, "Arthur Spear, Who Led Mattel through Fiscal Crises, Dies at 75," *The New York Times,* January 4, 1996.

[34] Ibid.

[35] Richard W. Stevenson, "More Trouble in Toyland," *The New York Times*, December 20, 1987.

fire from critics charging that the company was running sweatshops in Asia and employing underaged workers in Indonesia.

23   As a response to this public relations threat, Mattel's Global Manufacturing Principles (GMPs) were developed and introduced around the world. Highlights of the GMP standards are shown in Exhibit 5. These comprehensive GMPs provided a framework within which all manufacturing for Mattel must be conducted, regardless of whether it was done in their company-owned plants or in contractors' plants. These principles were supported and reinforced by an independent monitoring system, Mattel's Independent Monitoring Council (MIMCO), created to ensure that GMP standards were consistently met. MIMCO was headed by Dr. Prakash Sethi, a distinguished professor at Baruch College's Zicklin School of Business.

EXHIBIT 5   **Mattel's Global Manufacturing Principles**

Mattel's Global Manufacturing Principles (GMP) apply to all parties that manufacture, assemble, license, or distribute any product or package bearing any of the Mattel logos. GMP provides guidance and minimum standards for all manufacturing plants, assembly operations, and distribution centers that manufacture or distribute Mattel products. GMP requires safe and fair treatment of employees and that facilities protect the environment while respecting the cultural, ethnic, and philosophical differences of the countries where Mattel operates. GMP also requires internal and periodic independent monitoring of our performance and our partners' performance to the standards.

Mattel is committed to executing GMP in all areas of its business, and will only engage business partners who share our commitment to GMP. Mattel expects all its business partners to adhere to GMP, and will assist them in meeting GMP requirements. However, Mattel is prepared to end partnerships with those who do not comply. Mattel and its partners will operate their facilities in compliance with applicable laws and regulations. Mattel has defined the following overarching principles to which all facilities and partners are required to comply. These principles are dynamic and evolving to continually improve our efforts to ensure ongoing protection of employees and the environment. In addition, Mattel has developed a comprehensive and detailed set of underlying procedures and standards that enable us to apply and administer our GMP in the countries where we operate. The procedures and standards are updated and refined on an ongoing basis.

1. **Management Systems**
   a. Facilities must have systems in place to address labor, social, environmental, health, and safety issues.

2. **Wages and Working Hours**
   a. Employees must be paid for all hours worked. Wages for regular and overtime work must be compensated at the legally mandated rates.
   b. Wages must be paid in legal tender and at least monthly.
   c. Working hours must be in compliance with country and Mattel requirements.
   d. Regular and overtime working hours must be documented, verifiable, and accurately reflect all hours worked by employees.
   e. Overtime work must be voluntary.
   f. Employees must be provided with rest days in compliance with country and Mattel requirements.
   g. Payroll deductions must comply with applicable country and Mattel requirements.

3. **Age Requirements**
   a. All employees must meet the minimum age for employment as specified by country and Mattel requirements.

4. **Forced Labor**
   a. Employees must be employed of their own free will.
   b. Forced or prison labor must not be used to manufacture, assemble, or distribute any Mattel products.

EXHIBIT 5   Mattel's Global Manufacturing Principles (*Continued*)

5. Discrimination
  a. The facility must have policies on hiring, promotion, employee rights, and disciplinary practices that address discrimination.

6. Freedom of Expression and Association
  a. The facility must recognize all employees' rights to choose to engage in, or refrain from, lawful union activity and lawful collective bargaining through representatives selected according to applicable law.
  b. Management must create formal channels to encourage communications among all levels of management and employees on issues that impact their working and living conditions.

7. Living Conditions
  a. Dormitories must be separated from production and warehouse buildings.
  b. Dormitories and canteens must be safe, sanitary, and meet the basic needs of employees.

8. Workplace Safety
  a. The facility must have programs in place to address health and safety issues that exist in the workplace.

9. Health
  a. First aid and medical treatment must be available to all employees.
  b. Monitoring programs must be in place to ensure employees are not exposed to harmful working conditions.

10. Emergency Planning
  a. The facility must have programs and systems in place for dealing with emergencies such as fires, spills, and natural disasters.
  b. Emergency exit doors must be kept unlocked at all times when the building is occupied. Emergency exits must be clearly marked and free of obstructions.

11. Environmental Protection
  a. Facilities must have environmental programs in place to minimize their impact on the environment.

Source: Mattel.

24   This approach was effective and formed the basis of Mattel's sterling reputation in the industry. Mattel was the first global consumer products company to apply such a system to its facilities and core contractors on a worldwide basis. ". . . [The] fact is that Mattel— largely under Sethi's direction—has gone further than any other company to be a good corporate citizen with regard to its Chinese operations."[36] Given the legacy of pioneering collaboration with the Consumer Product Safety Commission and the ASTM to develop industry safety and testing standards, plus adherence to Mattel's GMPs and oversight by MIMCO, Mattel had earned its position as a role model in the toy industry for its worker health and safety and product safety practices.

25   Amerman was followed by Jill Barad, who was credited with building the Barbie brand from a dated doll generating $250 million in the mid-1980s to a collectible earning $1.9 billion in 1998 during her 18-year "storybook" career at Mattel. As CEO, Barad abandoned Amerman's focus on quarterly profits and shed unprofitable assets at a time when growth in Barbie sales was declining and Mattel continued to have a very limited new product pipeline. When Barad took over in 1997, Mattel had a $206 million profit; the following year they had a loss of $82.3 million.[37] She led the acquisition of the Learning Company, a company that controlled the market for educational software, in a $3.6 billion deal to secure Mattel's online, interactive, high-tech presence and to grow the top line.[38]

[36] Jonathan Dee, "A Toy Maker's Conscience," *The New York Times*, December 23, 2007.

[37] Ibid., p. 56.

[38] Barbara Kellerman, *Bad Leadership*, Boston: Harvard Business School Press, 2004, p. 55.

26   Analysts criticized Barad and Mattel for a lack of due diligence in the Learning Company acquisition, for overly aggressive estimates of growth revenue synergies from the deal, and for failure to take responsibility for the financial disaster the deal created.[39] Between 1999 and 2000, Mattel experienced a steady stream of executive departures. Roger Brunswick, managing partner of Hayes, Brunswick, and Partners commented, "In the end, she alienated the very individuals charged with helping her grow the company and deliver shareholder value."[40] Jill Barad was forced out in 2000.

MATTEL'S NEW MILLENNIUM

27   In May 2000, Robert Eckert took over as Mattel's CEO, and *BusinessWeek* called him the "anti-Barad."[41] He assumed the CEO role with no toy industry experience: Bob came from Kraft Foods, the only company he had ever worked for. He inherited a very troubled company, and many of the top management team had just left.[42] One of his first actions was to clean up the Learning Company fiasco. Eckert introduced a new vision for Mattel that focused on building brands of tried-and-true products—like Barbie, Hot Wheels, and Fisher-Price—cutting costs, and developing people.

28   When he took Mattel's helm, Eckert encountered low morale, an equally low stock price, and lack of accountability among his followers, the legacy of his predecessor. To remedy this, Eckert worked with a team of line managers to craft a set of new values for the company that conveyed collaboration. This well-respected CEO engaged the organization with a vision of greater collaboration, a vision that would eventually become known as *One Mattel*.[43] These values all built on the word play: *Play Fair, Play Together, Play with Passion, and Play to Grow*. Guided by these values, Mattel believed they would have to improve execution across all business segments, globalize into new markets, extend technologies and licenses, catch new trends with existing and future businesses, and develop people to carry out these missions. The spirit behind the strategies was to improve shareholder value by increasing revenues, operating profit margin, and ultimately cash flow.[44] Mattel's annual income statements for December 2003 through December 2007 are shown in Exhibit 6.

29   In line with Eckert's vision for cutting costs, in 2006 Mattel identified supply network initiatives to reduce manufacturing costs in response to the rising cost of material. These included ramping up lean manufacturing practices and optimizing distribution networks among other cost-saving initiatives.[45] Mattel also identified efforts to streamline the procure-to-pay process, including reducing cycle time for ordering and receiving goods. The interaction of these initiatives resulted in increased performance pressure on Mattel's Chinese contractors, including the Lee-Der Industrial Company plant, where the supply network was compromised by the use of lead paint on Sarge cars.

30   Mattel made about 65 percent of its toys in China, using a combination of company-run plants that focused on their most popular core products, and a network of contract manufacturers for the remainder of their production needs. They used this hybrid approach

[39] John W. Torgel, "Learning from Mattel," Tuck School of Business, Dartmouth (No. 1-0072), 2002.

[40] Byrne and Grover, "Mattel's Lack-of-Action Figures," *BusinessWeek*, February 21, 2000.

[41] Christopher Palmeri, "Mattel: Up the Hill Minus Jill," *BusinessWeek*, April 9, 2001.

[42] Robert Eckert, "Where Leadership Starts," *Harvard Business Review*, November 2001.

[43] Douglas A. Ready and Jay A. Conger, "Enabling Bold Visions," *Sloan Management Review*, Winter, Vol. 49, No. 2, 2008, pp. 70–76.

[44] http://www.financialexecutives.org/eweb/upload/chapter/austin/The%20Worlds%20Premier%20Toy%20Brands.htm.

[45] http://www.shareholder.com/mattel/downloads/Mattel_AnalystHandout_6-14-07.pdf.

EXHIBIT 6   Mattel's Annual Income Statements, December 2003–December 2007

(All dollar amounts in millions except per share amounts. Financial Year End: December)

	December 2007	December 2006	December 2005	December 2004	December 2003
Revenue	5,970.1	5,650.2	5,179.0	5,102.8	4,960.1
Cost of Goods Sold	3,192.8	3,038.4	2,806.1	2,692.1	2,530.8
Gross Profit	2,777.3	2,611.8	2,372.9	2,410.7	2,429.5
Gross Profit Margin	46.50%	46.20%	45.8%	47.20%	49.0%
SG&A	1,875.1	1,710.7	1,533.3	1,497.4	1,459.9
Depreciation & Amortization	172.1	172.3	175.0	182.5	183.8
Operating Income	730.1	728.8	664.5	730.8	785.7
Operating Margin	12.20%	12.90%	12.80%	14.30%	15.80%
Nonoperating Income	44.3	34.8	64.0	43.2	35.7
Nonoperating Expenses	71.0	79.8	76.5	77.8	80.6
Income Before Taxes	703.4	683.8	652.0	696.3	740.8
Income Taxes	103.4	90.8	235.0	123.5	203.2
Net Income After Taxes	600.0	592.9	417.0	572.7	537.5
Continuing Operations	600.0	592.9	417.0	572.7	537.5
Discontinued Operations	—	—	—	—	—
Total Operations	600.0	592.9	417.0	572.7	537.5
Total Net Income	600.0	592.9	417.0	572.7	537.5
Net Profit Margin	10.00%	10.50%	8.10%	11.20%	10.8%
Diluted EPS from Total Net Income ($)	1.5	1.5	1.0	1.4	1.2

Source: Mattel's Annual Reports.

to protect the brand of their core products. Mattel used a higher proportion of company-owned plants than the industry standard, which was, in effect, a higher cost method than using low-bid local manufacturers for all of their production.[46] About half of Mattel's toy revenue was derived from core products made in these company-run plants. When subassemblies and raw materials arrived at company-run plants, they were analyzed and tested for safety, either on site or in Mattel's test laboratories. As part of the independent monitoring process, Mattel's factories were inspected by independent auditors who posed result reports on the Internet for public viewing. Contract manufacturers had to comply with Mattel's strict quality and safety operating procedures and the GMPs, just like a company-run facility.[47]

31   Mattel competed on brand. In Mattel's public statements about quality, they promised:

> Mattel's reputation for product quality and safety is among its most valuable assets, and our commitment to product quality and safety is essential. ***Children's health, safety, and well-being are our primary concern.*** We could damage our consumers' trust if we sell products that do not meet our standards.

> Our commitment to product quality and safety is an integral part of the design, manufacturing, testing, and distribution processes. We will meet or exceed legal requirements and industry standards for product quality and safety. We strive to meet or exceed the expectations of our customers and consumers.

[46] Barboza and Storey, "Toymaking in China."

[47] Ibid.

Any compromise to product safety or quality must be immediately reported to Worldwide Quality Assurance.[48]

32   The United States, where Mattel designed and developed their toys, generated about 51 percent of their global sales revenue. The international segment made up the balance. The products marketed through the international segment were generally the same as those developed and marketed by the domestic segment with limited product localization. In China, for example, the Barbie sold in the United States was seen as too mature for little girls. As a consequence, Barbie in China was given a more juvenile appearance. Barbie was Mattel's largest and most profitable brand, but was experiencing declining sales. Unlike Barbie, Hot Wheels did not require local adaptation in China or most other international markets. Mattel was successful in extending existing brands; for example, Barbie movies on DVD, *Barbie Lives in Fairytopia,* a live touring stage show, or the Hot Wheels Hall of Fame exhibit at the Peterson Automotive Museum.

33   Mattel was the leading toy manufacturer for all children under eight years of age, primarily due to the strength of their Fisher-Price offerings. With children age 10 or older, however, Mattel lost considerable share to other competitors and non-toy activities.[49] All of Mattel's early innovations were developed internally. But they had relied on acquisitions and licensing over the past 40 years. In addition, all non-toy-related acquisitions and internal development ventures had failed.[50] By 2007, Mattel had a very limited presence in electronic entertainment, which their business intelligence told them was a very important growth segment.

TROUBLE IN TOYLAND REDUX

34   Jim Walter, a senior vice-president for worldwide quality assurance at Mattel, gave an interview to the *New York Times* on July 26, 2007. It was noted by media insiders that Mattel rarely gave media interviews. Walter claimed, "We are not perfect; we have holes . . . But we're doing more than anyone else."[51] Other toy manufacturers agreed. One week later, Mattel issued a press release announcing a voluntary recall of "some products made by a contract manufacturer in China that were produced using a non-approved paint pigment containing lead . . ."[52] In this release, they stated that this procedure was in violation of Mattel's standards. Walter commented, "We require our manufacturing partners to use paint from approved and certified suppliers and have procedures in place to test and verify, but in this particular case our procedures were not followed . . . We are investigating the cause to ensure such events do not reoccur."[53]

35   Mattel announced that they were conducting a thorough investigation of this problem, and would take appropriate action if they concluded that their safety procedures were knowingly ignored. Under CPSC rules, manufacturers were supposed to report all claims of potentially hazardous product defects within 24 hours. Mattel reportedly took months to gather information and privately investigate problems after becoming aware of them.

---

[48] http://www.mattel.com/about_us/Corp_Governance/ethics.asp#or_consumers.

[49] Babitch et al., "The Future of Play."

[50] Ibid.

[51] Ibid.

[52] http://www.shareholder.com/mattel/news/20070801-258085.cfm.

[53] Ibid.

Between August 14 and September 4, 2007, there were six separate CPSC recalls of Mattel products announced.[54] These included:

- Mattel Recalls Batman™ and One Piece™ Magnetic Action Figure Sets Due to Magnets Coming Loose (August 14, 2007)
- Mattel Recalls "Sarge" Die-Cast Toy Cars Due to Violation of Lead Safety Standard (August 14, 2007)
- Mattel Recalls Barbie and Tanner™ Magnetic Toys Due to Magnets Coming Loose (August 14, 2007)
- Mattel Recalls Doggie Day Care™ Magnetic Toys Due to Magnets Coming Loose (August 14, 2007)
- Additional Reports of Magnets Detaching from Polly Pocket Play Sets Prompts Expanded Recall by Mattel (August 14, 2007). This extends a November 21, 2006, original recall of Mattel's Polly Pocket Magnetic Play Sets.
- Mattel Recalls Various Barbie® Accessory Toys Due to Violation of Lead Paint Standard (September 4, 2007)

36   Mattel began working with "retailers worldwide to identify affected products, have them removed from retail shelves, and intercept incoming shipments and stop them from being sold."[55] In this same press release, Robert Eckert apologized, "We realize that parents trust us with what is most precious to them—their children. And we also recognize that trust is earned. Our goal is to correct this problem, improve our systems, and maintain the trust of the families that have allowed us to be part of their lives by acting responsibly and quickly to address their concerns."[56]

37   On September 4, 2007, Robert Eckert issued a statement, "As a result of our ongoing investigation, we discovered additional affected products. Consequently, several subcontractors are no longer manufacturing Mattel toys. We apologize again to everyone affected and promise that we will continue to focus on ensuring the safety and quality of our toys."[57] He added that Mattel had completed its testing program and spent more than 50,000 hours investigating its vendors and testing its toys in the preceding four-week period.[58] Of the 19 million-plus Mattel toys recalled, only 2.2 million of the recalls were because of lead paint. The rest of the recalls were the result of faulty design, the use of small magnets that could cause choking and internal injuries.[59]

38   Toys were pulled from retailers' shelves. A media frenzy ensued, and public pressure mounted. This resulted in Congressional hearings on toy safety, with a focus on protecting children from lead-tainted imports. Eckert testified to the House Subcommittee on Commerce, Trade and Consumer Protection of the Committee on Energy and Commerce, stating:

> Mattel has been manufacturing products and using contract vendors in China successfully and without significant manufacturing-related safety issues for more than 20 years...
> When Mattel does contract with vendors to manufacture toys, our contracts require that

---

[54] U.S. Consumer Product Safety Commission (http://www.cpsc.gov).

[55] Ibid.

[56] Ibid.

[57] http://www.truthout.org.issues_06/090507HB.html.

[58] Ibid.

[59] www.businessweek.com;bwdaily/dnflash/content;Sept2007/db20070921_569200. htm?cha=top+news_top+news+index_businessweek+exclusives.

the vendors comply with Mattel's quality and safety operating procedures and Global Manufacturing Principles ("GMP"), which reflect the company's commitment to responsible practices in areas such as employee health and safety, environmental management, and respect for the cultural, ethnic, and philosophical differences of the countries where Mattel operates.[60]

THE PERFECT STORM?

39 By the time the dust settled, Mattel had recalled 19 million toys made in China.[61] Mattel's stock price declined as they took a $40 million charge for recalls, and their costs increased.[62] Customers threatened to boycott Mattel and all toys made in China.[63] Bob Eckert had been called to testify before both U.S. House and Senate hearings on toy safety. In response to the hearing surrounding the recalls, Senator Sam Brownback commented, "Made in China has now become a warning label."[64] Despite industry pleas for voluntary compliance, the U.S. Senate voted by a large margin to enhance toy safety by passing a bill that would make the ASTM[65] International toy safety standard, F963, a mandatory requirement for all toys sold in the U.S.[66]

40 Chinese government officials saw Mattel's recall public relations approach as blaming China's manufacturers for what was primarily a Mattel design problem. This unfavorable publicity drew attention from Chinese regulators, and resulted in Mattel making a highly publicized public apology to China and China's quality watchdog chief, Li Changjiang.[67]

41 When it looked like nothing could get worse for Mattel, Congress sent a letter in January 2008 charging that Robert Eckert was not honoring the public commitment he had made to consumers during the initial recall incident. The text of this letter is presented in Exhibit 7. This tsunami of negative events left Mattel executives perplexed and reeling: How could this industry giant, a company so highly regarded as a toy industry model of corporate citizenship, find itself mired in such a controversy? What next steps should they take to recover from the crisis? What must they do to protect their brand? What should they do to restore their reputation? Was this crisis a major roadblock to being the world's premier toy brand "tomorrow"?

---

[60] Testimony to Subcommittee on Commerce, Trade and Consumer Protection of the Committee on Energy and Commerce, September 19, 2007.

[61] Steven G. Brant, "China's Quality Problem: A Long-Term vs. Short-Term Thinking Teachable Moment," *The Huffington Post*, 2007; Louise Story and David Barbosa, "Mattel Recalls 19 Million Toys Sent from China," *The New York Times*, 2007.

[62] http://caps.fool.com/Ticker/MAT.aspx.

[63] http://www.abc.net.au/news/stories/2007/10/23/2066950.htm; Bill Mah, "Recall Has Parents Mulling Toy Boycott," edmontonjournal.com,

[64] http://www.msnbc.msn.com/id/20738314/.

[65] ASTM International is one of the largest voluntary standards development organizations in the world, and is considered a trusted source for technical standards for materials, products, systems, and services. ASTM is known for high technical quality and market relevancy. ASTM International standards have an important role in the information infrastructure that guides design, manufacturing, and trade in the global economy.

[66] http://69.7.224.88/viewnews.aspx?newsID=1300.

[67] Andrew Clark, "Mattel: China Toy Scares Our Fault," *The Guardian*, 2007.

EXHIBIT 7 **Letter from Congress to Mattel, January 30, 2008**

Mr. Eckert:

We write you today not only as federal legislators, but as parents, grandparents, aunts, uncles, neighbors, and representatives of the children who find joy in the toys produced by Mattel. We are gravely concerned about the dangers posed to children by the use of lead in your company's products, and urge you, as a father yourself, to completely eliminate the use of lead in the toys produced by your company and all of its subsidiaries.

Specifically, we are disturbed by your lack of action upon the discovery that a red toy blood pressure cuff manufactured by Fisher Price, Mattel's subsidiary, contains high levels of lead; two such cuffs tested at 4,500 and 5,900 ppm of lead, respectively. It was not until Illinois State Attorney General Lisa Madigan notified you that the toys were in violation of Illinois state regulations that you took any action at all to protect our children, and said action was limited to removing the toy from the shelves of Illinois stores. We find this response to be deficient, and encourage you to immediately stop selling the red blood pressure cuff in all states. If this product is too dangerous for the children of Illinois, it is too dangerous for children in the rest of this country.

The effects of lead poisoning are irreversible and tragic, and every precaution should be taken in the manufacture of products intended for use by children—our most vulnerable population. The federal lead paint standard established nearly thirty years ago is 600 ppm. If 600 ppm is too high for lead paint, then surely lead levels in toys that are 800% to 900% of this standard are unacceptable.

The State of Illinois has taken a bold step in passing protective legislation on this issue, and other states and the federal government are examining legislation at least as strict as Illinois' extension of the 600 ppm limit to all toys, regardless of material. It is unfortunate, however, that toy manufacturers have not voluntarily enacted these standards on their own.

In an opinion statement published in the September 11, 2007, issue of the *Wall Street Journal* responding to criticism over recent recalls of numerous toys due to high levels of lead paint, you wrote:

> It is my sincere pledge that we will face this challenge with integrity and reaffirm that we will do the right thing. We will embrace this test of our company and the opportunity to become better . . . [M]y father encouraged me to earn his trust through my actions rather than just talk about what I was going to do… And it is on this principle that Mattel will move forward. We will earn back your trust with our deeds, not just with our words.

We encourage you to review your pledge and act accordingly by recalling the red blood pressure cuff. Furthermore, we challenge you to live up to your words and set a standard for the entire industry by completely eliminating the use of lead in all of the children's products manufactured by Mattel. When parents purchase a product from your company, they are not just purchasing a toy—they are putting their trust in an established brand that has historically been believed to provide merchandise that is safe for their children. We urge you to live up to this reputation.

Sincerely,

Neil Abercrombie	Keith Ellison	John B. Larson	Bobby L. Rush
Thomas H. Allen	Anna G. Eshoo	Barbara Lee	Linda T. Sanchez
Sanford D. Bishop, Jr.	Sam Farr	John Lewis	Janice D. Schakowsky
Corrine Brown	Chaka Fattah	Nita M. Lowey	Vic Snyder
G.K. Butterfield	Bob Filner	Edward J. Markey	Betty Sutton
Kathy Castor	Barney Frank	Doris O. Matsui	Bennie G. Thompson
Donna M. Christensen	Al Green	James P. McGovern	Debbie Wasserman
Yvette D. Clarke	Raul M. Grijalva	Kendrick B. Meek	Schultz
Wm. Lacy Clay	Luis V. Gutierrez	Dennnis Moor	Melvin L. Watt
Emanuel Cleaver	Phil Hare	James P. Moran	Henry A. Waxman
Steve Cohen	Baron P. Hill	Eleanor Holmes Norton	Robert Wexler
Elijah E. Cummings	Maurice D. Hinchey	Bill Pascrell, Jr.	Albert R. Wynn
Artur Davis	Sheila Jackson-Lee	David E. Price	
Diana DeGette	Carolyn C. Kilpatrick	Silvestre Reyes	
Rosa L. DeLauro	Dennis J. Kucinich	Steven R. Rothman	

Source: http://www.house.gov/list/press/md07_cummings/20080130mattel2.shtml.

Case 26

Scotts Miracle-Gro: *The Spreader Sourcing Decision*

John Gray

Michael Leiblein

1 As Bob Bawcombe drove to work on a warm California morning in June 2007, his mind was occupied with an upcoming meeting with the folks from the corporate office in Marysville, Ohio. Bawcombe was the director of operations of Scotts' Temecula plant. For over five years, he had been in charge of the Temecula manufacturing plant, which produced all of Scotts Miracle-Gro's domestic lawn seed and fertilizer spreaders (see Exhibit 1). As a result of the plant's location in Southern California, Bawcombe was under constant pressure to justify why Scotts should not offshore/outsource production of its spreaders to a low-wage manufacturing site, such as China.

COMPANY HISTORY

2 The Scotts Miracle-Gro Company (Scotts), based in Marysville, Ohio, was formed by a 1995 merger of Miracle-Gro and The Scotts Company. The merger made Scotts the largest company in the North American lawn and garden industry. It was the world's leading supplier and marketer of consumer products for do-it-yourself lawn and garden care, with products for professional horticulture as well.[1] In the 2007 fiscal year, Scotts had net sales of $2.7 billion (see Exhibits 2 and 3).

3 The Scotts Company was founded in 1868 by Orlando McLean Scott as a purveyor of weed-free seeds. By 1879, Scotts had diversified into distribution of horse-drawn farm equipment and also started a mail-order farm seed distribution channel. Scotts began offering grass seeds for lawns in 1907, distributing through retail channels beginning in 1924. In 1928, Scotts introduced Turf Builder®, the first fertilizer specifically designed for grass. Scotts started its spreader business with the introduction of drop spreaders in 1930; broadcast spreaders were rolled out in 1983. Scotts acquired Republic Tool & Manufacturing Company in 1992 and gained competencies in total quality control over

---

Professors John Gray and Michael Leiblein wrote this case with assistance from Shyam Karunakaran solely to provide material for class discussion. The authors do not intend to illustrate either effective or ineffective handling of a managerial situation. The authors may have disguised certain names and other identifying information to protect confidentiality.

Richard Ivey School of Business
The University of Western Ontario

Copyright © 2008, Ivey Management Services   Version: (A) 2009-06-22

[1] Scotts Miracle-Gro Corporate Overview — Corporate Profile, www.scotts.com/smg/, accessed May 31, 2007.

EXHIBIT 1
Scotts Miracle-Gro
Spreaders

Source: Scotts Miracle-Gro
company website, accessed
May 31, 2007.

Drop Spreaders		Scotts AccuGreen® 1000 Drop Spreader
		Scotts AccuGreen® 2000 Drop Spreader
		Scotts AccuGreen® 3000™ Deluxe Model Drop Spreader
Broadcast Spreaders		Scotts Basic Broadcast Spreader
		Scotts Standard Broadcast Spreader
		Scotts Deluxe™ EdgeGuard® Broadcast Spreader
Hand-Held Spreaders		Scotts Easy® Hand-Held Spreader
		Scotts HandyGreen® II Hand-Held Spreader

spreader manufacturing. Ownership of the firm changed hands several times, beginning in 1971 when ITT bought Scotts from the Scotts family. In 1986, a leveraged buy-out (LBO) made Scotts a private company again for a time, until 1992, when its stock started trading on the NASDAQ.

4   Miracle-Gro was founded in 1951 by Horace Hagedon. Unlike Scotts, Miracle-Gro had no internal production; all production was outsourced to contract manufacturers. Before the 1995 merger with Scotts, Miracle Gro was already a leading brand in the lawn care chemical industry. By early 2000, Scotts Miracle-Gro products were No. 1 in every major category and in virtually every major market in which they competed.[2]

---

[2] Scotts Miracle-Gro—Time Line and Company History, www.scotts.com, accessed May 31, 2007.

EXHIBIT 2   Scotts Miracle-Gro Annual Balance Sheet

As of (all numbers in millions of US$)	09/30/06	09/30/05	09/30/04	09/30/03	09/30/02
Assets					
Current Assets					
Cash	48.10	80.20	115.60	155.90	99.70
Marketable Securities	n/a	n/a	57.20	n/a	n/a
Receivables	380.40	323.30	292.40	290.50	249.90
Total Inventories	409.20	324.90	290.10	276.10	269.10
Raw Materials	105.80	77.50	72.80	72.40	72.50
Work In Progress	36.00	31.40	n/a	n/a	n/a
Finished Goods	267.40	216.00	217.30	203.70	196.60
Notes Receivable	n/a	n/a	n/a	n/a	n/a
Other Current Assets	104.30	59.40	75.00	90.10	111.40
Total Current Assets	942.00	787.80	830.30	812.60	730.10
Property, Plant & Equipment, Net	367.60	337.00	328.00	338.20	329.20
Property, Plant & Equipment, Gross	737.60	659.40	629.40	608.70	575.20
Accumulated Depreciation	370.00	322.40	301.40	270.50	246.00
Interest and Advance to Subsidiaries	n/a	n/a	n/a	n/a	n/a
Other Non-Current Assets	n/a	n/a	n/a	n/a	n/a
Deferred Charges	n/a	n/a	n/a	n/a	n/a
Intangibles	882.80	872.40	848.90	835.50	791.70
Deposits & Other Assets	25.20	21.70	40.60	44.00	50.40
Total Assets	**2,217.60**	**2,018.90**	**2,047.80**	**2,030.30**	**1,901.40**
Liabilities					
Current Liabilities					
Notes Payable	n/a	n/a	n/a	n/a	n/a
Accounts Payable	200.40	151.70	130.30	149.00	134.00
Current Long-Term Debt	6.00	11.10	22.10	55.40	98.20
Current Port. Cap Lease	n/a	n/a	n/a	n/a	n/a
Accrued Expense	289.80	323.40	281.20	243.80	219.60
Income Taxes	n/a	n/a	n/a	n/a	n/a
Other Current Liabilities	n/a	n/a	n/a	n/a	n/a
Total Current Liabilities	496.20	486.20	433.60	448.20	451.80
Mortgages	n/a	n/a	n/a	n/a	n/a
Deferred Charges/Inc.	49.20	4.50	18.60	n/a	n/a
Convertible Debt	n/a	n/a	n/a	n/a	n/a
Long-Term Debt	475.20	382.40	608.50	692.10	719.50
Non-Current Capital Leases	n/a	n/a	n/a	10.10	11.70
Other Long-Term Liabilities	115.30	119.60	112.50	151.70	124.50
Total Liabilities	**1,135.90**	**992.70**	**1,173.20**	**1,302.10**	**1,307.50**
Shareholder Equity					
Minority Interest	n/a	n/a	n/a	n/a	n/a
Preferred Stock	n/a	n/a	n/a	n/a	n/a
Common Stock	0.30	0.30	0.30	0.30	0.30
Capital Surplus	508.80	503.20	443.00	398.40	398.60
Retained Earnings	690.70	591.50	499.50	398.60	294.80
Treasury Stock	66.50	n/a	n/a	n/a	41.80
Other Liabilities	−51.60	−68.80	−68.20	−69.10	−58.00
Total Shareholders Equity	**1,081.70**	**1,026.20**	**874.60**	**728.20**	**593.90**
Total Liabilities & Shareholders Equity	**2,217.60**	**2,018.90**	**2,047.80**	**2,030.30**	**1,901.40**

Source: The Scotts Miracle-Gro Company annual reports.

EXHIBIT 3   Scotts Miracle-Gro Annual Income Statement

Period Ended (all numbers in millions of US$)	09/30/06	09/30/05	09/30/04	09/30/03	09/30/02
Net Sales	**2,697.10**	**2,369.30**	**2,106.50**	**1,887.70**	**1,748.70**
Cost of Goods Sold	1,741.20	1,508.90	1,314.10	1,198.80	1,112.10
Gross Profit	**955.90**	**860.40**	**792.40**	**688.90**	**636.60**
R & D Expenditure	n/a	n/a	n/a	n/a	n/a
Selling, General & Admin Expenses	711.30	667.00	516.90	493.60	432.20
Depreciation & Amortization	n/a	n/a	n/a	8.60	5.70
Non-Operating Income	7.90	7.50	−22.70	44.90	40.50
Interest Expense	39.60	42.80	94.30	69.20	76.30
Income Before Taxes	**212.90**	**158.10**	**158.50**	**162.40**	**162.90**
Provision For Income Taxes	80.20	57.70	58.00	59.20	61.90
Minority Interest	n/a	n/a	n/a	n/a	n/a
Realized Investment (Gain/Loss)	n/a	n/a	n/a	n/a	n/a
Other Income	n/a	n/a	n/a	n/a	n/a
Net Income Before Extra Items	132.70	100.40	100.50	103.20	101.00
Extra Items & Disc. Ops.	n/a	0.20	0.40	0.60	−18.50
Net Income	**132.70**	**100.60**	**100.90**	**103.80**	**82.50**

Source: The Scotts Miracle-Gro Company 2006 annual report.

TEMECULA OPERATIONS

5   The 1992 acquisition of Republic Tool & Manufacturing Company from the McRoskey family provided Scotts with a spreader manufacturing plant which occupied three buildings in Carlsbad, California. By 2000, the cost and inefficiencies associated with managing production across three independent buildings had spurred Scotts' management to explore alternative methods of producing or procuring spreaders. At that time, Scotts' senior management decided that a move to the current facilities in Temecula was the most efficient solution.

6   In 2001, Scotts leased its current 412,000-square foot facility for 15 years at an annual cost of $3 million.[3] The move allowed Scotts to consolidate production in one building to rationalize its production processes. While there were eight years left on the current lease, Scotts was fairly certain that it could terminate this lease quickly (in less than a year).

7   Although the decision had been made to keep the plant in California in 2000, the comparatively high plant and labor costs of the Temecula plant continued to create intense cost pressure. Over the 2002–2007 time period, Bawcombe and his leadership team had been largely successful in their efforts to improve productivity through continuous investment in product and process innovations (see Exhibit 5 for the current layout of the Temecula plant). Productivity improvements had averaged six per cent per year for the last few years and this trend was expected to continue for at least five more years before leveling off.

[3] All non-public financial, productivity and employment information has been disguised for this case.

The plant also had trained its 190 production line workers in lean management techniques and this effort had led to the identification of a number of workforce-driven improvement projects. Indeed, Bawcombe felt that these productivity improvements had allowed the Temecula plant to be cost competitive on a global basis and would continue to do so in the future:

> Our vision for the future involves making the plant as automated as possible and we are well on the way to achieving the goal. This would allow us to drastically cut labor costs and make our landed costs comparable to the landed costs of plants in China. My higher energy costs will be offset by their higher freight, inventory and quality costs. In the plant of the future we would need fewer assemblers and a greater number of machine technicians to maintain the plant. We are actively training and developing our human resources to meet this need.

8   The Temecula plant had built considerable general manufacturing skill. Bawcombe believed that this skill was responsible for a number of important process innovations. A good example of this sort of process innovation involved the development of a new hand spreader assembly process. The old process involved six people manually putting the product together in an assembly line. The hand spreader was recently redesigned to remove screw connectors and make all components pressure-fit. This allowed the plant to develop and build in-house an automated assembly line that required only four people. The plant had documented the assembly line design using computer-aided design (CAD). And, working in collaboration with corporate durables research and development (R&D), together they had greatly improved the design for manufacture of the spreaders. Bawcombe felt strongly that the development of this general manufacturing competence was intimately tied to the ability to continue the reduction of product costs going forward: ". . . this kind of innovation requires production capability to be in-house, so that Scotts retains the capability to innovate in production process and engage in design for manufacture. Our Quality Manager is a design engineer by trade, this is by choice not by accident."

9   The Temecula plant had also pioneered the use of "in-mold labeling," becoming one of the few facilities in the world to have "in-mold labeling" capability for injection molding of such a large product (the spreader hoppers). There was significant tacit knowledge in the ability to get in-mold labeling to work, although the plant was working to codify this process innovation. In-mold labeling allowed the label to be molded into the plastic product; this allowed for higher quality, as the labels would not fade, scratch or peel. The older method was called "hot stamping of labels." Hot stamping could result in lower quality, as the label was stuck on top of the plastic and could fade, peel or get scratched. This older process was still used for low-value products at Temecula and was the process that vendors would have readily available. While there were some within Scotts who felt that in-mold labeling was of little value to the end customer, there was discussion that the quality of "in-mold" labels could be a key part of a planned Scotts marketing campaign where messages on the spreader labels would be used to drive higher fertilizer/seed usage and sales. While neither the hand spreader assembly nor the in-mold labeling process innovations had been directly transferred to other Scotts manufacturing operations, the process improvement routines and skills developed in Temecula had been effectively utilized in Scotts' fertilizer packaging operations through benchmarking and the transfer of managers.

10   Bawcombe believed strongly that the product and process innovations in his plant were largely a function of manufacturing skills that his team had developed through prior experience. In an effort to maintain morale and avoid the loss of these skills and the associated problem-solving routines, the Temecula leadership team was especially careful to ensure that productivity improvements did not lead to firings. Instead, they used temporary workers and attrition to manage the declining demand for labor.

11 The main cost drivers of the Temecula plant (see Exhibit 4) were raw materials, labor, electricity and overhead (including building lease). Scotts used a discount rate of 15 per cent. Scotts spent capital to make the improvements in Temecula that it would not need to spend (directly) if it used a contract manufacturer. This had historically run about $500,000 per year. Given that contract manufacturers had lower labor costs and less incentive to invest in capital improvements, it was estimated that they would only spend about $300,000 per year in capital.

OUTSOURCING TO CHINA

12 Scotts had considerable experience sourcing components for its spreaders and had frequently considered the possibility of outsourcing the complete spreader manufacture and assembly to China. In fact, Scotts currently sourced the most complex components of the spreaders—related to the rotor assembly—from China. The molding of spreader buckets, the only non-assembly process occurring at Temecula, was a fairly simple process for

EXHIBIT 4 **Temecula Plant Cost Drivers**

Raw Materials:
The main raw material for Scotts was plastic resin. Plastic resin was a commodity and prices the world over were comparable. Although Scotts was able to obtain some volume discounts, similar discounts were obtained by any large plastic injection molding vendor. The Temecula plant had developed an extensive "regrind" process that allowed the Temecula plant to save annually an average of approximately $100,000* in raw materials costs, relative to a typical contract manufacturer.

Labor Costs:
Temecula employed 195 workers in its production process, at an average hourly rate of $16.25 (all inclusive). The labor rate at Scotts was increasing at three per cent per year. Scotts expected ongoing process and product innovations to increase productivity at an annual rate of six per cent for the next five years and then to settle to an annual increase of three per cent for another five years. Temecula also had 16 salaried employees, with fully loaded average salaries of $125,000.

Electricity Costs:
The Temecula plant currently used annually 8,000,000 kilo-watt hours. California electricity unit rates were currently at 16 cents/kilo-watt hour (plus a surcharge of 2.5 cents/kilo-watt hour until 2009). The electricity rate in California closely followed the trends of natural gas prices and was expected to increase by 50 per cent by 2017**. Scotts expected, through efficiency improvements, to be able to reduce the plant's electricity requirement to "cut in half" the expected electricity unit price increase—that is, the net electricity cost increase over the next 10 years was expected to be about 25 per cent.

Overhead Costs:
In addition to the building leasing costs, the Temecula plant absorbed $1 million of corporate overhead. Other assigned overhead costs amounted to 30 per cent of direct manufacturing costs (direct labor and electricity). Outsourcing Temecula would not be expected to reduce headcount in Marysville; therefore, the $1 million of corporate overhead would not be saved. But, the 30 per cent overhead would be saved if the plant were closed.

Source: Company records.

* As previously indicated, all non-public financial, productivity and employment information has been disguised for this case.
** U.S. Energy Information Administration.

EXHIBIT 5 **Temecula Plant Layout**

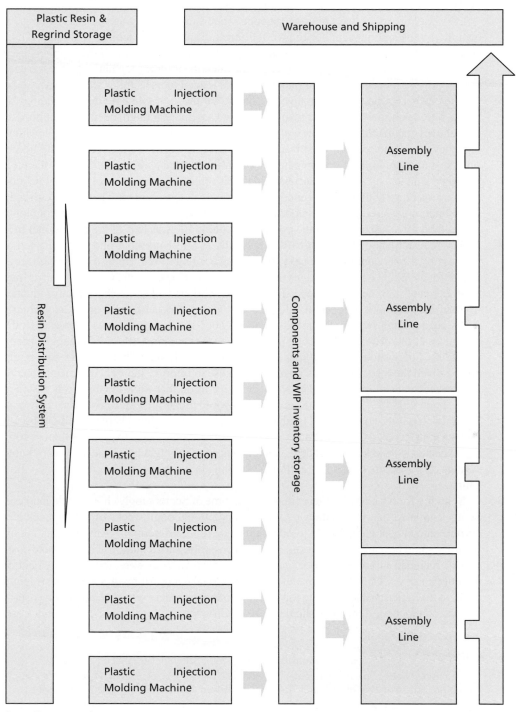

Source: Company records.

companies with experience in injection molding, with the exception of the in-mold labeling processes. Since the only product-specific component of the plastic injection molding process was the mold, the common practice when outsourcing was for the customer to own the molds and the supplier to own the injection molding machines and plant. Thus, customers might move the mold from one supplier to another, but only if the suppliers used a compatible injection molding machine. As the injection molding technology necessary for the hoppers was fairly mature, all major suppliers tended to use similar technology.

13   The one exception to this rule involved the use of the "in-mold labeling" technology. If Scotts were to outsource spreader manufacture and assembly, it might need to either provide the contract manufacturer with the equipment and know-how to perform "in-mold labeling" or remove this feature from its spreaders. Moreover, if Scotts were to provide the necessary "in-mold" training and equipment, it was unlikely that a chosen contract manufacturer would be able to use the molds currently in use at Temecula. New molds used for injection molding averaged about $40,000 and lasted approximately five years. There were currently 10 distinct molds used in Temecula in the injection molding for the "in-mold" technology; it would be safely assumed that the average remaining life was half of the total model life.

14   The relevant labor cost in China was currently at $0.91 per hour and was expected to increase by 40 per cent over the next 10 years, according to the Chinese Labor Ministry.[4] This estimate might be low, as wages increased almost 10 per cent in 2005 alone, up as high as 40 per cent in some companies.[5] The Chinese workers had somewhat lower productivity than U.S. workers, in general. Electricity in China was subsidized and was currently at 0.5 yuan per kilo-watt hour (approximately $0.065 per kilo-watt hour). Increases in the cost of coal, the main fuel used by China for power generation, suggested that electricity prices in China would rise by 20 per cent over the next decade. This estimate, too, might be low given the increasing pressure on the Chinese to improve their environmental record and recent trends in fuel costs. The lease for space to do this work in China was assumed to be about $200,000. These costs could be compared to the Temecula cost drivers given in Exhibit 4. If Scotts' entire annual production volume of approximately three million spreaders was transferred to China, the annual freight costs were expected to be $8 million in 2005 and expected to rise by three per cent annually. These costs might be partially offset by some savings off the approximately $1 million in shipping of components currently sourced from China.

15   Sourcing from China also meant that the lead time of Scotts supply chain would increase. Scotts estimated that it would have to hold an additional eight weeks of safety stock at a current annual cost of $460,000 to offset this lead time differential.[6] Any contract manufacturer would have management and oversight costs and earn a margin. The overhead costs (which included all salaried labor, maintenance, facility, etc.) were about 50 per cent of direct labor costs. The contract manufacturer would take a profit margin above costs; eight per cent was a reasonable estimate for this. And, of course, there would be transition costs—search, contracting, Temecula shutdown, etc. On-going, Scotts would have some costs

---

[4] Chinese Labor Ministry website, www.molss.gov.cn/gb/ywzn/gzfp.htm, accessed May 31, 2007.

[5] www.businessweek.com/magazine/content/06_13/b3977049.htm, accessed May 31, 2007; see also P. Beamish, "The High Cost of Cheap Chinese Labor," *Harvard Business Review*, June 2006. Reprint F0606D.

[6] This assumed that the contract manufacturer (CM) also engaged in level production, as Temecula did at the time of the case. While it was possible that a contract manufacturer could more closely match production with demand (perhaps by also producing, for example, toys, whose retail demand would peak late in the year versus spring), Scotts' current discussions with CMs indicated that the CMs would most likely also engage in level production.

(management time, travel) for managing the suppliers. Because spreaders were considered an agricultural product, Scotts would not have to pay duties and taxes when importing them. There was some (low) risk that this might change in the future.

16 Finally, Scotts' management anticipated that outsourcing would involve some additional general and administrative costs within its own organization. Scotts usually set up structured regular communication plans with its suppliers. Scotts had regular scheduled meetings and sent production plans (mostly in the form of purchase orders, POs) at regular intervals and avoided making changes to the POs, except in some extreme cases (sudden input/process/demand variation). Scotts also regularly qualified its suppliers and conducted weekly conference calls. These steps were taken to ensure that the supplier met Scotts' quality standards and used approved inputs and production processes. Despite these checks, Scotts occasionally faced issues with suppliers. The time required for transportation of spreaders from China to the United States and the batch nature of most supplier operations meant that any problems might not be detected until after a batch reached the United States and entire batches might have to be rejected or reworked.

17 Bawcombe feared that in today's meeting the corporate folks would push to outsource from China. Bawcombe was concerned about handing production over to another company and was prepared if needed to argue for another option. The alternative to outsourcing that Bawcombe was considering was the setting up of a Scotts production plant in China, i.e., to *offshore* spreader production. Setting up a plant in China would cost about $8 million and would take up to a year. Despite the high initial cost, this option offered the possible cost benefits associated with manufacturing in China, while allowing Scotts to continue to maintain direct control over its products and process.

18 One of Bawcombe's major concerns with either outsourcing or offshoring from China was uncertainty regarding the Chinese government's policy with respect to the yuan. Historically, the Chinese government had pegged the yuan to the U.S. dollar. This policy allowed only limited float in its price. The policy was controversial and a source of considerable inter-government talks. In 2007, the yuan-U.S. dollar exchange rate was 7.65 yuan/$. The market expectation was that the yuan would appreciate by about 20 per cent in the next five years,[7] although there was considerable uncertainty with the estimate. This appreciation would directly affect the cost of any product manufactured in China. If China were to allow the yuan to trade more freely, this appreciation would likely be magnified.

THE MEETING

19 Bawcombe welcomed his visitors from the corporate office, showed them some new innovations that the plant had implemented and took them to the conference room. When they got to the meeting, it was clear that the visitors had come to discuss the possibility of closing the Temecula plant. Bawcombe would do what was in the best interest of Scotts, but also wanted to keep Temecula open.

20 What should Scotts do?

[7] Bloomberg Yuan NDF (Non-denominated Futures).

Case 27

TiVo, Inc: *TiVo vs. Cable and Satellite DVR; Can TiVo Survive?*
Alan N. Hoffman, Rendy Halim, Rangki Son, and Suzanne Wong

BACKGROUND

"With TiVo, TV fits into your busy life, NOT the other way around"

1   The evolution history of Television started way back in 1939 with an original purpose of providing people with entertainment and enjoyment in life. It was then followed by an invention of the remote control in 1950 known as the "lazy bones." Perhaps, this has been one of the biggest breakthroughs and most influential forms of entertainment we all have appreciated and enjoyed up until now. However after the Lazy Bones was invented, the next generation of TV watching tools evolved; one of them was TiVo, every couch potato's dream. Thanks to two Silicon Valley veterans with their creative and smart ideas, they took the initiative to recreate innovative and advanced technology developments in a radically different approach. TiVo, was created not only just that entertainment, but "TV Your Way." Fundamentally designed, "With TiVo, TV fits into your busy life, NOT the other way around."

2   Now, many people may have heard the name TiVo . . . mentioned on popular TV shows, movies and many talk shows . . . even Oprah wonders in her September 2005 issue of her "O" magazine that why can't life be like TiVo . . . but not so many know what TiVo really is about.

ONCE UPON A TIVO . . .

3   Pioneered by Mike Ramsay and Jim Barton, TiVo redefined entertainment in many other ways, delivering the promise of technologies that were much hyped. Incorporated in Delaware and originally named their firm "Teleworld," the playback of TiVo started in August 4, 1997. As proposed, the original idea was to create a home network-based multimedia server where content to thin clients would stream out throughout the home. In order to build such product, solid software foundation is much needed and the device created has to operate flawlessly perfect, reliable and handle power failure gracefully for the consumers. At that time, both were still working in Silicon Graphics (SGI) and were very much involved in the entertainment industry. Jim Barton, though was involved with on-demand video system; he was the executive sponsor of an effort to port an open source system called Linux to the SGI Indy workstation, while Mike Ramsay was responsible for products that create movies' special effects for such companies as ILM and Pixar. With the combination of both worlds, these two SGI veterans thought Linux software would well serve TiVo as the operating system foundation. As for the hardware, it was designed solely by TiVo Inc and manufactured with the help of various OEMs including Philips, Sony, Hughes, Pioneer,

The authors would like to thank Audrey Ballara, Will Hoffman and Ann Hoffman for their research and contributions to this case. Please address all correspondence to: Dr. Alan N. Hoffman, MBA Program Director, LAC295D, Bentley College, 175 Forest Street, Waltham, MA 02452-4705, voice (781)891-2287, ahoffman@bentley.edu, fax (781)459-0335. Printed by permission of Dr. Alan N. Hoffman.

Toshiba, and Humax. Combined they created a product that is very much interactive with real people, delivering a commitment where those people will be able to take charge of their own entertainment whenever they want to and wherever they need to.

From the Server Room to the Living Room

4 Swaying from their original idea to create a home network device, they later developed the idea to record digitized video on a hardware storage drive. Inside the Silicon Valley headquarters of TiVo in Alviso, California, both veterans created a so called "fantasy living room," depicting a room full of executives who hope that will be a prototype for 100 million living rooms across North America. At that time, they both knew it would be so cool to exploit and develop the idea into an actual product with a promising future, a dream of most start-up companies. In the early days, Mike Ramsay said that they used to have thoughts of things like "Wow, you know, you can pause live television— isn't that a cool thing?" Jim Barton then got a computer to store a live TV signal and made it to play it back. Then . . . that was the start of TiVo—providing people with more than the original purpose of TV as just simply a tube to be watched, resulted with an invention to create the world's very first interactive entertainment network, where luxury of entertainment and control is in the viewers' own hands. As of March 31, 1999, TiVo shipped its first unit and because that day was a blue moon, an engineering staff code named TiVo's first version DVR as the "Blue Moon." Both Jim Barton and Mike Ramsay were psyched as the introduction to market a disruptive technology had just begun. Teleworld was then renamed to TiVo in July 1999. Now that the living room is filled only with an oval coffee table and a comfy chair just like any other living room in the households, the only objects that can be distinctively seen and left is what's on the table surface—a telephone and TiVo's distinctive peanut-shaped remote control. The sofa and chairs all face an entertainment center containing a big-screen television that is linked to several TiVo boxes (a few are available; a few are works in progress).

TIVO ACCLAMATION

5 Now where the success of on demand programs and online streaming are flocking TV networks, still many people have found DVR to be an essential part of their digital home entertainment center, catering more to people's viewing habits. Consumers would slip into stores such as big box retailers Best Buy, Circuit City, Target and Wal-Mart and sales people would refer them to TiVo as TiVo has been commonly associated as the "DVR." Reminiscing back to the history of DVR, TiVo was actually never a beginner, but ReplayTV. The two early consumer DVRs, ReplayTV and TiVo, both launched their product in 1999 Consumer Electronics Show in Las Vegas. ReplayTV won the "Best of Show" award in the video category and was later acquired by Sonic Blue and D&M Holdings later in the years. However, it wasn't ReplayTV, the pioneer of DVRs in the DVR industry, the brand that made it to the world producing a cult like product, but TiVo. TiVo's success also includes still currently being the only standalone DVR company in the industry. According to Forrester, from a scale of 1 to 5, TiVo's brand trust among regular users scores 4.2, while its brand potential among aspiring users scores A with 11.1 million potential users.

6 Spending approximately 13 months for full development of the first TiVo box, the wait was worthwhile as the revolutionary nature of TiVo won itself an Emmy award on August 19, 2006. This recognition was given to TiVo for providing innovative and interactive services that enhance television viewing to a whole new level. Other finalists for this particular Emmy award include AOL Music on Demand, CNN Enhanced and DirecTV Interactive Sports. With a cult-like product, TiVo has transformed into a verb. TiVo established a

top-notch brand that has become the "it" word among its fervidly loyal customers and even non-customers. In general, people would say "TiVo it," meaning to record or zap (make something disappear). A working wife, who has an important business dinner meeting that night and was rushing through the door, could speedily ask her husband "Could you TiVo Desperate Housewives for me tonight dear?" On the other hand, TiVo felt that this verb transformation will jeopordize TiVo and associate its products as a generic brand of DVR when people say, "I want two TiVo's." However, with all the TiVo buzz, TiVo became public on September 30th, 1999 at a price offering of $16 per share with a total of 5.5 million number of shares listed under the NASDAQ. On its way to the IPO, TiVo established one of the most rapid adoption rates in the history of consumer electronics. Quoted recently in an April 2007 article by PC World, TiVo became the third on the list of 50 best technology products of all time—saluted amazing products that changed our lives forever.

7   The acknowledgement has well served the young West Coast Company who is currently available in four countries which includes United States, United Kingdom, Canada and Taiwan. In addition, though it is not sold yet, TiVo's technology has been modified by end users so it could fit in another four countries such as Australia, New Zealand, Netherlands and South Africa. However TiVo has never come close to winning the number of customers (market share) nor generated a profit since it launched in 1997. Considered to be the best DVR system out there by variety of top notch publications such as *BusinessWeek, New York Times* and *Popular Science*, TiVo hit a 3 million subscriber milestone only by February, 18th, 2005. Not long after, TiVo finally made its first profitable quarter. TiVo's subscribers include diverse and loyal subscribers from the infamous Oprah Winfrey, Brad Pitt and entrepreneur Craig Newmark (the owner of Craigs List). Though, the business philosophy of TiVo is relatively simple: TiVo connects consumers to the digital entertainment they want, where, and when they want it.

THE BRAIN INSIDE THE BOX

"It's not TiVo unless it's a TiVo"

The Surf & Turf

8   As people's daily life became busier and demanded more and more to attain the pleasure of watching TV, Digital Video Recorders became the tool to suffice that trend. The trend resulted in audiences wanting to have more direct allegiance with particular programs. TiVo then revolutionized that new way to watch TV, with the introduction of the Digital Video Recording system (DVR). Hard as it seems to be described in a sentence or two, the best way to describe what TiVo really is, is by the things that it does.

9   The DVR platform has created massive opportunity for TiVo to continue developing creative and sophisticated applications, features and services. Unlike a VCR (videocassette recorder), TiVo as a Digital Video Recorder issues only Linux based software and allows users to capture any TV programming and record them into internal hard disk storage for later viewing. Its patented feature, "Trick Play" that allows viewers to stop, pause, rewind and slo-mo live shows are what TiVo is originally best at.

10   The TiVo device also allows users to watch their programs without having to watch the commercials if they don't want to. Users are exposed to promotional messages but are not forced to watch them. While this feature seems very attractive to consumers, understandably, not to television networks and advertising agencies. However, unlike ReplayTV that allows users to automatically and completely skip advertisements and was hit by several lawsuits by ad agencies and TV networks, TiVo managed to take a different approach.

11   With its inventive advertisement feature, TiVo offered to help, turning a difficult situation into a business opportunity, which has become TiVo's hallmark. TiVo surely knows that advertisements are a source of revenue. TiVo then started testing its "pop-up" feature. While recording or watching, there are some advertisements that pop up at the bottom of the TV screen. If a customer is interested in any of these advertisements, he has the ability to click to get more information about the product being advertised. People then have the choice to get advertisers' information or not depending on what they have interest in. "Product Watch" lets users choose the products, services, or even brands that interest them and it will automatically find and deliver the requested/relevant products straight to your list. Surprisingly, during the 2002 Super Bowl, TiVo tracked the viewing patterns of 10,000 of its subscribers and found that TiVo's instant replay feature was used more on certain commercials, notably the Pepsi ad with Britney Spears, than on the game itself. As of today, TiVo has included 70 "showcase" advertising campaigns in its TiVo platforms for companies such as Acura, Best Buy, BMW, Buick, Cadillac, Charles Schwab, Coca-Cola, Dell, General Motors, GMC, New Line Cinema, Nissan, Pioneer, Porsche, and Target.

12   Beyond the key functions above, there are much more for users to surf throughout the integral functionality of a TiVo device. While a "Season Pass Manager" is to avoid conflict resolution such as overlapping recordings, a "Wish List" platform allows viewers to store their search according to their specifics such as actor, keyword, director, etc. So far, no other companies have yet been able to match these two TiVo's recording features. In addition, the catchy remote control with its distinctive "Thumbs Up and Down" feature allows users to rate the shows they have watched purportedly for the use of others and themselves so that TiVo could assist and provide users with the movie similar to what they have rated. The remote itself has won design awards from the Consumer Electronics Association. Jakob Nielsen, a technology consultant of the Nielsen Norman Group, called the oversize yellow pause button in the middle of the remote "the most beautiful pause button I've ever seen." Steve Wozniak, the co-founder of Apple Computer mentioned "TiVo adjusts to my tastes" and that its remote has been the most ergonomic and easy to use one that he has had encountered in many years.

13   In addition, being portable is now the hottest thing in television right now. Nowadays, that people have yet become more tech savvy, "TiVoToGo," its newest feature launched in January 2005, allows users to connect their TiVo to a computer with an internet or a home network, transferring recorded shows from TiVo boxes to users' PCs. Then, through a software program developed with Sonic, customers are able to edit and conserve their TiVo files. Later in August 2005, TiVo released a software that allows customers to transfer MPEG2 video files from their PC to their TiVo boxes to play the video on the DVR.

14   TiVoToGo feature also includes TiVo's "Central Online" which allows users to schedule recordings on its website 24/7, and "MultiRoom Viewing" which allows users to transfer recordings between TiVo units in multiple rooms, download any programs in any format they want to into the TiVo box, and transfer them into a device such as an iPod, laptop or other mobile devices such as cellular phones. This provides the pleasure of viewing them anytime and anywhere the users desire to do so. On top of that, with the partnerships TiVo has established in regards to 3rd party network content, viewers now can access weather, traffic condition, even purchase a last minute movie ticket at Fandango.com and have the pleasure to enjoy "Amazon Unbox," allowing users to buy/rent the latest movies and TV shows to be downloaded into the TiVo box.

"Behind the Box"—The Hardware Anatomy of TiVo 101

15   So, many people would ask, how TiVo actually operates. "Even my mother can use TiVo with no problem!" This is the phrase that TiVo wants their people to say.

16   Technically speaking, installing TiVo units have been pretty much self explanatory because they are designed to be simple enough for everyone to install and operate. Parts that go into the device and its internal architecture have been made to be less complex. Online self installation guide with a step by step pictured instruction has been the tool to suffice complete this request, however, options do come in handy, with a teamed up "door to door" professional installation service with Best Buy or a set up appointment with 1-877-Geek Squad.

17   In basic sense, TiVo is simply a cable box, with hard drive that gives the ability to record, and the fancy user interface. The main idea at the beginning, however, was to free people up from being locked by the network schedule. With TiVo, the watchers can watch anytime they want with extra features such as, pause, rewind, fast forward, slow motion, and many other great features, including the commercial-free watching experience.

18   Initially, the box will receive the signals coming from cable, antenna, or satellite. Then the signals received by the box will be divided into many frequencies and selected with the tuner that is built-in the box. The signals with the right selected frequencies will be sent and encoded through the encoder, stored in the hard drive, and then decoded again for the watchers to view anytime.

19   TiVo's earlier model Series2 was supported with USB ports that have been integrated into the TiVo system to support network adapters which includes wired Ethernet and WiFi. It also provides the possibility to record over-the-air. The new TiVo series 3 has been built with two internal cable-ready tuners and it supports a single external cable or satellite box. As a result, TiVo gives the ability to record two shows at once, unlike other DVRs. Moreover, the latest version of the TiVo box has a 10/1000 Ethernet connection port and a SATA port which can support external storage hardware. It also has a HDMI plug which provides an interface between any compatible digital audio/video source, such as a DVD player, a PC, or a video game system. In other words, with the new TiVo box, customers don't even need their cable box anymore. Some recent models even contain DVD-R/RW drives which transfer recordings from the TiVo box to a DVD disc.

20   TiVo hardware can work as a normal digital recorder by itself. People might sometimes want to keep the hardware and cancel their subscriptions with TiVo, which is very damageable for the company revenue model.

What the Hack!

21   Where there is technology involved, there are incentives for hackers to challenge the system. Some people have hacked the TiVo boxes to improve the service, and to expand the recording capacity or/and storage. Others have aimed at making TiVo available in countries where TiVo is not currently available. In the latest version of TiVo, improved encryption of the hardware and software has made it more difficult for people to hack the systems.

THE TIVOPERATION—BEHIND THE SCENES . . .

". . . and I never miss an episode. TiVo takes care of the details"

Marketing:
Feel the Buzzzzzz—Hail Thy TiVo

22   When it comes to new technology, penetrating consumer markets is usually difficult as customers are slower to embrace new products than forecasters predict and opt to choose using old and easier technology like the VCRs. Mike Ramsay would get upset in the early days, when someone says, "oh, that's just like a VCR." He would then reply to them and say "no, no, no, no, no. It's much more than a VCR, it does this, it does that, let's personalize it

and all that stuff." At that point, it gets so difficult to describe what TiVo actually is, leading into a five to ten minute conversation instead of a 30 second TiVo pitch.

23   However, this problem has not hindered TiVo from being a great product. Early on, TiVo has tried the traditional way of getting the product across with a result of repetitive stumbles in marketing its products. The millions of dollars spent on advertisements did not help consumers understand what TiVo actually does. A customer claims, "I personally remember seeing TiVo ads on 'TV before I even knew what a TiVo was, and it took seven years for me to finally see one, in the flesh.' "

24   What makes TiVo DVRs different from other generic DVRs, can only be felt and experienced and not seen even though the feature differences can be seen in Exhibit 1. According to Gartner analyst Van Baker, "For cable and satellite DVRs, the interface stinks. They do a really bad job of it." TiVo would rally people to change their lives by continuously preaching its brand and products, creating cause and evangelism with a result of many people claiming TiVo changed their lives. According to a survey reported on the TiVo website, 98% of users said that they could not live without their TiVo.

25   The one word that explicitly describes the cult like product is "interactive" in many ways. So when TiVo subscribers feel the buzz, they show and tell, the story goes on and on and on. Between 1999 and 2000, TiVo's subscriptions increased by 86%. In addition to capitalizing on its tens of thousands of customer evangelists to move the product into the mainstream, TiVo's word-of-mouth strategy focuses on celebrity endorsements and television show product placement. The firm began giving its product away to such celebrities as Oprah, Sarah Michelle Gellar, Drew Bledsoe and many more, turning them into high-profile members of the cult, while Jay Leno and Rosie O'Donnell helped much influence TiVo's consumers in a very positive way.

The Market Research Team

26   The need to create such unique emotional connection between people and this product is significant to TiVo. Another way for a firm like TiVo to always be a step ahead and develop ways to improve and measure promotions and viewer behavior is to do continuous intensive market research. TiVo's market research team is considered as one of its functional units that are driving the company which includes Lieberman Research Worldwide and Nielson Media Research. With Lieberman, the first ever DVR based panel was established in August 2002. Internally, TiVo also has built a platform in their system that sends detailed information on its customers watching TV behavior back to TiVo. TiVo also fully embraced the community with its TiVo community and hackers programs so that TiVo research team know what people needs are, when and where they need them.

Financial:

Fast Forward or Rewind TiVo's Stock?

27   TiVo started with a price of $16 during its IPO in 1999. TiVo reached the highest in its stock price history after its IPO at $78.75 with its first eye catching ad "Hey, if you like us, TiVo us" which then became its first milestone. After the rush rapid growth, TiVo's stock price shot down to a price as low as $2.25, the lowest in history around 2002. TiVo's stock price then started to pick up in 2003 when FCC Chairman Michael Powell announced that he uses TiVo, claiming TiVo is a "God's Machine," and when White House Press Secretary Ari Fleischer was found too to be a loyal user of TiVo. Around mid 2003, TiVo hit its first 1 million subscribers, significantly increased its stock price to reach around $14.00/share then inched back down to a low $3.50 per share as a result from the resignation of its CEO, Mike Ramsay. With the new CEO in place, TiVo finally reached a 3 million subscribers milestone by mid 2005, reaching to a current average stock price of $6–$7 range per share. Now, the question is, how to appease investors without killing a feature that helps sell the product?

EXHIBIT 1

	TiVo Series2™ Boxes	Leading Cable Service DVR*	Satellite DVR**	DIRECTV DVR with TiVo ©
Record from multiple sources	Yes	No	No	No
	combine satellite, cable, or antenna, depending on product.	Digital cable only	Satellite only	DIRECTV only
Easy search:				
Find shows by title, actor, genre, or keyword	Yes	Titles only browsing only	Title, subject, and actor only	Yes
Online scheduling:				
Schedule recordings from the Internet	Yes	No	No	No
Dual Tuner:				
Record 2 shows at once[1]	Yes	Yes	Yes	Yes
Movie and TV Downloads:				
Purchase or rent 1000's of movies and television shows from Amazon Unbox and have them delivered directly to your television.[2]	Yes	No	No	No
Home Movie Sharing:				
Edit, enhance, and send movies and photo slideshows from your One True Media account to any broadband connected TiVo box.[3]	Yes	No	No	No
Online services:				
Yahoo! weather, traffic & digital photos, Internet Radio from Live365, Podcasts, & movie tickets from Fandango	Yes	Limited	Limited	No
Built-In Ethernet:				
Broadband-ready right out of the box—connecting to your home network is a snap[4]	Yes	No	No	No
TiVoToGo transfers to mobile devices:				
Transfer shows to your favorite portable devices, laptop or burn them to DVD.[3,5]	Yes	No	No	No
Home media features:				
Digital photos, digital music and more	Yes	No	No	No
Transfer shows between boxes:				
Record shows on one TV and watch them on another.[3]	Yes	No	No	No

*Leading cable services compared to Time Warner/Cox Communications Explorer® 8000™ DVR and Comcast DVR
**Leading satellite services compared to DISH Network 625 DVR
[1]On the TiVo® Series2™ DT DVR, you can record basic cable channels, or one basic cable and one digital cable channel, at once.
[2]Requires broadband cable modem or DSL connection.
[3]Requires your TiVo box to be connected to a home network wirelessly or via Ethernet
[4]Available on the new TiVo® Series2™ DT DVR and the TiVo® Series3™ DMR
[5]In order to burn TiVoToGo transfers to DVD you will need to purchase software from Roxio/Sonic Solutions.

Source: http://www.tivo.com/1.0.chart.asp

Multiroom Solutions

	Digeo/Moxi	Motorola	Scientific-Atlanta	Echostar	TiVo	Microsoft
Main DVR	Cable DVR*	Cable DVR†	Cable DVR†	Satellite DVR*	TiVo box	Media Center PC
Set-top box on additional TV(s)	IP terminal	Cable box‡	Cable box	None	TiVo box	XBox 360
How boxes share content	IP	IP	Digital broadcast	Analog broadcast	IP§	IP
Physical connection	Coax	Coax	Coax	Coax	Home network	Home network
Features available on additional TVs:						
Play back recorded programs	✓	✓	✓	✓	✓	✓
Record programs	✓	✓		✓	✓	✓
Pause programs	✓	✓		✓	✓	✓
View Internet content	✓	✕			✓	✓
View personal digital content	✕	✕			✓	✓

*New product specifically designed for multiroom use
†Standard cable DVR plus modifications for multiroom use
‡Requires additional IP dongle on standard digital set-top box
§Requires transferring files from one TiVo box to the other

"✕"= Available, but operators have not yet deployed

Source: Forrester Research Inc., 2006

TiVO DVRs

SAVE $150 INSTANTLY†

80-hr TiVo® Series2™ DT DVR

SAVE $150 INSTANTLY†

180-hr TiVo® Series2™ DT DVR

300-hr TiVo® Series3™ HD Digital Media Recorder

Comcast.

Motorola Set-Top Box

Scientific Atlanta Set-Top Box

DIRECTV®

Deconstructing TiVo

28   Since it was founded in 1997, TiVo has accumulated more than $400 million in losses. Looking at TiVo's revenues and costs structures in Exhibit 2, TiVo, an enigmatic company, has much divided its revenues and costs in variety of forms which includes service, technology, hardware and shared revenues. Being a company that lives under a great shadow of Wall Street pessimism, the question then becomes what value can TiVo add besides hyping their latest technology developments? Service revenues for example, TiVo needs to know what is the actual value of TiVo-owned subscribers and not TiVo's partnerships subscribers such as to DirecTV and Comcast. Deconstructing the value of just this one particular matter then leads to longer questions which includes, how long does a TiVo subscriber remain a subscriber, how much do each of them pay and are willing to pay, how much advertising revenue do users produce for every tag they click, moreover, how long and how can TiVo maintain its subscribers to be TiVo-owned subscribers?

29   In one way, the chicken and egg problem may have been the bulk of the TiVo's hardware revenues problem where people would say "What, huh, TiVo, personalizing your own TV network? What the hell are you talking about?," but not being able to gain the economies of scale that it desires, it should be TiVo's point of concern. Even though rebates are being offered, still, TiVo has not reached its price point that really attracts people. TiVo offers three types of boxes depending on the hours of programming storage capacity which range from an 80 hour TiVo Series to 300 hour TiVo Series HD. For the basic TiVo Series2 box of 80 hours and 180 hours has a one time fee of $99.99 and $199.99, while the HD TiVo box costs $799.99 with a 300 hours storage capacity.

30   TiVo also has been a heavy user of mail-in rebates which is reflected as one of their forms of revenues shown in Exhibit 2. According to *BusinessWeek,* $5 million in additional revenue was recognized because nearly half of TiVo's 100,000 new subscribers failed to apply for a $100 rebate. This slippage type of strategy is known to marketers as the "shoebox effect" and this usage of promotional practice has caused a large positive impact for TiVo.

Operation:

Research and Development—The "A" Team

31   Again, the word "interactive" is the buzz word. TiVo's R&D team makes sure that they build TiVo from the user's perspective and viewing habits. TiVo forms forums of communication through TiVo community.com and TiVo hackers. In this forum, criticisms are allowed and even encouraged, so long as they are constructive and help TiVo to grow. Users and aspiring users of TiVo are allowed to say what they like and dislike and voice what they expect to see TiVo in the future. Ideas generated through this forum will help TiVo's R&D team and developers to continuously be on hand and future innovaters accordingly to the need of people's ever changing lifestyle. TiVo is also concerned how its platform could actually be used the wrong way by kids these days. With this concern, TiVo has collaborated with parents to build a new feature called TiVo Parental Zone that allows parents to control what their kids are actually watching. Privacy concern has also been an issue nowadays in the advance technology industry. TiVo manages to protect its community regarding privacy concern by storing such information on a computer behind its "firewall" in a secure location, and often restricts the number of employees internally who can access such data.

32   Previously TiVo's R&D team only consists of contract based engineers; now, TiVo makes sure that its R&D team consists of a diverse, utmost creative and detailed staff engineers. Its intensive research principle is that benefits must extend existing people's behaviors. The design team has every little detail of steps to follow to fit the needs of lifestyle. As an example of TiVo's meticulous product design process, TiVo created a remote control that

EXHIBIT 2 Tivo Inc. Condensed Consolidated Statements of Operations (In thousands, except per share and share amounts) (unaudited)

	Three Months Ended October 31,		Nine Months Ended October 31,	
	2006	2005 Adjusted	2006	2005 Adjusted
Revenues				
Service and technology revenues	$ 52,616	$ 43,197	$ 160,605	$ 123,891
Hardware revenues	27,978	24,652	53,666	39,827
Rebates, revenue share, and other payments to channel	(14,934)	(18,234)	(32,932)	(27,860)
Net revenues	65,660	49,615	181,339	135,858
Cost of revenues				
Cost of service and technology revenues (1)	13,826	8,508	44,256	24,832
Cost of hardware revenues	31,925	24,667	68,678	48,006
Total cost of revenues	45,751	33,175	112,934	72,838
Gross margin	19,909	16,440	68,405	63,020
Research and development (1)	12,221	9,712	37,973	30,394
Sales and marketing (1)	10,123	10,006	25,856	24,410
General and administrative (1)	9,811	11,702	35,961	26,249
Total operating expenses	32,155	31,420	99,790	81,053
Loss from operations	(12,246)	(14,980)	(31,385)	(18,033)
Interest income	1,291	826	3,341	2,184
Interest expense and other	(133)	(10)	(165)	(13)
Loss before income taxes	(11,088)	(14,164)	(28,209)	(15,862)
Provision for income taxes	(1)	—	(35)	(51)
Net loss	$ (11,092)	$ (14,164)	$ (28,244)	$ (15,913)
Net loss per common share-basic and diluted	$ (0.12)	$ (0.17)	$ (0.32)	$ (0.19)
Weighted average common shares used to calculate basic and diluted net loss per share	91,930,061	84,200,655	87,680,571	83,362,402
(1) Includes stock-based compensation expense (benefit) as follows:				
Cost of service and technology revenues	$ 365	$ —	$ 1,035	$ —
Research and development	1,608	(6)	4,177	(131)
Sales and marketing	474	20	1,264	(20)
General and administrative	1,636	151	4,257	199

The accompanying notes are an integral part of these condensed consolidated statements.

combines personalization and interconnectivity. TiVo's remote has a feature of thumbs up and down to be clicked on for users to rate shows so that TiVo will know what to record. In addition, TiVo allows the Braille ability on its remote for eye impaired users. Other R&D processes includes product testing & development of its softwares and platforms, product

	1998	1999	2000	2001	2002	2003	2004	2005
Consolidated Statement of Operations Data: Revenues								
Service revenues	$ 3,782	$ 989	$ 19,297	$ 39,261	$ 61,560	$107,166	$167,194	
Technology revenues	$ —	$ —	$ 100	$ 20,909	$ 15,797	$ 8,310	$ 3,665	
Hardware revenues	$ —	$ —	$ —	$ 45,620	$ 72,882	$111,275	$ 72,093	
Rebates, revenue share, and other payment to the channel	$ (5,029)	$ (630)	$ —	$ (9,780)	$ (9,159)	$(54,696)	$(47,027)	
Net Revenues	$ (1,247)	$ 359	$ 19,397	$ 96,010	$141,080	$172,055	$195,925	
Cost and Expenses								
Cost of service revenues	$ 18,734	$ 1,719	$ 19,852	$ 17,119	$ 17,705	$ 29,360	$ 34,179	
Cost of technology revenues	$ —	$ —	$ 62	$ 8,033	$ 13,609	$ 6,575	$ 782	
Cost of hardware revenues	$ —	$ —	$ —	$ 44,647	$ 74,836	$120,323	$ 84,216	
Research and development	$ 25,070	$ 2,544	$ 27,205	$ 20,714	$ 22,167	$ 37,634	$ 41,087	
Sales and marketing	$ 151,658	$ 13,946	$ 104,897	$ 48,117	$ 18,947	$ 37,367	$ 35,047	
General and administrative	$ 15,537	$ 1,395	$ 18,875	$ 14,465	$ 16,296	$ 16,593	$ 38,018	
Total Costs	$ 210,999	$ 19,604	$ 170,891	$153,095	$163,560	$247,852	$233,329	
% Costs over Revenues	−16921%	5461%	881%	159%	116%	144%	119%	
Net Loss from operations	$(212,246)	$(19,245)	$(151,494)	$(57,085)	$(22,480)	$(75,797)	$(37,404)	

integration of software to satellite system and product integration such as the integration of a DVD burner and TiVo recorder. Besides developing its main products, the TiVo R&D team also tried to design platforms and technology that can be used with any other products and enhance the demand of TiVo's main products such as the ability to connect with computers, other home theater technologies and especially, cable and satellites.

33   Since the intensified competition exists in this DVR industry, TiVo found the need to patent its advance software and technology platform. TiVo licensed its TiVoToGo software to chip maker AMD, digital media software companies such as Sonic Solutions and giant companies such as Microsoft in order to enable video playback on pocket PCs and smart phones. As of today, TiVo has 85 patents granted and still 117 applications patents pending, which include domestic and foreign patents that further leave rivals scratching their heads. TiVo licenses its patents through several of its trusted partners such as Sony, Toshiba, Pioneer and DirecTV. TiVo believes that licensing its technology to third parties has been its best business model.

Executive Team & Management

34   TiVo's top management is always on hand with its operations and promotions. Former CEO, Mike Ramsay, would make overseas trips such as to Japan to conduct meetings and

TiVo Inc. Condensed Consolidated Balance Sheets (In thousands, except share amounts) (unaudited)

	October 31, 2006	January 31, 2006 Adjusted
ASSETS		
CURRENT ASSETS		
Cash and cash equivalents	$ 78,898	$ 85,298
Short-term investments	28,067	18,915
Accounts receivable, net of allowance for doubtful accounts of $121 and $56	27,300	20,111
Finished goods inventories	34,107	10,939
Prepaid expenses and other, current	4,327	8,744
Total current assets	172,699	144,007
LONG-TERM ASSETS		
Property and equipment, net	10,874	9,448
Purchased technology, capitalized software, and intangible assets, net	17,580	5,206
Prepaid expenses and other, long-term	597	347
Total long-term assets	29,051	15,001
Total assets	$ 201,750	$159,008
LIABILITIES AND STOCKHOLDERS' EQUITY/(DEFICIT)		
LIABILITIES		
CURRENT LIABILITIES		
Accounts Payable	$ 28,278	$ 24,050
Accrued liabilities	32,553	37,449
Deferred revenue, current	56,596	57,902
Total current liabilities	117,427	119,401
LONG-TERM LIABILITIES		
Deferred revenue, long-term	51,550	67,575
Deferred rent and other	2,208	1,404
Total long-term liabilities	53,758	68,979
Total liabilities	171,185	188,380
COMMITMENTS AND CONTINGENCIES (see Note 10)		
STOCKHOLDERS' EQUITY/(DEFICIT)		
Preferred stock, par value$ 0.001:		
Authorized shares are 10,000,000;		
Issued and outstanding shares-none	—	—
Common stock, par value$ 0.001:		
Authorized shares are 150,000,000;		
Issued shares are 96,922,295 and 85,376,191, respectively and outstanding shares are 96,841,792 and 85,376,191, respectively	97	85
Additional paid-in capital	753,373	667,055
Deferred compensation	—	(2,421)
Accumulated deficit	(722,335)	(694,091)
Less: Treasury stock, at cost - 80,503 shares	(570)	—
Total stockholders' equity (deficit)	30,565	(29,372)
Total liabilities and stockholders' equity (deficit)	$ 201,750	$159,008

seminars with consumer electronics makers. This effort is an attempt to convince the makers to embed TiVo's software into their products. In order to make sure everything goes well and accordingly, the ex-CEO has been focusing on maintaining partnerships. He would rarely be in his office, instead on the road talking to companies that can help TiVo build software and subscribers. However, many mistakes were made throughout his history being a CEO which includes employee layoffs twice in 2001. 80 employees (approx 25% of workforce) were laid off in 5th of Apr 2001 and 40 employees (approx 20% of workforce) were laid off in 31st Oct 2001. TiVo's previous CEO, Mike Ramsay was just an engineer on the block. He knows how to be creative and build great machines, but doesn't really know the industry very well, moreover manage the company and steer TiVo from drowning further. As a result, Mike Ramsay resigned in mid-2005; a change of CEO was implemented, where the new CEO hired was the former president of NBC Cable, Tom Rogers, a new strength to TiVo's management.

35   In addition, TiVo's Board of Directors consists of individuals from very diverse backgrounds and companies; however, this actually poses as one of TiVo's concern. TiVo needs more members that are from TiVo's industry related background and can influence future DVR/Cable industry; possibly they would make better decisions.

SLEEPING WITH THE ENEMIES

". . . So Long, TiVo! Hello DVR! . . ."

The Industry

36   The Digital Video Recorder or Personal Video Recorder market is located at the convergence of these 4 established industries: Broadcasting and TV, Software and Programming, Electronic Instrument, and Communications Equipment.

37   For TiVo, introducing a disruptive technology into the industry was full of obstacles. When a Digital Video Recording has the potential to be considered as a "disruptive technology," which means that the technology creates something new which "usurps existing products, services, and business model." According to Mike Ramsay, the DVR phenomenon has established that "people really want to take control of television, and if you give them control, they don't want you to take it back." Though TiVo has innovatively added all the great software, platforms and services that a standalone TiVo DVR has to offer, the viewing will not work / be greater without a connection to a cable network or satellite signals. Therefore, users who want a TiVo DVR will need to subscribe to TiVo, pay a onetime fee for the TiVo box and subscribe to companies that provides cable or satellite signals such as Comcast and DirecTV. Because this is the case, the TiVo DVR has made itself to be readily equipped with a built in cable-ready tuner for use with any external cable box or satellite receiver. TiVo has made many alliances and at the same time even competed with cable operators and satellite networks. With cable, satellite, and electronics companies pushing to have their own DVRs, the DVR industry is expected to grow rapidly.

38   Market share wise, TiVo claims to cover the entire US market.

Friends or Foe?

39   In 2000, AOL invested $200 million in TiVo and became the largest shareholder of the company and one of its main service partners. The deal allowed TiVo to release a box that provided both TiVo's capabilities and AOL services. Aside AOL, TiVo established other service partnerships. TiVo and Discovery Communication and NBC agreed on an $8.1 million deal in the form of advertising and promotional services. Later on, an additional $5 million was paid to NBC for promotions. It also collaborated on Research and Development and allowed

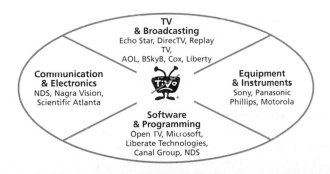

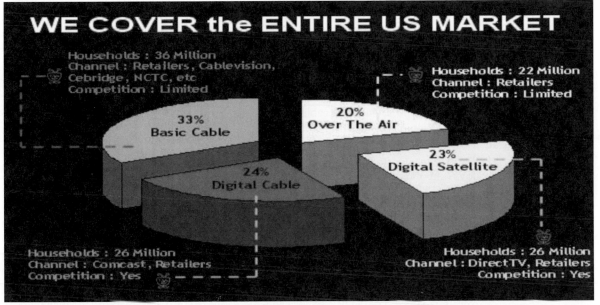

Source: Natexis Bleichroeder, Inc, July 2005.

40   TiVo to use a portion of its satellite network. AT&T helped TiVo to market and sell the service in Boston, Denver and Silicon Valley areas. BSkyB was the service partner for TiVo in the United Kingdom. Creative Artists Agency marketed and gave promotional support of the personal video recorder and was given in exchange 67,122 shares of preferred stock.

40   Despite all the partnerships that TiVo was able to enjoy, TiVo has actually been faced by a difficult challenge, that is cable and satellite operators who can be either TiVo's buddy or enemy—now that they offer digital video recorder-equipped set-top boxes of their own. Cable operators like Time Warner Cable and Cox Communications offer built-in DVR capability in set-top boxes and provide the equipment "free" to subscribers, and in late August 2003, Echostar announced a free DVR promotion, which was an unprecedented move in the industry. TiVo's fairly expensive retail priced unit could possibly jeopardize the company's ability to stay. There are relatively few cable and satellite providers, leaving TiVo with little power over them. These companies have the ability to dictate pricing of the TiVo technology because these huge cable companies can always develop or purchase their own generic DVR unit to market to their subscription base. Although TiVo had to give up a cut of profits to partners, still TiVo decided to have strategic relationship with competitors and cable companies for distribution and credit on its sales force.

41   Previously, DirecTV has been the backbone of TiVo, the service partner that has been fruit-fully fueling most of TiVo's growth. In addition, TiVo's current 4.4 million subscribers have

mostly come from its deal with DirecTV. As of early 2002, subscribers to TiVo service through DirecTV have increased from 230,000 to 2.1 million, representing more than half of all DVR subscriptions through satellite. Earlier on when DirecTV began the talk with TiVo, the satellite provider was already equipped with a DVR service through its partnership with Microsoft's Ultimate TV. For users to be able to watch their shows, subscriptions to DirecTV channels range from $29.99/month providing 40 channels to $65.99/month with over 250 channels.

42   Now that DirecTV is developing their own DVR device with the NDS Group and mentioned in 2005 that it would stop marketing and selling TiVo's digital recorders to its satellite TV subscribers starting in 2007, will TiVo become history? Though, DirecTV's DVR still costs users $299 onetime fee, but it includes unique features such as the ability to jump to a specific scene in the program as well as allowing users to pay for any downloaded pay-per-view movies only when they are being viewed. In 2006, TiVo and DirecTV reached a commercial extension agreement for three years. The agreement will allow existing DirecTV customers using the TiVo digital video recorder to continue to receive maintenance and support from DirecTV. As part of the agreement, TiVo and DirecTV also said they wouldn't sue each other over patent rights. Since the agreement with DirecTV was facing to expiration date, TiVo has been rushing to differentiate its product and struggling to strike other distribution deals.

43   In July 2000, Comcast, a cable operator, agreed to a trial offering TiVo boxes to its subscribers, hoping that the trial would lead to a bigger deal where Comcast would integrate TiVo software into Comcast cable boxes. Upon knowing it, Comcast balked and was unwilling to concede. In April 2001, when another trial was struck up to lead to a larger deal, TiVo laid off approximately 25% of its staff. November 2001, a full bloom of hope became hopeless when ATT Broadband agreed to offer TiVo DVRs to its customers with the fact that within a few weeks after, Comcast ended up killing the deal by acquiring the cable provider and its 14 million customers. In addition, in 2002, cable operators such as Comcast ended up developing their own DVR boxes with makers such as Motorola and Scientific Atlanta. However, similar to DirecTV, Comcast, the nation's cable company, announced in March 2005, that it would offer its customers a video recorder service from TiVo and even will allow TiVo to develop its software for Comcast's DVR platform. Comcast and TiVo agreed working to make TiVo's DVR service and interactive advertising capability (ad management system) available over Comcast's cable network and its set-top DVR boxes. This agreement also included that under TiVo brand name, the first of their co-developed products would be available in mid- to late-2006.

44   Subscriptions to Comcast's basic or standard cable cost users $8.63 or $52.55. To want to have a DVR feature, users need to add $13.94 with Comcast in addition to the subscriptions to TiVo which ranges from $12.95 to $16.95/month depending on the lifetime plan chosen that varies from one to three years. Due to the agreement with Comcast, TiVo's shares closed up nearly 75%, or $2.87 per share, to $6.70. Investors were positive about the news, some upgrading TiVo's investment rating from a sell to hold; even though, sparking investors had concern over TiVo's future, since DirecTV started using a second company, NDS, to provide DVR service, a deal with Comcast puts to rest some of those concerns by opening up a large new potential audience for TiVo's service. According to a filing with the SEC, TiVo receives an upfront payment from Comcast for creating a new DVR that works with Comcast's current service. TiVo also receives a recurring monthly fee for each Comcast subscriber who uses TiVo through Comcast.

45   Both TiVo's deal with a cable operator such as Comcast and a satellite broadcaster such as DirecTV were made merely because of the technological differences that can be tweaked around. Rolling out new technologies such as DVR, will be easier for satellite broadcasters because changes can be made in a central location. While as for cable operators, technology will have to be deployed gradually as they have different equipment in different areas. With all these deals, could TiVo's opportunities be beyond TV and that it helps TiVo to become what it has always wanted to be: a software provider?

46   In addition, with the hype of being portable, lately, TiVo and BellSouth FastAccess DSL agreed on a variety of co-marketing. With strong southeastern presence and renowned customer satisfaction of BellSouth, TiVo can turn a DSL Internet connection into a pipeline for video content delivered directly to the television. To expand program recording to a cellular phone, its latest TiVo Mobile feature, TiVo struck up a deal with Verizon to bring the digital video recording pioneer's capabilities beyond its set-top-boxes and the television, and directly to cell phones for the first time. In terms of contents, TiVo also has engaged in new partnerships with CBS Corp, Reuters Group PLC, and Forbes magazine, not to mention New York Times Co., National Basketball Association and some other firms. This will make "news and entertainment programs available for downloading onto TiVo's." International Creative Management is to recommend films, television shows and Internet videos that TiVo users can download onto their boxes. Finally TiVo has decided to open up to amateur videos through a deal with One True Media Inc., "an Internet start up that operates a Web Service designed to help users easily edit their raw footage into slick home movies.

THE TALKATIVO

". . . Bring 'em on! We are talking the HD language now . . . Yeah!."

HD Trend

47   High Definition sets in the entertainment industry are now the most important new consumer electronic items. HD products focus more toward quality of what is being seen and heard rather than the compactness like we saw a decade ago. High Definition sets include HDTV, HD broadcasting, HD DVD, HD Radio, HD Photo and even HD Audio.

48   Of which TiVo is linked particularly to, High Definition TV (HDTV) was first introduced in the United States during the 1990s and it is basically a digital television broadcasting system using a significantly higher resolution than the traditional formats such as NTSC, PAL and SECAM. The technology at that time was very expensive. Nowadays, as the prices have decreased, HDTV is going mainstream. A significant number of people have already bought HDTV; most people are planning to buy an HDTV soon. As of 2007, HDTVs are available in 24 million US households. By 2009, HDTV will have replaced all the old Standard Definition TVs. With the price of the hard-drive becoming lower and lower, and the increasing technology of HDTV, the demands for the HD products are also increasing multiple times. With HDTV, users are potentially being offered a much better picture quality than standard television, with greater picture on screen clarity and smoother motion, richer and more natural colors and surround sound.

HD TiVo

49   Lately, TiVo issued the TiVo Series3 which will allow customers to record HD television and digital cable. As people experience HDTV, TiVo service will be increasingly appealing. Once again, TiVo has set up the technological standards in the environment. The TiVo Series 3, HD version allows the consumers to do many additional great things and deliver both the audio and visual in HD.

50   TiVo realizes that great quality videos need to be supported by great quality audio, thus, they put a lot of efforts in the audio development, and received the certification of being the first digital media recorder to meet their performance standard in HDTV. THX is very well known to have developed highest standard of audio, mainly the surround systems in the entertainment, as well as the media industry.

TiVo SERIES 3

51   The new Hi-Def TiVo Series3 which is being sold for $799, has the ability to record two HD programs simultaneously while playing back a third previously recorded one. It also has two signal inputs and it accepts cable TV and over-the-air signals. It replaces the existing as well as the 30-second commercial skip. In addition, the new HD Tivo is different because there is no lifetime membership anymore for the HD TiVo compared to the older DVR products. Is this the shift of TiVo revenue model to aim at the subscription based revenue stream?

52   Despite that the capability of TiVo being able to record and playback at Hi-Def level, there are still many considerations for people before buying the TiVo. The downside of the HD TiVo, however, the price is overly expensive for most people especially when there are some DVRs being offered for free by the cable companies.

HD TiVENemies

53   Now that the HD trend is flocking the entertainment industry, TiVo competitors are also offering HD DVRs on their own and not just a DVR.

54   As for a cable operator such as Comcast, Comcast allows its subscribers to rent their DVR boxes for $13.94/month as they do not offer to sell their DVR boxes to their customers. With their HD DVR boxes manufactured by Motorola and Scientific Atlanta, users are able to navigate their own preferences just like using a TiVo, except that TiVo may have better and more features built into the TiVo boxes. Then with the Comcast DVR boxes, users will be able to watch the variety of cable channels offered by Comcast with an additional monthly subscription fee to cable channels.

55   Once a best friend, now may soon be a foe, DirecTV, a satellite operator, allows subscribers to add an additional DVR subscription service for $4.99 monthly on top of the chosen monthly subscription service package to DirecTV cable channels which ranges from $29.99 to $65.99. Same as Comcast not allowing users to keep their DVR boxes, if a user is in need of an HD DVR box, the user will need to pay an upfront cost of $299 with $100 rebate. As for the basic DVR, DirecTV charges $99.99 upfront cost.

REFERENCES

http://www.tivo.com/

http://en.wikipedia.org/wiki/TiVo

http://en.wikipedia.org/wiki/High-definition_television

http://egotron.com/ptv/ptvintro.htm

http://news.com.com/TiVo,+Comcast+reach+DVR+deal/2100-1041_3-5616961.html

http://news.com.com/TiVo+and+DirecTV+extend+contract/2100-1038_3-6060475.html

http://www.technologyreview.com

http://www.fastcompany.com/magazine/61/tivo.html

http://iinnovate.blogspot.com/2006/09/mike-ramsay-co-founder-of-tivo.html

http://www.acmqueue.org/modules.php?name=Content&pa=showpage&pid=53&page=7

http://www.internetnews.com/stats/article.php/3655331

http://thomashawk.com/2006/04/tivo-history-101-how-tivo-built-pvr_24.html

http://www.tvpredictions.com/tivohd030807.htm

http://www.tivocommunity.com/tivo-vb/showthread.php?threadid=151443

Case 28

Whole Foods Market 2007: *Will There Be Enough Organic Food to Satisfy the Growing Demand?*

Patricia Harasta and Alan N. Hoffman

1 Reflecting back over his three decades of experience in the grocery business, John Mackey smiled to himself over his previous successes. His entrepreneurial history began with a single store which he has now grown to the nation's leading natural food chain. While proud of the past, John had concerns about the future direction the Whole Foods Market chain should head. Whole Foods Market was an early entrant into the organic food market and they have used their early mover advantage to solidify their position and continue their steady growth.

2 In 2005 Whole Foods Market acquired the Wild Oats Food chain. Wild Oats operates 100 full-service stores in 24 states and Canada. With the changing economy and a more competitive industry landscape, John Mackey is uncertain about how to meet the company's aggressive growth targets. Whole Foods Market's objective is to reach $12 billion in revenue with 300+ stores by 2010 without sacrificing quality and their current reputation. This is not an easy task and John is unsure of the best way to proceed.

COMPANY BACKGROUND

3 Whole Foods carries both natural and organic food offering customers a wide variety of products. "Natural" refers to food that is free of growth hormones or antibiotics, where "certificated organic" food conforms to the standards, as defined by the U.S. Department of Agriculture in October 2002. Whole Foods Market® is the world's leading retailer of natural and organic foods, with 193 stores in 31 states and Canada and the United Kingdom. John Mackey, current president and cofounder of Whole Foods, opened "Safer Way" natural grocery store in 1978. The store had limited success as it was a small location allowing only for a limited selection, focusing entirely on vegetarian foods. John joined forces with Craig Weller and Mark Skiles, founders of "Clarksville Natural Grocery" (founded in 1979), to create Whole Foods Market. This joint venture took place in Austin, Texas, in 1980 resulting in a new company, a single natural food market with a staff of nineteen.

4 In addition to the supermarkets, Whole Foods owns and operates several subsidiaries. Allegro Coffee Company was formed in 1977 and purchased by Whole Foods Market in 1997 now acting as their coffee roasting and distribution center. Pigeon Cove is Whole Foods' seafood processing facility, which was founded in 1985 and known as M & S Seafood until 1990. Whole Foods purchased Pigeon Cove in 1996, located in Gloucester, MA. The company is now the only supermarket to own and operate a waterfront seafood facility. The last two subsidiaries are Produce Field Inspection Office and Select Fish, which is Whole Foods' West Coast seafood processing facility acquired in 2003. In addition to the above, the company has eight distribution centers, seven regional bake houses and four commissaries.

The authors would like to thank Ann Hoffman, Christopher Ferrari, Robert Marshall, Julie Giles, Jennifer Powers and Gretchen Alper for their research and contributions to this case.

Please address all correspondence to: Dr. Alan N. Hoffman, AGC 320, Department of Management, Bentley College, 175 Forest Street, Waltham, MA 02452-4705, voice (781) 891-2287, ahoffman@bentley.edu, fax (781) 459-0335. Printed by permission of Dr. Alan N. Hoffman, Bentley College.

5   "Whole Foods Market remains uniquely mission driven: The Company is highly selective about what they sell, dedicated to stringent quality standards, and committed to sustainable agriculture. They believe in a virtuous circle entwining the food chain, human beings and Mother Earth: each is reliant upon the others through a beautiful and delicate symbiosis." The message of preservation and sustainability are followed while providing high quality goods to customers and high profits to investors.

6   Whole Foods has grown over the years through mergers, acquisitions and several new store openings. Today, Whole Foods Market is the largest natural food supermarket in the United States. The company consists of 32,000 employees operating 193 stores in the United States, Canada and United Kingdom with an average store size of 32,000 square feet. While the majority of Whole Foods locations are in US, the company has made acquisitions expanding its presence in the UK. European expansion provides enormous potential growth due to the large population and it holds "a more sophisticated organic-foods market than US in terms of suppliers and acceptance by the public." Whole Foods targets their locations specifically by an area's demographics. The company targets locations where 40% or more of the residents have a college degree as they are more likely to be aware of nutritional issues.

WHOLE FOODS MARKET'S PHILOSOPHY

7   Their corporate website defines the company philosophy as follows, "Whole Foods Market's vision of a sustainable future means our children and grandchildren will be living in a world that values human creativity, diversity, and individual choice. Businesses will harness human and material resources without devaluing the integrity of the individual or the planet's ecosystems. Companies, governments, and institutions will be held accountable for their actions. People will better understand that all actions have repercussions and that planning and foresight coupled with hard work and flexibility can overcome almost any problem encountered. It will be a world that values education and a free exchange of ideas by an informed citizenry; where people are encouraged to discover, nurture, and share their life's passions."

8   While Whole Foods recognizes it is only a supermarket, they are working toward fulfilling their vision within the context of their industry. In addition to leading by example, they strive to conduct business in a manner consistent with their mission and vision. By offering minimally processed, high quality food, engaging in ethical business practices and providing a motivational, respectful work environment, the company believes they are on the path to a sustainable future.

9   Whole Foods incorporates the best practices of each location back into the chain. This can be seen in the company's store product expansion from dry goods to perishable produce, including meats, fish and prepared foods. The lessons learned at one location are absorbed by all, enabling the chain to maximize effectiveness and efficiency while offering a product line customers love. Whole Foods carries only natural and organic products. The best tasting and most nutritious food available is found in its purest state—unadulterated by artificial additives, sweeteners, colorings, and preservatives.

10   Whole Foods continually improves customer offerings, catering to its specific locations. Unlike business models for traditional grocery stores, Whole Foods' products differ by geographic regions and local farm specialties.

EMPLOYEE & CUSTOMER RELATIONS

11   Whole Foods encourages a team-based environment allowing each store to make independent decisions regarding its operations. Teams consist of up to eleven employees and a team leader. The team leaders typically head up one department or another. Each store employs

anywhere from 72 to 391 team members. The manager is referred to as the "store team leader." The "store team leader" is compensated by an Economic Value Added (EVA) bonus and is also eligible to receive stock options.

12 Whole Foods tries to instill a sense of purpose among its employees and has been named one of the "100 Best Companies to Work For in America" by *Fortune* Magazine for the past six years. In employee surveys, 90% of its team members stated that they always or frequently enjoy their job.

13 The company strives to take care of their customers, realizing they are the "lifeblood of our business," and the two are "interdependent on each other." Whole Foods' primary objective goes beyond 100% customer satisfaction with the goal to "delight" customers in every interaction.

COMPETITIVE ENVIRONMENT

Natural Products Sales Top $45 Billion in 2004

American shoppers spent nearly $45.8 billion on natural and organic products in 2004, according to research published in the *24th Annual Market Overview* in the June issue of *The Natural Foods Merchandiser*. In 2004, natural products sales increased 6.9% across all sales channels, including supermarkets, mass marketers, direct marketers, and the Internet. Sales of organic products rose 14.6% in natural products stores. As interest in low-carb diets waned, sales of organic baked goods rose 35%. Other fast-growing organic categories included meat, poultry and seafood, up 120%; coffee and cocoa, up 64%; and cookies, up 63%.

14 At the time of Whole Foods' inception, there was almost no competition with less than six other natural food stores in the United States. Today, the organic foods industry is growing and Whole Foods finds itself competing hard to maintain its elite presence. As the population has become increasingly concerned about their eating habits, natural food stores, such as Whole Foods, are flourishing. Other successful natural food grocery chains today include Trader Joe's Co., and Wild Oats Market.

15 Trader Joe's, originally known as Pronto Markets, was founded in 1958 in Los Angeles by Joe Coulombe. By expanding its presence and product offerings while maintaining high quality at low prices, the company has found its competitive niche. The company has 215 stores, primarily on the west and east coasts of the United States. The company "offers upscale grocery fare such as health foods, prepared meals, organic produce and nutritional supplements." A low cost structure allows Trader Joe's to offer competitive prices while still maintaining its margins. Trader Joe's stores have no service department and average just 10,000 square feet in store size. A privately held company, Trader Joe's enjoyed sales of $2.5 million in 2003, a 13.6% increase from 2002.

16 Additional competition has arisen from grocery stores, such as Stop 'N Shop and Shaw's, which now incorporate natural foods sections in their conventional stores, placing them in direct competition with Whole Foods. Because larger grocery chains have more flexibility in their product offerings, they are more likely to promote products through sales, a strategy Whole Foods rarely practices.

17 Despite being in a highly competitive industry, Whole Foods maintains its reputation as "the world's # 1 natural foods chain." As the demand for natural and organic food continues to grow, pressures on suppliers will rise. Only 3% of US farmland is organic so there is limited output. The increased demand for these products may further elevate prices or result in goods being out of stock, with possible price wars looming.

THE CHANGING GROCERY INDUSTRY

18   Before the emergence of the supermarket, the public was largely dependent upon specialty shops or street vendors for dairy products, meats, produce, and other household items. In the 1920s, chain stores began to threaten independent retailers by offering convenience and lower prices by procuring larger quantities of products. Appel explains that the emergence of the supermarkets in the 1930s was a result of three major changes in society:

1. The shift in population from rural to urban areas
2. An increase in disposable income
3. Increased mobility through ownership of automobiles.

19   Perhaps the earliest example of the supermarket as we know it today is King Kullen, "America's first supermarket," which was founded by Michael Cullen in 1930. "The essential key to his plan was volume, and he attained this through heavy advertising of low prices on nationally advertised merchandise." As the success of Cullen's strategy became evident, others such as Safeway, A&P, and Kroger adopted it as well. By the time the United States entered World War II, 9,000 supermarkets accounted for 25% of industry sales.

20   Low prices and convenience continue to be the dominant factors driving consumers to supermarkets today. The industry is characterized by low margins and continuous downward pressure on prices made evident by coupons, weekly specials, and rewards cards. Over the years firms have introduced subtle changes to the business model by providing additional conveniences, such as the inclusion of bakeries, banks, pharmacies, and even coffee houses co-located within the supermarket. Throughout their existence, supermarkets have also tried to cater to the changing tastes and preferences of society such as healthier diets, the Atkins diet, and low carbohydrate foods. The moderate changes to strategy within supermarkets have been imitated by competitors, which are returning the industry to a state of price competition. Supermarkets themselves now face additional competition from wholesalers such as Costco, BJ's and Sam's Club.

A DIFFERENT SHOPPING EXPERIENCE

21   The setup of the organic grocery store is a key component to Whole Foods' success. The store's setup and its products are carefully researched to ensure that they are meeting the demands of the local community. Locations are primarily in cities and are chosen for their large space and heavy foot traffic. According to Whole Foods' 10K, "approximately 88% of our existing stores are located in the top 50 statistical metropolitan areas." The company uses a specific formula to choose their store sites that is based upon several metrics, which include but are not limited to income levels, education, and population density.

22   Upon entering a Whole Foods supermarket, it becomes clear that the company attempts to sell the consumer on the entire experience. Team members (employees) are well trained and the stores themselves are immaculate. There are in-store chefs to help with recipes, wine tasting and food sampling. There are "Take Action food centers" where customers can access information on the issues that affect their food such as legislation and environmental factors. Some stores offer extra services such as home delivery, cooking classes, massages and valet parking. Whole Foods goes out of their way to appeal to the above-average income earner.

23   Whole Foods uses price as a marketing tool in a few select areas, as demonstrated by the 365 Whole Foods brand name products, priced less than similar organic products that are

carried within the store. However, the company does not use price to differentiate itself from competitors. Rather, Whole Foods focuses on quality and service as a means of standing out from the competition.

24   Whole Foods only spent 0.5% of their total sales from the fiscal year 2004 on advertising; they rely on other means to promote their stores. The company relies heavily on word-of-mouth advertising from their customers to help market themselves in the local community. They are also promoted in several health conscious magazines, and each store budgets for in-store advertising each fiscal year.

25   Whole Foods also gains recognition via their charitable contributions and the awareness that they bring to the treatment of animals. The company donates 5% of their after tax profits to not-for-profit charities. The company is also very active in establishing systems to make sure that the animals used in their products are treated humanely.

THE AGING BABY BOOMERS

26   The aging of the Baby Boomer generation will expand the senior demographic over the next decade as their children grow up and leave the nest. Urban singles are another group who has extra disposable income due to their lack of dependents. These two groups present an opportunity for growth for Whole Foods. Americans spent 7.2% of their total expenditures on food in 2001, making it the seventh highest category on which consumers spend their money. Additionally, US households with income of more than $100,000 per annum represent 22% of aggregate income today compared with 18% a decade ago.

27   This shift in demographics has created an expansion in the luxury store group, while slowing growth in the discount retail market. To that end, there is a gap in supermarket retailing between consumers who can only afford to shop at low cost providers, like Wal-Mart, and the population of consumers who prefer gourmet food and are willing to pay a premium for perceived higher quality. "The Baby Boomers are driving demand for organic food in general because they're health-conscious and can afford to pay higher prices" says Professor Steven G. Sapp, a sociologist at Iowa State University who studies consumer food behavior.

28   The perception that imported, delicatessen, exotic and organic foods are of higher quality, therefore commanding higher prices, continues to bode well for Whole Foods Market. As John Mackey, explains "we're changing the [grocery-shopping] experience so that people enjoy it. It's a richer, [more fun], more enjoyable experience. People don't shop our stores because we have low prices." The consumer focus on a healthy diet is not limited to food. More new diet plans emerged in America in the last half of the 20th century than in any other country. This trend has also increased the demand for nutritional supplements and vitamins.

29   In recent years, consumers have made a gradual move toward the use of fresher, healthier foods in their everyday diets. Consumption of fresh fruits and vegetables, pasta and other grain-based products has increased. This is evidenced by the aggressive expansion by consumer products companies into healthy food and natural and organic products. "Natural and organic products have crossed the chasm to mainstream America." The growing market can be attributed to the acceptance and widespread expansion of organic product offerings, beyond milk and dairy. Mainstream acceptance of the Whole Foods offering can be attributed to this shift in consumer food preferences as consumers continue to cite taste as the number one motivator for purchasing organic foods.

30   With a growing percentage of women working out of the home, the traditional role of home cooked meals, prepared from scratch, has waned. As fewer women have the time to devote to cooking, consumers are giving way to the trend of convenience through prepared foods. Sales of ready-to-eat meals have grown significantly. "The result is that grocers are

starting to specialize in quasi-restaurant food." Just as women entering the work force has propelled the sale of prepared foods; it has also increased consumer awareness of the need for the one-stop shopping experience. Hypermarkets such as Wal-Mart, that offer non-food items and more mainstream product lines, allow consumers to conduct more shopping in one place rather than moving from store to store.

31   The growth in sales of natural foods is expected to continue at the rate of 8–10% annually, according to the National Nutritional Foods Association. The sale of organic food has largely outpaced traditional grocery products due to consumer perception that organic food is healthier. The purchase of organic food is perceived to be beneficial to consumer health by 61% of consumers, according to a Food Marketing Institute (FMI)/*Prevention* magazine study. Americans believe organic food can help improve fitness and increase the longevity of life. Much of this perception has grown out of fear of how non-organic foods are treated with pesticides for growth and then preserved for sale. Therefore, an opportunity exists for Whole Foods to contribute to consumer awareness by funding non-profit organizations that focus on educating the public on the benefits of organic lifestyles.

OPERATIONS

32   Whole Foods purchases most of their products from regional and national suppliers. This allows the company to leverage its size in order to receive deep discounts and favorable terms with their vendors. The company still permits stores to purchase from local producers to keep the stores aligned with local food trends and is seen as supporting the community. The company owns two procurement centers and handles the majority of procurement and distribution themselves. Whole Foods also owns several regional bake houses, which distribute products to their stores. The largest independent vendor is United Natural Foods' which accounted for 20% of Whole Foods' total purchases for fiscal year 2004. Product categories at Whole Foods include, but are not limited to:

- Produce
- Seafood
- Grocery
- Meat and Poultry
- Bakery
- Prepared Foods and Catering
- Specialty (Beer, Wine and Cheese)
- Whole body (nutritional supplements, vitamins, body care and educational products such as books)
- Floral
- Pet Products
- Household Products

33   While Whole Foods carries all the items that one would expect to find in a grocery store (and plenty that one would not), their ". . . heavy emphasis on perishable foods is designed to appeal to both natural foods and gourmet shoppers." Perishable foods accounted for 67% of their retail sales in 2004 and are the core of Whole Foods' success. This is demonstrated by their own statement that, "We believe it is our strength of execution in perishables that has attracted many of our most loyal shoppers."

34   Whole Foods also provides fully cooked frozen meal options through their private label Whole Kitchen, to satisfy the demands of working families. For example, the Whole Foods

Market located in Woodland Hills, CA, has redesigned its prepared foods section more than three times in response to a 40% growth in prepared foods sales.

35   Whole Foods doesn't take just any product and put it on their shelves. In order to make it into the Whole Foods grocery store, products have to undergo a strict test to determine if they are "Whole Foods material." The quality standards that all potential Whole Foods products must meet include:

- Foods that are free of preservatives and other additives
- Foods that are fresh, wholesome and safe to eat
- Promote organically grown foods
- Foods and products that promote a healthy life

36   Meat and poultry products must adhere to a higher standard:

- No antibiotics or added growth hormones
- An affidavit from each producer that outlines the whole process of production and how the animals are treated
- An annual inspection of all producers by Whole Foods Market
- Successful completion of a third-party audit to attest to these findings

37   Also, due to the lack of available nutritional brands with a national identity, Whole Foods decided to enter into the private label product business. They currently have three private label products with a fourth program called Authentic Food Artisan, which promotes distinctive products that are certified organic. The three private label products: (1) 365 Everyday Value: A well recognized and trusted brand that meets the standards of Whole Foods and is less expensive than the regular product lines; (2)Whole Kids Organic: Healthy items that are directed at children; and (3) 365 Organic Everyday Value: All the benefits of organic food at reduced prices.

38   When opening a new store, Whole Foods stocks it with almost $700,000 worth of initial inventory, which their vendors partially finance. Like most conventional grocery stores, the majority of Whole Foods inventory is turned over fairly quickly; this is especially true of produce. Fresh organic produce is central to Whole Foods existence and turns over on a faster basis than other products.

FINANCIAL OPERATIONS

39   Whole Foods Market focuses on earning a profit while providing job security to its workforce to lay the foundation for future growth. The company is determined not to let profits deter the company from providing excellent service to its customers and quality work environment for its staff. Their mission statement defines their recipe for financial success.

> Whole Foods, Whole People, Whole Planet—emphasizes that our vision reaches far beyond just being a food retailer. Our success in fulfilling our vision is measured by customer satisfaction, Team Member excellence and happiness, return on capital investment, improvement in the state of the environment, and local and larger community support.

40   Whole Foods also caps the salary of its executives at no more than fourteen times that of the average annual salary of a Whole Foods' worker; this includes wages and incentive bonuses as well. The company also donates 5% of their after tax profits to non-profit organizations.

41   Over a five-year period from 2000 through 2004, the company experienced an 87% growth in sales, with sales reaching $3.86 billion in 2004. Annual sales increases during that period were equally dramatic: 24% in 2001, 18% in 2002, 17% in 2003 and 22% in 2004.

They achieved $5.6 billion in sales in 2006, which was up from $4.7 billion in 2005, resulting in a yearly increase of 19.2%. On average the company's sales have grown 19.4% over the past five years. In fiscal 2006, Whole Foods achieved 11% comparable-store sales growth (CSSG), which is well above the industry average. This growth is perhaps more impressive, given the relatively negative economic environment and recession in the United States.

42   Whole Foods strategy of expansion and acquisition has fueled growth in net income since the company's inception. This is particularly evident when looking at the net income growth in 2002 (24.47%), 2003 (22.72%) and 2004 (27.94%). In 2006 the company earned $204 million, a 50% increase from the $136 million it earned in 2005.

43   The ticker for Whole Foods, Inc., is WFMI. In reviewing the performance history of Whole Foods stock since its IPO reveals a mostly upward trend. The 10-year price trend shows the company increasing from under $10 per share to a high of over $100 per share, reflecting an increase of over 1,000%. In 2007, the stock has been on a downward trend due to slowing same store sales. The current price of $47 with 140 million shares outstanding gives the company a market valuation of $6.7 billion (Apr, 2007). As of 2006, Whole Foods had only $8.6 million in long-term debt, while having $256.2 million in cash and cash equivalent balances.

THE CODE OF CONDUCT

44   From its inception, the company has sought to be different from conventional grocery stores, with a heavy focus on ethics. Besides an emphasis on organic foods, the company has also established a contract of animal rights, which states the company will only do business with companies that treat their animals humanely. While they realize that animal products are vital to their business, they oppose animal cruelty.

45   The company has a unique fourteen-page Code of Conduct document that addresses the expected and desired behavior for its employees. The code is broken down into the following four sections:

- Potential Conflicts of Interest;
- Transactions or situations that should never occur;
- Situations where you may need the authorization of the Ethics Committee before proceeding; and finally
- Times when certain actions must be taken by executives of the company or team leaders of individual stores.

46   This Code of Conduct covers, in detail, the most likely scenarios a manager of a store might encounter. It includes several checklists, that are to be filled out on a regular, or at least an annual basis by team leaders and store managers. After completion, the checklists must be signed and submitted to corporate headquarters and copies retained on file in the store. They ensure that the ethics of Whole Foods are being followed by everyone. The ethical efforts of Whole Foods don't go unrecognized; they were ranked number 70 out of the "100 Best Corporate Citizens."

POSSIBLE SCARCE RESOURCES: PRIME LOCATIONS AND THE SUPPLY OF ORGANIC FOODS

47   Prime store locations and the supply of organic foods are potential scarce resources and could be problematic for Whole Foods Market in the future.

48   Whole Foods likes to establish a presence in highly affluent cities, where their target market resides. The majority of Whole Foods' customers are well-educated; thereby yielding high salaries enabling them to afford the company's higher prices. Whole Foods is particular when deciding on new locations, as location is extremely important for top and bottom line growth. However, there are a limited number of communities where 40% of the residents have college degrees.

49   Organic food is another possible scarce resource. Organic crops yield a lower quantity of output and are rarer, accounting for only 3% of US farmland usage. Strict government requirements must be satisfied; these are incredibly time consuming, more effort intensive, and more costly to adhere to. With increased demands from mainstream super markets also carrying organics, the demand for such products could outreach the limited supply. The market for organic foods grew from $2.9 billion in 2001 to $5.3 billion in 2004, an 80.5% increase in the three-year period. Currently, there are about 10,000 American farmers on about 2.3 million acres of land. Many companies have already started to look for resources outside of the US to meet its growing customer demands. As organics become more main stream, people are worried that standards will be lowered and farmers and businesses might resort to questionable farming practices. The Organic Trade Association estimates that the organic foods industry makes up about 2.5 percent of total US food sales. This figure is up from 0.8 percent in 1997, and represents annual sales increases of between 15 and 21 percent, compared to total US food sales of approximately 2 to 4 percent.

50   In 2005, consumer sales of organic foods totaled $13.8 billion. Whole Foods is the largest natural foods chain and with its acquisition of Wild Oats it now represents $3.2 billion of total organic food dollars. Together these two companies represent 47% of the US organic foods market. Roughly 46% of total organic food dollar volume was sold through the mass-market channel, which includes supermarkets/grocery stores, mass merchandisers, and club stores. The remaining 7% was made up of farmer's markets food service, and other non-retail sales. Whole Foods recognizes that the increased demand for organic foods may adversely affect their earnings and informs their investors as such. "Changes in the Availability of Quality Natural and Organic Products Could Impact Our Business. There is no assurance that quality natural and organic products will be available to meet our future needs. If conventional supermarkets increase their natural and organic product offerings or if new laws require the reformulation of certain products to meet tougher standards, the supply of these products may be constrained. Any significant disruption in the supply of quality natural and organic products could have a material impact on our overall sales and cost of goods."

EXHIBIT 1   Sales

	Sales (In Millions)						
Company	2000	2001	Growth%	2002	Growth%	2003	Growth%
Whole Foods Market[i]	$1,838.60	$2,272.20	23.60%	$2,690.50	18.40%	$3,148.60	17.00%
Trader Joe's Company[ii]	$1,670.00	$1,900.00	13.80%	$2,200.00	15.80%	$2,500.00	13.60%
Wild Oats Market[iii]	$838.10	$893.20	6.60%	$919.10	2.90%	$969.20	5.50%

[i]Hoovers Online: http://www.hoovers.com/whole-foods/−ID_10952−/free-co-factsheet.xhtml: December 1, 2004.
[ii]Hoovers Online: http://www.hoovers.com/trader-joe's-co/−ID-47619−/free-co-factsheet.xhtm: December 1, 2004.
[iii]Hoovers Online: http://www.hoovers.com/wild-oats-markets/−ID_41717−/fee-co-factsheet.xhtml: December 1, 2004.

WHOLE FOODS MARKET, INC. Unaudited Five-Year Historical Data[6]

	Avg Wkly Sales	Sales (000)	YOY Increase[1]	Comparable Store Sales Growth	2-Year Comps[2]	Identical Store Sales Growth	2-Year Idents[2]	Ending S.F.	YOY Increase	Wtd. Avg YOY Increase[3]	# of New Stores	Acquired Stores	Relocated/Closed Stores	Ending Store Count	Gross Margin	Store Contribution[4]
1Q02	$376,335	$ 780,799	21.3%	9.4%	16.7%	7.5%	14.0%	3,841,559	16.4%	18%	2	3	3	128	33.9%	8.6%
2Q02	$395,062	$ 622,789	20.5%	10.1%	19.7%	9.1%	17.3%	3,974,266	16.8%	16%	3	0	0	131	35.0%	10.3%
3Q02	$406,019	$ 648,763	21.1%	10.5%	20.7%	9.5%	18.2%	4,040,492	16.5%	17%	4	0	2	133	34.9%	10.0%
4Q02	$395,831	$ 638,124	19.9%	10.5%	20.7%	9.6%	18.4%	4,098,492	13.9%	16%	2	0	0	135	35.1%	9.6%
FY02	$392,837	$2,690,475	20.7%	10.0%	19.2%	8.7%	16.8%	4,098,492	13.9%	17%	11	3	5	135	34.6%	9.5%
1Q03	$414,571	$ 923,760	18.3%	10.5%	19.9%	10.1%	17.6%	4,287,368	11.6%	11%	5	0	0	140	34.0%	8.6%
2Q03	$422,554	$ 725,139	16.4%	7.0%	17.1%	6.4%	15.5%	4,423,052	11.3%	12%	3	0	0	143	34.4%	9.4%
3Q03	$432,906	$ 749,042	15.5%	7.6%	18.1%	7.0%	16.5%	4,463,883	10.5%	11%	1	0	0	144	34.5%	9.4%
4Q03	$429,020	$ 750,651	17.6%	8.8%	19.3%	8.3%	17.9%	4,545,433	10.9%	10%	3	0	2	145	34.2%	8.7%
FY03	$424,095	$3,148,593	17.0%	8.6%	18.6%	8.1%	16.8%	4,545,433	10.9%	11%	12	0	2	145	34.2%	9.0%
1Q04[5]	$478,666	$1,118,148	21.0%	14.7%	25.2%	14.3%	24.4%	4,578,933	6.8%	8%	1	0	0	146	34.4%	9.1%
2Q04[5]	$488,908	$ 902,140	24.4%	17.1%	24.1%	17.0%	23.4%	4,759,050	7.6%	7%	3	7	0	156	35.4%	9.9%
3Q04	$483,560	$ 917,355	22.5%	14.1%	21.7%	13.7%	20.7%	5,004,963	12.1%	9%	5	0	1	160	34.5%	9.1%
4Q04	$478,165	$ 927,306	23.5%	14.0%	22.8%	13.3%	21.6%	5,145,261	12.1%	13%	3	0	0	163	34.6%	8.6%
FY04	$482,061	$3,864,950	22.8%	14.9%	23.5%	14.5%	22.6%	5,145,261	12.1%	9%	12	7	1	163	34.7%	9.2%
1Q05	$516,277	$1,368,328	22.4%	11.4%	26.1%	10.7%	25.0%	5,258,601	14.8%	15%	3	0	0	166	34.6%	9.1%
2Q05	$539,003	$1,085,158	20.3%	11.6%	28.7%	10.2%	27.2%	5,399,604	13.5%	13%	4	0	2	168	35.7%	10.2%
3Q05	$556,912	$1,132,736	23.5%	15.2%	29.3%	13.2%	26.9%	5,536,424	10.6%	13%	3	0	1	170	35.2%	10.0%
4Q05	$541,987	$1,115,067	20.2%	13.4%	27.4%	11.9%	25.2%	5,819,413	13.1%	12%	5	0	0	175	35.3%	7.2%
FY05	$536,986	$4,701,289	21.6%	12.8%	27.8%	11.5%	26.0%	5,819,413	13.1%	13%	15	0	3	175	35.1%	9.1%
1Q06	$584,554	$1,666,953	21.8%	13.0%	24.4%	12.0%	22.7%	6,056,121	15.2%	15%	5	0	0	180	34.5%	9.0%
2Q06	$601,908	$1,311,520	20.9%	11.9%	23.6%	10.9%	21.1%	6,172,105	14.3%	14%	3	1	1	183	35.3%	10.1%
3Q06	$605,365	$1,337,885	18.1%	9.9%	25.1%	9.6%	22.8%	6,225,756	12.5%	14%	1	0	0	183	35.3%	10.2%
4Q06	$584,498	$1,291,017	15.8%	8.6%	22.0%	8.4%	20.3%	6,379,817	9.6%	11%	4	0	1	186	34.8%	9.2%
FY06	$593,439	$5,607,376	19.3%	11.0%	23.8%	10.3%	21.8%	6,376,817	9.6%	13%	13	1	3	186	35.0%	9.6%
1Q07	$619,966	$1,870,731	12.2%	7.0%	20.0%	6.2%	18.2%	6,581,347	8.7%	8%	4	0	1	189	34.3%	8.4%

[1] Excludes extra week in FY01

[2] Sum of two years of comparable and identical store sales increases

[3] Defined as increase in current year weighted average square footage over prior year weighted average square footage

[4] Defined as gross profit minus direct store expenses

[5] Results positively impacted by strikes at conventional grocery stores in Southern California for majority of Q1 and half of Q2

[6] Results in FY03–FY05 gross margins and store contribution are restated

Sales of a store are deemed to be "comparable" commencing in the fifty-third full week after the store was opened or acquired. Identical store sales exclude sales from remodels with expansions of square for greater than 20% and relocations. Store closed for seven or more days due to unusual events such as fires, snowstorms or hurricanes are excluded from the comparable and identical store base in the first week of closure until re-opened for a full fiscal week.

Whole Foods Market, Inc. Consolidated Quarterly Statements of Operations (In thousands, except per share amounts)

Fiscal Year 2006	1st Qtr January 15, 2006	2nd Qtr April 09, 2006	3rd Qtr July 02, 2006	4th Qtr September 24, 2006	YTD September 24, 2006
Sales	$1,666,953	$1,311,520	$1,337,886	$1,291,017	$5,607,376
Cost of goods sold and occupancy costs	1,092,018	848,020	866,260	841,436	3,647,734
Gross profit	574,935	463,500	471,626	449,581	1,959,642
Direct store expenses	424,438	330,470	335,555	331,505	1,421,968
Store contribution	150,497	133,030	136,071	118,076	537,674
General and administrative expenses	50,889	43,421	43,955	42,979	181,244
Operating income before pre-opening	99,608	89,609	92,116	75,097	356,430
Pre-opening expenses	7,823	5,696	6,604	11,935	32,058
Relocation costs	668	1,628	1,256	1,811	5,363
Operating income	91,117	82,285	84,256	61,351	319,009
Other income (expense):					
Interest expense	(3)	—	(8)	(21)	(32)
Investment and other income	6,082	4,068	5,581	5,005	20,736
Income before income taxes	97,196	86,353	89,829	66,335	339,713
Provision for income taxes	38,878	34,542	35,931	26,534	135,885
Net income	$ 58,318	$ 51,811	$ 53,898	$ 39,801	$ 203,828
Basic earnings per share	$ 0.42	$ 0.37	$ 0.38	$ 0.28	$ 1.46
Weighted average shares outstanding	137,532	139,450	140,712	140,215	139,328
Diluted earnings per share	$ 0.40	$ 0.36	$ 0.37	$ 0.28	$ 1.41
Weighted average shares outstanding, diluted basis	145,317	145,546	145,925	143,462	145,082
Dividends per share	$ 2.15	$ 0.15	$ 0.15	$ —	$ 2.45

The notes in the company's Form 10K for fiscal year 2005 are an integral part of these condensed consolidated financial statements.

Whole Foods Market, Inc. Consolidated Balance Sheets (In thousands) September 24, 2006, and September 25, 2005

Assets	2006	2005
Current assets:		
Cash and cash equivalents	$ 2,252	$ 308,524
Short-term investments—available-for-sale securities	193,847	—
Restricted cash	60,065	36,922
Trade accounts receivable	82,137	66,682
Merchandise inventories	203,727	174,848
Prepaid expenses and other current assets	33,804	45,965
Deferred income taxes	48,149	39,588
Total current assets	623,981	672,529
Property and equipment, net of accumulated depreciation and amortization	1,236,133	1,054,605
Goodwill	113,494	112,476
Intangible assets, net of accumulated amortization	34,767	21,990
Deferred income taxes	29,412	22,452
Other assets	5,209	5,244
Total assets	$ 2,042,996	$ 1,889,296

Liabilities and Shareholders' Equity	2006	2005
Current Liabilities		
Current installments of long-term debt and capital lease obligations	$ 49	$ 5,932
Trade accounts payable	121,857	103,348
Accrued payroll, bonus and other benefits due team members	153,014	126,981
Dividends payable	—	17,208
Other current liabilities	234,850	164,914
Total current liabilities	509,770	418,383
Long-term debt and capital lease obligations, less current installments	8,606	12,932
Deferred rent liability	120,421	91,775
Other long-term liabilities	56	530
Total liabilities	638,853	523,620
Shareholders' equity:		
Common stock, no par vale, 300,000 shares authorized; 142,198 and 136,017 shares issued 139,607 and 135,908 shares outstanding in 2006 and 2005, respectively	1,147,872	874,972
Common stock in treasury at cost	(99,964)	—
Accumulated other comprehensive income	6,975	4,405
Retained earnings	349,260	486,299
Total shareholders' equity	1,404,143	1,365,676
Commitments and contingencies		
Total liabilities and shareholders' equity	$ 2,042,996	$ 1,889,296

The accompanying notes are an integral part of these consolidated financial statements.

Case 29

J&J Electrical Contractors, Inc.: *Remaining Viable in a Highly Competitive Industry**

Olukemi Sawyerr Eke

Stanley C. Abraham

1 John (CEO) and Jean Abernathy (CFO), a husband and wife team, owned and operated J&J Electrical Contractors, Inc. (J&J).[1] J&J performed commercial, industrial, residential, and public electrical-contracting work. Electrical work entailed wiring and installing anything to do with power, lighting, or other electrical equipment and electrical contractors had to be licensed by the state of California. Often, electrical contractors were called to a job by a general contractor, who had overall responsibility for constructing a building or remodeling it. But they could also bid for projects independently, especially in the public sector.

2 By May 2006, John and Jean had successfully grown J&J from a company of three electricians, into one of 54 employees. They took the company to 2005 revenues of $5.22 million, a 75% growth over revenues of $2.98 million in 2001. J&J prided itself on its reputation for good customer service as reflected in this comment from John:

> Our most important accomplishment has been customer service. We have built our reputation on integrity, responsibility and reliability. Even though we are not always the cheapest, when customers hire J&J Electrical for a project they know what they are going to get; there are not a lot of surprises. When we do have a bad project, we never have to go to court. Instead of letting it go to our bonding company or walking away from the project and going into litigation, we just fix the problem, take the loss, and go on. You don't want to do that all the time, but sometimes you don't have a choice. So, we've built relationships that way. We have the same clients that we've dealt with since 1987, and we have continued to build clientele. So, our plan has been to focus on service and integrity.

3 Despite their success, however, the Abernathys were at a crossroad. Although J&J had experienced strong revenue growth, its net income after taxes (NIAT) had deteriorated over the past three years. According to John,

> Our sales have gone up, but profits have gone down because of the type of work we are doing. There are so many competitors coming into the electrical contracting market now as some of the other markets dry up. These firms think they can make an easy transition into this market, but they don't know the market and they put in low bids. When we submit bids, due to the increase in competition, our heart tells us to bid low, but our head tells us to bid the cost estimate. From experience we know what it takes to get the job done so we can only go down so low on our bids. We bid small projects that are several thousand dollars to projects that are over $2 million. We are doing all kinds of things including the smaller design and build projects. We have looked at where we have been the last five years and although we have been fortunate enough to increase sales a little bit, our profits have continued to slide. How to turn the ship around is a major challenge that we are facing.

*The names of the company and all its employees, including the owners, have been changed at the request of the company to preserve its anonymity. The financial statements remain intact.

[1] Interview, John and Jean Abernathy, May 25, 2006

4   While electrical-contracting firms focused in lots of different areas, the firm got to where it was by focusing in one area, modular classrooms for school districts, and found it difficult to change. The Abernathys were proud of how far they had taken the business; however, they also knew that the company faced some critical issues and problems that had to be addressed for its continued growth and success.

THE ELECTRICAL-CONTRACTING INDUSTRY: WHAT IT IS

5   The electrical-contracting industry was a segment of the construction industry. It mainly comprised establishments engaged in performing electrical work onsite, doing service maintenance, or selling and installing electrical equipment. Companies in the industry installed electric lights, power, electric wiring for construction projects, domestic exhaust fans, closed-circuit-video-surveillance systems, and communication wiring and cabling. In addition, they repaired or maintained electrical wiring (except for electrical transmission or distribution lines) and repaired and maintained communication and electrical equipment. Industry participants performed new work, additions, alterations, and maintenance and repairs.[2] The primary workers in the industry were journeymen electricians. In 2005, about 50% of electricians were employed in construction, 10% were self-employed, and 40% were distributed in various industries performing electrical-contracting-related work.[3] Over 74% of the companies in the industry had ten or fewer employees.[4] Many of the smaller local firms were nonunion and family-owned and -operated, similar to J&J. Electrical contractors typically performed the job at the construction site; however, sometimes they performed certain specialty jobs in their own shops.

6   Firms in the industry bid for public- or private-sector projects. Public-sector projects were publicly financed and usually designed to improve the existing infrastructure. Private-sector projects were privately financed projects. Public-sector projects were governed by multiple requirements and legislations, such as federal and state laws governing prevailing wages. Contractors in the State of California were required to pay the prevailing-wage rates on construction work greater than $25,000 and on alteration, demolition, repair, or maintenance work greater than $15,000.[5] Private-sector projects were governed by fewer laws and requirements. For example, private projects were not necessarily subject to competitive bidding and could be negotiated by the owner directly with a preferred contractor based on the contractor's reputation and performance on prior projects. Private-sector projects were also not governed by prevailing wage laws and firms could pay whatever the market would bear as long as it was above federal and state minimum-wage requirements. The minimum wage in California was $6.75 per hour in 2005.[6]

[2] Industry definition; U.S. Census Bureau. Industry statistics sampler NAICS 238210 Electrical Contractors. Retrieved on March 17, 2006, from http://www.census.gov/econ/census02/data/industry/E23821.HTM

[3] Reference for Business. *Encyclopedia of American Industries: Construction* Retrieved on March 17, 2006, from http://www.referenceforbusiness.com/industries/Construction/Electrical-Work.html

[4] U.S. Census Bureau. *2002 Economic Census Construction Series: Electrical Contractors.* Retrieved on March 17, 2006, from http://www.census.gov/prod/ec02/ec0223i238210.pdf

[5] California Department of Industrial Relations. Retrieved on May 1, 2008, from http://www.dir.ca.gov/dlsr/FAQ_Prevailing Wage.html

[6] UCBerkelyNews. Retrieved on May 5, 2008, from http://berkeley.edu/news/media/releases/2005/08/30_wage.shtml

THE ELECTRICAL-CONTRACTING INDUSTRY: CONDITIONS AFFECTING COMPETITION

7 Commercial and industrial new-building starts saw a major decline as a result of the recession of the early 2000s, although residential construction saw strong growth. The industry, which had been flat, began to see widespread growth in the mid-2000s. Electricians, to shield themselves against the downturns in the construction industry, began branching into systems work, which included low-voltage applications such as voice-data-communication lines and alarm systems. By 2002, standard electrical work accounted for 60% of industry sales, while systems work accounted for 33.5%.[7] The top two applications for electricians in the 2000s in the systems area were home-networking and security-systems installations.[8]

8 The number of renovations (remodeling and add-ons) in both the public- and private-sectors continued to increase. Because of increases in housing costs, many homeowners opted to renovate their homes instead of buying new homes. Beyond residential-renovation work, electrical contractors saw opportunities in the industrial- and commercial-conversion markets being driven primarily by code upgrades and technological advances. Existing power-distribution systems could not meet the demands for the greater number and variety of devices being used in buildings. Even newer buildings lacked the infrastructure necessary to take advantage of the advances in communications technology. State and local governments passed legislation to address the deficiencies in older buildings. For example, in California, several bond measures funded the renovation of public schools and universities to update them with the latest technology. Also, the state had mandated seismic compliance for older hospitals by 2010.[9] Finally, many cities were turning low-occupancy areas such as downtowns into residential areas by converting offices and industrial buildings into residential lofts and condominiums. These and other trends were providing firms in the industry with the opportunity to design and deliver renovation solutions to clients.

9 In addition to opportunities in renovation, the Energy Policy Act of 2005 provided additional opportunities for electrical-contracting firms. The Act provided tax incentives to individuals who installed energy-conservation equipment in their homes, including energy-efficient appliances and heating and cooling equipment, and who utilized alternative-energy sources such as solar or wind power.[10] Firms in the industry could provide services to make homes energy-efficient and to install alternative-energy installations such as solar photovoltaic electrical installations. In addition to individual incentives, the Act provided tax credits to businesses that installed qualified fuel cells, stationary micro-turbine power plants, and solar equipment as well as those who built energy-efficient residential and commercial buildings.[11]

---

[7] U.S. Census Bureau. *2002 Economic Census Construction Series: Electrical Contractors.* Retrieved on March 17, 2006, from http://www.census.gov/prod/ec02/ec0223i238210.pdf

[8] Ibid.

[9] Bremer, D. Renovation Revolution. Retrieved on March 17, 2006, from http://www.ecmag.com/editorial_detail.asp?id=1948

[10] Wikipedia. Energy Policy Act of 2005. Retrieved on April 18, 2006, from http://en.wikipedia.org/wiki/Energy_Policy_Act_of_2005

[11] Department of Energy. The Energy Policy Act of 2005: What the Energy Bill Means to You. Retrieved on April 18, 2006, from http://www.enrgy.gov/taxbreaks.htm

10   Energy costs and metal-price increases plagued the construction industry as these were critical in performing construction work. Crude oil closed above $70.00 per barrel for the first time in history in early second quarter 2006, and year-to-date prices had increased by 15%.[12] Copper, an essential component in electrical work, traded at $5,490 per metric ton with a year-to-date increase of 25%.[13] Economic growth continued to drive the demand for energy and metals and the associated need for infrastructure in Asia, particularly in China and India. The lack of investment in exploration and production of precious metals and the shortage of easy-to-tap sources led to supply shortages.[14] Increasing energy and material costs meant increasing production costs for electrical-contracting firms. Uncertainty associated with price increases meant greater difficulty in the estimating function. Also, substantial increases in costs translated into erosion of margins. The major cost components in electrical-contracting work were labor and materials which, combined, accounted for almost 70% of the total value of construction work.[15]

THE ELECTRICAL-CONTRACTING INDUSTRY: HOW CONTRACTS ARE WON OR LOST

11   Industry participants obtained work through intense competitive bidding, although private-sector projects could be negotiated contracts. Contracting agencies advertised the availability of projects and invited contractors to submit bids via a Notice to Contractors. Contractors obtained information regarding the availability of planned projects from multiple sources including local construction plan centers, local business journals, national/regional construction magazines, and contracting-agency information packages.[16] In addition, contractors could subscribe to multiple online sources and receive information regarding upcoming projects; J&J used a weekly construction magazine, *Southern California Construction Bulletin*, published by Reed Bulletin Construction Data (www.reedbulletin.com). Public-contracting agencies often required that contractors who planned to bid on their projects be prequalified, that is, be approved to construct a particular style of work up to a specified amount. For example, an agency might pre-qualify a contractor to perform concrete construction worth up to $350,000.[17]

12   Once the contractor had decided to bid on a project, he purchased plans and specifications for the project from the contracting agency who often sold the plans for the cost of duplicating. The contractor determined the cost of the project by breaking the job down into its component parts to begin the process of estimating. First, the contractor broke each bid item within the project proposal down into the operations that would be necessary to construct it. Second, he undertook quantity take-offs by determining the dimensions of

[12] Bhushan, B., and Davis, A. Oil Settles above $70 a Barrel, Despite Inventories at 8-Year High. *The Wall Street Journal Online*, April 18, 2006, p. A1. Retrieved on April 18, 2006, from http://online.wsj.com/article/SB114532452352528310.html

[13] Attwood, J. Prices of Silver, Copper Climb Again. *The Wall Street Journal Online*, April 3, 2006. Retrieved on April 18, 2006, from http://online.wsj.com/article/SB114402274202114826.html

[14] Davis, A. Rush of Investors to Commodities Fuels Gold Rally. *The Wall Street Journal Online*, April 11, 2006, page C1. Retrieved on April 18, 2006, from http://online.wsj.com/article/SB114468248061221847.html

[15] U.S. Census Bureau. *2002 Economic Census Construction Series: Electrical Contractors*. Retrieved on March 17, 2006, from http://www.census.gov/prod/ec02/ec0223i238210.pdf

[16] Andersen, D.G. (2000). Public Works Contracting: Start to Finish. BNi Building News, Anaheim, California.

[17] Ibid.

each item from the plan and calculating the quantity that would be required for the project. Finally, he determined the costs of labor, materials, equipment, and small tools and miscellaneous items associated with each operation of each bid item either from past experience if he had done a similar job or conceptually if he had no prior project-related experience. Powerful construction-estimating-software programs such as MasterBuilder had simplified the job-estimating function. Before finalizing the estimating process, the contractor typically participated in one or more job walks or site walks to get familiar with the project and identify any contingencies that might influence the cost of project execution. He could modify the estimated cost of the project based on additional or new information. Finally, the contractor determined the desired profit or risk margin to add to the estimate.[18]

13   The contractor prepared a bid which specified how much money it would cost him to complete the project. He submitted the bid in a sealed envelope by the bid deadline. As part of the bid-submission process the contractor submitted a Bid Bond which was a bidder's guarantee that it could perform the work at the bid price if its bid was selected. The contracting agency opened all the bids submitted for a particular project on the Bid Opening Day and publicly read them. The agency awarded the contract to the contractor who submitted the lowest bid price for the project. The contractor submitted performance and payment bonds and insurance information once awarded the contract.

14   Having the lowest price was only one of the variables that could win or lose a bid. A bid could be rendered non-responsive if it did not conform to all the requirements of the contracting agency. Bids were to be made on forms provided by the contracting agency, were submitted on a certain date, by a certain time in a certain place, had clear and exact photocopies, included the bid bond, etc. A bid could be rejected or considered non-responsive if it failed to meet any of these requirements. According to John:

> A lot of things go into how we get the bid besides just having the right price. Sometimes you turn in your envelope and if it does not have the category number of your bid they don't even open it. We bid 6 or 7 jobs a week in a really busy week; because of circumstances, we may land three jobs in a row. Sometimes you're the second bidder and you get the job because the lowest bidder got disqualified. Either they did not fill out the bid form correctly or did not have the signature or did not have the bond. So there are a lot of technicalities.

15   Construction contracts existed in many forms. Negotiated contracts, most commonly used in private-sector projects, involved the contracting agency negotiating directly with one or more contractors chosen on the basis of their reputations and overall quality of similar projects completed. Negotiated contracts had lower risks because the contractor was able to negotiate the contract costs. However, the contractor had to adhere to the contract amount specified in the contract once construction began. The typical profit margin for negotiated contracts was 5 to 15 percent. Fixed Price contracts, most commonly used in public-sector projects, involved contractors preparing estimates of the cost to complete a proposed project based on the requirements of the contracting agency. The lowest qualified bidder was awarded the contract. The contractor and the owner were not allowed to negotiate once the bid was accepted. Fixed Price contracts had the greatest reward and the most risk. If the estimates were accurate and the project managed efficiently, the profit margins could range from 5 to 25 percent; however, if the estimates were inaccurate and/or the project was managed inefficiently, the contractor absorbed the additional costs with no reimbursement from the owner.[19] As a result, estimating the bid price accurately was critical. Once the bid was accepted, a contractor was bound by the bid price and had to complete the project as

[18] Ibid.
[19] Ibid.

specified in its bid. Should anything change in the environment such as increased labor and/ or materials costs, the contractor had to absorb the increased costs. Alternately, if the price of materials and labor went down, the contractor would benefit by keeping the difference. Sometimes, a contractor was able to submit a change order to get the contracting agency to pay for the additional costs. However, as indicated by Jean, pursuing legitimate change orders could be difficult:

> Even with legitimate change orders we are having a hard time increasing the price of the project. Change orders have even gotten much more difficult, they are getting scrutinized so much more. We pursue legitimate change orders and everything is fine, but they limit you on how much they will allow you on your overhead and profit. It's all spelled out in the beginning; you know going in what they are going to give you. But the guys who are kind of shrewd, who understand how far they can go, they can make more money because they push the envelope by starting out with a low bid and then trying to recoup their costs by submitting change orders. The way I see it, life is too short to do that. If it is a legitimate change order we pursue it because we want everything we can get for it; if it is not, we are not going to fight it.

16   Contractors had difficulty pursuing change orders in both public- and private-sector projects. However, it was more of an issue in private-sector projects as the owners were highly leveraged financially and fought the contractor vigorously to have the contract stay within or below the original budget.[20] Legitimate change orders, although scrutinized, were often honored by public contracting agencies.

COMPETITION IN THE ELECTRICAL-CONTRACTING INDUSTRY

17   Competition in the electrical-contracting industry was intense in 2005, especially at the local level. Some of the larger national competitors located in Southern California included Bergelectric Corporation, Helix Electric, Inc., and Morrow-Meadows Corporation (MMC), all of which were privately held (see Exhibit 1). Bergelectric was founded in 1946 and was headquartered in Los Angeles. It focused on providing design-build and design-assist services for public-sector facilities such as schools and prisons and office buildings.[21] The company was ranked 11th in *Engineering News-Record*'s 2005 ranking of top 50 national electrical-contracting firms. It reported 2004 revenues of $300 million and had over 2,000 employees.[22] The company, in addition to its facilities in Los Angeles, had multiple locations in San Diego, Las Vegas, Portland, Sacramento, Orlando, Denver, Phoenix, and Raleigh.[23] Helix was ranked 14th of the top 50 national electrical-contracting firms in *Engineering News-Record*'s 2005 rankings.[24] The company was founded in 1985 and was privately held. It reported $186 million in sales in 2005. It specialized in commercial, hotel, design/build, retail, and high-density multi-unit residential projects.[25] Helix was headquartered in San Diego and operated primarily in California and Nevada.[26] Morrow-Meadows,

[20] Ibid.

[21] Hoovers. Bergelectric Corporation. Retrieved on March 17, 2006, from http://www.hoovers.com/ bergelectric/--ID_120418--/free-co-factsheet.xhtml

[22] Bergelectric Corporation. Retrieved on March 30, 2006, from http://www.bergelectric.com/ newaboutus.htm

[23] Ibid.

[24] Helix Electric, Inc. Retrieved on March 30, 2006, from http://www.helixelectric.com/

[25] Hoovers. Retrieved on March 17, 2006, from http://www.hoovers.com/free/search/simple/xmillion/ index.xhtml?query_string=electrical+contracting+&which=company&page=1&x=730&y=184

[26] Helix Electric, Inc. Retrieved on March 30, 2006, from http://www.helixelectric.com/

headquartered in the City of Industry, CA (near Los Angeles), reported 2005 revenues of $177.5 million and had 1,200 employees. The company specialized in data-communication and power-distribution systems for commercial and industrial facilities.[27] It had California locations in San Diego, San Francisco, and City of Industry, as well as locations in Oregon and Washington. The firm operated in Oregon and Washington as Cherry City Electric.[28]

18   J&J did not compete directly with the largest firms in the industry although most of them operated in multiple locations across the US and were thus well positioned to compete for jobs locally as well as nationally. Typical of over 70% of the firms in the industry, J&J competed only locally, primarily in the Inland Empire area of the Southern California region (an area about 40 miles east of Los Angeles). Some of the local competitors included Buck Electric, McBride Electric, Power Plus!, Daniel's Electrical Construction Company, and Champion Electric Inc., all of which were privately held (see Exhibit 1).

19   Buck Electric was founded in 1975 in Poway, CA. The company was a full-service electrical-contracting firm and it specialized in solar photovoltaic electrical installations, underground-cable installation, location, fault-detection and repair, conventional power systems including commercial and residential services, and custom lighting.[29] McBride Electric provided electrical, lighting, and data-cabling solutions to businesses across the nation. The company was founded in 1950 in Wichita, KS, and was headquartered in San Diego, CA. McBride had offices located in Texas, Georgia, Kansas, Colorado and California. It specialized in data-cabling services including the installation of Wi-Fi networks through its DataConnect unit.[30] Power Plus! specialized in providing expert utility solutions and turnkey services including temporary power generators, permanent electric, irrigation pedestals, street and landscape lighting, high-voltage overhead distribution, utility installations, utility consulting and design, co-generation, and grid-independent applications.[31] Power Plus! focused on serving the utility, construction, and "events" industries. It operated multiple Southern California locations plus operations in Las Vegas, NV, Houston, TX, and Phoenix, AZ. Power Plus! had over 30 years of industry experience in the Southern California market.[32]

20   Daniel Electrical Construction Company, a privately held, unionized company located in Fontana, CA, was founded in 1973 by Dan Bozick, its current CEO. The company provided a broad range of electrical-contracting services in both the public and private sectors throughout California.[33] In 1991, Glenn and Cynthia Rowden founded Champion Electric, Inc., in Riverside, CA, where the firm is still located. Glenn Rowden was the owner/president of Champion. The firm specialized in all aspects of electrical construction primarily in the Inland Empire area. The firm had 80 employees. On March 16, 2006, Champion Electric and Suburban Electric of San Bernardino, CA, merged under the Champion umbrella.[34]

---

[27] Hoovers. Morrow-Meadows Corporation. Retrieved on March 17, 2006, from http://www.hoovers.com/morrow-meadows/--ID_120330--/free-co-factsheet.xhtml

[28] Morrow-Meadow Corporation. Retrieved on March 30, 2006, from http://www.morrow-meadows.com/

[29] Buck Electric, Inc. Retrieved on March 30, 2006, from http://www.buckelectric.com/index.html

[30] McBride Electric. Retrieved on March 30, 2006, from http://www.mcbrideelectric.com

[31] Power Plus! Utility. Retrieved on March 30, 2006, from http://www.powerplusutility.com/corp.html

[32] Ibid.

[33] Daniel's Electrical Construction Company. Retrieved on May 18, 2006, from http://www.danielelectric.com

[34] Champion Electric, Inc. Retrieved on May 18, 2006, from http://www.championelec.com

EXHIBIT 1 Selected Southern California Competitors in the Electrical-Contracting Industry in 2005

Name	Headquarters	Specialty	Revenues (Millions)	Locations	Number of Employees
Bergelectric[a] Corporation	Los Angeles, CA	Design-build and design-assist services for public-sector facilities such as schools and prisons and office buildings	$300[b] (2004)	California, Oregon, Nevada, Arizona, Florida, Colorado, and N. Carolina	2,000
Helix Electric[c]	San Diego, CA	Commercial, hotel, design/build, retail, and high-density multi-unit residential projects	$186[d]	California, Nevada and Arizona	1,500
Morrow Meadows Corporation[e]	City of Industry, CA	Data-communication and power-distribution systems for commercial and industrial facilities	$177.5[f]	California, Oregon and Washington	1,200
McBride Electric[g]	San Diego, CA	Data-cabling services including the installation of Wi-Fi networks	n/a	California, Texas, Georgia, Kansas, Colorado	340
Champion Electric[h]	Riverside, CA	All aspects of electrical construction	n/a	California	80
J&J Electric, Inc.	Pomona, CA	Heavy industrial installations, commercial and office buildings, educational institutions, public works and many specialized systems including maintenance services	$5.22	California	54
Buck Electric[i]	Poway, CA	Solar photovoltaic electrical installations, underground-cable installation, location, fault-detection and repair, conventional power systems including commercial and residential services, and custom lighting	n/a	California	n/a
PowerPlus![j]	Anaheim, CA	Temporary power generators, permanent electric, irrigation pedestals, street and landscape lighting, high-voltage overhead distribution, utility installations, utility consulting and design, co-generation, and grid-independent applications	n/a	California, Nevada, Arizona, Texas	n/a
Daniel's Electric[k]	Fontana, CA	Electrical-contracting services in both the public and private sectors	n/a	California	n/a

[a]Bergelectric Corporation. Retrieved on March 30, 2006, from http://www.bergelectric.com/newaboutus.htm

[b]Hoovers. Bergelectric Corporation. Retrieved on March 17, 2006, from http://www.hoovers.com/bergelectric/--ID_120418--/free-co-factsheet.xhtml

[c]Helix Electric, Inc. Retrieved on March 30, 2006, from http://www.helixelectric.com

[d]Hoovers. Retrieved on March 17, 2006, from http://www.hoovers.com/free/search/simple/xmillion/index.xhtml?query_string=electrical+contracting+&which=company&page=1&x=730&y=184

[e]Morrow-Meadow Corporation. Retrieved on March 30, 2006, from http://www.morrow-meadows.com/

[f]Hoovers. Morrow-Meadows Corporation. Retrieved on March 17, 2006, from http://www.hoovers.com/morrow-meadows/--ID_120330--/free-co-factsheet.xhtml

[g]McBride Electric. Retrieved on March 30, 2006, from http://www.mcbrideelectric.com

[h]Champion Electric, Inc. Retrieved on May 18, 2006, from http://www.championelec.com

[i]Buck Electric, Inc. Retrieved on March 30, 2006, from http://www.buckelectric.com/index.html

[j]Power Plus! Utility. Retrieved on March 30, 2006, from http://www.powerplusutility.com/corp.html

[k]Daniel's Electrical Construction Company. Retrieved on May 18, 2006, from http://www.danielelectric.com

21   Besides competitors who provided only electrical-contracting services, J&J also competed with firms that performed electrical-contracting services in addition to work such as carpentry or masonry. John, in describing the competition, had this to say:

> Anybody who is bidding under the category of "electrical" is my competition. There are probably 10 to 15 that are right in our backyard here. There is a good core group that we deal with all the time . . . some are union contractors and others are non-union. We compete with them, it's friendly you know, and we feel that we have gained their respect. When they see J&J on the bid list they know it is going to be a competitive bid, they know we are not going to be the guys that are way down there, unless we made a mistake! We are going to be there, that is why our hit ratio is 1 out of 10 to 15 because we are bidding more with statistics instead of "I've got to get the job."

J&J ELECTRICAL CONTRACTORS, INC.: A SMALL FISH IN A BIG POND

22   In 1987, after several years of experience working as an estimator and sales manager for other electrical contractors, John decided to found his own company in Glendora (a city in the Inland Empire). He entered into partnership with Miriam Murray, the wife of an acquaintance, who contributed $50,000 to the new business. John bought out Miriam's interest in the business in 1991 and also purchased and relocated the firm to a facility in the nearby city of Ontario (about 40 miles east of Los Angeles). In 2004, John and Jean purchased a larger industrial unit in Pomona (about 10 miles west of Ontario) to accommodate the growing company and to take advantage of an attractive investment opportunity. They leased the Ontario facility to others. They remodeled and expanded the new facility to accommodate their needs. In May 2006, J&J had 42 electricians, 3 estimators/project managers (including John), a field superintendent, a purchasing agent, a warehouse manager, a driver and four corporate staff including Jean and Wyatt Johnson, the new Project Coordinator and Accounting Assistant. (See Exhibit 2 for the organizational chart.)

23   According to the 2000 census, the Inland Empire experienced the highest rate in population growth both in Southern California and statewide. The four-county area where J&J got most of its contracts experienced an average population growth rate of 20%, with Riverside

EXHIBIT 2
J&J Electrical Contractors, Inc. Organizational Chart

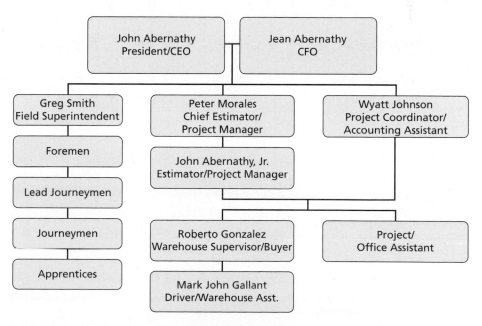

County experiencing the highest rate at 32%, San Bernardino County 20%, Orange County 18.1%, and Los Angeles County 7.4%. In addition, the area accounted for more than 35% of the new jobs in Southern California, 48% of all housing starts, and 75% of new industrial construction in the State of California.[35] With homes getting more expensive in Orange and Los Angeles Counties, more and more people were moving into San Bernardino and Riverside Counties. J&J bid on projects of up to $2 million. John Abernathy, Jr., joined the firm as an estimator/project manager upon graduating from college in 2004. The additional estimator/project manager enabled J&J to bid on larger projects.

THE CURRENT SITUATION: DECLINING PROFITABILITY

24   While J&J's revenues had seen strong growth over the past five years, its net income after taxes (NIAT) was flat or declining (see Exhibits 3 and 4 for the financial statements). The Abernathys identified two primary factors at the heart of this trend. The first was substantial

EXHIBIT 3   J&J Electrical Contractors, Inc. Statements of Income and Accumulated Adjustments

	2005	2004	2003	2002	2001
Net Sales	**$5,222,758**	**$5,089,078**	**$3,210,758**	**$3,448,654**	**$2,988,485**
Cost of sales	4,118,768	4,065,714	2,226,551	2,097,813	1,969,973
Gross profit	**1,103,990**	**1,023,364**	**984,207**	**1,350,841**	**1,018,512**
Operating Expenses	932,656	748,233	785,670	764,674	699,813
Income from Operations	**171,334**	**275,131**	**198,537**	**586,167**	**318,699**
Interest income	182	933	5,031	1,483	0
Pension Contribution	50,000	100,000	0	135,399	117,366
Contract Settlement	0	0	0	0	25,000
Loss on Sale of Assets	0	0	0	0	0
Other Income (Expenses)	16,401	0	0	0	
Income before income taxes (NIBT)	**137,917**	**176,064**	**203,568**	**452,251**	**226,333**
Provision for State Income Tax	987	4,169	4,292	4,453	4,219
Net income after taxes (NIAT)	**$ 136,930**	**$ 171,895**	**$ 199,276**	**$ 447,798**	**$ 222,114**
Accumulated Adjustments, Beginning of Year	692,040	636,146	734,370	430,572	248,058
Distributions	50,328	86,051	297,500	144,000	39,600
Accumulated Adjustments, End of Year	778,642	721,990	636,146	734,370	430,572
Income per Share (1,000 Shares Outstanding)	137	172	199	448	431

Source: J&J Electrical Contractors, Inc.

[35] Southern California Association of Governments. (n.d.). *Annual report.* Retrieved on July 29, 2005, from http://www.scag.ca.gov/census

EXHIBIT 4 **J&J Electrical Contractors, Inc. Consolidated Balance Sheet**
As of December 31, (amounts in dollars)

ASSETS	2005	2004	2003	2002	2001
Current assets					
Cash and cash equivalents	$ 95,891	$ 212,170	$(24,225)	$ 428,701	$ (35,791)
Accounts receivable (less allowable for doubtful accounts)	954,712	738,842	639,519	489,516	588,530
Costs and estimated earnings in excess of billings on uncompleted contracts	59,227	184,473	176,606	59,142	0
Inventories	7,360	5,000	5,000	5,000	5,000
Prepaid expenses and other	1149	559	16,700	3,304	7,880
Bonds					100
Total current assets	**1,118,339**	**1,141,044**	**813,600**	**985,663**	**565,719**
Fixed assets					
Autos and Trucks	239,572	214,147	182,423	156,032	148,077
Shop Equipment	24,794	24,794	13,661	13,661	13,661
Office Equipment	47,394	43,378	42,532	38,130	38,130
Leasehold Improvements	13,604	13,604	13,604	13,604	13,604
Accumulated Depreciation	(207,277)	(250,090)	(217,388)	(180,146)	(154,676)
Deferred Tax Assets	0	0	224	1667	1,667
Total fixed assets	**118,087**	**45,833**	**34,832**	**42,948**	**60,463**
Total Assets	**1,236,426**	**1,186,877**	**848,432**	**1,028,611**	**626,182**
LIABILITIES AND STOCKHOLDERS' EQUITY					
Liabilities					
Accounts Payable	$ 265,024	$ 131,297	$ 92,291	$ 43,801	$ 30,823
Accrued Payroll	18,213	14,972	2,709	22,335	21,006
Short-Term Debt	4,385	15,844	7,472	50,614	0
Billings in Excess of Costs and Estimated Earnings	82,661	192,274	38,184	27,419	117,366
Pension Contribution Due	50,000	100,000	0	135,399	0
Long-Term Debt	8,875	0	0	0	5,924
Other Liabilities	8,606	0	61,130	4,173	9,9991
Total Liabilities	**437,784**	**454,387**	**201,786**	**283,741**	**185,110**
Stockholders' Equity					
Capital Stock (15,000 authorized, 2000 issued and 1,000 outstanding)	20,000	20,000	20,000	20,000	20,000
Treasury Stock	0	(9,500)	(9,500)	(9,500)	(9,500)
Accumulated Adjustments (Retained Earnings)	778,642	721,990	636,146	734,370	430,572
Total Stockholders' Equity	**798,642**	**732,490**	**646,646**	**744,870**	**441,072**
Total Liabilities and Stockholders' Equity	**1,236,426**	**1,186,877**	**848,432**	**1,028,611**	**626,182**

Source: J&J Electrical Contractors, Inc.

increases in costs, especially the cost of materials and supplies; the second was J&J's mix of public and private work.

25   Cost increases were critical as materials accounted for 33% of the value of construction work.[36] According to John:

> In the last year and a half, construction costs have gone up. In any article you read they are 30% higher, and that was in concrete. All of our steel is going to China because it has an industrial revolution going on over there and is getting ready for the 2008 Olympics. So, when I buy my EMT pipe, my steel fittings, and my metal boxes, they have all gone up. Before, that stuff would be the same price for a year, no problem on our computer. Now they quote you prices for copper wire or PVC copper pipe that are good for the week or even the day. For a project we are doing up in the high desert, we bought over $50,000 worth of copper wire that is sitting in a warehouse at the wholesaler. I don't have to take it until next month; we paid it in March or April and they gave us 60 days. We were able to bill it to our client. He understood the circumstances and paid as long as we gave him the invoice. So, if you don't forecast, you're in trouble.

26   The unpredictability in the prices of essential commodities was particularly troubling as it made it more difficult to accurately estimate project costs. Firms in the industry obtained work primarily through intense competitive bidding. Thus, the estimating function was especially important because jobs bid too low resulted in losses and those bid too high resulted in failed bids.

27   The Abernathys hired Wyatt Johnson in January 2005 as Project Coordinator and Accounting Assistant. J&J installed a new computer system in June 2005 and began using Master Builder, a high-powered construction/accounting-software program. Jean worked closely with Wyatt to fully customize the system to meet J&J's needs. The system generated reports of all current jobs, projected monthly billings, current receivables, and other important data that form the basis for decision making. As a result of the new system and the estimation software, bid preparation became more precise. The firm was able to track dollars bid, when bid, and whether or not it won the bid. J&J was able to better track the cost of jobs, estimate more accurately the true overhead, and prepare bids that were competitive as well as provided margins that covered overhead and profits. According to John:

> Job-costing and accounting are like taking a snapshot of the company and being within a week of where you are—a week on labor and maybe three weeks on the material, because we don't want to enter the material every week. But before [the new system] it took a long time to find out where you were. Now we get cost reports. I can see how many hours I got in this job, and I can go back and try to hone in on it to see if I have some problems. So we start charting. We look to see what we have on the books in volume and in contracts. This helps us bid. We don't want to bid on work that will require us to take on more manpower between June and September [the summer rush] because between those months you're in trouble, that's where your profits go down. So, now we are looking strategically for projects that start in September through the fall and winter where we get slow. We are trying to get smarter.

28   According to John, some of the bids that J&J won in the last few years did not accurately reflect the true costs of the projects because the firm had difficulty producing accurate estimates. J&J typically added a percentage of the project cost for overhead and profit to each bid. However, because of the increased competition in the industry segment, J&J found that using this method did not produce competitive bids. In order to obtain more competitive

[36] U.S. Census Bureau. *2002 Economic Census Construction Series: Electrical Contractors.* Retrieved on March 17, 2006, from http://www.census.gov/prod/ec02/ec0223i238210.pdf

bids, the firm had to take much narrower margins which left very little room for error. Currently, J&J added 10% to each job for overhead and profit.

29   An additional challenge in the estimating function was that several of the bids had no provisions for contingencies; that is, a firm was unable to submit bids contingent on the conditions that were prevailing at the time the work was actually performed. Each project was governed by a standard construction-specification book that addressed the requirements for the project including what was to be constructed, how it was to be constructed, safety measures, materials to be used, applicable wage rates, insurance requirements, bond amounts, etc.[37] Electrical-contracting firms were obligated by the general conditions in the specification book in the bid-preparation process. This made it difficult to prepare bids based on the forecast prices for materials at the time the actual work was performed as opposed to when the bid was prepared. The firm pursued legitimate change orders; however, it was constrained as to how much was allowed for overhead and profit on the change orders. John believed that there was a need to tighten up the bid-preparation process in order to obtain more accurate cost estimates and boost overhead and profit.

30   The second factor contributing to the downward trend in profitability was J&J's mix of public and private work. In the early days, it focused primarily on private-sector projects in the Inland Empire. In the late nineties it saw an emerging opportunity in the public sector. The State of California adopted sweeping reforms to improve academic performance by requiring school districts to reduce class sizes in the early grades from 33 to no more than 20 students per class.[38] The resulting demand for classrooms prompted the Department of State Architect to endorse modular classrooms, which were portable buildings manufactured complete with heating and air conditioning, carpeting, and whiteboards.[39] J&J decided to fill the newly created and rapidly growing demand for the installation of modular classrooms. J&J was successful in competing for public-works projects in K–12, community colleges, and public and private universities in the Inland Empire. Over time, J&J's mix of public and private projects shifted to focus increasingly on public projects. In 2006, the company's ratio of public to private work was 9:1, that is, nine public projects to one private-sector project.

31   While both public- and private-sector projects were subject to competitive bidding, they differed in important respects. Competition for public work was primarily dependent on the bid price. John believed that on a scale of 1 to 10, J&J would score an 8 for price-competitiveness. J&J had developed important relationships in the business over the years; however, in public-sector work, relationships did not matter as much when it came to obtaining the job. According to John:

> I've got customers, school-district people, contractors, who would give me the job if they could. However, if it is over $15,000, it has to go to a competitive-bid process. That means they have to advertise it and it's got to be competitive. My best clients would want me to do the job but they can't. All they can do is give me notice maybe before it comes out in the publication, "hey this job's coming down the pipe, keep it in mind," and then I am like everybody else. I go and I buy my plans, I bid it, and I stand there with my envelope and that is it.

[37] See http://www.dot.ca.gov/hq/esc/oe/specifications/std_specs/2006_StdSpecs/2006_StdSpecs.doc for the State of California Standard Specification for Construction book.

[38] CSR Research Consortium. (1999). Class size reduction in California: Early findings signal promise and concerns. Retrieved on March 15, 2006, from http://www.classize.org/summary/97-98/summaryrpt.pdf

[39] EdSource Online. (1998). Portable school buildings: Scourge, saving grace, or just part of the solution? Retrieved on March 15, 2006, from http://www.edsource.org/pub_edfct_port.cfm

32   Public work was much more restrictive due in part to regulations related to prevailing wages, and tended to have lower profit margins. As a result, public projects had become increasingly less profitable. According to Jean:

> There is actually more profit in private-sector work. With the public work, you're paying your electricians prevailing wage as well, so they are getting a higher wage. It is so competitive that your profit margins are so much lower, and there is not a lot of room for error. So, when you get to the end of a project there are so many inspections, so many these and so many thats, and you see your profit just going down. You know, no matter how much you think you're on top of it, things can just change at the end. It is just harder.

33   Public work was becoming increasingly competitive. In the early days when J&J focused on commercial and industrial work, its hit rate (proportion of bids won relative to the number submitted) was 25%. The firm's current hit rate with public-sector work was 6–10%. Public projects also produced high receivables. Many school districts used construction-management companies to manage their projects. A common practice of these firms was to hold 10% of the total project value as retentions until the conclusion of the project. For example, for a $1 million project, the retention could be a substantial $100,000. Upon project completion, contractors were required to complete considerable close-out documentation to get the withheld money paid, taking as long as a year. This resulted in very high levels of accounts receivable for public-sector work.

34   Despite the problems associated with public projects, there were many opportunities in the state of California for public projects. Most school-district projects in California were funded from bond measures. The state of California in 2006 had $100 billion in school-construction bonds.[40] John felt that J&J still enjoyed substantial opportunities in the public sector, especially in community colleges. As he explained:

> Community Colleges! It's their turn. They seem to have gotten these bond measures passed. We just did a major job at a local college, the whole athletic field, and now we are doing another job there. We just finished a job at a second local college and they are asking us to bid more. So, there is money there. Now I am going to go into the colleges and maybe back off of the elementary and high schools.

35   The revenue generated in public projects was, as Jean put it, "as good as gold." Once a bid was submitted and accepted, the company knew it was guaranteed payment. Although it could take up to a year before the retentions were paid, they were still paid in full. The public-sector projects for which J&J competed were financed by voter-approved bond money which was available to satisfy the public agency's contract obligations. As indicated earlier, accurately estimated and properly managed public-sector projects often had greater returns than their private-sector negotiated-contract counterparts.

36   Another advantage of public projects was a greater confidence in the competitive bidding process. According to John:

> For the public projects, when you turn your bid in its sealed envelope you either get it or you don't. However, sometimes when we bid the general contractors unless you're the friend they can take your bid price and pass it on to somebody else. In the private sector, it is all about relationships. We are learning how to work the private sector, but it has come with some hard lessons.

37   In private-sector work, while price was important, there was greater opportunity to compete on the basis of reputation, relationships, and negotiation. J&J's investments in

[40] Davis, A. (2006). "Billions spent still not enough." *Contra Costa Times,* Tuesday, October 17, 2006. Retrieved on February 23, 2007, from http://www.contracostatimes.com/mld/cctimes/living/education/15778288.htm?template=contentModules/printstory.jsp

developing and maintaining strong personal relationships with its customers gave it a competitive advantage in the local area for private projects. According to John:

> Relationships and negotiation skills matter more with private projects than with public projects. If it is private money, someone is managing that money, be it the trustees or the general contractor working for that firm or the owner. They have budgets; the architect tells them how he thinks it should be. The difference is that competition is based not only on the price, but also on relationships and the ability to negotiate. For instance we have done a lot of work at the local university. We've built 70% of that campus and they are happy with us. Now we go in and negotiate with them. We can say to them you have a project coming up and we want to work with you on it. Of course we are going to give them a fair price. But lets say I am 3% higher than the lowest bidder, they can say I am going to give the contract to you because if I give it to this guy who I don't know that 3% is going to turn into 20% on the backside. Also, for private projects the owners can shrink the bid list. They put invited bidders only. There are about five or six general contractors that build all this retail stuff around us and they have their subcontractors. So, on private projects it is all relationships I am telling you. . . .

38   Private work was less restrictive, as it lacked the many rules and regulations that governed public sector work. According to John:

> The private work is still a construction project; you still have architects, engineers and you still do it the same way. It's just that on the operations side you don't have as much paperwork. All of the labor compliance and the payrolls are not as difficult. You don't have certified payroll every week, notarized certified billings, etc.; so, there is a lot of overhead time that goes into public work. In the private sector, we are still billing, we still invoice, and we still have payroll. But our payroll is lower. Electricians make less money in private work.

39   However, private-sector projects had added risks not associated with public-sector projects. The ability of private-project owners to meet their contract obligations was subject to the financial conditions of the firms and the vagaries of the economy. As indicated earlier, private project owners were often highly leveraged financially and sometimes had difficulty meeting their contract obligations. So, payment was not always guaranteed as was the case with public projects.

40   Construction was highly cyclical. During an economic boom, these firms were able to meet their contract obligations; however, during economic downturns, especially downturns in the housing market, they often had difficulty recouping their investments and meeting contract obligations.

THE FUTURE OF J&J: INCREASING PROFITABILITY

41   John and Jean faced some important decisions related to the future direction of the company. They needed to find a way to improve operating margins in the near term and grow the business in the long term. John favored greater growth and saw many opportunities that J&J could pursue, while Jean, on the other hand, favored more controlled growth with an emphasis on improving sales and margins, a more conservative approach.

42   John described his aspirations for J&J as follows:

> I would like to start or procure a low-voltage entity of J&J Electrical that does the structured cabling, fiber optics, category 5 wiring. Right now, we hire somebody else to do these. We go in and do all of the pipe work, the underground vaults and infrastructure, and then hire somebody, or somebody else comes in and they pull all of the fiber optics, etc. We don't have anyone trained to do that. I would like to find a small company or a mid-sized company that for some reason wants to sell, and buy it if we could, and operate that as a different entity of

J&J. It is another whole marketplace that is changing. I don't think if you get into that market that you're going to be on the outside looking in.

With the cost of homes going up so much, I see major remodeling of existing homes and businesses as another way for us to grow. People are going to get home-equity loans and be rebuilding or adding on. They say, well, it is too expensive to move. I have a client who is riding at the top of that and he is kind of pulling me along with it right now, and I think that we have to learn that. And we have to get technology into homes. It is so great that there are so many things in these smart homes. I just read an article yesterday that all the homes they are building now are all pre-wired for technology; they've got high technology, the high-span wire, and category 5 and 6 wiring. You can go in there and it's for high-speed Internet. All these homes that are built down here in Southern California, they all have structured cabling in there. Before, you [used to] go in and you do a home, you put the canned lights and all—it [cost] nothing, $2 or $3 per square foot. Now, that part goes up to $5 to $10 per square foot sometimes because of all the automated systems in there. So the profits are going up and all the guys who have been doing it all these years are making more money. Now, to try to get into [this market] will take us some time.

Another opportunity would be having another entity of J&J do small buildings and general building projects. We do a lot of modular-classroom buildings that are not elaborate. You do some grading, some plumbing, some asphalt work, some electrical, and we can get in and out and do it, but again that is a whole other entity of the company.

43   Jean, on the other hand, had a more conservative view:

I am opposed to [taking advantage of some growth opportunities] because I saw last year and the previous year that we had our struggles with profits. I want to see us working smarter and increasing our profits before branching out into something else. I want to take what we have here now and fix it and make it better before we diversify and go in another direction.

44   Although J&J had experienced strong revenue growth over the past four years, it had struggled with finding ways to increase profitability. After three straight years of declining net income after taxes (NIAT), John and Jean needed to reverse the course of J&J's profitability. In addition, the couple needed to find avenues for continued growth. Could J&J become profitable doing what it is currently doing? Should it change the ratio of public to private projects? Should it abandon public-works projects entirely and focus on private projects, or should it go in the direction of pursuing more community college and university bond projects, as John talked about? Should J&J even continue to operate as just an electrical contractor? Should it become a general contractor? Should it open a retail electrical-supply shop? Should it diversify into related areas of home audio or security systems, low-voltage installations, or the installation of alternative-energy-power sources, either by hiring individuals with those skills or acquiring a small company specialized in one of those areas? Should it expand into other high-growth areas in California and neighboring states? With such an array of possibilities, which direction should J&J take? Which option would help it most to get back on the road to profitability?

Case 30

Sula Vineyards

Raymond Lopez

Armand Gilinsky Jr.

Jigar Shah

Almost all my friends are in banking, consulting or the media. Originally they wondered why I wanted to head out to this godforsaken place. They looked at me as if I had gone mad—they thought I would lose my shirt![1]

1   In September 2007, Rajeev Samant could reflect on his California colleagues' reactions when he initially decided to return to his native India in the mid 1990s to grow grapes in order to produce and sell wine. He felt he had surmounted the risks of a new venture and successfully beat the odds to lead Sula Vineyards (Sula), an Indian winery, into the world wine producing market. Yet now his decade-old venture had reached a turning point. [Despite] Sula's growth in revenues since 2003, Rajeev felt that he faced several strategic and financing challenges. He could maintain current operations, accelerate growth, or position the company for sale to another beverage firm. Sula's early growth had been financed by debt as well as a private equity infusion in 2005, to supplement insufficient internally generated cash flows. To finance further expansion of winery capacity and inventories, new external funds would be needed soon.

2   Securing new funds at a reasonable cost could be critical to Sula's continued independence and ultimately determine its success in the marketplace for Indian wine. If Sula continued on its most recent growth trajectory, winery capacity would require incremental expansion, along with space for barrel aging of wine in inventory. These asset needs would, in turn, require additional external financing, since internally generated cash flows had not historically kept pace with either revenue or overall asset expansion and could not be expected to expand fast enough to support a forecast sales growth rate in the 20–25 percent range. Growth at these rates might not even enable Sula to maintain its current share of the rapidly expanding Indian domestic wine market. Additional infusions of equity could decrease Rajeev's share ownership and possibly lead to loss of control, while taking on new debt would increase Sula's financial risk lest future profits and cash flows not meet expectations.

[1] Mitra, S. 2005. "Wine Industry in Maharashtra: An Analysis," Markets and Regulations, Centre for Civil Society, 229.

RAJEEV SAMANT—AN UNLIKELY VINTNER

3 Born into an affluent Bombay family in 1968, young Rajeev came to the United States to study at Stanford University in Palo Alto, California. He majored in economics as an undergraduate, receiving his diploma in 1989. In 1990 he earned a master's degree in industrial engineering at Stanford and followed the lure of Silicon Valley by taking a job as one of Oracle's youngest financial managers.

4 Life styles in the Valley and the technology revolution of those years did not coincide with Rajeev's expectations and he quickly grew restless with a job that provided two weeks of vacation per year. Leaving Oracle after less than two years, he first traveled south to Mexico ("two months with a phrase book").[2]

5 In 1992, he read of his native India's decision to ease trade barriers with the rest of the world. "I was gripped by the excitement of those changes and wanted to go back to my country to help create job opportunities there."[3]

6 In mid 1993, Rajeev took a tour of his family's ancestral lands near the town of Nashik, approximately 120 miles northeast of Mumbai (then known as Bombay). See country and regional maps in Exhibit 1 and Exhibit 2. His father, a first-generation entrepreneur, accompanied him and discussed his plans to sell the 30-acre property. "It was so beautiful with gently rolling hills, a large lake and rich clay soil," Rajeev recalled. "I told him, 'wait!—don't sell it. I'd like to do something there.' "[4]

7 He felt the need to start something of his own. "There is a special, incomparable pride one takes in a self-started venture, a feeling of ownership that drives you to make it a success."[5] Over the next four years Rajeev became something of a gentleman farmer, studying the characteristics of the land as well as the climate of the region. His first experiment with agriculture entailed planting and harvesting alphonso mangos, followed by Thompson seedless grapes. The state of Maharashtra had been a leading producer of grapes in India for decades.[6]

8 Grape production in Maharashtra was extensive, with over 80,000 acres of vineyards producing almost one million tons of grapes annually. It was estimated that 99 percent of those grapes were used to make honey, crushes and jams or consumed fresh or dry. Nobody had really tried to grow wine grapes in that region, at least not commercially. The idea came to him: "If table grapes would grow there, why not grapes for fine wines?"[7] Some scientific analysis of extensive soil and climate data confirmed that the hot, dry days and cold nights of Nashik in the fall and winter months were similar to the summer growing environment of California's Sonoma Valley.[8]

9 In order to pursue his plan to go into the winemaking business, he needed a company. He formed a family corporation, Sula Vineyards, after his mother's name, Sulabha. Sula meant sun-like, he noted, "Sula represents the sun. When you think of wine you think of lovely grapes growing in the sun."[9]

---

[2] Rigoglioso, M. 2004. "The Mondavi of Mumbai," *Stanford Magazine,* January/February.

[3] Ibid.

[4] Ibid.

[5] Ibid.

[6] INSEAD Entrepreneurship Newsletter, January 2006.

[7] Rigoglioso, M. 2004. op. cit.

[8] Menon, P. 2003. "Giving an Indian Flavour to Wine," *Business Line,* May 19.

[9] Anon. 2001. "The Sunny Vintner," *Upper Crust,* January–March.

EXHIBIT 1 **Map of India**

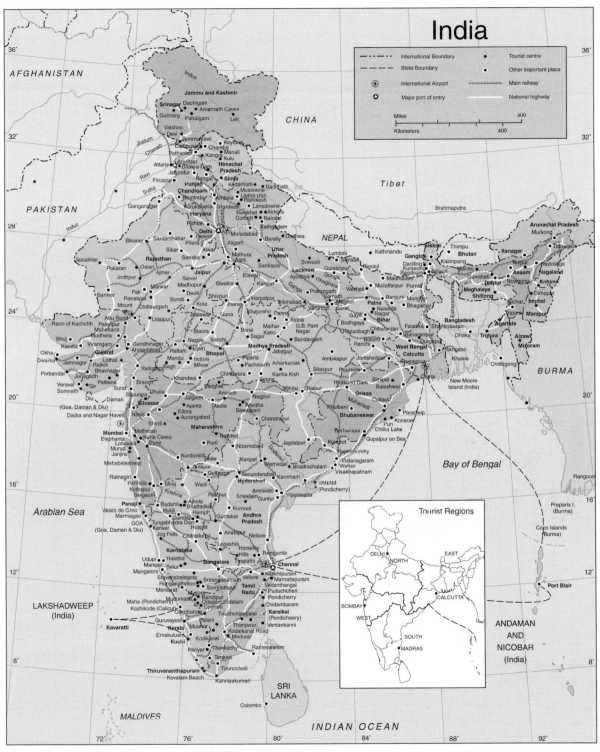

EXHIBIT 2   **District Map of Maharashtra**

Source: www.mapsofindia.com

LEARNING HOW TO GROW GRAPES—A CRITICAL COMPONENT ON THE ROAD TO SUCCESS

10   Without any knowledge of wine grape growing or the production of wine, Rajeev realized that expertise would be needed if his envisioned business project were to have any chance of success. Flying back to Northern California, Rajeev decided to team up with an expert. Through a variety of connections from his years in the area, he was ultimately introduced to Kerry Damskey, a Sonoma, California–based consultant. Kerry and his firm, Terroir, headquartered in Geyserville, had been overseeing winery startups and designing wine production systems for more than three decades. Kerry's firm was named after the French term, *terroir*. Terroir reflected the myriad of factors that affected growth in a vineyard: soil, elevation, climate, geographical features, orientation to the sun, and so forth. Some of Kerry's projects had borne fruit, resulting in production rates in excess of one million cases per year.

11   Kerry was at first skeptical when Rajeev outlined his proposal:

> When I was first approached, my initial reaction was, 'I didn't know they had wine in India.' Come on, it's the same latitude as Hawaii. It's tropical grape growing, and that just isn't done.

I quickly learned about the industry after my first visit in 1995. It was very exciting, a real adventure. My role here was to define the vision and create a road map.[10]

12   The peculiarities of the climate provided major challenges to the shared Rajeev-Kerry vision. Water was the most precious of all commodities, especially in the searing summer months in rural India. Sula's vineyards were located in a very suitable area, a short distance from the expansive Gangapure Lake and the shores of the Godavari River.[11] Irrigation of the fields presented few challenges. Nevertheless, dusty heat and dryness year round, alleviated by a monsoon between June and September, prevented the grape vines from undergoing their usual winter shut down in other regions of the world. To address this situation, workers had to prune vines after the harvest and save new shoots which became fruiting canes for the following year's crop.[12]

13   Around the world the best wines were usually made from grapes grown at higher latitudes, at least 35 degrees from the equator. The Nashik region was situated just 20 degrees north, so how, Rajeev wondered, could sophisticated wines be produced in such a hot climate? The answer lay in growing grapes in the winter months, after the monsoon season ended, usually late September to early October. From October through March, warm afternoons and cool nights approximated the climate of the Rhone Valley in summer, as well as that of Sonoma County in California. The strong sun resulted in increasing the sugar levels of wines (known in the wine industry as *brix*), but the night chill brought out the more subtle flavors of a wine made in a temperate climate.

14   Some adjustments to the area had to be made to approximate other grape growing regions. Vines were grown high and spread out to help dissipate heat and foster a leafier canopy. The soil needed to be graded into slopes so that there was adequate drainage during the monsoon season. Without this configuration, roots of the vines could become water logged and damaged, reducing grape production during the next growing season.[13]

15   Another challenge that could have slowed or even halted development of Sula's operations was the common, hidden cost of doing business in a country where *baksheesh* (bribery) was a way of life. Such practices were prohibited by law in most developed nations, and were considered a violation of the U.S. Foreign Corrupt Practices Act. Mindful of his U.S. experiences in conducting business in compliance with these standards, it took him almost two years, approximately 200 signatures, and perhaps a one-foot tall stack of documents to obtain permission to build a winery.

16   Despite the additional time needed to obtain licensing and planning permission, Rajeev earned respect for not taking shortcuts to developing grape growing activities and winery construction plans. Rajeev stated at the time, "To make beautiful wine, you need a beautiful winery."[15] A prominent Indian architect, Rahul Mehrotra, designed the main winery buildings and a four-bedroom ranch-style house (not owned by the company). This style was typical western Maharashtra, similar to Spanish architecture, with white-washed walls with sloping red tile roofs.[14]

[10] Mitra. 2005. op. cit., 227.

[11] Jung, C. 2003. "Stanford Alum Transforms Homeland's Wine Industry," *Business Today,* March 30.

[12] Restall, H. 2006. "Indo Vino Nouveau," *The Wall Street Journal,* May 17.

[13] Ibid.

[14] Mitra. 2005. op. cit., 227–228.

GRAPE TYPES AND WINE PRODUCTS

17   After analyzing the growing conditions of the region, Rajeev decided to plant Sauvignon Blanc, a classic grape from the Bordeaux region of France and Chenin Blanc, a classic grape from the Loire Valley of France. Neither of these varieties had ever been grown in India.

18   Rajeev's decision followed from a combination of both production and marketing considerations. These varietals were expected to grow well and the wine would stand up to the bold, spicy flavors of Indian cuisine. The target market was local, though the quality standards were world-class.[15]

19   Sula's grapevines were first planted in early 1997, with Sauvignon Blanc cuttings flown in from France and Chenin Blanc cuttings flown in from California. The vineyards produced their first grapes in 2000.

20   Planting vines and waiting for them to bear fruit in commercial quantities could take a few years. Rajeev decided to contract the original grape growing to local farmers in the region. This would generate a steady supply of grapes and lend a stimulus to the local rural economy. One kilogram of wine grapes retailed for over $0.70 per kg, while table grape farmers were lucky to get $0.35 per kg.[16]

21   Rajeev noted that winemaking was a challenging blend of art and science, a complicated process, from growing the raw materials, to processing, packaging, marketing and financing:

> It is a very capital-intensive business and all supplies have to be brought in. We import corks from Portugal, foil from Spain, yeast from Australia and barrels from France. The result was an indigenous product made with international techniques and know-how.[17]

22   Due to subtropical Indian weather conditions, stainless steel tanks required chilling jackets to optimize temperature and humidity during the fermenting process. Then the oak barrels mellowed the wine while adding other distinctive qualities. These had to be kept in climate controlled facilities, especially during the hot summer months.

23   Electric power would be required to keep facilities operating during those hot summer months. As supplies from the country's power grid were inherently unreliable, back-up generators would be needed to maintain operating efficiencies. Naturally, this added to the expenses of the fledgling firm, although all local competitors making similar wines in India faced power generation challenges.

24   The Rajeev-Kerry team had apparent success in matching wines to the Indian palates. Their decision to produce white wines was calculated to match India's fiery cuisine. The Sula Brut, a sparking wine, complemented *tandoori* dishes and *biryani*, as well as lighter Asian dishes such as *dim sum* and steamed seafood. The Chenin Blanc went well with salads and sweet and sour cuisines, such as Chinese, Southeast Asian and Gujarati. Sauvignon Blanc was a perfect accompaniment to coastal and southern-based coconut based curries and dishes flavored with coriander as well as spicier entrées.[18] The product line was quickly expanded to include a *methode champenoise* sparkling wine made with local table grapes and Chenin Blanc, and a blush Zinfandel made from grapes grown on the estate. To expand the firm's product portfolio, an imported Chilean Merlot was added, labeled Satoni. On the 300 acres acquired in 2004, the firm grew and introduced its first red wine, a Cabernet Sauvignon fleshed out with a small amount of Shiraz, also made from locally grown grapes.[19]

---

[15] Jung. 2003. op. cit.; and Menon. 2003. op. cit.

[16] Pal, A. 2003. "India's Wine Capital," *Business Today,* March 30.

[17] Menon. 2003. op. cit.

[18] Ibid.

[19] Mitra. 2005. op. cit., 227–228.

INDIA'S WINE INDUSTRY

25   India had been producing wine for more than 5,000 years.[19] Early European travelers to the courts of the Mughal emperors Akbar, Jehangir and Shah Jehan in the sixteenth and seventeenth centuries reported tasting wines from the royal vineyards. Under British influence in the nineteenth century, vineyards were established in Kashmir and at Baramati in Maharashtra. A number of Indian wines were exhibited and favorably received by visitors to the Great Calcutta Exhibition in 1884. However, for unknown reasons, Indian vineyards were destroyed in the 1890s.

26   Due to limited domestic consumption of wine and lack of availability of good quality wines made to international standards, not much research went into the industry and its grape growing activities. In the 1980s conventional wine grape production began as Indian markets opened to world trade and development.

27   Alok Chandra summarized the recent history of the Indian wine market in a 2006 *Business Standard* article.[20] The first wave of winemakers was known as "pioneers." Pioneers included Chateau Indage, in business since 1986, Grover Vineyards, established in 1992, and Sula, whose first wines were produced in 1999. The owners and managers of these firms were passionate about wine as a beverage and driven in their desires to expand the market for their products.

28   The second wave began in the state of Maharashtra in 2001, due to liberalization of a number of laws and regulations. With winery licenses easier to obtain, a number of new wineries were formed. Some of the larger ones included Vinsura, Flamingo, Renaissance, Sailo, ND, Mark Anthony, and Mohini.

29   By 2005 it was estimated that approximately 2,500 acres in Maharashtra and about 500 acres near Bangalore in Karnataka were dedicated to the production of wine grapes. Among these vineyards, 70 percent were in production while the remaining 30 percent were in the "establishment" stage and were expected to be producing within three years.

30   The third wave was just getting under way in 2006. It was characterized by the entry of major beverage companies and professionals that were well funded and knew quite well the spirits industry in India. They believed that the retail Indian wine market was on the verge of explosive growth and wanted to be there to participate in a meaningful way.[21] See Exhibit 3 and Exhibit 4 for Indian wine production trends and imports by wine type and price range.

31   In Maharashtra wine grapes were grown in three regions, Pune-Narayangaon, Nashik, and Sangli-Solapur. Estimated to reach full production by 2008, these regions could produce 15,000 tons of wine grapes ready for crushing each year, yielding an average of 9 million liters of wine, rising from approximately 5.4 million liters in 2005. Total Indian wine production in 2005 comprised 6.2 million liters, showing the importance of Maharastra to the industry.[21]

32   Production of wine was expected to continue to grow at 20 to 25 percent per year in volume and 25–30 percent per year in sales. In addition, imports of wine were also growing rapidly in response to the developing tastes and preferences of a growing portion of the Indian population. Of the thirty-eight private wineries operating in India in 2005, thirty-six were located in Maharastra, one in Karnataka, and one in Goa. Total winery investments in Maharashtra reached $18.14 million in 2004 and $25.47 million in 2005.[22]

[20] Chandra, A. 2006. "The Third Wave in India's Wine Industry," *Business Standard,* reprinted in *Sommelier India*/Blog, July 26.

[21] Ibid.

[22] Ibid.

EXHIBIT 3   Indian Wine Market—Domestic Production 2003–2007 (thousands of cases)

	2003	2004	2005	2006	2007
Sparkling Wines	35	35	46	56	64
Premium Still Wines	117	143	248	316	420
Economy Still Wines	234	240	390	470	547
Other	4	5	6	8	9
Total	390	423	690	850	1040
Industry Revenues (wholesale, in $ millions)	$12.00	$13.50	$22.20	$28.00	$35.00
Average Revenues/Case ($)	$30.77	$31.91	$32.17	$32.94	$33.63

Notes
Economy wines sold for under $5.00 per 750 ml per bottle
Premium wines sold for over $5.00 per 750 ml per bottle
One case contained twelve 750ml bottles
Sources: (1) Karibasappa, G. S., P. G. Adsule, S. D. Samant, and K. Banerjee, "About Wine: Present Scenario of the Wine Industry in India," June 25, 2006; and (2) Gupta, Nandini Sen and Chaitall Chakravarty, "Sparkling Time Ahead for Wine Industry," *The Economic Times,* reprinted in Sommelier India/Blog, November 6, 2006.

EXHIBIT 4   Indian Wine Market Imports 2003–2007 (thousands of cases)

	2003	2004	2005	2006	2007
Sparkling Wines	5	11	12	13	15
Premium Still Wines	53	63	66	71	79
Economy Still Wines	0	0	0	0	0
Other	1	1	1	1	1
Total	59	75	79	85	95
Industry Revenues (wholesale, in $ millions)	$12.00	$13.50	$22.20	$28.00	$35.00
Average Revenues/Case	$30.77	$31.91	$32.17	$32.94	$33.63

Sources: (1) Karibasappa, G. S., P. G. Adsule, S. D. Samant, and K. Banerjee, "About Wine: Present Scenario of the Wine Industry in India," June 25, 2006; and (2) Gupta, Nandini Sen and Chaitall Chakravarty, "Sparkling Time Ahead for Wine Industry," *The Economic Times*, reprinted in Sommelier India/Blog, November 6, 2006.

33   Of the 5.4 million liters of wine produced in Maharashtra in 2005, 2.54 million was red wine, 2.69 million was white wine, 0.15 million was sparkling and 0.04 million was rose (blush). In contrast, world production was 32 billion liters. This market share of .019 percent was miniscule compared to 17.5 percent for France, 16.6 percent for Italy, 10.9 percent for Spain and 6.9 percent for the U.S. There were at least two firms headquartered in the U.S. whose output exceeded that of India (Constellation Brands and E&J Gallo).[23]

34   Consumption of wine in India was concentrated in some of its major population centers. Analysts estimated that 39 percent was consumed in Mumbai, 23 percent in New Delhi, 9 percent in Bangalore and 9 percent in the tourist dominated state of Goa. All the rest of the country made up the last 20 percent.[24] The international exposure of these population centers was responsible for the developing taste for wine, by foreigners coming to India as well as Indians traveling abroad and then returning home.

35   Imports as well as domestic production rose rapidly to meet the growing demand; yet per capita consumption remained low, at only 0.07 liters per person per year, compared to 60–70 liters in France and Italy, 25 liters in the U.S., 20 liters in Australia and 0.4 liters in China.[25]

[23] Ibid.

[24] Chandran, R. 2005. "India Gets a Taste for Wine," *Sommelier India,* November 17.

[25] Ibid.

DRIVING GLOBAL DEMAND FOR INDIAN WINE

36   The Indian government planned to showcase "Wines of India" across the globe. The Agricultural and Processed Food Products Export Development Authority (APEDA) was developing a strategy and a campaign to support these initiatives. Wine had recently been exported to the U.S., where the product was being served in both Indian and Western restaurants. Exports were also going to France, Italy, Germany, the U.K. and Singapore, primary from production in Maharashtra.

37   APEDA's country wine promotion strategies included easing trade barriers and developing an awareness of Indian wine. These programs complemented efforts made by Rajeev at Sula and the Grover family of Grover Wines, to advertise and promote Indian wines. Other factors contributing to these efforts included changing life styles of the middle class in India, frequent travel abroad, the growth of women in the labor force, growing per capita income and international research on the health benefits of wine, consumed in moderation. Awareness of wine as a beverage of choice, especially table wine with meals, as well as the growing supply of domestic premium reds and whites, were contributing to the rapid acceptance and consumption.

38   Regulatory changes in 2001 in the state of Maharashtra resulted in a significant stimulus to wine demand in India. The state government declared winemaking a food processing industry, thus exempting it from excise duties as well as slashing sales taxes. Production costs of imported items (glass bottles, corks, yeast, etc.) were reduced along with the wholesale and retail prices of wine. Growth of quantity demanded accelerated, along with the other factors contributing to growing domestic consumption.[26]

39   In both 2004 and 2005, the Indian government made successive reductions of excise duty on imported wine, seen by industry observers as a major step to stimulate importation of international products. In early 2006, restrictions on the sale of wine in supermarkets were lifted, stimulating accessibility and demand for both domestic and imported products, although the legal drinking age in India remained twenty-five years in most states.

40   Infrastructure investment by the federal and state governments was needed, especially in the Mumbai-Pune-Nashik industrial corridor. Roads and reliable sources of electric power would assist everyone in the region. Diesel generators were used extensively for irrigation and other needs, a significant expense for vineyard operations.[27]

SULA VINEYARDS' OPERATING HISTORY

41   Sula Vineyards' groundbreaking for its first winery began in October 1998, and its first crush occurred in March 1999. The main cellar of the facility at that time did not yet have a roof, but that did not deter Rajeev from producing his first wines.[28] Sales were slow for the first six months, as only one truckload of wine was actually sold. The original winery had a capacity of 150,000 liters, or 200,000 bottles per year. By 2003, the cellar had a roof, and capacity increased threefold to 600,000 liters. In 2006 it reached 1.6 million liters, as the third-phase expansion was completed. Revenues had grown steadily to approximately $5 million in fiscal year 2006 (for the twelve months ending March 2006), with a target of $7 million in fiscal 2007.[29] See Exhibit 5, Exhibit 6, and Exhibit 7 showing

---

[26] Ibid.

[27] Anon. 2006. "The Hindu Interviews Rajeev Samant on Wine in India," *The Hindu,* reprinted in *Sommelier India*/Blog, November 24.

[28] "Sula Vineyards-India's Wine Pioneers—About the Company," www.sulavineyards.com.

[29] Verified by the casewriters via personal correspondence with company representative Ruth Dolla in September 2007 and subsequently with Rajeev Samant in September 2008.

EXHIBIT 5   Sula Vineyards Estimated Income Statements, 2003–2007 ($000)

	Year ending 31 March				
	2003	**2004**	**2005**	**2006**	**2007**
Revenue	$1,026	$2,297	$3,761	$4,946	$6,867
Cost of Goods Sold:					
Purchases	204	478	752	1,037	1,456
Manufacturing and Operating Expenses	227	488	786	1,034	1,380
Direct Labor	94	203	317	404	542
Cost of Goods Sold	525	1,169	1,855	2,475	3,378
Gross Margin	501	1,128	1,906	2,471	3,489
Administrative Expenses	117	277	421	583	728
Selling and Marketing Expenses	204	498	806	1,088	1,511
Sales Taxes	78	192	305	414	563
Total Expenses	399	967	1,532	2,085	2,802
Earnings before Interest, Taxes, Depreciation & Amortization (EBITDA)	102	161	374	386	687
Depreciation	33	52	65	81	131
Earnings before Interest & Taxes (EBIT)	69	109	309	305	556
Interest and Finance Costs	78	193	294	270	340
Profit before Taxes	(9)	(84)	15	35	216
Provision for Taxes (10%)	0	0	1	3	21
Net Income after Taxes	(9)	(84)	14	32	195

Source: Casewriters' estimates, based on comparable publicly traded Indian wine firms' statements, verified as representative of actual amounts by Sula Vineyards' management

the casewriters' estimated company financial statements for the 2003–2007 fiscal years, derived from comparable public Indian wineries.

42 Rajeev came to be dubbed "the Mondavi of Mumbai" by knowledgeable wine industry aficionados in the United States. These folks knew quite well what the legendary Robert Mondavi had accomplished for the wine industry in the U.S. From humble beginnings in the 1940s and 1950s he left his family business (Krug) to form the Robert Mondavi Company in the early 1960s. Almost single handedly he spread the word that wine could and should be an important component of fine dining. Via lectures, wine tastings, professional presentations, as well as incorporating innovative techniques into grape growing and wine production, Mondavi contributed to the growing U.S. per capita consumption of wine over several decades in the late twentieth century.

43 In his own way, Rajeev seemed to have taken a page out of Robert Mondavi's wine marketing book. He also sponsored wine tastings, presented at industry trade association conferences, and brought cutting-edge viticultural technology to what was still considered by many industry observers to be a nascent Indian wine industry. His decision to design wines to meet global standards of taste and quality convinced other Indian winemakers to follow suit. He formed a wine board to encourage other Indian firms to make quality wines and display their prowess in world markets. He maintained that, "We're going to need a group of good producers if India is going to be a contender in the world market. We have to do it together."[30]

[30] Rigoglioso, M. 2004. op. cit.

EXHIBIT 6 Sula Vineyards—Estimated Balance Sheets, 2003–2007 ($000s)

	Year ending 31 March				
	2003	**2004**	**2005**	**2006**	**2007**
Assets					
Current Assets					
Cash	$ 51	$ 77	$ 114	$ 142	$ 183
Accounts Receivable	196	463	788	1,091	1,455
Inventories	728	1,817	2,835	4,105	5,771
Loans & Advances	97	201	323	407	545
Total Current Assets	1,072	2,558	4,060	5,745	7,954
Fixed Assets					
Property, Plant & Equipment	863	1,542	1,877	3,386	4,253
Less; Accumulated Depreciation & Amortization	79	131	196	277	408
Net Property Plant & Equipment	784	1,411	1,681	3,109	3,845
Other Assets	11	21	38	51	63
Total Assets	$1,867	$3,990	$5,779	$8,905	$11,862
Liabilities and Capital					
Current Liabilities					
Accounts Payable	$ 42	$ 93	$ 152	$ 192	$ 282
Other Liabilities	12	32	46	63	96
Notes Payable (Bank)	838	1,721	2,563	2,660	4,011
Accrued Expenses	45	98	157	196	288
Total Current Liabilities	937	1,944	2,918	3,111	4,677
Secured Loans (Net)	900	2,100	2,900	2,300	3,500
Deferred Tax Liability (Net)	0	0	2	3	0
Total Long-Term Commitments	900	2,100	2,902	2,303	3,500
Equity					
Share Capital	200	200	200	300	300
Capital Surplus	400	400	400	3,800	3,800
Retained Earnings	(570)	(654)	(641)	(609)	(415)
Total Equity	30	(54)	(41)	3,491	3,685
Total Liabilities and Equity	$1,867	$3,990	$5,779	$8,905	$11,862

Source: Casewriters' estimates, based on comparable publicly traded Indian wine firms' statements, verified as representative of actual amounts by Sula Vineyards' management.

SULA'S FINANCIAL STRATEGY

44   After a few years of farming grapes, Rajeev formed Sula Vineyards with $1 million from family, friends, and bank loans. The firm's equity was 200,000 shares at $1 each, with $600,000 in loans from a diverse group of private lenders. The bank loan totaled $200,000.

45   Funds raised were used to build the first winery along with barrels for aging and a four-bedroom house. As success in the marketplace translated into growing sales, additional production capacity was needed. Financing for these fixed assets was through long-term

EXHIBIT 7   Sula Vineyards—Estimated Statements of Cash Flow, 2003–2007 ($000s)

	Year ending 31 March				
	2003	2004	2005	2006	2007
CASH FLOWS FROM OPERATING ACTIVITIES					
Net Income	$ (9)	$ (84)	$ 14	$ 32	$ 195
Depreciation	33	52	65	81	131
Increase in Receivables (Net)	(84)	(267)	(325)	(303)	(364)
Increase in Inventories	(37)	(1,089)	(1,018)	(1,270)	(1,666)
Increase in Loans and Advances	(48)	(104)	(122)	(84)	(138)
Increase in Accounts Payable	26	51	59	40	90
Increase in Other Liabilities	6	20	14	17	33
Increase in Bank Notes Payable	400	883	842	97	1,351
Increase in Accrued Expenses	22	53	59	39	92
Net Cash Provided (Used) by Operating Activities	309	(485)	(412)	(1,351)	(276)
CASH FLOWS FROM INVESTING ACTIVITIES					
Purchase of Property, Plant and Equipment	(482)	(679)	(335)	(1,509)	(867)
Other Assets	(8)	(10)	(17)	(13)	(12)
Net Cash Used for Investing Activities	(490)	(689)	(352)	(1,522)	(879)
CASH FLOWS FROM FINANCING ACTIVITIES					
Increase (Decrease) from Secured Loans	500	1,200	800	(600)	1,200
Increase (Decrease) from Deferred Tax Liability	0	0	2	1	(3)
Increase (Decrease) from Capital (Share and Surplus)	0	0	0	3,500	0
Net Cash Provided (Used) by Financing Activities	500	1,200	802	2,901	1,197
Net Change in Cash	319	26	38	28	42
Cash at the Beginning of the Year	71	390	416	454	482
Cash at the End of the Year	$390	$ 416	$ 454	$ 482	$ 523

Source: Casewriters' estimates, based on comparable publicly traded Indian wine firms' statements, verified as representative of actual amounts by Sula Vineyards' management.

loans backed by these facilities. Shorter-term borrowings were used to finance the growth in inventories.[31]

46   Due to successful marketing of the company's wine brands, by 2005 Sula's two wineries were operating at full capacity. Yet as positive and steadily growing profit levels had yet to be achieved, Sula's balance sheet seemed to be in need of strengthening. Company expansion had thus far been financed through borrowing, and lenders were voicing concern about the risks they were taking. Without an infusion of equity funding, Rajeev felt, further expansion might not be possible.[32] As the third Sula winery was already on the drawing board, Rajeev said,

> We [needed] quick access to funds. Wine is an extremely capital-intensive industry and we've been engaged almost consistently in construction, with demand showing no signs of slowing down. We've been borrowing heavily and the debt was making me feel uncomfortable, so

[31] Verified by the casewriters via personal correspondence with company representative Ruth Dolla in September 2007 and subsequently with Rajeev Samant in September 2008.

[32] Verified by the casewriters via personal correspondence with Rajeev Samant in September 2008.

we decided to divest through a preferential allotment of optionally convertible preference shares.[33]

47   In 2005, GEM India Advisors purchased shares representing one-third (33 per cent) of the ownership of Sula for $3.5 million, valuing the entity at $10.5 million. GEM was a private equity fund and its ownership covered only the Sula Vineyards winery operations. The original 30 acres of land, along with another 300 recently purchased acres, continued to be owned by the Samant family and associates. Funds from this transaction were earmarked to build the third state-of-the-art winery in Nashik and to pay down some existing debt.

48   Two key principals of GEM India Advisors were appointed to the Sula board of directors. Deepak Shahdadpuri was the founder and Managing Director of GEM, a private equity group that specialized in consumer centric growth equity investments in India. Also coming on board was Alok Sarna, an advisor to GEM and a former managing director at Morgan Stanley.

49   "The new partners are friends, wine lovers, but more importantly, they bring years of financial experience to the Sula board," commented Rajeev. "If I need to go for a public issue a year or year and a half from now, I'll have partners who have the right experience."[34]

FUTURE FINANCIAL AND STRATEGIC CHALLENGES

50   By 2007, two years after its infusion of private equity funding, important new challenges had to be addressed. In its early years, white wines had been the products of choice, primarily based upon Rajeev's expectations of domestic market demand for those wines. White wines could be produced and sold within a one year period since they required a relatively short period of time "in the oak barrels" for aging. They were "drunk young" and provided early cash flows that could be directed back into the business for repayment of debt or expansion into new markets with increasing production. Sula had also begun expanding its portfolio of brands and commenced production of a variety of red wines.

51   Exhibit 8, Exhibit 9, and Exhibit 10 present the casewriters' estimates of Sula's production and revenues from 2003–2007 by product type, illustrating the changing product mix. To enhance quality and support the growing image of the firm as a producer of a portfolio

[33] Singh, K. 2005. *Business Standard,* October 17. Regarding the issuance of these types of financial instruments, the laws were later amended by the Indian government: "With a view to mobilizing foreign investment through issue of preference shares, the Government of India (GOI) had [previously] permitted issuance of equity shares, preference shares, convertible preference shares by Indian companies to persons resident outside India in respect of financial projects/industries. The Reserve Bank of India on 8th June 2007 amended the guidelines applicable to foreign investment in preference shares. Pursuant to the revised guidelines, foreign investment from the issue of fully convertible preference shares would be treated as part of the share capital, which would be included in computing the sectoral caps on foreign equity . . . Foreign investments from the issue of non-convertible, optionally convertible or partially convertible preference shares, for which funds had been received on or after 1st May 2007, would be considered as debt and be required to conform with External Commercial Borrowings (ECB) guidelines/caps. Accordingly, all norms applicable to ECBs would apply to such preference shares." http://www.mondaq.com/article.asp?articleid=50634, accessed January 26, 2009.

[34] Singh, K. 2005. op. cit.

EXHIBIT 8   Sula Vineyards—Estimated Annual Production in Cases, 2003–2007

Product Categories	Year ending 31 March				
	2003	2004	2005	2006	2007
Whites					
Sauvignon Blanc	10,000	24,000	33,000	41,000	56,000
Chenin Blanc	8,000	15,500	27,000	33,500	43,000
White Zinfandel				2,000	4,000
Reds (See Note 1)					
Cabernet Sauvignon				3,000	5,000
Shiraz				2,000	4,000
Red Zinfandel				1,500	4,000
Chilean Merlot					
Import Satori	200	500	1,000		
Other					
Champagne Style Brut	2,000	4,000	6,500	8,000	9,000
Total Production	20,200	44,000	70,000	91,000	125,000
Winery Capacity					
Cases	66,666	66,666	66,666	83,333	177,750
Liters	600,000	600,000	600,000	750,000	1,600,000
Bottles	800,000	800,000	800,000	1,000,000	2,133,000

Note 1: Certain red wines require aging up to 24 months prior to sale, therefore, can be sold two to three years after date of production. For example, Cabernet Sauvignon and Shiraz produced in 2006 can be sold in 2008. Sales of red wines in years prior to 2008 are based on product purchased from other Indian vineyards.
Source: Casewriters' estimates, based on comparable publicly traded Indian wine firms' statements, verified as representative of actual amounts by Sula Vineyards' management.

EXHIBIT 9   Sula Vineyards—Estimated Revenues per Case, 2003–2007

Product Categories	Year ending 31 March				
	2003	2004	2005	2006	2007
Whites					
Sauvignon Blanc	$51.00	$52.50	$54.40	$55.30	$55.90
Chenin Blanc	$48.00	$49.30	$50.60	$51.10	$51.70
White Zinfandel				$47.90	$48.60
Reds (See Note 1)					
Cabernet Sauvignon			$57.20	$58.90	$59.20
Shiraz			$55.90	$56.80	$57.10
Red Zinfandel				$55.70	$56.10
Chilean Merlot					
Import Satori	$54.30	$55.80	$56.60		
Other					
Champagne Style Brut	$60.60	$61.20	$61.80	$62.20	$63.40
Average Price Per Case	$50.80	$52.20	$53.73	$54.36	$54.94
Total Production (cases)	20,200	44,000	70,000	91,000	125,000
Total Revenues	$1,026,060	$2,296,850	$3,761,400	$4,946,400	$6,867,300

Note 1: Certain red wines require aging up to 24 months prior to sale, therefore, can be sold two to three years after date of production. For example, Cabernet Sauvignon and Shiraz produced in 2006 can be sold in 2008. Sales of red wines in years prior to 2008 are based on product purchased from other Indian vineyards.
Source: Casewriters' estimates, based on comparable publicly traded Indian wine firms' statements, verified as representative of actual amounts by Sula Vineyards' management.

EXHIBIT 10 Sula Vineyards—Estimated Revenues by Product Category, 2003–2007

Product Categories	Year ending 31 March				
	2003	**2004**	**2005**	**2006**	**2007**
Whites					
Sauvignon Blanc	$510,000	$1,260,000	$1,795,200	$2,267,300	$3,130,400
Chenin Blanc	384,000	764,150	1,366,200	1,711,850	2,223,100
White Zinfandel				95,800	194,400
Reds					
Cabernet Sauvignon			85,800	176,700	296,000
Shiraz			55,900	113,600	228,400
Red Zinfandel				83,550	224,400
Chilean Merlot					
Import Satori	10,860	27,900	56,600		
Other					
Champagne Style Brut	121,200	244,800	401,700	497,600	570,600
Total Revenues	$1,026,060	$2,296,850	$3,761,400	$4,946,400	$6,867,300

Note 1: Certain red wines require aging up to 24 months prior to sale, so can be sold two to three years after date of production, for example, Cabernet Sauvignon and Shiraz produced in 2006 can be sold in 2008. Sales of red wines in years prior to 2008 are based on product purchased from other Indian vineyards.
Source: Casewriters' estimates, based on comparable publicly traded Indian wine firms' statements, verified as representative of actual amounts by Sula Vineyards' management

EXHIBIT 11 Sula Vineyards—Forecast Pricing Assumptions by Product Category 2008–2012

Product Categories	Year ending 31 March				
	2008	**2009**	**2010**	**2011**	**2012**
Whites					
Sauvignon Blanc	$57.30	$58.73	$60.20	$61.70	$63.25
Chenin Blanc	53.25	54.85	56.49	58.19	59.93
White Zinfandel	50.06	51.56	53.11	54.70	56.34
Reds					
Cabernet Sauvignon	$60.68	$62.20	$63.75	$65.35	$66.98
Shiraz	58.24	59.41	60.59	61.81	63.04
Red Zinfandel	57.22	58.37	59.53	60.72	61.94
Other					
Champagne Style Brut	$65.30	$67.26	$69.28	$71.36	$73.50

Source: Casewriters' estimates, verified as representative of actual amounts by Sula Vineyards' management

of fine premium wines, estate-grown red wines needed to remain in the barrel for two years or more. Financing a growing investment in longer term inventories posed a challenge for any premium wine producer, and Sula was no exception to this rule.

52   Rajeev identified his preliminary assumptions behind each forecast scenario for 2008–2012, shown in Exhibit 11, Exhibit 12, and Exhibit 13. He remained mindful of the fact that the impact of each growth plan would only be finalized after *pro forma* statements had been generated and analyzed. Using the assumptions and scenarios in Exhibits 11–13, he

EXHIBIT 12   Sula Vineyards—Pricing and Production Assumptions by Product Category, 2008–2012

Wine Varietal Categories	Growth Rates in Unit Prices	Growth Rates in Production		
		Scenario A	Scenario B	Scenario C
Whites				
Sauvignon Blanc	2.5%	6%	14%	23%
Chenin Blanc	3.0%	6%	14%	23%
White Zinfandel	3.0%	9%	20%	35%
Reds				
Cabernet Sauvignon	2.5%	20%	25%	35%
Shiraz	2.0%	10%	25%	30%
Red Zinfandel	2.0%	10%	25%	30%
Other				
Champagne Style Brut	3.0%	10%	20%	30%

Source: Casewriters' estimates, verified as representative of actual amounts by Sula Vineyards' management

EXHIBIT 13   Sula Vineyards—Assumptions for Pro Forma Income Statements and Balance Sheets, 2008–2012

	Scenario A	Scenario B	Scenario C
Income Statement (percentage of revenues)			
Revenues—to be estimated by you	21.0%	20.5%	20.0%
Cost of Goods Sold	20.0%	19.0%	18.0%
Manufacturing and Operating Expenses	8.0%	7.8%	7.6%
Employment Costs	10.5%	10.2%	7.6%
Administrative Expenses	21.5%	20.5%	20.0%
Selling and Marketing Expenses	8.3%	8.3%	8.3%
Sales Taxes			
Interest and Financing Costs = 7% of average borrowings			
Depreciation (see balance sheet)			
Provision for taxes = 10% of net income			
Balance Sheet (percentage of revenues except for P,P & E)	2.9%	2.7%	2.6%
Cash	22.0%	23.0%	24.0%
Accounts Receivable	81.0%	82.0%	83.0%
Inventories	8.0%	7.8%	7.6%
Loans and Advances			
Fixed Assets	66.0%	63.0%	59.0%
Property, Plant and Equipment	11 years	11 years	11 years
[Based on weighted average asset life, straight-line depreciation, in years]			
	1.0%	1.0%	0.9%
Other Assets	3.9%	4.0%	4.1%
Accounts Payable	1.3%	1.4%	1.4%
Other Liabilities	4.0%	4.2%	4.4%
Accrued Expenses			
	9.2%	9.6%	9.9%
Additional Funds Needed (AFN)	85.0%	90.0%	95.0%
Secured Debt (percentage of net PP& E)			

Source: Casewriter's estimates, verified as representative of actual amounts by Sula Vineyards' management prepared preliminary 2008–2012 forecasts for three growth scenarios (A, B, and C), shown in Exhibit 14, Exhibit 15, and Exhibit 16.

53   In order to reduce his anticipated financing needs, Rajeev could opt to lower his growth targets. If this path were followed, his promotional efforts on behalf of Sula and the Indian wine industry would probably also need to be decreased. Yet he remained confident that his company and the domestic wine industry were on the threshold of potentially explosive and sustainable growth, both for home sales and exports, over the decade to come. In any event, Rajeev needed to present a plan to finance Sula's future growth in consultation with

EXHIBIT 14   Sula Vineyards—Forecast Production and Revenues by Product, 2008–2012
Scenario A

	Year ending 31 March				
	2008	**2009**	**2010**	**2011**	**2012**
Annual Production in Cases:					
Whites					
Sauvignon Blanc	59,360	62,922	66,697	70,699	74,941
Chenin Blanc	45,580	48,315	51,214	54,287	57,544
White Zinfandel	4,360	4,752	5,180	5,646	6,154
	109,300	115,989	123,091	130,632	138,639
Reds					
Cabernet Sauvignon	6,000	7,200	8,640	10,368	12,442
Shiraz	4,400	4,840	5,324	5,856	6,442
Red Zinfandel	4,400	4,840	5,324	5,856	6,442
	14,800	16,880	19,288	22,081	25,326
Other					
Champagne Style Brut	9,900	10,890	11,979	13,177	14,495
Total Cases	134,000	143,759	154,358	165,889	178,459
Annual Revenues by Product:					
Whites					
Sauvignon Blanc	$3,401,180	$3,695,382	$4,015,032	$4,362,332	$4,739,674
Chenin Blanc	2,427,181	2,649,996	2,893,265	3,158,867	3,448,851
White Zinfandel	218,253	245,033	275,098	308,853	346,749
	6,046,613	6,590,410	7,183,396	7,830,052	8,535,274
Reds					
Cabernet Sauvignon	364,080	447,818	550,817	677,504	833,330
Shiraz	256,265	287,529	322,608	361,966	406,126
Red Zinfandel	251,777	282,494	316,958	355,627	399,013
	872,122	1,017,841	1,190,382	1,395,097	1,638,469
Other					
Champagne Style Brut	646,490	732,473	829,892	940,267	1,065,323
Total Revenues	$7,565,224	$8,340,724	$9,203,669	$10,165,416	$11,239,066

Source: Casewriters' estimates, verified as representative of actual amounts by Sula Vineyards' management.

EXHIBIT 15   Sula Vineyards—Forecast Production and Revenues by Product, 2008–2012 *Scenario B*

	Year ending 31 March				
	2008	**2009**	**2010**	**2011**	**2012**
Annual Production in Cases:					
Whites					
Sauvignon Blanc	63,840	72,778	82,966	94,582	107,823
Chenin Blanc	49,020	55,883	63,706	72,625	82,793
White Zinfandel	4,800	5,760	6,912	8,294	9,953
	117,660	134,420	153,585	175,501	200,569
Reds					
Cabernet Sauvignon	6,250	7,813	9,766	12,207	15,259
Shiraz	5,000	6,250	7,813	9,766	12,207
Red Zinfandel	5,000	6,250	7,813	9,766	12,207
	16,250	20,313	25,391	31,738	39,673
Other					
Champagne Style Brut	10,800	12,960	15,552	18,662	22,395
Total Cases	144,710	167,693	194,527	225,902	262,637
Annual Revenues by Product:					
Whites					
Sauvignon Blanc	$3,657,872	$4,274,224	$4,994,431	$5,835,992	$6,819,357
Chenin Blanc	2,610,364	3,065,089	3,599,028	4,225,979	4,962,144
White Zinfandel	240,278	296,984	367,072	453,701	560,775
	6,508,515	7,636,297	8,960,531	10,515,672	12,342,276
Reds					
Cabernet Sauvignon	379,250	485,914	622,577	797,677	1,022,024
Shiraz	291,210	371,293	473,398	603,583	769,568
Red Zinfandel	286,110	364,790	465,108	593,012	756,090
	956,570	1,221,997	1,561,083	1,994,272	2,547,683
Other					
Champagne Style Brut	705,262	871,703	1,077,425	1,331,698	1,645,978
Total Revenues	$8,170,346	$9,729,998	$11,599,040	$13,841,642	$16,535,937

Source: Casewriters' estimates, verified as representative of actual amounts by Sula Vineyards' management

his board of directors, notably Shahdadpuri and Sarna from GEM India Advisors. As he looked over the forecasts in preparation for his meeting with Sula's board in September 2007, Rajeev reflected,

> Looking back, the journey here has been challenging as well as incredibly rewarding. It's great to be my own boss—I travel to exciting places at short notice without worrying about my vacation day balance, because ultimately, I'm accountable to myself. I can't think of anyone who is happier with his/her job. Hugh Hefner, maybe.[35]

[35] Sula Vineyards' History, December 22, 2005, info.@dreyfusahby.com.

54   Rajeev needed to convince his board of the most advantageous way to finance future growth, ever mindful of his desire to continue to play a prominent role in the promotion of the Indian wine industry over the decade to come.

EXHIBIT 16   **Sula Vineyards—Forecast Production and Revenues by Product, 2008–2012**
Scenario C

	Year ending 31 March				
	2008	**2009**	**2010**	**2011**	**2012**
Annual Production in Cases:					
Whites					
Sauvignon Blanc	68,880	84,722	104,209	128,177	157,657
Chenin Blanc	52,890	65,055	80,017	98,421	121,058
White Zinfandel	5,400	7,290	9,842	13,286	17,936
	127,170	157,067	194,067	239,884	296,651
Reds					
Cabernet Sauvignon	6,750	9,113	12,302	16,608	22,420
Shiraz	5,200	6,760	8,788	11,424	14,852
Red Zinfandel	5,200	6,760	8,788	11,424	14,852
Other					
Champagne Style Brut	11,700	15,210	19,773	25,705	33,416
Total Cases	156,020	194,910	243,718	305,045	382,191
Annual Revenues by Product:					
Whites					
Sauvignon Blanc	$3,946,652	$4,975,741	$6,273,166	$7,908,894	$9,971,138
Chenin Blanc	2,816,445	3,568,155	4,520,495	5,727,015	7,255,556
White Zinfandel	270,313	375,871	522,648	726,742	1,010,535
	7,033,410	8,919,766	11,316,309	14,362,651	18,237,228
Reds					
Cabernet Sauvignon	409,590	566,770	784,268	1,085,231	1,501,689
Shiraz	302,858	401,590	532,509	706,106	936,297
Red Zinfandel	297,554	394,557	523,183	693,740	919,900
	1,010,003	1,362,918	1,839,960	2,485,078	3,357,885
Other					
Champagne Style Brut	764,033	1,023,041	1,369,852	1,834,231	2,456,036
Total Revenues	$8,807,447	$11,305,725	$14,526,120	$18,681,960	$24,051,149

Source: Casewriters' estimates, verified as representative of actual amounts by Sula Vineyards' management

Glossary

A

adaptive mode   The strategic formality associated with medium-sized firms that emphasize the incremental modification of existing competitive approaches.

adverse selection   An agency problem caused by the limited ability of stockholders to precisely determine the competencies and priorities of executives at the time they are hired.

agency costs   The cost of agency problems and the cost of actions taken to minimize them.

agency theory   A set of ideas on organizational control based on the belief that the separation of the ownership from management creates the potential for the wishes of owners to be ignored.

agile organization   A firm that identifies a set of business capabilities central to high-profitability operations and then builds a virtual organization around those capabilities, allowing the agile firm to build its business around the core, high-profitability information, services, and products. Creating an agile, virtual organization structure involves outsourcing, strategic alliances, a boundaryless learning approach, and Web-based organization.

ambidextrous organization   Organization structure most notable for its lack of structure wherein knowledge and getting it to the right place quickly is the key reason for organization. Managers become knowledge "nodes" through which intricate networks of personal relationships—inside and outside the formal organization—are constantly, and often informally, coordinated to bring together relevant know-how and successful action.

B

balanced scorecard   A management control system that enables companies to clarify their strategies, translate them into action, and provide quantitative feedback as to whether the strategy is creating value, leveraging core competencies, satisfying the company's customers, and generating a financial reward to its shareholders. A set of four measures directly linked to a company's strategy: financial performance, customer knowledge, internal business processes, and learning and growth.

bankruptcy   When a company is unable to pay its debts as they become due, or has more debts than assets.

benchmarking   Evaluating the sustainability of advantages against key competitors. Comparing the way a company performs a specific activity with a competitor or other company doing the same thing.

board of directors   The group of stockholder representatives and strategic managers responsible for overseeing the creation and accomplishment of the company mission.

boundaryless organization   Organizational structure that allows people to interface with others throughout the organization without need to wait for a hierarchy to regulate that interface across functional, business, and geographic boundaries.

breakthrough innovation   An innovation in a product, process, technology, or the cost associated with it that represents a quantum leap forward in one or more of these ways.

business model   A clear understanding of how the firms will generate profits and the strategic actions it must take to succeed over the long term.

business process outsourcing   Having an outside company manage numerous routine business management activities usually done by employees of the company such as HR, supply procurement, finance and accounting, customer care, supply-chain logistics, engineering, R&D, sales and marketing, facilities management, and management/development.

business process reengineering   A popular method by which organizations worldwide undergo restructuring efforts to remain competitive. It involves fundamental rethinking and radical redesigning of a business process so that a company can best create value for the customer by eliminating barriers that create distance between employees and customers.

C

cash cows   Businesses with a high market share in low-growth markets or industries.

CCC21   A world-famous, cost-oriented continuous improvement program at Toyota (Construction of Cost Competitiveness for the 21st Century).

chaebol   A Korean consortia financed through government banking groups to gain a strategic advantage.

company creed   A company's statement of its philosophy.

company mission   The unique purpose that sets a company apart from others of its type and identifies the scope of its operations in product, market, and technology terms.

concentrated growth   A grand strategy in which a firm directs its resources to the profitable growth of a single product, in a single market, with a single dominant technology.

concentric diversification   A grand strategy that involves the operation of a second business that benefits from access to the first firm's core competencies. A strategy that involves the acquisition of businesses that are related to the acquiring firm in terms of technology, markets, or products.

conglomerate diversification   A grand strategy that involves the acquisition of a business because it presents the most promising investment opportunity available. A strategy that involves acquiring or entering businesses unrelated to a firm's current technologies, markets, or products.

consortia   Large interlocking relationships between businesses of an industry.

continuous improvement   A form of strategic control in which managers are encouraged to be proactive in improving all operations of the firm. The process of relentlessly trying to find ways to improve and enhance a company's products and processes from design through assembly, sales, and service. It is called *kaizen* in Japanese. It is usually associated with incremental innovation.

core competence   A capability or skill that a firm emphasizes and excels in doing while in pursuit of its overall mission.

corporate social responsibility   The idea that business has a duty to serve society in general as well as the financial interest of stockholders.

D

dashboard   A user interface that organizes and presents information from multiple digital sources simultaneously in a user-designed format on the computer screen.

debt financing   Money "loaned" to an entrepreneur or business venture that must be repaid at some point in time.

declining industry   An industry in which the trend of total sales as an indicator of total demand for an industry's products or services among all the participants in the industry has started to drop from the last several years with the likelihood being that such a trend will continue indefinitely.

differentiation   A business strategy that seeks to build competitive advantage with its product or service by having it be "different" from other available competitive products based on features, performance, or other factors not directly related to cost and price. The difference would be one that would be hard to create and/or difficult to copy or imitate.

discretionary responsibilities   Responsibilities voluntarily assumed by a business, such as public relations, good citizenship, and full corporate responsibility.

disruptive innovation   A term to characterize breakthrough innovation popularized by Harvard Professor Clayton Christensen; usually shakes up or revolutionizes industries with which they are associated even though they often come from totally different origins or industry settings than the industry they "disrupt."

divestiture   A strategy that involves the sales of a firm or a major component of a firm.

divestiture strategy   A grand strategy that involves the sales of a firm or a major component of a firm.

divisional organizational structure   Structure in which a set of relatively autonomous units, or divisions, is governed by a central corporate office but where each operating division has its own functional specialists who provide products or services different from those of other divisions.

dogs   Low market share and low market growth businesses.

downsizing   Eliminating the number of employees, particularly middle management, in a company.

dynamic   The term that characterizes the constantly changing conditions that affect interrelated and interdependent strategic activities.

E

eco-efficiency   Company actions that produce more useful goods and services while continuously reducing resource consumption and pollution.

ecology   The relationships among human beings and other living things and the air, soil, and water that supports them.

economic responsibilities   The duty of managers, as agents of the company owners, to maximize stockholder wealth.

economies of scale   The savings that companies achieve because of increased volume.

emerging industry   An industry that has growing sales across all the companies in the industry based on growing demand for the relatively new products, technologies, and/or services made available by the firms participating in this industry.

empowerment   The act of allowing an individual or team the right and flexibility to make decisions and initiate action.

entrepreneurial mode   The informal, intuitive, and limited approach to strategic management associated with owner-managers of smaller firms.

entrepreneurship   The process of bringing together the creative and innovative ideas and actions with the management and organizational skills necessary to mobilize the appropriate people, money, and operating resources to meet an identifiable need and create wealth in the process.

equity financing   Money provided to a business venture that entitles the provider to rights or ownership in the venture and that is not expected to be repaid.

ethical responsibilities   The strategic managers' notion of right and proper business behavior.

ethical standards   A person's basis for differentiating right from wrong.

ethics   The moral principles that reflect society's beliefs about the actions of an individual or group that are right and wrong.

ethnocentric orientation   When the values and priorities of the parent organization guide the strategic decision making of all its international operations.

expert influence   The ability to direct and influence others because they defer to you based on your expertise or specialized knowledge that is related to the task, undertaking, or assignment in which they are involved.

external environment   The factors beyond the control of the firm that influence its choice of direction and action, organizational structure, and internal processes.

external interface boundaries   Formal and informal rules, locations, and protocol that separate and/or dictate the interaction between members of an organization and those outside the organization—customers, suppliers, partners, regulators, associations, and even competitors.

F

feedback   The analysis of postimplementation results that can be used to enhance future decision making.

formality   The degree to which participation, responsibility, authority, and discretion in decision making are specified in strategic management.

fragmented businesses   Businesses with many sources of advantage, but they are all small. They typically involve differentiated products with low brand loyalty, easily replicated technology, and minimal scale economies.

fragmented industry   An industry in which there are numerous competitors (providers of the same or similar products or services the industry involves) such that no single firm or small group of firms controls any significant share of the overall industry sales.

functional organizational structure   Structure in which the tasks, people, and technologies necessary to do the work of the business are divided into separate "functional" groups (e.g., marketing, operations, finance) with increasingly formal procedures for coordinating and integrating their activities to provide the business's products and services.

functional tactics   Detailed statements of the "means" or activities that will be used by a company to achieve short-term objectives and establish competitive advantage. Short-term, narrow-scoped plans of functional areas that detail the "means" or activities that a company will use to achieve short-term objectives.

G

generic strategy   A core idea about how a firm can best compete in the marketplace. Fundamental philosophical option for the design of strategies.

geocentric orientation   When an international firm adopts a systems approach to strategic decision making that emphasizes global integration.

geographic boundaries   Limitations on interaction and contact between people in a company based on being at different physical locations domestically and globally.

global industry   An industry in which competition crosses national borders on a worldwide basis.

globalization   The strategy of pursuing opportunities anywhere in the world that enable a firm to optimize its business functions in the countries in which it operates.

golden handcuffs   A form of executive compensation where compensation is deferred (either a restricted stock plan or bonus income deferred in a series of annual installments).

golden parachute   A form of bonus compensation designed to retain talented executives that calls for a substantial cash payment if the executive quits, is fired, or simply retires.

grand strategy   A master long-term plan that provides basic direction for major actions directed toward achieving long-term business objectives. The means by which objectives are achieved.

grand strategy clusters   Sets of grand strategies that may be more advantageous for firms to choose under one of four sets of conditions defined by market growth rate and the strength of the firm's competitive position.

grand strategy selection matrix   A four-cell matrix that helps managers choose among different and grand strategies based upon (1) whether the business is operating from a position of strength or weakness and (2) whether it must rely solely on its own internal resources versus having the option to acquire resources externally via merger or acquisition.

growth industry strategies   Business strategies that may be more advantageous for firms participating in rapidly growing industries and markets.

H

holding company structure   Structure in which the corporate entity is a broad collection of often unrelated businesses and divisions such that it (the corporate entity) acts as financial overseer "holding" the ownership interest in the various parts of the company, but has little direct managerial involvement.

horizontal boundaries   Rules of communication, access, and protocol for dealing with different departments or functions or processes within an organization.

horizontal integration   A grand strategy based on growth through the acquisition of one or more similar firms operating at the same stage of the production-marketing chain.

I

ideagora   A Web-enabled, virtual marketplace that connects people with unique ideas, talents, resources, or capabilities with companies seeking to address problems or potential innovations in a quick, competent manner.

implementation control   Management efforts designed to assess whether the overall strategy should be changed in light of results associated with the incremental actions that implement the overall strategy. These are usually associated with specific strategic thrusts or projects and with predetermined milestone reviews.

incremental innovation   Simple changes or adjustments in existing products, services, or processes.

industry   A group of companies that provide similar products and services.

industry environment   The general conditions for competition that influence all businesses that provide similar products and services.

information power   The ability to influence others based on your access to information and your control of dissemination of information that is important to subordinates and others yet not otherwise easily obtained.

innovation   A grand strategy that seeks to reap the premium margins associated with creation and customer acceptance of a new product or service. The initial commercialization of invention by producing and selling a new product, service, or process.

intangible assets   A firm's assets that you cannot touch or see but that are very often critical in creating competitive advantage: brand names, company reputation, organizational morale, technical knowledge, patents an a unique "bundle of resources"—tangible and intangible assets and organizational capabilities to make use of those assets.

intrapreneurship   A term associated with entrepreneurship in large established companies; the process of attempting to identify, encourage, enable, and assist entrepreneurship within a large, established company so as to create new products, processes, services, or improvements that become major new revenue streams and/or sources of cost savings for the company.

intrapreneurship freedom factors   Ten characteristics identified by Dr. Gordon Pinchot and elaborated upon by others that need to be present in large companies seeking to encourage and increase the level of intrapreneurship within their company.

invention   The creation of new products or processes through the development of new knowledge or from new combinations of knowledge.

isolating mechanisms   Characteristics that make resources difficult to imitate. In the resource-based view context these are physically unique resources, path-dependent resources, causal ambiguity, and economic deterrence.

J

joint venture   A grand strategy in which companies create a co-owned business that operates for their mutual benefit. Commercial companies created and operated for the benefit of the co-owners; usually two or more separate companies that come together to form the venture.

K

keiretsus   A Japanese consortia of businesses that is coordinated by a large trading company to gain a strategic advantage.

L

leadership development   The effort to familiarize future leaders with the skills important to the company and to develop exceptional leaders among the managers employed.

leader's vision   An articulation of a simple criterion or characterization of what a leader sees the company must become in order to establish and sustain global leadership. IBM's former CEO, Lou Gerstner, described IBM as needing to become the leader in "network-centric computing" is an example of such a characterization.

learning organization   Organization structured around the idea that it should be set up to enable learning, to share knowledge, to seek knowledge, and to create opportunities to create new knowledge. It would move into new markets to learn about those markets rather than simply to bring a brand to it, or find resources to exploit in it.

legal responsibilities   The firm's obligations to comply with the laws that regulate business activities.

liquidation   A strategy that involves closing down the operations of a business and selling its assets and operations to pay its debts and distribute any gains to stockholders.

long-term objectives   The results that an organization seeks to achieve over a multiyear period.

low-cost strategies   Business strategies that seek to establish long-term competitive advantages by emphasizing and perfecting value chain activities that can be achieved at costs substantially below what competitors are able to match on a sustained basis. This allows the firm, in turn, to compete primarily by charging a price lower than competitors can match and still stay in business.

M

market development   A grand strategy of marketing present products, often with only cosmetic modification, to customers in related marketing areas by adding channels of distribution or by changing the content of advertising or promotion.

market focus   A generic strategy that applies a differentiation strategy approach, or a low-cost strategy approach, or a combination—and does so solely in a narrow (or "focused") market niche rather than trying to do so across the broader market. The narrow focus may be geographically defined, or defined by product type features, or target customer type, or some combination of these.

market growth rate   The projected rate of sales growth for the market being served by a particular business.

matrix organizational structure   Structure in which functional and staff personnel are assigned to both a basic functional area and to a project or product manager. It provides dual channels of authority, performance responsibility, evaluation, and control.

mature industry strategies   Strategies used by firms competing in markets where the growth rate of that market from year to year has reached or is close to zero.

milestone reviews   Points in time, or at the completion of major parts of a bigger strategy, where managers have predetermined they will undertake a go–no go type of review regarding the underlying strategy associated with the bigger strategy.

modular organization   An organization structured via outsourcing where different parts of the tasks needed to provide the organization's product or service are done by a wide array of other organizations brought together to create a final product or service based on the combination of their separate, independent, self-contained skills and business capabilities.

moral hazard problem   An agency problem that occurs because owners have limited access to company information, making executives free to pursue their own interests.

moral rights approach   Judging the appropriateness of a particular action based on a goal to maintain the fundamental rights and privileges of individuals and groups.

multidomestic industry   An industry in which competition is segmented from country to country.

O

operating environment   Factors in the immediate competitive situation that affect a firm's success in acquiring needed resources.

opportunity   A major favorable situation in a firm's environment.

organizational capabilities   Skills (the ability and ways of combining assets, people, and processes) that a company uses to transform inputs into outputs.

organizational culture   The set of important assumptions and beliefs (often unstated) that members of an organization share in common.

organizational leadership   The process and practice by key executives of guiding and shepherding people in an organization toward a vision over time and developing that organization's future leadership and organization culture.

organizational structure   Refers to the formalized arrangements of interaction between and responsibility for the tasks, people, and resources in an organization.

outsourcing   Obtaining work previously done by employees inside the companies from sources outside the company.

P

parenting framework   The perspective that the role of corporate headquarters (the "parent") in multibusiness (the "children") companies is that of a parent sharing wisdom, insight, and guidance to help develop its various businesses to excel.

passion (of a leader)   A highly motivated sense of commitment to what you do and want to do.

patching   The process by which corporate executives routinely "remap" their businesses to match rapidly changing market opportunities—adding, splitting, transferring, exiting, or combining chunks of businesses.

peer influence   The ability to influence individual behavior among members of a group based on group norms, a group sense of what is the right thing or right way to do things, and the need to be valued and accepted by the group.

perseverance (of a leader)   The capacity to see a commitment through to completion long after most people would have stopped trying.

planning mode   The strategic formality associated with large firms that operate under a comprehensive, formal planning system.

policies   Broad, precedent-setting decisions that guide or substitute for repetitive or time-sensitive managerial decision making. Predetermined decisions that substitute for managerial discretion in repetitive decision making.

pollution   Threats to life-supporting ecology caused principally by human activities in an industrial society.

polycentric orientation   When the culture of the country in which the strategy is to be implemented is allowed to dominate a company's international decision-making process.

portfolio techniques   An approach pioneered by the Boston Consulting Group that attempted to help managers "balance" the flow of cash resources among their various businesses while also identifying their basic strategic purpose within the overall portfolio.

position power   The ability and right to influence and direct others based on the power associated with your formal position in the organization.

power curves   A power curve is a depiction of a fundamental structural trend that underlies an industry.

premise control   The systematic recognition and analysis of assumptions upon which a strategic plan is based, to determine if those assumptions remain valid in changing circumstances and in light of new information.

primary activities   The activities in a firm of those involved in the physical creation of the product, marketing and transfer to the buyer, and after-sale support.

principles (of a leader)   A leader's fundamental personal standards that guide her sense of honesty, integrity, and ethical behavior.

private equity   Money from private sources that is invested by a venture capital or private equity company in start-ups and other risky—but potentially very profitable—small and medium-size enterprises.

privatization   A restructuring in which the ownership structure of a publicly traded corporation is converted into a privately held company.

process   The flow of information through interrelated stages of analysis toward the achievement of an aim.

product development   A grand strategy that involves the substantial modification of existing products or the creation of new but related products that can be marketed to current customers through established channels.

product differentiation   The extent to which customers perceive differences among products and services.

product life cycle   A concept that describes a product's sales, profitability, and competencies that are key drivers of the success of that product as it moves through a sequence of stages from development and introduction to growth, maturity, decline, and eventual removal from a market.

product-team structure   Assigns functional managers and specialists (e.g., engineering, marketing, financial, R&D, operations) to a new product, project, or process team that is empowered to make major decisions about their performance responsibility, evaluation, and control.

punitive power   Ability to direct and influence others based on an ability to coerce and deliver punishment for mistakes or undesired actions by others, particularly subordinates.

Q

question marks   Businesses whose high growth rate gives them considerable appeal but whose low market share makes their profit potential uncertain.

R

referent influence   The ability to influence others derived from their strong desire to be associated with you, usually because they admire you, gain prestige or a sense of purpose by that association, or believe in your motivations.

regiocentric orientation   When a parent company blends its own predisposition with those of its international units to develop region sensitive strategies.

relative competitive position   The market share of a business divided by the market share of its largest competitor.

remote environment   Economic, social, political, technological, and ecological factors that originate beyond, and usually irrespective of, any single firm's operating situation.

resource-based view   A new perspective on understanding a firm's success based on how well the firm uses its internal resources. The underlying premise is that firms differ in fundamental ways because each firm possesses a unique "bundle of resources"—tangible and intangible assets and organizational capabilities to make use of those assets.

restricted stock   Stock given to an employee who is prohibited or "restricted" from selling the stock for a certain time period and not at all if the employee leaves the company before that time period.

restructuring   Redesigning an organizational structure with the intent of emphasizing and enabling activities most critical to a firm's strategy to function at maximum effectiveness.

retrenchment   A business strategy that involves cutting back on products, markets, operations, or other strategic commitments of the firm because its overall competitive position, or its financial situation, or both are not able to support the level of commitments to various markets or the resources needed to sustain or build its operations in some, usually declining or increasingly competitive, markets. Unlike liquidation, retrenchment would have the firm sell some assets, or ongoing operations, to rechannel proceeds to reduce overall debt and to support the firm's efforts to rebuild its future competitive posture.

reward power The ability to influence and direct others that comes from being able to confer rewards in return for desired actions or outcomes.

S

Sarbanes-Oxley Act of 2002 Law that revised and strengthened auditing and accounting standards.

self-management Allowing work groups or work teams to supervise and administer their work as a group or team without a direct supervisor exercising the supervisory role. These teams set parameters of their work, make decisions about work-related matters, and perform most of the managerial functions previously done by their direct supervisor.

short-term objective Measurable outcomes achievable or intended to be achieved in one year or less. Desired results that provide specific guidance for action during a period of one year or less.

simple organizational structure Structure in which there is an owner and a few employees and where the arrangement of tasks, responsibilities, and communication is highly informal and accomplished through direct supervision.

Six Sigma A continuous improvement program adopted by many companies in the last two decades that takes a very rigorous and analytical approach to quality and continuous improvement with an objective to improve profits through defect reduction, yield improvement, improved customer satisfaction, and best-in-class performance.

social audit An attempt to measure a company's actual social performance against its social objectives.

social justice approach Judging the appropriateness of a particular action based on equity, fairness, and impartiality in the distribution of rewards and costs among individuals and groups.

special alert control Management actions undertaken to thoroughly, and often very rapidly, reconsider a firm's strategy because of a sudden, unexpected event.

specialization businesses Businesses with many sources of advantage. Skills in achieving differentiation (product design, branding expertise, innovation, and perhaps scale) characterize winning specialization businesses.

speed-based strategies Business strategies built around functional capabilities and activities that allow the company to meet customer needs directly or indirectly more rapidly than its main competitors.

stakeholder activism Demands placed on a global firm by the stakeholders in the environments in which it operates.

stakeholders Influential people who are vitally interested in the actions of the business.

stalemate businesses Businesses with few sources of advantage, most of them small. Skills in operational efficiency, low overhead, and cost management are critical to profitability.

stars Businesses in rapidly growing markets with large market shares.

stock options The right, or "option," to purchase company stock at a fixed price at some future date.

strategic alliances Alliances with suppliers, partners, contractors, and other providers that allow partners in the alliance to focus on what they do best, farm out everything else, and quickly provide value to the customer. Partnerships that are distinguished from joint ventures because the companies involved do not take an equity position in one another.

strategic business unit An adaptation of the divisional structure in which various divisions or parts of divisions are grouped together based on some common strategic elements, usually linked to distinct product/market differences.

strategic control Management efforts to track a strategy as it is being implemented, detect problems or changes in its underlying premises, and make necessary adjustments.

strategic intent A leader's clear sense of where she wants to lead the company and what results she expects to achieve.

strategic management The set of decisions and actions that result in the formulation and implementation of plans designed to achieve a company's objectives.

strategic positioning The way a business is designed and positioned to serve target markets.

strategic processes Decision making, operational activities, and sales activities that are critical business processes.

strategic surveillance Management efforts to monitor a broad range of events inside and more often outside the firm that are likely to affect the course of its strategy over time.

strategic thrusts or projects Special efforts that are early steps in executing a broader strategy, usually involving significant resource commitments, yet where predetermined feedback will help management determine whether continuing to pursue the strategy is appropriate or whether it needs adjustment or major change.

strategy Large-scale, future-oriented plans for interacting with the competitive environment to achieve company objectives.

strength A resource advantage relative to competitors and the needs of the markets a firm serves or expects to serve.

structural attributes The enduring characteristics that give an industry its distinctive character.

support activities The activities in a firm that assist the firm as a whole by providing infrastructure or inputs that allow the primary activities to take place on an ongoing basis.

SWOT analysis SWOT is an acronym for the internal Strengths and Weaknesses of a firm, and the environmental Opportunities and Threats facing that firm. SWOT analysis is a technique through which managers create a quick overview of a company's strategic situation.

T

tangible assets The most easily identified assets, often found on a firm's balance sheet. They include production facilities, raw materials, financial resources, real estate, and computers.

technological forecasting   The quasi-science of anticipating environmental and competitive changes and estimating their importance to an organization's operations.

threat   A major unfavorable situation in a firm's environment.

three circles analysis   An internal analysis technique wherein strategists examine customers' needs, company offerings, and competitor's offerings to more clearly articulate what their company's competitive advantage is and how it differs from those of competitors while the strategists are in the midst of strategic analysis activities.

turnaround   A grand strategy of cost reduction and asset reduction by a company to survive and recover from declining profits.

U

utilitarian approach   Judging the appropriateness of a particular action based on a goal to provide the greatest good for the greatest number of people.

V

value chain   A perspective in which business is seen as a chain of activities that transforms inputs into outputs that customers value. Customer value derives from three basic sources: activities that differentiate the product, activities that lower its cost, and activities that meet the customer's need quickly.

value chain analysis   An analysis that attempts to understand how a business creates customer value by examining the contributions of different activities within the business to that value.

vertical boundaries   Limitations on interaction, contact, and access between operations and management personnel; between different levels of management; and between different organizational parts like corporate vs. divisional units.

vertical integration   A grand strategy based on the acquisition of firms that supply the acquiring firm with inputs such as raw materials or new customers for its outputs, such as warehouses for finished products.

virtual organization   Corporations whose structure has become an elaborate network of external and internal relationships. In effect, a temporary network of independent companies—suppliers, customers, subcontractors, and businesses around the core, high-profitability information, services, and products. Creating an agile, virtual organization structure involves outsourcing, strategic alliances, a boundaryless learning approach, and Web-based organization.

vision statement   A statement that presents a firm's strategic intent designed to focus the energies and resources of the company on achieving a desirable future.

volume businesses   Businesses that have few sources of advantage, but the size is large—typically the result of scale economies.

W

weakness   A limitation or deficiency in one or more resources or competencies relative to competitors that impedes a firm's effective performance.

Photo Credits

Chapter 1

© AP Photo/Paul Sakuma, p. 10.

Chapter 2

© AP Photo/Douglas Healey, p. 30.

Chapter 3

© AP Photo/Gene K. Puskar, p. 55.

© AP Photo/Fritz Reiss, p. 64.

© AP Photo/M. Spencer Green, p. 75.

Chapter 4

© AP Photo/M. Spencer Green, p. 90.

Chapter 5

© AP Photo/Peter Dejong, p. 132.

Chapter 6

© Julie Cordeiro/Boston Red Sox, p. 139.

Chapter 7

© AP Photo/Dave Koenig, p. 190.

© AP Photo/Atlanta Journal-Constitution, Kimberly Smith, p. 193.

Chapter 8

© AP Photo/Paul Sakuma, p. 217 (left).

© Kimberly White/Corbis, p. 217 (right).

© Yoshikazu Tsuno/AFP/Getty Images, p. 225.

Chapter 9

© AP Photo/Gautam Singh, p. 253.

Chapter 10

Courtesy of Symantec Corporation, p. 267.

© Monica M. Davey/Corbis, p. 273.

© Kim Kulish/Corbis, p. 286.

Chapter 11

Copyright © by The McGraw-Hill Companies, Inc. All rights reserved, p. 312.

Chapter 12

© AP Photo/Reed Saxon, p. 330.

© AP Photo/Mark Lennihan, p. 332.

Chapter 13

© Mike Simons/Getty Images. p. 358.

© AP Photo/Bell Atlantic, p. 367 top left.

© AP Photo/Paul Sakuma, p. 367 top right.

Courtesy of General Electric, p. 367, bottom left.

© AP Photo/Nati Harnik, p. 367, bottom right.

Chapter 14

Book cover of Taiichi Ohno's Workplace Management, © Gamba Press, 2007. Photo of cover: © Roberts Publishing Services, p. 372.

Courtesy of InnoCentive, Inc., p. 384.

Name Index

Page numbers followed by n refer to notes.

Subject Index

Case Study Index